Entrepreneurial Small Business

6e

Jerome A. Katz
Saint Louis University

Richard P. Green II
Texas A&M University–
San Antonio

ENTREPRENEURIAL SMALL BUSINESS

Published by McGraw Hill LLC, 1325 Avenue of the Americas, New York, NY 10121.

This book is printed on acid-free paper.

1 2 3 4 5 6 7 8 9 LWI 24 23 22 21 20

ISBN 978-1-260-57035-9
MHID 1-260-57035-5

Cover Image: *Makistock/Shutterstock*

mheducation.com/highered

To our parents, who gave us inspiration.

To our children, who gave us motivation.

To our spouses, who gave us dedication.

ABOUT THE AUTHORS

Courtesy of Jerome Katz

Jerome A. Katz

Jerome (Jerry) Katz is the Robert H. Brockhaus Endowed Chair in Entrepreneurship at the Richard A. Chaifetz School of Business, Saint Louis University. Prior to his coming to Saint Louis University he was an assistant professor of management at the Wharton School, University of Pennsylvania. Jerry holds a PhD in organizational psychology from the University of Michigan, and other graduate degrees from Harvard and the University of Memphis.

Throughout the years he has worked in or advised his family's businesses including stints working in the family's discount department store, sporting goods wholesaling, pharmacies, auto parts jobbing, and secondary-market wholesaling of frozen food. As a professor he has served as adviser to over 500 business plans developed by students at Saint Louis University, whose Entrepreneurship Program (which Jerry leads) has been nationally ranked every year since 1994.

He was also the founder and director of Saint Louis University's Billiken Angels Network, which was ranked by the *HALO Report* as one of the top angel groups in the United States. Earlier in his career he served as associate director for the Missouri State Small Business Development Centers. He has taught, trained, or consulted on entrepreneurship education and business development services in Germany, Spain, China, Portugal, Saudi Arabia, Korea, Sweden, Switzerland, the United Kingdom, Brazil, Singapore, Israel, Croatia, and the West Bank. His consulting firm, J. A. Katz & Associates, has a client list including the Soros, GE, Kauffman and Coleman Foundations, as well as the Korea Entrepreneurship Foundation, the Jerusalem Institute for Israel Studies, Sweden's Entrepreneurship and Small Business Research Institute, the International Labor Organization (ILO), RISEbusiness, the National Federation of Independent Business, the National Science Foundation, and the Committee of 200.

As a researcher, Jerry has done work on entrepreneurship, organizational emergence, opportunity analysis, and the discipline and infrastructure of entrepreneurship education. Today 8 of his papers can be found in 11 different compendia of "classic" works in entrepreneurship and small business. He was a co-recipient of the 2013 Foundational Paper Award of the Entrepreneurship Division of the Academy of Management, and Google Scholar reports Jerry's papers have been cited over 11,000 times. Jerry founded and edited two book series, *Advances in Entrepreneurship, Firm Emergence and Growth* (published by Emerald) and *Entrepreneurship and the Management of Growing Enterprises* (published by Sage) and has edited over a dozen special issues. He sits on the editorial boards of 11 journals: *Journal of Small Business Management, Entrepreneurship and Regional Development, International Journal of Entrepreneurship and Small Business, Journal of International Entrepreneurship, International Entrepreneurship and Management Journal, International Journal of Technoentrepreneurship, Experiential Entrepreneurship Exercises Journal, USASBE Annals of Entrepreneurship Education, Ekonomski Vjesnik Econviews, Journal of Entrepreneurship Education*, and *Entrepreneurship Education & Pedagogy*.

Following his parents' tradition of civic entrepreneurship, Jerry has served in a variety of roles including a governor of the Academy of Management, chair of the Entrepreneurship Division of the Academy of Management, and senior vice president for research and publications of the International Council for Small Business. He serves on a number of local, national, and international boards promoting entrepreneurship and entrepreneurship education and training for students and the general public.

For these efforts, he has been a recipient of more than a dozen major professional awards including Babson's Appel Prize for Entrepreneurship Education, the Family Firm Institute's LeVan Award for Interdisciplinary Contributions to Family Business, the Outstanding Lifetime Achievement Award given by the Academy of Management's Entrepreneurship Division, as well as Mentorship Awards from the Entrepreneurship Division of the Academy of Management, and from Saint Louis University's Graduate Student Association, and Saint Louis University's Chaifetz School of Business Alumni Award for Outstanding Educator. He was elected the fiftieth fellow of the U.S. Association for Small Business and Entrepreneurship.

Richard P. Green II

Richard Green is a successful serial entrepreneur who has started, built, and sold several businesses across an extraordinarily wide range of industries. His first business was an electrical sign repair company, which he began while an undergraduate student. Since then, Richard has started two other sign companies, a structural steel business, a manufacturer of stainless steel products, a real estate brokerage, a tax return preparation service, and a bed-and-breakfast. During the "go-go banking" years he held controlling interest in a state-chartered bank. More recently, Richard, with his long-time associate Richard Carter, conducted the start-up of Lineas Aereas Azteca (Azteca Airlines); served as co-owner with his spouse of a San Antonio bed-and-breakfast, the Adams House; and served as chief financial officer for a high-tech start-up, Celldyne Biopharma LLC. As a corporate entrepreneur, Richard has worked on expansion plans for companies as diverse as the Mexican airline Aerolineas Internacionales, Minneapolis-based Land O'Lakes, Inc., and the Venezuelan dairy Criozuca, S.A.

Courtesy of Richard P. Green II

Richard brings a similarly diverse set of skills to *ESB*, ranging from a pilot's license (he was a professional pilot, instructor, and check airman for TWA) to a CPA. A late-life PhD (from Saint Louis University), he has been an assistant and associate professor of accounting at the University of the Incarnate Word and Webster University, and is currently coordinator of the accounting program at Texas A&M University-San Antonio. His academic achievements are similarly impressive, with papers in the proceedings of North American Case Research Association (NACRA), American Accounting Association Midwest, the American Association for Accounting and Finance, and the International Council for Small Business, as well as journals such as the *Atlantic Economic Journal* and *Simulation & Gaming*. Richard also authored more than three dozen articles in popular magazines on topics ranging from personal computers to financial decision making. Richard is co-developer (with Jerry) of the measures for financial sophistication in the Panel Study of Entrepreneurial Dynamics, and is senior author of *Investigating Entrepreneurial Opportunities: A Practical Guide for Due Diligence* (Sage). He has received research grants from Pharmacia Corporation and the Kauffman Foundation.

Always active in professional and civic roles, Richard's contributions have ranged from serving as chair of the Airline Pilots Association's grievance committee to serving on the City of San Antonio's Air Transportation Advisory Committee. He is a member of the American Accounting Association, Academy of Management, United States Association for Small Business and Entrepreneurship, North American Case Writers Association, and the World Association for Case Method Research and Application.

PREFACE

This book got its start with a simple question from my mother, "What is the difference between what you teach and what your father did for a living?"

We were sitting *shiva* (which is the ancient Jewish tradition of mourning), in this case after the death of my father, a Polish immigrant to the United States who had been a small business owner for almost 50 years at the time of his death in 2003. When sitting *shiva* the immediate family mostly sits and reflects and prays for a week, so my mother, sister, and I had plenty of time to talk. And talking as we did, the question came up.

I gathered my thoughts for a minute. First off, I realized that throughout his life my father had picked up on my comments about the very rare high-growth, high-tech businesses that came through my class. Somehow he thought that was who I had as my run-of-the-mill student. That was funny to me, because in teaching entrepreneurship for nearly 20 years, fewer than a dozen of the several hundred business plans I worked on involved high-growth, high-tech firms.

But thinking about what my father heard, I realized that I talk about two sets of rules, one for when I have a potentially high-growth business and another for the more conventional businesses that most of my students start and that my own father had mastered three times in his life. The answer to my mother came out this way:

Conventional Small Businesses	**High-Growth Ventures**
Imitation	Novelty
Autonomy	Involve key others
Control as goal	Growth as goal
Financial independence	Wealth
Fund with your own money	Fund with other people's money
Cash flow as key	Profits as key
Cash crunch? Tighten belt	Cash crunch? Sell more

The list goes on, and you will have a chance to see it in Chapter 1. You will discover that the list exemplifies the prevention versus promotion focus discussed in Chapter 2, but this list gives you an idea of the difference. I told my mother that when I am teaching to students who have really big dreams, I try to get them to create businesses that would be innovative, using new technologies or markets. These would be businesses that could grow to be big businesses, creating major wealth for their founders. The founders are in it for the wealth. They expect to go after others' investment in the business and they expect to give away some of their autonomy along with their stock. My father's businesses were imitative, businesses like those already existing. He did the businesses to have a comfortable income and wanted to limit his growth to what he could comfortably control personally. No investors, no one second-guessing him. When times got tough, my father would cut his expenses; in a high-growth business that's when it needs to sell more. My father's business was built on his personal reputation, while high-growth firms try to maximize the reputation of the firm or its products.

I kept talking, but as I listened to myself, I realized that I had never seen a book that talked about small business the way I described it. I have students who have started such businesses–in fact, the vast majority of my students have started businesses in their own ways much like my father's three firms. I continue to help out those alums with advice, just as I did my father and his business. But in the end, what was important was that they *were* a different kind of business, and I felt that no book really addressed it that way anymore.

That was why I decided to write *this* book, and get Richard to join me in the effort. Why Richard? Because I knew a person with a story like his would make a great co-author for a book like this. His story goes like this:

> When Jerry first asked me if I would be interested in co-authoring a new small business management text, I was a bit reluctant. Where would I create time for such a daunting task? I asked myself. But when he described his vision–a text about starting

and managing the type of small businesses that we patronize every day—restaurants, beauty salons, plumbing companies, lawn care firms—I became enthusiastic. Yes, I definitely wanted to be part of a project that would deal with the 98 percent of businesses that start small and stay that way, not the 2 percent that become CNNs, Oracles, and Dells.

In many ways, I exemplify the type of entrepreneur for whom we wrote this book: people who start and operate the many ordinary enterprises with which you do business every day.

Unlike Jerry, I come from a family of employees. Neither of my grandfathers and none of my many uncles and aunts were ever business owners. My father began working as an employee while he was still in high school, and he continued as an employee until his retirement. I, on the other hand, started my first entrepreneurial enterprise the summer I was 12. I began my first "real" business the summer I was 18. In the years since, I have started several businesses and purchased three. In between businesses I have been, as my father and his father, an employee.

Not a single business that I have owned has ever been high tech, high growth, or even high innovation. I started every one either because I needed a source of income right then or because I expected to lose my current job very soon and didn't want to live on unemployment. I have been an owner-manager in the electrical sign business, structural steel erection, light manufacturing, consumer electronics retailing, real estate brokerage, construction, farming, and lodging.

Why so many businesses, you may ask. My mother probably would say that I have a short attention span. However, the real answer is that each time I started a business I took the first opportunity available, not necessarily the best opportunity. And what was the result? Some, such as the Grandview Sign Service Co., went broke (but not before it paid for flying lessons). Signgraphics, Inc. was sold. Paul's Sound Shop was a victim of recession. The real estate brokerage was financially very successful, but I hated the business. When my top-producing salesman finally passed his broker's exam, I eagerly made a deal for him to buy the company. I am still actively engaged in construction and in the lodging industry.

My interest in entrepreneurship as a field of study stems from this varied experience. I asked myself many questions, including, Why did I just make a living in the sign business, while Ted Turner made himself a billionaire from the same beginnings? Why is it that Paul's Sound Shop didn't become a retail behemoth as Best Buy did, although both started about the same time? And am I a success because I made money in several different businesses, or a failure because none became big businesses? This book is largely the result of my search for answers to these questions.

Together, Richard and I crafted our approach for *Entrepreneurial Small Business*, and as we will point up in the business planning chapter, all plans start with a vision.

The *ESB* Vision

In *Entrepreneurial Small Business*, you will not find a lot on venture capital, and very little on strategic concepts like "first to market." What you *will* find is a lot of coverage of the kinds of businesses most people (and especially most undergraduate and lifelong learning students) really *do* start—small businesses in traditional industries and markets. These businesses are vitally important—we will tell you why we think so in a moment—and helping them survive has long been an art. Today like never before that art is supplemented by science, and that is where your class—and this book—can help. In *ESB* we try to build a book that can combine the art of small business survival and the science of small business success. If you can get the benefit of both *before* you get into your business, you are likely to do better than those who have to get by with the advice they can catch on the fly as they get started.

ESB takes its information from the nearly 150 journals in entrepreneurship (https://sites.google.com/a/slu.edu/eweb/core-publications-in-entrepreneurship-and-related-fields); generating new understanding of what it takes to be successful from national studies like the Panel Study of Entrepreneurial Dynamics (PSED) at www.icpsr.umich.edu/icpsrweb/ICPSR/studies/37203, where we have the benefit of the experience and wisdom of Kelly Shaver (College of Charleston) to help generate many of the statistics we use in this volume. We also use the Kauffman Firm Study (www.kauffman.org/what-we-do/research/kauffman-firm-survey-series), their Indicators of Entrepreneurship (https://indicators.kauffman.org/), the surveys of the National Federation of Independent Business (www.nfib.com/foundations/research-center/monthly-reports/; http://www.411sbfacts.com/); global studies like the Global Entrepreneurship Monitor (GEM) at www.gemconsortium.org; the surveys conducted by the U.S. government (conveniently gathered together at www.nfib.com/foundations/research-center/additional-resources/data-sources/); and the best of modern wisdom from experts in entrepreneurship from government, media, business, and the Internet. The point of *ESB* is to get that knowledge and make it available to you, the small business owner of today or tomorrow. You and your business deserve every break you can get, and our economy and society *need* you to survive and succeed.

Why is that so important? It turns out that small business is essential for big business; it is essential for high-technology, high-growth business; and it is essential to our communities. In a world of relentless cost cutting and global competition, big businesses outsource everything but their most critical tasks. Often the best expertise, the best service, or sometimes even the best price exists in small businesses. Whether it is janitorial services or new product development, big businesses increasingly depend on small businesses to get their jobs done.

Small business is essential to our communities in much the same way. If you come from a small town or a neighborhood that gets bypassed by the big chains, you know how important small businesses can be. Without small businesses there might be *no* places to buy products or needed services. Big business and small communities depend on small business to get the job done.

For high-tech businesses the same argument can be made, but there is also another issue–that small business *defines* the community in important ways. If you work in IT, biotech, nanotech, medicine, media, or the like, when you finish your day in the lab or cubicle, where do you want to be? In a soulless, interchangeable town full of franchised outlets or a vibrant and diverse locale? These members of the "creative class," as Richard Florida[1] calls them, are demanding customers. They make their livings from their minds, and those minds crave stimulation, whether at work or at play. A big part of stimulation comes from being diverse, different, *special*, and that is where small businesses come into play. You can go to a dozen different small coffeebars and each is distinctive. Go to a dozen Starbucks and they are all pretty much the same. There are times when we all crave the expected, but the creative class also often craves the unexpected, and that is much more likely in small businesses than chains and large firms. No high-tech center can survive as a place to live without the excitement and variety a population of small businesses can provide.

The fact is that *every* small business is important for two reasons: first, because we can never be sure which ones are unimportant (if you can believe there could be such a thing), and second, it takes a lot of small businesses to support and enable one billion-dollar business.

For us, one of the lessons of the Panel Study of Entrepreneurial Dynamics (PSED) was that while high tech might be the ship folks hope will come in, for it to work that ship needs to be supported by an ocean of small businesses. Billion-dollar high-tech companies are rare. Less than 1 in 100,000 start-ups achieves that billion-dollar level. The irony is that *nobody* knows which of the next 100,000 start-ups is going to be that next billion-dollar business. All we can do is try and start as many as possible, knowing the more that get started, the greater the chance of that one breakthrough success.

The fact is that nearly every big business got its start as a small business. Hewlett-Packard really *did* start in a garage, and Walmart started small in rural Arkansas. They are giants today, but some part of their culture was defined in those early days when they were small businesses.

[1] R. L. Florida, *The Rise of the Creative Class: And How It's Transforming Work, Leisure, Community and Everyday Life* (New York: Basic Books, 2002).

When they started, none of their founders *knew* they were going to become billionaires, and neither did their investors, bankers, lawyers, or friends. You start your business, you take your chances, and the rest of us hope you make it.

In the meantime, however, those hundreds of thousands of start-ups literally help support big business and high-tech businesses. They do this by providing jobs and wages to half the country so people can buy things. They do this by providing products and services to big and high-tech businesses, and they do this by training and preparing the next generation of workers and owners. Small businesses for the past 25 years have been the major source of new jobs created in the United States. While Fortune 500 businesses have cut their payrolls by millions, the slack created has been filled by small businesses and especially those that grow to multiple sites or multiple shifts.

When you start on the path to creating your own small business, you make life better for us all. *Entrepreneurial Small Business* is dedicated to giving you the specific help you need to get started and be successful.

The Sixth Edition of *ESB*

In each edition of *Entrepreneurial Small Business* we try to follow a theme. The sixth edition's theme was "take it to the 'net." The Internet has made it possible for more people to share more ideas about entrepreneurship than ever before. For every major entrepreneurship magazine online, like Entrepreneur.com or Inc.com, there are hundreds of websites, blogs, and YouTube channels created by entrepreneurs and business experts with a laser-sharp focus on a few issues that are key to them. The goal for this book was to link students to the best of what's out there. Curation plays a big role in making the sixth edition of *ESB*.

We've added almost three dozen Learn More Online (LMO) boxes which contain some of the best sites on the web to learn more about topics in the text, or find applications or online services embodying the kinds of actions you need to take as a start-up entrepreneur. We've added over 100 new sites in the narrative of the text, and updated URLs for all of the more than 750 websites mentioned throughout the text. Building on thought leaders in entrepreneurship from *ESB*'s fifth edition like Eric Ries, Alex Osterwalder, Steve Blank, and Alex Bruton, we have added new leading-edge ideas like the PESO Model of Media from Gini Dietrich, IDEO's feasibility model, and Isaac Jeffries's fitting of it to the business model canvas, Brad Feld's vision of the structure of start-up communities, and Mike Moyer's Slicing Pie approach to figuring out equity for start-up teams.

As is true for every edition, there are updates throughout–updated numbers, counts, and statistics; updated URLs; updated and new examples; and updates on people from prior editions throughout this edition.

Instructors using *ESB* asked for even more skill modules and experiential exercises, and the sixth edition has 54 skill modules and 102 experiential exercises. Together these represent the largest number of behavioral activities ever gathered in a small business or entrepreneurship text.

We continue building on the great resources available to entrepreneurs from government and private sources. There include the blogs of Customerdevlabs.com, Justin Wilcox's remarkable efforts to make seeking out customers and workable ideas using the latest techniques and technology. But other examples abound, such as the canvases of BMfiddle.com, or the readily understandable approach to valuing businesses that comes from Valuations.com. We've added skill modules leveraging Facebook.com's Audience Insights and the newly revamped Census.gov data access web pages.

If you look closely at the materials from others we mention and include in the text, you may notice that while we use many of those ideas and techniques, we don't always follow their approach very closely. In the end, it comes from being true to our own philosophy. We started the preface by comparing traditional small businesses to high-growth firms. A lot of today's models think first of firms in the Silicon Valley, the world's greatest concentration of founders and investors pursuing high-growth entrepreneurship. But there are so many people creating and investing that no one has time for a business plan—to write them or to read them. People in Silicon Valley proclaim "the business plan is dead!" To match their pace you create a pitch deck, a business model canvas, and a set of financials. Internet-driven businesses are the bread-and-butter of Silicon Valley's industry.

But 99 percent of us starting businesses are not in Silicon Valley, and the vast majority of us are not starting Internet-driven or app businesses. We get funding from friends, family, and bankers, not venture capitalists roaming the coffeeshops. When regular people (and even most angels) in the rest of the country consider investing, they want to see a business plan. And for businesses that will take years to become successful—most manufacturing, most professions, most services, and even most retailing and wholesaling—you need to think through how you will operate and fund yourself for the years it will take until your business matures into its best self. An app can go from zero to operational in a weekend (that's what **StartupWeekend.org** and hackathons are all about; look at the story of **InvisibleGirlfriend.com**) and live through 10 iterations within the first week. An accounting firm, or a restaurant, or a new backpack will take longer to get going and be made successful.

In Silicon Valley, entrepreneurs are thick on the ground. There is expertise everywhere, so you ask for it, or trade for it, or buy it. In Silicon Valley you are known by the team you've assembled. The team is the best indicator of your business's capabilities. But in the rest of the country, the majority of businesses consist of only the entrepreneur, or the entrepreneur and one other person, and often while there are other entrepreneurs and help around, it takes a lot more effort to find them and get what you need. So an approach where you, the entrepreneur, have to be more self-reliant, more do-it-yourself, is essential to getting done the crucial jobs of starting a business everywhere but Silicon Valley. *ESB* talks about accounting, marketing, human resources, and a host of other topics in more depth than lean business practices or business model canvas approaches typically do. In the end, lean business practices are often all about the high-growth (aka "scalable") businesses, while *ESB* is focused on the traditional "main street" businesses that make up the bulk of our economy and our lives. Where lean approaches can help main street businesses, we use them. But we stay true to our focus on the businesses you are most likely to start.

As you will see in the acknowledgments, we get feedback from many professors, instructors, and students. We work hard to use these insights to improve the coverage, flow, and usefulness of the text for students and faculty alike. This involves a few major changes among many small changes such as these:

Chapter 1: The chapter is updated in terms of the statistics on small business and the websites, people, and businesses profiled. We've added material on the entrepreneurial process to help better explain our approach to the start-up process, and help those familiar with lean business practices get a feel for the *ESB* approach. We've also included a host of new examples in this chapter: Robin Rath of Pixel Press as our opening vignette, Jim McKelvey of Square replacing Paul McCartney as the CSI entrepreneur, Snapchat's founders replacing Jobs and Wozniak, and a new mini-case at the end of the chapter profiling Jolene Adams.

Chapter 2: This chapter talks about the personality of entrepreneurs, pretty much unchanged from the prior edition, except for the updating of stories, URLs, and statistics. We added a new opening vignette on Khalia Collier of the St. Louis Surge Women's Basketball Team; Learn More Online boxes on personality, competencies, women and minority businesses, second career and veteran entrepreneurs, and teams and family businesses; and new terms like *entrepreneurial mindset* and *micro-commitments*.

Chapter 3: This chapter is also updated in terms of the statistics on small business and the websites, people, and businesses profiled. We've updated the entrepreneurial environment model with the highly regarded work on entrepreneurial ecosystems by Brad Feld from his book *Startup Communities*. The chapter adds a skill module on using Flipboard for environmental scanning, and added Learn More Online boxes on daily news sources for entrepreneurs, finding help on using Facebook and Google advertising, and green/sustainable entrepreneurship. There is also a new Small Business Insight titled "The Dark Side of the Sharing Economy."

Chapter 4: Given this chapter received a major revamp for the fifth edition, the fundamentals remained the same. That said, we replaced the opening vignette with one about the multi-talented entrepreneur Mary Elizabeth Coleman. The RBI model used in the fifth edition was replaced by the better-known IDEO model for assessing initial feasibility. This also led to the addition of a new skill module applying the IDEO screen, and to some updates of the classic feasibility study outline. The chapter also added four Learn More Online boxes on creativity sites, customer-focused interviewing resources, online business model canvas resources, and landing page resources. New ideas included design thinking, retail arbitrage, customer job, and target market.

Chapter 5: Part-time businesses not only remain an important path to ownership, but are also increasing as a portion of all new business entrants. We replaced the opening vignette to tell the story of Carla Brauer and Dermestidarium Trophy Processing. This story is an exemplar of how a long-time avocation can change into a profitable business. Sections 5-1 and 5-2 were rewritten for clarity and better readability. We also added two Learn More Online boxes, one specifically relating to side businesses as part-time businesses. In addition, we updated the graphs and tables on numbers and types of business establishments, as well as several photos throughout the chapter.

Chapter 6: This chapter has been extensively reworked and topic order has been reorganized for more logical progression. A new opening vignette features Paul Hedrick and his boot company, Tecovas. The Small Business Insight was rewritten and uses Scratch Labs as an example of effectual reasoning. We have updated the text to include key terms *bootstrapping*, *bricolage*, and *lean practice*. Jasmine Adams and her start-up "Smudgies" is a new example for leveraging contingencies. Section 6-3, "Rewards and Pitfalls of Starting a New Business" has been revised and in addition, two Learn More Online boxes were added.

Chapter 7: In addition to general updating of statistics, stories, and websites mentioned, this chapter saw a new opening vignette, looking at the gift box company Greetabl (which will pop up in mentions in the rest of the book, up to the cover page of their design patent in Chapter 17). Perceptual mapping was replaced by "Mapping Your Distinctive Competence" which was originally step 1 from Skill Module 9.4 in *ESB* fifth edition. The skill modules, experiential exercises, and appendix in the chapter got revamped because of the change to Greetabl as well as changes in the U.S. Census's major data source for business, now called Census Business Builder. Skill Module 7.5 saw the addition of a Google Maps procedure for displaying your competitors.

Chapter 8: As you might guess, this chapter also received the general updating of statistics, stories, and websites mentioned. The RBI screen was replaced by the IDEO screen, but the biggest change was the replacement of the Colter Durham business plan with the plan from Red Jett Sweets, which first appeared in the fourth edition of *ESB* and was sorely missed by a lot of instructors. This version was completely rewritten to fit the 10+8 page model *ESB* now teaches. The chapter also added Learn More Online boxes on free online business planning programs, alternatives to PowerPoint for pitch decks and online résumé and cover letter builders, as well as terms like *traction*, *micro-commitments,* and *offering circulars.* A whole new section "Storytelling and the Art of the Pitch" tries to capture the art and science of getting your story out.

Chapter 9: In addition to the general updating of statistics, stories, and websites we've been doing for all the chapters, we worked to tighten up the customer section of this chapter, which received a major revision for the fifth edition. This included adding the section "Finding First Customers" along with changing the name of "The Perfect Customer" section to "Thinking about Customer Service" with a refocusing of some of the material in that section. This also led to adding a skill module on using Facebook Audience Insights. The "Segmenting Your Market" section from Chapter 10 (including the associated skill module "Identifying Target Market Segments" which is now Experiential Exercise 12) was moved here and integrated with the other customer-centric material, as was another Chapter 10 skill module "Finding Demographic Information by Zip Code." Some of the examples that were updated include 3-D printers and replacing MP3 players with Bluetooth speakers. The chapter includes new Learn More Online boxes on free online platforms for marketing surveys and free programs for 3-D model building. Skill Module 9.10 was retired in favor of Experiential Exercise 8.

Chapter 10: Structurally one of the biggest changes in *ESB*'s sixth edition was the rethinking of the promotion process of the 4 Ps of marketing. The field of marketing has coalesced around the PESO Model of Media developed by Gini Dietrich– reflecting paid, earned, shared, and owned forms of media, and their overlaps. The model really helps integrate traditional and social media and makes the options available to entrepreneurs and students much clearer than older models, so we replaced the earlier sections "Crafting Your Message" and "Conveying Your Message" with one section titled "Promotion Using the PESO Model." We moved substantial material from Chapter 11 such as "Brand and Organizational Identity" and sections from "Distribution" including "Direct Marketing," "Distribution Issues for Direct Marketing," and "Nondirect Distribution" to Chapter 10, integrating that material in the appropriate sections of the PESO Model, most often in paid media. Given these changes, we removed the section "Strategizing for Promotion." Learn More Online boxes included product review sites, affiliate marketing sites, and free customer relationship management (CRM) online services. There were also minor changes to Discussion Question 5 and Experiential Exercise 5. Experiential Exercise 3 from the fifth edition was moved to Chapter 9, Exercise 2.

Chapter 11: Aside from the general updating of statistics, stories, and websites, the biggest changes to this chapter were increased coverage of fulfillment by Amazon and its competitors (in the section formerly called "Nondirect Distribution" now renamed "Fulfillment and Nondirect Distribution"), and the addition of four Learn More Online boxes on coupon sites, loyalty program management platforms, economic development sites, incubator/accelerator/co-working directory sites, and online floor plan builder sites.

Chapter 12: This chapter received an overhaul, beginning with a new opening vignette highlighting Justin Beegel of Infographic World, Inc. The section "Why Accounting Is Important for Small Business Success" was rewritten for clarity and content. In "The Concepts That Make Accounting Work" we added qualitative characteristics of useful financial information as well as added an explanation of the greater claim creditors have on assets and rewrote the accounting equation. All accounting illustrations and financial reports were updated and now feature Red Jett Sweets, the company first introduced in Chapter 8. The industry links are current live sites and the "Accounting Systems for Small Business" section was rewritten to reflect current standards. We added a Learn More Online box with links specifically for tutorial sites for accounting purposes.

Chapter 13: This chapter, which deals with the issues of managing cash flows and completes the budget process, has been updated with a new vignette featuring the cautionary tale of Creatacor, Inc. All the learning objectives in this chapter have been rewritten and reorganized. Based on adopter feedback, the bank reconciliation section was moved to a new Appendix. Data on cash inventory were updated to 2019. The "Importance of Cash Management" section was renamed to specify cash, not just money, and we included a new introductory paragraph giving justification for the topic. In "Money In/Money Out," we updated data to reflect the most recent NFIB poll and also removed the dated Baby Einstein example. The "Managing Cash Flows" section offers a new explanation as to why this topic is important and a new exhibit from the Federal Reserve is included. The Learn More Online box provides links to discussion of providing discounts for prompt payment.

Chapter 14: The new opening vignette of this chapter tells the story of Bungii.com, a moving company that began when a college student in Kansas, Ben Jackson, got the idea for a business app that he believed could be developed into a profitable business. A new The Thoughtful Entrepreneur box titled "Royalty Financing" was added. The section "Gifts via Crowdfunding" was rewritten to be more consistent with current law and regulations. And, of course, data were consistently updated throughout the chapter to include prevalent information.

Chapter 15: In the fifth edition, for this chapter we added a section on the importance and value of documenting business processes. In this edition, we see a new opening vignette discussing inventory theft and the importance of protecting current assets, especially in small businesses. We added a relevant discussion on the risk of holding inventory. Skill Module 15.3 was removed along with the Small Business Insight "Outsourcing Blues." In the "Managing Operations" section we added a Learn More Online box with valuable links to various outsourcing services and manufacturing.

Chapter 16: Changes to this chapter include a new opening vignette focusing on the threat to small business computer systems caused by cyber criminals. New content was added to offer insight in dealing with cyber threats. The Small Business Insight box featuring Clint Eastwood was removed and we simplified the discussion of compliance with regulations. We added a new chart on the sources of theft in retail businesses and also new discussions on protecting businesses from theft and managing risks inventory. Several photos were also updated to give this chapter a fresher look.

Chapter 17: Given the updates in this chapter for the fifth edition, relatively little was done this time around, aside from the usual updating of statistics, stories, and websites. Skill Module 17.1 was revised and refocused on USA.gov instead of the NOLO.com website, and the knife sheath patent cover page from Hedgehog Leatherwork's Paul Scheiter was replaced by the cover page for the design patent for Greetabl's gift box developed by Joe Fischer. And in our discussion of intellectual property, we added how to register hashtags (e.g. #followme), along with updated instructions for USPTO's TESS database in Skill Module 17.2

Chapter 18: Like Chapter 17, this chapter saw general updating in the fifth edition, and little beyond the usual updating of statistics, stories, and websites was needed. The opening vignette, "Jesse Mecham and You Need A Budget," is new, as are the Learn More Online boxes added on job description websites and prehiring testing websites. A new section "Dividing Ownership in Nonfamily Start-Ups" was added after the section "Dividing Up Ownership and Dividends" which focuses on family firms. The new section builds on the work of Mike Moyer and his Slicing Pie model for allocating equity in bootstrapped start-ups.

When we look at the detailed list just discussed, for this edition about one-third of the ideas come from our own experience and discussions with our friends and colleagues at work. But it is important to recognize that the other two-thirds of the ideas, improvements, corrections, and revamps come from the suggestions of readers like you–faculty and students who are using *Entrepreneurial Small Business* to help them pursue their dreams of business ownership.

You are our target customer. Your satisfaction or dissatisfaction is central to our making this text work. Do you have a better idea about how to talk about something? Did we get something wrong? Is there something we're missing that could help others in their entrepreneurial quests? Tell us. Richard's email is richard.green@tamusa.edu and Jerome's is jerome.katz@slu.edu. We try to respond to all emails, and as you can see, we do try to improve the book based on your feedback.

The *ESB* Package

Professors reading this are probably wondering how all this translates into helping them teach their courses. One way we hope to help is through providing "imitation with a twist," which you will learn more about in Chapter 7. There are many other small business texts out there, and from an author's perspective they can be intimidating because so many of them *are* so good. So how can *ESB* expect to get your attention? As you will find as you look through the book, all the major topics you expect to see are present–that's the imitation that is basic to all mature industries (such as small business education).

What adds value are those aspects of the book that are distinctive–our "twists." We give the specifics on how to sell, how to negotiate, how to ask for help, and how to handle a crisis, building from the best of research and professional practice. You will see it in small touches in the chapters, like in our discussion of issues such as when you get or use gifts as a way to fund start-ups, or why an LLC should be your default legal form of organization. We tried hard to give students the easiest introduction possible to the potentially frightening issues of accounting and financial reports.

ESB is also the first book we know of that has devoted a chapter to the special needs and problems of part-time businesses. For this edition we have tried to cover the broadest possible range of writing projects used in small businesses—not just business plans, but feasibility analyses and industry analyses, and we've added business model canvases and IDEO screenings for rapid assessment of possibilities. We include real-life, high-quality *student-written* examples of the reports we expect students to work up as they start their business. And all the while we tried to keep the *ESB* vision in the forefront—asking ourselves what the absolutely critical things are for our students to know in order to start their small businesses and succeed in them despite a lot of competition. We have tried whenever possible to focus on providing only what is needed, and what would be relevant for the traditional small businesses our students most often start.

The *ESB* Role/Goal/Celebration

This book started with a wife and mother's simple question about the difference between the traditional small businesses her husband started and the high-growth ventures she heard about in her son's stories. Today there is a groundswell of converging ideas in business, economic development, job creation, and government showing us that the revitalization of those traditional small businesses is a key component of reviving our economies and communities.

That revival is more important than ever. Economists have shown us that over the past 50 years the percentage of self-employed people has gone down. With the baby boomer generation reaching retirement, even more small businesses will be closing in the next five years. At a time when entrepreneurship has never been more popular in the media and public thought, the number of people starting businesses seems to be steadily declining.

Some believe that it is too difficult to start the everyday sorts of small businesses. Some believe potential entrepreneurs are turned off by the riskiness of going into business. We continue to work on this book because we believe, and say repeatedly in the text, that "help helps." Research shows that entrepreneurs who get help do better and survive longer. They beat the odds and decrease the riskiness. The help can come from paid professionals, from free sources like the SBA, SBDCs, or SCORE, or from schools and training programs, or even books like this one. *ESB* is here to give you a start and point you to the other resources that can make your entrepreneurial dreams work out and be successful.

In many ways it has never been easier to start businesses. You can have a professional-looking online business operating in a couple of hours. With the baby boomer retirements at hand, literally millions of businesses would be available for purchase, with training thrown in by the founder and convenient terms to pay back the purchase from cash flow (doing it that way is preferable to shutting down a firm and letting employees and customers go). The same studies that show declines in everyday self-employment also say that high-growth businesses are growing in number. So the entrepreneurial world is full of opportunities, and books like this are intended as a gateway and support to those efforts of yours.

For students, we want *Entrepreneurial Small Business* to be your handbook, lightning rod, and motivator. When you read this book in your hands or online, mark it up! If something is important to the way you plan to run your business, dog-ear the page or print a copy from the online version to keep it with you. Write how something applies to your proposed or existing business. If you have not started a journal for business ideas, start using the margins or end pages of this book to hold them. If you are serious about becoming an entrepreneur and we did *our* job right, then success is measured in the material you keep and use from our book. If you are serious and the book did not do the job for you, let *us* know what we need to do better. We got this far on the wisdom of a network of a lot of students and faculty, and as you go through this semester, you become part of the network, too.

For faculty, our job as educators is not just to know about the fortunes of small business, and not just to help make this work, but to *celebrate* this. Academics have the power to legitimize through their acceptance and support, and they have the power to propagate through their contacts with hundreds of students and businesses a year. But most of all, we have the power to excite and to energize, most often through our own energy and support and occasionally even by the new opportunities and vistas we open for our students. You and all of us collectively have an important contribution to make to the revitalization of small business as a key component of the economy, just doing what you do every day.

We want to be a part of that effort with you—providing the examples to celebrate, the realities that help prepare our students for what they will face, and most of all the skills, knowledge, and resources that will prove to them that most critical of concepts in life and in small business success—"help helps."

We are the authors behind *Entrepreneurial Small Business.* We want to help. Let us know how we could do so better in the future. Welcome!

Jerome A. Katz
Saint Louis University
jerome.katz@slu.edu

Richard P. Green II
Texas A&M University–San Antonio
richard.green@tamusa.edu

ENTREPRENEURIAL SMALL BUSINESS:

Entrepreneurial Small Business provides students with a clear vision of small business as it really is today. It focuses on small businesses that students might actually start versus high-growth firms dependent on venture capital. It presents the *realities* small business owners face every day and strategies for those starting or maintaining a small business.

There are several chapters that emphasize the distinct focus of this book.

CHAPTER 5 Small Business Entry: Paths to Part-Time Entrepreneurship

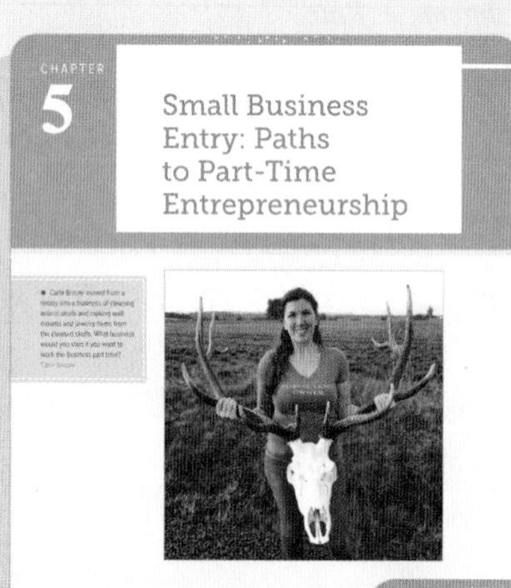

Chapter 5: Small Business Entry: Paths to Part-Time Entrepreneurship

Part-time businesses are tremendously important as they are a major portion of all current entrepreneurship, and it's the way most people enter into self-employment. This chapter discusses the benefits—and challenges—of part-time entrepreneurship.

SMALL BUSINESS REALITY: 75 percent of those starting a business already work full time for someone else and are pursuing their new business part time.

CHAPTER 10 Small Business Promotion: Capturing the Eyes of Your Market

Chapter 10: Small Business Promotion: Capturing the Eyes of Your Market

The key to building a successful business is to discover and meet customer needs. With this in hand, promoting your offering and its value to prospective customers is essential to making sales. This chapter shows how to build customer profiles, conduct unbiased interviews, translate these findings into value statements, and promote your firm, products, and services using social and conventional media.

SMALL BUSINESS REALITY: Today nearly all new start-ups rely on a social media strategy as an essential base on which to build their advertising, press relations, and public relations strategy.

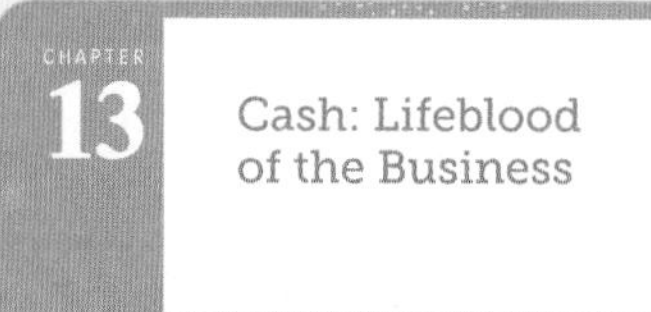

CHAPTER 13 Cash: Lifeblood of the Business

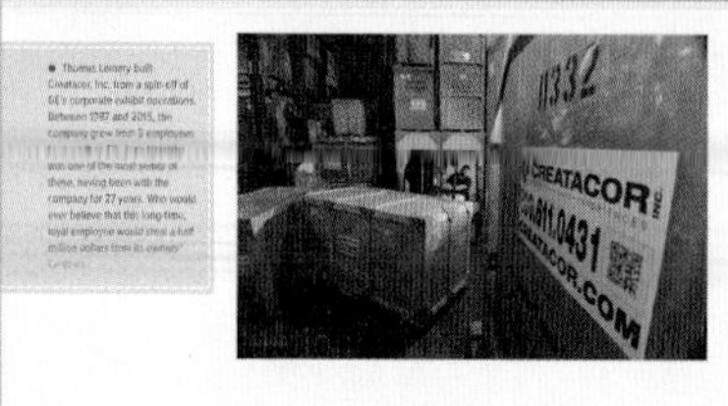

Chapter 13: Cash: Lifeblood of the Business

All small businesses must understand how to manage the business's cash flow. This chapter focuses on the basics of cash, budgets, shortages, and strategies to deal with cash flow problems.

SMALL BUSINESS REALITY: About 55 percent of small businesses that fail do so because of cash flow problems.

Finally . . . a book about the kinds of businesses your students are most likely to start!

Business Plans

Business model canvases and business plans are a part of every small business course. Even when a business plan may not be necessary to start your business, it remains critical to plan and understand your business in any circumstance.

CHAPTER 8

Business Plans: Seeing Audiences and Your Business Clearly

Chapter 8 includes practical information helpful to any small business owner, such as:

- The elevator pitch—how to quickly get people interested in your business.
- How to translate business model canvases (from Chapter 4) into business plan sections.
- How to write your executive summary—a key component of the business plan.
- Seven types of business plans and what components they should include.
- Tips on presenting your plan, such as the 13 slides of a business plan presentation.

Chapter appendixes contain samples of important business plan components:

IDEO Fast Screener (in Chapter 4)
Feasibility Plan (after Chapter 4)
Industry Analysis (after Chapter 7)
Cover Letter and Résumé (after Chapter 8)
Full Business Plan (after Chapter 8)

APPENDIX B

Red Jett Sweets Business Plan
May 2011

By: Natalie Gamez Meyer

This document contains confidential information belonging exclusively to Red Jett Sweets and its owners. Do not quote, copy, or distribute without permission.

[Note to students: The plan fits with the model presented in this chapter and came in at 4,081 words and 13 pages. That said, you will notice not every heading given in the textbook chapter is used here. If a section does not fit with your plan, it can be acceptable to leave it out. If you think moving a section will make the plan easier to read, that may work also. You should check with your instructor or an expert, though, to make sure you don't leave out a section important in your industry or to your readers. The cupcakery was opened, and was a finalist in Food Network's *Cupcake Wars*. You can see their original submission at www.youtube.com/watch?v=[illegible] and their competition at www.foodnetwork.com/shows/cupcake-wars/episodes/wicked. Red Jett Sweets closed in late 2013, as a walkaway (see Chapter 6) having no outstanding debts, with Natalie and Christina selling the firm's assets and going onto other businesses. Natalie is now the general manager for the Dallas-Fort Worth restaurant group Terra Mediterranean. She went from an independent to a corporate entrepreneur.]

Additional business plan supports include online examples of feasibility plans and business plans in the Connect Library. One online feasibility study and business plan focuses on the same company, allowing you to see how the business developed.

ESB Features

Practical Advice and Experiential Learning

To help students learn more about the benefits of small business ownership, as well as the challenges many small business owners face, *ESB* is full of practical advice and examples from true small businesses in a variety of industries. Its focus is to give students the tools and knowledge they need to go out and start their small business.

Along with over 100 end-of-chapter experiential exercises, 54 skill modules throughout the text give students the hands-on experience they need to start and manage a small business. *Together, these materials provide one of the largest collections of experiential learning techniques available from any text or online text alternative.*

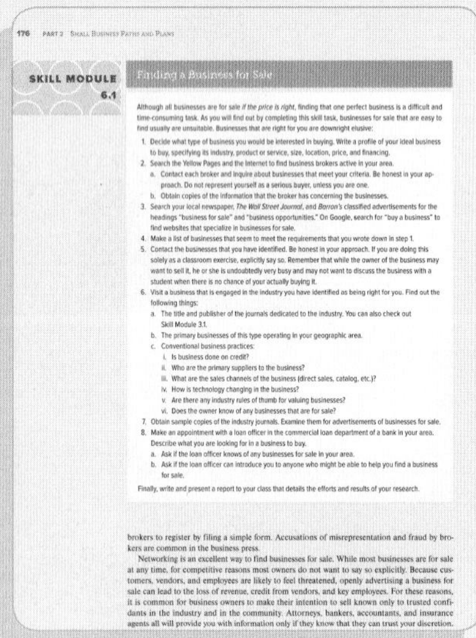

176 PART 2 SMALL BUSINESS PATHS AND PLANS

SKILL MODULE 6.1

Finding a Business for Sale

Although all businesses are for sale *if the price is right*, finding that one perfect business is a difficult and time-consuming task. As you will find out by completing this skill task, businesses for sale that are easy to find usually are unsuitable. Businesses that are right for you are downright elusive:

1. Decide what type of business you would be interested in buying. Write a profile of your ideal business to buy, specifying its industry, product or service, size, location, price, and financing.
2. Search the Yellow Pages and the Internet to find business brokers active in your area.
   a. Contact each broker and inquire about businesses that meet your criteria. Be honest in your approach. Do not represent yourself as a serious buyer, unless you are one.
   b. Obtain copies of the information that the broker has concerning the businesses.
3. Search your local newspaper, *The Wall Street Journal*, and *Barron's* classified advertisements for the headings "business for sale" and "business opportunities." On Google, search for "buy a business" to find websites that specialize in businesses for sale.
4. Make a list of businesses that seem to meet the requirements that you wrote down in step 1.
5. Contact the businesses that you have identified. Be honest in your approach. If you are doing this solely as a classroom exercise, explicitly say so. Remember that while the owner of the business may want to sell it, he or she is undoubtedly very busy and may not want to discuss the business with a student when there is no chance of your actually buying it.
6. Visit a business that is engaged in the industry you have identified as being right for you. Find out the following things:
   a. The title and publisher of the journals dedicated to the industry. You can also check out Skill Module 3.1.
   b. The primary businesses of this type operating in your geographic area.
   c. Conventional business practices:
      i. Is business done on credit?
      ii. Who are the primary suppliers to the business?
      iii. What are the sales channels of the business (direct sales, catalog, etc.)?
      iv. How is technology changing in the business?
      v. Are there any industry rules of thumb for valuing businesses?
      vi. Does the owner know of any businesses that are for sale?
7. Obtain sample copies of the industry journals. Examine them for advertisements of businesses for sale.
8. Make an appointment with a loan officer in the commercial loan department of a bank in your area. Describe what you are looking for in a business to buy.
   a. Ask if the loan officer knows of any businesses for sale in your area.
   b. Ask if the loan officer can introduce you to anyone who might be able to help you find a business for sale.

Finally, write and present a report to your class that details the efforts and results of your research.

brokers to register by filing a simple form. Accusations of misrepresentation and fraud by brokers are common in the business press.

Networking is an excellent way to find businesses for sale. While most businesses are for sale at any time, for competitive reasons most owners do not want to say so explicitly. Because customers, vendors, and employees are likely to feel threatened, openly advertising a business for sale can lead to the loss of revenue, credit from vendors, and key employees. For these reasons, it is common for business owners to make their intention to sell known only to trusted confidants in the industry and in the community. Attorneys, bankers, accountants, and insurance agents all will provide you with information only if they know that they can trust your discretion.

Skill Modules

Going beyond telling students what-to-do, *ESB's* skill modules give detailed how-to information on performing the key actions of successful entrepreneurs. These are resources that students can use in the course and that they can continue to use as they plan or grow their small business.

Examples include:

- Entrepreneurial Personality Overview
- Checking Ideas on the Web
- Short and Sweet Industry Analysis
- The Art of Closing
- Finding an Outsourcing Partner

Focus on Small Business

Each chapter opens with a vignette that highlights an entrepreneur and an aspect of a small business that relates to the chapter concepts. Discussion questions are included for students to consider as they read the chapter.

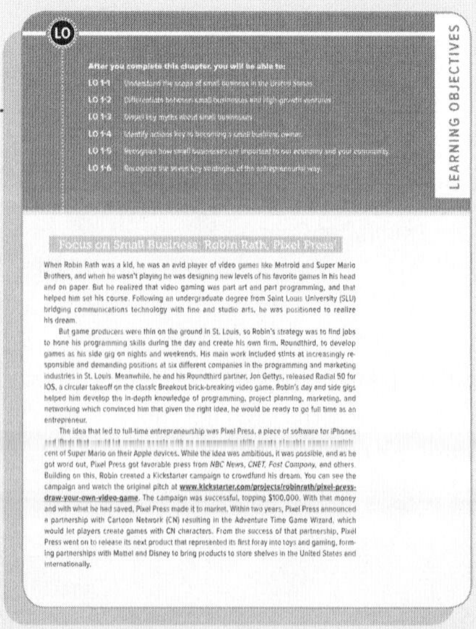

LO

LEARNING OBJECTIVES

After you complete this chapter, you will be able to:

LO 1-1 [illegible]

LO 1-2 [illegible]

LO 1-3 [illegible]

LO 1-4 [illegible]

LO 1-5 [illegible]

LO 1-6 [illegible]

Focus on Small Business: Robin Rath, Pixel Press

When Robin Rath was a kid, he was an avid player of video games like Metroid and Super Mario Brothers, and when he wasn't playing he was designing new levels of his favorite games in his head and on paper. But he realized that video gaming was part art and part programming, and that helped him set his course. Following an undergraduate degree from Saint Louis University (SLU) bridging communications technology with fine and studio arts, he was positioned to realize his dream.

But game producers were thin on the ground in St. Louis, so Robin's strategy was to find jobs to hone his programming skills during the day and create his own firm, Roundthird, to develop games as his side gig on nights and weekends. His main work included stints at increasingly responsible and demanding positions at six different companies in the programming and marketing industries in St. Louis. Meanwhile, he and his Roundthird partner, Jon Gettys, released Radial 50 for iOS, a circular takeoff on the classic Breakout brick-breaking video game. Robin's day and side gigs helped him develop the in-depth knowledge of programming, project planning, marketing, and networking which convinced him that given the right idea, he would be ready to go full time as an entrepreneur.

The idea that led to full-time entrepreneurship was Pixel Press, a piece of software for iPhones [illegible] cent of Super Mario on their Apple devices. While the idea was ambitious, it was possible, and as he got word out, Pixel Press got favorable press from *NBC News*, *CNET*, *Fast Company*, and others. Building on this, Robin created a Kickstarter campaign to crowdfund his dream. You can see the campaign and watch the original pitch at **www.kickstarter.com/projects/robinrath/pixel-press-draw-your-own-video-game**. The campaign was successful, topping $100,000. With that money and with what he had saved, Pixel Press made it to market. Within two years, Pixel Press announced a partnership with Cartoon Network (CN) resulting in the Adventure Time Game Wizard, which would let players create games with CN characters. From the success of that partnership, Pixel Press went on to release its next product that represented its first foray into toys and gaming, forming partnerships with Mattel and Disney to bring products to store shelves in the United States and internationally.

Small Business Insight Boxes

These boxes include "under the radar" advice from real small business owners and helpful statistics from small businesses around the country.

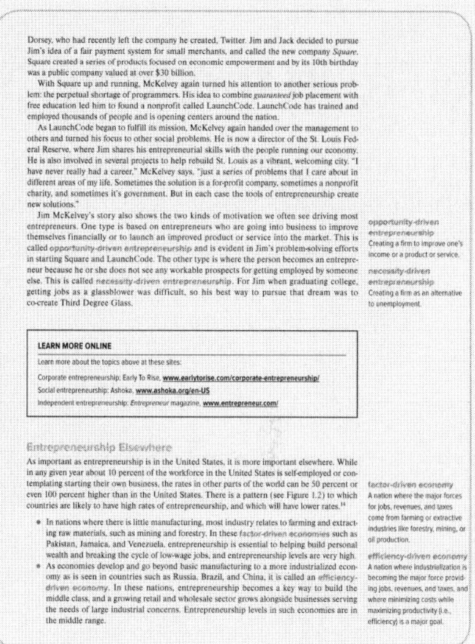

Learn More Online Boxes

Curating the best of the Internet, these boxes in every chapter provide links to more than 500 free online programs, sources of information, apps, and services that have been classroom-tested and found to be a help for student entrepreneurs and their businesses.

End-of-Chapter Materials

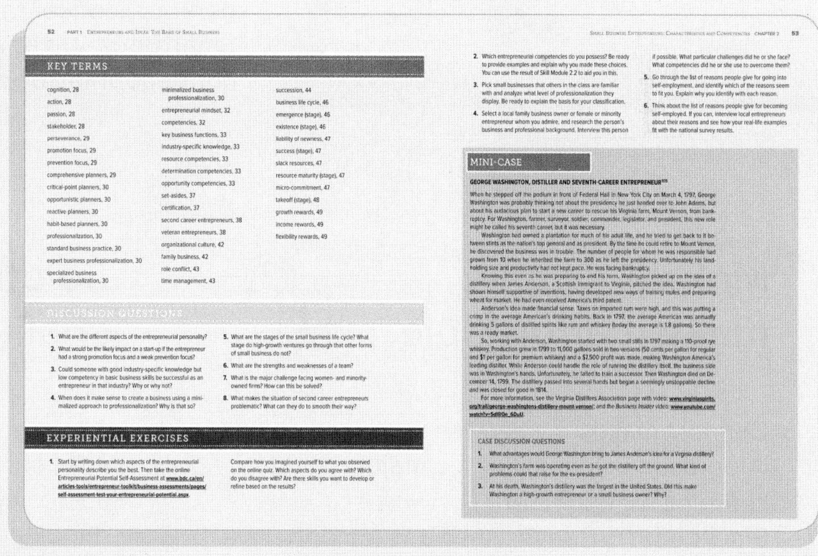

End-of-chapter materials include:

CHAPTER SUMMARY

An end-of-chapter summary is included, bulleted by chapter objectives, to help students review the chapter material and study for tests.

KEY TERMS

Important technical and professional terms are highlighted in the text and repeated here (and in the end-of-text Glossary) to help students identify and learn.

DISCUSSION QUESTIONS

Discussion questions are included in each chapter that can be given as assignments or that can be used for in-class discussion. Suggested answers are included in the Instructor's Manual.

EXPERIENTIAL EXERCISES

The experiential exercises include brief activities students can complete to get more information on the chapter topic, to look for additional resources, and to help build their competencies in a certain aspect of small business ownership.

MINI-CASE

A mini-case for each chapter is included as an additional opportunity for the student to apply the lessons of the chapter.

FOR INSTRUCTORS

You're in the driver's seat.

Want to build your own course? No problem. Prefer to use our turnkey, prebuilt course? Easy. Want to make changes throughout the semester? Sure. And you'll save time with Connect's auto-grading too.

65%

Less Time Grading

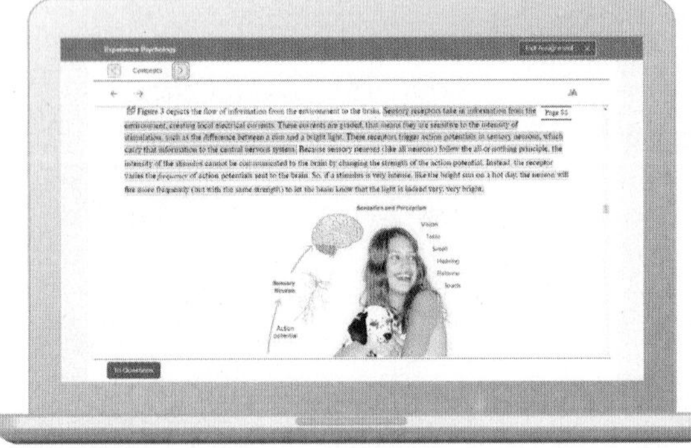

Laptop: McGraw-Hill; Woman/dog: George Doyle/Getty Images

They'll thank you for it.

Adaptive study resources like SmartBook® 2.0 help your students be better prepared in less time. You can transform your class time from dull definitions to dynamic debates. Find out more about the powerful personalized learning experience available in SmartBook 2.0 at **www.mheducation.com/highered/connect/smartbook**

Make it simple, make it affordable.

Connect makes it easy with seamless integration using any of the major Learning Management Systems—Blackboard®, Canvas, and D2L, among others—to let you organize your course in one convenient location. Give your students access to digital materials at a discount with our inclusive access program. Ask your McGraw-Hill representative for more information.

Padlock: Jobalou/Getty Images

Solutions for your challenges.

A product isn't a solution. Real solutions are affordable, reliable, and come with training and ongoing support when you need it and how you want it. Our Customer Experience Group can also help you troubleshoot tech problems—although Connect's 99% uptime means you might not need to call them. See for yourself at **status.mheducation.com**

Checkmark: Jobalou/Getty Images

FOR STUDENTS

Effective, efficient studying.

Connect helps you be more productive with your study time and get better grades using tools like SmartBook 2.0, which highlights key concepts and creates a personalized study plan. Connect sets you up for success, so you walk into class with confidence and walk out with better grades.

Study anytime, anywhere.

Download the free ReadAnywhere app and access your online eBook or SmartBook 2.0 assignments when it's convenient, even if you're offline. And since the app automatically syncs with your eBook and SmartBook 2.0 assignments in Connect, all of your work is available every time you open it. Find out more at **www.mheducation.com/readanywhere**

"I really liked this app—it made it easy to study when you don't have your text-book in front of you."

- Jordan Cunningham,
Eastern Washington University

Calendar: owattaphotos/Getty Images

No surprises.

The Connect Calendar and Reports tools keep you on track with the work you need to get done and your assignment scores. Life gets busy; Connect tools help you keep learning through it all.

Learning for everyone.

McGraw-Hill works directly with Accessibility Services Departments and faculty to meet the learning needs of all students. Please contact your Accessibility Services office and ask them to email accessibility@mheducation.com, or visit **www.mheducation.com/about/accessibility** for more information.

Top: Jenner Images/Getty Images, Left: Hero Images/Getty Images, Right: Hero Images/Getty Images

Additional Resources

Instructor Library

The Connect Instructor Library is your repository for additional resources to improve student engagement in and out of class. You can select and use any asset that enhances your lecture. The Connect Instructor Library includes the resources listed below.

INSTRUCTOR'S MANUAL

The Instructor's Manual includes lecture outlines, chapter summaries, descriptions of the text features, answers to end-of-chapter materials, additional activities, and references to relevant articles.

TEST BANK

The Test Bank includes multiple-choice, true–false, and short-answer questions, along with the correct answer and a rationale for the answer. The Test Bank is also available in a computerized version that allows you to add and edit questions.

POWERPOINTS

PowerPoint presentations for each chapter are available to instructors and students on the Online Learning Center. Included are figures from the text, lecture outline material, figures that expand concepts in the books, and questions that can be used in class.

Manager's Hot Seat

Now instructors can put students in the hot seat with access to an interactive program. Students watch real managers apply their years of experience when confronting unscripted issues. As the scenario unfolds, questions about how the manager is handling the situation pop up, forcing the student to make decisions along with the manager. At the end of the scenario, students watch a post-interview with the manager, view how their responses matched up to the manager's decisions. The Manager's Hot Seat videos are now available as assignments in Connect.

ACKNOWLEDGMENTS

This section is the one sure to get longer as a textbook revisions add up. We don't mind fighting for the space, because a text like *Entrepreneurial Small Business* could not be made without the contributions of a lot of people. Recognizing them here is a small recompense, but one we've valued in their works. It is also a lesson to you fledgling entrepreneurs out there–*all* ventures (and believe us, a textbook is a venture) require the support and advice of many other people to be successful. Here are the ones to whom we remain beholden.

Let's start with our mentors, professors who, through their academic lives, have served as inspiration to us all about the enduring importance of small business: Frank Hoy (Worcester Polytechnic Institute), Charles Matthews (University of Cincinnati), George Solomon (George Washington University), as well as three pioneering Coleman chairs, Gerry Hills (retired from Bradley University), Bob Brockhaus (retired from Saint Louis University), and Gerry Gunderson (retired from Beloit College).

There is also a group of faculty who were essential to *ESB* as it was developed and revised. Some of these started as doctoral students or protégés and are now long-established professionals and professors in their own right while others started as colleagues and remain friends long years later–Kathy Lund Dean (The Board of Trustees Distinguished Chair in Leadership and Ethics at Gustavus Adolphus College), Lisa Gundry (DePaul University), Janice Jackson (University of the District of Columbia), Gregory Konz SJ (Fairfield University), Laurel Boone JD (Saint Louis University), Scott Safranksi (retired from Saint Louis University), and Susan Peters (Thomas Family Center For Entrepreneurship Distinguished Professor at University of North Carolina at Pembroke). These people contributed much of the specialized expertise on which the text is built. Of course, the errors we have introduced over the years are our fault, not theirs.

At Saint Louis University, we use *ESB* in many of our classes, and the feedback SLU's Entrepreneurship Teaching Team provides us is invaluable. Over the past three years that team has included Professors Jintong Tang and Vince Volpe, and adjuncts Tim Hayden (Vivid Sky, FanzLive, Saint Louis University, and Stadia Ventures), Don Dent (Dent Consulting Group), Marian Nunn (Nunn Advisory Services), Steve Epner (The Start-up Within), Laura Burkemper (The Catalyst Center), Ron Roy (Wines That Rock), Rob Boyle (Saint Louis University), Beth Schulte (UHY LLP), Tim Murphy (Ziosk), Cyril Loum (Caring Ministries), Jason Bockman (Strange Donuts), Dave Finklang (Anders CPAs), Michael Black (Goliath Trucking), and Ken Herold (Thoughtware LLC and The Startup Within). We also benefit from a group of entrepreneurship-minded Saint Louis University faculty from across our campus called Coleman Fellows sponsored by the Coleman Foundation: Alesia Slocum, Amrita Chaturvedi, Andy Hall, Ann Scarlett, Bonnie Wilson, Constance Wagner, Dana Malkus, Dan Brewer, Dannielle Davis, David Barnett, Dorota Skowyra, Greg Beabout, Huliyar (Malik)Mallikarjuna, Jan McIntire-Strasburg, Jenna Gorlewicz, Jim Burwinkel, Jin Huang, Joanne Thanavaro, Krishnaswamy (Ravi) Ravindra, Katie Devany, Martin Brief, Michael Korybut, Michael Markee, Michael Swartwout, Mildred Mattfeldt-Beman, Patricia Lee, Ray LeBeau, Rebecca Lorenz, Sanjay Jayaram, Sarah Coffin, Scott Sell, Sridhar Condoor, Srikanth Gururajan, Steve Wernet, Steve Jenkins, Steven Howard, Whitney Linsenmeyer, and Yvette Liebesman.

We also want to thank a remarkable group of students, who agreed to share their work with you. Every business plan, industry analysis, marketing plan, and feasibility study you see in this book or on our website was authored by a student. This gives you a very realistic idea of what students *can* do using the ideas and approaches in *ESB*. Our thanks go out to our students and alums of the Entrepreneurship Program at Saint Louis University (in alphabetical order): Summer Albarcha, Beatrice Emmanuel, Tim Hayden, Corey James, Lachlan Johnson, James P. Keating, and Dan Watkins. As you would expect with our network of colleagues, there is also a host of students at other schools who contributed to the materials *you* see in *ESB*. These include Shannon Sheehee (California Polytechnic University-Pomona), Yong Xu (California Polytechnic University-Pomona), Mingkit "Jerry" Lai (California Polytechnic University-Pomona), and Laurel Ofstein (Western Michigan University). In particular we want to thank Natalie Gamez Meyer for her contribution of the Red Jett Sweets business plan that you will see in Chapter 8.

ESB also builds from an ongoing series of books and special issues edited or co-edited by Jerome Katz over the years, which includes the research series *Advances in Entrepreneurship, Firm Emergence and Growth* (published by Emerald), the text-supplement series *Entrepreneurship and the Management of Growing Enterprises* (published by Sage), and special issues of journals such as *Entrepreneurship: Theory & Practice, Entrepreneurship & Regional Development*, Academy of Management *Learning & Education*, and *Simulation & Gaming.* To the dozens of contributors, reviewers, and co-editors who made those publications possible and that information available, a collective thanks does not do justice, but is all that is possible. Theresa Welbourne (Alabama), Ron Mitchell (Texas Tech), Tom Lumpkin (Oklahoma), and Connie Marie Gaglio (San Francisco State) deserve special mention for their unique and repeated contributions to the informational underpinnings of *ESB.* Two names that deserves special mention, however, are Dean Shepherd (Notre Dame) and Andrew Corbett (Babson) whose work as authors and later as a co-editors of the Emerald series shaped many of the key ideas of *ESB.*

Evaluation is central to the professional approach, whether in small business or in publishing. One of McGraw-Hill's strengths is its unwavering professionalism in the pursuit of publishing. At first, it is frankly daunting. It seems that *every* detail of *every* aspect of a textbook is subject to review—and that perception turns out to be accurate. Yet it serves a purpose. When McGraw-Hill releases a textbook, it has been reviewed, rewritten, and refined until it is a truly first-class product. It is a time-consuming, painstaking, and often underappreciated effort, but it produces textbooks that you have to admire.

At the core of this effort are faculty. These faculty contributed feedback about chapters within the text, the text organization as a whole, and some reviewed the entire manuscript to help us develop the best product available for your small business course. For a text as complex and far ranging as *ESB*, a large, diverse, and committed set of faculty offering opinions and reviews is needed, and we were fortunate to have these dedicated colleagues willing to take time to help make this edition of *ESB* better. They have our thanks, and should have yours too, because without them, opening a book like *ESB* would be a game of chance. These faculty include:

Mary Ewanechko
Monroe Community College

Jonathan Krabill
Columbus State Community College

Terry Lowe
Illinois State University

Lisa McConnell
Oklahoma State University-Oklahoma City

Martin St. John
Westmoreland County Community College

McGraw-Hill went to extraordinary lengths to get feedback for the first through fifth editions, and the more than 155 faculty who contributed reviews and insights were central to the creation of a text that was useful from the start. It is on their contributions that this sixth edition is built. Those reviewers in whose debt we remain include David Aiken, Mark Andreason, Dave Arseneau, Jay Azriel, Calvin Bacon, Barrett Baebler, Kunal Banerji, Kevin Banning, Mike Bark, Kenneth Becker, Verona K. Beguin, James Bell, Jim Benton, Phil Bessler, George Blanc, Kay Blasingame-Boike, David Borst, Susan Bosco, Don Bradley, Steven Bradley, Harvey Bronstein, Mark Brostoff, Ingvild Brown, Russell Brown, Rochelle Brunson, Bob Bryant, Robert J. Calvin, Teresa Campbell, Sheri Carder, Kevin Carlson, Martha Carney, Shawn Carraher, Carol Carter, Ed Cerny, Robert Chelle, Jewel B. Cherry, Felipe Chia, John Christesen, Rod Christian, Michael Cicero, William Clark, Ed Cole, J. Robert Collins, Roy Cook, Dan Creed, Wayne Michael Dejnak, Christine DeLaTorre, Cory L. Dobbs, Michael Dougherty, Mike Drafke, Glenda Eckert, Micki Eisenman, Robert Ericksen, Mary Ewanechko, Michael Fathi, Mark Fenton, Gil Feiertag, Brian Fink, Dana Fladhammer, Rusty Freed, Leatrice Freer, Janice Gates, David Gay, Richard Gentry, Jim Giordano, Vada Grantham, Clark Hallpike, David Hansen, Donald Hardwick, Joe Hartnett, Gene Hastings, Brad D. Hays, Linda Hefferin, David Hensley, Diane Henslow, Kirk Heriot, Abel Hernandez, Anne Hernandez, Dorothy Hetmer-Hinds, Bob Hill, Mark Hoelsher, Edward Huff, Fred Hughes, Samira Hussein, Ralph Jagodka, Ken Jones, Lou Jourdan, Rusty

Juban, Linda Kice, Kelly Kilcrease, Jack Kirby, Larry Klatt, Mary Beth Klinger, Vicky Koonce, Jonathan Krabill, Scott Kunkel, William Laing, Ed Langlois, John Leaptrott, Les Ledger, Art Lekacos, Richard Lester, Paul James Londrigan, Terry Lowe, Luigi Lucaccini, Leyland Lucas, Shawna Mahaffey, Tim March, Greg McCann, Lisa McConnell, Joseph McDonnell, Pam McElligott, Norman McElvany, Jeffrey E. McGee, Clarence McMaster, Todd Mick, David M. Miller, Angela Mitchell, Douglas Moesel, Greg Moore, Mehdi Moutahir, John Mullane, Terry Noel, Don A. Okhomina Sr., Glenda Orosco, Eric Palmer, Gerald Perry, Fred Pragasm, Mark Pruett, Jude Rathburn, Deana Ray, William Rech, Levi Richard, Darlington Richards, Kenneth C. Robinson, Benjamin, Rockmore, Mary Ellen Rosetti, Matt Rutherford, John Sagi, Martin St. John, Tammy Schakett, Duane Schecter, Jim Schroeder, Gregory Schultz, Gerald Segal, Tom Severance, Owen Sevier, Martin St. John, Jack Sheeks, Cynthia Singer, Bernard Skown, Rick Smith, Bill Snider, Robert Sosna, Stuart Spero, William Steiden, Deborah Streeter, John Striebich, Ram Subramanian, James Swenson, Yvette Swint-Blakely, Vanessa Thomas, Sherry Tshibangu, Kathleen Voelker, Ken Walker, Frank Weidmann, Charles Wellens, Rebecca White, Jim Whitlock, Dennis Williams, Ira Wilsker, MaryLou Wilson, John Withey, Betty Wong, and Robert Zahrowski.

Penultimately, there is the team at McGraw-Hill. We had both written books before and thought we had some appreciation of the process of book publishing. However, publishing a *textbook* is a far cry from publishing text supplements or research tomes. In those cases, it is usually just words, with an occasional figure. For a textbook, it is figures, pictures, tables, key terms, URLs, cases of all different lengths, examples, discussion questions, experiential exercises, skill-building exercises, endnotes, business plans, manuals, website components, *and* words. And like a car assembled at one point where dozens of items miraculously come together, the assembly of a modern textbook is a similar experience.

Jennifer Blankenship served as our developmental editor—the person who has to check all the elements and bring them together at the end. She took on an awesome amount of responsibility for *ESB* late in the project, and made sure we were able to get this book to you on time and up to the usual high standards of McGraw-Hill. The job of a portfolio manager in a revision is that of the corporate entrepreneur or product champion, assembling the resources to make it happen, and motivating everyone to keep his or her eyes on the timeline, budget, book outline, and, oh, yes, the market. For *ESB 6e* that role was ably held by Laura Spell, who quietly went about keeping it all on track. Lisa Granger is now our marketing manager and the person responsible for the selling effort that got *ESB* into your hands. As such, she comes onboard late in the process, but at the critical time for the book's commercial success. In addition, there are people such as Mark Christianson, our program manager, Beth Blech, our designer, Maria McGreal and Emily Windelborn, our content project managers, and Traci Vaske, our content licensing specialist, who made all this possible. To each and every one of these fine publishing professionals, we offer our deepest appreciation. One other former McGraw-Hill professional, Ryan Blankenship, continues to have a special place in our hearts. He was the person who recognized the value of *ESB* and sold McGraw-Hill on our idea, and sold us on McGraw-Hill. We remain in his debt. What is wonderful is that our tie to Ryan was renewed in this edition through the involvement of his wife, Jennifer, as a developmental editor. We always feel our best when we know a Blankenship is looking after us.

Keeping with this networking idea, you will see that this book makes extensive use of several strategic partnerships. These include the Global Student Entrepreneur Awards program (www.gsea.org), which celebrates collegiate entrepreneurs, and the Panel Study of Entrepreneurial Dynamics. As the Internet becomes a more integral part of education, we have benefited from partnerships with websites that have developed great material that we use and build on in *ESB 6e.* These include Xtensio.com, which has a great free set of online templates of start-ups; BMfiddle.com, which makes available for free a broad range of business canvases; and Valuations.com, which offers a unique web-based model for computing business valuations.

In particular, there has been an outpouring of new insights on handling some of the toughest challenges in start-ups, and we've built on the works of several brilliant thinkers including Alex

Bruton (straightupbusiness.institute), whose model for linking feasibility analysis, business model canvases, and business plans we follow in this volume; Justin Wilcox (customerdevlabs.com), whose approaches to customer research offered new insights; Eric Ries, Steve Blank, and Bob Dorf, whose work on lean business practices and, in particular, the customer development approach helped us improve our marketing sections; Alex Osterwalder and Yves Pigneur and Ash Muraya, who through their business canvas approaches helped inform our own work; and John Mullins and Dileep Rao and the other faculty at Mike Morris's Experiential Classroom as well as Jerry's colleagues at the Billiken Angel Network, whose insights helped us take our financing chapter to the next level. We are grateful for the continuing support of *ESB* from all of these people. From examples such as these we hope you will see the practical value of strategic partnerships, which we talk about in Chapters 3 and 7. The fact is that we can show you more about the world of small business *because* of our partnerships, and that makes the book, and your experience, better.

Finally, *Entrepreneurial Small Business* will pass its thirteenth year of existence with this edition, and the thinking and talking about it stretches back almost 30 years, in classrooms, at meals, at social get-togethers, and over many, many phone calls, emails, presentations, and papers. What started as a labor of learning among professors and protégés became a labor of love among colleagues. Often this labor was possible because of time contributed by (or stolen from) families and significant others. The number of meals missed, calls taken over the family phone, late nights spent over the computer, or weekends spent at work over the past 30 years are innumerable. What those family members and significant others saw was the passion for discovery and the excitement of finding and telling others about a better way of doing things in small businesses or explaining small business. For all of the network, and especially the authors, that support was the critical enduring ingredient in making *Entrepreneurial Small Business* a reality. For that reason, we want to recognize the enormous emotional and motivational contributions made by Dave Peters, James F. Amrhein, Nora L. Peterson, Josh Katz, Lauren Katz, and Cheryl Nietfeldt.

BRIEF CONTENTS

CONTENTS

1

PART ONE

Entrepreneurs and Ideas: The Basis of Small Business

CHAPTER

1

Small Business: Varieties and Impacts

● Robin Rath of Pixel Press with kids drawing games to go into Pixel Press. How did he use his passion for video gaming to help him find his business idea?
Pixel Press

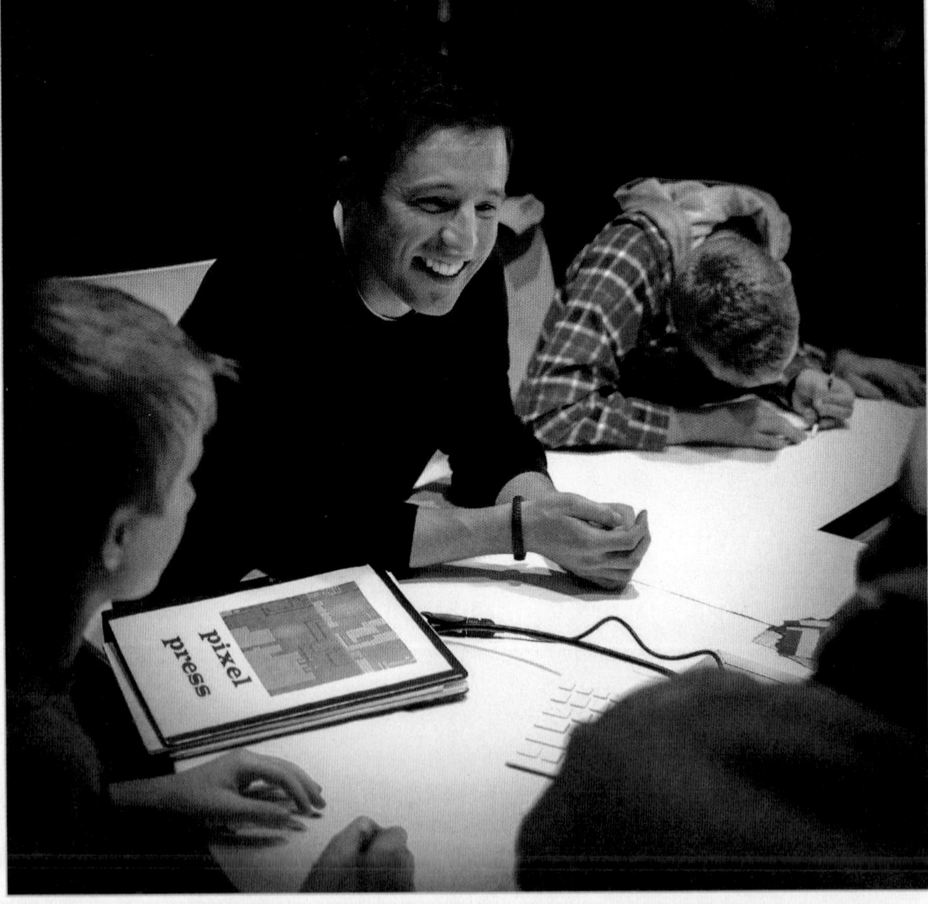

LEARNING OBJECTIVES

LO

After you complete this chapter, you will be able to:

LO 1-1 Understand the scope of small business in the United States.

LO 1-2 Differentiate between small businesses and high-growth ventures.

LO 1-3 Dispel key myths about small businesses.

LO 1-4 Identify actions key to becoming a small business owner.

LO 1-5 Recognize how small businesses are important to our economy and your community.

LO 1-6 Recognize the seven key strategies of the entrepreneurial way.

Focus on Small Business: Robin Rath, Pixel Press[1]

When Robin Rath was a kid, he was an avid player of video games like Metroid and Super Mario Brothers, and when he wasn't playing he was designing new levels of his favorite games in his head and on paper. But he realized that video gaming was part art and part programming, and that helped him set his course. Following an undergraduate degree from Saint Louis University (SLU) bridging communications technology with fine and studio arts, he was positioned to realize his dream.

But game producers were thin on the ground in St. Louis, so Robin's strategy was to find jobs to hone his programming skills during the day and create his own firm, Roundthird, to develop games as his side gig on nights and weekends. His main work included stints at increasingly responsible and demanding positions at six different companies in the programming and marketing industries in St. Louis. Meanwhile, he and his Roundthird partner, Jon Gettys, released Radial 50 for IOS, a circular takeoff on the classic Breakout brick-breaking video game. Robin's day and side gigs helped him develop the in-depth knowledge of programming, project planning, marketing, and networking which convinced him that given the right idea, he would be ready to go full time as an entrepreneur.

The idea that led to full-time entrepreneurship was Pixel Press, a piece of software for iPhones and iPads that would let regular people with no programming skills create playable games reminiscent of Super Mario on their Apple devices. While the idea was ambitious, it was possible, and as he got word out, Pixel Press got favorable press from *NBC News*, *CNET*, *Fast Company,* and others. Building on this, Robin created a Kickstarter campaign to crowdfund his dream. You can see the campaign and watch the original pitch at **www.kickstarter.com/projects/robinrath/pixel-press-draw-your-own-video-game**. The campaign was successful, topping $100,000. With that money and with what he had saved, Pixel Press made it to market. Within two years, Pixel Press announced a partnership with Cartoon Network (CN) resulting in the Adventure Time Game Wizard, which would let players create games with CN characters. From the success of that partnership, Pixel Press went on to release its next product that represented its first foray into toys and gaming, forming partnerships with Mattel and Disney to bring products to store shelves in the United States and internationally.

In speaking with Robin, he credits a constant presence of an entrepreneurial spirit around him from a young age and throughout his education: "Both of my parents were entrepreneurs and encouraged me early on in things like 'baseball card shops' not just in our basement but online as well, when making a website was still very hard. At SLU, I spent all four years as an intern in the Entrepreneurial Studies department and helped coordinate one of the country's first entrepreneurial awards hosted by SLU—the Global Student Entrepreneur Awards (GSEA). Seeing college students win $10,000 to help their business start was inspiring." Robin adds, "This also has motivated me to stay active with the Entrepreneurship Club at SLU, including all the work they do over the summer with high school students. Ultimately we are learning every day, and staying engaged at all levels helps me stay fresh and grounded."

DISCUSSION QUESTIONS

1. Do you think Robin was originally thinking about starting a business when he was working in programming and marketing positions in other people's companies?
2. What drove Robin to start a business of his own?
3. How important were contacts and connections to the growth of Robin's business?
4. Do you think Robin would credit his step-by-step approach with the success of his business? What is your opinion?

LO **1-1** Understand the scope of small business in the United States.

small business
Involves 1–50 people and has its owner managing the business on a day-to-day basis.

self-efficacy
A person's belief in his or her ability to achieve a goal.

Starting an Entrepreneurial Small Business: Four Key Ideas

Robin's story makes a simple point—you can start a **small business**, and there are ways to help you be a success at it. Consider the four key things that Robin did right:

1. **Believe that you can do this:** Robin's belief in himself and what needed to be done to make Pixel Press's app powered his efforts. That belief in yourself is called **self-efficacy**, and learning how to start a business in this class and from this book will help you build it for yourself.[2] Those who believe in themselves and in the passion of their beliefs are more likely to keep at it until they succeed.
2. **Planning + Action = Success:** A plan without action is futile. Actions without plans are usually wasted. Success comes from having the right sort of plan to get you to the right actions as quickly as possible. Like Robin, those who plan and act are the ones who most often succeed.[3]
3. **Help helps:** Successful entrepreneurs learn—from other entrepreneurs, from experts in their chosen field, from potential customers, or even from their professors![4] Skill Module 1.1 will help you find some of the best sources of help on the web. Remember, those who get help succeed bigger and more often.
4. **Do well. Do good:** In the long run, you will depend on partners, investors, employees, customers, and neighbors. If you always remember, as Robin has, to do good for others as you try to do well in your business, you'll feel better about your business and life, and those around you will too.[5]

entrepreneur
A person who owns or starts an organization, such as a business.

Entrepreneurial Small Business believes in the power of those four ideas, and we'll help you understand each of them and how to use them to make your entrepreneurial dreams come true. There are literally millions of those entrepreneurial dreams out there because there are so many ways to become an **entrepreneur**. Almost every year, while more than 400,000 new firms with employees are created, there can be 10 to 15 times that many new owner-only firms, so it is safe to say that there are 6 million new firms a year, and yours can be one of them.[6]

The Small Business Online Scavenger Hunt

SKILL MODULE 1.1

It can be mind-boggling to discover how much material is on the web ready to help aspiring entrepreneurs. To help you get a feel for what is out there, we have put together a web scavenger hunt focusing on key information. In a few cases you may have to register, but all registrations for websites listed here are free. Along the way you will get to peruse some of the "best of the best" entrepreneurship information on the web.

1. If you wanted to find stories about business in Albuquerque (or run the name of a business from there to see what it has done), which site would give you the biggest selection of local stories? **www.bizjournals.com**, **www.usatoday.com/money/business**, **www.wsj.com**.
2. Which of the following sites offers you a free online business plan maker? **www.usa.gov/business**, **www.sba.gov**, **www.entrepreneur.com**.
3. Which site can connect you to *free* local help for starting and growing your business? **www.nfib.com**, **www.sba.gov**, **www.inc.com**.
4. You can search for patents for free at **www.google.com/patents** or **www.uspto.gov**. Which will also let you search for trademarks?
5. If you want to find out what the profit margins are for businesses in the restaurant industry, which site would give you the answer? **www.sba.gov**, **www.entrepreneur.com**, **www.bizstats.com**.

By the time you have checked out these sites, you will be up to speed on some of the largest and most credible sets of free, high-quality small business information available today.

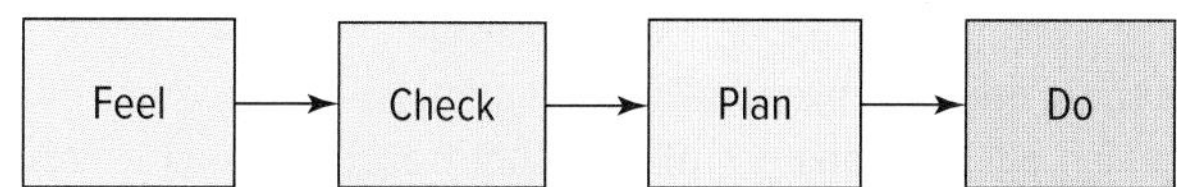

FIGURE 1.1
The Entrepreneurial Process

The vast majority of new firms go through similar start-up processes. The firms most likely to be successful follow a four-step process, shown in Figure 1.1.

- **Feel:** This is where the entrepreneur has a feeling–about maybe starting a business or maybe creating a particular product or service. This is what starts the founding process. We'll talk about entrepreneurs and the feelings leading to their business in Chapter 2.
- **Check:** Smart entrepreneurs check the likelihood for success of their idea through feasibility analyses (see Chapter 4) or customer development processes (see Chapter 9), repeating these until they have a winning and saleable idea.
- **Plan:** Getting from the idea to the business can be done by small-scale, part-time start-ups (see Chapter 5), lean business practices approaches (see Chapter 9), pilot testing (see Chapter 4), business modeling, or business plan creation (see Chapter 8).
- **Do:** Regardless of the type of planning approach you choose to implement your business activity, you will find that you need to refine your approach until you have a successful firm, including additional rounds of refinement and revising.

Entrepreneurs Are Everywhere

In addition to Robin Rath of Pixel Press, the United States had 15.5 million other full-time entrepreneurs working in 2015, according to the U.S. Census Bureau.[7] If we include people pursuing their entrepreneurial dreams on a part-time basis, we need to add another 50 million people.[8] What were they doing? Just about everything! Entrepreneurs could be found in almost every type of work there is, literally in hundreds of **occupations**. In fact, there are occupations

occupation
The type of activity a person does regularly for pay.

TABLE 1.1 The Top 10 Occupations for Entrepreneurs[9]

Top 10 Occupations with the Highest Number of Entrepreneurs		Top 10 Occupations with the Highest Percentage of Entrepreneurs	
Owner-managers	1,694,434	Farmers and Ranchers	86.4%
Construction	1,043,176	Medical Practitioners	75.2
Farmers	1,019,727	Movie Projectionists	72.6
Retailers	683,623	Artists	70.2
Drivers	450,709	Entertainers and Athletes	66.8
Child Care Workers	402,267	Salespeople	56.9
Real Estate Agents	376,834	Landscape Managers	56.3
Wholesalers	373,099	Photographers	56.2
Maintenance Workers	342,689	Service Managers	53.6
Lawyers	310,390	Furniture Finishers	52.9

Source: U.S. Census Bureau, Current Population Survey, March 2015, custom computation using DataFerrett by Jerome Katz.

goods or services
The tangible things (goods) or intangible commodities (services) created for sale.

firm
An organization that sells to or trades with others.

novelty
Characterized by being different or new.

imitative
Characterized by being like or copying something that already exists.

self-employed
Working for yourself.

founders
People who create or start new businesses.

franchise
A prepackaged business bought, rented, or leased from a company called a *franchisor*.

buyers
People who purchase an existing business.

heir
A person who becomes an owner through inheriting or being given a stake in a family business.

composed mostly of entrepreneurs. Table 1.1 shows the 10 occupations with the largest numbers of entrepreneurs as well as the 10 occupations with the highest percentages of entrepreneurs. Note that "owner-managers" are an occupation in their own right, but can appear in any other industry.

Notice that while there are entrepreneur-rich occupations that require college and even graduate school, there are also occupations popular with entrepreneurs with very basic entry requirements. What is most important here is finding something you want to do. When you decide on what your business is going to be, you are choosing your occupation. As the entrepreneur, you may be the owner of the business, but your occupation will depend on what type of **goods or services** you and your **firm** are producing. So the owner of an online store is a retailer, while the owner of a construction firm will be a construction manager. Robin Rath is an app maker because Pixel Press makes apps that he sells online. Whatever you want to do, there is probably a way to do it as an entrepreneur.

Truly entrepreneurial businesses are characterized by **novelty** in their products, services, or business models. Small businesses, on the other hand, are **imitative** in nature, with most small firms doing what other firms do, with only slight variations. But when we think about the people who start firms, the situations they face are situations of novelty. So whether he or she starts the successor to Amazon.com or the pizzeria on the corner, the person who starts a business is living the life of the entrepreneur. We recognize this distinction and address the challenges facing entrepreneurs, while focusing on the small businesses they plan to create or enter.

In *Entrepreneurial Small Business* we use the popular broad definition of *entrepreneur*[10]—anyone who owns a business is an entrepreneur. This, of course, means anyone who is a small business owner is an entrepreneur.[11] It also means that the **self-employed**, anyone who works for himself or herself instead of for others, is also an entrepreneur. As noted above, according to the Census Bureau, there were about 15.5 million full-time self-employed people in 2015. Including entrepreneurs who worked part time in 2015 added over another 50 million people to the number. Within the population of entrepreneurs, it is sometimes useful to split out certain groups. One of these is **founders**, the people who start a business, whether it is one of their own devising or a **franchise**, which is a prepackaged business you buy or lease from a franchisor. Other groups consist of **buyers**, those who purchase an existing business, or of **heirs**, those who inherit or are given a stake in the family business. These roles deal with the entry stage of

Entrepreneurs can be found in nearly every line of work there is. Into what occupation would your business put you?

ColorBlind Images/Blend Images LLC
Hero Images/Getty Images
Hero Images/Getty Images
Andersen Ross/Blend Images LLC

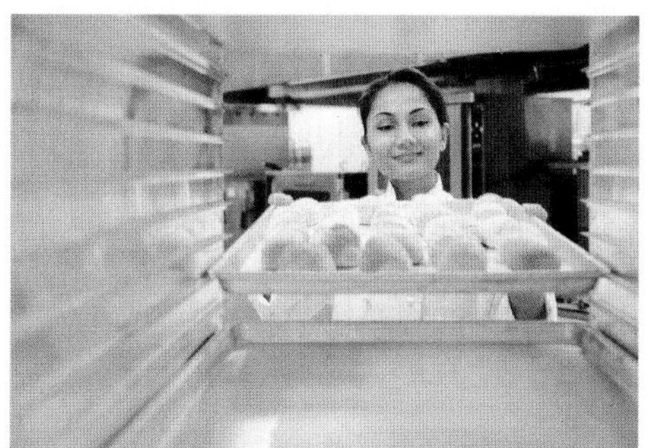

the business from the perspective of the entrepreneur. After entry, another role emerges, that of the owner-manager, the role in which most entrepreneurs spend their working lives. Throughout this text the terms *small business owner, entrepreneur,* and *self-employed* are used interchangeably. When founders or buyers or post-entry owner-managers are discussed, we specify which one is the focus.

CSI: Entrepreneurship

Notice that our definition of *entrepreneur* doesn't specify if the business is for-profit or nonprofit. The fact is that starting either type of organization involves the entrepreneurial process of founding. Self-employed founders of firms are involved in what we call **independent entrepreneurship**.

Founders of nonprofit organizations or for-profit **social ventures** are pursuing **social entrepreneurship.** These efforts involve creating new charitable and civic organizations that are financially self-sufficient like Bangladesh's Grameen Bank (which won the 2006 Nobel Peace Prize for making banking services designed to help the poor manage their money better), or for-profit companies that use much of their profit to fund charities such as Tom's Shoes with its "One for One" philosophy where for every pair of shoes you buy it donates a pair to children in need. Many people also include the founders of charities. When the social entrepreneur's focus is more specifically on the planet and ecological issues, we call it **sustainable entrepreneurship** or **green entrepreneurship**.

independent entrepreneurship
The form of entrepreneurship in which a person or group owns a for-profit business.

social ventures
Businesses that are organized as for-profit entities but are also solving or supporting solutions to social problems.

social entrepreneurship
The form of entrepreneurship involving the creation of self-sustaining charitable and civic organizations, for-profit organizations that invest significant profits in charitable activities, or the creators of nonprofit charitable or service organizations.

sustainable entrepreneurship
An approach to operating a firm or a line of business that identifies, creates, and exploits opportunities to make a profit in a way that can minimize the depletion of natural resources, maximize the use of a recycled material, or improve the environment.

green entrepreneurship
Another term for sustainable entrepreneurship taken from the popular belief that green is the color of a healthy environment, as in forests or fields.

corporate entrepreneurship The form of entrepreneurship that takes place in existing businesses around new products, services, or markets.

Economists talk about yet another type of entrepreneur, innovative individuals who are employed by others in existing companies. Such people are pursuing **corporate entrepreneurship** and estimates put the number of corporate entrepreneurs at about 80 percent that of self-employed entrepreneurs, or nearly 12 million Americans. In corporate entrepreneurship, the focus is typically on bringing new products or services to market, or opening up new markets for your firm. Famous examples of corporate entrepreneurship include the creation of new brands like Apple's iPhone or GM's green energy services. Companies rapidly expanding geographically, like Panera Bread or Planet Fitness, would also be a visible example depending on corporate entrepreneurs to open up new areas to their offerings.

CSI entrepreneurship Acronym for the three forms of entrepreneurship: corporate, social, and independent.

forms of entrepreneurship The settings in which the entrepreneurial effort takes place.

Together, corporate, social, and independent entrepreneurship represent what might be called **CSI entrepreneurship** or the three **forms of entrepreneurship**[12] and people move among the three forms more often than you might think. Consider Jim McKelvey, cofounder of Square.[13] You've probably paid for something with your credit card and had it swiped through a Square device. But Square was just another step along a winding, entrepreneurial path. After McKelvey graduated college (degrees in economics and computer science), he launched Mira, a software company. But Mira didn't make any money for its first five years, so McKelvey was forced to support himself by working as a glass artist. "Ironically, the only business I ever pursued primarily for the money was glassblowing." McKelvey recalls, "I became a glass artist simply to pay the bills. All the other organizations were created to solve a problem. I have always found problems to be the best motivators."

After Mira began to succeed, McKelvey was able to stop working in the studio just for the money, but continued to practice glassblowing as an artistic hobby. But glassblowing studios are rare and Jim was frustrated at the lack of access to both the tools and techniques. He resigned as CEO of Mira and cofounded Third Degree Glass Factory so he and others would have a place to create glass art in St. Louis. Third Degree pioneered the model combining education, production, and entertainment.

In 2006 Third Degree achieved international recognition after housing the Glass Art Society's annual conference, but by this time McKelvey's focus was on the problems of running a business and not making art. In 2008, Jim reconnected with one of Mira's early employees, Jack

Jim McKelvey has demonstrated CSI entrepreneurship as a cofounder of Third Degree Glass Factory, a makerspace for artists. He was cofounder of Square, and the person who created the iconic Square credit card reader. After Square's IPO, he served as a corporate entrepreneur. He also started LaunchCode, a nonprofit that teaches coding for free and helps graduates get jobs. His role there was as a social entrepreneur. You can see a video of McKelvey discussing this at **www.youtube.com/watch?v=wZFBvwm_CrY**.

Carl Juste/Miami Herald/TNS/Newscom
Jim McKelvey
Dawn Majors/St. Louis Post-Dispatch/MCT/Newscom

Dorsey, who had recently left the company he created, Twitter. Jim and Jack decided to pursue Jim's idea of a fair payment system for small merchants, and called the new company *Square*. Square created a series of products focused on economic empowerment and by its 10th birthday was a public company valued at over $30 billion.

With Square up and running, McKelvey again turned his attention to another serious problem: the perpetual shortage of programmers. His idea to combine *guaranteed* job placement with free education led him to found a nonprofit called LaunchCode. LaunchCode has trained and employed thousands of people and is opening centers around the nation.

As LaunchCode began to fulfill its mission, McKelvey again handed over the management to others and turned his focus to other social problems. He is now a director of the St. Louis Federal Reserve, where Jim shares his entrepreneurial skills with the people running our economy. He is also involved in several projects to help rebuild St. Louis as a vibrant, welcoming city. "I have never really had a career," McKelvey says, "just a series of problems that I care about in different areas of my life. Sometimes the solution is a for-profit company, sometimes a nonprofit charity, and sometimes it's government. But in each case the tools of entrepreneurship create new solutions."

Jim McKelvey's story also shows the two kinds of motivation we often see driving most entrepreneurs. One type is based on entrepreneurs who are going into business to improve themselves financially or to launch an improved product or service into the market. This is called **opportunity-driven entrepreneurship** and is evident in Jim's problem-solving efforts in starting Square and LaunchCode. The other type is where the person becomes an entrepreneur because he or she does not see any workable prospects for getting employed by someone else. This is called **necessity-driven entrepreneurship**. For Jim when graduating college, getting jobs as a glassblower was difficult, so his best way to pursue that dream was to co-create Third Degree Glass.

opportunity-driven entrepreneurship
Creating a firm to improve one's income or a product or service.

necessity-driven entrepreneurship
Creating a firm as an alternative to unemployment.

LEARN MORE ONLINE

Learn more about the topics above at these sites:

Corporate entrepreneurship: Early To Rise, **www.earlytorise.com/corporate-entrepreneurship/**

Social entrepreneurship: Ashoka, **www.ashoka.org/en-US**

Independent entrepreneurship: *Entrepreneur* magazine, **www.entrepreneur.com/**

Entrepreneurship Elsewhere

As important as entrepreneurship is in the United States, it is more important elsewhere. While in any given year about 10 percent of the workforce in the United States is self-employed or contemplating starting their own business, the rates in other parts of the world can be 50 percent or even 100 percent higher than in the United States. There is a pattern (see Figure 1.2) to which countries are likely to have high rates of entrepreneurship, and which will have lower rates.[14]

- In nations where there is little manufacturing, most industry relates to farming and extracting raw materials, such as mining and forestry. In these **factor-driven economies** such as Pakistan, Jamaica, and Venezuela, entrepreneurship is essential to helping build personal wealth and breaking the cycle of low-wage jobs, and entrepreneurship levels are very high.
- As economies develop and go beyond basic manufacturing to a more industrialized economy as is seen in countries such as Russia, Brazil, and China, it is called an **efficiency-driven economy**. In these nations, entrepreneurship becomes a key way to build the middle class, and a growing retail and wholesale sector grows alongside businesses serving the needs of large industrial concerns. Entrepreneurship levels in such economies are in the middle range.

factor-driven economy
A nation where the major forces for jobs, revenues, and taxes come from farming or extractive industries like forestry, mining, or oil production.

efficiency-driven economy
A nation where industrialization is becoming the major force providing jobs, revenues, and taxes, and where minimizing costs while maximizing productivity (i.e., efficiency) is a major goal.

FIGURE 1.2

Early-Stage Entrepreneurial Activity for 15 Nations in 2015, by Phase of Economic Development

Source: Custom tabulation of *2015–2016 GEM Global Report*, Table 5, p. 130, by Jerome Katz and Richard Green.

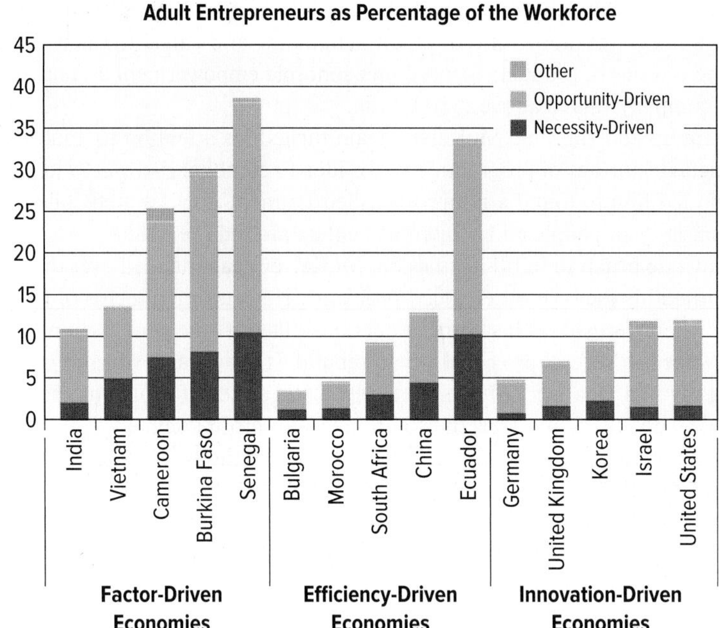

innovation-driven economy
A nation where the major forces for jobs, revenues, and taxes come from high-value-added production based on new ideas and technologies and from professional services based on higher education.

- **Innovation-driven economies** are focused on high-value-added manufacturing but are marked by a very large service sector providing high-end services to not only the resident population but also for export. Examples of such countries include Germany, the Republic of Korea, and the United States. Entrepreneurship levels in these countries average the lowest of the three types of economies.

The lesson here is that entrepreneurship is happening around the globe in virtually all types of economies, and as global trade (both face-to-face and web-based) increases, the impact of global entrepreneurship will be increasingly faced by entrepreneurs and their firms everywhere.

LEARN MORE ONLINE

Learn more about the topics above at these sites:

Global entrepreneurship: Global Entrepreneurship Monitor, **www.gemconsortium.org/**

Global entrepreneurship: Organization for Economic Cooperation and Development (OECD), **www.oecd.org/sdd/business-stats/**

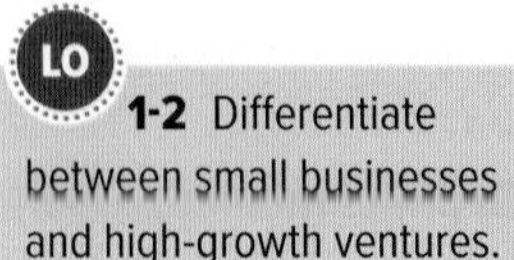
1-2 Differentiate between small businesses and high-growth ventures.

The Many Types of Entrepreneurial Small Businesses

small and medium enterprise (SME)
The international term for a small business.

You might be surprised to know that even with 15.5 million entrepreneurs out there, the number of firms is even greater–30.2 million in 2015![15] These firms are called many different things, such as **small and medium enterprises (SMEs)**, **independent small businesses**, or **owner-managed firms**. However they are labeled, there are more firms than entrepreneurs because many entrepreneurs become **serial entrepreneurs**[16] by starting additional businesses after their first one. As we will see a bit further into the chapter, this enormous population of

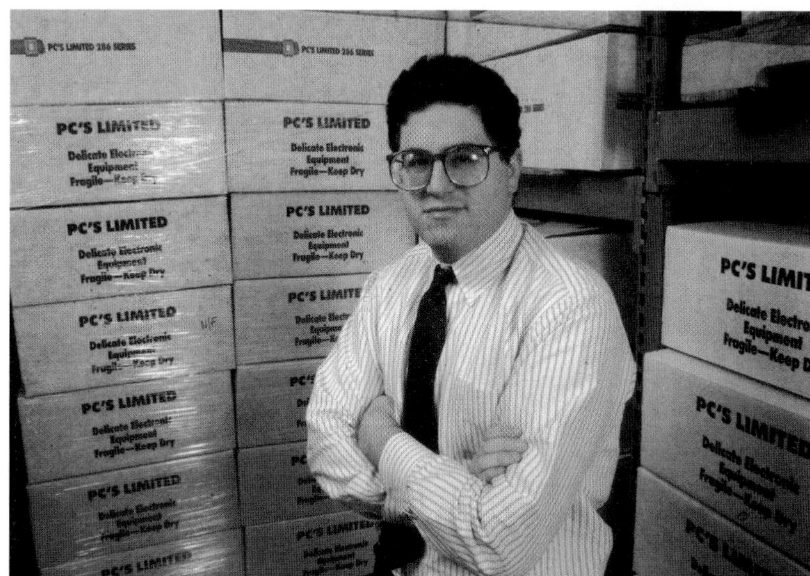

Michael Dell is well known now as the CEO of Dell Inc., a major industry leader in PC production. Before his success, though, Dell spearheaded at least three other much smaller businesses. What factors do you think led to Dell's decision to expand his earlier ventures and eventually to his successful capturing of the PC market?

Peter Silva/ZUMAPRESS/Newscom

small businesses is one of the major forces in the U.S. economy. But for now, just realize that you can pursue many dreams as an entrepreneur. No one is limiting you to just one. And after your first business, there is no telling how far you can go. Consider a nine-year-old Texan named Michael.

Michael started selling collectible stamps through the mail.[17] He typed his catalog one key at a time since he had never learned to type, and he made $2,000. His next business was selling newspaper subscriptions by phone from home; he made $18,000 on this venture. His third business was reselling IBM PCs from his dorm room at the University of Texas at a time when IBM was trying to limit sales to official IBM dealers like Sears and IBM's own personal computer stores.[18] It was Michael's fourth business, selling PCs, that we know today as Dell Inc. The nine-year-old was Michael Dell.

Michael Dell's four businesses point up the difference between small businesses and high-growth ventures. Both may be small when they start. However, small businesses are usually intended to remain small, generally a size that the owner feels comfortable controlling personally. For Michael Dell, his stamp, newspaper, and IBM PC resale businesses were designed to be small-scale operations that he could handle alone. He did everything himself, and he worked when he wanted to. The businesses were fairly conventional, with dozens or even hundreds of competitors all imitating one another.

High-growth ventures start small but are intended to grow rapidly, often requiring a team of partners or managers to handle the growth. When Dell got serious about the upgraded PC business, he created a company and started hiring others to help out. He moved from his dorm room to a commercial location, kept open regular hours, and started thinking about putting together a much bigger operation. That much bigger operation is the Dell Inc. known worldwide today. While the computer business as a whole was established, Dell's approach to assembly from highly standardized (and therefore low-cost) parts was fairly revolutionary, as was his use of mail-order and later telephone and web-based ordering. In his fourth business, Dell led the industry because of his **innovativeness**, and others imitated him.

The differences between small businesses and high-growth ventures aren't just semantic, they're fundamental, as shown in Table 1.2.

independent small business
A business owned by an individual or small group.

owner-managed firm
A business run by the individual who owns it.

serial entrepreneur
A person who opens multiple businesses throughout his or her career.

innovativeness
Refers to how important a role new ideas, products, services, processes, or markets play in an organization.

Entrepreneurs and Firm Growth Strategies

When creating his stamp business as a child and Dell Inc. as a young adult, Michael Dell had different goals and ambitions for each of these firms. As you can imagine, that kind of broad

TABLE 1.2 Differences between Small Businesses and High-Growth Ventures

	Small Businesses	High-Growth Ventures
Preferred funding source	Owner's own money	Other people's money
When the firm's in trouble	Cut costs	Sell more
What's more important	Sales	Marketing
Personal control preference	Retain autonomy	Involve key others
Focus	Efficiency	Effectiveness
Meta-strategy	Imitation	Novelty
External control preference	Control firm	Control market
Grow	When necessary	When possible
Human resources	Personalize	Professionalize
Acceptance	Personal validation	External legitimacy
What limits growth	Loss of control	Market response
Delegation orientation	Delegation is difficult	Delegation is essential

overall growth strategy
One of four general ways to position a business based on the rate and level of growth entrepreneurs anticipate for their firm.

lifestyle or part-time firm
A small business primarily intended to provide partial or subsistence financial support for the existing lifestyle of the owner, most often through operations that fit the owner's schedule and way of working.

traditional small business
A firm intended to provide a living income to the owner, and operating in a manner and on a schedule consistent with other firms in the industry and market.

high-performing small business
A firm intended to provide the owner with a high income through sales or profits superior to those of the traditional small business.

high-growth venture
A firm started with the intent of eventually going public, following the pattern of growth and operations of a big business.

unicorns
The most successful high-growth ventures, those with a valuation of $1 billion or more.

approach, called the **overall growth strategy**, represents another driver of the variety of entrepreneurship. The overall growth strategy describes the kind of business the owner or owners would like to have, from the perspective of how fast and to what level they would like the firm to grow. There are four generic growth strategies that account for nearly all businesses:

- **Lifestyle or part-time firms:** These typically have sales of $25,000 a year or less, which provide enough profit or salary to supplement an income but usually not enough on which to live. These businesses start and stay very small, often operating seasonally or when the owner wants to work in the business. Growth in these firms tends to quickly level off after the owners operate long enough to learn the basics of making money in their industry and setting. About 53 percent of all small businesses fall into this category including Michael Dell's first three businesses. (See Figure 1.3.)
- **Traditional small businesses:** These are the smallest full-time businesses, with schedules defined by customer, not owner, needs. Most often, these are one-site businesses with sales of between $25,000 and $100,000. Growth levels off after operations settle into a consistent, money-making pattern, generating enough income to provide a living for the owner and family. Around 22 percent of small businesses fall into this category.
- **High-performing small businesses:** These tend to level off after success defined by sales of between $100,000 and $1,000,000, depending on the industry. These firms grow at rates more like 5 to 15 percent a year, adding employees, and often growing through multiple locations and higher levels of professionalization in order to maximize their profitability over a long term while reaching a plateau that lets them remain manageably small. About 20 percent of businesses fall into this category, including Robin Rath's business.
- **High-growth ventures:** These aim to achieve growth rates of 25 percent or more a year, with sales of more than $1 million. The firms aim to become big businesses and pursue high levels of professionalization and external funding. Such firms represent about 5 percent of all businesses. At the tip of this group are firms called **unicorns**, like Uber and Airbnb, that have valuations of $1 billion or more. In January 2016, there were 174 unicorns in the United States.[19]

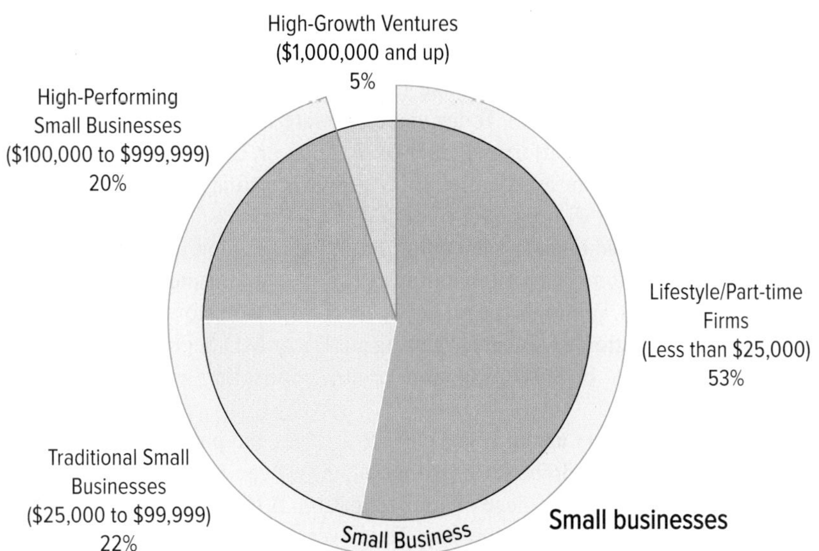

FIGURE 1.3

Types of Firms

Entrepreneurial Small Business focuses on the 95 percent of businesses outside the high-growth sector. These are what are often called **main street businesses** and include the lifestyle firms, the traditional small businesses, and the high-performing small businesses that represent the businesses most of us start and most of us deal with on a day-to-day basis.

main street businesses A popular term for small businesses reflecting the idea that these are the kinds of firms you would expect to find on the main street of a typical American city, and are the opposite of big business or "Wall Street" businesses.

LEARN MORE ONLINE

Learn more about the topics above at these sites:

Start-up businesses: Kauffman Indicators of Entrepreneurship, **https://indicators.kauffman.org/**

Main street businesses: Kauffman Index of Main Street Entrepreneurship, **www.kauffman.org/historical-kauffman-index/reports** (ended with 2017 data)

Data on small businesses: SBA's statistics page, **www.sba.gov/advocacy/firm-size-data**

Myths about Small Businesses

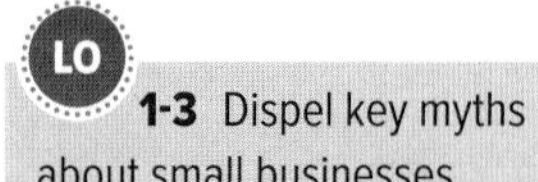
1-3 Dispel key myths about small businesses.

Here is a sobering truth: Although 56 percent of U.S. youth 15–25 years old polled in 2010 expressed an interest in becoming entrepreneurs, only 14.7 percent were actually doing anything to get a business started by 2018.[20] The challenges of small business scare off or derail people. For years potential entrepreneurs have mentioned problems like these:

- There's not enough financing.
- To make profits, you need to make something.
- If you fail, you can never try again.
- Students don't have the skills to start a business.
- Ninety percent of all new businesses fail within two years.

Over the past 10 years small business experts in academia and government have studied small business and potential entrepreneurs and learned that a lot of the challenges scaring people away from small business are the stuff of urban legends. Let's look at these five problems with the latest information.

1. **There's not enough financing:** The SBA reported that in its last survey of business owners almost 40 percent of solo entrepreneurs started their businesses with less than $5,000.[21] The SBA also reports that bank financing has been rising for 10 years, and the same is true for

crowdfunding
Funding a business online through the collective involvement of others who provide donations, loans, or investments.

P2P lending
Loans made from one or more individuals to the entrepreneur, rather than through a conventional bank. This can be as simple as a loan to a friend, or formally handled through a dedicated P2P website.

drop-shipping
A business in which you sell items in person or online, but you hold no inventory. You refer sales to a third party who handles the shipping, and very often the financial transaction, in your name.

bootstrapping
Using low-cost or free techniques to minimize your cost of doing business.

George Foreman: boxer to entrepreneur.

Cathrin Mueller/Bongarts/Getty Images

funding from family, friends, and angels.[22] New sources of financing like **crowdfunding** sites Kickstarter.com (which Robin Rath used in the vignette at the start of the chapter) and Indiegogo.com or **P2P lending** sites like Lendingclub.com or Upstart.com are providing alternatives to traditional banks.[23] Today you can create websites, blogs, and **drop-shipping** businesses for free using platforms like Wix, Weebly, or Ucraft[24] while **bootstrapping**[25] techniques like making your local coffee shop into your virtual office are increasingly popular as ways to get started without a lot of cash.

2. **To make profits, you need to make something:** From the recession in 2011 to 2015, Sageworks reported that of the 10 most profitable industries for small businesses, 9 were services like dentists, tax preparers, mining support services, credit counselors, insurance brokers, and legal and health practitioners. Whereas getting a DDS or MD degree takes years and tens of thousands of dollars, bookkeeping and credit counseling require little specialized training.[26]
3. **If you fail, you can never try again:** If you close a business and pay off your debts, you did not fail. If you learned how to do better next time, then you can honestly say you have paid (in dollars and hours) for another piece of your education. A large number of today's successful entrepreneurs had failures along the way. Today vegetarians who frequent restaurants are thankful for Paul Wenner's Gardenburgers, but few realize that Paul learned the food business by owning a restaurant that eventually went out of business. Other famous failures include Ray Kroc (famous for McDonald's, failed at real estate), Henry Ford (two failed auto companies before making Ford), and the founders of California Pizza Kitchens, Rick Rosenfield and Larry Flax, who previously failed at screenwriting, a regular Italian restaurant, and a mobile skateboard park.[27]
4. **Students (or moms or some other group) don't have the skills to start a business:**[28] It would be hard for an undergraduate to open a medical practice (watch *Doogie Howser, MD,* on Hulu.com if you want to see what this might have been like), but lots of students have useful business skills. If you are a student, you probably have a good idea what other students want to buy or have. That is the start of a retail business with a student market. If you have negotiating skills, the sky is the limit in retail and wholesaling, especially for products you already understand (T-shirts, energy drinks, backpacks, textbooks, etc.). In fact, you may have high-level but undocumented skills in developing websites or programming (like the founders of Facebook or Yahoo!). Competitions like the Global Student Entrepreneur Awards (www.gsea.org) or other award programs (Google "young entrepreneur competition" to find them) showcase dozens of highly successful students who started and grew their businesses. Any mompreneur has managed a household, negotiated for family purchases, and solved thousands of problems ranging from broken equipment to angry family members. It was more than enough to get Mary Kay's Mary Kay Ash, Body Shop's Anita Roddick, or Baby Einstein's Julie Aigner Clark started in small businesses that grew to be big ones. The same is true for any group–second career entrepreneurs include Josie Natori (investment banking to Natori lingerie), Jim Koch (consulting to brewing Samuel Adams beer), or George Foreman (boxer to entrepreneur).
5. **Ninety percent of all new businesses fail within two years:** This statement is wrong in two major ways. First, the percentage is wrong. Studies show that 69 percent of businesses are still going after 2 years, 51 percent are still going at 5 years, 34 percent make it past 10 years, and 25 percent survive 15 years. Second, looking at the businesses that close, the vast majority close but don't fail. Only one firm in three that closes was considered financially unsuccessful by its owner.[29]

Small Business Administration (SBA)
A part of the U.S. government that provides support and advocacy for small businesses.

Myths like these hold back many potential entrepreneurs. Knowing the truth is a powerful way to keep up your motivation for the undeniably tough work of starting your own business. When you encounter doomsayers, check out the facts at reputable sites like the U.S. **Small Business Administration (SBA)** at www.sba.gov (especially its FAQs) or in entrepreneur-focused magazines like *Inc., Fast Company,* or *Entrepreneur.* There you will find the facts you need, and the support and advice that underlies the idea that help helps.

LEARN MORE ONLINE

Learn more about the topics above at these sites:

SBA's small business FAQs: **www.sba.gov/advocacy/frequently-asked-questions-about-small-business**

SBA's small business finance FAQs: **www.sba.gov/sites/default/files/Finance-FAQ-2016_WEB.pdf**

Google search for reviews of free website companies: **www.google.com/search?q=free+websites+builder&oq=free+websites+builder**

Getting Started Now: Entry Competencies

LO **1-4** Identify actions key to becoming a small business owner.

There are a million things you *could* do to start a business, but which ones are best? Sometimes the answer will come to you in the form of an opportunity or offer, and sometimes you'll need to take the first steps yourself. In order to start a business, you need four elements to come together–boundary, resources, intention, and exchange.[30] This is referred to as the BRIE model, as shown in Figure 1.4.

A business needs the benefits of a *boundary*–something that sets it up as a firm, and sets it off from the buying or selling or bartering we all do occasionally. A boundary can be something as simple as a business name or government registration, a phone or email address dedicated to the business, or a specific location for the firm in a home, commercial space, or even on the Internet. Having a boundary gives you a place to locate and protect the resources you've gathered for the business. *Resources* include the product or service to be offered, informational resources on markets and running a business, financial resources, and human resources such as your own time to devote to the business or that of others working with you or for you.

Intention is the desire to start a business and is the most frequently occurring element of the BRIE model. Those 56 percent of young Americans who think about starting their own business are expressing their intentions. *Exchange* is also needed. This refers to moving resources, goods, or service to others in exchange for money or other resources. If the firm doesn't exchange with its environment, there is no "business" taking place.

The BRIE model factors outline the activities that need to take place to get a firm going. Skill Module 1.2 is a self-assessment that can help you recognize what important steps you have taken to start your business, and what remains to be done.

The BRIE model can help you deal with one of the biggest hurdles to starting a business. According to the experts, the biggest problem is simply inaction, as mentioned earlier. Stanford management professors Jeff Pfeffer and Bob Sutton[31] say that even when people know taking action would be in their own best interests, most people tend to procrastinate, sticking with inaction or doing familiar things that have not worked. Pfeffer and Sutton recommend taking small steps toward a goal as an easy way to start. The BRIE checklist gives you the kind of small steps that can make all the difference. Consider coming back to this checklist periodically to help assess your preparations for business and determine what you still need to do. Taking lots of small steps is a sure way to achieve your goals.

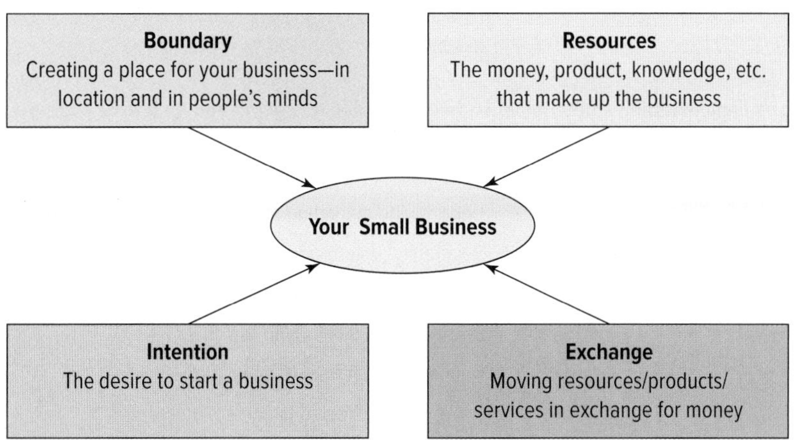

FIGURE 1.4

Four Elements Needed to Get Your Business Started (BRIE)

SKILL MODULE 1.2 BRIE Self-Assessment

The BRIE (boundary-resources-intention-exchange) model is a proven[32] and handy way to think about the activities necessary to get a business started. It also is a model that will come up again in later chapters of this book. How many of the items have you done so far to get your business started the right way?

The complete list of BRIE activities is given in the following table. Look at the BRIE list and check off actions you've taken already. Next to each item in parentheses are references that tell you in which chapter that topic is covered, in case you want to skip ahead to see how we suggest you do it. This exercise can help you think through which chapters are **most** important to you in preparing your business.

The list can also be scored as a checklist. Go through the list and check off which items you have already done in starting a business. Then write in the first column how many items of each BRIE category you've done so far. Once you are finished, you can see how to score the BRIE checklist at the end of the skill module.

BRIE Checklist

Boundary—creating a place for your business in space and in people's minds	
Number of boundary actions done	☐ Opening a bank account for the business (Ch. 13) ☐ Registering the business name with the state (Ch. 17) ☐ Creating business cards and/or stationery (Ch. 10) ☐ Purchasing a domain name (Ch. 10) ☐ Creating a business website (Ch. 10) ☐ Obtaining a business telephone line (Ch. 1) ☐ Identifying a place for the business at home or elsewhere (Ch. 11)
Resources—the things that make up the business, like money, products, knowledge, etc.	
Number of resource actions done	☐ Organizing a start-up team (Ch. 18) ☐ Obtaining copyright, patents, trademarks (Ch. 17) ☐ Purchasing raw materials, inventory, supplies (Ch. 15) ☐ Acquiring major items (equipment, facilities, property) (Ch. 15) ☐ Hiring employees and managers (who do not share ownership) (Ch. 18) ☐ Participating in classes or workshops on starting a business (If you are taking a small business course, you can check this item.) ☐ Participating in programs that help new businesses get established like SIFE, CEO, or SBIDA
Intention—demonstrating a determination to get the business going and for it to be successful	
Number of intention actions taken	☐ Thinking about the business (Ch. 4, 5, & 6) ☐ Undertaking marketing and promotional efforts (Ch. 7 & 10) ☐ Developing your product or service (Ch. 4 & 9) ☐ Beginning your full-time commitment to the business (> 35 hrs/wk) ☐ Preparing a business plan (Ch. 8) ☐ Defining market opportunities (Ch. 4) ☐ Developing projected financial statements (Ch. 7, 12, & 13)

Exchange—making investments in and sales from the business

Number of exchange actions done

- ☐ Generating sales revenue (Ch. 10)
- ☐ Arranging child care to work on business
- ☐ Establishing credit with a supplier (Ch. 14)
- ☐ Saving money to invest in the business (Ch. 12 & 14)
- ☐ Investing money in the business (Ch. 14)
- ☐ Seeking funds from financial institutions or others (Ch. 14)
- ☐ Seeking funds from spouse or household partner (Ch. 14)
- ☐ Seeking funds from current employer (Ch. 14)

The scoring is straightforward. At a minimum you need to have taken at least one action in each of the BRIE categories[33] to successfully start and grow a business. Business survival rates increase with the number of items checked across the different categories.[34] So people who can check three or four items in each BRIE category are more likely to have surviving and growing firms than those who check only one item per category. Having a BRIE category with nothing checked indicates that it is likely that something major is being overlooked, so the business is likely to fail. It is also important to balance BRIE activities. For example, having lots of boundary activities done and only a few exchange ones is likely to lead to an unbalanced approach to business and a lesser chance of survival.

Small Business and the Economy

LO **1-5** Recognize how small businesses are important to our economy and your community.

Small business is vitally important to your community and even to our economy. Part of this comes from the new things small businesses contribute to the economy, particularly new jobs and innovations, as well as the basics that small businesses provide for all of us–jobs, taxes, and products or services.

New Jobs

Since the 1970s big business has cut tens of millions of jobs. In the meantime, small business has added tens of millions of jobs. In the latest statistics, small businesses created 65.9 percent of the new jobs created since 2000.[35] When the Census Bureau looked more closely at the figures, it concluded that small business start-ups in the first two years of operation accounted for virtually all the net new jobs in America.[36] Small business *is* the engine of job generation, but it is important for existing jobs, too. Small businesses employ more than half of all Americans, providing wages, salaries, and the taxes those working people pay the government.[37]

One reason small businesses are a key employer is because they are more willing than most large businesses to offer jobs to people with atypical work histories or needs, like people new to the workforce, people with uneven employment histories, and people looking for part-time work. These employment issues are at the core of what makes small business attractive to local and state governments.

New Ideas

Small business is a key element of every nation's economy because it offers a very special environment in which the new can come into being. Austrian economist Joseph Schumpeter labeled this process **creative destruction.**[38] It refers to the way that newly created goods, services, or firms can hurt existing goods, services, or firms. For example, when a new restaurant opens in your neighborhood, people flock to it to find out what it's like. This helps the new restaurant, but it also causes the

creative destruction The way that newly created goods, services, or firms can hurt existing goods, services, or firms.

Snapchat cofounders Evan Spiegel and Bobby Murphy developed Snapchat's forerunner, Piccolo, while students at Stanford. They refined it and renamed it Snapchat, where it became the favorite social media platform of high schoolers and the industry leader for how to design mobile apps to be maximally involving. What kinds of innovations have you seen that make people say "I just gotta have it!"?

J. Emilio Flores/Corbis/Getty Images

other restaurants in the area to lose business, at least temporarily. One of the most famous examples of creative destruction is the personal computer, which started as a hobby that big business spurned.

Snapchat founders Evan Spiegel, Bobby Murphy, and Reggie Brown came up with one of the first apps that revolutionized how users interacted with their smartphones. Snapchat was designed to be used primarily on smartphones, and made better and more extensive use of smartphone features than anything ever before. While social media websites like Facebook already existed, Snapchat got more users to post, share, and look at more items on mobile screens than anyone ever had before. Instead of making posts permanent, they made posts vanish after being seen. Their innovative uses of smartphone technology (like drawing on top of photos or using gestures for nearly everything) changed how apps were designed, and increased user interaction with their mobile phones beyond what anyone had predicted.

Snapchat's innovations redrew the lines of the entire smartphone app industry, and it also created tremendous new wealth, utility, and innovation. Big business often has trouble with innovations that would eat away at existing business, but small, new businesses are more likely to see new revenues in innovations.

Why do so many innovations come from small business? Small business owners are freer of the judgments and social constraints of workers elsewhere.[39] To give you an idea how much more powerful innovation is in small business, the U.S. Small Business Administration reports that among firms that hold one or more patents, small businesses generate 16 times the number of patents per employee than do big businesses. And the patents produced in those small businesses are twice as likely to be among the top 1 percent of all patents cited by others.[40] That citation is a measure of the importance of the invention.

In the end, the freedom small business gives owners to pursue and perfect their dream creates the innovations from which we all benefit—not just major inventions like the personal computer, but whole classes of products such as snowboards (21-year-old Dimitrije Milovich in 1969),[41] earmuffs (15-year-old Chester Greenwood in 1858),[42] computer-controlled telephone systems (Krisztina Holly in 1992),[43] date rape drug testing coasters (Brian Glover, 35, and Francisco Guerra, 34, in 2002),[44] and Kitty Litter (Ed Lowe, 27, in 1947)[45] that were developed by innovative small business owners.

Think of the innovative contributions of small businesses in general and student-started small businesses in particular. Each group has made a tremendous difference in our industries, our economies, and our lives. Table 1.3 shows examples from both groups in eight different situations.

New Opportunities

People who own their own business are presented with tremendous opportunities—not only to improve their life and wealth, but also to help them move into and upward in the economy and society of the United States. The opportunities small business offers for getting into the economic mainstream of American life makes it attractive to people who foresee problems fitting into existing businesses—not only people with innovative ideas, but immigrants; people facing unusual schedules, demands, or limitations on their lives; and even people who need a second chance.[47] For many such people, small business *is* the best business opportunity.

Small businesses offer communities another type of opportunity—the opportunity to enjoy goods and services. Imagine a neighborhood or town without a grocery store or a pharmacy. In

TABLE 1.3 Major Inventions from Small Businesses and Student-Started Businesses[46]

Where Innovation Is Used	Innovations from Small Businesses	Innovations from Student-Started Small Businesses
Medicine	Heart valves (Demetre Nicoloff)	Video laryngoscope (Aircraft Medical)
Business Processes	Assembly lines (Olds)	JIT PC assembly (Dell)
Computing Hardware	Supercomputers (Cray)	Home computers (Apple)
Computing Software	Relational databases (Oracle)	Social networking (Facebook)
Everyday Technology	Photocopiers (Chester Carlson)	Google
Leisure	Outboard engines (Cameron Waterman)	Snowboards (Dimitrije Milovich)
Fashion	GORE-TEX (W. L. Gore)	Extreme custom nail polish (Dineh Mohajer)
Drinks	Snapple (Arnold Greenberg)	Kombucha (GT Dave)

Sources: *The State of Small Business: A Report of the President, 1994* (Washington, DC: U.S. Government Printing Office, 1995); Meinie Reid, "How a Shop Assistant Saw the Light and Saved Lives," *The Times,* July 17, 2008.

important ways, the town would not seem like a real community. A small grocery store, drugstore, hardware store, or gas station might be able to use its low overhead and capacity to adapt to local needs (e.g., a grocery store stocking a lot of fishing supplies to appeal to visiting fishing enthusiasts) to make a profit where larger chain stores could not.[48] For a small town or a neighborhood to be able to stand on its own, it needs a variety of businesses.[49]

Small businesses provide unexpected opportunities to large businesses and entrepreneurial high-growth firms. High-growth ventures and big businesses are like a giant boat, and where the boat sails, the economy sails along too. But for the boat to work, it has to be supported by deep water. The ocean supporting the boat consists of the tens of millions of small businesses. Without small businesses offering supporting services or offering to subcontract at low cost to the high-growth ventures and big businesses or creating the kinds of communities where creative and entrepreneurial people like to live,[50] those economic boats would lose their buoyancy or profitability and sink like stones. For example, industry giant Procter & Gamble outsourced the making of Ivory and other bar soaps to a small Canadian company, Trillium Health Care Products,[51] saving millions of dollars a year. In addition, big business depends on small business as a source of key ideas for new products. You might think this means high-tech inventions, but there is a lot of money to be made from everyday inventions. Consider the recent drink sensation Kombucha in the following Small Business Insight.

New Markets

One particular type of entrepreneurial opportunity comes from pursuing opportunities in other countries. Buying products or services outside your home country and selling them at home is called **importing**. Taking products and services made in your home country and selling them in other countries is called **exporting**.

importing
Buying products or services from a place not your home country, and selling them in your home country.

exporting
Taking products or services made in your home country and selling them in other countries.

Originally, small business was synonymous with local business. The vast majority of firms sold in their home communities, and it was a very rare firm that sold nationally. Through the beginning of the twentieth century, it was rare for small businesses to sell in any other country.

That is no longer true today. Small businesses account for 33.2 percent of the value of all goods and services exported from the United States, and represent 97.7 percent of all exporting firms. According to the U.S. government there were 280,229 small business exporters in 2016, and the average amount each firm exported was $1,530,891.[52] Generally most of these firms export on the basis of personal ties. An entrepreneur trades with the country of his birth, his

SMALL BUSINESS INSIGHT

SUCCESS: GT DAVE AND KOMBUCHA[53]

GT Dave's mom Laraine was battling breast cancer, and to help his mom at this awful time GT would make her kombucha tea (imagine a slightly bubbly bittersweet dark herbal tea) from the family's recipe. They learned about it through their lifelong involvement in Eastern philosophies. Laraine beat the cancer, and GT decided to offer the tea commercially.

At 15 he started mixing larger quantities of his tea, offering it in bottles and selling it locally in health food stores in his hometown of Los Angeles. He slowly grew the business to other health food stores in his area using nothing but his own money, profits from the business, and a $10,000 loan from his mother. While he tried to stay in high school, it was a tough go, and he left but kept working to get his GED and take community college classes.

Founder GT Dave proudly showing off his Synergy kombucha drink.

Ringo Chiu/ZUMA Wire/Alamy Live News/Alamy Stock Photo

Four years after he started the business, he got his two drink lines (Kombucha and a kombucha and fruit drink line called Synergy) into Whole Foods Stores across California. This watershed would move Kombucha to national distribution and the company took off from there. Today kombucha is a $600 million industry in the United States, with industry growth rates of nearly 20 percent a year. It is such an attractive market that Pepsi and Coke have bought some of GT's competitors to enter the space with products called KeVita and MOJO, respectively. Amid all this competition GT's company, GT's Living Foods, remains a family-owned business. It is widely seen as the most innovative company in the industry, with over 30 types of kombucha offerings, kefirs (a probiotic milk drink), yogurts and adaptogenic teas, and the industry sales leader, with more than half of the market. You can hear GT tell his story at **www.youtube.com/watch?v=VoG4RBmOLil**.

e-commerce
The general term for conducting business on the Internet.

virtual instant global entrepreneurship (VIGE)
A process that uses the Internet to quickly create businesses with a worldwide reach.

parents' birth, or where he has prior experience. The key for such exporters is the personal ties that make exporting predictable and safe.[54]

Another approach that has grown dramatically in the past 15 years is using **e-commerce**, particularly sites like eBay and Amazon, to handle global trade. The formal title for this is **virtual instant global entrepreneurship (VIGE)**.[55] VIGE depends on using websites like Amazon or eBay (for products) or Upwork (for services) to quickly establish a global presence. Many of these VIGE sites offer procedures, services, and web page templates that incorporate best practices for global trading. For example, eBay leads new sellers through the creation of seller and product descriptions found to be the most effective. Amazon, eBay, and Upwork also organize the sellers' accounts to handle international payments, shipping, insurance, and basic customer service issues. VIGE sites provide the assurance of honesty on the part of buyers and sellers, using rules, warrantees, and most of all, mutual ratings of buyers and sellers.

LEARN MORE ONLINE

Learn more about the topics above at these sites:

Importing and exporting: SBA's exporting page, **www.sba.gov/business-guide/grow-your-business/export-products**

Importing and exporting: The U.S. government's exporting page, **www.export.gov/**

Challenge and the Entrepreneurial Way

LO **1-6** Recognize the seven key strategies of the entrepreneurial way.

Entrepreneurs' stories usually tell us about challenges faced and overcome. What is fascinating if you hear enough stories is that there are some strategies that are used again and again. Knowing these strategies can help you achieve your own entrepreneurial dreams. What are the strategies? Some of them you have heard all your life; others might be new:

- **If you don't succeed the first time, try, try again:** This is called the strategy of **perseverance**, and has famous examples like Thomas Edison's testing of more than 8,000 different materials to find one that would work correctly for his lightbulb. Like Edison, it works only if you try different people, products, or pitches.
- **Scale back:** Maybe you have an idea but can't get the resources to get it started. Try scaling it back to the level of resources you currently have available. If you can't afford to open a restaurant, consider starting with a food truck or a catering service, or make yourself into a rent-a-chef service.
- **Bird in the hand:** Instead of planning a firm and then looking for resources, why not start with the resources you already have (knowledge, contacts, money, etc.) and think about what is the best use you can make of them? This is one of the strategies of the technique of **effectuation**, which will be covered in more detail in Chapter 6.[56]
- **Pivot:** Go ahead and start the business in any way you can and look for better opportunities as you go along. It happens all the time. William Wrigley Jr. started out selling soap and baking powder and, to get people's attention, he gave away gum as a promotional item. Wrigley switched to selling gum when he realized how popular a product his Juicy Fruit gum was.[57] This approach is also called the **corridor principle** because until you start going down the corridor (or in your case, doing your business) you can't tell what opportunities you might find.[58]
- **Take it on the road:** Sometimes the place you live isn't the best market for your product or service. Trying another market (in person or via the Internet) might help you find the traction you need to succeed.
- **Ask for help:** Today everyone can harness the wisdom of crowds, whether it is asking your personal and group connections on Facebook or LinkedIn for ideas, advice, opinions, or donations, or going to the many specialized websites out there for **crowdsourcing** such as Kickstarter.com (like Pixel Press did) or Indiegogo.com for funding or Coolbusinessideas.com or Quirky.com for finding or testing product ideas.
- **Plan to earn:** Think through your capabilities, prospects, and passions to find the best idea for you, and then plan for action to make it happen.

perseverance The behavior of continued effort to achieve a goal.

effectuation An approach used to create alternatives in uncertain environments.

corridor principle A theory in entrepreneurship and occupational theory that says that as you start pursuing one line of work or opportunity (which is like going down a corridor) you will encounter other opportunities.

crowdsourcing Techniques often based on Internet services to get opinions or ideas through the collective involvement of others.

In this chapter we have considered some of the key ideas and myths about small business. We have seen the work of founders of small businesses that stayed small and those that started small and grew larger. Either way, when small businesses are created, nearly every part of our society benefits–through new jobs, new ideas, and the new opportunities created for individuals, communities, and the economy. The key element in getting small businesses started is helping people who have the intention to start a business take the steps to get it done, and that is the goal of this text. If we can help you follow in the model of Robin Rath, you are certain to do well. He did.

Pixel Press, outlined in the vignette opening this chapter, obtained a lot of their startup funding from a crowdfunding campaign on Kickstarter.com, which is shown to the right. The materials you see here resulted in an oversubscription, raising $108,950 in a campaign seeking $100,000. People donating did not get equity, but gifts or consideration from Pixel Press. For example, a $1 donation got donors access to emailed updates and videos.

Pixel Press, "Kickstarter," https://www.kickstarter.com/projects/robinrath/pixel-press-draw-your-own-video-game.

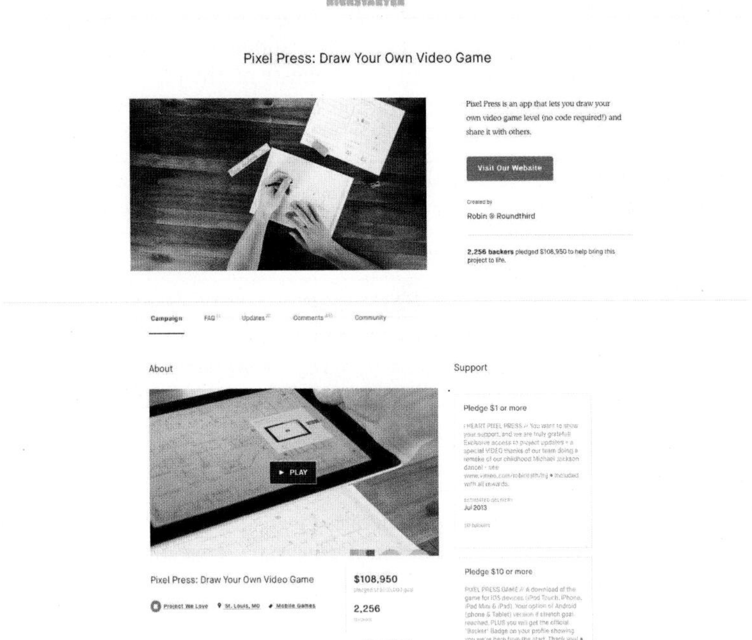

LEARN MORE ONLINE

Learn more about the topics above at these sites:

Inspirational images for entrepreneurs: Kauffman Foundation, **www.pinterest.com/kauffmanfdn/entrepreneurial-inspiration/?lp=true**

Inspirtational stories: *Entrepreneur* magazine, **www.entrepreneur.com/topic/inspiration**

Why firms fail: Autopsy.io, **http://autopsy.io/**

CHAPTER SUMMARY

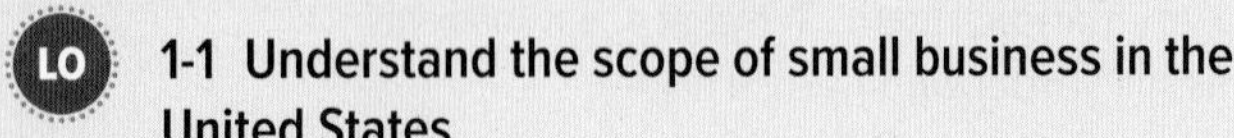

LO 1-1 Understand the scope of small business in the United States.

- The entrepreneurial process consists of four steps: feel, check, plan, do.
- There were 15.5 million entrepreneurs in the United States in 2015.
- About 50 million Americans were part-time entrepreneurs at the same time.
- Start-up success comes from combining planning and action, as well as believing in yourself.
- Getting help helps your chances of business survival.
- Successful entrepreneurs not only do well, they do good for others.
- An entrepreneur (alias *self-employed* or *owner* or *owner-manager* or *founder*) is someone who owns a business.
- An entrepreneur can create a new business or buy an existing business or a franchise.
- The CSI model describes how entrepreneurship plays out in our society through corporate, social, and independent entrepreneurship (which includes small business).

LO 1-2 Differentiate between small businesses and high-growth ventures.

- Small businesses form the economic core and largest segment of the economy.
- Small businesses range from low to moderate in innovativeness and growth rate.
- Small businesses are usually intended to remain small, generally a size that the owner feels comfortable controlling personally.
- High-growth ventures have high innovativeness and growth rates.

- Every owner has a chance to decide on his or her firm's approach to growth.
- Lifestyle/part-time firms start and remain small and centered on the owner's needs.
- Traditional small businesses are more customer-driven, but remain small and simple, providing an income for the owner.
- High-profit businesses add employees and locations in order to provide a substantial income to the owner.
- High-potential ventures attempt to grow enough to become a big business.

LO 1-3 Dispel key myths about small businesses.

- Dispelling the myths is important to supporting one's motivation to become an entrepreneur.
- *Myth 1:* There's not enough financing to start businesses. While we all would like more money, the vast majority of people starting small businesses report finding funding is not a problem.
- *Myth 2:* To make profits, you need to make something. Today the most profitable small businesses are typically in the service sector.
- *Myth 3:* If you fail, you can never try again. Lots of successful entrepreneurs have one or more failures in their background. If you pay off your debts and learn from the experience, you are positioned to try again.
- *Myth 4:* Students (or moms or some other group) don't have the skills to start a business. Facebook's Mark Zuckerberg was a student, Mary Kay's Mary Kay Ash a mother, and Samuel Adams's Jim Koch a consultant when they started their businesses. You could too.
- *Myth 5:* Ninety percent of new businesses fail within two years. In reality, 69 percent of new businesses are still going after two years.

LO 1-4 Identify actions key to becoming a small business owner.

- The BRIE (boundary-resources-intention-exchange) model describes the actions that need to take place for the business to be created in the earliest stage.
- The more BRIE activities that were pursued, the greater the likelihood of the new business surviving.
- The BRIE checklist gives easy-to-perform actions to help move prospective entrepreneurs from inaction to action.
- The BRIE actions also identify the competencies you need to master to get your business started.

LO 1-5 Recognize how small businesses are important to our economy and your community.

- Small businesses are important because they are the major source of new jobs in our economy.
- Small businesses are also the major source of innovations in society.
- Small businesses offer many benefits to localities including employment, taxes, new revenue inflow, support for other businesses, and visibility.
- Small business is also the major source for new opportunities, such as moving up in the economy and society, the opportunity for customers and businesses large and small to obtain needed goods and services.
- Exporting through VIGE and traditional approaches is a major economic force for small businesses worldwide.

LO 1-6 Recognize the seven key strategies of the entrepreneurial way.

- Persevere: When you don't succeed the first time, try, try again.
- Scale back: Start smaller and build up.
- Bird in the hand: Do the best you can with what you already have.
- Pivot: Start up and keep your eyes open for better opportunities along the way, then pivot into them.
- Take it on the road: Go where there is a receptive market.
- Ask for help: Get help from friends, from crowds; getting help helps.
- Plan to earn: Plan now to map your actions.

KEY TERMS

small business, 4
self-efficacy, 4
entrepreneur, 4
occupation, 5
goods or services, 6
firm, 6
novelty, 6
imitative, 6
self-employed, 6
founders, 6
franchise, 6
buyers, 6

heir, 6

independent entrepreneurship, 7

social ventures, 7

social entrepreneurship, 7

sustainable entrepreneurship, 7

green entrepreneurship, 7

corporate entrepreneurship, 8

CSI entrepreneurship, 8

forms of entrepreneurship, 8

opportunity-driven entrepreneurship, 9

necessity-driven entrepreneurship, 9

factor-driven economy, 9

efficiency-driven economy, 9

innovation-driven economy, 10

small and medium enterprise (SME), 10

independent small business, 11

owner-managed firm, 11

serial entrepreneur, 11

innovativeness, 11

overall growth strategy, 12

lifestyle or part-time firm, 12

traditional small business, 12

high-performing small business, 12

high-growth venture, 12

unicorns, 12

main street businesses, 13

crowdfunding, 14

P2P lending, 14

drop-shipping, 14

bootstrapping, 14

Small Business Administration (SBA), 14

creative destruction, 17

importing, 19

exporting, 19

e-commerce, 20

virtual instant global entrepreneurship (VIGE), 20

perseverance, 21

effectuation, 21

corridor principle, 21

crowdsourcing, 21

DISCUSSION QUESTIONS

1. Describe the population of small businesses in America. How many firms are there and how many new firms are started each year?
2. Why do you think 56 percent of 15- to 25-year-olds say they would *like* to start a small business, but only about 15 percent who express an interest actually do anything?
3. What are the differences between small businesses and high-growth ventures?
4. Describe the BRIE model and how it applies to creating a firm.
5. Why are small businesses better at innovation than large businesses?
6. Why is the presence of small businesses important for large businesses?
7. Take 10 businesses that operate in your community and categorize them in the appropriate type of overall growth strategy. Why did you put them there?
8. Many people think of the United States as one of the most entrepreneurial countries in the world. Are there other countries with higher levels of entrepreneurship? Name two and explain why their levels of entrepreneurship might be higher than that of the United States.
9. How does the story of Jim McKelvey reflect the key ethical idea of this chapter, "Do well. Do good"?

EXPERIENTIAL EXERCISES

1. Put this search into Google to find entrepreneurs from your school: "entrepreneur and [your school name] site: **linkedin.com**." Look at the first 100 names and see if you notice any patterns about what kinds of businesses they run. Your instructor might give you other aspects of their lives to look for.
2. Can you find examples of corporate, social, and independent entrepreneurs in your town? Are there examples of people who have done more than one type of entrepreneurship in their lives?
3. Check your state and locality's website(s) for information on programs that support economic development through small business creation and job creation. You can get a start at USA.gov's State Business Resources page: **www.usa.gov/state-business**. Pick a state and make a list of programs that might be worth looking into as you develop your business idea.

4. Look at the local newspaper's website, or the **bizjournals.com** website for the paper in your region. Search the terms "entrepreneur" and "small business owner" to find articles about local entrepreneurs. From this, compile a list of prospective local small business heroes and heroines to serve as role models and prospectors for local sources of help.

5. For students in your class thinking about (or in the process of) starting their own businesses, find out which of the BRIE items they have completed. Ask them which items they expect they will complete or get help on by taking this class.

MINI-CASE

CSI ENTREPRENEUR-TO-BE JOLENE ADAMS[59]

Jolene Adams was a student with an interest in helping fight "food insecurity" in St. Louis. Food insecurity can occur when people aren't getting enough food or are not sure they can afford or find enough food to feed their families, or when grocery stores are too far away for them to readily get to. Measured these ways, over 25 percent of the people in the city of St. Louis are food insecure or live in what are called "food deserts." You can check the USDA's food insecurity map at **www.ers.usda.gov/data-products/food-access-research-atlas/** for maps of food deserts at the neighborhood level.

Jolene wanted to help by creating a service to get low-cost or free food to people in neighborhoods with the highest food insecurity. She imagined a bus or truck fitted with shelves and bins containing food, which they would drive to those neighborhoods so people can shop near their homes.

She was trying to decide the best way to organize their business. There already was St. Louis Metro Market, a seasonal bus-based market organized as a nonprofit. You can see a video at **www.youtube.com/watch?v=ritl5ZwUK4I**. So, Jolene could approach them about starting a second bus, or staffing a second shift on their current bus. This could make her a corporate entrepreneur and part of an existing organization. She could create a new nonprofit organization for her bus or truck, making her a social entrepreneur. Or if she wants to, she could organize as a for-profit business, hopefully with low prices to help her customers, making her an independent entrepreneur.

Since the need was known to exist and solutions to the problem also were known, the initial question for Jolene was, what is the best way to approach the business?

See this YouTube news video on food deserts for more information: **www.youtube.com/watch?v=_lZwBMeogG8**.

CASE DISCUSSION QUESTIONS

1. What do you think are the advantages and disadvantages of the corporate, social, and independent entrepreneurial approaches outlined in the case?

2. How would you feel about being a corporate entrepreneur who is part of an existing organization? How about as an independent or social entrepreneur starting your own organization from scratch?

3. All businesses need to break even financially to be seen as workable. For-profit businesses also typically measure how much profit they make as one metric of their success. But businesses can also measure the impact they have on their communities, customers, economies, and environment. What kind of impact measure might it make sense to consider for the proposed market? Does it change depending on the kind of CSI entrepreneurship approach you choose?

CHAPTER

2

Small Business Entrepreneurs: Characteristics and Competencies

Being open to new opportunities and being willing to take on challenges are essential qualities for entrepreneurs like Khalia Collier to fulfill their career and life goals while also helping their home communities. What other entrepreneurial skills and qualities enabled Khalia to grow her business into what it is today?
Khalia Collier

LEARNING OBJECTIVES

After you complete this chapter, you will be able to:

LO 2-1 Recognize the key aspects of the entrepreneurial personality.

LO 2-2 Assess the operational competencies of the successful entrepreneur.

LO 2-3 Identify the challenges women and minority business owners face.

LO 2-4 Describe the situation of people who become second career (or veteran) entrepreneurs.

LO 2-5 Recognize the special nature of entrepreneurial teams.

LO 2-6 Describe the challenges of family business owners.

LO 2-7 Recognize the stages of development entrepreneurs and their firms go through.

LO 2-8 Discover the rewards entrepreneurs can achieve through their businesses.

Focus on Small Business: Women's Basketball Team Owner and General Manager Khalia Collier[1]

The City of St. Louis had been begging for a professional basketball team ever since the loss of the former ABA-NBA Spirits of St. Louis, back in 1976. Who knew that 35 years later a professional basketball team would once again reign in the city? Only this time, women's basketball would become the talk of the town.

Khalia Collier, a St. Louis native and former player, became one of the youngest sport team owners in the country in May 2011 after the 23-year-old bought out the ownership of the St. Louis Surge professional women's basketball team. Khalia began playing basketball at the age of five and fell in love with the game. Her talents on the court prompted her to become one of the top players in the region, setting several impressive records during her time as a student-athlete. She ultimately decided to commit to Columbia College and later Missouri Baptist University, both smaller universities where she would be able to continue playing varsity basketball while simultaneously dedicating herself to graduating with a degree in communication studies.

After graduation, Khalia began working for a Fortune 500 company, but she continued to play basketball when she could. Doing this, she discovered a semiprofessional women's basketball team, the St. Louis Surge. When Khalia thought about it a light bulb went off in her head as she instantly saw the potential the franchise had to thrive, and her natural ambition and grit took over. She felt her corporate experience, along with her passion for basketball, her family's entrepreneurial background, and her deep commitment to the city of St. Louis prepared her for the next phase of her life—becoming the owner and general manager of the St. Louis Surge.

In 2013 under Khalia's leadership the Surge began rebranding: new logo, staff, coaches, and roster. It was the beginning of a new chapter and a glimpse of what Khalia and the Surge would continue to build. She was determined to revolutionize the impact of sports in the community. To do so, Khalia took a creative approach by recruiting players that could serve as role models and mentors for the youth in the community. All players are required to obtain a college degree. Khalia thrust them into the community, arranging mandatory schedules for the players and herself to attend school appearances, host sports camps, provide community service, and participate in other local events. Building on this, Khalia secured several partnerships with local and national businesses to assist in brand expansion.

Khalia's strategy of growing the team by pursuing community engagement, promoting the development of leadership, and showing the importance of education embodies her personal philosophy and applies it to her team and community. Because of Khalia's drive and the ideas for improving the team, attendance at Surge games has grown from 50 or 60 when Khalia took over in 2011 to thousands of fans per game today. And on the court Khalia's Surge has won two national championships and has been four-time runner-ups in seven years. Her boundless energy and ability to see new opportunities keeps her charged up to continue making history.

For videos on Khalia Collier, see www.tedxstlouis.com/speakers/khalia-collier-owner-and-general-manager-st-louis-surge/ and www.youtube.com/watch?v=75mUw65WfkE.

DISCUSSION QUESTIONS

1. Why did Khalia Collier decide to become an entrepreneur?
2. What skills did she develop to become a successful entrepreneur?
3. What opportunities did Khalia find and pursue?

LO 2-1 Recognize the key aspects of the entrepreneurial personality.

The Psychology of Entrepreneurs

In the opening vignette, Khalia Collier displayed three of the key characteristics of successful entrepreneurs introduced in Chapter 1: She believed in herself and her ability to create a business that would let her do work she loved and help her community. She depended on help from family, friends, and associates to learn her business, and she persevered over several years until she achieved her goal. These are aspects of Khalia's behavior, her way of looking at and thinking about herself and her world, that are called **cognition**, and her visible **actions**. Is Khalia's pattern of entrepreneurial behavior the only type there is?

cognition
A person's way of perceiving and thinking about his or her experience.

action
The visible behavior a person takes.

The answer is that there is no one pattern of entrepreneurial behavior or entrepreneurial type. In Chapter 1 we categorized the entrepreneurs around the world into opportunity-driven and necessity-driven types. We talked about entrepreneurs in corporate, social, and independent settings and how their focuses differed. We even discussed the four kinds of overall growth strategies entrepreneurs typically design their businesses around. There are literally hundreds of ways to think about entrepreneurial personalities. That is good because it means there can be more than one personality type that can lead to success, and it increases the likelihood that there is an approach to entrepreneurship that will fit with your interests and style.

Successful entrepreneurial behavior leads to the creation of a new firm that meets the goals of the entrepreneur. For some entrepreneurial behaviors such as selling (think hard sell vs. softer sell) there is more than one way to do the job right. For other behaviors, there can be only one right way to do it (e.g., applying for a loan, registering a business). In this chapter we will consider the ways people are different, the ways they are the same, and close with a look at the patterns leading to successful entrepreneurial behavior for several distinct groups of entrepreneurs.

The Five Ps of Entrepreneurial Behavior

There are five aspects of behavior that most successful entrepreneurs display. These are not the only possible behaviors that you could consider, but they are behaviors that have been shown in the research to relate to success among entrepreneurs. The five behaviors include the following:

passion
An intense positive feeling an entrepreneur has toward the business or the idea behind the business.

stakeholder
A person, organization, or entity that has an interest or concern in a particular business or decision.

1. **Passion:** Passion is an intense positive feeling the entrepreneur has toward the business or even the idea behind the business. It comes from being actively involved in moving the business forward. Passion has multiple benefits, such as increasing your commitment to the business (which relates to perseverance), and inspiring key **stakeholders** like potential investors, employees, or subcontractors. Passion is displayed in three ways: (1) by looking at the challenges of the business in a creative way, (2) by being persistently focused on the

business, and (3) by being absorbed by the tasks and concerns of the business.[2] When we talk about entrepreneurs who "live for the business," we're talking about passion. When you see entrepreneurs get excited as they describe something about their business, we see and respond to their passion.

2. **Perseverance:** Perseverance is best thought of as a type of learned optimism,[3] the ability to stick with some activity even when it takes a long time, and when a successful or unsuccessful outcome is not immediately known. It is one of the most powerful contributors to entrepreneurial success like that of J. J. Rosen who literally taught himself programming to make his business work (see the following Small Business Insight).[4] In Chapter 1, we talked about the strategy of perseverance with the old expression "If you don't succeed the first time, try, try again." Trying again is the behavior behind perseverance, but requires thinking about what went wrong and what went right, and adjusting your next try to achieve a better result. Behind this thinking and behavior is the attitude of *learned optimism*, knowing that you can and will keep at this until you have mastered it.[5] The danger is to keep trying the same action repeatedly without learning. That is a problem behavior called *perseveration*.

perseverance
The ability to stick with some activity even when it takes a long time and its outcome is not immediately known.

3. **Promotion–Prevention Focus:** Most of us have some mix of two internal focuses (also called our regulatory focus), a **promotion focus** intent on maximizing gains, which gives us a bias toward pursuing opportunities likely to lead to those gains, and a **prevention focus** intent on minimizing losses, with a bias toward inaction or protective action.[6] Being a successful entrepreneur involves balancing the two focuses. In an established industry or a poor one, a prevention focus can work well, while a promotion focus can yield better results in richer, dynamic, uncertain environments or industries.[7] A reckless pursuit of opportunity may bankrupt your company, while a protection-at-all-costs focus may mean you will miss the opportunities necessary to keep cash flowing into your firm. Successful entrepreneurs deal with preventing problems by planning ahead of time and creating actions to avoid or deal with problems. For J. J. Rosen, keeping his day job until his software business took off was one way to protect his family and business. Those same successful entrepreneurs also plan where to find opportunities and how to pursue them. But planning is rarely perfect; you have to be ready to act when the situation demands it. Your own promotion-prevention balance is likely to come into play in those quick decision situations. Trust your plans, and where the plans don't have the answer, trust your "gut" or intuition. Entrepreneurs may have regrets about their choices, but they generally feel better having taken charge of the choice process.[8]

promotion focus
An entrepreneur's attention to maximizing gains and pursuing opportunities likely to lead to gains.

prevention focus
An entrepreneur's attention to minimizing losses, with a bias toward inaction or protective action to prevent loss.

4. **Planning Style:** There is more than one way to plan. In fact, there are five ways.[9] **Comprehensive planners** take a long-term view, develop long-range plans for all aspects of the business, are comfortable with planning, and act based on the plans they've developed.

comprehensive planners
Entrepreneurs who develop long-range plans for all aspects of the business.

Passion is an intense positive feeling about what you do, and this entrepreneur clearly has it. How do you display passion when you feel it?

Hero Images Inc./Alamy Stock Photo

critical-point planners Entrepreneurs who develop plans focused on the most important aspect of the business first.

opportunistic planners Entrepreneurs who start with a goal instead of a plan and look for opportunities to achieve it.

reactive planners Entrepreneurs with a passive approach, who wait for cues from the environment to determine what actions to take.

habit-based planners Entrepreneurs who do not plan, preferring to let all actions be dictated by their routines.

professionalization The extent to which a firm meets or exceeds the standard business practices for its industry.

standard business practice A business action that has been widely adopted within an industry or occupation.

expert business professionalization A situation that occurs when all the major functions of a firm are conducted according to the standard business practices of its industry.

specialized business professionalization A situation that occurs when businesses have founders or owners who are passionate about one or two of the key business functions, such as sales, operations, accounting, finance, or human resources, and pursues those functions in a professional manner.

minimalized business professionalization A situation that occurs when the entrepreneur does nearly everything in the simplest way possible, rather than in a professional way.

Critical-point planners plan around the most important aspect of the business first, act on it, and then consider if additional plans are needed. It is not a very long-term approach to planning. **Opportunistic planners** generally start with a goal and look for opportunities to achieve it. Once they find a good opportunity, even if it isn't the one related to their original goal, they act on it, so it is very short term in orientation. **Reactive planners** are completely passive, waiting for cues from the environment to determine what actions to take. Their focus is entirely short term, and there is little in the way of goals driving their efforts. They can make the most of a situation because there is no other plan competing for their attention. **Habit-based planners** do not really plan at all because their actions are dictated by their routines. They do today what they did yesterday. They don't plan, and they don't even tend to react to changes in their environments. Simply put, results from small business owners in countries around the world have shown that in terms of getting a start-up launched, keeping it going, and making a living from it, comprehensive planners do the best, followed by critical-point planners, and opportunistic planning types.[10] Reactive and habit planners generally do very poorly in business, even if they manage to get their firms started.

5. **Professionalization:** One hallmark of successful entrepreneurs is that they usually do at least one thing much better than average. That average is called a **standard business practice** and every industry has them. Doing that level or better is what professionalization is all about. There are three levels of professionalization: **expert business professionalization** when most aspects of the business meet or exceed the industry's standards, **specialized business professionalization** when one or two aspects of the business are at this level, or **minimalized business professionalization** when none of the aspects of the business achieve the industry standard. Consider the oldest professionalized firm in the world, the Zildjian Company. The company started in Turkey in 1623 with a formula for making an alloy ideal for cymbals. At this stage the company was specialized. In 1929, when Avedis

SMALL BUSINESS INSIGHT

J. J. ROSEN AND ATIBA SOFTWARE AND CONSULTING[11]

After graduating from Vanderbilt University in 1992 as a psychology major, J. J. Rosen landed his first job as a child-support coordinator for the Tennessee District Attorney General Conference, an administrative branch of the state's court system. As he closely observed the work processes, he soon realized that much of the work performed by the state's child-support collection agencies could be done more efficiently and effectively if it were computerized. There were just two problems—many of these agencies had no computers, and no specialized computer software existed to handle the type of functions needed by the organizations. J. J. set out to resolve this problem, fulfill a need, and take advantage of this potential business opportunity.

Here J. J. faced his third problem: While he had an idea for software, he did not know how to write a computer program. Driven to make his idea a reality, J. J. taught himself this skill. A few months later he had mastered programming well enough to create child-support services software that could track child-support payments and collection efforts. With this product, the Atiba Software and Consulting Company was born as a part-time venture. Promoting his software as a better idea and offering very low prices to get an initial customer base, he sold the software statewide. Soon his business was growing through word-of-mouth advertising, and he landed his first major client, Andersen Consulting, within a year of starting. Only then did J. J. quit his job in the district attorney's office and embark on his own business full time. By 2019 Atiba (atibasoftware.com) had more than 800 clients. For J. J., the idea drove the business, carefully.

Zildjian inherited the company, he moved it to America and applied his marketing, financial, and business knowledge to bring the firm up to the level of expert professionalization, where it remains today.[12]

Notice that these behaviors are relevant to more than starting a business. They are useful behaviors in business in general and even in life. If you are an employee, your bosses will want you to show passion (often called engagement) in the business, be persevering, and strike a balance of promotion and prevention. The fact that these five ideas are behaviors means that you can learn how to display them, even if it is not the way you were behaving originally. That is what education, skill development, and practice are all about. Each of these types of behavior can be assessed formally using psychological questionnaires, but you can make a general assessment with items like those in Skill Module 2.1.

Entrepreneurial Personality Overview[13]

SKILL MODULE 2.1

The complete assessment of each of the five Ps would require more than 100 questions, but you can get a very general sense of how you lean by answering and scoring the questions below.

In the following questions, determine how strongly you agree with the statement from 1 (Strongly Disagree) to 5 (Strongly Agree). If you are not sure, make your best guess.

	Strongly Disagree				Strongly Agree
1. I am better than my peers at being able to solve problems.	1	2	3	4	5
2. I am better than my peers at making money.	1	2	3	4	5
3. I am better than my peers at being creative.	1	2	3	4	5
4. I am better than my peers at getting people to agree with me.	1	2	3	4	5
5. I am really excited to be establishing a new company.	1	2	3	4	5
6. I am really energized by owning my company.	1	2	3	4	5
7. I am really in love with creating a new firm.	1	2	3	4	5
8. I am really excited to create something out of nothing.	1	2	3	4	5
9. I really enjoy nurturing a new business through its emerging success.	1	2	3	4	5
10. My personal philosophy is to do "whatever it takes" to establish my own business.	1	2	3	4	5
11. I would rather own my own business than earn a higher salary employed by someone else.	1	2	3	4	5
12. Owning my own business is more important than spending time with my family.	1	2	3	4	5
13. There is no limit to how long I would give a maximum effort to establish my business.	1	2	3	4	5
14. Overall, I am more oriented toward achieving success than preventing failure.	1	2	3	4	5
15. I often think about the person I would ideally like to be in the future.	1	2	3	4.	5
16. I frequently think about how I can prevent failures in my life.	1	2	3	4	5
17. I am anxious that I will fall short of my responsibilities and obligations.	1	2	3	4	5

For the next set of questions, rank them by putting a "1" by the statement that most closely fits your approach or belief, "2" by the next closest fit, and so on.

Rank (1–5)	
	A. I am most comfortable when I have planned for everything.
	B. If I've taken care of the biggest challenge, I feel my job is done.
	C. I am always looking for the next big thing, and when I find it I go for it.
	D. If someone offers me a good opportunity, I'll go for it.
	E. Whatever happens, I stick to what I have been doing all along.

For the next set of questions, rank them by putting a "1" by the statement that most closely fits your approach or belief, "2" by the next closest fit, and so on.

Rank (1–3)	
	F. I feel best when everything I do is done the best way possible.
	G. I think it is important to be known for doing one thing extremely well.
	H. I believe it is more important to get the job done than to try and make it perfect.

Scoring of the Entrepreneurial Personality Overview can be found in endnote 14.[14]

entrepreneurial mindset
The motivations, cognitions, attitudes, aptitudes, and behaviors that lead to a propensity to create solutions to problems or seek opportunities to do something new or better.

One other approach to thinking about the entrepreneurial personality that has seen a lot of attention recently is the idea of the **entrepreneurial mindset.**[15] In Google searches, it has eclipsed searches about entrepreneurial personality.[16] But at this point, there are multiple models for explaining and measuring the entrepreneurial mindset, like those of the Network for Teaching Entrepreneurship (NFTE), the Keen Engineering Entrepreneurship Network, the Gallup Organization's Builder Profile 10 (BP10), Eckerd College's Entrepreneurial Mindset Profile, and Mindcette.com's MindCette Entrepreneurial Test. Most require you to pay a fee in order to see your full results.

A free approximation comes from the Canadian government's Business Development Bank website. Google "bdc entrepreneurial self-assessment" to find it.[17] Its dimensions are pretty representative of the different models, consisting of motivations (need for achievement, power/control appeal, ambition, self-sufficiency), aptitudes (perseverance, self-confidence, tolerance toward ambiguity, creativity), and attitudes (acting on your destiny, action orientation).

LEARN MORE ONLINE

Learn more about the topics above at these sites:

UK universities' Entrepreneur Test (a relatively serious psychometric test): **www.psychometrictest.org.uk/entrepreneur-test/**

Harvard Business Review's entrepreneur test (gives you a general idea, not a full workup): **https://hbr.org/2010/02/should-you-be-an-entrepreneur**

competencies
Forms of business-related expertise.

Entrepreneurial Operational Competencies

LO **2-2** Assess the operational competencies of the successful entrepreneur.

All the aspects of the entrepreneurial personality depend on hard work, but there are other specific types of business-related expertise—called **competencies**—that appear repeatedly in successful entrepreneurs around the world.[18] While there could be as many competencies as there are personality types, theories, like the BRIE (boundary-resources-intention-exchange) model introduced in Chapter 1, help us focus on those few competencies that are essential to successfully starting and running a business. After you have read about these entrepreneurial competencies, use Skill Module 2.2 to assess your competencies.

The competency suggested by *boundary* in BRIE theory relates to the organizational and business processes of a firm. This type of expertise can be called *basic business competency*.[19] There are certain fundamental activities that all businesses must perform, which are called the **key business functions**, and include sales, operations (also called *production*), accounting, finance, and human resources. Getting organized and registered—which creates the boundary—is an example of an operations activity.

key business functions
Activities common to all businesses such as sales, operations (also called *production*), accounting, finance, and human resources.

There is also **industry-specific knowledge**. A restaurant really is different from a mechanic's shop or a computer store or a portrait studio. Each requires you to understand a particular industry and market, and each requires a very particular kind of skill. This was a large part of the reason that Khalia Collier, in the example at the start of this chapter, worked for others before going off on her own. Some of these skills focus on knowing your new business and its context (Chapters 5 and 6), having the kind of skills that fit the business, being able to diagnose your business's health (Chapters 8, 12, 16, and 17), and being able to see future business opportunities while doing your everyday work (Chapters 4 and 7).

Industry-specific knowledge
Activities, knowledge, and skills specific to businesses in a particular industry.

Resources lead to specific **resource competencies**.[20] For even the smallest part-time business, the entrepreneur needs to find or gain access to resources such as time, information, financing, space for the business, raw materials, and a variety of people (advisers, suppliers, service providers, customers). For J. J. Rosen of Atiba Software, getting the computer programming knowledge was critical. Knowing the best place to get raw materials or set up your operation, finding better information than your competition on your market, or having enough financing to ride out downturns in sales are examples of resources that could give you an advantage. You'll learn more about gathering resources in Chapters 5, 11, 13, 14, and 18.

resource competencies
The ability or skill of the entrepreneur at finding expendable components necessary to the operation of the business such as time, information, location, financing, raw materials, and expertise.

Intention reflects your determination to start your business and make it a success. These determination-driven skills can be called **determination competencies**[21] and are demonstrated by focusing on your business over other choices and being ready to find out about and do what it takes to pursue opportunities that will help get the business going. The entrepreneurs we have mentioned in this chapter—Collier and Rosen—displayed tremendous determination to do the work and stick with the business through thick and thin. Many of these determination competencies are essential to deciding if a business is feasible for you before you start a business, a topic that is covered in Chapter 4.

determination competencies
Skills identified with the energy and focus needed to bring a business into existence.

Exchange deals with the actual process of exploiting the opportunity for profit—which is a fancy way of saying "making sales." The competencies that make this work are called **opportunity competencies**,[22] which include identifying an opportunity, a product, or service idea that is likely to lead you to a profit and is ideally distinctive to your firm and, you hope, hard for others to copy. For Bill Gates when he developed Windows and J. J. Rosen when he developed Atiba, the opportunity each found was for creating software that would make life and work easier. You'll learn more about the opportunity process and protecting opportunities through strategic planning in Chapters 4 and 7, where we will discuss the strategy of imitation with a twist.

opportunity competencies
Skills necessary to identify and exploit elements of the business environment that can lead to a profitable and sustainable business.

Competency Self-Assessment

SKILL MODULE 2.2

In this exercise, rank your skill or competency at different types of business activities. The goal is to see where you feel you have strengths and on which competencies you need to work. For each skill, think of a person or a company that does a really good job at that activity. Then compare your own performance to it using one of four levels of competency: *needs development* means that you still have to learn the skill; *needs refinement* means that you have the rudiments of the skill, but still need to practice it and carefully check your performance; *competent* means you can perform the activity consistently and without mistakes;

excellent means you perform the activity as well as your role model, or nearly so. The categories of competencies are built from those listed in the text.

		Level of Competency			
Skill	Role Model	Needs Development	Needs Refinement	Competent	Excellent
Key Business Functions					
Sales					
Operations (production)					
Accounting					
Finance					
Human resources					
Industry-Specific Knowledge					
Industry expertise					
Industry skill					
Market knowledge					
Ability to diagnose					
Ability to see opportunities					
Resource Competencies					
Business information					
Business financing					
Space for the business					
Raw materials					
Support people					
Determination Competencies					
Business as primary focus					
Ability to manage time					
Ability to find/get help					
Ability to sustain relationships					
Willingness to act					
Opportunity Competencies					
Found profitable idea					
Idea imitates with a twist or is new, but tested					
Idea is hard to copy					

Entrepreneurs often find it useful to copy this list and ask people who know them well to fill it in with them in mind. Good examples can include business consultants or bankers, people who have worked with you, or even family members. Comparing what others see to what you see in yourself can help you put in perspective which skills need further development or better demonstration to others. In big business, such an approach is called "360-degree feedback," but it can also be applied in small businesses.

Research suggests that people can learn what they need to know to have adequate levels of expertise in all five competency areas. In fact, students who go through formal training or classes often score higher on the expertise tests than people running businesses.[23] In addition to training or classes, you can get consulting assistance from public or private sources, or you can even buy expertise in package form by adopting industry standard techniques. You can use state-of-the-art services or you can franchise.

The presence and absence of certain skills makes a tremendous difference in distinguishing those who start businesses from those who don't. But for those businesses that do get started, the amount of expertise is what distinguishes the more successful from the less successful firms. The concern about expertise leads to thinking about the level of professionalization you choose to use in your firm.

LEARN MORE ONLINE

Learn more about the topics above at these sites:

Infusionsoft's Entrepreneurial Type Test (a for-fun test): **https://quiz.infusionsoft.com/**
SBA's Small Business Readiness Assessment (checks a lot of the key issues): **https://eweb1.sba.gov/cams/training/business_primer/assessment.htm**

The Sociology of Entrepreneurs

Entrepreneurs can be as strongly affected by their social or sociological characteristics as by their personality characteristics.[24] These sociological characteristics relate to the social groups to which they belong. Family, gender, race, nationality, religion, age, and other types of group memberships, such as being a member of a team or a veteran, are typical examples. Some of these memberships are important enough that they are protected from discrimination by federal laws, and government and companies dealing with the government make special efforts to support members of those groups. Others lack such protections but are still powerful influences on the individual entrepreneur. The challenges members of these groups face share some similarities, as do the programs designed to support them. To get an idea of how this works, the following section considers entrepreneurs in family businesses and teams, women entrepreneurs, and second career entrepreneurs. While there are lessons and advice given for each of the groups, the lessons can apply to everyone–for example, the techniques of time management, which are discussed in the "Family Businesses" section, or the methods for managing idea ownership, discussed in the "Entrepreneurial Teams" section.

Women and Minorities in Small Business

LO **2-3** Identify the challenges women and minority business owners face.

Women-owned businesses are one of the fastest-growing sectors of all U.S. businesses.[25] Between 1997 and 2015, the number of private businesses with at least 51 percent female ownership increased by 74 percent, while the rate for firms overall was 51 percent.[26] Around 40 percent of all businesses are majority owned by women, with another 8 percent equally owned by women and men.[27]

Although in 2018 there were an estimated 12.3 million businesses owned by women, women-owned firms accounted for only 4.3 percent of small business revenue nationally.[28] Why the smaller impact? Generally it is explained by the kinds of occupations and industries women choose when starting their businesses. For example, Table 2.1 shows that more women choose service industries that tend to have lower average sales levels, while there are more men in construction and financial industries, which have higher average sales levels. Men also report more high-tech firms, as well as firms where technology is central to the business. Both are associated with higher firm sales.[29]

The entrepreneurs' goals in starting the business might also play a role. For example, men more often mention making money as a motivation, while women more often mention having flexibility for personal and family life. The overall growth strategies discussed in Chapter 1 also differ, with more women choosing single-person lifestyle firms over the small business forms that employ others. Along these strategy lines, women prefer less-risky firms, which also tend to be the firms with lower returns.[30] Another idea from Chapter 1 was whether the entrepreneur

TABLE 2.1 Percentage of Women Entrepreneurs in Different Industries, 2012[31]

Industries with More Women Than Average*	Percentage	Industries with Fewer Women Than Average*	Percentage
Health Care and Social Assistance (doctors, dentists, residential and child care)	52.8	Professional/Scientific/Technical Services (lawyers, CPAs, consulting)	29.2
Educational Services	44.9	Accommodation and Food Services	24.7
Personal Services (e.g., beauty salons, dry cleaners, auto repair, etc.)	41.6	Finance, Insurance, and Real Estate	19.7
Administrative Services	37.4	All Other Industries	18.9
Retail Trade	32.1	Construction	7.4
Arts, Entertainment, and Recreation	30.7		

*The average percentage of women across all industries was 30 percent.

Source: American Express OPEN, *The 2015 State of Women-Owned Businesses Report,* May 2015, www.womenable.com/content/userfiles/Amex_OPEN_State_of_WOBs_2015_Executive_Report_finalsm.pdf.

Women- and minority-owned businesses are rapidly increasing due to unprecedented educational and financial opportunities now available. What are some of the challenges you perceive still facing minority and women entrepreneurs?

LWA/Larry Williams/Blend Images LLC

chooses to start a business to pursue opportunity or out of necessity, here however American women and men report similar trends, with about 70 percent of each group mentioning opportunity.[32]

Representing approximately 29.3 percent of all U.S. businesses, the number of minority-owned firms has likewise grown explosively in recent years.[33] While the total number of U.S. self-employed edged up by less than 10 percent between 2007 and 2012, minority-owned businesses witnessed a remarkable 27 percent growth rate.[34]

What are the reasons for such phenomenal growth in the number of minority entrepreneurs? The establishment of both public and private funding and networking initiatives have helped level the business playing field for minority entrepreneurs by offering information, advice, and funding access. Another explanation lies in the growth of racial and ethnic groups within the U.S. population, a trend that is expected to continue. Hispanics represent 12 percent of all American business owners, Asians 7 percent, and African Americans 10 percent.[35]

Despite the growth in the number of women and minority entrepreneurs, both groups still face the challenge of access. Access refers to the simplest form of discrimination—often women- or minority-owned firms are simply excluded from the opportunities offered to firms owned by white males. This can result from the way that networks built from interpersonal relations in business exclude women and minorities. When business relationships build from shared hobbies, sports, or even college ties, social situations that are all male or largely white outside of work can lead to unintegrated business networks.

Access problems for women- and minority-owned small businesses crop up most often as discrimination in financing.[36] This means that they may not be given the same access to funds[37] or contracting opportunities[38] that white male-owned firms are given. For example, a national survey of small business finances found that minority business loan applicants were denied at twice the rate of whites, even though application rates did not vary by race.[39] The same study found that Asian and Hispanic business owners pay higher interest rates on their loans. These differences in loan denial rates and in interest rates occurred even when all business-related differences were considered.

There are two solutions for access-based challenges. One solution is institutional, when minority and women-owned small businesses pursue dedicated contracting funds, known as **set-asides**, among big companies and government agencies. The good news is that governments at all levels have special contracting opportunities for small businesses that are owned and operated by minorities or women. For example, the U.S. government allocated over $92 billion on set-aside-based contracts in 2015.[40] Big companies and those with government contracts also have similar programs, typically with two to three times as much money as the federal government allocates.[41] Qualification for set-asides requires certification as a business owned and operated by a woman, a minority, or a veteran (or combination).[42] For corporations, certification is handled by organizations that are not affiliated with the government or big business, such as the National Minority Supply and Diversity Council or the Women's Business Enterprise National Council. **Certification** consists of proving that the business is truly owned and operated by a woman or minority. A similar process is used by the U.S. government, with the Small Business Administration certifying firms for the SBA's 8(a) Business Development Program, whose details are online at the SBA site. It is also good to know that the Commerce Department has the Minority Business Development Agency (www.mbda.gov) that can provide help, along with local SBA, Service Corps of Retired Executives (SCORE), and Small Business Development Center offices.

set-asides
Government contracting funds that are earmarked for particular kinds of firms, such as small businesses, minority-owned firms, women-owned firms, and the like.

certification
An examination-based acknowledgment that the firm is owned and operated as specified.

Certification is not for every women- or minority-owned small business. For example, the SBA 8(a) and most corporate certification programs require a business to be in operation at least two years. As is true for any program involving government or big business, the small business needs to put more energy and resources into record keeping than it might otherwise do, especially businesses that opt for minimalized or specialized levels of professionalization. However, for those businesses that qualify, certification provides a ready means of access to opportunity and to networks of businesses and government agencies which can be leveraged to gain access to other sectors of business.

The second approach to solving problems of access is personal and involves making extra efforts to network. As discussed in Chapter 3, building a social network is central to business success. For minority- and women-owned businesses, networking is especially important because such firms need to network even more than other types of firms. While networking with other minority- or women-owned firms will feel comfortable, and lead to business within that group, the real gains in business require networking in more diverse and potentially less comfortable situations, such as industry and trade associations, chambers of commerce, and the like. Success comes from the number of different types of contacts one makes, and for a minority- or women-owned business, this requires having business contacts from other races, genders, ages, and sectors.

LEARN MORE ONLINE

Learn more about the topics above at these sites:

Small Business Administration's Office of Women's Business Ownership: **www.sba.gov/offices/headquarters/wbo**

American Express's Women's Business Initiative: **www.americanexpress.com/en-us/business/trends-and-insights/keywords/women-in-business/**

National Association of Women Business Owners: **www.nawbo.org/**

Fundera's 15 Resources for Women Entrepreneurs: **www.fundera.com/blog/business-resources-for-women-entrepreneurs**

Federal Reserve Bank Entrepreneurship Help: **www.kansascityfed.org/community/smallbusiness**

LO **2-4** Describe the situation of people who become second career (or veteran) entrepreneurs.

second career entrepreneur
Person who begins a business after having left, retired, or resigned from work. Can include veterans of the armed forces and civilians from a broad range of industries.

veteran entrepreneur
Individual who was formerly in military service who decides to become self-employed as a subsequent career. (Not to be confused with serial entrepreneur.)

Second Career and Veteran Entrepreneurs

A special group of entrepreneurs are called **second career entrepreneurs**—people who begin their businesses after having left, retired, or resigned from work. A related example of this are **veteran entrepreneurs**, who elect to become self-employed after their military service. Other examples include work in other profit or nonprofit organizations, or even when parents are no longer tied to caring for others at home.[43]

As increasing number of corporations merge, downsize, reorganize, and/or close altogether, many firms are offering attractive retirement packages to encourage employees to voluntarily leave the organization.[44] Workers are opting to accept generous offers to retire early (between ages 50 and 64). People's decisions of whether to return to work depend on their individual level of wealth (retirement income and savings), their health, and their work experience, as well as general economic conditions.[45] More older adults (62 and older) are becoming self-employed today than ever before. From 1988 to 2015 there was a 20 percent growth in entrepreneurship among seniors.[46]

About a third of the second career types younger than 62 who return to work decide to become self-employed.[47] Those who do face two challenges—adjusting to the entrepreneurial life and keeping personal finances out of the business.

Working for others for most of their life, second career entrepreneurs are likely to have gotten used to having many of the daily chores of running a business done for them. Even for former managers, the mechanics of getting the location cleaned or the payroll checks written may have been things they could take for granted. As entrepreneurs, they have to do these things themselves or arrange to have them done. All entrepreneurs have to get used to a do-it-yourself approach, but this is a particular challenge for second career entrepreneurs at first.

Second career entrepreneurs face distinctive challenges such as adjusting to the entrepreneurial life as they retrench themselves.

kali9/E+/Getty Images

The key for managing the demanding life of the entrepreneur is to get advice from people in your line of business, or from consultants (which can include the free consulting available through Small Business Development Centers, SCORE, or Veteran Business Centers) about the basic activities of the small business. Make sure you have all the demanding aspects of running a business covered. Pick one or two that are particularly hard or onerous and consider subcontracting those out in order to keep the early stage of the business manageable.

The second problem is keeping personal finances out of the business.[48] Often when individuals are mustered out, laid off, or given early retirement, they can receive lump-sum financial settlements. Frequently, people intending to become late career entrepreneurs plan to use a substantial portion of these funds to start the new business. Sometimes this happens because second career entrepreneurs see their personal funds as "easy money," funds that can be obtained quickly and without a lot of hassles. The problem is that many people who take the easy money are also taking the easy way out. They fail to carefully consider how they will invest the money in the business, and how it will be used. Taking the easy way out can often mean second career entrepreneurs underprepare for the rigors of business, and they are risking their retirement nest egg.

For second career entrepreneurs, the solution is to treat their own money as objectively as possible. Invest it only if you can make a strong case that the investment in the business is going to produce reasonable returns. Treat your own money as an outsider's investment. Do a business plan and consider seeking outside funding from friends and family to help keep you honest about the chances for the business.

Depending on how you ended up facing a second career, it can be made worse because of a loss of confidence.[49] This can come from being laid off, from the "up or out" rules for career military, from being outside the regular workforce for decades, or even from retirement. Regardless of the source, the change can make a tremendous difference in a person's level of confidence. Being given early retirement can be seen as a company's effort to replace expensive (if capable) older talent with junior people who work for less. But being laid off or downsized suggests that the person was expendable at best, deadwood at worst. The difference in labeling makes a difference in the second career entrepreneur's self-confidence.

When there are self-confidence issues, the first solution is to take some time to get over the shock to self-image. Counseling, whether job or psychological, can also help tremendously. When the person is ready, the solution often involves redefining one's life. The goal is to describe life in ways that help the individual take control over it. A layoff or mustering out becomes an indication that it was time to move on. A downsizing becomes something that occurs to those best able to land on their feet. In taking control over the past, it can become easier to assert control over the present and future.

The second self-confidence solution comes from networking. Entrepreneurs as a group are an energetic and optimistic group. Just talking to people you know, as Donna Herrle did (see the following Small Business Insight), or joining local entrepreneur organizations, such as the chamber of commerce or the local chapter of a trade or professional organization, can expose you to people full of energy and ideas. This is contagious, and as you hear the stories of persevering and overcoming challenges that abound among entrepreneurs, the possibilities for a successful entrepreneurial life seem to become more realistic.

LEARN MORE ONLINE

Learn more about the topics above at these sites:

Small Business Administration's veteran business page: **www.sba.gov/business-guide/grow-your-business/veteran-owned-businesses**

Veteran Entrepreneurs portal: **www.va.gov/osdbu/entrepreneur/**

AARP's Encore Entrepreneurs program: **www.aarp.org/work/on-the-job/info-08-2012/become-an-encore-entrepreneur.html**

SCORE's 50+ Entrepreneurs portal: **www.score.org/resources-encore-50-entrepreneurs**

Next Avenue start-up page: **www.nextavenue.org/category/starting-a-business/**

SMALL BUSINESS INSIGHT

DONNA HERRLE[50]

Imagine getting an invitation to a wine and cheese party for a new business, where the owner shows a "before" picture of herself in her corporate garb and an "after" picture of her in her home office, wearing pajamas and slippers, with the adage "change is good" over them both. That is what Donna Herrle sent to business acquaintances, friends, former co-workers, and family when she started her Pittsburgh graphic design business, Drawing Conclusions. A graphic designer and former sales manager of design and print services, she was out on her own after being laid off from corporate America at age 51. That layoff had set off alarm bells for Donna, who feared the loss of security a regular paycheck had brought her. At loose ends after the layoff, she also wondered what she should, or could, do.

Her turnaround and focus on starting Drawing Conclusions came about from talking to everyone she knew. She was surprised at how many others had been in or were facing the same situation, and the advice she got helped her make her own transition to self-employment. The advice she received again and again was to plan the business carefully and keep networking, and the work would come.

And the work came. One client brought a project to the wine and cheese party, based on Donna's graphically impressive invitation. Five more projects came in within 10 days of the party. Within a year she had over 50 clients and gross sales in six figures.

Entrepreneurship in Teams and Families

Stories about entrepreneurs can talk about the individual and their challenges in getting their business started, but the world has even more stories of entrepreneurs who did not start alone. For many, entrepreneurship starts with finding the right person to partner with, or even starting the business within the family. We talk more about that below.

Entrepreneurial Teams

LO 2-5 Recognize the special nature of entrepreneurial teams.

While the classic image of the entrepreneurial small business would involve the image of the solo entrepreneur, the modern reality is different. The majority of new businesses have a team of two or more co-owners, and the trend is toward even more businesses being developed by teams of entrepreneurs. Figure 2.1 shows you the breakdown from the Panel Study of Entrepreneurial Dynamics.

Most teams are family related. In fact, 53 percent of teams are spouses or life partners working together. Another 18 percent of the teams have different arrangements of family members working together, while only 15 percent of teams are composed of unrelated business associates.[51] That means about 400,000 new firms a year are started by teams, with about 320,000 started by family teams.[52]

Why so many teams? There are advantages to a team. When family members start a business, they start with already knowing and trusting each other. Teams are also likely to have more money, time, and expertise to put into a business. If the team members live together, they can save even more for the business.

When putting a team together it is important to work out key issues ahead of time. For example, team members might be putting different amounts of money or time into the business, but might be expecting identical returns, which creates an equity problem.[53] A team can also face conflict over idea ownership (see the Small Business Insight), shared goals, and how to make decisions, especially when the team is evenly split on choices.[54] Legal solutions to setting up partnerships are discussed in Chapter 17—being clear about responsibilities, trying to maintain boundaries between work and home, having outside advisers to help sort out thorny issues, as well as planning for how the firm might end or change[55]—work just as well for teams composed of unrelated individuals as they do for couple-based teams.

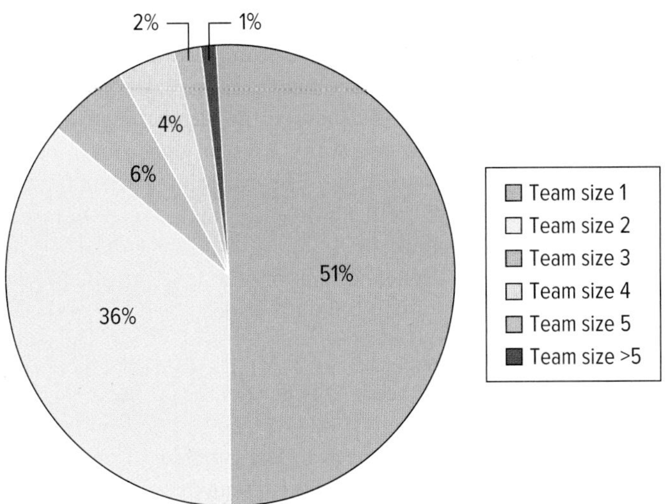

FIGURE 2.1

Number of Owners Involved in Start-Ups from the Panel Study of Entrepreneurial Dynamics

Source: Original analysis using PSED 1 and PSED 2 data (covering 1998 and 2006, N = 1749) done by Kelly Shaver, College of Charleston, for *Entrepreneurial Small Business*, February 2019.

SMALL BUSINESS INSIGHT

MANAGING IDEA OWNERSHIP ON A TEAM

In an entrepreneurship class students were supposed to work on teams around an idea. Greg, a student in the class, had an idea for an iPad stand with embedded lights that would pulse in time to music. He did a quick look online and did not find any such products available yet. The professor approved the idea as a project possibility for the class.

Greg described the idea to the class, and two other students, Nancy and Jim, joined the team. They all worked on the project and did the presentation for a grade. After that, Greg said he wanted to concentrate on getting into law school and was planning to put the idea on hold. Nancy, however, wanted to go ahead with the idea and kept working on it. When Greg found out, he went ballistic. "She stole my idea!," he would tell anyone who would listen.

The disputing alums came back to the professor. The first question was what was said to Nancy and Jim about ownership rights when they joined the team. It turns out Greg had not specified anything. In his own mind, however, Greg thought it should be obvious that the idea was his and that Jim and Nancy were contributing their labor for a grade. In Nancy's mind, it was clear that she and Jim were Greg's partners in the business, contributing their time, ideas, and sweat equity. Now they had to negotiate after the fact.

Ownership problems like this happen all the time in teams. The best way to handle it is to come out right at the start and specify or negotiate who owns what. There is no one "right" answer; it depends on how the group, and in this case their larger organization (the school), handles it. Some schools[56] maintain that all ideas generated for school projects belong to the school. Others say the idea belongs to the student, but in that case, which student?

Where there are no school rules defining "ownership," everything starts with the person who has the idea. If the person with the idea wants to keep absolute rights to the ownership, he or she should not take on other team members, or take on only members who agree (in writing) that the idea belongs to its inventor, even after noninventing students contribute their work to it. Why would students work without ownership? It can be for a grade or to save themselves from having to come up with their own idea for the class, or for the experience, or for the bragging rights of "I helped bring that to market." On the other hand, the noninventing but contributing students can try to negotiate some ownership rights. But whatever is decided, the students involved should make sure everyone has a copy of the agreement. Emailing the agreement is a good way to show everyone was sent it at the same time.

Note that teams in start-up businesses are not limited to the owners. A small business with full-time or part-time employees or contractors is a team, and the owner or owners and their outside advisers or board of directors are yet another team. In picking teams, it is often better to pick people based on their passion for the business or the idea behind the business, and expect to train people to do the work the way you want. This produces a stronger **organizational culture** and a more positive attitude in the firm.[57] The exception is when the firm needs specialized expertise the founder doesn't have. In that case, it still makes sense to hire the expert whose passion for the new business is the highest.

organizational culture
A set of shared beliefs, basic assumptions, or common, accepted ways of dealing with problems and challenges within a company that demonstrate how things get done.

There is a special case of organizational culture for start-ups, called entrepreneurial culture. There are a variety of approaches to thinking about the specifics,[58] but in the end there are five key elements:

- **Passion for the Mission:** The team needs to believe in the business, its goals, products, and services.
- **Passion for the Team:** Team members need to feel good about one another as people and professionals and want to help one another. It isn't enough to avoid toxic employees.[59]
- **Passion for the Customer:** A team that is always thinking about the customer and how to make their experience better will in turn make customers passionate about the company.
- **Passion for Innovation:** If the team is always thinking about making things better for customers, one another, the firm, and its offerings, it will mean the best days are always ahead of all.
- **Passion for Fairness:** At the bedrock, an organization that seeks to always be fair creates teams and individuals who emulate this, so that even when things don't go as planned, people have a basis for making decisions and knowing what is ultimately important.

In Chapter 18, we will talk more about how to select individuals for your firm, but the specific way you go about defining and making real your entrepreneurial culture will be an essential ingredient in picking and orienting the right people for your team and firm.

Family Businesses

LO **2-6** Describe the challenges of family business owners.

We think that the U.S. economy is built on an array of very large, publicly held companies–General Motors, Boeing, IBM, Bank of America, Exxon, and others–but this is only part of the picture. Many of America's largest companies–Mars, Hallmark, Dell, Motorola, Nordstrom, Campbell Soup, fully one-third of the S&P 500 companies–are family owned and managed.[60] Small and large, they make up over half the businesses in the United States historically and were the creators of well over half the new jobs in the United States.[61] But our interests are in those small businesses that are also family businesses, and those represent 39 percent of American businesses, or about 10.8 million firms. Defined as firms with a majority family ownership and direct daily family involvement, **family business** is a major economic force, employing 58 percent of America's total workforce.[62]

family business
A firm in which one family owns a majority stake and is involved in the daily management of the business.

Small, family-owned businesses have many advantages. If the business is managed at the top by a group of tight-knit family members, communication-based integration can be more effective and decision making can be easier and quicker.[63] A strong family bond can become a strong business culture, enabling members to make effective, coordinated decisions with little or no formal communication. Family members already have developed strong relationships and interact on a regular basis both in and outside the workplace. Families are a major source of funds and personnel for new small businesses,[64] providing a support network made up of people the entrepreneur knows and trusts. Family businesses are also a self-perpetuating source for future small businesses. Many new entrepreneurs have been raised in families in which one or both parents or other relatives owned a family business,[65] as you can see in the examples of the Ross and Enstrom families in the following Small Business Insight. As children of family business owners, these individuals learned how business works by observing their family at work. They gained early experiences that helped them develop the skills, competencies, and self-confidence that contributed to later decisions to become entrepreneurs and to their ability to succeed.[66] In fact, most entrepreneurs come from families of entrepreneurs.

SMALL BUSINESS INSIGHT

TWO ROUTES TO THE FAMILY BUSINESS[67]

Ross's Teal Lake Lodge and Teal Wing Golf Club is a family-owned business. Victoria Ross began helping wait tables at the Hayward, Wisconsin, resort when she was only 6 years old. By the time she was 18, she had moved into management positions. Having already earned her bachelor's degree in business administration, she is now working on her master's in global tourism. At 25, Victoria is ready to take over the family business.

Jamee Enstrom Simons took a different track to management of her family's business, Enstrom's Almond Toffee. She began working in the company when still a child, hand dipping chocolates after school. Jamee eventually became a registered nurse, but when her parents expressed interest in selling the company, she and her husband bought it in 1993. Under her leadership, sales revenues for Enstrom's Almond Toffee reached nearly $15 million in 2019.

Victoria Ross and Jamee Enstrom Simons both gained the confidence and skills they needed to succeed as small business owners from their early experiences in the families' businesses.

There are two challenges typical to family businesses—role conflict and succession.[68] **Role conflict** describes the kind of problem that arises when people have multiple responsibilities, such as parent and boss, and each makes different demands on them.[69] As a boss, you might want your daughter to stay at the store and work, while as a parent you might want your daughter to take time off to be with her own children. Role conflict is at its worst when people fail to recognize it. Often, reminding yourself and others that you face multiple, conflicting roles helps them understand the types of choices that must be made and the kinds of decisions that are most important.[70] For family business, the most effective approach for avoiding role conflict is to keep family issues out of the family business, as you can see in the case of Boyd Coffee (see the following Small Business Insight). Whenever possible, try and make decisions based on business necessities. When making a decision from a family perspective, broaden it to apply equally to nonfamily as well as family members. For example, if family members in the business can take off for their children's graduations, so should employees who are not part of the family.[71]

role conflict
The kind of problem that arises when people have multiple responsibilities, such as parent and boss, and the different responsibilities make different demands on them.

Role conflict breeds another unending problem—the shortage of time. Entrepreneurs are among the most rushed people in the workforce. Part of this comes from the responsibilities of ownership. Entrepreneurs are *always* working, even if it is just thinking about what to do next at work. Add family responsibilities, and schedule overload is almost a certainty. There are, however, a collection of techniques for **time management**, which can help meet the challenges of schedule overload. Consider these basic methods:

time management
The organizing process to help make the most efficient use of the day.

- **List**—Whether you use apps like Wunderlist, Evernote, or Todoist, a pad of paper, a specialized form like a Franklin Planner, or Microsoft Outlook's Task function, the key to staying on top of your responsibilities is to list them as soon as you get them. Then as you finish them, you can enjoy crossing them off the list.
- **123 Prioritize**—As you look at your list, prioritize your tasks based on their *importance* to your business and their *due date*. The most important tasks due soonest get a priority of 1. Tasks with lesser importance or a longer time to completion get ranked 2, and your "back burner" concerns get ranked 3. If there are tasks (of any level) that can be lumped together, so much the better. How do you decide importance? If the task will not help your business or family, it is probably not a priority 1 task.
- **Delegate**—Look at your task list and see which tasks you can get others to do for you (for free or at a price). When you're overloaded, getting more people on the job for you is a powerful way to get more done.

SMALL BUSINESS INSIGHT

BOYD COFFEE[72]

Boyd Coffee, started in 1900 in Portland, Oregon, had survived its first transition from founder P. D. Boyd to heir Rudy Boyd. Rudy's sons, David and Dick Boyd, grew up working in the family business. In 1975, Rudy officially retired, but he refused to leave the business. Even though David, the eldest son, became the CEO, Rudy stayed on as board chair and for many years he remained an active and influential presence around the company—often to the irritation of son David. A few years after Rudy's "retirement," the board of directors of Boyd Coffee—Rudy, his wife Ellen, David, and Dick, then president—voted 3–0 (with David abstaining) to remove David as CEO and name Dick the new CEO.

David and Dick believed the management change was based solely on members of the family taking sides in the David–Rudy conflict, rather than on sound business judgment. With the loss of the CEO position, David also wondered whether he had originally received the job because he had earned it through hard work and demonstrated ability or simply because of his name and family position as the eldest. Although after the awkward switch the brothers continued to work together for many years, their personal and professional relationships deteriorated to the point where they seldom communicated. The tension and lack of coordinated effort between the two inevitably led to the financial decline and instability of Boyd Coffee. Finally, in 1997, David threatened to dissolve the company. Only when faced with such a drastic possibility did the brothers begin the slow and difficult process of reconciliation.

With the assistance and guidance of outside advisers and consultants, the brothers have now made succession planning their top priority. They have established a family trust that allows younger family members the opportunity to leave home and develop their business skills and networks independently. The brothers also have encouraged their children to gain work experience outside the family business before deciding whether they want to return to work for the company, something the brothers never got to do.

- **Repeat**–Take a few minutes every day to repeat the above steps. It will save you time later.
- **Strategize**–Once a week, take a few minutes to look at the things you *didn't* do this week and check if you are overlooking something which could be important to your business, family, or yourself, but is getting overlooked in the short run. Entrepreneurs are notorious for overlooking their health and cheating themselves and their businesses out of time to think about the big picture and their firm's future. Ten minutes a week spent this way can make a world of difference.[73]

Thirty-nine percent of U.S. family-owned businesses are expected to face the retirement or semi-retirement of their CEO within the next 10 years. This statistic grows in importance if you factor in the idea that only one-third of family-owned businesses survive beyond the first generation.[74] Part of the problem can be an entrepreneur, like Rudy Boyd, who has difficulty letting go. Problems can arise when the owner cannot come to grips with retirement or envision someone else running the company.[75] Owners often resist giving up control and undermine–consciously or unconsciously–potential successors.[76] This is a problem because top managers at family firms tend to stay in their positions much longer than those at nonfamily firms. One study found that CEOs of family firms had an average tenure of 17 years as opposed to just 8 years for CEOs in other businesses.[77]

succession
The process of intergenerational transfer of a business.

When the current owners are ready to think about what follows them, we get into **succession**–the process of intergenerational transfer of a business. Often the lack of a clear succession plan is the death knell for those family firms facing their first intergenerational transition.[78] If the founder dies, becomes seriously ill, or is incapacitated before he or she can groom a successor, the new family leader may be suddenly thrust into the role before coming up to speed on vital company information and developing needed skills. Also, in the absence of a succession plan,

Planning together for the future is key to the success of family businesses. What other factors are important?

Ariel Skelley/Blend Images/Getty Images

private and public dissension among various factions of the family becomes more likely, negatively affecting operations within the firm, and may eventually cause the business to fail.[79]

As is true of so many things in a successful small business, the answer lies in taking a professional approach to the problem. In this case the professional approach involves crafting a succession plan like the one created by Boyd Coffee after Dick became president. Succession plans deal with the people who will take over, what roles they will fill, and what supports (such as training, outside assistance, voting power, resources control) they will receive.[80] Problems arise when there are no successors available within the family. One study found that only 5 percent of all entrepreneurs were able to rely on family members to take over.[81] Sometimes none of the children have an interest in the family business. The opposite problem arises in situations like that at Boyd Coffee when several family members believe they should take over the top spot and vie for the position to the detriment of both family and business. Problems like the Boyd Coffee competition remind us that it is important to plan how disputes will get resolved. Expect those disputes. The owners of a family business tend to be especially passionate about their enterprise, because they have a huge economic incentive to pay very close attention.[82]

One way to maximize communication in the succession process is to create a family council. A family council includes family members with immediate interests in the business (spouse, sisters and brothers, older children, etc.). The focus of council meetings is the business–family relationship. The meetings can also be a good forum for grappling with issues like role expectations, commitment, and personal responsibility.[83]

An advisory board, or a formal board of directors, can also contribute important skills and strategic direction. At Helzberg Diamonds, Barnett Helzberg Jr. set up a board to confront planning issues and to "help bring order (read *professionalization*) to the seat-of-the-pants decision making" at the firm. The board was critical to succession planning at Helzberg when trusted board members convinced Helzberg that he needed to step aside as president. He brought in someone else who had the skills to lead day-to-day operations while keeping the chairmanship himself.[84]

The key difference between a family council and a board of directors is that the function of the family council is to keep the family involved while the board is focused on running the business. The board includes significant nonfamily membership.[85] Careful use of a family council can also help by keeping family members involved in an appropriate way, allowing you more room to maintain a different balance with your board of directors.[86]

In addition, a good plan, like the one Boyd Coffee developed, also talks about the handling of the assets of the company in order to minimize the tax burden on the family and the firm and provide a suitable income for the former owner and his or her household. Because of the legal, tax, accounting, and leader development complexities, succession planning is best done with the advice of experts.[87] For family councils and boards of advisers, it is often helpful to get professional advice at the start, and then continue on your own. One organization that tracks experts in family business is the Family Firm Institute.

One special situation of the family business is the case of a married couple who jointly own and manage their business.[88] You need only consider the divorce rate in general to realize that marriage and business can be a volatile mixture. The problems of a lack of agreement, difficulty keeping business and family issues separate, and how to handle endings[89] are very much in evidence in couples' businesses, and the solutions are very much the same—being clear about responsibilities, trying to maintain boundaries between work and home, having outside advisers to help sort out thorny issues, and planning for how the firm might end or change.[90]

LEARN MORE ONLINE

Learn more about the topics above at these sites:

PricewaterhouseCooper's Family Business Survey: **www.pwc.com/us/en/industries/private-company-services/library/family-business-survey.html**

Family Firm Institute: **www.ffi.org/**

Marriage.com's Marriage and Entrepreneurs page: **www.marriage.com/blog/marriage-and-entrepreneurs/**

The Entrepreneurial Life and Its Rewards

So far in this chapter we have talked about the entrepreneur and his or her psychology and social setting, we have not talked about the reasons people mention for going into business for themselves and we also have not said anything about the life cycle of the firms entrepreneurs create, and that life cycle can have a profound influence on the life of the entrepreneur in their business. Both get covered below.

The Entrepreneurial Life Cycle

LO **2-7** Recognize the stages of development entrepreneurs and their firms go through.

Like every person, every small business is unique. But just as we all go through childhood and adolescence on the way to adulthood, so do entrepreneurs' small businesses. There is a lot of predictability in this growth process, and knowing the developmental stages of the **business life cycle** can help you better understand your business and your career as a small business owner. The small business life cycle is shown in Figure 2.2.

business life cycle
The sequence or pattern of developmental stages any business goes through during its life span.

Several models exist for the life cycle of the small business firm.[91] Each divides the stages a bit differently. But all models have the same general ideas: (1) there are multiple stages; (2) the key issues, actions, and lessons at each stage are different from the other stages; and (3) the level of risk the business faces changes from stage to stage.

For most small businesses, though, the usual sequence of stages is emergence, existence, survival, success, and resource maturity. Let's look at each of these stages to see what they involve for the small business and the key issue you can expect to face in each. These stages and business growth patterns are shown in Figure 2.2.[92]

emergence stage
The first stage of the small business life cycle, where the entrepreneur moves from thinking about starting the business to actually starting the business.

Emergence is the stage in which a person thinks about and takes actions toward starting a firm. Typically a lot more people think about starting a firm than actually take steps to do so. For example, in 2010, 56 percent of youth aged 15–25 expressed an interest in owning their own firm. But by 2018, only 13.6 percent were actually taking steps to start a firm.[93]

Getting from entrepreneurial thinking to entrepreneurial action is the challenge of the emergence stage.[94] Two techniques discussed in the book can help you move from thought to action. One is using the BRIE behaviors from Chapter 1 to start on the road to creating a firm. The other is to get into business part time (as discussed in Chapter 5) as a way to lay a foundation for future entrepreneurial action.

existence stage
The second stage of the business life cycle marked by the business being in operation but not yet stable in terms of markets, operations, or finances.

Existence is defined by having the business in operation, but not yet stable in terms of markets, operations, or finances. In 2017, according to the GEM studies, about 7.8 percent of Americans were involved with businesses in their existence stage. Existence is the second riskiest period after emergence. The reason risk is so high is that many business owners lack the key

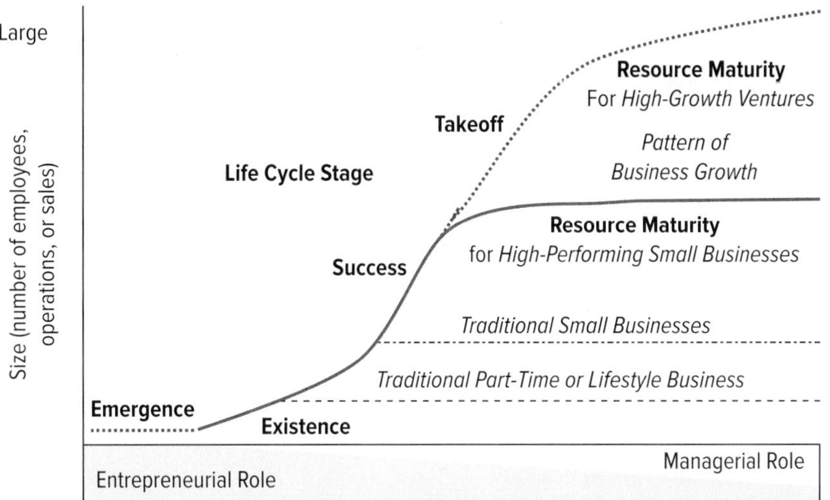

FIGURE 2.2

The Small Firm Life Cycle

Sources: Neil C. Churchill and Virginia L. Lewis adapted Greiner's model in "The Five Stages of Small Business Growth," *Harvard Business Review*, May–June 1983; William J. Baumol, "Entrepreneurship in Economic Theory," *American Economic Review* 58, no. 2 (May 1968), pp. 64–71; Gaylen Chandler and Steven H. Hanks, "Market Attractiveness, Resource-Based Capabilities: Venture Strategies and Venture Performance," *Journal of Business Venturing* 9, no. 4 (1994), pp. 331–349; Jerome Katz and William B. Gartner, "Properties of Emerging Organizations," *Academy of Management Review* 13, no. 3 (July 1988), pp. 429–441.

information or experiences they need in marketing, production, and management.[95] The problems of mastering these three areas form what are called the **liabilities of newness** for small businesses in their existence stage.

The solutions for liabilities of newness come from getting expertise as quickly as possible. For most owners of firms, personally getting more experience is risky because it takes too long. The safer way is to obtain help from others. As noted in Chapter 3, developing an extensive social network is essential for the success of any firm. Whether you use family, friends, industry contacts, or free or paid advisers, getting help helps you survive.

The **success** stage occurs once the firm is established in its market. Success stage firms show consistently growing financial performance, usually with slowly rising sales. Firms at this stage develop the information, skills, and most importantly the routines to grow the business's profits. Those profits aren't always taken in the form of money. Time off from work, a slower pace at work, or hiring additional personnel to take on more of the owner's tasks are all ways that these profits can be used to make the owner's life easier. Used that way, the extra profits are called **slack resources** by economists because they can be rechanneled into the business if needed. For most owners, though, these profits are called *flexibility*. All new businesses–from small businesses to high-growth firms–go through this stage. For most small business owners, this is a stage that lasts a long time. For the owners of high-growth businesses, this is a chance to catch their breath and lay the groundwork for the period of takeoff.

The **resource maturity** stage will follow the success stage for most firms. This stage is characterized by a stable level of sales and profits over several years. At this stage, the functional areas, the market, and the products or services are all being dealt with consistently and efficiently. The challenge of maturity is to avoid complacency. After years of consistency, customers and businesses can begin to take each other for granted. For your business, that can be deadly because a competitor can come to your customer, show personal interest and competitive products or services or prices, and take your customer away. Since the rule of thumb is that getting a new customer costs five times as much as keeping an existing customer,[96] every lost customer is important. How do you avoid customer complacency?

Supersales executive Zig Ziglar says he learned from Australian psychologist Joseph Braysich the four key components for staving off customer complacency–recency, frequency, potency, and recommendation.[97] Be in recent contact with your customers (recency), whether in person, by phone, or via the Internet. This is why you get so many emails and Facebook/Instagram notifications. Be in contact frequently (frequency); the more often they typically buy, the more frequently you want to touch base with them. When you do touch base with them, aim for something they will notice and remember (potency). This can be a personal connection or a message they can use or remember. The fourth is recommendation–either you recommending something to them or asking them to recommend your firm to others. This can include making **micro-commitments** such as favoriting or liking or retweeting a post.[98]

liability of newness
The set of risks faced by firms early in their life cycles that comes from a lack of knowledge by the owners about the business they are in and by customers about the new business.

success stage
The third stage of the business life cycle marked by the firm being established in its market, operation, and finances.

slack resources
Profits that are available to be used to satisfy the preferences of the owner in how the business is run.

resource maturity
The resource maturity stage is the most typical fourth stage of the small business. It is characterized by relatively stable or slowly rising sales and profits over several years. In a firm that has a takeoff stage following the success stage, the resource maturity stage occurs after takeoff.

micro-commitment
An online action that is quick and easy to make and connects you to the message, but does not require a substantial personal or financial commitment, such a liking or favoriting a post or reposting it to your own social media account.

takeoff
This stage occurs after the success stage for a small percentage of businesses. It is characterized by rapid growth (5–10 percent a month or more). When this growth levels off, the firm enters the resource maturity stage.

Although rare among small businesses, one possible variation is when the success stage leads into takeoff rather than resource maturity. The **takeoff** stage happens if a business embarks on a period of exceptional growth. For small businesses, it might come from landing an unexpectedly gigantic contract, expanding into multiple locations, or just being in the right place at the right time, as was the case when Square (from Chapter 1), Snapchat, or Instagram took off.

The challenge firms face in the possible takeoff stage is to understand the nature and demands of growth and get some control over it. Managing takeoff involves working extensively with potential sources of funding and other key resources, as well as working with markets outside and employees within the firm. It also often entails relearning the processes that led to this level of success; a growth-oriented firm often needs to do things differently from one content with maintaining a stable state. That was very much the case for the creator of the jack-o-lantern leaf bag (see the Small Business Insight). One example of this is outsourcing or

SMALL BUSINESS INSIGHT

SUCCESS = OPPORTUNITY + DANGER

Stuff-a-Pumpkins are the pumpkin-colored leaf bags you see on lawns around Halloween. You know the ones—they have a jack-o-lantern's face on them. They were the brainchild of Anita Dembiczak and Ben Zinbarg. Ben's company, Sun-Hill Industries, had been operating consistently for 17 years in Stamford, Connecticut. When he came up with the idea, he spent his own money to get the first run of bags made. They sold out instantly at the discount stores where he tried them out. The stores clamored for more and demanded immediate delivery! But Anita's, Ben's, and Sun-Hill's finances were tapped out, and the discount stores were months away from paying for the bags they'd sold. Ben went to his business banker, who refused to extend credit, even though he had contracts from big retailers. Twenty-three other banks also turned down Ben. He got the money needed to get out the next order by investing all his remaining personal money, securing a loan from a friend, and convincing suppliers and employees to delay receiving money owed them. He got the bags made and out to the retailers. But competitors meanwhile started to copy his bag, so he took the remaining money and started legal proceedings against these concept pirates.[99] Eventually Ben succeeded in getting the pirates on the run, but he probably came to a new understanding of why the Chinese term for crisis consists of the symbols for opportunity and danger.[100]

Geri Lavrov/Photographer's Choice RF/Getty Images

subcontracting for the growth-oriented firm to let the firm stay focused on its own key competencies. A growing nursery might subcontract out its bookkeeping and human resource functions so the managers at the nursery can focus on increasing sales and managing the expansion.

It is important to remember that most small businesses never go through the takeoff stage, and for those that do, the takeoff path often moves them into the high-growth firm model and away from small business. For firms that don't reach a possible takeoff stage situation, the jump is from the success stage to the resource maturity stage.

The lesson of the life cycle model of business is that much of your firm's development as a business is predictable within some broad terms. Knowing the stages of the life cycle and where your firm is among those stages can serve as a powerful reminder of the kinds of issues for which you need to watch. Knowing the different possible life cycle paths for the resource maturity stage makes it possible to clearly choose when to grow, and what to expect if a higher-growth approach is in the cards for your firm.

Rewards for Starting a Small Business

LO **2-8** Discover the rewards entrepreneurs can achieve through their businesses.

Why become an entrepreneur? If you said, "For the money," or, "To do things my way," you'd be right, but these are only a few of the reasons behind owning your own firm. We know that people go where they feel they have the best chance of getting the rewards they value most. The kinds of rewards people report are also fairly well known based on results reported from the Panel Study of Entrepreneurial Dynamics (PSED). The rewards mentioned by people in the process of starting their own firms are listed in Figure 2.3.

Nearly all entrepreneurs talk about three key rewards–flexibility, a livable income, and personal growth. These are covered in more detail below. There are two other rewards–building great wealth and creating products, which entrepreneurs mention more often than working people in general. There are also rewards that entrepreneurs mention *less often* than working people in general. These are social rewards, like the respect or admiration of others, or power over others, and family rewards, like continuing a family tradition in business. Those items are marked with an asterisk (*) in Figure 2.3. These "go it alone" tendencies are probably a good thing, because they help entrepreneurs keep some distance from others and pursue what they think is right.

The three most popular types of rewards for small business owners are growth, flexibility, and income. **Growth rewards** are what people get from facing and beating or learning from challenges. Self-professed computer nerd Marc Fleury's first venture went under with the dot-com bust.[101] His second business, The JBoss Group, was built around the challenges of going it alone financially while outperforming and outlasting his first venture. JBoss, which sells programming and support services, was successful from day one, and was eventually sold to Red Hat. Until then it was entirely self-funded.

growth rewards What people get from facing and beating challenges.

Income rewards refer to the money made from owning your own business. For more than three-quarters of entrepreneurs, this means seeking to match or slightly better the income you had before you started your own business. Only one entrepreneur in four says that she or he is seeking high income through her or his business. But entrepreneurs are looking in the right place. More than 75 percent of the millionaires in the United States are entrepreneurs.[102] Two-thirds of the millionaires are business owners, and one-third are self-employed professionals like doctors, lawyers, or therapists.

income rewards The money made by owning one's own business.

Flexibility rewards are perhaps the most rapidly growing type of reward. They refer to the ability of business owners to structure their lives in the way that best suits their needs. When Cyndi Crews was laid off from her work as an information technology resources manager of a large corporation, she bought a franchise of Schooley Mitchell Telecom Consultants. Today she advises companies on how to get the most from their telephone systems. She runs the business from her home in Lumberton, Texas, where she is able to set her own work schedule. This ensures her the flexibility she needs to take time off to be with her young son and husband.[103] Another variant of this is pursuing spiritual or religious goals through business. For example, Noah's Ark, a Kosher deli with branches in Teaneck, New Jersey, and New York

flexibility rewards The ability of business owners to structure life in the way that suits their needs best.

FIGURE 2.3

Rewards New Entrepreneurs Seek through Small Business[104]

Source: Nancy M. Carter, William B. Gartner, and Kelly G. Shaver, "Career Reasons," in William B. Gartner, Kelly G. Shaver, Nancy M. Carter, and Paul D. Reynolds (eds.), *Handbook of Entrepreneurial Dynamics: The Process of Business Creation* (Thousand Oaks, CA: Sage, 2004).

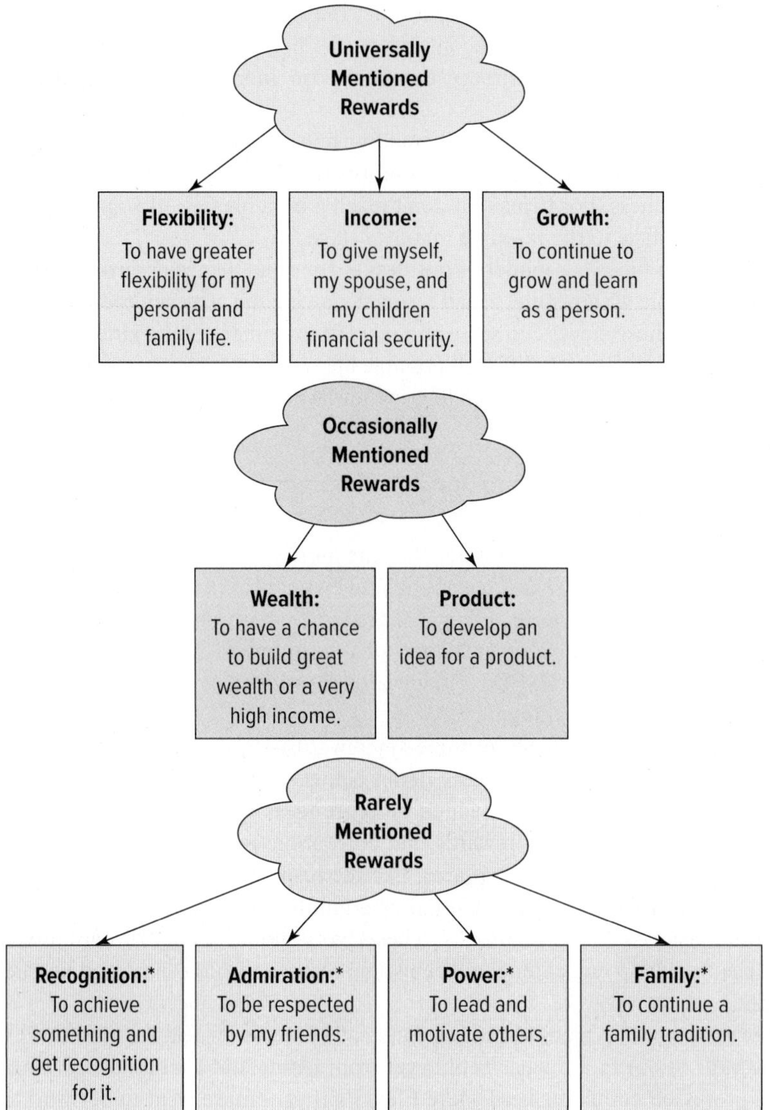

City, closes from 4 P.M. on Friday until 6:30 P.M. or so on Saturday night in observance of the Jewish Sabbath.

This chapter starts with the idea that while no single explanation can really cover all 15.5 million self-employed people in the United States, there *are* aspects of the entrepreneurial life that apply to many. Some of these are general ideas, such as the entrepreneurial career or the competencies needed to be successful in small business. There are also types of entrepreneurs that describe many, but not all, self-employed people. Whether we look at types like the lifestyle entrepreneur or high-performing small business owner, or if we look at demographic groups such as women or second career entrepreneurs, the more we know about people pursuing entrepreneurship, the better it is for identifying important issues in their business and personal lives. Every entrepreneur's story is uniquely his or her own, but across millions of entrepreneurs, there are some similarities, and these help make it easier to think about the entrepreneurial process and getting the right kind of help to entrepreneurs.

CHAPTER SUMMARY

LO 2-1 Recognize the key aspects of the entrepreneurial personality.

- In addition to self-efficacy from Chapter 1, there are five other key behaviors for entrepreneurial success.
- *Passion:* The intensely positive feeling entrepreneurs have for their business.
- *Perseverance:* The ability to stick to activities over long periods, even in the face of setbacks.
- *Promotion–Prevention Focus:* The behaviors related to pursuing gains and preventing losses.
- *Planning Style:* Ranging from comprehensive to habit-based, this reflects how much and about what you ordinarily plan.
- *Professionalization:* The extent to which an entrepreneur and their firm meets or exceeds the standard business practices for the industry.

LO 2-2 Assess the operational competencies of the successful entrepreneur.

- Forms of business-related expertise are called *competencies*.
- To be successful, an entrepreneur needs competency in the key business functions (e.g., sales, operations, etc.), industry-specific knowledge, resource competencies, determination competencies, and opportunity competencies.

LO 2-3 Identify the challenges women and minority business owners face.

- Women-owned and minority-owned businesses are growing at rates faster than other types of businesses.
- The major challenge facing these businesses is gaining access to opportunity.
- Access is achieved through networking and set-asides.

LO 2-4 Describe the situation of people who become second career (or veteran) entrepreneurs.

- Second career entrepreneurship happens when a person is laid off, downsized, given early retirement, leaves the military, or concludes taking care of family members in the home.
- The challenges facing second career entrepreneurs come from having to do everything themselves and using too much of their personal money too soon in the business.
- Having to do everything can be handled by identifying the tasks to be done ahead of time. Loss of confidence can be dealt with through taking time to heal and by networking with enthusiastic entrepreneurs. Second career entrepreneurs should use their own money only when it makes sense for the business, usually proven through a business plan.

LO 2-5 Recognize the special nature of entrepreneurial teams.

- The majority of businesses are started by teams.
- Spouses or life partners are the most common form of team.
- Couple teams can benefit from trust and financial flexibility.
- Typical problems include lack of agreement, separation of work and family issues, and handling of endings.
- Similar problems also crop up in non-spouse teams.

LO 2-6 Describe the challenges of family business owners.

- Family businesses are one of the major forms of small business.
- The major challenges facing the family business are role conflict, time management, and succession.
- All three challenges can be met through careful planning.
- Married couples and nonfamily partnerships face many of the same problems and solutions.

LO 2-7 Recognize the stages of development entrepreneurs and their firms go through.

- Every firm goes through a similar sequence of developmental stages.
- Emergence comes before the firm starts, followed by existence.
- Survival happens to most firms, as does resource maturity.
- Some firms experience the takeoff stage, but most do not.
- Each stage poses a distinct challenge to the small business and owner.

LO 2-8 Discover the rewards entrepreneurs can achieve through their businesses

- Nearly all people starting small businesses have flexibility, income, and growth as reasons for starting those businesses
- Small business owners are less motivated by social reasons (recognition, admiration, power, or family tradition) than the general public.
- While providing a good income is important to three-quarters of entrepreneurs, only one in four says generating great wealth is important.

KEY TERMS

cognition, 28
action, 28
passion, 28
stakeholder, 28
perseverance, 29
promotion focus, 29
prevention focus, 29
comprehensive planners, 29
critical-point planners, 30
opportunistic planners, 30
reactive planners, 30
habit-based planners, 30
professionalization, 30
standard business practice, 30
expert business professionalization, 30
specialized business professionalization, 30
minimalized business professionalization, 30
entrepreneurial mindset, 32
competencies, 32
key business functions, 33
industry-specific knowledge, 33
resource competencies, 33
determination competencies, 33
opportunity competencies, 33
set-asides, 37
certification, 37
second career entrepreneurs, 38
veteran entrepreneurs, 38
organizational culture, 42
family business, 42
role conflict, 43
time management, 43
succession, 44
business life cycle, 46
emergence (stage), 46
existence (stage), 46
liability of newness, 47
success (stage), 47
slack resources, 47
resource maturity (stage), 47
micro-commitment, 47
takeoff (stage), 48
growth rewards, 49
income rewards, 49
flexibility rewards, 49

DISCUSSION QUESTIONS

1. What are the different aspects of the entrepreneurial personality?
2. What would be the likely impact on a start-up if the entrepreneur had a strong promotion focus and a weak prevention focus?
3. Could someone with good industry-specific knowledge but low competency in basic business skills be successful as an entrepreneur in that industry? Why or why not?
4. When does it make sense to create a business using a minimalized approach to professionalization? Why is that so?
5. What are the stages of the small business life cycle? What stage do high-growth ventures go through that other forms of small business do not?
6. What are the strengths and weaknesses of a team?
7. What is the major challenge facing women- and minority-owned firms? How can this be solved?
8. What makes the situation of second career entrepreneurs problematic? What can they do to smooth their way?

EXPERIENTIAL EXERCISES

1. Start by writing down which aspects of the entrepreneurial personality describe you the best. Then take the online Entrepreneurial Potential Self-Assessment at **www.bdc.ca/en/articles-tools/entrepreneur-toolkit/business-assessments/pages/self-assessment-test-your-entrepreneurial-potential.aspx**. Compare how you imagined yourself to what you observed on the online quiz. Which aspects do you agree with? Which do you disagree with? Are there skills you want to develop or refine based on the results?

2. Which entrepreneurial competencies do you possess? Be ready to provide examples and explain why you made these choices. You can use the result of Skill Module 2.2 to aid you in this.
3. Pick small businesses that others in the class are familiar with and analyze what level of professionalization they display. Be ready to explain the basis for your classification.
4. Select a local family business owner or female or minority entrepreneur whom you admire, and research the person's business and professional background. Interview this person if possible. What particular challenges did he or she face? What competencies did he or she use to overcome them?
5. Go through the list of reasons people give for going into self-employment, and identify which of the reasons seem to fit you. Explain why you identify with each reason.
6. Think about the list of reasons people give for becoming self-employed. If you can, interview local entrepreneurs about their reasons and see how your real-life examples fit with the national survey results.

MINI-CASE

GEORGE WASHINGTON, DISTILLER AND SEVENTH-CAREER ENTREPRENEUR[105]

When he stepped off the podium in front of Federal Hall in New York City on March 4, 1797, George Washington was probably thinking not about the presidency he just handed over to John Adams, but about his audacious plan to start a new career to rescue his Virginia farm, Mount Vernon, from bankruptcy. For Washington, farmer, surveyor, soldier, commander, legislator, and president, this new role might be called his seventh career, but it was necessary.

Washington had owned a plantation for much of his adult life, and he tried to get back to it between stints as the nation's top general and as president. By the time he could retire to Mount Vernon, he discovered the business was in trouble. The number of people for whom he was responsible had grown from 10 when he inherited the farm to 300 as he left the presidency. Unfortunately his landholding size and productivity had not kept pace. He was facing bankruptcy.

Knowing this even as he was preparing to end his term, Washington picked up on the idea of a distillery when James Anderson, a Scottish immigrant to Virginia, pitched the idea. Washington had shown himself supportive of inventions, having developed new ways of training mules and preparing wheat for market. He had even received America's third patent.

Anderson's idea made financial sense. Taxes on imported rum were high, and this was putting a crimp in the average American's drinking habits. Back in 1797, the average American was annually drinking 5 gallons of distilled spirits like rum and whiskey (today the average is 1.8 gallons). So there was a ready market.

So, working with Anderson, Washington started with two small stills in 1797 making a 110-proof rye whiskey. Production grew in 1799 to 11,000 gallons sold in two versions (50 cents per gallon for regular and $1 per gallon for premium whiskey) and a $7,500 profit was made, making Washington America's leading distiller. While Anderson could handle the role of running the distillery itself, the business side was in Washington's hands. Unfortunately, he failed to train a successor. Then Washington died on December 14, 1799. The distillery passed into several hands but began a seemingly unstoppable decline and was closed for good in 1814.

For more information, see the Virginia Distillers Association page with video: **www.virginiaspirits.org/trail/george-washingtons-distillery-mount-vernon/**; and the *Business Insider* video: **www.youtube.com/watch?v=5dIROe_6DuU**.

CASE DISCUSSION QUESTIONS

1. What advantages would George Washington bring to James Anderson's idea for a Virginia distillery?
2. Washington's farm was operating even as he got the distillery off the ground. What kind of problems could that raise for the ex-president?
3. At his death, Washington's distillery was the largest in the United States. Did this make Washington a high-growth entrepreneur or a small business owner? Why?

CHAPTER

3 Small Business Environment: Managing External Relations

● Summer Albarcha became a fashion blogger to draw attention to stylish clothes for women who wanted to dress modestly. Fashion is just one area where there are personal, national, cultural, professional, and religious interests jostling for position in the environment. How can you better understand the environment to better understand the forces that can affect your business?
Kamran Jebreili/AP Images

LEARNING OBJECTIVES

After you complete this chapter, you will be able to:

LO 3-1 Describe the elements that make up the small business environment.

LO 3-2 Demonstrate your ability to scan the small business environment.

LO 3-3 Apply the techniques of building legitimacy for your organization.

LO 3-4 Navigate the techniques of social networking.

LO 3-5 Explain the basic skills for handling a crisis.

LO 3-6 Recognize how small businesses can achieve sustainability.

LO 3-7 Identify the major steps in making ethical decisions in small business.

Focus on Small Business: Summer Albarcha and the Controversial Skirt[1]

Sixteen-year-old Summer Albarcha was frustrated by how hard it was to find clothing that was modest but stylish, as befits a devout but contemporary Muslim woman. She decided to post items she found to Instagram to make it easier for other women to find great style. Her page **(www.instagram.com/summeralbarcha/)** grew to over 40,000 followers worldwide by 2014.

The summer before Summer started studying at Saint Louis University, the founders of Mimu Maxi, a comparable Jewish site, sent Summer one of their signature items. As *The Village Voice* put it, "On July 12, the [Mimu Maxi] fashion line and the blogger decided to do a little collaboration. Albarcha posted a photo of herself to Instagram wearing a lime-green Mimu Maxi skirt, paired with a white collared shirt, a few simple accessories, and of course, her hijab. It looked smashing. Mimu Maxi re-posted it to its Facebook page and to Instagram."[2]

That was when things got complicated. While many liked the look and the spirit of cooperation, a group of Mimu Maxi subscribers got tremendously upset that a Muslim was depicted on the site at a time when relations between Jews and Muslims in the Middle East were extremely strained. The Mimu Maxi sisters responded, defending the decision and talking about the shared desire for modesty in Jewish and Muslim traditions. The exchanges made not only *The Village Voice,* but *Look* magazine, *The Atlantic, The Daily Mail,* and a number of fashion blogs.

In the end, Summer saw the power of social media—for good or ill—and the need to be thoughtful about what she shares and how she shares it. The experience also reaffirmed for her the power of interfaith interaction, and the risk of facing opposition and even attack for doing something she believes in. But through the experience Summer also gained a new sense of empowerment, new Jewish followers, and other new fans of her sense of style, so that by February 2019, Summer's Instagram page had over 500,000 followers.

See Summer's YouTube channel at **www.youtube.com/channel/UCZaBtpOjMtP2gmLenyOGNIg**. To hear Summer talk about the Mimu Maxi story, see **www.youtube.com/watch?v=NFtl00mwy48**.

DISCUSSION QUESTIONS

1. How would you describe the different types of relationships between Mimu Maxi and Summer's Instagram page?

2. Do you think the extremely negative reactions from a subset of customers or followers is a typical response? If not, what do you imagine is typical?
3. How would you have handled the reactions of the upset followers?

LO 3-1 Describe the elements that make up the small business environment.

The Environment of Small Business

environment
The sum of all the forces outside the firm or entrepreneur.

organizational identity
Part of the BRIE model; composed of the name, description, and distinctive elements of a firm, such as trademarks, uniforms, logos, characters, and stories.

organizational culture
A set of shared beliefs, basic assumptions, or common, accepted ways of dealing with problems and challenges within a company that demonstrate how things get done.

The moment that reaction to the skirt photo made Summer focus more intently on what was happening around her, she became aware of the **environment**—all of the forces outside the firm or in this case the individual entrepreneur (or entrepreneur-to-be). In Summer's case, the environment was the source of her inspiration (if you recall the BRIE model from Chapter 1, the skirt would fall under resources), as well as the data from friends, family, co-workers, and the media giving her the background on the nature and scope of the problems with dressing modestly but stylishly in contemporary society.

Following the BRIE model in starting a business, the entrepreneur creates a boundary within the environment, setting his or her firm apart from the rest of the environment. In doing this, the entrepreneur gives the firm an **organizational identity**. Organizational identity is not just the name of a firm, but its basic description—what it does and where it does this. It can include formal elements like a registration with the state, or a website or email account with the firm's name on it, or a telephone number in the firm's name. But there are also important informal elements of identity. Often the firm and the entrepreneur are one and the same, but as the firm grows beyond the entrepreneur's direct personal control, for example, by adding a part-time employee or running an order-taking website 24/7, parts of the identity of the firm can grow beyond the entrepreneur alone.[3] And as the firm establishes a track record for performance, that performance along with the goods or services it creates become key elements of the firm's and entrepreneur's identity. For example, it is hard to think of Famous Amos without thinking about his cookies.

A key element of this organizational identity is its **organizational culture**, a set of shared beliefs or basic assumptions that demonstrate how things get done. Organizational culture also includes common, accepted ways of dealing with problems and challenges within a company.[4] For example, Brian and Lisa Jolles are the married co-owners of Jolles Insurance in Ellicott City, Maryland. They recognized that they needed to set an example of healthy living for their employees in order to promote wellness to their insurance customers. They did this by establishing exercise as part of the organization's culture. Employees are encouraged to walk during lunch to control stress and hunger. Wellness is so much a part of the culture that the Jolles run an adult exercise boot camp for employees, clients, neighbors, and friends three days a week, sponsor a website (www.wepromotehealth.com), and even sponsor a Health and Wellness Day at a local park, which initially drew 500 participants and since then has become a community-wide annual event.[5] Being a small business makes managing organizational culture easier than in larger businesses because, in a small business, there is a lot of flexibility in terms of roles and expected behaviors, especially when the business is first getting started.

In creating a firm using the BRIE model, the entrepreneur gathers resources from the environment. These can include information on how to do the business or whom to sell to, funding to run the business, space for the business, and raw materials for the business to use to make goods or deliver services. If the environment is rich with resources as it is during economic boom times, it can be easy to gather what is needed. In tougher times, such as during economic recessions, gathering resources can be harder. As entrepreneurs face resource constraints, they often learn to get by with less, or substitute a more readily obtained resource, or ask to borrow, rent, or trade for the resource. These techniques are called bootstrapping (which is covered in detail in Chapter 6) and are part of the culture of most successful start-ups.

The environment is at the core of exchange in the BRIE model, since exchange is literally the firm or entrepreneur dealing with the environment—buying, selling, or trading across the boundary of the firm. In the end, entrepreneurs carve a firm out of the environment by gathering resources, setting them up inside a boundary and trading or exchanging them across the boundary. In short, almost everything a firm does involves the environment. This chapter will help you understand more about the environment and its components, and how you can organize yourself and your firm to manage its relations with the environment.

The Elements of the Small Business Environment

Environment is a difficult concept to consider because it is so big. It literally includes the entire world outside yourself and your business. As an entrepreneur, or entrepreneur-to-be, how do you go about understanding it, much less using it to help focus and operate your business? The key is to have a model of the environment in mind, which can help you focus on a part of the world at a time.

You may have seen a diagram of the environment like the one in Figure 3.1 in your introductory business or management text. The different entities are examples of the potential stakeholders in your business—people, groups, and organizations who have a concern about your business. It makes sense to the environment and stakeholders here to think about how this applies to small businesses.

The **external environment** consists of everything outside the firm's boundary. When businesspeople talk about "the environment" and they are not talking about air, land, or water, this is the environment they are discussing. The easiest way to think about this very large entity is to break it into two parts. Those parts of the environment that directly and consistently touch on the firm are called the **task environment**, because these are the components that directly relate to your firm performing its basic business tasks. This part of the environment is made up of those people your firm deals with every day—customers, suppliers, distributors, professional supporters like accountants and lawyers, subcontractors, allies and corporate partners, unions and lenders—as well as important groups you may deal with directly less often, but that are always on your mind, like competitors, government, media, interest groups such as trade and professional associations, consumer groups, environmental groups, and so forth.

external environment
The forces, institutions, and people (i.e., the rest of the world) outside the boundary of the firm.

task environment
A part of the external environment made up of those components that the firm deals with directly such as customers, suppliers, consultants, media, interest groups, and the like.

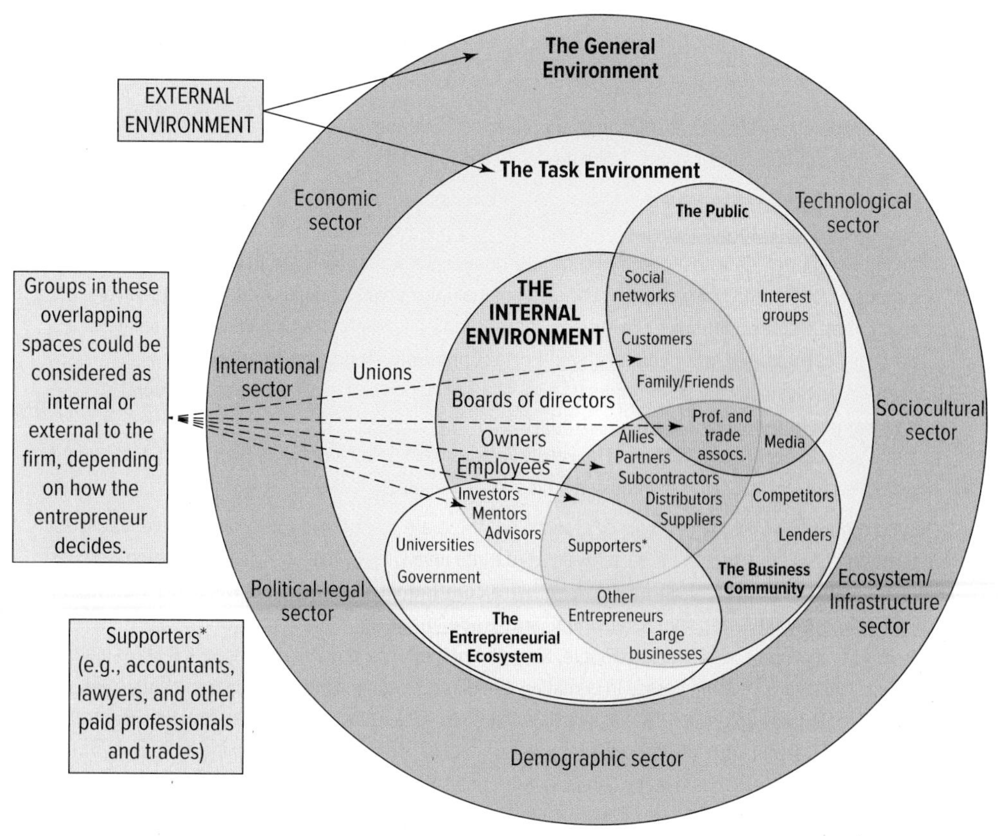

FIGURE 3.1

The Organization's Environment

Sources: Adapted from Angelo Kinicki and Brian K. Williams, *Management: A Practical Introduction* (New York: McGraw-Hill, 2009), p. 73; Brad Feld, *Startup Communities: Building an Entrepreneurial Ecosystem in Your City* (Hoboken, NJ: Wiley, 2012).

internal environment
The people and groups within the boundary of a firm, including the owners, managers, employees, and board members of the firm.

board of directors
A formal group within a company that is legally responsible for the decisions and actions of the company. The directors sit above the president or chief executive officer of the company.

trade magazines
The magazines that target specific industries and professions.

The **internal environment** is defined by those people who are directly involved in the organization and own or are employed by the firm. This includes the employees, but also the **board of directors** or advisory boards of the firm. Whether on the board of directors or not, your investors are part of the internal environment too. Contracted professionals like outside accountants or attorneys can be considered part of the internal or external environment, as can be subcontractors of the firm and firms with which you have formal contractual arrangements. Some companies will see customers as integral to the organization and count them in the internal environment, while other entrepreneurs will think of them as outside the firm. Similarly, in today's highly networked world, your social networks and personal networks could also be considered part of the internal or external environment. For all of these "either/or" situations, the key is how you closely you want your business involved with and how much you want to consider the ideas of these different groups. As an owner, your first responsibility should be to "your business." If these professionals, customers, and networks are groups to whom you feel responsibilities at a level similar to your employees, then you should think of them as part of your firm's internal environment. Otherwise, they are part of your external environment.

It helps to organize them into related communities, represented by circles shown in Figure 3.1. One community we often think of as the public, which includes your customers, their social networks, media, interest groups, and professional and trade associations. Because you deal with these groups on a consistent and ongoing basis, you may find yourself having trouble recognizing new trends or changes among these members of your task environment. One simple way to do this is to take some time to reflect on whether and how business and relations have changed with each group over the past 6 to 12 months. Another simple way is to look at the professional and **trade magazines** for their industries. You can find these publications using the techniques given in Skill Module 3.1. In particular, look for articles that include terms such as *trends* or *future* in the title. Another community is typically thought of as the business community, and includes the firms you partner with, do business with, and compete with. It also includes the large

SKILL MODULE 3.1 Finding Your Trade or Professional Association and Related Magazines

In this skill module we will start with finding your professional or trade organization, and with that information in hand, find that group's publications. There are four ways to find the organizations:

1. With over 35,000 local, regional, national, and international associations listed, the Directory of Associations (**directoryofassociations.com**) is a good place to start.
2. An industry portal is a website with capabilities for multiple groups like current members, potential members, media, and policy makers. Portals offer multiple services such as disseminating documents, chat rooms, discussion groups, registration services, databases, and the like. Wikipedia maintains a portal list at **https://en.wikipedia.org/wiki/Portal:Companies/Index_by_industry**.
3. If you are focused on consumer products, a list of associations and trade shows can be found at **www.marketing-mentor.com/pages/trade-list**.
4. If that does not work, most public and university libraries have Gale Publishing's *Directory of Associations,* which lists tens of thousands of trade and professional groups.

If you cannot find your trade group or association, there are three ways you could find the magazines that target specific industries and professions (called trade magazines). Two use an online search. The best online sources are WebWire's list at **www.webwire.com/IndustryList.asp** and Wikipedia's at **https://en.wikipedia.org/wiki/Category:Professional_and_trade_magazines**.

Or you can try a general search on Google. Enter the name of the product or service. If it takes multiple words, like "child care," put the phrase in quotation marks. Add a comma and the word *association*. For this example, Google turns up groups such as the National Child Care Association and the National Association for Family Child Care. In addition, printed directories of publications by Bacon Publishing or Burrelle's Information Services can be found on many libraries' reference shelves.

businesses and banks. A major part of that community are the paid professionals on whom you depend, like your accountants, lawyers, IT experts, and the like.

One part of the environment that is important for small business founders is called the **entrepreneurial ecosystem**.[6] These are the elements that make up the settings most helpful to promoting entrepreneurship. The specific parts of the environment of interest are the entrepreneurs in the community, the government, local universities, investors, mentors, service people (e.g., lawyers, accountants, etc.), and large companies. Having all these sources of help locally is the best, but using the Internet to link to mentors, university supports, or out-of-town investors can work, too.

The other, even larger part of the environment is called the **general environment**. It represents the major forces on the lives of people and institutions like businesses, and even nations. Some components of this environment are easy to understand and apply to small business. For example, the economic sector includes the trends and current conditions of the overall market for goods and services, the availability of equity and credit, and employment. The technological sector includes innovation, invention, and modernization. The sociocultural sector includes cultures often based on factors such as nationality or religion, and subcultures that are based on groups formed around shared interests within a larger culture. For example, think of the contributions of the hip-hop subculture to modern music and lifestyle marketing.

Hip-hop is a subculture that has made major impacts on fashion, design, language, and music. Part of the sociocultural sector, these subcultures shape new directions for entrepreneurship.

Comstock Images/SuperStock

The demographic sector includes trends in the mix of ages, races, and gender in society. For example, Jim Allsup had experience handling claims for Social Security, so he decided to start a business of his own using that experience. He did some research and discovered that as the baby boom generation (born 1946–1964) aged, the disability services market would grow right along with the retiree services market. From his work experience, he already knew that the Social Security Disability Insurance (SSDI) program was nearly impossible for people to deal with on their own, which delayed disability payments. He felt he could provide a valuable service to people to help them qualify faster for these payments, and in 1984 created Allsup, Inc. to do just that. Today, Allsup, Inc. is the nation's largest and most successful SSDI claims-assistance company, with over 300,000 claims processed.[7]

Another arena in the general environment is the political-legal sector. This sector reflects the broad trends affecting law, government, and politics, including changes in political parties and players, new legal and policy initiatives, and intersections of government, politics, or law with the other forces in the general environment. An example is when forces from the technological, economic, and international sectors led to the Affordable Care Act of 2010, a federally mandated changeover requiring everyone to have health insurance.

Finally, there is the ecosystem/infrastructure sector, which reflects the physical world in which we live. This sector includes the natural components such as raw materials, weather, and ecological forces, as well as created components such as cities, roads, and other elements of the infrastructure. Changes here are sometimes unpredictable, like the highly destructive Hurricane Florence of 2018, but sometimes more predictable, like the worldwide decrease in forested areas over the past 200 years.

entrepreneurial ecosystem
A specific configuration of the environment that reflects the components that are most central to developing a strong and active community of start-up businesses. The components are entrepreneurs, government, universities, investors, service people, mentors, and large organizations.

general environment
A part of the external environment made up of sectors of major forces that shape the people and institutions of the task and internal environments, such as the economic sector or the demographic sector.

Environmental Scanning for Small Businesses

LO **3-2** Demonstrate your ability to scan the small business environment.

Big corporations have whole departments focused on scanning the environment and the firm's competitors. Most small businesses cannot afford to try that approach, but they can benefit tremendously from even a small amount of environmental scanning such as those shown in

SKILL MODULE 3.2 Finding Out How the Small Business Economy Is Doing

A key element in environmental scanning is assessing the overall environment and its trends. There are several ways to do this, from the simple to the complex. Simple approaches use a single or small set of numbers, like the Kauffman Indicators of Entrepreneurship (**indicators.kauffman.org/**) or the National Federation of Independent Business's *Small Business Economic Trends* (**www.nfib.com/surveys/small-business-economic-trends/**), which offers its monthly Index of Small Business Optimism. For these, your greatest concern is the trend, and whether it is rising or falling. At the other extreme, the Small Business Administration's Office of Advocacy offers its *Quarterly Bulletins* (**www.sba.gov/advocacy/small-business-quarterly-bulletins**) with a compendium of measures and the SBA's own analysis of them. One other key source of data for your state is the Office of Advocacy's Small Business Profiles for the States and Territories (**www.sba.gov/category/advocacy-navigation-structure/research-and-statistics/state-economic-profiles**), but these report data from one or two years earlier. If you want to compare entrepreneurship in the United States to other countries, you can look at the annual Global Entrepreneurship Monitor's global reports at **www.gemconsortium.org/report**.

Skill Module 3.2. There are several low-cost and relatively fast ways to monitor the environment.[8] They include:

- Looking for trends and future-looking articles in the trade and professional press of your industry or those of members of your task environment (see Skill Module 3.1).
- Asking your customers, suppliers, banker, attorney, and accountants what they see on the horizon for business in general, for business in your community in general, or for your industry or line of business in particular.
- Keeping notes on the things that bother you about the way work is done now, or what bothers you about how something has changed (whether a product, service, or process you deal with), and periodically doing some fast research (typically searching on the web) on what causes it and how others feel about it. For opinion websites, see Google's customer opinion websites and you'll find up-to-date reviews of top sites.
- Use the Flipboard app (or go to **flipboard.com**) to create a free custom feed of news from all sorts of brand-name sources including major magazines, newspapers, and tech-, science- and entrepreneur-related magazines. Flipboard will let you tag, save, and share things you like, as well as create custom feed based on your interests (like science, sports, politics, design, health, etc.).Skill Module 3.3 will show you how to do this.

Bill Gates is famous as a trend-spotter (although he has made some bad calls too), but one of the tricks he swears by is "Think Week," where he goes away by himself and spends time thinking and researching to help him focus on what is coming and what is important to his business. Most of us can't afford a week off, but putting aside three to four hours every three months to review what you have noticed and what notes you have made can do a lot to achieve the major benefits of environmental scanning, and still leave time to get your own work done. Between those occasions, you can help make yourself aware by using apps like Flipboard to keep you up on what's happening in the world. Skill Module 3.3 shows you how to do this.

"real options" approach
An idea in entrepreneurship popularized by Rita Gunther McGrath and Ian Macmillan that suggests thinking of entrepreneurial opportunities (like start-ups) in terms similar to buying a stock option, putting a small amount of money down now to let you invest more at favorable rates later. This approach minimizes the amount you can lose and gives you a chance to make a decision later, based on the start-up's track record and prospects.

Do not be afraid to make a bad decision. The trick with all forward looking choices is to use a **"real options" approach.**[9] A real option is a choice you face to do or not do something. As an entrepreneur, you will often face situations like this. You may need to make a decision, but you often have time to research it or wait to see what happens. So to pursue a real options approach, you establish benchmarks to achieve, timetables for their achievement, and a formal review process to get you to make the tough "continue" or "stop" decisions. Microsoft initially dismissed the Internet, but it revisited its decision and changed course to make Internet Explorer the most used browser in the world.

Scan Your Environment with the Flipboard App

SKILL MODULE 3.3

Flipboard is a smartphone app that gives you a constant feed of news—global, national, business, technology, cultural, and more. The app and the news it posts are free, and you can customize your personal newsfeed with topics of interest to you. The initial list of topics runs close to 150 of them, with examples like style, science, sustainability, skateboarding, *Star Wars,* sleep, and space (just to sample the *s* category). The steps to start are simple:

1. Download and install the app on your smartphone and create your account.
2. Select topics you want to include in your personal feed (which shows up as "For You" on Flipboard's front page. Grab a few to get started. You can always go back and scroll through the full list and edit your choices. (Useful topics include #Startups, #Entrepreneurship, #Trends.)
3. Try a few things: Search for the name of your locality (for local news), people, or causes or companies you want to be kept up-to-date about.
4. Tweak your settings in order to get notifications for news for your topics of interest.
5. Check Flipboard when you have time or want to explore the world.
6. Also use features like saving to "magazines" you create to keep track of things of interest.

Beyond trend-spotting, the other key scanning ability is to find the resources you need from the environment to build your business. The key to identifying resources comes from the acronym PROFIT, which stands for the six types of resources:[10]

- **Property/Physical:** Buildings, land, equipment, raw materials
- **Relational:** Customers, networks, distributors, social capital
- **Organizational:** Systems, structures, operational procedures
- **Financial:** Money, lines of credit, crowdfunding, bartering
- **Intellectual (also known as Human):** Employees, contractors, advisers, consultants, and the skills the business needs or has
- **Technological:** Patents, trademarks, ideas, copyrights, licenses, access to technology or expertise networks

social capital
Characteristics of a business, such as trust, consistency, and networks, that represent potential social obligations that are assets of the firm or entrepreneur.

To be successful, a start-up needs some of each of the six types of resources. You start by thinking about what resources you have. If you're not sure, look at similar sorts of businesses and analyze their resources. You may not be able to see all of them, but it is a start, and as you analyze more competitors, you'll begin to see different types of resources. Then ask yourself what kinds would be useful for your business. From that list, go back to your environmental scanning and look for the resources you need in your internal, task, and general environments.

So now you know what the environment is, what its different components are, and how and where you might keep an eye on the environment to help you prepare for the future. That leaves open how you deal with the environment on a daily basis as you begin or run your business. In the next section we look at the major techniques for managing your relations with the environment.

LEARN MORE ONLINE

Learn more about the topics above at these sites:

Entrepreneur magazine (daily newsletter with general small business news): **http://link.entrepreneur.com/join/signup**

Innovation Daily newsletter (on entrepreneurship and innovation): **www.innovationamerica.us/**

CultureBanx newsletter (news with a minority focus): **www.culturebanx.com/**

Skills for Managing Relations with the Environment

Having learned about the different types and sectors of the environment, and the way to scan and analyze them, it only makes sense to look at how to apply that knowledge to help launch and grow your own small business. In this section we will introduce two approaches to managing relations with the environment, what is called **external relations**:

external relations
The general description for the processes and skills used in the management of a firm's interactions with people, organizations, and institutions outside of its boundary.

- Building legitimacy
- Developing your networks

The goal of any small business owner is to manage external relations in order to create social capital. Social capital includes characteristics of a business, like trust, consistency, and networks, that help make business operations smooth and efficient. Small businesses high in social capital are more trusted, checked up on less, treated more fairly by regulators, and given the benefit of the doubt when problems occur.[11] This social capital is capital in the same sense that cash or land can be. You can accumulate it or spend it, and the more of it you have, the greater the value of your firm. Social capital is the major component of what accountants call "goodwill," and you can find it on a business's balance sheet. Let us look at the techniques for managing external relations and building social capital.

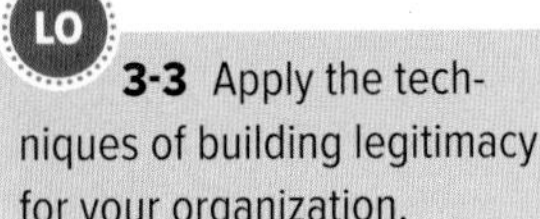

LO 3-3 Apply the techniques of building legitimacy for your organization.

Building Legitimacy

Legitimacy means that a firm is worthy of consideration or doing business with because of the impressions or opinions of customers, suppliers, investors, or competitors.[12] Gaining legitimacy is one of the top challenges facing new small businesses, but it can be especially difficult for entrepreneurs seen as "different"—women, minorities, home-based businesses, businesses started by young people, entrepreneurs introducing a new technology, or people new to the area or industry. Achieving legitimacy is also a major goal of all new businesses or of existing businesses that have gone through a significant change such as getting new owners or changing their product lines. Achieving legitimacy means building trust among customers and other key groups.

legitimacy
The belief that a firm is worthy of consideration or doing business with because of the impressions or opinions of customers, suppliers, investors, or competitors.

There are three general forms of legitimacy that you can develop—based on your people, based on your product, and based on your organization.[13] Each is discussed in the following tables.

Remember that often the owner *is* the business in many people's minds. So, he or she is the most important element of social capital to customers and supporters of a business, such as bankers, lawyers, and suppliers. Having people in the organization—an owner, employees, or even media spokespeople—whom customers know and respect increases the firm's legitimacy. Making sure the people of your business always work in the best, friendliest, and most professional way also helps build the business. Some of the major examples of people-based legitimacy are given in Table 3.1.

Also, many small business owners think that the most important source of legitimacy comes from an understanding of the product or service offered.[14] If customers do not understand it, the company is unlikely to get any customer attention because customers may not trust it. Fortunately, most small businesses offer products or services that customers are already familiar with (what we will call an "imitative strategy" in Chapter 7). The goal then becomes making sure the customer knows about the details of the product—its high quality and environmental friendliness, its competitive advantage, how to use it—and has the assurance that it will be backed up by the firm. Table 3.2 describes many forms of product-based legitimacy.

If the customer understands the product, the final key legitimacy factor is promoting knowledge about the organization itself. This might focus on telling about the history or visibility the firm already enjoys. It might come from published information that makes sure your firm looks like a substantial and professional business. Whatever gives customers confidence in the quality

TABLE 3.1 People-Based Legitimacy Indicators

People	More Legitimate	Less Legitimate
Goodwill	Have well-known or well-regarded owners, employees, supporters, or spokespeople	Lack well-known or well-regarded owners, employees, supporters, or spokespeople
Public recognition	Firm, owner, or employees receive awards (e.g., "Small Business of the Year") or make notable achievements outside the business (e.g., president of the PTA or BBB)	Have little or no public recognition
Product/service name recognition	Sell brand-name merchandise or services	Sell non-brand-name merchandise or services
Public reviews	Have more reviews and more stars on Yelp, Google, or other rating sites	Have fewer reviews and fewer stars on rating sites
Business network membership	Have membership in trade (e.g., National Restaurant Association) and business (e.g., BBB, NFIB, chamber of commerce) organizations	Have no memberships in trade and business organizations
Organizational size	Have employees	Have no employees
Attire	Wear uniforms or business attire	Wear casual attire

and survivability of the firm helps the selling process and in turn increases the all-important trust factor. Table 3.3 gives the key factors for organizational legitimacy.

Another approach to building organization-based legitimacy, which has grown in popularity since the original list was crafted, is the creation and display of a company code of ethics. In practice, good codes of ethics reflect the passions of the founder, the culture of the firm, and three classes of ethical standards found in research on existing codes of ethics.[15] These three classes are:

- Employees Should Be Dependable Organizational Citizens (e.g., finish your work, follow rules and orders, be on time, do not swear, dress appropriately, etc.)
- Do Not Do Anything That Will Harm the Organization (e.g., protect confidential information, do not take drugs, kickbacks, or company property, etc.)
- Be Good to Customers (e.g., be truthful, be helpful, listen attentively, etc.)

LO **3-4** Navigate the techniques of social networking.

Across these three types of legitimacy indicators there are 30 characteristics, and few small businesses incorporate all these elements. Most of the time the small business owner will pick 2 or 3 legitimacy-building features from each of the product, organizational, and people indicator listings and then work to implement them. Once implemented, they should be locked in. Part of legitimacy and building trust comes from the consistency of a firm's actions over time. Repeating one legitimacy characteristic daily does more to build your social capital than changing the legitimacy characteristics stressed by the firm in hopes of finding the perfect mix of characteristics.[16]

ISO
Stands for the International Organization for Standardization, and refers to certification for having met a standard of quality that is consistently evaluated around the world (see **www.iso.org**).

Baldrige Award
The Malcolm Baldrige National Quality Award is given by the U.S. government to businesses and nonprofit organizations that have been judged outstanding in seven measures of quality leadership; strategic planning; customer and market focus; measurement, analysis, and knowledge management; human resource focus; process management; and results (see **www.nist.gov/baldrige**).

TABLE 3.2 Product-Based Legitimacy Indicators

Product	More Legitimate	Less Legitimate
Customer assurance	Have publicly stated guarantees, bonding, try-before-you-buy policies and return policies, etc.	Have no publicly stated guarantees or return policies, etc.
Experiential supports	Offer documentation or demonstration	Do not offer documentation or demonstration
Customer service	Provide customer service live or online	Do not provide customer service live or online
Quality standards	Meet or exceed industry standards for quality	Fail to meet industry standards for quality
Environmental friendliness	Use recyclable materials, demonstrate green design, or have a low carbon footprint.	Show no concern for the environment or natural resources
Certifications	Are certified for **ISO**, **Baldrige Award**, minority or women-owned business, professional licensing	Are self-certified only
Testimonials	Present testimonials from customers satisfied with the product	Provide no information from users
Intellectual property	Have trademarks, service marks, patents, or copyrights	Have no trademarks, service marks, patents, or copyrights
Industry leadership	Set technological or service standards adopted by competitors	Use or provide common technologies or services
Media product/ service visibility	Achieve visibility for products/services through interviews, articles, placements, or columns in print or electronic media	Provide little or no visibility about products/ services in print or electronic media

Developing Your Networks

Another basis for building social capital is through building your network. There are two overlapping forms of network. Your *personal network* are people you have encountered in your everyday life—family, friends, classmates, workmates, and others you interact with in the physical world. Your *social network* are the people you know online.[17] Many of the people in your personal network may well be part of your social network, but you may know many more people through your social network than you might from your personal network. Knowing how to grow and sustain each is a key skill for any entrepreneur.

Both forms of networking are ways to work trust, reciprocity, and long-term relationships into your day-to-day business operations. They are ways to build your company's expertise by convincing others to share their skills and knowledge with your firm. The most successful owners are those who recognize that others have the expertise needed and establish relationships that give them the benefits of that expertise. In many of the stories of small business owners in this book you will see how success hinges on getting others to help you. You might be new to your business, industry, or locality, but, with the right expertise, your business can improve its chances of succeeding. The key is building a network of people who trust you and are willing to help you,[18] and who can depend on you for help and advice in return. Through this mutuality, social networking helps build long-lasting relationships.

TABLE 3.3 Organization-Based Legitimacy Indicators

Product	More Legitimate	Less Legitimate
Internet presence	Are on several platforms: website, Facebook, Instagram, Twitter, LinkedIn	Are on few or no Internet platforms
Firm name	The firm owns and uses its name as its domain name, e.g. Rabbitears Corp. is online as rabbitears.com	rabbitears.wordpress.com, rabbitears.wix.com, etc.
Media organization visibility	Achieve visibility through interviews, articles, or columns in print or electronic media about the organization	Receive little or no attention in print or electronic media about the organization
History	Have been in operation for a long time	Are new
Time commitment	Are a full-time organization	Are a part-time organization
Hours of operation	9–5, 9–9, 24/7	1–5, 6–9
Days of operation	M–F, 7 days a week	One day, weekends only
Phone line	Dedicated to business	Shared with home
Legal form	Corporation or LLC	Sole proprietorship or partnership
Physical setting	Commercial site like a store, office building, or mall	Home-based business; a business with no physical location; a business run out of a post office mailbox
Public listings	Google, Yelp, Yellow Pages, Dun & Bradstreet Business Profile, business directories	White Pages or none
Internet identity	Use business name (e.g., katz@esb.com)	Use generic name (e.g., katz@gmail.com)
Graphic design (business cards, stationery, websites, etc.)	Professionally done	Personally done
Partnering	Partners with known businesses	Partners with unknown businesses or no partnering
Dealer network membership	Authorized dealer or agent	Unauthorized, gray, or black market dealer or agent
Code of ethics	Adopt your industry's code of ethics, create one of your own, display the code	No code of ethics adopted

In both types of networking, you seek to build your reputation because reputation will have an impact on your community; if it is positive, it will increase trust and create a culture that enables people to make good decisions. Both forms of networking help all those aspects of small business by building your reputation as giving the most expert business goods or services and as being an important community resource. Effective networking of both types can help your long-term reputation as a business owner by showing others who you are[19]—a consistently top-notch community player.

TABLE 3.4 Sources for Network Connections

Family: Start here, and ask your parents, grandparents, and extended family. Include in-laws.

Friends and neighbors: Include your friends, and friends of friends.

Kids: Think about the people you've met through your children at their school and in their extracurricular activities.

Bank: You probably have a bank account, possibly several. Get to know your bankers and ask them for introductions or referrals.

Customer contacts: You are a customer, patient, or client to doctors, dentists, insurance agents, lawyers, and small business owners of all sorts. They know you and because they're in business, they may have the kind of contacts you need.

School: Think about students, faculty, and support organizations where you or your family have gone to school. Many colleges have alumni offices and entrepreneurship or small business development centers, and these can put you in touch with helpful others.

Hobbies: Hobbies often bring together people with diverse backgrounds. That makes them a great place for finding different sorts of contacts.

Business associations: Most communities have some form of chamber of commerce. Most industries and professions have associations. People join these in order to network. Ask the officers of the chamber of commerce or the association for referrals. Be willing to assist others who ask for your help.

Other organizations: Religious, civic, community, and political organizations often publish member lists. Go over these to see if you recall people who have the business ties or expertise you need.

Work: Consider co-workers, bosses, customers, suppliers, and people in other firms with whom you deal. Note that work contacts can be problematic. Check company rules or expectations first. Many firms consider such contacts a conflict of interest.

Small business support organizations: There are always organizations dedicated to small business such as the National Federation of Independent Business, National Small Business United, and the National Association for the Self-Employed. You can get lists of these by searching Google's directory for "small business associations." Many of these organizations have local chapters, and all encourage members to contact and help one another.

Developing Your Personal Networks

So, look at the contact list on your cell phone. Who is on it? What is your relationship with each person or organization? Those numbers are the easiest way to start thinking about and analyze your personal network. Table 3.4 talks about the major categories of your personal network. As you realize the types of personal network connections, you can better think about how to grow your personal networks.

What should you expect in terms of your personal network? Social psychologists tell us some basics, many of which we know from experience.[20] Not all contacts are equal. There are our closest friends, which can include family, and often number up to 5 people. Adding to this is the next layer of close friends, which might number as high as 10 to 15 people. General friends might number up to 50 people, and acquaintances up to 150. The more extroverted you are, the more likely you are to approximate these numbers; the more introverted, the smaller your circles will be at each level. The amount of time you spend will typically decrease as you go from inner to outer circles of friends. You may spend a few minutes each week, or even every day, with your closest friends, and connect with acquaintances by phone, email or social media only every month or two.

This sort of pattern was evident for entrepreneurs surveyed as part of the Panel Study of Entrepreneurial Dynamics (PSED). In the PSED, most prospective and early stage entrepreneurs reported having one or two people in their helping network, and they typically reported around three contacts a month across their whole network of folks providing help.[21] Information is the number one type of help sought from others, followed by introductions to others. Occasionally sought were requests for specific sorts of help—financing, business services, personal services, or resources.

Keep in mind the most powerful way to connect is face-to-face (about 34 times more powerful than email[22]). Phone is next and works best when the tone and context of your message needs to be heard. Email works if you're looking for a reaction or reply and the topic needs some explaining. If you need a reply but the thought is easily expressed, texting can work. Social media are the channels people view most irregularly, and they are also the channels that get the least consistent responses from recipients; so they are the least powerful way to ensure a connection to another person.[23]

Knowing whom to ask, what to ask for, and which channel to use when asking is only part of the story. The other part involves building the relationships and encouraging others to help you. One of the key parts of social networking is actually seeking the help or advice of others. Asking for help well is a skill. A little advance thinking and preparation can dramatically produce positive results. Skill Module 3.4 shows you one of the most successful methods for asking others for help.

Asking for Help

SKILL MODULE 3.4

The best people to ask for help are often the people who are the busiest. Knowing this, some small business owners shy away from imposing. In reality, there is no substitute for expertise, and getting it from others is one of the most efficient and effective ways to do it. Building on the ideas of Paula Caproni,[24] here is an eight-step approach to asking others for help:

- **Request from people you trust:** Either ask people who already know you, or establish a relationship with the people you want to ask before seeking help from them. This can be as little as a few minutes of talk to find common ground or common friends at a chamber of commerce reception, but it is an important foundation for the relationship.
- **Ask for specific behavior:** Your request is more likely to fit someone's schedule if it is specific and something that has a definite end. So, asking "How can I get an introduction to someone in purchasing at BigCorp?" is more likely to get a positive response than, "What can I do to sell more?"
- **Do not be defensive:** When explaining what you need, do not blame others for your needing help. And when asked questions by potential helpers, do not get upset or accusatory. Often they need to know what you have tried, how you did it, and how it worked out. They also often need to know what you are capable of doing, or what expertise you bring to the situation. Give concise answers and show your willingness to answer more. After all, they need the information to help you.
- **Do not overreact or underreact:** Think of your regular conversations with good customers or friends. That kind of give-and-take and that kind of emotional level is what a good asking-for-help exchange sounds like. While being brief is good—after all, time is money—if you sound like you are holding back or are unwilling to talk, it does not help build the relationship. On the other hand, going overboard with praise and information can come across as phony or irritating. Think of regular conversations, and try to emulate them here.
- **Summarize what was said to ensure understanding:** When your conversation is nearing the end, repeat what you understood as the advice. It is fine to put it in your own words. The goal here is for you and the person helping you to know that each of you understood the other. If you are going to try the advice on your own, you want to be certain you understand what to do, how to do it, and maybe even why to do it that way. Summarizing is a great way to confirm all that and show how attentive you have been.
- **Explain what you are going to do about feedback:** People you approach as experts often take part of their satisfaction from knowing that their expertise has made a difference—especially in your business, but at least in your thinking. If you can tell such people how you will use their help, it can provide them with an immediate reward. If you are not sure what action you will take, be honest about this, but also point to the new things you have learned or discovered from the help they offered.
- **Thank the person for the input:** This is in part providing an immediate payout to the person helping you, but also laying a foundation for future contact. Provide a simple thanks and mention how you hope to return the favor or help someday. A good handshake and a smile, and you are ready to get back to business.

(Continued)

- **Follow through:** It is always a good idea to inform people who tried to help you about how your efforts came out. Tell them how you solved your business problem in general terms. If their help was used, mention this. Thank them for their help (whether you used it or not). Finish with a mention of your appreciation of their help and your willingness to help them in the future.

mutuality
The action of each person helping another.

Remember, social networking makes a difference in how you'll conduct business every day. It means asking for help when you need it, respecting the other person's time and expertise, and most importantly being willing to reciprocate if asked. **Mutuality** is the idea and action of each person helping the other. Part of building social capital with social networking comes from the help people in the network can provide one another. Why help? Reasons may be making a new friend or making a friendship stronger, creating a relationship that can lead to future business or friendship, having a chance to demonstrate expertise, incurring a debt for future repayment, or even just wanting to help others. Helping others means you understand the idea of positive community impact, trust, and relationships–critical success factors in building an ethical business.

networking
Interacting with others in order to build relationships useful to a business.

Building social capital through social networking involves giving information, letting people know they belong, and providing social support and approval. You have to take the time to build and keep up your relationships with others in your network. This is called personal **networking**, which means small business owners interacting with others in order to build relationships useful to the business. Key skills for effective small business personal networking are given in Skill Module 3.5.

SKILL MODULE 3.5

Personal Networking Skills

Personal networking is a skill like any other. In business you often know the kind of situation you are about to go into or are likely to face. Knowing this, you can take several steps to prepare yourself to socialize with others as a basis for establishing a business relationship. Below are top suggestions of successful alums of our entrepreneurship program and the advice of experts.

Emily Muhoberac, COO of Sapper Consulting and Adjunct Faculty at Saint Louis University

- **Go with a friend.** While I think everyone should experience going to a networking event alone, you can ease your anxiety by attending your first event with a friend or colleague. Not only will this help you at the event, but it will also hold you accountable to actually attend (like a gym buddy).
- **Remember that networking might not help you now.** It's like investing time or money into most things that are worthwhile–you're not likely to see an immediate return. Many of the opportunities I've received came months or years after initially meeting the contact at an event.
- **Admit you don't know all the buzzwords and jargon.** Pretending to know what's going on won't make you look smarter, and won't help you out in the end. You'll end up either admitting you don't know at an inopportune time, or miss out on valuable knowledge that would have helped you grow.
- **Check the RSVP list to pre-network.** Most networking events have public RSVP lists where you can see who will be attending. Make connections before you get there, reaching out to guests that you'd like to talk to or have common interests via LinkedIn. Make a list for the meeting to help focus and remind you who you want to meet and why.

Byron Abrigg, Cofounder and COO at Mission Control GG

- **Play your student card.** There are very few executives or professionals who are not willing to give some time over a cup of coffee to offer some career advice and life lessons . . . because you're a student. As soon as you graduate, you are now a fellow professional out looking for something (a job, a promotion, etc.). Use your student card to get in as many conversations as possible while you can before it expires!
- **Ask for money, get advice; ask for advice, get money.** When networking, the only thing you should be looking for is advice. When you genuinely ask for input and advice, you build relationships and make others feel welcome and appreciated. It's only when you do this—build genuine relationships up front—that you can truly reap the dividends later. We raised our first $100K and lined up a dozen industry advisers for our first start-up simply off of genuine relationships we had built with people over the years where we never asked for anything but advice.

Advice from networking experts:[25]

- **Know who you are.** Craft a 30-second spot about yourself and your firm, and practice it until it sounds like a natural expression of your interests. This is often called an *elevator pitch*, and Chapter 8 (Business Plans) gives details on putting together a winning one.
- **Bone up on small talk.** What do you say after hello? A good place to start is to give your elevator pitch and close with why you were looking forward to meeting the person. If you think your business can help the other person's, talk about that. If the other person wants to limit the conversation to social topics, go with that. To help with chitchat in those situations, make sure you look at the local newspaper (sports section included) on the day of the event, and take a look at *The Wall Street Journal* or *USA Today* front page or your Flipboard feed if you can.
- **Do not forget why you're there.** People tend to gather in groups of like-minded folks. This can mean that all the golf players are together talking strokes, but it can be deadly if it means that all the women entrepreneurs are gathered together and not networking with the male business owners. If you are at a networking event and you start feeling comfortable, check to make sure it is not because you have actually stopped networking.
- **Make the connection.** The key to making networking work is to make the personal connection. Businesspeople *expect* to be approached by others at events. Do not be shy. Just walk up and say hello. If necessary, ask a friend or an event organizer to make the introduction, but, however you do it, meet the people.
- **Follow up.** After you meet someone at a networking event, periodically keep up the contact through emails, phone, mail, or personal contact. If you can offer help or information, that is the best reason to stay in touch.

Remember that the place to start thinking about your personal network is your cell phone contact list. A basic one is built into your phone, and it can connect to even more powerful versions in the cloud. If you use an Android phone, the cloud version is Google Contacts. For iPhone users it is Contacts on iCloud. If you have a version of Microsoft Office, you can use Outlook. The cell phone contact list can directly connect to programs that can help you build and manage your list, such as Camcard which scans business cards and adds them to your contact list, or full-fledged **customer relationship management (CRM)** software platforms like Zoho CRM, SuiteCRM or HubSpot which can let you organize your lists, get reminders when to re-contact someone, and create mailing labels.[26] Also note that your cell phone contact list can be connected to social networking apps like LinkedIn to help add more information to your regular contacts.

customer relationship management (CRM)
The process of tracking the customer's different contacts with the firm, and using these data to help improve sales as well as the customer's experience.

The goal is to make sure you keep track of your social and business contacts. The best approaches help you identify whom you need to contact to keep relationships fresh. This is because networking is one of the key skills for *all* business owners, female and male, minority and majority, high tech and no tech. Because in the end, business is all about making the sale and the sale depends on making a connection with customers, and that connection is what networking is all about.

Developing Your Social Networks

In personal networking most people probably top out around 150 or so friends and acquaintances. The power of social networking, however, becomes readily apparent because if all 150 friends and acquaintances are on a social media platform like LinkedIn or Facebook, and they have their 150 connections, you may be 1 connection away from 22,500 people! And broadcasting your interests to thousands, even millions, of people is much easier, faster and cheaper on social media platforms than in the world of personal networking. The challenge for entrepreneurs considering developing their social network is to decide which networks to pursue, and what is the best strategy to use.

The key factor for the small business owner is realizing where their target customers are. If you are looking to sell to consumers (a B2C business), then Facebook, YouTube, or Instagram are crucial to your strategy because they each have 1 billion users or more globally. YouTube is key if you generate videos, Instagram for photo-driven messaging, and Facebook handles both as well as textual messages. If your competitors have company pages on those platforms, you might want to consider setting up shop there too. If you are focused on selling to businesses (yours is then a B2B business), LinkedIn is the top platform. Note there are also dozens of specialized social media platforms that typically have smaller numbers of more highly active users, like Buzznet for music, Q&A platforms like Thumb or Ask.fm, or business platforms like Xing. Google "social media channels" to find the latest articles on different social media platforms.

A lot of entrepreneurs have their business on multiple platforms and many find Facebook, LinkedIn, and Twitter to be the "Big 3" of social networking. A number of businesses have a company or product page on Facebook and LinkedIn pages for the company, the owner, and even key employees. Today there are all sorts of free and freemium platforms to help you manage your message on multiple social media sites, such as Hootsuite.com and Buffer.com. These platforms let you create, schedule, and post one message on all your platforms, simplifying your ability to see and track what you are doing.

Regardless of the site or sites you use, there are four best practices that can help any online social networking effort become more successful (whether you are pursuing it online or in person):

- Make it easy for people to contact you (this often means giving one of your email or social network addresses).
- Take the initiative to ask others on the network (including colleagues from school and work, and friends and family) to link with you and then help them out online.
- Find and link up with network mavens–people who like to gather and share their enormous networks–and help out whenever you can.[27]
- Keep at it–successful online networking requires consistent involvement. It can be weekly, but it needs to be every week.

Electronic social networks are usually fast and easy to develop, as well as often free. Face-to-face social networks often have membership costs, but offer the all-important personal touch as well as those all-important local connections. When either type of social network works, it can produce results from unexpected sources. While the personal connection from face-to-face networking is always a great thing to have, if you cannot easily develop a large face-to-face network in your community, industry, or market, electronic social networking is the best way to go.

LEARN MORE ONLINE

Learn more about the topics above at these sites:

Facebook for Business advice search: **www.google.com/search?q=how+to+use+facebook+for+business**

Advertising on Google advice search: **www.google.com/search?q=advertising+on+google**

Advertising on LinkedIn advice search: **www.google.com/search?q=advertising+on+linkedin**

Skills for Making the Right Decision

As an entrepreneur you will make all sorts of decisions, from right now as you are thinking about the kind of business you want to start and how it will operate, and into the future as your business launches, grows, and hits the high and low points all businesses–and people–face. Thinking ahead of time about those decisions and situations can help you prepare yourself and your firm for the future. There are three areas where this is particularly important:

- Handling a crisis
- Achieving sustainability
- Making ethical decisions

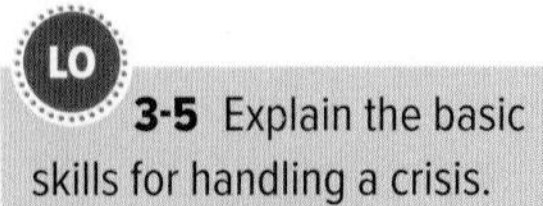

LO
3-5 Explain the basic skills for handling a crisis.

Handling a Crisis

While some challenges come slowly and give the small business owner a chance to think about how to choose, all businesses sooner or later face some sort of crisis. A crisis is a situation that poses a major problem for the business or its people, in which the survival of the business is at stake, and immediate action is necessary.[28] For owners, knowing what to do during a crisis is a very specialized and emotionally demanding form of decision making. Small business owners are optimists about their businesses, and it can be wrenching when something goes wrong. When the crisis is in full swing, knowing what to do is critical. The gold standard for crisis leadership comes from Norman Augustine,[29] former president of Lockheed Martin–a Fortune 500 company. Although originally given for large businesses, the six steps to follow can be readily adapted to small ones.[30]

The steps are:

1. Admit you're in trouble–quickly. It is better to say "If there is a problem, I will find it and fix it" than to delay an admission until fact-finding is done.
2. Get to the scene as soon as possible. Your job? Show caring and accountability.
3. Communicate facts you know (and those you don't) to employees, customers, and suppliers.
4. Have one person serve as the firm's spokesperson. It is best if it can be the owner, but an articulate employee, family member, or outside professional (e.g., lawyer) can stand in.
5. Separate crisis management from the everyday management of the firm. If you are doing both, try to take time to do each separately. Delegate as much as possible of the everyday management to employees or family while you concentrate on dealing with the crisis.
6. Deal with the crisis quickly. Take steps to solve the problem, and make the process of dealing with the problem as open as possible.

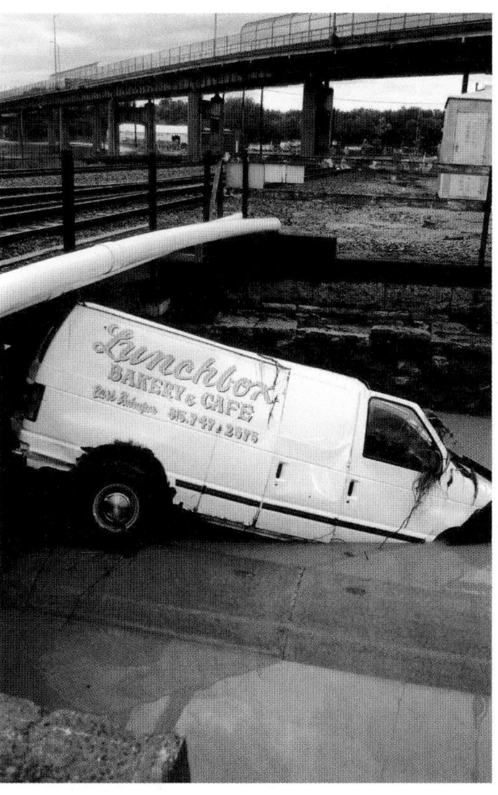

For a small business, an accident like this can become a crisis. Knowing what to do can help minimize its impact on your firm, customers, and employees.

Denise McCullough

Managing crisis is a difficult but necessary skill. Obviously, anticipating problems and avoiding them or handling them before they become major is a better approach, but only 1 business in 10 has a disaster or crisis plan.[31] To help small businesses with crisis planning the federal government has created a new website (www.ready.gov) to bring all these resources together in one location. The government recommends a three-step process for preparing for disasters:

1. Plan to stay in business (use a disaster plan like the SBA's from www.sba.gov/business-guide/manage-your-business/prepare-emergencies).
2. Talk to your people (plan with co-workers, practice your plans, and have a crisis communications approach in place). Include preparing a "dark website" with key information that you activate only during an emergency.[32]
3. Protect your investment (use insurance–see Chapter 16, backup procedures and supplies, etc.).

In the end, the best way to manage a crisis is to plan ahead, but in the middle of a crisis, the key for a small business owner is to keep calm, take care of the people involved, and keep people informed.

Achieving Sustainability

LO 3-6 Recognize how small businesses can achieve sustainability.

Researchers are finding human trash at the bottom of the oceans. Plastic grocery bags get caught on fences miles from cities. We are all seeing the problem of too much garbage and not enough recycling. *Sustainable entrepreneurship* is an approach to the operation of the firm, the line of business of the firm, or both, which identifies or creates and then exploits opportunities to make a profit in a manner that minimizes the depletion of natural resources, maximizes the use of recycled material, improves the environment, or achieves any combination of these outcomes. Positive outcomes along these lines are described as "greener," so the approach is also sometimes called *green entrepreneurship.*

As a nation, we have increased our greenness over the past 20 years through a variety of actions. We drive more fuel-efficient cars today because of government-mandated fuel efficiency standards. Companies and individuals do more recycling of trash. The latest effort to replace regular light bulbs with compact fluorescent and LED lights is another green effort.

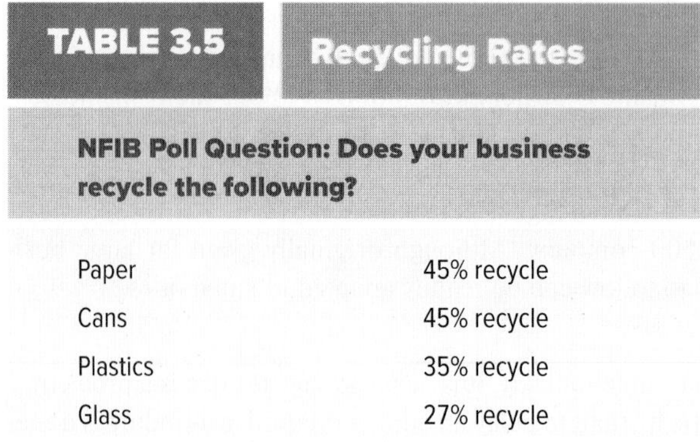

TABLE 3.5 Recycling Rates

NFIB Poll Question: Does your business recycle the following?	
Paper	45% recycle
Cans	45% recycle
Plastics	35% recycle
Glass	27% recycle

Source: National Federation of Independent Business, Small Business Poll, *Waste and Hazardous Materials* 7, no. 2 (2007). The U.S. Environmental Protection Agency believes the rates continue to rise.

Entrepreneurs can do quite a lot to manage their firm's impact on the environment. Recycling is one approach many businesses use. According to the National Federation of Independent Business (NFIB) poll, recycling among small businesses varies, depending on what is being recycled. Recycling rates for the major types of trash are given in Table 3.5.

A great way to start thinking about minimizing waste and environmental degradation is to run your thoughts about your business through a "green audit" like the one developed by the U.S. Environmental Protection Agency (www.epa.gov/compliance/audit-protocols) or those developed to obtain **ISO 14001 certification** for environmental management systems (try searching for "ISO 14001 checklist" to find out more). Minimizing paper use, using telecommuting and electronic communication, replacing paper copies with web-based documents, and buying products for the business made from recycled materials or products that can be recycled are all ways to create a more sustainable enterprise.

ISO 14001 certification
A certification awarded to organizations for creating and implementing an environmental management system that meets the requirement of the International Organization for Standardization.

The business itself can focus on ways to enhance others' sustainability efforts and make a profit doing it. Have you read about buildings in your area being LEED certified? It stands for Leadership in Energy and Environmental Design and is a certification standard from the U.S. Green Building Council for buildings that are more environmentally friendly (www.usgbc.org/leed). Construction companies have found this area to be a new source of sales and profits, as new buildings are designed to be more energy efficient and recyclable, and older buildings get retrofitted for energy savings and healthier internal environments. Similarly, green retailing, selling products that have a better environmental footprint, is a growing segment. Whether talking about greening your own business or making a profit from helping others get greener, sustainable entrepreneurship is another method for managing external relations with customers, governments, and the physical environment.

LEARN MORE ONLINE

Learn more about the topics above at these sites:

The EU's Green Entrepreneurship website: **greentproject.eu**

World Bank's green entrepreneurship page: **http://www.infodev.org/connecting-green-entrepreneurs**

Feedspot's list of green business blogs and websites: **https://blog.feedspot.com/green_business_blogs/**

LO **3-7** Identify the major steps in making ethical decisions in small business.

Making Ethical Decisions

Today so many of the issues that people have with business are ones with an ethical or moral element. Think about when you discovered Facebook was selling your personal data to companies for advertising purposes, or that some apps track your every swipe, or that a food company uses additives that lead to high blood pressure, or that a drug company uses animals for testing new products. How would you feel about a Coke machine that charges you more the hotter the outdoor temperature is?

ethics
A system of values that people consider in determining whether actions are right or wrong.

ethical dilemma
A situation that occurs when a person's values are in conflict, making it unclear whether a particular decision is the right thing to do.

Ethics comprise a system of values people use to determine whether actions are right or wrong. We consider ethics in determining whether a decision we are about to make is good or bad. And, we make judgments about actions–something is good or bad; someone is right or wrong–based on our own personal ethics. An **ethical dilemma** occurs when a person's values are in conflict, making it unclear whether a decision we're thinking about making is right or not.[33] An ethical dilemma also occurs when there are several different options for a decision we have to make and the best choice isn't clear. Of the many environment managing techniques discussed in this section, making ethical decisions is undoubtedly the hardest. Part of it is because the ethical problems that keep entrepreneurs up at night are ones for which there is not a satisfying yes or no answer.

LaRue Hosmer was initially a professor of entrepreneurship who came from a family logging business. He later turned his eye toward the challenge of making ethical decisions in business. He came up with a model widely used today, but it is focused more on big businesses than small ones. Adapting his approach[34] to small business, making ethical decisions involves three steps:

1. **Define:** Define the moral problem.
2. **Generate:** Generate alternatives that could meet the ethical, legal, and economic goals every business must balance.
3. **Implement:** Pick the best alternative you and your business can live with and implement it.

The model is given in Figure 3.2. As you might expect, although the steps sound easy, doing them well requires working through some complicated issues. Let us look at each step in turn.

Define the Moral Problem: To determine the moral dimension of a problem, you need to carefully think through the problem. For small businesses, there are typically four questions used to define the moral problem under consideration:

1. Who will be hurt (and how much)? Obviously more hurt is worse, but you also need to consider how likely recovery is and how long will it take to recover.
2. Who will benefit (and how much)? A tiny benefit for many is often of little use–think of those class action lawsuits that end up giving each of millions of claimants a few dollars off their next purchase. The overall size of the benefit needs to be weighed against the number who benefit, and balanced against the costs of the harm done to others by the solution.
3. What do you (or your firm) owe others? When you make a decision, it should reflect your real or presumed obligations to people and institutions in your firm and in its task environment. How you act under pressure is seen by many as the acid test of who you are and what your firm is about.
4. What do others owe you (or your firm)? Just as you and your firm make a commitment to others, they make commitments to you and your firm. Depending on the decision, there may be obligations from others or forms of support you can expect that help make doing the ethical thing easier on you or the other party involved.

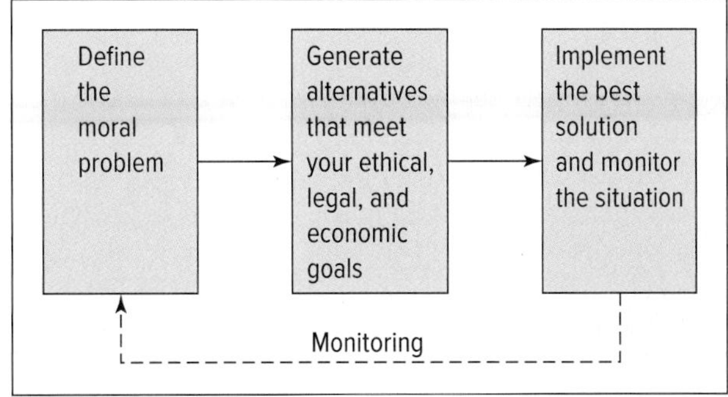

FIGURE 3.2

The Ethical Decision-Making Model for Small Business

Source: Adapted from LaRue T. Hosmer, *The Ethics of Management*, 6th ed. (Boston: McGraw-Hill/Irwin, 2008).

Generate Alternatives That Meet Your Ethical, Legal, and Economic Goals: Once you have defined the moral problem you face, you need to generate a variety of alternatives to handle it. These alternatives need to be evaluated to find the best one. At this stage, it makes sense to compare the alternatives to the ethical, legal, and economic standards of your firm, industry, and community.

Start with economic standards. Often economic dilemmas crop up in business because the answer sought by the other person would cost your business money. Sometimes the amount of money is more important symbolically than in reality. Have you seen a friend who will drive several miles to save a penny on a gallon of gas? Do the math. A typical gas tank size is 15 gallons and the average gas mileage of cars in the United States is 27.5 miles per gallon. If gas is $2.50 a gallon, then each mile costs 9 cents, and saving a penny a gallon makes economic sense only if the round-trip to the cheaper gas station is under 1.66 miles. Still, many people will pay more rather than feel they were taken advantage of.

That sense of being taken advantage of is a tough emotion to set aside, but in the end, part of being a professional in business, and part of being an honest decision maker requires that people do that. There is no easy way. It takes courage to do the right thing, and self-control to quash the emotional desire to lash out or get even.

Legal standards seem easy at first. If the answer is against the law, simply do not do it. But in reality, everyone's compliance with the law is less than perfect. Think about your classmates. How many occasionally drive above the speed limit? How many have a couple of pirated songs on their smartphone or iPod? Could one of your classmates with a part-time business have claimed more business expenses on a tax return than could be documented? Realize that even generally law-abiding people have their lapses. If the stakes or emotions are high enough, or the risk of being caught or being prosecuted is relatively low, people you would consider law-abiding could make a decision to do something illegal.

There are times when doing what is legally supported may not be the optimal solution. Consider EntreQuest (now called Shift - www.shiftthework.com), a Baltimore training firm with a famous example. When starting out, the two cofounders, Joe Mechlinski and Jason Pappas, heard through the grapevine that their first, biggest, and at that time only client was going to break its contract with EntreQuest. If that happened, Joe and Jason could take the client to court—but it would cost money, and even if they won, how would the client (or prospective clients) feel about EntreQuest? Jason and Joe had the law on their side, but decided to be proactive and meet with the client to find a better solution. It worked, and the resulting new contract made EntreQuest even bigger profits than before.[35]

So, when thinking through the legal standards, recognize that having the law on your side may feel good, but may not be workable as a solution. You can find yourself in the legal "right" but still unable to make a viable business decision by pursuing legal recourse. Still, the simple advice that you should not break the law knowingly and willfully makes a lot of sense as a legal standard for making moral decisions.

That leaves the ethical standard. Most professions (e.g., social workers, MDs, pharmacists, lawyers, etc.) and many occupation-specific organizations (e.g., Realtors®, Society of Professional Journalists, Association for Computing Machinery, etc.) have codes of ethics to help clarify their standards to members and the public. But there are several areas in business that do not have explicit standards, or that have standards but cannot enforce them on all members of an occupation.

caveat emptor
A Latin expression that means "let the buyer beware," which has been made into a philosophy sometimes used by businesses to put the burden for consumer protection onto the customer.

You can still see an occasional entrepreneur, corporate magnate, or economic pundit invoke the old Latin phrase **caveat emptor**, let the buyer beware. It gets repeated because it has popped up in legal cases, and the Latin makes it sound impressive, but as a legal principle, it has been routinely discredited.[36] Caveat emptor is often the first line of defense by rip-off artists, frauds, and producers of shoddy merchandise. Using it as a defense puts the entrepreneur who uses it, and, usually by association, the whole small business community, in a negative light. If you find businesses using caveat emptor as a principle, avoid them. If you have to deal with them, get everything in writing and watch them like a hawk. If they ask you if you trust them, use another famous line, from former president Ronald Reagan, "Trust, but verify."

The 40th president of the United States, Ronald Reagan, popularized the translation of a Soviet-era proverb "Trust, but verify." He used it on USSR premier Mikhail Gorbachev to get a workable deal banning intermediate range nuclear missiles. When looking for a workable deal of your own and getting hit with caveat emptor (let the buyer beware), hit back with Reagan's equally punchy "Trust, but verify," and follow your advice. Don't get caught unaware.

Dirck Halstead/The LIFE Images Collection/Getty Images

Assuming you realize the caveat emptor approach is not the way to go, you may still need to make a decision you believe is ethical. Here are four proven philosophies to try when you are thinking through alternatives to help you determine how ethical the choices are.

- **Am I treating others the way I would want to be treated?** You've probably heard of this one before. It's the **Golden Rule**, and almost every major religious tradition in the world has some version of it. Dumping toxic waste in someone's pond would be acceptable behavior if he or she could dump toxic waste in your pond. An unlikely example, but the point is that you need to think how you'd feel if someone took the same action *toward you* that you're thinking about taking. The Golden Rule can be one of the easiest ways to think about ethical dilemmas and potential solutions. It's a simple question: *Would I want to be treated in the way I am thinking about treating someone else?*

Golden Rule
An ethical model that suggests you treat others in the manner you wish to be treated.

- **Is my solution the best thing for the most people over the long term?** You may have heard of an idea called **utilitarianism**. Basically, it means that the action resulting in the greatest good for the greatest number of people is the right action to take. This idea has a strong community focus. One of the most important aspects of it is that you have to consider how your actions will affect other people. It's not about what's fun or quick in the short term but asks you to think about people's best interests down the road. If your solution means that many people will benefit from your actions, with acceptable costs to you, it's probably a good solution.

utilitarianism
An ethical model that supports seeking the greatest good for the greatest number of people.

- **What if everyone did what I want to do? What kind of world would it be?** Those questions in a nutshell are the idea of **universalism**, a code of right and wrong that everyone can see and follow. You may have read about universalism in philosophy class, since it's the brainchild of the German philosopher Immanuel Kant. You may have also heard it expanded by mothers everywhere. You get your ideas of right and wrong from your family, religion, education, and community. You can hear an example of this sort of thinking in real life in a lecture at Stanford by Heidi Roizen, https://ecorner.stanford.edu/in-brief/dont-compromise-your-ethics/.

universalism
An ethical model that suggests that there is a code of right and wrong that everyone can see and follow.

- **What if my decision were advertised on a billboard?** If you have tried ways to think this through and still can't decide whether what you plan to do is ethical, try the **billboard principle**. As the name implies, this asks whether you'd be comfortable having your decision (with your name, of course) advertised on a billboard for everyone you know to see. Picture it in your mind! Would you be proud to see your potential course of action up there in giant letters? Would you be ashamed? Would others think worse of you if they knew what you had done to resolve your ethical dilemma? Those questions are the heart of the billboard principle. Kim Polese explains this in a real-life example at https://ecorner.stanford.edu/video/ethics-in-business/.

billboard principle
An ethical model that asks whether someone would be comfortable having his or her decision and name advertised on a billboard for the public to see.

There are other ideas, which we have touched on earlier that can help, such as applying economic, legal, or ethical standards or trying to create win-win solutions. A lot of ethical behavior is about taking care of your employees, your customers, your community, your nation, your environment. You and your business are involved with each of these, and you look to each for something, so it is only fair to recognize that each of these entities may have expectations of what you will or should do.

Implement the Best Solution and Monitor the Situation: After running your list of alternative solutions through the philosophies and standards in the prior section, were you able to cross any off the list? You probably were. The four philosophies won't automatically give you the best solution to your dilemma, but they're where the rubber hits the road. If your potential solution can't pass and meet at least a couple of these philosophies, you need to rethink what you're about to do.

Occasionally you will be able to make a decision entirely on your own, with minimal emotional fallout, and make it stick for your firm. Saying no to a salesperson who suggests a kickback for extra discounts could be such a situation. Often, though, you will need to work through a solution with someone else.

In such ethically charged situations, the best outcome is a situation where both sides feel satisfied about (or at least about the same with) the result. In presenting your solution,[37] it works best to focus on what the customer or other party wanted and why. You should then make sure the other party accepts that basic review. Add what you were seeking and take questions if the other party has any. Then introduce your solution along with why you think it would fill both parties' needs. If the other side rejects it, rather than asking for an explanation of why, ask instead what part needs to be adjusted, and how the other party would recommend adjusting your offer. Do not be afraid to question the other side's reasoning, and be willing to suggest adjustments.

BATNA
An acronym for Best Alternative to a Negotiated Agreement in which the second-best outcome is identified by the parties in a negotiation to help clarify the value of achieving a successful negotiation.

If you get a response that seems to reject the entire proposal, ask if there is any point to start from so that you can build a better version. Bring up a point you took from the prior requests or suggestions, or one the other party seemed to approve of during your presentation. Starting from a small patch of common ground is not uncommon in negotiating sessions. If this does not work, be ready to talk about your **BATNA**, or Best Alternative to a Negotiated Agreement, and ask for his or hers. Often, the alternative to negotiating together can be "lumping it" (suffering with what aggravated you or the other party, possibly with loud complaints to others) if the amounts are small, or undertaking legal action if the amounts warrant legal fees or the hassles of enforcing small claims court decisions. When compared to the BATNA's of both parties, finding a solution together often makes more sense. If you'd like to learn more about the details of BATNA and how to apply it, you can check out a good video from Levesque and Associates at www.youtube.com/watch?v=oVGjuUjr2YI.

In cases like EntreQuest (Shift), the result is a win-win, with both sides happier for all the emotional trauma of the confrontation and discussions. But it is important to monitor the situation. In a world of smartphone users seeking reviews of nearly everything they might buy, the impact of a few bad reviews cannot be underestimated. And if the review goes viral, watch out! See the Small Business Insight on the following page about a video that went viral.

The idea of adding monitoring takes a page from decision-making theory, which usually includes a feedback loop to link the solution to the original problem. In the real world, often the first solution is not optimal, and you need to keep tracking it and revising it until it works well. In ethical decision making, the same thinking makes sense.

It is important to understand why acting in an ethical fashion is important. There are costs to firms for their illegal and even unethical behaviors. Research by Thomas, Schermerhorn, and Dienhart has shown that managers tend to focus on government fines and penalties, which have real but relatively small costs to the firm. What managers tend to underplay are results that are quieter, spread out over a longer term, and actually more damaging to the firm's reputation and finances, as seen in Figure 3.3. There is every reason to think that these results are as descriptive of small business owners as they are of managers in larger firms.

Before leaving the method for ethical decision making, it is worthwhile to look at one very special situation close to the heart of many small businesses–the problem of inventing a product or service too far ahead of its time. Small businesses are often the first to try something innovative.

Innovation is the creation of something new or trying something for the first time. Innovation also suggests that you're not sure how a new idea is going to turn out. Taking advantage of an innovative idea is often the reason small business owners start their business in the first place.[39] Sometimes small businesses become very successful at doing new things better than

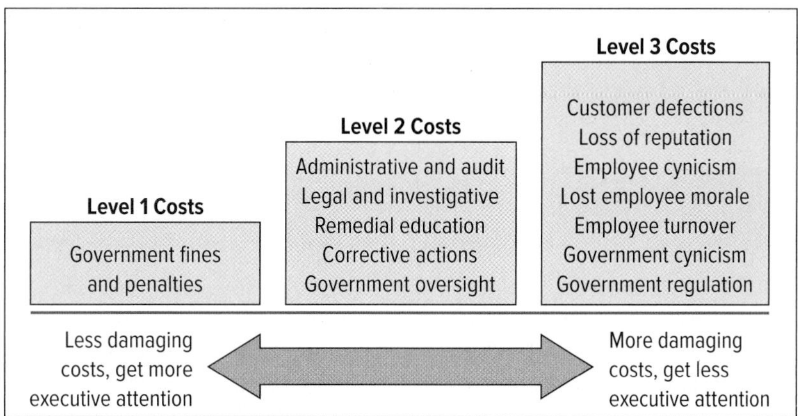

FIGURE 3.3

The Business Costs of Ethical Failures

Source: T. Thomas, J. Schermerhorn Jr., and J. Dienhart, "Strategic Leadership of Ethical Behavior in Business," *Academy of Management Executive* (May 2004), p. 58.

anyone else—and along the way may get into ethical hot water because of it, as sharing economy services like Uber and Airbnb have. See the Small Business Insight on the following page.

Ethical decision making probably represents one of the most complex and difficult kinds of external relations management situations you will have to face. Often the stakes may be as high as your reputation or even your entire business. You may feel under a lot of pressure. The approach we've shown you is considered one of the best ways to manage the procedure for finding an ethical solution.

You can also minimize the need for high-pressure ethical decision-making situations by integrating the lessons of legitimacy, networking, customer service, crisis management, sustainability, and ethical decision making into your everyday activities and into the structure of your business. How do you do this on an everyday basis? There are several approaches that can help:

1. Craft codes for legitimacy, networking, customer service, sustainability, crisis management, and ethical decision making that reflect the personal values you can live with and live up to. Don't get bogged down in details of what to permit or prohibit. Think about the general

VIRAL HORROR: THE BUSTED GUITAR[38]

Dave Carroll is a Canadian guitarist who leads the band Sons of Maxwell. He was flying on United Airlines from Halifax to Omaha in 2008 and checked his guitar as baggage (imagine trying to get it under the seat?). At the change of planes in Chicago, Dave heard passengers talking about guitars being tossed around outside, and his was one of them. When he picked it up in Omaha, it was so severely damaged it was unplayable. The repairs would cost $1,200, but by the time he had the estimate, United said he was too late to file it, and for months the airline refused all claims.

Frustrated, Dave ended up writing a song about his experience called "United Breaks Guitars" and the band posted a YouTube video about it (**www.youtube.com/watch?v=5YGc4zOqozo**). It went viral with 150,000 views within the first day, topping 500,000 within 3 days, 5 million within 60 days, and in August 2019 it had over 19 million views.

Unnerved by this, United tried to settle, but the damage was done. Initial sentiment was 50 to 1 in favor of Dave and his video, and today stands at about 60 to 1. The best United could do is show the video as part of internal training for its people on how *not* to do customer service. American Express reports that Millennials on average tell 15 people about their negative experience, while older groups will tell 11, so bad news will get around.

Today with Internet opinion sites like Google Maps and **Yelp.com**, and dedicated complaint sites like **Pissedconsumer.com** or even the good-old Better Business Bureau, it can be hard to track all the ways and places people can be talking about you. Only about a third of small businesses monitor their ratings. What do you think you will do?

SMALL BUSINESS INSIGHT

THE DARK SIDE OF THE SHARING ECONOMY

"Gypsy cabs" conjure up images of people using their cars illegally to transport people where they need to go. Gypsy cabs are not licensed by their locality. Their drivers aren't vetted by the cab authority or police. Nobody knows if their cars are safe. They aren't paying licensing fees to their localities, or abiding by the rules taxis have to follow, such as picking up everyone who asks for service. Today millions of Americans are self-employed as drivers with ride-sharing service platforms like Uber and Lyft. They don't think of themselves as illegal gypsy cabs, but despite the cute app, many of them have been.

Both ride-sharing companies use a policy of going into new markets unofficially at first, recruiting drivers online, and using locally targeted Facebook, Google, and other online ads to get people in that new market to download and use the app. During this "silent phase" for ride-sharing platforms, they are running a massive gypsy cab operation in those new markets. When localities notice and start legal action, the ride-sharing platforms alert riders and drivers to lobby to legalize the ride-sharing service locally. In some cities, like San Francisco and St. Louis, this worked in Uber's favor. In Austin and Anchorage, ride-sharing services were kicked out.[40]

Disrupting old models of doing business can lead to better services at lower prices, but that process of disrupting business can also disrupt our laws and communities. Part of entrepreneurs' responsibility is to think about what they are proposing to do and how.

Roman Tiraspolsky/Shutterstock

explanation of what you consider important in positively managing your firm's external relations. A real-life example of an ethical training effort at the high-tech start-up E.piphany can be found in a Stanford video at **https://ecorner.stanford.edu/video/company-ethics/**.

2. When hiring employees, subcontractors, or service providers, make sure you discuss with them your expectations about mutual responsibilities, ethics, and service levels.
3. When external relations lapses occur, if they are not so major that legal action or the demise of the firm is at stake, try to use them as learning experiences for the rest of the firm by talking openly about the issues. They make good opportunities to bring up your expectations again.
4. When counseling around external relations issues, try to use the following approach to help the learning occur:

   a. Do not get emotional. Talk through the issues calmly, even when it is hard.

b. Be specific about what the problem is and why it violates the way things are supposed to be done in the firm. Have the other person reason out loud why his or her behavior was a lapse to make sure he or she understands.
c. Once he or she understands, work on what future behavior should be (and why), as well as what needs to be done to make things right from the lapse.
d. Be consistent. Make sure everyone who has a lapse faces this process, and where consequences need to happen, they should be appropriate to the severity of the problem, specific to the problem, and the same for everyone who had that level of lapse.

5. Remember, you are the role model for ethics, social networking, and legitimacy. Employees, subcontractors, and even customers look at your approach as the role model for the way your business will approach these issues of managing external relations.[41]

Our goal in this section of the chapter is to give you some tools you can use to examine your problems and come to decisions you can be proud of. To accomplish that we have looked at the environment in which business operates, what makes it up, and how to analyze it and manage your external relations with it. The environment is critical to business–every business depends on the environment and a workable set of environmental conditions to get started, and from then on, many of the challenges, crises, and opportunities a firm faces come from the environment. But the lesson of this chapter is that while no one can really control the environment, it is possible to become better able to understand it. And through efforts such as developing social capital and planning ahead of time, small business owners can give themselves and their firms an edge when dealing with external environment.

CHAPTER SUMMARY

LO 3-1 Describe the elements that make up the small business environment.

- Everything outside the business is its environment.
- The internal environment consists of everyone within the firm.
- The task environment comprises those institutions the firm deals with directly.
- The general environment is the sectors shaping the larger world.
- Small businesses are constantly interacting with and being affected by the environment

LO 3-2 Demonstrate your ability to scan the small business environment.

- It is important for entrepreneurs to take time to scan the environment for trends and changes that could affect the business.
- Even simple environmental scanning approaches can achieve good results.

LO 3-3 Apply the techniques of building legitimacy for your organization.

- Legitimacy is others' belief that your firm is worthy of their business.
- Legitimacy can come from the way your firm deals with people, from the products or services you sell, and from the way you run your firm.
- Legitimacy (like social networking, crisis management, sustainability, and ethical decision making) is a way to build social capital with your environment.

LO 3-4 Navigate the techniques of social networking.

- Networking involves building relationships via mutual contact and help.
- You can connect through personal networking as well as social networking over the Internet.
- For personal networking, there are ways to optimize your inquiries for help.
- Personal networking is a skill you can practice and improve.
- Social media networking depends on your learning and leveraging the social networks where your customers already go.

LO 3-5 Explain the basic skills for handling a crisis.

- Crises are problems that risk a business's existence and require immediate action.
- There is a six-step process for handling a crisis taken from big business.

- Being honest and open is a big part of handling crises.
- The three steps of disaster preparedness are planning, talking to your people, and protecting your investment.

LO 3-6 Recognize how small businesses can achieve sustainability.

- Sustainable entrepreneurship seeks to run the business in a way that minimizes its impact on the environment.
- One way to minimize impact is through recycling.
- Another way is by creating green products or services.
- Using audits and certifications can help the firm be greener.

LO 3-7 Identify the major steps in making ethical decisions in small business.

- Ethics is a system of values that people use to determine whether actions are right or wrong.
- The three steps of ethical decision making are define the moral problem, generate alternatives, and implement the best solution.
- Workable solutions are those that meet your ethical, legal, and economic goals.
- The four philosophies you can use to check solutions are the Golden Rule, utilitarianism, universalism, and the billboard principle.
- Remember that innovations can lead to potentially risky ethical situations.

KEY TERMS

environment, 56
organizational identity, 56
organizational culture, 56
external environment, 57
task environment, 57
internal environment, 58
board of directors, 58
trade magazines, 58
entrepreneurial ecosystem, 59
general environment, 59
"real options" approach, 60
social capital, 61
external relations, 62
legitimacy, 62
ISO, 64
Baldrige Award, 64
mutuality, 68
networking, 68
customer relationship management, 69
ISO 14001 certification, 72
ethics, 73
ethical dilemma, 73
caveat emptor, 74
Golden Rule, 75
utilitarianism, 75
universalism, 75
billboard principle, 75
BATNA, 76

DISCUSSION QUESTIONS

1. What is the difference between the general environment and the task environment? Is it possible to say one is more important to a small business than the other?
2. In doing environmental scanning, the chapter mentions looking at the trade press and magazines outside your area of business, as well as asking customers, suppliers, your attorney, and your accountant for ideas about what is happening and what is coming next. If you have employees in your small business, should you ask them too? Why or why not?
3. What are the three general forms of legitimacy? Give two examples of ways to build legitimacy in each general form.
4. Why is a social network important for a small business?
5. Do you think that a small business could get by if it only did social networking using online sites like Facebook or LinkedIn? What would it miss by using this approach, and do you think it is important?
6. What are the three keys to success in building your network using a social networking website?
7. What are the six steps of handling a crisis?
8. How do the six steps of handling a crisis compare to the U.S. government's three-step approach to planning for disasters?
9. Why should small businesses make stronger efforts to achieve sustainability?
10. What are the three steps of ethical decision making?
11. What are the four philosophies you can use to evaluate alternatives you have generated to solve an ethical problem?

EXPERIENTIAL EXERCISES

1. Pick an existing business, or use one you own or are thinking about developing. For that business, identify at least two key players in at least two areas of its task environment (e.g., media and competitors). How did you determine which organizations fit? If you can, partner with another student to do the work on the same business and compare results.

2. Decide on three areas of the general environment you do not usually consider. Put together a profile of sources (online, print, or both) that you would use to do environmental scanning in those three areas, say every month during this class. One good source for each area is fine. Compare your general environment areas and sources to two others in the class. Arrange to compare findings after your first run-through of sources. In particular, what did you find that was "news" to you? What "news" did your classmates come up with for you?

3. Evaluate a franchise using the tables for the three forms of legitimacy. Go to the franchise's local operation to look around and check out the franchisor's website (e.g., **mcdonalds.com** for that chain). What forms of legitimacy are evident from your research? How positive a feeling does this give you about the firm?

4. Go to the websites of Facebook and LinkedIn. From what you can learn from the websites, how do these two social networking sites differ? Consider the market to which they are aiming, their relative sizes, and the kinds of methods they offer for online social networking. For a small business considering online social networking, which would you recommend first, and why?

5. Here are a set of challenging situations small business owners might find themselves facing. How would you handle them? Compare your solution to those of others in your class. When differences occur in the answers, what causes them?

   a. You own a dress shop specializing in prom dresses. A customer brings back a prom dress the week after her high school's prom. She swears she never wore the dress, but it seems to you that there were places where the dress shows wear or spots having been cleaned off. You have a "No Return" policy on the receipts and posted on the wall, but the customer says she will tell all her friends you were unfair if you do not refund her money.

   b. Last week one of your best employees asked to leave an hour early to take her spouse to the doctor. You said it was okay. Now another employee, who is an average but not great worker, is citing what happened last week and asking to be let go an hour early to go to "an appointment." The employee will not tell you what it is for.

   c. You need to buy office supplies. Do you go to Walmart with its visibly lower prices or the local office supply store, a small business like yours? Would it make a difference if the local office supply store bought from you?

6. When talking about codes of ethics, you were encouraged to do a Google search. One of the sites that may have turned up is the Center for the Study of Ethics in Professions at the Illinois Institute of Technology. Check out the site's collection of Codes of Ethics. Select one in an area that matches your small business interests (e.g., business, management, real estate, service, etc.) and look at one of the codes for that area. What do you need to do to prepare yourself to understand and follow that code when you enter your business?

7. You can complete and discuss the self-assessment below.

   Is your behavior ethical?

   For this exercise, you will be using the same set of statements twice. The first time you answer them, focus on your own behavior and the frequency with which you use it for each question. On the line before the question number, place number 1–4 that represents how often you did, do, or would do the behavior if you had the chance. These numbers will allow you to determine your level of ethics. You can be honest without fear of having to tell others in class of your score. *Sharing ethics scores is not part of the exercise.* The scale is:

   Frequently 1 2 3 4 Never

   The second time you use the same statements, focus on other people in an organization that you work for or have worked for. Place an O on the line after the number if you observed someone exhibiting this behavior. Also place an R on the line if you reported this behavior either within the organization or externally to some other person or organization.

1–4 O–R

College

____ 1. ____ Cheating on homework assignments.

____ 2. ____ Cheating on exams.

____ 3. ____ Turning in papers as your own work that were completed by someone else.

____ 4. ____ Helping someone do any of the above.

Job

____ 5. ____ Lying to others to get what you want or stay out of trouble.

____ 6. ____ Coming to work late and getting paid for it.

____ 7. ____ Leaving work early and getting paid for it.

____ 8. ____ Taking long breaks or lunches and getting paid for it.

____ 9. ____ Calling in sick to get a day off, when you are not sick.

____ 10. ____ Socializing rather than doing the work that should be done.

____ 11. ____ Doing personal work on company time.

____ 12. ____ Using the organization's phone to make personal calls.

____ 13. ____ Using the organization's computer and Internet access for personal use.

____ 14. ____ Using the company copier for personal use.

____ 15. ____ Using the company car for personal use.

____ 16. ____ Mailing personal things through the company mail.

____ 17. ____ Taking home company supplies and keeping them, or taking home company tools or equipment without permission for personal use and then returning them.

____ 18. ____ Giving company supplies or merchandise to friends or allowing them to take them without saying anything.

____ 19. ____ Putting in for reimbursement for meals and travel or other expenses that weren't actually eaten or taken.

____ 20. ____ Taking a spouse or friends out to eat and charging it to the company's expense account.

____ 21. ____ Taking a spouse or friend on business trips and charging the expense to the company.

____ 22. ____ Accepting gifts from customers or suppliers in exchange for giving them business.

____ 23. ____ Being pressured, or pressuring others, to sign documents containing false information.

____ 24. ____ Being pressured, or pressuring others, to sign documents you haven't read, knowing they may contain information or decisions that might be considered not in your or their best interest.

____ 25. ____ If you were to give this assessment to a person you work with whom you don't get along with very well, would she or he agree with your answers? Use a scale of 1–4 on the line before number 25.

Note to students: This self-assessment is not meant to be a precise measure of your ethical behavior. It is designed to get you thinking about ethics and your behavior and that of others from an ethical perspective. It is also designed to help you see situations in which you might have to think twice about your decision, because there is an ethical part to it. There is no right or wrong score. Another ethical issue of this exercise is your honesty when rating how often you might do these things—how honest were you?

Scoring: To determine your score, add the numbers from the 1–4 column for College and Job. Your total will be between 25 and 100. Place the number here ____ and on the continuum below that represents your score. The lower your score, the more you need to be thinking about the types of behavior you are doing in your organization.

Needs some thought A role model

25—30—40—50—60—70—80—90—100

Discussion Questions:

1. For the college items 1–4, who is harmed and who benefits from these behaviors?
2. For job items 5–24, select the three (circle their numbers) that you consider the most severe unethical behavior. Who is harmed and who benefits from these behaviors? Would it matter if they were in a small business or a big company? Why?
3. If you observed unethical behavior but didn't report it, why not? If you did report it, why? What was the result? Was it worth it to you to report the behavior?
4. As a small business manager, you know unethical behavior can threaten the company's existence. If you know some of the employees are stealing from the company, would you tell the owner? Why or why not?
5. If you were a small business owner and you caught your employee, who is also your friend, doing any of the three behaviors you circled in Question 2 (most severe), what would you do?

Application:

1. What did I learn from this exercise?
2. How might I use this self-understanding in the future if I own my own or manage a small business?
3. As a small business owner, what can I do to prevent unethical behavior?

MINI-CASE

TO RENT OR NOT TO RENT ON GAMEDAY[42]

Rami Casarda was a graduate student at Coastal University and the nominal head of a group of other grad students renting a house near the university's stadium, which has over 75,000 seats. With that capacity, you can imagine what gamedays at Coastal are like. The stadium is routinely sold out. Tailgate parties are everywhere. Porch parties from rental and owned houses spill out into front yards, and occasionally the street.

Hotels in the town of 35,000 are sold out months in advance, and at their top prices of the year. The challenge for many has been finding a place to stay. Person-to-person (P2P) providers like Airbnb and specialty football weekend competitors like **GamedayHousing.com** offer renters and owners a chance to make a little extra money offering a bed or room in their place. For Rami's house, one room rented for the 7 two-night stays of the home games would provide the house $11,200 after fees, or four months of house rent.

But they face challenges in two forms. One is legal. P2P ride services and overnight room rentals aren't legal in Coastal City. Police have ticketed Lyft and Uber drivers found on the road, but don't seem to have ticketed P2P rentals so far. But that said, there are only a few local listings on the P2P rental websites at this point.

The other challenge is more local. It involves worst-case guests, known in the business as "gameday moochers." They don't have gameday tickets and instead go around to tailgate and porch parties, grabbing free beer and food for hours on end. When the moochers return, they're often very drunk and very rowdy. Some sites let you add a security deposit to the rental fees, and other sites offer additional insurance, but there remains the hassle of proving the case and dealing with the guest during the problem period.

There is also a back-of-the-mind fear that rowdy guests returning late at night will draw the ire of neighbors in what is usually, even on gamedays, a relatively quiet residential neighborhood. This could lead to strained relations with neighbors, or at the worst, neighbors calling the police, and ensuring a ticket for illegal room rentals.

Rami and the housemates need to decide whether to list or not.

See related videos at **www.wcpo.com/money/consumer/dont-waste-your-money/airbnb-nightmare-mans-home-trashed-by-renters** and **www.wptv.com/news/region-s-palm-beach-county/boynton-beach/boynton-homeowner-takes-on-airbnb-over-damage**.

CASE DISCUSSION QUESTIONS

1. What advice do the four philosophies (Golden Rule, utilitarianism, universalism, billboard principle) offer for Rami's thinking?
2. What is your thinking about how the legal and local challenges noted above drive the decision? Which should take precedence and why?
3. When entrepreneurship is disruptive, it often runs ahead of existing laws. If you were the entrepreneur behind a new P2P rental site, should you operate everywhere? Should you not accept new rental locations in areas where their service is illegal? Do you think you can figure out where it is legal and where it is not? Should you depend on those offering rentals to know if what they are doing is legal? What do the four questions defining a moral problem tell you?

CHAPTER

4

Small Business Ideas: Creativity, Opportunity, and Feasibility

● Mary Elizabeth Coleman learned how to do feasibility analyses in her undergraduate entrepreneurship class. Years later, as a lawyer in private practice, she had an opportunity to revisit the skill for one of the largest law firms in St. Louis. How did Mary Elizabeth's experiences and education make her the right person for this entrepreneurial role?
Mary Elizabeth Coleman

LEARNING OBJECTIVES

After you complete this chapter, you will be able to:

LO 4-1 Identify strategies for innovation in your business.

LO 4-2 Recognize the sources of opportunity entrepreneurs draw on to get business ideas.

LO 4-3 Understand how creativity methods can help business owners recognize new opportunities.

LO 4-4 Understand the five pitfalls that hinder innovation.

LO 4-5 Identify how to screen ideas for business potential.

LO 4-6 Describe how to construct a business model canvas to assess the feasibility of your business idea.

LO 4-7 Describe how to conduct a comprehensive feasibility study for your business ideas.

LO 4-8 Recognize the value of building a creative culture in your business.

Focus on Small Business: Mary Elizabeth Coleman and the Feasibility Study[1]

Mary Elizabeth Coleman had her first business at 11, selling flower subscriptions to judges and attorneys in the courthouse of her hometown of Georgetown, Texas. She found out she needed an agricultural license to buy flowers wholesale, and thereby make a reasonable profit, but she couldn't afford it. Undaunted, she wrote Texas's agricultural commissioner, Rick Perry (later the governor of Texas, a presidential hopeful, and the secretary of energy) about the problem, and he personally paid for her license. Mary Elizabeth was growing into a person who gets thing done.

In her entrepreneurship classes at Saint Louis University she learned how to do feasibility studies as well as business plans, but her heart was still in those courthouses, so after college she married (her college sweetheart) and went to law school. From there she worked in law firms and then independently in her own law firm, doing business and taxable estate planning law.

Her old entrepreneurship professor[2] made her an interesting offer. He had been approached by the managing partner of Lewis Rice, one of the oldest and largest law firms in St. Louis, to recommend someone to do a feasibility study for a specialized law firm focused on estate planning. Clearly a lawyer who had done estate planning and had learned how to do feasibility studies would be the perfect person, and the professor recommended Mary Elizabeth. The two lawyers met, liked each other, and both liked the idea. As a result Mary Elizabeth had a consulting contract on top of her legal practice.

She performed what we call in this chapter a "classic feasibility analysis." She modeled a law office specializing in estate planning, looked at the market in St. Louis to determine the best locations to attract customers, and priced out what the offices, marketing efforts, and other costs would be. She used historical data to estimate revenues, and looked at the expertise and special services needed for such a business. She also studied how specialty legal clinics, like those for divorce or traffic tickets, were most professionally and profitably organized. She presented the ideas to the lawyer who hired her, and then to the partners. They were impressed, and decided to go ahead with the project, which they called TuckerAllen, and opened with five locations and the prospect for more.

Mary Elizabeth was also invited to serve as TuckerAllen's first CEO. She took the offer and became a corporate entrepreneur of this wholly owned subsidiary of the law firm. She was already a social entrepreneur. As a member of the Arnold, Missouri, city council, she was the driving force behind the creation of a co-working space called Corridor 55 (**www.arnoldmo.org/business/corridor-55/**), which was Missouri's first municipally owned co-working space. In whatever setting she finds herself, Mary Elizabeth keeps on coming up with new ideas. She is a great example of CSI entrepreneurship. With her latest role, as a member of the Missouri House of Representatives, there are sure to be some more new ideas coming out.

DISCUSSION QUESTIONS

1. How did Mary Elizabeth's education and experience help prepare her for this project?
2. What did Mary Elizabeth consider when performing her feasibility analysis of the estate law firm?
3. What other topics might you want to look into if you were doing the feasibility analysis?

opportunity recognition
Searching and capturing new ideas that lead to business opportunities. This process often involves creative thinking that leads to discovery of new and useful ideas.

LO **4-1** Identify strategies for innovation in your business.

Ideas, Opportunities, and Businesses

To many people, entrepreneurship is the pursuit of opportunity. What is an opportunity? There are literally dozens of definitions,[3] but they boil down to actions that you do or imagine doing in order to achieve some kind of business outcome. This can be creating a new product or service, or delivering an existing product or service where people will buy it or use it. Opportunities can be found (such as when an entrepreneur came across the bubbling spring that became Perrier water) or made (seeing someone toss a pie tin and making the toy version called the Frisbee). That search and capture of new ideas is called **opportunity recognition**, which researchers believe might be the most basic and important entrepreneurial behavior.[4]

entrepreneurial alertness
A special set of observational and thinking skills that help entrepreneurs identify good opportunities; the ability to notice things that have been overlooked, without actually launching a formal search for opportunities, and the motivation to look for opportunities.

imitative strategy
An overall strategic approach in which the entrepreneur does more or less what others are already doing.

incremental strategy
Taking an idea and offering a way to do something slightly better than it is done presently.

radical innovation strategy
Rejecting existing ideas, and presenting a way to do things differently.

LO **4-2** Recognize the sources of opportunity entrepreneurs draw on to get business ideas.

The exact reasons why entrepreneurs seem to be better able to find ideas that work are unclear. The notion of **entrepreneurial alertness** is one that has captured the attention of scholars in the field. This phrase means that entrepreneurs have a special set of observational and thinking skills that helps them identify good opportunities. Some scholars have suggested that entrepreneurs are able to notice things that have been overlooked, without actually launching a formal search for opportunities.[5] Others suggest that we also consider the motivations of entrepreneurs to search for new ideas.[6]

For example, Gaglio and Katz[7] found that serial entrepreneurs could come up with new ideas given nearly any situation. Sitting at an airport, these entrepreneurs might begin to look where lines are forming and wonder how to make money off that. Others could look at a collection of everyday items and in a few minutes they are thinking up ways to combine them to make a profit. Their use of the opportunity identification process tells us that being creative can become a way of life.

Gaglio and Katz found that these experienced entrepreneurs thought of different types of business ideas depending on the situation. Called the *opportunity identification process* (see Figure 4.1), it describes how the entrepreneur assesses whether the situation faced is one that is the same as it has been traditionally or if it is changing. Strategies that involve doing the same thing, or pursuing an **imitative strategy** (which is covered in detail in Chapter 7), or pursuing an **incremental strategy** make a lot of sense when the business or economy is continuing on a fairly steady course. Sometimes during these periods of stability, trying innovative ideas might help win more business from rivals, and "shake up" the industry, perhaps giving the innovator an advantage. During times of great change–whether from technological, political, economic, or cultural change–the potential for steady business declines, and the attractiveness of innovations increases. At times of great change, people become more willing to try extreme new ideas, so it becomes a great time to introduce extremely innovative ideas, also known as pursuing a **radical innovation strategy**.

Recall the four steps of the entrepreneurial process from Chapter 1–feel, check, plan, do. What entrepreneurs feel are the possibilities we call opportunities; it is their entrepreneurial alertness at work. Some are ones they see in front of them, like a new fashion that hasn't come to their community yet, and some they imagine, like when they have an idea for a product to solve a problem. When you think of it that way, you might conclude that there could be a lot of opportunities.

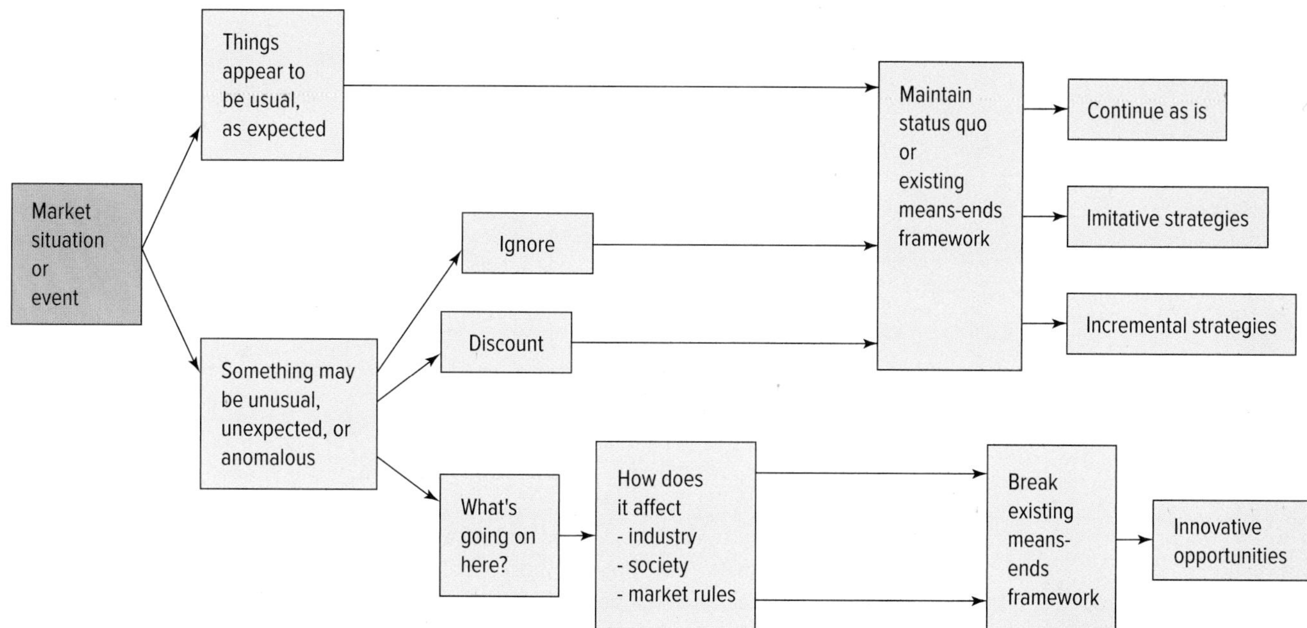

FIGURE 4.1

Opportunity Identification Process

Source: Adapted from C. M. Gaglio and J. A. Katz, "The Psychological Basis of Opportunity Identification: Entrepreneurial Alertness," *Small Business Economics* 16, no. 2, (March 2001), p. 99.

And not all opportunities are created equal. Trying to decide which opportunity to pursue can be tough. In big business, the rule of thumb is that it takes 3,000 initial ideas (or opportunities) to come up with one commercially successful product.[8] The secret of making this work is taking a second look at the opportunities to figure out which are best. Here is where the second stage—checking—comes in. In big business, doing some basic research on the idea eliminates 90 percent of the opportunities. Testing the remaining ideas in a very simple way eliminates 60 percent of those second-stage opportunities.

While the numbers for entrepreneurs haven't been tested yet, no one is suggesting an entrepreneur needs to think of 3,000 ideas to start. But any opportunity would benefit from being checked out. In this chapter, we will focus on finding and making opportunities and checking them out, so that when you get down to planning and doing, you're using your best idea.

There are two ways to think about opportunities and business creation:

1. One is the effectuation model of entrepreneurship mentioned in Chapter 1. In it you start with what you have—your skills, knowledge, and networks, and what needs you see that you can meet by using what you have. You talk to the people you know to find out if they can commit to your idea. If not, find out what they need, and which of those needs you can do something about.

If this approach sounds familiar, it is because that is probably the way your friends in high school got into business for themselves. Once they decided to earn some money, they took stock of what they knew (e.g., taking care of kids or yards) and checked to see if they could sell that to neighbors. But it's not just for high schoolers. It turns out that at least a subset of very successful serial entrepreneurs think the same way, but on a bigger scale, and you can too.[9] Using the four-step model, here is what happens:

- **Feel:** Recognize you want to do or make something through a business.
- **Check:** Assess what you know and who you know to determine your product or service and your customers.
- **Plan:** Offer your product or service to your customers and see if you get any sales.
- **Do:** If you get enough sales, keep going. If not, go back to the check step.

2. The second way to think about opportunities and business creation depends on your dreams or ideas about new or not-yet-created products or services. This is called the **causal model of entrepreneurship**. In this approach you think about what you need to do to cause your new product or service to come into existence. That may mean you have to learn new skills or find others to help you achieve your end, and doing that will probably take some additional time, perhaps some additional funding, and overcoming two risks—the risk that your

causal model of entrepreneurship
One of two approaches to thinking about entrepreneurship (the other is effectuation). The causal approach is one in which you want to create a particular product or service that does not yet exist, and to achieve that end, you have to cause the product or service to exist. This can mean you will have to learn new skills, or find others to help you achieve your end.

FIGURE 4.2

The Screening Process in the Causal Model of Entrepreneurship

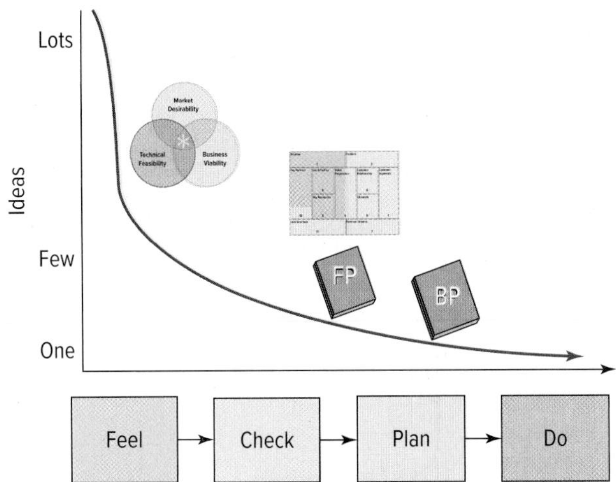

new product or service can't be created and even if it is created, that it isn't something that customers are willing to buy. Both of those risks can be decreased by thoroughly planning before you act, so the four-step process looks like this:

- **Feel:** Decide you have a great idea and want to go into business to make it happen.
- **Check:** Assess your ability to understand it and create it yourself. Get help if needed. Then assess the technical feasibility of the idea.
- **Plan:** If the idea is feasible, plan for making and selling it, checking with potential customers to make sure they will buy it. If you get enough interest, keep going. If not, got back to the check step.
- **Do:** Make the product or service and the company to sell it and get it into the market.

The model is shown graphically in Figure 4.2. The goal is to start with lots of ideas and narrow them down to a few ideas that you will test with techniques introduced in this chapter called an IDEO screen (the overlapping circles), business model canvas (the multicolored rectangles), or a feasibility plan (FP) until you find one that seems most promising, for which you do a business plan (BP). This approach gives you the best chance to think through the ideas, quickly evaluate them, and settle on the most promising one before starting the business.

We know that the effectual and causal approaches happen in real life. In the nationwide Panel Study of Entrepreneurial Dynamics (PSED),[10] a sample of 1,754 entrepreneurs were asked whether the decision or desire to start some kind of business (the effectuation approach) or the business idea (the causal approach) came first or if they combined the two. See the results in Table 4.1.

Given that effectual approaches depend on what and who you know, the path to business comes from self-analysis, but if you're taking a more causal approach, you might want to think about where you can look for ideas. Exhibit 4.1 gives you a set of sources anyone can immediately use.

These sources really do work. In the PSED, 480 entrepreneurs were asked "What led to your business idea?" Figure 4.3 presents the results of this question. Work experience in a particular industry or market was the most frequently mentioned source of ideas, followed by discussion with family and friends.

TABLE 4.1 What Came First for New Businesses

Business idea (causal)	36%
Decision/desire to start a business (effectual)	23%
Idea and decision were simultaneous (combined)	41%

Source: Original analysis using PSED 1 and PSED 2 data (covering 1998 and 2006, N = 1,767) done by Kelly Shaver, College of Charleston, for *Entrepreneurial Small Business*, February 2019.

EXHIBIT 4.1

Ten Sources of Business Ideas

1. **Work and personal experience:** Realizing frustrations or unfulfilled wishes from your life working or being a consumer.
2. **A similar business:** Seeing something new to you or your area, and thinking about importing or copying it.
   A. **Chance:** "Being in the right place at the right time." A lot of this can be **retail arbitrage**, buying closeouts at your local stores and selling at full price online[11] or buying up umbrellas and selling them on the street during rainstorms, or reselling tickets to sporting events or concerts.
3. **Family and friends:** Getting a great idea from family or friends.
4. **Education or expertise**: Applying what you've learned in school or developed on your own.
5. **Magazines:** Googling "top business ideas" or "new business ideas" to find articles and blogs talking about cool new business possibilities. Inc.com and Entrepreneur.com do these lists yearly.
6. **Idea sites:** Checking for ideas at halfbakery.com, coolbusinessideas.com, or ideaswatch.com, or searching online for "idea sites."
7. **Side gigs:** Driving for Uber or Lyft, renting rooms on Airbnb, selling your services on Fiverr.com or Upwork.com or to customers in your neighborhood or locally on Craigslist.org.
8. **Make and sell:** Making something and selling it locally, online (think Etsy.com), or at a market.
9. **Going online:** Seeing what is trending on social media, asking your online connections for ideas or needs, checking what's hot on Amazon or your favorite sites and seeing if there are ways to make a buck from that.

retail arbitrage
An approach to business where the entrepreneur buys something at a severely reduced retail price (like clearance or closeout merchandise from a retailer) and then resells it (most typically online) at a price closer to the typical retail price.

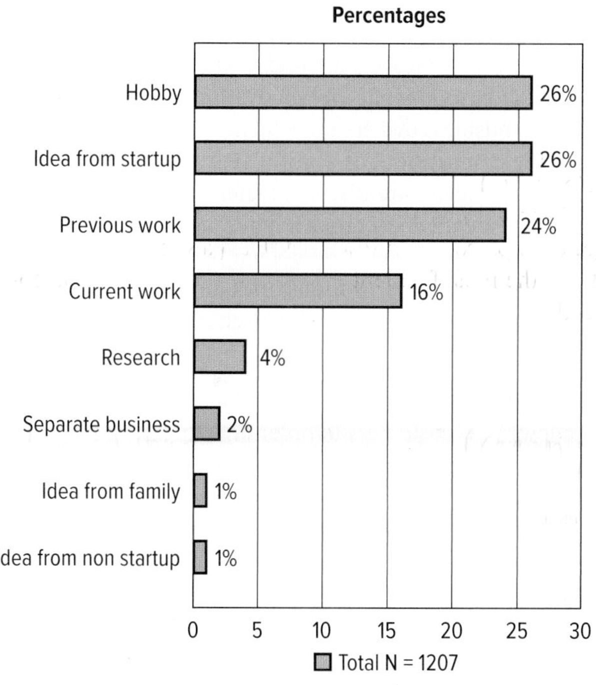

FIGURE 4.3

What Led to Your Business Idea?

Source: Original analysis using PSED 2 data (covering 2006, N = 1,207) done by Kelly Shaver, College of Charleston, for *Entrepreneurial Small Business*, February 2019.

Other powerful but rarely used sources of ideas are universities and government agencies. Both develop a tremendous range of new technologies or refinements of existing technologies, *but never do anything with them!* Major universities and government agencies, like NASA and the Departments of Agriculture and Defense, offer technological inventions for free to small businesses to develop. There are even government programs to help fund such efforts. The best place to start is Federal Labs (www.federallabs.org/), the centralized location for over 700 federal government technology producing programs. If you have a university nearby that has government-funded research, you can contact the technology transfer office and find out about inventions available for commercialization in your own backyard, or check out the website of the Association of University Technology Managers at www.aim.autm.net, or the multiuniversity iBridge Network at www.ibridgenetwork.org/.

license
A legal agreement granting you rights to use a particular piece of intellectual property.

Licensee
The person or firm that is obtaining the rights to use a particular piece of intellectual property.

Licensor
The person or organization that is offering the rights to use a particular piece of intellectual property.

royalty
A payment to a licensor based on the number or value of licensed items sold.

creativity
A process producing an idea or opportunity that is novel and useful, frequently derived from making connections among distinct ideas or opportunities.

What these organizations will offer you is an arrangement called licensing. A **license** is a legal agreement granting you rights to use a particular piece of intellectual property (for example, a technology). In return, you (the **licensee**) are required to pay the owner of the license (the **licensor**). These payments can consist of an up-front or annual flat licensing fee or a **royalty**, which is a payment per item sold. Often the licensor will provide access to the idea's creator to help make the move to market as successful as possible. Examples of licensed products you see every day include Dolby noise reduction, or Gatorade, or anything with a Disney or Coca-Cola or sports team logo on it, as well as products with famous characters from television shows, comics, or movies.

From Ideas to Opportunities through Creativity

LO **4-3** Understand how creativity methods can help business owners recognize new opportunities.

You might have a viable business idea, but is it the best one to pursue? Are you sure you have the right approach for making the most of the idea? Very often the first good idea an entrepreneur has is not necessarily the best one he or she will have. Before committing yourself to one viable idea, it is a good practice to take some time and see if you can take that viable idea and innovate on it to create an even better–more profitable, more distinctive, harder to copy–idea.

Why worry about being innovative in your approach? Consider the ease with which you can get data over the Internet on industries and markets, such as your competition, and how small business research and how-to articles are at your fingertips with many journals and magazines available over the web. Of course, everybody else who is thinking about starting a business similar to yours has this same information at his or her fingertips also.

brainstorming
A group thinking technique where you ask participants about a situation or a product or service. You ask them to tell you all the things that come to mind when they think of that situation, product, or service. You can ask for specifics, like ways to make something better, or ways to create new versions, or ways to imagine how it would be used at other times or in other situations. In this group discussion, criticism is suspended in order to generate the maximum number of ideas.

There are, however, some very creative methods you can use to help you generate ideas and opportunities that take you beyond what everybody else already knows. This is what can give you the innovative edge in business ownership, whether you are looking for ideas that are just a little bit different from the competition, or a world apart from what everybody else is doing or not even doing yet. These strategies are discussed later in the chapter. Figure 4.4 provides one tool you can use to help you identify new opportunities. It is based on the work of Alex Osborne, a pioneer in the field of **creativity**, who first coined the word **brainstorming** where a group tries to list as many ideas as possible, without critiquing or commenting. This other tool is known as SCAMPER, and it is an acronym for a set of cues that trigger new ideas for your business.

Substitute: Think of what you might substitute for something else to form a new idea. A feature that allows your customers to order directly from a website rather than visiting your store or ordering by mail is an example of substitution. Sometimes solutions derived through SCAMPER cues are very "way out" and lead people to some creative ideas for solving annoying problems. One city in the Netherlands, for example, was experiencing a growing litter problem (not unlike your own town or city, no doubt), and the civic leaders tried all the usual ways of fixing the problem: They increased the number of trash bins around the city, they posted signs reminding people not to litter, and they fined people for littering. Nothing seemed to help. Then they got a breakthrough idea: A tiny recording device was installed inside trash bins, and every time someone pushed the lid to deposit litter, a joke would play from the recorder! Not surprisingly, it was not too long before the litter problem declined.[12]

Idea Trigger: What opportunities can you think of that come as a result of substituting or replacing something that already exists?

Combine: Think of possible combinations you can make that result in something entirely different. Not long ago, if you wanted to buy a book you went to a store that typically carried only books, and if you wanted to buy a cup of coffee you went to a coffee shop, and if you wanted to hear music you went to a club or theater. Today, you can have all three under one roof at many establishments, including big ones such as Barnes & Noble, but also some smaller businesses such as Tattered Cover Book Stores in Denver, Colorado. Also, when you buy gasoline at the service station, you most likely can pick up some groceries along with basic auto supplies.

Idea Trigger: What separate products, services, or whole businesses can you put together to create another distinct business?

Adapt: Think about what could be adapted from products or services that already exist. Many successful businesses are founded on the concept of adaptation. It's a popular innovation strategy that can be just as effective, and much more likely in the real world, than business opportunities that are the result of radical innovations such as inventions. You may remember the original Book-of-the-Month Club that sent members a different book every month. What adaptations can you find? How about beer-of-the-month, pasta-of-the-month, and many other variations? Did you know that one day a manufacturer of toilet tissue received a shipment of paper that was too thick to use? The manufacturer could have thrown it out, but instead the manufacturer improvised, and paper towels were introduced! Sometimes adaptations occur when entrepreneurs try their best to work with scarce resources.

Idea Trigger: What could you adapt from other industries or fields to your business?

Magnify or modify: Taking an existing product and changing its appearance or adding more features or increasing the hours your store is open or making its advertising more dramatic are some ways you could magnify or modify your idea. For example, Ally Bank is a relatively small, new, online financial services company that is currently expanding nationally using ads proclaiming this in some very dramatic and humorous ways, poking fun at the traditional fees that banks and other financial service companies charge for checking accounts, for example. The goal is for such messages to be remembered by potential customers, and the effect is to make the business stick out among its competitors. There is much a small business can do to create memorable images and advertising for itself, and it does not need expensive television ads to do it. The letter *M* also can cue you to "minimize" something. The microchip industry was born, for example, when someone asked the question, "What if we shrunk them?"

Idea Trigger: What could I make more noticeable or dramatic, or different in some way from my competitors? It need not be in the product itself, but it could be the way you advertise or treat the customer during the transaction that becomes memorable.

Put to other uses: Think of ways you could generate a high number of opportunities for your product or service beyond what it is traditionally used for. A few years ago, Arm & Hammer Baking Soda was known as a product customers used by the teaspoonful every few weeks when they baked a batch of cookies or a cake. The problem for Arm & Hammer was that it wasn't selling a lot of boxes of the stuff since it tended to sit in people's kitchen cupboards for years. At 59 cents a box, that doesn't bring tremendous sales revenues. One day, the company brought together a group of employees and gave them the challenge to think of all the uses for baking soda (besides baking) that they could. Ideas took off, and today the company produces an entire line of baking soda–related products

S – Substitute

C – Combine

A – Adapt

M – Magnify or modify

P – Put to other uses

E – Eliminate

R – Rearrange

FIGURE 4.4

Using SCAMPER to Recognize Business Opportunities[13]

Source: Michael Michalko, *Thinkertoys: A Handbook of Business Creativity* (Berkeley, CA: Ten Speed Press, 1991).

that bring a handsome return in profits. Can you think of some? (*Hint:* Washing clothes, refrigerators that smell fresh, a product cats use, etc.)

Antoine Feuchtwanger sold frankfurters at the Chicago Exposition over 100 years ago, and his customers complained that they burnt their fingers when holding them. Fuerchtwanger tried gloves, but customers kept walking off with them. Finally, he took some rolls that a baker had made, cut them in half down the middle, and placed the frankfurters inside them. Hotdogs met buns, and today it's hard to imagine one without the other.

Idea Trigger: Suppose you learned that all the traditional uses for your product had disappeared and that you have trailer truckloads out back with tons of product. What other uses might there be? Aim for quantity, and allow outrageous ideas to flow along with more mundane ones. Who knows what new applications you may find.

Eliminate: Search for opportunities that arise when you get rid of something or stop doing something. What products or services emerged when these questions were asked: What if people didn't have to leave their houses to go grocery shopping? What if you could buy something (or do bank transactions) without leaving your car?

Idea Trigger: What could I get rid of or reduce that would eliminate something my customer has to do, and as a result give the customer more than he or she expected?

Rearrange or reverse: A generator is the reverse of a motor. Uber and ride-sharing services rearranged the process of getting a taxi, so instead of searching for a taxi stand or a taxi on the streets, you use your app to order one. Other examples include using reverse psychology or paradox to challenge old ways of thinking, for example, using stimulants to calm hyperactive children.

Idea Trigger: What can you rearrange or reorder in the way your product or service appears, or the way businesses in your industry usually look or are decorated or located?

SCAMPER is a very effective method for helping business owners and their employees come up with alternative solutions and opportunities. The method works because it helps you step outside the usual way you look at opportunities or try to solve problems. It offers cues that push you outside your traditional areas of expertise, to consider what interesting new forms might be out there that you could try.

Thinking of other ways to be creative, note that creative business owners similarly question and challenge the way things appear, to see if they can find a new way of doing things. When you see a highly innovative business, don't think that there is something especially magical or lucky about the entrepreneur or the situation. It's more likely that the person or team behind the

Arm & Hammer Baking Soda was put to another use when employees came up with absorbing refrigerator odors. What other uses can you imagine?

Bonnie-Kamin/PhotoEdit

business has been using a process for organizing creative thinking developed by Graham Wallas[14] consisting of four steps:

1. **Preparation**–Exploring the problem or opportunity from all directions.
2. **Incubation**–Thinking about the problem or opportunity in a "not-conscious" way, putting it on the back burner, so to speak.
3. **Illumination**–Bringing ideas together to spark new insights.
4. **Verification**–Testing the idea and reducing it to its most exact form.[15]

This process is very useful when you want to explore a business problem, such as why you lost a customer, or when you want to identify further opportunities for your business, such as new markets or features for your product line. If you can pinpoint what stage of the creative process you are in, you can guide yourself through to an innovative solution by looking at things from different perspectives and allowing the issue to simmer in the background for a bit. This technique has worked for many famous creative people–from Leonardo da Vinci to Albert Einstein.

Another variant of this approach is to turn the brainstorming process mentioned above on its ear. In **painstorming**, instead of asking for new ideas, ask people for pains or aggravations they face in a situation you choose. Even if people don't have ideas for what they want that's new, it is relatively easy to get almost anyone to tell you things that could be better in any situation. In starting with pains, you may be able to quickly come up with new ways to improve or even replace existing products and processes.

painstorming
A group thinking technique where you ask participants about a situation, product, or service they experienced. You ask them to tell you all the things about that experience that were suboptimal—what was wrong, what didn't work well, what caused pain or discomfort, what could have been better. Their results can help describe how to improve the product, service, or situation, or possibly even provide alternatives to the original.

LEARN MORE ONLINE

Learn more about the topics above at these sites:

Brainstorming techniques: **www.ideou.com/pages/brainstorming**

Painstorming techniques: **https://medium.com/@alyciadoxon/brainstorming-methods-pt-2-painstorming-80cd1fc50d4b**

Brainstorming with SCAMPER and related techniques: **https://medium.com/@gunsb002/structured-ideation-ad1388949a02**

Avoid Pitfalls

LO **4-4** Understand the five pitfalls that hinder innovation.

In your quest for new business ideas, from time to time you may catch yourself rejecting ideas or jumping on the first good idea you get because you are excited and there is no time to lose.

There are five major pitfalls[16] that business owners can become victim to when trying to become more innovative. See if you recognize the ones that apply to you and your business, so that you can sidestep them at every opportunity:

1. **Identifying the wrong problem:** When a problem doesn't stay solved or an opportunity doesn't pan out as expected, it could be that the wrong problem was defined. For example, a synthetic-fiber producer brought a group of employees together to help find ways to reduce the manufacturing costs of a particular product. After spending a few days brainstorming and finding that the problem was not leading them to any interesting or useful solutions, the employees turned the problem around and began developing ways to increase the sales of a highly profitable part of the product line. How were they able to change their focus in this way? They simply examined the problem within the broader context of profitability (instead of costs) and discovered that the real problem was low profits.
2. **Judging ideas too quickly:** At many business meetings when someone suggests a new idea or approach, often the first reaction you hear is, "We've tried that before and it didn't work," "The boss will never go for it," "It's not in the budget," or the frequently heard, "Yes, but . . ." People tend to judge ideas prematurely, before they take the time to ask, "What's right about this idea?" or "How could this idea be made better?"

3. **Stopping with the first good idea:** The first good idea you come up with is rarely the best. That's because it was the easiest to think of, and so there is little doubt that your competitors have already thought of it, too. Thinking of the 3,000 ideas for a successful product mentioned at the beginning of the chapter, it is easy to imagine that the very best ideas come a little later, after the ideas that are on the top of your mind come out. Using a tool such as SCAMPER, for example, encourages you to explore things more deeply than just rattling off the first thing you can think of and then doing that.
4. **Failing to act:** A colleague was passionate about Jamba Juice, a national chain that hadn't come to St. Louis yet. Anytime we traveled together, if there was a Jamba Juice, he'd find it and sit around talking about it. Knowing it was a franchise chain, I encouraged him to become the St. Louis franchisee. Although he was passionate about the product, he kept finding reasons not to try for the franchise. Ironically, another local found himself at loose ends when he lost his job as a top beer executive and ended up becoming the nation's largest Jamba Juice franchisee. Good opportunities have a way of coming into existence. It might be up to you to bring it to the market.
5. **Obeying rules that don't exist:** We sometimes put obstacles in front of ourselves because we think we can't do something, when in fact there is no reason we can't. Are you assuming that as the business owner you need to do all the work, or make all the sales calls, or solve everybody's problems (including your employees' or partners' problems)? Before you assume that you do, challenge the assumption.

Screen Ideas

LO **4-5** Identify how to screen ideas for business potential.

In the previous section we examined various ways you can search for your business idea or for ideas that improve existing products, services, or business processes. But recall that in big businesses, it can take 3,000 ideas to yield 1 commercially viable product. To increase their odds of finding a good idea, they take all the thoughts they came up with from the "feel" step of the entrepreneurial process, and put them through a "check." In this section we'll show you ways to do that checking for your ideas and opportunities.

We begin with some fundamental questions. Later in this chapter you will learn how to conduct a comprehensive feasibility analysis for your idea, a formal approach to assessing whether your idea is sound and could lead to a viable business. For now we offer a simple approach to help you quickly screen ideas.

In many cases you might be thinking about opening a service locally or starting a website or creating a basic consumer product. In all of these cases, it is likely that you can quickly and easily check out what is already out in the marketplace. The techniques are given in Skill Module 4.1. The fact that your idea is already out there is not necessarily a bad thing for you. You can check out what your competitors are doing and think about if you can do better. This can be by making a better product or service, or by doing a better job at marketing their product or service through some kind of contracting arrangement. If they've got something good, you might consider approaching them to become a distributor or agent selling their product or service in your locale. You could be in business tomorrow!

IDEO screen
A technique for conducting a fast initial analysis of ideas for their potential. An IDEO screen looks at three elements—market desirability, technical feasibility, and organizational viability.

design thinking
A customer-focused approach using interviews, observation, and exercises to create products and services that provide demonstrated evidence of solving customers' problems.

One of the simplest and fastest ways to screen ideas is what we will call the **IDEO screen**. IDEO is a consulting organization that is one of the creators of the approach called **design thinking**, which is a customer-focused approach to creating products and services that truly solve customers' problems. They recommend looking for ideas that are high in three elements, which are represented by the asterisk (*) in Figure 4.5:[17]

1. **Market Desirability:** Do people (your customers) really want the solution being offered?
2. **Technical Feasibility:** Can the solution really solve the problem, and can we make it?
3. **Business Viability:** Can we make the solution and make money doing it?

The questions can be answered in only a few words (think one Post-it Note per question), enough so someone can get a general idea of the answer. The IDEO screen for Pet Élan, whose feasibility study is shown later in the chapter, is included in Figure 4.5. Note that it was only one of many ideas entrepreneur Randy Miller came up with on the path to deciding on a business opportunity.

Checking Ideas on the Web

SKILL MODULE 4.1

When we think of a new idea, we generally assume that if it is new to us, it is new to the world. With the help of the Internet, we can now do a much better job of making sure that's true. Take the example of a book holder on an adjustable spring-loaded arm, like some types of desk lamps. It would let you read in bed at a comfortable angle without tiring your arms. Because you have not seen one before, it seems like it could be a new product idea.

Start your browser, point it to **google.com**, and type the product description "book holder for bed":

Google Inc.

In this case, the idea is popular enough that before we could type "bed," Google pulled it up as one of the more popular product searches. Going to the page will give you an idea of what kinds of holders already exist. Note that you might have to try several different ways to describe your product. For example, if you tried typing "spring-loaded book holder" you could get a different mix of products. So try to think of different ways to describe the product.

Realize that the existence of products like the one you imagined gives you a fast path to starting your business. Instead of manufacturing something (which will take your time and money), you can select the products you think would best fit your customers' needs, obtain the products from a wholesaler (or become a reseller with the manufacturer or wholesaler), and start selling overnight, with minimal up-front expenditure. If you can arrange to have the wholesaler or manufacturer or a third-party like Fulfillment by Amazon handle the drop-shipping, you can operate in an almost totally hands-off fashion.

If you are considering a service, like dog walking, the same basic approach applies. Bring up **maps.google.com** and put in the service and the zip code or locality where you would like to deliver the service. It should show you where potential competitors are located. Remember that many services are local, so if there is no one in your immediate vicinity, that may be enough space in which to get started.

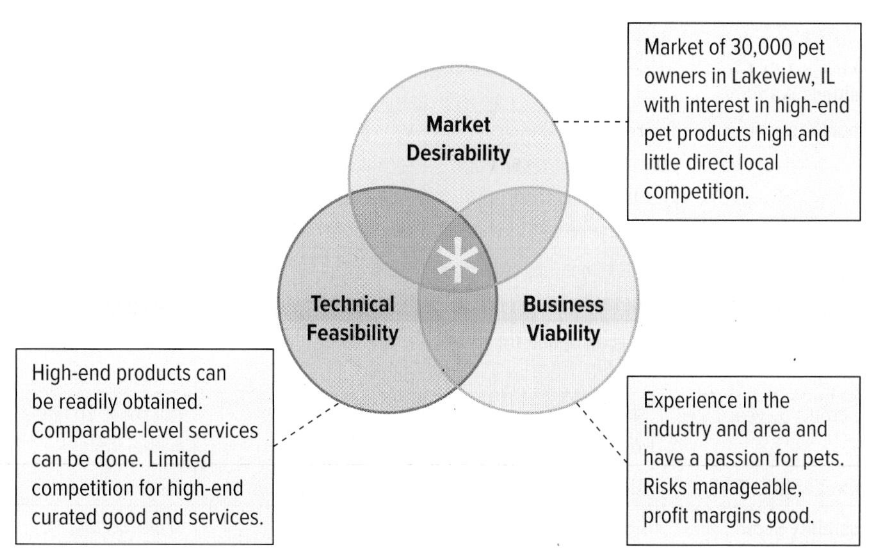

FIGURE 4.5 The Initial IDEO Screen for Pet Élan

However, if you are considering multiple ideas at the start of your screening process, it might help to put numbers to the analysis. Skill Module 4.2 provides a simple way to score initial ideas.

SKILL MODULE 4.2 Scoring Ideas in an IDEO Screen

The goal in screening (see Figure 4.2) is to narrow down the many ideas you have generated, make an initial assessment of them, and then do a more in-depth analysis of this smaller set of ideas using the business model canvas or classic feasibility study. Using the scoring matrix below is a three-step process:

Step 1: Score each idea on the 12 items in the table below. For each item, the score can be 1, 2, or 3, depending on which is the closest description of the idea at this time. If in doubt, use the lower score (this is a way to be conservative in your assessments).

Step 2: Total the scores from questions 1–4 to get the market impact score, which measures the acceptance and scale of your idea with potential buyers. Do the same for questions 5–12 to get the possibility score for that idea. The possibility score measures how possible the idea is given its complexity and your firm's capabilities.

Market Desirability	**Score 1**	**Score 2**	**Score 3**
1. Frequency of purchase	Buys it once	Return buyer for new versions	Repeat buyer for original purchase
2. Intensity of desire	Likes it	Loves it	Raving fan
3. Sales per week	100s of units	1,000s of units	10,000s of units
4. Customer testing	Real customers—directly asked about idea (family and friends asked do not count)	Real customers—given **"customer job"** interviews	> 20 real customers—given customer job interviews
Technical Feasibility			
5. Product	Would need to be built from scratch	Only needs customization or can be built using existing components	Already exists
6. Deployment	Requires new sales channels or efforts	Uses existing real-world channels and efforts	Uses existing Internet channels and efforts
7. Distinctive competence	Seen as "as good as the competition"	Seen as "better than the competition"	Seen as "the best choice by far"
8. Value proposition	Solves a part of the customer job	Solves majority of customer job	Directly and completely solves customer job
Business Viability			
9. Team	You need help with one or more of technical, sales, financial, or operations	You're "okay" at it all—technical, sales, financial, and operations	You're great at it all —technical, sales, financial, and operations
10. Risks (insurance, legal, technical, moral)	Risks not fully explored or managed	Major risks known and manageable	All risks known and manageable
11. Your passion for this	It is an option for you	It is what you want to do	It is a burning need for you to do this
12. Profits by year 2	Will cover firm's operating annual budget	Will cover 5 times annual budget	Will cover 10 times annual budget
Market Impact Score (Questions 1–4) (maximum = 12)			Score =
Possibility Score (Questions 5–12) (maximum = 24)			Score =

customer job
The term given to what a potential customer is trying to do—perform or complete some sort of task, solve some problem, or try to achieve some outcome. The target of the job is often the key to what a proposed product or service is intended to help.

Step 3: Plot the scores on the accompanying graph (or make your own with a 24 × 12 graph space).[18] The closer to the upper right the idea (the blue area), the better it is because of its high scores for possibility and market impact. Feel free to rethink or retool your ideas and rescore them to achieve an improved product or service. This is a very common practice, and one behind many of the best ideas. Of the things you can do, pursuing more customer interviews is often the key to making better solutions.

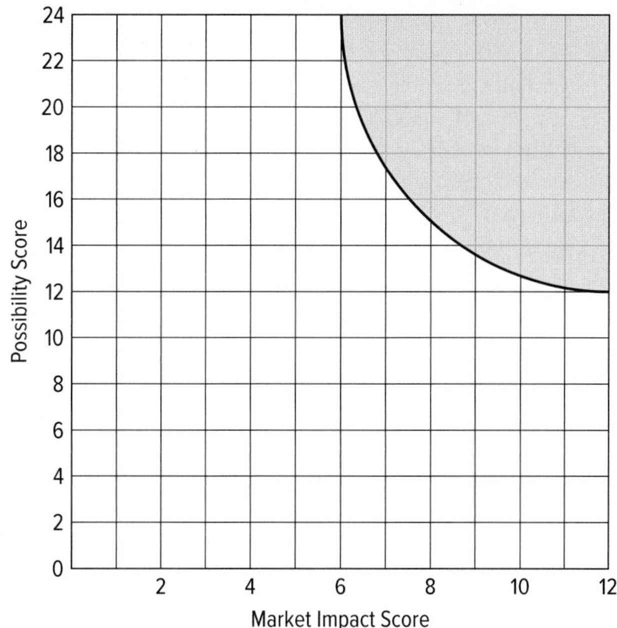

When Randy Miller scored his idea using the 12 questions his possibility scores were $1 + 3 + 2 + 2 + 1 + 2 + 2 + 2 = 15$ (out of 24) and his market impact scores were $3 + 2 + 1 + 1 = 7$ (out of 12), so he fell outside the blue high-impact area in the graph, but actually quite close to it, so the idea seemed worth considering, and perhaps worth doing some additional preliminary work to improve his customer interviews, making sure his risks are managed and help the idea work even better.

You might have noticed that the interviews getting the highest score in Skill Module 4.2 are "customer job" interviews. This style of interviewing has been developed by IDEO and several others, and it consists of your asking potential customers (family or friends don't work for this) about the problem they have, how they they have tried to solve it so far, and what are the good and bad aspects of that solution. Your goals are to find potential customers, learn their needs, how they meet their needs right now, and what they see as better potential solutions. In this approach, you do not tell them your idea for a product or service. You learn about their problems and the solutions tried first. If you offer your solution, there is too great a chance that they will tell you what they think you want to hear. At this point, you need some true leads more than reaffirmation of your own idea, if you want to have solid opportunities when you are done. You can learn about how to do such interviews in Skill Module 9.1. If you want even more suggestions for how to develop this key skill, look at the suggestions in the Learn More Online box below.

LEARN MORE ONLINE

Learn more about the topic above at these sites:

Talking to Humans free PDF ebook: **www.talkingtohumans.com**

Justin Wilcox's interviewing approach: **https://customerdevlabs.com/2013/11/05/how-i-interview-customers/**

Interviewing advice from the home of the business model canvas: **https://blog.strategyzer.com/posts/2015/11/26/a-quick-guide-for-asking-good-customer-questions**

When you are down to what you might think of as your leading idea, it is time to make your first deep-dive check. How best to do that depends on the type of idea.

Make Sure an Idea Is Feasible

Did you notice that the screening process doesn't ask you anything about money, like costs or sales? That is because trying to think through the finances is one of the more complex things to assess when thinking about a start-up. You need to do it eventually, but it is better to come up with interesting and potentially great ideas and then work through those "next-stage" sorts of issues, like financing.

feasibility
The extent to which an idea is viable and realistic and the extent to which you are aware of internal (to your business) and external (industry, market, and regulatory environment) forces that could affect your business.

In general, that next-step process after the IDEO screen is called testing the idea for its **feasibility**. Feasibility means the extent to which the idea is viable and realistic and the extent to which you are aware of internal (to your business) and external (industry, market, and regulatory environment) forces that could affect your business. In this section we will talk about the two major approaches to checking feasibility—the business model canvas process (also known as the online pilot test or the lean business practice), and the classic feasibility study.

The Business Model Canvas Approach

LO **4-6** Describe how to construct a business model canvas to assess the feasibility of your business idea.

Business models are ways to identify and organize key information on organizations and how they achieve their goals. There are literally hundreds of business models, both as analytic tools and as ways to do business. For example, the "razor and blades" business model explained how Gillette made money by selling razors cheaply but charging a *lot* more for razor blades—a model we all live with today. Think of how little you pay for your printer or smartphone up front, but how much you have to spend on printer ink or data plans to keep it useful!

business model
A way to identify and organize key information on a business and how it achieves its goals. Business models can be analytic tools (like a business model canvas) or a way to do business (like the "razor and blade" business model).

For our purposes, though, the focus is on the business model as an analytic tool. Figure 4.6 shows a variant of the popular business model canvas developed by Osterwalder and Pigneur with the IDEO overlay developed by Isaac Jeffries.[19] The business model canvas explores the 11 most important factors in developing a start-up that would appeal to customers, compete well, and generate a profit. The blue boxes within the canvas build on answers related to market desirability which you developed in your IDEO screen earlier in the process. The answers related to the technical feasibility you developed for the screen are applied in the red boxes, while the answers to the business viability items relate to the green boxes below. Let's consider each of the 11 boxes in the most likely order you would think about or encounter them,[20] which are the red numbers in Figure 4.6.

FIGURE 4.6

How the Business Model Canvas Builds from the IDEO Screen's Market Desirability (in blue), Technical Feasibility (in red), and Business Viability (in green)[21]

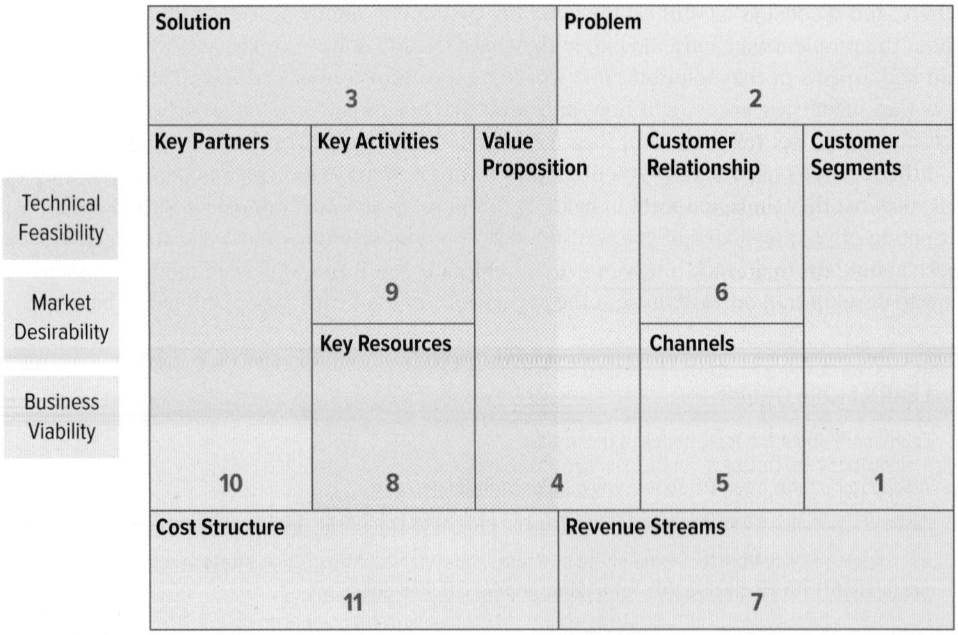

Legend: Technical Feasibility; Market Desirability; Business Viability

<table>
<tr><td colspan="2">Solution
3</td><td colspan="3">Problem
2</td></tr>
<tr><td rowspan="2">Key Partners
10</td><td>Key Activities
9</td><td rowspan="2">Value Proposition
4</td><td>Customer Relationship
6</td><td rowspan="2">Customer Segments
1</td></tr>
<tr><td>Key Resources
8</td><td>Channels
5</td></tr>
<tr><td colspan="2">Cost Structure
11</td><td colspan="3">Revenue Streams
7</td></tr>
</table>

1. **Customer Segments:** This builds from your customer workup in the screening process. Note there is often more than one type of customer (e.g., individuals vs. big corporations, athletes vs. nonathletes). Each type is called a **customer segment**, and each will have a different problem and need a solution and value proposition that fits his or her situation. So you are likely to end up having multiple copies of the canvas—one for each customer segment.
2. **Problem:** What problem (also called a **pain**) is faced by customers that you are seeking to solve? A variant of a pain is your customers' dreams of better ways or things, which we call a **gain**.
3. **Solution:** Here is where your offering goes—how you plan to handle the problem-solving pains or create gains for your customers.
4. **Value proposition** also comes from the screening, and will differ for each customer segment. What will make your solution the best available fit (i.e., the most valuable available alternative) to what the customer wants or needs? When you think of how your solution fits with the customer's job for each segment, you're considering issues related to market desirability. When you think how your solution value gives your firm a distinctive competence over competitors, you're considering issues related to technical feasibility.
5. **Channels:** How will you get your product or service to the customer? Selling directly is great (you control the process), but is often expensive or hard to get going. So if you're selling through others, how do you arrange to be heard and seen by your customers? Think of small hotels that use their websites (direct selling) but also sell through Expedia, Trivago, AAA, AARP, and others to get you to buy a room.
6. **Customer Relationships:** The best customers are ones that buy again and again and recommend you to their friends. The product or service is part of it, but most often it is the way you treat and take care of your customers that makes the greatest difference. How will you take the best care of your most important resource—your customer?
7. **Revenues:** How do you make money solving the problem and selling to your customers? How many different ways can you get revenues? **Freemium** models give you something and let you buy add-ons. Subscription models have ongoing streams. Big-ticket items like cars offer additional services such as financing, extended warranties, and dealer service to get more of your car dollars.
8. **Key Resources:** What great thing do you or your firm have that no one else does? Exclusive rights to the name of the latest rap star or the work of a rising manga artist? A lock on the only source of morel mushrooms in driving distance? A salesperson loved by everyone? A to-die-for clothing designer? The perfect location for your type of business? The best app programmer around? Remember from Chapter 3 the six types of resources? Any of them can give your firm its edge against the competition, and those resources are the key ones.
9. **Key Activities:** What will be the most important activities in your business—the ones most central to your doing the job right and making the firm successful? Take the value proposition and ask yourself what has to happen to deliver the value you're promising your customers. For a restaurant with a food focus, it means the food has to be the best it can be. For a restaurant that wants to be "the place to be," décor and location may be the keys to delivering on the promise.
10. **Key Partners:** Your team is the starting point for your partners. Your staff are key to the basic work of your business (they are in the green part of the box). But few start-ups can do everything themselves, so ask which individuals and organizations can help make you successful and able to deliver on the promise in your value proposition. Well-regarded suppliers of your raw materials, corporate partners that inspire confidence (e.g., IBM, Amazon), a well-connected attorney or accountant, an advisory board member known and respected by all—these are potential examples of key partners (in the red part of the box). Even a one-person business can have a village of key partners.
11. **Costs:** Many of the other boxes require actions or purchases to achieve their ends. When we consider all of those costs, and the other general costs of any start-up (salaries, filing fees, inventory or manufacturing costs, etc.), what are the costs? We compare these costs to the revenues and make our initial assessment of the profit potential of the business.

customer segment
A group or subgroup of potential purchasers that can be approached in a coherent manner.

pain
Any sort of problem, annoyance, source of aggravation, shortcoming, or suboptimal situation customers or potential customers face. It is one of two driving forces of creating new products or services, with the other driving force being gain.

gain
Any sort of outcome (a product, service, outcome, or situation) customers or potential customers would like to encounter or be able to depend on. It is one of two driving forces of creating new products or services, with the other driving force being pain.

value proposition
Small business owners' unique selling points (also known as benefits) that customers can expect from your goods or services, including benefits that differentiate your offering from those of the competition.

freemium
An approach to pricing, and a business model, that connects free and premium products or services. Typically a free version is offered and users have the option to pay to move up to premium features. Popular examples include Dropbox (5 GB of space for free, with more space or services at a price) and Angry Birds (free ad-supported version; paid version removes ads).

Figure 4.7 gives Pet Élan's business model canvas. To analyze feasibility using the canvas, we first compare the fit by customer segment to the value proposition, problem, and solution. The four should strongly reflect one another and reflect something customers in the segment will love

FIGURE 4.7

Pet Élan's Business Model Canvas

<table>
<tr><td colspan="3">Solution A more appealing Lakeview pet store offering upscale services, products (food, toys, and accessories), and pet community supports.</td><td colspan="2">Problem Pet owners who want to give their pets the very best can't readily or easily do so in Lakeview.</td></tr>
<tr><td rowspan="2">Key Partners
Local pet service providers (e.g., trainers). Local pet support organizations (e.g., Humane Society). SBDC or college for marketing help. High-end product suppliers.</td><td>Key Activities
Sell the right products with personalized service. Deliver high-end in-store services.</td><td rowspan="2">Value Proposition
We will be the place that pampers pets with upscale products and services, and supports community pet initiatives.</td><td>Customer Relationships
Owners serves you. Personal attention and recognition. Pet-friendly store. Active in local pet causes.</td><td rowspan="2">Customer Segments
Pet Pamperers: Higher income (>$50,000), in Lakeview, buy pet fashions, support pet-related causes.</td></tr>
<tr><td>Key Resources
Personal/local knowledge and connections. An excellent location and attractive store.</td><td>Channels
Store in Lakeview shopping area. Informational web-site. Partner referrals and mentions.</td></tr>
<tr><td colspan="3">Cost Structure
Storefront.
Equipment.
Inventory.
Owner does all.
~$50,000 to $80,000</td><td colspan="2">Revenue Streams
Product sales; in-house services; referral services; 50% plus margins, 6 days a week.
Sales projections needed.</td></tr>
</table>

and buy. If the customers do love it, we analyze the market factors, everything from value proposition to the right edge of the canvas, for their fit—are we doing everything we need to in order to connect with, sell to, satisfy, and keep the customer? For Pet Élan, the elements seem to fit, but it would be crucial to check with potential customers to make sure the concept is on track.

Then we look at the fit of the organizational factors (from the value proposition to the left edge of the canvas)—are we doing the right things in the best way possible with the best team and lowest cost to make the business itself a success? Again the fit seems to work, but making sure the key activities and solution fit what the customers want (seen in the *Value Proposition* box) needs checking with potential customers.

In reality, it is rare that a first-time canvas is seen as feasible right off the bat. That is all right. Canvases are made to be revised (use Post-it Notes at first—really!) so be ready to do it for every segment you have. Feel free to drop, add, or change segments. For Pet Élan, another segment consisted of customers who will do an occasional splurge on their pet—a reasonable market, but a less consistent source of revenues than the pet pamperers. Doing something great for one segment may be enough to make a good living and change your customers' worlds for the better. When you have a solid idea based on the business model canvas, the next step in the entrepreneurial process outlined in Chapter 1 is to create a business plan to map out and get control of the details of the business.[22]

LEARN MORE ONLINE

Learn more about the topics above at these sites:

Business model canvas starter video: **www.youtube.com/watch?v=QoAOzMTLP5s** (Strategyzer has more training videos on its channel)

Disney's business model canvas: **www.youtube.com/watch?v=Dqakc-VuKjs&t=35s**

Isaac Jeffries IDEO screen and business model canvas: **https://isaacjeffries.com/blog/2017/3/3/bmc-part-one-how-to-use-the-business-model-canvas?rq=lenses**

Canvanizer's free online business model canvas: **https://canvanizer.com/new/business-model-canvas**

BMfiddle's free online business model canvas: **https://bmfiddle.com/**

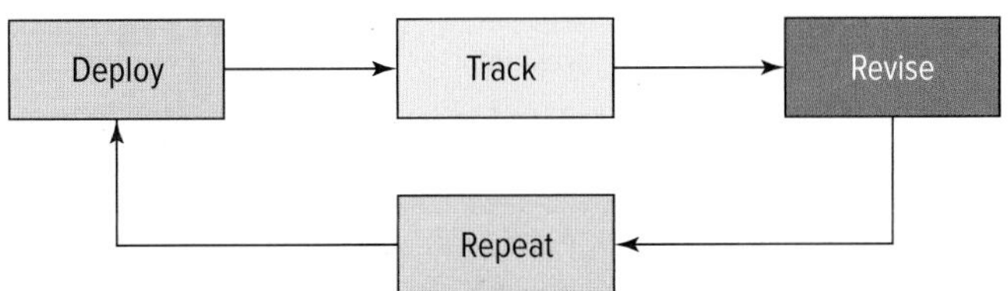

FIGURE 4.8

Online Pilot Testing Procedure

An interactive way to test the fit of the solution and value proposition to the customers is using a low-cost, low-risk approach for testing feasibility called an online **pilot test**, shown in Figure 4.8. In this approach, you deploy a basic informational website describing the products or services you want to offer, and start advertising it. You track the number of people who check out the site, where they came from, their demographics, and in particular the number who give their email address to be informed when the product or service is available (this is called the **conversion rate**). Typically two or more versions are run (called **A/B testing**).[23]

Based on the feedback from customers and visitors, you quickly fix (revise) what does not work and reinforce and promote those things that seem to work best. These changes are done quickly, usually over a few days, although if response is strong enough, over a few hours. This process gets repeated continuously until a highly accepted version of the idea emerges, or it becomes evident that the idea does not make a viable business regardless of the revisions tried. The strategy for using the online pilot test approach is to show potential partners, investors, or bankers that the idea can generate sales. In the spirit of "the proof is in the pudding," showing customer interest in potentially obtaining the actual product or service, and being able to say how many visitors became customers—the conversion rate— are powerful ways to prove your idea is potentially feasible. For small-scale ideas or those that lend themselves to a web-based approach, the online pilot test model can give powerful results quickly and painlessly.

pilot test
A preliminary run of a business, sales effort, program, or website with the goal of assessing how well the overall approach works and what problems it might have.

conversion rate
The measure of how many visitors to your website (or people who click on your online advertisement) are actually willing to make a commitment to the product or service promoted on the site.

A/B testing
A way to check customer reaction to websites describing your product or service. Two versions (version "A" and version "B") of the site are posted and are served up randomly to prospective customers. The version of the website that gets the most commitments from customers is the one kept and the less attractive site is revised and the two versions tested until one revision gets consistently superior customer reactions.

LEARN MORE ONLINE

Learn more about the topics above at these sites:

CXL's guide to A/B testing (and a free ebook): **https://conversionxl.com/blog/ab-testing-guide/**

Wix Academy's landing page advice: **https://academy.wix.com/en/landing-pages/what-is-a-landing-page** (Wix offers free websites for landing pages)

Unbounce's A/B testing advice page: **https://unbounce.com/a-b-testing/**

If you plan to go from an IDEO screen to a business model canvas to a business plan, you need to know that there is a lot more information in a classic feasibility study than in the business model canvas discussed above. But there is an expanded version of the canvas, called the business model environment, which captures and positions a lot of the data needed to build on in preparation for a business plan. Figure 4.9 shows the forces external to the firm that have an impact on the firm described in the canvas. The key trends and macroeconomic forces are introduced in Chapter 3. Industry and competitive analyses you'll learn more about in Chapter 7, while market forces will be considered in Chapter 10. You'll also see how these get handled in the business plan in Chapter 8.

feasibility study
Evaluates the potential of a business opportunity by studying five primary areas in depth: the overall business idea, the product/service, the industry and market, financial projections (profitability), and the plan for future action.

The Classic Feasibility Study

The other typical approach for evaluating ideas that survive your IDEO screen is called the **feasibility study**. Feasibility studies consist of careful investigation of five primary areas: the overall business idea, the product/service, the industry and market, financial projections (profitability), and the plan for future action. Within each of these areas you will examine the strengths and weaknesses (advantages and disadvantages) of your business opportunity. Exhibit 4.2 shows a descriptive outline of a feasibility study,[24] which includes a brief explanation of the areas that will help you decide whether your idea or opportunity can be a feasible business. A complete feasibility plan for Pet Élan is included in the appendix at the end of this chapter so you can see what it looks like in practice.

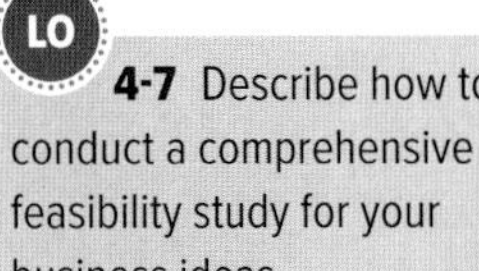

4-7 Describe how to conduct a comprehensive feasibility study for your business ideas.

FIGURE 4.9

The Business Model Environment

Source: Strategyzer, https://blog.strategyzer.com/posts/2015/10/14/how-to-scan-through-your-environments-disruptive-threats-and-opportunities.

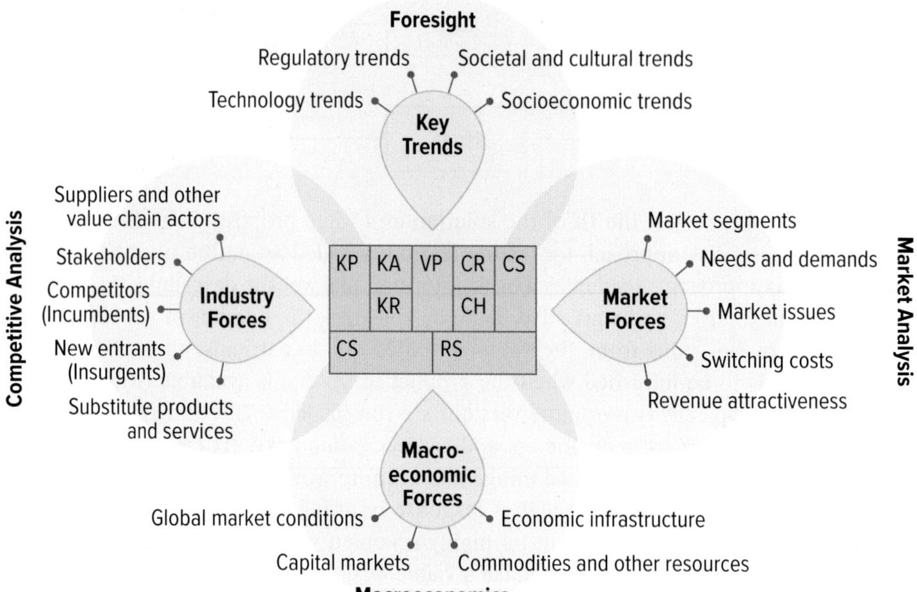

EXHIBIT 4.2

The Feasibility Study Outline

I. The Business Idea

- **Description of Your Business** What business are you *really* in? Describe your product or service in the most concise way you can, and think beyond the characteristics of the product or service to the *experience* that you hope the customer receives from buying the product or service.
- **Your Customers** Who are your customers? Demographic information tells you all about your customers' personal characteristics such as where they live, how much household income they have, and how many children they have. You can find very specific information in your library or online using zip code resource sites like www.zipwho.com, www.censusscope.org, or www.city-data.com. What are your customers' preferences, values, and attitudes that relate to your business? How will you find out what your customers think or intend to buy? How can you find out what problems they have, what they need, or what they want that they don't know yet! Use your creativity to learn as much as you can about your potential customers. If you have more than one **target market**, do this for each market segment. It's important to note the different benefits and limitations for each customer group. This is developed from the *Market Desirability* section in your IDEO screen.
- **Trends Related to the Product or Service** How will you keep your finger on the pulse of change in your product or service area? What trends are likely to occur in the way the product is used, or what features it offers, for example?

II. The Product/Service

- **Product/Service Description** What exactly are you offering? What are the unique features of the product or service? How do these features meet your customers' needs or preferences? Describe your product or service very simply, and use photos or drawings to illustrate how it works. This is developed from the *Technical Feasibility* in your IDEO screen.
- **The Competition** Who are your primary competitors, and what are their distinct advantages and disadvantages? Consider not only your direct competitors, but also

target market
A marketing term (also called serviceable obtainable market, or SOM) that refers to the group of customers in the area you plan to serve who would be likely to be interested in your product, or those of competitors. Target markets can refer to individuals or market groups called segments.

your indirect ones who might be selling a substitute for your product or service or bundling your product with something else they provide.

- **Competitive Advantage** After considering your competition, your offering, and your fit to the customer, what are your competitive advantages? Why do you believe they exist, and why do you think these will help you succeed in the marketplace?
- **Market Penetration** How will you reach your target customers? Will you be producing or subcontracting out the manufacturing or delivery of your product or service? List all the costs, including labor, supplies, shipping, repairs, and so forth. What forms of distribution or selling will you use? How will your potential customers become aware of your business? How will you advertise? What would your selling process look like in the different channels you have? What will your customer service look like?

III. The Business

- **Description of the Entrepreneur (or Team)** What do you bring to this idea or business? How well does this product or service fit with your knowledge, skills, abilities, networks, and experience? How determined are you to bring this product or service to market? If you are already in business, how does this idea fit with the other products or services you sell? This is developed from the *Technical Feasibility and Business Viability* sections in your IDEO screen.
- **Stage of Development** Is the product still in the idea stage, or is there a model or working prototype available? Have any samples been manufactured? If it is still in the idea or prototype stage, what is the time frame for getting it ready for production?
- **Legal Issues** List any patents, copyrights, trademarks, licenses, or domain names that apply to your product or service. If you are entering into a franchise agreement, partnerships, distributorships, and so on, these should be discussed in this section. Seek the assistance of patent attorneys or intellectual copyright specialists for assistance. Also list the government regulations you must adhere to, such as the FDA, EOA, OSHA, IRS, secretary of state, and research zoning restrictions carefully. If you will be home-based and your clients will be coming to your house, will this be impacted by your neighborhood's zoning restrictions? Note your legal form of organization and state of registry.
- **Insurance Requirements** Research the liability of your product or service and consult an insurance specialist to be sure you are protected adequately. This will depend on the nature of your business. A flower shop that sells floral arrangements is in a different liability situation than a pet grooming business, for example. If you have employees, you will need insurance to protect them from harm also, along with any insurance benefits you want to provide your staff.

IV. Future Action Plan

- **Summary Feasibility Evaluation** Considering everything you have discovered above, do you see this idea as holding enough possibility to be workable and successful that it warrants next steps? What is your basis for making this judgment? Likely outcomes are either confirming the idea as feasible, holding off concluding until you learn more, or realizing the idea is not feasible in its current form (which might prompt you to change your approach, try something else, or drop thinking about a business for now).
- **Next Steps** The direction this takes depends on the Summary Feasibility Evaluation above. If the idea is feasible, you will probably need to start working on a business plan and other start-up actions. If there are questions, you must list the research

(*Continued*)

you need to undertake to get answers. Pivoting your idea or thinking of new ideas or locations represent a different type of research. For all of these issues, list the individuals or groups you could consult for advice, or add an advisory board consisting of people with experience in your industry and professionals from other industries.

- **Start-Up Capital** If you see the business as feasible a key question is, how much money do you need to start the business? In addition to the cost of goods sold that you calculated and your marketing and administrative expenses, what additional costs do you have such as renting space, utility expenses, and salaries?
- **Sources of Start-Up Capital** Where can you obtain the money you need to start the business? Consider all the sources available to you such as personal savings, family and friends, bank loans, investors, and so on.

V. The Financial Projections

- **Assumptions** Put together a list of all the assumptions on which you are basing your financials—start-up and ongoing costs (also called operating expenses), pricing, sales projections and how you arrive at them, and how profits are computed. Do a breakeven analysis (see Chapter 13) somewhere in your financials, and also be sure to note somewhere what are your fixed and variable costs.
- **Summary Financial Table** Develop a basic three-year summary of your financials. The typical rows are: Revenues, Cost of Good Sold, Gross Margin, Operating Expenses, Net Profit (or loss) [which is figured pretax]. The development of these projections is detailed in Chapter 13.
- **Three-Year Detailed Financials** These are the detailed financials from which the three-year summary given above are based. The typical format is detailed in Chapter 13. Typically you will give monthly numbers for the first year and cumulative numbers for years 2 and 3.
- **Start-Up Budget** This listing gives the costs you will incur starting up your business, including legal costs and other professional fees, initial inventory or manufacturing costs, building and fixture costs, and technology costs.

In crafting a feasibility study, such as Pet Élan in the appendix at the end of this chapter, the goal is to assess if the idea can be profitably brought to market. The traditional problems facing new ideas are (1) the idea cannot be economically made into a product or service; (2) the resulting product or service works, but does not appeal to a large enough market (or is not worth enough to them) to make the effort profitable; and (3) the product or service works, has a market, and could be profitable, but you need to get additional people, funding, or other resources to make the idea into a business. Notice that each problem builds on the solution of the prior problem. As with idea screenings, having no solution for one of these problems may not spell the end of the process *if* you can use creative solution approaches like SCAMPER (introduced earlier in this chapter) to come up with a new way to resolve or sidestep problems.

As you can see, the business model canvas and the classic feasibility study produce very different results. The canvas can be made much more quickly, but if the idea proves feasible, the resulting business plan will require more work, especially on details like legal issues and the financials. But if you are considering a couple of ideas, a canvas can help you decide more quickly than a classic feasibility study and with a better overall assessment than the IDEO screen. When you have one idea, there is no substitute for the classic feasibility study, since it will get you to consider a much broader range of business issues and point you to the kinds of issues you will have to deal with in the business plan itself, saving you time when you do your plan. From the entrepreneurial process model in Chapter 1, either of these help you think about your business idea and both position you for your plan, so whichever approach you use, you'll be preparing yourself for the next step in the process of launching your start-up.

Often a feasibility study will lead to a decision either to keep pursuing the opportunity or to wait for a better time to move forward with the decision (perhaps in a better economy, or when the market matures, or after you get additional experience or training), or to stop working on the idea and look for something else. When you decide in a feasibility analysis to go with the idea, very often the next step is to begin working on a full business plan, which capitalizes on many of the things you have written about in the feasibility study. Business plans are more involved than feasibility analyses, and in Chapter 8 you will see not only how to create a business plan but also how business plans and feasibility studies relate to one another.

Ways to Keep On Being Creative

LO **4-8** Recognize the value of building a creative culture in your business.

Once you have generated your business ideas, screened them, and evaluated a few of them to find one that is feasible, you have completed the opportunity identification and evaluation process. But this process never really ends. Even after you are well on your way to starting a business and even after your business is successful and you have met your initial goals, the nature of entrepreneurship and small business is that you will always be on the lookout for new opportunities. Successful business owners never rest on their laurels and assume that, since they have achieved success, it will always be there. One of the pitfalls small business owners can fall into is to fail to build a company culture–a way of thinking and behaving–that encourages new ideas and embraces change. This is especially important if you employ or plan to employ other people. There is nothing as discouraging as working for someone who feels there is nothing new you can possibly contribute to the business. You would be surprised to learn how many business owners have this mentality. Here are some ways you can avoid this and build a company that is "idea prone." You will find that you can attract more creative employees and get more useful ideas out of them that affect your business's bottom line by following the recommendations given in Skill Module 4.3.

Great Ideas for Making Idea-Prone Companies

SKILL MODULE 4.3

1. Give yourself and your employees time to think of ideas. While it can seem that there is never enough time to get everything done and deadlines are always looming, you can't afford not to take the time to come up with new ideas. Allow even just a few minutes every day to discover what your customers or employees are thinking and what problems or frustrations they may be experiencing. Ask your employees what they are working on, where there may be problems, and what ideas they have for solving them.
2. Positively reinforce ideas[25]—avoid the automatic no. As discussed earlier, don't rush to judge ideas. It's the process of coming up with ideas that needs to be reinforced, not whether the idea is good. Evaluation can come later.
3. Look to unlikely sources of opportunities. You never know where creativity and innovation will emerge. Think beyond your age group, socioeconomic status, and education.
4. Get a room with a view. Give your employees—and yourself—varied experiences. Get away from the office, go visit customers, allow employees to learn one another's jobs, and so on. It enables people to get a different perspective, and it is when we can change our routine that breakthrough ideas often can be discovered.

An innovative company does not automatically develop out of an innovative business idea. You have to deliberately set your expectations and communicate them to your employees. Remember that recognition is fuel—it fans the fires of creativity and helps your business reach potentials that you may never have anticipated. Einstein said, "Creativity is contagious . . . pass it on." As the business owner, you are in a unique position to make sure that people's brains don't stop at your company's door.

Even if you are a solo small business owner, you can take steps to keep yourself in an innovative frame of mind.[26] Here are some techniques you can try as you practice the business of innovation on your own:

- Read magazines or trade journals outside your area.
- Invite someone you never included before to a meeting at which you are solving a problem or searching for a new opportunity. Try a supplier or a friend who works in a different field.
- Have a "scan the environment" day in which you discuss trends and happenings that could impact your business.
- Try a mini-internship. Ask a colleague or friend if you can spend a day at his or her business to see what you can learn that may be applicable to yours.
- Instead of trying to simply sell your product or service to customers, put yourself in their shoes and ask them what frustrates them most or what problems they cannot seem to solve that relate to your business.
- Redesign your work environment. Get a room with a view.[27] This doesn't have to cost a bundle in remodeling or even redecorating costs. Try to bring in some items from nature and add color and inspirational objects or quotations.

Innovation is at the heart of entrepreneurship because every time people start a business or become the owner of one, it is a new start and often a new experience for them. Some businesses are themselves built on new ideas or new twists on existing ideas. For these kinds of situations, taking some time before committing your money to think about which ideas make the most sense as a profit-maker can save a lot of grief later on. That is where the opportunity identification process, the idea screening process, and feasibility analysis come in to play. It is also true that one of the greatest challenges facing a business is getting control over the process of change—knowing when and how to change and try something new. Sometimes even thinking in new ways can be difficult, and that is when techniques like SCAMPER can make all the difference. The point is that while many people think innovation is a bolt from the blue, unpredictable and uncontrollable, in reality it is anything but that. That is good news because it means that one of the most powerful techniques for building your business is under your control.

CHAPTER SUMMARY

LO 4-1 Identify strategies for innovation in your business.

- Opportunity recognition is one of the most basic entrepreneurial behaviors.
- Entrepreneurial alertness means that entrepreneurs have a special set of observational and thinking skills that help them identify good opportunities.
- 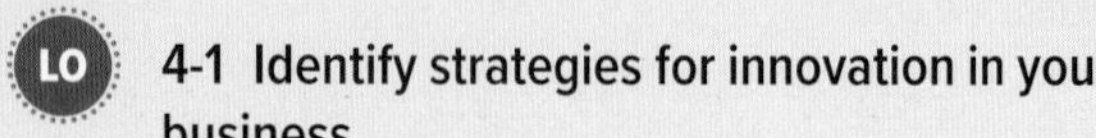
  There are three innovative strategies small business owners can select:
  - Imitative strategies take an idea that somebody else has already discovered and build a business around that idea.
  - Incremental strategies take an idea and offer a way to do something better than it is done now.
  - Radical innovation strategies reject existing ideas and present a way to do things differently.

LO 4-2 Recognize the sources of opportunity entrepreneurs draw on to get business ideas.

- In terms of the entrepreneurial process (feel, check, plan, do), entrepreneurs sense or feel the presence of opportunities as they begin the start-up process.
- It can take many ideas to find a potentially successful one. Big businesses need 3,000 ideas to get one successful product.
- Opportunities can be pursued in an effectual or causal way.
- Ideas for new businesses come from a great variety of sources. These include work and personal experience, imitation of a similar business, a chance happening, discussions with family and friends, education and experience, and online searches for "idea sites."

LO 4-3 Understand how creativity methods can help business owners recognize new opportunities.

- Creative methods help you identify opportunities beyond what everybody else already knows.
- SCAMPER is a tool you can use to trigger new opportunities for your business.
- The creative process has four stages: preparation, incubation, illumination, and verification.

LO 4-4 Understand the five pitfalls that hinder innovation.

- Identifying the wrong problem.
- Judging ideas and opportunities too quickly.
- Stopping with the first good idea.
- Failing to act.
- Obeying rules that don't exist.

LO 4-5 Identify how to screen ideas for business potential.

- The goal of the screening process is to quickly evaluate large numbers of ideas to eliminate those less likely to work for you.
- In assessing the potential viability of your business idea, there are three sets of questions to answer as part of an IDEO screen:
  - Market desirability: Do people (your customers) really want the solution being offered?
  - Technical feasibility: Can the solution really solve the problem, and can we make it?
  - Business viability: Can we make the solution and make money doing it?
- These questions can be evaluated qualitatively, quantitatively, or both.
- One of the keys to test these ideas is to perform customer job interviews with actual potential customers.

LO 4-6 Describe how to construct a business model canvas to assess the feasibility of your business idea.

- Business models are ways to identify and organize key information on organizations and how they achieve their goals.
- The business model canvas builds on an IDEO screen to generate a more in-depth look at the elements of the business and how they fit together.
- The goal of a canvas is to identify an opportunity that would appeal to customers, compete well, and generate a profit.
- Business model canvases are evaluated by the concreteness of their answers and the fit between subsets of the 11 boxes.
- For Internet-based sales and service businesses, it is possible to pilot test the idea online.
- An expansion of the canvas, called the business model environment, can help bridge the information from the canvas to that needed for business plans.

LO 4-7 Describe how to conduct a comprehensive feasibility study for your business ideas.

- Conduct an analysis to determine whether or not your business idea is feasible.
- Start with the business idea—your general business description, its customers, and the trends affecting customers now and into the future.
- Follow with the product or service: describe it in detail, tell us about the competition, what is your competitive advantage over them, and how you will go about marketing and selling your product or service.
- Next describe your business: Start with you and your team, the firm's stage of development, and the legal issues and insurance requirements you face.
- Conclude the narrative with your future action plan: Give your summary feasibility evaluation, your next steps, the start-up capital needed (if you intend to go ahead), and the sources for the capital.
- At the end put the financials: Start with the assumptions on which you are basing your financials, include a breakeven analysis and details of your fixed and variable costs, then include a summary of the three-year financials, and provide a spreadsheet with the detailed costs and revenues for the projected firm. This should be monthly for the first year, with aggregate totals for years 2 and 3. The financials should also include the start-up budget listing expenditures to get the business to opening day.

LO 4-8 Recognize the value of building a creative culture in your business.

- Build a company culture that values new ideas and embraces change.
- Create slack time to enable employees to think of new ideas.
- Positively reinforce ideas others bring to you.
- Look to unlikely sources of opportunities.
- Get a room with a view and establish an environment that stimulates innovation.
- Use techniques to help you get into an innovative frame of mind. Read outside your area, invite a "wild card" to a business meeting, have a "scan the environment" day, arrange a mini-internship, solve your customer's problem rather than selling a product, and redesign your work environment to stimulate your innovative skills.

KEY TERMS

opportunity recognition, 86
entrepreneurial alertness, 86
imitative strategy, 86
incremental strategy, 86
radical innovation strategy, 86
causal model of entrepreneurship, 87
retail arbitrage, 89
license, 90
licensee, 90
licensor, 90
royalty, 90
creativity, 90
brainstorming, 90
painstorming, 93
IDEO screen, 94
design thinking, 94
customer job, 96
feasibility, 98
business model, 98
customer segment, 99
pain, 99
gain, 99
value proposition, 99
freemium, 99
pilot test, 101
conversion rate, 101
A/B testing, 101
feasibility study, 101
target market, 102

DISCUSSION QUESTIONS

1. How do entrepreneurs recognize new ideas for their business?
2. What are some common ways you can search for new business opportunities?
3. What are the differences among imitation, incremental, and radical innovation strategies? How can you assess which one is right for your business?
4. How can entrepreneurs quickly screen large numbers of new ideas?
5. What is a business model canvas, and how do you use it to assess the potential of a business?
6. What should a good feasibility study contain? What questions can it help you answer to determine if your business idea is a sound one?
7. What pitfalls should you watch out for as you are searching for new opportunities?
8. How can entrepreneurs ensure that their business stays innovative and fresh? Why do you think some small businesses lose their creative edge as the business grows?

EXPERIENTIAL EXERCISES

1. As you go on errands or walk around your campus, notice all the things that you could improve. Make a list of things that frustrate you or things that could be made even better. Does your list surprise you in terms of how much you noticed? This is a variation of the painstorming technique.
2. List 15 new uses for a popular product or service. Try paper clips, or coffee mugs, or home delivery. Use SCAMPER to generate new uses and make connections to other uses.
3. Interview a local business owner and ask how he or she thought of the idea behind the business. How does the business develop new ideas now?
4. Do some research on innovative companies in your area. What sets them apart? How are they designed to take advantage of the innovativeness of their staffs?
5. Next time you are working on a problem or looking for new ideas (Your major in college? Where to move on campus? What do to this weekend?), go to a museum, a park, or anywhere outside the ordinary places you frequent. Were any new ideas suggested to you?
6. Keep a journal in which you can record your ideas as they come. Sometimes we get breakthrough ideas while our brain is incubating as we sleep. By the time we wake up in the morning we have lost them, so keep your journal near your bed.
7. Pick a business idea and research its industry and market. What did you learn? What are some creative questions you might ask about contemporary trends in this business? How could you find out the answers?

MINI-CASE

TIM HAYDEN AND THE MISSED HOME RUN[28]

Tim Hayden had been an avowed "sports fanatic" all his life. Friends could set their clocks by Tim. He was always watching games in the stands or on TV. Of all sports, he loved baseball the most. Sitting in the bleachers at the home of the St. Louis Cardinals, Busch Stadium, what he was sensing there distressed him. It seemed that fewer people were in the stands than in earlier years. He wished he could do something about it.

The final push to action for Tim came in 1998 when Mark McGwire crushed his 70th home run on his way to a baseball record. Tim and his father were sitting in the stands that historic night. However, they missed seeing the home run because they were standing in line at the concession stand.

As McGwire rounded the bases, Tim's friends at home were watching numerous instant replays from every conceivable camera angle while listening to the commentators talk about inside stories. In addition, they could see the exact positions of each pitch location and the in-depth scouting report on McGwire's home runs.

But here he was in the stadium, where he had paid good money for the ticket. And yet the best seat in the stadium was at home in front of his big-screen TV.

At that moment in 1998, Tim realized that others might be thinking the same way. He thought he finally knew one of the reasons why attendance was down. Sitting at home with a large-screen TV, the refrigerator nearby, the bathroom a few steps away, the seat comfortable and the room air-conditioned, how could the stadium compete? Television baseball had become so much more detailed and informative than the in-stadium variety, with last pitch graphics, hit location graphics, and detailed stats on all the players constantly shown on the big screen at home. The "best seat in the stadium" had indeed shifted to home, and the fans with it.

Tim sensed a business opportunity in that shift. Sports teams had to bring fans back to the stadiums, where teams make their most profit. He also realized that for a fan, there was an undeniable energy being among tens of thousands of fellow fans with the chance to personally see that once-in-a-lifetime play.

Being digitally savvy, he knew that combining a fan's personal cell phone, Wi-Fi, and a web-based application, he could bring the at-home experience into the stadium. Fans sitting in the stands could see any instant replay from dozens of camera angles, as well as all the cool graphics that you see on TV, with the ability to order food and drink to their seat, and maybe connect with other fans in the stadium. And even better, it could all be on-demand.

From his own pain, the feelings of other baseball fans, and over the next four years a careful study of the trends in the various sports leagues and televised sports, Tim Hayden realized that the enhanced digital experiences (they weren't as prevalent in 2002) and new TV graphic techniques of sports broadcasters had fundamentally changed the environment for sports watching. It also opened up a business opportunity.

CASE DISCUSSION QUESTIONS

1. Was the opportunity Tim was thinking about an imitative, incremental, or radical innovation strategy?
2. For Tim, which seemed to come first—thinking about creating a business, thinking about a business idea, or both at once?
3. Using the ideas in Exhibit 4.1, what were the sources of Tim's business idea?
4. What do you think was key to Tim's making the jump from a problem to a business opportunity?

APPENDIX

A Sample Feasibility Study

Pet Élan

I. THE BUSINESS IDEA

Description of Your Business

In recent years, there has been an increase in the number of households that have pets, especially dogs and cats. Further, there is emerging a steadily growing group of pet owners that is willing to purchase upscale, unique products for these important members of their family. Pet Élan is an upscale boutique for these discriminating pet owners in Lakeview, Illinois (zip code 60657). Pet Élan will offer high-quality pet products to discerning individuals who wish their pets to enjoy a healthy, fun, and elegant lifestyle while being pampered. By carefully selecting luxurious accessories made with superior materials, Pet Élan will provide an elite product line that celebrates the uniqueness of each animal's personality.

Your Customers

According to the American Pet Products Association (APPA; formerly called the American Pet Products Manufacturers Association), 68 percent of households in the United States own a pet, and 46 percent of households own more than one pet.[29] As income increases, the percentage of households with a dog increases as well.[30] In fact, 75 percent of the households with dogs have a combined income of greater than $35,000. This is consistent with the specific market profile of the clientele Pet Élan plans to target in the 60657 zip code.

There are 39,846 households in zip code 60657, with a median household income of $55,647.[31] Applying the APPA statistics, this means an estimate of 27,095 households with pets as our overall market, with 77.8 percent or 21,079 pet-owning households with an income greater than $35,000 as Pet Élan's target market, which is graphically shown in the pie chart.[32]

Household Income for Lakeview Residents

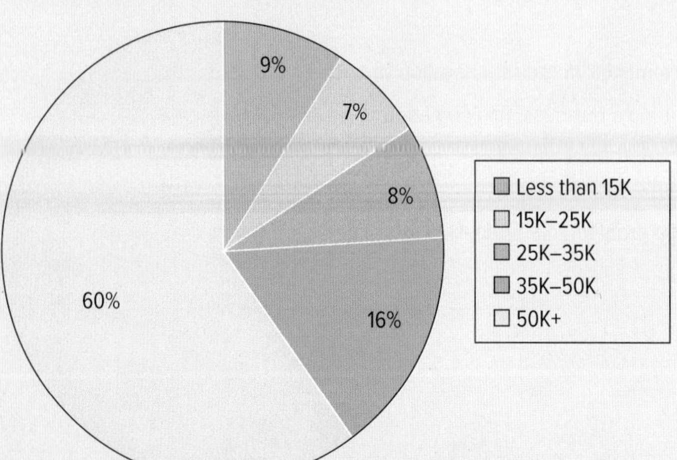

Trends Related to the Product or Service

Several studies show that pet ownership is at an all-time high and that people are taking better care of their pets and spending more money on them than previously. As a result, the pet products industry is booming. Americans spent a total of $34.4 billion on pet food, care, and supplies in 2004, and the industry is estimated to increase to $35.9 billion in 2005. Sixty-five percent of this estimated total was spent on food and supplies alone (*supplies also included medicine*).[33]

The upscale pet services industry was named as a hot market by *Entrepreneur* magazine in its annual prediction of the hottest business ideas for both 2004 and 2005.[34] The APPA also cites luxury, natural, and hygiene products as the top three among its top ten trends in pet gifts.[35] In fact, the APPA further notes that high-tech and high-end products such as tech-enabled dog collars are showing the most growth.[36] Similar to the human food industry, pet food trends are moving toward more organic and natural products. The Organic Trade Association reported that organic pet food sales are up by 63 percent from last year and are growing at almost three times the rate of human organic food sales.[37]

Despite this promising growth and if the economy contracts, customers may have less disposable income. The percentage they intended to spend on their cat or dog may be diverted for necessity purchases. However, according to pet industry analyst Julia Dvorko, "Owners tend to pamper their pets even when they have to cut back on [household] spending. After all, even during economic downturns, people give gifts to family members and buy special treats for their children."[38]

II. THE PRODUCT/SERVICE

Product/Service Description

Pet Élan will offer carefully selected premium products that promote a healthy, fun, and elegant lifestyle for dogs and cats. Our products are grouped into four primary categories: dietary products (pet foods by Newman's Own Organics,[39] Natura Pet Products,[40] Organix,[41] and snacks and treats from Old Mother Hubbard,[42] Three Dog Bakery,[43] Flint River Ranch,[44] and Howling Hound Bakery[45]) ; playtime products (dog toys for chewing, retrieving, tugging, and chasing, and cat toys for chasing and fetching from Happy Dog Toys,[46] KONG Toys,[47] and Fat Cat, Inc.[48]); travel accessories (leashes, collars, and travel bags); and home accessories (food and water bowls, pet furniture and pillows, and pet clothing from The Small Dog Company,[49] Dogz Togz,[50] and Ruff Ruff and Meow[51]).

The Competition

Pet Élan plans to open in the 60657 zip code area of Chicago, Illinois, locally known as Lakeview. There are 23 pet-related businesses in this zip code: 9 are veterinarians, 3 are pet sitting/walking services, 3 are pet grooming services, 3 are large chain pet stores (1 PetSmart, 2 Petco), 2 combination pet grooming/accessories stores, 1 combination boarding/training store, 1 pet adoption/accessories store, and 1 boutique called "Sam & Willy's: A Bow Meow Boutique."

While not competing directly in the 60657 area code market, national companies including Paul Mitchell and Origins are now offering lines of pet products ranging from dog shampoo, pet attire, and name-brand toys to gourmet treats and food.[52] Although these companies have recognizable brand identities, they do not specialize in the pet retail market. They do not carry a full line of pet products as Pet Élan will, and they cater more to impulse buyers rather than discerning pet owners.

The following table compares the strengths and weaknesses of a subset of the competitor pet stores in the 60657 zip code, as well as online retailers, and highlights the differentiating features of Pet Élan.

Online Stores

One of the largest threats to the luxury pet accessory industry is the presence of online stores. Pet Élan will compete with these online retailers, as well as other local pet stores. Consumers have the opportunity to comparison shop on the Internet, so Pet Élan will need to carefully determine the pricing strategy for each line of accessories to remain competitive. However, it is likely that pet owners will want to sample and view unique products we carry and will be willing to come to our store for its one-of-a-kind shopping experience—and bring their pets with them.

The rise of larger chain pet stores, like Petco and PetSmart, has made it much easier for pet owners to satisfy all their pet needs in one place. These stores are now offering pet apparel, pet furniture, and natural pet food. Pet Élan will offer a higher-quality, but more expensive, product mix that may overlap with these stores in some areas. To counter this, Pet Élan will showcase the products we carry that cannot be obtained at the larger retailers.

Competitive Advantage

Pet Élan's competitive advantage is quality and the ability to provide customers with the feeling that pampering their pets is an integral part of a healthy, fun, and contemporary lifestyle. Pet Élan must establish this reputation

Competitive Analysis of Pet Stores

Competitor Pet Stores in Zip Code	Strengths	Weaknesses	Differentiating Features of Pet Élan
Area pet grooming/accessories stores	• Customers shop while pets are groomed	• Limited selection • Pet grooming, not product sales, is core competency	• Core competency is selling luxury pet products and accessories
Petco[53]	• Brand identity • All-in-one stores • Wide selection • Online shopping	• Limited number of brands in pet clothing and accessories • Inexperienced sales associates	• Products are high end for discerning pet owners • Pet Élan builds personal relationships with customers
PetSmart[54]	• Brand identity • All-in-one stores • Wide selection • Online shopping	• More pet clothing and accessories brands than Petco, but not high-end brands • Inexperienced sales associates	• Products are high-end for discerning pet owners • Pet Élan builds personal relationships with customers
Sam & Willy's: A Bow Meow Boutique[55]	• Accessories and gifts in a boutique setting • Provides variety of organic pet food brands	• Static website • Sponsors local animal shelters but doesn't have social entrepreneurial mission	• Website provides tips and trends for hip pet owners • Five percent of pretax profits goes to a local no-kill animal shelter

through *high-quality products* and *selective advertising* and through *exceptional customer service.*

Market Penetration

Pet Élan will serve customers in a boutique setting where pets are welcome to browse along with their owners. The store will operate with a social entrepreneurial mission and will donate 5 percent of pretax profits to a local no-kill animal shelter. Consistent with this socially responsible mission, Pet Élan will work with other area pet-related businesses to form a network of highly qualified veterinarians, as well as well-established boarding, grooming, in-home sitting, and training service providers. By connecting Pet Élan customers with reliable service providers, Pet Élan will also benefit from the reciprocal referrals from these service providers.

Pet Élan will also maintain a website, but initially only to provide the location and hours of operation. As the business grows, the website could include tips and trends information for current and future consumers to keep up with the latest in pet fashion accessories. Pet Élan will seek assistance from a local college or Small Business Development Center for the website and marketing research assistance.

When the Pet Élan storefront opens, we plan to advertise by hosting a series of pet fashion shows, combined with an adoption event with local pet shelters. The events will raise awareness among clientele and would help a good cause. Until Pet Élan breaks even, the store will rely on the advertising and public relations from partnering with other service providers to draw customers into the store.

III. THE BUSINESS

Description of the Entrepreneur (or Team)

Randy Miller will be the owner of Pet Élan. Randy has been interested in pets since childhood, and has worked for vet clinics, the Humane Society, and a local zoo in pet care. Randy is currently employed full time at a local discount retailer. Randy's other retail experience includes work in local pet stores in animal care and sales, as well as retail experience at PetSmart. Randy's self-employment experience started as a teen, with child care and yard care businesses. Randy's education includes a BA in entrepreneurship from DePaul University. Although employed full time, Randy will leave to give 100 percent effort to the start-up of Pet Élan.

The owner will be the primary employee of Pet Élan for the first three months of operation. Beginning in the fourth month of operation, Pet Élan will hire one full-time sales associate. As the business grows, Pet Élan anticipates hiring a second full-time sales associate during the second year of operation. The full-time sales associates will assist the owner with customer service and other retail functions.

Stage of Development

Pet Élan is currently in the idea stage. This feasibility study is the first step in exploring the market potential for a luxury pet store. The current time frame for introducing Pet Élan is one year. Pet Élan has set the following milestones to accomplish prior to launch:

- Complete feasibility study: month 1.
- Begin and complete business plan and identify location: months 2–4.
- Pursue start-up capital: months 5–6.
- Receive start-up capital: month 7.
- Secure store location and secure appropriate permits: months 7–8.
- Plan and order inventory: month 9.
- Receive inventory and set up store: months 10–11.
- Store launch: month 12.

Legal Issues

Pet Élan will operate as a Sub-Chapter S Corporation to ensure limited personal liability and for tax advantages. Pet Élan will have one owner, who will have day-to-day responsibility for running the business. The corporation will receive all income generated by the business and pay the owner a salary and/or reinvest in the store. A board of directors will be appointed by the owner. The company will register its name with the state of Illinois, and buy the domain name petelan.com (or if it is not available, petelanlakeview.com).

Insurance Requirements

Pet Élan will purchase property and liability insurance policies to protect the corporation's assets.[56] As an employer, Pet Élan will also need to secure workers' compensation insurance and unemployment insurance.[57]

IV. FUTURE ACTION PLAN

Summary Feasibility Evaluation

Overall, the idea for Pet Élan seems feasible. Statistically, the Lakeview area should have a large number of high-income households with pets, and national market indications suggest these people would appreciate a premium pet products store like Pet Élan. Randy Miller has the requisite experience in retail and with pets to make this store workable, and the general model for such retailers is well established. Assuming he can get the bank loan (most likely as a personal loan), he should be able to start and make a go of the business.

Next Steps

To ensure the successful opening of Pet Élan, we must have a deeper understanding of the customer needs in the area. Conducting marketing research in the 60657 zip code area, using techniques such as surveys and/or focus groups of customers in Pet Élan's target market, could assess these needs. Pet Élan should also begin to approach other pet service providers in the area to explore potential partnership opportunities that could help raise awareness about both Pet Élan and the partnering business. This would also allow the owner of Pet Élan to form a network within the local pet products and services industry. With these steps completed, creating a business plan would be necessary to secure the loan and investors noted below. Pet Élan will review the initial draft of the business plan with a volunteer from the Service Corps of Retired Executives (SCORE) or the local Small Business Development Center.

Start-Up Capital

To start the business, Pet Élan will need to have enough start-up capital to cover leasing costs to secure the storefront location. The start-up capital will also need to cover insurance and operating expenses including appropriate licensing, store utilities, and professional services such as legal and accounting assistance. Initial inventory, as well as retail equipment needs (such as a cash register) will require a large initial investment. These needs will be funded through the start-up capital that Pet Élan secures prior to opening. The amount needed is estimated to be $70,000.

Sources of Start-Up Capital

The start-up capital of $70,000 is composed of 45 percent (or $31,500) of the owner's personal savings, 25 percent (or $17,500) of a bank loan, in addition to two equity investors (one family member of the owner and one local veterinarian), each with a 15 percent stake (or $10,500) in the company.

V. THE FINANCIAL PROJECTIONS

Assumptions

Pet Élan made the following assumptions in putting together the sales revenue forecast for the first three years of operations:

- Pet Élan will sign a three-year rental agreement for a 2,000-square-foot storefront location. The rental property will be priced at $35 per square foot, with an additional real estate tax of $9.50 per square foot per annum.
- Pet Élan will be open for business six days a week (Monday through Saturday) from ten o'clock in the morning until seven o'clock in the evening. The store will be closed on Sunday.
- The owner will be the primary employee of Pet Élan for the first three months of operation. Beginning in the fourth month of operation, Pet Élan will hire one full-time sales associate. As the business grows, Pet Élan anticipates hiring a second full-time sales associate during the second year of operation. The full-time sales associates will assist the owner with customer service and other retail functions.
- It is estimated that the average Pet Élan customer will spend $18 per visit and will visit the store, on average, two times per month.
- For purposes of this feasibility study, Pet Élan will assume a 54 percent margin on goods sold.
- As the customer base grows, Pet Élan will need to have a significantly higher amount of inventory on hand to support increased demand.
- Pet Élan will contribute 5 percent of pretax profits to a local no-kill animal shelter on a quarterly basis. This contribution has been accounted for in the pretax net profit (loss) forecast.
- Operational expenses include items such as rent, utilities, advertising costs, and professional services assistance.

Summary Financial Table

The Financials–Summary table below shows a detailed monthly spreadsheet for year 1 and aggregated spreadsheets for years 2 and 3.

Financials—Summary

	Year 1	Year 2	Year 3
Revenue	$296,740	$404,448	$458,304
Cost of goods sold	137,120	186,880	211,730
Gross margin	159,620	217,568	246,574
Operating expenses	$147,907	$190,881	$201,744
Net profit (loss) pretax	$ 11,713	$ 26,687	$ 44,830
Net profit (loss) pretax and post contribution (5%)	$ 11,127	$ 5,345	$ 42,589

Three-Year Detailed Financials

Financials—Years 1–3							
	Month 1 September	**Month 2 October**	**Month 3 November**	**Month 4 December**	**Month 5 January**	**Month 6 February**	**Month 7 March**
Sales	**$11,620**	**$16,900**	**$ 20,060**	**$27,460**	**$ 20,060**	**$21,120**	**$24,290**
Less cost of goods sold	$ 5,370	$ 7,810	$ 9,270	$ 12,690	$ 9,270	$ 9,760	$ 11,220
Gross margin	**$ 6,250**	**$ 9,090**	**$10,790**	**$14,770**	**$10,790**	**$11,360**	**$ 13,070**
Operating expenses							
Utilities	185	160	165	180	200	200	180
Salaries	2,500	2,500	2,500	2,500	2,500	2,500	2,500
Labor	—	—	—	2,125	2,125	2,125	2,125
Payroll taxes and benefits	313	313	313	578	578	578	578
Advertising	300	300	300	300	300	300	300
Website	20	20	20	20	20	20	20
Office supplies	150	75	50	50	50	50	50
Insurance	250	250	250	400	400	400	400
Maintenance and cleaning	50	50	50	50	50	50	50
Legal and accounting	350	350	350	350	350	350	350
Licenses	300	—	—	—	—	—	—
Bags, paper, etc.	150	150	200	250	250	250	300
Telephone	85	85	85	85	85	85	85
Miscellaneous	200	200	200	200	200	200	200
Rent	5,833	5,833	5,833	5,833	5,833	5,833	5,833
Total operating expenses (fixed costs):	**10,686**	**10,286**	**10,316**	**12,921**	**12,941**	**12,941**	**12,971**
Gross profit (loss)	**(4,436)**	**(1,196)**	**475**	**1,849**	**(2,151)**	**(1,581)**	**99**
Contribution to charity (5% of net):	—	—	***24***	***92***	—	—	***5***
Net profit (loss) pretax:	***(4,436)***	***(1,196)***	***451***	***1,756***	***(2,151)***	***(1,581)***	***94***
First year fixed costs (FC)			**$ 147,910**				
Contribution margin ratio (CMR) (sales – cogs)/sales)			**53.8%**				
Annual breakeven sales (FC/CMR)			**$274,970**				
Average monthly breakeven sales			**$22,910**				

Month 8 April	Month 9 May	Month 10 June	Month 11 July	Month 12 August	Total – Year 1	Total – Year 2	Total – Year 3
$26,400	**$28,510**	**$31,680**	**$35,900**	**$32,740**	**$296,740**	**$404,448**	**$458,304**
$ 2,200	$13,170	$14,640	$16,590	$15,130	$137,120	$186,880	$211,730
$14,200	**$15,340**	**$17,040**	**$19,310**	**$17,610**	**$159,620**	**$217,568**	**$246,574**
170	165	185	185	185	2,160	2,280	2,400
2,500	2,500	2,500	2,500	2,500	30,000	30,000	33,000
2,125	2,125	2,125	2,125	2,125	19,125	51,000	56,088
578	578	578	578	578	6,141	10,125	11,136
300	300	300	300	300	3,600	4,800	4,800
20	20	20	20	20	240	360	384
50	50	50	50	50	725	1,200	1,440
400	400	400	400	400	4,350	6,600	6,840
50	50	50	50	50	600	720	840
350	350	350	350	350	4,200	4,800	5,280
—	—	—	—	—	300	300	300
300	300	300	300	300	3,050	4,800	5,040
85	85	85	85	85	1,020	1,200	1,500
200	200	200	200	200	2,400	2,700	2,700
5,833	5,833	5,833	5,833	5,833	69,996	69,996	69,996
12,961	**12,956**	**12,976**	**12,976**	**12,976**	**147,907**	**190,881**	**201,744**
1,239	**2,384**	**4,064**	**6,334**	**4,634**	**11,713**	**26,687**	**44,830**
62	***119***	***203***	***317***	***232***	***586***	***1,334***	***2,242***
1,177	***2,265***	***3,861***	***6,017***	***4,402***	***$ 11,127***	***$ 25,345***	***$ 42,589***

Start-Up Budget

Initial Calculations

Cost Assumptions First Year of Operations

Fixed costs (FC)		Monthly	Annually
Lease payment ($35/sq. ft.)		$ 5,833	$ 70,000
Utilities		200	2,400
Insurance		833	10,000
Salary of owner		2,500	30,000
Salary of sales assistant		2,125	25,500
Advertising		200	2,400
General supplies		300	3,600
Professional services		667	8,000
Miscellaneous expenses		417	5,000
Website		20	240
Total		**13,095**	**157,140**
Variable costs (VC)		**Monthly**	**Annually**
Cost of goods sold		11,427	137,120
Total		**28,250**	**339,000**
Breakeven amount		**Monthly**	**Annually**
Contribution margin ratio (CMR)		53.8%	53.8%
Breakeven (FC/CMR)		$24,340	$292,082
	Daily	**Monthly**	**Annually**
Breakeven number of customers	45	1,352	486,803

Assumptions:

Rental location will be 2,000 sq. ft.

Average customer spends $18 per visit and comes to the store on average twice per month.

One-time start-up costs	
Licensing and permits	$ 300
Decorating	$ 800
Signage	$ 5,000
Beginning inventory	$40,000
Fixtures and equipment	$ 6,000
Professional fees (accountant, attorney)	$ 5,000
Total	**$ 57,100**

Source: This feasibility study, including text, art, and tables, was developed by Laurel Ofstein, a student at DePaul University in May 2005, under the direction of Professor Lisa Gundry of DePaul University. Reprinted with permission. It was revised in 2019 by Jerome Katz to reflect updated headings that fit better with the IDEO screen and business plan outline. Wherever possible, the text and numbers are the same as from the original study.

PART TWO

2

Small Business Paths and Plans

CHAPTER

5

Small Business Entry: Paths to Part-Time Entrepreneurship

● Carla Brauer moved from a hobby into a business of cleaning animal skulls and making wall mounts and jewelry items from the cleaned skulls. What business would you start if you want to work the business part time?
Carla Brauer

LEARNING OBJECTIVES

After you complete this chapter, you will be able to:

LO 5-1 Describe when and why part-time businesses are important.

LO 5-2 Describe the conditions that make part-time entrepreneurship a good decision.

LO 5-3 Describe the kinds of part-time entrepreneurship that exist.

LO 5-4 Describe the key factors to making a decision to go into part-time entrepreneurship.

LO 5-5 Use the BRIE model to describe what it takes to be successful in part-time entrepreneurship.

LO 5-6 Describe the advantages and pitfalls of delegating and outsourcing.

LO 5-7 Identify the ethical challenges of part-time entrepreneurship.

LO 5-8 Describe the challenges of moving from part-time to full-time entrepreneurship.

Focus on Small Business: Carla Brauer

In a way, it all began with a goat's head. Carla Brauer grew up in the city, but always dreamed of a country life. After college, she found work as a copy editor to be tedious, so she left the city for the boonies and found work on small farms. There, among other skills, she learned to humanely butcher animals grown specifically for that purpose. On a day dedicated to slaughtering some goats, one animal in particular had impressive large, symmetrical horns. Although, by her own admission, she really did not know how to go about it, she determined to de-flesh that goat's head, clean and bleach the bone, and turn it into a wall mount. She had absolutely no idea that she had just taken the first step in entering into a small business of making mounts of the heads of trophy animals.

Her approach to this process was to put the head into an unused fenced animal pen so that large scavengers could not carry it away, and then just wait for nature to take its course. This experiment soon had elements of a horror movie. Carla had vultures perching on top of the cage, and the rotting skull was covered in flies and developing maggots. The stench was nearly intolerable.

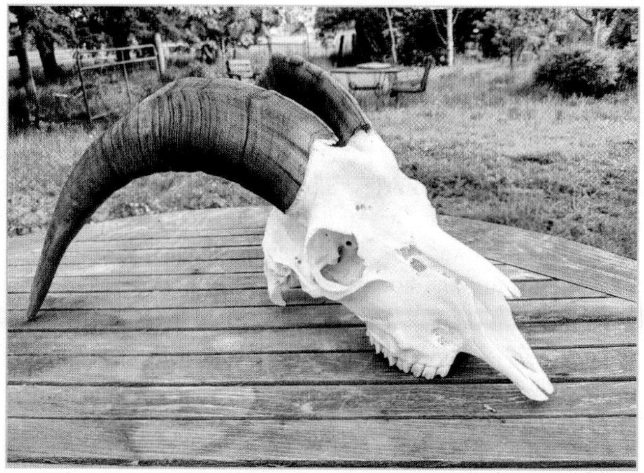

Goat skull with large symmetrical horns

Carla Brauer

But Carla persisted. She experimented with burying a head in an ant colony. Didn't work. No matter how energetic the ants, the results were unsatisfactory. So she tried boiling a head to soften the meat and sinews which she then tediously scraped from the skull. This process was both stinky and very messy. Carla soon realized if she was to continue this hobby, she had to find a better way.

One evening in an episode of the TV series *Bones* the leading character, Temperance Brennan, a forensic anthropologist, proceeded to clean skeletal remains by placing them into a terrarium with a bunch of dermestid beetles. Intrigued, Carla began conducting research into whether or not such an approach would actually work. Soon she discovered that not only were dermestid beetles commonly used for cleaning skeletal remains, but there is an active market for the beetles.

Soon she was equipped with a terrarium and a starter batch of beetles. Her first project for her new "employees" was to clean the head of a quail which had been farm raised and then butchered for its meat. This quail head was followed by the heads of a variety of animals. As her skill grew, so did her reputation. Friends asked her to make wall mounts of the special animals: a young person's first deer, a hunter's largest bull elk, even a bereaved owner's beloved pet. And so the business Dermestidarium was created.

After years of cleaning skulls and making mounts first as a hobby and later as a side hustle, Carla now maintains a part-time job in town and runs her skull-cleaning business as her primary enterprise.

DISCUSSION QUESTIONS

1. How would you handle the conflicting demands of being a loyal employee while at the same time running your own part time business?
2. What are the ethical concerns when you are working full time for one company and part time for yourself? How would you recommend managing these issues?
3. Carla Brauer currently is busiest during the fall and winter months of the hunting season. How might she obtain work to better utilize the time available during the rest of the year?

LEARN MORE ONLINE

Learn more about the topics above at these sites:

Dermestid beetles at work: **www.pbs.org/video/deep-look-hungry-beetles/**

Side hustles: **www.entrepreneur.com/article/325932** and **www.forbes.com/sites/abdoriani/2019/01/28/how-to-finally-turn-your-side-hustle-into-a-full-time-business/#69280250f139**

LO **5-1** Describe when and why part-time businesses are important.

Why Part-Time Businesses Are Important

Carla Brauer's experience is a common one. She graduated from college and proceeded to work for various businesses in her field. Later, while working a full-time job, she became dissatisfied and began to consider other opportunities. She found employment working on a small farm where she developed skills in horticulture and animal husbandry. This employment led her to become interested in a topic that was completely new to her: preserving animal parts as trophies. The interest became a hobby and the hobby became a part-time business which is now evolving into a successful full-time business.

part-time employment Working 35 or fewer hours a week.

full-time employment Working more than 35 hours a week.

When we talk about businesspeople like Brauer, we often use the terms **part-time employment** and **full-time employment**, which are usually understood to mean working 35 or fewer hours a week and working more than 35 hours a week, respectively. However, these terms do not cover the many patterns of employment available to entrepreneurs. In addition to working a specified number of hours each week, entrepreneurs may work on an occasional basis. Consider the people who buy and resell items on eBay, Etsy, or Craig's List websites. These entrepreneurs may not have regular "e-stores" but may sell items as the opportunity provides. And there are many artisans who sell their services or products only when they choose to. These are certainly not considered full-time businesses, but because they're not working regular hours they don't really fit the definition of either.

The great variety of ways people choose to conduct business makes it necessary to use additional terms to describe employment patterns. Businesses such as "**pop-up**" restaurants and pop-up retailers are often called **episodic businesses**. This is because the same business is run at differing locations and at differing times without having any permanent location or hours of operation. Episodic businesses offer many different services and products. For example, the college student who paints houses in the summer, the gardener who opens a produce stand during harvest, the hustler who sets up a fireworks stand each June, the vendor who follows a summer schedule of state and local fairs, or the skier who offers skiing lessons during the winter are all examples of episodic businesses.

pop-up business
A temporary business that offers services or products in a variety of locations for a brief period at a time. What characterizes a pop-up business from any other is its *temporary* nature.

episodic business
A temporary, project-based, or sporadically operating business.

Or, how would you describe an entrepreneur who keeps a job as an employee, but not necessarily a full-time job, while starting and running a business at the same time? In this case, the entrepreneur may work more than 35 hours per week in each job. Is this "double-time" employment?

No, a different name is needed.

Some are calling such employment patterns **hybrid entrepreneurship**.[1] If a person keeps a constant job as an employee and at the same time works at his or her own business, that person is a hybrid entrepreneur. But the number of hours worked at either is *not* what defines hybrid entrepreneurship.

hybrid entrepreneurship
The process of initiating a business while simultaneously remaining employed for wages or salary.

For this book, we will adopt the term **part-time business** to describe all the previously mentioned employment patterns. What matters in this definition is that the entrepreneur is *not* working full time at his or her own business but instead is working fewer than 35 hours per week, only a few days per month, or only during certain seasons. The person may or may not be keeping a full- or part-time position as an employee while running a part-time business.

part-time business
A business in which the owner either participates fewer than 35 hours per week or operates on a temporary or seasonal basis while maintaining employment elsewhere for wages or salary.

When you enter businesses as an entrepreneur, you are not required to work full time. There is no rule that says you must make your living from the business. You get to decide what is right for you. You may "go for broke" and risk all your resources on a full-time business. Or, you may just "hedge your bet" by keeping your day job while you feel your way into the business on a part-time basis.

Today, Carla Brauer keeps a part-time job, but also cleans and mounts animal skulls and other skeletal parts. As she is keeping a job for wages and at the same time working fewer than 35 hours a week at Dermestidarium, it is considered to be a part-time business.

This chapter focuses on part-time approaches to business. Why does it deserve a whole chapter? There are two reasons. First, most entrepreneurs start out working part time on their new business. According to the Panel Study of Entrepreneurial Dynamics (PSED), three-quarters of new businesses start on a part-time basis.[2] This includes the businesses shown in Table 5.1. The ease and low cost of entry and exit make part-time entrepreneurship a great way to try a variety of different businesses without "betting the farm" each time a new business is started.

TABLE 5.1 Famous Organizations Started by Part-Time Entrepreneurs[3]

Accion	Friendster
American Information Systems	Lionel Trains
Apple	Mary Kay Cosmetics
Dell	Microsoft
Facebook	Netscape
Ford Modeling Agency	Yahoo!

Sources: Joseph J. Fucini and Suzy Fucini, *Entrepreneurs: The Men and Women behind Famous Brand Names and How They Made It* (Boston: G. K. Hall, 1985); Brendan Howard, "Making Time: Not Ready for the Burden of a Full-Time Business? How Do Your Evenings and Weekends Look?," *Entrepreneur*, June 2000; Adam Cohen, *The Perfect Store: Inside eBay* (Boston: Back Bay Books, 2003).

volatility
The frequency of business starts and stops.

Second, the sheer number of part-time businesses makes them a major force in our economy, even if it is one we do not always recognize. Officially, of the 25.9 million small businesses in the United States in 2012, almost half (10.8 million) were part-time businesses.[4] However, that understates the situation. Many people jump into and out of self-employment (a change called **volatility** by economists) for a few weeks at a time, perhaps because they do project-based work like taking on a single consulting project in their spare time, or doing someone's taxes, or selling an item or two on eBay or at a garage sale. These very short-term projects get missed in the count of new business start-ups. The U.S. Census Bureau reported that during the first three quarters of 2018 approximately 300,000 new businesses were created each month.[5] This is about 3.5 million businesses per year—way more than the 1 million new starts counted by the Small Business Administration (SBA). The Business Formation Statistics (BFS) may itself underestimate the true number of annual business starts because it is based on the number of requests for new Employer Identification Numbers (EIN) from the IRS, and many episodic entrepreneurs, such as those selling products on eBay.com, simply report tax information using their own personal Social Security numbers.

LO **5-2** Describe the conditions that make part-time entrepreneurship a good decision.

When to Consider Part-Time Entrepreneurship

Many people assume that the one best way to go into business is to first write a detailed business plan, second raise capital, and third go into business full time from the start. In fact, this is exactly how most college courses in entrepreneurship present the process. There are good arguments for this approach to business entry, including the amount of thought and planning required to write a business plan, and the importance that angel investors, venture capitalists, banks, and other investors attach to a well-prepared business plan. However, starting or buying a full-time business entails a major commitment and is not always the best way to go about becoming an entrepreneur. And if you are not going to start a full-time business or ask other people for funding, a traditional business plan may not be needed.

There are four types of situations in which it makes good sense to first undertake a part-time business (see Figure 5.1). The first situation is where you are new to business in general and need to ***gain basic experience***. If you have not been involved in pricing, buying, and selling, learning how to do such things makes a lot of sense before launching the business of your dreams. You might want to obtain other types of experience before starting a full-scale business or writing a business plan. These can include experience in the industry, in the line of business, in the locality of the specific market you plan to serve, in managing cash, or in managing yourself in self-employment.

FIGURE 5.1

When to Consider a Part-Time Business

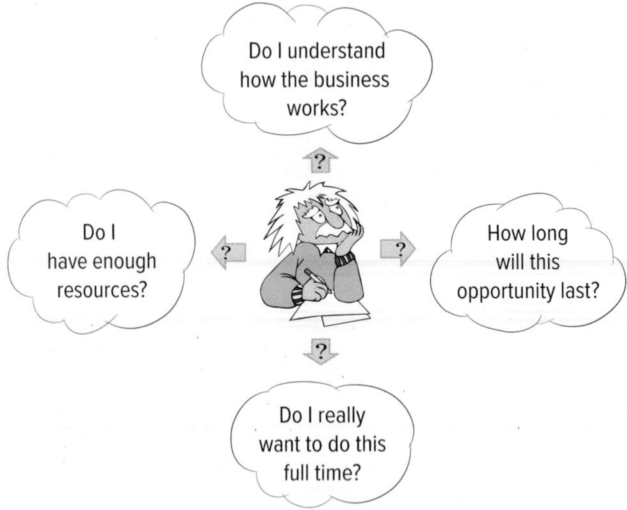

A second type of situation is one in which you ***lack the resources necessary*** to pursue a full-scale business or create a business plan. Time is probably the ultimate resource, and starting a business can tax it heavily. Estimates suggest that developing a business plan may take anywhere from 50 to 200 hours or more if you are new to business and working on your own.[6] Starting a full-time business can easily take 70 hours a week or more in its early stages. You might not be able to commit the time to work that many hours, so taking an easier path makes a lot of sense. Start-ups and purchases of full-time businesses also require substantial financial resources. When money is limited, starting out part time can greatly stretch those resources.

The third type of situation is ***a narrow window of opportunity***. For example, when teams are announced for tournaments like the NCAA Men's Basketball Tournament, there is suddenly a veritable flood on eBay of logo clothing and memorabilia from the selected teams. These eBay entrepreneurs are capitalizing on the increased interest in the newly announced teams. Within a few weeks, most of the selected teams will have lost and left the tournament, but in the meantime, they (and anything with their logo on it) are hot properties.

Part-time businesses can generally be created quickly. When the business situation does not allow enough time to do a business plan, pursuing a part-time business is often the only profitable way to seize the opportunity.

The fourth situation arises when you are ***uncertain about the demands*** of going into a full-time business. You may be concerned about whether or not you will actually like doing the activity as a business. As an example, Carla Brauer ultimately decided that she preferred being her own boss and creating a business was preferable to continuing to work as an employee. For her, the rewards of being in business make the demands of the business worthwhile.

LEARN MORE ONLINE

Learn more about the topics above at these sites:

Quitting Your Job to Start a Business: **www.entrepreneur.com/article/312133**

Quitting Your Day Job or Keeping It: **www.inc.com/melanie-curtin/should-you-quit-your-day-job-this-study-of-over-5000-entrepreneurs-has-a-surprising-answer.html**

What Kinds of Part-Time Entrepreneurship Exist?

LO **5-3** Describe the kinds of part-time entrepreneurship that exist.

In this section we will look at the kinds of part-time small business that exist in most industries—retailing, wholesaling, most services, and even manufacturing (because most part-time manufacturing is based on either an artisan's small-scale production of products or on subcontracted manufacturing). How do we know what are the most popular industries? Knowing that small businesses range from 97 to 99 percent of nearly every industry, a quick look at the number of firms in each can give us an idea. We can see a listing by industry in Table 5.2.

As you can see from Table 5-2 it is possible to have a part-time business in any industry, from accounting to zookeeping. Certainly, part time is more common in some industries, such as retail sales, than it is in others, such as mining or quarrying operations. Because of this, the rest of the chapter will be concerned with the common forms of part-time business, and not with specific industries. The most common forms of part-time businesses are:

- Home based.
- Internet informational websites.
- E-commerce and eBay websites.
- Home retail (home party, door-to-door selling, network marketing, stands).
- Pop-up.
- Mobile offices.
- Virtual offices, executive offices, and incubators.
- Consignments and agents.

TABLE 5.2 Size of U.S. Industries by Major Sector, Preliminary Data Third Quarter, 2015

NAICS*	Industry	No. of Establishments	Percentage
54–55–56	Professional & Business Services	1,739,828	19.1%
61–62	Education and Health Care	1,593,913	16.9
44–45	Retail Trade	1,047,401	11.5
81	Other Services (except Public Admin.)	829,262	9.1
71–72	Leisure and Hospitality	810,186	8.9
23	Construction	770,310	8.5
42	Wholesale Trade	624,052	6.9
52	Finance & Insurance	479,761	5.3
53	Real Estate, Rental, Leasing	369,802	4.1
48–49	Transportation & Warehousing	238,619	2.3
31–33	Manufacturing	342,991	3.8
51	Information	154,006	4.1
11	Agriculture, Forestry, Fishing, and Hunting	102,293	1.1
21	Mining, Quarrying, and Oil & Gas Extraction	35,942	0.4
22	Utilities	17,595	0.2
	Total	9,101,961	≈100%

*NAICS = North American Industry Classification System.

Source: U.S. Department of Labor, Bureau of Labor Statistics, "Industries at a Glance," www.bls.gov (accessed March 18, 2016). Special tabulation of the preliminary data third quarter by Richard Green.

Home-Based Businesses

Most part-time businesses start where you live—your home or dorm room—so home-based business is where we will start. The nature of part-time start-ups has changed in the past few years. Not so long ago, home businesses were strongly discouraged, if not outright banned in most towns and cities. The perception was that the increased traffic of a home-based business lowered the livability of residential areas. But this has changed because of increased use of the Internet as a source of information and as a method of communication. Today if you are trying to market beyond your immediate family, neighborhood, or circle of friends, you need to start your business with a web presence. Some businesses can in fact be done entirely on the web, and informational and e-commerce websites are the second and third business forms we will consider. The fourth start-up approach is a collection of other fast, low-cost approaches that can be helpful in a variety of situations. If you are looking for more ideas about the ways you can get started, consider jumping ahead to Chapter 11 which discusses some of the more involved techniques such as direct mail, telemarketing, and direct response advertising that can be used in particular situations for a part-time business.

Home might be where the heart is, but it is also where the part-time business starts. If yours is a retailing or wholesaling business, home is where you store your goods. If you are making furniture, toys, clothing, or food, it is probably where your work area is. And if you are in a service, it is where you retire to in order to get your work done. For nearly everyone, home is where you keep your office records, do your bookkeeping and taxes, and where you probably first receive your firm's mail. You may work away from home: In a section on location in Chapter 11 we consider service firms where you do part of your work at the client's location or at remote locations, but unless you get an office or other location from which you will base your business, you will probably start from home.

There were about 9.0 million home-based businesses in the United States in 2012,[7] and they represented 33 percent of all firms. The reason for these large numbers is that the home-based business meets at least two of the three criteria for start-up. It is inexpensive, since you are already living somewhere and you can quickly get your business going where you live. Although home-based businesses do not always give customers the strongest sense of legitimacy, the idea that a customer knows where the entrepreneur lives can be a point in favor of trusting in the potential permanence of the firm.

That said, with so great a number of firms, there are not many hard-and-fast rules that apply to everyone, but there are a few key ideas to keep in mind.[8] First and foremost is the location of your home-based business. Although the dining room table may be infrequently used, is it the best place for you to work? Even though anything *can* work, the following suggestions come from home-based entrepreneurs and are likely to make your life a lot easier.

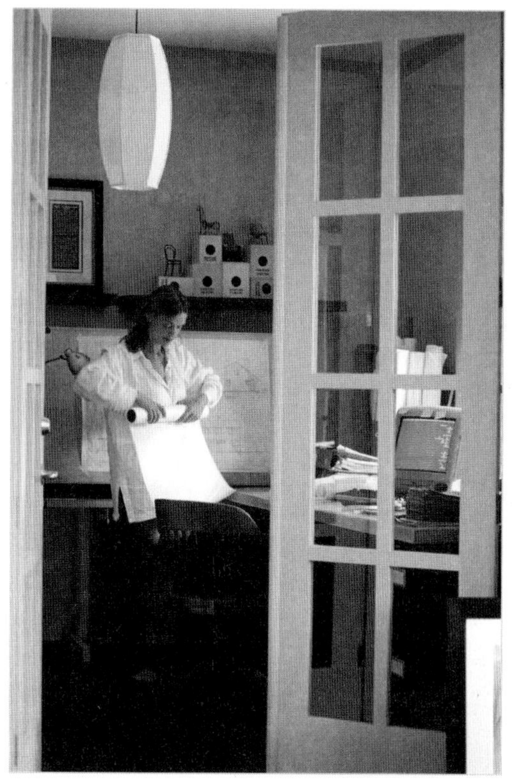

This is close to an ideal setup for a home office. There is space for files and equipment. The owner has the equipment needed to do her work, and there is a door to provide some quiet and privacy, but the glass lets her see what is going on at home, and lets her family know she is around.

Brand X/JupiterImages/Getty Images

According to home-based entrepreneurs, the greatest problems they face come when there are zoning challenges or family challenges to the business. Cities, counties, neighborhoods, apartment complexes, and dorms pass regulations that limit the ways residents can use or modify their space. The government restrictions are called **zoning laws**, while the ones set up by other organizations are called **covenants**. Unfortunately there is no comprehensive free online national listing of zoning regulations,[9] but there are public records, and these can often be found online on your city's or county's government website. Otherwise, the local chamber of commerce or the local library may have the basic information.

It is best to carefully check out the zoning and covenant situation before fully committing yourself to a home-based business. Most of us live in areas zoned as residential areas. Typically, it is not legal to have a home-based business in a residential area—even an online business.[10] It may be tempting to simply ignore such restrictions. Doing so, however, raises ethical issues and may cause the imposition of fines and penalties on your new business.

Usually people get into trouble only if a neighbor, landlord, or dorm staffer complains or it becomes apparent to police or other public service employees that "something" is going on at your home. In either situation, what causes the problem, and makes it stick, are aspects of your business that "change the residential character of the neighborhood" through increased traffic, noise, parked cars, or smells.

zoning laws
Government specifications for acceptable use of land and buildings in particular areas.

covenant
The limitations imposed on an individual's property by the neighborhood group.

variance
Permission from a government organization to act differently that the laws state.

To minimize problems, there are several alternatives.[11] If you are not concerned about the ethical implications, you can generally keep the web- and phone-based aspects of your business at home without neighbors becoming aware of (or disturbed by) your business—but be sure not to tell them you work from home! The way to handle large amounts of mail and packages is through the use of private mailboxes (from a company like PakMail, Mailboxes Etc., or Postal-Annex) and self-storage facilities (like Public Storage U-Haul, Storage USA, or similar local companies), rather than having them delivered to your home. Use the private mailbox address for your business on the web and on your stationery.

Another approach is to get permission—called a **variance**—to have your business operating from out of your home. Often there are local lawyers who specialize in real estate and zoning law, and they can advise you if a variance is a workable solution. While you can request a variance on your own, having a lawyer advocate for you can cost from hundreds to thousands of dollars, so this approach is only for those with determination and money.[12] The best way to find such a lawyer is through referrals from friends or businesspeople whose judgment you trust. If that does not work, or you want to check into the lawyers suggested to you, you can use an online directory such as Martindale.com or FindLaw.com to find and learn more about local lawyers.

● One of the greatest challenges to making a home office work is getting family and friends to give you the privacy and time alone to do the work you need to do. How could this father have avoided this situation?

JupiterImages/Getty Images

Once zoning is handled, think about issues inside your home. The following list touches on many of the issues home-based entrepreneurs find most important to running their business:

- Choose a work location inside your home that is away from noise, distractions, and family traffic. It helps you concentrate and sound businesslike when on the phone.
- Be realistic about the amount of space you'll need for your equipment.
- An office door can keep business separate from family and the rest of life.
- Try out your location for a day or two to check out noise, traffic patterns, lighting needs, and distractions.
- Don't overload on hours of work, or on snacks from the refrigerator down the hall.
- Set up your workday to minimize distractions from household or family chores and, as much as possible, stick to the plan.
- Consider hiring help to handle household or family chores to free up your time.
- Set the ground rules early and stick with them. Watch out for family, friends, and visitors who don't understand home-based businesses. When you run a home-based business you will find that working-outside-the-home parents, siblings, children, and friends don't understand that they can't drop off their ill or vacationing children so that they don't miss work. You'll be asked to do extra school or sports carpools, wait for service people, or other such things because of your at-home status.

Exhibit 5.1 summarizes the five most important issues that you should think about before you set up a home-based business.

Once you've chosen your location, you'll need equipment. You'll need a comfortable, usable desk and chair and adequate lighting. Consider the tasks you'll perform most frequently and check out the ergonomic options that will serve you the best. Although you can store files in cardboard boxes, an inexpensive filing cabinet would be so much simpler. Think about the layout of the furniture for access to proper lighting, phone jacks, and electrical outlets. You may need to supplement some or all of these.

Tools typically include a telephone (these days most often a cell phone), high-capacity Internet service (like cable or DSL or 5G Wi-Fi service for your laptop), a business email account, a high-speed desktop computer, a fax machine, a copier, and appropriate software (see Table 5.3 for high-quality free programs and services). These days many multipurpose devices combine a printer, copier, fax machine, and scanner into one piece of equipment, which reduces the amount of space you'll need. Consider the layout of the equipment and how you'll use each piece. You don't want to reach around your computer monitor to pick up the telephone or race across the room to catch printer pages.

EXHIBIT 5.1

Essential Questions to Answer for a Home Office

1. If you intend to deduct the expenses of your home office, can you comply with the regulatory standards?
   - Home office space must be regularly and exclusively used for business—no letting your preteen daughter use it for a weekend sleepover!
   - The home office must be your principal place of business, unless it is a freestanding structure such as a detached studio or a shed.
   - To be allowed to deduct home office expenses you must keep detailed records as listed in IRS Publication 587, Business Use of Your Home.
2. If you are going to use a home office, can you meet state, county, and municipal regulations?
   - Zoning must allow for home-based businesses.
   - If you use your home for producing, storing, or distributing any food or medicinal products you must conform to health, environmental (temperature and humidity), and safety regulations.
   - You will need to meet minimum standards for handicap accessibility, fire prevention, and liability insurance.
   - Home-based business are subject to the same licensing and inspection rules that apply if you have a remote location.
3. If you choose to have a home office, can you be productive in that space?
   - Interruptions from family members, neighbors, and pets must be kept to a minimum.
   - Distractions such as windows that overlook areas of high activity, television programs playing in other rooms, and squabbles among your children should be avoided.
   - You will need comfortable and sufficient work space such as a desk or a table.
   - You will need adequate storage, such as a fireproof file cabinet, for records and other documents.
   - In today's business world secure high-speed Internet access is essential. Dial-up will not do.
   - You may need space for an administrative assistant or other full-time help.
4. Will you be able to deal with clients, vendors, or employees in your home office?
   - A home-based business that deals with clients, such as an accounting, counseling, or therapy practice, should have a separate entrance from the one your family uses.
   - Unless you are 100 percent efficient in scheduling appointments, you will need an area where business visitors may wait comfortably.
   - If your home-based business requires team effort, you will need provision and space to hold meetings.
   - You must be able to meet minimum parking space regulations. Many cities stringently restrict on-street parking.
5. Will you be able to separate home and business life?
   - Home offices provide great temptation to devote all your time to work because they are "right there."
   - It can be very difficult to discipline yourself to keep regular office hours.
   - Spouses, children, and friends all have difficulty realizing that when you work in your home office, you really *are* working.

TABLE 5.3 Essential Free Software and Web Services for Small Businesses

	Open Source*	Web Based
Basic business suite (like Microsoft Office)	Openoffice.org; Libreoffice.org	Zoho.com (has CRM and other modules) Thinkfree.com
Project management (like Microsoft Project)	Projectlibre.org	Freedcamp.com Trello.com
Email (like Outlook)	Mozilla Thunderbird	Zimbra.com
Knowledge management (like PeopleSoft)	www.bitfarm-archiv.com/	Mediawiki.com
Customer relationship management (CRM)	SuiteCRM.com	Freecrm.com
Social networking	Elgg.org	LinkedIn.com
Financial projection creation	Exl-Plan Free, www.planware.org/exlfree.htm	SBA.gov/tools/business-plan
Accounting program (like QuickBooks)	Grisbi.org	Waveapps.com
PDF file creation (like Adobe Acrobat)	OpenOffice or PDFCreator, www.openoffice.org/; www.pdfforge.org/pdfcreator	Pdfonline.com
Desktop publishing (like Adobe PageMaker)	Scribus.net	www.fatpaint.com
Paint program (like Adobe Photoshop)	Getpaint.net; Gimp.org	Ipiccy.com

*All open source software offers versions that will run under Microsoft Windows. Many offer support for Macs and other platforms.

You'll want to have a separate business telephone line with an answering machine, voice mail, or virtual PBX service so that you can get those important calls after hours. Make sure your voice-mail message sounds businesslike and not like the message on your home answering machine. Consider a second phone line if you are limited to a modem-based Internet connection. Ideally, this space and its tools will be used only for your home-based office. In addition, totally separate space and equipment make tax deduction preparation much simpler.

When does a home-based business outgrow the home? For some companies, the answer is never. Some entrepreneurs opt for charging higher prices for their goods or services or limiting their sales so as not to outgrow the space available; being a home-based business is just too important to them to change. Others reinvest their profits into additions to their homes to accommodate their business growth or to upgrade to a roomier house with the extra space they need. Some die-hard home-based entrepreneurs faced with this decision have found creative ways of housing their staff and other operations in an outside office while continuing to telecommute as much as possible.[13]

More typically, a business will find the need for meeting rooms and employee accommodations or zoning restrictions will force the change. In other cases, family situations just aren't favorable to a home-based business. Some entrepreneurs find they aren't cut out for the solitude of working by themselves or find household chores, family, or other distractions disturb them too easily.

Home-based business is the easiest and fastest way to start a business, and the easiest and fastest type of business to move or close down. This ease of deployment, moving, and closing

Sometimes the success of a home-based business is what makes it necessary to move. This part-time entrepreneur's business completely overwhelmed the downstairs den. What started as a home office in the corner grew until it became an office warehouse and shipping center. How do you think her family is responding?

Paulaphoto/Shutterstock

make the home-based business one of the volatile forms of part-time business. Even so, it is the core and greatest common factor in business start-ups.

Internet Informational Websites[14]

Perhaps the biggest change in part-time self-employment in the past five years has been the growth of the Internet as a major method for conducting business. Most of us have bought something online, which is what is called **e-commerce**. But another type of website, the **informational website**, is an even more important type of site that informs possible customers about your firm. For a part-time entrepreneur, a website can become a 24-hour-a-day, 7-day-a-week source of information and prospects, if not sales.

e-commerce
The general term for conducting business on the Internet.

informational website
An Internet site designed to introduce and explain a business to others.

To get some idea about the power of the Internet for information and for e-commerce, consider this. Google now reports that it receives 40,000[15] searches per second worldwide. This calculates to over 1.3 trillion searches per year. Another way to look at this astounding number is it is equivalent to 187 searches made for each person: women, men, girls, and boys living today! The U.S. Census reported that e-commerce sales in 2018 were about $504 billion. This is more than 9 percent of the total retail sales reported.[16] But even this figure understates the real level of e-commerce sales. As David Evans et al. report, because of the way the Census Bureau calculates e-commerce totals, actual online retail sales are most likely understated, but by an amount that cannot be reliably estimated.[17]

Products like music and cell phones are examples of the kind of goods we buy as individuals. That type of e-commerce is called **business-to-consumer (B2C)**. There is another type called **business-to-business (B2B)** sales where one firm sells to another firm. While our personal experience is in the B2C marketplace, all of those sales on iTunes, eBay, Amazon, and the thousands of other online merchants account for only about 10 percent of all retail sales in the United States. For most of us, the B2B market is invisible, but when businesses buy, they buy big. In 2013, over 61 percent of all manufacturing sales were handled online as well as almost 47 percent of all wholesale trade between businesses.[18] You can see the difference, and the growth of these forms of e-commerce, in Figure 5.2. The moral of this story? B2C e-commerce is large, B2B e-commerce is larger, but using an informational website to inform customers–whether they are individuals or businesses–is huge and getting ever bigger! We can only guess what the percentages may be today.

business-to-consumer (B2C)
Business-to-consumer transactions using e-commerce.

business-to-business (B2B)
Business-to-business transactions using e-commerce.

The Internet's power comes from its being a very cost-effective and efficient way to contact your customers. With the Internet, a small, part-time, one-person operation can compete with a billion-dollar-a-year multinational. Whether your customers are other businesses or other **consumers**, getting a website together is essential.

consumer
A private individual or household that is the end user of (the entity that "consumes") a product or service.

FIGURE 5.2

E-commerce as Percentage of Total Sales 2002–2013

Source: U.S. Census Bureau, "U.S. Census Bureau 2012 E-commerce Multi-sector Data Tables," released May 22, 2014.

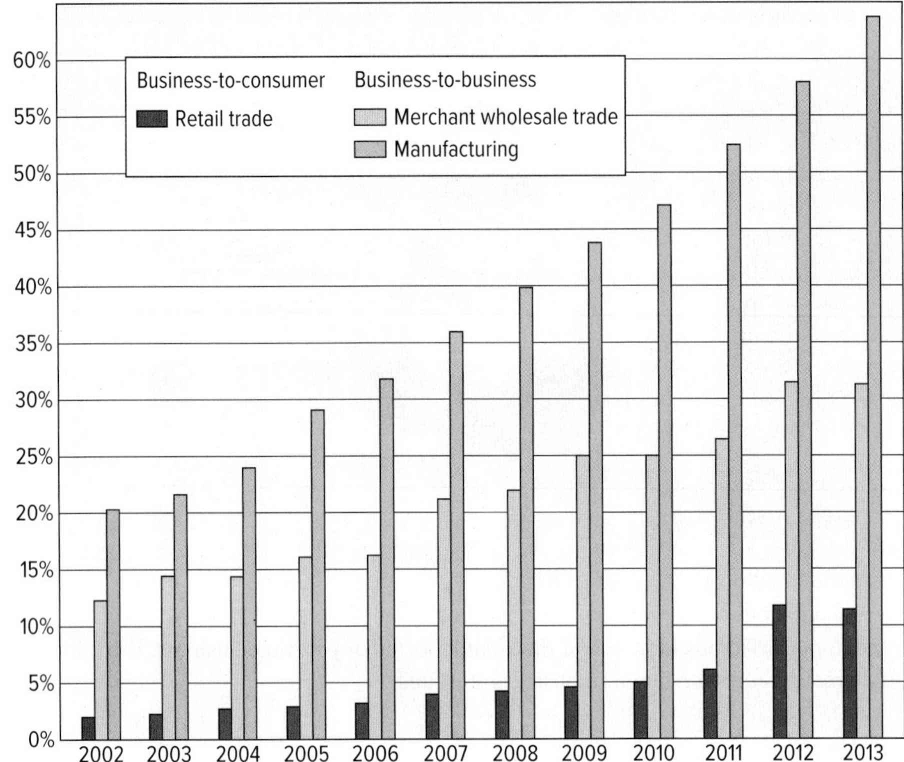

Most small businesses–even part time ones–need to have a website regardless of whether they use it for actual sales. First of all, potential customers will use it to find you. Second, if they've heard about you from something other than the Internet, they will use your site to find out more information about you and to decide if they want to actually contact you. Letrah International, a firm specializing in international consulting for design and engineering projects, knew it should have a website, but it was a low priority and was worked on only when something else did not come up. Dave Peters, the firm's vice president at that time, asked a firm in the United Arab Emirates if there was anything he could do to help convince the firm to accept Letrah's bid. The firm expressed concern that Letrah was not a real company because it didn't have a website, and "everybody knew real U.S. firms had websites." The website was running the following day.[19]

Letrah was able to develop and deploy an informational website in a matter of hours. That is not uncommon. The basics of an informational website can be set up within an hour. There are a number of very low-cost vendors, such as 1&1 IONIS (ionos.com), SiteBuilder.com, and GoDaddy.com, as well as the major web presence providers like Yahoo! and Google sites (just search Google for "cheap websites").

What you are looking for in a basic informational website package is a domain name of your own. Ideally you want your business's name in the domain name of your site. If you want to call your company Beachcomber Shoes, you would ideally look for the domain name beachcombershoes.com. If the dot-com version is not available, using *.net* or *.biz,* or *.us* might work for you. Otherwise you can tweak the domain name–for example, beachcombershoecompany.com or beachshoes.com. You want a name that reinforces your firm's name or your product's name, or something highly memorable, like ouch.com. Note that the price of domain names varies. An unregistered name is about $35 a year retail, but most of the discount website providers will charge as little as $10 a year, and some will include it for free when you buy a website (what they usually call a "hosting") package.

A hosting package for an informational site should include at least 1 gigabyte of traffic a month (this refers to people downloading your pages into their browser). It should give you at least 10 web pages of space to tell your story. It should also include templates to help you develop a website that has a professional look and an online website editor so you can make changes to your site without buying web-authoring software. The hosting package should also include at least five email accounts using your domain name (e.g., info@beachcombershoes.com, support@beachcombershoes.com, jane@beachcombershoes.com, etc.). While using Beachcombershoes@gmail.com (which is a free email service from Google) is good, having info@beachcombershoes.com is even better.

The material for your website can come from promotional material you have written. Every page should have the company name, your contact information (or a link to it), a site map link (which shows a directory of all your pages—don't worry, the template should generate this automatically), and a link back to the home page. Typically your home page (the first page people see when they type in your domain name) gives a quick (one or two paragraphs) introduction of the company and should prominently display your product or service. Other typical pages include:

- "About Us," which gives a brief background on the company and you.
- Product or service pages, which give a more detailed description of what you sell or what you do.
- Support page, which gives customers or potential customers information on how, and reassurance that, their problems with your product or service will get solved.
- Resources page, which typically gives general information (e.g., "Five things you should know about buying ______").
- Press or media page if you have received notice in the media.

Today many informational websites include the capability to add a **blog**, which is a web page in which entries are posted in reverse chronological order (i.e., the most recent at the top of the page). Many blogs let readers respond online, so the entrepreneur and the potential customers can interact directly. Today website packages include the ability to push content, like your blog, out to customers who register at your site. Some sites do this by using an **RSS feed**. *RSS* stands for "really simple syndication" and an RSS feed pushes or sends whatever web material you specify to subscribers to that feed. RSS feeds can be read in many browsers or with special readers.

blog
A web page in which entries are posted in reverse chronological order (i.e., the most recent at the top of the page).

RSS feed
An Internet messaging service that pushes (sends) whatever web material you specify to subscribers to that feed.

A similar approach uses an email mailing list to send emails or online newsletters (sometimes called e-newsletters) to people on your subscriber list. To read these, subscribers have to use an email program or a browser. Many web hosting packages offer a mailing list program as part of the package, but there are also for-fee specialized mailing list programs with more features, such as ConstantContact.com. The latest variation on push technology is Twitter.com. Twitter is a free service that lets a person send a 140-character-or-less message or **tweet** to people who subscribe to the person's Twitter account. You can see what Oprah is up to, or check out StockTwits.com, which uses tweets to inform members about up-to-the-second trends in the stock market.

tweet
A 140-character-or-less message sent using the Twitter web service.

Realize that while you can design your own site, there are also a lot of people who can do it for you, from your "techno-geek" teenage nephew who will do it for the cost of the latest computer game to firms that will not only design but also maintain your website for you—at a cost, of course. You can also hire professionals to set up and manage a site for you. Do a Google search for "managed e-commerce solutions."

There are volumes and volumes written about what things to consider when building your website. You probably have your own list of pet peeves about things some websites do that drive you crazy. That list is what you need to make sure your website does not have those elements, which probably include:

- Slow-loading graphics or pages.
- Too many layers of screens to get to what you want.
- Dead links within the website (when you see a "404 error").
- Hard-to-fill-in online forms.
- Pop-up ads.
- Pages that look or work "right" only in one type of browser.

But you are likely to have many other complaints. The trick is to think of them before you deploy your website, and you'll make your customers and prospective customers happier.

Once you've got your website up and running and it is a masterpiece in design, how do you get your customers to find it? The first way is **multichannel marketing**. Have your website listed on your business cards and every piece of paper, advertising, and the like. The second and equally important way is to get linked to other web pages. If you were in the target market for your product, what web pages would you visit? Figure out what these are and establish **reciprocal links**. In a reciprocal link, you display a link to another website and that website displays a similar link to yours. Scan chat rooms and other electronic message boards to see if people are looking for your type of product or service and post your website. Discover what sorts of electronic newsletters they might read and get a mention in them.[20]

multichannel marketing
The use of several different channels to reach your customers; for example, a website, direct mail, and traditional retailing.

reciprocal link
A listed, live connection to a different website, which in turn displays a similar link to the first website.

search engine optimization (SEO)
A general approach to website design intended to result in the site being displayed toward the beginning of a search engine's (e.g., Google, Yahoo!, etc.) listing for that term.

sponsored link
A form of paid advertising that gets your company's website at the top of a search list.

The third way is online searching. Searching online is how about 85 percent of Internet users find websites, but users will seldom go beyond the first couple of pages of a search.[21] There are several ways to get your site positioned so that a person searching is likely to see it. The technique, which is free, is called **search engine optimization (SEO)** and refers to designing a website so that search engines like Google, Bing, and Yahoo! are likely to rank your site high (closer to the first listing). Many web hosting packages include programs to help you edit your website to improve your ranking. There are also books on SEO and websites like SearchEngineGuide.com, SearchEngineWatch.com, and SubmitCorner.com that are devoted to telling you the hundreds of secrets to mastering SEO.

If you are willing to put up some money, you can pay for **sponsored links** (guaranteeing you a particular placement on the first page of a search) from the search engines at a manageable cost. Google and Yahoo! ask you what word you want to use and how much you are willing to pay (our suggestion is start with a low number). You then find out how often the word is used, and how often a searcher clicks on any sponsored link. Paying more will get your sponsored link closer to the top of the page. You can make multiple offers until you find one you can live with.[22] The problem you might face comes from what you sell. If you are a bookstore, the word "books" might come to mind, but that's true for lots of other bookstores, publishers, and other companies. Maybe "first editions" is more appropriate, if that is indeed what you sell.

On the other hand, if you sell something a bit more unusual like yo-yos, buying a sponsored link for "yo-yo" is likely to get you on a page with limited competition.[23] Watch for jargon; think of what the average searcher might enter. Your hosting service's SEO program or your own web page designer will understand where to place the keywords you select and can help you get listed on the major search engines. There are literally hundreds of search engines, but there are five major ones—Google, Microsoft Bing, Yahoo!, Ask Network, and AOL. The next six largest search engines share less than 1 percent of the searches. You can see their relative shares of the search business in Figure 5.3.

FIGURE 5.3

Search Engine Rankings—February 2016

Source: Data from comScore Releases, February 2016, U.S. Desktop Search Engine Rankings.

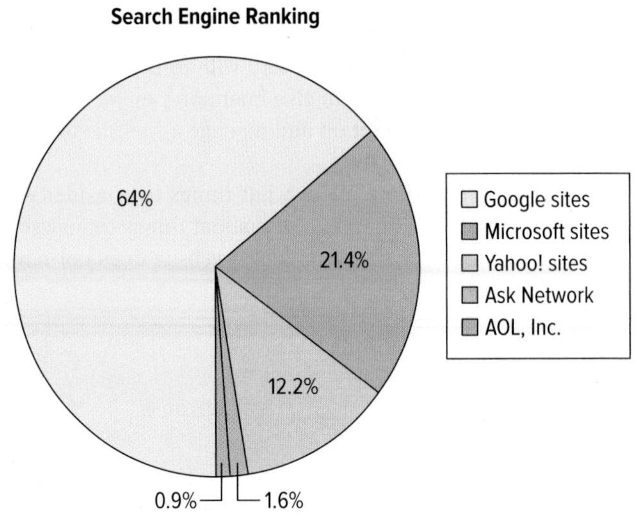

With all of these details revolving around making a truly effective informational website, you may wonder if it makes sense to do it yourself. As we have discussed, many $10-a-month web hosting packages will give you access to the tools to create a basic template-driven website and do the work necessary to perform SEO and will push your information to others via emails, RSS feeds, or Twitter tweets. The advantage is that you can deploy the site within hours and the cost is very low. The downside of template-based sites is that they can look similar to one another. On the other hand, having an e-commerce website created for you can be a $5,000 to $10,000 effort, and is likely to take a couple of weeks as you and your designer talk through draft versions of the site. One way to strike a balance between these two extremes is to commission custom graphics to use at the top of your online store's pages, and as a background. Another approach is to seek bids for your e-commerce store design on sites like Upwork.com or from local web designers.

For many part-time firms, an informational website is the essential starting point to get word out to the public, and to make your firm visible to those Internet search engines so many people use to find companies, goods, and services these days. Often, as the firm and its offerings mature, there is a benefit to moving beyond providing information via the web, and making it possible for customers to actually place their orders online. That takes you to the next step, e-commerce.

E-commerce and eBay Websites

How big is e-commerce and how fast is it growing? As noted earlier, there is a growing use of the Internet for e-commerce. The number of e-commerce sites, shown in Figure 5.4, passed 1 million in January 2009 and is estimated to be greater than 2.5 million today. Figure 5.2 showed how e-commerce sales were growing at a steady pace for B2C retail and wholesale sales, and growing at a much faster rate for B2B wholesale and manufacturing sales. E-commerce in 2013 was more than a $5.6 trillion sector of U.S. business.[24] So the answer is that e-commerce is big and getting bigger.

For part-time entrepreneurs, the lure of an e-commerce site is undeniable. Consider listing your products on the top two sites. There is no official count of eBay sellers, but Savanna Dance wrote in a user group posting that active eBay sellers number between 6.7 and 9.3 million in the United States alone.[25] Seven out of every eight sellers work on eBay only part time. The cost of

FIGURE 5.4

Growth of E-commerce Sites

Source: Numbers of Secure Sockets Layer (SSL) certificates issued since 2009 calculated by Richard Green from graph of percentage increase: http://news.netcraft.com/archives/2015/05/13/counting-ssl-certificates.html (accessed March 12, 2016).

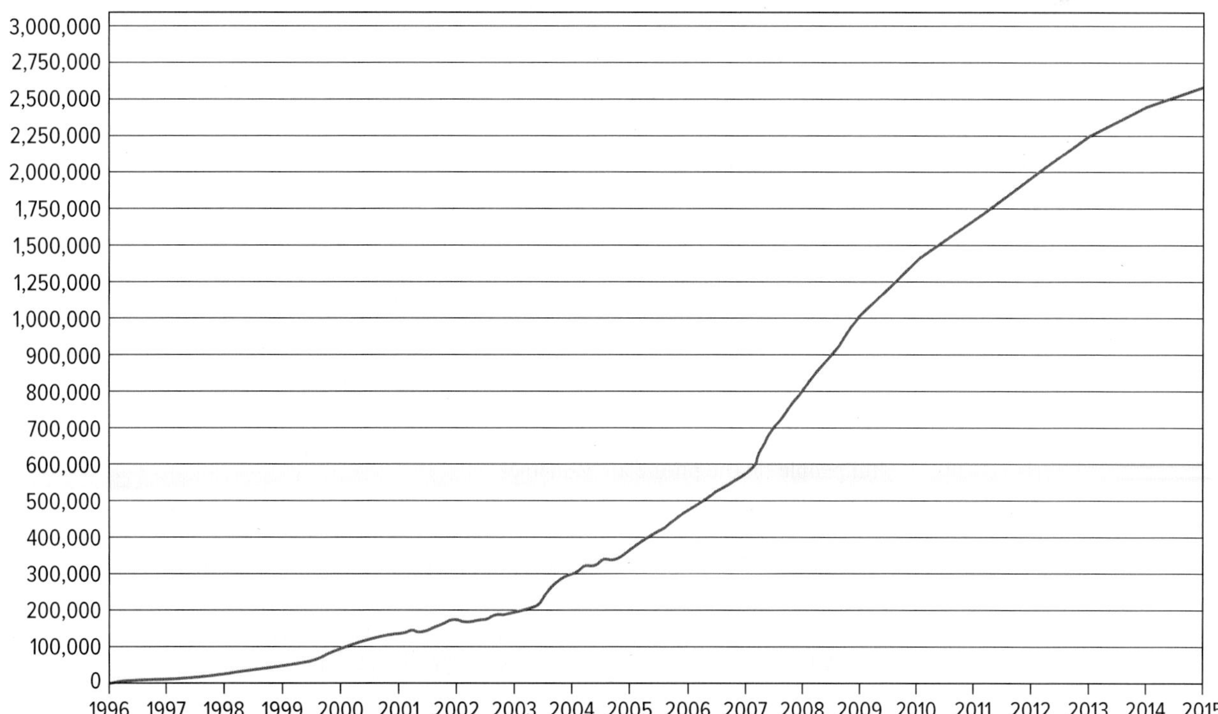

listing a $25 item on eBay is $1, plus an additional 8.75 percent of $25 if the item sells. The cost to open an eBay account? Nothing.[26] eBay's biggest competitor, Amazon, offers a similar deal with slightly different terms. Between the two sites, nearly a half-billion computer users visit one site or another during the year.

With numbers like those it is no wonder that e-commerce on the Internet is an attractive approach for entrepreneurs looking to create a business. This is especially true for part-time entrepreneurs. For part-time entrepreneurs the online approach makes a highly attractive opportunity because it offers the advantages of a large market, 24/7 availability of your products, and a start-up that is quickly done and potentially inexpensive. For many part-timers, the online approach provides a great way to learn the business and the market, establish your reputation and business track record, and lay a foundation for a full-time business. For entrepreneurs looking to prospect for the right type of business, the online sales approach makes it possible to try out a range of industries quickly and with minimal risk. For entrepreneurs with highly specialized products, the idea that low-cost listings on two sites could reach half of 1.1 *billion* Internet users worldwide[27] opens up sales possibilities like never before.

There are two major approaches to online selling. One is using Amazon, eBay, or another online site to showcase your goods and handle the selling and payment process. The other is to do this through a website of your own. The two approaches can be complementary. You can use eBay to introduce your product to a large audience, to find an initial selling price, and to learn more about customers and competitors. Once you are comfortable with how you must market your product, you can set up your own website as the primary point of sale and continue to use eBay to market to new customers.

Everything we have said so far about informational websites applies to a website enabled for e-commerce. Most of the hosting companies mentioned in this chapter can also provide you with an e-commerce site. In fact if you already have an informational site, they can set it up so everything you have posted to the web moves directly into the new, more capable site. What e-commerce sites add is the ability to create and maintain an online catalog of products, create new database entries for orders, and handle the payment for products or services. The more tools and services you need and the larger the catalogs you post, the more you will end up paying. It is worth doing some serious comparison shopping for hosting services. Conduct a Google search for "cheap e-commerce" and "free shopping cart" (a *shopping cart* is the electronic version of a catalog with an ordering system) to find a large number of possibilities. Many offer do-it-yourself software to make the design of websites and shopping carts easy.

In addition to the keys to designing an effective informational website covered previously, there are also two important financial issues to consider for entrepreneurs who create their own e-commerce websites: payments and chargebacks.

- **Payments:** Most online transactions use a credit card or an online payment system like PayPal (which originated as a division of eBay). There are fees for the transaction itself, and there are often fees for currency conversions, or guaranteed payments. Unless you as the seller buy a payment guarantee at the time of the transaction, services will also make a chargeback (see the next bullet point). Many online e-commerce packages come with a service that handles these transactions for a fee. Where you can specify another vendor, you may be able to get one that charges less. But as important as the fees charged is the service's handling of customer service. When problems crop up in payments, both buyers and sellers want to talk to a person immediately. Services with fast response rates and helpful people on the phone are valuable.
- **Chargebacks:** This is a fee the service charges you for any of a variety of problems related to the sale–for example, a lost, stolen, or fraudulent card was used, the customer reports nothing was received, the product was not the one promised, or there were problems with the product. While chargebacks in stores are around 0.1 percent of sales, online chargeback rates can be as much as five times higher.[28] Techniques to control this include using the Address Verification Service or verifying phone numbers or addresses yourself, getting proof of delivery from the carrier, and making sure your return policy is known by the customer before the sale is finalized.

eBay is a site offering a variety of ways to sell goods and services. To give you an idea of how varied are eBay's offerings, consider these ways eBay supports entrepreneurial efforts:

- For many interested in selling only a few items and moving to something else, eBay is like the largest consignment store or garage sale in the world. You can list a single item for sale without creating a website or a company to support your effort.
- You can create an online store within eBay complete with your own online catalog and ordering systems.
- eBay has 34 major categories of goods ranging from "collectibles," which includes the Pez containers many erroneously believe were eBay's first items, to "Business & Industrial," where you can buy 75-ton construction cranes.
- You can sell services through Upwork.com ranging from web design to business plans, accounting to translation, training to CAD projects, in a reverse auction format. In a **reverse auction**[29] the low bid gets the business.

reverse auction
An auction in which the low bid gets the business or wins.

Upwork.com adapts the eBay model to services. Businesses post projects, review bids, use the message boards to keep up-to-date, and can even pay online, all for a small fee Upwork collects once the provider is paid. Service providers are able to post information about their expertise and experience as well. Cheri Rychlee Tracy was looking for a web designer. Local companies wanted between $1,500 and $7,500. She was able to find a freelance designer on Upwork from the Ukraine for $750.[30]

While this section concentrates on eBay, it is important to know that there are competitors for every type of service eBay offers. Their traffic numbers may not match eBay's, but they may have a better audience for your purposes. For example, freelanceseek.com has a strong programming and online art focus, and is a site often used by people in the e-commerce industry. Competing sites include:

- For Upwork: Freelancer.com, Seek.com.
- For eBay's B2C auction services: Auction.com, Ioffer.com, uBid.com.
- For eBay's B2B auction services: Business.com.
- For eBay's online store services: Amazon.com, GoDaddy.com.

Using e-commerce services like eBay or Upwork can provide access to a wider range of vendors or service providers than most people would normally have. And many of the online services like eBay, Upwork, and Amazon provide detailed feedback and ratings from prior customers, so as a buyer you can have a higher level of assurance that the online company you are dealing with is on the up and up—but problems can crop up. Two of the greatest ones for vendors—chargebacks and payment problems—were mentioned. A customer can also face trouble, as seen in the following Small Business Insight.

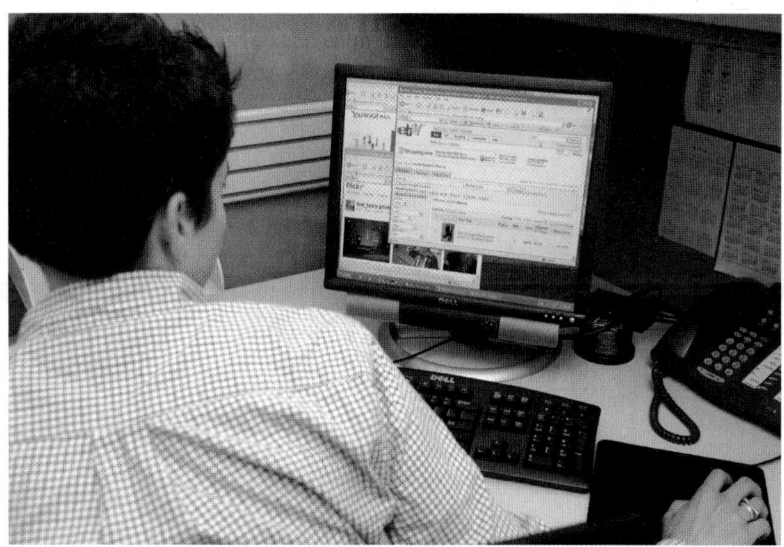

This entrepreneur is taking no risks with her product sales on eBay. Not only is she checking her product's listing for prospective buyers, she is also checking how her eBay online store is showing up in social media like Yahoo!'s groups and a set of photos of products she has uploaded to Flickr.

John Flournoy/McGraw-Hill Education

SMALL BUSINESS INSIGHT

MY PEOPLE MIGHT DESTROY YOUR WEBSITE

Henry Richardson was a professor at a small college and had an active consulting business. A lot of the materials he created for individual clients he rewrote in a more general form and sold as pamphlets, short reports, and self-published trade books. He had an informational website, but as the technology advanced he realized he could cut his production costs dramatically by selling his pamphlets, reports, and books as downloadable PDF files. To control this process he needed a different type of online store—one specialized for the electronic publishing industry. Such programs not only handle the order, but also control the downloading of files so that only bona fide customers can obtain the download. Not finding any electronic publishing sales packages he liked, he decided to have one custom designed.

Henry went onto **Elance.com** (now called **Upwork.com**) and put in a request for bids for his project. From the 23 responses (ranging from $11,800 to $450), Henry narrowed the field by looking at the customer ratings, track records, and portfolios of the companies. His chosen company had an American sales office and a team of programmers in India. Henry thought this would help provide better coordination for the project. The final negotiated price was $1,800.

Although the project was supposed to be completed in three weeks, Henry never heard from the U.S. or Indian offices, a definite bad sign. Henry got a call from the U.S. sales office in week 4 stating that the project was behind schedule but would be finished "soon." Excuses piled on for two more months. At the end of month 3, Henry sent an ultimatum to the vendor—finish the project or return the money.

This initiated a call from the Indian office. The company's manager said because they had done "work" on the project, they would refund $1,200, but only if Henry would give a positive review for the firm on Elance! When Henry asked what would happen if he gave an honest rating, the manager said he did not know how his programmers would take such an insult. They *might* just destroy Henry's existing informational website out of anger. Not wanting to spend his days protecting his website, Henry agreed. He later had a local programmer do the site for $4,000.

People who sell on eBay or competing auction site stores strongly suggest using the auction feature; after all, that is what most people think of when they go to the site. Sherry Chase of Fancy That! started an eBay store as a means of getting rid of excess merchandise from her store. She had tried her own website with virtually no luck at first. She found that eBay sales exceeded her expectations. She also found that by auctioning items and including her link in the auction description, she got people to her eBay store.[31]

eBay auctions themselves are legendary. On any day 12 million items are available with nearly 2 million new postings a day.[32] There are 150 new items for sale listed every minute, and 500 bids placed during that same minute. There are 69 million eBay users who spend $59 million a day.[33] The eBay method means you pay a fee for posting your product and a sales fee based on the final bid price when the item sells. You have the option of setting a bottom offer you will accept, a **reserve price** (if the bidding does not exceed the price, the sale will not go through), and the number of days the auction will run (out of several choices). Your posting can include pictures of the product and links to more data (like your website).

reserve price
A minimum acceptable selling price in an auction. If the bidding does not exceed the price, the sale will not go through.

eBay allows you a bit of anonymity—all buyers and sellers have screen names. Email addresses and limited personal information are given out only in certain circumstances. (Obviously, if you are a successful bidder, the seller needs to know to whom and where to send the merchandise.) eBay sellers may take checks, money orders, or credit cards, or accept payments through PayPal, eBay's own electronic payment system, reducing sellers' risk. eBay also allows buyers and sellers to post feedback about their transactions which produces a score that's displayed by the buyers' and sellers' screen names and allows others to get a feel for how reputable a certain buyer or seller is. This feedback is also available for the public to read. (See Skill Module 5.1 for more tips.)

Checklist for Maximizing Success on eBay[34]

SKILL MODULE 5.1

There are whole books written on how to do well on eBay, but what are the basics that can make the biggest difference? As you prepare for selling via eBay, test your ad and your approach to eBay selling against the checklist below.

DESCRIPTION

1. **Detailed Description?** Use detailed descriptions so that the buyer isn't expecting something different from what you are selling.
2. **Typppppos?** Watch out for misspellings and typos. Experienced eBay buyers use the search engine to find specific things and it won't find your misspelling. Besides, it doesn't look very professional.
3. **Factual Bad News Up Front?** Be honest and factual. Don't say "slight damage." Instead state that there is an 8-inch chip on the upper right-hand corner and a faint scratch along one side. The buyer can make an informed decision, and there are no surprises.
4. **Got a Positive Feedback Rating?** Since most buyers are somewhat reluctant about buying from a seller with no feedback, try buying for a while; your feedback rating will grow, and since there is no differentiation between buyer and seller feedback, this puts you in a better position as a seller.

PHOTOS

5. **Photo Present?** A picture is worth a thousand words.
6. **Photo Pretty?** Make sure the photo is not too dark or too light. Does it adequately display your product? Check out backgrounds, too. They can detract from the subject and might even show things you'd rather not display on the Internet.
7. **Photo Fast?** Don't use huge slow-to-download files.
8. **Photo Real?** Showing a photo of a box of commercial software is fine if that is what you are selling. If it is only the CD, without the box and the items included in it (like manuals, jewel cases, registration cards, etc.), it is better to take a photo of what exactly you are selling and include it on the eBay page.

COMPETITIVE ISSUES

9. **Price-Matched the Competition?** Check what the competition is doing to see if you even want to try eBay auctions. If your product (or something fairly similar) is selling on eBay for less than you need to meet your profit goals, find another way to get to your customers.
10. **Shipping Not a Rip-Off?** Be honest and up front about shipping. It is acceptable to charge for postage and a reasonable amount for shipping materials. If you are using recycled boxes, don't charge for them. Some sellers like to use a flat fee for all shipping charges (e.g., $5 per paperback book). Experienced eBay buyers will know that for regular U.S. media mail, that price is way out of line. If you're the only one selling that item, consumers may pay; but if there are a dozen others, they will shop around or reflect their concerns in the top bid they place.
11. **Terms Match the Competition?** When you find similar products being offered by competitors, make sure you have the same terms on your product page, so people searching on those terms find your page when they find your competitors'.
12. **Time Matches the Competition?** If you are using auctions, try to time your auctions to end after your competitors'. Remember that most people will lose in an auction. If you are offering a similar product, which comes up on the same search with similar costs and closing right after an auction from a popular seller, many buyers will bid on your offering.

SALES-RELATED SERVICES

13. **Email Ready?** If buyers have a question, they'll email you. Respond as soon as possible, at least within 24 hours. Don't post auction items just prior to going on vacation.
14. **Shipping Promptly?** Package well. Notify your buyers when things have been shipped. If you need to wait for a check to clear and you'll be gone a few days during that time, let them know. Most buyers are prepared to be reasonable if they know what's going on.

(continued)

15. **Quick Customer Response?** Customer service is very important. You want positive feedback. Dissatisfied buyers may either leave negative feedback or leave no feedback at all on your transaction.
16. **Gave Feedback Promptly?** Give feedback to your buyers, too. First, it helps them when making further purchases. Second, if you expect feedback yourself, do it for them. If they see you've posted positive feedback, they are more likely to do so themselves.

SCORING

Score 1 for each Yes answer and 0 for each No answer, then add up each category. 4 in a category is "Excellent," 3 is "Adequate," and 2 means "Needs Improvement." A score of 1 or zero in *any* category is "Not Ready for eBay," and you should hold off selling on eBay until you have raised your score in this category.

There are restrictions on the types of products that may be sold—for example, anything that is considered fraudulent, illegal, or harmful, as well as anything that infringes on patent or trademark rules. eBay does enforce this policy. For more detailed information about doing business on eBay, check the website www.ebay.com or look at one of the numerous books about eBay, such as *eBay for Dummies.*

Although the web traffic counts for eBay and Amazon are extremely high, a wise entrepreneur (even a part-time one) does not rely on customer searches on these sites alone to bring in business. The most successful web entrepreneurs keep using the multichannel marketing approach introduced earlier. Getting the name of your online store into newsletters (electronic or printed), newspapers, trade journals, blogs, or on mass media (local can be just as powerful as national) can help you promote your site to potential customers. Increasingly, entrepreneurs are using the social networking sites mentioned in Chapter 3, like Facebook, Instagram, and LinkedIn, to get the word out to friends of your firm as well as potential customers interested in what you or your firm has to say. A quick listing of the other places to promote your site is given in Figure 5.5.

FIGURE 5.5

Business Promotion Multichannels

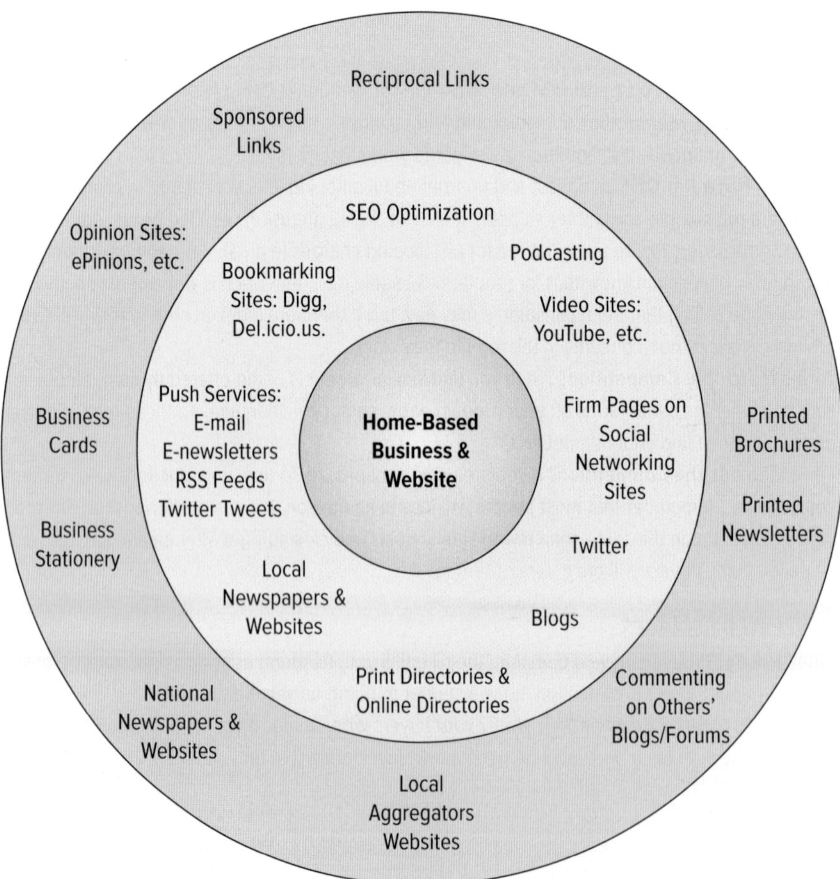

Figure 5.5 mentions a few other types of sites we have not discussed so far. These include free sites like the video site YouTube.com where you can post a video for free; bookmarking sites like Digg.com or Pinboard.in where you can identify websites and get these voted on or adopted by readers; and opinion sites where customers can post opinions about firms, products, and services. There is also a free way to get your name (and your business) known, and that is by making informed comments on blogs and discussion forums related to your business.

There are also several advertising channels that come with costs. Obviously, the traditional approaches to advertising, like business cards, stationery, printed newsletters, and brochures, cost money (although these days you can print just the quantity you need on a good color printer). There are also old media approaches that are still important. Local and national newspapers (like *The Wall Street Journal*) also have online versions (and online ads). The phone company's local directories also often come with an online version. There are also many specialized online directories, such as those of the Better Business Bureau (www.bbb.org).

Given the cost of getting into e-commerce, especially with sites like eBay, you can't argue with the resulting success stories. Mark and Robin LeVine sell more than $1 million per year of bubble wrap and other packing materials. Sarah Davis sells over $4 million annually of designer handbags. Although "eBay millionaires" are a minority of eBay sellers, these two examples are by no means unusual.[35] eBay is also successful for business-to-business selling, although it no longer maintains its business-specific pages.[36] Farmer Joel Holstad purchased a tractor, a combine, and a cherry picker for about half of what he expected to pay.

Home-based business and Internet business are the two core methods of getting started for part-time entrepreneurs. They can cover a wide variety of retail, wholesale, service, and even simple manufacturing situations (like artisans' work or custom electronics), but there are other approaches that offer quickly deployed, low-cost ways to start part-time businesses. Sometimes these approaches are next steps for home-based or Internet businesses, but in other cases, these approaches can be the first step for a part-time firm.

The Next Best Things to a Home-Based Business

Often, business success depends on getting close to the customer—close enough so the customer can see you, the entrepreneur, your product, or you delivering your service. As you'll learn in Chapter 11, you can go to your customer (as in the case of a repair service which works at the customer's site) or you can go to a mutually accessible location, like a store. There are several approaches closely identified with part-time businesses. Historically, two methods have been mentioned most often—home retail (which consists of home parties, door-to-door selling, and network marketing) and stands or kiosks.

Home Retail

At a **home party** the entrepreneur arranges a get-together at someone's home where participants can socialize and get acquainted with the entrepreneur and the products or services offered. Home party selling was pioneered (if not actually invented) by Frank Stanley Beveridge and Norman W. Squires who began selling Stanley Home Products by enticing homemakers to invite a small group of family, friends, and neighbors into their homes for a party.[37] At the party, the salesperson would demonstrate products and take orders for future delivery. Today this is a widely used technique with dozens of franchised sales operations for products such as Mary Kay Cosmetics and Tupperware.

home party
A business model in which the entrepreneur arranges a customer to host a party, inviting friends, family, and neighbors. During the party, the entrepreneur demonstrates products and accepts orders for future delivery.

The advantages of home retail businesses are the speed and ease of setup, the low cost of getting started, and the ability to do the work away from your home and employer, thus minimizing potential conflicts. The disadvantages come from always working "on the road," lacking a base from which you can organize and work, having a highly variable income, and finding ways for customers to get in touch with you (although cell phones and email have made a major difference).

You can arrange sales parties without selling a franchised product. One of the ways to make arrangements with minimal setup is to have the party at someone else's home. This person in return gets a portion of the proceeds in product discounts, products, or cash. You and the host work up a guest list, and the arrangements for refreshments and participation presents are agreed to in the early stages of the negotiation. Picking hosts with good contacts and a pleasant home is the key factor in party success. Often the opportunity for repeat customers and customers hosting later parties presents itself, and it's a great way to keep sales growing.

door-to-door selling
Door-to-door selling is the practice of taking product directly to the homes or places of business of potential customers and attempting to sell the product immediately.

In **door-to-door** selling, the retailer goes to the home to demonstrate and sell the product. Matching the product to the community is a key factor. For example, it is hard to find good prospects for buyers of seeds if you are working an apartment community. Think about the income and lifestyle of the community with respect to your product.

The fundamental success factor in door-to-door selling is closing the sale. *Closing* means getting the customers to agree to buy. Amazingly, asking the customers to buy is often all that is needed. If the answer is no, the natural comeback is to ask customers what they need to know or have in order to buy. If they tell you something they need, your job becomes trying to meet that need. Meanwhile you continue to ask if they are ready to buy. Only if you cannot meet a need of a particular customer do you give up and go to the next customer.[38]

network marketing
An approach to selling in which the salesperson recruits customers to become distributors of the product or service to others.

Another variation on the home model is **network marketing** efforts, also called multilevel marketing or MLM. These are organized through a parent organization; agents sell in part using in-home parties and person-to-person sales. The added twist is that current salespeople are invited to recruit additional new salespeople. The recruiter gets a commission from the sales made by his or her recruits. Everything mentioned previously also applies in network marketing, with the added need to carefully check into the parent organization and the terms of the recruiting. The extra caution is necessary because illegal pyramid schemes are often made to look like legal MLMs. For example, where the fees paid by newly recruited network members are paid directly to more senior network members, there is a good chance you are seeing an illegal pyramid scheme. You can check with the Federal Trade Commission (www.ftc.gov) and the Better Business Bureau (www.bbb.org).[39]

Stand Retail

Stand retailing–the roadside, flea market, farmers' market, or craft fair business–is one of the most ancient forms of small business. It is mentioned in the Bible, and marketplaces full of stands have been found in virtually all archeological digs. Today, stands tend to be either semi-permanent ones that remain in one place and are built to be sturdy, like a farmer's roadside stand, or movable ones that can be quickly assembled and disassembled for use in farmers' markets, flea markets, and craft fairs. To get started inexpensively, people often start selling from the back of their cars or using a folding table or blanket laid out with wares.

The advantage of stand businesses is that you can start with little investment. Stands can be a box or ground cloth. They also do not require a lot of investment in inventory. There are a variety of locations where a stand can be set up, such as flea markets. Stands can also be quickly established and easily ended as a business. Stands vary widely in the products they sell. The disadvantages of stands are the variable income they provide; the difficulty of making sure your stand and

This part-time business worker has his finger on the pulse of a niche market, capitalizing on the limitations experienced by people on the streets of New York who are hungry for a snack. His signs and position on a street corner create visibility and boost market desire for his products. His stand allows him to easily move elsewhere as he perceives needs. If you were positioning in a downtown for lunch and dinner traffic, how would you decide where to move your cart?

Jennifer Santolla/Alamy Stock Photo

business meet legal requirements such as compliance with registering, licensing, and zoning (for help with this look at the section "Exchange: Dealing with Others" later in the chapter); the problem of knowing how to price goods; and the building up of a customer base for your stand.

While stands can be among the least expensive ways to set up a shop, a high-end version exists too. It is the mall cart, if it is on wheels, or kiosk, when it is in a fixed location. Carts and kiosks cost between $2,000 and $10,000,[40] although carts can be rented from many malls. Carts and kiosks are often among the most expensive locations in the mall in terms of rent per square foot. A cart in a high-end mall like the Mall of America in Bloomington, Minnesota, can go for $2,300 or 15 percent of sales a month in rent.[41] Costs include rent (usually a percentage of sales with a base monthly rental), mall member fees, and cart design costs. On the other hand, carts can be rented for specific periods (holiday seasons, weekends). The advantage of carts and kiosks is that your products can be seen by more than 100,000 people a week as they walk through the mall. One idea to minimize rents is to consider placing your cart or kiosk away from the high-traffic locations, but near specific stores where your most likely customers would come from–for example, putting a trading card kiosk near a mall arcade or sporting goods store.[42]

The key success factor for a stand is having a location where there is enough foot or vehicle traffic to sustain the business. High traffic concentrations are why flea markets, farmers' markets, and craft fairs are popular locales for stands. However, even these locations will have traffic levels that vary. Try to locate on or near a major walkway, or near the food, entertainment, or major vendor areas to get the most traffic. Always make sure to keep your documentation (e.g., vendor's permits, licenses, tax numbers, etc.) handy for checks by police and venue officials.

The other success factor is inventory. You might be selling products you make yourself. The next best thing is to start with what you know. If you have seen someone's work and think it would sell, ask if you can be an agent or reseller. If you are looking for others' products to sell, there are a host of sources (like wholesalers shopify.com and Doba.com) or you can go online to search for products or services to resell at the Industrial Resource Network, or at Thomas Register's online site, which has a print version available in many libraries. You can also do a search online for the manufacturers of particular products.[43]

Pop-Up Businesses

One trend that we see increasing across the United States, Europe, New Zealand, and Australia is that of pop-ups. We see pop-up retail shops, pop-up restaurants, pop-up festivals, pop-up art galleries–the list seems endless. But what are these pop-ups that seem to be so much the trend today? According to Wikipedia (every college student's first-choice research tool): "Pop-up retail, also known as pop-up store (or pop-up shop in the UK, Australia, and Ireland), or flash retailing, is [the practice] of opening short-term sales spaces."[44]

Pop-up store in London, England.

singh_lens/Shutterstock

venue
A place where something takes place. For example, a theater is the venue for a play; a stadium is the venue for a football game.

What makes a pop-up a "pop-up" is that its **venue** is temporary—here today, but gone tomorrow. The space where a pop-up business is selling classic vinyl records today may well be the space where Halloween costumes are being sold tomorrow. Pop-up shops and restaurants are typically small, sometimes as small as a single shipping container.

One of the most interesting things about the pop-up fad is who is getting into it. It is not just individual entrepreneurs. City governments, colleges, arts alliances, charities, and many, many more organizations are either opening their own pop-up businesses or sponsoring venues in which entrepreneurs may open pop-up businesses. Cities as diverse as Leland, Mississippi, and San Antonio, Texas, sponsor pop-up business events. Leland, for example, holds an indoor pop-up event three times a year in conjunction with established festivals such as the "Frog Fest"[45] which is held annually in October to honor hometown artist Jim Henson, who created the Muppets. San Antonio's Center City Development and Operations Department (CCDO) offers no-cost short-term leases in various vacant downtown properties for pop-up businesses. The city also sponsors seasonal pop-ups along designated city streets and in neighborhoods popular with tourists.[46] The American Culinary Institute sponsors pop-up restaurants at all three of its campuses in Hyde Park, New York; Greystone, California; and San Antonio, Texas. The restaurants vary in cuisine, showing off the skills that students have mastered in their courses of study.[47] The Walker Art Center in Minneapolis, Minnesota, sponsored a pop-up art sale with items ranging from $2 to $12,000. The proceeds were split between the artists and the Art Center gift shop.[48] Goodwill Industries opens dozens of pop-up stores each year in cities all across America.

In a very real sense, the pop-up phenomenon is not new at all. In fact, it is very much like the stand retail discussed in the previous section. However, it is very much a part-time business. For part-timers the big advantage to a pop-up business is its extreme flexibility:

- Pop-ups do not have a fixed place of business.
- Pop-ups exist for only a short time—a few hours, a day, or a few weeks.
- Pop-ups are designed to be easy to set up and take down.
- Pop-ups can easily be set up in new locations.
- Pop-ups must be special, distinct from other permanent businesses.

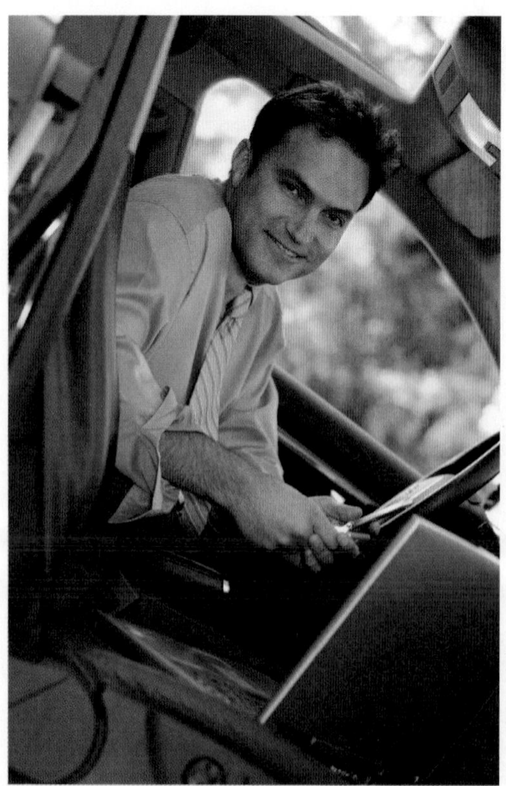

Today cell phones and laptops with wireless modems make it possible to run your business from your car. For a one-person, part-time business that wants to get close to customers, there is no better arrangement. What kind of features would you want in a car if you were going to use it as your primary office?

Comstock/Stockbyte/Getty Images

Mobile Offices

One recent survey suggested that one in six working Americans works from their cars or trucks. The kinds of jobs that involve face-to-face selling and client services are the ones most likely to be done from a car or truck. There are advantages to this approach. There is no rent, and car expenses can be deducted from tax returns. It places the entrepreneur close to the customer, and typically close to the entrepreneur's printed materials or tools.

The key to a mobile office is a cell phone and a laptop with Internet access and a printer (especially one that can be run from a USB port on the laptop). To keep everything powered, getting a power converter with a lighter plug will usually do the trick. What many mobile teleworkers initially forget is how important it is to have a comfortable place to write and mark up written reports—working behind the wheel gets old fast. Berny Coffee was an early entrepreneurial leader in teleworking. A yacht broker in Alexandria Bay, New York, Berny manages a network of 35 brokers from his car. The key for getting his work done is his cell phone, and a Wave Board wireless router, which connects him to Verizon's EvDO wireless network from wherever he is located. He runs it through a power converter plugged into his cigarette lighter. With the router working, he can even ditch his cell phone and call around the world for free using Skype. With this approach, Berny was even able to stay in business from Florida during a hurricane when people had no electricity and few cell phones worked.[49] These days, if you have a 3G or 4G cell phone or one of the 3G/4G wireless modems for your laptop, you should be able to mimic Berny's feat.

In terms of the car or truck, make sure it can accommodate you, all your equipment and files, and your telework equipment (and can handle the drain on the car's battery over the long term). It is also important that it provide adequate and comfortable accommodations for passengers. You may not drive them often, but you are likely to have them in the car for business discussions.

Virtual Offices, Executive Offices, and Incubators

When stresses in the home are making the home office problematic, but your business is not ready for a full-time rental, one approach is to look at outsourcing your office. A virtual office is actually the next step to most business web hosting packages. In addition to handling your emails and newsletters, a virtual office typically gives you access to your files, as well as web-based fax services and, most typically, full business telephone services including phone trees, voice-mail services, and often additional phone-based services such as reminders, and call forwarding based on the time of day. Major players include Regus.com, Onebox.com, and Hq.com.[50]

Executive offices provide small amounts of short-term space for an office or work area. They can be furnished or unfurnished, and provide basic utilities. They often have preferred vendor arrangements for phone services (which may not always be the best deal–keep using your cell phone) and low-cost shared services such as copying and telephone answering by a live receptionist. Regus and HQ also offer such services, as do InstantOffices.com and IntelligentOffice.com. A variant of these are called coworking spaces, which generally include a large open office space where you pay a daily, weekly, or monthly fee for access, and usually include all the Wi-Fi and coffee you can use, along with printers and copiers you can buy time on and bookable spaces for meetings. Google "coworking space directory" to start your search for one near you.

Another solution you might find interesting is to see if you can rent space in an **incubator**. Incubators are community-based organizations designed to help small businesses. For-profit incubators are very similar to executive office operations, although usually with somewhat lower prices. Nonprofit incubators are often sponsored by universities, economic development agencies, or localities themselves. They tend to offer heavily subsidized space, shared services like executive offices, and almost always offer on-site expert advice about running small businesses. The key online directory for incubators is run by the National Business Incubator Association at nbia.org.

incubator
A facility that offers subsidized space and business advice to companies in their earliest stages of operation.

Doing Business without a Business Organization: using Consignments and Agents

Artists, artisans, authors, inventors, small-scale manufacturers, and collectors of antiques or other collectibles all have one thing in common: They possess something they would benefit from selling. Often, these people start small part-time businesses to do that. With the advent of general selling platforms like eBay.com and specialty platforms like etsy.com, selling your work has never been easier. For inventors or **makers**, as they are known today, crowdsourcing platforms like quirky.com for idea generation and refinement or kickstarter.com or indiegogo.com for funding make it easier than ever to get your product together, both figuratively and literally.

maker
A modern term for an inventor, in particular, an inventor who uses modern techniques like 3-D software and 3-D printers or do-it-yourself electronics to create new items.

However, many others prefer to stick to their creating or discovering and let someone else handle the selling process. The kind of businesses that do this are called a variety of names such as consignment shops, auctioneers, or sales agents. Regardless of the name, the basic business model remains the same. The agent (we will use this term for the person running the consignment businesses) will take on the product of the creating or discovering or manufacturing part-time entrepreneur. Some agents charge a basic fee up front to cover initial expenses; some do not. All agents make an effort to sell the product they were given. When sold, the agent gets a portion of the sale price, with the remainder going to the part-time entrepreneur who employed the agent.

Let's look at two different types of consignment situations–eBay consignment shops and intellectual property agents. An eBay consignment shop starts with you dropping off your item. The consignment shop photographs the item, prepares a description, and posts it on eBay. When the item is sold, the shop ships it to the buyer and sends you your share of the sale price. There are several national franchise chains offering drop-off consignment services such as 877isoldit.com or sellforme.ebay.com. There are also hundreds of small, independent local consignment stores. An excellent listing of eBay drop-off stores can be found at drop-off-stores.com/. Although there is wide variation in pricing, the eBay consignment stores generally charge a percentage (around 40 percent for the smallest items, with less for larger sales) for their work.

intellectual property (IP) Property coming from some sort of original thought; for example, patents, trade secrets, trademarks, and copyrights.

Intellectual property (IP) refers to original works like inventions, visual and performing art works, books, and computer programs. We will learn about the many ways to legally protect IP in Chapter 17, but for now just think about how you might get money for some IP you have created. There are a variety of agents who specialize in different types of IP. Experts (often lawyers by training) called IP agents usually focus on placing inventions, computer programs, and manufactured products with companies willing to pay to add to their complement of new products. Sometimes companies will buy competing IP to prevent their competitors from getting it.

For works of art, there are a variety of specialized art agents. You have probably heard of book agents (also called literary or publishing agents), and there are similar types of agents for designs and paintings. Aaron McGruder created a comic strip called *The Boondocks.* Once he learned how hard it was to place a cartoon strip with newspapers and get a good deal doing so, he found the best artist agent he could to find the most motivated seller possible to help him structure a deal that got him the money, ownership, and editorial control he wanted.

Regardless of the type, you can find listings of agents through a Google search using the terms given previously. Finding the right agent for you requires some additional research. While an agent close to where you live means you would be able to meet face-to-face, local agents may lack the contacts in the major corporate, manufacturing, media, or artistic centers where your work could get its best offer. Some suggestions for how to find a good agent include:

- Check out the agent's biography and track record, as well as searching for articles confirming his or her accomplishments.
- Often there are a couple of local lawyers in the nearest big city who have experience dealing with agents from the major cities. It may be possible to get referrals from them.
- Don't be afraid to write someone in your field whom you respect and ask for his or her recommendation. The individual knows a bit about the business and may be able to give you some direction.
- Often faculty in your college or university may have experience with, or connections to, agents. Look for faculty who have done any mass media work (best-selling books, national TV, movies or radio, nationally sold designs or works of art, and faculty with patents, etc.).

In all forms of consignment relationships there are a few things you should always consider. For any consignment, make sure there is a written contract outlining what the consignment agent will do to sell your product, what the costs and fees are, and how they get paid (some will come out of the selling price, whereas others may be paid up front). It is also crucial to have a clear description of the product and any variations, parts, pieces, and manuals included. For physical products and works of art, the description should mention the condition of the items and any blemishes—photos help.[51]

The advantage of consignment approaches is that they permit full-time sales with only a part-time involvement from you, low setup cost, a low risk level, and the flexibility that comes from the variety of consignment agents and agencies available to you. The disadvantages can include little effort being put forth to sell your product, high potential for competing offerings, long amount of time before payouts, and lower profitability because of agent's fees.

LO 5-4 Describe the key factors to making a decision to go into part-time entrepreneurship.

Key Considerations for Success in Part-Time Entrepreneurship

When you decide to pursue part-time entrepreneurship, there are usually two major questions: What kind of product or service do you want to offer, and how do you want to organize your part-time business? Chapter 4 discussed the process for coming up with a good (and maybe even a creative) idea for your business. In this chapter we will focus more on how you would get that business started part time.

For the second question, about how to organize your business, there are usually three key considerations for part-time small business start-ups:

- The **cost to start up** your new part-time business.
- The **time to start up** your business.
- The **permanence** of the business you are creating.

cost to start up The amount of money it takes to start a new business.

time to start up How long it takes to start a new business.

permanance The impression of long-term continuity a business gives others.

For part-time businesses, you want a low cost of start-up, since you probably will not have a lot of money to invest, and may not get great returns to pay off expensive start-up efforts.

Time to start up is also best when shortest, since you are looking for a basic idea of what might and might not work. The more time and energy you spend preparing for a small-scale part-time business, the longer it takes to make a profit. The good news is that in most cases, the cost to start up and the time to market are closely related.

Permanence is related to the concept of legitimacy discussed in Chapter 3. For a small-scale, part-time firm, it may be hard to have a lot of the indicators of legitimacy. What customers want to know is that the firm is likely to be around for a while, to provide customer service and future sales. That is the fundamental idea of permanence. The three considerations are at the heart of most people's decisions about their mode of entry to part-time entrepreneurship.

Success Factors for Part-Time Businesses

LO **5-5** Use the BRIE model to describe what it takes to be successful in part-time entrepreneurship.

Research indicates that most service and retail firms typically start out as a hobby.[52] There are many different ways to start a part-time business. Consider, for example, the way Courtney Hennessey Hopson got Codi Jewelry going (see the Small Business Insight). The BRIE model introduced in Chapter 1 points out many of the key factors you need to think about. Intention is usually where part-time businesses start in the BRIE process, and we talked about key resources–such as inventory or competencies–earlier. Let's go further to address the two other aspects of the model for part-time businesses: boundary and exchange.

Boundary: Separating and Balancing Business and Home

Time is central to balancing home and business. It is important to organize a business around a schedule that makes sense for you. Internet-based businesses let you work anytime that is convenient for you. For Courtney, having time during Christmas break was critical. Operating on weekends at roadside stands or at flea markets or farmers' markets is the best way to structure time that is convenient for you and your customers.

Either way, time management, as discussed in Chapter 2, is the crucial skill for juggling your part-time business and the rest of your life. The key device for managing time is the to-do list. To be effective, the list needs to be with you at all times. You can get by with a small notepad, or can go for preprinted organizers, such as those from Day-Timer or Franklin Covey. Your smartphone almost certainly has a calendar that usually includes a way to post reminders or to-do lists. There are also free apps like Toodledo, Google Tasks, Remember The Milk, and others, often with smartphone and web versions so your list can always be a click away.

When using a to-do list, be sure to list the key information such as due dates and contact information if it applies. Most entrepreneurs find that it also helps to prioritize the list. One of the simplest ways to do this is 1-2-3 ordering. Those activities that are absolutely essential to your business or life are coded 1. Those that are current but of lesser importance or that can be rescheduled if necessary are assigned a 2. Activities that you want to do when you have some extra time or that have due dates far in the future get coded as 3. Typically, owners keep a to-do list of 6 to 20 items per week, and they reprioritize on a daily basis.[53]

For people with a part-time business, the to-do list includes items from business and personal life. For students, tests are probably a 1 priority. For parents, children's extracurricular activities are also 1s. Often family and personal lives make demands that put business and the rest of life in conflict.

SMALL BUSINESS INSIGHT

Courtney Hennessey Hopson and Codi Jewelry[54]

Courtney Hennessey Hopson of **CodiJewelry.com** did not intend to go into the jewelry business. It just grew. During Christmas break of her junior year at Saint Louis University, Courtney decided to make stretchy crystal bracelets for her friends as holiday presents. When she left the bead store, she had another problem—she had spent $400 on beads and string, and she needed to make the money back before her father found out. Courtney became a walking ad for her bracelets and sold them throughout the holiday, including at a family wake. Eventually the business grew to have in-person and online retail sales as well as wholesaling to stores, including Neiman Marcus. Eventually Courtney won a Global Student Entrepreneur Award for innovative thinking.

Courtney Hennessey Hopson, the founder of Codi Jewelry, began her small business part time out of the necessity to recover her Christmas gift-making costs. Like many others highlighted in this chapter, her part-time business afforded her the chance to earn a reasonable profit while carrying on with her other life priorities.

Courtney Hennessey Hopson

Having some general rules to help sort out these conflicting demands helps. Fred Kiesner, an entrepreneurship professor at Loyola Marymount College, suggests six key ideas:[55]

1. Do not waste time complaining; do something about a problem.
2. Do not aim for perfection; "good enough" really is good enough.
3. Do not dwell on the past; just plan to do better next time.
4. Minimize your time spent in meetings, or schedule meetings to be short.
5. Schedule and protect quality time with your family.
6. Schedule and protect some time for yourself to have fun.

The majority of part-time businesses are based in the home. The business takes space, uses resources the family also uses, and generally places stress on the household. Keeping a clean boundary, like an area known as the "business corner," helps make sure that family and business are protected from each other.

Exchange: Dealing with Others

There are two key groups outside your business with whom you must deal—government and customers. Even part-time businesses have to deal with government, and three issues pop up repeatedly: registration or licensing, taxes, and zoning which was discussed earlier in this chapter. For businesses run from a home or commercial venue like a fair or consignment shop, most states and localities require some form of **registration**, but the requirements vary so it is important to check. The U.S. government has a web page with links to state registration information at www.sba.gov/starting-business/choose-register-your-business. On the site, click on the menu item "Register your business." Note you might need to register your business name and possibly register your business with particular state agencies depending on your industry or occupation.[56] This is often called **licensing**. For example, home-based hairstylists need state licensing, and in many states home-based day-care providers need to get special registration and, in some cases, licensing.

registration
Information provided to the government concerning the existence of, name of, nature of, and contact information for your business.

licensing
Documented permission from the government to run your business.

Even when you do not have to register a business, you need to keep track of your sales in order to pay your income taxes later. Although taxes are discussed in Chapter 13, it is useful to mention here that you want to keep track of your costs, too, because if you itemize your deductions on Schedule C, you can deduct your costs from your income (and a lower income means lower taxes). In many states and localities you must also pay sales taxes, and these often need to be kept in a separate bank account and tracked as well. Often, flea markets and craft fairs include temporary local tax numbers in the booth rentals, but it is important to check.

Pricing and Costing

Because exchange is the way businesses make profits, it is important to price your goods or services to make profits likely. Folks working part time can be prone to underestimate their costs. Using things found around the house or neighborhood or not adequately considering the cost of the time you contribute are typically what lead to underestimating the cost of a product or service. Taking some time to think through the real cost of your product or service is critical to your success. Central to figuring the real cost is recognizing that your own time has value. When you price your product or service to pay yourself what you could get working part time for someone else, then you have achieved a real milestone on the road to growing your business.

Pricing is also often seen as a challenge by part-time businesses. Even if the business is part time, that does not mean the prices have to be cut-rate. One good way to get an idea of realistic pricing is to price competitors' offerings. Doing some window-shopping in person, via catalog, or on the Internet is the classic way. Once you know the kind of price your product or service can get and once you know your costs, then you are in a great position to know the kind of profit it's possible to make in your business.

What Are the Challenges of Being an Entrepreneur Part Time?

LO **5-6** Describe the advantages and pitfalls of delegating and outsourcing.

Four aspects of part-time entrepreneurship are very different from full-time business. Gaining legitimacy and trust among customers is discussed in Chapter 3. Three other key aspects remain: determining what you are able to delegate, the special ethical challenge that comes from juggling part-time entrepreneurship and other work, and the challenge you face when you try to move from part-time to full-time entrepreneurship.

Delegation and Outsourcing

For part-time entrepreneurs, time is the ultimate resource. While the most successful entrepreneurs in high-growth ventures are those who learn to get and leverage other people's money (OPM), for entrepreneurs in part-time businesses the key is leveraging other people's time (OPT). There are two major ways to do this—delegation and outsourcing. **Delegation** happens when you assign work to those over whom you have power, usually people you employ, those volunteering to help you out, or family members. When you employ outsiders who are not your employees to handle all or part of a functional area of your business, it is known as **outsourcing**.

delegation
The assignment of work to others over whom you have power.

outsourcing
Contracting with people or companies outside your business to do work for your business.

Delegation makes sense in two situations. The first is when others can do things better than you. For example, an entrepreneur who is a wizard at sales may be totally lost doing the books. The second is when you want your business to operate when you are not present, or operate in two places at once. If you have two people working in a store, you could be selling to two customers at once. Done well, delegation frees the owner to pursue those things that make the biggest difference in the business—key sales, strategic thinking, negotiating, or inventing. It is a powerful concept, and there are several tips that can help make any delegation effort more successful.[57]

- Start delegation with simple tasks to get you and your employees used to the process.
- Match the task to the person with the best skills and attitude for it.
- Solicit questions from your employees about the delegated work.
- Attach a motivating outcome to the delegated work—a chance to learn new skills or demonstrate leadership, increased visibility, or an opportunity to see more of the business or its customers.
- Allow time for the employees to learn the task and correct the inevitable early mistakes.
- Give employees feedback about their performance soon after they start.
- Hope for perfection in performance, but be satisfied with good enough.
- Once delegated, do not take back responsibilities. When problems arise, remedy them, rethink your approach, and retrain the employee.

Delegation is not for everyone and every situation. It makes the most sense when you have people who are good at their jobs and trustworthy, but with some additional steps, delegation can work in less than optimal situations. Even with these tips, being able to delegate depends on the owner's ability to trust others and on the quality of the people to whom the owner can delegate. When delegation is essential but it is hard to trust employees, checking up on an unpredictable schedule helps keep the employees on their toes and provides maximum assurance to the owner. When trust is high but employees lack skills, the owner should allow time to train them and monitor their work—frequently at first, but less often as they prove they know their jobs.

As noted earlier, when you employ outsiders who are not your employees to handle all or part of a functional area of your business, it is known as outsourcing. The most popular types of outsourcing among small businesses are shown in Figure 5.6.

FIGURE 5.6

Functions That Small Businesses Often Outsource

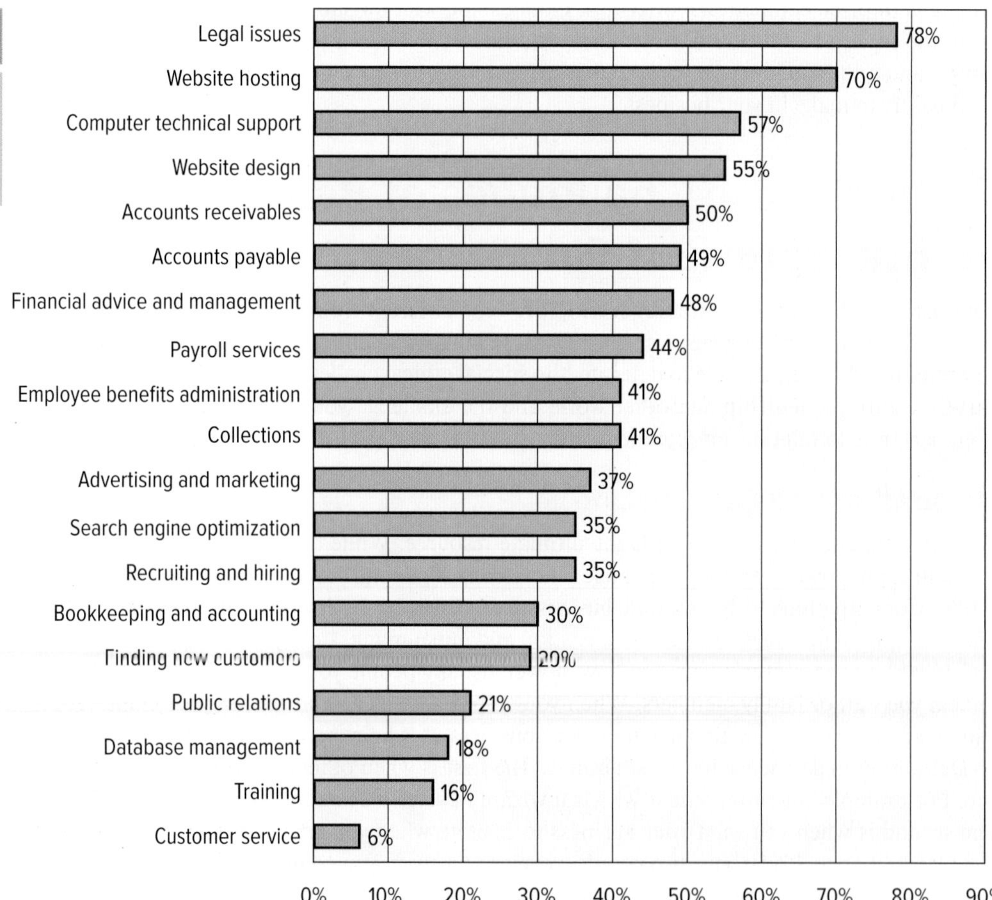

SMALL BUSINESS INSIGHT

Gourmet Gatherings[58]

Bibby Gignilliat has bounced from job to job. She was a programmer, bookseller, travel agent, bike tour guide leader, public relations representative, and marketing manager before she started as a cook teaching for HomeChef and later on San Francisco television. Her prior skills equipped her for a special project, using cooking as part of a team-building exercise for a group of lawyers, and later for a group of 40 businesspeople. This led to the idea for Gourmet Gatherings, which provides culinary entertainment "designed to inspire conviviality, camaraderie and confidence in people who appreciate good food."

Armed with a strong network of contacts, Bibby partnered with longtime friend Shannan Bishop (their fathers were partners in a brokerage business). Bibby's varied experience had an interesting side effect—she knew all the kinds of work she did not want to do. So she and Shannan outsourced every function of the business except the recipes and menus and leading the gatherings. Their financial, marketing, legal, and web work were all outsourced. They describe their role as "conducting a symphony of specialists" and argue that they could never have grown if they had to do everything themselves. Besides, it was the cooking that was fun, not the bookkeeping.

In the nineteenth and twentieth centuries, the idea behind automation was to save time. If you can get a computer program or another company to do work instead of you, you save time and that is good. Figure 5.6 shows that the most technical aspects of a business–issues such as law, computers, or financial records–are the areas in which outsourcing is most likely to occur. This provides some insight into how to think about outsourcing. In areas in which expertise is hard to come by, changes frequently, or is an important support to the functioning of the firm, it makes sense to outsource. The other key idea for outsourcing is to never outsource what *defines your distinctive competence*, what you think makes your business unique. Consider the example of Gourmet Gatherings in the Small Business Insight.

Gourmet Gatherings's "symphony of specialists" suggests the kind of careful involvement and oversight needed to make outsourcing work. Activities that are central to the strategy of the business, like cooking and running the cooking groups for Gourmet Gatherings, stay inside the firm. Activities that are not strategically critical are outsourced, especially when they can be done better or more cheaply by outside firms.

Ethics and Part-Time Small Business

LO **5-7** Identify the ethical challenges of part-time entrepreneurship.

It is impossible to gain legitimacy for your small business if your ethics are in question. There are two situations in which part-time entrepreneurs are particularly at risk: moonlighting and aggrandizing.

Moonlighting

Often, the most successful small businesses build from the business expertise and personal contacts of the entrepreneur. However, managing this without offending your current employer, or getting into legal or contractual trouble, is not easy. Working on your own part time after your regular job is called **moonlighting**, and it poses particular risks.

The major concerns are conflict of interest, cannibalizing sales, and poisoning the well. Conflict of interest crops up when people do work for their part-time business while they are at their full-time job, blurring the boundary between them. **Conflicts of interest** happen when what is best for your part-time business is different from what is best for your full-time employer or when people cannot be sure which of the two firms you represent. The key is to keep your full-time and part-time jobs clearly separate. For example, do not contact customers of your part-time business when you are at your full-time job.

moonlighting
Working on your own part time after your regular job.

conflict of interest
A situation in which a person faces two or more competing standards or goals.

cannibalizing
Taking business away from your employer.

Cannibalizing means taking business away from your employer. This can come from your taking sales away from your employer or taking working hours away to do your own business. This is a real problem if your part-time business is similar to your full-time occupation; for example, if you are a painter for a building contractor in your day job and do similar sorts of painting as your part-time moonlighting enterprise. In such cases, the usual course is to get your employer's approval at the start. This, however, may be easiest to get when the kinds of work you are doing, or the kind of clients you have, are *not* like those at your day job. In fact, it is often possible to get your boss to refer customers to you when they fit your type of schedule, pricing, or type of work a little better than that of the bigger enterprise.

poisoning the well
Creating a negative impression among your employers' customers.

Poisoning the well refers to creating a negative impression among your employers' customers. If you use your business contacts through your day job as the basis for your part-time self-employment, you will inevitably find some customers who do not want to hear your sales pitch. If, because of this, they tell your employer they are less likely to buy from him or her, your part-time business has hurt the full-time one. The traditional work-around for this is to develop a separate customer list without names from your full-time job and then wait for your employers' customers to ask you about this other business they hear you've started.

Aggrandizing

aggrandizing
Attempting to make your business or yourself seem more accomplished or grander than reality.

For a part-time small business, achieving legitimacy and business respect can become a driving force. Occasionally, the entrepreneur sees an opportunity that is possible, but a stretch. If it looks like a stretch to the customers, the entrepreneur may start thinking about making the firm seem bigger, more substantial, or more capable than it really is. This misleading impression, called **aggrandizing**, can spell the death of a firm if discovered at an inconvenient time. As discussed in the following Small Business Insight, this was the lesson Jeremy Barbera encountered in the early days of his business.

Jeremy "got away with it." He lied quickly and easily, no one checked up on his firm, and he was able to meet his obligations. However, if his aggrandizing had been exposed before he could prove himself, he would have lost all credibility. Jeremy says that an entrepreneur has to take risks to get ahead. When he started his firm, checking up on a firm required time-consuming investigations or credit reports, so Jeremy's risk was perhaps not so great. Today, with credit reports and business directories available online in seconds, the potential for being found out is much higher, and the risk is greater.

The most typical form of aggrandizement is implying that a firm is full time when it is only part time. Recall from Chapter 3 that it is hard for a part-time firm to achieve the legitimacy of a full-time firm, and there can be a strong temptation to make the firm sound like it is a regular nine-to-five business. Remember that in the end, however, the biggest risk is that of losing the trust of your current and potential customers. In a small business, especially a part-time one, the owner *is* the business. If you cannot trust the owner, you cannot trust the firm.

LO **5-8** Describe the challenges of moving from part-time to full-time entrepreneurship.

Moving from Part-Time to Full-Time Entrepreneurship

Some people start their businesses part time with hopes of moving to full-time operations when the time is right. For them, landing a major contract or sale may be the financial and marketing indicator of the right time. Others start part time and want to stay that way, and they can face challenges when they achieve success. The strains of producing goods or services for a voracious market can make staying part time difficult.

In deciding whether to make the move to full time, the key question is usually financial. If you are already employed full time somewhere else, the move to full-time entrepreneurship means taking a close look at your financial situation. Can you afford to go on your own? This means having enough to cover personal and family expenses (typically for six months), as well as business expenses (see the following Small Business Insight). There may also be new costs, as you scramble to replace employer-provided health insurance.

The way to determine the financial situation of a business is through crafting a business plan such as the one you will learn about in Chapter 8. Having a business plan helps you work out all

SMALL BUSINESS INSIGHT

METRO SERVICES GROUP INC.[59]

Trained as a physicist and employed by the National Aeronautics and Space Administration (NASA), Jeremy Barbera started Metro Services Group Inc. as a part-time business at his kitchen table with his "partner," his mutt Luka. Of the $900 he invested in the business, $200 went to rent a Madison Avenue mailing address at a local incubator to help his business look more professional. Selling direct marketing services to financial and entertainment firms, Jeremy was a one-person operation, but he consistently stretched the truth. For example, he used "we" and "us" when talking about the firm. He would promise a prospective client to have his secretary type up the proposal and courier it over before 5 P.M., but it was Jeremy who did both.

This once came close to backfiring. Jeremy had delivered the proposal in the afternoon, dressed as a delivery person, and reappeared the next morning for the follow-up meeting with the CEO, this time attired in suit and tie. An alert security guard informed the CEO's office that the delivery man claims to have a meeting with the CEO. Jeremy told the guard and CEO that the delivery man was his brother, down on his luck. Jeremy's favorite line was, "It all depends on the light you portray yourselves in." Jeremy made MSGI look bigger than it was until it landed its first contract—with American Express.

the major details of the business and how you plan to organize it as you are growing it. For example, Nancy Bombace of Mill Valley, California, took the time to do a business plan before taking her part-time honeymoon registry service, HoneyLuna, full time. By doing the plan, she learned she needed to keep her full-time job and run HoneyLuna on the side to make ends meet.[60] In addition, bankers, lawyers, big corporate customers, consultants, and potential investors will ask you for your business plan, so it makes sense to do one to show you have done your homework in starting a full-time business.

There are several ideas to keep in mind to help in this transition. First, it often makes sense to wait until there is a solid income likely for the business before moving over to full time. Second, make use of any transition services your former employer offers, such as COBRA health coverage (look at www.dol.gov/dol/topic/health-plans/cobra.htm to get information on this from the U.S. government). Third, recognize that initially at least you will spend nearly all your time running and marketing the business, so it makes sense to change over when your family and personal obligations are at their lowest and support from family and friends is at its highest.

Often people move into full-time entrepreneurship by building their part-time work to longer hours, until they have, in effect, two full-time jobs. Done this way, sleep, family, and personal time take a hit, but as a financially secure way to operate, the two jobs approach is great when done for short periods.[61]

Like the work of Nancy Bombace, Jeremy Barbera, or Courtney Hennessey Hopson, part-time entrepreneurship is around you all the time. Millions of people are working at part-time businesses of their own. Whether in retail or wholesale, selling services or products, they or their wares are in our stores and our markets, on our streets, and in our homes. Part-time entrepreneurship is important because it gives people a chance to learn the ropes in business and to test out their ideas. It also is often the only way people can engage in entrepreneurship amid their other responsibilities. Part-time entrepreneurship is important as a test bed for starting full-time, larger firms and as a means of self-reliance and self-expression. However, as long as a few minutes online or simply saying "I can do that for you" to a neighbor is all it takes to start a part-time business, it will remain an option that lots of potential entrepreneurs are certain not to overlook.

CHAPTER SUMMARY

LO 5-1 Describe when and why part-time businesses are important.

- Part-time businesses are important because the majority of new business start as part-time businesses.
- They are important because almost half of operating businesses are part time enterprises.

LO 5-2 Describe the conditions that make part-time entrepreneurship a good decision.

- It is a good decision when you need to gain basic experience.
- It is a good decision when you lack the resources for a full-time business.
- It is a good decision when you face a narrow window of opportunity.
- It is a good decision when you are concerned about the demands of going into full-time business.

LO 5-3 Describe the kinds of part-time entrepreneurship that exist.

- Businesses may be operated part time in any industry from accounting to zookeeping.
- Many part-time businesses are conducted from the entrepreneur's home.
- Most home retail businesses, such as home parties or network selling are operated on a part-time basis.
- Many other part-time businesses work from mobile offices, virtual offices, executive offices, and business incubators.
- Websites providing information or entertainment may be part-time businesses.
- E-commerce, including eBay and Amazon sellers, is often a part-time business.
- Pop-up businesses are usually part time.
- Services such as sales agents may be done on a part-time basis.
- Stand-based businesses, such as roadside stands, flea markets, farmers' markets, and fairs, are normally operated part time.

LO 5-4 Describe the key factors to making a decision to go into part-time entrepreneurship.

- You should consider the cost that will be required to start a part-time business.
- You should consider the amount of your time needed to start up your part-time business.
- You should consider the permanence of the business you are creating.

LO 5-5 Use the BRIE model to describe what it takes to be successful in part-time entrepreneurship.

- Use the BRIE model to help identify key boundary and exchange issues.
- *Boundary*—you need to manage your time carefully and keep business and home separate.
- *Exchange*—you will need to register with the government, pay your taxes, and comply with zoning regulations. You will also need to keep careful track of your costs including the cost of your own time.

LO 5-6 Describe the advantages and pitfalls of delegating and outsourcing.

- Delegation is getting others to do your work. It can help an entrepreneur get more done.
- Managing the delegated work and the people performing it is a key challenge for the entrepreneur.
- Outsourcing is paying experts to take on the functional tasks of your business.
- You may outsource to experts anything but the tasks that make your firm unique.

LO 5-7 Identify the ethical challenges of part-time entrepreneurship.

- The two ethical challenges of part-time businesses are moonlighting and aggrandizing.
- Moonlighting can result in cannibalizing sales from your employer or poisoning the well by making your employer's customers angry.
- Aggrandizing can happen when a part-time firm tries to present itself as a full-time one or a bigger one than it really is.

LO 5-8 Describe the challenges of moving from part-time to full-time entrepreneurship.

- The key challenges of moving to full-time self-employment are mainly financial.
- Do a business plan to assess your financial situation in the new business.
- When you make the move, do it when support from your family and previous employer are at their strongest.
- Consider increasing part-time work hours until you are working two full-time jobs, and then quit to devote your time to your full-time business.

KEY TERMS

part-time employment, 120
full-time employment, 120
pop-up business, 121
episodic business, 121
hybrid entrepreneurship, 121
part-time business, 121
volatility, 122
zoning laws, 125
covenant, 125
variance, 125
e-commerce, 129
informational website, 129
business-to-consumer (B2C), 129
business-to-business (B2B), 129
consumer, 129
blog, 131
RSS feed, 131
tweet, 131
multichannel marketing, 132
reciprocal link, 132
search engine optimization (SEO), 132
sponsored link, 132
reverse auction, 135
reserve price, 136
home party, 139
door-to-door selling, 140
network marketing, 140
venue, 142
incubator, 143
maker, 143
intellectual property (IP), 144
cost to start up, 145
time to start up, 145
permanence, 145
registration, 147
licensing, 147
delegation, 147
outsourcing, 147
moonlighting, 149
conflict of interest, 149
cannibalizing, 150
poisoning the well, 150
aggrandizing, 150

DISCUSSION QUESTIONS

1. What are the three situations in which it might make more sense to go into business part time rather than full time?
2. If you were going to start a home-based consulting business in a dorm room, what do you think would be the greatest challenge to face? What about if you were starting the same business from home?
3. The two major types of business websites are informational and e-commerce. What are the differences between them?
4. Is it possible to sell products on eBay without having an online store? What would be the advantages and disadvantages of doing so?
5. How would you use multichannel marketing to promote your part-time businesses? If you had to use one of the non-free approaches, which would you choose and why?
6. What are the differences between home party and door-to-door retailing?
7. When managing your time using a to-do list, how do you go about prioritizing the list? Why?
8. What kinds of tasks do small businesses most often outsource? Why do you think they are popular tasks to give to others?
9. Of the two ethical problems prevalent to part-time small businesses (moonlighting and aggrandizing), which do you think is the biggest problem for entrepreneurs? Why?

EXPERIENTIAL EXERCISES

1. Search for art fairs in your area using Google Maps. In the search box type "art fair" (leave off the quotes when you type) and the city and state you are checking on. When you look at the results, try the links for category searches to see if you get a narrower set.
2. Check the kind of licensing you need for a part-time business in your state. Go to **www.sba.gov/starting-business/business-licenses-permits**. Note that there are several different types of permits, licenses, and certifications needed from nearly every level of government. So start by looking at "Federal licenses and permits." See what requirements (if any), your type of firm has. Then click on "State licenses and permits" and select your state. The SBA site has links to the state office in charge of business licensing.
3. Research pricing your product or service electronically. Go to **eBay.com** (if you are selling a product) or **Upwork.com** (if you are selling a service) and enter the term for your product or service. From the resulting list, note the offerings that most closely match yours and check the prices posted. If possible, look for recent sales or contracts for your offering to see what people paid for the goods or services.
4. Create your own first-pass customer base. List family members; friends; people you know from religious, fraternal, civic, and school organizations; and people who provide you goods and services. Look at the list again and select five people who you think are most likely to know the kind of person you would imagine would make your best customer.
5. Create a to-do list for the upcoming week using the technique described in the chapter. Prioritize your tasks using the 1-2-3 method, and use the list for a week. Ask yourself if you felt having the list helped you remember better what you had to do and if it helped you better decide what to do and when to do it.
6. Do a Google search for "pop-up business guides." See if you can find a guide for your city or state. If not, what kind of help do you find?

MINI-CASE

TIM HAYDEN'S LAST VACATION

In the four years since missing St. Louis Cardinal Mark McGwire's 70th home run in St. Louis's Busch Stadium in 1998, Tim Hayden had been toying with the idea of creating some sort of electronic device to let people attending a sports event enjoy the same sort of video and informational graphics that people who watch the game at home enjoyed. He even figured out the technology needed. He would use a PDA with Wi-Fi capabilities, "hardened" through its construction and tough case to be able to withstand liquids and the kind of rough handling you would expect among spectators at a sporting event. He would call it SkyBOX. In his spare time, he pursued the SkyBOX idea with sports managers, advertisers, computer people, and with everyone he met.

A tech-savvy marketing manager by trade, Tim knew what the user interface would look like. Having no budget for his part-time business, he had to talk friends into putting together a flash graphic of what his service would look like. He had also thought about how he could make money with SkyBOX, and how he could get the major sports leagues to support the product.

Meanwhile, he continued his day job as the director of marketing and sales for a local advertising firm. He knew to make SkyBOX work he would need to leave his employer, but he wasn't sure how to decide. He was making good money and liked his work, but he was also likely to get moved from straight salary to more of a commission basis to help grow the business. He had a girlfriend. A lifelong St. Louisan, he had an active social life with his friends. He was close to his family, and they lived nearby.

The moment of truth came during a vacation Tim and his parents took in the summer of 2002 to visit family in Florida. Trading introductions around a pool, the man to Tim's right turned out to be the entrepreneur who founded the multimillion-dollar Val-Pak mailer business, Terry Loebel. Hearing about SkyBOX from Tim, Terry was relentless: "What's your business model?" "What's in it for the league and teams?" "Are you the right person to carry this off?" Under the hot sun, beers in hand, Tim and Terry went back and forth. In the end, Terry gave Tim a look that said, "You done good kid." A little while later, Terry left.

For the rest of the afternoon, Tim kept thinking, "I did it. I really did it!" He held his own and showed off his business well enough to impress a very successful entrepreneur. He knew his business, and he knew his stuff. Maybe he was ready to go for it full time.

Over dinner, he mentioned his experience to his parents—a corporate entrepreneur and a self-employed HR consultant. Suddenly a raft of questions hit him he wasn't prepared for, questions like "What will you live on?" and "What about your girlfriend?" With a lot more difficulty than that afternoon, Tim started answering questions. As he got more into it, he felt maybe he was on top of the personal dimension of the prospect of going full time.

CASE DISCUSSION QUESTIONS

1. People talk about entrepreneurs depending on luck. Tim saw Terry Loebel only that one time. Their conversation was one of the factors leading Tim to decide to go full time, starting his business as "Vivid Sky" with the initial product, "SkyBOX." Was it luck on Tim's part? Was there anything Tim was doing to improve his luck?
2. Tim had concentrated on mastering the business and technology angles of the SkyBOX, but was slightly taken aback when asked about how his personal life would change if he went into entrepreneurship full time. If you were contemplating a full-time entrepreneurial career, what are some of the personal considerations you think might be important?
3. Why would Tim's employer's plan to change business directions make becoming a full-time entrepreneur more attractive?
4. Tim felt he needed to go full time to take the SkyBOX "to the next level." Can you think of ways he could have continued building up the SkyBOX while sticking with a part-time approach? What would have been the downfalls?

CHAPTER

6

Small Business Entry: Paths to Entrepreneurship

● Paul Hedrick, born and reared in Texas, used his Harvard economics degree and skills learned at McKinsey & Co. and L Catterton Partners to create a new model business for providing high-quality cowboy boots at moderate prices. Paul Hedrick's Tecovas offers a selection of cowboy boot styles for men and women.
Hero Images/Getty Images

LEARNING OBJECTIVES

After you complete this chapter, you will be able to:

LO 6-1 Describe the strategies for going into an entrepreneurial business on a full-time basis.

LO 6-2 Describe five ways that people get into small business ownership.

LO 6-3 Compare the rewards with the pitfalls of starting a new business.

LO 6-4 Compare the advantages and disadvantages of purchasing a business franchise

LO 6-5 Compare the advantages and disadvantages of purchasing an existing business.

LO 6-6 Explain four methods for purchasing an existing business.

LO 6-7 Explain the issues of inheriting a family-owned business.

LO 6-8 Describe how hired managers become owners of small businesses.

LO 6-9 Identify the choices for exiting a business.

Focus on Small Business: Paul Hedrick, How I Got into This Business

After graduating from Harvard, Paul Hedrick took the conventional route for economics majors and accepted a job on Wall Street. After a while, he moved back to Texas where he was a management consultant. This led him to work for a private equity firm which took him back to New York. He was still dissatisfied, however, and soon was considering ways that he could go into business for himself.

The defining moment was the result of treating himself to a pair of high-quality cowboy boots. He was shocked at the price. They were the most expensive single item of clothing that he owned. He realized that there was a competitive opportunity to offer high-quality boots at a much lower price. With this realization Paul quit the job in New York and moved to Austin, Texas, and began planning for his new venture.

After several months of investigating the possibilities for direct-to-consumer selling of boots through vending at fairs, expos, trunk shows, and, of course, online he decided to take the plunge. His extensive research had disclosed that the leather and bootmaking capital is Léon, Mexico. He made an arrangement with an artisanal bootmaker and Tecovas, Inc. was in business.

For the next four years, Paul ran Tecovas as a one-person shop. Most of his sales were made online, but he also worked filling his car with boxes of boots and selling direct to customers at various events and weekend markets. At first he provided all capital for his start-up from his personal savings. But, as his business grew, more capital than he could provide became necessary to allow the business to succeed. In the fall of 2017, Paul received an investment of $2.6 million from an angel investor in order to expand his operations and to hire the necessary employees.

Today, Paul has expanded his product line to include men's jeans, leather luggage, and accessory items. All sales are direct-to-customer and made online.

DISCUSSION QUESTIONS

1. How did Paul Hedrick discover his entrepreneurial opportunity?
2. Would Tecovas have become successful more quickly if Paul had used angel and venture capital earlier?

3. Why does it make sense for a seller of high-quality boots to use online selling, exclusively?
4. What advice would you give to Paul Hedrick?

LO 6-1 Describe the strategies for going into an entrepreneurial business on a full-time basis.

Planning a Path into Business

Let's start with the assumption that you have decided to go into business for yourself.

OK, how will you accomplish this? What business do you want to enter? If you are a licensed electrician, becoming an independent subcontractor makes sense. If you are an accomplished cook and love preparing for and serving people, perhaps you might want to be in the restaurant business. If you are an experienced coder, it may be that creating a new app is your opportunity. Whichever set of talent, skills, and expertise you have, the path forward seems pretty clear: (1) choose your industry, (2) create a product or service, (3) test its feasibility, (4) determine the market, and (5) forecast sales and costs and from these specify the resources that you will need to turn your dream into reality.

causal (predictive) reasoning
The process of setting a goal and then determining the strategy and resources required to attain the goal.

As we described in Chapter 4, this form of planning is called **causal or predictive reasoning.** Causal reasoning has been the strategy for starting innumerable businesses and it is the method taught in almost every entrepreneurship class around the world. Causal reasoning is used to create a business plan. It is the type of reasoning that is used by business managers daily for making many business decisions, including such decisions as whether to buy or to make a product, enter or leave a particular market, and hire full-time or temporary employees. One great advantage of this type of reasoning is that it can be used in either case of going into business–that is, predictive reasoning is a useful technique regardless of whether you want to do business part time or full time.

But we know that business school entrepreneurship is not the only way to get into a successful business. As we also discussed in Chapter 4, many successful entrepreneurs have shown that they use a "backward" reasoning that was named **effectual reasoning** by Saras Sarasvathy of the University of Virginia.[1] Effectual reasoning begins with a consideration of what resources are available and what restraints there are on those resources. See the following Small Business Insight.

effectual reasoning
A logical process in which one analyzes the resources available and restraints on the use of resources to create an attainable goal.

If you think back to the PROFIT model in Chapter 3, you will realize that all entrepreneurs have at least four sets of resources immediately available to them: (1) financial–access to capital, (2) organizational–their own skills and abilities, (3) technological–their own knowledge, and (4) relational–their network of friends and business associates. An entrepreneur is using effectual reasoning when he or she begins to imagine what can be accomplished with the resources at hand. Ideas are evaluated for viability, often in a very small way that presents little risk of financial loss. Ideas that work lead to better ideas, plans, and goals. Ideas that fail are improved or thrown away. As the entrepreneur learns from experience and from interaction with customers, vendors, and mentors, it all comes together as a compelling story that serves to enlist others, create buzz, and bring the business to life.

Saras Sarasvathy has defined three principles that are critical in the process of effectual reasoning:

- Affordable loss
- Strategic partnerships
- Leveraging of contingencies

affordable loss
The minimum possible expenditure of capital and other resources in order to bring an entrepreneurial idea to market.

Affordable loss is the practice of bringing your product or your service to market with the minimum expenditure of capital, effort, and time. As Allen Lim and Ian MacGregor did, entrepreneurs who practice effectual reasoning will attempt to sell a product or service to some customer before it is even complete. They reason that if someone will buy it now, it must be at least potentially viable. Also, they will learn from both the selling process and the use that the customer has for the product. If the idea is a bomb, then the entrepreneur can walk away with very little loss and go on to the next idea without losing more than can be afforded.

SMALL BUSINESS INSIGHT

The Scratch Labs Story: Effectual Reasoning at Work

While Allen Lim, who holds a PhD in exercise physiology, was working with professional bikers as the team physiologist for Team RadioShack, he noticed that many of the riders complained about the sports drinks being used making them sick. When he found that diluting the drinks did not alleviate the problem, he began adding Alka-Seltzer Gold tabs (basically sodium citrate) to the diluted drinks. This did improve the situation, and Allen decided to do some further experimenting.

Allen Lim, cofounder and owner, and Ian MacGregor, cofounder and CEO of Skratch Labs.

Mary Mecklenburg

He teamed with Ian MacGregor, a retired American road racer with two Under 23 bicycling National Road Race championship wins. Together, they began to experiment with creating their own sports drink mix, aiming to create a recipe that first was an effective hydrator, second tasted good, and third did not make users ill.

Soon they had a formula that did all three, and they began making and distributing the mix. Initially, they used food-grade plastic buckets and a borrowed paint agitator to make the mix. This manual process was not sufficient to meet growing demand for the product, but neither could they find a commercial producer who would make the product for them in the relatively small quantity that they could sell.

This quandary was answered by a bit of good luck. Lim happened to meet Andy Rodriguez, president of All American Seasonings who just happened to be a bicycling enthusiast. Although Skratch Labs needed quantities that were not large enough to be economical for All American Seasonings to make, Rodriguez agreed to a trial contract, with Lim throwing in a deal sweetener in the form of a yellow jersey from the 2006 Tour de France autographed by Floyd Landis.

With the guarantee of sufficient product, Lim and McGregor continued their guerrilla marketing, going as far as handing out samples to bicyclers heading north out of Boulder, Colorado, on training rides.

Today Skratch Labs has a full line of hydration products, energy bars and chews, recovery mix, and of course, tee shirts, a cookbook, and gear for serious athletes.[2]

Jasmine Adams's business plan for her start-up, Smudgies, wins her $10,000.

©Margaret Fox

strategic partnerships Formal or informal relationships with customers, vendors, or mentors to ensure the success of an entrepreneurial venture.

Strategic partnerships can be either formal or informal relationships with other businesses and individuals who can provide support to your efforts at getting into business for yourself. Creating such partnerships early in the entrepreneurial process is often the key to ultimate success. These partnerships may be created intentionally or through serendipity. Lim and MacGregor provide an example of a strategic partnership that was formed at the point that luck and common sense came together. They were lucky to have met the president of American Seasonings who provided both advice and the first commercial-level production.

leveraging contingencies The practice of and ability to seize upon novel opportunities that become apparent during the conduct of business.

Leveraging contingencies is another way of saying "recognizing and using opportunities." While still in high school, Jasmine Adams just happened upon the nugget of her successful business. As she told the story, because she was a competitive swimmer, she usually had swimsuits lying around in her room. One morning she messed up applying her makeup. In a hurry, she grabbed the closest thing to wipe off the makeup and to clean her hands. That just happened to be an old swimsuit. It proved surprisingly effective, so she took some old swimsuits, cut them into pieces, and sewed the pieces into a double-sided square makeup cleaning cloth. Later she entered a business plan competition and her plan won a $10,000 prize. Today she has a business making the wipes while she attends college in Irving, Texas.[3]

Jasmine saw an opportunity, and she used materials (old swimsuits) and borrowed machinery (her mother's sewing machine) to start her business.

bootstrapping Using low-cost or free techniques to minimize your cost of doing business.

bricolage A word derived from the French verb *bricoler* ("to tinker"). In entrepreneurial usage bricolage refers to the process of analyzing the resources available and creating a product or service from them.

lean business practices An application created by Eric Ries that addresses the specifics of new business creation, particularly Internet-based businesses, where rapid experimentation and constant monitoring of viewers' choices are possible.

There are three other important ideas that fit into both the causal and the effectual approaches to entrepreneurship. These are **bootstrapping**, **bricolage**, and **lean business practices**. Bootstrapping got its name from an old description of a person who began poor and through persistence and self-reliance achieved unlikely success. Bricolage, which comes from a French word that means "to putter around," is the practice of making something from whatever you have at hand. In many ways, bricolage resembles the strategy of effectuation in that it means carefully considering the resources available, and then making something from them. Lean business practices refer to systematically eliminating waste of time, materials, and money throughout a business. The term *lean* first appeared in a 1990 book based on the Massachusetts Institute of Technology's 1980s study on the future of the automobile.[4]

Bootstrapping–finding a low-cost or no-cost way to do something–is especially important for firms early in their lives because one of the major threats to the survival of new firms is undercapitalization.[5] Businesses often run out of money before they become self-supporting. This can happen from a shortage of cash in the business or even from a shortage of cash in the owner's personal life, because for small businesses starting out the business and its owner are often drawing from the same resources.

Lean business practices include a set of tried-and-true methods that can lessen capital requirements and reduce cash outflows from the business. This reduces the financial risk of start-up and early operations when cash is often scarce. Lean and bootstrapping are similar in that both methods stress finding ways to achieve desired business goals and objectives when start-up capital is limited. Both lean operations and bootstrapping are based on and share three underlying ideas:

1. ***Waste not, want not.***[6] That this thought appears in a 1546 book published 18 years before Shakespeare was born tells you just how old this "newest" fashion is. Avoiding waste is one obvious way to achieve this, but so is borrowing something rather than renting it, and renting rather than buying. Making do with an older but free laptop would be another example, as would saving every penny you can.
2. ***Create, standardize, repeat.*** About the same time as Shakespeare was writing his famous plays, shipbuilders in Venice were creating ships made of standard parts. Using standard parts made building subsequent ships much faster and easier. You do this when you make a form letter to solicit customers, when you create a cell phone app that thousands of people can download, or when you buy in bulk to save money. Standardization of business processes leads to significant cost savings, increased competitiveness, and greater customer satisfaction.
3. ***Keep in touch.*** Central to lean business practices is being close to your customer. It helps you know if your product or service is doing its job. It alerts you to problems earlier so you can correct them, and it is just a good business practice in general. Customers and their needs change, and to keep up, you need to keep in touch. As you learn what is needed, adjust your product or service to optimally fit needs. Most cell phone apps get updated every few weeks. This is because as the app makers find out about bugs or glitches, they can fix them and get the fixed version out to users.

But bootstrapping and lean methods are not identical in either how people think about them or in how people actually put them to use. So it is a good idea to examine each method in some detail. We will discuss bootstrapping first. The key ideas of bootstrapping are simple:[7]

- Do without as long as you can.
- Cut your personal and business expenses to the bone (e.g., take no salary, work from home).
- If you need something, see if you can get it for free (like help from SCORE or former professors). If you cannot get it free, then borrow it, barter your time for it, rent it, or lease it before you buy it.
- If you need to buy outside services, consider offering ***equity*** instead of money, but be stingy with this.
- Before you buy anything, see if you can find a lower-cost alternative (e.g., a printing calculator and a lockbox instead of a cash register).
- When you do buy an asset, buy it used or at a deep discount, and always ask if you can stretch out your payments to minimize cash flow.
- If you need money, borrow it from yourself first, then from family, then friends, and after that, borrow from banks, or take credit card advances. Borrow from credit companies only if they are the sole place you can get money.
- Capture the capital tied up in your house by making first or second mortgages to get money for the business. Of course, you should do this only if you are comfortable risking your house.
- Minimize debt by using a cash card like American Express, which requires repayment in 30 days, instead of a credit card.
- Limit credit card purchases and keep your credit balance as clear as possible. Pay off the balance every month, if at all possible.
- And always, *always* keep track of your cash!

The key to making bootstrapping work is maximizing the value of low costs by obtaining free expertise. One way to do this is to set up an advisory board. Zoë Scharf and Joe Fischer, cofounders of Greetabl (see Chapter 7 opening vignette), recognized the value of finding advisers and were surprised at how easy it could be to find experts interested in helping a fledgling business. They were able to obtain lots of help from advisers while keeping their business small.

There are many people from whom you can get free expertise for your business, such as bankers, insurance agents, trade and professional association officers, former or retired entrepreneurs, and public business development organizations such as your local SCORE or Small Business Development Center.

One area of bootstrapping that is growing quickly is the availability of high-quality free software useful for small businesses. For example, 37signals.com, which has now grown into basecamp.com,[8] got started using free open source programs to build applications such as a project management program, which they offered for free over the Internet. Today, a small start-up can get even more of the tools it needs for free.Table 5.3 in the previous chapter lists several examples of such free programs. Note that in many cases you can use web-based programs (using an Internet connection) or have the free programs reside on your personal computer.[9]

For more free software explore the Free Software Directory project (directory.fsf.org/) and sourceforge.net. Note that free programs and websites often have limited support. However, many offer help files and discussion groups, and some offer email support if you can wait a day or more. If you choose a free program, consider picking one that offers pay-as-you-go support as an option, or better yet, bootstrap help by picking software or websites already used by friends.

What are now called lean methods were developed in Japan in the aftermath of World War II. Because consumer demand was very low in the war-ravaged country, manufacturers could not count on obtaining economy of scale through mass production. Nor could the cost of having high levels of inventory be tolerated. In response to these challenges, an engineer at the Toyota Motor Corporation, Taiichi Ohno, developed what came to be called the "Toyota Production System," or TPS. When the principles of TPS were brought to the United States, they were renamed "lean."

The critical insight of lean business practices is the recognition that customers are not willing to pay for everything a company does. If one supplier is wasteful in its production and distribution and attempts to be profitable by pricing its product and service high enough to cover these wasteful costs, other suppliers who are more frugal are given a critical competitive advantage in that they can be profitable at prices lower than those of their wasteful competition.

Those things that people are willing to pay for are called "value added." Things that customers will not pay for are subsequently referred to as "non-value added." It is just the nature of things that non-value-added practices eat up resources without providing any return for the owners of a business. Thus they are waste.

Lean principles started with a statement of seven areas of manufacturing in which non-value-added activities can take place. There are seven sources of the waste that lean management seeks to prevent (see Figure 6.1).

Although lean business practices have been applied to every phase of business operations, the set that you will find most interesting was developed and published by Eric Ries in his 2011 book *The Lean Startup*. The primary focus is to quickly produce what Ries calls a "**minimum viable product**." Of course, this approach applies to services as well as physical product. The minimum viable product is an early version that allows you to very quickly determine if there is a sustaining level of demand for your product. You collect feedback from your early customers, gaining "validated learning" about the business in its earliest days.

minimum viable product
A concept central to lean business practices where you make a minimum product, but one that can be sold. By selling to customers and collecting feedback, an entrepreneur can develop a product at minimum cost.

Ries provides the example of Zappos, the world's largest online shoe retailer. He tells how the founder, Nick Swinmurn, began with a very small experiment to find out if people were willing to buy shoes online. Swinmurn took pictures of shoes in local shoe stores. He then posted these photos online. When a customer ordered a pair of shoes, he went to the local shoe store, purchased the shoes at full retail price, and shipped them to the buyer. In this way, Swinmurn validated the viability of his vision for a business at very little cost and risk to himself.[10]

Because most beginning entrepreneurial businesses have limited resources, including cash, time, and experience, it is important that the resources that they do have be used very carefully.

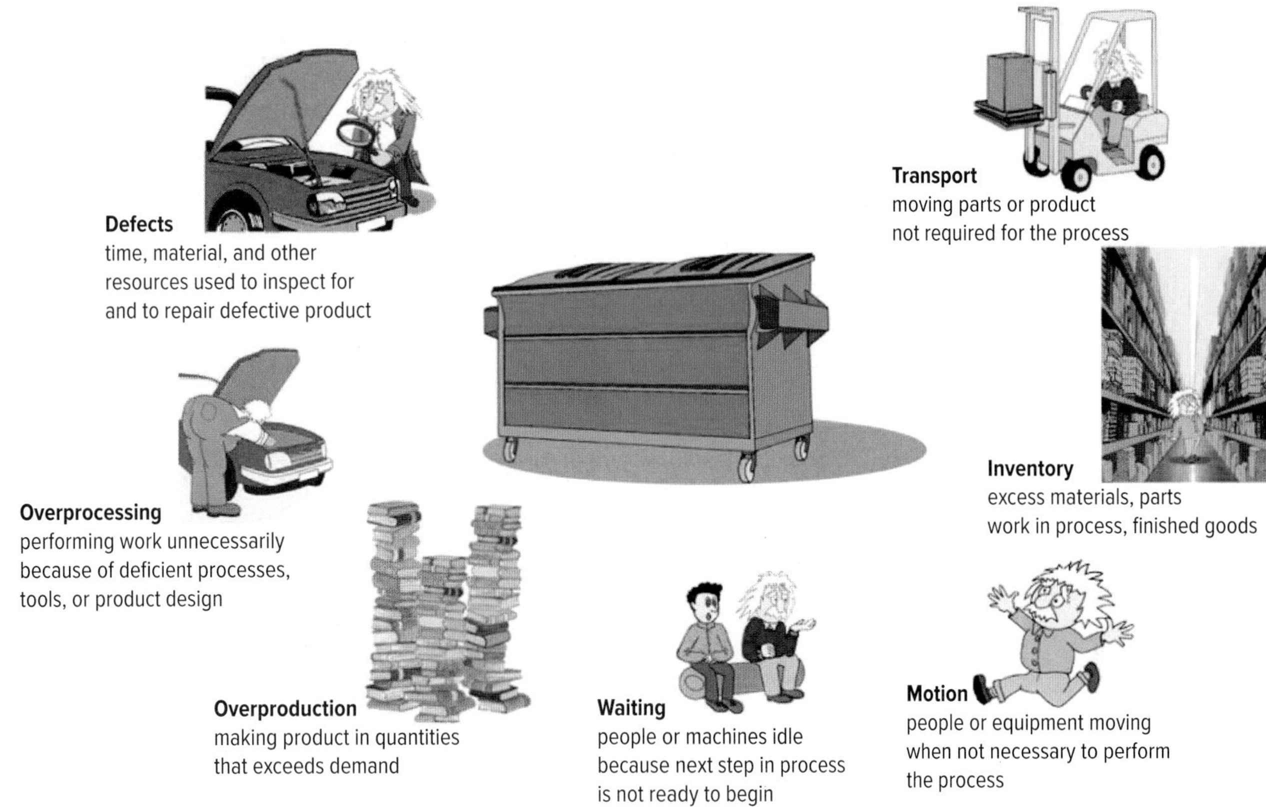
Defects
time, material, and other resources used to inspect for and to repair defective product
Transport
moving parts or product not required for the process
Overprocessing
performing work unnecessarily because of deficient processes, tools, or product design
Inventory
excess materials, parts work in process, finished goods
Overproduction
making product in quantities that exceeds demand
Waiting
people or machines idle because next step in process is not ready to begin
Motion
people or equipment moving when not necessary to perform the process

FIGURE 6.1

Lean Business Practices: Seven Sources of Waste

You can help ensure that you will have enough resources for success by carefully planning how you are going into business, then following the proven techniques of effectual planning, bootstrapping, bricolage, and lean business processes.

LEARN MORE ONLINE

You can learn more about the topics above at these sites:

Reasons for bootstrapping: **www.entrepreneur.com/article/315208**

Introduction to lean, six sigma, and lean six sigma: **www.greycampus.com/blog/quality-management/a-brief-introduction-to-lean-and-six-sigma-and-lean-six-sigma**

The Five Paths to Business Ownership

LO **6-2** Describe five ways that people get into small business ownership.

Despite the many unique stories that people tell about how they entered into business, when we examine enough of their stories it becomes evident that there are commonalities among them. In general, we find that every story of business entry can be placed into one of five general paths:

1. The entrepreneur started a completely new business.
2. Purchased franchise rights to an existing business.
3. Bought an already operating business.
4. Worked in a small business and eventually gained ownership.
5. Inherited a business from a family member.

But, of course, this is not the whole story. Starting a business, franchising a business, and buying a business may be done as either a part-time or full-time enterprise. The decision of whether

ACE Hardware: Jill Braaten/McGraw-Hill Education

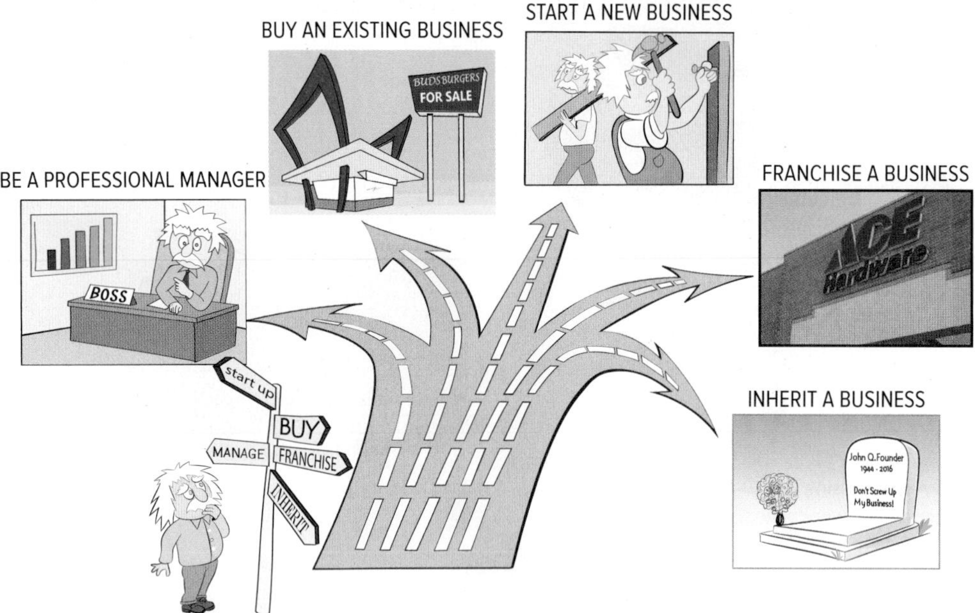

to jump in full time, or to dip your toes in the water by deliberately keeping your business small to start will require making many different decisions–how to plan for the business; how to finance it; what its physical location should be; how you will market it, and many more.

So, let's examine the basics of each of these five paths, then take a look at the pros and cons of starting on a part-time basis, or jumping in full time from the get-go.

LO 6-3 Compare the rewards with the pitfalls of starting a new business.

Starting a New Business

Starting a new business is at once the riskiest path into business and the path that promises the greatest rewards for success. The success rate of start-up businesses is a matter of some controversy. As we note in Chapter 1, numerous rigorous studies have found that fully 69 percent of businesses are still going after 2 years, 51 percent are still going after 5 years, 34 percent after 10 years, and 25 percent are still operating after 15 years.

Also, studies show that those businesses that get help last even longer. Eighty-seven percent of **start-ups** that begin in business incubators are still in operation 5 years later,[11] and the survival rates for students from entrepreneurship programs and entrepreneurs seeking help from Small Business Development Centers are about twice that of businesses in general.[12] Even for those who get help in starting their business, one must admire the courage and optimism of a person who chooses to start a new business (see Figure 6.2). Despite the rather high failure rate,

start-up
A new business that is started from scratch.

FIGURE 6.2

Survival Rate of Start-Up Businesses

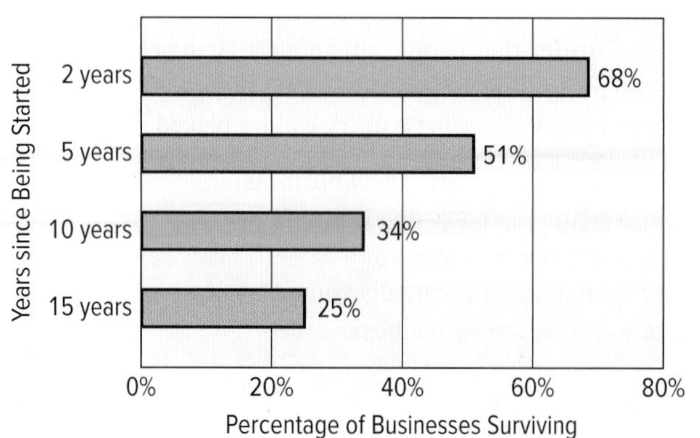

creating a start-up is not, as some maintain, a triumph of hope over reality. Many businesses that end do so not because they failed, but because the owner took advantage of a better opportunity.[13] The rewards, both financial and personal, of starting a successful new business can be most impressive.

Advantages of Start-Ups

There are many reasons that people choose to start a new business rather than purchasing an existing business, franchising, or being an employee:

- When you start a new business, you can "do it your way." There are no existing rules, processes, or culture that will be difficult to change.
- You will begin with a "clean slate." There are no existing employee problems, debts, lawsuits, contracts, or other legal commitments that must be satisfied.
- You have the opportunity to use the most up-to-date technologies. There are no "legacy" locations, buildings, equipment, or software that can hamper productivity.
- You can provide new, unique products or services that are not available from existing businesses or franchises. Existing businesses and franchises exist because of their success in providing proven products and services.
- You can deliberately keep the business small to limit the size of possible financial losses.
- You may take time to perfect your product, services, and processes.

Disadvantages of Start-Ups

Offsetting the advantages of starting a new business are several disadvantages (see the Small Business Insight):

- Your start-up business will have no initial name recognition. The lack of an accepted brand can put off potential customers.
- A start-up will require significant time to become established and provide positive cash flows.
- A start-up can be very difficult to finance. A new business will not have the existing **assets**, sales, and cash inflows that can be used to obtain financing for the business.
- A start-up usually cannot easily gain **revolving credit** from suppliers and financial institutions.
- A start-up may not have experienced managers and workers.
- Your start-up business will be faced with training employees and obtaining management support.

asset
Something the business owns that is expected to have economic value in the future.

revolving credit
A credit agreement that allows the borrower to pay all or part of the balance at any time; as the loan balance is paid off, it becomes available to be borrowed again.

Starting a New Business in an Existing Field

The vast majority of start-up businesses are "me-too" enterprises. The business idea is simply to create another occurrence of a common business: a hair salon, restaurant, bar or lounge, rock band, sign company, plumbing service, yard care, and so on. Starting a copycat business provides some protection from business failure. It is not necessary to define the business to the market because everyone knows what a hair salon, restaurant, or lounge provides.

On the other hand, this type of start-up can be very difficult to differentiate from other similar businesses. Often, the only competitive advantage may be the location of the start-up. This is why owners of common businesses go to so much effort to try to make a difference between their business and other, essentially identical, firms. An example is how Morton's of Chicago and Ruth's Chris Steak House operate. Careful sampling of each firm's steaks reveals no significant difference in price, quality, tenderness, size, or taste. The restaurants have similar menus and wine lists. Each, however, has distinctive interior decorating and presentation of its meals. Morton's brings a selection of huge uncooked steaks to each table for patrons to make their choices. The cooked steaks are served on oversized china plates. Ruth's Chris provides equally large steaks, selected from a printed menu, served on plates that are heated to a high temperature and coated in butter to create the trademark "sizzle."

SMALL BUSINESS INSIGHT

A FAILED START-UP—EVENTVUE

While still in college, Josh Fraser and his roommate, Rob Johnson, were contracted to develop a social networking app for a single business conference. The resulting product used information from the attendees' registration, thus achieving 100 percent inclusion for the conference.[14] Information included profile pictures, biographical information, and tags to allow users to sort on common interests, sessions to attend, and so on.

The partners put together a presentation of proposed features and were accepted by Techstars which provided mentoring and seed capital in the amount of $10,000. One of the mentors, Noah Kagan, agreed to use the product in an upcoming conference that he was producing. This led to a successful angel funding round in which approximately $500,000 was raised.[15]

EventVue was on its way.

But sales did not materialize. The product, as designed, worked only among registered attendees of any specific conference. Although the app was popular with conference attendees, it did not provide conference organizers any financial advantage. Rob Johnson wrote:

> Instead of investing in the production features to [enable] EventVue directly driving people to events (hindsight: mistake), we immediately went out and tried to sell the social network tool to conference organizers.[16]

The firm was rapidly running out of capital. Josh and Rob made a last-minute Hail Mary pass by attempting to address the issue of proving that the app had value for conference organizers who were the actual paying customers. Development proved to be much more difficult than the partners expected. Again they attempted to sell the app "as is," only to see sales remain elusive. As Rob wrote, "It really is too little, too late."[17]

The specific concept that leads to a start-up business usually comes from the experience of the person starting the business. Two-thirds of all start-ups are based on ideas from prior work experience, hobbies, and family businesses.[18] These businesses are generally more likely to succeed than are businesses based on ideas from other sources. Research into the indicators of successful start-ups shows that one of the best predictors of success is the level of experience of the **founders**. Random events, suggestions from friends and associates, and specific education courses are the sources of only a relatively few start-up ideas.

founders
People who create or start new businesses.

Increasing the Odds of Start-Up Success

accelerator
An organization that supports start-ups, typically of a particular type (e.g., Internet, biotech, fashion, sports, women-owned firms, etc.) with a financial investment, free or inexpensive office space, mentoring, a variety of free or low-cost support services, and other resources. The goal of an accelerator is to accelerate a start-up from its early stages to being ready to pitch for investment. Most accelerators take an equity stake in the companies they help.

The probability of creating a successful start-up is increased greatly when the founder has certain attributes and when the founder takes certain actions. Doing the following things has been shown to be the most effective route to success (see Exhibit 6.1).

- **Start the business in a business incubator or accelerator:** Business incubators and accelerators are organizations that provides financial, technical, and managerial help to start-up businesses. Most incubators are associated with economic development agencies, don't take equity in your business and are integrated into the community. Most accelerators take an equity stake in your business in return for a small amount of your stock, and are privately owned. Both connect entrepreneurs to angel investors, public grants for seed money, and technology support.

  Business incubators and accelerators are created to strengthen the local economy by helping create jobs through the establishment of successful small businesses. But incubators do much more than just create new jobs. They aid in the commercialization of new technologies, the revitalization of distressed neighborhoods, and the creation of wealth. The best incubators provide inexpensive office space with full-time on-site managers who

EXHIBIT 6.1

Top 12 Indicators of Start-Up Success

1. Start the business in a business incubator or accelerator.
2. Take part in a mentoring program.
3. Have a detailed start-up budget.
4. Produce a product or service for which there is a proven demand.
5. Secure outside investment.
6. Start with more than one founder.
7. Have experience managing small firms.
8. Have industry experience.
9. Have previous experience in creating a start-up business.
10. Choose a business that produces high margins.
11. Start the business with established customers.
12. Build trust in your "story."

can assist the entrepreneur in many ways. Incubator participants share common office services, such as telephone answering, and production and copying of documents. Perhaps most important, incubators provide legitimacy by furnishing the business with a location and with established business processes.

- **Take part in a mentoring program:** Successful business owners and corporate executives do well by doing good. They can, by helping others, in a way repay the many people who helped them achieve success. Executive volunteers contribute their time and energy to assisting start-up and struggling small businesses as a public service. Because of their experience, mentors can help you avoid mistakes and make good business decisions.
- **Have a detailed start-up budget:** The start-up phase is usually the most difficult time you will have in business. You are required to make myriad decisions concerning location, product, target market, promotion, sales, and all the facets of starting and operating a business. And you must juggle all these demands while simultaneously seeing that you have enough cash. A detailed start-up budget provides a road map for necessary spending during the startup phase, when cash inflows are likely to be small or nonexistent. Companies that carefully plan their start-up activities and avoid any unnecessary spending are much more likely to succeed.
- **Produce a product or service for which there is a proven demand:** It is an unfortunate fact that most new products and services fail to gain acceptance. NewProductWorks of Ann Arbor, Michigan, maintains a "failed product museum" that contains samples of over 73,000 items, all of which were commercial failures. During the dot-com bubble of 1998–2001, many businesses started with novel and completely untested products and services. Examples are Beenz.com, which was started to facilitate Internet transactions; webvan.com and shoplink.com, both of which sold groceries online for home delivery; and estamp.com, which offered online purchasing of U.S. postage, to be printed on the user's printer. All four of these businesses failed to gain success with their products. None of these businesses survived the dot-com bust of 2001, although the domain and patents of e-stamp.com were purchased by the currently operating company stamps.com.

  Large corporations, such as Procter & Gamble or Sony, spend millions of dollars annually testing the market acceptance of new products. Despite their huge resources and years of experience, they regularly introduce products that fail. (Are you old enough to remember "New Coke"?) Your start-up business will not have either the experience or the resources to absorb the loss from product failure. By producing a product or service for which there is a proven demand, the risk of product failure can be reduced or eliminated.
- **Secure outside investment:** Securing outside investment accomplishes two things: First, the process of obtaining investment funds means that your business will be critically examined by outsiders who have no vested interest in your idea, product, or service. Second, the fact

that you were able to convince outsiders to invest in your business indicates a level of belief in the business and you that provides legitimacy.

- **Start with more than one founder:** Starting with more than one founder provides the business with more experience, skills, and resources than can be furnished by a single individual. Having more founders in the business also provides an opportunity for **synergy**, in which the business results are greater than the sum of the input. Multiple founders can also provide a forum for examining ideas, evaluating information, and making good business decisions.

synergy
A combination in which the whole is greater than the sum of its component parts.

- **Have experience managing small firms:** Managing a small business requires attention very much like that displayed by a person spinning plates on sticks. As a performer must move quickly from plate to plate, many demands of small business management require that you have the ability to quickly move from task to task, without allowing any task to ultimately go uncompleted. The process can be overwhelming for inexperienced managers. Those entrepreneurs who have experience in small business management are more likely to be able to meet the many simultaneous demands of guiding a successful start-up than would a person new to small business.
- **Have industry experience:** Each industry has its own peculiarities. Only through experience can you learn the methods, sources, and markets for any specific one. Even simple tasks, such as buying necessary material, can be nearly impossible without industry knowledge. For example, suppose that you plan to start a quality steak house, similar to Ruth's Chris or Morton's of Chicago. Where do you buy prime beef of the required cut and quality? How do you cook the meat? Or, consider making high-tech, lightweight bicycles. Where can you buy titanium tubing? What does it cost? What do you need to cut, shape, and weld it? Are bicycles sold through wholesalers? Are they sold directly to bicycle shops? The less you know about something, the easier it appears to be. A true expert makes a task seem effortless. Watching Tiger Woods play golf might lead you to believe that it is an incredibly easy game. Just stand up, hit the ball, and watch it fly to the green. Sure it's easy: So why do fewer than 2 percent of golfers ever make a course par? The same is true of business. Businesspeople, such as Michael Dell, Scott McNealy, and Warren Buffett, make the process of succeeding in business seem effortless. But if you have been in the business, you know better. Being experienced won't make your start-up easy, but at least you have firsthand knowledge of how your industry works that will make your task easier.
- **Have previous experience in creating a start-up business:** "Nothing succeeds like success." In the 150 years since Dumas made this famous statement, it has come to be an unquestioned part of our language. It is just succinct enough, just truthful enough, to seem like a universal truth. For entrepreneurs, it is fortunate that the statement is also not completely true. Although one may learn from successes, most learners acquire expertise through a process of repetition, which only occasionally results in successes. One study of entrepreneurs who had successfully created a start-up business found that on average an entrepreneur suffered three start-up failures before achieving success. Thus it is more nearly correct to state that no entrepreneur succeeds without having prior experience in failing.
- **Choose a business that produces high margins:** High margins, the amount by which sales prices exceed product costs, provide a buffer for lots of mistakes. The single greatest hurdle to a successful start-up is obtaining and maintaining sufficient cash to support both operations and growth. When margins are low, loss of any one sale or customer has an immediate effect. However, the problem of replacing the lost margin is much easier if you have to make only one or two sales or get one or two new customers to make up for the lost business.
- **Start the business with established customers:** When you start with established customers, you know that you will immediately have cash inflows. There are basically three ways that you can go about obtaining committed customers prior to start-up: (1) You can start your new business as a **spin-off** from your current employer's business, (2) you can start a business to specifically go into competition with your employer, or (3) you can start a business to subcontract services to your employer or to other established businesses.

spin-off
A business that is created by separating part of an operating business into a separate entity.

Creating a spin-off is a regular business practice that is done by businesses of all sizes and at all stages of development. Some spin-offs are created to get rid of "non-core" activities. By disposing of the non-core activity, the parent firm reduces capital requirements and provides a tighter focus for management on the remaining businesses. Other spin-offs are created when the parent lacks either the interest or the resources to pursue the opportunity. By being spun off, the start-up can gain access to resources other than those of the parent.

Going into competition with your current employer is also a common practice. Of course, this almost always results in resentments and often ends in lawsuits over issues of trade secrets, rights to intellectual property, and abridgment of contractual provisions. You will have to make difficult ethical decisions. From a legal point of view, the contract between employer and employee is satisfied when all wages and other benefits have been paid in return for you accomplishing the tasks for which you were hired. Absent a specific contract providing otherwise, neither party, employer nor employee, is obligated beyond this exchange. However, not so easily answered are the questions: (1) Is it ethical to use your employment to build relationships with customers that subsequently can be used to start a new business? and (2) Is it ethical for you to use knowledge and skill received through training and education furnished by your employer to go into business competing with your employer?

Subcontracting services to an existing business is somewhere between doing a spin-off and starting a competing business. Services that are often contracted include sales, janitorial services, accounting, research, and product development. It is a common, accepted practice for the contractual relationship to be created prior to starting a business.

- **Build trust in your "story":** Building trust is essential to the success of all start-ups. You must be able to convince suppliers, employees, and, most importantly, customers that the business is now successful and will be in the future. Not only is there an understandable reluctance for people to be associated with a potential "loser," but customers, vendors, and employees all take risks by doing business with an unknown and unproven start-up.

  Suppliers are often reluctant to deal with start-ups, even if you make your purchases in cash. Most new businesses are small compared to established businesses in the same industry. There is a good reason why you, as the owner of a new business, would prefer to make numerous orders of small quantities of the goods and services you need. Doing so reduces cash flow requirements and reduces the risk of your being stuck with old or obsolete inventory. For the vendor, however, accepting your frequent small orders greatly increases the cost of providing goods and services to you. Most vendors, especially wholesalers, work on very small margins. The cost of accepting and filling numerous orders for a new customer may well make such business unprofitable. It is therefore essential that the vendor believes in your eventual success and that you will become a valuable customer in the future.

  Employees take on significant risks when they go to work for a start-up business. Not only may the start-up fail, but frequently the cash flow problems of start-ups cause payments for wages to be late or missed entirely. This is one reason why so many start-ups offer stock options and stock bonuses to employees. The start-up doesn't have enough cash to pay high wages right now, but if it's successful, employees will share the rewards in the future.

  Customers can similarly be at risk when purchasing from a start-up business. In the event that the start-up fails, there is no recourse for warranty problems, for maintenance, or for upgrades to the product. This risk is especially acute when the product or service of the start-up affects the core business of its customers. For example, the San Antonio Bed & Breakfast Association contracted with a start-up business to develop and maintain a web-based availability and reservation service for the association's members. The start-up failed during the dot-com bust of 2001. When problems with the system subsequently developed, there was no one to fix them. The system was complex and the source code incomprehensible. As a result, the association lost a core service that provided value to its members.

The issue of building trust in your story is a catch-22. If customers, vendors, and employees do not have trust in the entrepreneur and in the business, quite simply, there is no business. However, there must be a business, or you don't need customers, vendors, and employees. There are several ways for a start-up business to build trust and legitimacy, and these are detailed in Chapter 3. Specific examples for the kinds of businesses discussed in this chapter include obtaining a performance bond that will pay vendors and customers if your business fails. Restaurants, lodging establishments, barbers, hair salons, and other businesses that deal with issues of cleanliness as a business requirement can obtain licenses and join industry groups that perform inspections. Displaying licenses and certificates of inspection provides assurance that you are at least meeting minimum standards. Manufacturing businesses and construction businesses may hire engineers to certify design and construction details. Warranty service can be contracted to an independent company that specializes in providing such services. Rigorously maintaining business procedures that ensure on-time delivery of products and services and on-time payment of bills, wages, and loan payments will, in time, result in the start-up being trusted.

LEARN MORE ONLINE

Learn more about the topics above at this site:

U.S. Small Business Administration offers several free online courses about starting and growing a business: **www.sba.gov/learning-center**

LO **6-4** Compare the advantages and disadvantages of purchasing a business franchise

Franchising a Business

What Is Franchising?

franchise
A prepackaged business bought, rented, or leased from a company called a *franchisor*.

Franchising is a legal agreement that allows one business to be operated using the name and business procedures of another. The most ubiquitous **franchise** worldwide is McDonald's, which has over 30,000 restaurants in more than 100 countries. Approximately 85 percent of McDonald's restaurants are owned by independent businesspeople who operate them in a franchise relationship. The remainder are *company stores*, that is, stores that are owned and operated by the McDonald's Corporation.[19] Most franchisors are large businesses, most franchisees small: McDonald's Corporation is a large business; McDonald's franchisees are small businesses.

Franchises are agreements between two entities, (1) the franchisor who sets conditions and standards and who grants operating permissions, and (2) the franchisee, who pays a fee for the rights, and who agrees to abide by the conditions and standards.

Four elements are essential for an agreement to constitute a franchise:

1. The agreement provides the franchisee with a legal right to engage in the business of offering, selling, or distributing goods or services.
2. The agreement provides that the franchisee may engage in business using a marketing plan or system provided by the franchisor.
3. The agreement grants the franchisee use of a brand name, trademark, service mark, logo, or other commercial symbol that designates the franchisee as an affiliate of the franchisor.
4. The agreement requires the franchisee to pay a fee for the right to enter into the business.

The value of a franchise is determined by (1) the rights granted and (2) the cash flow potential to the franchisee. Each of these factors can be highly variable from one franchise to another. There are four basic forms of franchising:

trade name franchising
An agreement that provides to the franchisee only the rights to use the franchisor's trade name and/or trademarks.

product distribution franchising
An agreement that provides specific brand-name products that are resold by the franchisee in a specified territory.

conversion franchising
An agreement that provides an organization through which independent businesses may combine recourses.

1. **Trade name franchising** is an agreement that provides only the rights to use the franchisor's trade name and/or trademarks. Two examples of this are True Value Hardware and Associated Grocers, Inc.

2. **Product distribution franchising** provides the franchisee with specific brand named products, which are resold by the franchisee in a specified territory. Two examples of this type of franchising are Snap-On Tools and auto dealerships.
3. **Conversion franchising** provides an organization through which independent businesses may combine resources. An example is Century 21 Real Estate. Individual real estate businesses combine to create a nationwide brand name and enhanced advertising effectiveness.
4. **Business format franchising** is exemplified by the McDonald's Corporation. A McDonald's franchise includes the right to use McDonald's many trade names, specifications of the product to be sold, operating methods, marketing plan, and national advertising. Franchisees pay to the franchisor both an up-front fee to obtain the franchise rights and a percentage of gross sales.

Buying one of the top franchises, such as Ace Hardware or Jimmy John's Sandwiches, may be the right avenue for starting your own business if you want to lower some of the risks involved. Many franchised firms have been in business for a long time. Ace began business in 1924 and Jimmy John's in 1983. Franchising gives you the opportunity to cash in on an already developed product that has a proven market. However, drawbacks include having less creative control and greater reliance on your parent company's financial status. Does franchising appeal to you? Why or why not?

Jill Braaten/McGraw-Hill Education

In addition, some franchisors, such as Subway (sandwich shops), sell *master franchises* that require opening multiple stores within a specified area. Subway describes these franchisees as being "development agents." Master franchisees are required to open a minimum number of stores within a specified time period, which they may do by selling *subfranchises* within the development area.

Franchising has become the predominant method by which entrepreneurs open new businesses. Depending on who is doing the counting, somewhere between 1 in 10 and 1 in 8 businesses currently operating in the United States are franchised operations. Today, in addition to fast food, nearly every product or service from accounting to zoology is available from franchised businesses (see the Small Business Insight).

The most important reason that franchising has become such a successful way of doing business is that a well-run franchise offers a win–win situation for both the franchiser and the franchisee. Franchisers have the opportunity to experience high growth and rapid market penetration without having the requirement to raise capital in huge amounts and to obtain skilled, experienced managers in large numbers. Franchisees are able to partner with an established business that has proven success.

Franchising provides an entrepreneur with the opportunity to own a small business quickly while avoiding the high risks of a start-up. As we have discussed, starting a new business from zero is very expensive in terms of demands on the entrepreneur. Most start-ups have limited capital resources and very little room to make business mistakes while learning what is needed to make the business succeed. Franchisers have survived their own start-up phase of business and have determined the "recipe" for success. For this reason, franchises (on average) have lower failure rates and shorter times to achieve positive cash flows and business profits.

Advantages of Franchising

Let's take a look at the specific characteristics of franchises that offer such advantages to would-be entrepreneurs.

Having a Fully Developed System of Doing Business

Perhaps the single greatest advantage of a franchise is that it comes with a complete business system. Many franchises are actually "turnkey." That is, the franchiser oversees (or even manages) the selection of location, the construction of facilities, the acquisition and installation of necessary equipment, and the initial inventory with which to open business. Many franchises come complete with computer software for budgeting inventory control, ordering, point-of-sale computerized cash register, and complete accounting application. So, what does the franchisee do? First, the franchisee must, in one manner or another, pay for all these services. Second, the

business format franchising
An agreement that provides a complete business format, including trade name, operational procedures, marketing, and products or services to sell.

Small Business Insight

Entrepreneur's Franchise 500: Number 11 in 2019

James J. Liautaud (Jimmy John) started a sandwich shop in Elgin, Illinois, when he was only 19 years old. He had recently graduated from high school, and in his own words, "I graduated second to last in my high school class, so my options for college were slim to none." His father, an army veteran of the Korean War, wanted Jimmy to enlist. But Jimmy had other plans. He wanted to open a business. Finally, his father made him a deal: Dad would put up $25,000 to start a business. If Jimmy did not make a profit in his first year, then it would be the Army for him.

Jimmy's first restaurant

Courtesy Jimmy John's Franchise, LLC

Jimmy found a garage that had been remodeled for a pizza joint. The building was in Charleston, Illinois, in an area full of bars. Jimmy reasoned that the site was perfect. Charleston is a college town, home of Eastern Illinois University. College students drink in bars. When they drink they get hungry and there was Jimmy—selling gourmet subs.

Jimmy made that first-year profit and soon bought out his dad's share of the business. A few years later he had 160 sandwich shops, most of them franchised. In 2019, Jimmy John's was ranked 11th on the *Entrepreneur* Franchise 500 list and there are more than 2,800 Jimmy John's Sandwich Shops, with the number continuing to rise.[20]

franchisee will be required to complete training to become intimate with the details of the franchise business system. Third, the franchisee will be required to take an active part in opening and operating the franchise business.

Franchise Opportunities

There are more franchises available than you can count. Unlike finding a small business to buy, finding a franchise is easy. Every issue of *Entrepreneur* magazine contains the advertisements of dozens of franchisors eager to sell their franchises to you. Entrepreneur.com, the magazine's website, lists the top 500 franchises. The franchises are listed in rank by the number of new locations opened in the last year. The list of franchises is also broken down into more categories, including:

- Fastest-Growing Franchises
- Top New Franchises
- Best of the Best
- Top 10 Lists
- Top Home-Based Franchises
- Top Low-Cost Franchises
- Top Global Franchises

It is interesting that 8 of the top 10 franchises overall are in the service industry. The other two, which happen to be numbers one and two on the *Entrepreneur* Franchise 500 list, are the fast-food restaurants McDonald's and Dunkin'.[21]

If you don't find one you like in *Entrepreneur*, the Internet contains thousands of resources for identifying franchise opportunities. A Google search of the web using the terms "franchise opportunity" returned 132,000,000 pages.[22] Several of the highest listed pages were the sites of services that offer information concerning franchises of all types. Some offer free services; some charge a fee for information.

Among the 132,000,000 sites listed by Google are two U.S. government agencies, the Federal Trade Commission (FTC) and the Small Business Administration (SBA), a British government site, Business Link (www.businesslink.gov.uk), and an Australian site (Smallbusiness.gov.au). Similar government sources are available around the world.

Franchising's industry association, the International Franchise Association (IFA) (www.franchise.org) maintains a website that contains a database of over 800 franchises. The companies listed range from old familiars such as 7-Eleven stores to the really obscure such as Jetblack and Pop-A-Lock.

Once you've identified a potential franchise, you should perform due diligence, just as if you were buying an operating business. What you are most interested in with franchises is the stability, integrity, and financial performance of the franchisor. You really should interview current franchisees, and you should talk to competing franchisors and their franchisees. If you buy a franchise, you will invest thousands of hours and thousands of dollars. Be sure that it is really an opportunity for you and not just for the franchisor.

Legal Considerations

Before you sign on the dotted line, you should personally study two key documents you always receive from a franchisor—the uniform franchise offering circular (UFOC) and the franchise agreement. The UFOC is a standard document franchises use to explain their operations, requirements, and costs to potential franchisees. You can get a guide to help interpret the UFOC at the Federal Trade Commission site. The franchise agreement is the specific contract signed, often incorporating the information included in the UFOC. Both documents are complex. To make sure you have all your bases covered, it is important to get the opinion of an experienced franchise lawyer. You want to know several things, including (1) if and how you can transfer the franchise license to someone else, (2) how you may terminate the contract, (3) how the franchisor may terminate the contract, and (4) what disclosures you are required to make.

If the contract restricts or prohibits you from transferring the franchise to another or if it requires that you achieve unrealistic results to be able to renew, an unscrupulous franchisor has an opportunity to take over your successful business at a bargain price. Your blood, sweat, tears, and life savings will have gone for naught.

The contract must specify the conditions under which it may be terminated. There have been lawsuits and allegations of fraud against some franchisors because of contract provisions that prohibit the franchisee from terminating the contract, but give the franchisor permission to cancel without specifying cause or giving advance notice. If you can't terminate the contract in the case that the franchisor goes bankrupt, most likely you will also be forced out of business. See the Small Business Insight for an example of what can happen when a franchisor goes bankrupt.

SMALL BUSINESS INSIGHT

WHEN YOUR FRANCHISOR GOES BROKE[23]

Burt Benepal had just received a most unwelcome call. A business colleague reported that American Hospitality Concepts, Inc. had just declared bankruptcy. This news was delivered Friday the 13th, 2004, just before Benepal was to have opened his first-ever Ground Round Grill and Bar restaurant.

Because of the filing, American Hospitality had ordered all company-owned stores closed immediately. Timing could not have been worse for a restaurant. The announcement was delivered just as the Friday evening rush began. Diners were sent home with half-eaten meals in doggie bags. Over 3,000 employees were dismissed without any notice or severance pay. Their final paychecks bounced when they attempted to cash them.

Because he was a franchisee, Benepal did not necessarily have to stop work on his restaurant. However, he was under no illusion about the magnitude of the task facing him if he were to stay in business. He already had committed to a capital investment of $1 million. Would customers come to a restaurant that was involved in a bankruptcy?

"What should I do," he wondered.

In the subsequent weeks, struggling to stay in business, the franchisees organized. They formed a co-op, renegotiated contracts with suppliers, and even introduced a new low-carb menu to capitalize on the Atkins Diet fad. Soon they realized that they were not so bad off. They no longer had to pay royalties or toe the line to meet franchisor requirements. Soon they developed a plan to buy Ground Round out of bankruptcy. On July 7, 2004, their offer to the bankruptcy court was accepted. The franchisees were now the proud owners of Ground Round Grill and Bar, Inc.

What about Burt Benepal?

He finally opened his restaurant in Richmond, California. He opened five months later than he had planned, but at least it was open and successful. Benepal stated that he expected his first full year of sales to be almost $2 million. He was actively searching for a location for his next Ground Round to be opened in 2005. He had plans to open five more before the end of 2006.

In many ways, Benepal was incredibly fortunate. Often when franchisors go bankrupt, franchisees soon follow. Even in the Ground Round case, not all franchisees fared so well. Mike Metz, owner of three Ground Round restaurants in Pennsylvania, had a sales decrease of 20 percent. According to attorney Craig Tractenberg, several franchisees were forced into involuntary bankruptcy. Similar stories of failed franchisors abound. Have you ever heard of Chi-Chi's, Arthur Treacher's Fish and Chips, 50 Flavors in a Tub, Spud Nuts, or Minnie Pearl's Fried Chicken? Probably not, but they represent just a tiny fraction of the scores of failed franchisors who not only went out of business but who took hundreds of franchisees along with them.

Franchising has a long history of unscrupulous and fraudulent operations. Because of the many abuses, the U.S. government and the governments of all 50 states have passed regulatory legislation for franchisors. The minimum disclosure standards that a franchisor must meet are specified by Rule 436 of the Federal Trade Commission. Despite this law, however, abuses and frauds are still being perpetrated. In fact, the third item listed on the SBA's Hot List site is a document that details how to avoid being victimized by scam artists. In college terms, do your homework–know what the opportunity is and who the franchisors are. As is true of purchasing an operating business, caveat emptor.

LEARN MORE ONLINE

Learn more about the topics above at these sites:

Entrepreneur's Franchise Hub: **www.entrepreneur.com/franchises**

Traits needed to be a franchise owner: **www.forbes.com/sites/mikethorne/2018/05/18/do-you-have-what-it-takes-to-be-a-great-franchise-owner/#5f12d42e534d**

Buying an Existing Business

LO **6-5** Compare the advantages and disadvantages of purchasing an existing business.

The second most common way to enter small business management is to purchase an existing business. Buying an existing business has important advantages over creating a start-up. However, purchasing a business has its own unique set of risks.

Advantages of Purchasing an Existing Business

There are some advantages to buying an existing business:

- Established customers provide immediate sales and cash inflows. Because the business is already successful, it has proven that there is sufficient demand for its products and services to operate profitably.
- Business processes are already in place in an existing, operating business. This eliminates the need to hire employees, find vendors, set up accounting systems, and establish production processes.
- Purchasing a business often requires less cash outlay than does creating a start-up. The seller will often provide financing that makes it possible for you to buy the business.

Disadvantages of Purchasing an Existing Business

Disadvantages to buying an existing business include:

- Finding a successful business for sale that is appropriate for your experience, skills, and education is difficult and time-consuming.
- It is very difficult to determine what a small business is worth. The value of a small business can never be known with certainty. You must rely on analyses, comparisons, and estimates.
- Existing managers and employees may resist change. It can be very difficult to convince employees to adapt to new business methods, procedures, and processes that can provide increased profits.
- The reputation of the business may be a hindrance to future success. Sellers are usually reluctant to tell you about problems that the business has. Business owners are especially sensitive about discussing past disputes and lawsuits with vendors and customers.
- The business may be declining because of changes in technology.
- The facilities and equipment may be obsolete or in need of major repair.

Finding a Business to Buy

The first problem you must solve is finding a business for sale. Of course, you aren't looking for just any business. You are looking for one that is right for your own experience, education, and skills. The things that make a business appropriate for you are like those things that help create a successful start-up. The business should be in an industry in which you have experience. It should be producing a product or providing service that is in demand and that has high margins. Perhaps, most importantly, it should have adequate financing available so you can continue operations and make the business grow.

You will greatly increase your chances of finding the right business by using multiple sources. Make some calls: Contact business brokers and ply your own network. You should be actively reading advertising of businesses for sale in newspapers and magazines and on the Internet. You might consider asking your employer if his or her business is for sale. Keep in mind that *every* business is for sale at a high enough price. If you hear of a business that is interesting, contact the owners and ask what it would take to buy it.

Brokers advertise and facilitate the sale of businesses for a fee, usually a percentage of the ultimate selling price. Most states have laws that require brokers to work solely for the interest of the seller and to obtain the highest selling price possible. This creates a conflict of interest between the broker and you. The broker is trying to get the highest price. You're trying to get the lowest.

The quality of broker services ranges from excellent to outright rip-offs. Only a few states have any education or licensing requirements, although some, such as Illinois, do require business

SKILL MODULE 6.1 Finding a Business for Sale

Although all businesses are for sale *if the price is right*, finding that one perfect business is a difficult and time-consuming task. As you will find out by completing this skill task, businesses for sale that are easy to find usually are unsuitable. Businesses that are right for you are downright elusive:

1. Decide what type of business you would be interested in buying. Write a profile of your ideal business to buy, specifying its industry, product or service, size, location, price, and financing.
2. Search the Yellow Pages and the Internet to find business brokers active in your area.
   a. Contact each broker and inquire about businesses that meet your criteria. Be honest in your approach. Do not represent yourself as a serious buyer, unless you are one.
   b. Obtain copies of the information that the broker has concerning the businesses.
3. Search your local newspaper, *The Wall Street Journal*, and *Barron's* classified advertisements for the headings "business for sale" and "business opportunities." On Google, search for "buy a business" to find websites that specialize in businesses for sale.
4. Make a list of businesses that seem to meet the requirements that you wrote down in step 1.
5. Contact the businesses that you have identified. Be honest in your approach. If you are doing this solely as a classroom exercise, explicitly say so. Remember that while the owner of the business may want to sell it, he or she is undoubtedly very busy and may not want to discuss the business with a student when there is no chance of your actually buying it.
6. Visit a business that is engaged in the industry you have identified as being right for you. Find out the following things:
   a. The title and publisher of the journals dedicated to the industry. You can also check out Skill Module 3.1.
   b. The primary businesses of this type operating in your geographic area.
   c. Conventional business practices:
      i. Is business done on credit?
      ii. Who are the primary suppliers to the business?
      iii. What are the sales channels of the business (direct sales, catalog, etc.)?
      iv. How is technology changing in the business?
      v. Are there any industry rules of thumb for valuing businesses?
      vi. Does the owner know of any businesses that are for sale?
7. Obtain sample copies of the industry journals. Examine them for advertisements of businesses for sale.
8. Make an appointment with a loan officer in the commercial loan department of a bank in your area. Describe what you are looking for in a business to buy.
   a. Ask if the loan officer knows of any businesses for sale in your area.
   b. Ask if the loan officer can introduce you to anyone who might be able to help you find a business for sale.

Finally, write and present a report to your class that details the efforts and results of your research.

brokers to register by filing a simple form. Accusations of misrepresentation and fraud by brokers are common in the business press.

Networking is an excellent way to find businesses for sale. While most businesses are for sale at any time, for competitive reasons most owners do not want to say so explicitly. Because customers, vendors, and employees are likely to feel threatened, openly advertising a business for sale can lead to the loss of revenue, credit from vendors, and key employees. For these reasons, it is common for business owners to make their intention to sell known only to trusted confidants in the industry and in the community. Attorneys, bankers, accountants, and insurance agents all will provide you with information only if they know that they can trust your discretion. You can usually get solid leads just by telling other businesspeople that you're interested in buying a business.

There is a trade journal for every industry that exists. The replacement window industry looks through *Fenestration Review*. The electric sign industry is energized by *Signs of the Times*. People in the mortuary business bone up with *Embalmer* and *American Funeral Director*. The folks who process dead and decomposing animals into usable products digest *Render* magazine. The construction industry digs *Rock and Dirt*. No matter what type of business you might be considering, there is a magazine for it. They all have advertisements of businesses for sale. Skill Module 3.1 details how to find professional associations and trade magazines.

The Internet also has numerous sites that advertise businesses for sale. A search using Google with the keyword "business" and the phrase "for sale" resulted in over *700 million* pages listed. None of the advertisements that were inspected during the research for this book provided the name or the exact location of the advertised business. Rather, the sites have various ways you can obtain additional information. Some provide a link by which you can request more information. A very few listed phone numbers you can call. Others require becoming a member and paying a fee for access.

There is a trade journal for every industry.

Sources: *Signs of the Times* April; *Funeral Business Advisor*; *Fenestration Review*.

Your current employer is probably a ready source of information about businesses for sale in your industry. Most managers of small businesses are members of formal and informal groups of businesspeople, for example, the chamber of commerce, Rotary, Kiwanis, and other groups that have meetings and provide resources. Also, your employer probably has information about competitors and vendors in the area.

Investigating Entrepreneurial Opportunities: Performing Due Diligence

Suppose you've actually found a business you'd like to buy. Your job has just begun. Finding an appropriate business is merely the first, and easiest, step in the process. Buying a business is a lot like getting married–it is easy to get into, but if it turns out bad, it's very hard to get out. Now that you've found that "perfect" business, you must make an exhaustive investigation to tell if it is really suitable. Unlike residential real estate, which is highly regulated in the United States, sellers of businesses are not legally required to make disclosures of impairments or deficiencies. If you are outside the United States, your laws may be different. For example, in Canada, sales of businesses for a price less than $200,000 are tightly regulated. Sales for amounts greater than $200,000 are not regulated at all. As in the United States, it is *your* responsibility to fully investigate the business and to come to your own independent evaluation of its value.

Due diligence is the process of investigating to determine the full and complete implications of buying a business. During the process of due diligence every aspect of the business is examined in exacting detail. Nothing is taken for granted. No statement is accepted without evidence. Evidence is, itself, substantiated with sources external to the company. Properly performing due diligence minimizes the risk of failure and maximizes the probability of success by identifying the strengths and weaknesses of the business.

due diligence
The process of investigating a business to determine its value and potential for investment.

When a business is to be acquired, there is a clear order of steps that should be followed:

1. Conduct extensive interviews with the sellers of the business.
2. Study the financial reports and other records of the business.

3. Make a personal examination of the site (or sites) of the business.
4. Interview customers and suppliers of the business.
5. Develop a detailed business plan for the acquisition.
6. Negotiate an appropriate price for the business, based on the business plan projections.
7. Obtain sufficient capital to purchase and operate the business.

The first five steps together make up the process of due diligence.[24]

caveat emptor
A Latin expression that means "let the buyer beware," which has been made into a philosophy sometimes used by businesses to put the burden for consumer protection onto the customer.

A basic tenet of business law is **caveat emptor**, or "let the buyer beware." This does not mean that a seller can freely lie to you about the business. Deliberate misrepresentations can lead to lawsuits and may be prosecuted as fraud. However, except for specific representations by the seller, you are responsible for understanding the condition and the facts of the business. It's kind of a "don't ask–don't tell." If you don't ask the right questions, the seller has no obligation to tell you the right answers. Thus, as the buyer, you must determine how the business is currently being operated, and you must substantiate (or disprove) representations made by the seller regarding the existence and value of assets, liabilities, financial performance, and the condition of the business.

Due diligence has two primary goals. *First*, you are attempting to find any wrongdoing: (1) fraud committed by the owners or managers; (2) misrepresentations of the sellers, such as improperly recognized revenues or expenses; and (3) missing information, including pending or threatened litigation, technological obsolescence of equipment, processes, product, or service, and unpaid taxes. *Second*, you are trying to find any inefficiencies, unnoticed opportunities, waste, and mismanagement. The first goal is information that greatly affects the value of the business and the advisability of purchasing it. The second goal is how you, as a new owner, can make changes to increase its value. Both goals can give you a negotiating advantage.

The first information that you get is usually a set of financial statements. There are four reasons why this is so: (1) the seller usually has financial statements available and incurs little added cost in providing them, (2) you, as a businessperson, are most likely familiar with financial statements and can extract useful information from them, (3) financial statements are accepted as representative of the business by bankers and investors, and (4) financial statements are considered to be indicators of future business results.

Financial statements should include (1) a balance sheet, (2) an income statement, and (3) a statement of cash flows. You should also examine the federal and state tax returns for at least the last five years. Information forms for partnerships, corporations, or limited liability companies should be examined also. Any financial statement prepared by or for the seller must be treated with skepticism. Some financial statements that you see will have been subjected to rigorous examination by professionals outside the business; some will have been dashed off by the owner at midnight on April 15. To be believable, the statements must be substantiated by external sources.

When you examine the income statement, you should focus on corroborating the amount and timing of revenues and expenses. Be aware that the income statements of small businesses are commonly misstated. To avoid taxes, owners often charge personal expenses to the business, such as cars, country club memberships, travel, and even home office expenses. On the other hand, when preparing to sell the business, owners are motivated to overstate revenues and understate expenses to show the highest profit.

intangibles
Assets, such as patents or trademarks, and liabilities, such as accounts payable, that have no physical existence.

Balance sheet items that are likely to be misstated are intangibles, that is, things that have no physical existence, but rather are legal rights and obligations. **Intangibles** include accounts receivable, patents, licenses, and liabilities. Assets claimed on the balance sheet must be examined to ensure that they exist and that the stated value is reasonable. Because liabilities are legal requirements to give up economic value in the future, such as debts for borrowed money or merchandise purchased on account, your risk is that there will be liabilities that are not disclosed. Your problem is that you are attempting to prove the absence of something. Once the examination is complete, you should adjust the amounts, contents, and format of the statements to reflect what you have discovered through due diligence.

During due diligence you should also try to answer many nonfinancial questions. Why is the business for sale? Who are key employees? What is the extent of obsolescence of equipment and key technologies? What are the prospects for the firm's products and services? What opportunities can the firm reasonably expect to have in the near future?

Determining the Value of the Business

After you have completed a thorough and exacting investigation, you need to analyze all the information you have gathered. This is the time to consult with your business, financial, and legal advisers to arrive at an estimate of the value of the business. Outside advisers are impartial and are more likely to see the bad things about the business than are you. You should make a decision to actually attempt to buy the business only after the evaluation process is complete.

It is very difficult to place a value on a small business. The most theoretically rigorous method of valuing an ongoing business, using **discounted cash flows**, is based on estimates of future cash outflows and inflows, given the change in ownership. Making such estimates is highly problematic. Because of these difficulties, it is common to use other, less rigorous methods to place a value on a business, such as asset valuation, comparable sales, financial ratios, or industry heuristics.

discounted cash flows
Cash flows that have been reduced in value because they are to be received in the future.

Discounted Cash Flow Methodology

Discounted cash flow analysis is based on the concept that the longer you have to wait to receive money, the less valuable it is right now. The application of discounted cash flows to business valuation is similar to having an annuity. An annuity consists of some amount of money which is invested to earn interest. The interest that is earned and a portion of the capital invested is then paid back to the holder of the annuity in a series of equal cash payments. In a similar way, when one buys a business, an investment is made. The business then should provide a return sufficient to repay the investment and also provide a return on that investment.

A detailed explanation of the use and calculation of discounted cash flows is presented in the appendix to Chapter 15.

Asset Valuation Methodology

Asset valuation methods are based on the assumption that a business is worth the value of its assets minus the value of any liabilities. There are two major problems with using asset valuation methodologies. First, such estimates do not consider the value of an ongoing firm over the value of its identifiable assets; for example, the value of an established restaurant over the value of the building, signage, equipment, and fixtures. Second, it is very difficult and time consuming to separately identify and estimate the values of all the assets of a business–imagine a hardware store with tens of thousands of items.

There are three methods commonly used to estimate the value of a firm's assets, book value, net realizable value, and replacement value.

Book value is the original acquisition cost of the asset, minus all depreciation expense recognized to date. There are three major problems with using book value:

book value
The difference between the original acquisition cost and the amount of accumulated depreciation.

1. The original cost of an asset might bear no relation to its current value–for example, a computer bought five years ago may be worth next to nothing today.
2. Depreciation is an arbitrary, although systematic, method of transferring asset value to expense. Depreciation makes no attempt to measure actual loss of value of an asset. For example, for income tax purposes, a new car is depreciated over a five-year period, where in fact it loses 40 percent of its value when you drive it off the lot, but may well have significant cash value at the end of the depreciation period.
3. Internally developed assets, such as patents, trademarks, and trade secrets, do not have book value. For an example, consider the Coca-Cola Company. Its single greatest asset is its rights to the names "Coca-Cola" and "Coke." However, if you examine the annual statement of the company, you will discover that no value for this right is shown in the balance sheet. To address such problems, you must make adjustments to the value of assets that are obviously worth more or less than their book values.

Net realizable value is an estimate of the amount for which an asset would sell, less the costs of selling it. If you were selling a building, the cost of selling would be the money spent on the real estate agent, advertising, and preparing the building for display.

net realizable value
The amount for which an asset will sell, less the costs of selling.

Replacement value is an estimate of what an identical asset would cost to be acquired and readied for service. Net realizable value is usually significantly less than the replacement value of any specific asset.

replacement value
The cost to acquire an essentially identical asset.

Comparable Sales

Comparable sales of other firms in the same industry are commonly used to estimate the value of a business. This method has two major problems. First, no two firms are exactly alike. Second, there are often no recent sales to use for comparison. But there are online sites like Valuations.com and Bizbuysell.com, or check if your library has access to DealStats (formerly Pratt's Stats) or BIZCOMPS database.

Financial Ratios

Financial ratios are often used to place a value on businesses because industry ratios are independent of the size of the business. For example, the percentage food cost for the entire Pizza Hut chain is essentially the same as that of an independent pizza restaurant. Using financial ratios requires that you have an estimate of future income and tax flows. Businesses are never identical. At the minimum they occupy different locations. At the other extreme, they may be different in all measurable aspects: location, size, gross sales, profitability, condition of markets, and physical assets. The best source of industry financial ratios is from data collected by industry associations or industry statistic providers, such as Bizminer or Bizbuysell.com.

Some of the commonly used ratios are:

earnings multiple
The ratio of the value of a firm to its annual earnings.

The **earnings multiple** ratio is simply firm value divided by actual or expected annual earnings. Multiplying forecast earnings by the earnings multiple provides a quick estimate of firm value. You can try using this approach with the valuation calculator at www.bizex.net/business-valuation-tool or see how it is used for computing Private Company Comparables in the Valuations.com Skill Module 6.2.

SKILL MODULE 6.2

Estimating a Business's Valuation on Valuations.com

Valuations.com is a free website that lets you create a valuation report for any sort of business. Getting started requires only three pieces of information: the business's industry, its annual sales for the latest year, and a general idea of the growth rate of the business. You'll need to create a free account first. For this example, imagine an online retailing business selling $50,000 worth of products last year, with pretty stable sales. Typing "online sales" into the "What does your company do?" brings up a number of options. For our business, the closest is "Electronic Shopping and Mail-Order Houses." We'll pick "Stable Company" for the growth rate, so the initial screen looks like this:

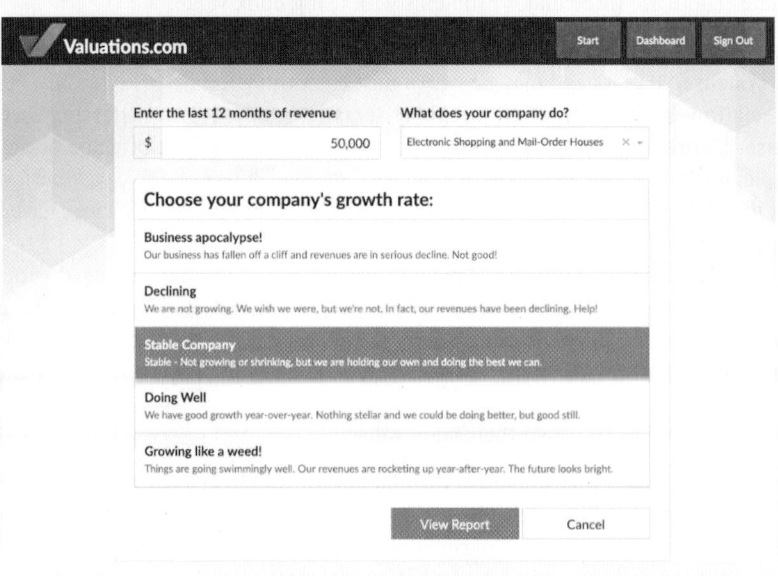

Valuations.com

Choose "View Report." On the resulting report, you can see options for the discounted cash flow (DCF) model described above as well as two versions of the comparable sales approach. Given we are talking about small businesses, we'll choose the "Private Company Comparables" tab, which gives a suggested valuation of $18,422. This number is higher than Valuations.com's computed estimate of $12,000 because of differences in the data sources. Note that you can adjust the descriptions for your firm with the sliders toward the top of the page for profit margins and estimated annual growth rates.

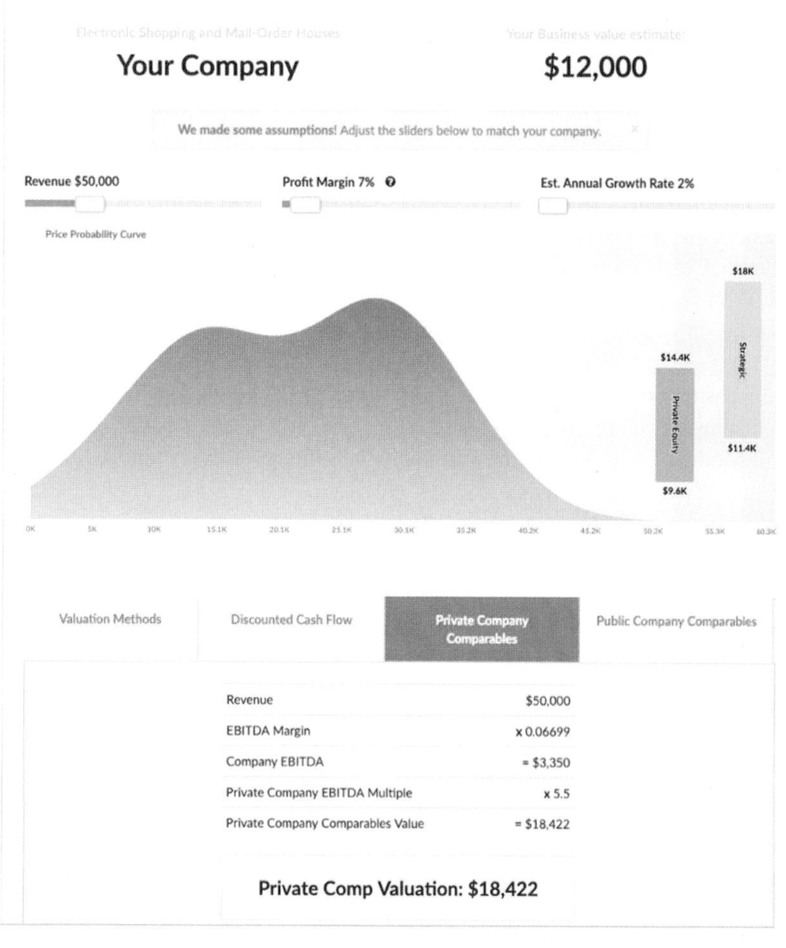

Valuations.com

These Private Company Comparables are based on actual sales of existing companies. There isn't a straightforward way to assess the valuation of a new start-up. But an imperfect workaround is to take the numbers from year 3 of your business plan's financial projections, and use those to get an idea of the valuation of your proposed business, **if** you reach your projected sales, profit, and growth levels **and** you don't have any other major problems facing the firm.

Pretax return on assets (ROA) is calculated by dividing earnings before income tax by asset value. Multiplying forecast earnings by the pretax ROA gives an estimate of net asset value, or total asset value minus liabilities.

Net income to equity is determined by dividing income by the equity owners have in the business. To estimate firm value, you must multiply your estimate of future earnings by the ratio. This ratio, however, can seriously understate firm value because it does not include the value of borrowed capital.

Net income to (equity + debt) is an extension of net income to equity that explicitly includes the value of borrowed capital as a component of firm value.

Income capitalization is calculated by dividing projected net income excluding depreciation, interest, and owner draws, by the best return that you could expect to obtain in other investments. For example, if you are forecasting that you will have a net income of $66,000 and your cost of capital is 11 percent then the estimated value of the business would be $600,000 ($66,000/0.11).

Industry Heuristics

heuristic
A commonsense rule; a rule of thumb.

Industry **heuristics** are simply rules of thumb that are commonly used to estimate firm value in relation to some easily observable characteristic of the business. Industry heuristics are similar to comparable sales in that they represent the combined experience of people active in the industry. For example, in the bed and breakfast and small inn industry, two heuristics are often used to estimate the value of an operating inn. The first is that an inn should sell for approximately $100,000 per rental room. The second is that an inn should sell for approximately four times its annual gross revenue.

Industry heuristics can be amazingly accurate. In a recent survey of 300 inns, the Professional Association of Innkeepers International found that the average selling prices of inns between 2000 and 2002 was $99,300 per guest room. The average gross revenue multiplier was 4.3.[25] Similar heuristics exist for nearly all industries and are usually available from the group's trade association. You've seen how to find associations in Chapter 3. You can also look at online sources like bizstats.com/reports/valuation-rule-thumb.php[26] or Business Valuation Resources (www.bvresources.com) for selected heuristics.

A useful website for making basic valuation efforts is valuations.com, which prepares free reports on a business's valuation based on key information you input (sales, growth rate, and industry).Skill Module 6.2 shows you how to create and interpret those reports.

LO **6-6** Explain four methods for purchasing an existing business.

Structuring the Deal

point of indifference
The price at which a buyer is indifferent about buying or not buying the business.

A buyer and seller get together to negotiate the final price for a business. The buyer should have performed the due diligence procedure and be confident about the assessment of the condition and value of the business. Along the way you, as the buyer, should have decided on the absolute highest price that you would be willing to pay. That highest price is called your **point of indifference**[27] in the negotiation process. The term comes from the idea that once that price is reached, you should be indifferent as to whether or not a deal is made.

Of course, you'll open negotiations with a price substantially lower than your point of indifference. The purpose of opening low is twofold: (1) you want to make the purchase at the lowest price possible, and (2) you recognize that the seller assumes that any opening offer is less than what you are actually willing to pay. A low opening bid allows both parties room to reach a compromise satisfactory to both.

In addition to negotiating for price, you also negotiate about the terms of the sale. When you are buying a business, everything is negotiable, not just the price. In fact, the terms of the acquisition, such as seller financing, payment periods, noncompete agreements, and the exact details of what is being acquired, all interact to affect the price that you are willing to pay and that the seller will accept. There are four basic ways that a business may be bought: (1) you may buy out the seller's interest in the business; (2) you may **buy in** by acquiring some, but not all, of the ownership; (3) you may *buy only the key assets* of the business such as the inventory or equipment of the business, and not the business itself; and (4) you may **take over** a public business by buying a controlling interest of its stock.

buy-in
The purchase of substantially less than 100 percent of a business.

takeover
The seizing of control of a business by purchasing its stock to be able to select the board of directors.

buyout
The purchase of substantially all of an existing business.

Buyouts

Buyouts are restricted to businesses that have a formal legal form of organization, including corporations, limited liability companies, and some partnerships. Legal business organizations are artificial entities that exist separately from the owners. Buyouts are accomplished through purchasing the ownership interest in the entity. Technically, partnerships and sole proprietorships do not exist separately from the owners and thus cannot be purchased. Rather, the assets of the business must be purchased and the liabilities assumed in a process called *key resource acquisition* or *bulk asset sale.* The subsequent business is considered to be a new entity different from the selling entity. In practice, partnerships can continue in existence despite a change in ownership. Sole proprietorships cannot.

The primary advantage to a buyout is simplicity. The seller must only transfer his or her stock to the purchaser to complete the transaction. The business continues as an entity, owning its assets and maintaining responsibility for its liabilities. The primary disadvantage to a buyout is that all liabilities are transferred, including potential lawsuits that arise from actions and transactions that took place prior to the change in ownership. This has, as in the case of the widespread class-action suits concerning asbestos, led to bankruptcy for the purchaser.

A buyout may take place all at once, with all stock being transferred at a single point in time. Sometimes buyouts are made with ownership being transferred over some agreed-upon time range. Buyouts made by employees are examples of changes of ownership over time. Employee buyouts were made legal in 1974 when employee stock ownership plan regulations were codified into law. An employee buyout occurs when the owners of a company sell a majority of stock to the employees through an **employee stock ownership plan (ESOP)** as was provided in the 1974 legislation. ESOPs are complicated transactions that require highly skilled professionals to implement them.

employee stock ownership plan (ESOP)
A formalized legal method to transfer some or all of the ownership of a business to its employees.

Buy-Ins

A buy-in results when someone acquires only part of the ownership of an existing business. Any amount of ownership may be considered a buy-in, as long as less than 100 percent of the ownership is transferred. Buy-ins can be made in any form of business. Technically, if one buys into a sole proprietorship, it becomes a partnership. Corporations and limited liability companies may continue without a change of the form of entity.

There are two advantages to making a buy-in: (1) a buy-in allows the purchaser to leverage inside knowledge, and (2) it aids in keeping key employees. The seller and the managers of a successful business, by definition, have experience in operating that business profitably. The buyer, no matter how expert, does not have the same depth of knowledge of the business being purchased. One great threat to the buyer of a business is that employees who are key to its operations will leave the business. Keeping the current owner as an active participant of the business reassures employees that large changes are not likely to occur.

The disadvantages of a buy-in are the same as the advantages: the prior owner and management remain with the business. This often causes friction when the new owner wishes to make changes, and the old owner and managers do not.

Key Resource Acquisitions

Key resource acquisitions, also called *bulk asset purchases*, are the only way a sole proprietorship may be purchased. This technique may also be used with any other form of business. As the name implies, key resource acquisitions comprise purchasing only the assets of the business. Usually, the seller will keep any cash and receivables and will retain responsibility for some short-term liabilities such as notes payable.

As we saw earlier, the most difficult issue in purchasing a business using this method is assigning a value to the intangible assets, such as the value of the business name, the value of having an ongoing business, the value of established relationships, and so forth. The value of the business in excess of the value of the identifiable assets is called *goodwill*. You should attempt to recognize a minimum amount of goodwill. One advantage of business ownership is the ability to shelter income by using noncash deductions to reduce income taxes. Prior to 2002, a business could reduce income taxes by deducting goodwill over a period of years. However, businesses purchased after December 15, 2002, are prohibited from deducting for goodwill.[28] Thus the more of the business's value that is recognized as goodwill, the less income can be sheltered from income tax.

Key resource allocation provides one important advantage. Because only the assets are acquired, the subsequent business, regardless of its legal form, is not responsible for any of the acts or transactions made prior to purchasing the business. Although this does not completely relieve the successor business from all prior liabilities, it does protect it from action concerning any noncollateralized liabilities, such as a line of credit or a personal loan of the seller.

Takeovers

Takeovers are possible only in businesses that have stock that is freely transferable without the permission of management or other owners. In other words, only corporations and certain partnerships can, under any circumstance, be acquired in a takeover process. A takeover comprises purchasing enough of the target business's stock to gain control of the board of directors of the business. In a takeover, the buyer (often called a *raider*) seizes control of the business without the permission of all owners. Sometimes only a few owners are involved, as takeovers can often be accomplished by purchasing or even borrowing a relatively small percentage of outstanding stock.

Takeovers are hostile events. There is the threat that current management will be replaced. Occasionally, the raider will explicitly state that the intention of the takeover is to sell off portions of the business, or even to liquidate it completely. In these circumstances, current management is likely to make strenuous efforts to prevent the takeover from occurring.

Because of the requirement that stock be freely transferable, only a few small businesses are vulnerable to hostile takeovers. Accomplishing a takeover of a small business is likely to result in the loss of key employees and the resentment and resistance of those employees who remain. As a result of these limitations and problems, takeovers are usually done on medium to large businesses. Only rarely does anyone acquire a small business through a hostile takeover.

LO **6-7** Explain the issues of inheriting a family-owned business.

Inheriting a Business

Unless your parents or grandparents are small business owners, you might think that this section does not apply to you. However, the fact that you are taking this course indicates that you have some interest in becoming a business owner yourself. Thus, someday you may well find yourself on the other end of the inheritance process: You may be the founder who wishes to pass your business to your heirs. Whether you are inheriting a business or bequeathing a business, you face the same problems of passing ownership. Only your point of view changes.

In Chapter 2, we introduced the topic of family businesses. As we pointed out there, family-owned businesses make up a huge percentage of all businesses in the United States. In fact, this pattern holds throughout the world. Ownership of all these millions of businesses can potentially be passed through family succession, for example, by being inherited in one form or another.

Family Businesses Succession

Inheritance is not restricted to parent-child or grandparent-grandchild. Family businesses can be, and often are, passed from the current owner-manager to nieces, nephews, cousins, or in-laws.

One of the most difficult things that you will ever have to do is make a successful ownership transition. Turning over management authority is not easy for most founders, nor is it easy for the heir of the founder to assume the authority. However, if the firm is to prosper, you've got to find a way to do it. Research shows that family-owned businesses usually fail after the death or retirement of the founder. Fewer than 30 percent are successfully transferred to a second generation. Fewer than 13 percent succeed long enough to be inherited by the third.[29] Family businesses that successfully make the transition do so by taking specific actions to organize the business and ensure that it can run profitably when the founder is gone.

Developing a Formal Management Structure

To make the transition, you will have to establish a formal management structure. You will need to develop a comprehensive business plan that states clear goals and objectives. Most difficult, you must be able to clearly see the strengths and weaknesses of family members who will remain in the business.[30] You must then hire professional managers to run those functions that family members cannot. Once successors have been selected, they must be educated in all parts of the family business to develop experience and skills.

Whether you are the founder or the successor, you face an overwhelming task. The founder must impart his or her unique knowledge, skill, and experience that has made the business successful. The successor must learn all these things. While this is happening the founder and successor will have to work closely together.[31] There always will be issues of who is in charge. No matter the skills and experience of the successor, as long as the founder is active in the business, many people will automatically turn to him or her for decisions.

Succession Issues for the Founder

To ensure that your business survives after you're gone, you must be proactive in bringing selected family members into the business as soon as you can.[32] The issue that must be faced in this process is selecting the appropriate family members. All members of the family business, whether being active in management roles or simply being silent owners, should have an open and ongoing dialog about the strategy, goals, and operations of the business. If you, as the founder-manager, take part in family dialogs about the business, you will gain insight into their values, ideas, and goals. Although family members usually share a set of basic values, there is inevitably some diversity in motivations and personal goals. This diversity can be a positive advantage when it brings new thinking to the management of your business. On the other hand, it can be a source of divisiveness that can lead to a failure to cooperate or even to angry confrontations to the point of mutual lawsuits among family members. Handling conflict in families is a topic covered in Chapter 18.

To avoid having the diversity of values, goals, and motivators from becoming the source of such intrafamily strife, you and the other family business members should respect one another's differences by:

- Being certain that all family members know and accept that they are not forced to enter the management of the business if they don't want to.
- Providing each member of the family business with the opportunity to obtain education and experience outside the business. Working in other businesses will provide knowledge and skills that cannot be provided solely from within the family business.
- Allowing each family member who does wish to enter the business to find out and do those functions and activities that he or she does best.
- Not assuming that the leadership of the business must come from within the family. Being part of the family does not guarantee business leadership skills.

Once you have brought a family member into the firm, you must provide opportunities for learning and growth. This is achieved by deliberately and methodically sharing both responsibility and authority. Often, the founder of a small business finds it very difficult to give up decision-making authority to family members, especially to children and grandchildren. Regardless, you have to "let go" and allow family members that you bring into the business to use their knowledge, skills, and experience to make decisions in the areas where they have special competence. It is only by doing that you and your heirs can develop stronger management skills necessary to ensure the future success of the business.

Successfully bringing family members into the firm, allowing them to find their areas of special abilities, and sharing both responsibility and authority for management decision making is an essential first step. Next, you need to set up specific avenues of access among family members to be able to share their ideas and challenges. One way to achieve this goal is to set up regular "family board" meetings–meetings where each family member listens carefully to the others, and each has a chance to express specific concerns. Openness and regularity in intrafamily communications ensure that you will develop your family managers into a learning community that will benefit from each other's mistakes and successes.

You should write out your specific decisions and desires concerning who inherits what. You should then personally inform everyone who is affected by your decisions. You must also explicitly state the reasons for selecting any one family member over another when there is competition for a specific job in the business. All too commonly the heir not selected challenges the succession after the founder dies. When this happens, the business often fails, and only the lawyers win.[33]

Succession Issues for the Successor

To ensure that the business thrives after you've taken over, you must be able to gain the loyalty of other family members, professional managers, and employees. You will be treading a fine line between acceding to the wishes of the founder, and making changes as all dynamic businesses require. When changes are necessary, you should take the time to involve as many of those affected as possible in the decision process. It is important that you neither allow the business to become fossilized–a monument to the founder–nor present yourself in such way that you are perceived as an "upstart"–determined to erase all signs of the founder.

In the best of all possible worlds, you will have started working in the family business while you were quite young. As you aged and matured, you would have been given increasingly more difficult and important tasks to complete. You would have worked in all parts of the company, from the most menial to the most demanding. As you learned these tasks, you would have been provided the same performance evaluations, training, and mentoring as would be provided to any employee being groomed for greater responsibilities.

Such a gradual and growing role in the business goes a long way toward reducing suspicion and resentment of workers that the "boss's kid" is being given the position despite any lack of competency. (Assuming, of course, that you are actually competent.) As you, the successor-to-be, gain greater responsibility and authority you will also gain experience and skills in the multiple activities and functions of the firm. Although the responsibility for teaching and grooming the successor lies with the founder, you, the successor, have a responsibility to know and to master the areas that are essential to the success of the business.

These essential skills include (but are not limited to):

- *Technical knowledge*–You must understand the science, technology, and methodology of the industry of which the business is part.
- *Financial knowledge*–You must understand the financial needs and resources of the business and industry, and be competent to negotiate with lenders, investors, vendors, and customers.
- *People skills*–You must be able to effectively deal with people, with other family members in the business, with employees, suppliers, regulators, and, most importantly, with customers.
- *Leadership skills*–You must be able to communicate your vision for the company to family members and to employees, getting them to "buy in" and make the business goals their goals.
- *Knowledge of your own limitations*–Nobody can know and be expert at everything. You must know your weaknesses, and be quick to obtain assistance in those areas.

Finally, you must determine just how final authority will be passed to you. Business succession is not always the result of the death of the founder. Often the founder simply realizes that it is time to "pass the torch" to the next generation. Your problem, as the successor, is to understand and to be comfortable with the role, if any, that the founder is to play in the business once you take over. Often, the founder takes an executive position, such as board chair, while the successor becomes chief executive officer. Sometimes, however, strong-willed founders just can't keep from meddling. When this is the situation it is probably best that the founder leave the business altogether and allow the successor space to create his or her own management style in the business.

Ownership Transfer

Whether you are the founder or the successor, you certainly do not want to wait until the founder dies to transfer ownership. If you are the founder, once you're dead, your desires become irrelevant. If you are the successor, once the founder is dead, there is no authority figure who can help with issues of control and strategy. Rather than waiting for the founder to die, you should assist in completing a comprehensive estate-planning process while the founder is still healthy and in charge.[34] In most cases, a gradual transfer of ownership is preferable to a single inheritance.[35] This strategy may not be appropriate, however, if there are multiple heirs. Of greatest importance is determining who gets voting stock. If the heirs who are not involved in management receive voting stock, issues of who is in control can arise because of jealousy and intrafamily rivalries.

There is no easy answer to these issues. In fact, the transfer of ownership is highly complex and is unique to each family business. The larger and more successful your business is, the more complex and difficult the problem becomes. Using experts in law, accounting, and business can help identify the potential problems and help organize solutions. For family business succession plans, using specialists is essential. For family business experts, the major professional association is the Family Firm Institute. There are several organizations for business brokers; you can find them in the Google directory by entering "business broker association." In any case, it always pays to ask other entrepreneurs and advisers such as lawyers and accountants if they have recommendations and personal experience with these experts. Involving specialists also sends a clear message to creditors and suppliers that both old and new owners are determined to make a success of the transition.

Professional Management of Small Business

LO **6-8** Describe how hired managers become owners of small businesses.

As small businesses grow, the requirements of managing them increase proportionately. If a business grows large enough, no matter how experienced or talented a business owner is, eventually the demands of managing will become too great to be handled alone. At this point, one of two things happens: (1) the business starts to decline, or (2) professional managers are hired to share the management load.

In the terms of small business, professional management is not an issue of education, titles, or credentials. A professional manager of a small business is one who has the experience and skills to use a systematic approach to analyzing and solving business problems.

These kinds of people are not easy to find. You may have to look to other businesses in your industry for experienced managers who are seeking new challenges and opportunities. You may find such people working for your vendors or your customers. In an ideal world these people would already be working among your employees, people who, because of their individual drive, personality, and skills, have learned your business quickly, and have taken on responsibility and authority.

An opportunity for you to get into small business while avoiding the many risks of start-ups or franchises, and at the same time avoid the difficulties of raising capital to buy an existing business, is to go to work for the business as a hired manager. If you have the skills and experience of a professional manager that will allow you to be hired, taking the position will provide a unique perspective of the business from the inside. Should the business prove to be one that you want to own, you are in a position to understand the business's worth and to negotiate terms that make it possible for you to acquire it.

Employee managers of small firms are often would-be entrepreneurs. The set of management skills needed to be an effective manager of small business is very similar, if not identical, to the set needed to be an effective business founder or owner. Because of this, it is common for a manager to become an owner—either of your business or of a competing business. Entry into ownership is accomplished through all the ways discussed in this chapter, including leaving employment to start up a new business, buying out or buying into an existing business, or contracting a franchise relationship.

There are only five paths of entry into small business management, although the details of how any one person gets started are unique. You may start a business, franchise a business, buy an existing business, inherit a business, or be employed as a manager in a business. Getting into business, for all its difficulties and problems, however, is the easiest part of small business management. Making the business successful and finding a graceful and appropriate way to get out is the true challenge, and that is what we look at in later chapters.

transfer
An endgame strategy in which ownership is moved from one person or group to another.

termination
An endgame strategy in which the owner closes down a business.

sell off
A type of business transfer where the seller gets only a fraction of the value of the business. This is most often done to maintain employment for the staff and service for the customers, but the business can generate only a small amount of profit with which the original owner can be paid, or the new owner does not have much money to buy the business.

How to Get Out of Your Business

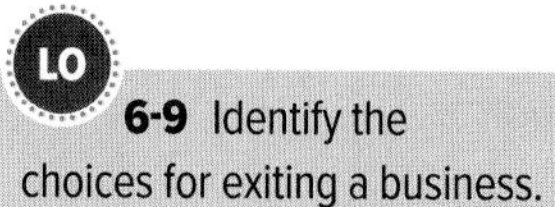
LO **6-9** Identify the choices for exiting a business.

Here is the flip side of starting a business, that of getting out of the business when the time comes. We briefly discussed some issues that entrepreneurs face when they bequeath a business to their heirs, but in fact, there are even more ways to get out of business than there are to get in. Many small businesses are just "put to sleep" by their owners when a better opportunity occurs. Others are sold—to outside investors, other entrepreneurs, employees, other existing businesses. It is unfortunate that a few go through formal bankruptcy and liquidation.

Figure 6.3 shows the range of outcomes from best to worst. Succession is one of a range of alternatives for **transferring** or **terminating** a firm. In any year, there are roughly 900,000 family business successions taking place. In addition to succession, the other way to benefit from the transfer is to sell the business to someone else. There are roughly 1 million business sales each year. In addition to the profitable types of business sales, when the purchase price represents only a token amount, the transfer is called a **sell off**, and where the old owner gets no payment, in effect giving the firm away, it is called a **pass off**. These approaches accounted for nearly 40 percent of family business transfers.[36]

Terminations represent about 1.8 million firms a year.[37] Closing the business with no outstanding debts is referred to as a **walkaway**. More than one-third of the closing firms annually take this approach.[38] As the owner who is closing the business faces more debts, the typical

pass off
A type of business transfer where the owner gives the business to someone else without a payment. This is most often done to maintain employment for the staff and service for the customers, but the business is not profitable enough to give the original owner any revenue.

walkaway
Business termination in which the entrepreneur ends the business with its obligations met.

FIGURE 6.3

The Hierarchy of Business Outcomes

workout
A form of business termination in which the firm's legal or financial obligations are not fully met at closing.

bankruptcy
An extreme form of business termination that uses a legal method for closing a business and paying off creditors when debts are substantially greater than assets.

serial entrepreneur
A person who opens multiple businesses throughout his or her career.

approach is to arrange a **workout**, where the owner takes another job and pays offs the remaining debts of the business. More than one-half of all business closings are workouts.[39] In the worst case, the owner of a failed business, with too much debt to realistically pay back, faces the prospect of **bankruptcy**, a legal method for closing a business and paying off creditors in extreme situations. Bankruptcy will be covered in Chapters 13 and 14, and it is very rare with only 22,245 businesses filing for bankruptcy in 2018.[40]

The smartest entrepreneurs will think about exit strategies from the start, especially those seeking angel or venture capital, because those investors will want an exit to get back their investments and profits. In reality, though, most entrepreneurs don't take outside investment, and for them, exiting the business comes up late in the process. But even starting late, it is possible to plan and take steps to improve your chances of selling the firm.[41] Of the 4 million firms that will change hands or close down this year, almost half will make the entrepreneurs richer, through sale and succession. Another quarter of the entrepreneurs will have benefited from their businesses, and walk away ready to start their next firm. And start them they do. There is a special term for those owners who start multiple businesses in their careers—**serial entrepreneurs**.

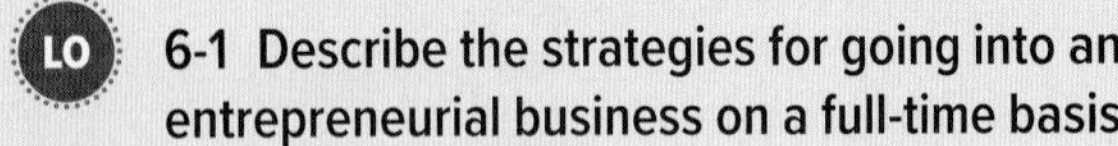

CHAPTER SUMMARY

LO 6-1 Describe the strategies for going into an entrepreneurial business on a full-time basis.

- People may set a goal for a business and then determine the resources that will be required to reach the goal. This is referred to as "causal or predictive reasoning."
- People may assess the assets available to them and the limits under which they must operate to establish the goal to be obtained and the methods of reaching the goal. This is referred to as "effectuation."

LO 6-2 Describe five ways that people get into small business ownership.

- You may start a new business.
- You may franchise a business.
- You may buy an existing business.
- You may inherit a business.
- You may be hired to be the professional manager of a small business.

LO 6-3 Compare the rewards with the pitfalls of starting a new business.

- **Advantages:**
  - A start-up begins with a clean slate and provides the owner with the opportunity to use the most up-to-date technologies and new unique products or services.
  - It can be deliberately kept small to limit possible losses.
- **Disadvantages:**
  - A start-up business has no initial name recognition and will require significant time to become established.
  - It can be very difficult to finance.
  - It cannot easily gain credit.
  - It may not have experienced managers and workers.

- Starting a new business from scratch can be made easier by using methods to reduce initial capital requirements and to gain access to business and industry experience, such as starting a business in your home to reduce start-up costs, having a partner to share capital, and making an alliance with your current employer to gain access to industry sources.

LO 6-4 Compare the advantages and disadvantages of purchasing a business franchise.

- Franchising is a legal agreement that allows a business to be operated using the name and business procedures of another firm.
- There are four basic forms of franchising:
  - Trade name
  - Product distribution
  - Conversion
  - Business format
- Master franchises require opening multiple stores within a specified area.
- **Advantages:**
  - A franchise has a proven successful business model.
  - A franchise includes training and management support.
  - You face less risk than in starting a new business or acquiring an operating business.
- **Disadvantages:**
  - You have little control of business marketing and operations.
  - Your success is determined to a large extent by the success of the franchisor.

LO 6-5 Compare the advantages and disadvantages of purchasing an existing business.

- **Advantages:**
  - Established customers provide immediate sales and cash inflows.
  - Business processes are already in place in an existing business.
  - Purchasing a business often requires less cash outlay than does creating a start-up.
- **Disadvantages:**
  - It is very difficult to determine the value of a small business.
  - Existing managers and employees may resist change.
  - The reputation of the business may be a hindrance to future success.
  - The business may be declining because of changes in technology.
  - The facilities of the business may be obsolete or in need or major repair.
- There are multiple sources to help find businesses for sale, including:
  - Business brokers
  - Networking in the industry of interest
  - Advertising of businesses for sale
  - Your current employer's business
- You must do an exhaustive investigation to determine a business's suitability and value.

LO 6-6 Explain four methods for purchasing an existing business.

- Buyouts are restricted to businesses that have a formal legal form of organization, including corporations, limited liability companies, and partnerships.
- A buy-in involves acquiring only part of the ownership of an existing business.
- Key resource acquisitions, also called bulk asset purchases, are the only manner in which a sole proprietorship may be purchased.
- A takeover involves purchasing enough of the target business's stock to gain control of the board of directors of the business.

LO 6-7 Explain the issues of inheriting a family-owned business.

- Family-owned businesses tend to fail after the death or retirement of the founder.
- Those family businesses that make the transition from the founder to the next generation take specific actions to organize the business.

LO 6-8 Describe how hired managers become owners of small businesses.

- Entry into ownership by employee managers may be accomplished in three ways: leaving present employment to start up a new business, buying out or buying into a business, or contracting a franchise relationship.

LO 6-9 Identify the choices for exiting the business.

- Exit strategies include terminations and transfers.
- Strategies like walkaways and pass offs don't produce financial outcomes for the original owners.
- Other types of business exit produce revenue for owners.
- Owners may work out outstanding debts or face bankruptcy.
- Smart owners plan ahead for their exit.

KEY TERMS

causal (predictive) reasoning, 158
effectual reasoning, 158
affordable loss, 158
strategic partnerships, 160
leverage contingencies, 160
bootstrapping, 160
bricolage, 160
lean business practices, 160
minimum viable product, 162
start-up, 164
asset, 165
revolving credit, 165
founders, 166
accelerator, 166
synergy, 168
spin-off, 168
franchise, 170
trade name franchising, 170
product distribution franchising, 170
conversion franchising, 170
business format franchising, 171
due diligence, 177
caveat emptor, 178
intangibles, 178
discounted cash flows, 179
book value, 179
net realizable value, 179
replacement value, 179
earnings multiple, 180
heuristic, 182
point of indifference, 182
buy-in, 182
takeover, 182
buyout, 182
employee stock ownership plan (ESOP), 183
transfer, 187
termination, 187
sell off, 187
pass off, 187
walkaway, 187
workout, 188
bankruptcy, 188
serial entrepreneur, 188

DISCUSSION QUESTIONS

1. What is the best way to get into business? Why do you think so?
2. If you were able to enter into any small business that you desired, what things would you look for in the business?
3. Suppose you had arranged enough capital so that you could either buy into an existing Outback Steak House or could start your own independent steak house restaurant. What are the advantages and disadvantages of each alternative? Which would you prefer and why?
4. Suppose that you have developed an idea for a new business service. You have limited capital and you do not want to drop out of college. How might you successfully start up a new business using your idea?
5. One evening when you went to pick up your child at the KinderKare, the owner mentioned to you that she would like to sell the business. You have always wanted to run a day-care facility and would like to try to buy her business. What facts should you consider in making this decision?
6. After discussing the KinderKare purchase with your banker, you decide to make a determined effort to purchase the business. To make a good decision, what information must you have, and how will you get it?
7. Based on the information you developed, you have decided that the maximum value of the KinderKare including the building and lot is $350,000. You have $35,000 that you inherited from your favorite great aunt. Your parents have promised to invest $35,000. Based on the $70,000 that you have available, the bank has promised to make you an SBA guaranteed loan of $70,000. What are your options if you wish to pursue this opportunity?
8. You took a job bagging coffee for a business that purchases directly from Guatemalan farmers, thereby getting the coffee at a bargain price, while still paying the farmers above market for the coffee. Working with all that caffeine has you charged up about going into business for yourself. The owner is only 60 years old, but he has told you that he'd like to slow down. He has offered to sell you all or part of the business. What things should you consider in making a decision about what to do?

EXPERIENTIAL EXERCISES

1. Using the resources of your library, find the name and address of an active business broker in your area. Arrange an interview with the broker. Write a report detailing what methods the broker uses to place a value on a business for sale.

2. Find out how the owner of the business where you are employed got into business.

3. Visit the Small Business Administration website franchising page at **www.sba.gov/starting-business/how-start-business/business-types/franchise-businesses**. Using the links on that site, find a franchise business that you believe might be successful were you to buy it. Contact the franchisor, explain your interest, and find out the specifics of the franchise opportunity. Report your findings to your class.

MINI-CASE

TOO HOT TO HOLD

Gwendolyn Bonnefille, a single mother, is barely scraping by. Although she earns a fair salary working in the accounts receivable department of a local business, she has to pay for child care for her two children, Samantha who is five and Merlin who is three. While surfing the web, under a listing titled "businesses that can be moved," she found for sale a business that makes a great hot sauce called Caterwauling Coyote, with the slogan, "You'll howl at the moon!" The sauce is made in the owner's kitchen, bottled, labeled, and then delivered to gift and specialty shops in southern Texas. The equipment to make the sauce is commercial quality and appears to be in good condition.

The business financial statements and the owner's 1040 Schedule C business tax returns do not agree. The financial statements show that in the most recent year the business earned $60,000 on sales of $200,000. The 1040 Schedule C shows a profit of only $10,000, and a zero tax liability because of deducting losses suffered in prior years. The sellers are asking $240,000 for the business. They are willing to finance $190,000 at 10 percent for 15 years.

When Gwendolyn sat down with the owner, Sylvester Gatos, he attempted to explain the discrepancy between the accounting and the tax returns.

"You see," Sly said, "there are two things. First, some of the expenses on the schedule C aren't really business expenses, if you know what I mean. Second, when we did the income statement, we took out depreciation, interest, property tax, and the money that we used from the business because a buyer will not have those expenses."

CASE DISCUSSION QUESTIONS

1. What do you think about Sly's explanation of the differences between his income statement and his 1040 Schedule C?

2. Suppose that the income statement is reasonably accurate. What do you think about the purchase price?

3. What information should Gwendolyn obtain before making a decision to purchase the business?

CHAPTER

7

Small Business Strategies: Imitation with a Twist

● Joe Fischer and Zoë Scharf took time to understand the industry they were planning to go into as well as their market. How did this thorough analysis lead to their success in a market dominated by big companies?
Greetabl

LEARNING OBJECTIVES

After you complete this chapter, you will be able to:

LO 7-1 Describe the decisions needed to establish a foundation for strategic planning.

LO 7-2 Identify the forms of imitative and innovative businesses.

LO 7-3 Articulate the benefits that win over customers.

LO 7-4 Assess how industry changes affect strategy.

LO 7-5 Explain the major strategies of business—differentiation, cost, and focus.

LO 7-6 Determine how to sustain competitive advantage through attracting customers and discouraging competition.

Focus on Small Business: Joe Fischer, Zoë Scharf, and the Strategy Behind Greetabl[1]

"*We help people make people smile*"—Zoë Scharf, Greetabl cofounder

For most of his 20s and early 30s, Joe Fischer found himself in recurring situations—a friend's wedding for example. He found he had this need for something that would make his gift of money stand out from the pile of physical greeting cards, online e-cards, and social media wishes his friend was going to get. He imagined a small box with beautiful designs and places you can write your message, into which he could put his gift.

Joe started shopping craft stores for tools and materials to make box prototypes and started looking into the greeting card industry. He found IBISWorld's report on the greeting card industry.[2] It reported that small new specialty greeting card companies were taking share away from Hallmark and American Greetings, as were digital card companies.

Joe imagined his distinctive competence. As he put it, "Relationships matter, and how we celebrate important events in our loved ones' lives matters too. Our fondest memories didn't occur in the digital world, and neither should our best friends' celebrations." The IBISWorld report argued there were opportunities for greeting card manufacturers whose products were innovative, high-quality, and customizable. That was the opportunity he would pursue.

Joe had been working by himself on the idea, even to the point of cutting out the corner of a used Honey Nut Cheerios box to make a prototype of the gift box he imagined. Knowing this, around this time friends connected him to Zoë Scharf, a graphic designer. Together they built on Joe's initial idea and the industry research he found to create the original Greetabl, an attractive box in the $5–$7 range, which could contain a present or gift card, and gave the buyer room to write personal messages to the recipient. You would order them online or get them in gift shops. You would fill in the custom messages, fold it together, and send the Greetabl in its own mailing box. Together Joe and Zoë launched Greetabl and the product, joining other small niche start-ups challenging giants Hallmark and American Greetings, whose combined revenues were over $4 billion.

The first version of Greetabl made it to market as a customizable gift box. You could order it online or buy it in gift, card, and specialty stores, fill it with your gift, write out your message on the box, and mail or give it to the recipient. Customer response was good, but founders Joe and Zoë felt it could be better, so they talked to customers. They found out purchasers didn't want to take their boxes to the post office to get the right postage. They found out some buyers had trouble putting the box together, and many wanted help on what to put into the box.

So, they revamped Greetabl to be a one-stop shop that was entirely online. Joe and Zoë's second version of Greetabl would handle everything including writing the message and mailing. They were expanding their offerings, adding services to the products they launched, and finding more ways to differentiate themselves from the big card companies and their niche competitors.

See the Greetabl video at **www.youtube.com/watch?time_continue=40&v=CoWIJ41y8Bk**.

DISCUSSION QUESTIONS

1. Did Joe start with the idea for his business or with the goal of starting a business?
2. What was the role of the IBISWorld industry analysis in the creation of Greetabl?
3. What kind of strategy did Joe and Zoë plan for Greetabl?

LO **7-1** Describe the decisions needed to establish a foundation for strategic planning.

Strategy in the Small Business

Strategy is the idea and actions that explain how a firm will make its profit. Whether you know it or not, all small businesses have a strategy. The strategy may be a blueprint for planning or a standard to compare actions against. Either way, strategy defines for you, your customers, and your competition how your business operates.

Good strategy leads to greater chances for survival and higher profits for a small business. What makes a strategy good is its fit to the particulars of your business and the resources you can bring to it. In this chapter, we consider how strategy can be created and applied to help your business be its best.

Strategy in small business is special because most small businesses are more imitative than innovative. If you are opening a home day-care center, a machine shop, an Italian restaurant, or an online collectible figurine store, these types of businesses already exist. You can find examples, books, and often even magazines to study, as well as trade and professional associations to join. There are special strategies that aim to help imitative businesses be successful.

Getting to the useful strategies for a small business is a four-step process. Figure 7.1 shows the strategic planning process for small businesses. The first step involves reviewing and confirming the goals that define your firm and knowing your *magic number*. The second step is where you consider your customers and the benefits you want to offer them and plot these out against competitors in a procedure called *distinctive competence*. The third step is to study the dynamics and trends of your industry using a technique called *industry analysis* in order to identify the best way and time to enter business. The fourth step involves building on the prior three steps to determine the best strategic direction and strategy for the firm. After this four-step process, there is a continuing effort called *post start-up* which aims to refine your firm's strategies and tactics in order to maintain a competitive advantage.

As you can see in Figure 7.1, strategy builds on four key types of decisions you make about your firm. These may be made formally or informally in your opportunity analysis or feasibility analysis. These decisions are:

1. The major goals you set for your firm.
2. The types of customers you seek and what benefits you plan to offer them.
3. The stage and trend of your chosen industry.
4. The specific generic and supra-strategies you choose to pursue.

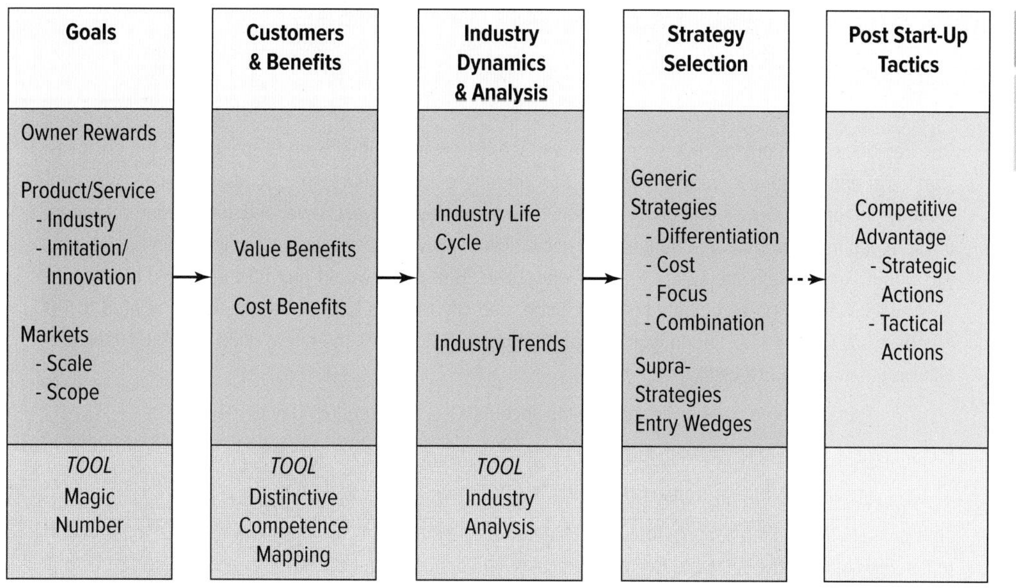

FIGURE 7.1

The Small Business Strategy Process

Goals: The First Step of Strategic Planning

Before getting into industry analysis, you as the entrepreneur need to make some very basic decisions about your goals for your prospective business–you, your idea, and your firm. These **goal** decisions will set the stage for the kind of business you will have and are the foundation for further analyses. There are five initial key goal decisions:

goal An intended outcome for your business.

1. As owner, what do you expect out of the business?
2. What is your *product or service* idea (and its industry)?
3. For your product or service, how *innovative or imitative* will you be?
4. *Scale:* Whom do you plan to sell to–everyone or targeted markets?
5. *Scope:* Where do you plan to sell–locally, regionally, nationally, globally?

Owner Rewards

For a small business that is starting out, all strategy starts with the owner. As owner, what do *you* want out of your business? In Chapter 2 we introduced the rewards sought by entrepreneurs from their businesses. Some, like flexibility, personal growth, and a solid personal income, were pretty universal. Skill Module 7.1 looks at how you can determine your **magic number**, which is the income you personally seek from the business. Knowing that number from the start, you are better able to evaluate if your proposed business can deliver on that very basic need that everyone reports needing. Other rewards like great wealth and developing a new product or service are mentioned occasionally, while recognition, admiration, power, and family tradition get mentioned least often of all rewards. For Greetabl, the original reward was to generate a product that would solve a problem Joe Fischer repeatedly experienced and felt others shared.

magic number The posttax income the entrepreneur personally seeks from the business.

Whatever the reward or rewards you seek–it is fine to want more than one–it should be central to your creating the business. In a very real sense, what you want from the business *is* the core of your and your firm's strategy. It is the "why" that drives the process of entrepreneurship.

Product/Service Idea and Industry

Along with this pursuit of rewards, there is often an idea for the business. Recall in Chapter 4 we saw that 36 percent of businesses start with an idea that energizes the entrepreneur to start a firm. For 23 percent, the desire to start their own business comes first, while for 41 percent, the idea and the desire to start a business are simultaneous.[3] Greetabl was one of those cases where the idea (the box) came first. Whichever applies in your case, the fact is that the idea for a

SKILL MODULE 7.1 Finding Your Magic Number

One key decision all prospective entrepreneurs face is how much they want to make from the business. That's the entrepreneur's "magic number." For full-time entrepreneurs, that number should cover your monthly personal expenses and give you some leftover money to invest, save, and add to your enjoyment of life. If you have ever made a budget, you know how to arrive at that number. For this example, assume you would like to take home $24,000 a year, after taxes. How much would your business need to pay you?

A quick way to figure combined federal, state, and city taxes is to check the numbers related to Tax Freedom Day from the Tax Foundation (**taxfoundation.org**). For 2019, the rate was 29 percent, so the pretax computation would look like:

Pretax income = (Your desired posttax income)/(1 – Tax Freedom Day percentage rate)

For our example, it would look like this:

Pretax income = $24,000 / (1 – 0.29) = $33,802

That is what you would receive before the business taxes are paid. In your feasibility analysis you probably got an idea of what the costs are for your particular type of business. Let's say they are around 75 percent, not including any salary for you. At that level, for you to be able to take home $33,802, your firm would need to sell the amount in the equation (which is the same type of computation as we did on pretax income) below:

Company sales = $33,802 / (1 – 0.75) = $135,208

Now you have a starting goal. Here are some basic ideas on what it would take to achieve those sales:

Business	Unit Sale	Number of Units	Number per Day
Web design	$50/hour	2,704 hours	11 hours/day
Greetabl box	$5/unit	27,042 units	108 units/day

The Number per Day gives you an idea of what you need to accomplish each day. For the web design business, we are looking at 250 days a year (5 days a week for 50 weeks). For the original Greetabl box, we are figuring while an online store is open year-round, fulfilling orders is done on a 5-day-a-week basis (so 250 working days again). As you can see from this analysis, the web designer is clearly facing a challenge. She will need to scale back her financial goals, or increase her prices, or rethink her approach in other ways, since few people want to work 11 hours every day. But that is fine; if a few minutes with a pencil and paper can help you get a sense of the task in front of you, it is time well spent.

What is your magic number?

product or service and the idea to start a business to earn rewards make up the core of strategy—what you plan to do and why you are doing that. The process for evaluating ideas, called the feasibility study, was detailed in Chapter 4. For the purposes of this chapter, we will assume you know your idea is feasible.

Some entrepreneurs may start a firm to get the product or service out, while others may create the product or service and have agents find firms to use it, which is the consignment process described in Chapter 5. Either way, the idea gets made real as a *product* (something physical a customer buys) or a *service* (activities undertaken on a customer's behalf). It is possible to combine products and services, like a GM auto that comes with the OnStar cell phone service. You can learn more about that in Chapter 9.

industry
The general name for the line of product or service being sold, or the firms in that line of business.

If you have in mind a product or service, you also have an industry. **Industry** is the general name for the line of product or service being sold. Examples include the restaurant industry, the computer consulting industry, and the collectible doll industry. In addition to a name, industries have numeric codes, North American Industry Classification System (NAICS) codes,[4] which are discussed below. Industry is vitally important to your core strategy decisions because simply put, there are industries that are more profitable than others.

In fact, picking the right industry is key to the success of your small business. Stanley and Danko,[5] in *The Millionaire Next Door,* point out that two-thirds of all millionaires are self-employed. They say that the key to being successful is selecting an industry that offers good potential for making a profit and attractive opportunities to work with a minimum of risk and competition. These industries are described as having high *industry attractiveness.* Stanley and Danko were surprised to discover that most millionaires who owned businesses are in industries like scrap metal, coal mining, and dry cleaning. It turns out that industries that are attractive from a profit-making sense may not be the industries thought of as attractive places to work. But choosing one of these attractive industries can do a lot to help your firm survive and you to be successful.

Industries that do well in good times and poor historically include financial firms tied to banking, health-related firms, insurance firms (especially related to health), and business consulting.[6] When talking about the small business myths in Chapter 1, other occupations that came up included bookkeeping, credit counseling, and tax preparation.[7] Figure 7.2 gives information about a number of industry sectors and some popular individual businesses to help you get an idea of the relative attractiveness of industries (based on their profitability), and the expected level of sales.

If you know the industry's code number (see Skill Module 7.2 to find out how to do this), you can find out a tremendous amount of information about the industry. This is because most information is coded using the industry number. From the work done by marketing researchers Stanley and Danko[8] as well as Bizminer.com and others, we know there are between 15,000 to 30,000 different industries in the United States.

There are two major classification systems that code industries: the new NAICS and the better-known SIC. SIC codes have four digits; NAICS have six. NAICS covers more industries and more of the newer types of industries. Skill Module 7.2 gives you help in finding the NAICS and SIC codes for the industry for your business.

The key to finding information about industries is knowing how to check the information, and NAICS codes are essential to that. It is also important to know that there are no "safe" industries. In much the same way that families and societies are living things—things that are born, mature, and can die—industries can be considered living too. When you were in kindergarten, coffee shops were a dead industry in most of the country. However, today, with Starbucks, Panera Bread, Seattle's Best, and a host of independent coffee shops blanketing the country, the industry has been revived through franchises, company-owned stores, and innovative independents.

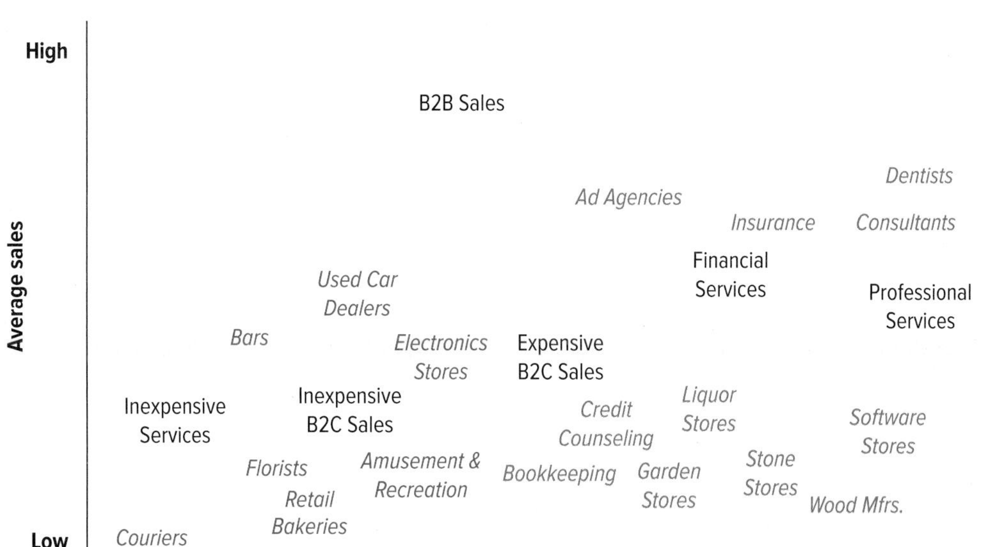

FIGURE 7.2

Attractiveness of Selected Industries and Lines of Business

Note: Industries shown in blue are the most profitable, while industries shown in red are the least profitable. Averages for major industrial sectors are shown in black.

SKILL MODULE 7.2 Finding Your Firm's Industry

The government organizes firms by their industry and gives each industry a formal name and numerical code. That coding system is called the North American Industry Classification System: United States, 2012 (NAICS, 2012). Knowing the formal name and NAICS number can help you find a wealth of government data on your target industry.

It's easiest to search online using the Census Business Builder. Go to **cbb.census.gov** and find the text box that says "or Search for your type of business." Enter the name of your industry. For today's example, think about opening a hamburger and fries sort of restaurant to compete with McDonald's in your little corner of Texas. For our example, you could start typing "restaurant" and you'll begin to see all sorts of industries with those letters in the name.

Scroll down and you will see "Limited-service restaurants," which is what we're seeking. Its NAICS code is 722513. In this case, *Limited Service Restaurants* are what the government calls fast-food restaurants. Click on the hot link, and you'll find yourself looking at a hotlink saying "You selected; Fast Food." If you look to the right, there is question 2. Where are you considering locating the business?" Here you can type in the location of interest to you and generate a map or report with information on that industry in the locality you pick.

Let's type *San Antonio* and choose "San Antonio city, Texas." Then pick "Create Report." The resulting report will have a section "My Potential Customers" (the people of San Antonio), a section called the "Business Summary" about the fast-food sector in San Antonio, and a section titled "Consumer Spending" which includes the section "Consumer expenditures per household on Dining out (food away from home)."

The Business Summary includes information on businesses with employees (and if there are owner-only businesses, called nonemployer businesses, they get listed separately), business revenues, exports, and workforce data. Depending on the industry and locality, some sections of the report may be empty.

For example, in this report San Antonio, Texas, had 1,136 fast-food restaurants (establishments), employing 25,608 people, or 23 employees per establishment, who were paid on average $12,807. You can check out the population per restaurant, the range of sizes of restaurants, and their legal form of organization. You can even compare your proposed business to the state and national statistics by checking the graphs that accompany this table. The latest data reported were from 2016.

Armed with the NAICS codes, you can go to library and online sources listed later in the chapter in Table 7.1 to find more detailed information about the industry you're thinking of entering.

Imitation and Innovation

LO **7-2** Identify the forms of imitative and innovative businesses.

This chapter's subtitle is "Imitation with a Twist." The idea reflects the fact that for most small businesses, the owner wants to be a lot like others in the industry, but not exactly like them. Owners who elect to imitate their **competitors** still want to have *something* that distinguishes them from the others–something that makes the owner's firm special and better. That special and better element–that innovation amid a lot of imitation–gives us the kind of entrepreneurial thinking behind the chapter title.

competitor
Any other business in the same industry as yours.

imitative strategy
An overall strategic approach in which the entrepreneur does more or less what others are already doing.

innovative strategy
An overall strategic approach in which a firm seeks to do something that is very different from what others in the industry are doing.

The choice between imitation and innovation is truly important and often overlooked. Businesses, especially new firms, can do more or less what others are already doing–an **imitative strategy**–or they can start doing something that is very different from what others do–an **innovative strategy**. Imitation is the classic small business strategy. We know from the PSED that almost two-thirds of people starting businesses today plan to use imitation as their approach.[9]

There are several advantages to using an imitative strategy.[10] You benefit from being able to buy existing technologies, such as industrial grade washing machines for a laundromat, web servers for a hosting service, or calligraphy pens for greeting card publishing. Architects, builders, real estate agents, zoning boards, equipment manufacturers, equipment servicing companies, and banks are more likely to understand the industry and what is expected. Because of this, they can give you firm estimates of costs and schedules. With imitative approaches, there is also the possibility to buy existing businesses.

Perhaps the key benefit of an imitative strategy comes from your customers. Chances are they already know about the kind of product or service you are offering. This means your marketing efforts can focus on the benefits you offer instead of explaining the product itself.

When you elect an innovative strategy, you have the benefit of making your business precisely fit your own ideas and preferences. Take the example of snowboards. When Dimitrije Milovich built the first modern snowboard in 1969, he not only had to have the product available for purchase, but he also had to inform the customers that such a product existed and how it could be used. With highly innovative businesses, there is often not much opportunity to sell the business, and the owner spends a lot of energy in creating the processes and markets as well as informing suppliers, resellers, and investors about the new product or service.

In practice, most firms use imitation plus or minus one **degree of similarity**. Imitation minus one degree of similarity would be the business equivalent of cloning. It is franchising, first discussed in Chapter 6, in which you purchase a precise and complete copy of an existing business from the franchisor. Imitation itself involves patterning a business on existing firms and processes. Your imitation is not likely to match the precision or completeness of copying seen in franchising, since you are unlikely to have all the information about the model businesses or processes. You may also adapt your business to fit local situations or your current situation. You might pattern your new Italian restaurant after the Olive Garden, but you end up buying your equipment and food from different sources and add local favorites, such as toasted ravioli in St. Louis, barbeque pizza in Memphis, or deep-dish pizza in Chicago. This approach is called **parallel competition**.

Imitation plus one degree of similarity is where you look at existing businesses and pattern yourself after them, with the exception of one or two key areas in which you seek to do things in a new, and hopefully better, way. This is called **incremental innovation** and is second only to parallel competition in frequency. You have seen it in the fast-food business where Burger King told customers "have it your way." This approach was bettered by Wendy's, which offered custom-built hamburgers that were, in addition, "hot and juicy." Hardee's moved into the fray with supersized custom burgers. Each company makes custom-built hamburgers, but each added a small innovation to differentiate it from its competition. Small businesses do the same thing, whether they are offering haircuts or golf clubs.

The last type is **pure innovation**, also called a **blue ocean strategy**, which results in a new product or service. These situations are rare. Typically with a new product or service, you also have a unique setting. For example, consider Cirque du Soleil, which started as a French Canadian circus, but transformed itself into what it calls a "contemporary circus." This means that each show is a theatrical performance, building each program on a unique theme and musical score. While the human acts common to circuses, like acrobats, clowns, and aerialists, are present, there are no animals. Instead of targeting children and families, Cirque aims for adults and corporate clients looking for a unique, live entertainment experience for which they are prepared

degree of similarity
The extent to which a product or service is like another.

parallel competition
An imitative business that competes locally with others in the same industry.

incremental innovation
An overall strategic approach in which a firm patterns itself on other firms, with the exception of one or two key areas.

pure innovation
The process of creating new products or services, which results in a previously unseen product or service.

blue ocean strategy
A strategy based on creating a new product or service that has no competitors.

Cirque du Soleil upended the classic idea of a circus with a more theatrical, themed and musical experience. What kinds of marketing challenges might a pure innovation product or service pose to a small business owner?

PA Images/Alamy Stock Photo

to pay several times more per ticket than traditional circuses. At a time when traditional circuses are deteriorating (with Ringling Brothers Barnum and Bailey closing in 2017 after 148 years), in 2019 Cirque du Soleil is running 10 different shows around the world, and inspiring a new generation of contemporary circuses like Circus Smirkus or the Pickle Family Circus. It has achieved this by getting out of a crowded, eat-your-competitor "red ocean" and aiming for a "blue ocean" of uncontested market space.[11]

These ideas lead to a simple set of strategic moves that can help you think about how to compete better as an imitator. Think of the case of the upstart Netflix, which became a major player in the video rental business, but was a relative latecomer.[12]

- Parallel innovation
  - Use the standard-setter's approach for lower start-up costs: Blockbuster set the standard, so the software and basic inventory for video rental existed.
  - Don't make the mistakes the leader is making: Blockbuster customers complained about lack of selection and out-of-stock movies, so Netflix had a larger selection and arranged to avoid stock-outs.
- Incremental innovation
  - Take it to the next level: Pick one area important to customers to do much better than the pioneer. You can be easier, cheaper, or offer higher quality. Netflix offered avid movie renters a better financial deal and better selection.
  - Borrow from outside: If another industry has a solution that works (and people know about and like), imitate that idea in your home industry. Netflix married the book clubs' use of mail and the video rental model of Blockbuster.

Remember that a lot of research shows that imitators do better than pioneers in the long run.[13] For example, we know Boeing, Microsoft, and Google, but these are all imitative companies. The pioneers in their industries were companies like Wright or Curtis (airplanes), Digital Research (PC operating systems), Wandex (web searching), and Overture (keyword ad sales). When you do imitation well, it can do well by you.

To Whom Will You Sell?

A **market** is the business term for the population of customers for your product or service. If you know your market inside and out, you are likely to know much of the key information for how to be successful in your line of business. Many of the decisions related to markets will be covered in Part 3 of this textbook. But there are two strategic decisions about your market in general that you need to make early in the process of going into business. One of these is the **scale** of the market, which is the size of the market—whether you plan to aim for a mass market or a niche market. The other is the **scope** of the market, which defines the geographic range covered by the market—from local to global.

market
The business term for the population of customers for your product or service.

scale
A characteristic of a market that describes the size of the market—a mass market or a niche market.

scope
A characteristic of a market that defines the geographic range covered by the market—from local to global.

mass market
A customer group that involves large portions of the population.

niche market
A narrowly defined segment of the population that is likely to share interests or concerns.

Scale: Mass or Niche

When you think about the market for your product or service, you typically have two choices. A **mass market** is a market that involves large portions of the population—all men, all women, all teens, all elderly, all families, all manufacturers, all restaurants. Mass markets are broad, and a mass-market approach targets the entire market.

A **niche market** is a narrowly defined segment of the population that is likely to share interests or concerns—25- to 34-year-old women, families with twins, student athletes, Italian restaurants, manufacturers in your city. Niche markets are specific and narrow, and in a niche market approach, you try to target only customers in the niche.

Most industries have both mass and niche markets. For example, the greeting card industry has mass-market giants like Hallmark and American Greetings, which advertise nationally on TV (a sure sign of a mass marketer). However, the industry is also full of niche markets. For example, Maria Peevey and Lisa Bicker started SimplyShe with greeting cards targeting women going through trying life experiences such as breakups, motherhood, or weddings. Having identified their niche and its needs, they market their cards through specialty fashion boutiques such as Henri Bendel, as well as online.[14]

Scope: Local to Global

Market scope is related to market scale. Market scope refers to the geography of your target market. It can be local (like a neighborhood or a city), regional (e.g., a metropolitan area or a state), national, international (usually meaning two to a few countries), or global (meaning everywhere). Owners of the businesses studied in the PSED[15] were asked how much of their business they thought would come from each of the geographic categories. Overall, they estimated that 58 percent of sales would be local (within 20 miles), 30 percent would be regional (from 21 to 100 miles), 22 percent would be national (from 100 miles out to the rest of the United States), and only 4 percent would be international (outside the United States).

Market scope is important for two reasons. First, knowing your market scope helps you decide where to focus your sales and advertising efforts. The second benefit is that knowing your target market gives you a way to determine which potential competitors you need to worry about most, namely those also in your market scope.

In the goal step, the key is to bring together the decisions that underlie the business you hope to own. This starts with you and the rewards you seek; the product or service you plan to offer for sale to achieve those rewards; and the industry and markets with which you and your firm will plan to deal. Armed with this basic understanding of your firm, you are ready to begin developing a strategy to achieve your goals. Very often, it starts with a closer consideration of your potential customers and what you can do with your product or service to best catch their attention.

Customers and Benefits: The Second Step of Strategic Planning

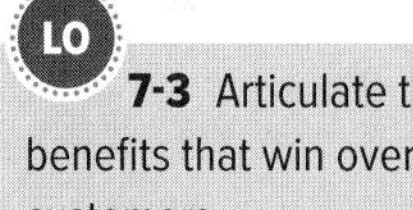

7-3 Articulate the benefits that win over customers.

Strategy and marketing are closely connected in the planning and everyday operation of any business because together they define the who, how, and why of the business's operations. As noted earlier, strategy is the idea and actions that explain how a business makes its profits, while **marketing** is the actions of a business related to promoting and selling goods or services. Both strategy and marketing are defined in large part by the specific products or services being sold, but they focus on different aspects. As Figure 7.3 shows, marketing focuses on the customers with the key being the goods' or services' **value proposition**, while strategy focuses on the competition, with the key being the goods', services', or firm's **competitive advantage** over the other firms.

marketing
The actions of a business related to promoting and selling products or services.

value proposition
Small business owners' unique selling points (also known as benefits) that customers can expect from your goods or services, including benefits that differentiate your offering from those of the competition.

competitive advantage
The particular way a firm implements customer benefits that keeps the firm ahead of other firms in the industry.

This chapter concentrates on building the right side of Figure 7.3, while the chapters in Part 3 will focus on the left side of the figure. But to figure out the competitive advantage, we need to look at something central to the market and the strategy—the benefits the goods or services offer.

So, in this second step of the strategic planning process, the focus is on the kinds of customers you want to sell to and the benefits that will attract them. Just as there are industries that offer better and worse opportunities, there are customers whom entrepreneurs prefer. Customers who offer the kinds of rewards you are seeking are generally those you are most likely to view positively. If you are interested in great wealth, having customers who are themselves wealthy and not very sensitive to price issues would be seen as rewarding. If growth is your goal, having customers from whom you can learn and who expect things to be constantly new and improved will help you meet your goal. There are also some types of customers often seen as particularly attractive. These include:

- *Corporate customers:* Look at Figure 7.2 and compare the B2B (wholesale) to B2C (retail) sales. Selling to other businesses may produce greater profits.
- *Loyal customers:* Loyal customers return and are already presold, making your life easier. They also refer friends, another source of revenue.
- *Local customers:* This was originally true because as the owner you could keep tabs on the satisfaction of local customers more easily than distant ones; but in the digital age, it is less about geographic proximity than about you taking the time to stay in touch with your customers.
- *Passionate customers:* People who are not just loyal but are likely to rave about your business are likely to generate more potential customers than any other type.

FIGURE 7.3

How Strategy and Marketing Relate

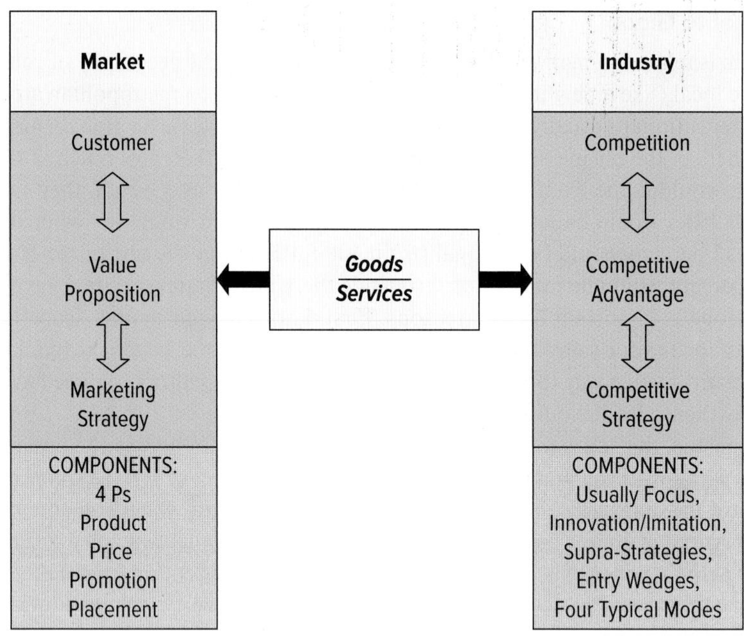

There are literally dozens of beliefs about the best customers. Most of them have at least a germ of truth about them. You can learn about the types of customers in your intended line of business by talking to other entrepreneurs already in the business, and by researching the business in the trade press (to find these, refer back to Skill Module 3.1). Look for terms like "customer profile" and "preferred customers" as well as articles about "loyalty programs" and "repeat customers." These articles are most likely to have information about the most prized customers in your proposed line of business.

The point is that thinking ahead about the kinds of customers with whom you want to deal is the best way to orient your strategic planning process toward finding those customers when you get to picking a strategy. As you decide on the types of customers you want to encounter, your next step is thinking about the kind of benefits you can offer them to help meet their needs with your product or service.

Value and Cost Benefits

Benefits are characteristics of a product or service that the target customers would consider worthwhile, such as low cost or high quality. The best way to identify desirable benefits is through potential customers. You can do this directly through interviews, focus groups, or questionnaires (see Chapter 9 for more details on how to do this), or indirectly through reviewing websites using the techniques given in Skill Module 7.3. Ratings and complaints for products and companies can give you valuable information on what benefits people want, and might want more of. Usually the benefits focus on value added to the product or service or on the cost of the product or service.

Benefits are usually characterized as value benefits or cost benefits. A *value benefit* displays characteristics related to the nature of the product or service itself. Things like quality, fashion, and reputation are elements that give a product or service value in the eyes of the customer. A complete list is given in Exhibit 7.1 on value and cost benefits.[17] Value benefits are important because they are almost always what lead to higher prices and higher profits. For example, McDonald's Big Mac often costs $2 more than its double cheeseburger. The difference between them are some sesame seeds, a third piece of bun between the top and bottom patty, the "special" Big Mac sauce, and some lettuce. Both have two all-beef patties, two buns, and cheese, which you would figure (correctly) are the major costs of the sandwiches. But people pay far more for the Big Mac and pay it far more often. Next time, ask your friends why they do that. The answers you will get will tell you a lot about value benefits, and how much people will pay for them.

Checking Customer Opinions Online

SKILL MODULE 7.3

Today there are many ways to quickly assemble information about products or services from customers from online sources. For this exercise, imagine you would like to produce and market a new iPhone case. The following list will point you to online sources you can use to build a profile of customers and their opinions. The list starts with the most direct ways to find opinions, and shows more complex ways to find opinions as you work your way down the list.

1. **Amazon.com** should be your first stop because it does an outstanding job of soliciting and displaying large numbers of customer ratings on a wide range of products. Competitors like **eBay.com** or **shopping.google.com** can also be worth checking.
2. When you have a particular product or service in mind, try to start with a website that specializes in it (or type the product name into Google).
3. You can go to the major customer opinion sites to see if they have anything on iPhone cases. Googling "top customer opinion websites" will get you articles giving lists and reviews of the best such websites. **Yelp.com**, **Tripadvisor.com**, and **AngiesList.com** are also important sources for customer opinions about services.
4. Most manufacturers provide a customer opinion web page and from that you can learn a wealth of information about your competitors' products.
5. Finally, you can look for blogs on the subject. Typing "iPhone case blogs" into Google or Yahoo! will point to blogs with individuals passionate about a variety of topics and who along the way mention iPhone cases.

With these reviews, you look for themes about what satisfies and dissatisfies customers. What these reviews miss are potential customers—people who did not buy. On the other hand, those who provide reviews tend to be the more passionate customers—pro or con. You can get a wealth of information from dozens of people for free in a matter of minutes.

Beware that one problem is the "fake review," often gushingly positive reviews that turn out to have been written by the manufacturer or reseller. That is why it is important to get reviews and comments from different sites and keep an eye out for similar-sounding reviews. You can get help assessing reviews using sites like **www.fakespot.com**.[16] When presenting your results, list the sites you visited and the number of customer reviews you analyzed. You can use the value benefits list to categorize your findings, or make a set of categories that fit the special features of your product or service.

Finding online reviews can be fast and easy, but it helps when you supplement this with in-person reviews of users to get a better "feel" for how consumers think about the product. We will talk more about this sort of research in Part 3 of the text.

While *value benefits* refer to what the customer senses in the product or service, *cost benefits* refer to the ways by which a firm can keep costs low for the customer. These include scale and scope savings. It is often important for customers to know one of these cost benefit reasons why a product or service has a low price so that they do not erroneously conclude that your firm has cut price by cutting quality.

These two burgers have very similar costs for raw materials and preparation, but one costs $2 more than the other because of the value benefits it offers.

(left): Ingram Publishing/SuperStock; (right): P Maxwell/Shutterstock

EXHIBIT 7.1

Value and Cost Benefits

1. Value Benefits

Quality: Offering a quality level others do not. It can be the highest quality, just enough quality to meet the basic need, or a bit more quality than is typical for the price. Offering guarantees and warranties also reflects quality benefits.

Style: Items that are beautiful, fashionable, popular, or otherwise aesthetically pleasing.

Delivery: Sometimes simply offering delivery is enough, but other times you may need to deliver quickly, on schedule, or where others do not.

Service: Examples include the go-the-extra-mile sort, the personalized know-your-customer's-name sort, the we-serve-you-in-one-minute sort, or even the service-after-the-sale sort.

Technology: You can offer state-of-the-art or leading-edge technology, technology that others do not have, or technology that automates or simplifies tasks or that meets industry standards. Offering complementary technology such as voice mail or answering machines to people with telephones also fits in here.

Shopping ease: Providing one-stop shopping; having all of a product line; making ordering, returning, or upgrading easy for the customer are all benefits.

Personalization: This can come in building custom products or services, or personalizing the customer experience.

Assurance: Offering guarantees, warranties, or service that takes the risk out of buying your product or service.

Place: Being conveniently local is one example. Being willing to sell and deliver where others do not is another.

Credit: One key benefit small businesses offer customers can be extending credit where larger firms and chain stores will not.

Brand/reputation: This can come from the products or services that you offer, or from your own firm's reputation.

Belonging: Some products confer value because they make the customer part of a larger group, such as a member of a club or an online gaming community.

Altruism: If your product helps the community, a group, the environment, or the world, it is a benefit.

2. Cost Benefits

Lower costs: Operating from your home, getting family members to contribute their time for free, or selling something you've already gotten your value out of are all examples of ways small businesses keep their costs low.

Scale savings: Buying in volume usually produces savings, so some firms buy in bulk and sell or repackage in smaller amounts, passing along some of the cost savings.

Scope savings: A multifunction printer has a broad scope—it combines a printer, a scanner, and a fax machine into one box. This is because they can share parts, and this sharing results in lower costs.

Learning: As a firm gets more experience, it can often work with fewer mistakes and greater efficiencies, thereby lowering costs.

Organizational practices: Possibly a small business has automated or professionalized or mastered a product or service to the extent it can do it more cheaply than others.

Benefits are central to how you appeal to your target customer base. Picking benefits customers find attractive makes your firm attractive to them. Picking customer-desired benefits that your competitors do not offer is a powerful way to make your firm stand out from the competition. Benefits drive your firm's offering to its customers and influence every part of the strategy process. As we will see later, benefits can be combined to offer themed strategic packages.

Offering the benefits your customers want opens up the possibility of your being able to charge a premium price and make higher profits, since people are willing to pay for value-based benefits they desire. Having cost-based benefits can also increase profits by lowering your cost of doing business, and thereby increasing your margin relative to your competition's. Therefore, it is easy to see how benefits help you select a strategy that improves your firm's profitability.

As you decide what benefits to offer, you open up the possibility of using a powerful strategic analysis tool called a **distinctive competence map. Distinctive competence** maps are a graphic display of your firm's product or service, compared to that of your competitors. You map the features and benefits you offer, and your competitors offer. It often helps to use the value and cost-related ideas from the list in Exhibit 7.1 to get started, but feel free to include ideas you come up with and also the ideas you hear from customers or prospective customers.

Core competencies are those skills that you and pretty much all of your competitors have. Every fast-food burger place you know about has similar core competencies around making burgers, fries, and shakes, serving you quickly, and handling dine-in, drive-through, and online ordering. But they also have features that differentiate them. As we noted, this becomes Burger King's "have it your way" model for customization, or Wendy's "hot and juicy" burgers, or Hardee's supersized burgers, or McDonald's value menu. Those differentiating features are how the firms describe their distinctive competence, or specialty. To stand out in any industry, you need to meet the core competencies of your competitors, but also offer something distinctive that you do well. Here is where "imitation with a twist" meets "distinctive competence." Skill Module 7.4 takes you through developing a distinctive competence map.

distinctive competence map
A graphic display that compares your company's product or service to that of your competitors, in order to identify your core (shared) competencies and those unique to you and to your competitor.

distinctive competence
Those features, benefits, or aspect of your business that are unique to your firm, or more strongly identified with your firm than with your competitors. This is the specialty for which your firm is best known.

core competency
The main work of a firm in a particular line of business.

SKILL MODULE 7.4

Mapping Your Distinctive Competence

Mapping your distinctive competence is done in comparison to your competitors. Mapping it works best with sticky notes or pencil or chalk. You will be moving things around.

Start with the two overlapping circles, you and your competitors' firms:

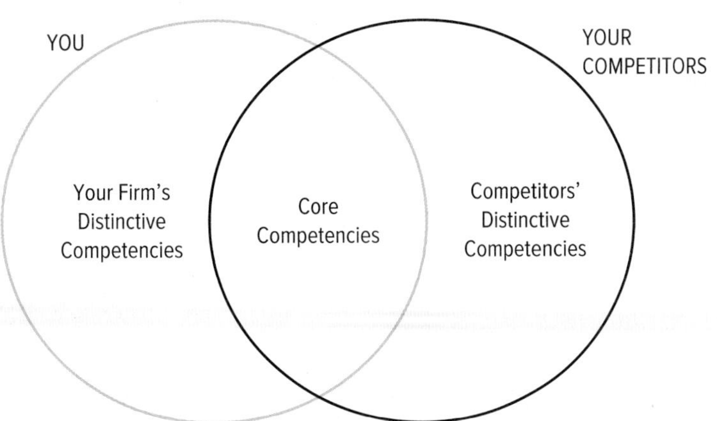

- Start with the "YOU" circle, listing the features and benefits of the product or service you are considering. You can use examples from Exhibit 7.1 and add-in other features and benefits in your own

(Continued)

words, or those of customers or prospective customers. Repeat this in the "YOUR COMPETITORS" circle for competitors' similar offerings. It may help to focus if you start by considering only the competitor you think will be the most likely choice of your customers.

- Move entries for features you both have into the overlapping area for now. That area represents the core competency of firms in your industry, the basic features or benefits or actions that anyone in your industry must have to be successful.
- What is left in each circle are the distinctive competencies of your firm and your competitors'. The distinctive competencies in your circle are the key factors in describing the competitive advantage you offer your customers.
- Save your results because you will use them again in Skill Module 9.8 "Coordinating Your Distinctive Competence and Value Proposition."

In the end, the set of benefits you offer your customers will probably look a lot like what your competitors offer. The key is to have one or more benefits that are important to your customers that your competitors don't offer. *Those* benefits represent your competitive advantage, which we will come back to at the end of the chapter.

LO **7-4** Assess how industry changes affect strategy.

Industry Dynamics and Analysis: The Third Step of Strategic Planning

industry dynamics
Changes in competitors, sales, and profits in an industry over time.

introduction stage
The life cycle stage in which the product or service is being invented and initially developed.

growth stage
An industry life cycle stage in which customer purchases increase at a dramatic rate.

Industry refers not only to your product or service, but also to all the firms selling that product or service; in other words, your competitors. In setting strategy you need to look at your competitors in order to best position your firm, but you also want to look at the changes in competitors, sales, and profits in your industry—what are called the **industry dynamics**—to make sure it is a good time to enter it.

It turns out the fortunes of industries move in a predictable way. Figure 7.4 shows the two ways the number of firms in an industry change.[18] Most industries' **introduction stage** starts with only a few firms. These firms elected to be innovative in their approach, making a new product or offering a new service. The number of firms typically grows slowly at first. Sales are probably small, and most customers are largely unaware of the offering. When enough customers have bought the product so that it begins to draw the attention of the general public, there are two possibilities for the **growth stage**. Most products and services tend to grow at a regular rate, one at which the growth in the number of firms more or less meets customer demand. However, some products or services turn out to be extremely popular or "hot" and grow very rapidly. In

FIGURE 7.4
The Industry Life Cycle

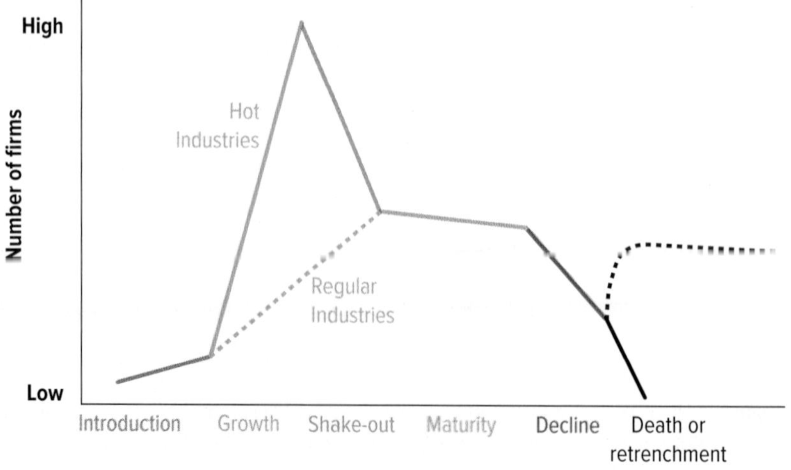

these cases, the original firms are unable to keep up with consumer demand. Other firms jump in to take advantage of the growth; this stage is often called the **boom**. Firms begin to compete on features and price, and there may seem to be an explosion of choices. Eventually, all such booms come to an end, and there is a stage called the **shake-out** in which many of the firms close down. This phase ends as the rapid die-off of firms stops.

Whether through slow and steady growth or a boom and shake-out cycle, the industry eventually reaches a relatively stable number of firms, with minor variations and a slow drop in numbers. This is called the **maturity stage**. Eventually mature industries begin a **decline stage**. Some industries face death, while others find new life in a process called **retrenchment**. We will look at those stages later in this chapter.

Starting early is not always a guarantee of eventual success. Consider cars—the original car companies were small businesses. Charles and Frank Duryea, brothers who created a family business, made the first production car in the United States in 1893. Firms from the start-up stage included Duryea, Winton, and Studebaker as well as Olds, Cadillac, and Ford. The boom started in 1905 and went to 1915 with over 75 auto manufacturers, many of them still small businesses. In the shake-out during World War I, the number dropped into the teens, settling into the maturity phase of the Big 3 (GM, Ford, and Fiat Chrysler) who survived into the twenty-first century.

Industry dynamics are important in telling you and potential partners or investors about the prospects for the industry as a whole. Obviously it is easier to sell people on your business when the whole industry is growing. If the industry is not growing there are still ways to be successful, but as a start-up you need to have worked through these ahead of time. After the 9/11 attacks, many airlines gave up routes due to the downturn in air travel. This market relinquishment opened up opportunities for new small airlines in the cities abandoned by the major airlines. Remember, there are small businesses started in every industry at every stage of the industry life cycle. Knowing where your industry is in the life cycle helps you craft the best strategy for success.

boom
A type of life cycle growth stage marked by a very rapid increase in sales in a relatively short time.

shake-out
A type of life cycle stage following a boom in which there is a rapid decrease in the number of firms in an industry.

maturity stage
The third life cycle stage, marked by a stabilization of demand, with firms in the industry moving to stabilize or improve profits through cost strategies.

decline stage
A life cycle stage in which sales and profits of the firm begin a falling trend.

retrenchment
An organizational life cycle stage in which established firms must find new approaches to improve the business and its chances for survival.

Tool: Industry Analysis

Armed with the concepts and preliminary information about the product/service and the market, you are ready to do a preliminary industry analysis. **Industry analysis (IA)** is a research process that provides the entrepreneur with key information about the industry, such as its current situation and trends. Most entrepreneurs initially do an IA to find out what the profits are in an industry in order to better estimate possible financial returns. Taking this one step further, finding out how those profits are generated often makes the difference between success and failure. Armed with this information, the entrepreneur can tell if the industry is growing, stable, or in decline and what the degree of competition is. Skill Module 7.5 provides a how-to description for gathering the key types of information needed to perform an industry analysis. It also explains how the information is useful. For a complete example of an industry analysis, see this chapter's appendix.

industry analysis (IA)
A research process that provides the entrepreneur with key information about the industry, such as its current situation and trends.

Short and Sweet Industry Analysis

SKILL MODULE 7.5

The basics of industry analysis (IA) consist of knowing seven pieces of information:

1. **NAICS number and description (online):** Getting this information is detailed in Skill Module 7.2. It is important to know this number in order to search for other information about the firm.
2. **Industry size over time (online):** Getting this information is detailed in Skill Module 7.2 for 2016 data for San Antonio, but the Census Business Builder can also generate data for any industry across all of the United States. These numbers tell you the *overall trend* (growing, stable, declining).
3. **Profitability:** Profits are key. You can get the basic information for a wide variety of industries from the **BizStats.com** website under "Sole Proprietor." Select the description of your business (you will find restaurants listed under "Accommodation-Food services-Drinking Places" and then "Food Services-Drinking Places"). Look for **gross profit** (what is left after deducting the cost of goods sold) and

(Continued)

gross profit
Funds left over after deducting the cost of goods sold.

net profit
The amount of money left after operating expenses are deducted from the business.

profit before taxes
The amount of profit earned by a business before calculating the amount of income tax owed.

net profit (what is left after deducting the operating expenses of the business). You can get more detailed reports for more individual industries for a fee from the Risk Management Association (RMA) or Bizminer websites, or you can check if your school or local library has a copy of the RMA's *Annual Statement Studies: Financial Ratio Benchmarks*. One valuable number you can find in the RMA report is the **profit before taxes**, which represents the amount of money the owners take out of the firm annually and on which they pay taxes. When the business can sustain it, owners tend to put their salaries in the operating expense category. However, if the firm cannot afford the owners' salaries, the only income is the profit before taxes.

4. **How profits are made (interview or articles):** Armed with the previously listed information, you can look for the last piece of the puzzle—*how* profits are made. It isn't always obvious. McDonald's single biggest source of profit is real estate; GM's is financing! Toy stores make almost all their profit during the Christmas shopping season. There are usually four activities to evaluate. One is what can be done to generate more sales. Second is a judgment of whether it is possible to charge a premium for a product or service. Third is how to keep the cost of goods or services below the industry's average. Fourth is looking at ways to keep operating expenses below industry averages. Small businesses may use one or more of these approaches. Finding out which get used and the specifics of how they are used generally requires either talking to people in the industry or checking out the industry press. Skill Module 3.1 talks about where to find the trade and professional press for particular industries. If you go the interview route, you can talk to people at companies in the industry. Among the owners most willing to talk are those who have been officers in trade and professional associations or owners of businesses who would not see you as competition, such as owners in other cities. Whenever possible, try to get at least five different sources to make sure you know what is really going on.
5. **Target market competitor concentration (directory checking):** By looking at the listings for local and commercial directories, companies' websites, and map searches such as **maps.google.com**, you can get an idea of the market scope and scale of the businesses with whom you'll be competing. For example, keeping with our fast-food theme, type into Google Maps "fast food restaurants near San Antonio, TX 78205." You'll see a map and listing of restaurants, which you can use to count those places you see as competitors. By getting the number that matches your firm in scale and scope, you can get a clear idea of the concentration of competitors in your segment of the industry—and whom you will need to keep an eye on.
6. **Analysis:** In general, the data you have gathered are put into a report, which helps readers understand what the numbers mean for the industry under consideration. When analyzing the industry, give an overview of the industry (e.g., growing, stable, declining, does it have any major segments like fine-dining versus quick-service restaurants) in words and numbers, its size and profitability (as well as the trends for each over the past three to five years), and the major strategies by which businesses in the industry make money (e.g., cost or differentiation strategies; see the section "Strategy Selection: The Fourth Step in Strategic Planning" later in this chapter).
7. **Sources:** Let readers know where you obtained your information (e.g., books, websites, or personal interviews). It is important to assure them of the quality of your work. Without sources, you could be accused of plagiarism.

What are you looking for in your industry analysis? You want a business that can help you meet the magic number you determined earlier in the chapter. In looking at the other numbers in the industry analysis, you may see ways to cut costs, or leverage friends or expertise or other resources available to you to make your business more profitable than the average one. That can be a tremendously useful finding.

Knowing the stage and trend in the industry is important to thinking about how you will enter the industry. Going into an established industry means it is easy to find locations, equipment, and experienced people (think pizza parlors). Going into an industry early may mean you have to spend more time and money doing things for yourself. It is better to know these things early. If the analysis tells you that you are facing a lot of competition, you want to pay particular attention in building or rebuilding your perceptual map to find a set of benefits that will help your firm stand out. All in all, an industry analysis is central to your plotting of your firm's strategy.

Table 7.1 provides a listing of many of the key databases used in assembling industry analyses. Some are online, while others are in book form and available in local libraries. Armed with the information from your industry analysis, you are in a better position to decide if the industry

TABLE 7.1 Sources of Data for Industry Analysis

Free Online Sources

BizStats.com—Offers profit and cost information for about 100 industries dominated by small businesses. Also has balance sheets and income statements as well as a calculator to project financials from the firm's sales and legal form of organization. BizStats has a for-fee companion called Bizminer (see below).

Bureau of Labor Statistics Consumer Expenditure Survey (www.bls.gov/cex/)—One of the few databases that tracks buying habits (expenditures) of American consumers (families and individuals). Useful for determining market size. Also includes income and demographic information on consumers. Note that these data are now included in the Census Business Builder reports.

Census Business Builder (cbb.census.gov)—We've already mentioned this in Skill Module 7.2. To see output, look at the appendix at the end of this chapter.

data.census.gov—Scroll down and click on the industry you are considering under "Industry and NAICS codes." You'll see a list of data types you can explore including tables, maps, and pages. The pages show the latest statistics available from the government.

www.clustermapping.us—A free resource from Harvard and the U.S. government's Economic Development Administration. Learn more about it in Experiential Exercise 5 at the end of this chapter.

Sources Likely to Be Found in a Library

Standard and Poor's Industry Surveys—These give you the overall trend in narrative and statistical terms for 52 major industries.

Encyclopedia of American Industries—Provides detailed rundowns on major industries. Names leaders and gives upcoming trends as well as historic ones. Has two volumes, one for manufacturing and one for all other industries. (Also available online as the Gale Business Insights database.)

Industry Norms and Key Business Ratios and *RMA Annual Statement Studies*—Each of these two competing products offers a rundown of the financials for hundreds of industries, along with the key ratios (see Chapter 15 for more detail on this).

Market Share Reporter—Compiles market share data on products and services for public and private (i.e., small business) companies.

For-Fee (Not Free) Online Sources (many school and local libraries already have access to these databases, so check with yours)

Bizminer.com—Bizminer covers over 15,000 industries including those most dominated by small business. For example, Bizminer has reports on more than a dozen types of restaurants and has similar coverage in other industries. In addition to financials, Bizminer offers market reports for thousands of industries in hundreds of U.S. communities.

Gale Business Insights—Database with an extensive listing of industries (along with industry reports), companies, and news articles linked to specific firms. Listings of small businesses give names, locations, and in some cases sales figures. Competing databases with similar types of data (but in less organized form) include Lexis and ABI/Inform. Your library may have the hard copy version of this, the *Encyclopedia of American Industries*.

IBISWorld—Covers 700 industries in the United States and provides industry strategies, along with economic and big-picture market projections.

Mintel Reports—Covers United States and Europe with an emphasis on marketing research (versus industry analysis), such as giving consumer segments and purchasing habits in covered lines of business.

meets your needs for income (which comes from profits and operating revenues), financial growth (depending on the trend of the industry as a whole), and competitive challenge (depending on the number and concentration of competitors). It can also help you determine if you have or can get the expertise needed to run a profitable business (comparing how profits are made to how you would run your business if you started now). If the IA outcomes do not look promising, there are thousands of other industries to try, and it is time to think about what you can offer to attract customers to your business.

LO 7-5 Explain the major strategies of business—differentiation, cost, and focus.

generic strategies
Three widely applicable classic strategies for businesses of all types—differentiation, cost, and focus.

differentiation strategy
A type of generic strategy aimed at clarifying how one product is unlike another in a mass market.

cost strategy
A generic strategy aimed at mass markets in which a firm offers a combination of cost benefits that appeals to the customer.

focus strategy
A generic strategy that targets a portion of the market, called a *segment* or *niche*.

Strategy Selection: The Fourth Step in Strategic Planning

There are three classic strategies for businesses of all types—differentiation, cost, and focus.[19] Because they are so widely applicable, they are called **generic strategies. Differentiation strategies** are aimed at mass markets—situations in which nearly everyone might buy your product or service. With this strategy, you try to show how your firm offers some combination of value benefits that is different from and better for the customer than those offered by competitors.

Relatively few small businesses use differentiation strategies because it is hard for small businesses to have the resources to pursue mass markets. It happens most often when a small business offers a mass-market product or service locally. For example, a gas station offers a mass-market service, but its sales are naturally limited to a particular location. This business reality sets boundaries for where the firm competes, which help target advertising and pricing.

Cost strategies are also aimed at mass markets. In a cost strategy, you try to show how your firm offers a combination of cost benefits that appeal to the customer. Small businesses in a variety of industries make use of mass-market cost strategies. Typically, this comes when the small business can pursue a very low cost operation. For example, one gravel supplier in Memphis, Tennessee, was the undisputed low-cost provider. His secret? A farmer by trade, he discovered gravel under one of his farm fields. He sold directly to the users, cutting out intermediaries and their costs.

Focus strategies target a portion of the market, called a *segment* or *niche*. Instead of selling mass-market gravel for everyone, a focus strategy might target people seeking decorative gravel. For example, Scott Stone Company in Mebane, North Carolina, offers 20 different types of gravel that differ in color, stone size, and durability. By ensuring the quality and consistency of the gravel and knowing which types work best in specialized settings, such as oriental gardens or waterscapes, Scott Stone offers customers products and expertise not readily available elsewhere.

Small businesses often use a combination strategy that can use aspects of differentiation or cost approaches that are reformulated for the niche market. You identify a focus or combination strategy by figuring out what benefits your market most wants. This can be done by asking customers outright, through surveys, or by looking at what is working among your competitors locally or in more advanced markets. Often you will find that your market seems to want several benefits at once.

Building from this, strategy researchers such as Dean Shepherd and Mark Shanley as well as Michael Porter have identified classic benefit combinations that they call *supra-strategies*[20] which are given in Exhibit 7.2. All are designed to work where there are many small businesses in an industry, along with a few larger firms.

Tightly managed decentralization can also work in more conventional firms too. The Menlove family mastered the auto business in southern Utah with a Dodge dealership that started in 1962. Family members opened a Toyota dealership in 1986, and a Mitsubishi-Subaru dealership in 2002. Each one was highly rated in customer satisfaction and sales volume. Part of the underlying reason for their success was their ability to transplant the skills they mastered in the first

EXHIBIT 7.2

11 Small Business Supra-Strategies

Craftsmanship: Specialized product, localized business operations, high levels of craftsmanship (versus competitors with scale economies).

Customization: Short delivery times, custom features, short production runs, high quality (versus products that are mass produced).

Supersupport: Extensive, intensive, and personalized after-sales service.

Serving the underserved/interstices: Targeting markets forgotten by larger competitors.

Elite: High-quality products with high prices, backed up by high expenditures for advertising and R&D (versus mass-market products).

Single-mindedness: Developing and demonstrating exceptional expertise in one product or service (versus competitors with broad approaches or product lines).

Comprehensiveness: Offering one-stop shopping with complete inventory, immediate delivery, knowledgeable staff, and the major supporting services in one location.

Formula facilities: Use a prepackaged business (like a McDonald's franchise or a preconfigured restaurant package from Sysco) to offer a better or more consistent product or service.

Bare bones or no-frills: Keep prices super low by cutting back on décor (think warehouse stores), hours (think weekends only or flea markets), or employees.

Cutting out the intermediary: Today farmers at their roadside stands and bands selling their own tracks online are able to sell at lower prices and still make more money by eliminating wholesalers' and retailers' markups.[21]

Tightly manage decentralization: Once you know how to efficiently run one type of business, it often becomes easier to open related firms. This is especially common for Internet businesses.

dealership. The quality of the operations and customer reactions were fundamental to the selling of the chain of dealerships in 2011.[22]

Armed with these strategic choices, it is possible to profile the most typical modes for new businesses. Table 7.2 shows four types of start-ups and outlines how they align with the scope, generic strategies, imitation-innovation choice, and supra-strategies discussed earlier.

It might help to think about how Table 7.2 applies in a particular industry. Let's look at Italian restaurants (part of NAICS 72211). There are probably several Italian restaurants where you live or go to school. If you think about it, the vast majority offer the same sorts of dishes. They are fundamentally imitators of one another. Most of them differentiate themselves based on one or two menu items (one has cannoli, another has Italian wedding cake, etc.). That is their craftsmanship. Another may differentiate on the basis of atmosphere (i.e., best place to take a date) or location (close enough to walk to from class). They probably have nearly identical kitchens and bought most of their furniture and serving ware from the same restaurant supply store. That is their formula facility. Together, these restaurants are classic imitators.

There is also probably another Italian restaurant known as the place to go toward the end of the month, when money is tight. The menu has the same sort of items, but the quality of the ingredients may be less (e.g., more like institutional food) or the décor may be nothing to look at, but the prices are always low. That restaurant is your classic cost leader.

Last, think about the Italian restaurant that has the most different menu. It may be hard to find a marinara sauce on the menu. The décor may look more at home in a Scandinavian restaurant, and the menu may change with the season and what looks good locally. Here you have a firm pursuing an innovator strategy. It may appeal only to a few individuals. Because the food

TABLE 7.2 Typical Modes for Small Business Start-Ups

	Classic Imitator	Internet Imitator	Classic Cost Leader	Classic Innovator
Market Scope	Niche	Niche or mass	Niche	Niche
Optimal Strategy	Focus (differentiation)	Focus (differentiation or cost)	Focus (cost)	Focus (differentiation)
Imitation–Innovation	Imitation	Imitation	Imitation	Innovation
Organizational Goal	Match competition with one element different	Match competition but be online	Lowest price	Master technology
Supra-Strategy	Craftsmanship; formula facilities	Comprehensiveness (inventory); cutting out the intermediary; serving the underserved	Bare bones; cutting out the intermediary; single-mindedness (cost)	Elite; single-mindedness; supersupport
Attractiveness	Moderate to low	Moderate to low	Low	Moderate to high
Life Cycle Stage	All	All	All except introduction	Introduction, growth, or retrenchment

varies so much, they are more willing to tweak recipes to fit the customer's wishes. Some of the equipment in the kitchen or the seating area will probably be different from what the other local Italian restaurants have. That too is part of the innovator strategy. Innovators either grow enough to become mainstream, or they die out fairly quickly.

Innovators may also come along as drivers of the retrenchment of an industry. The growth of northern Italian cuisine (think Italian without red sauce) revitalized the Italian restaurant industry by expanding the menu and reenergizing bored customers to come back and learn about new dishes. The growth of the wine industry in the United States also led to a revitalization of Italian eating. The Internet version of the Italian restaurant is the online ordering system pioneered by big chains like Pizza Hut, but is now available for small restaurants everywhere. The food is the same. The prices are the same, but the difference is the ability to order online. For some other businesses, the online inventory may be larger than the one at the store, because the entrepreneur can fill an online order through their supplier, without adding to their own inventory. So it is possible to be more comprehensive online than in the store.

Most of the time your preferences for a particular type of business or industry and the industry analysis you perform are closely tied together. But there are times when opportunities pop up unexpectedly, and suddenly you can find yourself trying to decide if the opportunity is the right business and industry for you. This ability to quickly pivot is one of the classic strengths of the entrepreneur. Retired entrepreneurship professor Karl Vesper[23] named these opportunities **entry wedges**, and he identified seven that come up again and again:

entry wedge
An opportunity that makes it possible for a new business to gain a foothold in a market.

- **Supply shortages:** Supply shortages occur when a new product is in demand. The target audience is leading-edge buyers who are willing to pay a premium to be the first to have the product. This is a short-term market and one that changes rapidly. The key benefits are delivery, shopping ease, and style.
- **Unutilized resources:** Unutilized resources can be a physical resource like gravel in a farm field or even entire inner cities (see the following Small Business Insight). It can also be a human resource. Tax Resources, Inc. was started in 1988 by people experienced in dealing with the IRS in order to advise taxpayers on legal strategies to minimize their taxes or handle audits.[24] The key benefits are lower costs, scale savings, or organizational practices.
- **Customer contracting:** Customer contracting occurs when a customer, most often a business, is willing to sign a contract with a small business to ensure a product or service. Because big businesses frequently downsize, they have ongoing needs to outsource work. Former employees are often the preferred source for independent subcontractors. The key

benefits are quality, delivery, technology, shopping ease, brand/reputation, and assurance. Style and personalization are often factors too.

- **Second sourcing:** Second sourcing seeks out customers who are already being serviced by another firm. The strategy is to offer customers a second place to obtain goods or services. Often the advantage the small business offers is being locally based. Second sourcing provides the customer with greater certainty of supplies or services, and at its best provides a competitive pressure to keep both suppliers providing the best service and prices. Like customer contracting, the key benefits are quality, delivery, technology, shopping ease, brand/reputation, and assurance.
- **Market relinquishment:** Market relinquishment occurs when business firms leave a market. As the need for the major airlines to fill every seat on every flight has grown, those airlines have pulled out of markets where they can't fill a full-sized plane. For small commuter airlines, these market relinquishments have been opportunities to expand and provide ongoing service to smaller airports with their smaller planes. Key benefits are place, shopping ease, quality, delivery, and service.
- **Favored purchasing:** Favored purchasing occurs because government agencies, government-sponsored commercial contracts, and many big businesses have policies that provide for set-asides or quotas for purchases from small businesses, minority businesses, and disadvantaged businesses (see the Small Business Insight below). You can find out more at the SBA's online government contracting site (www.sba.gov/contracting). Key benefits are quality, delivery, service, assurance, place, and belonging.
- **Government rules:** Rule changes by the government can help small firms compete. For example, when the Environmental Protection Agency let small construction firms out of some of the water pollution treatment requirements that large firms must face, it gave the small businesses a savings of $1.5 billion, which made them more competitive. The Regulatory Flexibility Act of 1980 drives many of these rule changes in government.[25] Key benefits here are technology, service, personalization, lower costs, and organizational practices.

The industry analysis helps confirm that you have chosen the right industry, and also where your competitors are and the current industry stage. That and your own decisions earlier about the scope of your business and whether you plan to pursue an imitative or innovative strategy give you the fundamentals for deciding the type of small business strategy that makes the most sense for your start-up. With that information in mind, it is time to think about how you will set up your firm to implement the strategy.

SMALL BUSINESS INSIGHT

INITIATIVE FOR A COMPETITIVE INNER CITY (ICIC)

Joe Vazquez's undergrad degree was in accounting, and he spent years as an auditor in the construction industry.[26] He burned out on 80-hour weeks, and joined his father-in-law's construction firm, but in 2008, during the recession, he decided to start his own construction company, Vazquez Commercial Construction (VCC). He leveraged government contracting and certification opportunities he learned about from Missouri's Procurement Technical Assistance Centers (most states have similar organizations) including HUBZone, SBA 8(a), Minority Business Enterprise, Disadvantaged Business Enterprise, and Small Disadvantaged Business certifications—all of which give his firm increased opportunities to land government contracts. This meant that he went from $38,000 in 2008, to 25 federal projects worth $1.3 million in 2013, to $30 million and a spot as the number six fastest-growing minority business in America in *Fortune* magazine's ICIC Inner City 100 list for 2018.

Post Start-Up Tactics

LO 7-6 Determine how to sustain competitive advantage through attracting customers and discouraging competition.

The goal of strategy after the start-up stage is to maximize profits (or any other reward you specify as meeting your criteria for success) and protect your business from the competition. To secure success, there is a step you need to take past picking and implementing the right strategy. It is the step of securing *competitive advantage.* Competitive advantage is the particular way you implement your customer benefits that keeps your firm ahead of other firms in your industry or market. Competitive advantage is your firm's edge in meeting and beating the competition.

It can be harder than it looks. Why? In part because most small businesses face a lot more forms of competition than they initially realize. Strategy guru Michael Porter[27] identifies five different sources of competition for any business (see Figure 7.5). One set of sources come from the **supply chain** you face, literally where you get your raw materials and where your finished goods or services go, namely, your customers. The other set of sources come from within your industry, from existing competitors (rivals), other start-ups like your business, and the alternatives and substitutes your customers have been using instead of your product so far.

suppy chain
A way to think about the line of distribution of a product from its start as materials outside the target firm, to its handling in the target firm, to its handling by sellers, with placement into the hands of customers.

Imagine you plan to start a web development firm in Pocatello, Idaho. The first place to look at for competitive threats are *existing firms* in your industry. Pretty much all the other web developers in the Pocatello vicinity pose the threat of *rivalry.* Since web development is even being taught in high schools, another potential competitive threat will be potential or *new entrants,* other web development firms that open after yours. If you think about why people come to a web developer, you realize that there is a very broad threat of *substitutes* with which you compete. Prepackaged website templates are offered by many hosting services, companies like Wix.com, GoDaddy.com and Amazon.com sell whole e-commerce sites already laid out using templates, and people can buy their own templates from companies on the Internet like websitetemplates.com or even freewebsitetemplates.com. But *customers* can substitute whole other approaches, so you compete with free blogs from Blogger.com and WordPress.com, and the growing possibility of running a company site from Facebook.com and other social networking sites.

strategic actions
Competitive responses requiring a major commitment of resources.

tactical actions
Competitive responses with low resource requirements.

Part of what will make your web development firm special might be the advanced services you offer. Perhaps you licensed one of the large archives of photos to include in your customers' websites. If your *supplier* of photos raises prices, your profits could take a hit. Similarly, if your customers have done their homework and checked out what other local developers offer and are charging.

These five–rivals, entrants, substitutes, suppliers, and customers–are aspects of your industry that can change your profitability and give an edge to any of the many types of competitors you face. The major ways you cope with these competitive pressures is by undertaking some combination of **strategic actions** and **tactical actions**. Exhibit 7.3 shows some of the best-known examples of each type. Generally strategic actions require more time, money, and specialized expertise (which collectively are known as your firm's resources) than most tactical actions. That means a tactical response is most often your first response, with strategic actions building behind the scenes.

FIGURE 7.5

Porter's Five-Forces Model of Industry Competition

Source: Adapted by the authors from *Competitive Strategy: Techniques for Analyzing Industries and Competitors* by Michael E. Porter. (New York: Free Press, 1988).

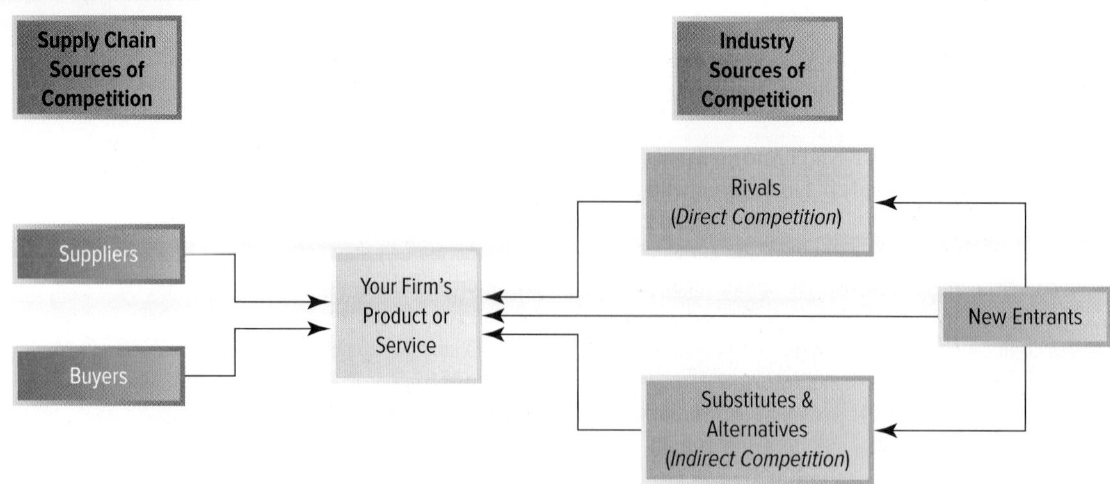

EXHIBIT 7.3

Strategic and Tactical Competitive Actions

	Specific Actions	Examples
Strategic actions		
	Entering new markets	Make geographic expansions Go global directly, by agents or by joint ventures Expand into neglected markets Target rivals' markets Target new demographics Expand Internet markets
	New product introductions	Imitate rivals' products Address gaps in quality Leverage new technologies Leverage brand name with related products Protect innovation with patents or trademarks Offer stripped-down versions as loss leaders Introduce older products in less sophisticated markets
	Changing production capacity	Create overcapacity Option others' capacity to keep it out of competitors' hands Tie up raw materials sources Tie up preferred suppliers and distributors Stimulate demand by limiting capacity Seek production certifications (e.g., ISO 9000)
	Mergers/alliances	Acquire/partner with competitors to reduce competition Flank your primary competitor by connecting with their competitors in other industries Tie up key supplies through alliances Obtain new technology/intellectual property Facilitate new market entry Seek protective legislation Seek favorable standards
Tactical actions		
	Price cutting (or increases)	Maintain low price dominance Offer discounts and rebates Offer incentives (e.g., frequent flyer miles) Enhance offering to move upscale
	Product/service enhancements	Address gaps in service Expand warranties Make incremental product improvements Co-package your product with related ones Bundle multiple products together Add online components or expansions for the product
	Increased marketing efforts	Use guerrilla marketing Conduct selective attacks Change product packaging Use new marketing channels Promote stories of customer and employees Offer altruistic benefits—going greener, charity contributions, etc. Tie customers in via social media
	New distribution channels	Access suppliers directly Access customers directly Develop multiple points of contact with customers Expand Internet presence

Sources: Adapted from G. Dess, A. Eisner, G. McNamara, Strategic Management: Text and Cases, 10th. ed. (McGraw-Hill, 2019), Exhibit 8.2, p. 300; M. J. Chen and D. C. Hambrick, "Speed, Stealth, and Selective Attack: How Small Firms Differ from Large Firms in Competitive Behavior," *Academy of Management Journal* 38, no. 2 (April 1, 1995), pp. 453–482; M. Davies, "Sales Promotions as a Competitive Strategy," *Management Decision* 30, no. 7 (December 31, 1992), www.emeraldinsight.com/journals.htm?articleid=864603&show=abstract (accessed June 20, 2012); W. J. Ferrier, K. G. Smith, and C. M. Grimm, "The Role of Competitive Action in Market Share Erosion and Industry Dethronement: A Study of Industry Leaders and Challengers," *Academy of Management Journal* 42, no. 4 (1999), pp. 372–388; R. A. Garda, "Use Tactical Pricing to Uncover Hidden Profits," *Journal of Business Strategy* 12, no. 5 (December 31, 1991), pp. 17–23.

From all this, you can see that strategy represents the way by which an entrepreneur plots a path to success. For strategy to work, it needs to draw on most of the elements discussed in the chapter. When Joe and Zoë were putting together the idea for Greetabl.com, they were trying to strategize the right way. You know by now that they did an industry analysis that led them to see that Greetabl had a chance in the greeting card market at the small firm side of it where distinctiveness and customization were important. So when it came to imitative-innovative, they went more innovative—when they thought about Porter's strategy types they went with focus, with more of a differentiation approach. While there wasn't an entry wedge to leverage, their supra-strategy was customization (of messages and graphics and later adding pictures) and a single-minded approach. This positioned them as using the typical mode of a classic imitator. And they continued to refine their strategy based on how their product did, what customers did and said, and how their competitors and the rest of their industry changed.

Long term or short, every small business has a strategy, and successful small businesses have strategies that fit their industry, market, and resources. Strategy is one of those areas in which you can take charge and think through the options available to you and your firm. For all the ideas on which strategy touches, in the end there are some straightforward ways to help you decide on strategies, such as industry analyses and perceptual maps. These analysis techniques can help you narrow down your choices to a model of strategy that can help you succeed. For the vast majority of small businesses, the most powerful technique is to pursue an imitative strategy. By following the industry standard practices, with only one or two innovations to differentiate your firm from others, you can gain many of the benefits of established businesses and industries and still benefit from the power of innovation along smaller lines, which can make a real difference for your customers. For many owners, strategy *is* the grand game of business, but it is a game in which winning can make a major difference in the success of your firm and your life.

CHAPTER SUMMARY

LO 7-1 Describe the decisions needed to establish a foundation for strategic planning.

- Strategy is the idea and actions that explain how the firm will make its profit.
- Strategic planning for small business is a four-step process.
- Consider the rewards you seek from your business when crafting and evaluating strategies.
- Choose whether your firm will focus on a mass or niche scale and a scope ranging from local to global.

LO 7-2 Identify the forms of imitative and innovative businesses.

- Imitation is the classic strategy of small businesses.
- An imitative approach lets you build on existing products, services, and markets.
- An innovative approach lets you build a business in your own unique way.

LO 7-3 Articulate the benefits that win over customers.

- Industry focuses on competing firms. Marketing focuses on your customers.
- Benefits are desirable characteristics of a product or service.
- Benefits can target value, such as quality or style, as well as cost.
- Situations and benefits can help clarify entry wedges that can offer exceptional profits.

LO 7-4 Assess how industry changes affect strategy.

- A successful start-up depends on knowing the industry's stage.
- Access to support depends on the industry's performance trend.
- An industry analysis combines trend, stage, and profit data to assess the firm's chances in a particular industry at a particular time.

7-5 Explain the major strategies of business—differentiation, cost, and focus.

- There are three generic business strategies—differentiation, cost, and focus.
- Most small businesses use a focus strategy, targeting a niche by combining cost or differentiation approaches.
- Particular combinations of benefits are called supra-strategies.

7-6 Determine how to sustain competitive advantage through attracting customers and discouraging competition.

- Competitive advantage is your firm's edge in meeting and beating the competition.
- Operating businesses deal with competition through a combination of strategic actions and tactical actions.

KEY TERMS

goal, 195
magic number, 195
industry, 196
competitor, 198
imitative strategy, 198
innovative strategy, 198
degree of similarity, 199
parallel competition, 199
incremental innovation, 199
pure innovation, 199
blue ocean strategy, 199
market, 200
scale, 200
scope, 200
mass market, 200
niche market, 200
marketing, 201
value proposition, 201
competitive advantage, 201
distinctive competence map, 205
distinctive competence, 205
core competency, 205
industry dynamics, 206
introduction stage, 206
growth stage, 206
boom, 207
shake-out, 207
maturity stage, 207
decline stage, 207
retrenchment, 207
industry analysis (IA), 207
gross profit, 208
net profit, 208
profit before taxes, 208
generic strategies, 210
differentiation strategy, 210
cost strategy, 210
focus strategy, 210
entry wedge, 212
supply chain, 214
strategic actions, 214
tactical actions, 214

DISCUSSION QUESTIONS

1. The book asserts that "All strategy starts with the owner." Many of the gurus of strategy say strategy starts with the environment outside the firm. Which do you think is true? Be ready to back it up.
2. A lot of famous entrepreneurs brag how innovative their product is, when it is fundamentally like the competition, although better in one way or another. How do you classify such entrepreneurs in terms of the imitation–innovation balance?
3. Imagine you have developed a new two-way GPS system for trucks and their dispatchers. Trucking companies are all over the country. So are you looking at a mass market? Why or why not?
4. What are the differences between imitative and innovative strategies? Which is more likely to be something a small business can pursue?

5. Pick a small business with which all of the class is familiar. Discuss what are the customer benefits that business is trying to offer. Could they do a better job if they chose some other benefit?
6. Small businesses that pursue a cost (or cost focus) strategy often do so by using a location in a very low-rent district, with the store itself made up of used furniture, no decorations, and a no-frills atmosphere. What is the problem with such an approach? Can you think of other ways to achieve low cost without encountering similar problems?
7. What is the competitive advantage of a business, and how does it lead to success?
8. In the life cycle of an industry, how can you tell when it has left the introductory stage and entered the growth stage?

EXPERIENTIAL EXERCISES

1. Get the industry statistics you need from the government. Go to Census Business Builder page (**cbb.census.gov**) and look up "Lawn and Garden Equipment and Supplies Stores" (NAICS 4442). Our goal is to get the info on stores in Vermont. So type "Vermont" in the "State, County, City/Town or ZIP Code" box on the right and then click "Create Report" to see the statewide numbers. How many stores with employees were there statewide at the last count?
2. Look at local hamburger restaurants. How do they pursue imitative strategies, and where do they offer their innovations?
3. Pick five online businesses in the same industry. From their websites, see if you can identify what *they* think is their competitive advantage. Do you agree with their assessment? Why or why not?
4. Think of the life cycle of an industry. Give examples of industries that are at the different stages, and be ready to defend your classification.
5. You can get an overview of a lot of US industries at **www.clustermapping.us**. For example, imagine you're interested in selling something online. If you put "commerce" into the search box at the top right corner of the site, you can choose from several forms of "Distribution and Electronic Commerce" from the drop-down box that appears. Pick the item for "Electronic and Catalog Shopping." You can pick an economic region from the map. For this example, pick Omaha, NE, and then click on "Go to Region Dashboard" and scroll down until you find the link to "Dive into This Region's Clusters." On the resulting page you will find employment in different industries. Look for "Distribution and Electronic Commerce" in the bar chart of "Private, Non-Agricultural Employment." Click on the bar for "Distribution and Electronic Commerce" and you will see local employment in that industry. You can get employment figures for earlier years by changing the year on the time bar above the bar chart. You can also find out wages for people in the industry by clicking on "Wages" above the time bar (there are also options to learn about job creation and other characteristics of the different industries in the Omaha region). You can try this site with just about any industry that interests you, for example restaurants (which come up as "Hospitality Establishments").

MINI-CASE

ANALYZING TO FIND A PATH FORWARD

Ronnie Scales had his heart set on an Internet consulting business specializing in search engine optimization (SEO), which involves designing websites with characteristics that help them appear high up in search result displays. Being on the first screen that people see can be worth a lot to a company selling on the web.

Ronnie had a strong background, with a bachelor's degree in management information systems (MIS) with a marketing minor from a university in his hometown of Dallas. He had worked in the university's lab, and had done web design and SEO for campus organizations, local nonprofits, and a few students with online businesses. When he tried a distinctive competence map with the features and benefits he and his competitors offered, such as expertise, his firm did not do well. After all, he was new to the industry so his experience was not as great as a lot of his competitors. Also, since SEO can be done remotely, he was competing with firms in India and eastern Europe who charged less than he did. He felt there had to be some advantages of being physically near the customers, but he was not sure how to leverage it.

What sort of tactics could he use to better position his SEO business for success in such a crowded industry?

CASE DISCUSSION QUESTIONS

1. Considering the Porter model, from what sectors would Ronnie's competitors be coming? What kinds of threats do they pose to his business?
2. Pick two tactics from the list in Exhibit 7.3 and explain how they could be applied to Ronnie's business. Explain why you think those tactics would work.
3. Industry experts say that SEO is an industry on the rise. What are the implications for Ronnie as he plans to run his business?

APPENDIX

Five Steps to an Industry Analysis

Retail Shoe Store

HOW-TO'S

Step 1: The Right Data for Your Industry

The first order of business is to find the NAICS code and Census Business Builder for your industry of interest. This is done by going to the website cbb.census.gov. Plug in your keyword, in this case "shoe store," and you will see shoe stores in general are NAICS code 4482. Usually the longer the number, the narrower the slice of an industry, and the fewer the number of firms, but these may be a closer match to your goal. The numbers and graphics you will see when you do this might look different from those in this Appendix. This is most likely to be because the government is using newer data.

Step 2: Industry Size

The Business Builder tells us there were 24,693 establishments (aka firms) in the United States in 2017. Type "St. Louis" in the location box and choose "St. Louis city" and then click "Create Report." In the report, scroll down to the "Business Summary" section. You'll see there were 19 employer establishments in 2017.

Double-click on the "Employer establishments" box (which has a blue background in the graphic below) and the graphic to the right will change to reflect the number of employer establishments from 2013 to 2017. If you click on a column in the graph, it will show you the number for that year, for example, 16 stores in 2013. That change from 16 to 19 stores from 2013 to 2017 gives us one measure of industry size trend. You can repeat this process with any of the measures.

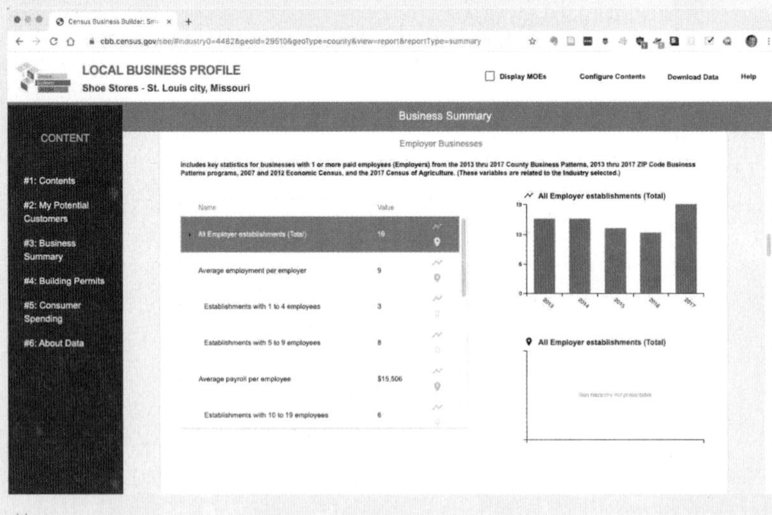

cbb.census.gov

If you scroll down the page in the Census Business Builder, you will see a section titled "Business Revenue," another way to say "sales." The default configuration shows the "Average revenue per employer" for 2007 and 2012 (the latest two Economic Census results available at that time). Again, clicking on the graphs gives you the actual numbers, $814,000 in 2007 and $844,000 in 2012. These numbers give you another measure of industry size and its trend. The graph in the lower right even gives you the 2012 comparable numbers for Missouri and the United States as a whole.

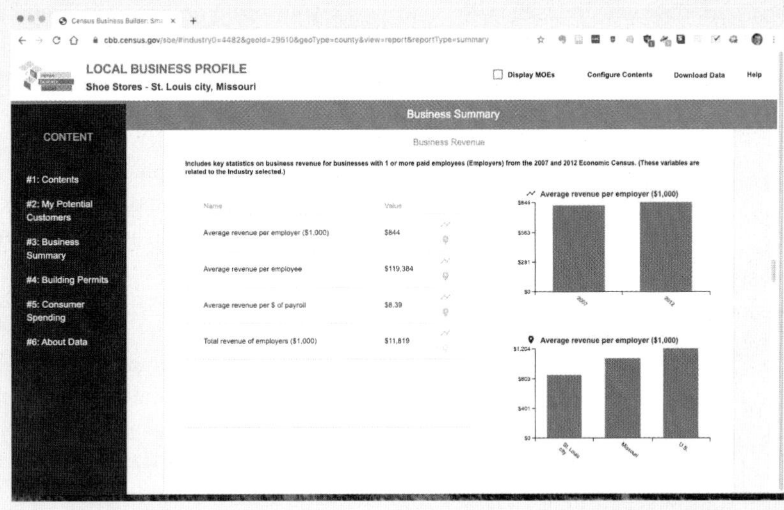

cbb.census.gov

Step 3: Profitability

Step 3 starts with going to the BizStats.com website and clicking "Sole Proprietor" from the top line menu. On the list of industries, select "Retail." In this case, a retail shoe store would fall under the category "Clothing-Accessories." Click on the link and you will be taken to the report.

The BizStat report in March 2019 showed numbers from 2016 of gross profit 51.62 percent, total expenses 46.61 percent, leaving a net profit of 5.01 percent. It then also gives you a line "Direct Labor and NP" (net profit), which reflects that a sole proprietor might be paying themselves a salary in addition to the profits made. That number is 14.62 percent.

Remember that these BizStat numbers give you an average based on a variety of different types of clothing stores. So it still makes sense to get specific numbers for shoe stores (including corporations, partnerships, and sole proprietorships), and you should still get the BizMiner or Risk Management Association data.

Go to the library to find information about the profitability of the retail shoe industry next. Using the RMA's *Annual Statement Studies: Financial Ratio Benchmarks,* the following information was gathered for the smallest stores, with zero to $500,000 in sales in 2018–2019, in NAICS code 448210.

Gross profit 42.9 percent

Operating expenses 41.2 percent

Operating profit 1.7 percent

All other expenses 1.1 percent

Profit before taxes 0.7 percent

Note that the RMA numbers are more specific to the shoe store segment than the BizStats.com numbers; also the numbers are more pessimistic. The rule of thumb in business is to use the most conservative or most pessimistic figures. In this case, the most conservative figures come from RMA, and are specific to your industry. From this you would conclude that the profit picture for the shoe store industry is potentially problematic. When looking at the RMA data, look at the financials for the larger shoe stores. You'll quickly see that the largest stores ($10–$50 million in sales) are more profitable. Note that the BizStats numbers suggest there might be some *other* type of clothing store that is posting superior profits, and looking for that type of business might make sense.

Step 4: Ways to Make Profits

Information about making profits can be found by looking at trade articles and information or doing actual interviews. The following information came from two sources: One source is a trade site, National Shoe Retail Association (to find its material, Google "profitability site: nsra.org"—by the way, this technique can work for all sorts of organizations whose website address you know), and the other is from the home business site www.PowerHomeBiz.com. The answers to four key questions on profitability are as follows:

- First is the question, What can be done to generate more sales?
  - Excellent service.
  - Courteous and well-trained staff.
  - Diversity in product selection.
  - Competitive pricing.
  - Functional store design.
  - Location, location, location (more heavily populated cities have greater demands for shoes).
- Second is a judgment of whether it is possible to charge a premium for a product or service.
  - Depends on the market that you are catering to. If it is high end, then your target customer has the means to spend more money on more expensive (brand-name) shoes. Also, if the store is located where families have higher discretionary income, the demand for brand-name shoes will be higher.
- Third is how to keep the cost of goods or services below the industry's average.
  - Put adequate stock control in place to reduce inventory costs and increase stock turns. Loss prevention is critical in any retail establishment, as theft and shrinkage represent lost dollars for the retailer. Have systematized procedures for doing physical counts of your inventory as well as clear policies on employee theft. It is also important to choose styles that are hot to the consumer to avoid inventory costs.
  - Another cost-saving tactic is to use "in store" completion dates on all orders (i.e. when you require the order to be on your premises). Start negotiating on everything received past completion date.
- Fourth is to look at ways to keep operating expenses below industry averages.
  - Always check your freight expenses against the freight charge on the packing slip. It is usually different. Charge the difference back to the vendor.
  - Join forces with other same brand concept stores for savings on your direct mail advertising. In direct mail, the higher the quantity printed, the lower the cost per unit. There are additional savings to be realized in the cost of mailing if all pieces are sent from the same location. Savings can be substantial.
  - Use co-op dollars to reduce costs. Use some of your co-op dollars to co-brand with suppliers on things like business cards, shopping bags, and so on.
  - If you're doing a profit and loss statement monthly, consider doing it quarterly. Chances are you are simply putting it in a file anyway and are not adjusting the operating budget that often. This can trim the accounting bill considerably.
  - Negotiating better terms and rates with your bankers and other service providers can really save on fees. For example, go to other banks to get competitive rates and then renegotiate with your bank or change banks. For a bank, this applies to bank transaction fees as well as interest and credit terms.
  - Bid or get multiple estimates for things like construction/repair projects, insurance, contract services (i.e., refuse removal), and so forth.

Step 5: Competitor Concentration

The last step is using a directory provider to find out how many competitors there are in an area. Using the Census Business Builder mentioned above, there were 130 stores in St. Louis County in 2016. Alternatively you can use YP.com's online yellow pages directory or Google maps to find shoe stores. YP.com reported there are 208 retail shoe establishments in the St. Louis metropolitan area (which is larger than just St. Louis County alone).

ANALYSIS

Overview

It seems as though the retail shoe industry is growing slowly. From 2013 to 2017 the number of stores in the industry increased by 19 percent. The RMA statistics suggest that small shoe stores are at a particular disadvantage in the industry, trailing the largest stores in sales and profits. We can conclude that the retail shoe industry is very competitive, and for small start-ups, it is essential to be able to distinguish themselves in a mature market.

Profitability

While the gross profit for this industry looks very good compared to other similar businesses (at 42.9 percent), operating profit and profit before taxes are low. Therefore, to be successful in this industry it is important to differentiate and focus on customer service and other approaches which add value. Also, an owner should do everything possible to cut the cost of goods sold and expenses. Taken together, these strategies might result in a profitable firm, but it will be a highly risky venture.

Differentiation and Cost

There are several ways to differentiate in the retail shoe business. There are many different categories for retail shoes. An owner could choose to focus on men's or women's shoes, kids' shoes, or athletic shoes or include all these categories in one store. Then within these categories, there is low end, one price and discount, mass designer, and high end. Again, the shoe business is very competitive, so it is important to choose an image and stick to this image to establish and build a reputation with customers.

Once the image is established, there are six areas that must be covered to be successful and maintain a foothold in the industry. They are as follows:

- Excellent service–many a customer is won over by receiving great service.
- Courteous, honest, and well-trained staff.
- Diversity in product selection–offer a wide range of shoes appropriate for the surrounding environment. For example, if the location is near a beach, be sure to include plenty of sandals, thongs, and flip-flops in the inventory.
- Competitive pricing–be competitive with other stores in the area to maintain a loyal customer base.
- Functional store design so that customers may move around with ease.
- Location, location, location–locations in or near heavily populated cities tend to have higher sales.

Incorporating these elements well, along with a differentiating image, will help an owner have strong placement and be most able to compete effectively in the industry. It would seem that with a solid business plan, a marketing edge, and great location, while a retail shoe business could be risky, it could also be viable and rewarding.

SOURCES

"Bright Ideas" from National Shoe Retailers Association's February 2005 Conference, www.nsra.org/brightideas.pdf.

Jenny Fulbright, *Starting a Shoe Retail Store,* www.powerhomebiz.com/business-ideas/succeed-in-the-shoe-store-retail-business.htm (accessed April 10, 2016).

Risk Management Association, "RMAU Online: Annual Statement Studies–Industry Data 448210–Shoe Stores," https://rmau-org.ezp.slu.edu/industry/detail?indCode=448210&leftnavmenuid=3 (accessed March 25, 2019).

U.S. Census, Census Business Builder (NAICS 44821), https://cbb.census.gov/sbe/# (accessed March 25, 2019).

Note: This industry analysis was originally written by Beatrice Emmanuel of Saint Louis University under the direction of Professor Jerome Katz. It was updated in April 2019 by Professor Katz to reflect the latest data and new Census data sources.

CHAPTER

8

Business Plans: Seeing Audiences and Your Business Clearly

● Krista Clement was a lifelong basketball player who enjoyed giving back to the communities in which she lived. When she came up with an idea to track student-athlete volunteering hours, she created a business plan that described the idea and the resulting business for investors and accelerators.
Krista Clement and Helper Helper

LEARNING OBJECTIVES

After you complete this chapter, you will be able to:

LO 8-1 Understand why and when to develop a business plan.

LO 8-2 Know how to tell the business plan story.

LO 8-3 Learn the major sections of the business plan.

LO 8-4 Focus business plan sections to meet specific needs.

LO 8-5 Identify the major risks to business plan success.

LO 8-6 Master pitching your business plan to others.

Focus on Small Business: Krista Clement and Helper Helper[1]

For Krista Clement, basketball *was* life. A player since she was four, she grew up in a small town in northern Michigan and got a basketball scholarship to the University of Michigan after winning a state championship and being awarded "Miss Basketball," a recognition given to the best player in the state. She played for the University of Michigan (UM), serving as the captain of her team all four years. She loved playing, being with her team, and doing things with them, both on and off the court.

Given the University of Michigan's ethos of social responsibility, the basketball team was expected to volunteer in the Ann Arbor community. For example, Krista mentored students at elementary schools and visited Mott's Children's Hospital as a volunteer. Other UM athletic teams did likewise, and it was a point of pride for student-athletes and teams to engage in the local community. Krista thought finding a way to track this volunteerism and help student-athletes engage even more might be worthwhile.

Krista found out that the Athletic Department at UM was spending a lot of time tracking volunteer hours and coordinating events. Most of the tracking was imprecise, with lots of student-athlete hours not being recorded, and it was a struggle to get every student involved. Most records consisted of paper forms, sign-up sheets, and word of mouth communication. She had an idea for a better way.

Her answer was Helper Helper, a subscription service for colleges and universities that would give every student-athlete at the college a smartphone app which could help them find volunteering opportunities, log-in when they arrive to volunteer, log-out when they're done, and track their volunteer hours. The web-enabled database behind Helper Helper would track not only the individual student's hours, but the hours for every student and every team, and it could generate exactly the sort of reports wanted by the NCAA, the colleges and universities, and the student-athletes themselves.

The idea for Helper Helper was first developed as a feasibility study and then a business plan at Saint Louis University (SLU). The plan was used to raise money for app development, and SLU's Billiken Angel Network was one of the first groups to invest in the business based on the business plan. The plan was also the basis for Helper Helper winning Arch Grants and MergeLane accelerator applications. Informational versions of the plan were also used with programming companies to help them understand Krista's idea and approach.

Within a few months of Helper Helper's opening, it became the go-to app for the NCAA's *Team Works* Competition, in which NCAA schools compete in terms of the number of volunteer hours completed by their student-athletes. Today, Helper Helper is used in over 400 schools and tracks over 1 million hours of volunteering each year!

DISCUSSION QUESTIONS

1. What were the different uses to which Krista put her business plan?
2. What other purposes might a business plan be used for?
3. What might you put into a plan to answer the concerns of investors?
4. How often do you think a business plan might need to be changed?
5. How might a feasibility study help you in creating a business plan?

LO **8-1** Understand why and when to develop a business plan.

Business Plan Background

Krista Clement had recognized a great opportunity, but turning that opportunity into a going business concern would take a lot of planning. This was especially true because while Krista knew what Helper Helper would need to do, she couldn't do the programming herself and would need to find people to do it. Also, the business would take significant funding in order to get the equipment needed to make Helper Helper work. When you are serious about your business or when a lot of money of your own or someone else's is at stake, creating a business plan is perhaps the most critical activity you can undertake. The plan is important, but what is even more important is the understanding you get from the planning process. This chapter will help you understand the thinking behind business plans and how to make and present your own.

business plan
A document designed to detail the *major* characteristics of a firm—its product or service, its industry, its market, its manner of operating (production, marketing, management), and its financial outcomes on the firm's *present* and *future*.

external legitimacy
The extent to which a small business is taken for granted, accepted, or treated as viable by organizations or people outside the small business or the owner's family.

A **business plan** is a document designed to detail the *major* characteristics of a firm—its product or service, its industry, its market, its manner of operating (production, marketing, management), and its financial outcomes with an emphasis on the firm's *present* and *future*.

There are two circumstances under which creating a business plan is absolutely necessary. One is when outsiders expect it. This is called **external legitimacy**. Creating a business plan is the acknowledged best way to build external legitimacy for your firm. When you are seeking outside support—whether financial or expert—you do a business plan to signal your professionalism and how serious you are about the business. Investors, whether they are venture capitalists, informal investors (called *angels*), government bureaucrats, bankers, or your two great-aunts, are going to expect to see a business plan before considering investing in your business.[2] If you are pursuing a partnership or joint venture with a larger firm, a plan is the only way you are going to get the attention of outsiders. The kinds of benefits these different groups look for in a plan are given in Table 8.1.

Keep in mind how business plans get used. The most common use of business plans is when you are raising money for your business. In that case, the plan becomes a way to introduce your idea, your business, yourself, and your deal to the reader. The plan is a sales document, but also the first installment in the relationship you are hoping to build with an investor. You want your plan to be easy to read, to make clear who you are and what you are offering, both as your goods or service and as a potential investment. Remember that many potential investors, especially family and friends, may not have an extensive background in your proposed business, so the plan needs to explain how your industry (i.e., you versus your competitors) works and how your business fits into and builds its opportunities in its market (i.e., with your customers).

The items for each type of audience in Table 8.1 can help remind you what parts of your plan are crucial for the intended audience. It is not uncommon to have different types of plans for different audiences. Your Aunt Mary may not be into the social media industry, but she wants to know how long you'll need her money and what she will get in return. And if she refers the plan to her accountant or attorney for an opinion, he or she will want to know these things for sure.

TABLE 8.1 Concerns of Different Business Plan Audiences[3]

Audience	Concerns
Family and friend investors	Amounts and schedules for returns
	Stability of firm
	Funds use
	Your investment
Silent partners/angel investors	Growth rate
	Market
	Business team
	Amounts and schedules for returns
Joint venture partners	Fit between the firms
	Competitive advantage
	Benefits
	Intellectual property protection
	R&D
Bankers	Cash flow and cash cycle
	Asset/collateral base
	Long-term prospects
Government agencies and institutions	Compliance with regulations and laws
	Monitoring compliance
Potential customers	Service/product quality
	Benefits
	Competitive advantage
	Responsiveness to customers
Key employees	Stability of firm
	Growth (as applies to increased opportunities within the firm)
	Long-term prospects

On the other hand, if you are presenting to accomplished angel investors individually or in groups, they will want to know a great deal about your business market potential. They want it to be big to ensure the high returns they demand for their investment. They will want to know the projected growth rate, and because they probably don't know you as well as Aunt Mary does, they will want a lot of information about you and your team, since most angel investment can be based as much on the investor's assessment of a venture team as on the product itself.[4] Most angels believe a winning team can make the most of nearly any situation.

Remember that while Aunt Mary and the angels will require a full business plan (as we call it in Table 8.5), other investors listed in Table 8.1 would not expect to see everything about your business. For example, you might develop a version of the plan for potential key employees or key suppliers. Neither would expect to see your financials, but both would want to know what the business is about, who is in your market, and who is on the firm's team already. So when putting your plan together, flip between Tables 8.1 and 8.5 to make sure you get the right sections (from Table 8.5) and emphasize the right issues (from Table 8.1) to get the most from your business planning effort.

pitch deck
The name of a slideshow presentation that summarizes a business or more often a business plan.

internal understanding
The extent to which employees, investors, and family members involved in the business know the business's purposes and operations.

As the lean business practices method has become more widespread, you will hear from followers of that approach that "the business plan is dead." They argue that all investors want to see is a **pitch deck**, maybe a business model canvas, and maybe a set of financials. Lean business practices started in Silicon Valley, and in that one very special place, business plans *aren't* needed—the investors in the Valley generally know the people they're hearing from and those people's track record or supporters. They have so many deals coming in (50 percent of all venture capital deals and 20–25 percent of all angel deals nationally come from California,[5] with more than three-quarters from Silicon Valley alone) that they claim they don't have time to deal with business plans. So savvy Silicon Valley entrepreneurs give the Silicon Valley investors what they want—pitch decks.

A platform for pitch decks, DocSend, commissioned a study in 2015 looking at the pitch decks that led to funding. In following up with the Harvard professor who did the study, while few of the pitch decks that got funding had business plans, almost all were app and Internet companies in Silicon Valley. Asked what happens in Boston, the professor replied that for apps and Internet companies, a business plan is sometimes not needed, but even there, some Boston investors wanted to see a plan before investing. For *all* other industries, a business plan was essential to being considered.[6] For the rest of the country, for the rest of funding (including bank loans, most angel investors, and most venture capitalists), and for virtually all industries with the possible exceptions of app making and Internet firms, a business plan *is* needed.

Even for lean business practices followers, and everyone else, there is a second circumstance under which a business plan is needed: for **internal understanding**. This is when you want to get all the aspects of the business clear in your mind and the minds of others in the business, such as your partners or your key employees. For example, the La Terrasse restaurant in Philadelphia survived more than 30 years because it had an extensive business plan. It talked about the history and vision of the restaurant and included a detailed operational plan covering everything from table layouts to techniques for minimizing waste. For new hires, the plan offered insight and specific information on the La Terrasse way of doing things.

Is a business plan absolutely essential? If you are seeking a banker, investor, or partner, yes. Generally if you need outside support to get a business going, those you are seeking support from will want to see a business plan—and you will want to make sure the plan addresses their concerns.

Also, if you are trying to start or run your business in a professional or ambitious way, a business plan is vitally important. It is true that some of the most famous entrepreneurial firms—Microsoft, Dell, Facebook, Holiday Inn—started without business plans. On the other hand, there are a lot more famous firms that started from the business plan—Amazon, Apple, eBay, Red Hat, Xerox, and Federal Express to name a few.[7] When *Inc.* magazine polled 500 owners of high-performing small businesses, 54 percent had a formal plan and 41 percent did not.[8] But even many of those who did not have a written plan had a plan in their heads with occasional parts written out, which is what Mark Zuckerberg had for Facebook. Typically, the higher-performing firms in any industry (measured in profits) tend to be those who engage in formal planning.[9]

It is important to know that research suggests that firms without a business plan are more likely to close down than firms with plans.[10] While having a business plan does not guarantee higher profits,[11] it is essential to qualify to be considered by business professionals for investments, loans, or credit lines. For example, Apple and Microsoft drafted business plans when they wanted to go for venture capital funds.[12]

These days there are more ways to plan than ever before. You've seen in earlier chapters techniques like the IDEO screen, the business model canvas, and the feasibility study. These embody different types of planning processes, focusing on particular aspects of the proposed business, and the undeniable fact is that regardless of the exact types of plans an entrepreneur pursues, engaging in the process of planning—even if it is only in your head[13] —is what helps you avoid problems and think about the best way to move your business along. In your head or on paper, sooner or later most businesses need to do some sort of plan.

The Business Plan Story: Starting Small and Building Up[14]

LO 8-2 Know how to tell the business plan story.

Business plans are a type of story. In a business plan, you tell the reader about a future place—your business. Every business plan is a bit like fiction. The best fictional stories are based on what exists now, as a good business plan should be. The business plan tells a story that starts in the here and now and builds believably toward a better future.

Good storytellers know that you make the story fit the audience's time. Sometimes you have only a moment to get the story of your business across; sometimes you have hours. Entrepreneurs need to have a variety of versions of their business's story available.

Figure 8.1 shows the path or sequence of presentations entrepreneurs may create when planning to go into business. When you have only a moment to talk, your vision statement or a tagline you've developed is the way to go.[15] When you have more time to talk about your business, longer and longer presentations are possible. These range from the two-sentence concept all the way to the 18-page business plan. The four types of business planning presentations are (1) vision statements, (2) elevator pitches, (3) executive summaries, and (4) business plans. We tell you how to do each in the following sections.

The Vision Statement

A firm's vision statement is perhaps its most important single idea held by the owner and employees.[16] The **vision statement** is a very simple 5- to 10-word sentence or, better yet, a **tagline** that expresses the fundamental idea or goal of the firm. As strategy professors Greg Dess and Tom Lumpkin suggest, a vision statement is supposed to be inspiring, overarching, and long term.[17] When Bill Gates and Paul Allen started Microsoft as teenagers, their vision was "a computer on every desk—running Microsoft software."[18] At the time, personal computers were being constructed by hobbyists and even lacked keyboards! So you can easily see how visionary their vision statement was.

vision statement
A very simple 5- to 10-word sentence or tagline that expresses the fundamental idea or goal of the firm.

tagline
Memorable catchphrase that captures the key idea of a business, its service, product, or customer (also known as a slogan).

Taglines or slogans or what Guy Kawasaki calls a mantra are a good way to present vision statements because a good tagline or mantra is brief and memorable. The tagline can also serve as the company's vision statement.[19] Some examples of good taglines encompassing the firm's vision statement are:

- Book Passage (Corte Madera, California): The Bay Area's Liveliest Bookstore.
- Crum Electric Supply (Casper, Wyoming): Plug into Quality—People, Products, Service.
- Progressive Insulation & Windows (Chatsworth, California): Total Living Comfort.

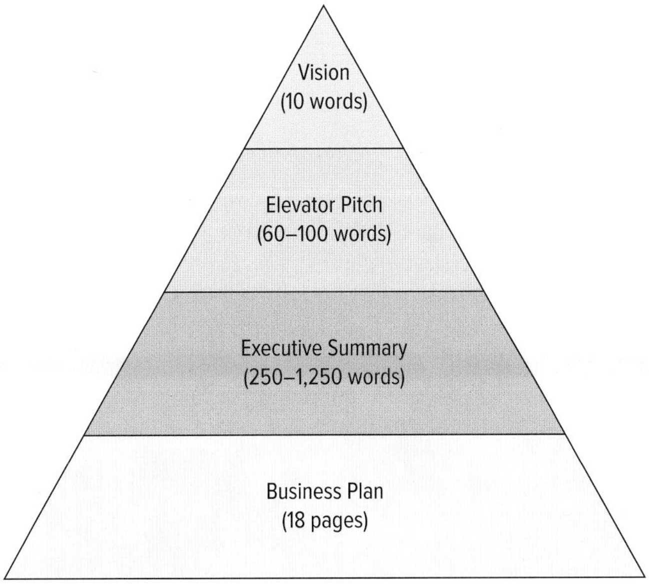

Vision
(10 words)

Elevator Pitch
(60–100 words)

Executive Summary
(250–1,250 words)

Business Plan
(18 pages)

FIGURE 8.1

The Path to the Business Plan

mission statement
A paragraph that describes the firm's goals and competitive advantages.

Related to the vision statement is a **mission statement**, which is typically longer (20–50 words) and often adds the firm's competitive advantage, which we discussed in Chapter 7. However, mission statements fell out of favor as they became too much like one another and too full of business jargon. Poking fun at these, sites like https://lotta.se/mission-statement-generator/ offer randomly generated mission statements that do not sound unreasonable. As a result, many small businesses drop the mission statement, moving from a vision to an elevator pitch.

The Elevator Pitch

elevator pitch
A 30-second (100 words or less) action-oriented description of a business designed to sell the idea of the business to another.

An **elevator pitch** is an action-oriented description of your business that is somewhat longer than a vision statement or tagline. It is designed to open the door to a more in-depth dialogue. Even when it doesn't lead to any sales at that moment, this information about your business should be memorable enough so that the listener can tell others about your business. The idea of the elevator pitch is that you are alone with a prospective customer or investor for the length of an elevator ride, say, around 30 seconds.[20] That comes out to 100 words or less. This description is used in one-on-one business settings and when someone asks for more detail after hearing your concept. In a time when politicians develop sound-bites and a good phrase can make a product (Altoids, for example, are "curiously strong"), having a high-quality elevator pitch for your business, like the following one for a cupcake truck, is more important than ever.[21]

> Is there any dessert that can offer the variety, innovation or eat-it-anytime satisfaction of a cupcake? Red Jett Sweets is Fort Worth's first mobile cupcakery, delivering freshly-baked traditional favorites like Red Velvet, seasonal treats like Peter Pumpkin and unique specialties like Beloved Banana Foster to multiple locations every day. We offer cupcakes with home delivery, special orders, gift wrapping, private parties, and customization. You look like you could use a cupcake. What can we offer you?

The Red Jett elevator pitch leads with the hook–luring us to think about cupcakes right off the bat. It follows up with the solution: Red Jett's offerings of traditional, seasonal, and specialty types of fresh cupcakes. For a familiar type of business like this one, you talk about what makes your firm unique or superior to the competition, in this case, the ability to go to multiple locations, delivery, and custom order and service. If your pitch were for a new type of service, you would want to give the listener more details about how it works than may otherwise appear in an elevator pitch. The pitch includes supportive details such as it being the first mobile cupcakery providing freshly baked favorites in unique flavors. And it ends with an ask or sales pitch. This

Going up? Each year, Saint Louis University's Chaifetz Center for Entrepreneurship holds its national Real Elevator Pitch competition. Real students with real business opportunities submit their pitches online. The best are invited to St. Louis to pitch to real investors in real elevators in Missouri's second-tallest building. Could you convince an investor to meet with you during a 40-second ride covering 42 stories? To see the competition in action, visit vimeo.com/125537474.

Saint Louis University

could also be where you close asking for money from seed investors. This is about 80 words and would take about half a minute to say. Listeners might be customers or investors, but either way, the goal is to sell them on the idea and their need for it. With this background, Skill Module 8.1 explains how to craft an elevator pitch.

How to Write Your Elevator Pitch

SKILL MODULE 8.1

Elevator pitches have four success factors: hook, solution, support, and ask.

First, find a *hook*—describe a problem you or the listener would face in a way that people would remember and take to heart. "Did you ever have trouble learning something?" Everyone has had that problem. "Big government couldn't find new small businesses to help." The terms are familiar and we could see the possible problem. "Imagine you have a beautiful 1967 Corvette but it has a busted water pump." People could imagine a classic old Corvette, so this would work too.

Second, focus on the *solution* your product or service serves for the customer. Do not talk skills ("I am a graphic designer"); talk about how you make customers happy ("I produce designs that sell books!") or what you can do for them ("We take care of all your online marketing needs").

Stan Mandel at Wake Forest University created the first elevator pitch competition, so he knows pitches. He suggests using analogies. If you're planning a website that connects people who love the outdoors with landowners who want to rent their properties for the day, you might say, "We will be the Airbnb for the outdoors."[22] It helps people quickly understand your firm. Great pitches or concepts aim to get the listener to ask questions or take some other form of "next step." Stan suggests different pitches for different sorts of audiences—investors, customers, suppliers, and so forth.

Third, provide *support* to prove to your listener that your solution is worthwhile. **Traction** with customers (whether sales figures, number of users, number of transactions) is often the best. Awards, recommendations, or high-star ratings by customers, experts, or the media can also help. Mentioning things like patents (even if they're pending) or leading-edge, industry-leading, pioneering, proprietary, or proven technologies can also help.

traction
Those characteristics of your business that show it is making progress, such as making sales, recruiting customers, being sold in more locations, or achieving milestones that reflect a firm's growth or development.

Finally, always close with an *ask*. This can be a request to purchase, an offer to tell more about your business, a follow-up meeting, a referral to someone who might benefit from your offering or help you or your business in some other way. If nothing else, ask how you can help the listener. There are two goals you can seek in your ask: One is to get the listener to make some sort of **micro-commitment** in favor of your business. Getting the listener to take a small step can reflect movement that will lead to sales down the road. The other is to build your network. Perhaps this person doesn't need what you are offering, but might know someone who would. You never can tell.

micro-commitment
An online action that is quick and easy to make and connects you to the message, but does not require a substantial personal or financial commitment, such a liking or favoriting a post or reposting it to your own social media account.

Once your elevator pitch is written, you need to become conversationally perfect in your delivery. You want to be able to give the pitch or concept dozens, even hundreds of times. Yet it is important that the pitch does not sound memorized. It needs to sound like regular conversation, preferably a conversation whose topic excites you. To achieve this, you must master the material and then keep working on it so that it becomes a natural part of who you are and what you say to others. Have family and friends listen to it. Consider using a video camera to see how natural you seem when making the pitch. Remember, the elevator pitch is often the first real insight people have about your business, so it is essential to have a pitch that flows and sells for you.

Realize that the goal in an elevator pitch is to start a connection. Even if you are asking the listener to buy, it is unlikely he or she will do so from a 30-second pitch. What is more likely—and what you should aim for—is to use the pitch as a first step in connecting with the listener. Exchanging cards, getting invited to his or her office to talk, grabbing a coffee, or even getting a call or email in the future are all considered outstanding outcomes from a pitch.

What do you do if the listener says he or she is not interested (or doesn't say anything)? There are two options: You can ask if he or she knows someone who might benefit from your product or service. If the answer is yes, ask for a referral. The other option (which also works if the listener doesn't provide a referral) is to ask if there is something you can do to help him or her, if you haven't asked earlier. Either way, a thank you at the end is always a good idea.

The Executive Summary

executive summary
A one- to two-page (250–500 words) overview of the business, its business model, market, expectations, and immediate goals. It is typically put at the start of a business plan and is the most popular summary form for a business plan.

An **executive summary** is the key component of the written business plan because it is the one element that nearly everyone will read first when they receive a plan. If the executive summary is part of the full business plan, it is typically one page long. A freestanding executive summary can go as long as five pages. Either way, an executive summary is an overview of the business, its business model, market, expectations, and immediate goals. (See Exhibit 8.1.) Executive summaries remain the most popular item to send people who ask about your business. They comprise the core of a business plan presentation and form the basis for additional discussion when someone asks for more detail. Executive summaries are written in a formal style, suitable for investors, lawyers, and bankers to read. They give much more detail about the business than the vision statement or elevator pitch. Executive summaries are usually organized in a series of short paragraphs (three or four sentences) and typically cover five key topics. These topics are:

- **Problem:** Describes the need for the product or service.
- **Product:** Describes the product or service and how it is used.
- **Market:** Describes the size and characteristics of the customer group and how they will buy the product or service (e.g., in person, online, catalog).
- **Competitive advantages:** Explain what makes the product or service unique, often in terms of an entry wedge.
- **Business/team:** Describes the current stage of the business, the timeline, and the team behind the product.
- **Financial summary:** Gives sales, growth, and profitability information, and if funding is sought, an overview of that.

The order for the topics in an executive summary is not fixed, although most experienced readers will be looking for the same items–markets, advantages, financials, and management. The summary is probably the single most important written part of the business plan for two reasons. First, it is the single most widely distributed written description of the business. Second, all readers of a business plan typically start with the executive summary, and then go on to the section where they can best apply their expertise. For example, accountants typically go to the financial projections after they've read the executive summary.

It also is typical to include the key numbers for the business such as industry size, customer base, number of employees, or projected sales. However, it is important to make sure that the numbers can be supported by a trustworthy source. Examples of such sources include the government, industry associations, and major commercial sources such as Dun & Bradstreet, the Risk Management Association, BizStats, or Bizminer. The sources may be included in the executive summary or made available to readers in footnotes.

EXHIBIT 8.1

Executive Summary for Red Jett Sweets (with Sections Identified)

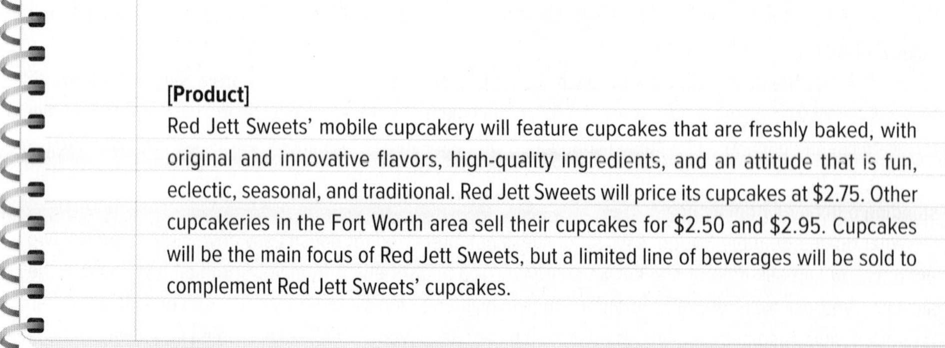

[Product]

Red Jett Sweets' mobile cupcakery will feature cupcakes that are freshly baked, with original and innovative flavors, high-quality ingredients, and an attitude that is fun, eclectic, seasonal, and traditional. Red Jett Sweets will price its cupcakes at $2.75. Other cupcakeries in the Fort Worth area sell their cupcakes for $2.50 and $2.95. Cupcakes will be the main focus of Red Jett Sweets, but a limited line of beverages will be sold to complement Red Jett Sweets' cupcakes.

[Market]

Red Jett Sweets' primary target market includes people aged 25 to 44 with household incomes of $75,000 or higher. Secondary target markets include people in younger (16–24) and older (45–54) age groups with household incomes between $40,000 and $75,000. Red Jett Sweets' primary trading area will be west Fort Worth. In the 2001 census, the total number of households in our primary target market was approximately 29,000. The total number of households in both the primary and secondary target markets was 60,000.

Red Jett Sweets' management and staff will provide customer service that is friendly and helpful, but not pressured, with an emphasis on building ongoing relationships. The mobile cupcakery will provide extensive client service offerings such as home delivery, special orders, gift wrapping, private parties, and customization. The mobile cupcakery design will create an inviting atmosphere that customers will enjoy visiting. Red Jett Sweets will focus on promotional strategies based on personal relationships, word of mouth, and social media marketing.

[Competitive Advantage]

Red Jett has three competitive advantages—our cupcakes, our location, and our social media efforts. We will offer our customers the greatest variety of products, best customer service, and best mobile food truck environment and experience, all available in accessible locations without paying more than at other storefronts in the area. Our mobility also means we are able to deliver larger orders. We will also have the most active Facebook and web media effort among competitors.

[Business and Team]

Red Jett Sweets, Inc. is a Subchapter S corporation opening a mobile cupcakery in August 2011. Red Jett Sweets will build a reputation in Fort Worth as one of the best cupcakeries in the area. Red Jett Sweets will provide its clients with innovative flavors, high-quality ingredients, and the highest level of customer service and satisfaction found anywhere.

At the heart of Red Jett Sweets are the owners, Christina Meyer and Natalie Gamez Meyer. They will be responsible for all aspects of product selection, client relations, and day-to-day operations. Ms. Meyer has previous experience starting and running a small business, where she has demonstrated talent in most of the activities required to manage a small business. Ms. Gamez Meyer has worked at many businesses in the restaurant industry and still maintains many connections in the industry. She is very detail oriented and well organized, and has a passion for baking.

[Financial Summary]

Red Jett Sweets expects to achieve sales revenues of $48,379 in the first year and up to $167,723 by the third year. It may be possible to achieve higher sales than this conservative estimate, which is equivalent to 160 cupcakes a day from August to December. Break-even sales for the first year are $80,358 or 29,221 cupcakes. Net income after taxes is projected to be ($17,003) in the first year and over $19,500 by the third year. Note that during these first three years of business, the break-even sales is raised and net income is significantly lowered due to purchases of equipment and amortization of intangible assets related to Red Jett Sweets' start-up.

Ms. Meyer's initial equity investment of $50,000 will fund the start-up of Red Jett Sweets. This includes $29,000 for the mobile cupcakery and small renovations; $13,000 in working capital; and $8,000 for marketing, equipment and R&D. **[626 words]**

LO **8-3** Learn the major sections of the business plan.

The Business Plan

The business plan remains the standard for describing the business in detail. It takes all the elements introduced so far and includes them in a complete description of the major elements of the business. The eight parts of the full business plan are detailed here and outlined in Table 8.2. The full (or classic) business plan contains a cover page, table of contents, a maximum of 10 single-spaced pages of text (around 3,500–4,000 words),[23] and 7 pages of appendixes that include the financials for a total of 18 pages.[24]

While the expected length of a plan is widely known, there are no "plan police."[25] Plans can be longer or shorter if needed. For example, a plan for any business whose product or service is new, even revolutionary, may need more pages to explain the product, service, or approach. However, recall from our discussion of strategy that most small businesses are more imitative than innovative. When you are going into an imitative business, your business plan might be shortened. Where the type of business is well established, such as a dry cleaner or word processing service, the market is well defined and well known, and the entrepreneur comes to the business with experience in the industry, the amount of necessary description could drop. In such cases, you might be

TABLE 8.2 Business Plan Outline[26]

1. Cover letter (1 page, but is separate from plan)
2. Title page and table of contents (2 pages, not counted toward limit)
3. Executive summary (1 page)
4. The company, product/service, and industry (2 pages total)
    - 4a. Company description (1 paragraph)
        - 4a1. Vision statement
        - 4a2. Company background
    - 4b. Product/service and industry (1–2 pages)
        - 4b1. Product/service description and value proposition
        - 4b2. Industry description
5. The market (3–4 pages total)
    - 5a. Market and target customer (1–2 pages)
    - 5b. Competition and competitive advantage (1 page)
    - 5c. Marketing strategy (1 page)
        - 5c1. Overall strategy
        - 5c2. Sales plan
        - 5c3. Competitive plan
        - 5c4. R&D/growth plan or next steps
6. The organization (1 page total)
    - 6a. Legal and organizational structures and IP and locations
    - 6b. Key personnel
    - 6c. Key partners, advisers, and related service providers
    - 6d. Key activities and operations
7. Financial summary: sales, profits, "the ask and deal" (1 page total)
8. The appendixes (typically 7 pages maximum)
    - 8a. Financial statements (3 pages): income statement, cash flow projection, balance sheet, start-up costs, assumptions, schedule
    - 8b. Supports: owner 1-paragraph biographies, product or service pictures, details or specifications, indicators of success

submitting a 2- to 3-page executive summary of the business, along with the financials and appendix. Table 8.2 summarizes the classic business plan in outline form, and page budgets are given for each content section. Note that the page budgets for items 3 through 7 total 8 to 9 pages. The leftover 1 to 2 pages available to you can be used to strengthen any of the regular portions of the plan, or bring up material you might otherwise put in the appendix to help better tell your story.

If you have tried the techniques introduced in Chapter 4 to screen your ideas and assess their feasibility, you've already done a significant portion of the thinking and writing you will need for the business plan. Table 8.3 shows how the sections from an IDEO screen, business model canvas, or feasibility study align with the sections of a business plan shown previously.

As you move through the different write-ups for your business ideas, you generally are adding detail to the ideas and its components. You are also building key details on how your idea will get translated into a specific business. These details are important. McDonald's and Red Robin are both hamburger restaurants, but their details differ dramatically. Let's look at the parts of the business plan from the start.

TABLE 8.3 Comparison of Business Write-Ups

IDEO Screen	Business Model Canvas	Feasibility Study	Full or Classic Business Plan
			1. Cover letter 2. Title page 3. Executive summary
Technical Feasibility	Problem Solution	1. Business idea 1.1 Business description 1.2 You, your firm, and your fit 2. The product/service 2.3 Stage of development 2.6 Trends related to product/service 2.7 Product/service delivery costs	4. The company and product/service 4a. Company description 4a1. Vision statement 4a2. Company background 4b. Product/service and industry 4b1. Product/service description (and value proposition)
Technical Feasibility	Value proposition	2.1 Unique features: Benefits 2.2 Unique features: Limitations	4b1. (Product/service description (and value proposition)
Market Desirability	Customer segments	3. Industry and market 3.2 Market potential for industry 3.4 Customers	5. The market 5a. Market and target customer
Market Desirability	Customer relationships Channels	3.5 Market penetration	5c. Marketing strategy 5c2. Sales plan
Technical Feasibility	Distinctive competence	3. Industry and market 3.1 Current industry 3.3 Competition	4b2. Industry description 5b. Competition and competitive advantage 5c1. Overall strategy 5c3. Competitive plan
Business Viability	Key resources Key partners	2.4 Legal restrictions and rights 2.5 Insurance requirements	6. The organization 6a. Legal and organizational structures and IP and locations 6b. Key personnel 6c. Key partners, advisers, and related service providers
	Key activities		6d. Key activities and operations

(Continued)

TABLE 8.3 *(Continued)*

IDEO Screen	Business Model Canvas	Feasibility Study	Full or Classic Business Plan
Business Viability	Cost structure Revenue streams	4.6 Profitability 5.1 Start-up capital 5.2 Sources of start-up capital 5.5 Support needed	7. Financial summary—sales, profits, "the ask and deal"
		5. Future action plan 5.3 Further information needed 5.4 Writing a business plan	5c4. R&D/growth plan or next steps
		4. Financial projections 4.1 Pricing 4.2 Sales revenue forecast 4.3 Cost forecast 4.4 Gross profit 4.5 Operating expenses	8. Appendixes 8a. Financial statements: income statement, cash flow projection, balance sheet, start-up costs, assumptions, schedule
			8b. Supports: owner 1-paragraph biographies, product or service pictures, details or specifications, indicators of success

Cover Letter

When you send a business plan to someone, it is a good business practice to include a cover letter. A **cover letter** is a one-page document that introduces the business plan and owner and indicates why the recipient is being asked to read the plan. It is typically the first written material someone sees about your business, so it needs to look and sound just right. The specifics of writing a cover letter are provided in Skill Module 8.2 in Appendix A of this chapter, along with an example of a cover letter. Traditionally cover letters were done on business stationery (also called *letterhead*), but today, with most business plans being submitted electronically, it is most typical to write a cover letter as email. If you go that route and you have a **signature block** for your business, include that.

cover letter
A one-page document on business stationery (also called *letterhead*) that introduces the business plan and the business owner to the recipient and indicates why the recipient is being asked to read the plan.

signature block
A snippet of text (or text and images), typically inserted at the bottom of an email, that contains contact information for the sender of the email.

Title Page

The title page typically contains the following information:

- Company name (usually in large type, with a logo if you have one).
- Contact information (owner name[s], company address, telephone and fax numbers, email, website, and social media addresses).
- Date this version of the plan was completed.
- Proprietary statement to protect your ideas: For example, "*This document contains confidential and proprietary information belonging exclusively to [your company's name goes here]. Do not copy, scan, fax, reproduce, or distribute without permission.*" On the line following this statement there may be a copy number unique to each copy of the plan. This helps you keep tabs on individual copies.

There are three other possible items to include on the title page. One might be a securities disclaimer. If you are using a business plan to seek individual investors, it is important to state the following on the title page: "*This is a business plan. It does not imply an offering of securities.*" Typically this comes after or as part of the proprietary statement. The disclaimer is needed to comply with Securities and Exchange Commission (SEC) rulings. Another item to include is the name of the person who prepared the business plan, if it is someone other than the owner. The third possible item for inclusion is a notice of copyright for the plan or trademark for your brand name or logo, if you choose to pursue those forms of intellectual property protection. You can learn more about those in Chapter 17.

Table of Contents

The table of contents typically puts the major section headings (e.g., executive summary, company, market, etc.) in boldface type and the sections underneath each in regular type. Page numbers are given for every component, including financial statements and appendixes. Remember to put page numbers on every page of the business plan, even the financials. Typically, the table of contents is combined with the title page or starts the second page of the plan packet.

Executive Summary

Many entrepreneurs write the one-page executive summary first, using it as a guide, and then write the rest of the plan. (We discussed the executive summary earlier in this chapter.) Covering the major sections outlined in Table 8.2 is the usual strategy–company, product/service, industry, market and target customer, competitive advantage, marketing strategy, organization, and financial summary where each is a sentence or two. In general, it is common to come back and revise the executive summary as your thinking changes as your write your plan, so it is the first and also the last item you will edit in your plan.

Company, Product/Service, and Industry

The first section of a business plan tells the story of your product or service, and the company that will deliver it. It usually consists of two subsections–one that provides an overall description of the business and another focusing on its product or service. The sections can come in either order.

Company Description (1 paragraph)

Typically this paragraph gives the vision or tagline of the company and a brief description of the business–its age, current status (start-up, seed stage, ongoing, expansion, and so on), and location, as well as the markets it serves or plans to serve. The firm's most recent milestone achieved is often mentioned (received initial investments, finalized product design, tested a prototype, completed market testing, made first sales, and so on). For an existing business, the history of the business is briefly covered here.

Product/Service and Value Proposition (1–2 pages)

In many ways this is the most important section of the plan because it is where readers come to understand what your business is all about–the product or service. Today this most often starts with a description of the problem (pain) you are trying to solve or the benefit you're hoping to deliver to the customer (gain). You then introduce your product or service as the solution, and explain how it works and how it delivers on the need. The description is often bolstered by a graphic of the product to help readers better visualize it.

These descriptions are rooted in the idea of the value proposition introduced in Chapter 4 and the value benefits to the customer (quality, style, delivery, service, technology, shopping ease, personalization, assurance, place, credit, brand/reputation, belonging, and altruism) discussed in Chapter 7.[27] The product's or service's competitive advantage is also mentioned here. Additionally, if the product or service has protection through a **proprietary technology** or from patent, trademark, or copyright, you mention it here.

proprietary technology
A product or service or an aspect of one that is kept as a trade secret or is protected legally using patent, copyright, trademark, or service mark.

Industry (1 paragraph)

The paragraph usually has the industry's formal name (possibly including its NAICS number), its size (in number of firms and sales), and whether the industry is growing, stable, or in decline (with some measure of this). Much of this information comes from the industry analysis, also discussed in Chapter 7.

The Market

The market section talks about your customers—who they are and what they are like, who else is pursuing them, and how you plan to get and keep your customers. The market section builds on material you may have developed in the IDEO, business model canvas, and feasibility analyses you've done earlier (see Chapter 4), the industry analysis (see Chapter 7), and the marketing efforts plan (see Chapters 9, 10, and 11).

Market and Target Customer (1–2 pages)

As you can probably tell from the amount of space allocated, this is the second most important part of your business plan, because it tells us who will buy your product or service. The market refers to the total population of people or firms to whom you plan to sell. Markets are usually described in terms of their size (both in numbers of customers and size of sales) and scope (local, regional, national, international, global). The major ways the market is organized, what are called channels in the business model canvas, are also covered. Professional, trade, or industry associations, special-interest clubs, major national gatherings, and media dedicated to the market (e.g., *Restaurant Business* magazine for restaurant owners, or *Scrapbooking & Beyond* magazine for people who are into scrapbooking) are all relevant.

The target customer section focuses attention on the individual who would buy your product or service. Target customers are described in terms of demographics (such as age, gender, education, income, experience), their relation to the product or service (will they use it themselves, gift it, resell it, etc.), how often they buy (once a day, once a week, twice a month, every three years, once in a lifetime, etc.), their past experience with your kind of product or service (new user, prior user of competitor's product, prior user of your product), and what they are looking for when buying your product or service. Often target audiences are described in terms of the marketing funnel introduced in Chapter 10. What target customers are looking for should be based on discussions with potential customers, and it hopefully matches closely with the value benefits your product offers. Providing a comparison of the two is often a good idea.

It is very common to have multiple target audiences, also called customer segments. When this is the case, you should provide a separate description of each one. It often helps to give each target group a specific name when you refer to them in the rest of the business plan. For scrapbookers, the target audiences have names like "kiddies," "moms," "grandmoms," "hobbyists," and "historians." Since your marketing plan can differ dramatically among the different groups—imagine how to sell to "kiddies" and "historians"—you want to have an easy way to differentiate them. There are several ways to develop these, such as empathy maps, user personas, and value canvases, which will be discussed in Chapter 9.

Competition and Competitive Advantage (1 page)

Consider doing this section with a half-page of text and a half-page table. The table identifies the major competitors for your market by name. Remember from Chapter 7, the vast majority of businesses are imitative in nature, not new, and rarely disruptively new. If you think you don't have competition, think again! What do your customers use to achieve your goal now? Find those firms or products and list them here. Other columns mention market shares, price, competitive strength, and competitive weakness.

The accompanying paragraph summarizes the table's results and focuses on your firm's competitive advantage—what makes your product or service or firm unique—and how your competitive advantage gives you an opportunity to win sales from competing firms. Often this information is based on material gathered from the industry analysis (see Chapter 7). Some people prefer having this section included in the industry section. That works, too. The advantage of having it here is that it connects your market description to what you will do to sell your product or service against the competition.

Marketing Strategy (1 page)

A good marketing strategy section focuses on three ideas: (1) the overall strategy your firm pursues in the market, (2) the sales plan that shows the specific ways you apply strategy to secure sales from your customers, and (3) the longer-term competitive plan that shows how you protect your firm from efforts of the competition to unseat you. Many of the specifics are built from the ideas you develop in the marketing chapters of the book, Chapters 9, 10, and 11.

The overall strategy paragraph is a short one that discusses your generic strategy (differentiation, cost, focus) as well as any supra-strategies (craftsmanship, customization, etc.) or fragmented industry strategies (no-frills, formula facilities, etc.) you pursue. Explain here how each is used in your firm and in your sales efforts.

The sales plan paragraph addresses the day-to-day specifics of how sales are achieved. It builds on the value benefits being sought by your customers and shows how these are turned into promotional efforts, pricing and incentive programs, distribution techniques, and location. Most of all, it emphasizes the way you or your employees go about selling. Examples of advertising materials, displays, coupons, social media campaigns, or the like are useful and typically mentioned here, but details are put in an appendix. The proof that your approach is working comes from sales made using these approaches, so the strongest sales plans talk positively about the results of pilot tests, **presellling** efforts, or conventional sales already made. Being able to name customers (especially repeat customers) really builds up this section.

preselling
Involves introducing your future product to potential customers and taking orders for later delivery.

R&D/Growth Plan or Next Steps (1–2 paragraphs)

Over the longer term, even with a clear competitive advantage, a sound strategy, and a good sales plan, your competitors are not likely to give up the market. They will fight back. When they do that, trying to match your sales plan features or competitive advantage, what are you keeping in reserve to help you fight back? Here is where you want to have several additional strategies that play against weaknesses in the competition, or further improve your product or service. These can include protections through patents and intellectual property protection or relationships with powerful partners. You may have contracts that tie customers to you long term, but most often advantages come from bringing out improved versions of your product or service before the competition introduces its own improved product or service.

Having these improvements ready requires some preparation on your part. In a business, this is often called **research and development (R&D)** or the *growth plan*. Most business plans add a section on R&D or growth here to explain how they are working to maintain an in-depth competitive advantage, with one or more additional generations of products or services ready to be used, or quickly brought to market, in order to keep the competition one generation behind your firm in meeting customer needs. Growth plans often talk about longer-term partnerships to be sought, new markets to be pursued, or ways to leverage the firm's assets, for example through licensing or franchising. Even for a firm at its earliest stage, before you know what your competitors' reactions will be, this section can be used to tell the steps your firm will be taking in the next few months to become established, beyond the specifics described in the rest of the plan. The R&D or growth or next step paragraph can occur in this section, or at the end of the plan as a means of outlining the business's future.

research and development (R&D)
The part of a business (and a business plan) that is focused on creating new products or services and preparing new technologies, ideas, products, or services for the firm's market.

The Organization

In this section you lay out the components and supports for the firm itself. So far you have covered the product and the customer. The goal for this section is to convince the reader that the business will be successful because it has access to high-quality people both within the firm and within the larger business community, and the organization itself is structured to make the best use of those people.

Legal and Organizational Structures and IP and Locations (1 paragraph)

This subsection describes the legal form of the business (LLC, C corporation, sole proprietorship, etc.) and where it is formally registered (topics discussed in Chapter 17) and located (both physically and on the Internet). If the firm has acquired licenses or certifications they are mentioned here, along with the firm's intellectual property protections, such as patents, trademarks, and trade secrets. If some of these are in process, mention that.

Key Personnel (1–2 paragraphs)

By now you have sold people on your vision, mission, product, service, competitive advantage, and even your sales approach. It is now time to sell the most important single element in the business plan–you! In any business and any business plan, everything hinges on the quality of the entrepreneur behind it. If we do not have confidence in the entrepreneur, there is no way to have confidence in the other parts of the plan. The goal for the key personnel subsection is to inspire that confidence in your reader.

Who are your key personnel? Any owners or senior managers count, as do people who will be handling key aspects of the business. For example, a salesperson with an extensive customer base would be a key employee, as would an employee who is locally famous for a skill the business will use. Often businesses have a circle of outsiders involved. This might include a local media personality who will be promoting your business, or the inventor or holder of a patent or trademark you are using, or the owner of a key outside venture partner.

While you might put in the résumés of one or two key people in the appendix if you have the space, typically the key personnel are each described in a two- to three-sentence description. Simply put, the goal is to impress the reader. What is impressive? Accomplishments, and the closer these are to the business, the better. Having been successful in the business in this industry in another firm or in your own firm (if this plan is for an existing business rather than a startup) is the best proof. Having been successful in another line of business is a good second choice. Having experience in sales is always useful, as is experience managing projects or people.

Whenever possible talk about accomplishments rather than just experience. Achieving some mark of distinction, such as being a store's top salesperson, is best, followed by years of experience in some aspect of business, followed by education. Sometimes giving the specifics of the accomplishment does the job, even if no award was given. For example, being able to say "In my five years at Hobbyco, my sales increased an average of 50 percent a year" shows your sales abilities are improving, which is good.

When looking for accomplishments, do not limit yourself to business. Particularly for students and stay-at-home spouses, there are often organizational accomplishments that are relevant. Activities undertaken or managed for schools, churches, social organizations, civic organizations, or community groups are often important indicators of expertise. For example, managing a team during a fund-raising event may help prove your skills in people management and making quick decisions.

Often this section concludes with a sentence or two that makes clear how many employees there are and whether they are full time or part time, permanent or seasonal, family or nonfamily.

Related Service Providers (1 paragraph)

These days, small businesses are rarely alone, and the quality of the professionals surrounding you tells people a lot about how good you might be. Taking a paragraph or two to identify your bank and banker, your attorney and legal firm, accountant or bookkeeper, and other consultants can help show that you have high-quality supports. If you have major relationships established with well-known suppliers or customers, list these here also. If you have a board of directors, members can be mentioned here or under key personnel. If you have a board of advisers made up of people who are not owners, they would be listed here.

Key Activities and Operations (1 paragraph)

Many times your business will operate in very standard ways. For example, most restaurants literally buy their kitchens and dining products from the same catalogs or showrooms. Letting people know that you will operate in a familiar way is useful. That said, the "imitation with a twist" strategy we recommend suggests that there be something in how you operate, or in your business model, or in your product or service that is distinctive, and this is a place to show how that twist plays out. Also, if there are key activities–things you must get right to be successful–or specialized operations that you want investors or partners to know about to prove you have mastered your business, this is a place to put that information.

The Financial Summary

The one-page financial summary section starts with a paragraph (often with a summary table) showing the overall financial results (in sales and profits). It is followed by "the ask," which is what you are seeking from others, the use of the investment funds, and the projected returns. For all types of business plans, a set of financial reports or projections then follows as the central component of the appendix. For the summary and the full financials themselves, it is always important to develop them in the most conservative way possible—never overstate your sales or profits, always explain the assumptions you are making, and provide (or be ready to give) the source for every number you include. It is usually better to include fewer numbers, but ones you understand inside-out, rather than having lots of numbers, but knowing only in a general way how you arrived at them.

"The ask" paragraph typically talks about how much money is needed and how the funds will be used. This paragraph goes on to address any prior or existing investments and the current ownership situation. Then it explains the funding type being offered to investors (see Chapter 14), giving the price and the kinds of assurances offered (e.g., seats on the board of directors, buy-sell agreements, etc.). Here the plan details how investors will be able to sell or redeem their funding in order to harvest their money tied up in your business, and exit the business. The best plans explain how investors will be assured that management will be responsive to investor concerns.

The Appendixes

The financial statements expected include (1) income statements (also called a P&L for profit and loss) and its assumptions; (2) cash flow and its assumptions; and (3) balance sheet and its assumptions. For start-up businesses, it is also common to include a listing of the expenses incurred in the start-up process.

For an existing business, the financials report the last two years of actual data, and then offer three-year projections for the income, cash flow, and balance sheet. For a start-up business, the tradition is to offer three years of data projections. If you will take three or more years to show a profit, it makes sense to give projections for five years. In either case, income and cash flow are given monthly for the first year, and annually for the second and later years. Think in terms of a layout described in Exhibit 8.2.

Note that each of the financial statements also includes its assumptions. Included as endnotes or footnotes, the assumptions are often considered to be the most important part of the financials. Assumptions explain how the computations are made, which items are included or excluded, and whether there are any special considerations underlying the particular numbers. For example, key assumptions include how sales are computed, which items are expensed versus depreciated, and how inventory and business valuations are made.

A schedule of the major milestones or benchmarks the company plans to achieve is often included in the financials section, typically toward the end. If significant milestones or

EXHIBIT 8.2

Financials Layout for a Typical Business Plan

Page 1:	Income statement and cash flow tables (year 1 by month, years 2–3 [or 2–5] by year). Assumptions given in endnotes or footnotes.
Page 2:	Balance sheet for years 1–3 (or 1–5) by year. Assumptions given in endnotes or footnotes.
	Start-up cost budget. Assumptions given in endnotes or footnotes.
Page 3:	Overflow from financial statements, footnotes or endnotes.
	Timeline or milestone list.
Pages 4–7:	Supporting materials that can help you tell your story better. (See the bulleted list below.)

benchmarks have already been achieved, these can top off the schedule, so readers can see how the firm has progressed.

With approximately three pages used for financials, you have up to four pages left for appendixes. The ones you select depend on what you are trying to highlight in your business plan. They can include:

- Product or service pictures or specifications (important when you stress features or style, or when your product or service is not familiar to readers).
- Copies of signed contracts, letters of intent or commitment, or contingency contracts from customers or investors (useful to show acceptance).
- Results of marketing studies or pilot sales efforts (useful for showing market acceptance).
- Industry reports (if there is significant information not included in the plan).
- Price lists for products or services.
- Floor plans of the location, if it is central to the business (e.g., a manufacturing facility or restaurant).
- Advertising copy, such ads, logos, catalog pages, brochures, sales letters, or press releases.
- Customer or spokesperson testimonials.
- Letters of opinion from intellectual property attorneys on prospects for patent or trademark protection or from manufacturers or consulting engineers about the viability of production processes for the product.
- More detailed biographies of principals, or a one-page version of the owner's résumé (see Skill Module 8.3 in Appendix A of this chapter).

If readers want to know more about something that is not in the plan, they will ask you for the additional information. So do not worry too much about the many possible appendixes you cannot include. The goal of appendixes is to provide the most essential supporting information that helps detail the key selling points of your plan.

The Mechanics of a Business Plan

Most people use the outline and notes in this chapter to write a business plan from scratch. They talk with their team, their instructor, and their mentors about which parts of the plan to include or skip, and which parts to add material for greater clarity or impact. Other people prefer to start with the structure you get when you use a business plan writing program. The best-known commercial program is LivePlan.com from Palo Alto Software. The best-known free programs are given in the "Learn More Online" box below. While there is a lot of similarity between the formats of those online plans and the plan in this chapter, there are some differences of coverage and order. Table 8.4 compares the coverage of the model in this chapter (the ESB plan), the Red Jett Sweets example plan in Appendix B, the SBA's business plan model, and LivePlan.

Consider using Table 8.4 to help you think about different ways to order your own plan and to think more broadly about what you want to see in your plan to make the best impression on the people reading it. You might also want to compare the plans in the table to other online options for business plans, such as those shown below.

LEARN MORE ONLINE

Learn more about the topics above at these sites:

Purdue's INventure plan (free): **www.purdue.edu/newventure/**

TD Bank plan (free): **www.tdbank.com/small_business/create-business-plan.html**

StratPad (free plan for college students and start-ups): **www.stratpad.com/stratpad-college/**

Business plan tool from Wells Fargo (free): **https://bizplantool.com/**

FormSwift plan (free): **https://formswift.com/business-plan**

TABLE 8.4 Comparison of Business Plan Models

ESB	Red Jett Sweets	SBA	LivePlan
1. **Cover letter**			
2. **Title page**	1. **Title page**	1. **Cover page**	
3. **Executive summary**	2. **Executive summary**	2. **Executive summary** 2.1 Product 2.2 Customers 2.3 What drives us	1. **Executive summary** 1a. Opportunity: Problem and solution Target market Competition Why us? 1b. Expectations: Forecast Financing needed
4. **The company and product or service** 4a. Company description 4a1. Vision statement 4a2. Company background 4b. Product/service and industry 4b1. Product/service description 4b2. Industry description	3. **The Company** 3a. Company description 3b. Mission statement/ value proposition 3c. Products 3b. Industry	5. **Product/service line** 5.1 Product or service 5.2 Pricing structure 5.3 Product/service life cycle	2. **Opportunity** 2a. Problem and solution: Problem worth solving Our solution Company history*
5. **The market** 5a. Market and target customer	4. **The Market** 4a. Market & target customer 4b. Mobile cupcakery placement strategies	4. **Marketing research** 4.1 Industry 4.2 Customers	**Opportunity** 2b. Target market: Market size and segments
5b. Competition and competitive advantage	5. **The Competition** 5a. Competitive 5b. Competitive advantage	4.3 Competitors 4.4 Competitive advantage	2c. Competition: Current alternatives Our advantages
5c. Marketing strategy 5c1. Overall strategy 5c2. Sales plan 5c3. Competitive plan	6. **Marketing Strategy** 6a. Marketing objectives 6b. Sales plan	6. **Marketing and sales** 6.1 Growth strategy 6.2 Communication 6.3 Prospects	3. **Execution** 3a. Marketing and sales: Marketing plan Sales plan
6. **The organization** 6a. Legal and organizational structures and IP and locations	7. **The Organization** 7a. Legal issues	3. **Company description** 3.1 Mission statement 3.3 Legal structure 4.5 Regulation 5.4 Intellectual property rights	4. **Company** 4a. Overview: Ownership and structure Intellectual property* Regulatory requirements* 3. **Execution** 3b. Operations: Location and facilities
6b. Key personnel 6c. Key partners, advisers, and related service providers	7b. Key personnel	3.2 Principal members	4b. Team: Management team Advisers Partners and resources*

(Continued)

TABLE 8.4 (Continued)

ESB	Red Jett Sweets	SBA	LivePlan
6d. Key activities and operations	7c. Key operations	[No equivalent section. You will need to add this.]	3. **Execution** 3b. Operations: Technology Equipment and tools 3c. Milestones and metrics: Milestones table Key metrics
7. **Financial summary—sales, profits, "the ask and deal"**	8. **Financial summary**	[No equivalent section. You will need to add this.]	4. **Financial Plan** 4b. Financing: Use of funds Sources of funds Statements Exit strategy* 4b1. Product/service description
5c4. R&D/growth plan or next steps		5.5 Research and development	
8. **Appendixes** 8a. Financial statements: income statement, cash flow projection, balance sheet, start-up costs, assumptions, schedule	9. **Appendices** 9a. Appendix A: Financials 9a1. Start-up costs 9a2. Break even sales 9a3. Financial projections	6. **Financial projections** 6.1 Profit and loss 6.2 Cash flow 6.3 Balance sheet 6.4 Break-even 6.5 Financial assumptions	4. **Financial Plan** 4a. Forecast: Key assumptions Revenue by month Expenses by month Net profit (or loss) by year 4c. Statements: Profit and loss statement Balance sheet Cash flow statement
8b. Supports: owner 1-paragraph biographies, product or service pictures, details or specifications, indicators of success	9b. Appendix B: Supports 9b1. Owners biographies 9b2. Mobile cupcakery 9b3. Product photos 9b4. Rack card - cupcake menu	[No equivalent section. You will need to add this.]	[No equivalent section. You will need to add this.]

*In LivePlan, these items can be added into the plan. They are not part of the basic plan outline.

Note: Items in **bold** are section headings.

At this point, you might think the writing of the business plan is done, but there is still work to be done assembling it. Plans are typically delivered as an 8 1/2-by-11-inch document or electronically as an Adobe Acrobat PDF file (that includes your financials and appendixes integrated into the single document[28]), which has been carefulee and repetedly checked to eliminate spelling and grammer mistakes [see how much a couple of spelling mistakes stand out and make you think less of the project?]. In these days of 140-character messages sent on the fly, everyone's spelling has suffered, but if your plan's words are problematic, readers may also think your numbers, or worse yet your ideas, will also be full of mistakes.

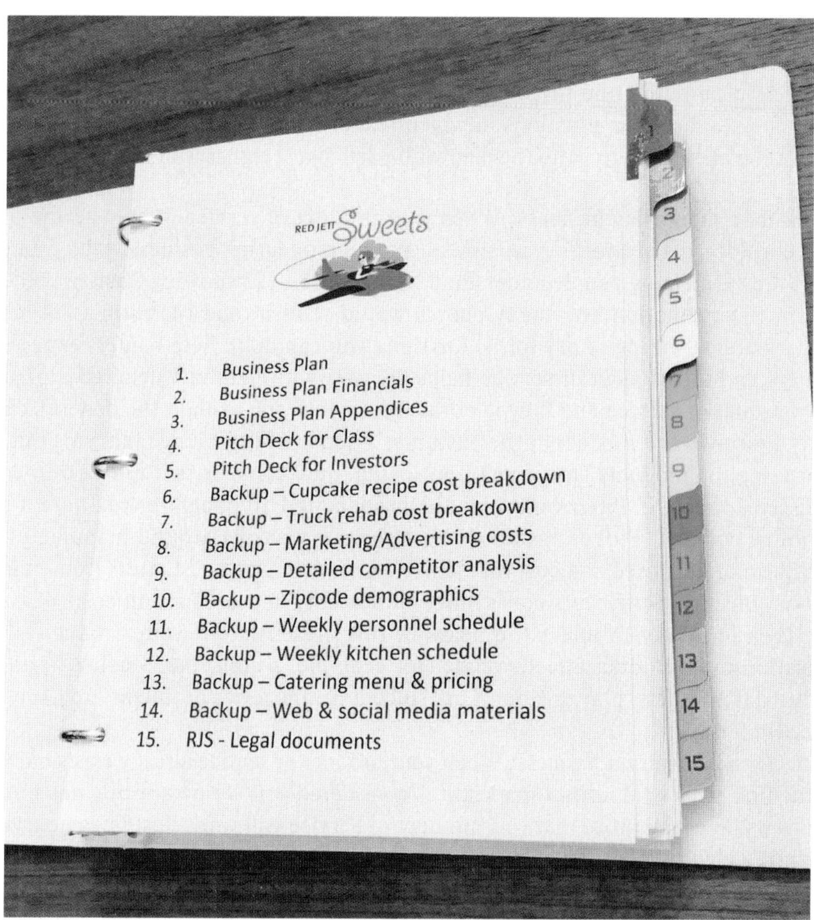

Three-rIng-binder version of your business plan with tabs for major sections and subsections.

Jerome Katz

Along these lines, make sure you have checked that all pages are included and cleanly printed. While your own copy of the plan will be in a loose-leaf binder to make insertions and deletions easy, the copies you give out should be spiral bound (so they lay flat when opened). Covers should be sturdy to protect the plan from the inevitable coffee stains of business. Cover letters are typically clipped to the cover, rather than included in the plan itself, so the reader opens the plan to see the title page.

There are typically two versions of any business plan: the one you give others and the one you keep for yourself. The difference is what is included in each. As we've said, the plan you give others is 18 pages long. That plan becomes the basis for your personal copy, but you add to your personal copy the material on which you built your plan, things like the detailed market study or competitive analysis, the detailed product comparison, the details of your pricing or costing model for your financials, the agreements you have struck with partners, leases, intellectual property filings, the interviews you have conducted as you built your plan, or if you are already in business your customer lists or accounting records–in short, anything a potential investor or partner might ask of you to back up what you have included in your plan.

As you can tell, this means your personal copy of the plan is probably a good-sized three-ring binder, ideally with tabs for each section of the plan and even for the major documents within each tab. This is the copy of the plan you take with you when you present. Why a three-ring binder rather than a copy on your laptop or tablet? Because any panel of investors will want different items at about the same time, and a laptop can be used by only one person at a time. The paper copies can also be easily handed out, or spread out and compared. The electronic version of the three-ring binder is called a **data room**, and is what you share with potential financiers when they are looking at nearly every aspect of your business in-depth as they consider investing, a process known as **due diligence**. You can create a data room by creating private folders in Google Drive or Dropbox and sharing the URL with those considering your business, or use dedicated data room services like Box.com or one of its several competitors.[29]

data room
An online repository (e.g., Dropbox, Box, ShareVault) for the documentation that backs up and details the specifics of your business and business plan. The contents of the data room are very similar to those of the three-ring-binder personal edition of the plan held and used by the founder.

due diligence
The process of investigating a business to determine its value and potential for investment.

LO **8-4** Focus business plan sections to meet specific needs.

Focusing Your Business Plan

To be successful in telling the firm's story, a business plan needs to match the needs of the reader. Businesses face four situations in which reader needs are specific enough and distinct enough that it makes sense to write the plan with particular emphases in mind.

pioneering business
A firm whose product or service is new to the industry or is itself creating a new industry.

test marketing
Selling your product or service in a limited area, for a limited time.

new entrant business
A firm whose product or service is established elsewhere, but is new to this market.

- **Plans for a pioneering business:** When your product or service is truly new to everyone, it is considered a **pioneering business**. With a pioneering business, your greatest problems are (1) helping people understand how it works, (2) showing them how they would use it, (3) estimating how many people would want it, and (4) estimating how much they would be willing to pay for it. Anything you can do to help readers experience and understand the product or service helps demystify it. Plan on a detailed explanation of the product or service and how it works. Make sure you explain the benefits customers would receive, and talk about the customer's personal experience in trying out, buying, and using the product. The value of preselling, pilot tests, or **test marketing** cannot be stressed enough. If 100 people tried the product and 10 bought it, you have a powerful proof of concept. Pioneering products also face a hurdle around manufacturing–can they be manufactured at a cost that leaves a chance for profit? Letters from manufacturers or consulting engineers confirming the viability and production costs of your product go a long way to alleviating fears in this area. Also, if your product is a minor variation on a product already made (for example, a consumer version of an existing industrial product), play this point up, since it means fewer problems are likely for your specific product.
- **Plans for a new entrant business:** When your product or service already exists but your *firm* is the first of its kind in your market, it is considered a **new entrant business**. As such it is always harder to prove that your product or service will work. Just imagine trying to explain the idea of a $5 cup of coffee to people who had never heard of Starbucks! In response, help make the product or service seem more familiar by detailing how it is used by customers, and give more background on how the product or service has done in other markets, especially markets similar to yours. Also emphasize existing operations in your industry analysis. Seeing that it has worked elsewhere takes much of the mystery out of the question of whether it would work where you plan to market it.
- **Plans for an existing business:** Occasionally, entrepreneurs start a business before they write a plan for it. When writing a plan for an existing business, you have the benefit of knowing the history, the existing market, and the financial track record of the firm. These form a foundation for the plan, so the projections about future markets, sales, and profits should clearly build on these historical facts. It can make sense to gather information on existing customers to help clearly define the market, and often suppliers and trade associations can provide more in-depth information on market shares and competitors. Existing firms have assets to protect, such as the customer list, the firm's name, and any intellectual properties it has developed (e.g., a patented way of performing work, a trademark, a copyrighted report, a recipe protected as a trade secret). Showing how you plan to protect and perhaps even make additional profits from your intellectual property (e.g., through licensing patents or trademarks) strengthens the plan, as does talking about new ideas for increasing sales, which typically appears in the research and development section.
- **Plans for a business with significant government involvement:** Some businesses depend on government approvals to go forward. Examples include salvage yards, garbage dumps, companies using toxic chemicals, nursing homes, service stations, and even in many places, day-care centers. When government gets involved in a major way, for example, having to approve the business license, zoning, or environmental impact, delays are inevitable. You need to build a plan that anticipates delays and either works around the parts of the business requiring approvals or is able to go into a type of sleep mode, using as few resources as possible until approval arrives. Working around approvals usually hinges on selling services or products that are part of the business but do not require specific approval. For

someone starting a service station, it may be possible to do minor car repairs such as oil changes, detailing, or tune-ups at the customer's home or workplace. This helps spread the word, build a customer base, improve skills, and keep cash flowing until approval for the service station comes.

Once you have written the complete business plan, you are positioned to create special-purpose versions of the plan to meet the needs of a wide variety of people important to your business. Usually these special-purpose plans use a subset of the total plan. In addition to the full business plan described previously, there are seven other special-purpose types of plan:[30]

- If you intend to send your plan to professional funding sources such as private banks, investment clubs, or venture capital firms, it is common to send what is called a *mini-plan* or a **screening plan**. The idea is to give the basic overview of the firm and a detailed look at the financials. This is because funding sources typically start their decision process with clear ideas about the industry and the profit levels they want to pursue. Screening plans usually consist of the cover letter, title page, executive summary, and financials sections of the business plan. The only time any appendixes would be included is when it is important to prove the viability of contracts, intellectual property protection, or the product's ability to be manufactured. A screening plan can also be a useful way to get into the planning process. Michael McMyne won one of the Global Student Entrepreneur Awards for his consulting business. When he started, all he used was his executive summary and the financials.[31]

screening plan
Also called a *mini-plan*, gives the basic overview of the firm and a detailed look at the financials.

- You may find that the business plan has a lot of information you would like to share with potential customers or suppliers, but you do not want them to see your financials. One variant of the traditional business plan is called the informational plan. **Informational plans** typically consist of company and organization sections. The cover letter, title page, executive summary, and table of contents are typically revised to reflect the differences. Relevant appendixes might also be included, such as detailed product descriptions or price lists.

informational plan
A business plan that gives potential customers or suppliers information about the company and its product or service.

- A special form of informational plan posted on the Internet is the **proof-of-concept website**. This kind of site is designed to solicit information on customer interest. They are particularly useful for demonstrating a technology or service that is new or novel or to reach a market that is very widely spread out, making conventional promotional techniques too expensive. The goal is to inform customers and partners about the firm and the product, so proof-of-concept websites consist of the vision and mission statements, the product/service description, and often an animated or interactive demonstration of the product or service. Short biographies of the key personnel replace résumés, and the site may also have price or product lists or testimonials. The site itself tracks information about the viewers. Visitors are asked for feedback on the concept and are offered the chance to be kept up-to-date as the product nears the market.

proof-of-concept website
An Internet-based type of business plan providing information or demonstration of a product or service designed to solicit information on customer interest.

- In seeking a marketing or joint venture partner or a key employee, you need to provide more of an idea about your market and approach to it. In the early stages of finding a partner, however, it is usually too soon to share your detailed financial information. As a result, a **key employee/partner plan** (also called a *summary plan, concept plan*, or *idea plan*) can be drawn up to include all the materials of an informational plan, plus the market section and critical risks subsection of the regular business plan.

key employee/partner plan
A business plan that provides information on the company, product/service, market, and critical risks to prospective business or marketing partners or to prospective key employees.

- An **invention plan** focuses on the market and operationalization of a new invention. Inventions are typically licensed to others, so the organization section simply describes the inventor and any business the inventor runs, to provide background. The product or service being invented is given a very detailed description, with diagrams or pictures to help the licensee understand it. While the plan helps explain the market and competition to the prospective licensee, the marketing strategy is not typically included. Legal issues tend to focus on intellectual property protection (e.g., patents, trademarks, etc.) instead of on the legal form of organization, and the financials are limited to the prospective deal and risks, since the invention does not come with a firm that creates sales.

invention plan
A business plan that provides information to potential licensees. Invention plans focus on the details of an invention, including intellectual property rights.

operational plan
A business plan designed to be used internally for management purposes.

private placement memorandum (PPM)
A specialized legal form of business plan crafted by lawyers for the purpose of soliciting formal investments.

offering circular (OC)
A legal document required by firms seeking funding through equity crowdfunding platforms created under the JOBS Act. An OC contains SEC required forms, an offering memorandum (which is almost identical to a PPM), and the financial statements of the firm.

- There are only two types of plans that actually add material to a full business plan. **Operational plans** are designed to be used as working documents within a business. So in addition to all the material typically included in a full business plan, an operational plan includes detailed specifications of the major techniques, methods, recipes, formula, and sources used by the firm to do its work.
- The other type of plan that adds to a business plan is a **private placement memorandum (PPM)** or an **offering circular (OC)** for equity crowdfunding under the JOBS Act. PPMs and OCs are the official versions of a business plan offered to potential investors. As such, it is a legal document, and should be drafted by a lawyer. PPMs/OCs build on a business plan, using information about the company, products and services, strategy and operations, and competition. There are also sections on the risks facing the business, the people and partnerships, the deal being offered, the financial statements, and the planned use of the investment money, although these are often longer (for the risks section, much longer) than in a business plan. There are also sections unique to a PPM/OC such as a plan for the description and distribution of shares, compensation of managers and officials, and even the articles and bylaws of the corporation. In short, PPMs/OCs are complex and exacting and should be left to lawyers. However, the basis for a PPM/OC is the business plan that you create.

Table 8.5 provides an easy way to compare the different types of special-purpose plans and the components they take from the full business plan. Even though the table shows the business plan sections and subsections usually included, it is important to keep the specifics of your business and your readers in mind. If sections of the business plan seem inappropriate for your type of business or for the specific readers who will see the plan, it makes sense to leave them out. The business plan is first and foremost a sales document, and tailoring the plan's "pitch" to the specifics of your business and the readership is always a smart move.

LO **8-5** Identify the major risks to business plan success.

The Most Common Critical Risks in a Plan

risks
The parts of a business or business plan that expose the firm to any kind of loss—profits, sales, reputation, assets, customers, and so on.

working capital
The cash immediately available to the firm for the day-to-day expenses and operations of the firm.

Every business faces **risks** in the real world, so every business plan needs to spend some time addressing them.[32] The exact issues raised by business experts, bankers, lawyers, and investors are often specific to your plan, but the themes they consider in assessing risks are actually quite common. Knowing these risk themes, you can go through your business plan, identify the risks, and determine how you want to handle them, the way the founder of Daniel J. Watkins Photography did (see the following Small Business Insight). Each of the risks can be handled, but the best test is to have people in your target audiences give you feedback on your plan.

1. **Overstated numbers:** Examples include sales or profits that are too optimistic, owner salaries above the minimum needed to live when the firm is just starting out.
2. **Numbers that are wrong:** Examples include balance sheets that do not balance, numbers in the financials that do not flow from one section to the next, no assumptions given for the financials, and ratios that do not match RMA or other standards (Standard & Poors, Bizminer), with no explanation given for the differences.
3. **Inadequate cushion:** The number one killer of young firms? Not enough money. Having enough cash (called **working capital**) to survive three to six months goes a long way to avoiding this risk.
4. **Inadequate payback:** There are always opportunities out there; is yours worth someone's time, energy, and (maybe) money? Any plan that does not clearly specify the key paybacks to readers will fail to sell them on the idea. Don't offer an investor a 10 percent return when corporate bonds offer nearly that with little risk of default.
5. **Narrative and financials that do not fit:** If you have a plan that calls for a large marketing campaign, but financials do not show costs for one, there is a problem.
6. **No direct customer connection:** If it sounds like you have not actually talked to potential customers about your product/service, readers will consider that a major problem.

TABLE 8.5 Types of Business Plans

Business Plan Sections	Full Business Plan	Operational Plan	Invention Plan	Key Employee/ Partner Plan	Informational Plan	Proof-of-Concept Website	Screening Plan
1. Cover letter	X	X	X	M	M		M
2. Title page	X	X	X	M	M		M
3. Table of contents	X	X	X	M	M		
4. Executive summary	X	X	X	X	M		X
5. The company	X	X	M	X	X		
5a. Company description	X	X	M	X	X	X	
5a1. Vision statement	X	X		X	X	X	
5a2. Mission statement	X	X		X	X	X	
5a3. Objectives (optional)	X	X		X	X		
5a4. Company background	X	X	M	X	X	X	
5b. Product/service and industry	X	X	X	X	X	X	
5b1. Product/service description	X	X	X	X	X	X	
5b2. Industry description	X	X	X	X	X		
6. The market	X	X	X	X			
6a. Market and target customer	X	X	X	X			
6b. Competition and competitive advantage	X	X	X	X			
6c. Marketing strategy	X	X		X			
6c1. Overall strategy	X	X		X			
6c2. Sales plan	X	X		X			
6c3. Competitive plan	X	X		X			
6c4. R&D/growth plan	X	X	X	X			

(Continued)

TABLE 8.5 *(Continued)*

Business Plan Sections	Full Business Plan	Operational Plan	Invention Plan	Key Employee/ Partner Plan	Informational Plan	Proof-of-Concept Website	Screening Plan
7. The organization	X	X		X	X		
7a. Legal and organizational structures	X	X	M	X	X		
7b. Key personnel	X	X	X	X	X		
7c. Related service providers	X	X	X	X	X		
7d. Location	X	X		X	X		
8. The financials	X	X					X
8a. Critical risks	X	X	X	X			X
8b. The deal	X	X	X				
8c. Income statement	X	X					X
8d. Cash flow projection	X	X					X
8e. Balance sheet	X	X					X
8f. Start-up budget	0	0					
8g. Assumptions	X	X	M				X
8h. Schedule	X	X	X				X
9. The appendixes	X	X					
9a. Owner's résumé	X	X		0	0	M	0
9b. Popular appendixes	X	X		0	0	0	0
10. Detailed specifications of work	0	X					

Note: X = Included; M = Included in modified form; O = Optionally included. PPMs and OCs are not included since they are done only by lawyers.

SMALL BUSINESS INSIGHT

ANALYZING RISKS AT DANIEL J. WATKINS PHOTOGRAPHY

Daniel J. Watkins Photography

Award-winning photographer Daniel J. Watkins started two businesses in the last decade—one succeeded and one failed. In that first business, sales never seemed to take off, and the financial health of the business was not as clearly known as it should have been. Dan feels the major difference between the two was the presence of what he called "a good solid business plan" for the second business. Dan argues that a thorough business plan can turn great ideas into reality because it forces you, the prospective entrepreneur, to take a close 360-degree look at your business ideas. For Dan the plan became a basis for evaluation as his business grew, with detailed sections on the market, how to sell to them, and the financial projections those sales should generate. He knew he was getting the hang of business when the second business venture became profitable in the exact year, quarter, and month that his original business plan had forecast it would. The one element of the plan Dan credits with the most importance was the critical risks section. Dan claims, "If I hadn't considered some of the potential pitfalls associated with my original business ideas, my business venture probably wouldn't have been successful or profitable at all." For Dan, the plan made all the difference, and the critical risks section made the plan.

7. **Uncertain sales (especially conversion rates):** You need to prove your sales estimate. The best way is to know your *conversion rate* (alias *hit rate*), which is the percentage of people who buy out of the total population of people you approach. You get this from test marketing or preselling (introducing your product to potential customers and taking orders for later delivery).
8. **Overlooked competition:** You do not want to overlook a major player in your industry. If a search on the web or in a phonebook can turn one up you could be in trouble. Also be broad in your search for competitors. For example, a student claimed there was no competition for his wireless cell phone headset because he didn't use Bluetooth, but the Bluetooth headset makers could quickly change radio types if it made business sense. Recall Porter's five forces (rivals, substitutes/alternatives, buyers, suppliers, new entrants) to find competitors.

9. **Experience deficits:** Do you (or someone else in your firm) have experience in (a) the line of business, (b) the industry, (c) the locality, (d) managing?[33] Have it, find it, or say how you'll learn it.
10. **"What" problems:** For the product or service, make sure it is explained clearly enough so anyone could understand it. Also make sure the plan (or cover letter) is clear about what is being asked of the reader (e.g., invest, make a loan, give feedback, partner, etc.).
11. **Deadly aggravations:** Looking and sounding professional is key. A plan with misspellings looks amateurish. Lacking a table of contents or page numbers in the plan makes life harder for people you want to impress. Selling instead of summarizing in the executive summary comes across as hucksterism.

Ideally, you should have a circle of advisers who can review the plan and help identify the critical risks and your coverage of them. This circle might include successful entrepreneurs you know, lawyers, or accountants. Other good resources include the free consultants from the Service Corps of Retired Executives (SCORE), available via www.score.org, or your local Small Business Development Center (www.sba.gov/sbdc). There are even websites that make it possible for you to get a preliminary analysis of your plan. The SBA has an online self-assessment (https://eweb1.sba.gov/cams/training/business_primer/assessment.htm) that is keyed to SBA resources and is suitable for a wide range of businesses. To get a quick check of your major financial measures, you can use the BizStats website (www.bizstats.com). The key is to get as much feedback as possible before sending it out in hopes of money, sales, or people.

LO 8-6 Master pitching your business plan to others.

Pitching Your Plan

pitch
The name given to the formal presentation of a slideshow summarizing your business plan given before judges or potential investors or partners.

When it works, a written business plan is the way to get on the schedule of someone who can provide the money, the expertise, or the markets you seek. In such cases, the written plan is followed by a chance for you to make a formal presentation of your plan and answer questions about it. This presentation is called a pitch, and the slideshow you have created for the **pitch** is called your pitch deck. The pitch, like the plan itself, has a very clear tradition about how it is supposed to be done. Knowing this tradition can help you quickly learn what is expected when pitching a plan to others.

A business plan presentation or pitch usually lasts 10–15 minutes, followed by 15 or more minutes for questions. Usually the pitch provides an overview of the key points of the business plan—a chance to sell your ideas and, most of all, a chance to sell yourself.

A major part of any business plan presentation is a chance for the listener to form an opinion about you as an entrepreneur. The key things an influential person looks for in you

Presenting your business plan as often as possible, to fellow students like you see here or to businesspeople, can help you become a more polished and professional presenter. What is the biggest challenge you feel you face in pitching your plan to others?

ColorBlind Images/Blend Images LLC

are (1) your passion for the business, (2) your expertise about the business and the plan, (3) how professional you are in your work, and (4) how easy it would be to work with you. How do you show these?

- **Passion for the business:** When pitching, do not read. Think of yourself as telling a story–a fascinating story–about your business. Help listeners understand why you are excited about the business, proud of it, and ready to stake your reputation and assets on it. Learn your pitch so well that it comes out as an often-repeated, beloved story, not as a prepared statement. This is the point where watching pitches on *Shark Tank* can prepare you for the real world.
- **Expertise about the business and the plan:** Practice answering questions about the plan. Expect really tough questions. Assume people do not trust your assumptions when they first read them. Be ready to explain where you get your assumptions, your numbers, and your ideas. Be ready to mention sources. Be ready with comparisons to competitors and their offerings. (This is where your three-ring binder with the backup information becomes invaluable to you.) Know how every number in the plan came about and what it means. For example, it is not uncommon for a banker to ask, "In your cash flow statement for April in the first year, you say you will be spending $1,140 on sales promotion expenses. How did you get that number–and isn't it a bit high?" It is better to have less material and know it backward and forward than to have material in the plan you do not totally understand.
- **How professional you are in your work:** Your plan should look professionally done. It should be neat and orderly, with perfect spelling and grammar. When you present it, you should be in business attire, clean and pressed. Carry copies of your presentation slides to give the listeners. And have copies of your slides on USB so that you can present no matter what technology is available. Have business cards ready, and bring a couple extra copies of the plan in case someone unexpected comes to the presentation. Meet all those attending the presentation with a smile and a firm handshake. Give them your card and take theirs if they offer one in return. Make sure you know the names of all the people in the room, and their position, so if there is a part of the plan you think might be of interest to them, you can mention it.
- **How easy it would be to work with you:** Typically when you are presenting a business plan, you are doing it with the goal of establishing an ongoing relationship with the listener. All relationships carry an element of liking. It is easier to see yourself establishing a relationship with someone you like than with someone you do not like. Part of the goal in the presentation is to get the listeners to like you. How? The techniques are simple–use eye contact, use people's names, remember what they might be interested in or in what they have shown an interest before, smile, and above all, be honest. When they ask tough questions, try not to get nervous, upset, angry, or defensive. If you do not have the answer, tell them so honestly, make a note about their question and name (do it right then–it gives them confidence you're taking them seriously), and tell the person you will get back to him or her with the answer. Then make sure you deliver on this promise! Recognize that tough questions are the listeners' way of making sure they–and you–are protected from risks.

It may be hard to accept it when you are pitching, but no matter what the outcome, there are two points in the presentation where your listeners will be giving you value: in the questions they ask you and in the feedback they give you at the end of the session. Make sure you have someone taking notes for you (you will be busy answering questions) or ask if you can record the Q&A session on your smartphone (make sure you have an app for it). Knowing what kinds of questions are being asked can help you prepare for the next time, and can also inform you on how best to revise the plan. Recalling what the feedback was regarding you and your plan also gives you a powerful leg up for your next presentation. If the listeners offer feedback after your presentation is over, take notes or see if you can record that too.

Typically the presentation follows the content of the business plan. For different audiences, for example, potential partners or customers, you delete slides–just as you delete sections in the business plans for partnering or customer information plans.

Crafting Your Pitch Deck

Probably no part of the business plan experience has changed as much in the past few years as the creation of pitch decks. Part of this comes from research. Online pitch deck sites like DocSend.com or DocDroid.net track how long viewers spend on slides, and in what order they look at slides.[34] Online displays of pitch decks reflect one of the two ways they get seen. The other (and more common) way is a face-to-face presentation between the start-up's entrepreneur and a judge in the classroom or a potential investor or partner outside of school. For either setting, the contents of a solid pitch deck are very well known. Exhibit 8.3 gives the specifics on the content of the slides and what you talk about when presenting the slides. Each category has one slide, unless noted otherwise. This approach leads to a 15–17 basic slide deck. By the way, the typical font size is 30 points or larger for text and 44 points or larger for titles.

EXHIBIT 8.3

Pitch Deck Slide Categories

1. **Introductory Slide:** This slide has your firm's name and the names of the owners and presenters. It introduces your firm by name, as well as you and any other people from your firm whom you have brought with you.
2. **Company Purpose Slide:** While showing this slide, you thank your listeners for the opportunity to present and explain the purpose of the business as well as the purpose of this presentation of the plan (e.g., financial, partnering).
3. **Problem Slide:** This slide tries to make real to the listener what is the problem customers face or what is missing from their experiences. The more important this is, the better. Sometimes the problem is given in the form of a user's experience.
4. **Solution Slide:** This slide demonstrates how your product or service solves the problem or provides a much-needed benefit. Sometime entrepreneurs will skip this slide in favor of the product slide doing double duty.
5. **Product Slide(s) (1–2):** Often it is useful to go into more detail on your product or service—how it works or its details. Your goal is to give the listener an in-depth understanding and create a positive attitude toward your product or service.
6. **Why Now Slide:** What makes this point in time the right one for your business idea? New problems? New technologies? Failures of competitors? Legal changes? Something missing locally?
7. **Market Size Slide:** This slide gives the size of the overall market (customers/sales) as well as the specific target market you can sell to, address, or service.
8. **Business Model Slides (2–3):** There is often more than one slide in this category. Building on the market size, this section explains how you will market, distribute, and get sales made, with an eye toward how you will generate revenues and profits.
9. **Competition Slide(s) (1–2):** One slide identifies the major competing firms or products/services and shows how you compare to them. A second slide usually shows how you will successfully compete against these firms and what is your general strategy and distinctive competence.
10. **Team Slide(s) (1–2):** Investors invest in people as much as in ideas. This slide presents the key people with the one or two skills they have that are most persuasive in proving their expertise or their contributions to the business. If you have partnerships or alliances with names the listeners would know and respect, these can be included (often as corporate logos) and briefly mentioned on an additional slide.
11. **Financials Slide:** Here you give the sales, breakeven, and profit projections for the firm for the period covered in the plan. Be prepared to mention the worst-case scenario

projections if asked, but explain why you think the numbers on the screen are the most likely ones.

12. **The Ask and the Deal Slide:** "The ask" can be funding, partnership, mentoring, network access, or just general support and feedback. Give this line in your most confident and sales-oriented manner and mention that you believe you have shown this in today's presentation. Include a line on the slide with the request from the listener ("Distribute our product," "Line of credit of $100,000," "Investment of $50,000," "Mentor our firm on selling to corporations"). In covering this, explain briefly what the use of the listener's resources will be. There should also be a line on the slide for what is offered in return (for the items above—the opportunity to grow sales, savings moved to a bank, stock in the firm for investors, or a chance to help a great young firm grow). This is what is called "The Deal" by investors.
13. **Closing Slide:** Slide decks end with a slide that says thanks and asks for questions.

Storytelling and the Art of the Pitch

The hook-solution-support-ask model we introduced for the elevator pitch can be easily expanded to handle the pitch deck. The greater time available to you when pitching means you can engage in telling more of a story about your recognizing and solving the problem, and a lot more about the company you have developed to implement your solution. These stories tend to fall into one of several **storytelling arcs**. The model we use is based on one of the oldest and best-known models, Aristotle's Three-Act Structure.[35]

storytelling arcs
There are several classic structures to stories, such as beginning, middle, and end, or a multiple-step journey, or a situation-complication-resolution.

- Act I—The Beginning: You set up the story
  - The arc starts with the hook, which gives listeners a little bit of introduction about you and how you came to recognize a problem in the world or something you felt needs to be done. This is the first effort to introduce a little bit of drama in your story.
- Act II—The Middle: You introduce the inciting incident and action rising to the solution
  - You tell listeners about the problem, who has it, the problem's size, and why it needs to be solved. This part of the story is intended to make listeners realize that something needs to be done—it builds up the drama in your story.
  - You introduce what the solution is, the story of how you arrived at the solution, and why it helps solve the problem. The drama in this part of the story comes from your efforts to solve the problem, why it is a good solution, and why now is the time to solve the problem.
- Act III—The End: You tell listeners the rest of the story and conclude
  - You add the supports that tell listeners about the business you have created to make the solution available. Here the drama is replaced by parts of the story that help listeners feel good about your firm's ability to keep solving the problem.
  - Having heard the story's hook, problem, solution, and supports, listeners should be ready to hear you ask for the kind of help you want from them. Since this is you asking listeners to consider doing something, it shifts the drama from you to them, and your asking them for something should help them increase their own level of readiness, if for no other reason than you are asking for a response from them.
  - Finally you offer a closing that brings the story to its conclusion, typically one that ties back to the beginning, thanks listeners for listening, and opens the floor for questions and responses from them.

If you look at Figure 8.2 you can see how the four sections of an elevator pitch relate to the elements of the storytelling arc and to the slides of a typical pitch deck shown in Exhibit 8.3. The figure also shows how the drama level increases and changes as you tell your firm's story.

FIGURE 8.2

The Storytelling Arc and Its Relation to Elevator Pitches and Pitch Deck Slides

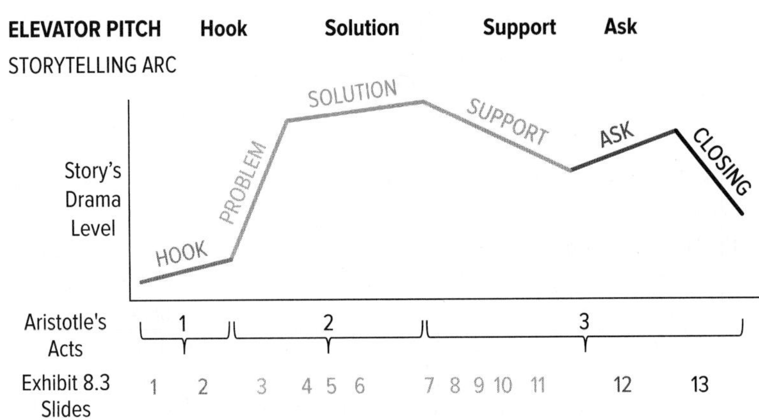

The drama shouldn't be coming from your voice (we are not talking about screaming about the problem!) but rather from the nature of the story itself. Most of us, when hearing about a problem, want to see it get resolved. If a solution was not obvious, we appreciate it more, and if you ask us for something, we typically will give it some thought. These are the natural elements of drama that we expect when we find ourselves in the role of a listener. Use it to your advantage.

The Mechanics of Pitching

Like the three-ring-binder version of the business plan containing additional appendixes and background research and material on the business, the pitch deck you take with you in reality is likely to have a lot more slides than the ones shown in Exhibit 8.3. A 15-slide basic pitch deck can often have 25 or more additional slides prepared to answer questions likely to come up, or provide additional depth on the topic raised in the plan or pitch. There is nothing that proves your mastery of your business and the pitching process like being asked a question and pulling up a prepared slide with the answer.

The mechanics of pitching typically involves presenting your pitch deck using your own laptop or tablet, or one at the location where you are pitching. In designing your pitch deck, it is worth taking time to think about how easy it will be for listeners to see your slides. If you're using a laptop or tablet, small type on a slide becomes a hindrance to your pitching. When most people see a slide dense with words or numbers, they tune out the speaker to take a few seconds to figure out what is on the slide–that's the power of visual stimuli working. To have people focus on you and what you are saying, craft slides with few words or numbers.

If you are creating a pitch deck for online access, an almost opposite set of rules apply. Since you won't be there to explain what is on the slide, you need to create the pitch deck that can convey your thinking without you being there. In this case, having more words on each slide is acceptable, and adding enough slides to make sure people understand the basics of your business is fine. Unlike the pitch deck for a 10-minute presentation, which has a natural limit on how many slides you can cover, the online pitch deck is less constrained. That said, the DocSend study reported that investors looking at pitch decks online spent only 3 minutes and 44 seconds on average looking at a pitch deck!

One other mechanical aspect of the pitch deck is the specific program and templates you use for the pitch deck. When you are starting out, using PowerPoint or Keynote to outline your thinking is fine, but as you move closer to presenting for real, you want to "up your game" in terms of the quality of the slides (see the Small Business Insight for an example of this).

LEARN MORE ONLINE

Learn more about the topics above at these sites:

Slides with visual design elements: **www.canva.com, www.beautiful.ai**

Slide backgrounds that match keywords: **https://haikudeck.com**

Keynote, Mac's equivalent of PowerPoint: **www.apple.com/keynote**

Explainer videos: **www.moovly.com**

Circular (vs. linear) models with zooming: **https://prezi.com**

Working from outlines: **https://slidebean.com**

SMALL BUSINESS INSIGHT

THREE GENERATIONS OF A PITCH DECK

Holly Faivre, Lauren Hoffmann, and Jackie Price were working on a product called "Good For U," a superfood additive for smoothies and yogurt. Over the course of a semester in the business plan class, their pitch deck went through several iterations. The three key stages are shown here for the product slide.

Initially, they started by outlining ideas. This was a bare-bones effort to help get the ideas down on the version 1 slide.

As they became more confident about the content, they sought to make the slide more attractive and professional. Using Google Slides, they added pictures they found on the Internet, as you can see below in version 2.

Our Product

- Seeds, fruits, vegetables, and other superfoods
- Pureed
- Supplements your other foods
- 12 oz jar
- Flavors
  - Acai Blueberry
  - Matcha Kale
  - Cacao Sweet Potato

Version 1: The initial product slide.

Version 2: The revised product slide.

Lauren had a friend, Jessica Burgess, who was a graphic designer, and they worked out a trade—a revamped slide deck in return for a home-cooked dinner. The change from "You" to "U" came from a trademark conflict the team discovered. Version 3 shows the resulting final design used in the presentation to judges.

Version 3: The final product slide. GOOD For U

This sort of revision process is typical of the development of pitch decks. If you don't have access to graphic designers, consider looking for professionally designed templates for pitch decks. PowerPoint, Keynote, and Google Slides offer pitch deck and business plan templates. Try Googling "pitch deck templates free" for others.

Closing Thoughts on Business Plans

Business, and the understanding of business you get from business plan writing, changes. Sometimes it changes quickly as you achieve new things or learn new things (including errors that crept into the plan you just finished). This means that parts of your plan may change from week to week. You handle this by creating handouts with the new information. These can be mailed to people reading your plan, or handed to them at the presentation. If there are detailed parts of your plan that you have left out, such as a market survey or a detailed cost breakdown, it makes a lot of sense to make copies to use as handouts during a presentation or question-and-answer period.

Dwight Eisenhower was not only the 34th U.S. president, but he was also the general who planned the most daring effort in all of World War II, the D-Day landing. A master planner, Eisenhower said, "I have always found that plans are useless, but planning is indispensable." The best way to think about the business plan is as a way to get yourself to think through your entire business. Some parts will be so easy that you can instantly know how everything works. Things in the business you imitate from others are classic examples. For other aspects of the business, planning may become the way you get a handle on the complexities and risks you face.[36] Some results of the planning process you will write down. Other parts will be kept in your head, ready to be used or amended as circumstances require. Many of the parts of the plan will quickly become outdated or need to be changed or adapted as the business is in operation.[37] In fact, the Eisenhower quote makes sense in another way too—business planning is a process you continue throughout your firm's life. Plans, once done, get revisited. Sometimes this is done formally, but more often you informally compare reality with the plan. See the Small Business Insight for more business planning words of wisdom.

SMALL BUSINESS INSIGHT

WISDOM FROM THE FRONT LINES

Those of us teaching at Saint Louis University have asked for short takes from students after the smoke clears from their business plan presentations. Here are some of the most memorable observations and thoughts:

- I nailed my numbers, but this entrepreneur failed my plan because I misspelled his name in the cover letter! It is a lot like playing poker for the first time, but you're playing against pros [for this student, bankers and angels] that have been doing this for years. You've got to bring your "A" game or it's all over!
- Before you start pitching, walk over, look them in the eye, smile, and introduce yourself. It makes them more like regular people.
- You don't have to have everything in the plan, just as long as you have it with you when you present. [This student's partner added—"And have it where you can find it. Tell your students, USE TABS!"]
- When they challenged me and I knew I was right, I stood my ground, but I was polite about it. I think that got me their respect.
- After a while, the judges could figure out which member of our team wasn't "into" the plan and they just kept hounding that person.
- Passion pays! If you don't come across as totally believing in your plan, nobody will. Pitch it like your life depends upon it. My grade did!
- How can an inexperienced kid stand up to those old guys? I figured I've got energy. I've got fresh knowledge. I've got a world of supporters I can get to on the web, and nobody knows my business or cares about my business more than me. If they don't like it, I've got years to go find someone who does.
- The best plan is one where you've already got sales. If you've got sales, you've proven everything. If you've got sales, you've got cash and you've got real financials, not financial projections. I got sales, so I had it made.
- Like my mom always says, where there is a will, there is a way.

However you approach it, the idea of business planning is a powerful one, helping you imagine and then realize the business the way you want it to be. The techniques that contribute to creating a business plan—forming vision statements, elevator pitches, financials, and pitch decks—can be used as stand-alone activities that help you meet the many demands you face as an aspiring entrepreneur. Whether you become an avid business planner or not, the process of business planning goes a long way to helping firms survive and prosper.

CHAPTER SUMMARY

LO 8-1 Understand why and when to develop a business plan.

- Plans are done for external legitimacy and/or internal understanding.
- Plans are sometimes essential, and are often linked to improved firm survival.
- Different audiences seek different goals when reading business plans.

LO 8-2 Know how to tell the business plan story.

- The business plan is a story you write about your firm.
- The story gets told in different ways and lengths, from vision statements, to elevator pitches, to executive summaries, to full business plans.

LO 8-3 Learn the major sections of the business plan.

- The business plan gives the complete story of the firm and its major elements: company, product/service, industry, market and target customer, competitive advantage, marketing strategy, organization, and financials.
- It is a maximum of 18 pages long, with a cover page, 10 pages of text, and up to 7 pages of supporting material.
- Business plans build from the IDEO screens, canvases, and feasibility analyses you have already done.

LO 8-4 Focus business plan sections to meet specific needs.

- A business plan is often modified for special circumstances the firm faces, such as pioneering technology, new markets, established operations, or significant government involvement.
- Parts of a business plan are often combined to create shorter plans for particular audiences such as investors, partners, or others.

LO 8-5 Identify the major risks to business plan success.

- All business plans face risks; part of the role of the business plan is to explain how the firm will handle these risks.
- The risks come from numbers or assertions that are not adequately explained or supported.

LO 8-6 Master pitching your business plan to others.

- Most business plans are presented to others using a pitch deck.
- Listeners check presentations for the presenter's passion, expertise, professionalism, and potential as a colleague.

KEY TERMS

business plan, 226
external legitimacy, 226
pitch deck, 228
internal understanding, 228
vision statement, 229
tagline, 229
mission statement, 230
elevator pitch, 230
traction, 231
micro-commitment, 231
executive summary, 232
cover letter, 236

signature block, 236
proprietary technology, 237
preselling, 239
research and development (R&D), 239
data room, 245
due diligence, 245
pioneering business, 246
test marketing, 246
new entrant business, 246
screening plan, 247
informational plan, 247
proof-of-concept website, 247
key employee/partner plan, 247
invention plan, 247
operational plan, 248
private placement memorandum (PPM), 248
offering circular (OC), 248
risks, 248
working capital, 248
pitch, 252
storytelling arcs, 255

DISCUSSION QUESTIONS

1. What are the reasons to write a business plan?
2. Imagine you were presenting your plan to a consultant who specializes in your industry. Your goal is to get her help. Using the ideas in Table 8.1, what kinds of issues do you think would be of interest to her as she reads your plan?
3. You are going to attend an after-work gathering sponsored by your local chamber of commerce. Which of the types of short business plan presentations (vision statement, elevator pitch, executive summary, pitch deck) will you prepare for use, and when will you use them?
4. What is the most important part of a business plan in general? Considering the way you plan to use your business plan, what will be the most important part of it?
5. What are the differences in a business plan for a start-up pizza business and for an existing pizza business?
6. Students know people, including some who might invest in your business. What kind of business plan (e.g., informational, screening, key employee, full) would you give to other students?
7. For a business plan being put together by a student in his late teens or early 20s, what are the most likely risks?
8. Passion is clearly important in the business plan presentation. How can you display your passion for the business during the presentation?
9. What can you do to make the business plan easy to read and understand?

EXPERIENTIAL EXERCISES

1. **Evaluating a Business Plan:** The goal of this exercise is to help you get used to scoring business plans the way bankers and investors do in the real world. Most financial professionals have checklists and scoring sheets that convert their accumulated wisdom into the factors that make a difference. Knowing how this scoring works can help entrepreneurs bulletproof their plan, identifying problems before outsiders see them.

   For this exercise, let's build on the IDEO screen, adding from the business plan outline. In evaluating each of these items in the Business Plan Report Card, give it a grade based on this rubric:

   A: I would sign on the dotted line and give them what they want right now!

   B: No signature. I would take them out to dinner to "ask a couple of questions."

   C: No dinner. Coffee, free refills. I have a lot of questions.

   D: Nothing to eat or drink. I am detecting major flaws.

   F: You're wasting my time. You're embarrassing yourself. Get out of here.

   Circle your grade in each category and your overall grade for the plan.

BUSINESS PLAN REPORT CARD

Item	Component	Grade
Market Desirability:	1. People want this	A B C D F
	2. Marketing/sales process sound	A B C D F
	3. Better than competitors	A B C D F
Technical Feasibility:	4. Will work and cost as predicted	A B C D F
	5. Operations are defined	A B C D F
Business Viability:	6. The firm will succeed as described	A B C D F
	7. Have excellent team and advisers	A B C D F
	8. Legal and intellectual property covered	A B C D F
	9. Financials make sense	A B C D F
OVERALL EVALUATION OF THE BUSINESS PLAN		A B C D F

A. Now read through the Red Jett Sweets business plan included in Appendix B of this chapter.

B. After reading the plan, fill in a grade for each of the rows.

C. Be ready to discuss your findings (and defend your grading) in class. Give some thought to what could be done better in the plan to achieve a higher score.

Your score will vary from those of others in the class. You will find that some of the difference comes from how closely people read the plan and the Report Card. There will be times when everyone will agree on what was read, but disagree on the meaning or score. That happens in business too. That is why it is important to try out your plan repeatedly. Just because one person or firm or bank said no does not mean that everyone will see it or score it the same way.

2. **Searching Business Plan Archives:** See if you can find a plan for your business at one of the business plan archive sites, because there is no shortage of business plans available for review on the Internet. For example, the commercial site behind Business Plan Pro and LivePlan (which is sometimes bundled with this textbook) offers over 500 example business plans (**www.bplans.com/sample_business_plans.php**). This is the site the SBA refers people to when they seek example plans.

MINI-CASE

LOFT IN SPACE[38]

A student at the University of Nebraska–Lincoln (UNL), Michael Cain, built a loft for his dorm room bed. Others asked him to build one for them, and he started to think about making a business out of it. He had put together his marketing plan in his head and had even begun to think about operational details that would help make his business more efficient. He knew he needed to get some sort of official approval, since his business would be on campus. So he started checking with university officials about setting up his business, but it was here that he started hitting problems, such as:

- He could not run the business out of his dorm room.
- He couldn't use his UNL telephone or email account for the business.
- His firm needed a $1 million liability policy to work on campus.

He needed to be able to address these problems and make sure the solutions would leave him with a profitable business.

CASE DISCUSSION QUESTIONS

1. If he was going to build a business plan to present to the university administrators, what type of plan should he develop (following the types mentioned in Table 8.5)?
2. What parts of the plan should he make sure are included?
3. What solutions would you suggest for his three problems?

APPENDIX A

Example Cover Letter and Résumé

SKILL MODULE 8.2

How to Write a Cover Letter

We all know that first impressions are important. For business plans, the first impression is made by the cover letter, so having a good one-page letter is vital. Fortunately, writing a good cover letter is easy.

Step 1: Get the recipient's email and address information. Find out the proper name, title, and address of the person to whom you are sending the plan. Check the company's website, the individual's LinkedIn page, or call or email this person's office to get the right information if you are not sure.

Step 2: Draft your letter. There is a classic format for cover letters.

a. **Salutation:** "Dear Mr. Monroe," "Dear Ms. Craft," or "Dear Dr. Jones" is how cover letters typically start. If you have a long-standing personal relationship with the reader, you can start informally, like "Dear Chris."

b. **First paragraph:** Here you introduce yourself and your business ("I am Edward Blankenship, owner of PROmote Advertising"). You explain how you got the recipient's name ("Brigit Hawkins at Security Bank suggested I contact you," or "I am contacting you in your role as president of the Northside Investment Group").

c. **Second paragraph:** Here you explain your company in a little greater detail. Typically this will be a variation of your vision statement in the first sentence ("PROmote specializes in increasing sales of small-lot professional and technical books through market expansion"). The next sentence describes the product or service in a sales-oriented manner ("PROmote's expertise gets books into specialty bookstores, online bookstores, and professional and trade association booklists for new sales"). The third sentence points up your competitive advantage, or what makes your product, service, or firm special ("PROmote is the only company in the industry that targets small-lot professional books on behalf of the authors, helping them increase sales").

d. **Third paragraph:** Here you describe the current situation of the company and explain what you are seeking from the recipient ("PROmote is in start-up phase, having completed its pilot tests and secured its first customers. PROmote is currently seeking a $20,000 line of credit. I would appreciate your consideration of the attached business plan"). The typical requests are for investment, lines of credit, partnering or joint ventures, sales, or feedback on those areas of the plan in which the recipient is expert.

e. **Fourth paragraph:** In closing, you thank the recipient for his or her consideration, let the reader know you are available to answer any questions, and close with a mention of your future action, such as a promise to contact the recipient within a week.

f. **Signature block:** Typically you sign off with "Sincerely," and your name the way it appears in the business plan.

Step 3: Proofread. A cover letter with misspellings or grammatical errors sends the worst possible first impression. If the cover letter has problems, imagine what the plan must look like!

Step 4: Attach, double-check, and send. Make sure you have attached the business plan and anything else you've mentioned in the cover letter. Double-check the cover letter one more time before you send it off. CC or BCC yourself so you can make sure it was sent.

Example Cover Letter

Mr. Michael Hansen
Vice President for New Accounts
Bank New Narwhal
1234 Main Street
Anchorage, AK 99501

Dear Mr. Hansen,

I am Abe Zabrowski, the founder of a new painting inspection company, Surety Inspections, LLC. I have been doing my personal banking at BNN for several years, and so you were the first person I thought about when considering establishing a business line of credit.

Surety Inspections evaluates the completeness and quality of commercial painting projects for the clients of painting companies. Because commercial painting is difficult to evaluate, we offer an objective evaluation to painting customers to make sure everything is done according to specifications, or industry standards. Our clients are industrial plants, commercial firms, and government organizations that buy major painting projects. We are the only full-time professional painting inspection business in Alaska, with most of our competition consisting of painting firms that work between jobs. As such, we offer a more consistent and higher-quality evaluation, and we are always available for inspections.

While we have funded our initial equipment and operations, it is possible that we will need a line of credit to draw against when we must rent or buy equipment specific to particular contracts, or to pay for travel and lodging for contract work away from Anchorage. Since work in our industry is paid for after the report is delivered, we could incur costs early in a project and need credit. We are looking to secure a $10,000 line of credit. We can offer the firm's equipment as collateral, and we would be willing to discuss other forms of collateral or conditions that would make this workable. You will see that my credit rating and bank history are very solid.

Thank you for your consideration. I am available to answer any questions you have. Please call me at 907-555-1213. I will call you later this week to schedule an appointment to discuss my business and what BNN can do to help me grow it.

Sincerely,

Abe Zabrowski, CEO
Surety Inspections, LLC

How to Write a Résumé

SKILL MODULE 8.3

Résumés are among the most popular and most frequently changed documents a student or businessperson ever writes. There are many forms of résumé, and many ways to prepare one. Every college's career center has booklets and workshops on résumé-building, and most will be glad to review any résumé you put together. Microsoft Word includes résumé templates.

Simply put, résumés are summaries of you and your accomplishments. There is a strong business norm that résumés should be limited to one page. Résumés typically start with a block at the top identifying you: name, address, phone, email. By the way, make sure your phone's voice-mail message and your email address sound "businesslike." An email address like **xtremedrift@hotties.com** is better replaced by jsmith1811 (or even better, your own regular name) at one of the free email sites such as Gmail, Outlook Mail, or Yahoo! Mail. Consider a site that lets you use your own name.

After the identification block, it is good for students and those changing jobs to include a "Skills" section. Go beyond school-based skills. The ability to sell, to work in a team, to lead others, to communicate, to organize, to work exceptionally hard, or to solve problems for yourself or others count as much as knowing financial modeling or web design. For any skill you list here, be ready to back it up with specific examples of when you demonstrated this skill.

For students (or newly graduated students) usually the next section is "Education" because it is the most important section. For people in the workplace already, "Work Experience" is usually here. Both sections are presented in reverse chronological order (i.e., most recent first). Entries give the college, its city, and your graduation month and year (even if it is in the future). On the next line, give your degree and major. If you have a good GPA (grade point average), put it in too. Generally, you do not list high schools, only colleges and up.

The "Work Experience" section is similar. For each company you worked for—in reverse chronological order—put your position, the company, city, state, and starting and ending dates. On the next line put two to four bullet points explaining what you achieved at work. We understand most jobs; what helps is for you to tell us how you helped the company and did superior work.

The last section covers any honors or awards you've received or earned (like Dean's List, scholarships, honorary society memberships, elected or appointed positions, etc.). Like in "Work Experience," give the organization on the first line, then bullets with the honor or award on the subsequent line.

The content of résumés change often, so keep in mind the following example résumé. Make sure the résumé is easy to read (use 11- or 12-point type) and scan (keep colors and fancy formatting to a minimum). And remember, the purpose of a résumé is to sell you! There are also free online résumé builders available to help you build and format your résumé so it looks professional. Be sure you can download the resulting résumé as a DOC or PDF file for your own use.

LEARN MORE ONLINE

Learn more about the topics above at these sites:

Online résumé builder and cover letter builder: **www.resume.com, www.resumebuilder.org**

Résumé builder with student résumé option: **https://resumebuild.com**

Example Résumé[39]

DANIELLE SHERWOOD
123 University Drive
St. Louis, MO 63101
(314) 555-XXXX
dsherwood@ggg.com

SKILLS

- Able to plan and organize self, others, and operations.
- Exceptional sales ability.
- Capable leader and team member.
- Excellent presentation and communications skills.

EDUCATION

Saint Louis University, St. Louis, MO, May 2019
Bachelor of Science in Entrepreneurship, Minor in Marketing, GPA: 3.6/4.0

WORK EXPERIENCE

Owner, CardinalAngelSales, St. Louis, MO, 2017-Present

- eBay Gold level reseller specializing in St. Louis Cardinals memorabilia and logo wear.
- Grew sales to over $15,000 in year 1, with a 99.8 percent customer approval rating.

Student Intern, Saint Louis University, St. Louis, MO, 2015-2019
- Partner with program director in writing and editing brochures and advertisements on leadership.
- Trained 10 new student employees and facilitated orientation on job duties.
- Generated new ideas to update department's website.

Sales Associate, May Company, St. Louis, MO, 2014-2015
- Sold merchandise to clients, increasing monthly sales by 25 percent.
- Resolved customer complaints and problems in a positive manner.
- Implemented customer service questionnaire which helped improve buyer satisfaction.

HONORS/ACTIVITIES

Collegiate Entrepreneurs Organization
- Vice President, Membership (2018-2019)
- Textfile Shift Manager (2017-2018)

Alpha Delta Pi
- President (2018-2019)
- Philanthropic Chairperson (2017-2018)

APPENDIX B

Red Jett Sweets Business Plan

May 2011

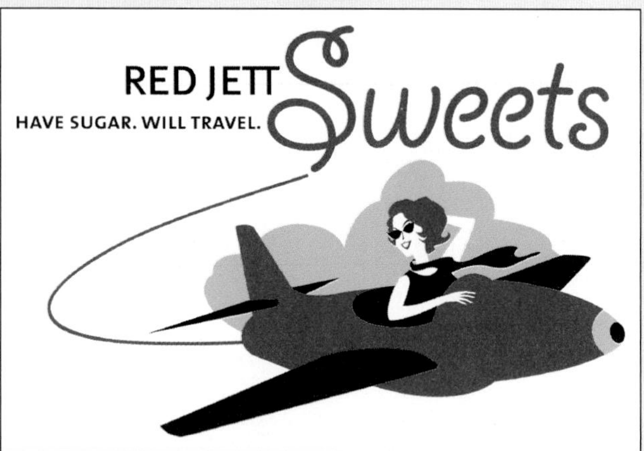

By: Natalie Gamez Meyer

This document contains confidential information belonging exclusively to Red Jett Sweets and its owners. Do not quote, copy, or distribute without permission.

[Note to students: The plan fits with the model presented in this chapter and came in at 4,081 words and 13 pages. That said, you will notice not every heading given in the textbook chapter is used here. If a section does not fit with your plan, it can be acceptable to leave it out. If you think moving a section will make the plan easier to read, that may work also. You should check with your instructor or an expert, though, to make sure you don't leave out a section important in your industry or to your readers. The cupcakery was opened, and was a finalist in Food Network's *Cupcake Wars.* You can see their original submission at www.youtube.com/watch?v=CLrUdsWecDo and their competition at www.foodnetwork.com/shows/cupcake-wars/episodes/wicked. Red Jett Sweets closed in late 2013, as a walkaway (see Chapter 6) having no outstanding debts, with Natalie and Christina selling the firm's assets and going onto other businesses. Natalie is now the general manager for the Dallas-Fort Worth restaurant group Terra Mediterranean. She went from an independent to a corporate entrepreneur.]

TABLE OF CONTENTS

EXECUTIVE SUMMARY

Red Jett Sweets

Red Jett Sweets, Inc. is a Subchapter S corporation opening a mobile cupcakery in August 2011. Red Jett Sweets will build a reputation in Fort Worth as one of the best cupcakeries in the area. Red Jett Sweets will provide its clients with innovative flavors, high quality ingredients, and the highest level of customer service and satisfaction found anywhere.

The mobile cupcakery will feature cupcakes that are freshly baked, original and innovative flavors, high quality ingredients, and that are fun, eclectic, seasonal, and traditional. Although Red Jett Sweets is targeting individuals with the disposable income to buy cupcakes, the mobile cupcakery will be welcoming a wide variety of income levels by competitively pricing cupcakes at $2.75. Other cupcakeries in the Fort Worth area sell their cupcakes for $2.50 and $2.95. Cupcakes will be the main focus of Red Jett Sweets, but a limited line of beverages will be sold to complement Red Jett Sweets' cupcakes.

Red Jett Sweets' management and staff will provide customer service that is friendly and helpful, but not pressured, with an emphasis on building ongoing relationships. The mobile cupcakery will provide extensive client service offerings such as home delivery, special orders, gift wrapping, private parties, and customization. The mobile cupcakery design will create an inviting atmosphere that customers will enjoy visiting.

Management

At the heart of Red Jett Sweets are the owners, Christina Meyer and Natalie Gamez Meyer. They will be responsible for all aspects of product selection, client relations, and day-to-day operations. Ms. Meyer has previous experience starting and running a small business, where she has demonstrated talent in most of the activities required to manage a small business. Ms. Gamez has worked at many businesses in the restaurant industry and still maintains many connections in the industry. She is very detail oriented and well organized,and has a passion for baking.

Target Market

Red Jett Sweets' primary target market includes people, ages 25 to 44, with household incomes of $75,000 or higher. Secondary target markets include people in younger (16-24) and older (45-54) age groups with household incomes between $40,000 and $75,000. Red Jett Sweets' primary trading area will be West Fort Worth. In the 2001 census, the total number of households in our primary target market was approximately 29,000. The total number of households in both the primary and secondary target markets was 60,000.

Competitive Positioning

Similar businesses exist in other cities, but when Red Jett Sweets opens it will be the first and only mobile cupcakery in Fort Worth. Its customers will enjoy the best variety of products, best customer service, and best mobile food tuck environment and experience, all available in accessible locations without paying more than at other storefronts in the area.

Some existing local cupcakeries, such as Cupcake Cottage and J' Raes, offer similar cupcakes to Red Jett Sweets', but do not sell their products via a mobile cupcakery. A growing trend, over two-thousand mobile and cart food vendors covered U.S. street corners and parking lots in 2010, with $163 million in sales revenue nationwide.

Red Jett Sweets will focus on promotional strategies based on personal relationships, word of mouth, and social media marketing. Red Jett Sweets will use a client database to notify clients when new flavors become available. The mobile cupcakery will host events such as a large opening party with local newspapers and magazines invited to cover it, and special events with 10-15% of profits donated to local charities and organizations. Ms. Meyer and Ms. Gamez will leverage their diverse personal networks to build awareness and interest in Red Jett Sweets before and after the mobile cupcakery opens.

Projected Sales and Income

Red Jett Sweets expects to achieve sales revenues of $48,379 in the first year and up to $167,723 by the third year. It may be possible to achieve higher sales than this conservative estimate, which is equivalent to 160 cupcakes a day from August to December. This is lower than reported sales at similar cupcakeries in other cities. The local market is large enough to support a higher level of growth.

Break-even sales for the first year are $80,358 or 29,221 cupcakes. Net income after taxes is projected to be ($17,003) in the first year and over $19,500 by the third year. Note that during these first three years of business, the break-even sales is raised and net income is significantly lowered due to purchases of equipment and amortization of intangible assets related to Red Jett Sweets' start-up.

Financing

Ms. Meyer's initial equity investment of $50,000 will fund the start-up of Red Jett Sweets. This includes $29,000 for the mobile cupcakery and small renovations; $3,000 for marketing and advertising materials; $2,500 for equipment; $2,500 for research, development of recipes, and direct labor hours associated with the two; $13,000 in working capital.

THE COMPANY

Company Description

Red Jett Sweets, Inc., is a start-up company in Fort Worth, Texas, opening a mobile cupcakery in August 2011. The company, which is a subchapter S corporation, and the mobile cupcakery are both referred to as Red Jett Sweets throughout the business plan.

Mission Statement/Value Proposition

Red Jett Sweets shares moments of joy with its customers by providing mouth-watering, quality cupcakes that delight the senses of young and old alike. Red Jett Sweets will be the premier mobile cupcake business in the area, widely known for its unique vehicle that offers convenient street sales and that delivers creative custom designs for special events.

PRODUCTS

At Red Jett Sweets we are intent on baking a cupcake that sends mind, body, and soul to a whole new place. Whether you are a traditionalist or an adventurer, you will find a cupcake for every craving. We offer a number of crowd-pleasing flavors on a regular basis as well as a rotating menu of featured cupcakes that simply sparkle with innovation and wit. We will have crowd-pleasing daily flavors such as our signature Red Jett Velvet cupcake, as well as a rotating menu of featured cupcakes that simply sparkle with innovation with flavors such as Beloved Banana Foster and seasonal flavors like Peter Pumpkin at Halloween. All our cupcakes will be priced at $2.75. We will also serve a variety of beverages that complement the taste of our signature cupcakes. We will have our everyday beverages, as well as seasonal beverages, including: waters, milk and lemonade. For details of all of these, see our menu on the Rack Card in Appendix B(4) and photos of some of our cupcakes in Appendix B(3). We will offer services such as catering for private parties, special orders, delivery and gift packaging.

Industry

Red Jett Sweets functions predominately as part of the food truck industry (NAICS code 722330), although it is sometimes treated as part of the bakery (pastry) industry (NAICS code 311811). Over two-thousand mobile and cart food vendors covered U.S. street corners and parking lots in 2010. Also, in 2010, mobile food operations were estimated to have earned $163 million in sales revenue nationwide. Sales in Texas in 2007 were $22,004,000, across 94 mobile food service vendors according to the 2007 Economic Census of the USA.[40] Nationally, the market for pastry and baked good has expanded over the past 10 years. This growth was in part due to an increase in public awareness because of media coverage, such as The Food Network and TLC food shows. Consequently, this has led to an increase in demand for premium bakery products such as what Red Jett Sweets offers its customers.

THE MARKET

Market & Target Customer

Red Jett Sweets is a Fort Worth based business, with a Total Available Market (TAM) of 195,078 households (averaging 2.62 people each), according to the 2000 Census. The Serviceable Available Market (SAM), or primary trading area, consists of 59,590 households. These are within a five-mile radius west Fort Worth roughly centered at the intersection of Hulen Street and Vickery Avenue. This area includes 10 zip codes 76102, 76104, 76107, 76109, 76110, 76114, 76115, 76116, 76132, 76133. Figure 8.3 maps out the area, showing the target zip codes in red. The Service Obtainable Market (SOM) for our upscale product is households with incomes over $75,000 annually, and there are 28,941 such households in this area.

Within Red Jett Sweets' SAM and SOM the primary target market includes people, ages 25 to 44, with household incomes of $75,000 or higher. The SAM or secondary target markets adds people in younger (16–24) and older (45 and up) age groups and with household incomes between $40,000 and $75,000. We have chosen these groups as our primary target market because of the disposable income the age group of 25–44 has and also because they are still young enough to be following current trends. The secondary market is important because the age group of 16–24 follows trends and social media more than any other age group and the 45 and up age group has the desirable disposable income and will appreciate our charitable donations.

Mobile Cupcakery Placement Strategies

Red Jett Sweets will choose locations based on the type of people in the area and the amount of traffic in that area. We will focus mainly on areas around Texas Christian University (TCU), downtown Fort Worth, and southwest Fort Worth, specifically Hulen St. and Bryant Irvin Blvd. which have high levels of street traffic (e.g. around Cousins BBQ). These streets specifically have high traffic levels from 2:30 p.m. to 4:30 p.m. The types of families who attend these schools are mostly in our primary targeted income levels. For all of these locations, the hours of operation are flexible and could change on a day-to-day basis depending on customer habits and events around town.

Competition

While there are no mobile cupcakeries in the Dallas-Fort Worth area, there are four "brick and mortar" cupcakeries (mostly in the Arlington Heights area), shown in Table 8.6 below. All of these brick-and-mortar stores have the advantage of being in a known location at all times, but also cannot be where the biggest concentrations of customers might

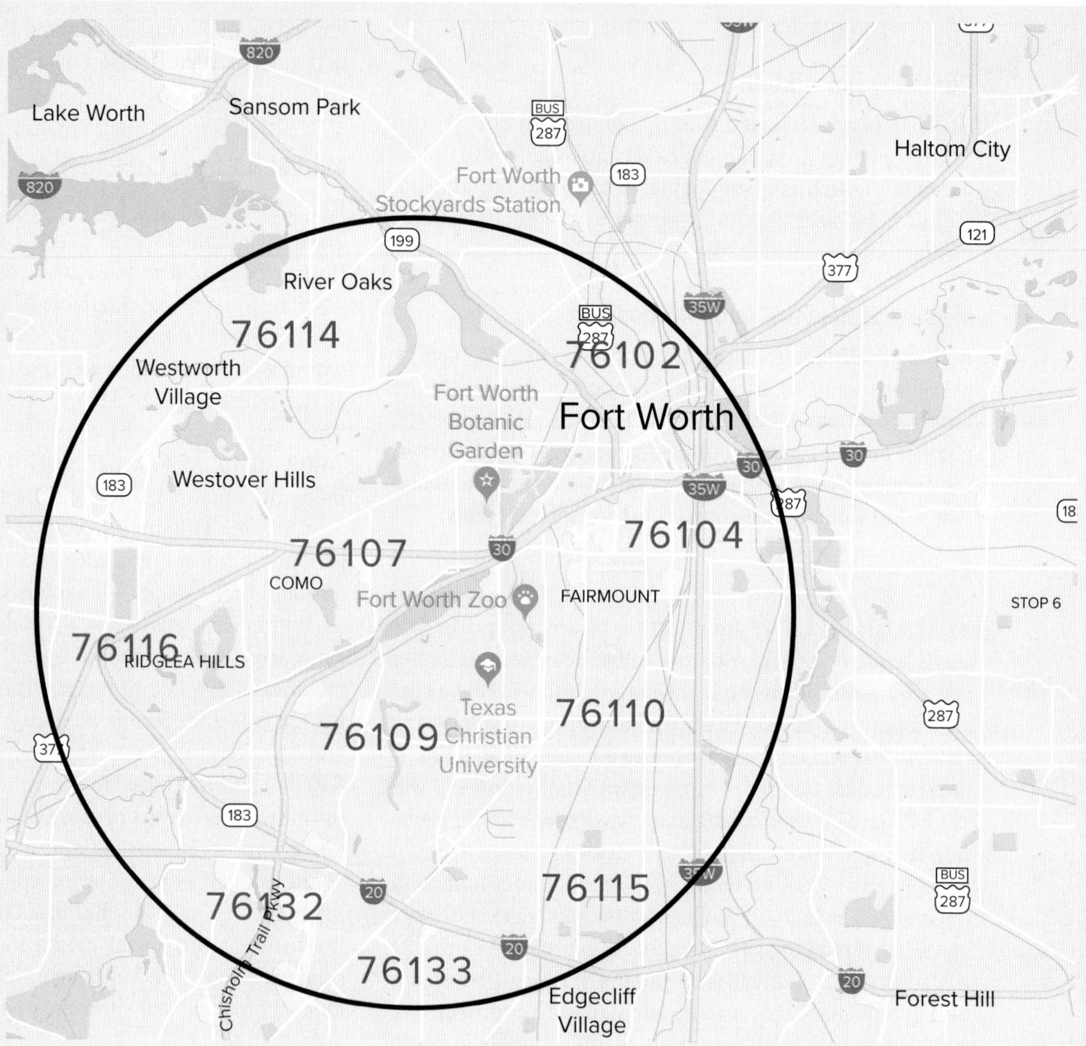

FIGURE 8.3

RED JETT SWEETS MARKET AREA.

Five-mile radius map of the Red Jett Sweets Market Area (Primary Zip Codes in red)

[Google Maps]

be. All of these competitors and Red Jett create product daily from scratch, with high-quality ingredients, but none of the competition will have the variety of cupcakes Red Jett Sweets offers on a daily basis. Red Jett Sweets will also sell at a price advantage to all but J Rae's. Red Jett Sweets will also be on Facebook, which is only used by Cupcake Cottage.

While there are five special-order cupcake businesses (Sugar Lush, Le Chat Noir, Blue Bonnet, Nothing Bunt Cakes, McKinley's) and three cake shops (Sublime, Crème de la Crème, Couture) in our five-mile radius, both types of competitors have bigger minimum purchases than Red Jett Sweets and more limited cupcake offerings, so they pose less of a competitive issue.

Competitive Advantage

Red Jett has three competitive advantages—our cupcakes, our location and our social media efforts. We will offer the broadest range of cupcakes in the area, the most

TABLE 8.6 Red Jett Competitive Matrix

	Red Jett	Cupcake Cottage	J Rae's	Ultimate Cupcake	Leah's Sweet Treats
Location Strategy	Mobile	Fixed	Fixed	Fixed with delivery	Fixed
Cupcake Focus	Yes	Yes	No	Yes	No
Facebook/Web Presence	F/W	F/W	W	W	W
Price	$2.75	$2.95	$2.50	$3.00	$2.92

customization options, and will be the cupcake innovation leader in the Fort Worth market with more variety and more new and seasonal flavors than anyone else. Red Jett Sweets will be the only business able to change location on a fixed schedule (which can be adjusted when advantageous) to be where the largest concentration of customers is at every time of the day. This will build on co-locating where crowds are, such as where other food trucks congregate, major local events and eateries like Cousins BBQ as well as the TCU campus. We have partnerships with other food truck owners and Cousins BBQ to assure we will be where the food trucks gather. In addition, we will build arrangements with local party planners to provide custom cupcakes for events. Our mobility also means we are able to deliver larger orders. We will also have the most active social media effort among competitors.

MARKETING STRATEGY

Marketing Objectives

- Build Awareness. Various communication tools will be used to create awareness of Red Jett Sweets in the target markets and trading areas and to attract the attention and interest of potential clients.
- Convert Sales. When potential customers visit the mobile cupcakery, Red Jett Sweets' personal selling techniques, delicious cupcakes, and inviting environment will encourage customers to revisit to make purchases. The events that Red Jett Sweets will host will also create a setting in which clients are more likely to buy.
- Exceed Expectations. Red Jett Sweets will pursue customer service excellence to ensure that each customer leaves fully satisfied. Such customers are more likely to become loyal, repeat customers and to encourage others to visit our mobile cupcakery.
- Build Loyalty. Red Jett Sweets will maintain its relationships with customers after they leave the mobile cupcakery, encouraging them to not only become repeat customers, but also to build an emotional investment in the mobile cupcakery and their relationship with the owners. Such loyalty will help Red Jett Sweets maintain its customer base in the face of increasing future competition. Red Jett Sweets will do this by keeping a client database and interacting with customers on various social media channels.

Sales Plan

- Word of Mouth: Interest in Red Jett Sweets has already been spreading by word of mouth a year before the truck will open. In the long term, word of mouth will be the single most important means of building awareness and attracting new customers. Red Jett Sweets will further encourage word of mouth once the mobile cupcakery opens by exceeding customers' expectations, building loyalty, hosting events, and providing customers with delicious cupcakes that invite the question, "Where did you get that?"
- Personal Networks: Ms. Meyer has developed an extensive personal network through her social, professional, and volunteer activities. She will ask friends and associates to help spread the word about Red Jett Sweets around Fort Worth and Tarrant County, including specifically targeted social groups such as local country clubs, parents at Fort Worth Academy, and Junior League. Ms. Gamez will help target the target age group of 16–24 through her connections at Trinity Valley School, All Saints Episcopal School, and Fort Worth Country Day School. She will also help target parents at these schools. During May 2011 Ms. Meyer will order a set of stylish T-shirts with Red Jett Sweets' logo and give them to friends to wear around town.
- Charitable Donations: We will donate cupcakes to local charities and nonprofit organizations, to be viewed as a socially responsible and community-oriented company. We might also partner with a local business, organization, or school to allow Red Jett Sweets to park on its premises and donate a portion of sales from that day to the organization. By donating only some of our cupcakes, instead of money, we will be exposing ourselves to a new customer base while making a good impression on the community.
- Guerrilla Marketing: We will look for opportunities that are unconventional, interactive, and catches consumers at unexpected places. This goal is to create a unique, thought provoking, image that creates buzz to pass along via word of mouth.
- Search Engine Optimization: These services ensure that www.redjettsweets.com will be more visible to consumers on search platforms and that the website will generate more hits. We will use keywords, such as "cupcakes," "Fort Worth cupcakes," "mobile cupcakeries," "Fort Worth food trucks," "cupcake truck," etc.
- Digital Marketing: In addition to our website, www.redjettsweets.com, we will use the full range of social media platforms (Facebook, Twitter, Foursquare, Yelp, Instagram) to inform customers where we are at any time, what flavors we feature that day, and other cupcake news. We will also consider using social coupon sites like Groupon, and email

campaigns to our customers. We also own www.redjetsweets.com as a redirect in case of misspellings.

- Print Marketing: We will pursue articles about our cupcakes and truck in local magazines and newspapers and consider paid ads when it makes sense. We will have business cards at the truck and at events, along with rack cards and table toppers. The owners and friends may have car magnets promoting Redd Jett Sweets. The truck will have a full wrap with logo and contact information, and all boxes and containers will have custom stickers.

THE ORGANIZATION

Legal Issues

Red Jett Sweets, Inc., is a subchapter S corporation (S-Corp) registered in the state of Texas. This form was selected because S-Corp profits and losses are taxed only once. The relevant permits for the business include Fort Worth Business License and Health Permit, Tax ID number, Food Manager's Permit, Food Handler's Permit, Mobile Unit Permit, Texas Manufacturing Permit (TDSHS). We also possess and will maintain the currency of the materials needed for the Fort Worth mobile vending certification. We also hold full insurance (liability, interruption, property) for our kitchen, food and mobile operations.

Intellectual Property: Red Jett Sweets' name and logo will be trademarked in the state of Texas and Federally. We may consider trademarking some cupcake flavors in the future. The URL and most likely misspelling are already owned. All social media and advertising material will be copyrighted. The recipes and customer lists will be treated as trade secrets.

Key Personnel

At the heart of Red Jett Sweets are the owners, Christina Meyer and Natalie Gamez Meyer. They will be responsible for all aspects of product selection, client relations, and day-to-day operations. Ms. Meyer has previous experience starting and running a small business. She has a strong passion for the business and swiftly builds personal connections and maintains strong relationships with people. Ms. Gamez has worked at many businesses in the restaurant industry and still maintains many connections in the industry. She is very detail oriented and well organized and has a passion for baking.

Other Key People: Red Jett Sweets will be staffed with a baking assistant and eventually one or two sales associates, selected for their genuine enthusiasm for our business. Ms. Meyer and Ms. Gamez have established relationships with several additional outside consultants, including an insurance agent (Eric Jones), attorney (Aaron Moses), and graphic/website designer (Amy Devine). Their accountant, Diane Hanley CPA, will play an active role in financial management and reporting in the first year. Red Jett Sweets is currently looking for members to be on an advisory board.

Key Operations

Mobile Cupcakery: Red Jett Sweets recently purchased a mobile cupcakery from Rosie's Cakes in Denver, Colorado. It is a 1997 Chevy 3500 Box Truck with 48,000 miles. The truck has had two previous owners. Rosie's Cakes, the most recent previous owner, owned the truck for less than a year and put fewer than 1,000 miles on the truck. Rosie's Cakes sold their truck because they could not handle the level of business generated by the mobile truck and the additional special orders. The owner of Rosie's Cakes felt it was more beneficial to sell the truck and to focus on special order business. Refer to Appendix B(2) for photos of the truck and also for a layout of what Red Jett Sweets' mobile cupcakery will look like. We will use Square or its equivalent for credit card purchases.

Kitchen: Red Jett Sweets will be renting an offsite kitchen in Fort Worth to bake the cupcakes. The kitchen is located at 7455 South Hulen Street #120 Fort Worth, TX 76133. This kitchen is owned by All in Good Taste, a Fort Worth catering company. We will be paying a monthly all-inclusive rent of $1,000 for full use of the kitchen, most equipment, utility payments, cleaning supplies, etc. from 12:00 a.m. to 11:00 a.m.

FINANCIAL SUMMARY

Red Jett Sweets expects to achieve sales revenues of $48,379 in the first year and up to $167,723 by the third year. It may be possible to achieve higher sales than this conservative estimate, which is equivalent to 160 cupcakes a day from August to December. This is lower than reported sales at similar cupcakeries in other cities. The local market is large enough to support a higher level of growth.

Break-even sales for the first year are $80,358 or 29,221 cupcakes. Net income after taxes is projected to be ($17,003) in the first year and over $19,500 by the third year. Note that during these first three years of business, the break-even sales is raised and net income is significantly lowered due to purchases of equipment and amortization of intangible assets related to Red Jett Sweets' start-up.

Ms. Meyer's initial equity investment of $50,000 will fund the start-up of Red Jett Sweets. This includes $29,000 for the mobile cupcakery and small renovations; $3,000 for marketing and advertising materials; $2,500 for equipment; $2,500 for research, development of recipes, and direct labor hours associated with the two; $13,000 in working capital.

APPENDICES

Appendix A: Financials

RED JETT Sweets

Start-up Costs	
Sources:	**Amount:**
Equity Investment	50,000
(Christina Meyer)	
Total	50,000
Uses:	**Amount:**
Mobile Cupcakery	29,000
Website & Marketing Materials	3,000
Equipment	2,500
Research & Development	2,500
Working Capital	13,000
Total	50,000

Break Even Sales for 2011	
Equity Investment (Not including working capital)	37,000
Rent	8,290
Telephone	1,520
Transportation	2,403
Insurance	2,000
Legal/Permits & Accounting	3,088
Marketing	2,864
Repairs	1,000
Payroll Taxes	2,082
Total Costs for 2011	60,247
Selling Price per Cupcake	2.75
Cost per Cupcake	0.25026782
Contribution Margin per Cupcake	2.0617635
Break Even Sales for 2011 (Cupcakes)	29,221
Break Even in Sales for 2011 ($)	80,3581.15
Working days per month	25
Months per year	12
Working days per year	300
Break Even Sales per Day	97.40

RED JETT Sweets

Key Assumptions for Business Plan	
1	The sales from the mobile cupcakery van will begin in August, 2011.
2	Each month's sales will be a specific number of cupcakes sold.
3	All sales will be made to individual customers from the mobile cupcakery van.
4	Price of a single cupcake in $2.75
5	Variable cost (ingredients & consumables) total $0.68 per sale.
6	All cupcakes have the same cost of goods sold.
7	50% of sales will be cash, the remainder will be credit card purchases.
8	Credit card processing fee is calculated on gross sale, including sales tax.
9	Any ending inventory of cupcakes will be donated to a food bank. The cost will be absorbed in a spoilage allowance of 3% of COGS for the period's sales.
10	All raw materials (flour, sugar, butter, icings, flavorings, and other miscellaneous consumables) are purchased and consumed in full each month.
11	Revolving credit will be used as needed to maintain a non-zero cash balance.
12	Revolving credit is at 10% annual interest.
13	Interest is paid monthly.
14	Principle is repaid when cash balance allows.
15	Depreciation expense recognition begins in August, when the equipment is actually first placed in service.
16	Depreciation method is 7-year straight line.

Income Statements

RED JETT SWEETS, Inc.
YEAR 1 Income Statement (accrual basis)

	January	February	March	April	May	June	July	August	September	October	November	December	Total
REVENUES													
Unit sales	145	218	145	291	291	218	218	2,983	2,983	2,983	2,983	2,712	16,170
Cash sales	$ 427	$ 641	$ 427	$ 856	$ 856	$ 641	$ 641	$4,389	$4,389	$4,389	$4,389	$4,389	26,434
Credit card sales	$ —	$ —	$ —	$ —	$ —	$ —	$ —	$4,389	$4,389	$4,389	$4,389	$4,389	21,945
Gross Sales	427	641	427	856	856	641	641	8,778	8,778	8,778	8,778	8,778	48,379
Less:													
Credit card fees	—	—	—	—	—	—	—	88	88	88	88	88	439
Spoilage & over production	3	5	3	6	6	5	5	61	61	61	61	56	333
Sales tax collected	30	45	30	60	60	45	45	615	615	615	615	615	3,390
Net sales revenue	394	591	394	790	790	591	591	8,014	8,014	8,014	8,014	8,019	44,217
Less cost of goods sold	99	149	99	198	198	149	149	2,029	2,029	2,029	2,029	1,845	11,002
Gross margin	295	442	295	592	592	442	442	5,985	5,985	5,985	5,985	6,174	33,215
Sales, general, & administrative													
Salaries & Wages	480	480	480	480	480	480	480	4,141	4,141	4,141	4,141	4,141	24,065
Payroll taxes/benefits	42	42	42	42	42	42	42	358	358	358	358	358	2,084
Rent	420	280	420	490	560	560	560	1,000	1,000	1,000	1,000	1,000	8,290
Web site, marketing	1,900	100	100	100	100	100	100	100	100	100	100	100	3,000
Telephone	310	110	110	110	110	110	110	110	110	110	110	110	1,520
Transportation						343	343	343	343	343	343	343	2,403
Insurance	167	167	167	167	167	167	167	167	167	167	167	167	2,000
Research & recipe development	313	313	313	313	313	313	313						2,188
Legal & Accounting	2,703	35	35	35	35	35	35	35	35	35	35	35	3,088
Depreciation expense								316	316	316	316	316	1,580
Total SG & A	6,334	1,526	1,666	1,736	1,806	2,150	2,150	6,570	6,570	6,570	6,570	6,570	50,218
Operating income	(6,039)	(1,084)	(1,371)	(1,144)	(1,214)	(1,708)	(1,708)	(585)	(585)	(585)	(585)	(396)	(17,003)
Interest Expense													
Net income before taxes	(6,039)	(1,084)	(1,371)	(1,144)	(1,214)	(1,708)	(1,708)	(585)	(585)	(585)	(585)	(396)	(17,003)

RED JETT Sweets

Income Statement for the Year Ending December 31, 2012	
Revenues	
Unit sales	48,000
Cash sales	$ 70,620
Credit card sales	$ 70,620
Gross Sales	141,240
Less:	
Credit card fees	1,412
Spoilage & over production	980
Sales tax collected	9,887
Net sales revenue	128,961
Less cost of goods sold	32,640
Gross margin	96,321
Sales, general, & administrative	
Salaries & Wages	49,680
Payroll taxes/benefits	3,478
Rent	12,000
Web site, marketing	1,900
Telephone	310
Transportation	2,500
Insurance	3,500
Research & recipe development	2,000
Legal & Accounting	2,800
Depreciation expense	3,792
Total SG & A	81,960
Operating income	14,361
Interest Expense	
Net income before taxes	14,361

RED JETT Sweets

Income Statement for the Year Ending December 31, 2013	
Revenues	
Unit sales	57,000
Cash sales	$ 83,862
Credit card sales	$ 83,862
Gross Sales	167,723
Less:	
Credit card fees	1,677
Spoilage & over production	1,163
Sales tax collected	11,741
Net sales revenue	153,142
Less cost of goods sold	38,760
Gross margin	114,382
Sales, general, & administrative	
Salaries & Wages	60,000
Payroll taxes/benefits	4,200
Rent	13,200
Web site, marketing	1,900
Telephone	310
Transportation	2,500
Insurance	3,500
Research & recipe development	2,400
Legal & Accounting	3,000
Depreciation expense	3,792
Total SG & A	94,802
Operating income	19,580
Interest Expense	
Net income before taxes	19,580

Cash Flow Statements

RED JETT SWEETS, Inc.
CASH FLOW—Year 1

	January	February	March	April	May	June	July	August	September	October	November	December
Cash flow from operations												
Cash received from customers	424	636	424	850	850	636	636	8,717	8,717	8,717	8,717	8,722
Cash paid to vendors	—	—	—	—	—	—	—	88	88	88	88	88
credit card providers												
sales tax paid to Texas	30	45	30	60	60	45	45	615	615	615	615	615
raw materials used in production	99	149	99	198	198	149	149	2,029	2,029	2,029	2,029	1,845
Salaries & Wages	480	480	480	480	480	480	480	4,141	4,141	4,141	4,141	4,141
Payroll taxes/benefits	42	42	42	42	42	42	42	358	358	358	358	358
Rent	420	280	420	490	560	560	560	1,000	1,000	1,000	1,000	1,000
Web site, marketing	1,900	100	100	100	100	100	100	100	100	100	100	100
Telephone	310	110	110	110	110	110	110	110	110	110	110	110
Transportation	—	—	—	—	—	343	343	343	343	343	343	343
Insurance	167	167	167	167	167	167	167	167	167	167	167	167
Research & recipe development	313	313	313	313	313	313	313	—	—	—	—	—
Legal & Accounting	2,703	35	35	35	35	35	35	35	35	35	35	35
Net cash flows from operations	(6,039)	(1,084)	(1,371)	(1,144)	(1,214)	(1,708)	(1,708)	(269)	(269)	(269)	(269)	(80)
Cash flow from investing activities												
Purchase of Equipment	(31,500)											
Cash flow from financing activities												
Investment by owners	50,000											
Cash received from borrowing												
Cash paid on loans	50,000											
Net cash flow from long-term financing activities												
Beginning cash	—	12,461	11,377	10,006	8,861	7,647	5,940	4,232	3,963	3,695	3,426	3,157
Net cash increase (decrease)	12,461	(1,084)	(1,371)	(1,144)	(1,214)	(1,708)	(1,708)	(269)	(269)	(269)	(269)	(80)
Ending cash	12,461	11,377	10,006	8,861	7,647	5,940	4,232	3,963	3,695	3,426	3,157	3,077

RED JETT Sweets

Statement of Cash Flows
for the year ending Dec 31, 2012

Cash flow from operations	
Cash received from customers	140,260
Cash paid to vendors	
credit card providers	1,412
sales tax paid to Texas	9,887
raw materials used in production	32,640
Salaries & Wages	49,680
Payroll taxes/benefits	3,478
Rent	12,000
Web site, marketing	1,900
Telephone	310
Transportation	2,500
Insurance	3,500
Research & recipe development	2,000
Legal & Accounting	2,800
Net cash flows from operations	18,153
Cash flow from investing activities	
Purchase of Equipment	- 0 -
Cash flow from financing activities	
Investment by owners	- 0 -
Cash received from borrowing	
Cash paid on loans	
Net cash flow from financing activities	- 0 -
Beginning cash	3,077
Net cash increase (decrease)	18,153
Ending cash	21,230

RED JETT Sweets

Statement of Cash Flows
for the year ending Dec 31, 2013

Cash flow from operations	
Cash received from customers	166,560
Cash paid to vendors	
credit card providers	1,677
sales tax paid to Texas	11,741
raw materials used in production	38,760
Salaries & Wages	60,000
Payroll taxes/benefits	4,200
Rent	13,200
Web site, marketing	1,900
Telephone	310
Transportation	2,500
Insurance	3,500
Research & recipe development	2,400
Legal & Accounting	3,000
Net cash flows from operations	23,372
Cash flow from investing activities	
Purchase of Equipment	- 0 -
Cash flow from financing activities	
Investment by owners	- 0 -
Cash received from borrowing	
Cash paid on loans	
Net cash flow from financing activities	- 0 -
Beginning cash	21,230
Net cash increase (decrease)	23,372
Ending cash	44,602

Balance Sheets

RED JETT Sweets

Balance Sheet as of December 31, 2011	
Current Assets	
Cash	3,077
Total Current Assets	3,077
Long-term assets	
Equipment	31,500
Less accum. depreciation	1,580
Net Long-term assets	29,920
Total Assets	32,997
Liabilities	
Total liabilities	- 0 -
Equity	
Investment by owner (common stk.)	50,000
Retained earnings (loss)	(17,003)
Net equity	32,997
Total liabilities & equity	32,997

RED JETT Sweets

Balance Sheet as of December 31, 2012	
Current Assets	
Cash	21,230
Total Current Assets	21,230
Long-term assets	
Equipment	31,500
Less accum. depreciation	5,372
Net Long-term assets	26,128
Total Assets	47,358
Liabilities	
Total liabilities	- 0 -
Equity	
Investment by owner (common stk.)	50,000
Retained earnings (loss)	(2,642)
Net equity	47,358
Total liabilities & equity	47,358

RED JETT Sweets

Balance Sheet as of December 31, 2013	
Current Assets	
Cash	44,602
Total Current Assets	44,602
Long-term assets	
Equipment	31,500
Less accum. depreciation	9,164
Net Long-term assets	22,336
Total Assets	66,938
Liabilities	
Total liabilities	- 0 -
Equity	
Investment by owner (common stk.)	50,000
Retained earnings (loss)	16,938
Net equity	66,938
Total liabilities & equity	66,938

Appendix B: Supports

(1) Owners Biographies

Ms. Christina Jett Meyer: Ms. Meyer has served as a sales associate, store manager, vice-president of operations across fashion and supplement industries. In 2004, Ms. Meyer opened She Boutique. She personally launched the store for women's clothing and accessories with annual sales of $1,200 per sq ft. Ms. Meyer was successful in building a large customer base through effective branding and marketing. She also organized innovative series of themed special events that generated high sales and positive word of mouth. Ms. Meyer has developed diverse personal networks in the Fort Worth community through activities such as her extensive volunteer work with Fort Worth Academy and her acting roles with the Fort Worth Theater and Circle Theater. She will leverage these networks to help implement relationship based marketing strategies for Red Jett Sweets.

Ms. Natalie Gamez Meyer: Ms. Gamez has several years of experience in the restaurant industry. She has worked in many different areas in the industry. She has perfected her customer service, time management, and organizational skills that will be critical to the success of Red Jett Sweets. Ms. Gamez will be graduating from Saint Louis University in May 2011 and will use the accounting, marketing, and financial skill she learned to help Red Jett Sweets thrive. Ms. Gamez also has many ties to the community and will also utilize these relationships to Red Jett Sweets' advantage. Ms. Gamez will be actively involved in the day-to-day operations of Red Jett Sweets and is fully committed to dedicating time and effort to make Red Jett Sweets a successful business.

(2) Mobile Cupcakery

Natalie Gamez Meyer

(3) Product Photos

Natalie Gamez Meyer

(4) Rack Card–Cupcake Menu

Cupcake Love *let us explain...*

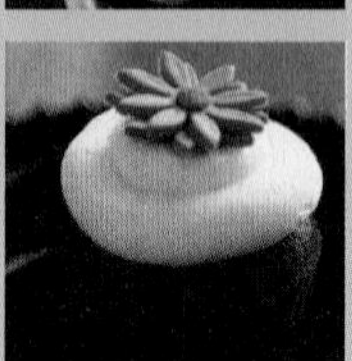

At **Red Jett Sweets** we're intent on baking a cupcake that sends mind, body, and soul to a whole new pleasure center!

Whether you're a traditionalist or an adventurer, you'll find a cupcake for every craving. Crowd-pleasing flavors as well as a rotating menu of special feature cupcakes that boast innovative taste combinations, each one guaranteed to delight your palette.

So the next time you want to **woo or wow**, share the love and let us bring dessert_

RED JETT SWEETS
HAVE SUGAR. WILL TRAVEL
817 458 6150
WWW.REDJETTSWEETS.COM

RED JETT SWEETS
Check out some of the cupcakes we've featured:

- ★ **Chocolate Echo**
  dark chocolate espresso cake + buttercream
- ★ **Red Jett Velvet**
  red velvet cake + cream cheese icing
- ★ **Strawberry Champagne - cheers!**
  strawberry champagne cake + buttercream with dark chocolate drizzle
- ★ **Beloved Banana Foster**
  banana cake + buttercream with caramel drizzle
- ★ **Dulce de leche**
  3-milk cake, caramel center + cream cheese icing
- ★ **Gingerbread Hug**
  gingerbread cake + cinnamon cream cheese icing
- ★ **Cocoa Peppermint Cloud**
  Chocolate cake + peppermint buttercream
- ★ **Peter Pumpkin**
  pumpkin spiced cake + cream cheese icing

PRICED JUST RIGHT
Red Jett Sweet cupcakes are classically sized and priced at $25 per dozen.
For special events and quantities exceeding 100, please call for pricing.

HERE'S HOW TO ORDER
Feel free to call or send us an e-mail:
817.458.6150 / orders@redjettsweets.com

Please include your name and phone number so we may contact you to complete your order.
All major credit cards accepted.

RED JETT SWEETS
HAVE SUGAR. WILL TRAVEL
817 458 6150 / WWW.REDJETTSWEETS.COM
Check out our website for all the latest updates, featured cupcake flavors, and news about our grand opening later this year!

Natalie Gamez Meyer

3

PART THREE

Marketing in the Small Business

CHAPTER

9

Small Business Marketing: Customers and Products

● How has the pricing strategy most likely changed for Greetabl as the company has expanded? What might be the future challenges in terms of pricing and continuing to deliver customized products to its customers?
Greetabl

LEARNING OBJECTIVES

After you complete this chapter, you will be able to:

LO 9-1 Recognize the steps of the marketing process.

LO 9-2 Use customer roles and profiles to help define the target market.

LO 9-3 Segment and further define your target audience.

LO 9-4 Recognize the major methods for conducting marketing research.

LO 9-5 Develop your value proposition.

LO 9-6 Understand how to organize marketing plans.

LO 9-7 Recognize the characteristics of goods and services.

LO 9-8 Define the total product.

LO 9-9 Differentiate the stages of new product development.

LO 9-10 Consider the impact of the product life cycle.

Focus on Small Business: Revisiting Greetabl[1]

Greetabl started as a decorated gift box to use in place of a greeting card (see "Focus on Small Business: Joe Fischer, Zoë Scharf, and the Strategy behind Greetabl" at the start of Chapter 7). Developed by Joe Fischer and Zoë Scharf, the original Greetabl was sold online and in card and specialty shops. Based on research with customers, in its second version, Greetabl became an online-only service that would let you customize the box with your own message and photos, all for $5–$7.

As sales grew for the second version of Greetabl, so did their customer research. They came to build a profile of their core customer, someone they called "Emily the Giver." These were women 25–45, who tended to give many gifts to friends and family over the year—for birthdays, "thinking of you" gifts, and special occasions. These women were busy looking for ways to say and show they care, but looking for ways that were stylish, thoughtful, distinctive, customizable, and that fit within their price range—something that was "just right" in size and price, a concept they identified as the Gifting Gap: giving a gift and card that falls in the $15–$30 range. Emily the Giver and people like her would be Greetabl's new focus. As Joe put it, "we would niche down to scale up."

This research launched the third version of Greetabl. Joe and Zoë partnered with another printer who could quickly print custom messages and photos on selected panels of every box. Greetabl would offer a curated range of curated gifts for all sorts of occasions and tastes to fill those boxes (and increase its profit levels per order). Think specialty candies and chocolates (like the "Lucky Guy" brownie in the photo above), unique teas, jewelry and pins, small ceramics, cosmetics, bath bombs, and of course a tremendous range of gift card possibilities. Greetabl worked to get orders into the mail within two-days—the fastest in the industry. It added reminder services, online address books, and subscription memberships to its website to make it easier for "the givers" to make Greetabl their go-to place for gifts.

Even with hundreds of thousands of units shipped, Joe and Zoë still continue their customer research. They have realized that industries exist where their marketing consists of relationships with people–think creative industries like photographers, designers, marketers, and wedding planners. For that segment Greetabl's specialized business-focused services can make it easier than ever to give distinctive gifts, messages, and experiences to their own customers. Joe and Zoë's latest strategy is to apply everything they've learned to help these professionals grow their businesses, deliver great experiences, and save them time and money through features like discounted shipping and additional customizations.

The following video describes version 3 of Greetabl and describes how version 4 will work: www.youtube.com/watch?v=nTHszWYFq8Q. See other Greetabl videos at www.youtube.com/user/greetabl/videos.

DISCUSSION QUESTIONS

1. How would you describe the pricing approaches used by Greetabl when it started and as it grew?
2. What differences do you imagine exist between Greetabl's Emily the Giver and business-focused customer types?
3. How would you find customers for Greetabl's Emily the Giver and Insider customer types?

The Marketing Process

LO 9-1 Recognize the steps of the marketing process.

The story of Joe and Zoë and Greetabl's offerings shows the power of marketing in the entrepreneurial small business. What exactly is marketing? Marketing is the process of planning and executing the factors of product, price, promotion, and placement to satisfy the goals of the entrepreneur and the organization. It is often confused with selling. Selling is the actual effort to pitch a product to a customer. Sales are essential to the business because sales are the major way any business makes money. But marketing's goal is to lay out the best way to get sales, and set up the conditions so selling will be as successful as possible. The selling act and the marketing process need each other for the small business to be successful. Product, price, promotion, and placement mentioned previously are called the **4 Ps of marketing** or the *marketing mix*. The next section of the book covers these 4 Ps as well as marketing plans, starting with product.

4 Ps of marketing
The four major components of a marketing effort—product, price, promotion, and placement. Sometimes called the marketing mix.

From an entrepreneur's perspective, marketing is all about connecting your customer to your product or service. As you can see in Figure 9.1, the first step in this process is connecting the two through the value proposition. The second step applies the value proposition to the mechanics of making the connection through the 4 Ps of marketing (product, price, promotion, placement). The point of all this is simple–generating sales of the product or service for the firm.

FIGURE 9.1

The Marketing Process

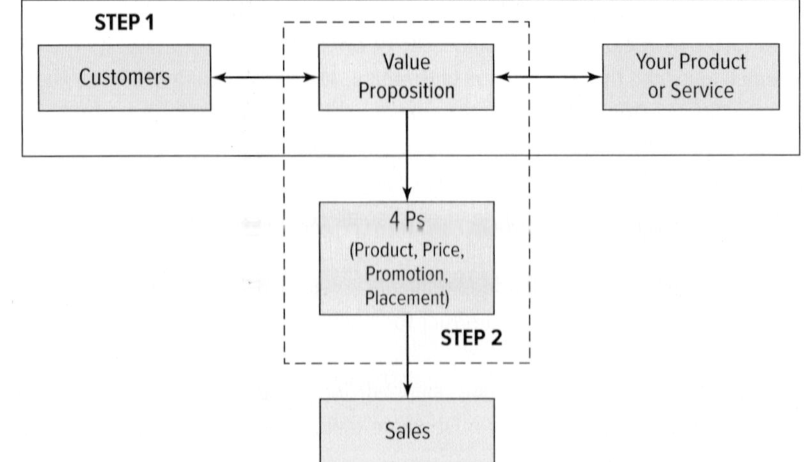

TABLE 9.1 Sources of Ideas for PSED Entrepreneurs

From within themselves	
My experience in a particular industry or market	54.1%
Thinking about a problem	28.5%
Knowledge or expertise with technology	25.8%
Developed from another idea I was considering	24.1%
Hobby or recreational pastime	26.0%
From others	
Discussions with my friends and family	44.1%
Discussions with potential or existing customers	29.4%
Discussions with existing suppliers or distributors	14.3%
Discussions with potential or existing investors/lenders	8.0%

Note: Multiple responses were permitted so totals do not add up to 100 percent.

Source: Custom compilation from the PSED 1 survey performed by Kelly Shaver, February 2019.

In this chapter we will go through step 1, focusing on the customer, product, and value proposition. This will also cover the first of the 4 Ps–product. The later chapters will cover the remaining 3 Ps.

In Chapter 4 we saw that some entrepreneurs interviewed by the PSED study got an idea for a product or service first, some decided they wanted to start a business first, and some saw both at the same time. We asked those entrepreneurs where their product or service idea came from. As you can see in Table 9.1, sometimes the idea seems to come to them based on their own thoughts and experiences, and sometimes it comes from listening to others. And a subset of entrepreneurs used both–which is the approach we recommend as the most effective.

The approach where the entrepreneur comes up with the idea on his or her own is often called the **product development process**, while the approach based on discussions with others is often called the **customer development process**. The difference between the two comes from the central or driving focus of the process. In the product development process, the focus is on the product itself, whether it is new or just the newest iteration of an existing product. This was Joe Fischer's and Zoë Sharf's experience in creating the Greetabl box, and then eventually starting their company. Perfecting the product or the innovation within the product is the central focus. In the customer development process, focus is on the customer, specifically on meeting the need of the customer, hopefully in a way that leads to a new product or service for the firm.

product development process
The procedure to organize and pursue the creation of new goods or services.

customer development process
The procedure to organize and pursue the finding, obtaining, and keeping of new customers.

Each approach has value and limitations. When an entrepreneur is far ahead of customers in terms of thinking of solutions, it might make sense to trust your own "gut," but it helps if you are a genius. When Steve Jobs saw a Xerox prototype computer whose screen mirrored the printed page and could be edited, he knew that was the direction he had to take Apple, whose current computer, the Apple][+ (Apple 2+), could edit only a line of text at a time. The new idea was so hard for personal computer users to understand that few liked the idea when Jobs explained it to them. But when the original Macintosh computers came out, the what-you-see-is-what-you-get approach made such perfect sense to people who shared Jobs's graphical orientation that the new computer immediately found a niche market in the visual, design, and publishing communities, and grew to almost universal acceptance within a decade.

Many entrepreneurs are absolutely convinced that like in the movie *Field of Dreams*, "if you build it, they will come." Such entrepreneurs believe they have a better idea, and if only they create the perfect embodiment of their idea, customers will flock to make it a success. But the statistics show this approach doesn't work out often in the real world–few of us are the next Steve Jobs. For example, the U.S. Patent Office issues about 100,000 patents a year–the proof that an idea is truly original–but only about 0.1 percent of those are profitable.[2] In a typical year, over

50,000 new products will be introduced in the U.S. market. Of those introduced by big businesses, the survival rate is between 20 and 55 percent after two years, while for small businesses the survival rate is estimated at closer to 5 percent.[3] In reality, the solution is to engage customers as early in the product development process as possible, as we will see.

The customer development process starts with the pains and gains of customers as noted in Chapter 4. Understanding how these occur and are dealt with today become a basis for designing new products or services to better resolve the pains or gains than what customers use now. The challenge for entrepreneurs is picking the right customers and the right pains and gains. Everyone has unresolved pains and unfulfilled gains, but as an entrepreneur, the ones that are important to your business are those people will pay well for. University of Southern California professor Tom O'Malia has a saying "contracts, not compliments," and it points to the need to have a solution to customer needs that they are willing to pay for. Getting rave reviews or millions of free users for solving their problem doesn't help if it doesn't lead to your ability to make the profits you and your firm needs.

For example, consider the app business. In early 2016, 94 percent of all the money spent on iPhone/iPad paid or freemium apps in the Apple App Store went to 623 publishers, with 61,677 other app makers fighting over the remaining 6 percent.[4] This meant that each of the 61,677 app makers on average had a market share of 0.0001 percent each, and an average of $1,391 in revenue. But the reality for the vast majority of app developers is that even with 1 million or more downloads of a free basic app, when less than 1 percent of these users are willing to pay to buy the full-featured app or pay to upgrade the app through in-app purchases,[5] few app makers can get enough royalties to live on. Many of these app developers have created something a lot of users download, like, and enjoy, but the app makers haven't created apps that users are willing to pay for. So a strictly customer-driven approach may not always work either.

In the end, products and customers have to be developed in a hand-in-hand manner. Let's start by looking at what we mean when we talk about a product or service, and then look in-depth at the product development process.

LO 9-2 Use customer roles and profiles to help define the target market.

Understanding the Customer

For an entrepreneur, understanding your customer is truly essential. While we are all customers in our everyday activities, most of us don't think about being a customer, so when we switch to being an entrepreneur, it helps to have an idea how to think about customers. In this section, we will introduce the different customer roles, how to initially learn from your customers, and how to use both of these pieces of information to identify the people who can most benefit from your business, your target customers.

end user
A customer role that describes the person who eventually makes actual use of a product or service in his or her personal or work life.

purchaser
A customer role that describes an individual or institution that pays for or obtains a product or service.

decision maker
A customer role that describes a person in an organization who is responsible for choosing which product or service will be obtained.

influencer
A customer role describing a person or group who can make credible or recognized suggestions or recommendations to others regarding purchase choices.

Customer Roles

As customers ourselves, our first thought is that the customer is the person who buys something. That can be true, but determining who is your customer can be far more complex. To help clarify this, let's think of the roles tied into buying and using products or services.

- When you buy it yourself and use it yourself, you are the **end user**, and the **purchaser**.
- But when you are buying something for someone else, you're still the purchaser, but the end user is the person receiving the present.
- In sales to organizations (e.g., groups, families, or businesses), this happens all the time where the organization has a person or office who handles purchasing goods and services for end users.
- In organizations, yet another person may be the **decision maker** who determines which product or service will be bought for the end users, and then tells the purchaser to place the order.
- For individuals or organizations, an important additional role is played by the **influencers**, people or groups with the ability to make suggestions or recommendations to people in any of these roles.

Understanding these roles and how they relate is essential to understanding who your customer is. Very often, especially for products or services you are selling to organizations, you will have multiple customers in the organization–the end user, the purchaser, the decision maker, and the influencers. On the other hand, selling to individuals on the Internet can be a very direct process, where the end user and the purchaser are one and the same. But even here, there are often influencers in the mix, such as referring websites, online recommendations, or the suggestions of family, friends, or social media connections.

The other reason it is useful to think about these customer roles is to use the roles to help you understand and map out the **purchasing process** for your proposed product or service. This initially consists of two questions: (1) How does the individual or organization use these roles to make purchasing decisions? (2) Who is in each role and what is important to them in making those decisions? The answers to these questions will be important to your promotion and sales efforts later. Closely related to this is the idea of the customers' **budget cycle** (for major purchases this is sometimes called the capital budgeting cycle), which in turn focuses on two more questions: (3) Can the customers afford to buy your product or service right when you pitch to them? (4) If the purchase price is above that level and they need to budget for it, when do you need to pitch to them so they can make their decision, and when will they actually be able to buy from you? These answers will help you schedule your sales efforts and help you set your pricing. To help you better understand your customer, we recommend building a customer profile next.

purchasing process
The sequence of steps an individual or organization goes through in making a decision to buy a product or service.

budget cycle
A term applied to the schedule and the process for setting the schedule for making purchases by an individual or an organization.

Initial Customer Profiles

The most important initial piece of information for the start-up entrepreneur thinking about selling to a customer is understanding at a deep or gut level what the customer is like. Possibly the single most important idea that has come from the lean business practices process is the adage "get out of the building!" The idea behind the phrase is that wisdom about your customers and their needs and wants can only come when you engage potential customers–lots of them–face-to-face. Another element of the lean startup is to develop a **customer profile** (also called a customer persona or user persona). This should be the first step in doing any research on your customers and their needs. Later steps, outlined below, can involve surveys and secondary (archival) research, but these first face-to-face interviews are what give you a deep, personal understanding of your customers, which the other approaches don't do well.

customer profile
A detailed description of an archetypal or hypothetical potential customer for a product or service, also called a customer persona.

The process for a start-up should begin with face-to-face interviews with people you have identified as potential customers. The goal in these interviews is to get an unbiased sense of the ways potential customers think about dealing with the issue your product or service helps resolve or improve. The unbiased aspect is crucial. Asking people if they would like your product or service will get you a lot of people trying not to hurt your feelings. Gathering biased information now means you are likely to draw the wrong conclusions about your offering later, at best costing you time and money to fix, and at worst meaning you won't really be able to find customers who want what your product or service offers, and your business crashes. Learning how to do this is the purpose of Skill Module 9.1.

You analyze the results by first looking at the problems your interviewees were trying to solve (question 1). This is often called the **customer job**.[6] Questions 1, 2, and 3 tell you about the pains your customers are experiencing or the gains they wish they could achieve. Question 4 tells you about the ways they try to deal with the pain or gain right now, while question 5 tells you where there is a possibility for something better. Together, the answers to these questions help you understand how your potential customers are thinking about the situation. If they are spending time and money on alternatives that they don't think do the job, then their pain can point you in the right direction for developing a product that might resonate.

customer job
The term given to what a potential customer is trying to do—perform or complete some sort of task, solve some problem, or try to achieve some outcome. The target of the job is often the key to what a proposed product or service is intended to help.

You take these answers and the demographics and build one or more customer profiles to translate the results into a personal example of the kind of people you will keep in mind as your develop and sell your product. The resulting report is often done as a single-page profile, shown

SKILL MODULE 9.1

Interviewing Customers in an Unbiased Way

One of the best examples of how to do unbiased interviewing comes from marketing expert Justin Wilcox of Customer Development Labs (**http://customerdevlabs.com/2013/11/05/how-i-interview-customers/**). He proposes a five-question survey, what he calls his "customer interview script":

1. What's the hardest part about [**problem context**]?
2. Can you tell me about the last time that happened?
3. Why was that hard?
4. What, if anything, have you done to solve that problem?
5. What don't you love about the solutions you've tried?

Justin points out that the hardest part of preparing the interview is figuring out what the problem context is. He says you should look for a situation that occurs frequently enough or is painful enough for the interviewee to warrant solving. So if you imagine yourself building Yelp for Vegetarians, don't ask "What's the hardest part about finding a good vegetarian restaurant in a new city?" That question telegraphs what your product is. Asking "What's the hardest part about being a vegetarian?" is so broad you could get lots of irrelevant answers. A good balance would be asking "What's the hardest part about eating out as a vegetarian?" You can learn more from his website and the video explaining his approach.

Justin also offers a free online script generator at **http://customerdevlabs.com/script/**. He includes a video explaining how to use the generator. Armed with this script, your next goal is to go out and interview potential customers (your instructor will give you a target number). Record the interviews so you can catch everything (your smartphone probably has a recording app), or take detailed notes on each person, including his or her demographics and how you can get back in touch with the individual.

in Skill Module 9.2, and again in Skill Module 9.6 when you build on the customer's job to craft your value proposition.

pivot
Typically, a term describing a change of direction in the thinking of an entrepreneur or a firm, often based on new data or other findings.

What if your unbiased customer interviews show your basic idea for a business doesn't hit a responsive cord? There are two possibilities: (1) change or **pivot** your product or service to better fit with what customers are talking about, or (2) change or pivot your customer base to find people who would be willing to buy what you propose. If neither works, you probably need to look at another business idea. But if your interviews show a path to creating a worthwhile

SKILL MODULE 9.2

Creating a Basic Customer Profile

You can build a basic customer profile with sections corresponding to the issues raised earlier: (1) the customer job, (2) pains, and gains, (3) how strongly he or she feels about the pain/gain, (4) how the customer deals with getting the job done now, (5) a demographics section including basics about the person (age, family situation, work, (6) customer job specifics (how often does it happen, where), and (7) the purchasing process and budget cycle for solutions to the customer job.

For these sections, you pretty much fill in the information from the interviews. In doing many interviews you're looking for recurring customer thoughts, issues that have the greatest potential for satisfying a larger share of the market (aka more sales!).

When you have this information, you apply your creativity to create three more elements: (1) The customer story should be a short paragraph that helps you get a feeling for the customer, pulling together what is on this page, and including special or unique points not covered elsewhere. They help you understand the person and his or her situation around the customer job in as close to the customer's own words as possible. (2) A quote, picture, or both helps remind you of what drives them. (3) A name for the profile helps it become your in-house shorthand for categorizing them, like "Emily the Giver" or "new mom."

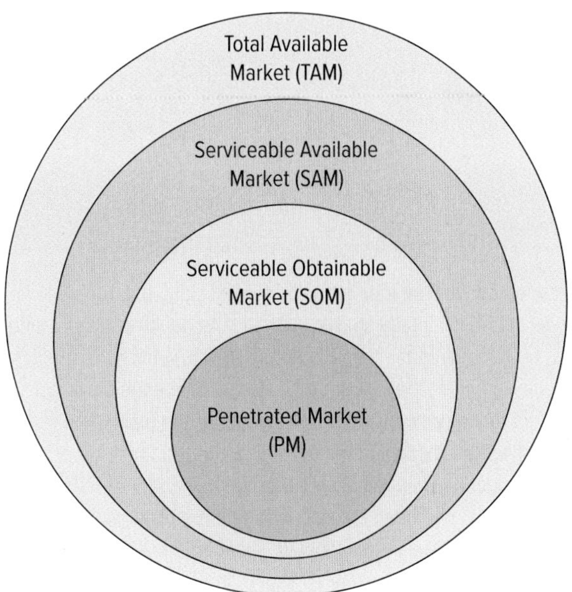

FIGURE 9.2

Nested Types of Markets

product or service, it is time to do an even bigger customer research effort using all the tools at your disposal, which we cover next.

Target Market

The point of identifying the customer roles and building the customer profile is to help you clarify exactly who would be the best customer for your business–the person who would be helped most by the product or service you're offering, and because of this would be your best and most loyal customer. That "perfect fit" customer is called your target market.

Target and Other Markets

Target market is the name given to one of a set of nested terms for the market sizes, from most general to most specific. The terms are shown in Figure 9.2:

- **Total available market (TAM):** This represents everyone who might consider the product or service you're offering.
- **Serviceable available market (SAM):** This represents customers within your geographic reach. If you depend on local traffic, it might be your neighborhood, city, or region. If you're online, it could be as large as your TAM.
- **Serviceable obtainable market (SOM):** This is also called your target market and represents the customers that you think would be interested in your particular product or service. This is almost always first based on the pains they are suffering or the gains they aspire to acquire, but it can also be refined by other demographic, attitudinal, or behavioral qualities like their income, their fashion sense, their participation in particular activities, or even being close by.
- **Penetrated market (PM):** If your business is operating, your actual number of customers divided by the target market tells us how much of the market you have attained so far, and how many people are available to be sold to.

There can be more than one target market, when your product or service could be used by groups different enough that they may like your offering for different reasons (a famous one went "tastes great" versus "less filling"), requiring different promotional efforts. These are called customer segments, and we will go into segmentation analyses in Chapter 10.

The Target Customer

In reality, most entrepreneurs start out with an idea who their target customer "is." The quotation marks are there because most of the time, as entrepreneurs begin to research with

total available market (TAM)
A marketing term that refers to all of the people or organizations (in one nation, region, or the world) who might consider a product or service being offered.

serviceable available market (SAM)
A marketing term that refers to the customers within the geographic reach of a firm.

serviceable obtainable market (SOM)
A marketing term (also called the target market) that represents the customers that a firm expects to be interested in its particular product or service, and able to be serviced by the firm.

penetrated market (PM)
A marketing term that describes the actual number of customers of an operating firm, divided by the size of the target market, which gives a percentage of the market the firm (or product/service) has attained so far.

SMALL BUSINESS INSIGHT

REFINING A TARGET MARKET

One of our students started out with an idea for a social messaging app for students studying abroad. His initial target market was students already studying abroad. As he interviewed students who had been or currently were abroad, he discovered the time to capture the students as customers was when they were still at their home colleges, planning their trips. So he started to change his target to students planning to go abroad. As he switched to interviewing students currently in the planning process for studying abroad, he found out these students primarily depend on the suggestions of their school's study abroad office.

Armed with this knowledge, he changed his focus to the managers of college study abroad offices. As he interviewed those managers, he added a school-to-student-studying-abroad messaging feature to his product. As his interviewees told him about competing services in the industry who were mostly targeting the larger state schools and wealthiest private colleges, he narrowed the focus of his target market to Catholic colleges. As a student in a Catholic college, he better understood that market than colleges in general and it was easier for him as a Catholic school student to get time with study abroad administrators at other Catholic colleges. His competitors didn't have these colleges in their sights—yet!

customers, doing the initial interviews and building the customer profile, they refine or even change their description of the target customer. A typical example is given in the Small Business Insight.

Finding the right target customer is crucial to your success in building a business. So as you move from your first guess to your first data-based findings, you will begin to see more possibilities for who could be your target customer. How can you decide? There are several ways:

1. **Benefit Matching:** The more closely customers' needs/pains/gains align with the features or benefits of your product or service, the happier they will be. You can find the categories of benefits in Chapter 7.
2. **Long-term value (LTV)** or **customer lifetime value (CLV):** A repeat customer will give you more revenue than one who buys from you only once. A customer who buys the premium product will give you more profits than one who buys the basic version. A customer who buys the product and add-ons like accessories or warranties will give you more profits than one who sticks only to the product itself. Going after the customer who will bring the most revenue and profit to your firm is a time-honored way to target. You can compute LTV by taking (a) the size of your average sale to the type of customer you're focusing on, times (b) the number of repeat sales per period of time–weeks, months, years, times (c) the number of time periods you expect to keep these customers, times (d) the profit margin. For Starbucks in 2004 (when it released these data publicly), this was (a) $5.90 times (b) 4.2 visits per week times (c) 52 weeks times 20 years times (d) 21.3 percent profit margins led to $5,489 in profits per customer based on sales of $25,771.[7]
3. **Influencer Impact:** A customer who buys your product or service and likes it is good, but one who spreads his or her message of happiness to the rest of the world, through word of mouth or social media, can lead to increased sales from customers you might not have known to target.
4. **Minimizing Churn:** Keeping existing customers is usually more valuable than trying to find and attract new ones. To compute your churn rate, count the number of customers you get over a period of time (a day, week, month, year–depending on your sales cycle). The percentage who never come back is your churn rate.

long-term value (LTV)
A marketing concept that refers to the revenue (or profit) generated by one customer over his or her lifetime dealing with one firm. Higher long-term value is usually preferred. LTV is also known as customer lifetime value or CLV.

customer lifetime value
A marketing concept that refers to the revenue (or profit) generated by one customer over his or her lifetime dealing with one firm. Higher long-term value is usually preferred. CLV is also known as long-term value or LTV.

churn
The turnover rate for your customers—the percentage of customers you typically lose after their first purchase from you.

In deciding on whom to target, keep in mind that there can occur for some businesses a "perfect storm" of benefit, influence, and long-term value, and these often characterize your perfect customer.

TABLE 9.2 Three Ways to Find First Customers

	Pros	Cons
Family and friends: You know them; they like you; find in person and on social media.	They'll buy because they like you. They'll buy when you ask. You know who they are.	May not really need or use the product. If same last name, less useful for testimonials and sharing.
Early adopters: Love new things; find them shopping (Sharper Image, Best Buy) or online (The Grommet, SkyMall) where new ideas and products are offered.	They are most likely to make an impulse buy if it is new and seems interesting or useful.	Only 16 percent of all customers are early adopters, so finding them is harder. May not have the greatest need for product.
People in pain: Think who has the biggest need—for moms of babies think baby stores, for little league products go to local games and fields.	Because they are facing the customer job and the pain tied to it, they can appreciate your product the most and can offer the most useful feedback.	Even harder to find. How many moms going into toy stores have the problem your new baby bib solves? The baby food aisle at the supermarket would be better.

Finding First Customers

For entrepreneurs in a start-up, finding those first customers is a key challenge. You have to start somewhere, and it could make good sense to believe that having any sales is a good thing, but in reality, having good sales is what is most important in those early days. What makes a sale "good"? Getting revenue from customers is a good thing, but in reality, especially in the early days of your business, what is probably more important to you are the nonfinancial benefits. Three come to mind: (1) **feedback**: you want to know how well your product or service works for the customer, how well it meets their needs, what they like and dislike about what you offer, and if they would buy it again or recommend it to others; (2) **testimonials**: statements they make that they will let you publicly repeat and attribute to them; and (3) **sharing**: where they post positive comments about your product or service to their social media accounts. There are also three typical places to go for first customers, which are outlined in Table 9.2.

feedback
The process of communicating within or to the organization about how the outputs worked or were received.

testimonial
Statement made that is allowed to be publicly repeated and attributed to the person that made it.

Looking at Table 9.2, you can see why finding people in pain could be the best (even if it is the hardest) way to go. Getting feedback from such people may be more important than the cash, so discounting or even giving away your product could be worthwhile if you can get permission to follow up with the customer. Those first customers, regardless of how you find them, who give you feedback, testimonials, and sharing are your best initial prospects for "perfect customers." Taking care of them is what we will talk about next.

Thinking about Customer Service

Know that not all customers are created equal. Business is a relationship, and like all our other relationships, there are degrees of closeness. Customers can love your business, like it, feel neutral about it, or dislike it. Obviously having people who are positively disposed toward your firm is what you want. In fact, the hallmark of the most successful start-ups is customers who are passionate fans of the business. Most of the greatest brands are successful because of a small, but steadfast and vocal, cadre of passionate fans. Think of people raving about Starbucks, Ben and Jerry's, Whole Foods, iPhones, or any of a thousand performers, movies, or shows.

What makes a passionate fan of your business? It can be a product that resonates powerfully, like the iPhone does for a segment of customers, but more often, it is a solid product or service wrapped up in an organizational culture or way of life that creates an enduring emotional connection with the customer. The hallmarks of this, which we might call **outstanding customer service**, include:[8]

outstanding customer service
The idea of "going all out" for the customer or providing over-the-top service, not just the basic help, professionalism, and friendliness we all expect in any business transaction; an employee or manager who is trying to make sure the customer walks away with an exceptional experience.

- Show interest in and concern for everyone in your business—customers, employees, suppliers, and the community alike.
- Go the extra mile for these people. You've heard of Zappos's and Nordstrom's return policies because customers are so impressed by them.

- Take time to be nice to all these people. A famous book is *Hug Your Customers* by Jack Mitchell, but it applies to everyone you deal with.
- Be honest and open in how you operate.
- When mistakes are made, fix them. Dave Sinclair, a St. Louis car dealer, had nailed this when he made his motto "If the car you buy from me isn't right, we'll make it right, free."
- Keep in mind the SERVICE acronym (social, enthusiastic, responsible, vibrant, intelligent, courteous, engaged) as a way to recall (and teach your employees) what outstanding customer service entails.

Realize that small businesses have a natural advantage in connecting to their target customers and making them into fans. Why? Because your customers can talk directly to the CEO of the business. Because a small business can change quicker than a big firm. Because each customer is probably more important to the small firm starting out than for a bigger, established business. For many entrepreneurs engaged in their start-up, there are so many things to do and so many things to learn and relearn that it can become too easy to forget about the customers, or take them for granted, as some of the businesses did in the following Small Business Insight.

SMALL BUSINESS INSIGHT

Generating Value for Customers

I had the misfortune to have to replace my air conditioner in the middle of a St. Louis summer. Dutifully I called three firms. One was the firm I had been dealing with for years. Another had good referrals from friends, and the third, Indoor Comfort Team (www.indoorcomfortteam.com), had won a local service award. All three responded promptly, came out to my house quickly, and gave me their estimate. The friend's referral emailed me a PDF invoice that was clearly just typed in MS Word. The price was given, and a line said "Warranty included." The long-time connection left a two-color proposal with about 10 of 20 boxes checked off showing what the company would be doing and four items showing what the warranties would be.

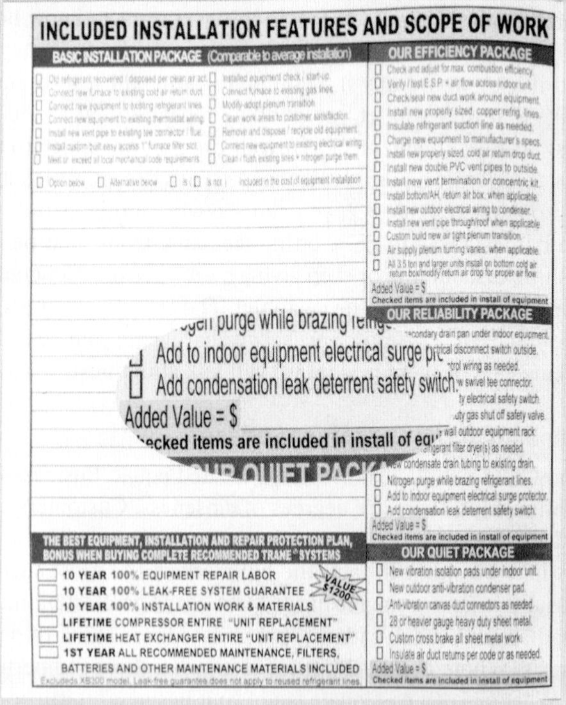

INCLUDED INSTALLATION FEATURES AND SCOPE OF WORK

BASIC INSTALLATION PACKAGE (Comparable to average installation)

OUR EFFICIENCY PACKAGE

- ☐ Check and adjust for max. combustion efficiency
- ☐ Verify / test E.S.P. + air flow across indoor unit
- ☐ Check/seal new duct work around equipment
- ☐ Install new properly sized, copper refrig. lines
- ☐ Insulate refrigerant suction line as needed
- ☐ Charge new equipment to manufacturer's specs
- ☐ Install new properly sized, cold air return drop duct
- ☐ Install new double PVC vent pipes to outside
- ☐ Install new vent termination or concentric kit
- ☐ Install bottom/AH, return air box, when applicable
- ☐ Install new outdoor electrical wiring to condenser
- ☐ Install new vent pipe through/roof when applicable
- ☐ Custom build new air tight plenum transition
- ☐ Air supply plenum turning vanes, when applicable
- ☐ All 3.5 ton and larger units install on bottom cold air return box/modify return air drop for proper air flow

Added Value = $

Checked items are included in install of equipment

OUR RELIABILITY PACKAGE

- ☐ Nitrogen purge while brazing refrigerant lines.
- ☐ Add to indoor equipment electrical surge protector.
- ☐ Add condensation leak deterrent safety switch.

Added Value = $

Checked items are included in install of equipment

OUR QUIET PACKAGE

- ☐ New vibration isolation pads under indoor unit.
- ☐ New outdoor anti-vibration condenser pad.
- ☐ Anti-vibration canvas duct connectors as needed.
- ☐ 28 or heavier gauge heavy duty sheet metal.
- ☐ Custom cross brake all sheet metal work.
- ☐ Insulate air duct returns per code or as needed.

Added Value = $

Checked items are included in install of equipment

THE BEST EQUIPMENT, INSTALLATION AND REPAIR PROTECTION PLAN, BONUS WHEN BUYING COMPLETE RECOMMENDED TRANE® SYSTEMS

- ☐ 10 YEAR 100% EQUIPMENT REPAIR LABOR
- ☐ 10 YEAR 100% LEAK-FREE SYSTEM GUARANTEE
- ☐ 10 YEAR 100% INSTALLATION WORK & MATERIALS
- ☐ LIFETIME COMPRESSOR ENTIRE "UNIT REPLACEMENT"
- ☐ LIFETIME HEAT EXCHANGER ENTIRE "UNIT REPLACEMENT"
- ☐ 1ST YEAR ALL RECOMMENDED MAINTENANCE, FILTERS, BATTERIES AND OTHER MAINTENANCE MATERIALS INCLUDED

VALUE $1200

Excludeds XB300 model. Leak-free guarantee does not apply to reused refrigerant lines.

A high-value job estimate. The enlarged circle gives you an idea of what all those lines of text represent.

Mark Dierker/McGraw-Hill Education

The award winner had me floored. The proposal form was six colors, showed "good," "better," and "best" options, and had nearly 60 check boxes, which the sales rep went over with me to show all the things the company would do and what it would check and double-check. The rep mentioned twice as many warranties as my long-term provider.

Note that all three firms had the same potential. They are in the same business, with pretty much the same products. When I explained to my long-term provider why I was going with Indoor Comfort Team, the entrepreneur told me, "But we will do all the things the other guys say they will." However, the award winner had taken the time to think through all of those steps, package them nicely, and go through them with me, the customer, to ensure what I was getting. By doing this the rep was actually *creating value*, helping me learn more about what I was trying to do, and in doing that, helping me appreciate his thoroughness and professionalism.

Passionate customers are beneficial in a variety of ways. They are most likely to buy again and again. They are more likely to share their passion for your business with family, friends, co-workers, and online pals. They are more likely to closely watch what your firm does and are the first to give you feedback and their ideas for new products or services. Their passion for your firm will empower and reward you and your employees, and because passion is contagious, passionate customers raise the positivism other customers feel. That is why creating a passionate core of target customers is so important to having a truly successful business, and achieving that depends on your creating a culture that puts customers first, as a unending reminder to you and your team what you *want* to do for your customers and your company.

With your customer profiles, target markets, and segments defined, you are positioned to do a deeper dive into your market, an approach called marketing research.

Segmenting Your Market

LO **9-3** Segment and further define your target audience.

It is easy to say that "everyone" will buy your idea, but that is true for very few products or services. Think of your circle of friends. How many foods or drinks or movies do you all agree on? How would those choices play with your parents? In reality, most products and services work best with particular markets. The successful entrepreneur leverages this idea to identify the best market (or markets) for their good or service.

That leveraging process is called **market segmentation**. **Segmenting** is simply a way to divide the total market—everyone in the world, essentially—into manageable pieces that have some common characteristics. Your **target market** is the segment or segments you select on which to concentrate your marketing efforts. A marketer can choose more than one target market, but financial, resource, or time constraints may mean that a smaller business can concentrate its efforts on only one target market at the beginning and consider additional ones later. Marketers use information on the target market's wants and needs in order to tailor the product or service, as well as its price, distribution, and promotion.[9] Sources of these wants and needs can be the customer interviews, customer profiles described above, and marketing research described next.

market segmentation
The process of dividing the market into groups that have somewhat homogeneous needs for a product or service.

segmentation
The process of dividing the market into smaller portions of people who have common characteristics.

target market
A marketing term (also called serviceable obtainable market, or SOM) that refers to the group of customers in the area you plan to serve who would be likely to be interested in your product, or those of competitors. Target markets can refer to individuals or market groups called segments.

Although you could divide by virtually any method imaginable (by middle initial, month of birth, number of cavities, last book read, etc.), marketers tell us to look for segments that are likely to have similar needs and buying behavior. There are several classic methods for segmenting customers:

- *Geographic segmentation*: Many businesses, large or small, choose to operate in one place, and even the biggest multinationals choose a manageable number of countries.[10] People who live in cities often have different needs from those in rural areas. People who live in Minnesota have different needs from those in Arizona, particularly in the winter. New Yorkers have different preferences from Los Angelinos. Many service industries have no choice but to segment geographically; if your car wash is located in Lubbock, you aren't going to attract too many customers from other cities.
- *Demographic segmentation*: Teenagers have different needs from toddlers, and both differ from seniors. Where and how people shop and what they buy varies because of income, ethnicity, gender identification, education level, marital status, and virtually any demographic variable you choose (see Figure 9.3). Life cycle position—unmarried, married without children, married with small children, married with teenage children, empty nesters, retirees, and so on—also determines the types of products a person may be interested in buying.

- *Benefit segmentation*: Recall the discussion of benefits in Chapter 7. Customers can be divided into groups based on what benefits they seek when making product or service decisions. For example, one customer buys a certain brand of toothpaste because it is a cavity fighter. Another customer wants the toothpaste that gives him fresher breath. A third may be looking for whitening power, while a fourth may want something that fights plaque. Many cars are segmented this way—speed, safety, capacity, and the like. Frequently used categories include those shoppers interested in a good value versus those more interested in reputation and prestige—think of Walmart shoppers versus those frequenting designer dress shops and how Target tries to position themselves as just a little more fashionable than Walmart.
- *Psychographic segmentation*: Another category for segmenting has to do with an individual's personality, attitudes, concerns, choices and behaviors. Adventure seekers buy different products (or for different reasons) than more timid people. Hobbies, sports interests, religion, cultural interests, and similar individual factors can determine the likelihood of people purchasing certain products. Where benefit segmentation looks at the products' features, psychographic segmentation looks at what drives the person, for example health concerns (so plaque fighting is important) vs. social concerns (where bad breath is the focus). It is typical to combine these types of segmentation approaches. For example, the Beacon Street Girls (p. 314-316) products were segmented by gender (girls) and age (9-13). In addition, the fact that they were into values and community service would be a form of benefit segmentation. Beacon Street Girls also had primary and secondary target markets—the girls and their parents as the primary target and secondarily other gift-givers. Even here, the different segments may buy the same product for different reasons.

predetermined market segments
Professionally compiled target audiences based on shared demographic, financial, shopping, and psychographic characteristics.

In fact, there are companies who have spent millions creating specialized customer profiles based on combinations; these are often called **predetermined market segments**. Claritas (which used to be a part of Nielsen, a company you probably recall is famous for television ratings) has several types of segmentation analyses. The one that fits for most consumer-oriented firms is called PRIZM (https://claritas360.claritas.com/mybestsegments/#zipLookup). For nearly any zip code in the United States, PRIZM can tell you the predominant groups in it.

PRIZM, for example, will identify the five largest market segments within a specific zip code for free. For each segment, PRIZM provides a free, detailed rundown about the buying habits and demographics of this group. The information in these predetermined market segments can help you identify the financial and shopping characteristics of the group, which can be difficult questions to ask people face-to-face. These segments can also be a useful check on your own analyses of your target market.

A competitor to PRIZM is Esri's Tapestry model (www.esri.com/data/tapestry). Tapestry provides descriptions of its segments, as well as the opportunity to see some data for free by zip code. Additional data require a fee.

FIGURE 9.3

Target Market Ads

These Burger King ads are aimed at targeting two different markets. Can you identify which market(s) each ad is geared toward? Is each ad successful in meeting its market's needs? Why or why not?

Images Courtesy of The Advertising Archives

Why don't we recommend using these carefully crafted segments first? Because the essential strength of small business owners is that they are close to their customers. Good entrepreneurs understand their customers and their needs at a personal level. It actually hurts your ability to define your own target market if you first rely on some other group's or firm's idea of who the target audiences are. The only certain way for you to know your customers is to start looking for them personally, finding out what they are like personally, and hearing what they have to say personally. Then you have a basis for deciding if and how these predetermined market segments fit any of your real customers. If they do, then these commercial products can help you know more about your customers, but they can never really replace the knowledge you first build about your customers on your own.

A Segmentation Example

Let's imagine you live in Phoenix, Arizona. You are bilingual in English and Spanish, and you want to start a day-care center with a bilingual focus. You have done some customer interviews and found there are families interested in this.

From your interviews you have created a customer profile. The Juarez family wants to find a day-care center for little Tomas. The family speaks a mix of English and Spanish at home and wants the children to be comfortable in both languages. Good news! At your center he is not likely to be misunderstood. Other benefits include being able to leave instructions in English or Spanish or having children get a mix of both cultures, such as holiday and birthday celebrations, stories that are read, decorating colors, the day-care center's name, and such. From the interviews, it was also clear that these features would appeal to secondary-market families where parents speak English and Spanish and even all-English-speaking families who want their children to be bilingual. The challenge facing you is deciding where to put your center to get the largest number of customers.

Applying this profile, think about who is your market. For starters, it is small children, or at least, the parents of small children. You have segmented by life cycle position; that is, you have eliminated children, teenagers, senior citizens, and parents of older children. But this really does not eliminate very many potential customers. How else could you limit your potential customers? Given the bilingual interests, you are probably looking at families (primarily Hispanic) with moderate income and above, figuring that families need to be rich enough to afford your service but not so rich as to hire nannies. Given people don't like to drive their children all over town, you need to pick a location close to families who would be in your target market segment. It is possible to do this sort of demographic segmentation research on the Internet, as shown in Skill Module 9.3.

What are the benefits to both your primary- and secondary-market customers if you open a bilingual day-care center in the middle of a largely Hispanic neighborhood? How would you promote to both of these markets?

Andrew Resek/McGraw-Hill Education

SKILL MODULE 9.3 Finding Demographic Information by Zip Code

There are several websites that offer breakdowns of demographic information organized by city or even zip code, such as **www.zipwho.com** and **www.city-data.com.** When looking for basic information on potential customers, this kind of information can be extremely valuable.

We've talked about a bilingual children's day-care center in Phoenix. The primary target market is Hispanic families with children and working parents. One way to advertise to these parents would be to do a traditional flyer, like those mailed out by Valpak and similar companies. For such coupon-sized flyers, you can select the zip codes in which your target audience would receive them. So in Phoenix, which zip codes would it be?

For this search we will use **www.zipwho.com** because it provides the most ability to specify demographics and localities in searching. Selecting Arizona and typing in "Phoenix" gets us precisely where we want to be. Because we are looking for Hispanic families we selected "Hispanic Ethnicity (%)." While there isn't a demographic category on **zipwho.com** for families with children, instead we used "Average Family Size," figuring families with children will be larger, and there we'll accept the default values. We will also look for "Median Income" to identify families with more money to spend on day care.

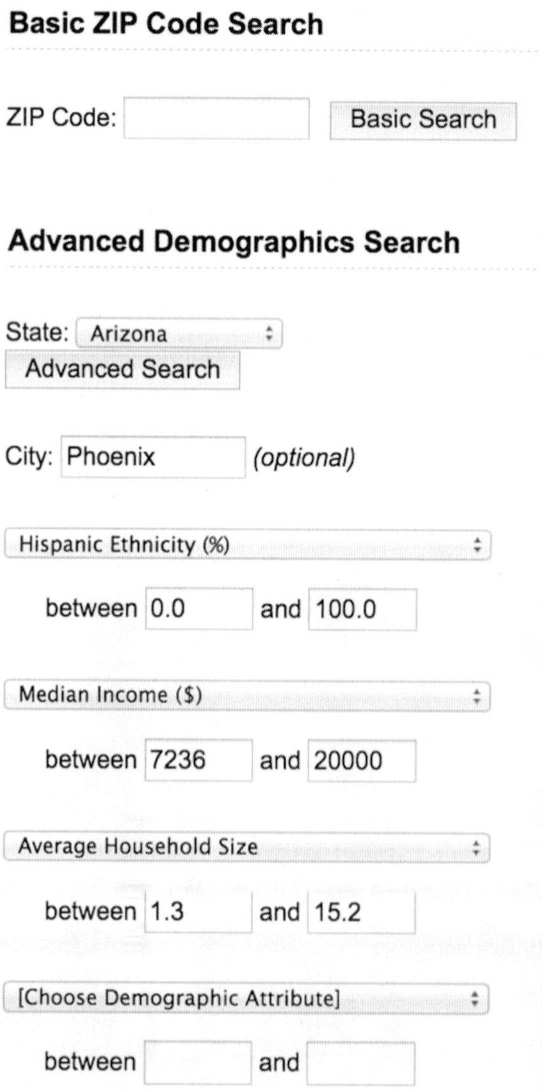

Basic ZIP Code Search

ZIP Code: [ ] Basic Search

Advanced Demographics Search

State: Arizona
Advanced Search

City: Phoenix *(optional)*

Hispanic Ethnicity (%)

between 0.0 and 100.0

Median Income ($)

between 7236 and 20000

Average Household Size

between 1.3 and 15.2

[Choose Demographic Attribute]

between [ ] and [ ]

ZipWho

The result is a list of 38 Phoenix zip codes ranked by median income. The zip code with the highest income and highest Hispanic ethnicity is 85037, with an income of $49,101, 41.5 percent Hispanic ethnicity, and 3.3 people per household.

	Location	Hispanic Ethnicity (%)	Median Income ($) ▼	Average Household Size
1.	85045 Phoenix, AZ	6.6	105,090	2.9
2.	85054 Phoenix, AZ	4.6	87,106	2.7
3.	85048 Phoenix, AZ	7.9	82,865	2.8
4.	85028 Phoenix, AZ	6.0	65,427	2.5
5.	85050 Phoenix, AZ	6.6	64,971	2.6
6.	85044 Phoenix, AZ	9.7	60,095	2.3
7.	85024 Phoenix, AZ	8.7	56,463	2.5
8.	85037 Phoenix, AZ	41.5	49,101	3.3
9.	85053 Phoenix	13.4	46,422	2.6

ZipWho

For each zip code, there is a hotlink that takes us to a demographic breakdown of the area. Let's look at the number 8 zip code on the above list, 85037. Click on 85037 and you will see the statistical profile below.

85037: Phoenix, AZ

		National Percentile Rank (0-99)	
Median Income ($)	49,101	73	
Cost Of Living Index	102.5	52	
Median Mortgage To Income Ratio (%)	22.1	64	
Owner Occupied Homes (%)	83.6	76	
Median Rooms In Home	5.5	54	
College Degree (%)	11.7	30	
Professional (%)	22.2	22	
Population	33,208	89	
Average Household Size	3.3	96	TOP 10%
Median Age	27.2	3	BOTTOM 10%
Male To Female Ratio (%)	98.9	80	
Married (%)	59.7	41	
Divorced (%)	11.6	79	
White (%)	45.6	11	
Black (%)	7.5	73	
Asian (%)	1.8	77	
Hispanic Ethnicity (%)	41.5	95	TOP 10%

ZipWho

(Continued)

The population in this area is well-off, with income in the 73rd percentile (meaning only 27 percent of Americans are making more than the median income in this zip code). Household size is even higher, at the 96th percentile. So it is likely the people in this community have children, and should probably be able to afford child care. Note also that this zip code has a good-sized population, 33,208 (41.5 percent Hispanic), so there would be more people to respond to zip code–focused advertising efforts. This number is important because direct mail firms usually have minimums, for example, 10,000 households at, say, 4 cents per home; making sure you can make back your $400 initial outlay is a key consideration.

This is where the marketing funnel described in Chapter 10 comes into play. So you send out to 10,000 households. If the funnel's return rate holds, you could get 20 customers, 10 of whom would be loyal. To make this advertising program work, you would need to make a $20 profit from each of the 20 initial customer families.

Repeat this with the other zip codes in the listing and identify at least two zip codes that you think look promising, with a large enough number of Hispanic families in the area and an area with a high enough family income to give the mail-out the possibility of being financially worthwhile.

By the way, you can see many of these Census statistics graphically mapped at **www.city-data.com**, but it doesn't let you select multiple factors at the same time.

Given this process you have a target zip code, 85037. With that information, you can go to PRIZM and check into the predetermined market segments of the community. PRIZM will identify the five largest market segments within a specific zip code for free. For each segment, PRIZM provides a free, detailed rundown about the buying habits and demographics of this group.

For zip code 85037, all of the five top segments according to PRIZM are ones with kids (Multi-Culti Families, Multi-Culti Mosaic, Pools & Patios, Second City Startups, and Up-and-Comers). See the photo of the PRIZM results below. As noted earlier, using predetermined market segments can help you understand your target market in new ways, but the key always is the information you personally obtain from the prospective customers you interview.

While defining your target market is important, it also pays to think about secondary target markets.[11] Remember that for Beacon Street Girls the secondary market were friends and grandparents of the girls, a potential likely source of revenue (pages 314–316). These are customers who might be interested in using your product or service, but are not whom you probably start out targeting. You need to at least consider who they are and how you might respond

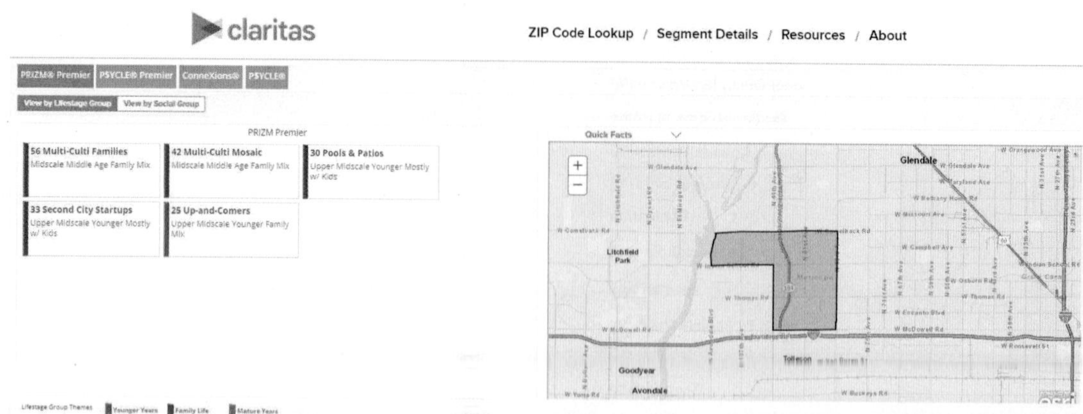

This is the breakdown for the 85037 zip code in Phoenix using Claritas's segmentation model, PRIZM, found at https://claritas360.claritas.com/mybestsegments/#zipLookup. The profiles on the left side are 5 of 66 different consumer segments based on extensive research. Why should predetermined market segments like the one shown here be used only after you've identified and learned firsthand about your target market?

claritas

to them, and certainly keep them in mind for future expansion. For example, what will you do if Chinese parents call your day-care center and ask if they can enroll their child so that she might learn more Spanish along with her English? Roy "Bud" Davis, one of the cofounders of Bert and Bud's Vintage Coffins (www.vintagecoffins.com), builds custom coffins designed to be works of art that make a statement about the person who will be buried in them. His target market is wealthier people over age 55 who have "an independent streak, a sense of humor about their mortality, and the practicality to plan ahead." He found secondary target markets in Civil War reenactors who want authentic-looking recreations of historical caskets, heavy metal music fans who use them as beds, and pet owners looking for a way to remember a special pet.[12]

Why bother with all of this targeting? The main reason is so that you don't waste a lot of effort and money. Once you know who your target market is, you can determine their purchasing behavior. You can find out where people in that group shop, where they are likely to see your advertisements (e.g., what television shows they watch, what magazines they read, what websites they visit, etc.), what prices they expect, what messages are likely to appeal to them—in short, everything you need to know to successfully market to them. If you are trying to sell handmade baby clothes, you could buy a banner ad on the CNN website, but one on the Mommy Mall website is less likely to be wasted on nonpurchasers. It's just logical to be where your potential customers are.[13]

From the information you gather from your interviews and the data you can develop from these data sources, you can think through how well you know your customers, and what you still want to learn from them. No commercial survey and most initial customer interviews answer all the questions any entrepreneur wants answered before they start spending their money and making their key decisions. So all this research helps you decide what *else* you need to know, and it help you decide on the topics you want to pursue in your own marketing research efforts. The goal is to know everything you need to about your customers to know who your key target market segments are, where are they, what will they like about your offering, and where they get the information they use to make purchase decisions.

Marketing Research

LO **9-4** Recognize the major methods for conducting marketing research.

While the customer profiling method mentioned previously is essential to give you a personal, gut-level understanding of your customer, when you have to start thinking about customer groups that may be counted in the thousands or millions, there is nothing like solid research to give entrepreneurs and investors confidence that a plan will actually work. Getting these facts is called marketing research.[14] **Marketing research** can verify the size of the potential market. It can show what the competitors are doing correctly or what their weaknesses are. It can also reveal where potential customers are likely to shop, likely to see advertisements (as well as how they feel about different sources and types of advertisements), and what they consider a reasonable price. You may believe that your product or service has some tremendous advantages over the competition, but marketing research might show you that the customers really aren't willing to switch providers, do not think your features are worth the extra cost, or do not even like these features at all. Without this sort of information, you cannot put together a coherent business plan.[15] Marketing research is where and how you get the facts to support your plan and the proof that what you are planning to do has a reasonably good chance of succeeding.

marketing research
Systematic collection and interpretation of data to support future marketing decisions.

Research falls into two major categories. **Primary research** is research gathered to answer a specific marketing question. **Secondary research** is research already gathered for some other reason than your specific question, but can be just as useful. We will cover each next.

primary research
An approach to researching based on the gathering of new information, using techniques such as interviewing, surveying, and observation.

secondary research
An approach to researching based on the use of existing information, often from government, commercial, or academic databases and research efforts.

Primary Research

Primary data are specific to the problem you are solving. When you did the customer profile interviews, you were conducting primary research. In primary research, you decide what you need to know and how to get that information. This information is extremely current, but it can often take somewhat more time and money to gather it. There are marketing research firms that could do this for you, but the cost—usually several tens of thousands of dollars—tends to put it out of

TABLE 9.3 Cost Comparisons for Various Survey Methods[16]

	Mail	Phone	Online
Setup	$40,000	$6,000	$1,500
Invitations	34,800	66,667	500
Processing	38,560	72,000	0
Total	$113,360.00	$144,667	$2,000
Cost per response	$4.72	$6.03	$0.08

Note: Based on 12 surveys with 2,000 responses each.

reach for small businesses. A much more reasonable option is an online survey. (See Table 9.3 for some cost comparisons.)

There are several forms of primary research. You were introduced to interviewing in the discussion about building customer profiles. Other techniques include observation, focus groups, and surveying.

Observation

ethnographic research Data gathered by simple observation—seeing what consumers do, rather than asking them.

There are a number of methods for gathering data in primary research. One category consists of observation methods. For example, I could go to the local grocery store and watch people shop. I could make lists of the products they choose and the time they spend making decisions.[17] This is called **ethnographic research** and has its place. For example, if I was considering opening a restaurant in a particular location, I could stand in front of the location and count foot and automobile traffic. I could visit a competitive restaurant and observe what people ordered, how long they stayed, and the time of day they visited. I could listen to the customers' comments about what they like or don't like.[18] A great free resource is Giff Constable's book *Talking to Humans* which details the how's and why's of this approach, and it is available to students and faculty for free online at www.talkingtohumans.com/.

Focus Groups

focus group A form of data gathering from a small group led by a moderator.

Another method is the **focus group**, which is a small group (8 to 12 people) that is asked to meet to discuss a series of questions about a particular product or service. A skilled researcher, who can make sure the questions are asked the right way and the data are systematically collected, conducts these meetings. Because participants are often paid for their time, this can be an expensive prospect for many small businesses.[19]

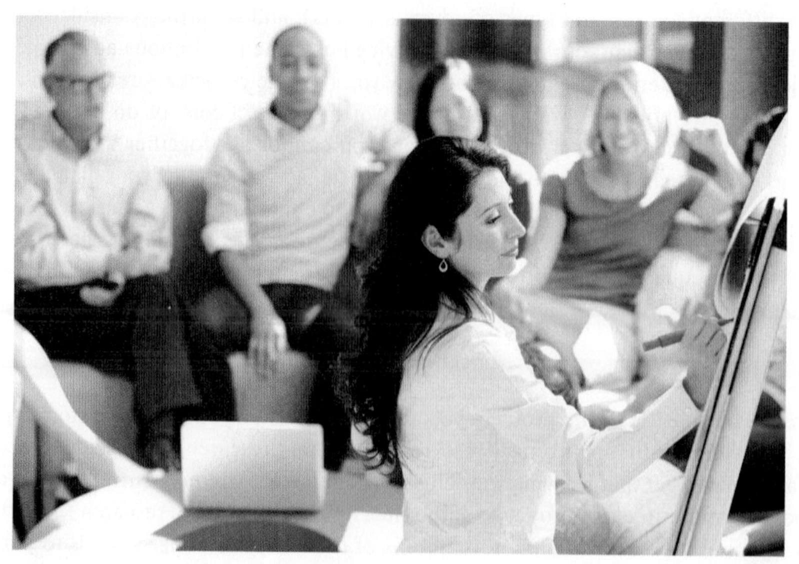

In a focus group, the goal is to get participants to talk about their impressions of a product, service, company, or concept. How would you select focus group participants to give you the best feedback for your business idea?

Monkey Business Images/123RF

On the other hand, gathering a few friends and neighbors over for dinner and quizzing them on their ideas about your product may be just as productive, if not quite so formal, but with friends, you always need to worry about how much they are trying to avoid hurting your feelings. (See Skill Module 9.4 for a brief explanation of how to conduct a focus group.) This more informal approach is also a good way to test your questions to make sure your audience understands exactly what you are asking. That is especially important with closed-ended questions, because there may be alternatives you hadn't considered or ambiguities you hadn't noticed. (This is sort of like the yes/no question, "Have you stopped spanking your children?" How do you answer that if you *never* spanked them?)

Surveying

A most typical data-gathering tool when you are looking to gather information from large numbers of people is the **survey**—some form of questionnaire. The questions may be asked in person, on the telephone, by mail, or online. In person tends to be the most expensive method, with telephone coming in second, followed by mail and online, as shown in Table 9.3. On the other hand, mail has the lowest return rate and does not allow for much flexibility. In person, you can

Survey
A data-collection method using a questionnaire—in person, on the phone, on paper, or on the Internet.

How to Conduct a Focus Group

SKILL MODULE 9.4

Focus groups are one of the most widely used techniques for getting information, especially at early stages, when you may not know everything you need to know about your product, service, or market. While it is probably best to have professionals run your focus group, you can do a passable job on your own if you follow these steps:

1. **Background:** Take a look at a book on how to conduct a focus group to familiarize yourself with the technique. Some examples are books like *Focus Groups: A Practical Guide for Applied Research* by Richard A. Krueger and Mary Anne Casey (Thousand Oaks, CA: Sage, 2000), or his online guide at **www.eiu.edu/ihec/Krueger-FocusGroupInterviews.pdf**. Or see the University of Kansas's web page on conducting focus groups (**http://ctb.ku.edu/en/table-of-contents/assessment/assessing-community-needs-and-resources/conduct-focus-groups/main**).
2. **Questions:** Determine the three things you'd like to know about how potential customers think about their purchases of your product or service. Aim for open-ended questions.
3. **Moderator:** To help people feel at ease, it is better to get someone other than you to moderate the focus group. If you have a friend with experience, that's great. If not, a friend who works as a salesperson, especially the sort who travels, has many of the needed skills, such as getting people to explain their reservations, dealing with a variety of customer reactions, and thinking on his or her feet. You can also check with the local university to see if there are students or professors with experience whom you can hire.
4. **Location:** Get a location that is comfortable and offers few distractions. In order to hear what is going on, buy or borrow a child's in-room monitor, so you can listen from a distance to the focus group as it happens. Get a tape recorder to save all the comments.
5. **Participants:** Think in terms of friends and friends of friends. Look for people who like to talk and are likely buyers of your product or service or who are already using a competitor's product or service. Offering dinner and perhaps a small gift or a drawing for a larger gift is suitable for this kind of setting.
6. **Scheduling:** Aim for a two-hour block of time. Take a break after around 60–75 minutes so you can talk to the moderator if you need to adjust the questions or probe for answers. Greet the participants as they arrive and leave, and be ready to answer their questions. It is a nice touch to come in and answer participant questions at the end of the session, if you can do it graciously and without sounding defensive.
7. **Analysis:** Have an adviser or mentor listen to the recording separately from you, and discuss what he or she noticed and what you did. Where possible, build a poll of responses to see how many people felt one way or another. Be on the lookout for concerns or problems people raised.

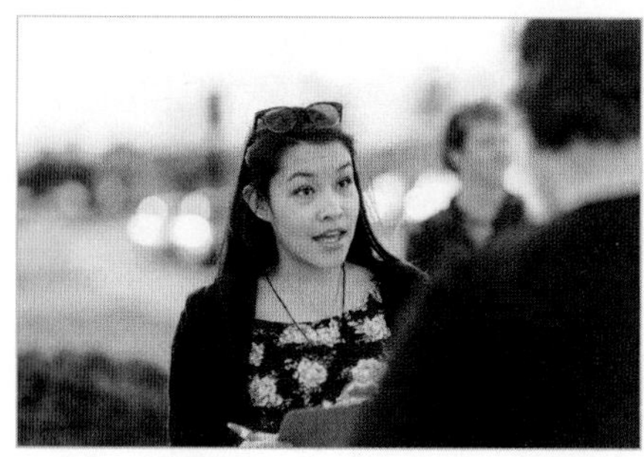

Surveys can be done online, by mail, on the phone, or in person like the entrepreneur and prospective customer here. What kinds of questions would work well in face-to-face interviews?

Marc Romanelli/Blend Images/Getty Images

ask for clarification, have people expand on their answer, or even change the next question based on the response. Online surveys are easy to get started, and can be extremely inexpensive. That said, getting people to respond to online surveys is a particular challenge. For all types of surveys, it can help to use multiple screens of questions, so respondents get to the right questions for them based on their responses to earlier questions (known in online survey terms as *branching*). For example, if a respondent is currently not using a particular product, the next questions he or she sees may go after the reasons for not using it. If respondents do currently use the product, the next questions may ask about their current provider.[20]

Having a set of predetermined written questions has certain advantages whether responses are oral or in writing. If you ask the same questions of each respondent, you can accurately compare answers and even statistically analyze these answers. You can come up with an average answer or compare answers between two (or more) specific groups (and conduct more complex statistical analysis, if the situation warrants it).

For example, suppose you ask people to rate your product on a scale of 1 to 10. The average rating might be 6.5, with 10 being high. This is nice information to know, but what could you find out by reexamining the data? What is the range of answers? If it is 5 to 8, you know that most people have similar feelings about your product—better than average but not perfect, with those at the 8 level being relatively pleased. It might take just a few tweaks of your product to move that average up to 7.5 or higher.

What if the range were from 1 to 10? Now you have people who love your product and others who hate it. It would likely take tremendous changes to convert those 1s to higher scores, and those changes might end up alienating the 10s. You now have a whole different scenario from when the range was small. What if you subdivided the answers based on some demographic value? For example, maybe you could sort by sex, age, wealth, or race. If you subdivide your answers into male and female, for example, you might find out that the average male response was 3.4, while the average female response was 7.8. If your product were a new skin lotion with a floral fragrance, you would expect women to like it better than men. If you thought the fragrance was neutral (and you should have asked this in your questionnaire), maybe you will want to revise the scent or simply focus on the target market that likes it, the women.

scalar question
Question that is answered by some sort of scale; for example, "On a scale of 1 to 5, how do you like this book?"

dichotomous question
Question that has only two possible choices; for example, "Have you shopped here before?"

categorical question
Question that is answered by selecting the proper category; for example, "What is your ethnicity? White, African American, Hispanic, Asian, American Indian, Other."

open-ended question
Question that allows respondents to express themselves as they choose; for example, "What do you like about this book?"

There are two major types of questions used in surveys: open- and closed-ended questions. One frequent type of closed-ended question—the **scalar question**—was illustrated earlier: "On a scale of 1 to 5, how would you rate XYZ?" **Dichotomous questions** are those with two choices—gender, employed or not, and so on. **Categorical questions** give you several predetermined groups from which to choose—for example, age levels (under 20, 20 to 29, 30 to 39, etc.). **Open-ended questions** allow the interviewees to answer any way they wish. Instead of asking "Do you like XYZ?" (a question that can be answered yes or no) you could ask, "What are the advantages of XYZ?"

With closed-ended questions, which can be answered only in certain ways, it is much easier to compare groups and to statistically analyze. However, they can limit the information you get. Let's say that your research shows that many people are concerned with the quality of their lawn service. What does this mean? One woman may believe that the trimming isn't as accurate as she would like, while a man is upset because the service ruined his in-ground sprinkler system. A simple 1-5 scalar, closed-ended question wouldn't capture this information. Open-ended questions—"What do you dislike about your current lawn service?"—would.[21]

Open-ended questions, which can be answered in many ways, can help you find new niches and perfect your product or service before you introduce it. Stephanie Kellar (www.lashoutpro.com) had an idea for a new eyelash curler. She posted open-ended questions on a Usenet newsgroup called alt.fashion. In just a few months, she had collected information from over 100 people with minimal effort. She also used this venue to find people willing to test her new product in the development phase.[22] Today Stephanie would use Facebook or Twitter, but the process would work just as well.

As Kellar found out, polling a group of consumers with common interests on the Internet is an inexpensive way to do marketing research and to find potential new customers for both test markets and the real thing. Today you can post questions on your social media accounts, or on sites like Quora.com to get answers, or you can use paid samples on Amazon Mechanical Turk, SurveyMonkey.com, Qualtrics.com, AYTM.com (Ask Your Target Market), and GutCheckIt.com. These services can generate results in one to two days based on your criteria, often for $500 or less. A great example of this using Amazon Mechanical Turk can be found online at https://customerdevlabs.com/2012/08/21/using-mturk-to-interview-100-customers-in-4-hours/.

Open-ended questions provide data that are more difficult to tabulate; they take considerably more time to ask and evaluate, and answers can be difficult to compare. For example, if you asked "How often would you use this product?" you might get answers such as "some of the time," "two or three times a month," or "whenever I have guests." Are those answers the same? If not, which one reflects a heavier user? In this case, a categorical question (once a month, 2-3 times a month, 4-5 times a month, etc.) would be easier to interpret. Open-ended questions are best for gathering preliminary information, when samples are small and when there are data that are difficult to get any other way. You can get a feel for the strengths and weaknesses of each type of question from Experiential Exercise 11 at the end of the chapter.

Last, you need to recognize that there is no such thing as perfect information. People say one thing and do another. They may like your product but consider it a luxury item that they may or may not purchase. Things are constantly changing, and no one can understand all the interrelationships and how they might affect a business. There are always more questions that could be asked, and more data that could be collected. Look for support for your ideas, but understand that the best you can do is make a good, educated guess.

There are volumes written on how to write good questions and how to gather and analyze data scientifically. If you are expecting people to invest huge sums of money in your business, your data had better be accurate and correctly gathered (see the Small Business Insight). In order to accomplish this, study a good marketing research text or hire or enlist outside help. Most small businesses don't need to be quite so formal; potential investors will let you know where they need more information and what they want to see.

Today there are multiple online survey platforms that can help you put together professional-looking marketing surveys for free on the web, your smartphone, or even on your Facebook page. They will often have example surveys put together by their experts to help you get started. Most will let you obtain responses for free from 100 people (in some cases more). The Learn More Online box below lists websites where you can build and distribute your surveys for free (some limitations apply). As you understand the sort of questions you would like to ask, you could build your own free survey with unlimited numbers of questions and respondents using Google Forms.

SMALL BUSINESS INSIGHT

GRANDKIDS[23]

Irene Viento thought she had done things right. She decided to start a retail outlet, GrandKids, to target grandparents—especially those who had money to buy extra special things for their grandchildren. Viento had experience with this target group, being a grandmother herself. She studied the demographics of Pelham, New York, her hometown, and relying on school data and information from an advertising circular company, she estimated that there were about 10,000 families in the area. Although there were 10 direct competitors within eight miles, there were none in Pelham, an upscale New York City suburb. She found a location just outside of town and started her business in 1994, but she had to close her doors by 1997. Basically, her research was flawed: Pelham had only slightly more than 3,200 families and the largest age group was in the 22–49 range—not the grandparents Viento needed. She also didn't know whether her potential customers were willing to drive to her out-of-town location, and if they were, wouldn't they be just as apt to visit her competitors?

LEARN MORE ONLINE

Learn more about the topics above at these sites:

Survio product evaluation survey: **www.survio.com/survey-template/product-evaluation-survey**

Sogo product evaluation survey template: **www.sogosurvey.com/survey-templates/customer/product-evaluation-survey/?type=individual**

Typeform customer feedback form template: **www.typeform.com/templates/t/customer-feedback/**

Facebook survey: **www.facebook.com/simple.surveys/**

Other sources include your local Small Business Administration office or SCORE (www.score.org) office, a marketing professor at your school, or a school marketing club. Also note that colleges often offer students free access to online survey platforms such as Qualtrics, which has an excellent product evaluation template.

Secondary Research

Secondary research refers to using existing data or databases to gather information on the topic of interest to you. Every Google search you do is an example of secondary research–Google finds information based on your search query and you look for relevant data in the lists of links Google gives you. As you can see, secondary research is often free and quick; there is no need to design questions and gather information yourself. Problems with secondary data, which apply to your Google results too, include that the data may not be timely and you don't always know why the data were gathered and whether they were gathered correctly (biases). Sometimes it is hard to find the exact details you need. But because of its ready availability, speed, and potential for using high-quality data, secondary research is always a good approach to use and will often be able to at least tell you if you are in the ballpark.

The challenge in secondary analysis is finding good data, meaning data that are gathered in an unbiased way, reported fairly, and are considered by knowledgeable people to be reputable. The most useful websites for finding fast and reliable secondary data for marketing research include:

- BizStats.com: Benchmarks, statistics, and financials for industries and the economy.
- Economic Census (www.census.gov/programs-surveys/economic-census.html: Sales, payrolls, employees for all industries. Also contains considerable detail on costs and characteristics (e.g., type of cuisine for restaurants) for individual industries.
- Expenses and Expenditures: The old business expenses survey covering wholesale, retail, and some service industries has been replaced and the new surveys are available at www.census.gov/topics/business-economy/expenses.html. The successors to the Capital Expenditures Survey covering major expenditures for most industries and the survey on Information and Communications Technology Expenditures are also found on this page.
- E-Commerce Statistics (www.census.gov/programs-surveys/e-stats.html): Overviews of performance and prospects of the Internet industry.
- Population and Household Statistics: Following the technique used in Skill Module 11.2, you can look at a wide variety of household statistics obtained by the government (e.g., income, education, computer ownership, health insurance, housing costs, number and age of family members, etc.) and made available to us on the Census website as well as on many commercial websites, including some free ones like www.zipWho.com and www.City-Data.com.

Commercial services that offer information (and in some cases may be the only source for the data you need) abound. Check with your school's library to see which databases they subscribe to and obtain a quick introduction to using them from your library's reference librarian. Examples include Mintel.com (focused largely on consumer data), IBISWorld.com (focused largely on industry information), Freedonia.com (B2B focus), or Statista.com as well as general-purpose business data sources like LexisNexis or ProQuest's ABI/Inform (www.proquest.com/products-services/abi_inform_complete.html).

Supplementing these commercial databases are free databases on the major social media sites which can give you extraordinarily detailed information on users of the specific social media platforms, like Facebook and Instagram as well as Google sites. You can learn more about these at https://adespresso.com/guides/. Skill Module 9.5 below shows how to use Facebook's Audience Insights to zero in on customers of companies you might consider competing with.

Let us take a moment and see how you can use these resources to determine the three most important numbers for a marketing plan—the total size of the market (in terms of sales, or failing that, customers) for the geographic area of your focus, the typical price of a product or service like yours, and the typical profitability of that product or service.

Using Facebook Audience Insights

SKILL MODULE 9.5

For this exercise you need to have a Facebook account. Google "Facebook audience insights" or go directly to **www.facebook.com/business/insights/tools/audience-insights**. You'll need to sign in to your Facebook account to get to the page.

1. From the "Choose an Audience to Start" box select "Everyone on Facebook":

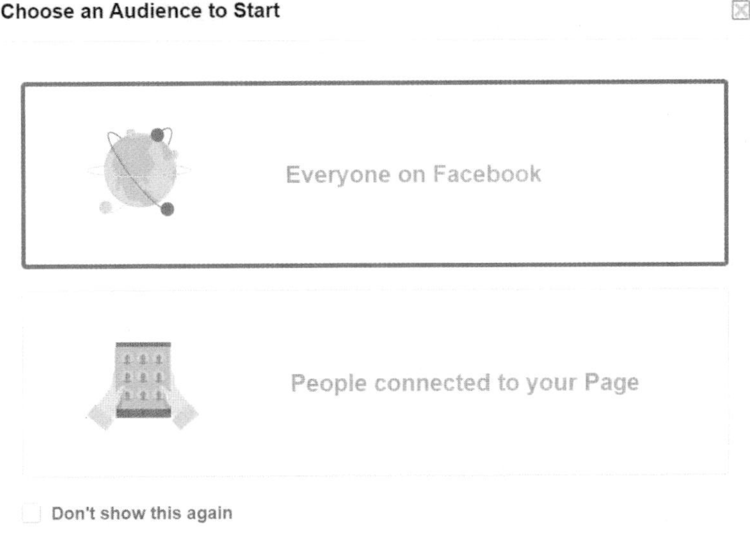

Facebook

2. For now, let's keep the "All United States" as location. Note the size of the (New Audience), which is 150–200 million people. This is the number of people who use Facebook in the United States in a typical month.

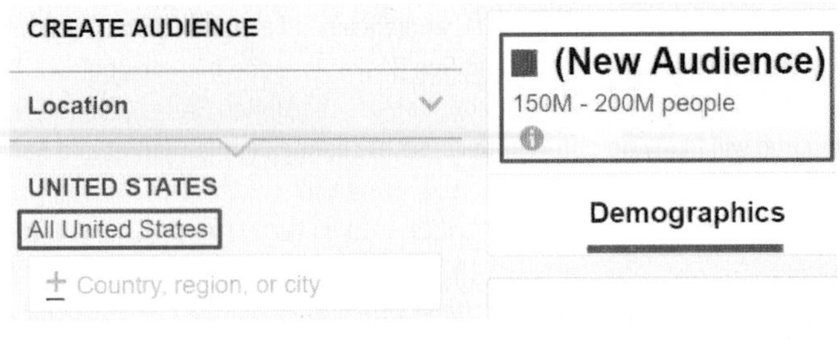

Facebook

(Continued)

3. Note you can select Facebook users by age, gender, interests, connections (to your Facebook page), or other "Advanced" ways like work, education, or life events:

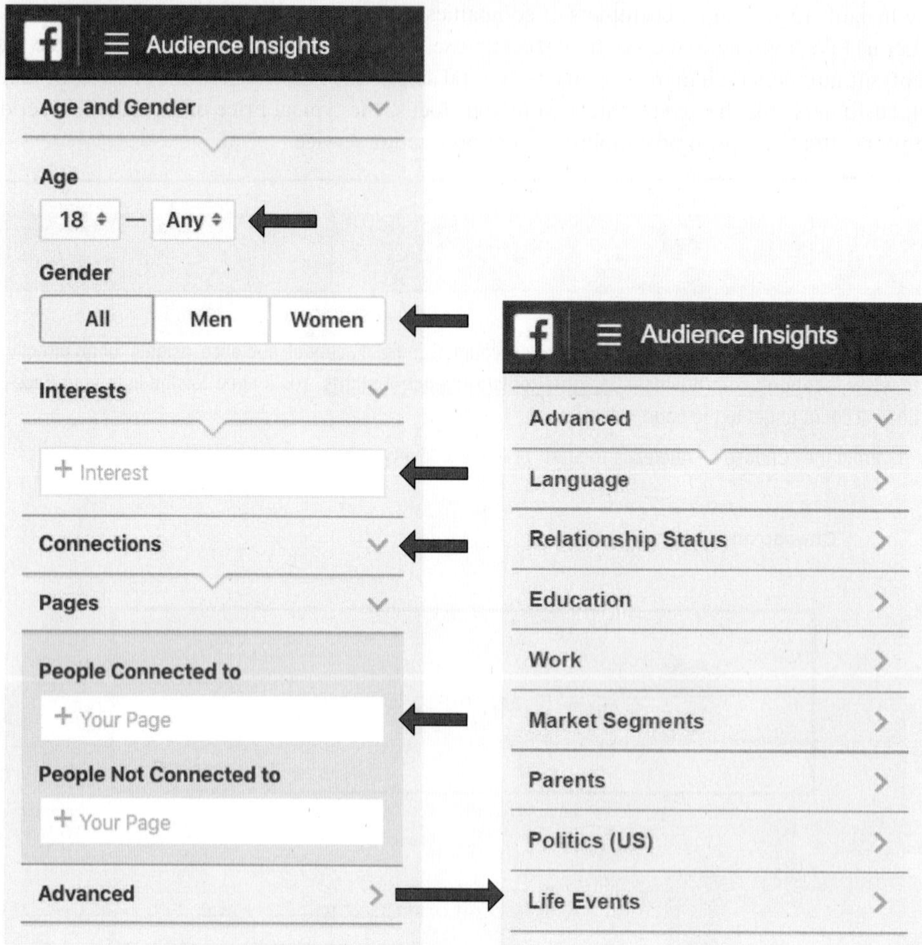

Facebook

4. Let's get to work. Our focus is on a prepared meal kit using hyperlocal ingredients intended to launch in the St. Louis market, and would initially be aiming at people from 20 to 44. It would be called "LouBox" after St. Louisans' slang for their town.
5. The key for this (as for so many Facebook searches) is in the "Interests" box. Let's start by typing in "meal kits." No matches appear so the term just sits there. Hitting return does nothing. We hit a dead-end, but there are alternatives. So, let's try the names of some of the biggest meal kit makers in the United States, starting with *Blue Apron*. Google "meal kits." For this Skill Module we chose **www.pcmag.com/picks/the-best-meal-kit-delivery-services** for the list and tried all the names. The ones that had matches (i.e., audiences) in Facebook were AmazonFresh, Blue Apron, HelloFresh, Home Chef, Plated, and Sun Basket (see the blue box below). These result in an audience of several million people a month across the United States (see the red box; the numbers you find will likely be different because of changes in the market and Facebook):

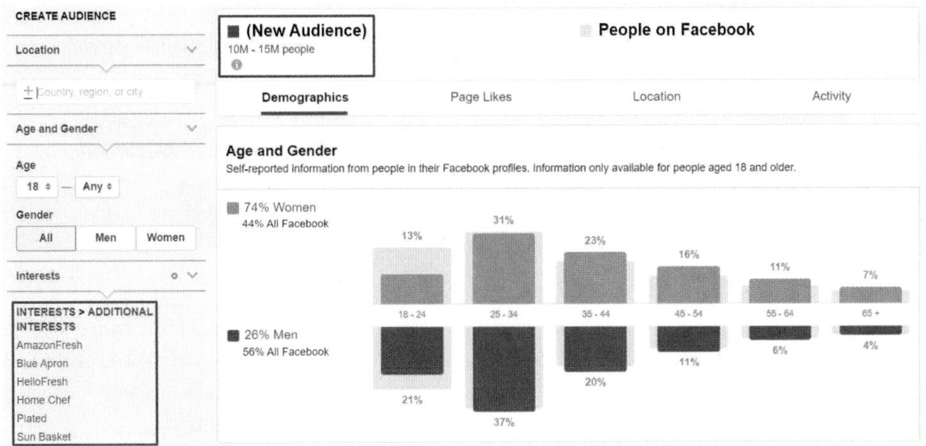

Facebook

6. Let's narrow this down to the St. Louis market. In the "Location" box, type in "St. Louis" and select it from the resulting drop-down menu:

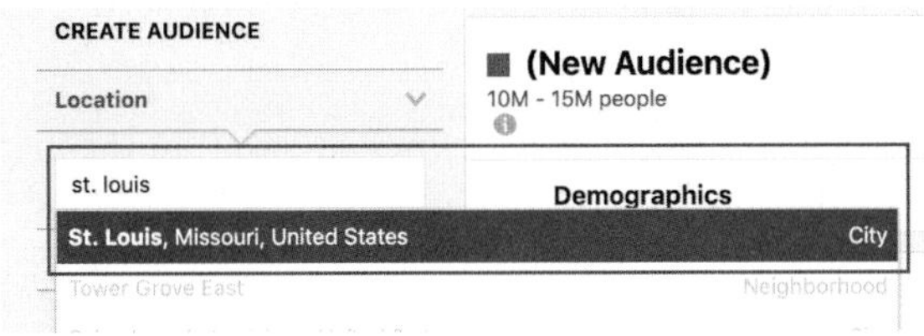

Facebook

This produces a market of tens of thousands of people a month:

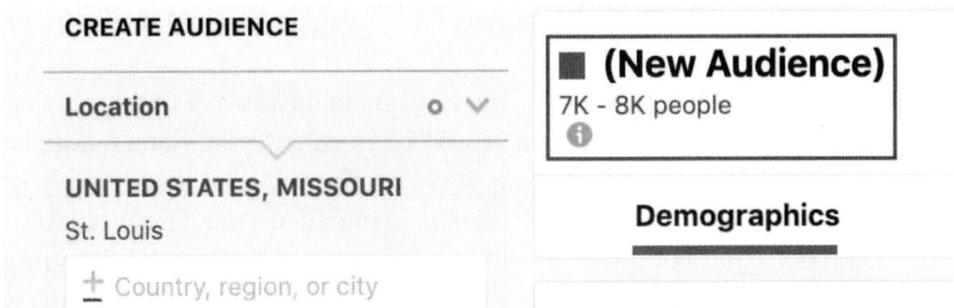

Facebook

7. You could refine the ages to the 20–44 age range, which will reduce the audience of Facebook users every month:

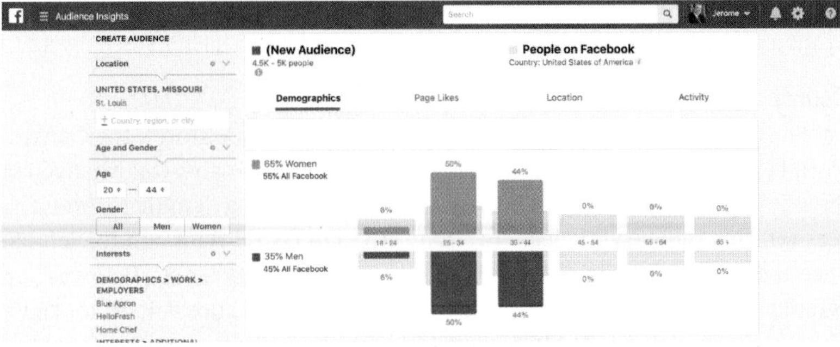

Facebook

(Continued)

8. You can save your work, and name the audience you've create, to make it easier when you come back. Use the menu above the "CREATE AUDIENCE" label:

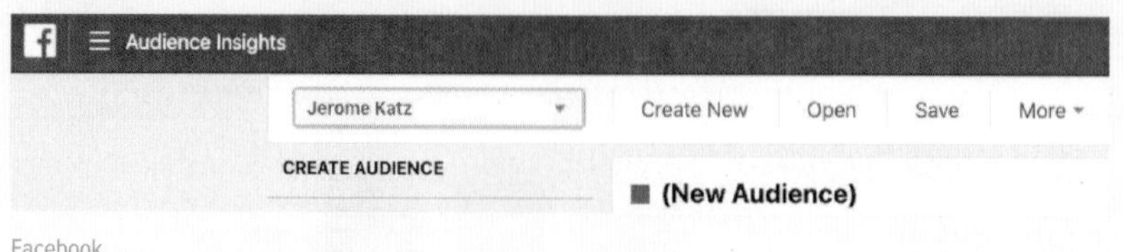

Facebook

9. You can check out the many hotlinks on the page to learn all sorts of details about your targeted audience, such as what sites they like for different categories and what are their most-liked pages (under the "Page Likes" tab). For a great example of how to use the range of data Audience Insights can provide, look at **https://adespresso.com/blog/facebook-audience-insights/**.

Size of Market

Market size is typically given in one of two ways—the number of people in a market or the number of businesses in the industry. We'll show you how to do both next.

People Counts

Recall we introduced the TAM/SAM/SOM set of nested terms for the market sizes earlier. The terms are described again here, but this time we've added examples based on the idea of a high-end women's shoe store in St. Louis (like one developed in the Chapter 7 Appendix) to show how size counts work:

- Total available market (TAM): This represents everyone who might consider the product or service you're offering. For a U.S.-based women's shoe store, the TAM is 50.8 percent of 327 million people in the United States, or 166 million women, based on statistics from the U.S. Census Bureau's QuickFacts page: www.census.gov/quickfacts/fact/table/US/PST045218.
- Serviceable available market (SAM): This represents customers within your geographic reach. For the women's shoe store, this would be in general the female population of St. Louis, or 159,082, which we can get using www.city-data.com/city/St.-Louis-Missouri.html
- Serviceable obtainable market (SOM): This is also called your target market and represents the customers that you think would be interested in your particular product or service. For the high-end women's shoe store, the SOM would probably be women with higher incomes. Use www.city-data.com/income/income-St.-Louis-Missouri.html to get income figures for St. Louis. For St. Louis, we see that the median income is $41,441 and 13 percent of households have incomes of $75,000 or more (which would be one way to think about high-income). Taking 13 percent of 159,082 women in St. Louis would result in a SOM of 20,681 women.
- Penetrated market (PM): Doesn't apply because your store hasn't started yet.

Business Counts

When you are looking at a store level (for example, a women's shoe store), the Census's Industry Statistics Portal (https://census.gov/econ/isp/index.php) can often give you what you want. Enter the NAICS code 448210, and you will be taken to a page showing "Guide to All Census Bureau Data Sources for This Industry." Select "ECONOMIC DATA IN AFF" on the left-hand sidebar and you'll see the page shown in Figure 9.4. Choose "County Business Patterns" and the line with "Geography Area Series: County Business Patterns." For Figure 9.4. we looked at the 2016 data. For shoe stores in general (NAICS code 448210), there were 24,693 shoe stores across the United States in 2016. You can look at Skill Module 7.2 "Finding Your Firm's Industry" in for details on finding NAICS codes. These stores employed 238,361 people (9.65 employees per store on average), and paid these folks $4,005,605,000 in payroll or $16,805992 each, which suggests these were mostly part-time positions.[24]

FIGURE 9.4

Selecting the 2016 Country Business Patterns Report on Shoe Stores from the Census Industry Statistics Portal

Source: United States Census Bureau

Notice that we did not find any measures of the number of customers. The Census Bureau has revenues for businesses in the Economic Census as well as the County Business Pattern reports mentioned above. Revenues for local businesses in your industry can be found in the Census Business Builder (https://cbb.census.gov). You can also look at commercial databases like Mintel or contact one of the trade associations (e.g., National Shoe Retailers Organization, found using a Google search for two words–"association" and "shoe"). You could also look for a trade magazine on the shoe or fashion or athletic wear industry and find a report on the industry (these often occur yearly in a particular issue).

Prices

The easiest way to find selling prices for products these days is on the Internet. Sites abound for consumer products, like Google shopping (www.google.com/shopping) or Amazon.com. Today even industrial products can be found using these comparison shopping engines, although there are specialty sites like Purchasing.com, or eBay Business & Industrial (www.ebay.com/rpp/business-industrial). For services, there are sites like Upwork.com, Freelancer.com, Fiverr.com, or Workhoppers.com that sell services online and give you some idea about prices, although these will be far more variable. Typically you can see what contracts have been posted, and get an idea of the basic charges for services. A better approach is to ask potential customers what they are currently paying (and what they get for their money).

Profitability

While the profitability of any particular store is nearly impossible to find, industry standards for profitability are easier than most people realize. For example, we have talked repeatedly about BizStats.com. Go there and look at the benchmark box at the lower half of the page, then scroll down to the closest category. In the "Annual Sales" box enter $1000000 as the average sales for your proposed shoe store. Select "Corporations" as the form of business and click "Submit." The major industry is "Retail Trade" and the specific industry is "Clothing-Clothing accessories stores." The resulting table tells you the net profit is 15.33 percent.

This number is a ballpark estimate, since it is not specific to shoe stores, much less women's shoe stores, and does not even consider location. The numbers it gives are averages. More important to your plans, the profits reflect an average of stores where the vast majority of them are older and more experienced than you are at this point. As a result, the 15.33 percent tells us what you *could* make once you learned the business and solved the problems that others have mastered. Still, as a starting point, the BizStats numbers can give you an idea.

It is wise not to depend entirely on one source when performing secondary analysis. In fact, there are other, more detailed sources available in your college or public library. These include the Risk Management Association's (formerly Robert Morris Associates) *Annual Statement Studies*, Dun & Bradstreet's *Industry Norms and Key Business Ratios*, or Leo Troy's annual *Almanac of Business and Industrial Financial Ratios.* All of these sources offer breakdowns of financial information based on the sales of firms, which can help you get a better idea of costs for the newest and smallest businesses. Also, they are widely recognized and respected by bankers, and are probably the sources for the financial ratios and sales numbers they will look up when they benchmark your business, so it makes sense to check those sources too.

LO **9-5** Develop your value proposition.

The Basics: Crafting Your Value Proposition

value proposition
Small business owners' unique selling points (also known as benefits) that customers can expect from your goods or services, including benefits that differentiate your offering from those of the competition.

Chapter 7 introduced the idea of value and cost benefit. This will be further developed by talking about your total product later in this chapter. But to give you an early glimpse of what will be discussed, your total product is not just the bare-bones object or service you provide, but what it means to your customers. You don't just do a great job cleaning houses; you provide free time to your customers. You don't just sell desks; you handcraft beautiful and functional desks in exotic woods. You can talk about your competitive edge—what you do better than your competition—or your distinctive competence—what you do that no one else does, but what is missing when we talk about those competencies is the benefit to the customer of all that capability. The relation of product or company capabilities to customer pains and gains is the **value proposition**[25] you offer your customer. Skill Module 9.6 shows you how to organize your value proposition and relate it to your customer profile.

SKILL MODULE 9.6 Customer-Focused Value Proposition Design

The customer profile you created in Skill Module 9.2 becomes the basis for this exercise. In that profile, you talk about the job the customer is trying to get done, and the pains and gains he or she feels while trying to do the job. Using the graphic for the Strategyzer Value Proposition Canvas,[26] we can map them, putting each idea on a separate sticky note in the sections of the right-hand circle.

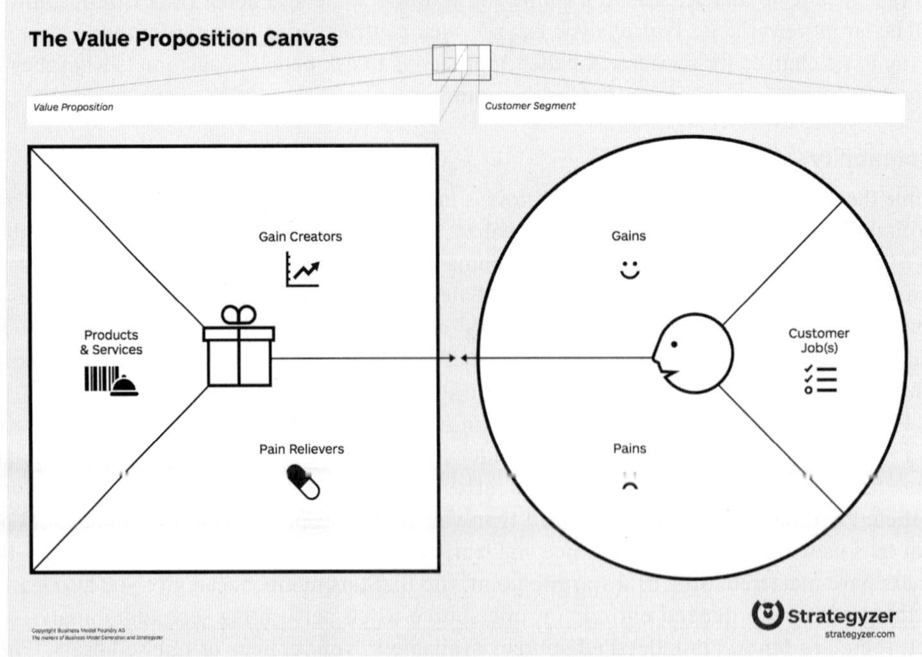

Source: Strategyzer, http://businessmodelgeneration.com/canvas/vpc.

The second step is putting your proposed product or service in the left-hand section of the left-hand box. Then add sticky notes with the specific benefits you will offer, split into "gain creators" and "pain relievers."

Your three tests of this approach are (1) how closely your product or service fits the customer job, (2) how many customer pains you solve, and (3) how many customer gains you can provide. Your goal is to have a product/service that closely fits the customer segment's situation. Exceeding what the customer wants is great, but you want to make sure you cover the major pains and gains they report. With this in hand, you can move onto crafting your value proposition as you will describe it in your marketing efforts.

Source: Strategyzer, http://businessmodelgeneration.com/canvas/vpc

The chances are that there is more than one feature or benefit in the "Your Value Proposition" section. The challenge now is to boil down those multiple items to one short value proposition mantra. Recall we introduced the idea of mantras in Chapter 8. Value propositions are generally focused similarly–one clear idea that describes the benefit you offer your customer and powerfully resonates with them. Note we say *benefit* and not *feature*. Customers buy a product or service because of the benefits they get from using your offering to get their job done.[27] To get to your value proposition mantra, list those needs only you meet and look for a way to draw a commonality from among them. If it helps, BMWs offer superior pickup and handling over any competitor; how does the automaker combine those? Remember its tagline: BMW–the ultimate driving machine.

There are several useful ways to craft mantras.[28] Think of Red Jett Sweets from the business plan at the end of Chapter 8. Given the cupcakes were made of the finest ingredients, were rich and tasty, and were certain to satisfy your cravings, the company's mantra could have been: "Red Jett Sweets are Godivas of the bakery world." A slightly different approach comes from Steve Blank who tells us to do something along the lines of "We help X do Y by doing Z." For Red Jett Sweets, this would have been stated as "Red Jett Sweets satisfies your desert cravings." Eric Sink suggests a model based on Superlative (why) - Label (what) - Qualifier (who), so Red Jett Sweets would have come out as "The finest cupcakes for the best times." Some entrepreneurs prefer a longer value proposition in order to cover points they think are worth including, like competitive advantage. Skill Module 9.7 gives the details of how to craft a longer value proposition.

Developing a Value Proposition

SKILL MODULE 9.7

Choose one small retail business (e.g., children's clothing store, pet store, independently owned hair salon, restaurant, etc.). Using promotional and advertising material, level of service, in-store displays, location, and any other information available (website), create a value proposition for that business. The goal of this value proposition is to create and occupy a space inside the target customer's head. Create a value proposition for your chosen small retail business by replacing the text in parentheses below as it reflects the product, market, and strategy.

- **For** (target customer)
- **Who** (statement of the need or opportunity)
- **The** (retail business name) **is a** (product or service category)
- **That** (statement of key benefit—that is, compelling reason to buy/purchase)
- **Unlike** (primary competitive alternative)
- **Our business** (statement of primary differentiation)
- **Is available** (where)

This would be the workup for Red Jett Sweets: "For the person who wants a moment of sweet indulgence, Red Jett Sweets provides traditional and unique cupcakes that can fulfill any taste and make any moment brighter."

Now place the answers in paragraph format to arrive at the overall value proposition. Feel free to share your perception of the proposition with the actual small business owner.

There is one more important way to think about the value proposition, and that is in comparison to competing firms and their products and services. You might recall Figure 7.3, which showed the relationship between your product or service, your market, and your industry. Part of that depended on the distinctive competence of your firm, your product or service, which was covered in Chapters 4 and 7. The other part depended on the value proposition. The final goal for developing and testing your value proposition is how it stacks up against and will compete against the other offerings available to your customers. Here we will analyze both value proposition and distinctive competence using a mapping technique shown in Skill Module 9.8.

SKILL MODULE 9.8 Coordinating Your Distinctive Competence and Value Proposition[29]

Start with the results of Skill Module 7.4 Mapping Your Distinctive Competence. Recall that you built out two circles:

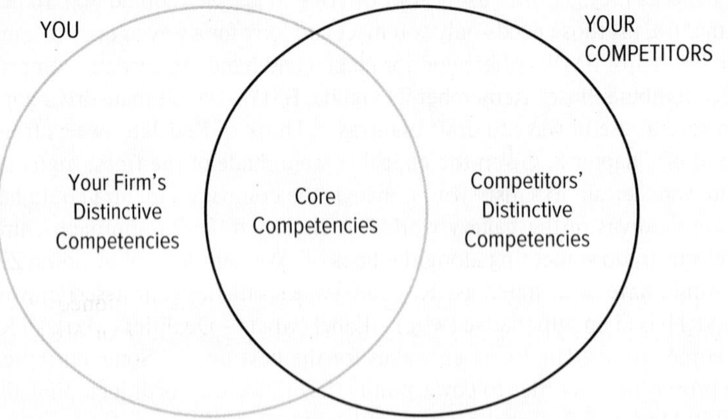

- Now you add the "CUSTOMER" circle, overlapping the first two circles, to your map. Get ready to move features around!

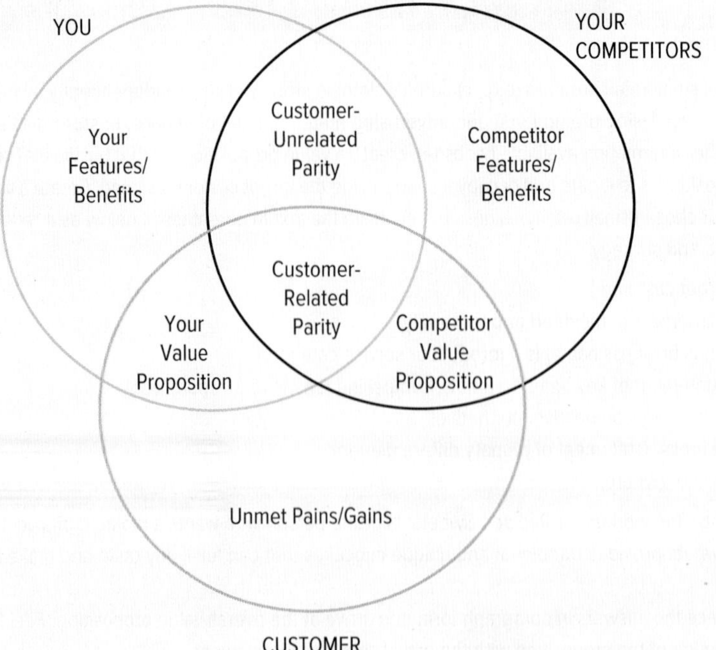

- Start in the "CUSTOMER" circle by listing all the pains and gains your target customers have and the benefits they are seeking, based on your research. These would be summarized in your customer profile from Skill Module 9.2 and mapped out in Skill Module 9.6.
- Next, go to the items in the core competency overlapping section. Features or benefits that meet the pains or gains of customers get moved to the "Customer-Related Parity" section. *Parity* means being basically equal. These are features customers want, and you and your competitors have them.
- The remaining items are ones where you and your competitors have parity, but these features or benefits aren't relevant to these target customers. If you have multiple customer segments, some of those features might be important to them. If not, these could be features that might be left out in future versions of the offering.
- Those features or benefits customers want, that your competitor has but you don't, go into the "Competitor Value Proposition" section. These are where you could lose customers, and one of the places to look to in the future to decide what features or benefits to add.
- Those features or benefits customers want that only you offer represent "Your Value Proposition." These are the most important features or benefits to stress in your branding, messaging, and marketing because these are important to your customers, and **not** met by your competitors. They are distinctive to you!
- What remains in the "CUSTOMER" circle are pains and gains, or needs and wants, that neither you nor your competitors currently meet. Those represent a potentially powerful set of opportunities to grow your offering in future versions.

With your value proposition developed, mapped to the customer, and mapped against the competition with your distinctive competencies identified, you are positioned now to think about your customer development process, which will structure the rest of your marketing effort.

Planning for Marketing

LO **9-6** Understand how to organize marketing plans.

In the following chapters you will learn about the 4 Ps of marketing—product, promotion, price, and placement. The goal is to create the specifics of the marketing strategy you will use to generate sales for your business. So business plans always have a marketing section. The content follows this chapter. Often the plan will describe the customer and their pains or gains (in the problem section) and the solution you propose—your product or service. So the parts that come out in the marketing section of your plan usually focus on how marketing will get done in terms of promotion, price, and placement—which reflects location and distribution.

Marketing is one of the basic building blocks for your business plan and your road map to what you want to do; it can't be set in concrete.[30] Successful businesses are constantly tweaking their marketing to accommodate necessary adjustments found during evaluation and control reviews, or to reflect new research, changes in the environment, changes in competition, new target markets, new opportunities in promotion, new anything.[31] In addition, on a regular basis (at least once a year)[32] you should take the time to decide what you want to accomplish next—increase sales, introduce a new product, move into a new market, and the like—and revise your marketing plan to reflect this next step. Caryl Felicetta started her business, The Argyle Studio, an advertising and graphic design firm, without a marketing plan. After a year of haphazard growth, she and her partner did their first systematic review and marketing plan. With this plan, their business grew by 100 percent the next year and has averaged about 50 percent growth each year after that.[33]

While our focus is on building a marketing plan section for your business plan, you will also be doing the lion's share of the work you need for a stand-alone marketing plan. If you have already started your business, or are doing a business where you don't expect to do a full business plan, a stand-alone marketing plan might be useful as a way to better strategize about how you

TABLE 9.4 Marketing Plan Outline

	Stand-Alone Marketing Plan	Marketing Section of a Business Plan
1. Table of contents	X	
2. Executive summary	X	
3. Company description, vision, background	X	(earlier in plan)
4. Product/service and Industry	X	(earlier in plan)
a. Product/service description	X	(earlier in plan)
b. Value proposition	X	(earlier in plan)
c. Industry description	X	(earlier in plan)
5. Marketing analysis	X	X
a. Market and target customer	X	X
b. Competition and competitive advantage	X	X
c. Marketing strategy	X	X
I. Overall strategy	X	X
II. Pricing strategy	X	X
III. Promotion strategy	X	X
IV. Place/distribution strategy	X	X
d. Competitive plan (reaction to competitors)	X	X
e. R&D growth plan or next steps	X	X
6. Marketing budget and projections	X	
7. Evaluation and control	X	
8. Appendixes	X	

will get sales. Table 9.4 shows what each of these would require. Keep the table in mind as you discover the elements of marketing, and think about how you would apply them in your business, and in your business plan.

Don't underestimate the power of marketing plans. For start-ups, they help define how the firm will build its brand and relationship with customers. For established businesses, the marketing plan becomes a key step in imagining how a firm might reposition itself and maintain its most important relationship, the one it has with customers. You've seen one famous example of this as Dove soap changed its advertising from using professional models to using regular people to promote its products as part of its "Campaign for Real Beauty." Crafting and implementing a marketing plan with the new approach gave Dove a way to think through the issues in the change, and implement a new advertising model that led to greatly increased sales, and customers who became much more passionate about its brand of soap. The soap remained the same; it was the marketing change that made the difference, and that change depended on a detailed marketing plan.[34]

If you are uncomfortable with the prospect of doing a marketing plan yourself, there's low-cost help for you available in a number of ways. First, try the Small Business Administration (www.sba.gov) or the Service Corps of Retired Executives (SCORE) (www.score.org) for advice. *Entrepreneur* magazine (www.entrepreneur.com) has examples and a number of worksheets you can use to help you gather and organize your information. Last, contact a local community, technical, or four-year college (small business or entrepreneurship department if it has one; otherwise, the marketing department) or campus club in those areas and offer your company as a class project.[35] (A small donation to the class or club should be considered.)

Product

Goods versus Services

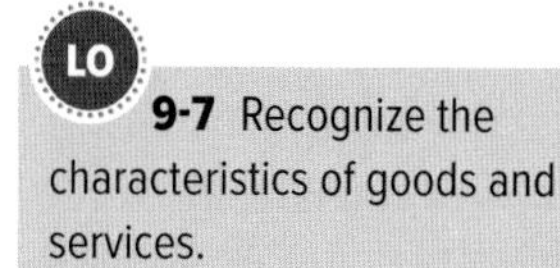

9-7 Recognize the characteristics of goods and services.

A *product*, in general terms, is anything that is offered to the market to satisfy consumer wants, needs, and demands. This can include **goods** (like Red Jett Sweets's cupcakes, a car, a can of green beans, a DVD), **services** (haircut, divorce), people (political candidates, celebrities), and ideas (a political platform, an environmental message). Most people's first thoughts are to think in terms of goods or services, but these days most of the things sold are combinations of the two (see Figure 9.5) along what is called the *goods-services continuum*.

goods
Physical products.

services
Nonphysical products.

tangibility
An item's capability of being touched, seen, tasted, or felt.

Let's talk autos for example. If you need transportation customized to your needs, you could start with buying a car. That seems at first to be a pure good, but it is not likely to be. The car has **tangibility**; it is something you can touch, but your check also covered the cost of a warranty on the car, which is a service, and something intangible. If you included a satellite radio, or a cell service like OnStar, or an extended warranty, you have bought more services. Still, the vast majority of what you are paying for is for the car itself, so most car purchases would be an example of a *good-dominated product*.

But what if, instead of buying the car, you lease it. Then the leasing company owns the car and you are getting the use of it (a service). While you have the car you are responsible for gas and maintenance, so you are taking care of the tangible product, but it is in the context of the lease. Leasing a car is an example of a *hybrid* good and service combination.

Taking this a step further, think about renting a car. The rental company takes care of maintenance and may even take care of the gas. You just pay and drive. New hourly rental car businesses like ZipCar.com and Share-Now.com rent you a car for 1 to 24 hours at a time and include all services, including insurance. With this model, the car becomes something more along the lines of a mobility service you control, or what marketers would call a *service-dominated product*.

At the other extreme, there is the pure service of a cab. You get in and get transported to the destination of your choice. A car is involved, but it is in no way your car. You pay for the service only. The cab driver is responsible for everything else. This is something close to a *pure service* and since by paying for the service you have nothing physical, that service you bought was an intangible product, whereas buying the car gave you a tangible product. Looking at these different types of personal transportation, you can probably see differences in how you would market them to customers. You may recall how these different products have been marketed to you (leasing versus buying, renting versus taking cabs, etc.).

There are other differences among the five types of product. Car rentals show the problem of the **perishability** of services. If a cab goes without a fare for an hour, that is one hour of revenue that is lost forever–it literally perished. For the car sitting on the dealer's lot, whether it sells today or tomorrow, the dealer will recoup pretty much the full value of the car. These cars are nonperishable goods. That cab ride is also an example of the **inseparability** of services. The service you bought, the cab ride, can get delivered only when you get in the cab. The service, and your consumption of the service, happen at the same time so they cannot be separated. On the other hand, goods have separability of production and consumption. The car you bought could be a week old or six months old. For goods, production and consumption can be separated in time.

perishability
A service exhibits perishability in that if it is not used when offered, it cannot be saved for later use.

inseparability
A quality of a service in which the service being done cannot be disconnected from the provider of the service.

heterogeneity
A quality of a service in which each time it is provided it will be slightly different from the previous time.

The fourth characteristic differentiating goods and services is **heterogeneity**. Products are generally thought of as homogeneous or consistent. They should have the same quality every time you buy one. Services, however, can be more heterogeneous. The quality of your haircut

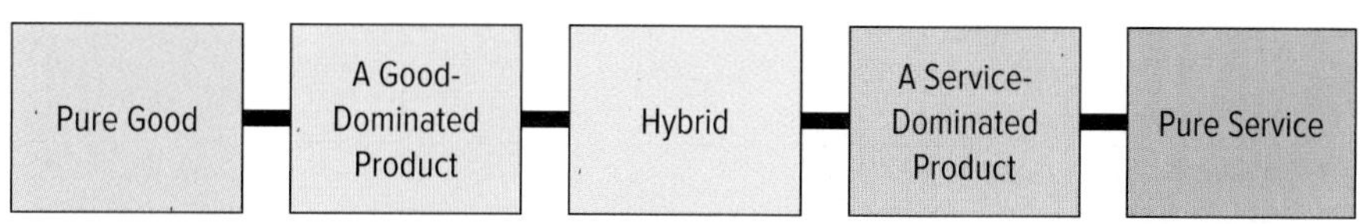

FIGURE 9.5
Goods–Services Continuum

ZipCar autos for rent include all related services, such as insurance, making these cars a service-dominated product.

Scott Mullen/Bloomberg/Getty Images

depends on which shop you visit and which stylist you use, and may even vary day to day depending on the mood of the stylist, how busy the day has been, whether you are the first or last client, and a hundred other factors. To solve this challenge, service firms use employee training, identical—or nearly identical—store layouts, employee uniforms, services offered, prices, automation, and the like to reduce heterogeneity.

Those combinations fall between pure goods and pure services and have names, shown in Figure 9.5. The combinations also differ in how much they have of each of four characteristics. For most businesses, like Red Jett Sweets, there are elements of both goods and services in nearly every offering. You can test out your ability to handle these issues by trying Skill Module 9.9. For almost every industry, there are ways to offer your customer a good, a service, or a mixture of the two. In reality most of what we buy, and what small businesses make, are combinations of goods and services. Knowing, understanding, and playing around with the particular blend of goods and services in your particular offering helps you find your product's differential advantage and communicate it better to customers.

This restaurant is not making money from empty seats at the counter. Those empty seats reflect the perishability of service businesses. Those lost meals can never be made up. What other services do you see as highly perishable?

Image Source/Getty Images

Facing Intangibility and Perishability

SKILL MODULE 9.9

Because service industry businesses are so diverse, there can be no hard-and-fast list of characteristics to use in facing intangibility and perishability. For example, we want a quick-service restaurant (like McDonald's or your local small business equivalent) to provide a meal in a couple of minutes, but at a premium restaurant (like Ruth's Chris Steak House or your local small business equivalent) we expect more leisurely service. Similarly, most of us want that meal at pretty much the same time, so restaurants often are their busiest around noon or 6:00 P.M. That time sensitivity means that restaurant sittings are perishable. If you had an empty table at lunch, you'll never make up that money again.

So put on your thinking cap and work in a team to come up with some ways to handle the problems of intangibility and perishability in one of the following service industries:

A restaurant specializing in soup
A website specializing in self-recorded music
A bookkeeping firm
A housekeeping service
A rooftop cell-phone tower rental service
An online sporting goods retailer
An 800-number health advice service
A home-based child care service
A house-sitting service
A business consultancy specializing in tax advice

For intangibility, what kinds of symbols would help make your service seem more tangible to potential customers, and what kinds of qualities would help strengthen the customer benefit or value of the service? Test these out with other groups in class.

For perishability, identify if there are times of peak demand for the service, and if there are limits to how many customers you can serve at once. If there are peak times or customer service limits, explain how you would organize your business to get the largest sales possible. Test these out with other groups in class.

The Total Product Approach

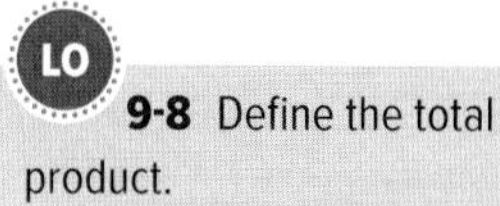

9-8 Define the total product.

Most products are combinations of goods and services. They have differing degrees of perishability, tangibility, heterogeneity, and inseparability. Understanding these characteristics of your good or service will help you better match it to your customers' needs and differentiate your product from those of competitors. But there can be aspects of your product that even you as its creator or distributor do not know about.

In marketing, this is the difference between the total product and the augmented or core products. The **total product** includes the entire bundle of products and services that you offer, but is based not only on what you as the small business owner thinks about the product, but also about how customers think about it. An Alabama bottlemaking company discovered that one of the top 10 reasons customers liked its 16- and 20-ounce screw-top plastic bottles was because, when filled with water and enough rocks to sink the bottle, it makes a safer toilet tank space filler than bricks, which can break down when left in water for years. People learned about this on several green living blogs.

total product
The entire bundle of products, services, and meanings of your offering; includes extras like service, warranty, or delivery, as well as what the product means to the customer.

We often know less than we think we do about customers, co-workers, or even those close to us. Try Skill Module 9.10 to test this out.

The total product is how your customers describe your good or service, but there are two other ways to describe your product. What you describe as your product or service is your **augmented product** and has features that differentiate it from the competition. These features can include brand names, quality levels, packaging, and specific features of your product.

augmented product
Core product plus features that tend to differentiate it from the competition.

SKILL MODULE 9.10

Learning about the Total Product of You

Marketing is all about getting people to like your product enough to buy it. In a way, we market ourselves to others, doing a little bit of selling of ourselves in the hopes of getting another person to like us. When they do end up liking us, is it for the reason we pitched to them?

This one is simple. Pick your spouse, boyfriend, or girlfriend and make a note to yourself why he or she likes or loves you. You can put down as many reasons as you want. This is your augmented product. Put away the note and, when you have a chance, ask why he or she likes you. If he or she gives you more than one reason, there is a very good chance it will be one not on your list. Those unlisted items are what distinguish the total product of "you" from the augmented product you described in your note to yourself. When you have a product for your business, repeat the procedure, this time asking customers why they like it. You will likely see the same thing happen.

In practice, it might sound like this when you are asked "What do you do?" "I run the Happy Housekeeper, a housecleaning business in the greater Chicago area."

core product
The basic description of what a product is—a bar of soap, a housecleaning service, and so on.

Underneath the total product and the augmented product lies the **core product**, which is the basic description of what your company does. It is a variation of the NAICS code or industry description we discussed in Chapter 7. The company Red Jett Sweets's core product was cupcakes, the bottlemaker makes bottles, and the Happy Housekeeper is in the housecleaning industry. It is the most general description of your business, and the one that captures the smallest amount of what is special about your business.

Why is the total product in particular important for you as a small business owner? First of all, your product means more to a consumer than just the core component. Sure, a housekeeper will clean your house, but this will give the consumer additional leisure time, might be a status symbol, and probably has other meanings for your customers. Merry Maids sends its personnel to your house in a distinctive van with the company's name plastered all over it; when your neighbors see the van in your driveway, they know that you are important/rich/busy enough to be able to afford this service.

Second, as a small business owner, using the total product approach can help you get inside your customers' heads and figure out the most cost-effective "bundle" of value and cost benefits (see Chapter 7) to give your target market. Last, when you're designing the rest of your marketing plan, knowing what your product really "means" to consumers will help you set an appropriate price (Would driving a BMW mean as much if it cost only $10,000?), design effective advertising ("We give you valuable free time" versus "We clean your house"), and select the distribution chain that will successfully carry out some of your service components (such as delivery, installation, repairs, etc.).

LO 9-9 Differentiate the stages of new product development.

New Product Development Process

An old *Far Side* cartoon describes an early (as in the cave dweller era) business failure. The product? Porcupine on a stick. Although meant as a joke, it should remind any entrepreneur that every product idea needs to go through the development process (illustrated in Figure 9.6) before it gets introduced. This process may take a few hours for simple products that are similar to existing products (commonly referred to as **me-too products**) or may take years and years of preparation and testing, such as introducing a new pharmaceutical product. For me-too products, steps may even be skipped.

me-too products
Products essentially similar to something already on the market.

Regardless of the pace you are able to move at, this is a necessary process; as noted earlier, the U.S. Patent Office issues about 100,000 patents a year, but only about 0.1 percent of those are profitable. Marketing and new product experts believe that most of the small business failures could have been avoided by following the new product development (NPD) process.[36]

As discussed in Chapters 4 and 7, most businesses are imitative in nature, so the vast majority of new ideas for such businesses will be me-too products. If people are already using white ear

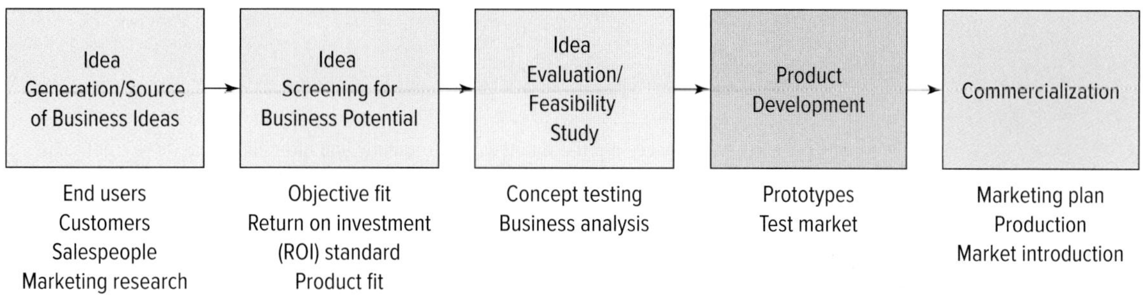

FIGURE 9.6

Stages of New Product Development

buds for their music players, might they buy other colors? Probably, and the most likely colors are ones that match their clothes or their already-purchased music player cases. Does this require a lot of testing? Probably not.[37] Most of the testing has already been done and public acceptance is pretty much ensured. Your me-too product needs to have a differential advantage over your competition–otherwise, why would you introduce it?–and this advantage may be the only thing you need to test. Customers are familiar with the product category, and some of them may already have been thinking about what they'd like to see different about the product or service. Much of the up-front testing can simply be polling existing users of the product and suggesting to them what you might see as an improvement. "I see you are using XYZ; what if I was able to sell you the same thing, but deliver and install it (or add or change features, etc.)?" Open-ended questions ("If you could change one thing about XYZ, what would it be?") might confirm your potential improvement, might point out other new ideas, and won't necessarily tip off the competition as to what you are planning to do.

For goods, there is a cost for design and manufacturing as well as a delay, so trying out new products is more of a gamble. For service firms, it can be easier. Should a restaurant offer low-carb pasta? The cost is probably a case of pasta, or an even smaller amount of soy flour (used instead of the regular seminola flour) to make your own fresh. If no one likes it, it vanishes from the menu and blackboard. Cost? Twenty dollars for the case of pasta and reprinting the menus to drop low-carb pasta.

For small businesses planning to pursue an NPD effort for a highly innovative product, the steps start with the process described in Chapter 4; let's review them briefly.

Idea Generation[38]

Behind every great product is a great idea. The difficult question is where do you get the ideas? The traditional first idea generator–and often what gets an entrepreneur started–is something they need or want themselves and either can't find or can't find the way they want it. The new way to find opportunities is through the use of the SCAMPER approach as discussed in Chapter 4. Skill Module 9.11 provides you with an example of how to implement a simple SCAMPER application.

Idea Screening

Idea screening is the process of selecting the most promising ideas to be further evaluated for feasibility. Chapter 4 introduced the IDEO screening model that identifies what factors are important to consider when screening ideas to find the most promising ones. For each idea, these are the customer desirability, the technical feasibility, and the business viability.

Typically, the smartest idea is to generate multiple ideas and compare them head-to-head to help clarify what characteristics are important and which idea has the greatest potential. This comparison approach is shown in Exhibit 9.1 and is very simple. The ideas are listed across the top of the grid, and the important factors are listed vertically. Each idea is given a numerical score for each of the factors, and the scores are totaled. While you are likely to be one of the screeners, it is fine to let others in on this. One model created by World Innovation Network that is used by Innovative Product Technologies (www.inventone.com/) has purchasing managers

SKILL MODULE 9.11

Creating Your Idea Notebook

There are many products and services out there that we use regularly and often think that there's got to be a better way. Even with products and services we like, we can often think of improvements that we'd like to see:

1. Make a list of about 10 products or services you believe could be improved.
2. Specify exactly what it is about each one that you do not like.
3. Select 3 or 4 of the products or services and think of ways that would "fix" the "defect." (Assume you have relatively unlimited money and technology.) Use the SCAMPER approach.
4. Talk to several friends and brainstorm to see if they have similar opinions about the product or service. Ask their opinion of your solutions and if they have any other ideas.
5. Add all these to your "idea" notebook—and who knows?

Many new products or services are "invented" because someone was unhappy with the available alternatives. Sometimes the technology isn't there yet; sometimes the solutions are too expensive to implement or make the product too expensive. Others are just waiting for someone to do something.

evaluating a product. You can have friends with business expertise or people in the target market look and offer their opinions. Done this way, it is possible to screen out the less promising ideas and identify the ideas you want to take to the next stage, idea evaluation.

Idea Evaluation

Idea evaluation is an exhaustive process of specifying the details of each idea's technological feasibility, its cost, how it can be marketed, and its market potential. Additionally, you should

EXHIBIT 9.1

Idea Screening Comparison

Factor	Scale	Idea 1	Idea 2	Idea 3	Idea 4
Offering—Innovative	1 (Low)–5 (High)	2	3	4	5
Offering—Uniqueness	1 (Low)–5 (High)	4	2	1	4
Customer—Market Need	1 (Low)–5 (High)	5	2	5	5
Customer—Market Size	1 (Small)–5 (Large)	3	2	1	3
Value Proposition Strength	1 (No) and 5 (Yes)	1	2	5	2
People—Quality	1 (Low)–5 (High)	1	2	2	5
Distinctive Competence	1 (Low)–5 (High)	5	2	2	5
Other Resources Needed?	Count of Resource Types Needed	2	2	1	2
Total		**23**	**17**	**21**	**31**

consider how the idea fits with the mission and goals of your business. A basic tool for idea evaluation is the feasibility analysis introduced in Chapter 4. Recall the components of a feasibility analysis: (I) The Business Idea, (II) The Product/Service, (III) The Business, (IV) Future Action Plan, and (V) The Financial Projections. These topics follow on those you considered in the idea screening, but cover them in greater depth, based on library and Internet research, as well as discussions with experts and potential customers. As we saw in Chapter 4, while the hoped-for result is that the idea can be profitably produced and sold to a large and eager market, the more typical outcome of a feasibility analysis is one of these three:

1. The idea cannot be economically made into a product or service.
2. The resulting product or service works, but does not appeal to a large enough market (or is not worth enough to them) to make the effort profitable.
3. The product or service works, has a market, and could be profitable, but you need to get additional people, funding, or other resources to make the idea into a successful business.

Feasibility analysis is an essential step in the new product development process because it precedes a potentially large investment of your time and money into the creation of the key product or service of your business. Making sure the underlying concept is financially and competitively feasible is an important safeguard of your precious resources, and an important double-check of your own initial positive impression of an idea.

Product Development

Concepts that survive to this stage are ready for formal development. The first versions are called **prototypes**, or minimum viable products, and are used in further consumer testing.

prototype
The name given to the first model of a product or service. Some prototypes may be functioning, but built in a way that no consumer would buy it (e.g., with exposed wires and sharp edges) but shows the product can do what is promised. Some prototypes look like the final product, but might not be functional. Prototypes are made to prove aspects of the idea and are seen as the first stop along the path of product/service creation.

If you are just starting out (rather than adding a product to your product line), you may need to get a prototype made. Prototypes can be expensive, but there are a few shortcuts you can try. Study the manufacturing process necessary to make your product and see if you can't come up with a simplified "desktop" version. This is especially useful if you need to go through several iterations to debug your process. Jorge Lahens did just this to prototype a fragrance tab that hooks onto dog collars. He used Thomas Register (www.thomasnet.com/) to find companies dealing with scented plastics and learned all he could from them. He perused *Inventor's Digest* (www.inventorsdigest.com) and found information about how to set up a small-scale manufacturing model for just a few hundred dollars. Other sources of information include local inventor's clubs which are listed at the United Inventor's Association's[39] website (www.uiausa.org) and *The Inventor's Handbook* which is available online for free from the Lemelson-MIT Program (http://lemelson.mit.edu/search-resources/45).

For many, getting a prototype or sample built is the toughest hurdle. One suggestion is to rough something out using products from home, or a craft or art store. Seen at a distance, it will

Rapid prototyping machines, like the one pictured, can create a wide variety of products to help potential customers and investors get a clear sense of what the entrepreneur is marketing.

Izabela Habur/E+/Getty Images

help customers visualize without having full details. Today, 3-D printers are widely and inexpensively available. Colleges, makerspaces, copy centers, commercial prototypers, even libraries offer inexpensive access. You can Google "find 3d printers near me" to get started. Today there are multiple free online and downloadable open source programs for 3-D drawing (the Learn More Online box below) that can produce the drawings necessary for a rapid prototype to be built. One advantage of a 3-D printed prototype is that if you get suggestions from prospective customers about how to change the product for the better, you can quickly and relatively inexpensively revise and print the next edition of the prototype. You can get a great online introduction to 3-D modeling and printing at https://diy.org/skills/rapidprototyper. Google "3D libraries" to find repositories of 3-D designs for hundreds of thousands of items; it can give you a leg-up on your creation process.

LEARN MORE ONLINE

Learn more about the topics above at these sites:

SketchUp online service with free personal accounts: **Sketchup.com/plans-and-pricing/sketchup-free**

Blender free, open-source, downloadable, community supported: **www.blender.org**

K-3D free, open-source, downloadable, community supported: **www.k-3d.org**

If a university approach is not workable, realize that you can make prototypes out of anything. Joe Fischer used a cereal box to prototype Greetabl. You can wrap any box with your message to help people imagine it. You can use LEGOs, Popsicle sticks, pipe cleaners, and things you have around your room or house to prototype. You can ask others for help or advice (or materials). Prototypes don't have to be elegant. Their purpose is to give the observer an idea what the product might be like.

For services, the same ideas apply. You develop your service, often first with example projects you think of yourself, or creating a mock-up as in the case of a website. Make sure you set up the website so that it is not indexed by search engines until you are ready to start selling.

Internet-based and app-based businesses are special cases of a service business because they are susceptible to the minimum viable product approach. In this, based on your customer research, you create the simplest Internet or app service that meets the needs of your target customers. You make it available (putting it online, or posting it to the Apple or Google play stores) and seek feedback from users while watching download and usage statistics. As you discover what needs to be fixed or changed, you quickly (literally within hours or days) create an updated version and post that, continuing this process until your Internet or app offering meets your goals for success. In one sense, these Internet or app businesses are like product businesses in that the ability to deliver the product often depends on having the programming expertise to create the app or website. That said, many basic websites, including blogs and e-commerce sites, can be built using attractive existing templates available from major hosting firms such as 1and1.com, goDaddy.com, or wordpress.com. In addition, basic apps can be built using templates or prebuilt apps from Xamarin.com, ibuildapp.com, or outsystems.com. You can find more firms in each of these areas with a quick online search for "blogging platforms," "e-commerce platforms," or "built apps."

Once the prototype is developed and tested, the product is ready for test marketing. Test marketing involves selling the prototype in either a real or simulated market environment. Standard test marketing introduces the product and the marketing strategy in the actual environment. Small businesses, for financial reasons, primarily choose smaller local markets and conduct fewer tests than their larger counterparts. While test marketing can reduce the potential for failure and can identify weaknesses in the product, advertising, price, or distribution method, there are also opportunities for astute competitors to "steal" your ideas and launch before you do. More recently, simulated test markets have also been computer-generated. This is relatively safe from competitive interference, but, the biggest problem with simulations is that they are artificial and do not always reflect actual buying behavior. Also, for small businesses, simulations may be expensive—especially the traditional method.

Depending on your product, offering to deliver a service or giving samples to friends and family may be a convenient option for getting a test market type of feedback. They are less likely to tell your competitor, but they may try to spare your feelings if they don't like your product. If appropriate for your product and if you are patient, you could pass out samples or provide the services to friends and family and then wait to see if they come back asking for more or refer friends to you; that's a sure sign they liked it. Then see if they'll pay you the next time they want a replacement.

You may also be able to find (or belong to) a group that is willing to try your product and report back to you about how it works.[40] Sometimes nonprofit groups (a church's Ladies Aid, Friends of the Library, or something similar) might be willing to be a test market in order to gain a small donation toward one of their causes. If you are offering a service, they may be willing to let you test it out on them for free. Maybe the product would be appropriate for use at one of their activities, such as trying out your environmentally friendly detergent at a series of church suppers. Be sure to select a nonprofit that represents your target market as much as possible.

One of the ways to leverage social media is to invite participants in the test-marketing effort to share their opinions on a private group on Facebook[41] or LinkedIn. As they post their observations and see what others think, they are more likely to mention their experiences, and the exclusivity of their involvement as a tester becomes an additional benefit.

If you're not in business—or if you are in a very different business—prototyping and test marketing services are very difficult. Simulations work in some cases. Focus groups and concept testing, as discussed earlier in this chapter, work in others.

Commercialization

Commercialization is the process of making the new product available to consumers. In reality, most businesses creating a new product will not face problems with this step. If a rapid prototyping model can be developed, the molds for manufacturing can be made inexpensively by most modern manufacturers. However, if your product requires a truly innovative manufacturing process, you are looking at what is likely to be a multimillion-dollar undertaking. This is relatively rare.

commercialization
The process of making the new products ready for use by consumers by achieving standards of durability and performance suitable for the market and comparable to (if not better than) the competition.

When the technology underlying the product comes from a university- or government-funded research effort, the small business may be able to get government financial assistance for commercialization through the Small Business Innovation Research (SBIR) and the Small Business Technology Transfer (STTR) programs. Even adding qualifying intellectual property from a government-backed project to an existing technology you are developing might qualify your business for SBIR/STTR funding. Find out more at www.sbir.gov.

Even with support, commercialization is a risky process. Many weaker ideas have dropped out of consideration by the point of commercialization, but still only about 60 percent of all new product launches are successful.[42] To play in this league, a small business may need to rent or purchase manufacturing space and equipment. Large companies may spend between $10 million and $200 million for advertising, promotion, and other marketing efforts during the first year of a product's introduction.[43] A small business, especially a young one, cannot afford to spend that much money. That does not mean, however, that a small business cannot compete. (See the Small Business Insight box in Chapter 11, "The Story of Kryptonite.") By using contract manufacturers (see www.mfg.com for an extensive listing) you are utilizing the consignment approach discussed in Chapter 5, so look at the advice on making the most of these sorts of arrangements.[44]

If you are doing it all yourself, know that smaller firms generally introduce their products city by city or region by region in a gradual fashion until their potential market is covered—a limited rollout. Mistakes made in earlier markets can be addressed before rolling out to additional markets. However, limited rollouts also have the problem of allowing competitors to anticipate your movement into their markets and to counterattack.

Before leaving commercialization, think about the augmented product idea introduced earlier in the chapter. Whatever your new product is, me-too or radically innovative, the key is going to be having something unique about it that separates it from everything out there. The Innovation Index[45] shows that since 1990, innovative products ran well under 10 percent of all new products

FIGURE 9.7

The Product Life Cycle

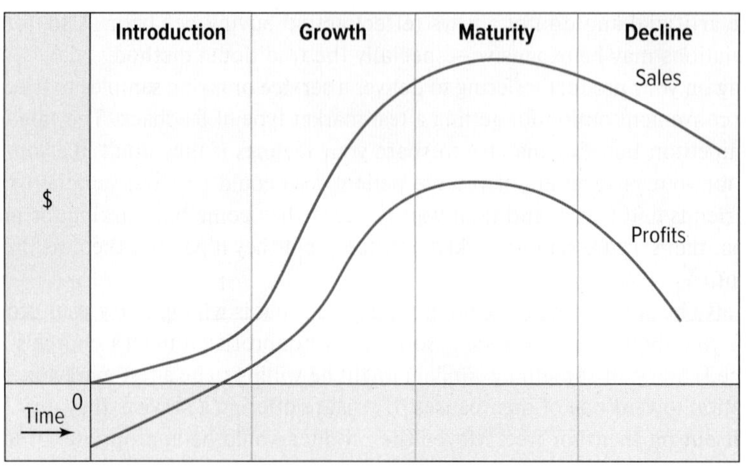

introduced–and the index includes as innovative things such as reaching an unmet market, repositioning of a product, or even creative new uses. The point is that you can do–and probably will do–a me-too product, but it better have something unique about it that separates it from everything out there or you won't even get it on the store shelves.[46]

LO 9-10 Consider the impact of the product life cycle.

Product Life Cycle[47]

Just as firms go through life cycles, so do the products and services within them. Since the stages for products are very similar to those for firms, we will quickly review the four stages (Figure 9.7) in terms of their implications for managing your firm's growth.

Stage 1—Introduction

Most small businesses can only afford to launch a product on a small scale, so naturally the sales are low and profits not likely when a product emerges into the market. In fact, many traditional marketing techniques described will depress profits at the start more than they will at later stages. For all the marketing money being spent, the risks from competition in the introduction stage are generally low since most competitors will wait to see if your product is a threat and has staying power before they act.

From a marketing standpoint, the more innovative the product, the slower the sales because fewer customers are comfortable with such products. Me-too products have an easier time gaining customer acceptance. Either way, the best sales method is to focus on the *relative advantage* your product has over the competition. When possible show how easy the product is to use, and how easily or well it coexists with the other products the customer owns. For people who like listening to music from their smartphone, headphones were a way to listen wherever they were. Then along came earbuds, noise-cancelling earbuds and headphones. The cost of basic headphones and earbuds have dropped as the new products came to market and the number of headphone and earbud users skyrocketed, Along these lines, providing samples or demonstration opportunities will also help seed the product during this phase.[48]

It should be noted that not all products survive the introduction phase of the product life cycle. Some products may take too long to begin making a profit because of high marketing expenses. Other products simply never catch on with consumers and never sell enough to cover their costs. And in reality many products in this stage get revised based on customer reactions and reasons behind lost sales. For online services, such revisions can be done on an almost daily basis, and very inexpensively. For products, the revision process can take weeks and cost thousands of dollars. Either way it gets done, products that are successful move on to the growth stage.

Stage 2—Growth

Like its firm counterparts of success and takeoff stages, during the growth stage acceptance of the product (whether innovative or imitative) increases rapidly. Think about Twitter. Although founded in July 2006, it had about 500,000 visitors by the end of 2007, 4.5 million visitors by December 2009, and over 500 million visitors by May 2012, to 2.8 billion visitors by May 2016 and almost 4 billion in May 2019. While Twitter doesn't charge for products that are sold, sales and profits during this stage grow at higher rates than at any other part of the product life cycle. Prices tend to drop as production becomes more efficient and competition increases.

From a marketing standpoint, consumers are aware of your product and know how it will make their lives better. Products nearly fly off the shelf. During this stage, advertising and promotion are much less critical than in the introduction stage, but keeping up with production and ensuring good distribution become more critical. Often a particular toy becomes "hot" and production has a tough time keeping up with demand. At times like that, a $20 doll can go for $200 on eBay. Other marketing goals during this time are to maximize your market share and keep ahead of competitors, so this is when you try to get into *all* the markets you can nationally (or internationally).

Stage 3—Maturity

Once the rapid growth begins to slow down, the product enters the *maturity stage*.

During this stage sales will level off, and profits follow suit, but remember, both should be at fairly high levels. Keeping both at that fairly high level is the challenge the small business faces. Since there are few new users for the product, most gains in market share are made by stealing customers from competitors. So you'll focus on defending the market share you have. As weaker competitors start to leave the market, you'll have opportunities to take their "leftover" customers.

For example, think about docking/charging stations with expansion speakers for iPhones and iPods. The first ones came out in 2012, with different ones being proclaimed "hot products" by industry experts. The growth phase came then, and with the growing opportunities, so came competitors. In 2016 a quick check of Amazon.com showed over 148,000 products. At that point, it was the peak for the speakers, which would signal that the maturity phase would be starting. The number of customers will probably remain flat for a while, and the number of competitors will go down because of increasing competition. Competition will increase because many of the people who want a speaker will already have one, so there are fewer customers and greater competition for the ones left.

What can we expect for maturity-stage products? Price competition starts to rise, and manufacturers find ways to cut costs or introduce new features to keep or gain market share. Something as simple as coming out with new speakers in colors may spark customer interest and keep or gain market share. But the truly smart companies already realize it is critical to have new ideas in the pipeline now and to get them ready for commercialization. Later in this stage, you will see products available through outlets and outlet sites like Overstock.com. As of May 2019, Overstock.com had over 441 different bluetooth speakers available for sale.

Apple iPhone bluetooth speakers went through a fast three-year sprint from introduction to maturity due to rapid adoption and rapid innovation. What other products or services can you think of that are in the growth stage?

pianodiaphragm/Shutterstock

Techniques used to bolster sales during this period include:

- Advertisements become reminder ads or extol new uses for the product; for example, Chex cereal being promoted as a party mix, rather than only as a breakfast food.
- Promotions (coupons, rebates, multipacks, etc.) flourish.
- Companies reposition brands to appeal to new markets, for example, Rembrandt toothpaste repositioned its product from being a smoker's toothpaste to a low-abrasion, whitening toothpaste for kids.[49]

A product can stay in the maturity stage for a long period of time. While the technology of the product may be older, the product is comfortable for the consumer. A quality product that inspires brand loyalty, such as Murphy's Oil Soap, can remain in the maturity stage for decades.

Stage 4—Decline

Once a product begins its permanent decline, this decline can be slow or fast, steady or unsteady. The bluetooth speakers dropped from 148,000 products on Amazon in 2016 to only 5,000 by 2020. This decline may come from competition in the mature industry, the introduction of a new technology, such as MP3s replacing music CDs, and before that vinyl records, or digital televisions replacing analog ones with 4K TV's replacing the original digital ones. The decline may also be caused by a shift in consumer preferences, such as bell-bottom jeans going out of style.

Whatever the reason for the decline, the characteristics of the decline stage remain the same. Both sales and profits fall during this stage. Advertising and promotion expenses are usually nearly eliminated at this point. Companies pare back their product lines and don't market to less profitable segments in order to cut costs and squeeze as much profit out of the final stage as possible. Tab, a popular diet soda in the early 1980s, is now available in only certain locations with highly loyal consumers, such as Cincinnati, New York, Atlanta, Phoenix, and Houston.[50]

Some products' decline is permanent. For example, with the switch in the United States to digital television in 2009, the analog television is pretty much dead as a product. On the other hand, many products go into decline, only to be resurrected in the future as styles come back to old standards, or when a company finds a new way to revitalize the product. Or consider the old disc-shaped record. The staple of music from the late nineteenth century held on until the early 1990s, surviving challenges by eight-track and cassette tapes, when it was eclipsed by the digital compact disc and later by MP3 files with online delivery via new retailers like iTunes and Rhapsody. But hard-core audiophiles started going back to traditional records in the twenty-first century, with 16-fold increases in sales from 2007 to 2018.[51] The willingness to sell individual songs revitalized that type of music retailing. Similarly, hot rods were popular in the 1950s but became very much a niche product, carried along by that generation. But for the manufacturers of car customization and performance equipment, video games like Grand Theft Auto and movies like *The Fast and the Furious* spurred a widespread renewal of their industry as "rice burners or "rice rockets" became the hot rods of the new millennium.

Service Life Cycle

While services do in fact go through the same four stages–introduction, growth, maturity, and decline–it can be somewhat easier to extend the life cycle and to virtually eliminate the decline stage of a service. Primarily, this is because services are often much easier to change "on the run." You can add and remove items from menus, change service levels, add additional services, revamp your website, and otherwise modify your service bundle more quickly than those who are manufacturing products. You can go with a gluten-free menu to accommodate the current diet fads, just about as fast as you can have new menus printed or change your "daily specials" chalkboard. You can attend a seminar or course to learn about adding

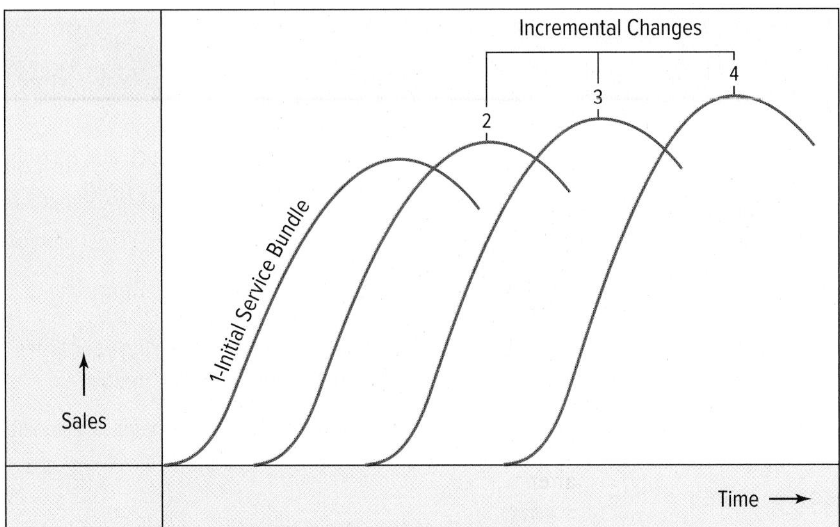

FIGURE 9.8

Service Life Cycle

new skills and offer that service to your accounting or legal clients. Service changes can be done relatively quickly and, if they don't work out well, they can be removed just as quickly.

This process of on-the-run changes means that your service is starting new life cycles with each tweaking of its existing offering. The curves will look more like those in Figure 9.8, where curve 1 is the initial service bundle and curves 2–4 represent the incremental changes. While a major change (like from Italian food from Chinese) can bring a firm almost back to the starting point, in most other cases, the new service is on top of all existing services–has no impact on existing services–like adding a manicurist to your hair salon.

Similar to products, new services will take a little time to attract customers, and initial advertising efforts will be to educate your clients as to the benefits of this service (or, perhaps, that you now offer this service). As sales seem to level off, continue to remind your customers that you offer the service and why it's better than that of your competition. Eventually, as sales drop off, eliminate the service totally or perform it only for those "old time" customers who ask for it.

Using the Product Life Cycle[52]

Many of the challenges in using the firm life cycle or the industry life cycle from Chapter 7 apply to using the product life cycle. It is hard to know exactly where in a cycle a particular product or service might be. Let's say Twitter's visit numbers grew by only 5 million from December 2011 to March 2012, but then dropped by over 4 million in April. Is Twitter reaching maturity or is it a minor slowdown in a meteoric rise? No one at the time could tell for sure. A marketer must weigh many things before trying to decide what phase a product is in. Moreover, products often experience a "revival" as new generations discover them. Brands such as Oxydol, Fanta, Breck, and Ovaltine, after near extinction, are experiencing new popularity.[53] Tattoo shops, a service that was nearly extinct, have started a new life cycle as styles have changed.

At the other extreme, products like Murphy's Oil Soap mentioned earlier, or Morton Salt, or Coca-Cola–have lasted for decades and show no signs of stopping. The bottom line is that you must be aware of the product life cycle and consider where your product might be and what that means, but you should understand that the determination can be imperfect and somewhat unpredictable. You should keep trying to decipher the life cycle stage because using the product life cycle gives you, as the entrepreneur, a way to think about your product, customers, and competition. If you follow the advice given here, it can help identify many of the likely issues and offer advice on how to handle these challenges in marketing your product.

CHAPTER SUMMARY

LO 9-1 Recognize the steps of the marketing process.

- Marketing involves connecting your customer to your product or service.
- Connecting these through the value proposition is the first step of the marketing process.
- Using the value proposition to craft the 4 Ps of marketing is the second step.

LO 9-2 Use customer roles and profiles to help define the target market.

- Customers can hold many roles such as end users, purchasers, decision makers, and influencers.
- Customer profiles are created to help understand the types of customers.
- Initial research on customers is usually done with personal interviews organized to give unbiased information.
- These profiles are used to help define the target customer.

LO 9-3 Segment and further define your target audience.

- Aim for a narrow segment (or portion) of the market.
- Develop a profile of the needs of your target market.
- Match your product or service and promotion to your target market's needs.

LO 9-4 Recognize the major methods for conducting marketing research.

- Primary data are data that you gather to answer your current questions.
  - Primary data can be gathered through observation, focus groups, or questionnaires.
  - Questionnaires can be administered via mail, phone, Internet, or in person and can consist of closed-ended or open-ended questions.
- Secondary research are data that are already gathered for some other purpose than the question you are trying to answer.
  - Internet, libraries, newspapers, and magazines offer free data; data are also for sale and can range from relatively inexpensive to very expensive.
  - While using secondary data is quick and often free, they may not give you exactly what you need.

LO 9-5 Develop your value proposition.

- Build your value proposition by analyzing your firm's distinctive competence and customer needs.
- Create a mantra and a one-paragraph value proposition.

LO 9-6 Understand how to organize marketing plans.

- In addition to developing the marketing section of a business plan, with a little additional work it is possible to create a stand-alone marketing plan for your business.

LO 9-7 Recognize the characteristics of goods and services.

- Goods differ from services in tangibility, inseparability, perishability, and heterogeneity.
- Very few true goods or services exist; most products fall somewhere along a goods–services continuum and have components of each.

LO 9-8 Define the total product.

- A product is a bundle of services and goods and has three basic levels: core, augmented, and total product.
- Understanding the total product allows you to concentrate on the features and aspects important to the customer and to coordinate your other marketing activities.

LO 9-9 Differentiate the stages of new product development.

- The stages include idea generation, idea screening, idea evaluation, product development, and commercialization.
- During the product development phase, prototypes can be developed in order to do additional screening, and test markets or test market simulations can be run.
- The last stage, commercialization, involves developing the final marketing plan, getting the product into production, and the start of sales.

- "Me-toos" are products similar to competitive products that need a much-abbreviated new product development cycle. In this case, only the aspects that are different from competition need to be tested.

LO 9-10 Consider the impact of the product life cycle.

- The stages of the product life cycle include introduction, growth, maturity, and decline.
- From a marketing viewpoint, the different stages tell us about the competition and how to focus the individual elements of the marketing plan—product, price, promotion, and placement.
- As services are usually more able to make incremental changes almost continually, the service life cycle is more typified by a series of mini–product life cycles.

KEY TERMS

4 Ps of marketing, 284
product development process, 285
customer development process, 285
end user, 286
purchaser, 286
decision maker, 286
influencer, 286
purchasing process, 287
budget cycle, 287
customer profile, 287
customer job, 287
pivot, 288
total available market (TAM), 289
serviceable available market (SAM), 289
serviceable obtainable market (SOM), 289
penetrated market (PM), 289
long-term value (LTV), 290
customer lifetime value (CLV), 290
churn, 290
feedback, 291
testimonial, 291
outstanding customer service, 291
market segmentation, 293
segmentation, 293
target market, 293
predetermined market segments, 294
marketing research, 299
primary research, 299
secondary research, 299
ethnographic research, 300
focus group, 300
survey, 301
scalar question, 302
dichotomous question, 302
categorical question, 302
open-ended question, 302
value proposition, 310
goods, 315
services, 315
tangibility, 315
perishability, 315
inseparability, 315
heterogeneity, 315
total product, 317
augmented product, 317
core product, 318
me-too products, 318
prototype, 321
commercialization, 323

DISCUSSION QUESTIONS

1. How do the risks differ when you start your business using a purely product development process approach versus a purely customer development process approach?
2. What are the customer roles and what does the person in each role do?
3. What are the elements that go into a customer profile and why is each useful?
4. What is the target market and how does it differ from the other types of markets (TAM, SAM, SOM, PM)?
5. What are some of the ways that you could use secondary research to better understand the various segments of your market and to develop promotional materials?
6. What sorts of primary data could you collect using observation for your car wash?

7. Create a questionnaire that could be used to gather data for your car wash. Use both closed- and open-ended questions.

8. A college education comes pretty close to being a true service. Discuss the four main characteristics of service—intangibility, inseparability, perishability, and heterogeneity—as they pertain to a college education.

9. What is the core component, the augmented product, and the total product sold at your college or university? How does it differ from your institution to others in the area?

10. List all the products/services you have seen lately that are promoted as new, different, improved, or otherwise changed from what has been available before. What percentage of these are actually me-too products? Identify the differential advantages these companies believe they have over the competition.

EXPERIENTIAL EXERCISES

1. Visit your school's library or your local public library and investigate the reference section. Make a list of resources that might be useful if you were opening a new dry cleaning business.

2. Try **https://claritas360.claritas.com/mybestsegments/** and look for the *Zip Code Lookup*. For this exercise use the zip code around Contra Costa Community College, 94806. Compare the first listed segment on the PRIZM and P$YCLE lists. How do their approaches to describing people in that segment differ? Which would be more useful to you, and why? Feel free to repeat this for the zip code you are interested in for your business.

3. Select a local shopping mall to do some observation and primary data collecting. (Try a food court or bench in a waiting area where you can be comfortable and unobtrusive.) Make a list of the sorts of observational data you could collect.

4. Interview someone at the company where you work. What kind of marketing plan does the company have (formal, informal, detailed, etc.)? How often is it reviewed?

5. At this time, you are fairly experienced with college education. What do you suggest could be done in order to reduce intangibility, inseparability, perishability, and heterogeneity of this service?

6. With a group of friends, brainstorm a list of ideas for a service you could provide for your college professors. Design an idea checklist to evaluate this list.

7. Select a service you know. Brainstorm a list of potential incremental changes—whether technologically feasible or not—that might extend the product life cycle for it over the next several years.

8. Go to a product idea site like **www.ideaswatch.com** (lists of sites is available at **www.ideaconnection.com/ideasites/** and **www.quora.com/What-websites-let-people-share-discuss-and-rate-ideas**). Grab an idea and work with one or more people to think about who might be the target market for that product or service.

9. Prototype by creating a box for your product: Paper over a box (e.g., a cereal box, a gift box, a small shipping box, etc.) and draw, write, paste things you print, add stickers or whatever you can to convey what your product or service does to the potential customer. Revise as you think necessary. When done, share it with potential customers and get their reactions. Revise the box as you learn more about what you want to do for customers.

10. Prototype by creating a nonworking model of your product: In the old days people would do this out of bars of soap (Ivory was big and easy to work with), Play-Doh, clay, wood, block, LEGOs, or things found around the house, school, or workshop. Today we can add 3-D printing, using free software like SketchUp, Blender, or K-3D to make it. Consider grabbing something similar from the "thingiverse"—a repository of more than 1.4 million 3-D designs you can download and modify for free—to get started, tweaking the design to make it fit your vision. If you don't have access to a 3-D printer, share the design with potential customers instead.

11. With a partner, design two questionnaires about a service business you are considering—dry cleaning, restaurant, and so on. One questionnaire should have only open-ended questions, while the other one should ask similar things using closed-ended questions. Each of you should submit your questions (orally, in writing, or online) to 10 people (different sets of people). Compare your results. What are the pros and cons of each set of data?

12. Look for segment-focused ads by browsing through magazines that appeal to very different audiences, for example, different ethnic groups *(Latina, Ebony)*, different age groups *(AARP Magazine, Seventeen)*, different hobbies or sports *(Skiing, American Philatelist, Opera Today)*, different income levels *(Forbes, Affordable Housing Finance)*, different sexes—or gendered orientations *(GQ, Ladies Home Journal, Out, Girlfriend)*, different life stages *(Brides, Pregnancy, AARP Magazine)*, and the like. Review the ads and look for clues that would cause you to believe that the ad is focused at a particular group. Show several of these ads—without identifying the magazine—and see if your classmates can determine the possible target market. Figure 9.3 shows a couple of examples.

MINI-CASE

YAK MILK[54]

Dongzhou Gongbu saw a golden opportunity, only he wasn't quite sure what to do with it at first. A native Tibetan, he had worked in the Chinese government for a number of years and had witnessed the difficulties the Chinese government was facing feeding its people. While China is quite a large country, over 60 percent of its landmass is unsuitable for agriculture. Those areas that are suitable are also where China's huge population lives, further reducing available land. Dongzhou remembered the vast Tibetan plateau dotted with yak, the only animal suited to the severe climate found there, and knew there had to be a solution.

Yak are "low-maintenance" animals needing no feed that they can't gather themselves and living on the open range herded by nomadic Tibetans. While yak are milk producers, the quantities produced are much less than that produced by dairy cattle. In addition, because of its remoteness, bringing milk from the plateau to the population centers is an expensive proposition. A quick look at the prices on existing milk products and yak milk cost structure showed that yak milk just couldn't compete, because it would need to be about 50 percent more expensive than cow's milk.

Dongzhou didn't let this stop him, though. He consulted a specialist and found that yak milk was higher in certain nutrients than cow's milk. In addition, the Tibetan plateau is well respected in China for being pollution-free. Dongzhou capitalized on these features, plus the fact that the yak were truly organically raised and revered in Chinese mythology. He positioned his product not as just another milk but as an extremely healthy alternative to other products—almost a nutritional drink—and priced it at a premium level.

CASE DISCUSSION QUESTIONS

1. How did Dongzhou Gongbu "discover" his new product?
2. What was his "total product"?
3. Who do you imagine is the target market for yak milk?
4. How might he use this in advertising?
5. Can you think of another product that is basically the same as the competition and has been positioned much differently in order to command a higher price?

CHAPTER

10 Small Business Promotion: Capturing the Eyes of Your Market

● Addie Swartz's lifestyle brand, Beacon Street Girls, is aimed at two market audiences. What challenges are posed to this small business by its double-pronged approach? How might this approach work to Swartz's advantage?
Source: B*tween Productions, Inc.

LEARNING OBJECTIVES

After you complete this chapter, you will be able to:

LO 10-1 Describe the marketing funnel and the stages in the customer development process.

LO 10-2 Recognize the PESO model of the promotional media landscape.

LO 10-3 Apply the key skills involved in personal selling, especially closing the sale.

LO 10-4 Recognize the major approaches to customer retention.

LO 10-5 Identify sales forecasting methods.

Focus on Small Business: Addie Swartz and Accessories for Girls Who Are "between Toys and Boys"[1]

As Addie Swartz's two daughters approached the pivotal "tween" years, she—like many mothers—struggled to find something to help her girls bridge the gap between Barbie and Beyoncé. Frustration stoked her entrepreneurial spirit, and the Beacon Street Girls, a new lifestyle brand for girls ages 9 to 13, was born.

NO DOLLS OR ICONS

The Beacon Street Girls invites tweens into a rich and exciting contemporary world in which values matter, friendships are everything, and community service is important.

In promoting the brand, Swartz comments that all of Beacon Street Girls's marketing initiatives need to understand and speak to two audiences: tween girls and their parents/older gift-buying relatives. Their goals are to:

- Build awareness among stakeholders.
- Create interest and desire in tweens to engage with the brand and share with their peers.
- Drive customers into the stores to seek and purchase Beacon Street Girls products.
- Encourage tweens and their parents to come to the website.

Marketing programs are aimed to promote retailer presence, push to the web, and leverage the tween consumer to promote the brand via web-based viral marketing programs. In describing her market further, Swartz divides the market into two segments, the primary and secondary. The primary market consists of girls ages 9–13 years, with the "sweet spot" being the older 11- to 12-year-old tween. These girls are entering middle school, a time of new friendships, body changes, and growing-up experiences. They are media-savvy, looking for fun and possibilities, admiring of teenagers, but still want to be kids. They are in the early stages of navigating the often rocky waters of adolescence and desperately want to fit in. The secondary market consists of their mothers, fathers, aunts, uncles, and grandmothers who seek positive role models and messages for their daughters/relatives.

DISCUSSION QUESTIONS

1. What are some ways that Beacon Street Girls can promote its brand in order to meet the company's goals?
2. What ways can Beacon Street Girls market to the tween girls?
3. How can it also reach the parents of the tweens? In what ways is the marketing message different or the same?
4. How can Addie Swartz continually develop and promote the brand that has meaningful, value-driven tween girl properties that are also relevant, cool, and realistic?

LO 10-1 Describe the marketing funnel and the stages in the customer development process.

The Need for Promotion

In Chapter 9 we talked about two processes for approaching new firms, products, and services. One was the product development process. The other was the customer development process, which we will discuss further here.

In order for customers to purchase your goods and services, you must first go to them. You need to advertise and actively promote your business before you can expect inquiries into what you have to offer. While there are a handful of promotional means that are standard for all business ventures, entrepreneurs' limit to promotions is their own creativity.

For a long time, the process of selling to customers has been thought of as a funnel, like the one shown in Figure 10.1. The idea is that to some extent, marketing is a game of numbers. To get people to buy what you are offering, you first need to make an impression on them, letting them know who you are and what you are offering. Those who have some interest become your **sales leads** and the most interested ones become your **prospects** for a sale. So at a

impression
What it is called when someone notices a promotional effort.

sales leads
People who receive a promotional impression and who give some thought to buying the product.

FIGURE 10.1

The Promotion Process and the Marketing Funnel

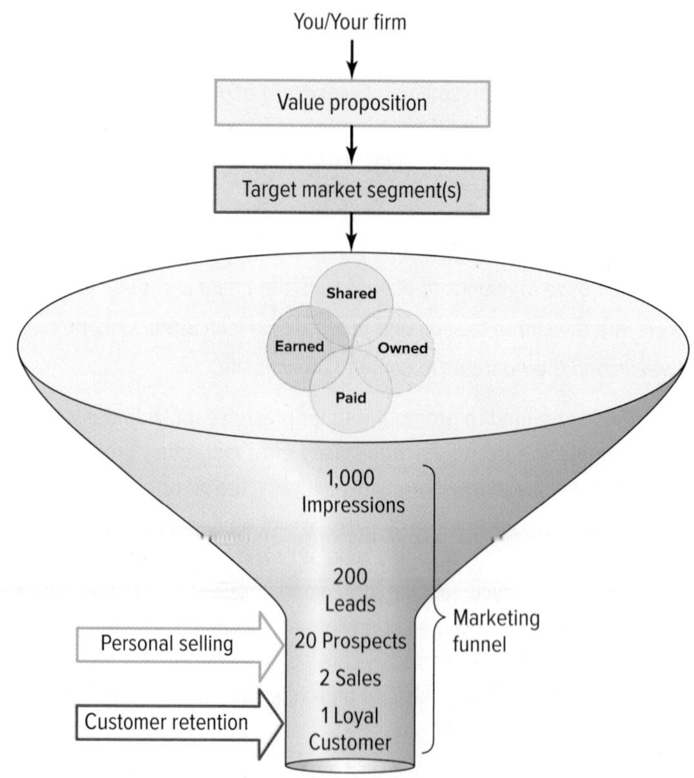

fundamental level, promotion drives sales. How many prospects? Marketers talk about the **marketing funnel**, a rule of thumb about how many prospective customers it takes to find one who will actually make a purchase. For mass-market advertising the typical ratio is 500 to 1, while for Internet advertising, it is 1,000 to 1.[2] Figure 10.1 graphically shows you the promotion process and how the marketing funnel fits into it.

prospects
Sales leads who actually make some sort of effort to learn more about the product, service, or business in anticipation of a possible purchase.

marketing funnel
The rule of thumb in marketing that it takes a large number of people to be made aware of your product in order to find a purchaser.

The marketing funnel still works to give a sense of the contributing factors in promotion and sales, and a sense of the numbers, but Silicon Valley serial entrepreneurs Steve Blank and Bob Dorf came up with a more inclusive approach for the customer development process. In their approach, there are major goals: (1) get customers, (2) keep customers, and (3) grow customers. This builds on the idea that finding new customers can cost 5, 10, even 25 times as much as getting sales from an existing customer, depending on your industry and sales model. Or try it this way—what is the easiest way to increase your profits 100 percent? According to the research, just keep one more customer out of every 20 (i.e., increase your retained customers by 5 percent).[3]

That ability to increase sales resulted in Blank and Dorf creating a new funnel, which focuses on ways to grow sales to existing customers. The resulting double-sided funnel is seen in Figure 10.2. It expands "customer retention" from Figure 10.1 to reflect a range of specific steps you can take as an entrepreneur.

The steps in the "Get Customers" funnel on the left are the same as are found in the traditional sales funnel. They build from the same advertising, public relations, sales promotion, social media, and direct marketing efforts shown in Figure 10.1. The steps are:

- **Awareness:** Is the process of getting your message out as much as you can to your target market, or if you are unsure about your target market, to the people in your intended service area. Your goal is to get a subset of the people who see your message to take the next step and express interest.
- **Interest:** Is the process of prospective customers taking some action to learn more about the product, service, or your company. This can be through looking at your website, catalog, or store. It could be from checking for more information from third-party sources such as friends, family, review websites, magazines, or the like. The goal is for potential customers to get the information that leads them to include your product, service, or firm as one of the prospective purchases they are thinking about.
- **Consideration:** Is the process of getting into the prospective customer's final list of brands of products or services they are considering for purchase, and doing what you can to help

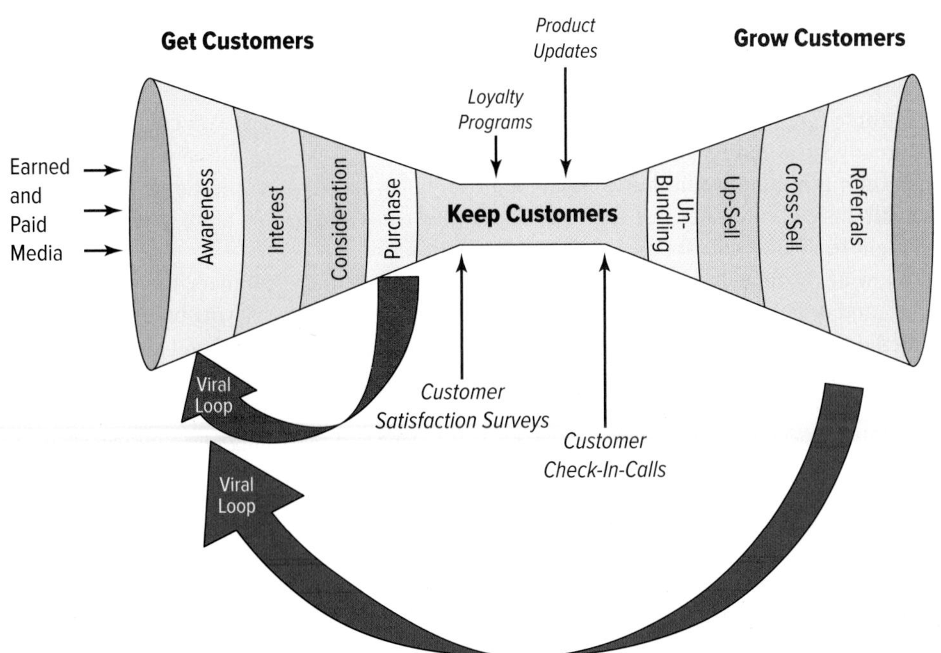

FIGURE 10.2

The Customer Development Funnel for Physical Products

Taken from Figure 4.11 of *The Start-Up Owner's Manual*, ©2016, Steve Blank and Bob Dorf, used with permission.

FIGURE 10.3

The Customer Development Funnel for Web/Mobile Products

Taken from Figure 4.17 of *The Start-Up Owner's Manual*, ©2016, Steve Blank and Bob Dorf, used with permission.

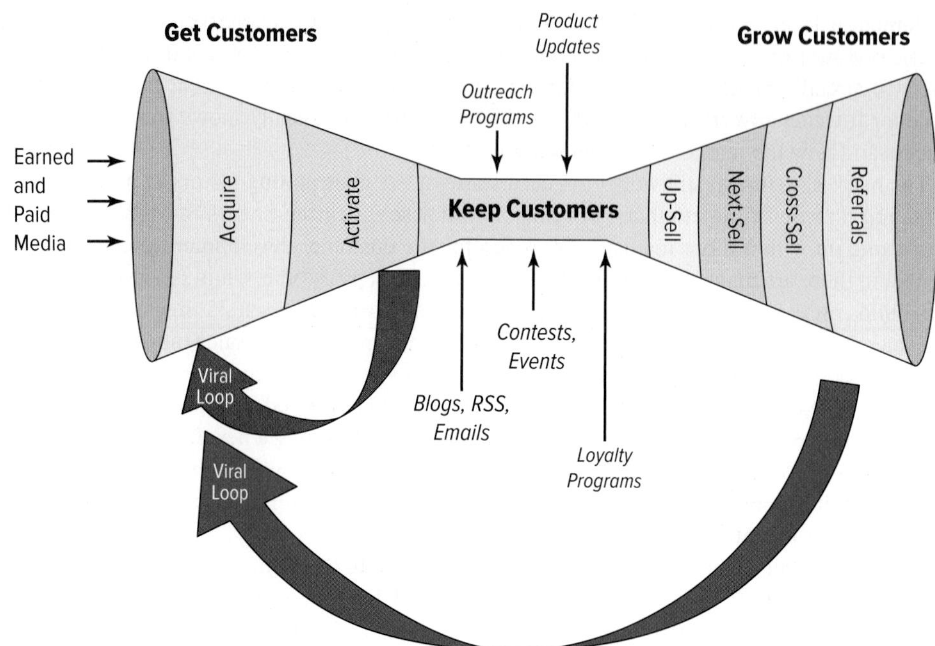

tip their decision in your favor, through customer contact, providing information, experience with the product (e.g., samples, test-drives, etc.), or pricing information, including discounts and coupons if you use these in your business.

- **Purchase:** This is the end of the initial promotional funnel, where a person buys your product or service and becomes a customer of your firm.

We will cover the Keep Customers and Grow Customers sections of the funnel later in the chapter when we discuss customer retention methods.

The model is designed for selling goods and services in the physical world, where you actually can hold the product in your hands, or have the service delivered by a person at some physical location (a store, shop, or your home). There is a slightly different version of the Blank and Dorf funnel for Internet-based businesses, shown in Figure 10.3.

The left-hand-side funnel has only two steps, **acquire** customers, usually through web and phone contacts (although traditional media may be the source by which prospective customers hear about you), and **activate** a customer, which can be as simple as their signing up for a website, or giving their email address or phone number.

All three funnels illustrate selling to the general public, but what if you could target people you already know have a reason to be interested in your goods or services? Maybe one or two people in a thousand would buy a baseball glove, but what if you could target people playing baseball? Instead of 2 sales per 1,000, with *qualified leads* like people already playing baseball, you might be able to sell 10 times as many gloves, or more.

Following the funnels, in this chapter we will talk about getting customers, defining your target market, and determining how to identify segments like those already playing baseball. We discuss the methods of promotion including social media, public relations, and press relations. We then get into the methods of selling to and keeping customers, and focus on a discussion on managing post-sale relations in order to grow sales. The end of the chapter includes a deeper dive into predicting sales, which is useful when you are creating business plans and marketing plans for your firm.

LO 10-2 Recognize the PESO model of the promotional media landscape.

Promotion Using the PESO Model

American consumers are bombarded by messages all day. For example, a Yankelovich Advertising Agency study reported the average person was exposed to 5,000 ad messages a day.[4] However, many of us screen out most of the commercials we see or hear. Even when an advertisement catches our eye, we are likely to spend only a few seconds at most considering it unless it is of special importance to us. For example, if you are in the new car market, the car advertisements suddenly become more visible to you. But even when you are interested and move down the marketing funnel from having an impression to becoming a sales lead, you may have a poor recall of any ads you've seen. Was it the funny ad or the one with the special effects? Ad recall is a major problem for all advertisers.

The bottom line consists of two questions: How can you get the attention of your potential customer? If a potential customer sees or hears your message and walks away with only one thought about your firm, your product, or your service, what do you want that to be?

The how has been addressed somewhat by thoroughly investigating your target market and finding out what they like. This will give us a good idea of where they are likely to be exposed to our messages. This will also give us a good idea of how our messages should be designed.[5] So if you did a good job on the target market analysis introduced earlier, you should know where they look and what they want. That leaves crafting a message that fits their needs.

The PESO Model of the Media Landscape

Once upon a time, that is before the Internet, the media landscape was pretty small and manageable. There were four national networks (ABC, CBS, NBC, and PBS), a dozen radio stations, one or two newspapers in your town, fewer than 100 national magazines, of which only about a dozen printed regional editions in which a small business might imagine **advertising**. In your neighborhood you could pass out flyers or try mailers, use signage, sponsor a team or something at school or church, and of course hope for positive word of mouth. If you were lucky, occasionally a local TV or radio station or newspaper might mention you in an article. Today is very different.

For starters, customers are being bombarded by more than 5,000 messages a day, as noted above. There are more than 1,000 U.S. cable channels, hundreds of pay-per-view and streaming services, 7,167 magazines in the United States, 1.6 billion websites of which 200 million are active worldwide, 2.46 billion social media users worldwide (all of whom have pages), 31 million bloggers in the United States, and 1,276 newspapers in the United States (nearly all of which can serve ads to specific localities).[6]

There is a flood of information and messaging, and for the entrepreneur, the challenge is getting heard by potential customers–in particular, those people who are most likely to want your product or service. One way to make sense of this gigantic media landscape is to use a model that helps you organize media opportunities.

One of the best models was developed by Gini Dietrich, head of the Chicago-based marketing firm Arment Dietrich,[7] called the PESO model. *PESO* stands for the four major types of media: *p*aid, *e*arned, *s*hared, and *o*wned. Figure 10.4 shows the model graphically and labels the four circles and the key overlaps. Like other popular models, PESO has spawned a lot of variations, and the model we use here is a hybrid building on Dietrich's original thinking.[8]

In using the PESO model, we will start with a simple way to order our approach. Most of Dietrich's clients are pretty well-off financially, so it makes sense that she started her model with **paid media**. But we will start with a focus on **owned media**, which includes your websites, newsletters, emails, signage, and the like, because that is where you establish your business's media presence. We'll focus on **shared media** second, because getting onto social media is free (and free is best when starting out and not having a lot of money) and helps connect you to your initial customers and the friends they share with. Third will be **earned media**, which is public relations and press relations and garnering what we will call "free ink." This is easier when you have established credibility through your growing base of friends on shared media. Fourth will be paid media, which refers to all the different forms of paid advertising you can buy. We put it last because it works best when you know who your customers are, and where they go on the vast media landscape, so you can target your ad buys as precisely (and cheaply) as possible.

As you read about the PESO model you may find that an item, such as contests, might show up in several places. That is OK. The model's purpose is to help you think of the different ways

advertising
Often used to support the corporate identity and value propositions that are established through public relations efforts. Part of conveying your message to your customers, advertising outlets include newspapers, magazines, billboards, television, and Internet banner ads, to name a few.

paid media
Generally referred to as bought or paid advertising, paid media are promotions where your firm pays another for the placement and distribution of the material.

owned media
These are promotional materials directly and wholly owned by your company, like your name, your websites, your signage, and the like.

shared media
Generally called word-of-mouth or referral advertising, these are promotional mentions of your brand, firm, product, services, or user experiences with them made by customers and others and posted or shared through their social media sites.

earned media
Generally what has been called publicity or press or public relations, these refer to do-it-yourself and paid efforts to get the message of your brand, business, product, or service out to the general public or the mass media (TV, radio, print) in hopes it gets repeated by them.

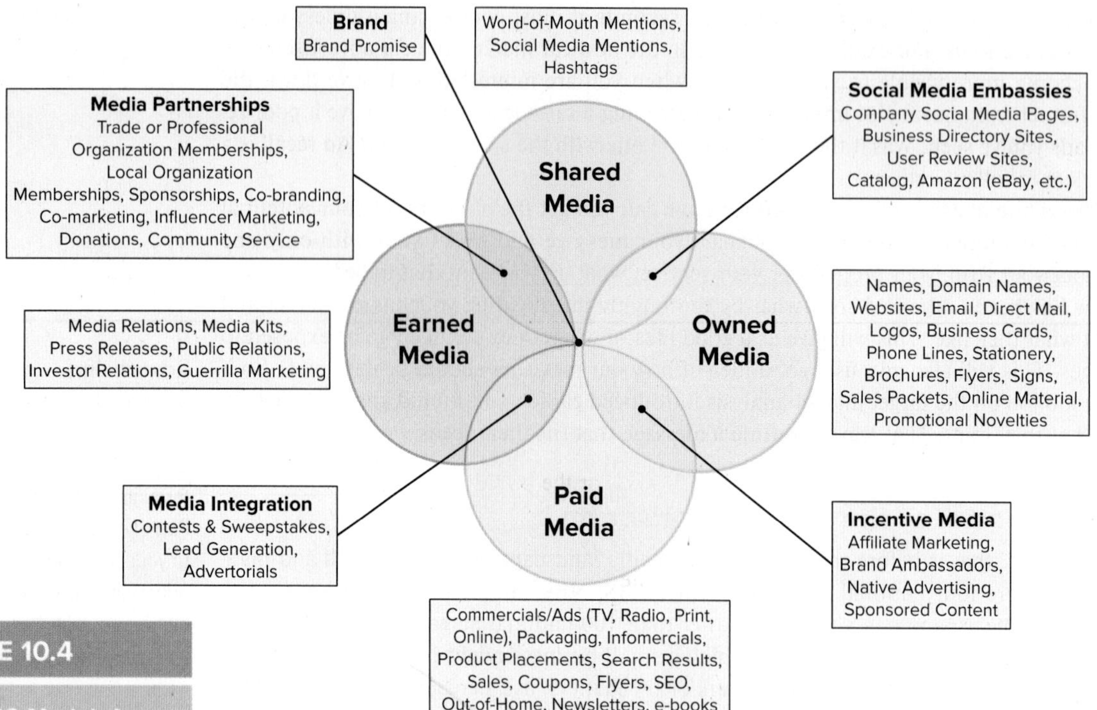

FIGURE 10.4

The PESO Model: A Hybrid Model of How to Think about the Media Landscape

Source: Adapted from G. Dietrich, "The Four Different Types of Media," *Spin Sucks*, June 24, 2013.

you can promote your business. Items don't need to fit in only one category. What is important is that you think about the kinds of media available to you, what is called the **promotional mix** of techniques you will use to get customers to notice your business.

The overlaps of the circles also have a special meaning. The owned-shared overlap is where your **social media embassies** (your firm's pages on social media platforms) exist and are your gateways to shared content. The shared-earned overlap is where your **media partnerships** with companies, influencers, and media organizations reside. The earned-paid media overlap is called **media integration** and is where you develop contests, advertorials, lead generation efforts, and influencer-directed campaigns. The paid-owned media overlap is where **incentive media** based efforts are the focus, such as sponsorships, affiliate marketing efforts, brand ambassadors, and related types.

At the very center of the PESO model is where your brand and your organizational identity goes, and it is where everything starts. Your owned media is based on the brand you are seeking to promote, and that brand is the living manifestation of your firm's identity—it is who you are and what you, your firm, and its products or services are all about. So we will start building out the PESO model with brand, and then talk about owned, shared, earned, and paid media.

promotional mix
How much of each message conveyance you will use to sell your product as well as your objective in using each one.

social media embassies
These combine elements of owned and shared media and represent the social media platforms on which your brand, business, products, or services have a formal presence (like a company page). The page belongs to you, but it exists on a media platform that you don't own or control.

Your Brand: The Start of It All

What is a **brand**? At first glance a brand may seem like the name a firm puts on itself and its products to differentiate them from competitors' offerings. But in reality it is more than that. Coca-Cola is one of the best-known and best-thought-of brands in the world, and a former president of the company, Muhtar Kent, is famous for the quote "A brand is a promise. A good brand is a promise kept." One of the most important jobs of the entrepreneur of a start-up is to craft a brand message that reflects what the firm is about.

Think about your customer interviews. If your brand were to promise something to help meet the customers' pains and needs, what would that be? A natural response for many entrepreneurs would be something along the lines of "It would be a product (or service) that does. . . ." While it might be the natural first response, from a branding standpoint it is too limiting. Your product or service will probably evolve, so your brand would need to change to reflect this.

A better approach is to think about what *underlies* your brand. You have probably had personal experience with Disney movies, shows, games, books, and perhaps even theme parks.

So take a second and think about what the Disney brand means to you. Following is how Disney executive Roy Disney (who was Walt Disney's nephew) thought about it:

> The Walt Disney Company is more than just a business. It is an authentic American icon—which is to say that over the years it has come to stand for something real and meaningful and worthwhile to millions of people of all ages and backgrounds around the world. This is not something you can describe easily on a balance sheet, but it is tangible enough. Indeed, it is the foundation on which everything we have accomplished as a company—both artistically and financially—is based. I believe our mission has always been to be bringers of joy, to be affirmers of the good in each of us, to be—in subtle ways—teachers. To speak, as Walt once put it, "not to children but to the child in each of us." We do this through great storytelling, by giving our guests a few hours in another world where their cares can be momentarily put aside, by creating memories that will remain with them forever. This is the core of what we've come to call "Disney."[9]

Notice Disney doesn't talk about the films, the books, or the parks. He talks about how the work they do provides benefits to their customers (which are called "guests" in Disney-speak). The characters of the Disney stories will change. New technologies will mean Disney will come to us in different channels and ways, but the brand's message, and promise, remains the same. Skill Module 10.1 explains how to craft a brand promise.

media partnerships
These occur at the overlap of shared and earned media and represent the paid and unpaid arrangements made by your brand, company, product, or service with outside individuals or organizations to promote your brand to the public or their own social media or public bases. These partnerships include influencer marketing (also called brand ambassadors), trade and professional organizational memberships, local organization memberships, sponsorships, co-branding, co-advertising, donations, and community service.

Creating Your Brand Promise[10]

SKILL MODULE 10.1

Establishing a brand can be as simple as being able to say what you are promising to deliver to your customers—the benefits or help that you give us and we should expect from you. This is called your **brand promise**. This reflects what *you, your firm, and your employees will strive to do* for the customer. The focus of the promise is keyed to an emotional outcome you want to achieve in customers through your action. Given this, the template for a brand promise is simple. As practitioner Sue Kirchner put it, your brand promise in effect says how "We are the company that does X (achieves the emotional result) for Y (the customer) because we do Z (the action you take).[11]

It differs from the customer job because the job looks at what the customer is trying to get done. Similarly, it differs from the value proposition (Chapters 4 and 9) and mantra (Chapter 8), which focus on what pains and gains your product or service solve. And it differs from your competitive advantage (Chapter 7), which is what your firm does better than the competition. Ideally, the value proposition, mantra, and competitive advantage for any of your product or service offerings should be a natural extension of the brand and the brand promise.

media integration
The overlap of paid and earned media is based on generating leads through three paid types of efforts: advertorials (editorials written by a company as a type of ad), lead generation purchases (e.g., mailing or subscriber lists or contests), and contests or sweepstakes.

incentive media
The overlap of paid and owned media reflects the partnerships where you are paying for connections useful to your business. This includes affiliate marketing, brand ambassadors, native advertising, and sponsored content.

Small businesses actually have natural advantages in branding. For these businesses, the entrepreneur is close to the customer. A brand can be close to a personal promise, one more likely to be believed, and one that can be acted on or repaired immediately. The basic brand promise is that your product and service will work as indicated. Your gas powers my car. Your cleaning of my house leaves it clean and shiny.

But you also have the potential of going beyond this basic promise. How do you go above and beyond? A family-owned chain of country restaurants called Lambert's Cafe started in Sikeston, Missouri, in 1942. While they seem at first glance similar to Cracker Barrel restaurants, Lambert's has a following that is legendary. Motorcycle clubs, busloads of seniors and churchgoers, truckers, tourists, and classic American food fans will travel hundreds of miles out of their way each weekend to grab a meal at Lambert's. Its approach was and remains enormous portions of staples, cooked traditionally, and served with all-you-can-eat pass-around side dishes and hot rolls thrown across the room to you. Its three restaurants themselves are gigantic, but usually have lines out the door. Its founder, Norman Ray Lambert, built the brand with "Our simple but powerful rule: Always give you, our guest, more than you expect to get."[12]

brand
The name a firm puts on itself and its products to differentiate them from competitors' offerings.

brand promise
The gains provided (i.e., the benefits) or the help given (i.e., the pains removed) by the product or service your firm offers.

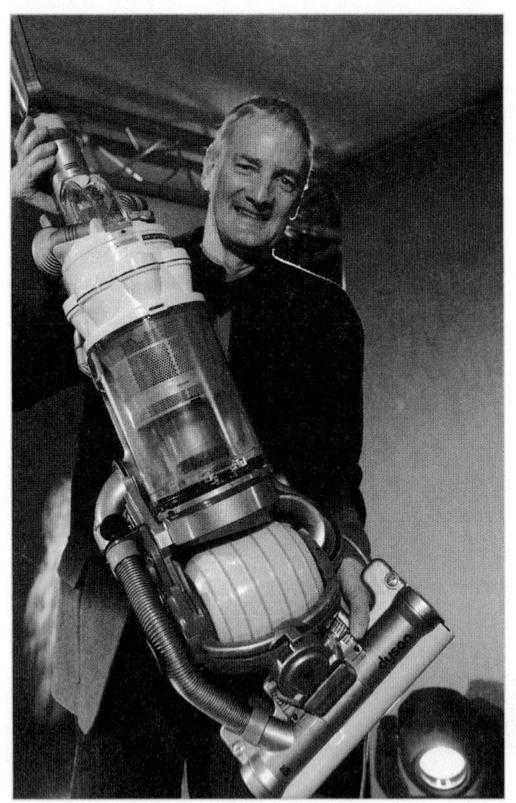

James Dyson's face, voice, and identity as the founder of Dyson, Inc. are as much a part of his firm's brand as Dyson, Inc.'s innovative products.

Bruno Vincent/Getty Images

Branding builds from what you can do for the customer (the value proposition), what you can do better than others (your competitive advantage or distinctive competence), and what you personally want your firm to represent. It is something you need to do because if you don't build and promote a brand of your own, you leave open the potential for your competitors to create a brand image of your firm in customers' minds.[13]

Keep in mind that at a basic level, as the entrepreneur, owner, and founder, to many people you are the brand. What would Dyson vacuum cleaners be without the on-screen presence of inventor James Dyson? If chef Emeril left his restaurant, wouldn't you feel something important was missing? For small businesses, the entrepreneur and the business often start out as one and the same. As the business adds employees, the importance of the owner declines, but realize that the brand you have created will always be dependent on you. When Vince Shlomi, the pitchman for the ShamWow towels, was arrested for a hotel room brawl in Miami, his mugshots made the celebrity TV shows and magazines. Can you imagine how the ShamWow's target market reacted? Remember, for your small business you are part of the brand, even when you have been careful not to put your name on the business.

As you develop your brand and brand identity, you come to know yourself and your business well enough to start the process of building the business out in the media landscape. And as we said earlier, that starts with a focus on your owned media.

Owned Media

Once you have come to an idea about what you want your firm's brand to be, you are in the position to start crafting your firm's organizational identity (introduced in Chapter 3) and the many forms of owned media. Organizational identity starts with the names of your business, product, or service, and these days often includes logos, symbols, characters, slogans, **hashtags**, uniforms, and packaging. Picking names that can work across all these different forms can be more complex than you might think, and we will introduce some of the key issues to think about next. Once you have the names created, they become the basis for creating your business identity.

hashtag
A term developed to be easily searched on the Internet. Hashtags are words or multiword phrases (without spaces) preceded by a "#" sign (called a hash) that is associated with an idea, person, product, service, brand, firm, event, or the like.

Picking Names

Your brand's name sets the product's personality and helps separate it from competitors.[14] For some small firms the brand name and the company name may be the same—especially if you are a service (Speedy Dry Cleaning) or have a limited product line (e.g., Beyond Clothing). There are certain guidelines for coming up with good names, but there are many exceptions. Here are some things to keep in mind:

- The first thought for many entrepreneurs is to name the firm after themselves. While that is not necessarily a problem, it is also not very clear to potential customers what it is that you do. What is the Smith Company? What products can I find at Brown's Emporium? Consider adding another descriptive word to your name—Smith Machining Company will attract a whole different clientele from Smith Beauty Supply. This typically isn't a problem with a product because we usually add the product category: Smith Dishwashing Detergent.
- Another issue with using your name concerns how to handle the name if you decide to sell the company. The new buyer of Smith Machining Company will become tired of explaining that there is no longer any Mr. or Ms. Smith with the business. If you decide later to reenter the business (or any business), your name is now on someone else's business; while "Smith" is common enough, customers may wonder why Mr. John Cuttlebrink doesn't work at John Cuttlebrink Machining Company. In addition, should the new owners have a bad reputation, it's your name that will be smeared.
- Is your name appropriate? If your name is Payne, you might not want to use it for a dental clinic. How many other firms are using the same name (with or without additional

descriptors), and will that cause confusion? (City or place names can get overused as well.) Maybe you are the only Srivhantinivasthian in the phone book, but will your customers remember your name or be able to spell or pronounce it? Maybe you should consider a nickname or a first name, or forget vanity for now and go with something else.

- Be careful about infringing on trademarks. Even names relatively close can cause you trouble. Dr. Peter wouldn't work for a soft drink, but it could be used for other products.
- Something that describes your firm or product and is easy to remember is ideal. While plain-old "Discount Furniture" certainly fills that bill, "Cheap Seats" is a little catchier and more memorable. Be careful, though: This technique isn't appropriate for every type of business. "Divorce Depot" or "Bankruptcy Barn" probably won't convince potential clients that you're a serious, competent attorney.
- Creative spellings are eye-catching, but don't go overboard; "Myk's Otto Groj" is certainly different, but Mike's customers won't have an easy time finding him in the phone book or on the Internet when they need their cars repaired. Product brand names, too, are often evocative of the benefits they offer–Vaseline Intensive Care–but they may also be simple names–Dove, Zest, and so on. The same guidelines about being relatively easy to spell (not too creative) and to pronounce apply here as well.
- Beware of selecting a name that's too narrow to allow your firm to grow. "Just Jams and Jelly" might work right now, but what happens when you expand into candy, juices, pies, and the like?
- Check that the name can be used as your firm's name on the Internet. If you decide on Rachel's Dog Care Products as your name you will want to be able to buy the domain name www.rachelsdogcareproducts.com or www.rachelsdogcare.com for your website and email address.

Of course, many firms use one name for their company and a separate brand name for their products. Procter & Gamble doesn't use its company name on a single item. Kraft uses its name on some products (cheese, for example) and not others (Jell-O). The nice thing about separating your company name from your brand name is that if you have a product that doesn't take off–or fails catastrophically–you can drop that product line with minimal impact to the company image. Dropping New Coke was a bigger problem for Coca-Cola than dropping the Edsel was for Ford Motor Company. The same basic rules apply here as well: Catchy, easy to spell and pronounce, and descriptive are usually the best options.[15]

The Forms of Owned Media

So when you have worked out your organizational identity and brand, with all its meanings and promises, it is time to turn those important ideas into the basic items of your firm's owned media. While some elements are free, others will take some money up front. The following bulleted items list the key elements of creating your corporate identity:

- **Domain name, website, email, and app:** Today the selection of a company name that can become your **domain name** (what is typed after *www* in a web address) is essential to building your corporate identity. Most website packages will also let you use the domain name for your emails, so Jerome@Telesell.com becomes your email instead of Jerome6073@gmail.com. Using your domain name in your email address makes it look more professional and helps reinforce your company's identity. The details of selling via mail and email is discussed in the Chapter 11 section "Direct Mail and Its Variants."

  You can check if prospective names are available at at www.whois.net or at most web hosting companies' websites (search for "cheap web hosting" to find one), but if you find that a name you like is available, plan to buy it that day. There are firms paying each day to see what names were looked for, and they buy the names to resell them to you! Search for "cheap domains" to find low-cost domain name vendors. Many web hosting companies will give you the domain name free with a web hosting package. Unless you're planning to do e-commerce from day one, you can open up a "starter" type website (usually around five pages) for a low fee and upgrade as you get an idea of what your business really needs.[16]

domain name
The specific name of an Internet site, consisting of a name followed by *.com*, *.net*, or a similar code.

- **Logo:** Armed with your domain name and email you can start making business cards, and then websites and brochures (the print equivalent of your website). If you think a professional-looking logo would help, there are free do-it-yourself sites like www.logomaker.com or www.freelogodesign.org, or you can post for proposed logos on a site like www.upwork.com and offer a price ($25 is typical) for the logo you select. Most marketing and web design firms can help you in this area as well.
- **Phone lines:** You need that phone number to include on your business card and website. Think about getting a number that reflects your business–one tile company snagged a phone number it could display as 555-868-TILE (8453). One free service to consider is Google Voice, which will let you program one number to ring in multiple places or across multiple phones–or your PC or tablet. With these basics in place, you can get down to the serious business of advertising your product and service offerings.
- **Business cards and stationery:** These should have your firm's name, address, phone, website, and email address at a minimum. If you have the space, adding your slogan, Facebook, Twitter, or other company pages can be good ideas. Your business card may very well be your first advertisement. Use every opportunity to pass it out, not only to potential customers but also to friends and family who may also pass along your card (word-of-mouth advertising). Many places offer bulletin boards where you can post your card. Place several if permitted, in case a potential customer takes one. Your stationery puts your name and message in front of potential clients, existing clients, suppliers, and others. You need stationery and business cards anyway; you might as well make them work for you.
- **Brochures and flyers:** These pieces can be produced on your computer and printed with good results on most color desktop printers. Or they can be run off rather inexpensively at many copy centers. Both will give more information about your firm and products than your business card. The brochures and flyers can be as simple as a photocopied takeout menu or as complex as glossy four-color printed mini-catalogs. They can be passed out, posted on bulletin boards, enclosed in other mailings, or mass-mailed by themselves. We go more in-depth on catalogs and related techniques in Chapter 11.
- **Sales packets or marketing kits:** These materials provide potential customers an education in your product or service, including stories of customers whose problems were solved, FAQs (frequently asked questions), as well as a page on your products or services, and a page on you and your firm. These sheets can be printed on nice paper and put into a pocket folder with a sticker with your firm's name and address on it. If you're lucky, you may also be able to add customer-generated content to your site (a shared media on your owned site).
- **Online sales support materials:** Companies put a variety of materials on their websites to help potential and current customers connect to the products, services, and people. They include videos (think ads, how-to's speeches done by your experts and leaders, reposts of local TV news stories, etc.), newsletters, blogs, infographics, customer stories, employee stories, case studies, research, white papers, e-books, and pretty much anything people might see about your business or your thinking.
- **Signs:** Signs are also a form of advertising. They need to be large enough to be read by passing traffic and should reflect your firm. Homemade signs do not indicate high quality and professionalism. Consider lighting it at night–a must if you do business in evening hours. Changing messages keeps your customers' interest.[17]
- **Packaging:** For products, the packaging is the major way you market to purchasers. It is where you tell your brand story, the benefits you provide and the details of your product (e.g., ingredients, dimensions, etc.). Packaging can also include point-of-sale displays, racks, special signage, coupons, and the like. We discuss some examples of this in Chapter 11's coverage of direct sales techniques.
- **Promotional novelties**: Novelties range from key chains, pens, and coffee mugs to more expensive embossed briefcases and the like. Something like a pen or small calendar can be produced with your company's name and slogan for pennies in quantity. Fancier items may be given to key customers or potential key customers or as gifts to your employees. T-shirts, golf shirts, or other clothing can be given as gifts or worn by employees and your message

Entrepreneurs have promoted their businesses for ages. This sign is ageless, although depending on where you are, it might mean you are about to enter a coffee shop or a tea room, but either way it still works today. What kind of eye-catching sign could you create for your business?

tonyz20/Shutterstock

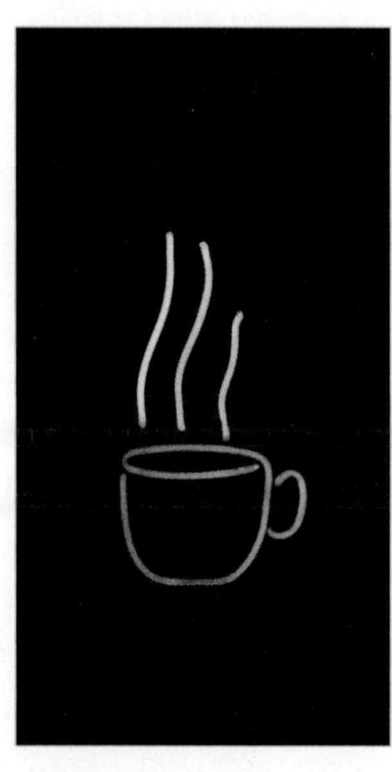

goes wherever the clothes are worn. Staples developed a whole marketing plan around the **succinct message** "Staples: That was easy" and created the Easy Button. This promotional novelty was so successful that it now sells the buttons in its stores.[18]

succinct message
The key point in as few and as memorable words as possible.

Social Media Embassies

The overlap of owned media and shared media is one of the most important parts of any small business's media strategy; it is where your firm has its own branded page on the different social media sites. There are your "embassies" on social media sites owned by firms like Facebook and Google. This includes the classic social media sites like Facebook, Twitter, LinkedIn, YouTube, Pinterest, Instagram, Vine, Google Currents, Snapchat, Periscope, and SlideShare. It includes **business directory sites** such as Google, Yahoo!, and yellowpages.com. It also includes **user review sites** like Yelp, Choice, Trustpilot, and others,[19] They also include catalogs, both online and in print, which are discussed in Chapter 11, and the 800-pound gorillas of retail, online sales platforms like Amazon, eBay, Etsy, and others, which combine online catalogs and extensive user ratings, Q&A, and comments rivaling other types of social media platforms.

For the sites that are most popular with your customers, you will want to keep an eye on the online feeds. Postings to these sites can give you an early warning of potential problems, and gives you a platform from which to handle the problem. Solving a problem on your social platform will be seen by other customers and build your credibility and their trust in you. Even when things are going well online, responding positively to customers who post rewards them and increases everyone's engagement with your business. Most of these platforms will send you notifications of new postings to help you stay on top, or you can use a **social media management platform** like Hootsuite.com, or even pay a customer, friend, or family member to keep an eye on the sites for you and alert you when action is needed.

business directory sites
Online services that provide the equivalent of the old telephone directory, listing businesses, their websites, phone numbers, and other information for prospective customers.

user review sites
Online sites where customers and users of products and services can post their opinions, rating, and experiences for others to see. Smart companies track these sites and respond to customers' reviews on these sites.

Shared Media

Shared media is the ultimate form of free advertising. It happens when people post on their personal social media accounts about your firm or its products or services. Talking to friends, family, or co-workers is what you hope for. If you ask most service providers how they get business, the answer is usually referrals or **word of mouth**.[20] Carter Prescott, head of New York–based Carter Communications, which provides high-level writing and speaking services for Fortune 500 clients, doesn't even have a listed phone number. "I've never needed one," she says. "It's better to have people call you on their own, rather than soliciting calls anyway. You get a better client that way." She gets calls only when a current client gives her number to a potential client.

A word-of-mouth-related opportunity is when customers share their stories about your business. This can happen in person or online on social media sites where there is the possibility of buzz or **viral marketing**. You or one of your customers may post a message, picture, or video on their own account (or your business's Facebook or Twitter account). When a potential customer hears of the business from a trusted friend, a connection is established that cannot be matched by advertising or other marketing methods. If others start sharing, you benefit. If the sharing becomes explosive, with thousands or even millions of people seeing and sharing the material, you've "gone viral." That is the home run of Internet and word-of-mouth marketing.

Creating and leveraging hashtags is a popular way to increase the viral impact of your business. Hashtags are words with an added "#" at the front. They can get added to social media posts, and are searchable and countable across different social media platforms. Google "small business hashtags" to see the range possible. Thinking of gyms and personal trainers, these could include terms like #fitnessfriday, #wellnesswednesday, #getfit, #workout, #crossfit, and more that you would include in your social media postings. The goal is to use hashtags that connect with how your customers might think of your business. As you create hashtags of your own, you can register them at twubs.com to show when you started using it. It is possible to trademark a hashtag, but the idea is to make hashtags as available as possible to get the broadest awareness and use.

Some say that going viral can only occur naturally. But it may be possible for you to get a small-scale virus going. For example, imagine our day-care center owner posts on her Facebook page a short video titled "How to get your child ready for his or her first day at day care." The customers on the Facebook page like it enough to pass it on to their friends, who pass it on, and suddenly a reporter at the local TV station sees it and asks the owner for an interview. In the

social media management platform
An online service that captures and displays the feeds from your social media platforms and makes it easy to post across multiple platforms, schedule posts on different platforms, and help you see social media statistics. Free and freemium examples include Hootsuite, Buffer, Tweetdeck, SocialOomph, and Followerwonk.

word of mouth
A means of spreading information about your business through the comments friends and customers make to other potential customers.

viral marketing
Any electronic equivalent of word-of-mouth advertising, in which the advertiser's message spreads quickly and widely via email, website, blogs, and other online tools.

interview, the reporter mentions the video and links to it from the TV station's website. Suddenly the owner is the top day-care expert in Phoenix. Think about that when you see the local news.

Media Partnerships

Just as individuals are better off when they band together, so are businesses. There are all sorts of membership organizations for businesses–chambers of commerce or local business organizations that focus on all firms in a particular geographic area, **trade or professional associations** (see Skill Module 3.1) who focus on people in particular lines of work (e.g., all auto repair shops, or all physical therapists), organizations that focus on political issues such as international trade, climate change, safety, taxation, or improving transportation systems. Firms may join these efforts, and even display their membership on their websites and in their publications. For the firm, it provides access to a network with shared interests and knowledge, and can be a way to learn about the leading-edge and best practices in their own field. Note some of these memberships cost, but increasingly, memberships (especially for Internet-based organizations) are based more on a freemium model where donations or memberships are optional.

trade association
(also known as *professional association*). A group of people in the same industry who band together to gather and share information and present and represent the industry to the public and government.

sponsorships
Paying for a local organization's needs in exchange for recognition.

co-branding
When two companies or brands combine to create a new product or service that combines both brands, such as Nike's LeBron sneakers.

co-marketing
A type of media partnership where two products jointly pay to advertise together. Usually this is when customers use the two products together, like chips and salsa.

influencer
A customer role describing a person or group who can make credible or recognized suggestions or recommendations to others regarding purchase choices.

But there are a multitude of other ways to partner. Consider the photo below of a street fair. How did it come about? Quite often, it is the store owners on the street who decide to jointly throw and promote the fair as a way to promote their businesses to a bigger audience in a bigger way. For them this form of advertising is called a **sponsorship**. The more businesses involved, the more sharing of the news, the more customers involved, and the more booths selling products or services, which draw even bigger crowds.

There are other forms of media partnership. Consider the business that lets you put up a poster for your product or service in its window, or the restaurant that mentions you as a food provider on its menu. Any mention of your firm, your product, or your service by another organization is a type of promotional partnership. These efforts can get much more involved. For example, **co-branding** occurs where two companies combine their products. Nike's LeBron Soldier sneakers are an example of co-branding between the person and the manufacturer. A variant of this is **co-marketing** where two companies with similar audiences combine their marketing efforts to improve their impact. A famous example was a 2018 Super Bowl ad for Doritos and Mountain Dew, www.youtube.com/watch?v=rZh_CbcVe7M.

A key type of media partnership comes from dealing with **influencers.** These are people producing content on social media platforms with the idea of getting a circle of readers and subscribers far beyond their personal circle of friends. This can be organized as a blog, a YouTube channel (which may also be called a vlog), or a profile on Instagram, Snapchat, or Facebook. Influencers talk about products and services, and they are generally very open to considering new things. You can find influencers by asking your customers for the people they follow, or you can Google it (using our day care example, type in "top parent influencers phoenix" and you'll see things like "The 10 Best Mom Blogs in Phoenix." Or try Googling "blog directory." You can also use influencer management platforms such as AspireIQ.com, Buzzsumo.com, or Dealspotr.com.[21]

Street Fair in Seattle
Most times, these fairs are put together by vendors on the hosting street, as a partnership that leads to more business for everyone.

Tom Mareschal/Alamy Stock Photo

Influencers get segmented by the size of their networks—macro-influencers have more than 10,000 subscribers, micro-influencers fewer. As you might guess, shout-outs by macro-influencers will cost more, but think about who your target audience is.[22] A micro-influencer might be the best fit for your intended audience. And not all influencers need to be paid all the time. If the influencer believes in your product or service, or in you because of your approach or message, the influencer may promote your brand for free, thinking it will benefit his or her subscribers. Internet marketer Kipp Bodnar[23] suggests providing blog-ready materials like answers to a blogger's readers' likely questions, aggregating and interpreting industry statistics, or making lists or charts the blogger can quickly incorporate in the next posting (e.g., "Top 5 Items for Your Preschooler's Backpack").

If you can get the bloggers or other influencers to like your product or service, they are more likely to mention it. Sending them your press release (more on that follows) might work if it is relevant, but a sample of your product might be better. Do some research on the sites to decide which to target. You can get some idea about the range of these sort of sites from the Learn More Online box below.[24]

LEARN MORE ONLINE

Below are major influencer sites for a variety of industries:

Urban life: **http://coolhunting.com**

Furniture: **http://mocoloco.com**

Tools: **http://kk.org/cooltools/**

Fashion: **www.refinery29.com**

Luxury items: **http://pursuitist.com**

Electronics: **http://gizmodo.com** or **https://thewirecutter.com**

Green products: **www.treehugger.com**

The whole idea of connecting businesses to blogs has itself spawned entrepreneurship opportunities. There are sites where entrepreneurs can solicit and pay for blog posts. Examples include Payu2blog.com, Seekvisibility.com, and Blogsvertise.com—which are blog focused but not free for all services. These firms connect entrepreneurs hoping to be featured on blogs with bloggers who don't mind some extra cash for mentioning their products. These firms state that they ask bloggers for an honest review; the companies don't specify whether the content needs to be positive. In other words, you can even get paid for complaining about a product or service.[25]

There are other types of media partnerships that can be important not only for promotion but also because of the things you believe are important. For example, what charities or causes are important to you, your employees, or your customers? You might partner by promoting their events and campaigns. In return, you may be displayed or mentioned as a supporter.

donations
Monetary or other gifts to organizations or people who are in need.

Donations are the other paying forward approach, and do not need to be millions of dollars. Small businesses can give their time, their connections, their services, or products. We've all seen small businesses performing **community service** helping clean up a site, or staff a tent at a public event. We've seen a firm sponsor employees reading to older adults, or supporting scout troops or athletic teams or programs. Groceries and restaurants routinely donate food at the end of the day. An in-kind donation of product, service, or cash to a charity event may get your name in the program. Doing good this way may not result in instant publicity, but can be worked into company history or biographical information and is an example of a **virtuous cycle**.[26]

community service
Activities undertaken to help support, repair or improve the community, its institutions, infrastructures, or people. Examples include clean-up days, disaster relief, or helping-your-neighbor efforts, among others.

virtuous cycle
Situations where one good turn invites a another one from someone else are called virtuous cycles.

Earned Media

Earned media occurs when other organizations (like corporations or mass media outlets) talk about you, your firm, or your products or services and you didn't pay them directly for the mentions (those instances are paid media, which is discussed later). Getting other people in the media to talk about you and your business is one of the best ways to get potential customers'

free ink
Mentions of your company or products in the media for which your firm did not pay.

attention. Since the days of newspapers, this has been called **free ink** because getting the local gossip columnist to mention your restaurant got your name in ink but didn't cost you hard dollars (although it might have meant the gossip columnist got a free meal from you).

In reality, like so much of the media landscape, you can do it yourself, generally for no cost but your time, or you can pay others to assist you or take it over entirely. But today there are more ways than ever to get free ink, and it goes far beyond newspapers. In addition to influencer and partner relations already discussed, there are three types of earned media we will talk about here: media relations, public relations, and investor relations. In Chapter 11 we will cover guerrilla marketing.

newsworthy events
To garner serious attention from the media and the public, a news story needs to deliver certain essentials that will hold their attention and keep your news in their thoughts. It should have public recognition, importance, and interest.

Media Relations The basics of getting free ink dovetail nicely with the ideas behind building press relations. These generally relate to paid media–TV, radio, newspapers, newsletters, and magazines in particular–but your goal is to get free ink from them. Like bloggers, the easier you make it for the press to find and create the story, the more likely they are to use it. For the press, a key issue is how **newsworthy** your material is. A news story needs to deliver certain essentials that will hold readers' attention and keep your news (and the press outlet's brand) in their thoughts. It should have public recognition, public importance, or public interest. These are detailed in Exhibit 10.1.

Even though something is "new," it might not have enough of the three "essentials" above to grab the attention you had hoped. For example, most hires don't hold importance for the media. Even new products aren't newsworthy unless they are something new and innovative on the market. Since you are a small firm and perhaps local in scope, national media are probably a tougher sale for you (unless you have invented the next Google, YouTube, or other breakthrough technology). But most communities have local media outlets promoting local businesses. Local television stations like to feature stories as fillers in their newscasts–especially if the story is newsworthy, of human interest, humorous, or generally "feel-good." Look at the example tied to Red Jett Sweets's "Cupcake Wars" participation at www.youtube.com/watch?v=sxD82ooE38U. Note that your professional or trade magazines are always looking for stories from firms in their target industry, and are a good place to get broad exposure, especially if you're selling to businesses. Refer back to Skill Module 3.1 to find those sources.

EXHIBIT 10.1

The Three Factors of Newsworthiness

1. **Public recognition**
   - **Issue recognition**: Have you solved a problem, maybe even one they didn't know about until now?
   - **Trendiness**: What's new and great?
   - **Famous faces**: People you should know about.
   - **Proximity**: Important things near you.
2. **Public importance**
   - **Power**: Changes in current or future leaders.
   - **Currency**: What's happening now?
3. **Public interest**
   - **Good story**: A situation full of drama.
   - **Human interest**: A character or situation to which we can personally relate.
   - **Visuals**: Fires, fashion, kids, animals, action—the things that make for good photos and videos.
   - **Cultural resonance**: A moment likely to be remembered by us all or one that captures a moment of time we'll appreciate.

As we did when we profiled your customers, make a list of these media and then determine which ones are most likely to carry the sorts of news you offer. Treat them as if they are your customers. Find out the main contact people, their phone numbers, and do a Google search to see what stories they cover and find out more about them. See if you can identify any preferences they have as to how they like the information delivered (hint: it is usually on their website). Some will prefer that you write the story and let them edit. Others will prefer to send out their own reporters. Many major media outlets have a **media kit** (also called a *press kit*) on their website that provides their publication schedule, topics, readership, and ad rates.[27] You can see an example at mediakit.inc.com.

These days, small and start-up businesses can (and should) make something similar to share with the media to let them know all about your business. We'll call these **business profile kits**. The typical small business profile kit includes brochures, business cards, product information, and other materials that can provide background material for a reporter. It is usually built around a new press release that you think would be of interest to the media outlet. If done in print or email, it should include a letter of introduction and may include a brief history of the firm (sometimes called the "about us" page), and information about the owner and other key managers. Include other press releases, articles, and newspaper clippings and other materials about the firm. Consider including a "frequently asked questions" page, information about awards, audio and videos of television, or radio interviews. If appropriate, include samples of your products, camera-ready logo art, statistics specific to your industry or target market, photos, and even an order form–it could be your next customer![28] Whenever you run across a new media outlet appropriate to your clientele, send them your business profile kit.

The other piece of material you will want to develop is the **press release**, which is usually the centerpiece of your business profile kit, and the reason it is being sent out when it is to the intended recipients (i.e., you want them to do a newsworthy story about your firm, right about now). The press release is the key method for telling your business story.[29] Entrepreneurs can use the AIDA (attention, interest, desire, and action) formula to write press releases well.

media kit
A type of specialized web page or sales-material-based package (hard copy or PDF) sent to media outlets that is focused on telling them about your company and its story. These are often built around a press release for something of potential current interest to the media outlet. Also called a *press kit*.

business profile kit
The name for the media kit you create for your own business (to distinguish it in your mind from the media kits of other organizations).

press release
A written announcement intended to draw news media attention to a specific event.

- **Attention:** Get their attention with a catchy headline. Something clever or a play on words may do the trick. It needs to be short–no longer than 10 words and preferably less. Sometimes a subtitle may be used, especially if the attention-getting title may not give enough information. For example, "Udderly Delicious: Dairy Marketing in Venezuela"[30] is the example of a clever title–a pun–and a subtitle to explain what the article is really about. Try to strike an emotional chord with your readers. Empathize or address a problem they have and you may draw their attention further.[31]
- **Interest:** While the title should start to pique their interest, the opening paragraph should really capture them. This first paragraph should include the *who, what, when, where, why*, and *how* of the story. If you are really good, you can get all that in the opening sentence. The idea is to "hook" them and get them to read further.
- **Desire:** Now provide the meat of the press release–details that tell us more about the opening information and increase our interest. Depending on what your press release is about, this could include features of your new products, or some biographical information on the new person you hired. Start with the most important information in the story because editors frequently delete ending materials to fit space. Quotes from key people from outside the company can imply third-party endorsements.
- **Action:** At the end you put contact information. Where can they find out more about your wonderful new product, your exciting new vice president, or this fantastic company that just won an award? The goal is to get them to be potential clients; kind of hard if they don't know where to find you!

These days there are online templates to help you write your press release like toolkit.prnewswire.com/pressreleasewizard. Once you have developed your press release, there are a variety of websites that can assist you in sending or emailing your press release to the appropriate media. These include:

- Your local TV and radio stations, newspapers (including neighborhood and business or specialty newspapers if they're relevant to what you're offering).

- In terms of regional and national notice you can try:
  - Press release sites: Google "press release sites" and look for free and paid services.
  - Newspapers: ABYZ News Links (www.abyznewslinks.com) contains links to more than 17,200 newspapers and other news sources from around the world.
  - Blogs: Blogarama.com has hundreds of thousands of blogs categorized, and you can Google "blog directory" to find others.[32] To see one approach to getting out press releases to bloggers, look at Justin Wilcox's own blog post on Customerdevlabs.com.[33]

There are other forms for sharing your story and ideas with the public and professional media. These include providing interviews or brief podcasts in areas where you would be expected to be expert, or offering a tour of your facility or some place newsworthy (e.g., you have a cleaning service and you offer to let a TV camera crew join you to see the first assessment of flood damage of a home). The goal is to get the attention of the press, and the more innovative you can be, the better your chances. Novelty sells!

Public Relations Public relations includes publicity and other forms of communication so that the public and important stakeholders gets a favorable opinion about your firm. This list includes government, education systems, special-interest groups, neighbors to the firm, competition, other business in general, employees and potential employees, investors, and, of course, potential clients. That's a lot of places to build a favorable view.

It isn't an easy or straightforward process. Many people regard public relations stories skeptically: "Of course they will tell us only the good things and not the bad." Some feel that these stories are a thinly veiled advertisement. Also, these are very difficult to control. A firm may spend many hours and resources developing and submitting press releases or other publicity and the news media may never use them. Or, often worse yet, the news media will edit the press release to the point that the original intent is totally distorted.

Public relations are those things you do to help create a favorable opinion of your firm in the mind of people in general. For most businesses, the more people who know about your business the better, but this works only if people have a positive opinion about your firm. Often it is easy to do things that help get you a favorable opinion from others. Activities you undertake that show your willingness to help others, through pitching in or sharing time or expertise, can do a lot to build favorable public opinion.

For example, we talked about donations and community service above. Similarly, sponsorships can be a good way to get the word out about your firm. Your budget will not cover renaming a local major league baseball stadium, but it might put your name on the back of a T-ball team's uniforms in a neighborhood where your target market lives and plays. This spreads

This basketball tournament will raise money for and awareness of the needs of amputees, and was put on by an entrepreneur whose friend is an amputee. What other ways can small businesses generate positive publicity?

Realistic Reflections

goodwill among the local community and might even be picked up in the press. If a community group has a program that would attract your target market, approach the group about sponsorship. Unexpected money is often the most persuasive to sponsored organizations.

There is another approach for building positive public awareness of your business—creating a publicity event. This works best if it is tied into what you sell. Additionally, it is likely to get more press if the idea is not seen as self-promotion. For example, Immaculate Baking Company baked the world's largest cookie—100 feet in diameter and 40,000 pounds. This put it in the *Guinness Book of World Records* but also generated publicity. What made it even better was that Immaculate Baking tied this into a fundraiser for the construction of a local folk art museum. Sales went from about $500,000 to over $7 million and the museum gained $20,000 in donations.[34] Even simple approaches can pay handsome dividends. Hold an open house or a tour. Have a booth at a local street fair. Celebrate Grover Cleveland's birthday with special activities throughout the day. You can even hold seminars or programs on issues of immediate interest when your firm has topical expertise, or you can give your site to the media as a place to film outside the studio, but if you do, make sure your signs are visible. These approaches are not the only ones possible. Others can be found in the following The Thoughtful Entrepreneur.

Investor Relations Investor relations apply the above ideas to a group crucial to your business' survival—your investors. Even if you don't have actual equity investors, you are certain to have a group of stakeholders in your business. These include investors, advisers, mentors, companies with whom you have important relationships (your largest customer, a key supplier, etc.). Your goal with these stakeholders is to convey the good news about your business, show how you appreciate and use their support, and if there are things you want them to know or be aware of, let them know before the general public finds out.

THE THOUGHTFUL ENTREPRENEUR

TIPS FOR GENERATING PUBLICITY[35]

OK, you are convinced that publicity is great for your firm; what can you do that's newsworthy and likely to be picked up by the news media? The following are based on suggestions by Margie Fisher, the president of Zable Fisher Public Relations:

- Create a holiday: Why shouldn't February be National Roofing Month—even if it's only on your signs, banners, and advertising?
- Write a book: So what if it is self-published and you give it away rather than sell it? It still establishes you as an expert.
- Apply for business awards and send out press releases when you win.
- Get on a reality show or game show: Even a three-sentence introduction can mention that you are the owner of XZY Plumbing in Sarasota, Florida.
- Put on an educational workshop: Ginger's Quilt Shop of Upland, California, offers all sorts of free or reduced price classes in quilting or related activities and if you happen to want to buy your supplies at her shop, that's fine.
- Produce a printed or electronic newsletter: Realtors are great at sending out newsletters all about buying, maintaining, and selling houses and just mentioning that if your plans include buying or selling, to let them know.
- Create a contest with a twist: A camera shop could run a contest for the worst picture ever taken. A veterinarian could offer a free checkup for the homeliest pet.
- Do pro bono work: Clients who get your service for free also practice word-of-mouth advertising.

Most often investor relations in small businesses tends to build from personal contacts, supplemented by emails, often with supporting documents. The goal is to keep investors and other stakeholders up-to-speed on your business, its successes and challenges. For investors, you have a fiduciary responsibility to inform them, because they own a part of your business. For nonequity stakeholders, if you are concerned something is happening or is about to happen that will complicate your relationship with them, it is better to alert them about the pending challenge and explain how you plan to handle it. When possible, you try and do this before it becomes a crisis, but if it does become a crisis, recall the six steps for handling them introduced in Chapter 3.

It helps to communicate on a standard schedule. Two, 3, or 4 times a year is typical, while some firms may connect monthly. If something comes up, don't wait for the regular posting, get the word out. In terms of impact, a face-to-face meeting is best, followed by a phone call, or an email. Tweets and text messages probably will not give you the space to get your point across.

In your regular communications,[36] you want to share the firm's wins. You want to remind them of your firm's purpose and passions. Talk about the value you provide over and above financial returns. Invite them to reach out to you with any questions or thoughts. And always ask if there is something you can do for them.

Media Integration

This category comes from the overlap of earned media and paid media, and represents efforts you pay for to help generate earned media attention. One example you have no doubt seen are contests or sweepstakes sponsored by companies. Today using social media, it is easier than ever to set up a contest on Facebook, Instagram, or Snapchat (or use contest platforms like Sideqik, Wyng, or Woobox to automate this process across platforms), get the word out to your own network, encourage respondents to share your contest link with their friends, and alert relevant influencers about the contest in hopes they mention it. For these efforts, your goal should be getting new prospects or customers and growing your engagement with your existing customers.

Prizes need to be credible—think of a free cupcake from Red Jett Sweets in Chapter 8. Think about what you want beyond an email address; consider asking for submissions like fan photos, fun photos, testimonials, new taglines, or other materials to use in your own social media and advertising.[37] To give you an idea of how this works, Todd Giannattasio described in *Entrepreneur* magazine a contest he ran for a client who had a candy shop and was giving away candy as prizes. The campaign resulted in 623 signups, but 1,851 friends of these people also participated. A campaign costing $101.08 for paid promotion on social media generated 2,474 signups or 4 cents a sign-up.[38]

lead generation The promotional technique of obtaining prospective customers through paid and unpaid efforts to obtain contact information from people with the plan to send these prospects advertisements or other messages in hopes of getting them to become customers.

advertorial Typically a paid advertisement from a company written in the form of an editorial, making the company's point about an issue, and published in the mass media.

OOH Stands for "out of home" and refers to advertising people will encounter when away from home. This includes posters, digital and print ads in transit shelters, at airports and venues with major foot traffic, and digital and conventional billboards and signage.

Contests are a specific form of the key media integration technique of **lead generation** which involves paying for mailing lists of potential customers, or selecting target markets or buying subscriber lists on social media sites to whom advertisements will be shown. These techniques can be free (think of gathering addresses or business cards at an event) or paid, as in the case of custom mailing lists (search for "mailing list suppliers" or "mailing list brokers" to find these).[39] The other media integration technique is placing **advertorials,** editorial-like articles paid for by your business, making a case for something important to your firm and hopefully a subset of your current or future customers.[40]

Paid Media

Because of the Internet, today's entrepreneurs have never had so many ways to promote their businesses. Traditional media like advertisements in magazines and on billboards can now appear all over web pages. Commercials on TV can also appear on the web on YouTube, Facebook, and more. Door hangers with your coupon can be supplemented with local campaigns on Groupon, Facebook, or Google My Business to focus on particular cities or even neighborhoods. There are more places to put the name of your firm or product than ever before—from every square inch of a NASCAR racer's uniform, to the poles of turnstiles at the amusement park, to pop-ups inside your YouTube video. Table 10.1 gives you an overview of the many forms of paid media available to you.

TABLE 10.1 Traditional and Online Promotional Techniques

Promotional Video (Good for Building Awareness)	Traditional Media	Online Equivalent
Commercials	1-, 5-, 10-, 15-, 30-, 60-second spots	Online/social media video
On-screen logo overlays	Overlayed on-screen ads	Overlay ads in videos, hotlinked logos in videos and photos
Dedicated programming	Infomercials	Online infomercials (same placements as commercials), podcasts, e-books, white papers
Product placements	In movies, on TV, cable, streaming services, and pay- per-view	In online games, videos
Audio		
Radio	Commercials, infomercials	Audio commercials, infomercials, podcasts
Print (Best for Complex Information)		
Forms with company identity	Stationery, business cards, business forms	Company website, Facebook page, LinkedIn page, Twitter page, custom URLs for these, custom emails with firm's name
Ads	1/8- to full-page ads	Online ads
Paid specially placed ads	Newspaper or magazine ads placed by section and day/edition, code for ad responses, phonebook ads	Online ads placed by search results or matched to content (e.g., Google AdWords, Facebook ads), track click-through rates, cookies, or code for ad responses, targeted email, opt-in options on websites
Search results	Phonebooks	Websites appearing as a result of a search (called "organic" results if they come up on their own, "paid" or "sponsored" if you pay for first-screen placement)
Included ads	Blown-in/copackaged ads	Pop-up ads
Classified ads	Classified ads	Craigslist (and competitors') ads, newspapers' online ads
Customer newsletters	Mailed newsletters	Emailed/online newsletters, RSS feeds, blogs, Facebook postings, Twitter tweets
Sponsorships	Sponsorship in ads and commercials	Sponsorship on websites, emails, videos, links, online games
Sales promotions	Coupons (in newspaper, Valpak, etc.), customer sales mailings, contests, sweepstakes, etc.	Online coupons (Retailmenot, Coupons.com, or Groupon), emailed sale announcements, online contests and sweepstakes
Locational Promotion		
Basic location design	Store, storefront	Website, store pages on Google, Yelp, Bing, Yellowpages.com, Facebook, etc.
In-store promotions	Sales displays, in-store coupons, in-store scannable QR codes	Pop-up displays and coupons, store-specific mobile apps with coupons and sale info
OOH (out-of-home) ad placements	Shelter ads, wall posters, transit placements, digital place ads, billboards	Search engine results placements and portal ads
Network Advertising		
Referral promotions	Coupons for friends, shopping together specials	Invite/refer a friend, share links, Facebook "Likes," Twitter hashtags, social bookmarking (e.g., Digg, Reddit)
Mass exposure	Billboards	Banner ads on major websites and search engine results
Reciprocal advertising	Reciprocal ads	Reciprocal links

As you can imagine, given the enormous number of ways to advertise it is impossible to give you detailed information on the ins and outs of each type of advertising technique. In fact there are semester-long courses in advertising in most business programs, with whole textbooks going through the many forms. You can get a lot of information online from reputable sources such as **www.entrepreneur.com**, **www.inc.com**, **www.mashable.com**, and **https://ducttapemarketing.com/blog/**. What we can do here and in our more detailed discussion of advertising in Chapter 11 is help get you started in advertising your business. So we will talk about the first steps you take—those you need to pay for and those you can do for free.

From your prior workups of customer interviews, customer profile, value proposition, target market, and market segmentation, you should have a clear idea of your intended audience. You should have some idea of where they get their information—from TV, radio, newspapers, magazines, direct advertising like mail, or the Internet—and how much they use and trust each of these vehicles. From this, you can begin to think about how to structure your mix as soon as you add one more item—price!

Advertising costs are usually based on cost per thousand (CPM—the *M* is the Latin *mille* or thousand). Figure 10.5 shows you CPMs for a number of different forms of paid advertising. What the chart doesn't show, but you need to keep in mind, is that one ad impression is unlikely to do the job. Marketers talk about needing 15 to 20 impressions for people in the general audience to notice and remember who you are. This is why you will notice that commercials are repeated so often on TV and radio. The companies are trying to get enough impressions to you so that you recall their product.

Taking a look at the graphic and knowing the underlying need for ad repetitions, you can quickly see that major advertising campaigns using traditional media are problematic for small businesses—they are just too costly for most start-ups. How can you build an advertising campaign on a limited budget?

For companies whose products have a regional, national, or global audience, there is no real competition to the Internet, with the possible exception of a Yellow Pages listing. You need to

FIGURE 10.5

Cost per 1,000 Impressions for a Variety of Paid Media Used in Promotional Campaigns

Source: "PJ Solomon US Major Media CPM Comparison," *The Media Monthly*, March 2019, p. 124, www.pjsolomon.com/wp-content/uploads/2019/03/March-2019-PJ-SOLOMON-Media-Monthly.pdf.

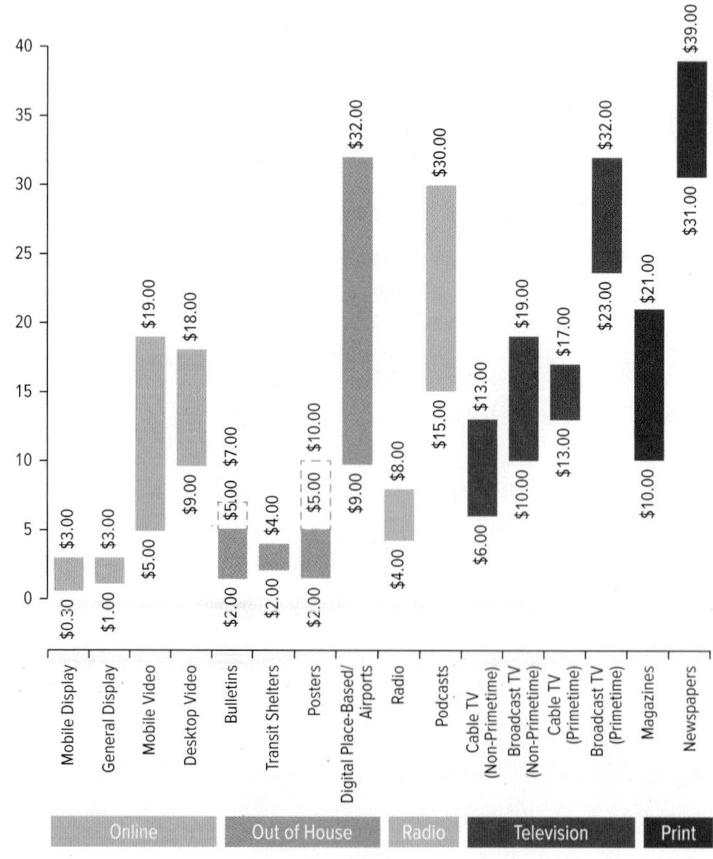

consider putting your company on the major web services your customers are likely to use: search engines like Google, Bing, and Yahoo!, and social media sites like Facebook, LinkedIn, Twitter, Pinterest, Instagram, and Snapchat. Some will let you put up a business page for free; some will charge. All will charge you for ads, but it could be worth it, depending on how you approach it. Your ad could be seen by millions around the world every hour, or by a few hundred people in your town searching for your keyword. Even without paid ads, your business website on say, Facebook, could help you. If a customer of yours "Likes" your Facebook page, all of his or her Facebook connections will see that, which can explosively add to your growth. Typically your pages on these social networking websites always link back to your main website, so that customers can easily use all your web resources and grow their connection to your business.

But because those paid Internet ads depend on how often they get shown, you will want to limit who sees the ad to people in particular localities, or people who have searched for a term linked to your product, or people online on certain days or times of day. You will be able to check how many people react to the ad by their click-through rate, the frequency with which they click your ad for more information or to buy the product. You can also test multiple forms of the ad in a day (called A/B testing), and adjust the ad as you learn what works best with your target audience. The key to this is using the existing business services on the major websites, like Google Analytics, which is shown in Skill Module 10.2.

Getting Started with Google Analytics

SKILL MODULE 10.2

The real value of Internet advertising is that you can see how it works, so you can tell what attracts customers and what they do on your site. Google (**support.google.com/analytics**) and Facebook (**www.facebook.com/business**) have developed extensive websites full of articles and videos to help you develop, deploy, and understand how your marketing efforts work on their platforms. Instagram, Pinterest, and Twitter also offer services, but generally it works best to learn the basics on Google or Facebook and then use the more bare-bones approaches of the other sites.[41] A great site with guides for Google, Facebook, and Instagram is **https://adespresso.com/guides/**.

For Google, there are two related sites you'll want to work with: Google Analytics and Google AdWords (**ads.google.com**). You will need to register for both, but registration is free. Start with Analytics, which tells you who has visited your website. It will know because your first step is to paste code from Analytics on every page of your site you want to track. Step two is to set goals for your online campaign (e.g., get people to view at least two pages on your site, sell to 1 visitor out of 100, etc.). The measurements for these goals are often called **key performance indicators (KPIs)**.

Step three is to add in Google AdWords. AdWords lets you analyze keywords (including those used by your competitors) and purchase ads on Google, which can be based on very specific keywords, demographics (age, gender, location, etc.), and interest profiles such as gamers or parents. Competing sites offer similar capabilities. Note that you can use the AdWords app to research keywords to help optimize your own site's search engine position without having to buy AdWords. There are also independent sources like **keywordtool.io** or **www.wordstream.com/keywords**.

The fourth step is to return to Google Analytics to track and analyze your results. Analytics will show your **organic traffic**, the people who came to your site without you paying for the link that brought them there, as well as traffic brought in from your paid-for sources. It will show actions in the site and the demographics of the people who showed up.

You can learn more about this (and even get online training leading to certification) at **support.google.com/analytics**. To learn more about online marketing in general, you can download the e-book *eMarketing: The Essential Guide to Marketing in a Digital World* for free at **https://open.umn.edu/opentextbooks/textbooks/emarketing-the-essential-guide-to-marketing-in-a-digital-world**, or try some of these how-to sites recommended by entrepreneur and social media expert Ron Roy of **Winesthatrock.com**:

- **SocialBakers.com:** Lots of social media insight, marketing tips, and case studies.
- **SocialMediaExaminer.com:** One of the best "how-to" social media websites.
- **KissMetrics.com:** Tracking tools if you want to take your social reach to the next level.

key performance indicators (KPIs)
Measures or metrics that identify the outcomes that are most important to the success of a business. While outcomes like sales or products produced are KPIs, events leading up to these are also usually considered key, like customers coming to your store or website for sales, or number of products started.

organic traffic
People who come to your website based on their own actions (e.g., typing in your URL, clicking on a link mentioning your site on a web page, or clicking on a search engine finding based on where your site naturally—or "organically"—appears in the search results) where you have not paid for the link. It is also called *unpaid search*.

Services like Google AdWords and Facebook for Business let you focus your paid ads in a relatively small geographic area. Recall we explored how to do this using Facebook Audience Insights in Skill Module 9.5. Services like Valpak and competing local coupon-mailing or door-hanging services offer a similar service using traditional print media. For our day-care center, we could use Google AdWords for people searching for "day care" or "child care" in the local area and supplement that with mailed coupons in areas of town we know have families with children. We could then supplement these with the free techniques discussed next. We also could check locally for neighborhood newspapers where we might place ads, as well as church and school newsletters, which tend to be very low cost.

But as great as web-based advertising is, it is worthwhile only if your intended target audience is on the Internet on sites where you can advertise to them. The story of AO Rafting in the following Small Business Insight shows a powerful way to leverage the web. For our day-care

SMALL BUSINESS INSIGHT

Whitewater Marketing[42]

Digital Vision/Getty Images

A business website doesn't win awards because it has cool features and bells and whistles that are part of many websites. It has to work for both the customers and the company. Rated as one of the top sites according to *Inc.* magazine, that's what really distinguishes the website of AO Rafting (**www.aorafting.com**). Established by a schoolteacher over 50 years ago, the company All-Outdoors Whitewater Rafting, or AO Rafting, is a multigenerational family business. It's a regional company in a seasonal business, with about $2 million in annual revenues and fewer than 20 permanent employees year-round. However, during its eight-month annual season, AO Rafting employs more than 100 people including some 75 part-time guides. Based in Walnut Creek and Lotus, California, right by the mother lode that drew the forty-niners out west for the Gold Rush, this business seems isolated, deep in canyon country. Yet, it has built a web presence that puts to shame a lot of other small businesses that may be more tech-savvy and have greater resources. Prospective customers can tour the Klamath and Tuolumne Rivers through the site's virtual tours. They can also plan trips right on the site, check the availability of tours, make reservations, access real-time information on water conditions, refer the company to friends, and find discounts on trips. The site has virtually replaced almost all the traditional marketing and promotion that All-Outdoors Whitewater Rafting used to do.

center in Phoenix, we could limit online ads to people in Phoenix who search for terms such as "day care."

When you think about spending money to buy advertising space, especially when we are talking about traditional media like TV, radio, and print, it can make a lot of sense to also allocate some money to have advertising professionals prepare your ads. There are small advertising and marketing agencies virtually everywhere (and if you are comfortable working with an online ad agency, they literally could be virtually everywhere). Most good ones will show you a portfolio of their work, and hopefully you can check them out with their other clients. Most will also give you a cost estimate to help you determine quickly if you can afford them.

This can also apply to your Internet ads, especially if you are planning to develop videos or want interactive websites with state-of-the art graphics, or if having a stylish site is central to the image you want your firm to project. Otherwise, many people using the Internet seem to prefer the less professional ads that give you the sense of a personal connection to the entrepreneur at some other computer on the World Wide Web. On the other hand, you may want to hire some professional help in order to make your website appear high up on search results, through the techniques of **search engine optimization (SEO)**. Identifying the best **keywords and description tags** to your web pages can be extremely useful, especially if you are new to the intricacies of the World Wide Web.

But a key decision is who and how often your Internet pages will get checked and refreshed. While these sites are free and interactive, giving you a way to exchange ideas and opinions with one another, if you are going to be serious about using these free networks, you need to be consistent about living up to your social obligations. Checking Facebook, LinkedIn, or Twitter every morning and afternoon is necessary, and you need to not only check what is happening, but to keep the site's content fresh with new postings at least a couple of times a week. A dormant Facebook or Twitter account actually hurts your business reputation because it seems like you don't care.

search engine optimization (SEO)
Techniques applied to web pages in order to obtain favorable placement on Internet search page results.

keywords and description tags
Terms included in the hidden portion of a web page (called the *document head*) that are used by search engines such as Yahoo! and Google to describe your website and evaluate its focus and category placement.

Incentive Media

This, the last of the nine elements of the PESO model, focuses on the overlap between paid media and owned media. Incentive media most often represent partnerships where you are paying for connections useful to your business. The best known and perhaps the biggest of all forms is called **affiliate marketing**. You have probably read about a cool product or service online, and clicked on the hotlink to learn more about it, or even buy it. That link took you to a special version of the product/service page to make your purchase. The place you saw the original mention of the item was on the affiliate's site. The page where you bought the item is on the retailer's site, and the retailer pays a flat fee or a percentage of the sale price to the affiliate for every sale that comes through that particular hotlink.

You can create an affiliate program and detail it on a page on your website. To get an idea what to offer as payment for a sale based on an affiliate link, consider looking at the affiliate pay rates of major companies like Amazon or Walmart. Rates often vary based on the type of product or service (e.g., 1 percent for video games versus 10 percent for contact lenses). You can also decide if you pay only for sales, or for lesser categories like new additions to your email list. Affiliates usually add a cookie to people who click the link, to identify their site as the source for your customer, and you can set how long the cookie remains active. As you probably gather, there can be a lot of complexity. There are sites you can access to learn about creating your own affiliate marketing program, or as is the case so often on the Internet, someone offers a service to do this for you. You can find these in the Learn More Online box below. Many of them offer for-fee affiliate marketing managment services.

affiliate marketing
Partnerships between firms where a firm (often a content creator) mentions the product or service of another firm. That mention includes a link to purchase the product or service, and each time the link is clicked and produces the agreed-upon outcome (seeing the website, having a cookie placed, leaving their email, requesting information, buying the product) the content creator gets paid by the other firm.

LEARN MORE ONLINE

Learn more about the topics above at these sites:

AM Navigator: **www.amnavigator.com/**

Affiliate Programs: **www.affiliateprograms.com/**

How Stuff Works: **https://money.howstuffworks.com/affiliate-program.htm**

You can also become an affiliate of companies offering products or services you think your customers or viewers might find interesting. Googling "best affiliate marketing programs" will point you to lists of potential partners.

brand ambassador
A person who represents your brand, company, product, or service to others to increase brand awareness, sales, and positive attitudes among the public. They can be paid or volunteer. They often receive your products and services to use and show off to the public. Also called a spokesperson.

Related to affiliates are **brand ambassadors**. These are people who represent your brand, company, product, or service to the public. The goal is for the ambassador to display, use, or talk positively about your offerings to build a positive public awareness of them. Ambassadors can be paid or volunteer, but either way, you provide them with your products or services so they can display and talk about them in person and online. You may know someone who is well known in your market, and you can ask him or her to become your ambassador. For example, basketball star Jayson Tatum came from St. Louis, and grew up loving Imo's thin-crust pizza. He mentioned it during the NBA draft and generated a mini-blizzard of notoriety for the chain. Imo's then asked Tatum to be its brand ambassador and spokesperson.[43]

But there are also local talent agencies that can connect you to local celebrities who might be looking for promotional gigs, and of course there are always online services. We talked about some of these (like Buzzsumo.com) above as a means to recruit influencers, and a brand ambassador or spokesperson is a different, usually more long-term, form of contracting with an influencer. In addition to those platforms, there are dedicated brand ambassador platforms like www.getambassador.com, www.crewfire.com (check out the guides under their "Resources" tab) and brandchamp.io.

native advertising
Native advertising are forms of ads inserted into the regular flow of noncommercial web pages so that it appears to be "native" to the page. The FTC regulates that native advertising carry an identifier (such as "Sponsored" in front of the item) to show it is an ad and not a statement by the page's content creator.

The other forms of incentive media typically focus on printed content. Did you ever notice items on social media feeds or web pages that say "Sponsored" or "Recommended For You" or "From Our Advertisers"? These are all ways to insert ads into pages that aren't intended to be primarily commercial. They are called **native advertising**, and are one of the frontiers in online ads. The goal in native ads is for the ad to blend into the regular content of the page. FTC rules, though, require some indication that it is an ad–for example, the "Recommended for You" tag you see. Online ad platforms discussed above can set you up with native postings.[44]

sponsored content
Sponsored content is material you develop or have developed to present to customers information about your company, brand, products, or services. Links to this material are placed on other people or brand websites or social media feeds, in hopes potential customers will click on the links and learn more about your offering.

A variation of this is called **sponsored content**. Typically, sponsored content refers to articles, videos, blogs, or downloadable materials that promote your brand, business, product, or service. The sponsored content is clearly associated with your business, and will carry your firm's name on it, but it will be linked to spots on the pages of other people and companies. Like native advertising, you may see "Brought to you by" or "Presented by" as a way to identify sponsored content (versus content created by the owner of the site).

There you have it! Nine basic ways to think about promoting your business. The challenge is always to find the method that connects you to the largest number of customers who will buy from you, and do so at the lowest cost. The goal is simple. The options available to you to achieve it are many. But note that there is a lot you can learn for free online to either do it yourself, or split the work with platforms or professionals (or a mix of both).

Developing Your Promotion Strategy

One lesson you've probably pulled from this section is that there is a lot you can do to promote your business. So much so that having a plan is crucial. We talked in Chapter 9 about the marketing plan that is part of your business plan, but backing up that one-page of overall strategy should be a detailed listing of the goals, types of activities, and anticipated outcomes of your marketing efforts.

media content strategy plan
A document, for the managers and employees of the firm to see, that details the specifics of the firm's marketing efforts including the goals, target audiences, distribution channels, keywords, content types, calendar, publishing procedures, action items, KPIs, and analytics across all the different types of marketing efforts the firm will attempt.

These are the major components of your **media content strategy plan**. In addition to the goals, activities, and outcomes, other information you would want to include are what kinds of promotional efforts you will do, the schedule for doing them, the publishing procedures you will use, your budget and costs (including which marketing efforts will be free and which will be paid for), and how you will measure if your goals are being met (through KPIs and reviews of your process as well as the trends and analytics you track).

Once again, it is worth noting that there are so many ways to promote your business that it can be hard to decide where to start. For most start-ups, it makes the most sense to focus on brand and owned media, which are necessary to get your business started and established. Initially branch out into shared media through your social media embassies because it is cheap and involves keeping you close to your customers, which is essential to learning your business and market. Keep your eyes open to opportunities for partnerships and earned media, especially the free, low-cost ones or do-it-yourself sort, to get a broader exposure. Look for people you know who might become partners, affiliates, or influencers on your behalf. And as you get experience with these you will be better able to make informed choices about the types and amounts of media integrations, paid media, and incentive media you want to use to boost what you are already achieving.

Having a great product or service does not do you or your business any good if potential customers do not know about it. Getting the word out about your business and its offerings is the purpose of promotion in small business. The avenues for getting the word out are fairly well known—current or potential customers, the press, and these days the Internet—but because everyone knows those avenues, crafting and distributing a message that people will notice and respond to amid all the ads they face is an ever-increasing challenge. This chapter focuses on preparing you with the basic skills of press and public relations, as well as advice on what makes promotion efforts pay off. Armed with these ideas, you *can* make your business stand out and be noticed. The other key role of this chapter is to discuss the specifics of selling—how to get started and how to close sales. In the end, sales are everything because everything in business depends on sales. If you can master promotion and selling, your business will have gone much of the way toward eventual success.

The Process of Personal Selling[45]

LO **10-3** Apply the key skills involved in personal selling, especially closing the sale.

One of the most important jobs an entrepreneur can do is being a good salesperson for his or her product or service. Who knows more about your firm than you do? Who believes in it so much to put all the time and effort into getting it launched?

Personal selling has the advantage that you can be flexible in your presentation. If the current customer is a technophobe, emphasize ease of use. If he loves technology, let him know that he'll be on the cutting edge. Personal selling allows you to find out the buyers' main concerns and address them; in advertising you can only guess. Personal selling allows you to find out from clients what future features they may want to see.

personal selling
The process of selling your products and services; includes prospect and evaluate, prepare, present, close, and follow up.

While selling may be thought of as an art, there is a general formula for generating interest in your product or service:

1. **Prospect and evaluate:** A good salesperson will collect background information and prepare to present. This could start months ahead of a sales call by making sure that you are thoroughly informed about your product and what it can or cannot do. Of course, the entrepreneur knows all that but may need to study up on some of the technical terms used in the field. In hiring a new salesperson, this step may be lengthier. In addition, putting together a list of potential clients (called "prospecting") takes place. Here is another case when thoroughly knowing your target market is key and critical. In some firms, this may be as simple as who walks in the door. How do you find these prospects? Here's where using a referral form can be a good idea. Ask all satisfied customers of the names of people they know who may potentially need or want your product. Customers may prospect themselves by asking

Entrepreneurs are, in a sense, always selling their company, product, or service. Being skilled in personal selling is important for many reasons. What elements of the process of personal selling are you confident in? Are there elements you think you need to practice?

Hero Images/Getty Images

for more information after finding your website or responding to a direct mail advertisement. You may buy mailing lists of prospective clients as well. (See Chapter 11 for more information about direct mail and mailing lists.)

2. **Prepare:** Preparation means finding out what you can about the clients before approaching them. In business-to-business selling, you may be able to check out their website and find out more about what sorts of products the potential clients make. This will help you decide how you may want to pitch your product. What seems to be critical to them? Is it state-of-the-art technology or quality or cost? Prequalifying means cleaning up your list to remove potential clients that are unable or unlikely to buy your product. The reasons for excluding will vary from firm to firm but might include financial status, having just purchased a competitive product, legal issues (e.g., to whom you can or cannot sell), and the like. At the end of this phase, the initial contact is made or the appointment is set up. Once again, check your intended sales pitch for jargon or terms and phrases the customer is unlikely to understand. You want your argument to be compelling and logical for the customer and the sooner the customer can see the potential advantages, the more likely you are to successfully close the sale. What do you offer that is better than the competition? Go back to your value proposition and make sure you are correctly communicating it.[46] This stage is certainly a bit harder than consumer selling where the potential customers may often just walk into your place of business. Some of the best salespeople for handling these sorts of clients are found in the computer and electronics industry. They usually start off with a few questions to hone in on information to help them make their pitch: "Will you use your new computer for gaming, Internet searching, or word processing?" "Do you have a budget in mind?" "Who will be using this computer: you or your child?"
3. **Present:** During the presentation phase, the salesperson presents a logical and compelling argument for purchasing the product. The more information the salesperson is able to obtain in the preparation phase, the better she or he is able to address potential concerns and point out specific features. Most salespeople emphasize the needs or wants their product can satisfy. You don't sell features; you sell benefits. Presentations should be rehearsed and facts memorized, but the presentation should never appear canned. A good salesperson can and will adapt his presentation to his audience. Note that this is similar to suggestions in Chapter 8 on how to prepare and present an elevator pitch. It is much the same type of selling. Establishing a personal relationship helps. Take an interest in what clients like. Be prepared to spend a few minutes in idle chit-chat, but don't waste their time. If they want to chat, fine, but when they want to get down to business, switch gears immediately. For walk-in clients, introduce yourself and if they give you their name, use it. Find out a little bit about them in the approach (remember the computer salesperson mentioned previously). Try to establish rapport—an emotional connection between you and the other person. Even simple statements like "I know what you mean; I hate that, too" make clients feel that you understand. Use technological language appropriate for your audience.
4. **Close:** As you begin to wrap up your presentation, you will likely encounter objections as customers also anticipate the close of the sales pitch and the coming request for purchase. Customers nearly always have objections and the good salesperson is prepared to answer these objections. "Certainly the price is higher than our competitor's, but we have 20 percent less downtime, making our product much more cost-effective." Once the material has been presented and the objections answered, the salesperson needs to close the sale. The close is the commitment from the customer. There are a number of techniques including:

   - **Trial close** ("Which credit card would you like to use to pay for that?")
   - **Assumptive close** ("I'll just need your credit card for payment.")
   - **Urgency close** ("This rate will end at the end of the day.")
   - **Alternate choice close** ("Would you prefer the standard or deluxe model?")
   - **Chances-are close** (Customer asks to think about it and you say, "What are the chances you will buy later?")
   - **Make-a-suggestion close** (Offer a waffling customer suggestions on why it is a good idea to buy.)

- **Try-before-you-buy close** (Offer a trial period, if your business can handle that.)
- **What-will-it-take close** (Ask "What will it take to close this deal?")

Additional closing techniques are discussed in Skill Module 10.3.

The Art of Closing[47]

SKILL MODULE 10.3

Columnist Cord Cooper of *Investor's Business Daily* has made a career of gathering tips on closing sales. His suggestions include:

- **"Restate the need."** As Barbara Corcoran, chair of The Corcoran Group, a $2.5 billion New York City real estate firm and author of the book *Use What You've Got,* suggests to get the customer's requirements and restate them. If you can do a better job of explaining the customer's needs, so much the better.
- **Listen.** It seems obvious, but it is the key to everything. Don't interrupt and listen for what seems important to the customer. Note needs your product can meet (and those it can't) and include the former in your response.
- **Ask, "When would you want it?"** This question is a great way to determine the degree of urgency the customer faces. Something needed "tomorrow" means making the sale now and could help the customer feel better.
- **Get feedback.** The more a customer will tell you about what he or she likes and dislikes, the better you can tailor your sales effort.
- **Handle buyer's remorse.** If someone is buying a big-ticket item, he or she might get nervous about the money being spent. While you're there, reinforce the customer's desire for the product by going over the benefits. Consider telling him or her of others' positive experiences, and think about calling the customer the next day to reinforce the benefits and value.
- **Sell the result.** Show customers specific beneficial outcomes from their use of your product.
- **Use more than one outcome.** High-quality items last longer and are more prestigious—use both benefits if they fit your customer's needs. Consider outcomes like service, delivery, financing terms, warranties, and extras in addition to cost.
- **Take strategic advantage.** This is done in several ways. Bring along your assistant to show you're important and to have another pair of eyes. Ask to be last so you don't have to compete with anyone else. And above all, practice. "Role-playing puts your inhibitions to rest and results in a well-prepared, confident delivery," says Corcoran, who started her firm with just $1,000.
- **Be patient.** Often if you ask for a decision before the customer is ready, the answer is "no."
- **Accumulate "yeses."** The more items you and the customer agree on, the more likely he or she is to agree to the sale. Arrange the discussion of needs and benefits to generate a lot of information, and a lot of yeses.
- **Counter positively.** When you hear something that makes you want to say "no," or "yes, but . . . ," instead try to phrase your response as "yes, and . . ." to show agreement.

5. **Follow up:** Finally, the close is not the end of the sale. The important objective of following up is to make your customers feel at ease. Do this by staying with the clients for a few minutes postsale and get to know them. Have you ever bought something only to start second-guessing yourself in a couple days? Maybe you should have at least checked out the competition? Maybe you should have waited until it was on sale? This is known as **cognitive dissonance** and happens frequently especially with more expensive items or purchases that are considered risky. A good salesperson will often contact you during this time to reiterate all the good qualities of your purchase and to reassure you that you did indeed make a good decision. This is also a good time to ask for referrals. Follow-up may also include activities from others in your firm such as installation, warranty work, financing, and the like. Building long-term relationships is the key to successful business and taking care of a customer postpurchase goes a long way to building them.[48]

cognitive dissonance Doubt that occurs after a purchase has been made. An inconsistency between experience and belief.

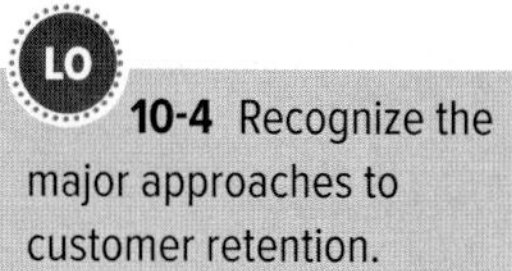
10-4 Recognize the major approaches to customer retention.

Customer Retention: Keeping and Growing Customers after the Sale

Every sale gives you the most valuable resource any business can get—a customer. It sounds obvious, but once you have been in business awhile you will learn that it is easier and more profitable to sell to existing customers than to prospect and attempt to sell to people who are not your customers. The founder of the modern quality movement, W. Edwards Deming, put it this way, "Profit in business comes from repeat customers; customers that boast about your product and service, and that bring friends with them." How much easier is it to sell to existing customers? Literally five times easier, according to the research. Research shows it costs five times as much to get a purchase from a new customer compared to an existing one.[49]

customer retention (CR) Techniques that focus on efforts to promote satisfaction with and interest in the firm.

customer relationship management (CRM) The process of tracking the customer's different contacts with the firm, and using these data to help improve sales as well as the customer's experience.

The name for the general approach to keeping customers is called **customer retention (CR)**. CR focuses on satisfying your customers after the sale, and managing your marketing efforts with customers to maximize their loyalty to and purchases from your business. There are three major elements to CR these days. One is handling problems that crop up after a sale. The second is called **customer relationship management (CRM)**, which focuses on the longer-term monitoring and promotion of customer interest and loyalty. The third is growing customer sales, which builds from the customer development model of Blank and Dorf and the lean business practices movement.

Handling Postsale Problems

In Chapter 9 we talked about how customer service is one of the truisms of why small businesses are better than large ones, and even how small firms can achieve outstanding customer service. But in reality the hardest time to maintain good, much less outstanding, customer service is when dealing with postsale complaints. Small business is usually a personal business, so it is hard not to take complaints personally. But in the end, the ultimate test of any business is how it handles adversity, and complaints are probably the most frequent example of that ultimate test.

Bill Gates said, "Your most unhappy customers are your greatest source of learning." He had a point. Research has shown that anywhere from 68 to 96 percent of dissatisfied customers don't report their dissatisfaction.[50] One 2015 study showed that 19 percent of dissatisfied customers contacted their retailers, but 81 percent didn't and of that latter group, at least 32 percent were reporting their negative experiences to others and finding other retailers.[51] Why would they think this way? Of the 81 percent, three out of five of them felt it was not worth the trouble, while two out of five felt it wouldn't do any good. So given how few upset customers complain to the firms, those that do are giving you a real chance to improve your operations, and to keep this customer and probably other, quieter ones, too.

In reality, some complaints are justified[52]—a product or service arrived late, did not live up to (or worse yet match) the description, did not reflect the quoted price or discounts, was lower quality than the customer was led to expect, or was delivered by an impolite, uncaring, or unprofessional worker. A famous customer service thought came from Donald Porter, a vice president of British Airways, but it works equally well in small business: "Customers don't expect you to be perfect. They do expect you to fix things when they go wrong." Exhibit 10.2 gives you a four-step approach to dealing with these difficult situations.

Your goal as the owner is at a minimum to come to an arrangement that the customer thinks is fair. In reality, creating a solution that renews the customer's belief in your business is a better solution. Why take the extra step? Keep in mind the value of a lifetime of this customer's purchases to help you realize how far you should go to keep him or her happy. Think about how far negative opinions or even grudging acceptance travels in these days of social media. It has never been easier to upset a customer and have him or her spread that negativity to friends and the wider public.

EXHIBIT 10.2

Four Steps to Handling Postsale Problems[53]

1. **Prepare yourself and listen.** When you realize you are facing an angry customer, put yourself in a calm state of mind. Be open to the customer. As hard as it may seem, don't get defensive—don't take it personally. The more open and sympathetic you are, the better the chances for a positive outcome. If you're caught off-guard, you'll have to do this preparation in real time, in your head, but get yourself ready first.
2. **Accurately reflect.** Once you've gotten yourself in a position to listen, accept the customer's anger and ask him or her to tell you all about it. This is the first stage of defusing the situation. When you can repeat back what happened and how the customer sees it, and he or she agrees that you've "got it," you're ready to go to the next step.
3. **Apologize and start generating solutions.** Sincerely apologize for the problem, even if you feel it wasn't entirely your firm's (or your) fault. This is the second stage of defusing the situation. Doing this positions you to start working on solutions, preferably with the customer. That solution-seeking is the third stage of defusing.
4. **Implement and follow up.** When you have a solution you can both accept, implement it immediately. Give yourself a few minutes alone to recover. Then, a few days (no more than a week) later, call the customer (it's more personal than emailing and the customer's voice will give you clues as to his or her feelings) to see how things are going. If you can offer an incentive to deal with your firm again (like a discount on a future purchase), do so, or at least ask the customer to ask for you the next time so you can take care of him or her.

But it is also true that you will face customers with unjustified complaints. There is no magic phrase that disarms these explosive situations.[54] Your job is to remain calm and stay focused on what you are willing to do. Some ways to handle this sort of problem include:

- Appeal to the customers' sense of fair play, saying you want to do what is right.
- Consider offering a compromise, giving them some (but not all) of what they seek.
- Suggest involving a third party like the Better Business Bureau to arbitrate.
- Consider politely standing firm only when the facts unquestionably back you up.
- Also consider politely giving in even when the demand is clearly unreasonable. Think about the stories you've heard about companies that go above and beyond, like Nordstrom taking back a customer's "recently" purchased tires (even though Nordstrom itself has never sold tires).[55] Such stories do more to build everyone else's confidence in your firm than the cost of fixing the problem.

When handling these complaints as a small business owner, it does not work to talk about "company policy" as a reason for inaction–as owner, you make the policies. It also never works to lose your cool and yell. It backs the customer into a corner (where you are likely to lose business if nothing else) and makes you look less professional. Finally, it does not work to argue with a customer. Winning these sorts of arguments may mean the end of the relationship with the customer. Know that dealing with postsale problems can make a major difference. Recall those 19 percent who complain. When the company solves the problem, 86 percent stay,[56] and we know from other research those who stay are more likely to buy more in the future.

Upset customers, like this woman, can get overwrought. How can you handle postsale problems when they arise?

ximagination/123RF

In the end, marketing is about sales, and in most businesses, the goal is to sell to the same customers again and again, as well as to get those customers to recommend your business to their network. Doing this well over the long run requires not only mastering the 4 Ps (product, promotion, price, and placement), but also handling postsale complaints. Your goal is to have satisfied customers, and in the end that is what business is all about. As Babson's Jeff Timmons says, "Happiness is a positive cash flow." And nothing generates cash like sales.

For most start-ups, the keys to building a strong customer base are to work your original customer base by increasing market penetration and product expansion. We'll talk next about ways to build a customer relationship management approach that does just that.

CRM in Two Steps

Entrepreneurs have always tracked their customers. It could be as simple as a 3 × 5 index card with the customer's name and contact information on it, the customer's family members' names, perhaps their sizes, and what major items they've bought and when. Today, of course, we use computers or web-based services to handle these kinds of chores, but the basic ideas remain the same, and the analysis of customer data is easier and more powerful than the previous generation of entrepreneurs could have imagined. This modern computerized approach is called customer relationship management (CRM). As in the old days, the necessities are pretty much the same: (1) gathering the data and (2) analyzing the data. Where there has been rapid growth in recent years has been in thinking about how to build on CRM-driven marketing efforts to increase sales, which we will cover in a later section.

Step 1: Gathering the Data

The key to CRM is the data on current or prospective customers. Given the power of repeat selling, the most valuable data come from your existing customers. For all existing customers you want two kinds of data—contact data and performance data. Contact data give you the particulars on your customers while performance data give you information on the date and type of contact, since in many sales situations it can take repeated contacts before a sale is made.

Some of this information might be entered by the customer, for example, when buying online or filling out a delivery form in your store, or it could be done by you or an employee. As noted, when you are building a prospect database for your CRM efforts, the names and contact data usually come from a variety of sources outside your firm.

There is no need to build a CRM program. You can get high-quality CRM programs for free. If you want to see what the high-end CRM looks like, check out Salesforce.com (a commercial product) or the free CRMs listed in the accompanying "Learn More Online" box.

LEARN MORE ONLINE

Learn more about the topics above at these sites:

HubSpot (free for any number of users): **www.hubspot.com**

Agile CRM (free for any number of users): **www.agilecrm.com**

Zoho CRM (free for three users): **www.zoho.com**

In effect, a CRM is a beefed-up version of your smartphone's address book or your email contact list. In fact, most CRM programs let you import your contact list or address book to help get your CRM database going. They also can usually import spreadsheets and data in other forms. These CRMs are beefed-up in that they add dozens of additional fields that help you track and classify the people you engage in business. You can get a sense of the kinds of information a CRM is organized to handle in Table 10.2. For example, customers are often tracked by where they are in the buying process shown in the funnels at the start of the chapter (impressions/awareness, leads/interest, prospects/consideration, sales/purchase). Don't worry, most entrepreneurs leave a lot of fields empty—at least at first—until you decide what is important to you. That importance comes up in terms of the reports that CRM programs let you run: the analysis step.

TABLE 10.2 Example: Types of Key Data in a CRM Database

Contact data

- Person and firm
  - Unique customer ID number
  - Basic address book/contact card information
  - Basic firm information (name, contact information, etc.)
  - Basic demographics (age, gender, and other data specific to your business, such as sizes for clothing firms, education for professional training firms, etc.)
- Source
  - Sales
  - Referral from customer (give customer ID)
  - Mailing list (specify which one)

Performance data

- Purchases: product/service, quantity, price, discounts, date, sales setting (online, in-store, at a show or fair, etc.), related purchases (e.g., delivery, setup, refills, warranty)
- Nonpurchase events: Other visits without purchases, website visits without purchases, telephone contacts, other contacts
- Follow-ups: Actions, date, future actions, customer reactions
- Follow-throughs: Actions, date, future actions, customer reactions

Step 2: Analyzing the Data

There are three general types of reports that you are likely to be interested in. Each CRM has different names for the categories, but the specific report names tend to be very similar. The types are:

1. **Customer vector reports** let you summarize information by date, by product or service being sold, by groups or segments of customers (e.g., all firms in NAICS 453310–antique dealers, all customers from California), or by the purchases of an individual person or firm.
2. **Sales process reports** summarize data based on where customers are in the sales process (impressions/awareness, leads/interest, prospects/consideration, sales/purchase) and what you have done with these individuals. In particular, tracking prospects and leads is essential to get an early sense of where sales are likely to be going.
3. **Sales outcome reports** summarize issues around the actual sales, like the amount, how long it took from first contact to completed sale (called the sales cycle), and the eventual conversion rates.

customer vector report
A type of CRM report that segments by customer (or customer group) on purchases or dates of purchase.

Reports such as these can help you decide how to operate several key aspects of your marketing effort. If you track sales by purchase basis, you can tell which of your advertising efforts resulted in the most sales, so it makes it easier to decide which marketing efforts to continue or expand as in the case of the Union National Community Bank in the accompanying Small Business Insight. If you link sales and purchase basis to the type of customer (by industry, location, education, or age) you might figure out how to better target ads or promotions to particular types of customers. If you look at customer source basis and purchase, you might be able to tell which mailing lists produce the best returns. You could also find a product that has low quality by tracking sales organized by product and customer satisfaction. As these varied examples show, the possibilities are nearly endless, even with basic data.

But perhaps the simplest and most important analysis is sales by customer. In marketing, there is a strong belief that 20 percent of your customers give you 80 percent of your sales. The key is identifying which customers are in that 20 percent and once you have, doing everything you can to keep them, and keep them happy. In the hustle and bustle of the day, you might come to believe that the loudest or most demanding people are your biggest customers, but often a sales-by-customer analysis lets you identify quiet, easygoing customers who are nonetheless major purchasers, and who are the ones you would otherwise be most likely to overlook.

SMALL BUSINESS INSIGHT

UNION NATIONAL COMMUNITY BANK[57]

Union National Community Bank (UNCB) in tiny Mount Joy, Pennsylvania, was founded in 1853 and pretty much had the local market to itself until the big national banks moved in during the 1990s. Facing competitors offering more and better services and lower rates, UNCB lost customers. Although it lowered its loan rates and offered higher returns for deposits, it could not make up the lost business. Then the bank installed a CRM system and had a revelation when it saw a report of customers segmented by how profitable they were. With this information in hand, the bank identified the customers most important to the bottom line, and offered those people more of the services they had shown they liked. Less profitable customers were directed to services like electronic banking, which in turn helped make even this segment profitable. The CRM approach helped turn around the bank's fortunes, with more than $1 million in increased revenue and a profit increase of 35 percent. For the bank, CRM made a big difference.

Customer analysis can get significantly more complex, and there are whole courses and segments of the marketing profession focused on performing and interpreting those complex analyses. However, you can get your own 80 percent of benefit from performing the simple basic 20 percent of analysis outlined here.

Growing Customer Sales

The goal of all this data gathering and analysis is to increase your sales and help make your marketing efforts as economical as possible. The proof of a CRM effort is seen in (1) higher levels of customer loyalty in existing customers, (2) higher levels of purchasing from your existing customers, and (3) more tracked prospects making initial purchases from you. The techniques for managing current and prospective customers are actually very similar, and tie together many of the techniques we have talked about throughout this section of the book.

Fundamentally, the keys to customer service are follow-through and follow-up. *Follow-through* refers to doing what you said you would do. If a customer mentions a concern or problem, you will of course try to fix it. But too often entrepreneurs or their employees can get rushed, and delay or even forget about what they promised customers. If you remember to keep up your CRM database (which is the biggest problem for entrepreneurs), a good CRM system will remind you of the promises you have made.

Follow-up refers to the contacts you periodically make with customers in order to remind them of your business, and your interest in their business. This can be done through personal contacts by phone, mail, or personal visits, although increasingly contact is done electronically through emails, electronic newsletters, discussion lists, or interactive web services like blogs or wikis.

The advantage of the electronic approaches is they can dramatically lower the cost of marketing efforts by saving you printing and mailing costs. Additionally, electronic marketing aids can get into your customers' hands in minutes or hours rather than days. The interactive approaches also give you a chance to hear ideas and concerns from customers directly and immediately, giving you a chance to resolve problems quickly and even get new prospects for products and services to offer from those who have the need. The essential aspect of follow-up is to take the initiative to stay in contact.

But realize that as you tie more of your marketing efforts (e.g., email campaigns, trade show lists, referrals, etc.) into your CRM, you can begin to significantly expand the kinds of marketing you can pursue. You can move beyond existing customers to focus more on new markets and new products. There are four approaches to growing your business, seen in Figure 10.6. Selling the same products to the same customers is called a **market penetration** approach, while selling the same customers a new product is called **product expansion**. When selling to your existing customers, you have the benefit of being able to use data you have gathered in your prior customer contacts.

market penetration
A strategy whose goal is growth, based on selling more of the firm's product or service to the existing customer base.

product expansion
A strategy whose goal is growth, based on selling existing customers a product or service they have never bought before.

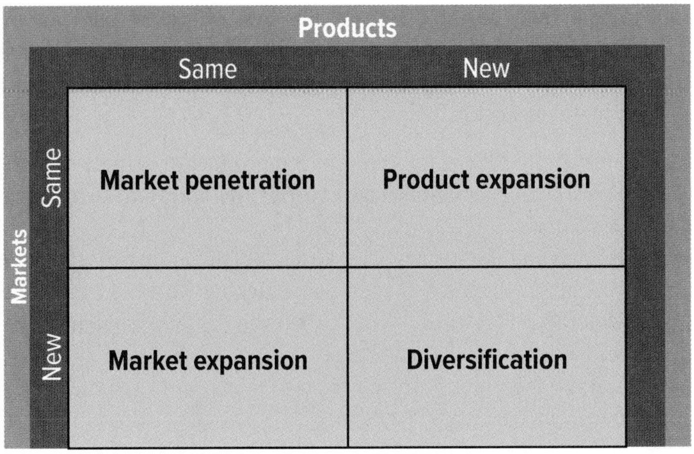

Markets \ Products	Same	New
Same	**Market penetration**	**Product expansion**
New	**Market expansion**	**Diversification**

FIGURE 10.6

The Strategies of Market Growth

Source: William O. Bearden, Thomas N. Ingram, and Raymond W. Laforge, *Marketing: Principles and Perspectives*, 4th ed. (Burr Ridge, IL: McGraw-Hill/Irwin, 2004), p. 57.

If you are looking at people who have not been customers, you might seek a **market expansion** strategy to sell your existing products to them (this is where prospecting comes in), or a **diversification** strategy if you are trying to sell them newly developed products (e.g., your new lines). In such cases, you might get prospects' contact information from referrals by existing customers (the approach likely to give you the best results), purchases of mailing or customer lists from marketing list big businesses like Dun & Bradstreet or Donnelly or from smaller specialized list firms such as Direct Media or USADATA, or from organizations whose members might be particularly interested in your product or service (e.g., a local kennel club's member list if you had a pet grooming business). Wherever you get the information, it goes into your CRM to generate new reports to help plot the best places to grow your business.

market expansion
A strategy whose goal is growth, based on selling in areas or to groups previously not served by the business.

diversification
A strategy whose goal is growth based on adding new products or services to the firm's existing collection of offerings.

The Mechanics of Growing Customer Sales

Think back to the customer development model double funnels in Figures 10.2 and 10.3 at the beginning of this chapter. We discussed the "Get Customers" or promotion portion earlier. Here is where we look at one of the lean business practices' contribution to small business in general, giving us a better way to visualize and think about the steps in growing our connection and sales to our existing customers. Recall that increasing sales to existing customers is the fastest and least expensive road to higher profits. Remember that the more you build relationships and sales through keeping your customers happy and their needs met, the more likely they are to recommend you to their connections, further building sales at next to no cost. It is the best way to grow your business and profits.

"Keep Customers" in the middle section of the physical products funnel reflects a time when you take steps to hold onto existing customers to get them to continue to buy your product and hopefully recommend it to friends and employers. This typically involves four kinds of activities: (1) creating and deploying (or selling) product updates; (2) checking-in with customers by phone, email, or social media as we talked about follow-up and follow-through; (3) asking customers to participate in customer satisfaction surveys by phone, email, or online; and (4) operating loyalty programs where customers get points or benefits for actions related to what they've bought which can lead to additional free or discounted gifts, accessories, updates, or other promotions.[58] Loyalty programs and other types of sales promotion are discussed in more detail in Chapter 11 as part of pricing.

Keeping customers in the online world involves using similar approaches such as product updates and loyalty programs, but also including new approaches like (1) blogs, RSS feeds, emails, and feeds through social media outlets or phone text messages; (2) contests and online or real-world events to involve customers; and (3) outreach programs. These approaches are more or less online versions of check-in programs, based in part on the greater ability to track customers' interactions with your website so you can identify who has and hasn't used your service. You can follow up with welcome emails, how-to guides, and even phone calls to help the customer start using the service. Note that these online channel approaches can be adapted for physical channels, and the reverse is true too. Think of McDonald's Monopoly game–a contest run by a company in the physical channel.

Steve Blank and Bob Dorf's "Grow Customers" section of the funnels represents a clean and simple model to show how existing customers can be approached to grow sales.[59] They have already committed to your firm, and to your products or services. If you've done a good job of connecting and listening to your customers, they should have a favorable attitude toward your firm and offerings. This primes the pump for additional sales to them. These additional sales can take four forms in the physical world:

unbundle
To break apart a product or service into components.

up-selling
Selling additional accessories or higher-quality versions of the product at a higher cost.

cross-selling
To sell related products.

referrals
Getting customers to refer their friends to you.

- *Unbundling:* To **unbundle** means to break apart a product or service into components. An example would be for your cable package to offer the ability to drop news or children's networks to get a savings.
- **Up-selling**: This is selling additional accessories or higher-quality (and probably higher-profit) versions of the product at a higher cost. Sticking with the example of cable, when they ask if you want the NFL All-Game package on top of your regular sports channels, the company is up-selling you.
- **Cross-selling**: To cross-sell means to sell related products. For cable services, the typical cross-selling comes from adding on deals for Internet access or landline telephone.
- **Referrals:** Getting customers to refer their friends to you is a major way to grow sales because those friends are hearing about you from a source they trust. One of the findings that made social media valuable to entrepreneurs was learning how powerful friend referrals are on future sales to those people. Rewarding current customers for referring new customers to you is a great way to build sales inexpensively, and further tie current customers closer to your business.

In the online world, the right-hand side of the funnel also has familiar concepts like Up-Sell, Cross-Sell, and Referral, but also adds Next-Sell, which are your attempts to prime customers to make their next purchase. Examples include reminding you how long it has been since your last purchase of a perishable or expendable product (like an air conditioner filter), or offering customers an automatic reorder service for scheduled shipments of perishable/expendable products.

The point is that whether you are thinking big picture and seeking new places to sell, like through market expansions or new product offerings, or going deeper into your existing customer base to leverage your relationships to deepen connections and sales, the entrepreneur can always find new ways to grow his or her business. That's what the goal of marketing is all about. As you think about these efforts, one of the biggest challenges for the entrepreneur is estimating what those possible sales will be. The firm's ability to imagine and deal with the future depends on it, and that is what we will cover next.

LO **10-5** Identify sales forecasting methods.

Sales Forecasting[60]

One of the most important pieces of the marketing efforts, and the part that will feed directly into your financial projections for your business (or your business plan), is knowing what your sales will be. Sales determine your profitability and, ultimately, whether you will stay in business or not. Sales projections are also the basis for estimating how much money you will generate in the near future. If your forecast is off, your firm could run out of money earlier than expected. So sales forecasts are vitally important.

The CRM services mentioned in the prior section actually come with sales forecasting modules that can look at your sales for the past week, month, or quarter and project forward. This is exactly the process used by existing companies—basing sales forecasts on what are called historical sales; but since you're new, you can't do that. Fortunately, there are also much simpler ways of coming up with reasonably good initial estimates, such as the one shown in Skill Module 10.4 and the techniques described next.

Some products or services are tied to others. For example, if your company lays sod for new lawns, you can estimate the total market by looking at projected new homes being built in your geographic area. From there, you'll need to calculate what percentage of that market you can get. In other words, what's the competition like, and how do you measure up? If the market is underserved and all the competition is relatively equal in terms of size, product, price, service, and such, you might be able to divide the total market by the number of competitors, and maybe deduct a percentage "just to be safe" since you are relatively new. For example, perhaps the three existing firms will cover 85 percent of the business, and you'll only get 15 percent the first year. On the other hand, if you, or your competitor, offer unique products or services or have other advantages

Sales Forecasting from a Fixed Inventory

SKILL MODULE 10.4

Let's start with a simple reselling example. You will buy St. Louis Cardinals Adjustable Baseball Caps (with the MLB logo sticker showing it is official) from a St. Louis area Walmart. The caps retail for $5.00, but you talked the store manager into giving you a deal on 100 of them for $4.25 each.

Go to **shopping.google.com** and type in "St. Louis Cardinals Cap." In summer 2019 around 350 possibilities came up, with prices ranging from $5.00 to $62.19.

Now look at the types of caps being offered. The red cap you got from Walmart is the most distinctive of the types, and let's say that only two vendors sell a similar cap. One is on eBay and the other is available at an online store. Both sell the cap at $9.98, shipping included. This is your baseline price, unless you think you can sell at a premium. Since you have 100 caps, your forecast is how long it will take to sell them. You can track the cap seller on eBay to see how long it takes for the "in stock" number to drop, and then multiply that number of days by 100 to figure how long you can expect your stock to last. (If you track sales of the other types of caps, you can learn which are the most in demand and perhaps buy a different type of cap next time.)

You could speed up your sales by going to stores around the Cardinals' stadium on game day and selling the store owner some additional caps, or (if your peddler's license is valid) even sell caps outside the stadium itself. At $10.00 a cap you will be undercutting the competition, and should be able to sell all 100 in one afternoon or evening game. A quick Google check shows the stadium seats 44,494, and most games are at 70 percent capacity, so you're looking at 31,146 people. If one person in 311 buys your hats, you'll sell out in one game. By the way, if you're selling out too fast, raise the prices until your hats keep moving, but at a 100-hats-a-game rate.

(or disadvantages), these can factor in. Using the same example, if you are the only firm offering in-ground sprinkler installation as well, you may be able to capture a larger portion of the market, or maybe most of a subsection of the market—in this case, perhaps the more expensive homes.

Some products are not tied as neatly to others. If you are opening a restaurant, looking at the number of people who eat out in your particular geographic area won't cut it. Some folks eat only fast food. Others don't like Chinese cuisine. Some go out only for breakfast. As a result, there are many different types of restaurant customers.

This is a good situation for some marketing research. You could conduct traffic counts during the hours you'll be open. You could stop a number of people to ask them how often they eat out and what type of restaurant they are likely to choose (and whether they think they'd like to try yours—a little word-of-mouth advertising). You could stop by your competition and see how long the waiting lists are or pick up a menu and see what prices they are charging. From these items you can get an idea of how many customers you might get.[61] This is certainly "softer" than the first method of estimating and is slightly more subject to error (both overestimation and underestimation). However, for most products this is the best information you can get.

This is also the time to verify that the potential market you've identified meets your capacity. If your restaurant will serve only 120 people over the hours you are open and the potential market is 300, you need to use your capacity figure, *not* your potential market figure. (You may also want to consider a larger space, more tables, more hours, more staff, or other ways of handling this unexpected extra market, if not immediately, at least for the future.) On the other hand, if your potential market is only 50, is that enough to be profitable? (Or can you lease a smaller, less expensive place or cut costs elsewhere to make your business profitable?)

One of the key issues in determining your number of customers is assessing your **hit rate**, how many prospects you need to approach in order to make one sale. In our baseball cap example, with 31,146 people in the stadium, how many people pass by the seller (impressions), how many notice the hat stand (leads), and how many stop to check out the hats (prospects). How many of the prospects actually buy a hat? That is the hit rate. It is better to do even a small-scale sales effort to get a realistic sense of your hit rate than guess about this crucial metric. It is important because the hit rate is a key factor in your eventual financial projections.

hit rate
How many prospects or leads you need to approach in order to make one sale. Also called the *conversion rate*.

Once you have figured out the number of possible customers and your hit rate, the next step is to estimate the average amount of sales per customer. This is usually a little easier; if your lunch prices range from $10 to $15, you could select the average price, or, more conservatively, assume everyone will eat the least expensive meal.

If you are selling a product, see what competitive products are going for in the market. Using traditional retailers and distributors nearly always quadruples the price you set "at the factory." You know what your costs will be and you know what profit you need; does this price the product beyond the competition? If so, can you find a way to convince your customers of your extra value, to cut your costs in production, or to use a different distribution channel? (More about that is covered in the other marketing chapters.) Are your prices below that of the competition? While this doesn't sound like it could be a problem, it might be a signal for you to double-check all your assumptions to make sure you didn't miss an important step. (Also, lower prices sometimes cause customers to doubt the quality; you expect more from a $10 T-shirt than from a $2 one.)

bot
A web-based program that uses artificial intelligence techniques to automate tasks such as searches.

If you are selling online, a search will bring up competitive products. Or use some of the pricing **bots** such as Google product (google.com/shopping), eBay.com, and Amazon.com for products, or Upwork.com or and Fiverr.com for services to come up with the best prices.[62] For other products, try an Internet search of "your product price bot." If your prices seem too high or too low, rethink how you calculated your costs, your product, and your method of distribution, or determine how you can create enough value for your customer to choose you over the competitive products out there.

When you have the estimated number of prospective customers, the hit rate for sales, and the amount of each sale, you have the basic numbers for creating your sales forecast:

$$\textit{Prospective customers} \times \textit{Hit rate} \times \textit{Sale amount} = \textit{Sales forecast}$$

In many cases, the best sales forecast you can come up with is another educated guess. Consider the assumptions you made and try to justify why you made them. Try to anticipate questions that you will be asked and consider your answers beforehand. In some cases you may want to look at several levels of sales forecast—an optimistic, average, and pessimistic view.[63]

With these numbers for sales forecasts, another good check on your business sense is to compare the sales projection to your cost of marketing, advertising, and selling. If your sales aren't covering these sales-related costs, it's a clear message to change your marketing efforts or find different customers.[64]

When making those first sales estimates, although you might want to be optimistic when talking to potential investors, when it is your business and your budget on the line it is better to have a conservative (i.e., low) sales projection initially and base your upcoming expenditures on that lower number than believe your optimistic estimate, and spend based on it happening, only to discover you've spent money you haven't made yet. If "Happiness is a positive cash flow," make sure the sales estimate you believe will be a positive one—low, maybe, but a low but real number is better than being broke.

CHAPTER SUMMARY

LO 10-1 Describe the marketing funnel and the stages in the customer development process.

- The marketing funnel relates promotional impressions to firm sales.
- The value of promotion is directly tied to the sales it produces.
- The customer development process funnels expand on the classic marketing funnel.

LO 10-2 Recognize the PESO Model of the promotional media landscape.

- PESO stands for *paid*, *earned*, *shared* and *owned* media.
- Brand is at the center of the PESO model and drives it.
- Owned media represent identity and promotional materials that belong to your firm, like name, websites, logos, locations, and your own marketing materials.
- Social media embassies combine owned and shared media and are your company and product pages on social media sites.
- Shared media are when customers and others mention your business and their experience of it on any social media platform.
- Partnerships combine shared and earned media and represent situations where your business works with other organizations in joint efforts such as co-branding, influencer marketing, donations, or community service.
- Earned media (aka publicity or free ink) are mentions of your business in mass media or among the public for which you did not directly pay.

- Media integration combines earned media and paid media and represents efforts you pay for to generate earned media attention, such as contests, lead generation, and advertorials.
- Paid media describe the many forms of paid advertising in print, TV, radio, cable, out-of-home, and Internet platforms.
- Incentive media combine paid and owned media and refer to paid representatives of your business, like brand ambassadors, affiliate programs, native advertising, and sponsored content.

LO 10-3 Apply the key skills involved in personal selling, especially closing the sale.

- Recognize the importance of personal selling.
- Key processes of personal selling include prospect and evaluate, prepare, present, and close.
- The art of closing the sale includes:
  - Restate the need. "When would you want it?"
  - Get feedback. Forewarn customers about buyer's remorse.
  - Practice.
  - If your buyer gets cold feet, unfurl more benefits.
  - Weigh the angles before you start. Don't outbid yourself when bidding on a project—counter with care.
  - Accumulate "yeses."
  - Follow up the sale (in order to stimulate referrals, encourage repurchasing, and prevent cognitive dissonance).

10-4 Recognize the major approaches to customer retention.

- Handling complaints impersonally but empathetically is a particular challenge in small businesses.
- The goal in resolving all complaints is to keep good customers satisfied with your firm.
- Postsale success depends on customer relationship management (CRM), driven by keeping and analyzing data on existing and prospective customers.
- Market expansion, market penetration, product expansion, and diversification are strategies for market growth.
- Utilizing techniques to keep customers engaged and loyal, and grow additional sales to them is key to firm success.

10-5 Identify sales forecasting methods.

- If your product or service is a component of another product or tied directly to another product or service, your estimated sales can be calculated as a portion of this known number.
- Most products and services, however, will require "softer" estimates such as traffic counts or questionnaire results.
- Getting a "hit rate" based on some real-world experience will be crucial to making good sales forecasts.
- This sales forecast is critical to and must be checked against your capacity and cost of sales.

KEY TERMS

brand ambassadors, 356
native advertising, 356
sponsored content, 356
media content strategy plan, 356
personal selling, 357
cognitive dissonance, 359
customer retention (CR), 360
customer relationship management (CRM), 360
customer vector report, 363
market penetration, 364
product expansion, 364
market expansion, 365
diversification, 365
unbundle, 366
up-selling, 366
cross-selling, 366
referrals, 366
hit rate, 367
bot, 368

DISCUSSION QUESTIONS

1. What are some ways that you see small business owners promote their products or services? Provide examples of your perception of their value proposition to each of the markets they are currently targeting. In your opinion, how effective do you think some of their messages are?
2. In your opinion, what do you think is the most effective and efficient way for small business owners to promote and market their products or services? Why?
3. How have you seen the use of referrals and word-of-mouth advertising work to the benefit of a small business owner? Provide examples. How have these methods worked in reverse (to the disadvantage of the owner, but possibly to the benefit of the competition)?
4. Recall the last time you purchased a product or service from a small firm. Did it use any of the techniques or skills involved in personal selling? How did the salesperson close the sale with you?
5. Imagine a brand-new customer of your online e-book service had bought an e-book and a day later emails you she wants a refund, saying the e-book didn't open and she no longer wants to see it. Others have been able to open it and so can you. You suspect she is just pirating the e-book and wants her money back. How would you resolve her complaint? If the DVD had an obvious problem opening on some computers (say one using a non-Adobe PDF reader), would it make any difference in how you would resolve the complaint?
6. Think about your product or service. How can you extend your offerings to better keep and grow your customers?

EXPERIENTIAL EXERCISES

1. Collect promotional materials from a small business in your area. These can include coupons, loyalty programs, special tie-ins, special events, advertisements, or any other promotional materials. Using these materials, answer the following questions:
   - What is the owner trying to achieve with these promotions? What are the goals and objectives of each? If you take the various promotions as a portfolio, what overall goal do they have?
   - What incentives (for the customer) are embedded in the promotion materials?
   - What business image or business characteristics do these promotions convey or imply?
   - Assuming limited funds, how would you improve the promotions for this business? Be sure to tie your ideas to specific goals.
2. Create a Google AdWords account at **www.google.com/adwords** (it's free), and load the keyword tool. Enter the keyword "day care" to see the kinds of related search terms come up, and the level of competition for ads using the different search terms. How could you limit the keywords you buy to minimize your cost and maximize your impact?
3. Go to **www.ionos.com/** to find out what it would cost for a domain name and a basic website. When asked for a desired web address, give a made-up name (not one you might want to buy later on) and see what it would cost to register the name for the different top-level domains (.com, .net, .biz, etc.). Also price the business websites to see what is offered, and how those might expand your marketing opportunities.
4. Read your local newspaper for information about a small business that you think stems from a publicity effort (e.g., new location or management, product line shift or

expansion, special events, or promotions). Compare the information in the article to website information and to business advertisements for the same business. What are the differences and similarities? Advantages and disadvantages (for the business and for the customer)?

5. *Inc.* magazine is a leading resource for small businesses. Download its media kit at **https://mediakit.inc.com/**. Based on the information in the kit, what approach would work best for you—email using the magazine's dedicated email subscriber list or its e-newsletter subscriber list?

6. Imagine that you own a small independent bookstore. You are holding a special reading and book signing by a well-known author:

   a. Describe what your goal(s) might be in arranging this event.

   b. Write a press release for the event.

   c. What other events might support the same goal(s)?

   d. Describe how you might use this information in crafting a newspaper advertisement for the store.

   e. Compare the press release, the ad, and any other events arranged in terms of overall promotional strategy for the store.

MINI-CASE

GOING VIRAL MAKES FOR A HEALTHIER FIRM[65]

Dr. Bob Wagstaff (a biochemist and nutritionist) developed the Orabrush to scrape bad breath–causing particles off the tongue. He got the Orabrush patented and approved by the FDA. He got it manufactured and worked hard to get it onto the shelves of drugstores and supermarkets. He had some success with smaller chains, but sales were below his expectations. He tried making an infomercial, which cost him around $40,000, but it produced only a few hundred more Orabrush sales. Thinking bigger marketing clout would make the product into a success, he tried marketing the patent to oral hygiene companies, but no one took him up on his offer.

He went to a marketing class at Brigham Young University and received advice from students in the class. He hoped that the young people could tell him how to sell more Orabrushes over the Internet. A survey a class team conducted showed 92 percent of the respondents wouldn't buy an Orabrush online, and the students on the team concluded that the Internet approach was not workable. However, another student in the class, Jeffrey Harmon, had a different interpretation. Jeffrey suggested that with millions of people watching videos on the Internet every day, getting 8 percent of that group to buy an Orabrush would still be an enormous market. After class "Dr. Bob" asked Jeffrey to help him market Orabrush on the web, giving Jeffrey his old motorcycle as payment. Jeffrey recruited a co-worker named Austin Craig to be the video's pitchman for $100. He got scriptwriter friend Joel Ackerman to write the script and film major Devin Graham to film the video. Total cost? About $500. It was actually recorded in the back room of a pool hall—so that really is a clinking sound in the background of the video. The video went viral on YouTube, racking up millions of views and igniting sales of the Orabrush, with close to 1 million brushes sold over the next two years.

Note: Videos related to the case include *Story of Orabrush*, www.youtube.com/watch?v=p4tuTi8_z6Q; original YouTube video: www.youtube.com/watch?v=nFeb6YBftHE.

CASE DISCUSSION QUESTIONS

1. Why do you think a YouTube video worked better than a professionally done infomercial?
2. How were Dr. Bob and Jeffrey able to get so much done for so little money? How could you apply this in starting your own business?
3. Dr. Bob had tried traditional media and pursuing traditional outlets for the Orabrush. Why do you think his sales were not up to his expectations?
4. Explain how having 8 percent of the potential market to draw from could still be a worthwhile strategy for a small business.

CHAPTER 11

Small Business Pricing, Distribution, and Location

● Steve Niewulis's original marketing efforts focused on major sports stores. When that wasn't successful, he altered the way he marketed his product. Can you think of other methods that he might have employed to create interest in his product?
BLOOMimage/Getty Images

LEARNING OBJECTIVES

After you complete this chapter, you will be able to:

LO 11-1 Understand why pricing is an important but complex and difficult task for small business.

LO 11-2 Recognize the different pricing strategies that could apply to your product or service.

LO 11-3 Understand the types of sales promotion available to small businesses.

LO 11-4 Recognize the different types of direct marketing and their pros and cons.

LO 11-5 Learn how to do nondirect distribution.

LO 11-6 Differentiate the types of international strategies.

LO 11-7 Identify the factors to consider in selecting your business location.

LO 11-8 Recognize the key issues in leasing.

LO 11-9 Know what to look for in evaluating a potential site layout.

Focus on Small Business: Steve Niewulis and Tap It![1]

Steve Niewulis, a minor league baseball player, came up with a solution to a problem all baseball players have—keeping the baseball bat handle dry between pitches. He invented Just Tap It!, a rosin bag attached to a wristband so a player could dry the bat handle between pitches. While it seemed like the perfect product for all the major sports stores, the stores were not interested because they prefer to buy from companies with several products in their product lines. Undeterred, he began attending trade shows and association meetings for high school coaches, tennis association meetings, and other similar venues. He was able to set up a booth displaying his product for just a few hundred dollars, and he created interest, recognition, and sales. At one show, he met up with Baseball Express, a catalog that targets high school, college, and minor league teams. Since he already had orders and customers using the product, he was able to show Baseball Express that this was a product it should carry. As a result, Niewulis sold thousands of Tap It! units not only to baseball players, but also to athletes who participate in other sports such as basketball, tennis, golf, and rock climbing.

DISCUSSION QUESTIONS

1. Niewulis's original intent was to market to major sports stores. How would you describe the market he finally targeted? Is there a commonality?
2. What other methods could Niewulis use to get this product to his customers?
3. Would this method have worked as well had the product been something like baked goods? Or mural painting? What methods would work better for these sorts of products?

LO **11-1** Understand why pricing is an important but complex and difficult task for small business.

Pricing

The act of writing down a price on a tag and putting it on your product is one of the easiest and most quickly done actions an entrepreneur can take. But for most entrepreneurs, setting a price for your good or service is one of the toughest decisions you will face. This is because price is central to how much you can make on each sale and that relates to your personal income. It can also determine how many sales you are likely to make. In addition, price can convey a sense about the quality of your firm and your product like the Kryptonite lock in the following Small Business Insight. So setting a price can be emotionally difficult.

It is also subject to various complexities and a lot of second-guessing. Since most goods and services are imitative, there are competing alternatives in the marketplace, so many potential customers have an idea of what something should cost. There are computations you can do to help inform your decisions, but they take a bit of time and thought. However, computations cannot provide hard and fast answers because they are subject to the quality of the data put in, the assumptions you make and their fit to the reality of your firm, and the interpretation of the resulting answers. Price also depends on your magic number and strategy (see Chapter 7), your target audience and value proposition (see Chapter 9), and the costs of your business (see Chapter 12).

optimum price
The highest price that will produce your desired level of sales in your intended market.

Simply put, your fundamental goal should be setting the **optimum price**, the price that would generate the most income possible for the product or service you are selling over the course of a year. If your sales are less than you expect, you will end up asking yourself, "Are my prices too high?" On the other hand, if sales are exceeding expectations, you will end up asking, "Are my prices too low? Am I leaving money on the table?" There are four key factors for determining an optimum price:

1. **Demand for the product or service:** Where demand is high, you can charge a premium. Where it is low, you need to consider lowering prices to keep cash flowing into the business.
2. **Value delivered to the customer:** You can buy hair-coloring kits at the supermarket for $8, and a single use of professional products would not cost more, but having a professional do the job with professional products and expertise can easily cost 10 times as much–and many people gladly pay it.
3. **Prices set by competing firms:** If a liter of Coke costs a dollar, few are likely to pay $2 for a liter of Pepsi.
4. **Your business strategy and product placement:** A company that prides itself on an environmentally conscious approach to manufacturing probably would not choose to use cheaper, unrecycled components, even if it helped profits.

Failing to set the right price is one of the greatest problems facing small businesses. Why does this happen? Often entrepreneurs set prices using some more or less arbitrary heuristic, or rule of thumb. In other words, they guess at what the best price should be using some formula such as "add 40 percent to what I pay for the product," or "set prices so that the cost of the food on the plate is no more than 35 percent of the menu price." But is that rule of thumb any good? Does it apply to the specifics of your business? Are you willing to risk your income and survival on that rule of thumb? A much better approach for you is to take the time to understand pricing, develop that optimum price, and then monitor and adjust it to work for you and your business.

In the following sections we will talk about the key ideas behind setting a price that is advantageous for you. We will start by talking about the fundamentals of setting a price–margin pricing and elasticity, value and contextual factors–and follow it up with a rundown of the amazing number of different tactics for adjusting price to fit the many situations your firm may face once it is in operation.

The Fundamentals of Pricing: Margin Pricing and Elasticity

Recall in Chapter 7 we showed you how to find your magic number: the posttax income you wanted from your business. In that example, a person who wanted $24,000 a year after taxes would need annual sales of $135,208. If you imagine yourself in a five-day-a-week business (i.e., 250 working days a year), that would work out to $541 of sales per day. Here is where you start making decisions.

SMALL BUSINESS INSIGHT

The Story of Kryptonite[2]

How do you build a strong brand on a small budget? The Kryptonite Lock Company (**www.kryptonitelock.com/**) has found the answer and now owns more than 60 percent of the North American bike lock market.

Back in 1972, Michael Zane founded Kryptonite and created a unique premium-priced "U-shaped" lock that changed the face of bicycle locks forever. By mid-1972, Kryptonite was so convinced of its product's superiority that it began offering the first antitheft guarantee to protect against bike theft caused by lock failure.

In the early 1980s, the U-shaped locks were gaining acceptance as a strong security measure. Additionally, with its commitment to creating high-quality products, Kryptonite rose to become the leader of bike security technology. Competitors then began to aggressively target the company and captured the low-end market. Kryptonite's response was to introduce the lower-cost KryptoLok in 1988, again increasing market share. The KryptoLok helped offer a wider range of products at different price points.

In 1989, with the increased popularity of mountain bikes, Kryptonite introduced the ATB (all-terrain bike) model, further diversifying its product offerings. In 1992, the Evolution 2000 was introduced with a stronger Kryptonite steel.

In 1994, in response to a new method New York City thieves were using to break locks, the New York Lock was introduced with a flurry of hype. Zane locked up his own bike on the streets of New York and sat in a surveillance van for 48 hours with a *New York Post* reporter. Together they watched as several would-be thieves tried unsuccessfully to steal his bike.

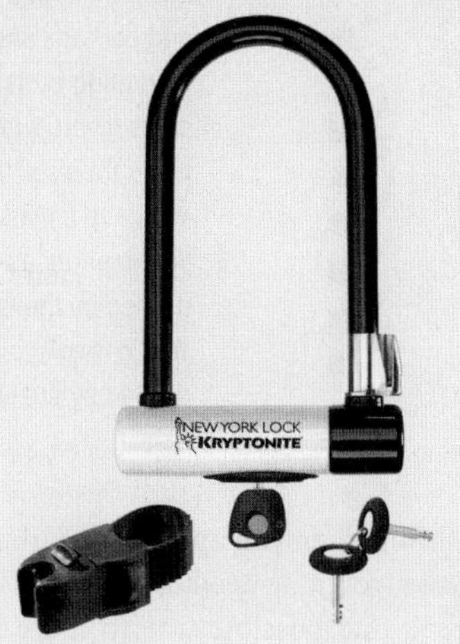

Kryptonite's rise from idea stage to its current status of multimillion-dollar market leader is a story of consistently innovative product development, competitive pricing, and creative marketing. How does Kryptonite's story reflect product development and pricing?

Now known for product innovation and attention to customer needs, Kryptonite continues to add new products and sustain their premium price. In addition to bike locks, Kryptonite offers a complete line of security devices for motorcycles, sporting goods, skis, and snowboards as well as travelers' security locks, and it sells these products in over 50 countries. Attention to detail and to changing customer needs has earned Kryptonite the reputation as the number one bike lock brand in the world. Not bad for a bearded kid who started with only a VW van and a big idea.

Imagine you were selling custom-designed T-shirts and your first thought was to price them at $20 each, based on what you've paid for similar T-shirts in the past. Exhibit 11.1 shows you the costs. To get to your $541 in sales you would need to be able to sell 28 T-shirts a day—more than 3 T-shirts every hour! This assumes you are selling online or in-person wherever you are so you don't have to add costs for rent, displays, and the other things that go with a storefront.

The method shown in Exhibit 11.1 is an example of what is called **markup pricing** and is probably the most widely used of the many pricing methods out there. Knowing your costs and the **markup**—what you would like (or need) to make from each sale—gets to the fundamentals of pricing and relating prices to your business. The computations also tell you what your margin of profit is, and that number is one asked by bankers and is one of the numbers you can often find in industry statistics, so it is a good number to know.

markup pricing
A price-setting method where an amount is added to the cost of a product to set the retail price and provide a profit.

markup
The amount an entrepreneur adds to costs to provide a profit.

EXHIBIT 11.1

Computing Margin and Markup

You can easily purchase all-cotton T-shirts for a unit price of	$3.00
Equipment, ink, and your time to screen them will add perhaps another	$2.50
Marketing costs (mostly flyers and a couple of shirts given away)	$0.50
If you then sell the shirts for	$20.00
You have a markup of $20.00 – 6.00 =	$14.00
Your markup as a percentage is the markup divided by the cost:	$14.00/6.00 or 233 percent
Your **margin** on sales of the markup divided by the sales price:	$14.00/20.00 or 70 percent

margin
The amount of profit, usually stated as a percentage of the total price.

But when you apply the markup model and then figure out what your daily sales would need to be, you may need to refigure. If selling 3 $20 T-shirts an hour sounds like a difficult-to-achieve goal, one possible way to increase sales is to drop the price, figuring the less expensive the T-shirt, the more people will be willing to buy them. If you drop the price to $10, you might think that more people will be willing to buy them. But at $10 each, you will need to sell 55 T-shirts a day or nearly 7 per hour.

elasticity
From economics, the idea that the market's demand for a product or service is sensitive to changes in its price.

inelastic product
Product for which there are few substitutes and for which a change in price makes very little difference in quantity purchased.

elastic product
Product for which there are any number of substitutes and for which a change in price makes a difference in quantity purchased.

If the idea of dropping the price to increase sales makes sense to you, congratulations! You understand what the economists call price **elasticity**. Something that is essential to how you live and does not have many substitutes or alternatives is called an **inelastic product**. Housing, basic food, basic clothing, basic transportation, and utilities are examples. The T-shirts you are planning to sell go beyond basic clothing and fall into the category of an **elastic product**, which has a lot of substitutes–cheaper T-shirts, used T-shirts, other types of shirts, shirts hidden deep in your closet, and so on.

Economists have figured out that when you increase the price for an inelastic product, people might cut back, but only a little. Think about what happens to your driving when gas prices go up sharply–you cut back on your driving as much as you can, but you are stuck buying that high-priced gas. When you cut back on an elastic product, like your T-shirt, people buy a lot less. You might buy one T-shirt a month at $10 each, but at $20 you might not be willing to buy it at all, or if you are willing you will probably want to save up to buy it. The difference in elasticity is why in bad times you see clothing stores close down more often than you see gas stations close.

Figure 11.1 shows the difference in elasticity for your elastic product of T-shirts and for the inelastic product of gasoline. The difference in the slopes of the lines can help you think about the impact of dropping or raising the price. Remember to keep in mind how the general economy is affecting your customers. If money is tight, they will respond to price increases for elastic products much more negatively because that is where their needs are more flexible, or elastic.

law of supply and demand
The economic theory that describes how the demand for products (or services) and the supply of them affect each other.

price gouging
Charging an outrageously high price for something.

You've heard about the **law of supply and demand** and this is where it applies in business. When the supply of a product or service is generally enough to meet the customer demand for it, the price is stable and, over the long term, pretty average. If the supply suddenly shrinks (e.g., imports of basic T-shirts you sell in your business dry up because of a trade embargo, a typhoon, or any other reason), the prices go up. If demand suddenly grows (everyone wants to wear a red T-shirt on Monday to show support for the hometown team), the prices are likely to go up. While there is an ethical (and sometimes a legal) issue in charging too much in such situations–what is called **price gouging**–having a reasonable increase is expected. Figuring out what is "reasonable" is a case of looking at what your competitors are doing, considering what you feel is ethically right, and being ready to adjust your prices as you gain insight into the situation.

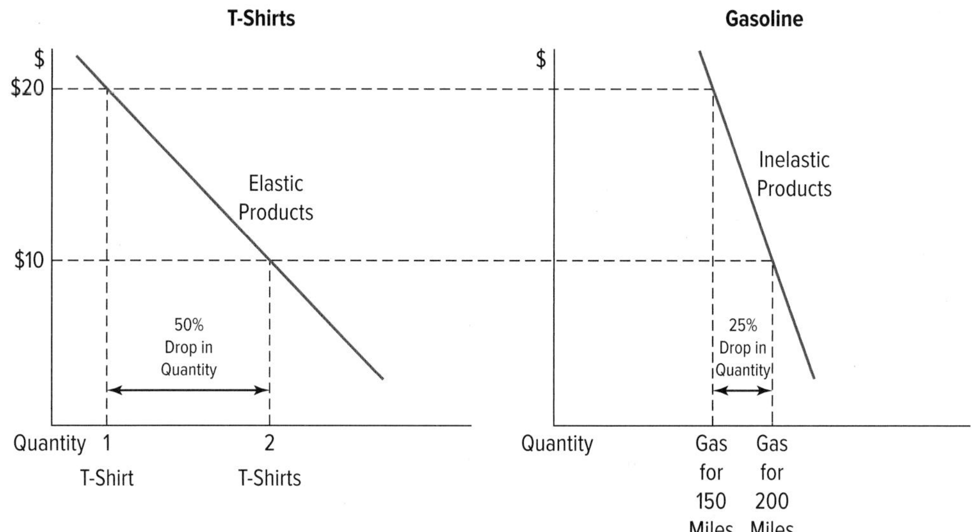

FIGURE 11.1

Pricing Elasticity

So as an entrepreneur, you can adjust your prices based on supply and demand, but you also need to keep an eye on the competition. As we noted earlier, if a liter of Coke costs a dollar in the store, few are likely to pay $2 for a liter of Pepsi in the store. But as an entrepreneur you have the potential to make choices that may justify a $2 price, for example, selling ice-cold liters of Pepsi on the street corner across from the baseball stadium on the afternoon of a game. Demand will be up because of the heat, and your $2 price might still look like a good value compared to soda prices inside the stadium.

As you can see, being an economic theory and not a law of nature, the predictive power of elasticity and the law of supply and demand can get watered down by a host of possible factors. Coke and Pepsi are brands people know about so they know what they are buying when they get a liter. T-shirts, however, are another matter. If you begin selling T-shirts for $20 and you don't get enough sales, you might want to see what happens when you drop the price of the T-shirts from $20 to $10. Sales may go up because of the lower price, but it is also possible that some customers will assume that you have started compromising on quality (maybe getting cheaper T-shirts on which to put your designs). Taking the price of the shirt as an indicator of quality, they may decide to buy fewer shirts at $10 than at $20. That means to make elasticity work, you need to also keep in mind the value people see in your product. Let's look at how that gets figured into pricing.

Gasoline is a product with almost no substitutes. If you need to drive, you need gas, no matter how high the price. That makes gasoline an inelastic product. Even when expensive, you will buy it.

Roberto Westbrook/Spaces Images/Blend Images LLC

The Fundamentals of Pricing: Value

Elasticity is an important indicator, but it is not the only one you ought to consider. T-shirts and gasoline are products that almost everyone buys, and whose sales result in a lot of competition and price pressure. However, there are other markets and products for which people will pay extra. Remember in Chapter 7 we talked about value and cost benefits. Those value benefits now come back into play as you think about price. We know that people will pay more for a product of high quality or high stylishness or leading-edge technology. That is why we all know that an iPhone typically costs more than the competing Android phone. But small businesses can offer products with the same sort of appeal.

Let's consider the example of Screaming Eagle wines from Napa Valley, California. This small business follows a strategy of deliberately remaining a limited producer of fine wines. The demand for high-end wines is so high that the winery sells solely by subscription. Even at $850 per bottle for newly released vintages, there is a waiting list of people wanting to be placed on the customer subscription list. There certainly is no pressure for the winery to reduce prices, as it currently sells its entire output before it is even bottled. In fact, there is pretty good evidence that Screaming Eagle could increase the winery price substantially and still sell its entire 600- to 850-case output before it is released. You need only do a Google search for "Screaming Eagle wine"

Screaming Eagle sells its wines for $850 a bottle and sells all its wine before it is even bottled. How do you think it can do such a great job of convincing customers to pay a superpremium price?

Source: Screaming Eagle

to see that there is a very vigorous secondary resale demand. You will find individual bottles of older vintages of the wine priced over $5,000.[3]

The value delivered to the customer is second in order of importance to the pricing decision. How can a boutique winery like Screaming Eagle charge $850 for a bottle of wine?[4] The answer is that the price customers are willing to pay is determined by their perception of value received. From the consumer's point of view, top-flight vintners are selling much more than a mere bottle of fine wine. They are also selling exclusivity. Only a few, very rich people can buy Screaming Eagle directly from the winery, and they can buy it if, and only if, they have been accepted to the subscription list. Also consider: "Would the wine have the very high demand that it currently enjoys if it were priced at a more 'reasonable' rate, say $50 per bottle?" Certainly it would not. The extravagant price is actually part of what creates and maintains the high demand.

In addition to demand and value provided, you must consider the prices set by your competition.[5] It is often tempting to set your price lower than that of your competitor in the hope that you can pull away some of her customers. This is often self-defeating for two reasons. First, if you lower your price, your revenue will decline as a percentage of your total sales. Often, the increase in sales is insufficient to make up for the lost revenue. Second, if your strategy works, it will not be long before your competitor realizes the drop in sales and lowers prices to meet yours. You both end up with lower prices, and no more volume than before the price cut. The issues of deliberately lowering prices for strategic reasons are discussed in detail later in this chapter.

The opposing temptation is to set your prices higher than that of your competition. For wines, the First Growth (Grand Cru) wines of Bordeaux actually sell for even more than $850, so why not raise the price of Screaming Eagle? For that matter, bottles of Screaming Eagle wine sell for more than $2,000 on wine-searcher.com all the time. The problem with this reasoning is that it is backward: it is considering the firm's competitive position from only the owner's point of view. A much better approach would be to determine what features your customers are actually willing to pay for. Setting prices higher than the competition without providing customers with the perception of receiving greater value can only lead to lower overall volume. For Screaming Eagle's connoisseur customers, a Grand Cru is an even better wine, so it should cost more. Someday Screaming Eagle may have the vintage that makes the breakthrough in the world of wines, matching Bordeaux's best, and it is then it could safely raise its prices and keep its customers happy.

With the lesson of Screaming Eagle wines in mind, go back to the list of value benefits in Chapter 7 and ask yourself if there is a way to tap into them to make a case for higher price. For the T-shirts, having designs by a known local artist or band or offbeat designs featuring local schools could make it work. If you work it right, value benefits can turn into higher prices for your products.

The Fundamentals of Pricing: Contextual Factors[6]

The discussion up to here has covered why pricing is so important and the major factors that determine prices. Issues of the effects of demand and value on pricing were analyzed. All this is necessary information for you to be able to set prices. However, it does not explain the "nuts and bolts" of how to use the information to actually set a price. Of course, one reason that this discussion is necessarily general and not specific is that the details of determining the "right" price differ among industries and businesses. Still, some practices are valid across industries.

As we've said, your first task must be to decide what is the optimum price. This can be a very different number among similar businesses, depending on specific business goals. If you are operating profitably near your business's maximum capacity, the right price is most likely the one that maximizes the probability of a sale without leaving money on the table. For example, if your restaurant and bar is the "in" place to be, and you cannot even begin to handle those Friday and Saturday night crowds, you just might want to impose a cover charge. Or if your business is the patent holder of a biopharmaceutical that will grow hair on bald men's pates, you will initially set the price so high that only a few can afford it. Then, as the patent approaches its termination, you will lower the price to capture the maximum market and to establish a barrier to the entry of generic manufacturers.[7]

If you are operating below capacity, the right price might be one that is low enough to fill your production capacity and keep your key employees working. If you could throw a bowling ball through your restaurant without hitting anyone on a Friday night, you will want to consider $10 pitchers of margaritas, or perhaps (if local regulation allows) a "ladies drink free."

If you are trying to make your business grow, or if you are at the point that you are preparing to exit your business, the right price is the one necessary to capture a desired market share or to meet a specific profit target, given an anticipated level of sales volume.

Once you have decided what your pricing goals are, the next logical step is to examine the existing market prices for similar products and services. You should also make a comparison list of the similarities and differences among your competitors' offerings. We've gone through examples such as distinctive competence maps (Skill Module 7.4), coordinating your distinctive competence with your value proposition (Skill Module 9.7), or the idea comparison matrix shown in Exhibit 9.1 (replace only "Idea 1" with your offering, and the other ideas with your competitors' offering). If at all possible, you should attempt to determine which features of your competitors' products and services are actually desired by customers. This process will provide you with a range of prices and features to which you can compare your own product.

Now is the time to consider your business costs. The question that you must answer is, "Can I make a profit at the price that will meet sales volume goals?" If the answer is yes, you have established an acceptable base price. From this price, you can then experiment a bit. You probably should start by deliberately setting your price above the acceptable base. Too often start-ups price themselves too low, which doesn't account for the mistakes and learning that will take place at the business's start, and keeps the potential profits too low. The kindhearted buyer in the following Small Business Insight is not the kind of customer you can depend on to let you know you've priced too low. Most customers will just buy you out of your product or service and let you find out you're not going to make a profit for all the business you've done.

SMALL BUSINESS INSIGHT

BLUE WATER BOATWORKS

Blue Water Boatworks was started by Saint Louis University student JP Keating. It provided boat cleaning and detailing services to individuals, marinas, and boat dealers. An issue arose for the company when one of the biggest boat dealers negotiated a price for detailing dozens of boats in preparation for a boat show. With Blue Water in its start-up phase, JP was overjoyed to get the contract, and set a price based on his costs of materials and time. Being a student, he didn't think his time was worth that much. He set the cost at $100 for a 15-foot boat, and adjusted it as boat length became longer.

The boat dealer figured that it cost him almost $300 to detail the 15-footer in his organization. A part of him wanted to in lock JP for a long-term contract to get a great deal. But the dealer also realized he would be taking advantage of JP, and once JP realized he had massively underpriced his service, he would not be a willing contractor.

The dealer called JP over to the office and showed him what it really cost to detail a boat. He worked with JP to come up with a more realistic price, one that would help JP stay motivated and grow his business. In the business plan, JP set the price at $350. He felt he could charge more than the in-house cost because as a specialist, he could do a better job. In addition, he offered boat owners convenience, doing the detailing on the owner's schedule. For the boat dealer, this meant being able to do two things at once—a real help as the big boat show approached. He was glad to pay the $350, but JP gave him a discount price of $300 out of respect for the dealer's honesty and help.

JP was lucky to find such an ethical first customer. But from then on, he always worked through the mechanics of setting his prices before talking to customers.

If your initial price needs to be adjusted, you will face much less customer dissatisfaction if your response is to lower your price rather than to raise it. If the answer is no, however, you are going to have to consider how you can lower your costs to the point that you can make a profit at the price that you have determined to be the "right" one.

Your Company Objectives[8]

For most small businesses, the early years are survival years and the tendency is to sell your product for whatever you can get for it. Sure, you'd like $5,000 per desk, but if someone offers you $3,000, well, at least it'll help you to meet this week's payroll. While it may be a fact of life at certain times, it shouldn't be your firm's pricing objective.

More commonly, firms set prices to maximize profits or to increase market share. Increasing market share usually means pricing toward the low end of the competition in order to take market share from the competition. This strategy becomes more popular as a product reaches the maturity phase of the product life cycle. However, this shouldn't be an objective for a small business for several reasons.[9] Bigger, better-established companies have deep pockets, and often more geographic diversity, and larger product lines than you do. They can match or undercut your price in a heartbeat—even sell below cost because they're supported by sales of other products or in other regions.[10] Another reason why a small firm shouldn't try to compete on price is that it probably won't be working at full capacity for some time. Your building rent is the same whether you are producing at top speed or working only a few hours a week. If you cut your prices too low, you won't be able to cover costs during your nonproductive times. When you are up to full speed, you could drop your prices, or you might find other ways to please your customers, such as including free delivery or other services, and leave your price alone.[11]

Maximizing profits is a much better option for the small firm. This doesn't mean that you need to have the most expensive product out there unless you're worth it, but it does mean that your price should be above the average price.[12] First, this simply adds to your profit. If your business is profitable, a one dollar increase in price will add one dollar to profit. Second, as a small business you do not have the volume of sales that would allow profitable operation with low margins.

Studies have also shown that companies that compete on product innovation and high quality achieve higher growth than those that try to compete on price. Firms that compete on price even tend to experience negative growth.[13] Another study of 1,000 firms shows that a 1 percent price increase converted to a 12 percent increase in profitability, all else being the same.[14] There are times and places to compete on price, but exhaust all other strategies first.

One more example: J. David Allen, director of a large entrepreneurship center, once owned a company that sold dominoes. He barely sold any at $3 per box. Then he added a design for the Texas Sesquicentennial and couldn't keep them on the shelf at $19.95.[15] The product cost roughly the same—adding the design had minimal impact—but look at the difference in the profit. Be different, be better, but don't be too cheap. And remember: It's always easier to lower prices than it is to raise them.[16]

Marketing Strategy

Your price must be consistent with the rest of your marketing strategy. If you are advertising high quality or prestige but price your product lower than the competition, your customers will be confused at best, or at worst simply not believe your ads. If you're trying to get into Walmart, you don't want to have Rodeo Drive prices. If you package in a plain cardboard box, you're hinting at a different price point from a silk-lined, leather case. If you are making custom desks, they had better be higher priced than the pressed board, assemble-it-yourself ones you find at the discount stores. Consistency is key.

Channels of Distribution

Everyone who handles your product will be expecting to make something from it. If you are using a traditional retailer, your product may go through several intermediaries (see the "Distribution" section of this chapter for more information) before getting on the shelf. The end price to your customer might be four times from what *you* got. This is called *price escalation.* You need to make sure that once all those involved get their cut, your product is still priced correctly to reach your target market. If the distribution costs price you out of the market, you may want to sell direct.

Competition

We've talked a bit about pricing in relation to your competition, but you can't just look at the competition's price ranges and pick something at, oh, about 75 percent of maximum. Just as yours is, your competitors' products are a "bundle of satisfactions." How do their product bundles match up to yours? You may make athletic shoes just as good as Nike's, but you don't provide the prestige of the Nike logo (at least not when you're new). What other "extras" do customers get from your competition–additional service, brand recognition, prestige, bragging rights, comfort of knowing a big company will back up the product, and others? These intangible things are hard to price, but you need to think about how your product or service matches up to theirs.[17]

Ultra Pearls, sold by Dan and Russell Schlueter, offers the ultimate in cat litter control. How does the Schlueter pricing strategy reinforce the product's known benefits?

Mark Dierker/McGraw-Hill Education

Dan and Russell Schlueter sell pet products, including Ultra Pearls and Crystal Clear Litter Pearls. This cat litter offers a significant benefit over ordinary litters. About 4 pounds of the Schlueters' product lasts as long as 28 pounds of other litters. When competing brands sold 14-pound bags for $6 to $7, the Schlueters priced their 4-pound bag at $14 to $16. Their 4-pound bag lasts a month–the same as two bags of the other litter. Still, they're at a premium to the competition. Which would you rather carry from the store–28 pounds of the old stuff or 4 pounds of Ultra Pearls? Add some awards from *Cat Fancy* magazine and PetSmart Outstanding Technology Achievement Award and in less than five years their company has become a $10 million plus business.[18]

Legal and Regulatory Issues

There's a plethora of items that can fall under legal and regulatory issues. There are laws, for example, against price fixing and other collusion among competitors. The government sometimes establishes "acceptable" prices or price minimums or maximums–especially if you are selling to the government. Some forms of price discrimination are illegal.[19] It's OK to lower your prices during happy hour (effectively discriminating against those who work during that time period), but you can't charge different prices to customers of different races. You can offer a senior citizen's discount, but you can't charge a "skinny person" premium. In most states you must collect sales tax for retail purchases. Usually, however, you are not required to do so for mail order and Internet sales. Sometimes there are special taxes or fees that must be collected, such as deposits or hazardous waste handling fees. Talk to your accountant and your attorney about specific rules pertaining to your product or service.[20]

The Pricing Toolbox

LO **11-2** Recognize the different pricing strategies that could apply to your product or service.

You should now know what influences the setting of prices based on your magic number, your costs, the value you can offer, the elasticities of the market, and the contextual factors from your business environment. You should have a basic idea of *your* costs and needs, but there is still one key group that needs to be considered–your customers. For most people, their reaction to the prices they see is as much about their own perceptions and psychology as about the major market forces. In this section we provide you with the tools to make that final pricing decision, adding to the mix the customer's psychology and the myriad of techniques that can help you couch a price in *just* the right way to appeal to your intended customer. Then we will give you practical examples of how pricing works when selling a product and a service.

Pricing Psychology: How Customers Perceive Prices

When you shop for products, you look at a price and make a judgment as to whether this is a fair price or too low or too high. Where you shop and under what circumstances you shop can also influence this judgment. We expect different prices at different places. We expect to pay more for emergency plumbing repairs or for certain conveniences. If your needs change, your willingness to pay changes. A submarine sandwich has little value to you if you have just completed a five-course meal, but if you haven't eaten in two days, you might pay almost anything for it (even though it is exactly the same sandwich).

internal reference price A consumer's mental image of what a product's price should be based on experience and the consumer's estimate of what the comparative value might be.

external reference price An estimation of what a price should be based on information external to a consumer, such as advice, advertisements, or comparison shopping.

Consumers have what are known as internal and external reference prices. Basically these are expectations about what a price should be, based on their own knowledge (**internal reference pricing**) or from gathering information from outside sources (**external reference pricing**). External reference prices may come from looking at competitive ads, researching on the Internet, visiting several stores, or asking friends. Consumers will also pick up on external clues. If the product is sold at Walmart, they will expect to pay less than if it's sold at an upscale department store (expectations based on where it is bought). A Rolex watch sold by a street vendor in Beijing should cost less than a Rolex at Tiffany's in New York City (expectations based on perception of the likely quality and authenticity). You'd expect lower prices at a "going out of business" sale than at a "back to school" sale (perception of motivation of the seller–how eager he or she is to sell).

Consumers' internal reference price may be based on the last time they purchased something, recollections of what they might have read or heard in the past, their understanding of how much it would cost to make it (it's made in China, so it should be inexpensive; it's gold-plated, so it'll cost more), or their perception of the value the product has. If the last time you went to the movies you paid $4 for a ticket and today you find out it costs $10, you might just wait for the video to come out. (You're forgetting that the last time you went to the movies was 10 years ago.)

Perception of value varies from person to person. For example, if you can clean your apartment in two hours and figure your time is worth $10 an hour, you won't want to pay someone else $30 to do it for you. On the other hand, if it takes you four hours or if you figure your time is worth $20 per hour, then $30 sounds like a good deal. It doesn't need to be purely financially motivated either. If you find cleaning relaxing and a break from your regular job while other people rank it as their absolute least favorite thing to do, they are willing to pay something while you may be willing to pay nothing at all. Skills may be involved: Some people might be able to figure their taxes themselves; others may find any math involving more than three digits beyond their capabilities.

Expectations of future prices may be internal or external. The newspaper says interest rates are going up; consumers may decide to pay a bit more to get their new house now while rates are low. You're going to the Bahamas next November; you'll wait for the end-of-the-season sales to buy your vacation clothes because you remember end-of-the-season sales from past experience.

Consumers also have a price range of acceptability. Any price within this range is really OK with them. How wide the range is varies by product, by consumer, and by situation. This price range of acceptability tends to be the inelastic parts–the "sticky" parts–of the elasticity curves.

Setting a price somewhat above the competitive midpoint has a psychological impact on buyers.[21] If three sweaters appear to be identical but are priced at $30, $40, and $50, you are likely to feel that the more expensive one is of higher quality.[22] You can explore this in Skill Module 11.1.

How you define your product determines your competitive advantage and affects your price. When you get right down to it, there are only two competitive advantages: your product or service must be better (quality, features, distribution, etc.) or cheaper. Being better is sustainable, but someone else can always match or beat your price.[23]

Customers who are attracted to low prices will not be loyal and will switch as soon as something cheaper comes along.[24] Customers will always pay more for a product or service that stands out from the crowd. Treehouse Cuts Salons is a children's hair salon that has chairs designed as Barbie jeeps and other kid-friendly items such as televisions or Sony PlayStations at each chair. The salon charges about 30 percent more than the competition, but parents are willing to spend the money to make their child's haircutting experience more pleasant.[25] Consumers perceive Treehouse Cuts as a better value–regardless of the actual price.

Pricing Strategies[26]

We have discussed all the "externalities" that can affect your price. These set the limits for what you are able to do with your pricing strategies. For example, if the government has set a price

Pricing Psychology

SKILL MODULE 11.1

Customers often view pricing as a proxy for quality, especially when it is difficult for them to truly evaluate the products:

1. Tell your friends that you are conducting a taste test and provide three samples of the same product in containers marked A, B, and C. (Choose products for which brands are not easily visually detected, such as pasta, soft drinks, etc.)
2. Predetermine three price points: one that is about average for the product, one that is relatively high compared to the competition, and one that would reflect the "discount" brand price.
3. As your friends sample each of the three, give them some data about the product. Include exactly the same data about each—in a different order—except for the suggested retail price. (For example, soft drink A might be sugar-free, vitamin-fortified, cola-based, only 1 calorie, manufactured in the United States, and available locally for 50 cents. Sample B sells for 75 cents and is cola-based, and is manufactured in the United States as well. It has only 1 calorie and is sugar-free and vitamin-fortified. Sample C is an American, cola-based, vitamin-fortified soft drink with no calories. It retails for $1 and is sugar-free as well.)
4. Allow your friends to taste each product once, and do not permit them to go back and resample. Between samples, provide a sip of water or a cracker to remove any lingering taste—anything to separate the three samples slightly.
5. After tasting all three, ask them to discuss each one, stating what they did or did not like about the product.
6. If done in a classroom setting, provide a score sheet for each student to rate the product.
7. Often you will find that the more expensive product's characteristics are rated higher.

Note: This test often works with similar results on other "quality indicators" such as the store where something is purchased (the item bought at Walmart versus an upscale department store) or the country of origin (products from a country with a good reputation versus a less-developed country; for example, wine from France or Bulgaria).

maximum, you may not be able to use a skimming or premium price strategy–strategies that mean setting prices relatively high compared to the competition. If you have determined that the price range of acceptability for a large pizza is between $8 and $15 and your costs determine that you need to charge $20, then the premium pricing route–with creating the correct mind-set through other parts of the marketing mix–is almost imperative.

To reiterate, it's almost always a bad idea for a small firm to try to compete on price. Competing on price may lead to a price war in which you just don't have the staying power of a big firm. Lower prices are "throwing away" profit you really need. They can signal your customers that your product isn't as high quality as your competitors'. There are, however, plenty of strategies available to small businesses that you can use as successfully as the larger firms.[27]

Skimming[28]

Skimming is charging the highest price the market will bear. This technique is usually possible only if you are absolutely the first product or service of your type in the market, and only if it's something people really want. Companies sometimes use this strategy in order to recoup research and development costs or heavy marketing expenses. If your product or service is truly innovative and at the beginning of the product life cycle (little or no competition)–for instance, 8K television–and if you can convince customers to try it through effective advertising, then skimming may be an option. This method will attract competition, so it's not a long-term strategy.

skimming
Setting a price at the highest level the market will bear, usually because there is no competition at the time.

Prestige or Premium Pricing[29]

Just as setting your prices low signals low quality, having a high price can signal great quality and an item that is prestigious to own.[30] When a consumer has difficulty assessing the quality of the item—for example, the first time he or she purchases a product in that category—price is used as a proxy for quality. Similarly with prestige. Consider average computer buyers: Do they really understand RAM and ROM and gigabytes and all those other terms or do they have the vague impression that "bigger is better"? The same goes for the price; that more expensive computer just *has* to be better than the less expensive, no-name brand. (If you needed a root canal, would you rather go to a dentist who says it'll cost several hundred dollars or one who states he or she can do it for $49?) Certainly most everyone would agree that a Toyota Corolla is a good-quality automobile, but if you ask people what kind of car they aspire to own, you'll hear Jaguar, BMW, Mercedes. It's a prestige thing determined partly by a higher price tag.

prestige pricing
Setting a price above that of the competition to indicate your product is a status symbol.

premium pricing
Setting a price above that of the competition to indicate a higher quality.

Generally **prestige pricing** is for an item considered a status symbol, such as a Rolex watch, a Mercedes automobile, or the Remy Martin cognac shown in Figure 11.2. **Premium pricing** is used for nonstatus symbol types of products, such as toothpaste, shampoo, or laundry detergent, as in the example of Tide presenting itself as a premium-priced detergent in Figure 11.2. The general idea behind both approaches is the same.

A few warnings. If you are going to go for the high-end market, remember what we say about marketing mix consistency: Make sure your product, packaging, advertising, and distribution—in short, everything—match your price. If your product or service quality isn't appropriate, you'll not only fail to get a second chance, but you'll also generate a lot of bad word of mouth as well. And you may not want to be the very highest out there; a Lamborghini and a Jaguar are both prestigious cars, but the Jaguar market is much larger.

Odd-Even Pricing[31]

odd-even pricing
Setting a price that ends in the number 5, 7, or 9.

Odd-even pricing simply means setting a price that ends with a 9, 7, or 5. For example, don't charge $100; charge $99.99 (or $99.97 or $99.95). Numbers that are multiples of 10 are a psychological hurdle for consumers. Therefore, $9.99 seems much cheaper than $10, and the difference between $9.99 and $10 feels greater than the difference between $9.99 and $9.98. Consumers will set price limits in their minds; they'll want to spend under $1,000 for a new computer. They may spend $999, before taxes and other extras are added on, and they'll feel that they've succeeded in meeting their budget—and will brag to their friends that they were able to buy "all this for under a grand."[32] Does odd-even pricing work? A recent study showed that when an identical dress was priced at $34, $39, and $44, a third more dresses were sold at $39 than at either of the other two prices.[33]

FIGURE 11.2

Prestige/Premium Pricing Ad[34]

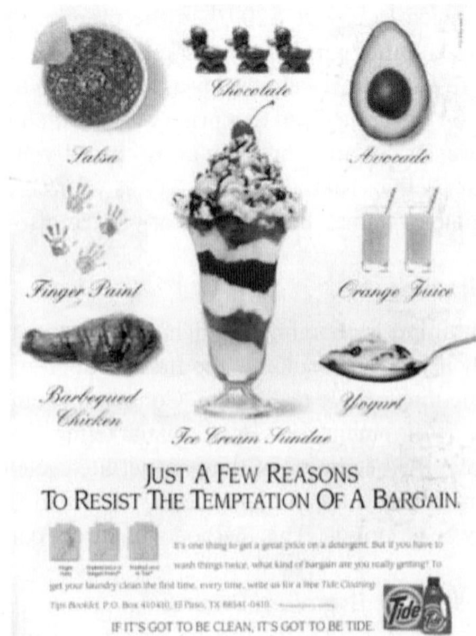

Image Courtesy of The Advertising Archives; Procter & Gamble

Partitioned Pricing

Partitioned pricing is alluded to in the previous computer example–setting a base price and charging extra for all other components. You set the price for the main component–a computer for $999–but just about everything else you need is extra. You need a printer? That's another $100. How about cables to connect the printer to the computer? That's $29.95. Did you realize you could increase your computer's memory, add a read/write CD burner, or a DVD player? They cost more, of course. Extended warranty? $79.95. Don't you want to scan photos, add a digital camera, and upgrade to a flat-screen monitor? What about some ink cartridges for that new printer? And several different kinds of paper? Don't forget to check out our excellent selection of software on your way up to the checkout. That $999 computer may end up costing twice that much (or more) before the consumer gets out the door.

partitioned pricing
Setting the price for a base item and then charging extra for each additional component.

Partitioned pricing works because once consumers make a decision that a certain product is the one they want, they are very reluctant to change their mind. It's sort of like saying that they made a bad decision or decided too quickly. They don't want to look stupid or cheap or settle for something less than they really "deserve." A number of products are sold that way: shipping, extended warranties, installation, training, additional services, and the like are not often included in the final price.

Captive Pricing

For certain products and services, **captive pricing** works well. In captive pricing, you sell something, usually a base system, at a relatively low price, but the expendables it uses are relatively expensive. Computer printers are usually priced low for the technology–sometimes even thrown in for free when you buy a computer–but the cost of the replacement ink cartridges is high. By the time you purchase three or four, you've spent more money for them than the price of the printer. For services, something you can offer a low price for, such as first-time membership to a health club, can be a candidate for captive pricing. Any extra classes, sauna, massage, and the like can be higher priced and more profitable. Although it's true that customers could get a massage elsewhere, they have already purchased this membership and it's convenient. The whole freemium approach, which has been mentioned earlier in the text, is a model of captive pricing often used in the app business.

captive pricing
Setting the price for an item relatively low and then charging much higher prices for the expendables it uses.

Price Lining

Price lining is an attempt to appeal to several different markets. In this situation, you might have three models of your product or service price to appeal to the high-, mid-, and low-end market. You might have a computer with all the bells and whistles priced at or near the top of the competitive price range, a bare-bones, stripped-down version priced at or near the bottom, and a third model at a midrange price with midrange features. This way you appeal to customers with different budgets and different needs. Even if it's a product without a lot of features to add or remove, price lining can work. Next time you are at the store, find all the Procter & Gamble or Unilever products in the shampoo or laundry detergent aisle; they'll have products at every price point with different brand names. For example, Unilever manufactures both Suave hair care products at the low price end and Tresemmé products at the high price end. Procter & Gamble has Gain (low price) and Cheer (high price) laundry detergents.

price lining
The practice of setting (usually) three price points: good quality, better quality, best quality.

Price-Lowering Techniques[35]

Even though all-out price competition is not usually the best strategy for smaller businesses, there are times when a company needs to reduce its prices in order to attract more business, smooth service cycles, build loyalty, move excess inventories, alleviate temporary cash flow problems, and the like. *Sale* is a powerful term. A recent study shows that even just the word *sale* can drive up demand by 50 percent without any actual price change.[36] The following techniques generally can be used without starting price wars or reducing the quality perception of your product or service. The complete list is given in Table 11.1. Some of the less obvious techniques get a bit more coverage next.

TABLE 11.1 Pricing Strategies

Pricing Technique	Description	Example
Secondary market pricing	One price for the primary market and a different one for secondary markets.	Computer priced at $2,000 for U.S. business markets and at $1,500 in Mexico.
Periodic discounting	Patterned or systematic price reduction.	Holiday sale, back-to-school sale.
Random discounting	Nonsystematic price reduction.	Sales without a discernable pattern.
Price skimming	Charging the absolute highest possible price due to inelastic demand.	Prices of plasma televisions.
Off-peak pricing	Lower prices during off-peak periods in order to even out purchases.	Happy hours or late-night specials at restaurants.
Loss leaders	Selling a name brand at or near cost in order to attract traffic to a retailer.	Target selling Pampers at cost and locating them at the back of the store, hoping a customer might pick up other items while in the store.
Price discrimination	Charging different prices to different groups, usually to attract a different demographic.	Senior citizens' discounts.
Penetration pricing	Setting a low price in order to get market share.	A later entrant into the market may set prices below all competition in order to steal market share.
Limit pricing	Extremely low penetration price to discourage competitors from entering a market.	Instead of skimming, the first on the market may price just above cost until it feels the competition has given up on the market.
Price signaling	Setting a high price on a product in order to imply high quality or similar quality to a competitor.	If I set my price the same as Levi's jeans, people will assume they are the same quality.
Going rate	At or near industry average.	Competitors price from $5.00 to $10.00 and your price is $7.50.
Captive pricing	Selling one item at a very low price (even below cost) when there are necessary supplies that you can sell for a high price.	Low-price ink-jet printers, but high-priced replacement ink cartridges.
Bait pricing	Advertising an inexpensive product and placing it near better, more expensive models. The idea is to get the consumer to buy up. Sometimes the product will be intentionally ugly—unpopular color, etc.	The ad shows a $300 computer, but to see it you have to walk by all the other computers that have many more features, better quality, etc.
Reference pricing	Two similar products displayed side-by-side in ad or at the store but at different prices. Implies the same product but at a better price.	Walmart brand aspirin next to Bayer, but at half the price.
Everyday low price	Implying that the price stated is always low and it's always a good deal.	The Walmart strategy; even when its prices are higher than the competition's, the consumers feel that they are not.
Odd-even pricing	Ending a price with a 9, 7, or 5.	A book that is $69.99.
Customary pricing	Prices based on tradition; it's very difficult to raise above this limit.	Penny gumball machines, 50-cent candy bars.
Prestige/premium pricing	Setting a high price to imply that this product is a status symbol and/or of much better quality than others.	Pricing of luxury cars, the best perfumes.
Professional pricing	Fees set by doctors, lawyers, and other similar professionals that tend to be uniform in a geographic region.	Lasik eye surgery runs between $1,000 and $3,000 at most eye doctors.
Product line pricing	Selling products at different price points to attract the low-, mid-, and high-end customers.	Marriott hotels are high priced, but the Marriott Courtyards are moderately priced.

Pricing Technique	Description	Example
Bundling/bonus pack/ multipack	Putting two or more of the same or different products or services together and selling for a price somewhat under the products' individual prices.	An oil change is $49 and tire rotation is $69, but if you do them both, it will cost only $99.
Partitioned pricing	Pricing each piece separately; the consumer gets "hooked" on the core component and then pays extra for everything else needed.	The computer is only $699, but the printer is another $100 and cables are $30 and the modem is. . . .
Coupons/rebates	Temporary price-reduction strategies.	This coupon is worth $1 off the next visit.
Loyalty programs	A reward given to repeat customers.	Buy nine sandwiches and the tenth one is free.
Referral discounts	A reward to customers who encourage others to buy from you.	If one of your friends signs up at our health club, you'll get one month free.

Periodic and Random Discounting

Periodic discounting refers to sales that happen regularly, such as the January White Sale or the special on Christmas cards on December 26. You may need to do one of these to keep up with your competition, since savvy customers often expect these sales. An alternative is **random discounting** where you run a sale unexpectedly. Random discounts shouldn't be too frequent because consumers begin to realize if they stock up in this sales period, they can probably wait until the next sales period.

periodic discounting
Sales conducted at predictable intervals, such as before major holidays.

random discounting
A sale run on a schedule that is unpredictable to the customer.

Off-Peak Pricing

Where does happy hour drink pricing fall in all of these techniques? It is an example of **off-peak pricing**. Services have busy periods and slow periods. Restaurants give wait staff split shifts with time off between lunch and dinner, but not every service can do this. By putting on a sale during slack periods, you may cover part of the cost of staying open. Happy hours are designed to attract business in the late afternoon slump just before the dinner crowd arrives. The reverse of this is *peak pricing*. Hotels charge more during their busy tourist season for example. Movie tickets also cost more on weekends. When demand is higher, people are less concerned about paying a premium to get the service when they want it.

off-peak pricing
Charging lower prices at certain times to encourage customers to come during slack periods.

Bundling or Multiple-Packs or Bonus-Packs Pricing

This works equally well for services or products. Let's say a haircut is $25 and coloring is $50. For this week, if you do both you'll pay only $60. The beauty salon has "**bundled**" haircuts and coloring for a price lower than the two would cost separately.[37] This technique is particularly effective for promoting the sales of a second product or service that might not be doing as well or is newly introduced. This can also be a way to increase sales when reversed, as in the example of unbundling products, which is one of the ways to increase sales when retaining customers in the customer development funnel of Blank and Dorf.

A variation of this is selling **multiple or bonus packs**, such as buying five bottles of hand lotion for the price of three–the kind of packaging that has made Sam's Club so famous. People are creatures of habit, and the more you can get them to use your product, the more likely they are to internalize it–it becomes their brand.

bundling
Combining two or more products in one unit and pricing it less than if the units were sold separately.

multiple or bonus pack
Combining more than one unit of the same product and pricing it lower than if each unit were sold separately.

Pricing in Practice

Price setting is one of the more complex decisions an entrepreneur faces. It certainly is one of the most studied, and it is one of the most crucial. So let's look at how entrepreneurs use these materials and their own judgment in setting prices. We saw one example previously in the chapter with our T-shirt entrepreneur. We will return to that example of selling something tangible and also include an example for a service.

Pricing T-Shirts

In Exhibit 11.1 we saw our T-shirt entrepreneur–let's call her Janeen–pick a price of $20 a shirt for online and in-person sales. Janeen's quick check of the Internet showed her that a lot of designed T-shirts are in the $15 to $20 range, and a check of local stores showed a range from $15 to about $25. Taken together, this gave her some confidence in her $20 price. To finalize her price and make it more attractive, she applied the technique of odd-even pricing to price her T-shirts at $19.99, and then, exercising her entrepreneurial judgment, dropped the price further to $19.89. This had the benefit of odd-even pricing, seemed just a little less expensive than the competition, and would fit with some of her plans for future shirts and branding efforts. Janeen thought 1989 was a good year for what she felt was important: world changes that promoted freedom, like the Solidarity movement getting elected in Poland, apartheid starting to be dismantled in South Africa, Israel and the PLO starting their talks, and the first Chinese youth promoting freedom taking to the streets. She is toying with the name "1989 Tees" or "89 Tees" since the domain names are available, and it would reflect some of what makes her T-shirts special.

She is also looking for opportunities to build her brand using price. She hopes to connect with a local band and sell T-shirts with the band's logo. She realizes that means the band will get a cut, and some online research and discussion with friends in the local music scene tell her their share would be about $2 to $3 per shirt, with part paid up front, which she can't afford right now. On the other hand, if she gets the deal and can sell at the band's local shows, she can sell the $20 tees for $24.89 or even $29.89, with $1 a shirt going to the owner of the local venue and another dollar going to the band itself. She is also thinking about when to offer a sale, like when she opens up, or for a week early in the Christmas season to grab shoppers early. For those sales, she will be aiming for $17.89 (the year George Washington takes office, first Congress convenes, France gets rid of feudalism) and if she is closing out a shirt, $9.89, even though she cannot think of anything freedom-related in that year.

Pricing Web Design Services

Antonio has designed websites for friends and students starting businesses from their dorm rooms, but now that he's graduating, Antonio wants to make web design his business. He found a calculator for helping him set rates[38] and went through the computations. Central to this was the belief that starting out, he would be able to sell only half of his available hours, with the rest taken up with business upkeep, and for a start-up marketing the business to drum up sales. After figuring out his own needs (rent, food, insurance, etc.) and his business expenses, he came up with a breakeven rate of $45.21 an hour, but if he wanted to make a target $20,000 profit for the year, he would need to charge $66.49 an hour. The summary of his computations are included in Exhibit 11.2. His first thought was to drop his hoped-for profit down to $10,000 for the year, which brought his target rate to $55.85 an hour, which Antonio rounded up to $60 an hour.

EXHIBIT 11.2

Computing Hourly Rates

Business costs	$11,500
Personal costs	$31,000
Desired profit/year	$20,000
Target income	$62,500
Billable hours/year	940 (235 days × 8 hours/day × 50% unbillable hours)
Breakeven hourly rate	$45.21 (Business costs + Personal costs/940)
Target hourly rate	$66.49 ($62,500/940)

What does this exercise do for him? Antonio now knows the lowest price he can take and cover his costs is $45.21 an hour. He knows that his target hourly rate should be $60 an hour. This computation was the equivalent of what Janeen did in Exhibit 11.1. How do these numbers work when we factor in the real-world issues? Antonio found results online from a 2014 survey of web design prices that ranged from $25 an hour to $350 an hour with an average of $68 an hour.[39] If Antonio were starting today, he'd look for the current costs. In addition, when Antonio looked online for local competitors, those who gave rates generally had rates of $70 to $90 an hour, so he thought his numbers were good for now but that he would keep evaluating them.

But web design is sold two ways. One is based on an hourly rate, while the other is based on selling a package of services at a fixed price. Antonio checked online (an online search of "web design calculator") and found several online design quote wizards.[40] Antonio built a model package consisting of the items in Exhibit 11.3, which is what he thought a business might want in their first professionally designed website.

For the kind of package he thought he could sell locally, the cost range the wizard produced was between $1,423 and $6,934. No local companies posted package rates, so while Antonio did not have a solid basis for estimating how his prices stacked up locally, he also thought he might be able to aggressively market a package price to fill the opening left by his competition. He decided on a package price of $4,500, which put him in the midrange for this type of service. Notice that this works out to $56.25 an hour, which is very close to the hourly rate he computed separately, and which he knows fits with what local competitors are charging.

With Antonio's $4,500 package, he has some other options open. He obviously could apply odd-even pricing to make the price $4,499. Another method that fits well is partitioned pricing, adding additional desirable services to the basic package at different price points, like a basic blog for $150, or $750 to add an iPhone or Android app, or a complete e-commerce shopping cart for an additional $2,000. He will also offer different types of postinstallation supports, as well as web server packages so he can be their one-stop for all web needs.

Antonio was lucky to find a website that goes through the types of work possible and provides estimates of how long each takes, but you need to take those estimates with some skepticism. For

EXHIBIT 11.3

Antonio's Basic Professional Website Package

Completely custom site	15 hours
Custom graphics	5 hours
Integrate 7 pages of typed content (2 hrs/page)	14 hours
Mobile Friendly (Responsive Design)	7 hours
Contact form	3 hours
Site search	4 hours
Google AdSense integration	2 hours
Traffic statistic reports	1 hour
MetaTag keyword optimization	5 hours
Search engine submission	3 hours
Twitter integration	3 hours
Facebook page	5 hours
Total number of hours	67 hours
Estimated budget	$1,423–$6,934
Estimated average	$3,685

Source: Computed using the web design wizard at www.designquote.net/html/dq_estimate_wizard.cfm.

example, DesignQuote estimates the time to make a Flash banner is 4 hours, but Antonio has not used Flash very much so he could easily spend 12 hours making his first banner. The best basis is to use your own experience, but when you have to use estimates from others, always treat them as tentative and be quick to adjust your estimates and rates based on your own experience. Some other ways to find out what competitors are charging is to ask their customers. Telling someone you liked their website and asking who did it and for how much can help you get a feel for local costs. But in the end, there is no substitute for building estimated costs from your real-life experience. Taking on jobs for free to build your reputation, to create a portfolio of projects, and to give you a more solid basis for estimating your costs is a good idea to build many service-oriented businesses.

Pricing Strategy Wrap-Up

Entrepreneurs agonize about price, but perhaps for the wrong reason. Too often owners figure since they run a small business, their prices should be smaller too. But that is highly dangerous. Ellen Rohr, the financial management expert at *Entrepreneur* magazine, estimates that 99 out of 100 small businesses in financial difficulties have set their prices too low.[41] As this chapter has tried to show, it makes more sense to find ways to charge more than to charge less. And when it's all said and done, only 15 to 35 percent of consumers decide on a product using price as the number one factor, depending on the product. In fact, nearly 80 percent cannot accurately recall the price on something they purchased a week ago.[42]

So, goal number one in pricing is to set the price as high as you think you can, using your competition and customers' responses as a check. If the higher price was working, but has tapered off, consider pursuing goal number two—use the pricing strategies given in Table 11.1 to drive more sales. Customers recognize sales for what they are, a temporary reduction in price, and these won't tarnish your product image. Even if the competition matches a sale or offers some other promotion to match your offering, it's not as aggressive an action as a price war. Your customers will feel smart about buying something at a better price, and even if your prices are higher than the competition's and you offer a sale that brings you in line with its pricing, customers are still likely to buy from you—all else being equal—and feel they got a great deal.[43]

Believe it or not, Table 11.1 only scratches the surface of pricing strategies. If you are fascinated by these, grab a marketing textbook and learn about even more methods for saying "sale!" New pricing strategy ideas crop up all the time. For example, Amazon, Priceline, and eBay let the customer set the price,[44] so there are always new methods to learn about.

To wrap up this chapter, remember that the marketing effort in small businesses starts with the idea for the product or service and builds from there to include the key benefits that customers will want, the price they are willing to pay, and also some larger issues such as innovativeness and where the product or service is in terms of its life cycle. Together, these issues can help you craft a pricing strategy that can lead you to success. Even if your product or service is imitative, your profits do not need to be. The secret is in understanding the market, the cost of doing business, and the prices your customers are willing to pay.

Sales Promotions

LO **11-3** Understand the types of sales promotion available to small businesses.

Sales promotion, along with advertising, press/public relations, personal selling, and direct marketing, is one of the major forms of marketing. Sales promotions are a form of communication that encourages the customer to take immediate action. Good examples of sales promotions include:

sales promotion
A form of communication that encourages the customer to act immediately, such as coupons, sales, or contests.

- Discounting techniques like coupons, rebates, discounts, buy-one-get-one promotions, and of course the unending garden-variety sort of sale.
- Introductory techniques like giveaways, samples, and tastings to help introduce your offering to potential customers for subsequent purchase.
- Contest techniques like sweepstakes, contests, and games that introduce your brand to customers without an immediate call to purchase.
- Loyalty techniques like referral programs, social media likes, and customer loyalty programs to increase the stickiness of your brand among customers.

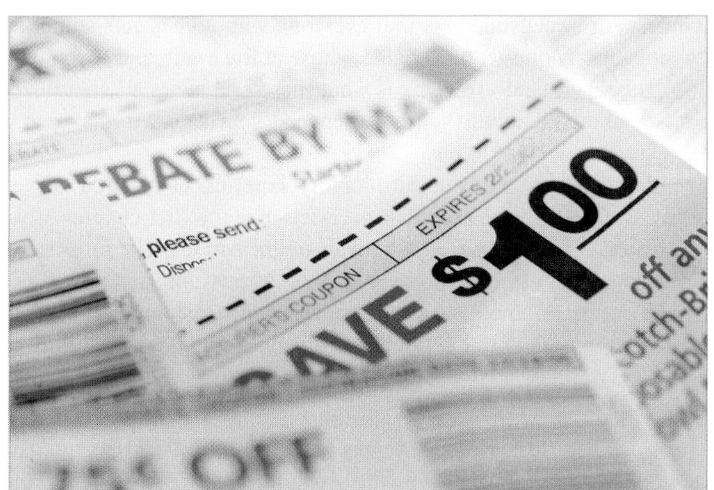

Coupons are one of several sales promotion techniques small businesses can use. These coupons were sent by mail, but you can also provide coupons online through your firm's website or coupon aggregator sites like Dontpayfull.com or DealCatcher.

Tom Grill/Getty Images

As you might recall from Chapter 10, many of these techniques pop up in the "Keep Customers" part of the customer development model funnel. The techniques of sales promotion range from inexpensive (sales flyers photocopied) to expensive (all-expenses-paid vacations). They are relatively easy to manage (sales and coupons) to much more complex (contests and sweepstakes). When using contests and coupons, it is a good idea to check into local and state laws, since there are some places that prohibit or limit how these are used. For example, if you use a sweepstakes in Florida or New York, you need to post a bond equal to the amount of the prizes.[45]

Discounting Techniques

A variety of methods are used to reduce prices and promote sales. Most coupons are delivered in newspapers (80 percent)[46] or magazines; by mail; on packages, handbills, or door hangers; on the Internet; and in person. The higher the value of the coupon, the more likely it is to be redeemed. But even so, coupon redemption runs only 2 percent in the United States. About 64 percent of all Americans are willing to switch brands if they have a coupon.[47] Coupons are a great way to get people to try new products as well (reduces the risk). Even if coupons aren't redeemed, they serve an advertising purpose. Consumers see them and their brain registers a lower price. Even if they forget to clip the coupon or use it, their subconscious remembers the product favorably. In the same way, a rebate—even one that is not redeemed—leaves people with the impression they saved (or could save) money.

Rebates are so powerful that many people, seeing there is a rebate on a product, might buy it even though it was not something they were in the market for at the time.[48] Loyalty programs are intended to tie customers to your business. Most often, these take the form of a card (see Figure 11.3) on which each purchase is stamped, and when a certain number of purchases or visits have occurred, the customer gets a free service, a discount, or a gift. Again, people may lose or not use the card in their purse, or wallet, but in their minds they hold the perception that they are getting a good deal. If that's not a good enough incentive for you, how about the fact that 45 percent of all consumers spend more money in stores with loyalty programs?[49]

FIGURE 11.3

Typical Loyalty Program

Loyalty programs, like this one for Costa Coffee, are intended to increase the retention and spending of your customers.

Realimage/Alamy Stock Photo

Introductory Techniques[50]

The key for giveaways, samples, and tastings is promotion in advance to get people aware and likely to attend the event, or scheduling the event for a location sure to have a good crowd of your target market. Consider placing signs to guide participants to your site, and make sure the site, the offering, and the staff are presented as attractively and positively as possible—this will be the first time many potential customers will be seeing your business, so they will be forming their first impressions. Bring plenty and give it out freely. The whole idea around this type of promotional effort (unlike contests or sweepstakes) is that everyone who comes gets something. Offer coupons giving discounts or buy-one-get-one deals to those at the event, and if you can sell the product there (or book the service), do so! That is what these events are all about. Consider getting people to post to social media about their experience at your event. It is a great way to build a customer base.

It can be exceptionally easy to create introductory experiences on the Internet. Often these involve giving away samples of your product or service–like the first chapter of your new book, or a checklist (with answers) from your new book or online service. The same suggestions apply: You want your offering on the Internet to look as good as possible, and you want to promote it widely through your own social media accounts, relevant bloggers and websites catering to your audience, and maybe even with online ads focused on your target market.

Contest Techniques[51]

In contests, people compete for a prize, whereas in sweepstakes, winners are usually drawn in some usually random fashion. In some ways, the preparation for these is a bit more complex. To protect yourself and your reputation, you need to think through and post the rules for the contest or sweepstakes. What are the dates? What do you promise to do and what do you promise to offer? You also want to think about how much you will be asking of participants for them to qualify for a shot at the prize–giving an email address? Answering a couple of questions to help you in your marketing efforts? Offering slogans, logos, photos, social media postings? If you have them contributing something to your firm, you want to make sure you have the rights to use the information or material in the future.

These techniques can be used to generate leads for future sales, or as an incentive to existing customers to remind them about your firm and get them active with it once again. As with the other sales promotion techniques, you want to have your advertising effort planned well ahead of the contest, to drive as much traffic to your content (and your business) as possible.

Loyalty Techniques

Loyalty programs are generally thought of as a rewards program that benefits returning customers. They can offer rewards like free or discounted merchandise, special events, or coupons or special deals with partner firms. You can manage these yourself (search online for "loyalty program software"), or there are online services that will run your loyalty or referral program for you (for a fee, of course). There are several highly rated platforms for managing loyalty programs (and other elements of sales in your business) as reported by Capterra. For a few examples of services with freemium models (which are often the best place for small businesses to start) see the Learn More Online box below.

LEARN MORE ONLINE

Learn more about loyalty programs at these sites:

Capterra's List of Customer Loyalty Programs: **www.capterra.com/small-business-loyalty-programs-software**

Tango Card: **tangocard.com**

NiceJob: **get.nicejob.co**

In fact, a lot of companies offering gift cards also offer loyalty card programs. Advice for making a loyalty program work well includes keeping it simple, having tiers so customers can grow in the program, matching benefits to what customers value, and above all, tracking the program to make sure it is helping you keep and develop your most committed customers.[52] If you have multiple customer segments, you might benefit from multiple loyalty programs.

referral discount
A discount given to a customer who refers a friend to the business.

A variation on the loyalty discount is the **referral discount**, in which a current customer refers a new customer to use the service or buy the product. The older customer then gets a discount for referring the new business. Since, for services, the recommendation of a friend or relative is often a deciding factor in a purchase or in trying a new service, referral bonuses can be a powerful technique.

The growth of social media has made it easier than ever to connect with customers and get customers to refer their friends to your business. Getting customers to like your latest social media post means their friends will see the post, and your business. It is a simple, free, and powerful way to generate referrals. But for this approach to be the basis for your loyalty program (where the customers get some sort of benefit for posting) or referral program (where customers get a benefit when friends come to your business) requires some thinking ahead of time. It can be as simple as thinking through what customers would want, and what you want them to tell others about. But it will also depend on how your firm rewards customers who like you. Rewards can be emotional, liking them back, which doesn't take a lot to set up, or tangible, such as discounts or points toward some reward, which you will want to be conscientious about tracking. Keys for referral programs are similar to those for loyalty programs, but take extra steps to promote the best referrers to the rest of your customers to inspire them to participate too.[53]

Distribution[54]

LO **11-4** Recognize the different types of direct marketing and their pros and cons.

Other chapters have answered a lot of the *who, what, when, why,* and *how* questions about small business; the rest of this chapter deals primarily with the *where*. There are two basic *where* questions to be considered. The first one is, "Where are my customers?" In answering this question, you are primarily interested in figuring out how to get your product or service to them so that they have the opportunity to buy it. *Distribution* is the process of getting your product to the customer. The second question is, "Where should I be?" This question can be closely tied to the first–if your business is a restaurant, you need to be exactly where the customers are. Other businesses can be located at a distance from their customers–and often find advantages in doing so.

To help explain why **channels** are important to your marketing strategy and profits, think about the implications of the different channels shown in Figure 11.4. They differ in terms of the number of intermediaries between you and the eventual customer. Keep in mind that every one of the intermediaries will want to make a profit for selling your product or service, so they will each add their share to the price you sold to them. Assume you created a product that cost you $5 to make and sold it to an agent or to a retailer for $10 to resell. They want their profits, so they mark up the price to $20.

Realize that the more intermediaries you add, the higher the eventual price of your product. Also keep in mind that all of your profits are based on your first sale of the product. Hold that thought a second.

As the **manufacturer** of the good or service, you have the ability to set the **manufacturer's suggested retail price** of your product. To do this, you need to think of how many intermediaries are likely to be in the channels for your product. In the previous example, with a single

channels
People and firms who connect producers of goods and services with customers.

manufacturer
The entity that produces a product or service to be sold.

manufacturer's suggested retail price
A target price set by a manufacturer for a product or service intended to provide profit for each intermediary in the distribution channel.

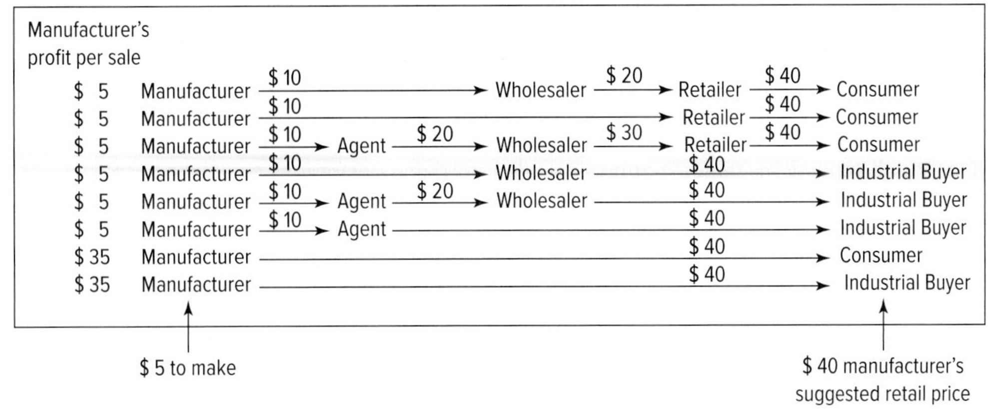

FIGURE 11.4

Typical Distribution Channels

direct sales
Methods of going directly to your customer in order to sell your product. Vending machines, door-to-door salespeople, leasing space at a craft fair, farmer's markets, party sales, and most industrial sales are methods of direct selling.

direct marketing
Selling your goods or services to consumers without intermediaries, typically to select customer groups and typically with tracking of the results.

intermediary, your $5 product costs end consumers $20. That approach is called **direct sales** and is part of **direct marketing**. But what if there is a second intermediary, for example, from you to a wholesaler or distributor, who in turns sells to retailers? Not everyone doubles the price they paid for a product, but for this exercise, if they do double the price, then your $5 product costs consumers $40. If your product is popular, then everyone is happy–the consumers certainly are and because of their happiness, the retailers, wholesalers, and you are probably happy, too.

Because of the math of intermediaries in channels, the possibilities for direct marketing become more and more attractive. Why? Well, it would not be fair to all those intermediaries if you sold your product to the public for $10. In fact, doing so would pretty well ensure that few intermediaries could compete with you and make a profit. But because you have set the retail price at $40 to keep your intermediaries happy, you too would sell to the public for $40, in which case instead of your usual $5 profit per product sold to other resellers, you are suddenly making $35 profit per sale! Done this way, your resellers are happy and not overly worried about you as a competitor, and you are happy because direct sales can be some of the most profitable ways for you to make sales. We go into direct marketing and direct sales next.

Direct Marketing

For many entrepreneurs–and larger firms as well–direct marketing is the way to go. Direct marketing refers to sales where the entrepreneur is selling to the end user of the product or service without any other sales intermediaries involved. It can be as simple as the child who sets up a lemonade stand in front of her home, or as complex as a four-color printed catalog with a mass mailing. Direct marketing can be relatively inexpensive. It also provides more control over where your product or service goes, the information that gets passed along to the consumer, how the product is used, and final pricing. In Chapter 5 you were introduced to several forms of direct marketing through the Internet, including eBay. Even having learned these, there remain about as many forms of direct marketing as there are entrepreneurial ideas, and some of the more common ones are discussed here.

Word of Mouth[55]

This is a great way to get customers and is usually the first technique an entrepreneur uses. Word of mouth[56] is discussed in detail in Chapter 10.

Direct Sales

Direct sales (industrial, door-to-door, party sales, vending) can take several forms. This is the primary way of selling to businesses. A salesperson (often you) contacts industries, churches, schools–whatever type of business is likely to use your product or service–directly. The salesperson meets with the decision maker, presents the product, and hopefully makes a sale.

The lemonade stand mentioned is also a form of direct sales, albeit a little less professional than you may want to be. A more polished approach is a booth at a local fair, cultural event, flea market, craft fair (all of which are discussed in Chapter 5), trade show, or association event. The cost of leasing space can be less than $100 for a local flea market to hundreds of thousands of dollars for a major space at a national trade show. For a flea market, a simple card table may be appropriate, while the cost of a professional booth at a major trade show could easily top $100,000. The key here is to pick the event most likely to attract your target market and least likely to make a serious dent in your pocketbook. Start small and move up as you get more sales revenues.

Some of the other techniques discussed in Chapter 5 that are also direct sales methods include door-to-door sales (remember the Avon lady?), party sales (think Amway, Younique, or Mary Kay),[57] and vending machines. For products that need demonstrations or detailed explanations, door-to-door selling allows you to show consumers how your product works in their home. Part of the success of home sales is that it is hard for consumers to say no after the salesperson has spent some time in their home–it's just not hospitable. This method is made more difficult these days with dual-income families because evenings are usually the only time to catch people. Consumers are often reluctant to invite strangers into their home, but you might be able to at least introduce yourself and leave behind information about your product or service. Avon used to sell predominately through door-to-door sales but has branched out into Internet, mail order, and mall kiosks sales in order to combat declining door-to-door sales for the reasons just mentioned.

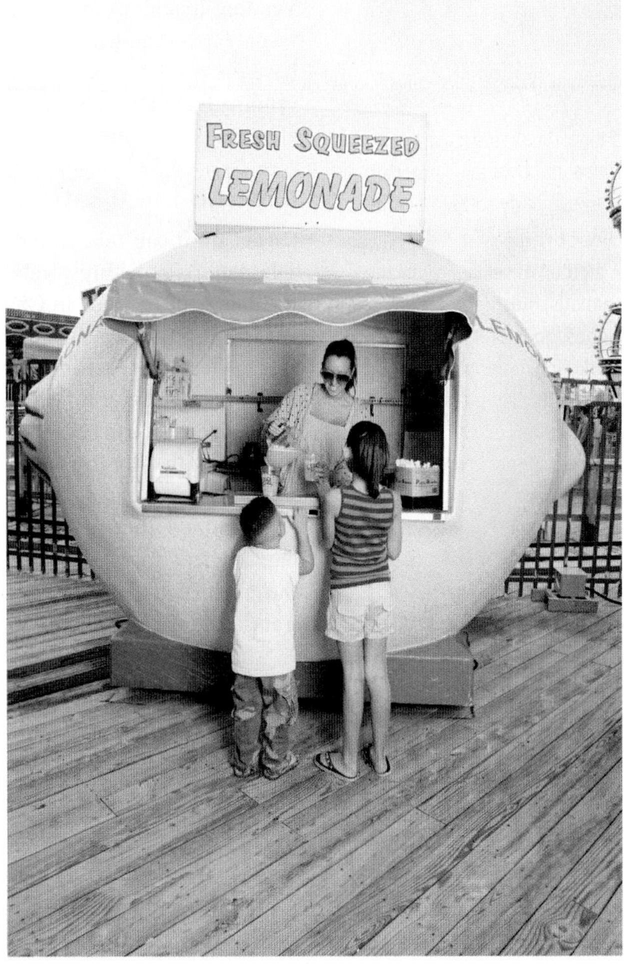

Whether it is your first effort at a lemonade stand at home or your tenth stand at a top tourist attraction, direct sales is the basis of most entrepreneurs' retailing efforts. Did you try direct sales while growing up?

Paul Bradbury/Caia Image/Glow Images; Image Source

Party sales usually require a range of similar items to be sold, and this kind of selling is not appropriate for every product. Typically, a host invites a number of friends and family members to his or her house while a company representative (you, at first) demonstrates the product. Samples of the products as well as catalogs are available for all the guests to browse through, and orders are taken at the party for later delivery. Typical party sales products include everything from laundry aids to makeup to lingerie to cookware to housewares. Two of the disadvantages are the sanctity of the home and the reluctance of people to open up their homes to strangers (salespeople). As these parties take several hours of a salesperson's time and can usually be held only in the evening, one person is limited to how many parties (sales) a week he or she can handle. Generally, the successful companies using this method have hundreds of salespeople who earn a percentage of each sale they make. Many entrepreneurial firms have grown tremendously from a party sales approach–Mary Kay, Amway, Pampered Chef, and others.[58]

Trade shows and expositions are powerful direct marketing techniques for many businesses, like Steve Niewulis from the chapter's opening vignette used. Almost every industry has a trade show where firms in the industry come together to learn about the latest ideas and offerings. Search online for "trade show directory" to find listings for your industry and see Skill Module 3.1. For consumers, there are a host of expositions like house and garden shows, baby shows, car shows, boat shows, outdoor shows, and the like. You can find them by searching online for "exposition directory." The advantage of trade shows and expositions is that nearly everyone attending can be a member of your target market, so it is a great place to prospect for business and engage with a lot of potential customers in a very short time. It is also a great way to see your competition up close to better understand what you're up against.

Vending machines aren't appropriate for every product, but they do offer the flexibility of having your product available around the clock and at convenient locations for your customers.

Vending machines are typical for less expensive convenience products. The key to success is volume achieved with machines located everywhere. People are willing to pay extra in order to have the product readily available. Compare the price of a can of your favorite beverage from a vending machine to what you would pay in the grocery store. The disadvantages of vending machines are their high maintenance and vulnerability to vandalism.

Direct Mail and Its Variants[59]

direct mail
A method of selling in which catalogs, brochures, letters, videos, and other pieces of marketing materials are mailed directly to customers from which they can mail in, call in, or email an order. Direct faxing and direct emailing are more modern forms of direct mail.

mail order
Sales made from ads in newspapers or magazines, with purchases taken online or by phone as well as by mail.

Direct mail can take many forms—postcards, catalogs of your products, videos, **mail orders**, sales letters, brochures, leaflets, emails, and many others. A variant of this, Internet-based direct mailing, is introduced in Chapter 5.

There are several advantages to the direct mail approaches: the ability to sell on your schedule, low costs for getting started (especially if you sell your goods online), the ability to get by without major inventory investments, and the potential for selling to large markets. It plays well with customers too because they tend not to see direct mail as a form of home invasion (as they often do with door-to-door sales or telemarketing); they can read it at their leisure, and they have something they can set aside until they need it.

Of course, there are challenges to this approach including adequate preparation before selling, the need for writing and photography skills, and a way to get customers' attention. Perhaps the greatest challenge is the need to find the right market for your offering. In direct mail, market translates into getting the right mailing list or sales vehicle.

There are many companies that will sell you a list of addresses (even a list already typed on labels), and these are often available for virtually any target market you may choose. The cost of these lists can vary, but current rates are about $60 to $75 per 1,000 names. Try InfoUSA.com (as shown in Skill Module 11.2) or Focus USA (www.focus-usa.com), or do an Internet search for direct mail lists. Also, professional organizations, churches, and clubs sometimes will sell their mailing lists for relatively modest fees.

SKILL MODULE 11.2

Building a Mailing List

Recall in Chapter 10 we talked about a bilingual day-care center in zip code 85037 in the Phoenix area. If you wanted to send out a flyer or invitation to the families with children in the zip code, it is possible. Go to **www.infousa.com** and click on "Consumer Lists." When you've read the background info, click on the "Get Started" button. Now you will see a box asking if you want leads for mailing, calling, or both. Let's pick mailing for this exercise, and accept the default "Very Little Risk" deliverability option. Then select "ZIP Codes" and type in 85037 as in the following screenshot:

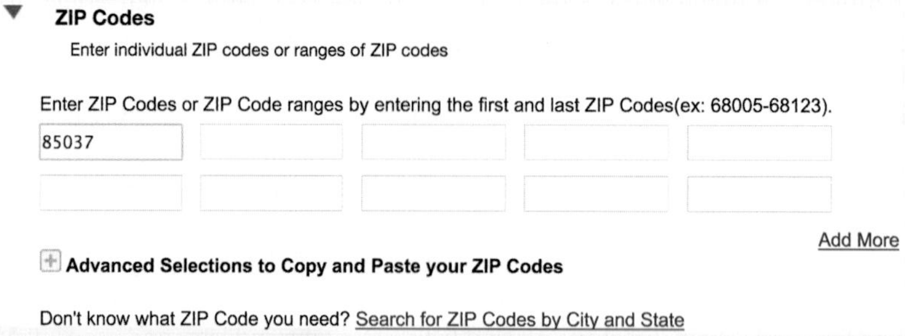

▼ **ZIP Codes**
Enter individual ZIP codes or ranges of ZIP codes

Enter ZIP Codes or ZIP Code ranges by entering the first and last ZIP Codes(ex: 68005-68123).

85037

Add More

⊞ **Advanced Selections to Copy and Paste your ZIP Codes**

Don't know what ZIP Code you need? Search for ZIP Codes by City and State

InfoUSA

Click the "Update Count" button in the upper right of the screen to find out how many addresses are in this zip code (12,369 in November 2019). Since we want households with children, click on the "Optional" tab where the first set of variables include "Children." Click on "Households With Children" and hit the "Update Count" button. The count becomes 3,854 leads. Let's limit age from zero to 5, so the count becomes 1,371 leads. Hit the "See Price" button to learn how much you'd spend for these labels. You'll need to sign up (which is free) to get the quote, which is $233.07, or 16 cents a household.

The other major technique for generating lists of mail or email addresses is to create landing pages offering potential customers something of value in return for their contact information. Search for *free landing pages* to find places (many offering advice and free templates) to host a landing page. Announce them on social media to get the word out for free.

There are also other low-budget ways of getting a mailing list. Often membership rosters are distributed to members of certain organizations. If such an organization meets your target market, you can have the list for the price of membership. One caution, though: Sometimes members are expressly forbidden to use these lists in any commercial way. Check with the organization if you can send a mailing with an article that would be of value to most members, and limit your advertising to mentioning who you are, your business name, and website or Facebook page. If the article truly is useful, your product or service is one that a number of these members are likely to want, and your mailing isn't too much of a commercial, they may very well say it's okay.

Those sales vehicles already mentioned refer to the magazines, newspapers, or websites you select to display your mail order ads. If you are targeting doctors, advertising in the local newspaper would get you most of them, but you also would be paying for the ad to be seen by 98 percent of the readers who are not doctors. There are magazines and websites that focus on particular groups. These include the trade magazines you learned to find in Skill Module 3.1. For websites, a quick Google search of "doctor's websites" will get you started. You can use a service like Similarweb.com to check on the overall traffic to sites, although the magazines and sites themselves should give prospective advertisers like you more detailed information on their visitors.

The other challenges mentioned relate to preparing an ad that does a good job of answering the customers' questions and entices them to buy. There are best practices for writing copy for ads and they are discussed in Skill Module 11.3.

Making Mail Order Ads Work[60]

SKILL MODULE 11.3

WRITING AD COPY

1. **Headlines are key:** Focus on the customer's needs, benefits, problems, or goals. Keep the headline short—five words or less. Scan the mail order ads of your newspaper or magazines to see what attracts your attention, and check the headlines of your competitors. Unless your company name is famous, its name should not go in the headline.
2. **Put the payoff up front:** If the customers don't see the payoff to them for using your product in the first sentence or two, they will give up and look elsewhere.
3. **Offer incentives:** In the body of your ad, consider putting in a discount ("Save 20 percent if you mention this ad!") or coupon to spur customers to action. Put an end date on the offer to move them along. A variation of this is to register customers in a drawing for a prize. This helps keep promotion costs down.
4. **Add visuals:** While adding pictures can be prohibitively expensive, check out lower-cost options such as different font styles or sizes to make your ad distinctive. Sometimes line drawings are possible, and they are usually less expensive than photos.

PLACING ADS

1. **Place newspaper ads:** You can always place classified ads, but for ongoing sales, you will want to use column ads in the regular sections of the paper. Think about what section of the paper is the one most likely to be read by your customers. Also, think in terms of what days of the week make sense. If the big automotive ads are in the Wednesday paper, that may be when you want to advertise your car repair service.
2. **Find magazines:** In order to find the appropriate newspapers in which to place your ads, consider the following: **usnpl.com** or **magazine-directory.com**. At your library, you can find hard-copy magazine directories from Oxbridge, Burelle, and Bacon.
3. **Get the media kit:** Contact the magazine or newspaper of interest and ask for its media kit. These kits tell you about the types of ads, placement options, and costs. They're a great way to get an understanding of the basics of the ad business.
4. **Monitor:** Put a code in every ad, and ask customers for the code in their orders. That way you can track which ads work best for you.

Everyone is familiar with catalogs. They offer customers a description and often a picture of the product and tell the customer how to order it by mail, phone, or online. Catalogs are usually targeted at particular types of consumers and focus on particular types of products.

You can start a catalog of your own. Depending on the size and quality of the catalog, costs for print versions start at around 50 cents each and can rapidly go up to $2, $5, or more. With modern printing systems, there often is not a minimum number of catalogs you will have to order. Still, online catalogs are a less expensive approach. Creating and disseminating a catalog online saves you the cost of printing and mailing. Generally, web hosting services offer shopping baskets that are in fact online catalog-making programs.

However, most part-time entrepreneurs typically try to get their products into existing catalogs. Here the catalog firms function as your first customer; you want to convince them to carry your product. You can find catalogs through the www.catalogs.com site or from print directories in the reference section of your local library.

When you have found the catalogs, try to obtain copies and check to see how your product would fit. Once you've identified your target catalogs, the key person you will be trying to find (by phone, mail, or online at the websites) is called a *buyer.* For the bigger catalogs there will be several buyers, each specializing in a few product areas. Buyers usually require pictures of the product, and some will want to see the actual product. Buyers are used to buying based on preproduction models and prototypes. This works well with part-time entrepreneurs trying to maintain a microinventory. A **microinventory** is a set of goods or services that consists of only one or a few items. Microinventories are the small business's answer to **just-in-time (JIT) inventory** methods in big business. In microinventories, you try to buy your product or prepare your service only after you get an order. For this to work, you need a stable, consistent, and secure source of inventory supply.

microinventory
The purchase of inventory only after a sale is made; very typical with Internet firms.

just-in-time (JIT) inventory
The practice of purchasing and accepting delivery of inventory only after it has been sold to the final customer.

When possible, try to talk to the buyers by phone first to make sure your product would fit their needs. Also make sure you check out each catalog's requirements for companies listing with them. There are many factors to consider such as whether the catalog charges for a listing; whether it holds the inventory (and if so has it bought it), or does it expect you to drop-ship it; and whether the catalog gets an exclusive on your product and the right of first refusal for future versions or even your entire line. While these are policies held by thousands of catalogs, there are always other catalogs with different policies so negotiation may be possible. Also, check out the catalog with the Better Business Bureau (www.bbb.org) to make sure it has a solid track record among entrepreneurs like you. Entrepreneurs typically send buyers a packet with ad copy and pictures of the product. It often helps to provide different versions of the ad copy and different pictures to maximize the chance buyers see something they like. If possible (or if asked), send a sample product.

It is rare that catalog sales, like most business-to-business sales, are immediately successful. Be prepared to come back repeatedly to catalogs that best fit your product or market. Persistence shows you are serious about the business.

Also, think about local wholesalers. The phone book or business directory at the library can point you to wholesalers who supply local businesses with products. If you know a business your product would fit, you can ask the owner who the wholesaler is and build on that. The materials developed for the catalogs work in terms of introducing your product to wholesalers too. The product description and photo for a catalog can quickly be made into an offering circular that you send to wholesalers to test their interest.

Three other direct mail sorts of activities are worth mentioning: direct faxing, email, and daily coupon sites like Groupon. Particularly for business sales, direct faxing can be a way of reaching potential clients. Fax numbers can be obtained in the same way as mailing lists. Unfortunately, frequently faxes are of relatively poor quality, and often the person receiving the fax is not a decision maker. With some specific exceptions, where faxes are still common, this approach is generally on its way out.

Anyone who has an email account is subject to this form of direct mail, commonly known as *spam.* Email addresses can be purchased just as can regular addresses from the same companies. There is also inexpensive software (do a search for "email marketing software") that can easily generate millions of possible addresses. Email is one of the least expensive forms of direct mail, and the cost per recipient is by far the lowest. There is now a nationwide CAN-SPAM Act (search online for details) that specifies the rules direct marketers have to consider, and other nations have their own rules too.[61]

However, in some cases state laws are more stringent and must be followed as well. For example, in California, the email must state "ADV" in the subject line.[62] Most of the requirements of the national law are fairly straightforward:

- Don't in any way falsely misrepresent who you are, where the email is from, or that the email is anything other than a sales pitch.
- Randomly generated email addresses or harvested email addresses are not to be used.
- All emails should allow recipients the opportunity to "opt-out" of receiving further email correspondence from you—and you must obey their wishes on this.[63]

Spam is a hot topic and legislation changes are likely, so be sure to check on current rules. "Opt-in" email, where recipients allow you to email them, is legal and much more acceptable to the potential client.

One of the areas of explosive growth on the Internet has been around daily deal sites. Groupon.com was the first to strike it big, but today there are literally hundreds of sites. There are two major types. One is coupon sites, where you can buy a coupon that entitles customers to a discount on a product or (more often) a service, for example, getting a $50 massage for $10. These are intended largely as a way to build awareness of and traffic to your business. But be ready to manage a major spike in customer demand immediately after a coupon comes out. Many businesses find that they have trouble meeting demand if there are too many coupons in customers' hands.

The other type of deal site is called a group buying site or deal-of-the-day site, like livingsocial.com, which usually offers viewers a chance to buy a product at a discount. This is a way to get rid of excess inventory, but keep in mind that the discount levels for such sites can be very high, squeezing the profit margin severely. For either type of daily deal site, make sure that you can limit the numbers of coupons or products that you offer. Also look for sites that have success with your type of offering and your target market. Today there are thousands of local sites, and they, as well as most of the major national daily deal sites, will let you focus your listing in particular geographic areas. See the Learn More Online box below to find websites to list your coupons and deals of the day.

LEARN MORE ONLINE

Learn more about the topics above at these sites:

Gottadeal, for deals and coupons: **www.gottadeal.com/**

Coupon Website Directory: **www.couponwebsitedirectory.com/**

MyCoupons: **www.mycoupons.com/**

Telemarketing

We have all received telephone calls from salespeople (or worse yet, recorded messages) wanting to sell us everything from aluminum siding to vacations. While most consumers find this method particularly annoying, **telemarketing** still remains a viable form of direct marketing because it works. It is, however, the most expensive form of direct marketing. The best way to handle this is through the national Do Not Call registry maintained by the FTC at https://telemarketing.donotcall.gov/ for sellers. Target market telephone lists may be purchased from the same companies as mail or email addresses—theoretically cleansed of all do-not-call registrants.

telemarketing
Contact via telephone for the express purpose of selling a product or service. Telemarketing can either be inbound (customer calls company) or outbound (company calls customer).

Inbound telemarketing is a different story. Here, the customer calls the manufacturer or service provider. This may be in response to a direct mail piece, direct response advertising, or other methods. A major consideration for the entrepreneur is handling the phone lines. Your California customer calling at 8 P.M. reaches your home in Connecticut at midnight. This is where voice mail with a message stating working hours (located far from your bedroom or with the sound turned off) is a necessity.

If inbound telemarketing is your primary way of doing business and if there are enough calls (and profit) to warrant it, there are firms that will answer these calls for you. You can find them by searching online for "call center services." Generally these firms can take orders or send on additional information; more technical problems or special situations will require your personal attention. The cost varies, again based on the amount of service and volume of calls. These centers can also provide services in several languages if this is critical for your firm.

Direct Response Advertising

direct response advertising
Placing an advertisement in a magazine or newspaper, on television or radio, or in any other media. The ad contains an order blank with a phone number and email or regular mail address with the intent of having the customer place an immediate order.

In **direct response advertising**, you place an ad somewhere—magazine, newspaper, radio, billboard, or television, for example—that includes a phone number, email address, or snail mail address and wait for the orders to come in. (Placing a website in the ad is technically part of Internet marketing, which we get to in a moment.) This can be as simple as a classified ad in the newspaper or as elaborate as a half-hour infomercial—and the costs associated vary as much as the type of ads. A chart showing the cost per thousand (CPM) for a variety of media is given in Figure 10.5.

The pros and cons of your media choice are just about what you'd expect. Television can be expensive, but it attracts a large audience and is a good way to demonstrate what your product is capable of doing. Try cable channels for the cheapest rates. Many stations offer discounted advertising for small businesses. This might not amount to much more than an announcer reading your ad over the credits of the local news, but it's a starting point.

Some of the home shopping networks may be appropriate if your product meets their criteria. These networks publish their standards on their websites and may offer days for inventors to demonstrate their products to studio personnel—a chance to sell your concept. Products that work well are those that have a wide appeal and have advantages that are easy to demonstrate, like the Floppy Sprinkler (see the Small Business Insight below).

A magazine allows for very specific targeting—a hobby, sporting interest, a certain age, or other demographic group—and often offers classified type ads (less expensive) or multipage, full-color ads (much more expensive). Newspapers allow geographic segmentation; that is, they are a great source if you want to attract people in a specific geographic region (think restaurant, day-care center, and the like).

Magazines are also very appropriate places for direct response advertising for business-to-business selling. Virtually every industry, trade, and profession has a magazine dedicated to it.

SMALL BUSINESS INSIGHT

FLOPPY SPRINKLER USA[64]

Jeff Pettit, the founder of Floppy Sprinkler USA, LLC (**www.floppysprinkler.com**), used television to get the word out about his unique water sprinkler called Rain on Demand. The idea was so different from traditional water sprinklers that a demonstration seemed the logical way to convince customers of the product's worth. Pettit found information for submitting ideas on the QVC website (**www.qvc.com**) and got his opportunity. His company started in 2000. With the QVC push, sales reached $250,000 by 2002. Today, his product is patented in 34 countries and is being marketed worldwide by a South African firm that has licensed the rights to the product. Today it sells it not only as an improved lawn sprinkler, but a water-saving, yield-increasing irrigation system for farms—a highly lucrative additional market.

Finding the correct one and placing your direct response ads will give you high contact with your target market. Try *Gale's Directory of Publications and Broadcast Media* or the *Encyclopedia of Associations*, probably at your library, for lists of industry trade magazines and trade associations. You can also refer back to Skill Module 3.1 for some help along these lines.

Radio ads provide both geographic and demographic segmentation; if you custom-design cowboy boots or train horses, a radio ad on the local country western station might be just the right place. On the other hand, radio audiences are generally highly distracted; people listen to the radio while driving or doing housework or other tasks and might not be able to drop everything to write down your phone number. Billboards reach local people but do not permit a lot of details. Other possibilities include signs in buses and cabs or at bus stops.

For a start in direct response advertising, consider a classified-type ad–no pictures, limited graphics (if any), and relatively low cost. If your target market is a specific geographic region, newspapers might work best. If it is specific to a hobby, job, sport, or other interest, try a magazine catering to that interest. If the budget allows, try a quarter- or half-page ad with some color or modest graphics. Magazines will sell you an eighth- or sixteenth-page ad.

Remember that there are also the relatively low-cost methods of Internet advertising such as videos, blogsites, postings on Facebook or Twitter, and a host of other techniques (described in Chapter 10) that can be as effective or even more so than the traditional marketing vehicles.[65]

Guerrilla Marketing[66]

guerrilla marketing
The use of creative and relatively inexpensive ways to reach your customer. Examples include doorknob hangers, flyers under windshield wipers, T-shirts, balloons, and messages written on sidewalks.

Guerrilla marketing is a relatively new concept in marketing but the start-up company's best friend. *Guerrilla marketing* is a term for unusual and nearly free advertising. While it can be simply advertising–stating why your product or service is great–it's extremely effective as direct response advertising when you add your phone number, address, website, or other contact information. Guerrilla marketing includes everything from placing flyers under windshield wipers of cars to waving signs at passing cars to hanging information on doorknobs to placing business cards on bulletin boards at the grocery store - or even making a personal appeal to a key influencer as in the case of Courtney Hennessy in the Small Business Insight. For the cost of copying and a bit of shoe leather, you can get your message out to a lot of potential customers. Then again, if you aren't interested in delivering the message yourself (How valuable is your time?), there are many companies that will do this for you, such as www.globalflyerdistribution.com or a local service. Often local newspapers will let you distribute newspaper "ride-along" advertisements, doorknob hangers, flyers, or product samples to selected target neighborhoods. It will even design and print your advertisements for you for an extra fee.

The key here is to catch the customer's attention. We talked earlier about daily deal coupon sites, but when it comes to couponing, there are a myriad of ways to get the word out to your consumers. Susan P., moving into a new house in a new subdivision, became part of the target market for landscapers, house cleaners, blind and drapery manufacturers, pool installers, satellite television installers, painters, decorators, local restaurants and merchants, and a plethora of other such small businesses. Daily there are several pieces of advertising trying to get her attention. A few–very few–are slick four-color brochures or in-mail catalogs and coupons. The majority are low budget or homemade. What attracts her attention? "Coupons are a good bet; I'll try out a restaurant or neighborhood merchant if I get a discount or free dessert or some other gift. Others that catch my eye are those that are different. For example, a landscaper left his business card–just like several dozen before and after him–but his was in a small plastic sandwich bag with a few samples of decorative gravel and bark. It cost him only the time to make these, but this was much more appealing than just sticking a business card in my door." In another case, a decorator printed her ad on a wallpaper sample–colorful and different![67]

Find unusual and unique places to display your products. Can you wear your own creations? Can you pass out samples of your homemade fudge to your bridge club? Could you display your product alongside complementary products or services, such as a custom jewelry maker who arranges to display her product at the checkout counter of a local hairstylist, with both of them splitting the profits. Give your product as gifts, along with your business card or other contact information, and encourage the recipients to pass along that information to anyone who asks. A

Guerrilla marketing, as in the photo, gains potential customer attention while helping small businesses keep down marketing costs. Which guerrilla options seem most effective to you, and why? Do you see any ethical concerns with guerrilla marketing techniques?

Courtesy of The Michael Alan Group

variant of this is to try a barter arrangement with local TV and radio stations. You give them your product or service for free or at a significant discount in return for their mentioning it, or preferably endorsing it, on the air. All of these approaches share the common quality of guerrilla marketing—they are low-cost ways to gain a potentially high impact on your market.

Multichannel Marketing

multichannel marketing The use of several different channels to reach your customers; for example, a website, direct mail, and traditional retailing.

The term **multichannel marketing** refers to using several outlets for contacting your customers. If you include in your classified ad your phone number, your website, and your email address, then you are a multichannel marketer. One customer may pick up the phone. Others will

SMALL BUSINESS INSIGHT

COURTNEY HENNESSEY REVISITED—GUERRILLA GURU[68]

We met Courtney Hennessey Hopson of Codi Jewelry (**www.codijewelry.com**) for the first time in Chapter 5. While Courtney might not have realized that she was a guerrilla marketing expert, her experience speaks for itself. Her first products were stretchy bead bracelets, and she generated interest by wearing them around town. People would ask about them, and she'd take orders. If they didn't place an immediate order, she had business cards to pass out "for future reference." She gave out business cards with all her sales, too, so her customers could pass them along to people who commented on their new jewelry. One of these cards ended up with a Neiman Marcus associate, which resulted in several trunk shows at the store, where she was allowed to present her merchandise directly to the jewelry buyers. One of her more unusual marketplaces—and possibly a marketing first—was her great aunt's wake where she brought samples of her jewelry and walked away with $800 in orders. During a vacation in the Bahamas, she happened to be eating at the same restaurant as Regis Philbin, host of one of the top morning talk shows of the time, *Live with Regis and Kelly*, and worked up the courage to approach him with her story and samples of her jewelry for his wife, daughters, and cohost Kelly. Regis presented the necklace to Kelly during the show, telling the story about Codi Jewelry, resulting in well over 100,000 hits on her website the next week. None of these "marketing ploys" cost her very much, but all were incredibly successful at generating publicity for her firm and getting resulting orders.

email or browse your website. This simply allows your customers to contact you in the way they feel most comfortable. Having your phone number, website address, and email address on your packaging ensures that your customer can find you again should a retail outlet decide not to carry your product any longer.[69]

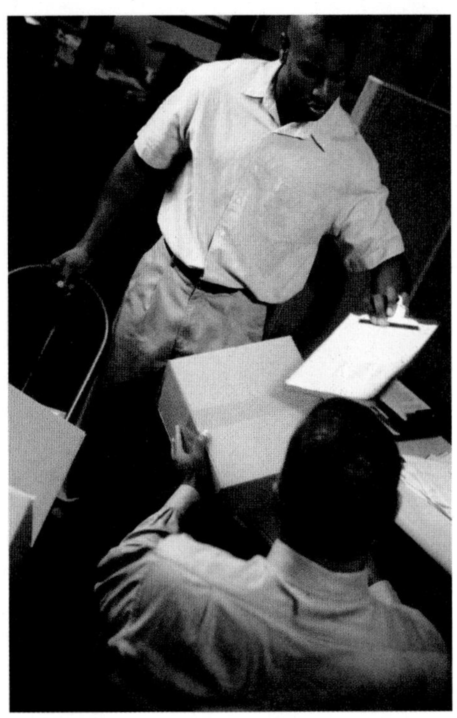

● Arranging for fast and low-cost delivery is essential to successful distribution. Where would you go to compare shipping costs?

Ingram Publishing

Distribution Issues for Direct Marketing

Even when your shippers pay postage, you'll need to know where to go to find the information you need to add that to the amount the seller pays. You'll need a decent postage scale and rate tables. These tables can be downloaded from UPS (www.ups.com), Federal Express (www.fedex.com), or the U.S. Postal Service (www.usps.com), and there are commercial sources to help small businesses streamline their shipping by helping you compute costs and compare and manage services, like shipworks.com. *Tip:* Charge a shipping and handling fee that includes postage as well as packaging materials. Most catalogs have a shipping and handling fee based on the dollar amount of the order. These companies also offer tracking software that can be downloaded and installed on your computer to track your shipments.

For small businesses handling their own shipping, in addition to issues of cost,[70] there are issues of which services you want a shipping company to offer you and your customer, such as tracking and insurance. There are also issues of pickup and delivery times. You may have a tiered approach to shipping; for example, using the USPS for regular deliveries that are not time-sensitive; a local courier, package delivery, or taxi service for local rush deliveries (at a much higher cost to the customer, of course); and another service for overseas deliveries. As is often the case in small business, a bit of research up front can help you save time, money, and aggravation down the line.[71]

Fulfillment and Nondirect Distribution

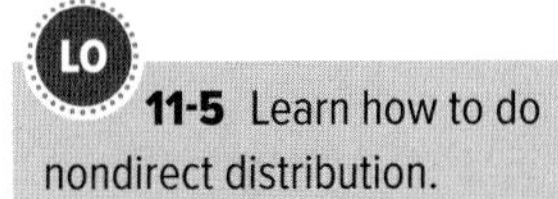

LO 11-5 Learn how to do nondirect distribution.

In Figure 11.4 you saw **wholesaler**, retailer, and **agent**. These, along with distributors and a dozen or so others not mentioned, are commonly referred to as *intermediaries*. Intermediaries—frequently small businesses themselves—provide the service of getting the product to the end consumer, including such functions as inventory control, advertising and promotion, delivery and warranty services, to name a few. For these services, they take a percentage of the profit. As a result, the final price the end user must pay is often four (or more) times the manufacturing cost.

How do you find out which distribution channel is correct for your product? For many startups, the simplest initial answer (next to doing it yourself) is to use a fulfillment center. You have probably noticed when buying something on Amazon and some of the products say "Fulfilled by Amazon." For these products, the retailer keeps inventory in one or more of Amazon's over 200 fulfillment centers. These centers warehouse the retailer's products, pack and ship them, and send an automated email to customers to let them know the product is on its way. Other services Amazon and its competitors provide include processing credit cards, supplying inventory levels to your website, reordering products, offering call center services, and handling returns.[72] Fees vary, but you want them to fit into the "shipping and handling" fees you plan to charge customers; generally they should be less than 10 percent of sales plus freight costs. Distributors are a good idea if you want to offer a whole line of products that you don't have to buy or warehouse. In this case, the distributor services several **retailers** or **e-tailers**.[73]

While Amazon is one of the largest fulfillment services in the world, it is far from the only one. To find others (including some in your locality), type "fulfillment center lists" into your favorite search engine and start checking out sites. There are few business equivalents of *Consumer Reports*, so you will have to do your homework to find the best services for you. Remember to check out your finalists with BBB.org to make sure they have a good record dealing with other businesses.[74]

Another way to find an intermediary is to start at the end and work your way up by asking each link from whom they buy.[75] At that point, you can determine other wholesalers or distributors that carry similar products and begin interviewing them to find the best fit for your product and target market. Another way to locate possible distributors is to attend trade shows. The

wholesaler
An intermediary business that buys (typically in large quantities) and sells (typically in smaller quantities) to businesses rather than consumers.

agent
An intermediary business that represents a manufacturer's product or service to other business-to-business intermediary firms.

retailer
An intermediary business that sells to consumers or end users of a product (typically in single or small quantities).

e-tailer
An electronic retailer; a store that exists only on the Internet.

Manufacturers' Agents National Association publishes a *Directory of Manufacturers' Sales Agencies*, available in many libraries.

Unfortunately for the entrepreneur, many distributors and wholesalers are not interested in taking on a start-up product. They are concerned about an unproven source and market, setup charges, and a multitude of other possible problems. On the other hand, talking to distributors—especially in product development stages—may often give you ideas on what to do and what not to do.

One way to get a distributor interested in trying your product is to be able to prove that it does sell. In this case, you may have to convince a single retailer to give the product a try. Dr. Bob Wagstaff, the inventor of the Orabrush, had gotten it into stores by literally walking in and talking to managers. As noted in the following Small Business Insight, he faced a rocky road but persevered, working his way through the system.

Getting your product into a catalog may also convince a distributor that it's a product worth taking, but how do you get into that catalog? One way is by showing your product at trade shows and gaining sales and recognition. This is the route that Steve Niewulis from the chapter's opening vignette used.

Another way to get into a catalog is to find one that carries the type of product you have and for about the price you'll want to charge. Call for its guidelines for submitting new products and follow the information you get carefully. If you aren't already receiving such a catalog, you can check out resources such as the *National Directory of Catalogs* or *The Catalog of Catalogs VI: The Complete Mail-Order Directory* in your local library. Some will charge you a fee for warehousing your product, while others will simply pass the orders along to you.[76]

SMALL BUSINESS INSIGHT

How Orabrush Pitched Itself into Walmart[77]

You recall from Chapter 10 how Orabrush went from an also-ran on the toothbrush aisle to the darling of the Internet when its YouTube went viral. Online sales skyrocketed, but the firm still had trouble getting the Orabrush into major chain stores. Its target was Walmart, the nation's largest retailer. It turns out the Walmarts around Provo, Utah, where Dr. Bob Wagstaff lived and worked, had Orabrush on sale in their stores. A Walmart manager took the plunge, and other local Walmart managers liked the point-of-sale display and the product enough that they brought them into their stores, too. Those managers recommended Orabrush to Walmart's headquarters. Orabrush sent the buyer at Walmart a customized video on DVD, with statistics, media coverage, and customer comments, but no decision was coming. In the end, they decided to build some support around Walmart headquarters. They created a Facebook ad (tied to a video, of course) saying Walmart employees had bad breath and needed the Orabrush, which ought to be sold at Walmart. They targeted Walmart employees around Bentonville, Arkansas, where the headquarters is. After spending $28 on Facebook ads, they got the email they were hoping for, asking if Orabrush could deliver 735,000 Orabrushes in a couple of months—and stop the Facebook ad.

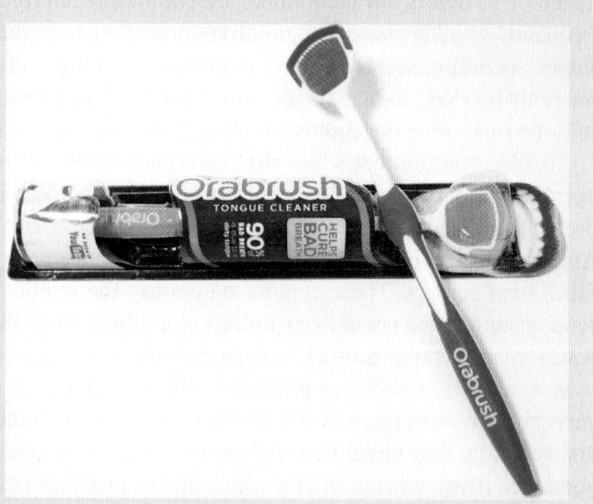

Mark Dierker/McGraw-Hill Education

Virtually every industry, sport, hobby, or interest has its own trade shows and events. Regional events are usually a better place for the entrepreneur because you have lower expenses and less competition. Hit the library or Internet to find them, and be sure to have all the answers about cost, delivery, product advantages, and the like.

If catalog sales do not feel right and retailers do not seem interested in your product, an e-tailer[78] might be willing to take a chance. Because of e-tailers' low overhead and unlimited shelf space, they can afford to take a chance on an unknown firm or product. Sometimes they will carry inventory, but often they just pass the orders on to you for fulfillment. You can find potential sites by doing an Internet search for "e-tailer." Sometimes they will post information on how to submit product ideas, while other times be prepared to dig for phone numbers and names. Craig Winchell, the inventor of Conscience, an interactive board game for teaching children right and wrong, tried the American International Toy Fair, a trade show, with disappointing results. He found that EToys was willing to take a chance. EToys's initial order was six games in 1998; in 1999, Winchell shipped close to 10,000 units.[79] With the kickstart from the EToys sales, by 2007 Conscience was sold at 10 online catalog sites and more than 10 retailers in the United States and Bermuda. In the end, though, Craig felt the board game would not give him the financial independence he needed. Today you can find Conscience on sale at several Internet sites, but Craig remains an entrepreneur making his money as a management consultant in Dallas. Companies like Pipecandy.com provide some lists of e-tailers online, and *Internet Retailer* magazine publishes an annual list of the top 1,000 leading vendors.

International Strategies

LO **11-6** Differentiate the types of international strategies.

When you are struggling to get through that first year of business, international sales are about the last thing on your mind. The U.S. Department of Commerce, however, indicates that large companies account for only about 2 percent of all exporters, meaning the other 98 percent of the exporters are small businesses.[80]

Entrepreneurs typically fall into three categories. There are those who realistically will never go international (for example, a restaurant owner or dry cleaner working from a single site). There are those who intentionally start international businesses[81] (for example, import-export businesses), such as Peter P., the director of procurement for a Russian trading company, who saw a trading opportunity with the opening up of eastern Europe and the former Soviet Union. Educated in the United States, he is of Ukrainian descent and speaks both Russian and Ukrainian.[82] Last, there are those who think international business might be something they'll do someday way off in the future. This section is primarily for the last two categories.

Thanks to the Internet, once a company has a website it is essentially an international business, a whole new breed of firms known as **born internationals.**[83] Potential foreign customers see the website and before you know it—or before you are prepared—the first international order rolls in. Even "website-free" companies aren't exempt. A foreign visitor comes across your products and sees a need for it in his or her country, and here comes that order.

born international
A new firm that opens a website immediately, thus being exposed to customers from around the world.

Some international orders aren't all that difficult to handle. If the order is small enough, if the product or service is not highly regulated domestically, and if the country is one with which the United States has rather liberal trade such as Canada, the order processing may offer few or no headaches. The customer may use a credit card or international money order, and the product ships in the mail without much more effort than figuring the extra postage. That's OK for the occasional order, but more complex situations will require more time and effort on the part of the entrepreneur. The ideal situation is to consider and prepare an international strategy before it becomes a hit-and-miss method that is too cumbersome or before serious and costly mistakes are made.

Entrepreneurs have available to them the same options as large companies including wholly owned subsidiaries, joint ventures, licensing, franchising, and exporting. For most, though, an export strategy is sufficient and is all that is covered in this section. It's usually inexpensive, quick to start, easy to change, and less risky than other ventures. It has the additional advantage of allowing the entrepreneur the opportunity to learn about doing business abroad in case the company reaches the point of moving further. For U.S. entrepreneurs, the U.S. government offers detailed and useful help for exporters, including seminars and other training, export assistance, websites and reports, financing, insurance, and legal and collection assistance.

Exporting[84]

Putting together an export strategy involves answering three questions:

1. Are we ready?
2. Where should we go?
3. Whom do we contact there?

There are many sources for assistance in answering these questions, and many good ones are free or almost free. One excellent resource is the U.S. Commerce Department's Export.gov site which offers advice by country and industry and online market intelligence on potential markets, and links to services offered across the Federal government to help entrepreneurs export.

Question 1: Are you ready to export? Exporting requires a different kind of thinking and preparation from selling locally or even nationally. Are you going to target one country, a region, or the whole world? Do you know what customers want? Do you know what the import requirements are? What aspects will you handle, and which ones will you contract out? Are you ready for the costs and headaches of exporting? To see how you are coming along, you can check your readiness online at the U.S. government's exporting site (www.export.gov), which provides extensive exporting basics.

Consider your product as well. Will your U.S.-designed product fit an international lifestyle or needs? Clothing sizes differ–both in how they are numbered and what the sizes mean. A woman's medium in the United States is an XXL in mainland China. Electrical currents differ, as do various other safety and product standards, and the United States is one of only two countries that's not on the metric system.[85]

There are several ways you can export. One is to use online services such as eBay. Approximately 58 percent of eBay's sales are out of country.[86] If you're handling your international business this way, a lot of the rest of this section isn't really for you until you want or need to change methods. Another is to work from personal contacts gained through school, travel, or family. Most exporting small businesses start with countries where they have had personal experience or support.[87] These two methods are called **direct exporting**, since you are selling *directly* to foreign buyers or distributors.

direct exporting
Exporting using no intermediaries.

indirect exporting
Exporting using intermediaries such as agents, export management companies, or export trading companies.

freight forwarders
Firms specializing in arranging international shipments—packaging, transportation, and paperwork.

If you want to use outside experts, there are three intermediaries who can help. With **indirect exporting**, you use agents, export management companies, or export trading companies as intermediaries to handle most of the exporting process. Direct exporters can also get help from freight forwarders. **Freight forwarders** are specialists in export-related activities including tariff schedules, shipping, insurance, packing, transportation arrangements, customs clearing, and other export details. (By the way, many agents, export management companies, export trading companies, and freight forwarders are themselves small businesses. They know exactly what problems you've faced and are much easier to approach than some megacompany.) The Small Business Administration's Export Assistance Centers (www.sba.gov/tools/local-assistance/eac) can help you find one.

Question 2: Where should we go? The United Nations has 193 member countries in the world; chances are not all of them are right for your product. Even if your product should have wide appeal, it makes good sense to pick one or two as first markets. One of the safest bets is to consider countries that are similar to the United States–Canada, United Kingdom, Australia, for example. In those countries you have few language issues, the culture is pretty close to the U.S. culture, the governments and economies are stable, and the people there are likely to want or need about the same kinds of products as people in the United States do. Should you decide to go further afield, those are the same sorts of things you want to look for–language and culture issues, government and legal situations, economic situations, and people's wants and needs. Here's a good time to use those personal contacts mentioned earlier; if they live there, they are likely to be able to tell you if the product makes sense or not.

International marketing research isn't cheap and can be difficult to do. Contacts are a valuable resource. Additionally, the U.S. government and world trade centers can give a lot of free or low-cost assistance. See Table 11.2 for a list of some of the major ones.

TABLE 11.2 Sources of Export Assistance

Agency	Website	Assistance Offered
Small Business Association	www.sba.gov	U.S. Export Assistance Centers offer help in virtually all areas of exporting, much for free or at very low costs.
U.S. Department of Commerce	www.export.gov	U.S. government's main exporting site with extensive exporting basics. This extensive guide is available for downloading and contains virtually everything a beginning exporter needs to know. Includes copies of most paperwork and how to fill it out.
Regional U.S. Department of Commerce offices	www.export.gov/locations/	Offer export seminars on various topics; many are free or under $50.
Ex-Im Bank	www.exim.gov	Offers seminars on export financing.
Bureau of Industry and Security	www.bis.doc.gov	Offers seminars on export licensing and compliance issues.
International Trade Administration	www.trade.gov/	Has detailed information about U.S. trading partners.
World Trade Centers Association	www.wtca.org	Networks hundreds of local world trade centers, which provide export–import assistance.
State and local governments		Often offer convenient seminars and other export assistance programs.

Question 3: Whom do we contact there? You may already have international contacts through school, friends, travel, or other methods. If so, you're ahead of the game. Even if they cannot help you with specific questions, they probably know someone who can. On the other hand, if you do not have any contacts, many of the government services you have already used can provide lists of potential intermediaries or end users. In addition to the free services available, U.S. Commercial Service (www.trade.gov/cs/) provides a number of levels of fee-based customized services. For $750, it offers its International Partner Search service, which will identify up to five potential businesses to work with you as licensees, agents, distributors, or strategic partners, and prequalify them based on your criteria. The government's www.export.gov site offers a database of sales leads that can be searched for free by industry, region, or country. It is also the point of contact for catalog exhibitions that can get your product or service catalogs into the hands of potential buyers in specific markets (or at specific trade shows) overseas. The Commercial Service has local offices all over the country, which can point you to international trade efforts based out of your locality.

Other good ways to make international contacts are to participate in trade shows and trade missions. In a trade mission, a U.S. government official takes a small group of business owners to different foreign countries in order to help establish relationships and promote exporting. There are not a lot of these missions, and they are usually specific to a particular type of business and region of the world, so they are not always appropriate. At an international trade fair, similar to domestic trade fairs, you have a booth displaying your products or services and the opportunity for exposure to thousands of potential clients. Again, some fairs are industry-specific, while others are more general. The U.S. government often has a U.S. pavilion featuring export-oriented companies. These companies may have the opportunity to tie into other U.S. government services such as meeting with local U.S. embassy officials, prearranged meetings with qualified customers, market research information, trade barrier information, transportation and customs information, and assistance and access to U.S. trade show experts. Even if you can't exhibit in the fair, attending the fair may give you a chance to meet the sort of people you need to know.

Exporting is a major way for small businesses to grow, and today there are more resources than ever before to help you find markets overseas. What would be some of the first websites you would check to find help?

Maxx-Studio/Shutterstock

The U.S. government through www.export.gov also provides such services as printed and video catalogs, online databases, and personalized (fee-based) contact services. U.S. Commercial Service will also assist a company in arranging private promotional activities, including exhibitions, press releases, and receptions when appropriate.

Still another way is to look for foreign companies with a resident representative in the United States, a type of private importing agent. Often these representatives are interested in bringing U.S. products back to their home countries and will already have a good idea if your product is right, and how to promote and distribute it.[88] To find these resident representatives, try a Google search with the terms "resident representative" or "U.S. importing site."

The next step is to export your products. But there are a few other things to consider first. Pricing becomes complicated as you need to cover transportation, the additional documents you may need, possible tariffs (taxes on incoming goods), potential currency valuation changes, the cost of converting currencies, and the additional packaging necessary to ship abroad. The importer usually covers foreign taxes, tariffs, additional shipping charges, port handling fees, and the like, but this must be carefully spelled out in your contracts in order to avoid potential differences of opinion.

Shipping documentation and other paperwork are very specific to the product and the country to which it is going. The International Trade Administration (www.trade.gov) provides extensive information about tariffs, taxes, specific country information, and other general exporting information. The U.S. Country Commercial guides also provide some assistance in this area, as do some country government websites. The Bureau of Export Administration provides information about when export licensing is necessary and also information on exporting of politically sensitive products.

There are a variety of payment procedures available. The easiest for you is to require up-front cash payment prior to shipment (or credit card if appropriate). This eliminates your risk, but puts the customer at risk. Providing credit to your customers reverses the risk, and puts it all on you. Both of these are possible methods of receiving payments, but less often used. More typical methods include **letters of credit** or **documentary drafts**. In both cases, the payment procedure now includes four parties–you, your customer, and both of your banks–and payments are made upon proper presentation of certain documents, including the letter of credit or draft, bills of lading, and other paperwork. Although the system is somewhat complex, it provides a lower level of risk for all parties than cash in advance or an open account. You can find assistance about these methods at your current bank.

letter of credit
A document issued by a bank that guarantees a buyer's payment for a specified period of time upon compliance with specified terms.

documentary draft
A draft that can be exercised only when presented with specified shipping documents.

Financing and insurance become important because of the length of time it may take for international payments to be processed and the risk of default, as well as the difficulty of recovery in case of default in international transactions. The Small Business Administration (www.sba.gov), the Export-Import Bank (EXIM Bank) (www.exim.gov), and the Overseas Private Investment Corporation (www.opic.gov) provide loans and insurance to cover exporting. In some cases, these loans may also be used to finance trade show participation, to translate brochures and catalogs for international distribution, to renovate or expand existing facilities necessary to produce products for export, to set up lines of credit for potential customers, to provide export working capital, and to provide funding for developing an export program.

Last is the consideration of conflict resolution. Although the possibility exists for pirating, product misuse, and other unfortunate occurrences, the primary areas for conflict resolution include nonpayment and contract default issues. There is no universal court of law that can handle these situations. The U.S. Department of Commerce can provide advice and offer reputable local counsel, but only for sizable losses, typically several thousand dollars or more. The U.S. Council for International Business (USCIF) is the U.S. National Committee to the International Chamber of Commerce (ICC) (www.uscib.org/icc-dispute-resolution/) which provides international arbitration services and offers some other suggestions. But arbitration, too, is costly and probably not worthwhile unless the loss is significant. This difficulty in international dispute resolution underscores the need to carefully select partners and to do a thorough job of prescreening. This is an area in which various government agencies can help you. The U.S. Commerce Department, for example, prequalifies potential customers in many cases prior to recommending them; you should check the particular program specifics to verify. EXIM Bank provides credit information on potential customers and, as mentioned earlier, many agencies provide insurance for export payments.

Importing

Importing strategy is similar to exporting, but with the buyers and sellers reversed. Instead of customers to buy your products, you are looking for sources to sell products to you (which, of course, you'll eventually resell). If you have the opportunity to travel abroad, look for products that are selling well in the country you're visiting and aren't available in the United States or products that are considerably cheaper than similar ones found in the United States (labor and manufacturing costs are often cheaper in other countries than the United States). Trade mission and domestic and international trade shows are also good sources. If you can't travel, ask your international contacts for this information. Next, find out who manufactures them and write the manufacturer a letter, introducing yourself and your company and the potential you see in your market for its product. You're selling yourself, so be sure to tell the producer why you are the best person or company to be representing the product (i.e., experience in that product or in importing, contacts and distribution systems already in place, familiarity with the market, etc.). International mail can be painfully slow, so a fax or email letter is probably best. Also, avoid slang terms (e.g., "your product is da bomb!") and idiomatic expressions (like "break the ice") that are likely to be misunderstood. Since English is rapidly becoming the language of business, a translation is usually not necessary. Follow up with a phone call or visit in which you can pitch the specifics of your marketing plan for the product.[89] One way to conduct international calls and video calls for free is to register for Skype (www.skype.com) and Google Voice (www.google.com/voice). If you and the overseas company both use either of these programs, having long conversations to get an understanding of each other will not pose a financial problem.

With importing, many of the paperwork and insurance details will be your source's responsibility. Import buying works the same way as export selling, that is, the same sorts of paperwork and procedures are followed only in reverse.

Concluding Thoughts on International Business

One of the major mistakes commonly made by U.S. businesspeople (entrepreneurs or major companies) is being insensitive to cultural differences. You're likely to make some mistakes, but take time to learn at least the basics about the culture you're dealing with to avoid the biggest errors. Travel guides and U.S. government country reports often offer brief cultural assistance as do books such as *Kiss, Bow or Shake Hands,* and a plethora of "doing business in . . ." guides.[90]

Although international business might seem a little daunting with all the paperwork and regulations, small businesses just like yours do it every day. There's a lot of free or very inexpensive help out there; make use of it.

LO **11-7** Identify the factors to consider in selecting your business location.

Location

When you ask real estate agents the best three things to look for in a house, they will tell you "Location, location, location." The same holds true in your business. What location—in particular, *good* location—means for your business is highly dependent on what your business is, the amount of money you can afford to budget for it, your particular business philosophy, and the marketing niche you are seeking. Let's start with some general information about location, then move onto specific issues for services (including retailing) and manufacturing businesses. We then discuss some specific choices such as site selection and layout and the buy, build, or lease option.

The first choice, and often only choice, for many entrepreneurs is their hometown because it offers convenience and a familiar setting, and it eliminates a lot of possible family issues. There may also be valid business reasons for this choice: The local banker knows you and is more likely to loan you money; you know your market—the potential customers in the area—and understand their wants and needs; you have seen an unmet need that you can fill; and, for many entrepreneurs, friends and family (usually local) are often the first customers and are great at spreading the word about your business. (Remember that word of mouth is often the first method of getting to your customers.)

There may also be some compelling reasons to consider a different location. What are the business laws like in your area? Local zoning ordinances specify what sorts of businesses are allowed and not allowed in specific locations.[91] Certain types of businesses—usually those deemed hazardous or noisy—may be banned or severely restricted. State and local pollution standards, workers' compensation, wage rates, and other such legislation might increase the cost of doing business to the point that other locations become much more favorable. State and local taxes in particular vary considerably from state to state. For example, Wyoming has no personal or corporate income tax, while California has relatively high rates. On the other hand, certain locations often offer attractive incentives for new businesses ranging from tax credits to low-interest loans, from favorable business laws to business incubators (discussed later). Most of this information can be found on the Internet. See the Learn More Online box below for additional information on economic development in your area.

LEARN MORE ONLINE

Learn more about the topics above at these sites:

U.S. government: **www.usa.gov/state-business?source=busa**

U.S. Small Business Administration: **www.sba.gov/local-assistance/find/**

Site Selection magazine: **www.siteselection.com**

Listing of U.S. chambers of commerce: **www.officialusa.com/stateguides/chambers/**

Other reasons to consider other locations are tied to your customer. Your hometown may not be the best place for you to find your target market customers. Are you close to the people who will use your product or service? Other considerations include population growth or decline (especially in your target sector), income levels, and predicted increases or decreases in income. Is the location expanding economically or slowly dying? Perhaps the best source for this information is the U.S. Census Bureau's Census Business Builder (https://cbb.census.gov/sbe/#). State and local municipality business development offices may also carry such information, but they are likely to be slanted toward attracting new businesses. Being positioned to benefit your customer can also be key. For example, Zappos's first distribution hub was placed in Louisville, Kentucky, to be close to a major UPS air cargo hub in order to speed delivery.

Also consider the type of business you are planning. Do you need skilled labor? If so, what areas will provide you with the necessary employees? Do you need to be near raw materials or particular methods of transportation? These issues will help determine your choices. Where are your competitors? Certain industries tend to be clustered in certain regions where they can make efficient use of services and employees. Think of California's Silicon Valley or the financial district of New York City.

Doing business in your hometown may be perfectly appropriate; however, the cost of moving a company—whether across town or across the country—can be very expensive. It pays to plan ahead.

Service Firms

There are three typical locations for services: at the client's location, at a mutually accessible location, and at your firm's location. Traditionally, services may have been tied to one or another of these, but marketing niches have been carved out by people daring to be different. Typically, dry cleaning and restaurant dining are services provided at a place accessible to both parties, but some dry cleaners now offer pickup and delivery from the client's home, and with services like Grubhub.com and Doordash.com not only pizza restaurants offer delivery these days. Thanks to the Internet, video rental like Netflix.com and other services are handled electronically, and the customer and service provider may never meet face-to-face. Whatever innovative niche you select, there are a few things to keep in mind.

At the Client's Location

Typically, these services include things such as house or office cleaning, pest control, remodeling, lawn and gardening services, carpet cleaning, and similar services that must be performed at the client's location. Business headquarters can be a home office with enough room to store and maintain any necessary equipment used in the service. Reliable transportation, preferably modified to organize and store tools efficiently, may be required for your business (see Small Business Insight below). More importantly, the range of your client's locations must be planned to prevent transportation times from being unmanageable. For example, facing a one-hour drive to a client's location might mean you have tied up two hours in commuting. If you cannot charge for travel and do not have other clients nearby, it means you have two hours in which you cannot make any money that day.

If you've done your homework carefully, you already know the geographic area(s) most likely to use your service. Certain services may be organized into a rotating schedule. For example, a house cleaning service may clean a certain set of neighborhoods on Monday, different set on Tuesday, and so on. In other cases, more remote clients may be charged a transportation fee. In some cases, a mileage fee may be appropriate for your business (delivery services, for example).

As the firm grows, it may outgrow its home-based headquarters. As your clients seldom, if ever, visit you, you have more latitude in where you can be located and the ability to seek out low-cost space (see the site selection section). Reasonable distance to the clients and adequate storage room for your expanded fleet and equipment are key to choosing a site.

SMALL BUSINESS INSIGHT

LINDZEY PATTERSON AND HOME COOKING

Lindzey Patterson had a real passion for cooking. Even as she was finishing her degree at Saint Louis University, she was planning her next classes at a local cooking school. Her idea was to offer cooking classes in the client's own kitchen. Her business could operate from a van equipped with her cooking equipment and refrigerators for storing food. Reservations could be handled by cell phone. This way, Lindzey had taken a business usually based in a mutually accessible location and made it into a business conducted at the customer's location. In doing so she was able to minimize her costs and personalize her service, called Home Cooking. This, in turn, served as the launch pad for her next business, Coffee Girls Cafe in Kansas City. Today she consults other start-ups in the restaurant industry.

Finding a truly convenient space is one of the challenges of placing one's business in a mutually accessible location. In the example pictured, the owners offer an expanded product line to attract passersby on a busy downtown street. Locating several different kinds of related items in one street-front store gives customers the ability to shop for several needs at one time and place.

Kelly/Mooney Photography/Getty Images

Mutually Accessible Location

Services using this approach often have too much specialized equipment to be readily transported and a need for at least some client involvement. Barbershops, dentist offices, and restaurants are services typically located at a site that is extremely convenient for the client and reasonably so for the owner and employees.

Even though your service may be traditionally located in a mutually accessible area, consider what you might do to make it home based (see Chapter 5). Your watch repair shop might generate clientele by being located in a shopping center, but will the added sales be offset by the high cost of rent, utilities, insurance, and other payments? Can you offer pickup and delivery and do the work at home? Your restaurant idea might work as a catering service. Instead of a specialized clothing shop, why not try mail order or Internet-based sales? FoxPaw (www.foxpaw.com) is a cell phone repair service in St. Louis that has over 20 automated kiosks for dropoff and pickup across the metropolitan region to be close to the customer.

Remote Location

In this type of service, face-to-face meetings with the client are infrequent. Typical services that meet this criterion include medical transcription, data processing, fulfillment centers, and some consulting work. These services generally are ideal for home-based businesses. Certain services, for example, fulfillment centers, generally take more space—at the minimum, an attic, garage, or basement. The biggest advantage of these sorts of businesses is that they can be located anywhere in the world. U.S. hospitals, for instance, use medical transcription services located in India. One such company, InfoFlow/TSVI, operates from a U.S. sales base (which makes handling calls from U.S. hospitals easier) with transcription being done in India, managed there by a co-owner who is a cousin and long-time friend of one of the two American owners.[92] Other than perhaps some initial sales meetings, all business is transacted via phone, fax, electronic exchanges, or mail.

Manufacturers

What if you are selling a product and not a service? What are your considerations about location now? Where you make the product is really dependent on the product. Some products that do not require a lot of specialized or bulky equipment can be produced at home unless zoning ordinances forbid it. In addition to whatever office space is needed, adequate work space is also required. The basement, a garage, or a home workshop may be adequate for some time. As business expands and as you add employees, it will become awkward if not illegal to continue production at home (see Chapter 5).

Some products require bulky and specialized equipment, utility demands atypical of homes, or sizable warehousing requirements and are never suitable for home businesses. Certain production characteristics–for example, use of hazardous materials and materials with strong odors or noisy operations–may make a home-based business undesirable. Many cities have zoning ordinances prohibiting manufacturing in residential areas. When you start to hire employees, providing the amenities they will expect or that are required by law will usually require moving the business from your home.

One emerging trend are rentable manufacturing spaces. Examples include makerspaces (https://makerspaces.make.co/), which are high-tech workshops with 3-D printers as well as traditional tools; hackerspaces (https://wiki.hackerspaces.org/List_of_ALL_Hacker_Spaces), which focus on programming and app development; or community kitchens–also called shared use kitchens (search for either term online or try rentthiskitchen.com). Local business incubators may also have rentable manufacturing facilities.

Contract manufacturing might be a better option, at least for a while. In this case, a firm with the capabilities to produce your product is contracted to manufacture it for you, usually for a flat per unit fee and a possible setup charge. Some firms will also assist in marketing and sales as well. Trade magazines in your field often list ads for contract manufacturers, or Google "contract manufacturing directory." An interesting possibility here is to use **sheltered workshops** to perform light manufacturing or assembly sorts of businesses. These workshops exist in nearly every state and offer very competitive pricing, often including tax benefits for the business.

contract manufacturing
An existing firm with the correct manufacturing capabilities makes your product for you.

sheltered workshop
A nonprofit organization or institution that provides business services by using workers who have disabilities or who are rehabilitated.

Site Selection

Once you have determined the general location of your business, you need to determine the exact location for your operation. What you should look for falls into three main categories: home-based businesses (covered in Chapter 5), high customer contact (e.g., retail), and low customer contact (e.g., manufacturing). Each has certain criteria to be considered.

High Customer Contact Businesses

Businesses with high customer contact include such diverse operations as medical or legal offices, restaurants, retail establishments, dry cleaners, and other businesses that are highly dependent on being convenient to the customer. For these operations, there are three critical site selection considerations: traffic, customer ease, and competition.[93]

First of all, you want a site that is convenient to your target market and to enough of the customers to make you profitable. If you are considering a franchise, many will offer site criteria to help you make your selection. If you are going it alone, consider the population density of the area and how many of the people in the area meet your target market criteria. The U.S. Census Bureau website and a number of free nongovernment sites like www.zipwho.com and www.city-data.com can be a good starting place for free information (see Skill Module 9.3). If plowing through the Census Bureau website doesn't get you what you want, several commercial services mentioned in Chapter 10 including PRIZM and Esri will sell you data about the population in a particular zip code for several hundred dollars. More detailed and specific commercial information is also available and can range in price from several thousand dollars to over $100,000 and is probably not an option for most entrepreneurs.[94] Again, the website of *Site Selection* magazine (www.siteselection.com) mentioned earlier has tools and additional articles that can help.

Another consideration is the presence of **traffic generators** in the area. These are other businesses that draw customers to the area and may include supermarkets, office complexes, schools, and malls. If the customers are drawn there, for example, to grocery shop, they will be more likely to come by your business too. Reflect on the type of customer you are seeking and the likelihood of these businesses in attracting them. If you want a teen customer, a location near a high school or a mall works well. If you are looking for evening clientele, offices that close at five aren't the right traffic generators for you. Drive around likely areas and locate possible sites. Visit during the hours you anticipate to be peak times for your business and evaluate foot and car traffic.[95] Look at the crowds or lines in similar businesses and decide whether there is room for you. If most businesses seem empty, you probably will be too.

traffic generators
Other businesses that bring customers (generate traffic) to the area.

Intersections of major streets offer high automobile traffic, but because of divided roads and other barriers, they may not make it easy for your customers to get to you. Businesses along interstates have high visibility, but the frontage roads can be so convoluted that the clients seek easier-to-get-to competitors. Even some malls and shopping centers have such tortuous access problems that customers avoid them when possible. Sometimes entry is easy, but getting out is difficult. For example, no signals for left turns when most of the traffic needs to head in that direction can turn off customers.

Parking is also an issue as seen in the Small Business Insight below. Is it conveniently located to your place of business? Do customers need to cross busy streets to get to you? Is parking free or paid? Are parking areas well lit and safe? Are there wheelchair ramps or other accommodations for customers who are disabled?

Customers have strong ideas about how far they should have to drive for things. These vary somewhat from major metropolitan areas to more rural towns and from one region of the United States to another. Generally convenience stores, fast-food restaurants, and gas stations need to be close to consumers. Grocery stores and banks can be somewhat farther away, but not much. Discount stores and midscale restaurants can be even farther away, while specialty stores, upscale restaurants, and malls can be relatively remote. Where does your business fit? How far are customers willing to drive to get to you?

Malls are great traffic generators, but space at malls is costly. If it is appropriate for your product, you might consider a kiosk or cart in the mall as a way of testing the market and location without making a large investment.[96] Neighborhood shopping centers (those anchored by a supermarket, drugstore, or major retailer) or strip centers (shopping centers without major anchors) are more modestly priced, but lack the drawing power of malls.[97]

Generally, competition in the area can draw away valuable clients, but this is not true in every case. Many cities have a restaurant row, an antique district, or an automobile mile (as well as other business types) where many competitors cluster. Clients wish to comparison shop or have choices and are drawn to areas where they can see several similar businesses at one time. Locating far from these will mean that you are free from competition, but this benefit may easily be offset by the cost of attracting customers to a different place. Additionally, you can capitalize on competitive advertisements that bring potential customers to the area. Your competitor's high-budget TV ad might get customers to the neighborhood, but the "sale" sign in your window may get them to stop at your place instead.

Another instance when you want to be near competitors is when your business provides a strong contrast to the competition in the area. Do you offer better assistance, additional services, unique advantages, or other benefits that can easily be seen by customers? They may be drawn to the area by a well-known competitor's name, but they may select your establishment instead because of what you offer that differentiates you.

SMALL BUSINESS INSIGHT

STEAK-OUT RESTAURANT[98]

Mark Dukes thought he'd found the perfect location for a restaurant that specialized in the delivery of burgers, chicken, and steaks when he found a location in the middle of the University of Tennessee in Knoxville. Students are always hungry and love delivery. However, during school breaks there are no orders—and also no employees. In addition, there was no parking at his location on campus. After seven years of struggling, Mark moved his failing franchise off-campus to a freestanding building with a parking lot. His sales went up 100 percent. He still delivered to students, but he got a lot of community business, and a family order would average $30 compared to the student order of $7 or $8. Today he also owns several Steak-Out franchise outlets and Fork River Foods, Inc.

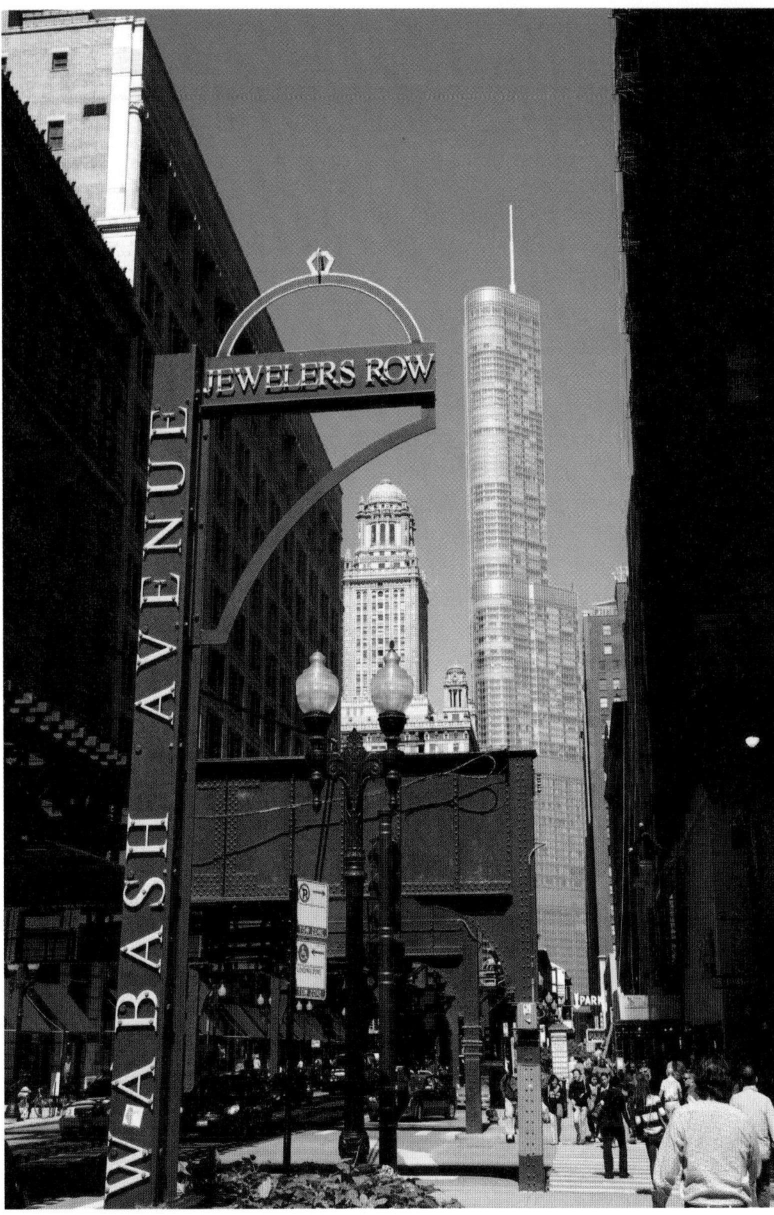

Chicago's Jewelers Row is an example of clustered competitors whose proximity to each other gives customers added convenience and more options. What are some reasons you can think of that illustrate how clustering helps bring more interest and business to an entire area?

Peter Ptschelinzew/Alamy Stock Photo

Low Customer Contact Businesses

Generally low customer contact businesses are manufacturing businesses, the headquarters of client location-based services, or remote location services. Customer access is relatively unimportant. More critical are access for your employees, reasonable cost, and the space necessary to do your business. Certain manufacturing operations will need adequate utilities and specialized transportation too.

Unless you plan to use some of this space as a high-traffic showroom, commercial space in a business park or light industrial park might be appropriate. These parks are located near major transportation routes, often have rail spurs, and are designed for industrial utilities; that is, they have adequate electricity, gas, water, waste water treatment, and the like. Frequently, support businesses will be located in or near the park such as warehousing, shipping firms, copy centers, and office supply stores. Industrial or business park space tends to be cheaper in smaller cities and rural towns than in major metropolitan areas. If distribution to customers can be arranged, these locations are certainly cost-effective.

Some major metropolitan areas offer specialized zones where special support is provided to companies locating there. These are sometimes called *empowerment zones* or may be economic development zones. These zones, often in economically depressed areas, offer businesses low-cost space and tax advantages for locating there. For more information, check with your local government or SBDC. You can also see www.rd.usda.gov/programs-services/all-programs/business-programs or www.siteselection.com for different incentive programs to promote businesses moving to certain locations.

A third possibility is a business incubator. The International Business Incubator Association (InBIA) (inbia.org) shows over 400 business incubators in North America sponsored by government, universities, or private investment groups. These business incubators are specifically designed for the entrepreneur, and, in addition to relatively low cost space, they offer a multitude of small business support services. These services range from copy machines, faxes, and conference rooms to accounting, finance, and consulting services. Since the building is populated by other entrepreneurs, it's a great place to talk to others who might have had some of the same problems or to brainstorm new ideas. Most incubators require a stake in your company in exchange for their assistance—maybe as much as 50 percent—and often have quite a bit to say about how you run your business. Opinion is mixed on how much real help a company can get; just like all businesses, there are better and worse incubators, so do your homework.[99]

accelerator
An organization that supports start-ups, typically of a particular type (e.g., Internet, biotech, fashion, sports, women-owned firms, etc.) with a financial investment, free or inexpensive office space, mentoring, a variety of free or low-cost support services, and other resources. The goal of an accelerator is to accelerate a start-up from its early stages to being ready to pitch for investment. Most accelerators take an equity stake in the companies they help.

co-working space
A type of "incubator lite" offering low-cost shared space and basic business services (Wi-Fi, desks, coffee, conference room, copier, etc.) for a daily, weekly, or monthly rental fee. Unlike incubators, co-working spaces rarely get any equity in the businesses using the space.

A variant of the incubator is an **accelerator**. Accelerators generally focus on helping one type of business (e.g., Internet, biotech, financial tech, toys, fashion, etc.) accelerate their move from start-up to being ready to pitch for investor dollars. Accelerators generally offer cash investment, space, mentoring, and free or low-cost access to professionals like lawyers and accountants. In return, they get a stake in your business. You can find lists of accelerators in the Learn More Online box.

There has also emerged in many locales settings called **co-working spaces** which many consider a type of "incubator lite." These spaces usually offer the basic amenities needed for modern Internet-based work (desks, chairs, copiers, a conference room, and of course, coffee and fast Wi-Fi) in a setting much a library's main room. Directories of the spaces are given in the Learn More Online box. Entrepreneurs rent access by the day, week, or month, and that is all the co-working space gets. Co-working spaces rarely get equity in the businesses they house.

LEARN MORE ONLINE

Learn more about the topics above at these sites:

Business incubators: **http://exchange.inbia.org/network/findacompany**

Accelerators: **www.seed-db.com/accelerators**
http://gan.co/
www.galidata.org/accelerators/directory/

Co-working spaces: **http://wiki.coworking.org/**
https://www.coworker.com/
https://findworkspaces.com/

General Comments on Site Selection

How do you go about finding potential sites? Looking for "for sale" and "for rent" signs is a start, but not all space will be advertised that way. Just as a good real estate agent can warn you about the proposed freeway project going through the backyard of the house you are considering or let you know about houses not yet listed but likely to be, an experienced real estate broker will also be able to assist you in your search for your business location. Many have relationships with landlords that can work to your benefit. They are also likely to have at least some of the market statistics you may need to help you decide if the location is right for your business.[100] Level with them about what you can spend. You have your business plan and know the cost per square foot you can afford and be profitable. If you are looking at property more expensive than that, you'll need to cut corners elsewhere.[101]

Leasing

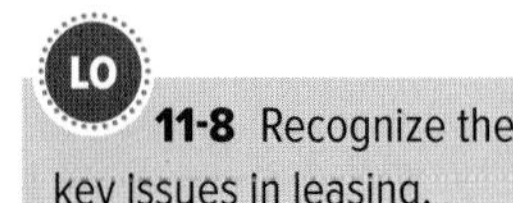

11-8 Recognize the key issues in leasing.

It is rare that a small business start-up buys its first location. The reason is financial. It takes a lot of money to buy a place, and beyond that a long-term commitment to pay for it. For most small businesses, it is not a worthwhile risk. It makes more sense to rent or lease your facility to leave more money for other aspects of the business. But leasing is one of the most complex of the issues an entrepreneur faces when starting a business.

In reality, most landlords (especially those from big national commercial real estate and mall companies) have fairly standard contracts that they don't like to change. These typically start out as very pro-landlord. That said, in many cases they are also likely to accept certain standard clauses that are more tenant-friendly. However, it is unlikely they will offer those. You will need to ask for them. In this section you will learn about the major types of tenant-friendly clauses you might want to seek. However, it makes tremendous sense to get a real estate lawyer involved to help you. He or she should be able to tell you what kinds of clauses are typical, who else offers them in your area, and if there are any other likely traps in the lease. You can learn how to choose a lawyer in Chapter 17.

You should begin the leasing process by looking for locations. You can start using the local newspaper's or business journal's classified ads for commercial real estate. If you know of a great location, but there is no "for rent" or "for lease" on it, consider asking the owner or current renter about subleasing a portion of the location. If your product or service complements the current tenant, you could find a home. Local real estate websites may also have listings, and there are national websites like LoopNet.com which compile listings from a variety of sources. You may contact a real estate agent with commercial experience to help you, but make sure you know how the agent is making his or her money. You want the agent to work in your best interests.

It helps to have two or three possibilities identified before you begin negotiating leases. This is a use of the idea of the power of rivalry from Chapter 7. This gives you a basis for comparison, and an alternative for leasing when negotiating. But note that the more alike the properties, the greater your power at the negotiating table. Also, if you are opening a franchised operation, you will want to contact your franchisor before you start looking for locations. Most franchisors have specifications for locations, and advice on costs and other features. They often have a lease review department to help you with this process.[102]

The best way to start thinking about the clauses is to separate them into those clauses related to choosing a property, day-to-day operations, and endings. In reality, though, all of these clauses will get negotiated when you and the landlord discuss the lease agreement.

There are several issues that could pop up as you are narrowing your choices and trying to decide which location and deal is the best for you. These are:[103]

- **"As is" versus compliant property:** If the location has problems, who should fix them? The landlord would like to have you do it, and will try to push you to accept the property "as is." You, of course, want the landlord to fix it before you move in, so you would ask the property to be "in compliance with all applicable laws, rules, and regulations." Realize that the landlord will get back the money paid for repairs eventually, through fees or higher rents, but it can save you money on the front end.
- **HVAC:** This is the commercial jargon for "heating, ventilation, and air conditioning." It can be the most expensive type of repair, and since it is mechanical, one of the types most likely to go wrong. The landlord wants it to be your responsibility. You want it to be the landlord's. This is particularly important if the location has a central air system so everyone shares the same air conditioner and heating equipment. This type of equipment needs to be the landlord's responsibility. For any type of equipment, you want the landlord to at least guarantee the first year of operation.
- **Signs:** Called "signage" in the business, it can be on the street, on the building, or around the door. You probably have ideas for your signs. If you are a franchise, you face signage requirements from the franchisor. You want a landlord who will work with you on the size, placement, and visibility of signs. Make sure you have written agreement on the signs and, if possible, a clause that says approval cannot be unreasonably denied for future changes.

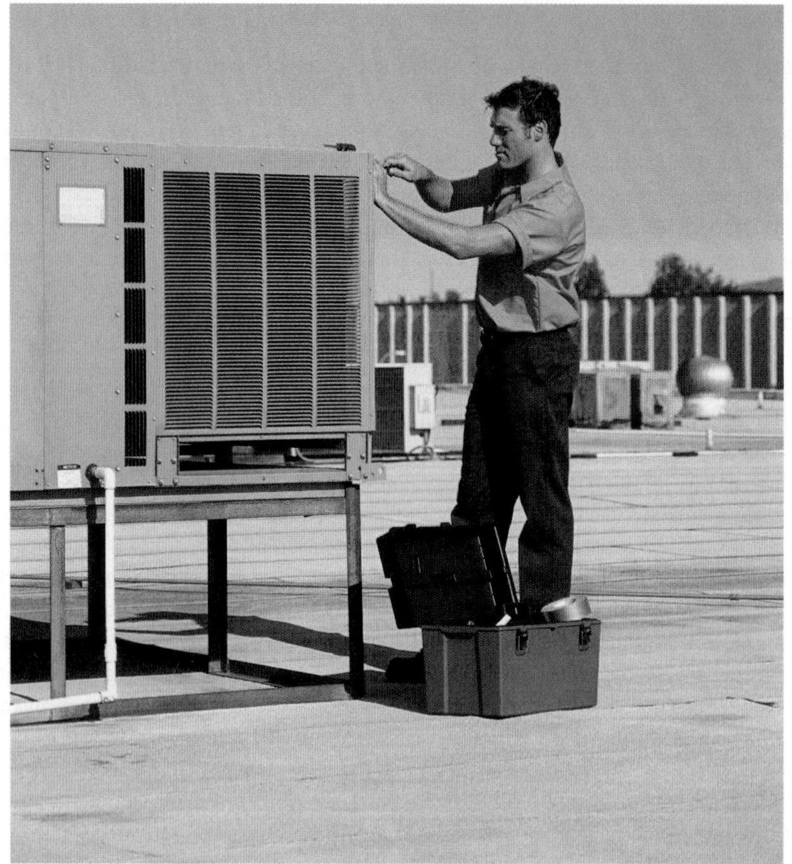

This is what no one wants to see—repairs needed for an air conditioner. But who is going to pay for it? What kind of air conditioners are likely to be your responsibility?

Fuse/Getty Images

There are other benefits possible if you know to ask for them. Often these are called concessions. Examples include "leasehold improvements," which are permanent changes made to the location to fit your business's needs, like bringing in a higher voltage power outlet or new drainage. You cover these by seeking a "tenant improvement allowance" or "construction allowance" which are rent dollars (typically $5 to $25 a square foot) you can put into improving your location.[104] This amount should be based on a firm estimate from a construction professional. Another concession is a "rent-free use period" which covers the time while you prepare your location prior to opening.

As you start thinking about how you would operate day-to-day, there will be several different issues you will face. These include:

- **Hidden charges:** Many leases include charges that do not have to be listed in the term sheet given you for the property. An example is a monthly operating expense. This may be justified. You may be leasing a thousand feet of space, but there are also common areas, restrooms, parking and the like that the landlord keeps up for everyone. Ask specifically for a list of all expenses or charges for which you will be liable, and compare to other locations. Also make sure to learn the conditions under which you can lose all or part of your security deposit.
- **Use of premises:** You specify in the lease what you will sell or do at the leased location, but too exact a description could prevent you from expanding the products or services you offer. Try to add the clause "and related goods and services" to any description you give to provide reasonable flexibility.
- **Noncompete:** If you have a pet store in a strip mall, you'd like to be the only one there. For many types of businesses, you negotiate a clause limiting the landlord's ability to lease to a competing business. This can be just for your facility or for a radius. You should expect to

pay for the exclusivity and the farther you want it, the more it will cost. Note that competition in terms of different types of restaurants, or another store selling some of your products, is still likely.

- **Hours of operation:** Mall landlords want stores open the same hours and days, and landlords of other types of properties may have some of the same desires. You need to negotiate times that fit your business model. Look for stores in the landlord's properties that match your hours. Pointing out those firms helps here.
- **Rent default:** When you are late paying rent, all sorts of penalties and problems emerge. It also hurts your credit rating. Some leases require the renter to keep track. Ask to change the lease to specify the landlord needs to alert you immediately on the rent due date in written or telephonic (usually fax) or email form, and get the 5- to 10-day default period for paying rent before default starts from that notice.
- **Moves and remodels:** There may be a clause that gives the landlord the right to move your business elsewhere, at their discretion. If this is to update or repair an area, fine, but what if it is to get a higher-paying tenant in your space? Set time limits and return rights on any forced move. Similarly, if the landlord decides to remodel, you should not have to pay for it.

As an entrepreneur negotiating a lease, you need to prepare for the good and the bad as time moves along. The good is the prospect your business grows and you need more space. The bad is that your business doesn't do well, and you need to get out of your lease before the end of the term. Dealing with these issues is like worrying about a prenuptial agreement while you are taken with the romance of getting married. It might be painful to imagine, but it is important to keeping what is yours.

If your business falters, you are obligated to continue paying your monthly rent and fees for the duration of the lease. A landlord has the power to let you out of a lease, but he or she is only likely to do this if a better tenant is lined up. Once you tell your landlord you may need to vacate the premises, she or he is supposed to look for a replacement tenant, but not all do, or do a good job of it. If you can find a replacement tenant, it can help this process along, but you need to make sure there is a clause that lets you sublease the property, and further, that the landlord can't unreasonably deny the sublease. If your pet store is closing, finding a dress shop is probably reasonable (as long as it doesn't violate some other tenant's noncompete clause), but finding an adult book store is probably not a reasonable replacement.

Three other ways to handle an early termination are to set up a short-term (e.g., 6 months) lease initially, ask for a bailout clause, or for a "cap" or limit on how long you need to continue paying rent. The bailout clause lets you out of the lease if sales do not meet an agreed-to level. You negotiate this with the landlord up front. To understand a cap, think about a three-year lease. If you close down after only 6 months, you are still obligated to pay 30 more months' rent. With a one-year cap you are obligated to pay only 6 months' more rent. This is like a type of insurance, and like insurance policies, you will probably have to pay a slightly higher rent from the start to cover this possibility.

Realize there can be problems you face caused by the property itself. What if you move into a shopping center or mall with a major chain like Lowe's, Target, or Macy's. Part of what you are paying a premium for is the traffic and reputation these anchor stores bring. What if they leave? Your location's quality could dramatically drop. To get out of your lease under these unfortunate circumstances, you want to ask for a cotenancy clause.

Although we've segmented a renter's concerns by stage of the leasing process, all of these issues need to be negotiated at the start when crafting a lease. Landlords often start with a lease they call "standard," but nearly everything about it can be negotiated. However, be fair; the space may mean a lot to you but it is a drop in the bucket to large commercial realtors. You can learn more about negotiating in general in Chapter 17, but there are some special considerations for lease negotiations. Because so many aspects are potentially negotiable and areas have different norms for what are typical tenant-friendly clauses, work with a real estate lawyer of your own to help you in the negotiation and phrasing of the lease terms.

Build, Buy, or Lease[105]

Ultimately, there are three choices available to the business: build, buy, or lease. Building has the advantage of having the perfect layout in the perfect location and the street appeal of a new building, but it is costly and slow. Buying something already in existence shortens the time and may be somewhat cheaper, but any remodeling or retrofitting that needs to be done may overshadow any time or money savings. In both cases, though, business owners have an asset that they can leverage, as well as the depreciation tax advantage. They have the flexibility to make the changes they need and know what the long-term costs will be.

Leasing, which we detailed earlier in the chapter, is an option with a considerably lower initial cash outlay, and it is often the only feasible choice for new businesses. Lease expenses are deductible business expenses. One of the main downsides of leasing is that you are usually limited in the renovations you can do. Another one is that leases tend to get higher with each renewal contract, and your landlord may choose not to extend a lease, forcing you to move before you are ready to do so.

The issues of location and distribution are decisions that business owners make only occasionally. Many businesses operate from the same location for their entire existence. Distribution decisions may come up more often. For example, a business started on eBay develops its own website and then grows into a store in the city's commercial center. Regardless of how often these decisions are made, they are central to the success of the small business because placing a business in the right location and equipping it with the right channels of distribution are essential to finding and connecting with customers. Done right, managing the issues of location and distribution can turn an average firm into a major success.

LO 11-9 Know what to look for in evaluating a potential site layout.

Layout

Since so much of this is particular to the type of business you are in, what you'll read below is a general guide. Check out competitors or similar types of businesses to see what you like and don't like, what seems to work well, and what seems to cause a lot of problems. In addition, certain categories–restaurants and retailing, for example–have numerous books from college textbooks to do-it-yourself books, like the "For Dummies" series. Try your local library or bookstore.

The layout of a potential site must be considered carefully. Is the building setup appropriate for your use? A restaurant will have different needs than a retail area or a manufacturing plant. The amount of area allocated to the "front room" (e.g., eating or retail areas) versus "back room" (storage, kitchen, warehouse, and office areas) needs to be adequate for the purpose of your business. If you are operating a restaurant or retail operation, how important is space in the front room? A coffee shop or fast-food restaurant squeezes in more customers per square foot than a gourmet restaurant. Do you need specialized areas, such as a kitchen or laboratory that are expensive to retrofit into existing buildings? Is there adequate storage area? How much dock space is appropriate for your business? A manufacturing firm usually needs more dock space and storage than a retailer or a restaurant, while a service company may need very little of either. Retail operations need display windows, while manufacturers do not. For restaurants or other services, this need varies. Is there room for expansion should the business grow? Remember: Moving can be expensive. A good strategy is to rough out the desired layout of your operation on graph paper to get a basic idea of the square footage needed and how it should look. What exactly you want may not be out there, but you'll be able to see what's close and what's impossible to live with.

Consider the amenities that are already there. Carpeting may be appropriate for a retail area and perhaps the office or dining area of a restaurant, but not appropriate for manufacturing or cooking areas. What about the walls? What sort of ceilings and lighting is appropriate? Again, a visit to the competition will help you decide what works and what doesn't, as well as where you want to be different.

Check the exterior, too. Is the building attractive and inviting? Are the sidewalks and landscaped areas in decent shape? Is parking adequate, well lit, and safe? Is employee parking separate from customer parking? What about accessibility for people with disabilities? The 1990 Americans with Disabilities Act (ADA) specifies that businesses (with few exceptions) must accommodate persons with disabilities. Many buildings have been brought up to code, and all new construction should meet the requirements of this act, but keep your eyes open.

Once the building has been selected, how you lay out the interior also needs to be considered. While retailers, restaurants, offices, and manufacturers all have different layout needs and considerations, two facts hold true: (1) layouts need to be designed to eliminate unnecessary and excessive employee movement, and (2) layouts say something about who you are to your customers, employees, and visitors. In retailing, this last factor is called *atmospherics.* While the opportunities for variation are limitless, let's consider the major types of retail and manufacturing layouts as well as what atmospherics might mean to a business.

Traditionally, manufacturing processes are laid out in one of two formats: production line layout and process layout, as displayed in Figure 11.5. In the production line layout, material flows in on one side of the operation and continues to the other end of the operation. Most assembly manufacturing is done this way, often with conveyors moving subassemblies from one station to another. Although a rather rigid flow, it works well for mass production and high-volume manufacturing. The second method, process layout, groups similar machines/or functions together, not unlike a typical machine shop. This format is much more appropriate for lower-volume, flexible manufacturing.

There are also two traditional layouts for retail operations, which are shown in Figure 11.6. The first one, the grid layout, has aisles running from the front of the store to the back like the typical grocery, discount, or convenience store. It's a very efficient and organized layout, although it lacks some visual impact. The second layout, the free-form layout, alleviates this problem. In this layout, the store is laid out in sections with aisles that angle or meander through the store. This is the layout more typically found in upscale department stores, clothing stores, and the like.

Atmospherics include all the ambience items that might be considered in your business. An upscale women's clothing store is likely to have wider aisles, deep carpeting, soft "elevator music," indirect lighting, and, perhaps, a lightly perfumed aroma. These are appropriate atmospherics for the target market. A shop catering to edgy teen fashions may be done in black and chrome with loud rock or alternative music and strobe or black lights. Both of these send a message about whom the store is likely to appeal to. Restaurants use atmospherics, too. Compare a family restaurant to a gourmet restaurant to an ethnic restaurant. Services and the office and public areas of manufacturing firms do this as well in their choice of colors, furniture styles, and background music.[106]

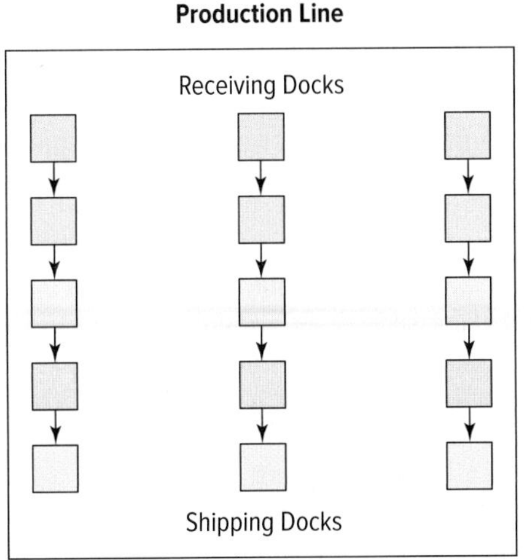

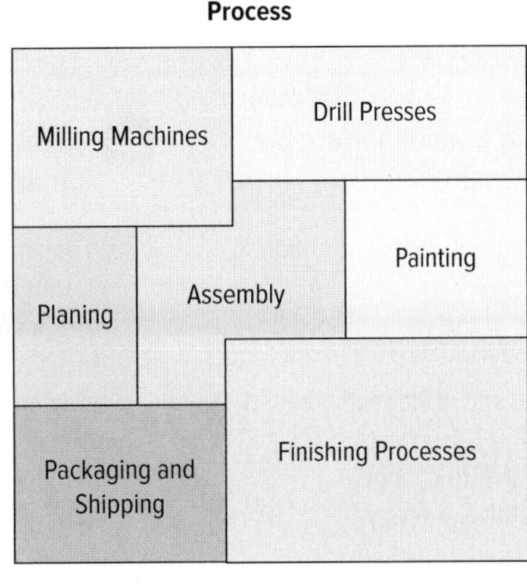

FIGURE 11.5

Typical Manufacturing Layouts

FIGURE 11.6

Typical Retail Layouts

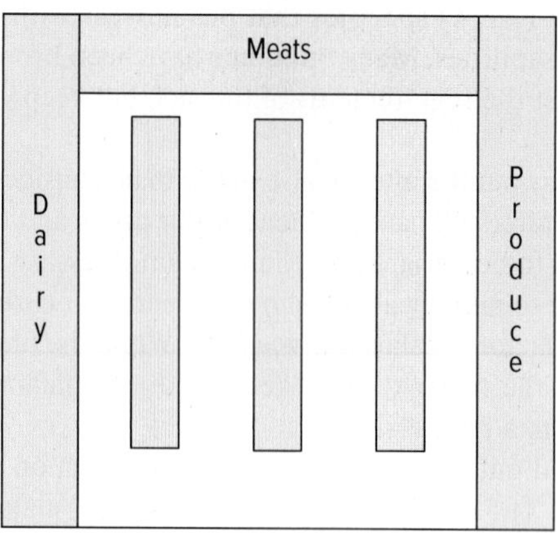

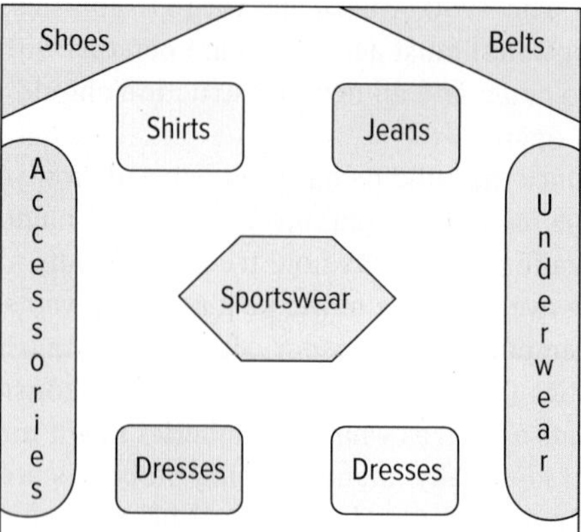

The good news is that there are a number of online business floor plan design programs. Some of these programs offer professionally designed templates for particular types of businesses, which can help you see how experts recommend setting up a layout, and this can help you decide how to do the best you can from the start. Several online building plan maker services have free trial periods, or are free in general. Check out the Learn More Online box for details.

LEARN MORE ONLINE

Learn more about the topics above at these sites:

RoomSketcher: **https://planner.roomsketcher.com/**

Gliffy (gives students up to four years of free use): **https://support.gliffy.com/hc/en-us/articles/217895678**

Lucidchart (has a free plan with a limit to how complex your design is): **www.lucidchart.com/users/registerLevel#/pricing**

CHAPTER SUMMARY

11-1 Understand why pricing is an important but difficult task for small business.

- Owners of small businesses give a great deal of attention to issues of pricing.
- The price of a product is a function of the value placed on the product by the customer.
- Price is directly related to revenue, and is indirectly related to volume.
- Price is the easiest marketing variable to change.
- Price is an essential part of competitive strategy.

11-2 Recognize the different pricing strategies that could apply to your product or service.

- Products tend to be price elastic or inelastic; that is, the quantity sold may vary considerably due to changes in price (elastic) or not (inelastic).
- Prices are also influenced by the effects of the law of supply and demand, the margins you set, and the value you can show to your customers.
- In addition to costs and consumers, price setting is influenced by five other factors: company objectives, marketing strategy, channels of distribution, competition, and legal and regulatory restrictions.

LO 11-3 Understand the types of sales promotion available to small businesses.

- Consumer psychology has an impact on pricing as well. Through a number of ways, consumers get ideas about what is an acceptable price and what is not.
- Firms may use a variety of different pricing strategies. Some of the more common ones include skimming, prestige or premium pricing, odd-even pricing, partitioned pricing, captive pricing, and price lining.
- Dropped prices are hard to raise. Rather than dropping prices, firms should consider using periodic or random discounting, off-peak pricing, bundling, coupons, rebates, and referral discounts.
- There are different methods for setting product prices, hourly rates, and service package prices.

LO 11-4 Recognize the different types of direct marketing and their pros and cons.

- Word of mouth is a good starting point and is low cost, but is not controllable and is limited in reach.
- Direct sales fall into a variety of categories: word of mouth, personal contact, door-to-door, party sales, trade shows and exhibitions, and vending machines.
- Direct mail encompasses catalogs, flyers, letters, videos, mail order, and anything else that can be mailed, faxed, called, or emailed.
- Telemarketing has two forms: outbound (calling the customer) and inbound (customer calling your firm).
- Direct response advertising is any ad that prompts the consumer to make contact with the company by phone, mail, or email.
- *Guerrilla marketing* is a term used to describe extremely low-cost or free alternative marketing. It covers things such as doorknob hangers or flyers stuck under windshield wipers.
- Multichannel marketing refers to giving your customers multiple ways of contacting you—phone, website, or mail-in order forms, for example.
- Direct selling distribution supports include Federal Express, UPS, and the U.S. Postal Service who offer shipping software and services for small businesses, with fulfillment centers or distribution center partners for larger shippers.

LO 11-5 Learn how to do nondirect distribution.

- Nondirect distribution requires using wholesalers, distributors, or retailers as well as other intermediaries.
- The appropriate channel may be discovered by tracing similar products back to their sources.
- Getting distributors interested may mean starting with direct sales through catalogs or trade shows to establish your product, demand, and reputation.
- E-tailers—Internet stores—may be willing to take on unknown suppliers and products because they have low overhead.

LO 11-6 Differentiate the types of international strategies.

- Entrepreneurs generally fall into three categories in using international strategies: some will always remain local; some are founded specifically to be international; and most believe that international business might be right for them someday, but do not worry about it until that day comes.
- Small businesses have the same options as large businesses in the international area (licensing, joint ventures, etc.) but most will start with—and may always stay with—an exporting strategy.
- Exporting has four main steps: (1) determining whether you're ready to export, (2) determining where to export, (3) determining whom to contact, and (4) determining how to begin.
- Importing: While many of the steps are similar to those for exporting, it is important to know how to find potential products to import and how to make the initial contacts.

LO 11-7 Identify the factors to consider in selecting your business location.

- Although most entrepreneurs assume they'll operate in their hometown, this isn't always the best location for their businesses. Consider the business climate, where your customers are, and proximity to key resources for your business.
- Service firms may perform work at the client's location, at a mutually accessible location, or can be remotely located and have limited customer interface.
- Manufacturers may be home based, but most will be located away from the home. Contract manufacturing is a low-cost way to get started.
- Site selection choices include home-based businesses, high customer contact locations, and low customer contact locations.
- High customer contact considerations include traffic, customer ease, and competition.
- Low customer contact settings include business and light industrial parks, business development zones, and business incubators, accelerators, and co-working spaces.

LO 11-8 Recognize the key issues in leasing.

- Standard leases are designed to be landlord-friendly.
- Entrepreneurs seek changes, added clauses, or concessions to make the lease fit their needs and circumstances.

- There are issues around choosing a property, operating the firm, and terminating the business that need to be negotiated up front.
- The changes, clauses, and concessions typical in one situation or locality will differ from another.
- Because leases are so complex, the help of a real estate attorney is essential.
- You can lease, buy, or build (in order of up-front costs).

11-9 Know what to look for in evaluating a potential site layout.

- Consider the physical layout and size of the building, its amenities, and its exterior. What changes or improvements will be needed, and who will have to pay?
- Manufacturing typically is laid out in one of two ways: production line or process layout.
- Retailing also has two primary layouts: grid or free form.
- Atmospherics tell customers a lot about your business and the type of customers you are likely to service.

KEY TERMS

optimum price, 374
markup pricing, 375
markup, 375
margin, 376
elasticity, 376
inelastic product, 376
elastic product, 376
law of supply and demand, 376
price gouging, 376
internal reference price, 382
external reference price, 382
skimming, 383
prestige pricing, 384
premium pricing, 384
odd-even pricing, 384
partitioned pricing, 385
captive pricing, 385
price lining, 385
periodic discounting, 387
random discounting, 387
off-peak pricing, 387
bundling, 387
multiple or bonus pack, 387
sales promotion, 390
referral discount, 392
channels, 393
manufacturer, 393
manufacturer's suggested retail price, 393
direct sales, 394
direct marketing, 394
direct mail, 396
mail order, 396
microinventory, 398
just-in-time (JIT) inventory, 398
telemarketing, 399
direct response advertising, 400
guerrilla marketing, 401
multichannel marketing, 402
wholesaler, 403
agent, 403
retailer, 403
e-tailer, 403
born international, 405
direct exporting, 406
indirect exporting, 406
freight forwarders, 406
letter of credit, 408
documentary draft, 408
contract manufacturing, 413
sheltered workshop, 413
traffic generators, 413
accelerator, 416
co-working space, 416

DISCUSSION QUESTIONS

1. Suppose you are operating a copy service. You learn that FedEx Office is going to open an outlet just a few blocks away. You are concerned that you cannot compete with the marketing power of FedEx. What is likely to happen to your business if you lower your prices and place colorful advertising banners in the windows announcing the lowered prices?

2. While displaying at a craft fair, a representative of a mail order catalog company wants to put your product in the

catalog. It will pay you $40 and mark up the product to $55 for the catalog. It estimates that your market share could be substantial and should be dependent only on your production output. You decide to quit your real job and devote all your time to making wreaths, but you want to match your current $50,000 salary. You really don't want to work more than 40 hours per week in actual wreath manufacturing (assume all paperwork, material purchasing, and such takes place beyond those 40 hours). You want four weeks a year for vacation, holidays, and sick days or personal days. Taking into consideration time constraints, the price you will get from the catalog company, and your revised costs, does this make sense?

3. Why do owners and managers of small businesses spend so much time on pricing issues?
4. Some of the most innovative start-ups have been firms that have dared to buck tradition in their distribution choices, like **Netflix.com** which initially distributed rental videos through the mail from its website, and now streams live. Select four small businesses and come up with unique distribution systems for them. Beyond the differential advantage, what other advantages might a better distribution system give a firm?
5. The chapter mentioned several unique guerrilla marketing pieces that stood out from the rest—the landscaper who used a plastic sandwich bag of decorative stones with his business card and the decorator whose ad was on a wallpaper scrap. Come up with two or three innovative ways of presenting your message.
6. What direct response ads can you recall seeing or hearing lately? Which ones were more effective? Why?
7. Assume you have developed innovative new business software and want to sell it internationally. Without doing any research, come up with a list of likely countries. Why did you choose the ones you did? If the product had been a nutrition bar or soft drink, would the list be different? Why?

EXPERIENTIAL EXERCISES

1. For one week collect all the coupons you find in newspapers, magazines, mail, and so on. What percentage are for products or services or brands that you would actually buy? Typically, how many coupons do you use in a week? Pull all the coupons for one product category and visit a store. Are there other brands of that same product that do not have coupons? Is the store engaging in any other methods to attract customers—rebates, sales, contests, multipacks, and so on?
2. Paul Scheiter's firm, **HedgehogLeatherworks.com**, makes high-end sheaths for knives. One of his customers, Ian Atkinson, is a big fan and also a leatherworker, and provided his analysis of the pricing behind one the Hedgehog's most popular sheaths. See the video at **www.youtube.com/watch?v=NYqmSzx_LRs**. Based on this example, explain in your own words how elements like design and quality of construction make a product worth more than just the cost of raw materials and an hourly wage for leatherworking. The first 14 minutes give you the pricing discussion. The last 7 minutes show you what you would have to do to make a similar sheath of your own.
3. Choose a business that you might someday like to start. Try the **www.infousa.com** website described in Skill Module 11.2 and locate a list that you feel would be appropriate to reach your market. Which list did you select and why? What would it cost?
4. Select a major high customer contact business category (restaurant, retail, dry cleaning, hair salon, etc.) and visit two or more different providers. What do you see in their store layout that seems to work well? What suggestions do you have for things that might work better?
5. Visit two stores, one where you belong to the target market and one where you do not. Make a list of all the atmospherics you detect and explain how they appeal to the target market.
6. Keep a list of direct marketing you experience for a week. Which messages did you find particularly appealing? Why? Which ones were you more likely to ignore?

MINI-CASE

THE MULTIPLE MARKETING EFFORTS OF FLIPOUTZ[107]

After creating Flipoutz (**flipoutz.blogspot.com**, **facebook.com/flipoutz**) in 2008, we applied to *Shark Tank* and we knew the "sharks" would want to see impressive sales of our wristband with coins you could flip out and trade with other kids. We used the traditional routes such as using social media, hiring a sales representative to focus on small retail and independent toy stores, and attending trade shows, but we also tried our own unique approach.

We created the "Flipoutz Kidz Force" to teach kids about entrepreneurship using our products to create their own business. They could buy Flipoutz wholesale or use our sample kit to take orders, then become a brand ambassador to sell to their friends and keep all of the profits! Each child that joined Kidz Force participated in weekly conference calls, received monthly newsletters, and got a training binder that taught the children how to become a brand ambassador. It was also important to us that we use Kidz Force to teach entrepreneurial skills, so our newsletter and calls focused on how kids could grow their business, as well as tips on making presentations and problem solving.

Our marketing had to follow the Children's Online Privacy Protection Act (COPPA) which regulates how businesses can interact with kids online. Although it required a substantial investment, we subscribed to a service that provided constant oversight of our online activities to ensure COPPA compliance, as well as a state-of-the-art technology for our website that flagged bad words, slang words, and personally identifiable information.

Since we had to be careful about marketing to kids directly in the digital world, we let our Kidz Force ambassadors reach our end users—the kids! An important note is that we were careful to make sure involvement in Kidz Force was conditioned on having a parent or teacher as an initial contact and sponsor. This guaranteed our investment as well as keeping us COPPA compliant.

We also focused on trade shows such as the Chicago Toy and Game Fair, the New York Toy Fair, the Southern Christmas Show, and the Atlanta International Gift Market to get into stores. We even brought Flipoutz to local events of all sizes, from the small Irmo Okra Festival to the giant South Carolina State Fair! My siblings and I worked five or six trade shows and festivals a year and found that our young age (8, 12, and 14 at the time) was a great way to attract buyers to our booth. We also made ourselves available to promote the product in stores. Small retailers often took us up on the offer and appreciated the extra marketing help.

Through these efforts, we were eventually carried in over 300 independent retail stores across the country. After appearing as the first children to pitch in the *Shark Tank* and seal a deal with three "sharks," we became visible to kids all across the nation who were excited to do what we were doing and become a part of Kidz Force!

CASE DISCUSSION QUESTIONS

1. Why do you think Flipoutz used so many different types of marketing? What were the different marketing techniques contributing to sales?
2. Using kids as brand ambassadors is particularly complex because of the COPPA regulations, but in looking for brand ambassadors in general, what would you look for in a person?
3. For Flipoutz, personal selling was done in multiple venues, to multiple audiences. How would you vary your sales pitch for Flipoutz when talking to prospective kid brand ambassadors, small retailers, and sharks on *Shark Tank*?

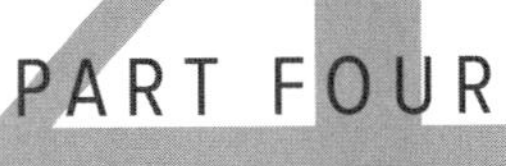

PART FOUR

Accounting, Cash, and Finance in the Small Business

CHAPTER 12

Small Business Accounting: Projecting and Evaluating Performance

● Justin Beegel quit his day job to go full time as an entrepreneur in his bootstrapped business. Within the first year on his own, he got into a position where he did not have enough cash to pay the bills. He had not paid enough attention to record-keeping and reporting systems. He thought, "I'll be out of business in 30 days!"

How would you respond to a critical financial position such as Justin's?

Infographic World, Inc.

Justin Beegel of Infographic World, Inc.

igw The Visual Marketing Agency

LEARNING OBJECTIVES

After you complete this chapter, you will be able to:

LO 12-1 Describe the basic concepts of accounting.

LO 12-2 Specify the requirements for a small business accounting system.

LO 12-3 Explain the content and format of common financial statements.

LO 12-4 Use accounting information as a tool for managing your business effectively.

LO 12-5 Create a set of appropriate budgets that support developing pro forma financial statements for your business plan.

LO 12-6 Use accounting information to make better business decisions.

Focus on Small Business: Justin Beegel of Infographic World, Inc.

Infographic World, Inc.'s story reads like a Hollywood script for a stereotypical "by-his-bootstraps" movie about a struggling businessperson. Justin Beegel, fresh out of Binghampton University with a new MBA to post on his wall, went to work for as the social media manager for Hachette Filipacchi Media—the publishers of *Woman's Day, Elle, Road and Track, and Car and Driver* magazines.[1] While working for Hachette Filipacchi, Justin began working a side gig for extra money. Soon the side gig had grown to the point that he was in effect working two full-time jobs. In an article for the Young Entrepreneur Council (YEC) Justin wrote, "I was working until 6 pm at the day job, and 5 am on the side business."[2]

Justin quit his day job and went full time into his start-up, Infographic World, Inc. This was a gutsy move—he had no significant savings and took no partners to provide funding.[3] And, by his own words, the business very nearly failed soon after start-up.

Justin is quoted as saying, "there is no better teacher than failure."[4] His first failure in the start-up came within the first year of operation. One day while he was printing invoices from vendors he suddenly realized that he did not have enough cash to pay the amounts that were due. He had largely ignored the need for accurate record keeping and for timely reports to help him direct and control his business. He wrote, "I had virtually no systems . . . to track . . . how much was coming in . . . how much I would need to pay."[5]

In his desperation Justin turned to his father, who had often been his mentor. With his father's help, he began to make a plan to work himself out of the hole.[6] His solution was twofold. First, to address the cash flow problem, he would establish and enforce specific payment terms with his vendors and also with his clients. Second, he would establish the necessary procedures and systems to ensure that he had the information needed to plan, direct, and control the finances of Infographic World, Inc.[7]

Today, some 10 years later, Infographic World, Inc., now renamed IGW, focuses on all things concerned with visual marketing. The company is highly successful, having won many awards for its eye-catching infographics and visual marketing campaigns. IGW has worked with a wide range of businesses, from newly funded star-ups to Fortune 100 corporations. In 2015 it was named one of *Entrepreneur* magazine's "30 Startups to Watch."

DISCUSSION QUESTIONS

1. Why did Justin Beegel run out of money to pay his bills?
2. What would you do differently from what Justin did when confronted with a financial crisis?
3. Does a good accounting system guarantee entrepreneurial success?
4. In what ways does an inadequate accounting system impede entrepreneurial success?

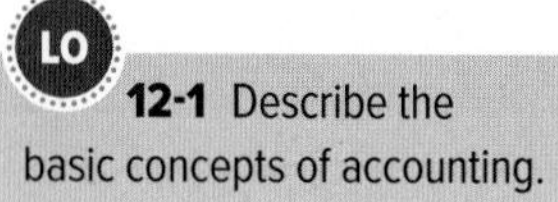
LO
12-1 Describe the basic concepts of accounting.

Why Accounting Is Important for Small Business Success

You probably really dislike having to deal with accounting. This is certainly understandable: You are interested in creating and running a business, and not very interested in spending time dealing with the details of what the business did in the past. You may think, "Time spent on boring accounting tasks could be so much better used for planning and selling your business concept!" You are not alone in having this opinion. Few students of entrepreneurship are fond of the topic of accounting.

So why do it?

There are several compelling reasons to become familiar with the process and the uses of accounting for small businesses:

1. Investors will not even consider funding your concept unless you provide specific accounting information in an accepted format.
2. Bankers will not loan money to a business that has no formal financial statements.
3. You absolutely cannot know how your business is doing without accounting information.
4. Business planning and controlling cannot be done without accounting information.

An essential part of business is generating profits to increase the wealth of its owners. Many businesses have owners who are not active in the running of the business and, because of this, do not have a firsthand knowledge of the profits (or losses) that the business is generating. These owners demand that the owner-managers who are actually running the business provide accurate and timely reports of the operations. Keeping careful records of financial transactions makes it possible for both active and absentee owners to have the information that they need.

In addition to owners, there are many other entities that have an interest in the results of the business. These include bankers and other lenders, who want to be assured that the business can repay loans, and governmental agencies that want to ensure that proper taxes are paid and specific regulations are followed.

Accounting is an essential tool for successfully doing management tasks. If you do not have a reliable accounting system that produces timely reports, you must rely on guesses and hopes when you make business decisions. Similarly, there is no substitute for having specific performance goals and accurate reports to be able to analyze current operations and make effective plans for future operations.

To understand the essential place of accounting in creating and operating a successful small business, we need to see just what accounting really is and what it really does.

The first thing that you need to understand is that there are three types of accounting you will need to use in your business: (1) **financial accounting**, (2) **managerial accounting**, and (3) **tax accounting**. Let's take a look at each of these types of accounting, concentrating on how they are used to help you succeed in your small business.

financial accounting
A formal, rule-based set of accounting principles and procedures intended for use by outside owners, investors, banks, and regulators.

managerial accounting
Accounting methods that are specifically intended to be used by managers for planning, directing, and controlling a business.

tax accounting
An accounting approach based on specific accounting requirements set by governmental taxing agencies.

Financial Accounting

When most people use the term *accounting* they are really referring to financial accounting, which is based on a set of rules called **generally accepted accounting principles (GAAP)** that detail specific methods of keeping records of financial transactions; of placing the transactions into categories; and of producing specific financial reports that consist of:

(1) How profitable the business is.
(2) The value of the things that the business owns and who has a claim on that value.
(3) How much and from where money was received and how much and to whom money was paid.

These three financial reports are called the **income statement**, **balance sheet**, and **statement of cash flows**, or *cash flow statement*, respectively. Note that each of these financial reports presents information about things that have already happened. Product and services were sold. Various expenses were incurred. The difference between the amount of sales and the amount of expenses is the profit of the business. Things were acquired so that the business would be able to provide product and services to customers. Cash was collected and paid out. But all of these things happened *before* the financial statements were created. So you might ask, "If financial accounting deals only with things that have already happened, just what use can it be to me?"

The short answer is that financial accounting does not have a lot of value for running the day-to-day activities of a business. Financial accounting was created and is conducted for the benefit of owners of the business who are not involved in the management or operations of the business. In other words, financial accounting is for investors and financers, not for managers. But you are more than a manager, you are also both an owner and an investor. As owner, investor, and manager, financial accounting information is relevant to many tasks that you must perform such as convincing people to invest in your business or convincing bankers to loan money to your business.

generally accepted accounting principles (GAAP)
The standardized rules for accounting procedures set out by the Financial Accounting Standards Board and used in all audits and submissions of accounting reports to the government.

income statement
A statement that lists revenues and expenses and shows the amount of profit a business makes for a specified period of time.

balance sheet
A statement of what a business owns (assets), what it owes to others (liabilities), and how much value the owners have invested in it (equity).

statement of cash flows
A statement of the sources and uses of cash in a business for a specific period of time. Also called a cash flow statement.

Managerial Accounting

Managerial accounting has very little resemblance to financial accounting except for the case when managerial accounting is being used for planning future business operations. Managerial accounting is forward-looking where financial accounting is concerned only with the past. Managerial accounting has no set of formal rules. In fact, managers may do any accounting process, any analysis, any forecast that they please. The issue is not what is permissible. The issue is what is valuable. If the benefit of any managerial accounting task is greater than the cost of doing that task, then it should be done.

One of the most valuable functions of managerial accounting is planning for future business activities. This is done through a process that is often called **standard budgeting**, or **profit planning**. Because managers are familiar with the format of accounting statements, these plans usually are produced so that they look very much like an income statement, balance sheet, and cash flow statement. This method of organizing and formatting business planning is called **pro forma financial statements**. However, the final product of this process is not just a spending plan as you might make for your family. Rather, it is a detailed plan for future operations and is the standard against which actual results are compared to assess the performance of individual managers, operations, departments, and divisions. We will examine the details of business planning later in this chapter.

standard budgeting
A method for business forecasting and control in which specific expected volumes and prices per unit are used

profit planning
The process of creating a set of interconnected budgets that combine into a master budget that can be used for assessing and controlling the business processes.

pro forma financial statements
Planning documents for future business activities that are formatted to look like the common financial statements of the income statement, balance sheet, and statement of cash flows.

Tax Accounting

Tax accounting is done by following the tax laws and regulations that are made by various governments. The final product of tax accounting is a set of returns, forms, and schedules. There are many different business taxes, including federal income tax, state income tax, employment taxes, inventory tax, excise taxes, and various use taxes including sales tax and, in some countries, value-added tax. The primary value of tax accounting for a business is to avoid penalties for noncompliance and to legally minimize how much money it has to pay in taxes.

The Concepts That Make Accounting Work

Summa de
Arithmetica geo
metria. Proportioni: et proportionalita:
Continentia de tutta lopera:

● First Edition of the *Summa de Arithmetica*

UtCon Collection/Alamy Stock Photo

Financial accounting, which is what most people mean when they use the term *accounting*, is based on just a few basic assumptions that have been developed over thousands of years. We have 8,000-year-old accounting records from Mesopotamia. The Greeks and the Romans each had detailed rules for accounting to be sure that the proper taxes were paid. But accounting as we do it today really began about 600 years ago in the trading city-states of what is now Italy. The oldest textbook of accounting principles like those in use today is the *Summa de Arithmetica, Geometria, Proportioni et Proportionalità,* written by Luca Pacioli and published in 1494. The *Summa*, pictured here, is probably the most expensive accounting textbook in existence. A copy was recently listed on Biblio.com for a mere $200,000.

The assumptions that underlie accounting are very basic:

1. A business is an entity that is separate from its owners.
2. An operating business will continue in business.
3. Accounting information is valuable only if it is useful for the owners and managers of the business.
4. Creditors (lenders and suppliers) have claim on business assets that must be satisfied before any claim of an owner.
5. The claims of creditors and owners cannot be greater in total than the asset value of a business. This is called the accounting equation, and is explained below.

Let's consider each of these assumptions, then see how they combine to form the system of accounting that is in use across the world today.

Business Entity Concept

business entity concept
The concept that a business has an existence separate from that of its owners.

Because of the **business entity concept**, it is possible to separate business transactions from your own personal transactions. Thus, we can distinguish between money that your business borrows, and money that you borrow for personal needs. It is the business entity concept that underlies the legal forms of establishing businesses such as corporations, limited partnerships, and limited liability companies. (These are explained in detail in Chapter 17.) The business entity concept is implicit in all business regulation. Violating it can be a criminal offense.

As detailed in the Small Business Insight box, Mr. Padilla learned this the hard way. He carelessly accounted for funds that he had received for specific business purposes. In doing so, he "mixed" the investors' money into money that he held in his personal bank accounts. This practice is called commingling and although it is not uncommon in small businesses, it really should not be done. While there is no specific law prohibiting such commingling, it can be used in court as evidence of an intent to defraud.

Going Concern Concept

going concern concept
The accounting concept that a business is expected to continue in existence for the foreseeable future.

The assumption that a successful business will stay in business enables long-range planning and strategy. Accounting assumes that this year's business results will affect next year's, and that the intent of business is to make money over a period of many years. The **going concern concept** also implies that, as a separate entity, the business may continue in business even if it is sold to other owners.

Qualitative Characteristics of Useful Financial Information

The Financial Accounting Standards Board (FASB) is the body that establishes and maintains standards for financial accounting. Its publication, *Statement of Financial Accounting Concepts*

SMALL BUSINESS INSIGHT

DOES IT BELONG TO THE BUSINESS, OR IS IT MINE?

Mauro Padilla III, a San Antonio, Texas, builder, ran afoul of the law because of bad accounting, said his lawyer Adam Cortez.[8] U.S. Attorney James Blankinship agreed, writing in a presentencing court filing that more than $18 million of down payments and loan proceeds from different projects had been commingled with Padilla's own funds to the point that it was impossible to determine from the bank records what belonged to Padilla and what belonged to the various projects.

Cortez conceded that there should have been better segregation of the funds. But he also maintained that the failure was, in his words, "not a federal crime . . . just bad accounting."[9]

In this case bad accounting, specifically not keeping a "bright line" between business funds and personal funds (a violation of the business entity concept), led to very serious results. Padilla received a 12-year prison sentence, 5 years of supervised release, and was ordered to pay more than $6 million in restitution to banks and investors.[10]

Mauro Padilla III leaving the federal courthouse in San Antonio, Texas.

JOHN DAVENPORT, SAN ANTONIO EXPRESS-NEWS

No. 8, published in August of 2018, states in part that useful accounting information is "relevant and faithfully represent(s) what it purports to represent." The *Statement* further holds that usefulness of of the information is enhanced "if it is comparable, verifiable, timely, and understandable."[11]

The Greater Claim to Assets of Creditors

Laws regulating the disposition of the assets of debtors were developed in medieval Italy. At that time, the concept of corporations had not yet been developed, and thus all owners of a business were individually and as a group responsible for repayment of loans. The early Italian laws, developed primarily in Venice and Genoa, allowed creditors to seize the assets of the debtor-owners, sell the assets, and satisfy the claims of the creditors. If any money was left over after the claims were satisfied, it was returned to the debtor-owners. This basic process is still followed today, some 600 years after it was invented.

The Accounting Equation

accounting equation The statement that assets equal liabilities plus owners' equity (Assets = Liabilities + Owners' Equity).

asset Something the business owns that is expected to have economic value in the future.

owners' equity The difference between assets and liabilities of a business.

Financial accounting is based on a very simple equation called the **accounting equation.**

$$\text{Assets} = \text{Liabilities} + \text{Owners' equity}$$

The equation follows logically from the assumptions discussed in the paragraphs, above. If the business is an identifiable entity that exists apart from its owners, then the value of the business is the sum of the values of everything the business owns. The name for what a business owns is **asset.**

Owners of a business **do not own** the assets of the business. The business itself owns them. Rather, the owners of the business have a **claim on the assets** of the business. This claim is called **owners' equity.**

This does sound unnecessarily complicated. The best way to explain it is by using a simile. A business can be thought of as a container that holds (1) the money provided by owners, (2) things that the business has bought or built, and (3) things that the business controls because of contracts and laws. Look at the illustration below. The box represents the business Red Jett Sweets, Inc. This box (the business) currently holds $50,000 of cash, which was given to the business by the business' co-owner, Christina Meyer. Christina does not own the money any longer. She gave that money to the business. Christina has a claim on the value of the money and that claim is called **equity.**

FIGURE 12.1

Business as a Container of Asset

Courtesy of Natalie Gamez Meyer

The Balance Sheet

Remember, this is only a simile. Real businesses are much more than cardboard boxes and entrepreneurial owners are much more than sources of money for the business. Also, the accounting report does not look anything like the cartoon. For example, the balance sheet to report the equity transaction between Christina and Red Jett Sweets would look like this:

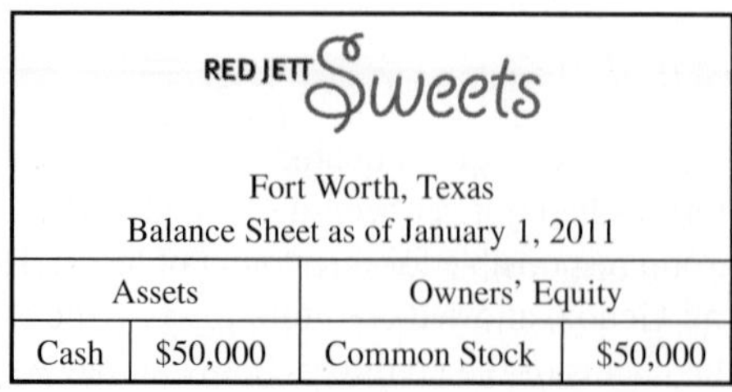
RED JETT Sweets

Fort Worth, Texas

Balance Sheet as of January 1, 2011

Assets		Owners' Equity	
Cash	$50,000	Common Stock	$50,000

Of all the concepts and ideas of accounting, the accounting equation is the simplest, but least understood. The entire system of accounting entries, reports, and financial statements is developed from this simple equation. The accounting equation is the method that is used to place these records into understandable categories that are useful for managing your business.

Up to here, we have seen the term **liabilities** but it has not been defined. To complete the discussion of the use of the accounting equation you need to understand the meaning of liabilities. Liabilities are legally enforceable obligations that will require the business to give up assets or to forego receiving assets in the future. Again, this probably make more sense if we use the earlier simile.

liabilities
Legal obligations to give up things of value in the future.

Suppose that Red Jett Sweets begins business. The managers make a decision that to conserve limited cash, the mobile cupcakery food truck will be purchased using a loan from a bank. Red Jett negotiates a contract to purchase the cupcakery for the expected $29,000, but borrows $23,000 to complete the transaction. At the same time, management acquires bakery equipment by paying $2,500 cash.

How does this show up in Red Jett's balance sheet?

RED JETT Sweets

Fort Worth, Texas
Balance Sheet as of January 31, 2011

Assets		**Liabilities**	
Current Assets		**Current Liabilities**	
Cash	$41,500		- 0 -
Long-Term Assets		**Long-Term Liabilities**	
Bakery Equipment	2,500	Long-term loan	$23,000
Mobile Food Truck	29,000		
Total Long-Term Assets	31,500	**Owners' Equity**	
		Common Stock	$50,000
Total Assets	$73,000	**Total Liabilities & Equity**	$73,000

As you can see, Red Jett had to make a down payment of $6,000 to buy the food truck. At the same time, the bank provided $23,000 which was immediately paid to the seller of the truck. This leaves Red Jett with $44,000 in cash and the owner of a long-term asset (the food truck) with the value of $29,000. The bank's claim on the assets of Red Jett is in the amount of $23,000 and is listed as a long-term liability. Red Jett still has a $50,000 claim on the assets of Red Jett made up of the $6,000 equity in the truck, $2,500 of bakery equipment, and the $41,500 in cash.

The important thing to consider is that the sum of the assets of the business, or $73,000, is ***exactly*** equal to the sum of the claims of the creditors and the owners.

Costs, Revenues, and Expenses

To explain revenues and expenses it is best to continue our example. Suppose that, having started the business and purchased inventory, Red Jett now purchases raw materials for a total price of $2,040 **on account**, then bakes and sells 3,000 cupcakes at $2.75 each on account to a local group for the group's spring fund-raiser.

on account
Merchandise purchased or sold with payment due in the future, usually within one month.

Recognize that no cash has changed hands. Red Jett purchased supplies on account which means that the company is allowed to take the goods and to pay for them later, usually within one month. Similarly, Red Jett sold the cupcakes on account which means that the buyer was allowed to take the cupcakes and has promised to pay for them in the future.

Red Jett Sweets received raw cupcake ingredients and gave up a promise to pay for them within a month. The company then turned around and received the customer's promise to pay

expense
A decrease in owners' equity caused by consuming your product or service.

cost of goods sold
An expense recognized at the time of a sale of merchandise in the amount of the cost of the merchandise to the seller.

revenue
An increase in owners' equity caused by selling your product or service.

retained earnings
(1) The sum of all the profits and losses that the business experiences from formation. (2) A balance sheet item in owners' equity that reflects the wealth created by the business from its formation.

and in exchange gave up the completed cupcakes. In accounting terms Red Jett has incurred an **expense**, called **cost of goods sold** in the amount of $2,040 and realized a **revenue** in the amount of $8,250. The difference between the revenue and the expense is a profit of $6,210, which will be reported on the balance sheet as **retained earnings**.

RED JETT Sweets

Fort Worth, Texas
Balance Sheet as of January 31, 2011

Assets		**Liabilities**	
Current Assets		**Current Liabilities**	
Cash	$41,500	Accounts Payable	$ 2,040
Accounts receivable	8,250	**Long-Term Liabilities**	
Total Current Assets	49,750	Long-term loan	$23,000
		Total Liabilities	25,040
Long-Term Assets		**Owners' Equity**	
Bakery Equipment	2,500	Common stock	$50,000
Mobile Food Truck	29,000	Retained earnings	6,210
Total Long-Term Assets	31,500	**Total Equity**	56,210
Total Assets	81,250	**Total Liabilities & Equity**	81,250

Now we can see the differences among costs, revenues, and expenses. Costs are the value of whatever you give up to get what you need or want. Revenue is an increase in owners' equity that is the result of selling your product or service. Expenses are reductions in owners' equity that recognize the value of goods (inventory) and services (labor) used to produce your product or service.

Let's suppose that Red Jett collects the invoice due from its customer and pays the bill that it owes to the manufacturer. If it were to use the balance sheet format to record these transactions, the balance sheet would look like this:

RED JETT Sweets

Fort Worth, Texas
Balance Sheet as of February 28, 2011

Assets		Liabilities	
Current Assets		Short-Term Liabilities	
Cash	$41,500	Accounts Payable	- 0 -
Plus invoice collected	8,250		
Minus bill paid	(2,040)	Long-Term Liabilities	
Total Cash	47,710	Loan on food truck	23,000
Accounts receivable	- 0 -		
Inventory	- 0 -		
Total Current Assets	$47,710	Total Liabilities	$23,000
Long-Term Assets		Owners' Equity	
Bakery Equipment	2,500	Common stock	50,000
Mobile Food Truck	29,000	Retained earnings	6,210
Total Assets	$79,210	Total Liabilities & Equity	$79,210

As you can see, this balance sheet is getting really messy. If we continue to record transactions in this way it will soon be nearly impossible to understand. Just imagine a year's worth of sales and expenses being recorded as in the previous example. So, as a matter of practicality, transactions are not actually entered directly into the balance sheet. Rather, we create an **account**. An account is simply a record of transactions that are similar in nature. Thus we have an account for sales revenue where we record each sale as it is made. Similarly, we have an account for wage expense in which we record wages as they are incurred. At the end of the accounting period, whether it is a day, a month, a quarter, or a year, we simply add up all revenues and all expenses. We then subtract expenses from revenues and the remainder is our profit (or our loss if it is a negative number).

The accounts that are not revenue and expenses (such as cash, accounts receivable, notes payable, etc.) are called **permanent accounts** and are kept in balance all the time. So, at any time the receivables account, for example, will show the sum of all credit that has been given to customers and all collections that have been made from customers.

account
In terms of accounting practice, an account is a chronological list of all additions to and subtractions from a single type of asset (e.g., cash, receivables, loans outstanding).

permanent accounts
The accounts of assets, liabilities, and owners' equity, excluding accounts for revenues and expenses.

Why Do Accounting?

There are only two reasons to do accounting: first, to produce information that is useful to you for managing your business; and second, to meet legal or contractual requirements. To be useful, information must be accurate and relevant.[12] One way to help ensure that your accounting information is accurate is by using a computerized accounting program, as discussed in the following section. Relevance of information must be evaluated for each decision as it is made. If having the information helps you make a smarter decision, a faster decision, or a decision you feel more comfortable about, then the information was relevant.

Skill Module 12.1 illustrates the issues discussed in this section.

Why Does Accounting Matter?

SKILL MODULE 12.1

Suppose you are operating a buffalo wings restaurant, and you purchase a high-capacity fryer. You have estimated the following costs of operating your restaurant for one month:

Variable costs:	
Food (chicken, potatoes, etc.)	$15,000
Beverages (soda, tea, beer)	4,500
Supplies (napkins, cleaning materials, etc.)	2,000
Labor	21,600
Total monthly variable costs	$43,100
Fixed costs (rent, insurance, depreciation, etc.)	$21,900

Now suppose that you are currently using a battery of three fryers that you originally bought used for $4,000. Because the purchase price was small, you recognized the entire $4,000 cost of the fryer as an expense in the year it was purchased.

The Vulcan representative is trying to sell you a new four-basket computer-controlled battery fryer. The purchase price is $25,000 and the costs of shipping, installation, and testing will be $5,500. The representative has shown you how the new fryer, because of its improved insulation, safety features, and cooking capacity, will save you $1,000 per month in reduced electricity use and lowered insurance premiums. The fryer also has much greater capacity than the one you are currently using, so you will be able to cook more wings and serve more people.

MACRS rate
An Internal Revenue Service acronym for the Modified Accelerated Cost Recovery System. The MACRS approach lets taxpayers depreciate more of the cost earlier in the life of a capital expense.

depreciation
Regular and systematic reduction in income that transfers asset value to expense over time.

You have spoken with your accountant, and she told you that for tax purposes the fryer will have to be depreciated in six years, using the five-year **MACRS rate** set by the IRS. The amount of **depreciation** expense you will recognize will be as follows:

Year	Depreciation
1	$6,100
2	9,760
3	5,856
4	3,513
5	3,513
6	1,758

1. What is the cost of buying the new fryer?
2. How will your expenses change if you buy the fryer?
3. How will your fixed costs per year change if you buy the fryer?
4. If you predict that sales will increase by 10 percent per year, should you buy the fryer?
5. Suppose that your accountant called you and said that the fryer could be depreciated for seven years, using straight line depreciation of $4,357 per year for the first six years and $4,358 in the last year. Would this change your decision of whether to buy the fryer?
6. Under what conditions is the amount of depreciation expense relevant to deciding whether to buy the fryer?

Your instructor may provide you with a suggested solution for this skill module.

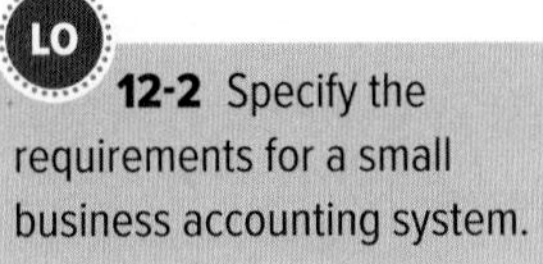

LO
12-2 Specify the requirements for a small business accounting system.

Accounting Systems for Small Business

The primary reason to acquire and use a computerized accounting system is to ensure the accuracy of your accounting information. Computerized systems also simplify the accounting process by providing automatic error checking, entry screens that look like the common business forms, and automatic production of financial statements and management reports.

The small business systems that are most commonly being used in the United States today are QuickBooks, Xero, MYOB, Sage BusinessWorks, and Microsoft Dynamics.[13] That said, the market for computerized accounting programs for small businesses is in a state of turmoil. The entry of cloud-based accounting programs which are paid for on a subscription basis has changed everything. This revolution, if not begun by, was at least accelerated by Xero, which is based in New Zealand. Founded in 2006, the company today claims over 600,000 paid users. It also claims to have a dominant market share in Australia, New Zealand, and Great Britain. However, Xero also has a significant user base in the United States.[14] Its rapid entry prompted Intuit, the owner of QuickBooks, to completely overhaul its own online accounting program to be competitive.[15]

Key Software for Small Business Accounting Systems

1. QuickBooks (www.quickbooks.com/)
2. Xero (www.xero.com)
3. MYOB (www.myob.com)
4. Sage BusinessWorks (www.sage.com)
5. Microsoft Dynamics (www.microsoft.com/en-us/dynamics/erp-gp-overview.aspx)

The market for accounting programs is highly concentrated. QuickBooks is reported to have approximately 75 percent of the market for accounting systems for small business. The remainder of the market is divided among at least 75 different computerized accounting programs, ranging alphabetically from Accounting Edge to Zoho Books.[16] And the number of entrants is growing. So you now have options for small business accounting systems ranging from free-to-use cloud-based open-source programs (GnuCash, SQL-Ledger, xTuple PostBooks, etc.) to mammoth enterprise resource planning systems such as Oracle ERP Cloud and SAP Business One. The cost to use the programs ranges from free for the open-source programs, to less than $10 per month for programs like Xero, to thousands of dollars for the large ERP systems.

All of these systems will more or less automatically produce financial reports that meet legal requirements for content and format. Still, as with any computer program, you will have to invest some time in learning to use it effectively. All of these accounting programs are user-friendly, although each has its irritating quirks. They can be mastered in a short time, generally a matter of a few hours. Most community colleges offer night and weekend classes in QuickBooks and Sage Accounting, and you may have (or have even taken) similar courses at your school. There are also numerous online sites that offer tutorials. Each program itself includes a tutorial, help files, and a printed manual to help you master its use.

LEARN MORE ONLINE

Learn more about the topics above at these sites:

QuickBooks: **https://quickbooks.intuit.com/tutorials/all-quickbooks-tutorials/**

Xero: **www.xero.com/us/training/small-business/**

MYOB: **https://academy.myob.com/**

To ensure that your accounting information is accurate, reliable, and useful, the accounting system that you choose should easily and efficiently accomplish the following tasks:

- Provide a simple, easy-to-understand user interface.
- Have an exhaustive context-sensitive help function.
- Produce an income statement that clearly lists revenues and expenses by appropriate categories for your industry and type of business.
- Produce a classified balance sheet that clearly shows the financial position of your business.
- Facilitate the development of a cash budget.
- Facilitate the task of developing operating and investment budgets.
- Produce financial statements in approved formats to be furnished to outside investors, bankers, and regulators.
- Produce multiple-year comparison financial statements for management use.
- Provide a method for you to define and produce custom reports to meet your management needs.
- Be able to export financial data in a form that can be used by your accountant and can be imported into tax preparation and spreadsheet programs.
- Maintain an internal "audit trail" that records all entries and changes to the accounting system in order to facilitate the identification and correction of errors.
- Enforce security measures to reduce the opportunity for employee misuse or fraud.
- Have provisions that will either allow the program to grow with your business or to easily export its data into programs that can handle larger businesses.

Setting Up an Accounting System

Your specific accounting needs are largely determined by the industry you're in and by the size of your business. The smallest businesses often need little in the way of accounting records beyond an accurate check register. As businesses become larger, the difficulty of any one person being able to remember all its details increases exponentially. When a business is large enough to have one or more employees, formal record keeping is a must.

Regardless of your business's size, the one essential element of an accounting system is *cash accounting* that is accurate, easy to use, and tracks all checks written and all deposits made.

As your business grows the following accounting functions will become important to your success:

- *Accounts receivable* records if you provide credit to your customers. Accurate and timely accounts receivable records are essential for making decisions concerning the extension of credit. Accurate records also help produce accurate billing of customers, and thus help maintain good customer relations.
- *Accounts payable* records to track what you owe and to make timely payments in order to capture prompt pay discounts and to maintain a good credit rating for your business.
- *Payroll* records to ensure that payroll and employment taxes are kept current.
- *Fixed asset* accounting that automatically calculates and accumulates depreciation.
- *Inventory* accounting that facilitates maintaining the appropriate levels of inventory and aids in calculation of appropriate stocking and reorder levels.
- *Credit card sales* function to enable reconciling your sales records with the amount of discount and chargebacks taken by your credit card provider.
- *Insurance register* to ease the problems of keeping necessary insurance coverage current and in force.
- *Investment* records if your business keeps surplus cash invested in securities.
- *Leasehold* records if your business has made improvements to leased property or equipment.

The actual task of setting up a computerized accounting system for your business is quite easy if you understand accounting a bit. You do not need to be an expert. The small business accounting systems listed earlier include all the functions that you are likely to need. Additionally, each program has a method to establish a set of records that is appropriate for your specific business. Should you have a business that is unique, setting up a set of records from scratch usually takes less than an hour. QuickBooks and Sage Accounting each include an "interview" function that will guide you through the setup process by furnishing a series of questions and prompts.

But what if you are not sure that you can set up an accounting system properly? You can get help for free from your local Small Business Development Center (www.sba.gov/tools/local-assistance/sbdc) or SCORE (the Service Corps of Retired Executives, www.score.org/). Alternatively, for a small fee (generally $200 to $1,000) many certified public accountants (CPAs) will set up any of these accounting programs for your specific needs. You can find CPAs in your phone book (hard copy or online) or even through Google searches for "accounting consultant." As when you choose any other professional (such as doctors or lawyers), it makes sense to check with others about a professional before making a major commitment.

Setting up your accounting system can be outsourced to consultants who are expert in the accounting system you chose. QuickBooks has an online directory of certified consultants. The directory (http://proadvisor.intuit.com/search/index-standalone.html?v2#/) can be searched using your zip code and the distance you are willing to go to find a consultant. Sage offers a similar service (www.sage.com/us/accountant/locator), but lists consultants as being expert in either accounting, the Sage accounting application, or both. As with the QuickBooks site, search is done by zip code and distance. Microsoft also provides a guide to consultants for Dynamics (www.microsoft.com/en-us/dynamics/partners.aspx). As you might expect given the cost and complexity of Dynamics, the Microsoft site allows you to search not only by zip code and distance, but also by your business need and industry. If you are still not sure about which consultant you need, Microsoft provides a page for you to complete and then the company will match you with a consultant who has the expertise you need. One-Write does not provide information about consultants for its accounting programs, but a Google search returned almost 400,000 "hits." Be aware that there is no standard pricing for consultant services so you will have to do some comparison shopping and perhaps some negotiation to retain the right consultant for your accounting needs.

Financial Reports

LO 12-3 Explain the content and format of common financial statements.

The final output of a computer system is a set of **financial statements** and reports. Although there is certainly room for you to customize financial reports in many ways, the overall content and form of financial statements have been made standard by long usage. Bankers and investors are familiar and comfortable with standard financial statements. When you apply for a loan or seek equity investment, you will be expected to present financial information in the format and containing the information that is standard for your industry.

financial statements Formal summaries of the content of an accounting system's records of transactions.

There are six common financial statements:

- Income statement
- Statement of comprehensive income
- Statement of retained earnings
- Statement of owners' equity
- Balance sheet
- Cash flow statement[17]

> While there are six financial statements, most small businesses will actually use only three: (1) income statement, (2) balance sheet, and (3) statement of cash flows. The statement of comprehensive income will apply to your business only if you deal in financial derivatives. The statements of retained earnings and owners' equity are usually simply incorporated into the balance sheet.

To the uninitiated these financial statements can seem almost as strange as Egyptian hieroglyphs, but in reality each type is similar in concept and operation to financial records we use in everyday life (see Figure 12.2):

- Think of your checking account or the account tied to your debit card. You put money in and write checks or use your debit card to take money out. The record of the deposits and withdrawals are similar to the format of the income statement.
- The exact amount you have in the account at any moment depends on the deposits credited to your account (which can take anything from minutes to days, depending on how you made the deposit and the speed of your bank) and which checks have been handled by the bank. Figuring that exact amount (which some people do with their check registers or by keeping a running tally in their heads) is the idea behind the statement of cash flow.

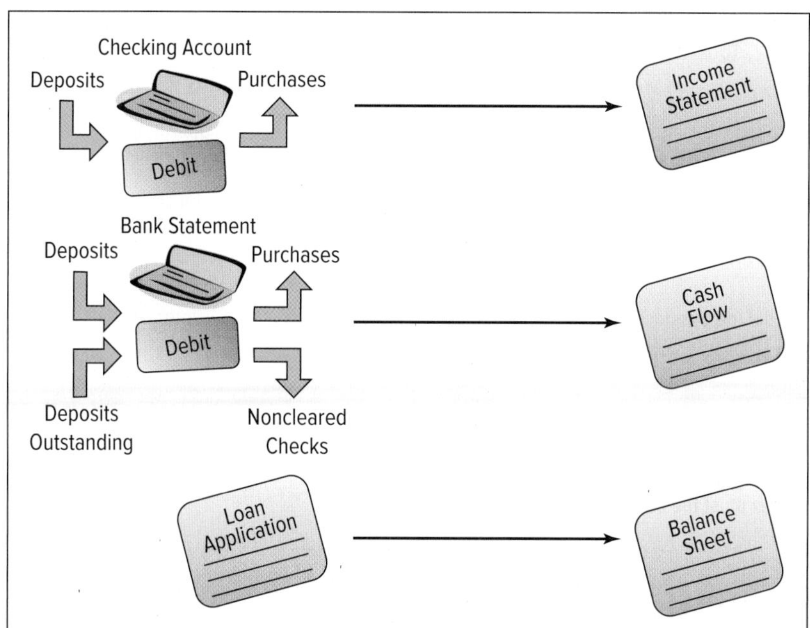

FIGURE 12.2 Everyday Financial Documents and Similar Financial Reports

- The monthly bank statement gives you the check and deposit information as well as any fees the bank charged you or interest it paid into your account. That parallels the statement of **retained earnings**.
- When you apply for a student loan or for a loan to purchase a car, you must fill out a loan application. This form asks you to list what you own and how much it is worth. It also asks you to list all debts you owe to others. This is very similar to the balance sheet on which financial accounting is based.

retained earnings
The sum of all profits and losses, less all dividends paid since the beginning of the business.

articulate
The concept that information flows from the income statement through the statements of retained earnings and owners' equity to the balance sheet.

The important thing about these financial statements is that they **articulate**, that is, information flows from the income statement through the statement of retained earnings, the statement of owners' equity to the balance sheet. Information from the income statement and the balance sheet flows to the cash flow statement.

To illustrate the content and format of the financial statements, we will use the Red Jett Sweets, Inc. business plan projections for its first year of operation, 2011. Later in this chapter and in Chapter 13 we will use projections that we have created to show you how to create financial projections. These illustrations are based on Red Jett's business plan except that we have, for illustration only, added an assumption that Red Jett will maintain a beginning and ending inventory of raw materials (flour, sugar, butter, etc.). This added assumption is being made solely for the purpose of being able to demonstrate budgeting techniques when inventories are part of your business.

Income Statement

The **income statement** is the primary source of information about a business's profitability. The income statement shows the amount of revenues earned minus its expenses which equals net income:

$$\text{Revenues} - \text{Expenses} = \text{Net income}$$

All income statements follow the same simple general format. Reading from the top down, the income statement presents answers to the questions shown in Figure 12.3.

FIGURE 12.3

Organization of the Income Statement

Question	Income Statement Content
How much did the business sell?	Sales
minus	
What did the product sold cost the business?	Cost of goods sold
equals	
How much is available to pay expenses and pay profits?	Gross margin
minus	
How much did the business use in its operations?	Operating expenses
equals	
How much income did the business produce?	Operating income
minus	
What costs did the business have for financing?	Interest expense
equals	
How much income did the business earn before taxes?	Net income before tax
minus	
How much tax must the business pay?	Income tax
equals	
How much profit did the business make?	Net income

The usefulness of the income statement for managing a small business is related to the amount of detail available in the statement. There are two formats for income statements: (1) a *single-step* format, illustrated in Figure 12.4A, which provides little detail—it simply lists all revenues and gains together, then lists all expenses and losses together; and (2) a *multiple-step* format, illustrated in Figure 12.4B, which lists revenues from operations separately from other income and gains.

Most owners and managers of small businesses prefer the multiple-step format because of its greater detail. Notice that in Figure 12.4B operating loss of $17,003 is reported separately from

FIGURE 12.4A

Typical Single-Step Format Income Statement

RED JETT Sweets

Income Statement for the Year Ending Dec. 31, 2011	
Revenues and gains	
Sales revenue	$48,379
Expenses & losses	
Cost of goods sold	15,164
Sales, general, and administrative	50,218
Provision for income tax	- 0 -
Net income	($17,003)

FIGURE 12.4B

Typical Multiple-Step Income Statement

RED JETT Sweets

Income Statement for the year ending Dec. 31, 2011	
Revenues and gains	
Sales revenue	$48,379
less fees, spoilage, sales tax collected	4,162
Net sales revenue	44,217
less cost of goods sold	11,002
Gross margin	33,215
Sales, general, & administrative expenses	
Salaries & Wages	26,149
Rent	8,290
Web site, telephone, marketing	4,520
Transportation	2,403
Insurance	2,000
Research & recipe development	2,188
Legal & Accounting	3,088
Depreciation expense	1,580
Total SG & A	50,218
Operating income	(17,003)
Provision for income taxes	- 0 -
Net income	($17,003)

Gross margin is stated specifically.

Marketing, advertising, and cost of selling is specified.

Operating income is reported.

any nonoperating gains or losses. The two most commonly used computerized accounting systems for small businesses, QuickBooks and Sage Accounting, produce income statements in the multiple-step format by default.

Difficulties in Understanding the Income Statement

There are two typical difficulties that arise in understanding and interpreting the income statements. First, there are disagreements about *what* exactly should be reported as revenue. The second problem arises from disputes over *when* to recognize revenues.[18]

Suppose your business is a water park that is open for only 120 days between June and September. In late fall you run a promotion to sell season tickets as holiday gifts. Through this promotion, you sell for cash $200,000 worth of season tickets. Have you realized a revenue? No, to be recognized as revenue, you must have earned the money. This means that even though you have $200,000 in your bank account, it really isn't yours until the holders of season passes use them to visit the park. In fact, the amount of the season passes would be shown on your balance sheet as a liability–you owe the pass holders either access to the park or their money back.

Similar problems arise in determining the amounts and timing of gains, losses, and expenses. Suppose your business sells motor scooters. Customers who buy one will expect to receive a warranty. If they have a problem within the warranty period, they will expect that the scooter will be promptly repaired or replaced. So how much expense should you recognize for warranty? And when should you recognize it? When you sell the scooter, or when it comes back for repair? The amount of warranty cost and the timing of returns are not known at the time of sale.

Despite the difficulties and limitations of the income statement, it provides valuable information. Most small businesses do not have any difficulty deciding how much and when revenues and expenses occur. In many small businesses, all sales to customers are made either for cash or as credit card transactions that are essentially the same as cash. Subscriptions and warranties are not an issue. So in many cases, the income statement of a small business is a reliable report of just how well the business is doing in producing profits.

Use of the Income Statement

operating income
The amount of income earned by the regular operations of the business.

The income statement is used by you, by lenders, and by investors to analyze the effectiveness of business operations. **Operating income** is the most used item on the statement. It represents just how well management achieved sales and controlled costs to produce profits. Lenders use operating income as a measure of how much debt a business can support. Interest is deductible for determining income tax, therefore net income before tax is available to make interest payments. Equity investors similarly look to operating income as an indication of future sales, so operating income becomes a favorite indicator of the value of their investment.

Because the income statement is of great interest to owners, investors, and lenders, it is often deliberately misstated. The Small Business Insight box illustrates how easily the income statement can deliberately made misleading. Certainly, such manipulation of the income statement is unethical. If done with intent to defraud, it is illegal.

Balance Sheet

The **balance sheet**, also called the *Statement of Financial Position*, presents a "snapshot" of the financial holdings and liabilities at the close of business on a specified date. The balance sheet explicitly details the accounting equation for your business. The balance sheet provides answers to the questions shown in Figure 12.5.

The usefulness of the balance sheet is determined by the detail it includes. As shown in Figure 12.5, the minimum level of detail is to report both assets and liabilities in two categories: current, which will either produce or use cash within a year, and long term, which will convert to cash over a period of time greater than one year. However, your balance sheet may be made in greater detail if there is a need to do so. A common practice is to present multiyear balance sheets to facilitate analysis. Figure 12.6 shows the most common format for single-period balance sheets.

SMALL BUSINESS INSIGHT

. . . BUT IS IT *RIGHT*?

ETHICAL ISSUES WITH THE INCOME STATEMENT

The characteristics that sometimes make the income statement hard to understand also provide temptation to "fudge" the numbers. Consider the example of a water park in the previous section. If you are applying for a loan to install a new water slide, you can easily "clean up" your financial statements to appear to be a better credit risk.

How?

It's easy. Just state the $200,000 of advance sales as being a revenue. You instantly reduce the amount of liabilities and simultaneously increase owners' equity. Here is an example:

Honest Financials

Income Statement for November 2020	
Sales	–0–
Expenses	10,000
Net income	(10,000)

Balance Sheet as of November 30, 2020	
Current assets	
Cash	$ 200,000
Current liabilities	
Accounts payable	10,000
Unearned income	200,000
Owners' equity	(10,000)
Total liabilities & equity	200,000

Misstated Financials

Income Statement for November 2020	
Sales	200,000
Expenses	10,000
Net income	190,000

Balance Sheet as of November 30, 2020	
Current assets	
Cash	$ 200,000
Current liabilities	
Accounts payable	10,000
Owners' Equity	190,000
Total liabilities & equity	200,000

Of course, any change in your financial statements has many implications; consider what effect changing your income statement from a loss of $10,000 to a profit of $190,000 would have on income taxes. In this case you would end up paying taxes on $190,000 in the current year. This would be a very expensive way to get a loan.

It could work the other way, though. You could immediately recognize warranty expense, for example, and reduce stated income and thus the amount of tax due. But remember: the IRS takes a dim view of manipulating your financial statements to reduce your income tax.

So, the question remains, "Just because you can make your business results look better, should you?"

FIGURE 12.5

Organization of a Typical Balance Sheet

What does the business own that can be turned into cash in one year?	Current assets
plus	
What does the business own that will produce revenues for more than one year?	Fixed assets
plus	
What other things does the business own (investments, patents, copyrights)?	Other assets
equals	
What is the value of everything the business owns?	Total assets
plus	
What does the business owe to others that must be paid within one year?	Current liabilities
plus	
What does the business owe to others that must be paid more than one year from now?	Long-term liabilities
plus	
How much is the business worth to its owners?	Owners' equity
equals	
Does the total of liabilities and equity equal total assets?	Total liabilities and equity

FIGURE 12.6

Typical Balance Sheet

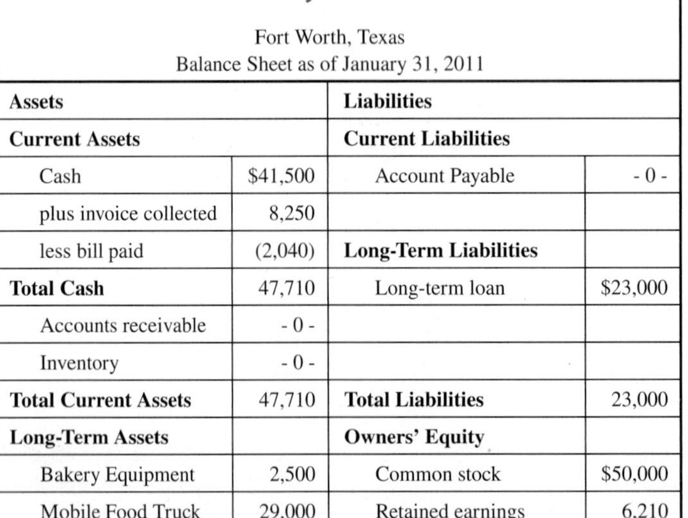

RED JETT Sweets

Fort Worth, Texas
Balance Sheet as of January 31, 2011

Assets		Liabilities	
Current Assets		**Current Liabilities**	
Cash	$41,500	Account Payable	- 0 -
plus invoice collected	8,250		
less bill paid	(2,040)	**Long-Term Liabilities**	
Total Cash	47,710	Long-term loan	$23,000
Accounts receivable	- 0 -		
Inventory	- 0 -		
Total Current Assets	47,710	**Total Liabilities**	23,000
Long-Term Assets		**Owners' Equity**	
Bakery Equipment	2,500	Common stock	$50,000
Mobile Food Truck	29,000	Retained earnings	6,210
Total Long-Term Assets	31,500	**Total Equity**	56,210
Total Assets	79,210	**Total Liabilities & Equity**	79,210

Use of the Balance Sheet

The information in the balance sheet is used to determine the liquidity, financial flexibility, and financial strength of the business, which are detailed below. These measures of a business's financial position are used by owners, lenders, and equity investors in making financial and investment decisions.

Liquidity is a measure of the expected time before an asset can be converted into cash, and of the expected time before a liability must be paid. A completely liquid asset is one that can be converted instantly to cash, at its full value.[19] Cash is the most liquid of assets, as it does not have to be converted. An illiquid asset *cannot* be sold quickly without suffering a significant discount from its true value. Specialized machinery is not a liquid asset. Certainly, given enough time, specialized machinery that is not technologically obsolete can be sold. However, it is not likely to be sold quickly, and is quite likely that when sold, it will sell for only a portion of its true value as a productive asset. Think of a hot rod automobile. You might spend $20,000 or more building it. But if you must sell it, you are unlikely to get more than a tiny fraction of your cost. The same is true for any custom asset, and the more illiquid it is, the greater the discount.

liquidity
A measure of how quickly a company can raise money through internal sources by converting assets to cash.

Liquidity is a measure of the ability of a business to meet both short-term and long-term obligations. Lenders are concerned with liquidity because it indicates the level of risk that a loan will not be repaid as contracted. Equity investors are concerned with liquidity because it affects a business's ability to pay dividends.

The most common ratio used to estimate liquidity is the **current ratio**. The current ratio is calculated by dividing the value of current assets (those assets expected to be converted to cash within one year) by the value of current liabilities (those liabilities that must be paid within one year). The rule of thumb for evaluating current ratio is that the minimum acceptable ratio is 2.0, and higher is better. The calculation and use of financial ratios are discussed in detail in Chapter 14.

current ratio
The value of current assets divided by current liabilities.

Financial flexibility is an indicator of the business's ability to manage cash flows so that the company has the financial ability to respond appropriately if an unexpected opportunity or problem arises. There are no accepted financial ratios that are indicators of financial flexibility. Financial flexibility is a matter of judgment, usually based on experience. What owners, managers, bankers, and investors look for to help indicate levels of financial flexibility include (1) the ability to sell non-operating assets, (2) the ability to obtain loans or to sell additional stock, and (3) the ability to increase efficiency and to lower costs of operation.[20] You can see that what is similar across the three indicators is the business's ability to rapidly and efficiently raise additional capital.

financial flexibility
A business's ability to manage cash flows in such a manner that the company can respond appropriately to unexpected opportunities and needs.

The **financial strength** of the business is also a matter of informed judgment. The balance sheet provides information about the nature of the assets and liabilities of the business. In evaluating financial strength, more cash and cash equivalents indicate higher strength. Current assets that comprise cash, short-term investments, and accounts receivable are more indicative of strength than are inventories and prepaid expenses. In fact, excessive amounts of inventory in the current assets are indicative of management problems and financial weakness. For example, a large inventory may indicate lagging sales or products that have become obsolete or fallen out of favor with customers–all indicators of out-of-touch management. Long-term assets that are relatively new, low current liabilities, low long-term debt, and fully funded retirement plans for employees are all indicative of financial strength.

financial strength
The ability of a business to survive adverse financial events.

Problems in Interpreting Balance Sheet Information

For all its usefulness to the owners and managers of businesses, the balance sheet has several limitations. First, all values listed in a balance sheet are *historical* values–the cost of the asset when it was acquired. In the case of long-lived assets, such as land, buildings, and equipment, the value recorded in the accounting records can be widely different from the asset's current value. Given even a small level of inflation, the original cost of such assets is likely to be a much smaller number of dollars than its current value. On the other hand, cash is always current. This means that ratios such as return on assets (current income/net average asset value) have a current value as numerator and a denominator that, at best, is measured in older dollars of greater purchasing power. At the extreme, the true value of the asset may have changed because of changes in population density, demographics, highway access, and economic development.

Additionally, every balance sheet typically contains estimated amounts, such as an allowance for estimated loss from uncollectible accounts receivable, an allowance for estimated warranty cost, accumulated depreciation, depletion, amortization, and income taxes. Sometimes these estimates can be significantly wrong, such as when an unexpected product defect appears.

Finally, certain assets and liabilities are omitted from the balance sheet. Assets that are not listed include the value of licenses, established business with vendors, established customers, organizational knowledge and expertise, employee loyalty and morale, and research and development. When such assets represent a major strength of your company, the balance sheet will under report your firm's financial strength.

Despite its problems, the balance sheet provides essential information for outside investors. Investors who would buy equity want to know the value of the assets of the business and what claims exist on those assets. Bankers look to the balance sheet to estimate the likely future cash flows that will be available to repay the loan. Skill Module 12.2 gives an example of how the information in the balance sheet is used by lenders.

Cash Flow Statement

You compute the **cash flow statement** in order to see the sources and uses of cash by the business. Cash flow statements can be either direct statements or indirect statements. The direct statement is developed solely from the cash records of the business (only those things bought

SKILL MODULE 12.2

Applying for a Loan

You are going to apply for a loan for your business. Your banker told you that you will need to bring him a set of financial statements that show your business income, your business's financial position (balance sheet), and your cash flows for the year to date. To complete this task, you have collected the following information from your accounting records, which you keep manually in a three-ring binder.

Use the information to make a balance sheet in the format shown in Figure 12.6.

Account	Balance
Accounts payable	$ 2,500
Accounts receivable	5,000
Building and equipment	112,000
Note to bank	27,500
Customer deposits	3,000
Cash	15,000
Accumulated depreciation	35,000
Capital portion of owners' equity	50,000
Retained earnings	14,000

1. What is the amount of current and long-term assets that you have?
2. Can you pledge the retained earnings of $14,000 as collateral for the new loan? Why or why not?
3. Calculate the current ratio. Using the rule of thumb given in the text, is this a good or bad ratio?
4. Why would the current ratio matter to your banker?

Your instructor may provide you with a sample solution for this skill module.

and sold). GAAP (generally accepted accounting principles) now specifies that the direct method should be used.

The indirect statement of cash flows starts with net income and adjusts the accruals and deferrals to provide cash flow information that can be easily reconciled to the other financial statements. Most owners, lenders, and investors prefer the indirect method because it explicitly links net income and the balance sheet to cash flows.

There are six items that must be reported in the statement of cash flows (see Figure 12.7A):

1. Cash flows from operating activities.
2. Cash flows from investing activities.
3. Cash flows from financing activities.
4. Net effect of foreign exchange rates.
5. Net change in cash balance during the period.
6. Noncash investing and financing activities.

FIGURE 12.7A

Organization of the Cash Flow Statement

Question	Cash Flow Content
Cash flows from operating activities	
1. How much money did I receive from my customers?	Cash collected from customers
2. How much did I pay for merchandise?	(Cash paid for merchandise)
3. How much did I pay for leased equipment?	(Cash paid for equipment leases)
4. How much did I pay my employees?	(Cash paid for wages and salaries)
5. How much did I pay for other expenses?	(Cash paid for miscellaneous expenses)
6. How much cash did I receive from interest earned?	Interest received
7. How much did I pay in interest on borrowed funds?	(Interest paid)
8. How much cash was provided (used) by operations?	Net cash provided (used) by operating activities
Cash flows from investing activities	
9. How much cash did I receive (use) from disposing of obsolete or surplus equipment?	Cash proceeds (use) from disposal of equipment
10. How much did I use in paying credit deposits?	(Cash paid in security deposits)
11. How much cash did I receive from selling stock in another company?	Cash proceeds from security sales
12. How much cash did I pay to acquire equipment?	(Acquisition of equipment)
Cash flows from financing activities	
13. How much money did I invest in my own business?	Owner's contributions
14. How much did I borrow from banks?	Proceeds from bank loans
15. How much did I pay back to banks on loans?	(Principal payments on bank loans)
16. How much money did I take out of the business for personal use?	(Owner's draws)
Net effect of foreign exchange rates	
17. How much money did I gain (lose) through foreign currency conversions?	Gain (loss) due to foreign currency exchanges
Net increase (decrease) in cash	
18. Do I have more or (less) cash now than at the beginning of the year?	Net increase (decrease) in cash
Noncash investing and financing activities	
19. What was the value of barter transactions that I made?	Schedule of noncash investing and financing activities

Common *cash inflows* (receipts) and *outflows* (payments) are shown in Figure 12.7B.

The actual predicted cash flow for Red Jett for January 2011 is shown below. Compare the line items in the Red Jett cash flow statement to the items listed in Figure 12.7A, above.

RED JETT Sweets

Fort Worth, Texas
Cash Flows for the Month of January 2011

Cash received from customers	$ 424
Cash paid to vendors	
credit card providers	-
sales tax paid to Texas	30
raw materials used in production	99
Salaries & Wages	480
Payroll taxes/benefits	42
Rent	420
Web site, marketing	1,900
Telephone	310
Transportation	-
Insurance	167
Research & recipe development	313
Legal & Accounting	2,703
Net cash flows from operations	(6,039)
Cash flow from investing activities	
Purchase of Equipment	(31,500)
Cash flow from financing activities	
Investment by owners	50,000
Cash received from borrowing	
Cash paid on loans	
Net cash flow from long-term financing activities	50,000
Beginning cash	-
Net cash increase(decrease)	12,461
Ending cash	$ 12,461

operating activities
Activities involved in producing and selling goods and services.

investing activities
The purchase and sale of land, buildings, equipment, and securities.

financing activities
Activities through which cash is obtained from and paid to lenders, owners, and investors.

Operating activities include all the functions that are performed to create your product or service. Thus the receipt of cash from customers is an operating activity. Funds received from obtaining a loan at a bank is not an operating activity; rather, it is a financing activity.

Investing activities include the acquisition and disposal of property, plant, equipment, and investment securities of other firms. The outflows are the cash investments made by the business to acquire noncash assets. Investing outflows arise from the sale or disposal of noncash assets acquired from prior investments.

Financing activities are those actions taken by management to finance the operations of the business. Thus cash inflows come only from investments by owners and from money borrowed

FIGURE 12.7B

Typical Cash Inflows and Outflows on the Cash Flow Statement

Inflows	Outflows
Cash Flows from Operating Activities	
1. Cash received from customers	1. Cash paid to purchase inventory
2. Interest received on accounts receivable	2. Salaries and wages
3. Dividends received on investments in other firms	3. Cash paid for rent, utilities, royalties, and license fees
4. Cash refunds from vendors	4. Income taxes, duties, and fines
5. All interest received from loans to other entities	5. All interest paid on liabilities
Cash Flows from Investing Activities	
1. Disposal of property, plant, and equipment	1. Acquisition of property, plant, and equipment
2. Disposal of investment securities	2. Acquisition of investment securities
3. Receipt of the capital amount of loans made to customers and vendors	3. Loans made to other entities
	4. Acquisition of assets other than inventories
Cash Flows from Financing Activities	
1. Cash received from owners of the business	1. Cash paid to owners as dividends and draws
2. Cash received from borrowing	2. Cash paid to acquire the firm's own stock
	3. Repayment of the principal of borrowed funds

through notes, mortgages, and bonds. Cash outflows from financing activities comprise capital repaid to owners and repayment of the principal amount of borrowings.

Net effect of foreign exchange rates is becoming ever more important to small businesses. The Internet has opened foreign trade to businesses of all sizes. Exchange rates often vary rapidly, affecting the value of contracts and sales made in currencies other than the currency of the home nation of the business.

Net change in cash balance simply reconciles the net increase or decrease with the beginning cash balance and the ending cash balance.

Noncash investing and financing comprise transactions in which an exchange of value other than cash takes place. An example of a noncash transaction is when a debt is settled by issuing stock to the creditor. These types of transactions are rarely made by small businesses. A more common transaction for small businesses is a barter transaction, which is discussed in detail in Chapter 13.

Uses of Financial Accounting

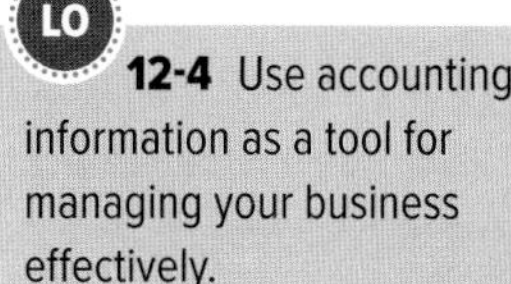

12-4 Use accounting information as a tool for managing your business effectively.

Although financial accounting is not specifically designed for management purposes, it can be a highly valuable aid in decision making. Financial and business managers are familiar with the format, content, and interpretation of financial statements. Obtaining loans, answering Internal Revenue Service inquiries, and satisfying the reporting requirements of regulatory agencies are all made easier when an appropriate set of financial statements is provided.

As the accounting scandals of recent years have made evident, the existence of financial accounting statements, even when audited by major accounting firms, does not guarantee that the representations of management are complete, accurate, or even true. In this respect, financial accounting is much like a lock on the door. A lock will keep honest people honest. Crooks, on the other hand, will pick the lock, jimmy a window, or find another entry to commit burglary. Similarly, a business manager who is determined to commit fraud might be inconvenienced by accounting standards, but will find some way to do the crime.

Thinking about the lock idea, if you have locked something, doesn't it just make sense to double-check that the lock is in fact locked? Doing that just shows a healthy skepticism. Similarly for owners and managers of small businesses, all representations by owners, managers, employees, and providers of business outsourcing should be examined with an attitude of informed professional skepticism. It's just a healthy attitude to have.

Reporting to Outsiders

The greatest value of financial accounting for small business owners and managers is reporting the results of operations and the financial condition of the business to entities outside the business. Outsiders can include absentee owners,[21] creditors and lenders, unions, and taxing and regulatory agencies. Each of these groups has some interest in the conduct of the business. Each has either or both legal rights and political power to enforce honest disclosure of your business's finances. You are less likely to be accused of misrepresentation if your disclosures comply with accepted accounting principles.

Record Keeping

The primary criteria for a small business's record-keeping system are (1) simplicity of use, (2) accuracy of detail, (3) timeliness of reports, (4) understandability to the manager of the business, and (5) security of data. An appropriate accounting system keeps records of the details of financial transactions that facilitate the task of corroborating the conduct of the business. The most convincing evidence that can be provided to outsiders is a set of complete and accurate records that can be substantiated by third-party sources.

Taxation

Current Internal Revenue Service (IRS) regulations require that employers withhold federal income, social security (FICA), and Medicare taxes from the wages of each employee. Employers must also pay the federal unemployment tax (FUTA). The amount withheld, and the employer's share of taxes, must be paid to the IRS regularly, on a schedule determined by the amount of withholding. At the year's end, each employer is required to submit summaries of each employee's total earnings and withholdings for the year and to report the information to the IRS and to each employee on a Form W-2. This process can be automated by using one of the small business computerized accounting systems mentioned earlier.

Similarly, businesses need to pay taxes each year, and having the financial records makes the task dramatically easier. In fact, many of the computerized accounting packages have tax modules or are designed to feed information to tax programs such as Intuit's TurboTax or H&R Block's suite of tax preparation programs.

Control of Receivables

Accounts receivable–money owed your business by customers–are often the key to survival. An appropriate record-keeping system provides detailed reports of amounts due from customers including purchases, payments, and current contact information. The key in controlling receivables is to have them *aged*, by sorting them into groups of those that are 30, 60, 90, and over 90 days past due. If you don't receive payment when due, you should take immediate and appropriate action to collect it. Often businesses step up collection efforts when the receivables are more than 30 days overdue, with many businesses treating receivables more than 90 days old as delinquent. In such cases the owners may refer the account to a collection agency or even factor the account, selling it (at a substantial discount) to a company that will take aggressive actions to collect the entire amount owed and keep all the money it obtains.

Analysis of Business Operations

Your accounting records contain information that can be easily used for analysis of the results and state of your business. Experience in your business provides a benchmark to which all items may be compared. Those items that appear unrealistic—either too high or too low—should be carefully examined. The examination should attempt to answer the following:

- What are the appropriate levels of sales and expenses?
- Why do certain expenses appear too high or too low?
- Can any expenses be reduced or eliminated?
- Are profits appropriate for your investment, risk, time, and effort?

The use of financial accounting ratios for evaluating performance, controlling, and directing is discussed more fully in Chapter 14.

Uses of Managerial Accounting

Managerial accounting is a set of forward-looking accounting procedures and techniques that is used as tool for effective management. Mastering certain managerial accounting techniques will make you a better small business manager. The techniques of managerial accounting will help you become more accurate at forecasting profits, planning operations, and conserving scarce resources. Managerial accounting information and reports are used in the conduct of all managerial functions: planning, organizing, staffing, directing, and controlling.

Managerial accounting is based on understanding how costs change as a result of business changes. Some costs, such as the cost of food for a restaurant, change because of increases or decreases in the number of people who dine there. If you sell more steaks to customers, you must buy more steaks from your meat supplier. Other costs, such as rent on your building, do not change when you sell more or when you sell less. Rent is usually determined by a contract called a lease. For most stores outside of malls, leases have a specified term (for example, one year) during which rent will not change.

Many things both external and internal to the business can cause costs to change. External forces that cause cost changes can be anything from inflation, to changes in supply and demand, to economic shocks such as war. Internal forces are functions of how your business works. Consider a commuter airline. The amount of fuel used changes as a result of how long, how high, how fast the airplane is flown, and how much it weighs. Flying a long trip at a low altitude and a high speed will use much more fuel than flying a short trip at high altitude and low speed. The cost of fuel, therefore, changes with (1) **external factors**, the cost per gallon that you have to pay; and (2) **internal factors**, how you decide to operate your planes. Other costs of your airline will change according to the operating decisions you make. For example, the costs of landing the airplane are caused by the cost of a landing fee at the airport, wear on the tires and brakes, and fees for parking and using airport facilities. Costs for ticket agents, baggage handlers, and on-ground fleet service are largely driven by the number of airports that the airline serves.

external (cost) factors
Aspects of the world outside the business that could cause the business's costs to change.

internal (cost) factors
Aspects of or choices within the business that could cause the business's costs to change.

Notice that none of the costs for this commuter airline are related to the revenues paid by passengers. Pilots and flight attendants are paid the same even if there are no paying passengers on board. Landing costs are priced by the landing, no matter how many passengers are aboard, and no matter what they paid for a ticket. Costs for ground crew are determined by how many people are working and how many hours they work, not how many passengers they help.

Management cannot quickly adjust to changes in the factors that cause most of the costs of operating an airline. Management is restricted by the characteristics of the airplanes operated, government regulation, and contractual obligations. It is fortunate for owners of small businesses that their costs usually are not so complex and difficult to predict. In fact, many familiar businesses have cost structures that make cost planning both possible and valuable.

There are two managerial accounting procedures that depend on being able to forecast future revenues and expenses. These are (1) **cost-volume-profit** analysis and (2) the **budget cycle** process. We will discuss each of these below.

cost-volume-profit analysis
A method for planning operations necessary to attain a specific profit goal. Break-even analysis is a specific application of cost-profit-volume analysis.

budget cycle
A term applied to the schedule and the process for setting the schedule for making purchases by an individual or an organization.

Cost-Volume-Profit Analysis

Many new entrepreneurs and also many established business managers use cost-volume-profit analysis because it is easy to calculate and is easy to adjust for a range of assumptions.

variable costs
Those costs that change with each unit produced, for example, raw materials.

fixed costs
Those costs that remain constant regardless of quantity of output, for example, rent.

total cost
Total costs are simply the sum of all costs that are incurred within an accounting period. For the purposes of cost-volume-profit analysis, total costs are set equal to the sum of fixed costs and variable costs.

Cost-volume-profit analysis is based on sorting costs into only two categories: **variable costs** and **fixed costs. Total cost** is then the sum of fixed costs and variable costs. To make this analysis, all costs that change with changes in output (which can be units made, units sold, or sales revenue) are called variable costs. All other costs, those that do not change because of changes in output, are called fixed costs.

Using Red Jett Sweets as our example, variable costs include the cost of the ingredients of the cupcakes (the more cupcakes made, the more flour, butter, and so on is used). But the cost of the mobile cupcakery, itself, is a fixed cost. The food truck will have the same depreciation and the same interest and insurance expense regardless of whether or not any cupcakes are made.

If we take a look at the proforma income statement that is part of the Red Jett business plan, we can easily categorize the fixed and variable costs as shown in Exhibit 12-1.

It is important to understand that fixed costs are paid whether you sell or make one product, one million products, or no products. Fixed costs include such things as rent, insurance, interest, and depreciation.

Variable costs, however, are the costs directly related to the production or sale of one item. For example, Red Jett's cost for flour, butter, milk, and flavorings will increase with each cupcake that is baked.

As is the case for Red Jett, most manufacturing, wholesale, and retail businesses usually have variable costs for the goods they sell. In contrast, many service businesses have very few variable costs. For example, costs for a provider of cloud services, such as Rackspace are primarily the cost of the fixed investment in computers, data storage devices, and the "wiring" that allows access by customers. There is very little cost to adding a customer. Rackspace has already invested in the computers and programs. Energy cost is not appreciably affected, nor will Rackspace have to hire additional personnel.

Expendables are often variable costs. Expendables (also called indirect materials) are products used in the sales, manufacturing, or delivery that are not part of the finished product. An order of a dozen cupcakes will require a carton and packing materials in order to be shipped. This cost is not part of the product, but is necessary for distribution.

Once the costs of a business have been placed into the categories of fixed and variable costs, it becomes possible, indeed it is easy, to calculate just how much product must be sold to reach a breakeven point where revenues exactly equal expenses.

To accomplish a breakeven analysis, we need to simply solve a simple profit equation as is shown in Figure 12.8. The numbers used are from the Red Jett Sweets business plan projections for the month of August 2011.

EXHIBIT 12.1

Expense (cost items)

Credit card fees	variable
Spoilage & overproduction	variable
Cost of goods sold	variable
Salaries & wages	fixed
Payroll taxes/benefits	fixed
Rent	fixed
Website, marketing	fixed
Telephone	fixed
Transportation	fixed
Insurance	fixed
Legal & accounting	fixed
Depreciation expense	fixed
Interest expense	fixed

At breakeven, revenue exactly equals total costs, thus:				
Revenue	=	Variable cost	+	Fixed cost
Units sold × Price	=	Units sold × Unit variable cost	+	Fixed cost
Units sold × $2.75	–	Units sold × $0.68	=	$6,750
		Units sold × ($2.75 – $0.68)	=	$6,750
		Units sold × ($2.07)	=	$6,750
		Units sold	=	$6,750/$2.07
		Units sold at breakeven		3,261 cupcakes

Note that the calculation for breakeven sales is actually 3,260.87 However, only whole units can be sold, so the breakeven quantity is rounded up.

FIGURE 12.8

Breakeven Analysis for Red Jett Sweets, Inc. for One Month

Examine the way that the equation for breakeven is simplified at the next-to-last line in Figure 12.8. Notice that the final simplification is calculated as:

Breakeven in units = Fixed costs for the period/(Price of one unit – Variable cost of one unit)

The expression "Price of one unit – Variable cost of one unit" is called the contribution margin. You will usually see the equation for breakeven in units stated as "Breakeven = Fixed cost/Contribution margin" which is more succinct.

The breakeven equation may be extended to allow for calculating the necessary level of sales to reach any desired profit. The logic of breakeven is that it is the level of sales where profit equals zero. It follows then that simply by adding the desired profit in dollars to the fixed cost in dollars and then dividing the sum by the contribution margin will provide the unit sales needed to attain that profit.

Unit sales to attain a specific dollar profit = (Fixed cost + Desired profit)/Contribution margin

To illustrate this, assume that Red Jett wishes to make a profit of $1,000 in one month. The equation to calculate the unit sales necessary to do this is:

Unit sales to have a $1,000 profit = (Fixed costs + 1,000)/$2.07

Unit sales to have a $1,000 profit = ($7,750)/$2.07

Unit sales to have a $1,000 profit = 3,744 cupcakes

Let's create a graph of the CVP revenue and total cost lines. This graph is shown in Figure 12.9.

Note that the two lines, revenues and total cost, cross at the point where units equal 3,261 cupcakes and dollars equal $8,968. This is the breakeven point.

The gold-colored vertical and horizontal lines show that at 3,745 unit sales, revenues equal $10,300 (the point where the gold line intersects the revenue line) and total costs equal $9,300 (the point where the gold line intersects the total cost line). Profit is the vertical distance in the green-colored area which is the difference between total revenues and total costs, or a profit of $1,000.

The cost-volume-profit analysis is an example of one type of **sensitivity analysis.** Once you have entered the data into a spreadsheet program, you can easily change your estimate of unit price and total costs to immediately see the effect on profitability.

Key Points to Remember

- Fixed costs remain constant in total, but variable costs increase as output increases and decrease if output decreases. The more cupcakes that Red Jett sells, the less its fixed cost per item becomes, but variable cost per item is unchanged.

FIGURE 12.9

Cost-Volume-Profit Graph for Red Jett Sweets, Inc.

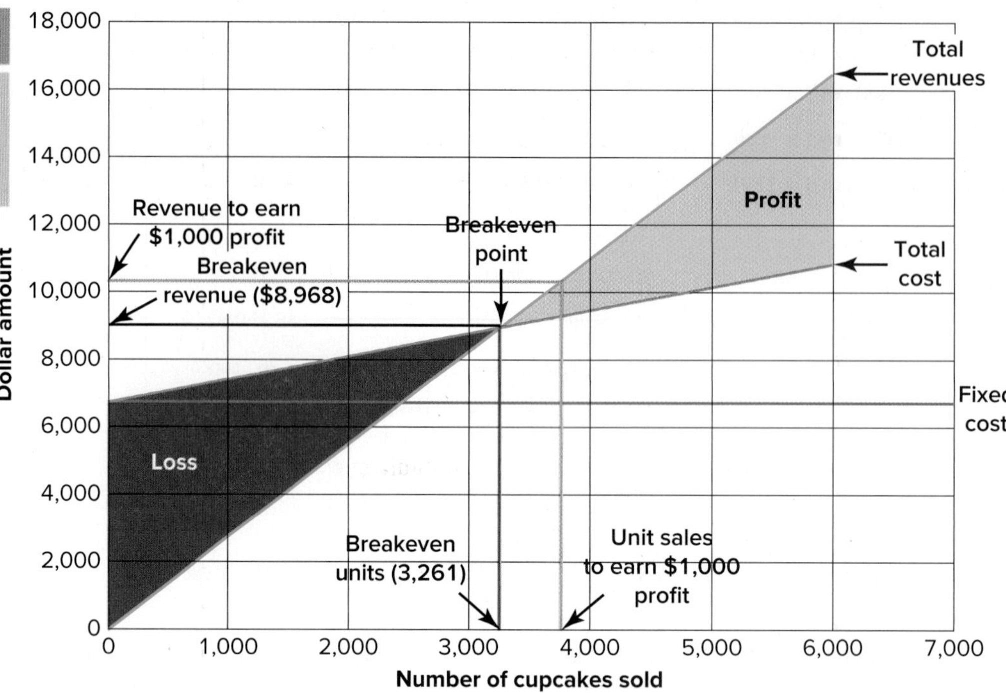

- The breakeven equation simplifies to: **Breakeven = Fixed costs/Contribution margin of one unit**.
- The output level necessary to attain any specific profit goal is calculated by adding the desired profit to the fixed cost then dividing the sum by the contribution margin of one unit.

The next important managerial accounting use for small businesses is the budgeting process, which we will discuss as the next topic.

LO **12-5** Create a set of appropriate budgets that support developing pro forma financial statements for your business plan.

Preparing Pro Forma Financial Statements for Your Business Plan

The most common model used for small business planning is the familiar business plan, like those described in Chapter 8. Looked at from the perspective of managerial accounting, a business plan specifies the amounts and types of inputs required to achieve a set of desired outcomes. It is based on assumptions concerning how costs will change in response to changes in the business operations, how risks can be controlled, and what opportunities can be taken.

The financial projections in your business plan are a form of a budget which can easily be expanded to be useful for day-to-day management of your business. In fact, the budgeting techniques we show here use exactly the same estimates and calculations as you must make to create pro forma financial statements for a business plan. The budgets here, however, have the advantage of being comprised of a series of small, easy-to-understand schedules. When they are linked and printed as a single set of financial statements, they are identical to the familiar business plan pro forma statements.

Planning/Budgeting

Strategic planning, as discussed in Chapter 7, results in statements that are expressed in broad terms. For example, your strategic marketing position may be a price strategy, a luxury strategy, or a value strategy. However, if your broad strategic goals are to be achieved, you must take specific tactical steps. Budgeting is the process through which strategy is mapped into a series of tactical and operational actions.[22]

The process of achieving your strategic goals requires complex activities, cooperation among the people in your business, and the use of significant valuable resources. You will be better able to direct all this if you have a documented quantitative plan of action for your business. Such a plan is called a **budget**.

budget
A financial plan for the future based on a single level of operations; a quantitative expression of the use of resources necessary to achieve a business's strategic goals.

Once a budget has been prepared, it becomes a standard against which performance can be measured.[23] Your budget establishes resource restraints within which your managers and employees must operate. Your budget becomes the basis for controlling activities and the use of resources. By constantly comparing actual performance to budgeted amounts, determining the causes of the inevitable differences, taking necessary corrective action, and providing feedback concerning performance, you may ensure that you attain your business goals.

Despite the many benefits to comprehensive budgeting, few small business owners consistently budget.[24] Those who do create budgets often set them aside in the rush of business activities.[25]

Let's face it, budgeting is seen by many entrepreneurs as a tedious and difficult job. We are going to try to convince you otherwise. In fact, business planning is a *simple* process of applying your knowledge of your business to make estimates of future operations and results. In many ways it is little more than an expanded application of the breakeven analysis that was discussed earlier. However, business planning uses more detail than breakeven analysis, and thus provides a basis for analyzing, directing, and controlling your day-to-day business operations at the level of detail that is most effective for you. Budgeting provides an organized and consistent platform for providing necessary information for effective management.

The first step in budgeting depends on where you are in your business. If you are operating an established business with a history of operations, you should start with a sales forecast. If, however, you are at the earliest planning stages forecasting sales may not be possible. As we mention in the discussion of cost-volume-profit analysis, it may be more practical if you budget your forecast expenses, then return to the sales forecast and see just what results from various forecasts of sales volume.

From the sales forecast, and from your knowledge of cost behaviors, collections, payments, and expenses, a complete business plan will be developed. Although this sounds daunting, in practice, you can adjust the level of detail you need to provide a comprehensive budget that is both compact and understandable.

The Process of Budgeting to Produce Pro Forma Financial Statements

The single most common mistake that most entrepreneurial students make when they attempt to produce a business plan is to furnish pro forma financial statements that are internally inconsistent. The accounting process is structured such that information flows from one financial statement into another financial statement and thus can be reconciled to each other. This relationship among the financial statements is called articulation. Properly prepared financial statements agree such that net income can be adjusted for accruals and deferrals to determine cash flows from operations. The cash flow statement provides the ending cash balance for the balance sheet. Net income from the current period is transferred into retained earnings on the balance sheet.

If you follow the very simple process illustrated here, you will be able to produce a set of pro forma financial statements that are consistent, accurate, and easy to modify as your business plan evolves.

To illustrate just how easy this process is, we will use the information from Red Jett Sweets's business plan, but will follow a logical set of steps that will end in the familiar financial statements: income statement, balance sheet, and statement of cash flows. We will do this by completing a set of very small schedules which we call budgets. Table 12.1 lists the most commonly used of these budgets for a manufacturing business and a merchandising business.

To start this process, refer to the financial assumptions in the Red Jett business plan. The only change we make from these original assumptions is to provide for an ending balance of raw materials. This allows illustrating the budgeting method. For this exercise, we will prepare a set of budgets as if we were planning for the last quarter of mobile cupcakery sales. As you will see, the process is exactly the same whether you are budgeting for a single month, a quarter, or a year.

TABLE 12.1 Useful Budgets and Schedules

Budget for a Manufacturing Business	Budget for a Retail or Wholesale Business
1. Sales budget	1. Sales budget
2. Production budget	2. Purchases budget
3. Direct materials budget	3. Cost of goods sold budget
4. Direct labor budget	4. Labor budget
5. Manufacturing overhead budget	5. Overhead budget
6. Cost of goods manufactured and sold budget	6. Selling and administrative budget
7. Selling and administrative expense budget	7. Cash receipts budget
8. Cash receipts budget	8. Cash disbursements budget
9. Cash disbursements budget	9. Cash budget
10. Cash budget	10. Budgeted income statement
11. Budgeted income statement	11. Pro forma cash flow statement
12. Pro forma cash flow statement	12. Pro forma balance sheet
13. Pro forma balance sheet	

The diagram in Figure 12.10 illustrates how a comprehensive (or "master") budget is developed from basic inputs (sales forecast, assumptions, existing financial facts, and current plans for development and growth) through detailed item budgets to a final pro forma budget plan. The individual detailed budgets are discussed in this chapter.

You may create as many or as few supplemental budgets and schedules as you need to model your business. The budgets and schedules that you will find most useful are listed in Table 12.1.

Completing a Master Budget

As you will have to do when you develop your own business plan, the owners of Red Jett Sweets, Inc. had to make a set of assumptions about how their business would work. Some of the assumptions that they made were to simplify the task of planning. Other assumptions, however, are unique to the business. The Red Jett business plan specifically states that the company will not maintain any inventory of ready-to-sell cupcakes beyond the day they are actually baked.

FIGURE 12.10 Budgeting Relationships

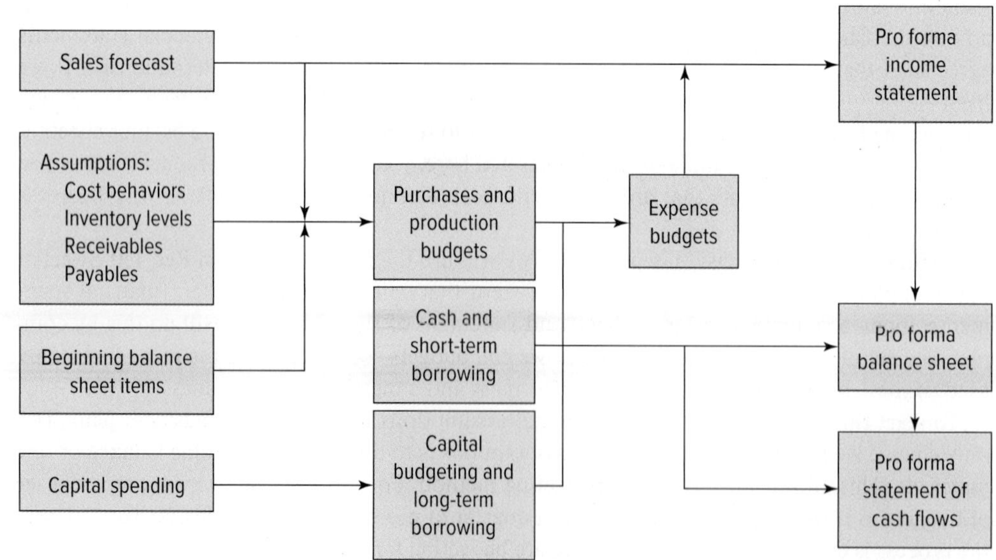

TABLE 12.2 Sales Budget Fourth Quarter, 2011

RED JETT Sweets

Sales Budget
Fourth Quarter, 2011

REVENUES	October	November	December	Quarter 4	January
Unit sales	2,983	2,983	2,983	8,949	3,000
Sales price (including sales tax rounded)	$ 2.94	$ 2.94	$ 2.94	$ 2.94	$ 2.94
Cash sales	4,389	4,389	4,389	13,167	4,414
Credit card sales	4,389	4,389	4,389	13,167	4,414
Gross Sales	8,778	8,778	8,778	26,334	8,828
Less:					
Credit card fees	88	88	88	263	88
Spoilage & over production	61	61	61	183	62
Sales tax collected	615	615	615	1,845	618
Net sales revenue	8,014	8,014	8,014	24,042	8,060

All unsold cupcakes are to be donated to charity at the end of each day. Also, the plan provides for a minimum of productive assets. The kitchen and ovens are rented. Only a limited number of baking pans, mixing bowls, and other cooking tools are to be acquired. Thus, even though the Red Jett business combines elements of both a manufacturing business and a merchandising business, the plan is unique to Red Jett and cannot easily be adapted to other businesses.

Therefore, to provide you with as useful an example as possible, one which can be easily modified to fit a wide variety of businesses, we will follow the Red Jett business plan, except for the assumption that an inventory of raw materials will be kept on hand. This will allow us to present a teaching case that will include assumptions that are more generally applicable to the most common small businesses.

The Sales Budget

The first step in preparing a master budget is to prepare a sales budget. The sales budget, illustrated in Table 12.2, shows the projected future level of sales in units multiplied by the sales price per unit. Chapter 10 discusses the many methods you may use to project future sales, but for this exercise we are simply using the original projections from the Red Jett Sweets, Inc. business plan. To complete the last quarter's budgets, we need a sales projection for January 2012. While the Red Jett financials do not provide a specific number for January, the year's projected sales is 48,000 units, or an average of 4,000 units per month. Because January is usually not a good month for food truck sales, we will assume target sales for January 2012 of 3,000 units.

This may not seem to be very realistic, but remember that all the numbers both in an initial business plan and in later budgets are based on lots of estimates. There simply is no way that you are ever going to estimate the exact "correct" amount. For the purposes of planning, controlling, and directing, it is sufficient for any small business to carry calculations only to whole dollar amounts, or even to round to the nearest one hundred dollars.

The Purchases Budget

Once sales have been projected, the next step is to plan for inventory purchases.

The business plan for Red Jett Sweets specifically states that all raw materials are consumed in the month that they are purchased and that all unsold cupcakes are donated to charity each day. Because of these assumptions the business plan does not provide for ending inventories of either raw materials or completed cupcakes.

Solely for the purpose of illustrating the budgeting techniques, here we will change the assumption for raw materials to plan to have 20 percent of the next month's needs in inventory at the end of each month. Thus, we assume that at the end of September there are enough raw materials of flour, sugar, milk, eggs, and butter to meet 20 percent of October's planned production.

Also, we are budgeting raw materials in only dollar amounts. This is because Red Jett's financials are silent on the quantities of the raw materials that will be needed. The budgeting process is exactly the same for budgeting for physical quantities of materials as for budgeting for dollars. So, if you wish to budget in physical quantities for your business plan, you need only use the same format shown here. After all, a dollar is nothing but a quantity of money.

There are almost as many patterns of buying and holding inventory as there are businesses that need inventory. Restaurants and bars usually purchase food and alcoholic beverages, especially meats, fish, and beer, two or three times per week. It is common for restaurant food suppliers to require payment in cash when the goods are delivered. The common practice for consumer electronics (stereos, DVD players, car radios, etc.) is for the retailer to place annual orders for products that will come in the form of only a few future deliveries. This annual ordering is often done at the winter Consumer Electronics Trade Show, held in Chicago every January.

Most often, a wholesale business will start each month with some amount of inventory already in hand (as much as 60 percent of projected sales) and the rest is ordered for delivery in that month.

TABLE 12.3 **Purchases Budget in Dollar Amounts Fourth Quarter, 2011**

RED JETT Sweets

Purchases Budget in Dollar Amounts
Fourth Quarter 2011

	October	November	December	Quarter 4	January
Unit sales	2,983	2,983	2,983	8,949	3,000
Raw materials per unit	$0.68	$0.68	$0.68	$0.68	$0.68
Materials needed for production	2,028	2,028	2,028	6,085	2,040
Plus desired ending inventory	406	406	408	408	
Materials required	2,434	2,397	2,252	6,309	
Less beginning inventory	406	406	406	406	
Inventory to be purchased	$2,028	$2,028	$2,028	$6,087	

Note that the amount needed is the sum of the amount for production plus desired ending inventory

Note also that there is $406 worth of inventory on hand at the beginning of October. This amount does not have to be purchased

Also note that Nov ending inventory is Dec beginning inventory

The purchases budget (Table 12.3) shows the number of units that are expected to be acquired during the budget period. The specific number of units that must be bought in each period is a function of how many units are on hand at the beginning of the period, how many are projected to be sold, and the desired number of units to be left over in inventory at the end of the period.

This simple formula is used over and over to produce most of the schedules of a master budget:

Amount to be bought = Amount to be used + Desired ending amount – Beginning amount

Other inventory items to be purchased are estimated in exactly the same manner.

The Cost of Goods Sold Budget

The cost of goods sold budget (Table 12.4) is very simple for Red Jett Sweets. Because the business plan states that all cupcakes made in a day will be consumed completely by sales and by giving any remaining inventory to a shelter, the amount of material used is directly proportional to gross sales. Thus the budget is simply the number of cupcakes to be made multiplied by the variable cost per cupcake.

TABLE 12.4 Cost of Goods Sold Budget

RED JETT Sweets

Cost of Goods Sold Budget (Dollar Amounts)
Fourth Quarter, 2011

	October	November	December	Quarter 4
Unit sales	2,983	2,983	2,983	8,949
Unit cost of goods sold	$0.68	$0.68	$0.68	$0.68
Total cost of goods sold	2,028	2,028	2,028	6,085

The Inventory Budget

An inventory budget combines a purchases budget with a cost of goods sold budget. This is done solely to simplify the budget process where the business does not maintain significant inventories. In the case of Red Jett Sweets, the only inventory is raw materials, the amount of which is negligible.

The managers of Red Jett Sweets, Inc. have decided that the value of calculating the cost of goods sold is less than the added complexity and expense that the process entails. And, of course, the Red Jett business plan specifies that all materials will be purchased and consumed within the same period which makes an inventory budget unnecessary.

The Labor Budget

The labor budget (Table 12.5) shows both the amount and cost of labor needed to meet output goals. Red Jett makes an assumption that both wages and salaries will be the same each month and will increase year-over-year proportionally to the anticipated increase in gross sales.

There are small businesses, especially online businesses, that have very little cost of labor. In such cases, management often chooses not to show labor as a separate amount and includes it in administrative or overhead costs because the cost of separate budgeting and accounting for these processes is greater than the value of separate accounting for these processes for the management of the firm.

So, how would you predict labor costs if they do vary with the amount of output? First, you would have to estimate the amount of production labor required for each unit of production. Second, you would then multiply the unit labor cost times the number of units actually

TABLE 12.5 Labor Budget

RED JETT Sweets

Salary and Wages Budget				
	October	November	December	Quarter 4
Salary and Wages	4,141	4,141	4,141	12,423
Total cost of Salaries and Wages	4,141	4,141	4,141	12,423

produced. A common way to make this estimate is to take total annual estimated production labor costs and divide it by total annual estimated units of output. This provides a reasonable estimate of labor cost per unit.

The Selling, General, and Administrative Expense Budget

It is common to combine all costs of selling into a single SG&A budget. This is the method in the Red Jett example, as shown in Table 12.6.

Budgeted Income Statement

The budgets that have been completed to this point can now be combined into a pro forma budgeted income statement. It is common to create the budgeted income statement for the first year of a business plan in a monthly format as is shown here. The second and third years are usually presented as one-year projections. Table 12.7 illustrates this convention by showing each month, October through December, separately, followed by the summation of these months in the column labeled "Quarter 1."

Thus the detailed planning that is included in the budget is condensed for the income statement. The entire budgeted income statement is based on the assumption that all budgeted items,

TABLE 12.6 Selling, General, and Administrative Expense Budget

RED JETT Sweets

Selling, General, and Administrative Budget				
Selling, general, & administrative	October	November	December	Quarter 4
Salaries & Wages	4,141	4,141	4,141	12,423
Payroll taxes/benefits	358	358	358	1,074
Rent	1,000	1,000	1,000	3,000
Web site, marketing	100	100	100	300
Telephone	110	110	110	330
Transportation	343	343	343	1,030
Insurance	167	167	167	500
Legal & Accounting	35	35	35	105
Depreciation expense	316	316	316	948
Total selling, general & administrative	6,570	6,570	6,570	19,710

TABLE 12.7 Budgeted Income Statement

RED JETT Sweets

Budgeted Income Statement
for the Fourth Quarter, 2011

	October	November	December	Quarter 1
Gross Sales Revenue	8,778	8,778	8,778	26,334
Less				
Credit card fees	88	88	88	263
Spoilage & over production	61	61	56	178
Sales tax collected	615	615	615	1,845
Net sales revenue	8,014	8,014	8,019	24,048
Less cost of goods sold	2,029	2,029	1,845	5,903
Gross margin	5,985	5,985	6,174	18,145
Sales, general, & administrative				
Salaries & Wages	4,141	4,141	4,141	12,423
Payroll taxes/benefits	358	358	358	1,074
Rent	1,000	1,000	1,000	3,000
Web site, marketing, & telephone	210	210	210	630
Insurance	167	167	167	500
Legal & Accounting	35	35	35	105
Transportation	343	343	343	1,030
Depreciation expense	316	316	316	948
Total SG & A	6,570	6,570	6,570	19,710
Net income before taxes	(585)	(585)	(396)	(1,565)

sales, production, purchasing, labor, and SG&A will be incurred exactly as planned in the supporting budgets. During the year, comparisons of actual results are made to the budgeted items. If the budget is met, then the projected profit will be realized.

Completing a Comprehensive Budget

The final schedules to be completed to produce a master budget are (1) a cash receipts budget, (2) a cash disbursements budget, and (3) a cash budget. From these schedules, a pro forma cash flow statement and a pro forma projected balance sheet are prepared.

The management of cash is so important to small business that it deserves a chapter to itself. Therefore, the discussion of cash and cash budgeting is included in the next chapter.

Controlling

Managerial accounting, primarily through the budget process, provides information that allows managers to determine how well the business is doing in attaining its goals. This is done by comparing actual results to budgeted results. The difference between actual and budget is called a **variance**. Management can determine where the business is not meeting goals through examining a report of variances.

variance
The difference between an actual and budgeted revenue or cost.

Variances should be evaluated to determine the significance of a particular difference from the original budget. Small variances from budget are expected to occur, as the budget is a collection of estimates. No business manager, in fact, no person, no computer, is capable of making estimates that are exactly what future results will be. For this reason it is customary for management to determine a range of acceptable variances. Individual variances that fall within the predetermined acceptable range are ignored. Variances that exceed the acceptable range are examined in detail, with the manager tracing the activities that drive the cost to determine the cause of the variance and appropriate methods to deal with it.

variance analysis
The process of determining the effect of price and quantity changes on revenues and expenses.

Variance analysis is a topic that is simple in concept but complex in execution. At the variance analysis' most basic level, variances occur because of one of two events: (1) prices are different from what was estimated, or (2) quantities are different from what was estimated.[26]

Variances can be constructed to show two things: (1) the effect of changes in prices and (2) the effect of changes in the quantity used or produced. You can learn more about variance analysis from the McGraw-Hill textbook by Ray Garrison et al., *Managerial Accounting,* 15th edition.

Decision Making

LO **12-6** Use accounting information to make better business decisions.

Managers have five primary functions in a business: planning, organizing, staffing, directing, and controlling the combined efforts of the firm. Each of these functions requires making decisions, both large and small. The primary purpose of managerial accounting is to support good decision making.

To use accounting information for decision making, you need to have some understanding of the processes by which people make decisions.

All current theories of decision making are based on the belief that people are rational, that is, people think, reason, and consider alternatives before they act. Although this assumption may be a bit optimistic, it applies (or *should* apply) to decision making in business situations. The assumption of rationality itself comes in several "flavors." At one extreme are theories that assume that the human mind has essentially unlimited reasoning powers. At the other extreme are theories that assume that people have limited abilities to obtain and process information.

The theories of unlimited reasoning powers have been largely discredited. Research shows that people use incomplete information and incomplete analyses of alternatives to make decisions. Today, it is generally assumed that people are inefficient processors of information. Theories based on the assumption of limited human abilities are called *bounded rationality models.*[27] One implication of the assumption that people are limited in their ability to use information is that the more information available to be included into the decision process, the less efficient that process will be.

Thus to make good decisions we need (1) good information, (2) efficient ways to condense information so it is understandable, and (3) methods to help compare alternatives.

Both financial and managerial accounting are methodologies that reduce the complexity of the information used to make business decisions. By definition, accounting deals with only financial information. By limiting the information being considered to financial concerns, the complexity of the alternatives is reduced. Accounting further reduces information complexity by evaluating information for relevance to the decision to be made. For financial purposes, any decision that was made in the past cannot be changed and is therefore irrelevant to any decision to be made today. Information that is the same for two or more alternatives cannot be used to choose between them. For these reasons, accounting decision support is based solely on the differences in expected financial outcomes among identified alternatives.

Examining some of the common management decisions that can be aided by the use of accounting information and procedures will illustrate these concepts.

investment
An asset that is acquired for the purpose of either generating future incomes and cash flows or appreciating in value to provide an increase in future wealth.

Investments are a constant management problem. To reduce the difficulty of choosing from among investment alternatives, accounting has developed two basic methodologies to reduce the magnitude and complexity of the information that must be considered in making an appropriate decision.

The first of these simplification methods is called *differential revenues and expenses.* This methodology comprises estimating the *changes* in revenues and expenses from current operating results that will occur if each alternative is taken. The decision rule that is applied is to accept the investment that produces the greatest profit.

The second simplification method is called **net present value (NPV)** analysis. NPV analyses are based on the concept that a dollar to be received right now has more utility (value) than does a dollar to be received at some time in the future. To perform NPV analyses, only cash flows are considered. The decision rule is to accept the largest positive NPV. The theory and application of NPV is covered in detail in Appendix B of Chapter 15.

net present value (NPV)
The difference between the present value of cash inflows and the present value of cash outflows over a specified period of time.

Outsourcing requires that a decision be made whether the business should make a component of its own product or purchase the component from another business. As is done in investment decisions, accounting information relevant to the decision is reduced to differential revenues and costs, or to cash flows. Depending on the methodology chosen, either the differential profits (losses) or the net present value of each alternative is calculated. Once the information is developed, decision rules are applied.[28]

outsourcing
Contracting with people or companies outside your business to do work for your business.

A simple example of an outsourcing decision is the provision of salad for a local restaurant. Suppose that the restaurant is a barbeque that serves cole slaw as its only salad. The restaurant may either make the slaw on premises at a cost of $2.87 per pound or purchase it from a wholesaler at $2.40 per pound. Should you make the slaw or purchase the slaw? A superficial examination of the problem would indicate that purchasing it is less expensive. Examining only the differential costs offers a very different conclusion (see Exhibit 12.2).

The difference arises from the fact that fixed costs will not change if the decision is made to purchase the slaw. By definition, fixed costs are costs that do not change with changes in output (here output is slaw). As a result, the amount of fixed cost allocated to making slaw is irrelevant to the decision. If you have trouble understanding this, simply put a line for fixed cost into the previous decision criteria. Put the allocated amount of $1.00 in the columns for making and buying the slaw. Add the columns and see if your decision would change.

Accounting is useful for managers of small businesses, for record keeping, for reporting to absentee owners and other stakeholders, for substantiating assertions made to regulators and taxing agencies, for support of the five functions of management, and for decision making. Accounting information is a financial model of the operations of the business and provides a wealth of useful reports, analyses, and measures that are valuable to the management of small businesses. Accounting is a rich source of information. It is not, however, the only source of information needed by managers.

EXHIBIT 12.2

Using Differential Costs to Make an Outsourcing Decision: Make or Buy?

Current Costs to Make Slaw on Premises	
Pounds of slaw served per month	900
Materials per pound	$0.87
Direct labor per pound (2.4 hrs @ $10 per 30 lbs.)	0.80
Variable overhead per pound	0.20
Allocated fixed costs per pound	1.00
Total cost per pound	$2.87

Differential Costs between Alternatives	**Alternatives**	
	Make	Buy
Materials	$0.87	–0–
Direct labor	0.80	–0–
Variable overhead	0.20	–0–
Purchase price	–0–	2.40
Total	$1.87	$2.40

CHAPTER SUMMARY

LO 12-1 Describe the basic concepts of accounting.

- Accounting matters to small businesses because:
  - Accounting proves what your business did financially.
  - Accounting shows how much your business is worth.
  - Banks, creditors, development agencies, and investors require accounting statements.
  - Accounting provides easy-to-understand plans for business operations.
  - Accounting provides information about how your business is doing.
- There are three types of accounting:
  - Managerial accounting attempts to predict the results of management decisions.
  - Tax accounting is used to produce tax returns and schedules.
  - Financial accounting is a formal, rule-based system intended primarily for absentee owners, bankers, investors, and regulators.
- Accounting is based on a few basic concepts:
  - A business is believed to have an existence that is separate and different from the owner's (business entity concept).
  - Because a business exists, it is expected to continue to exist (going concept).
  - The accounting equation is simply an expression of the commonsense statement that your net worth is whatever is left over after all your debts are paid.
- To use accounting effectively for management purposes, you must understand the difference between costs and expenses:
  - Costs are real changes in the value of what you own.
  - Expenses are simply entries made in your accounting system to record your use of goods and services in the conduct of your business.
- There are only two reasons to do accounting:
  - To produce information that is useful to you for managing your business.
  - To meet legal or contractual requirements.

LO 12-2 Specify the requirements for a small business accounting system.

- The primary reason to acquire and use a computerized accounting system in your business is to ensure the accuracy of your accounting information.
- Your accounting system should easily and efficiently accomplish the following tasks:
  - Provide a simple, easy-to-understand user interface.
  - Have an exhaustive context-sensitive help function.
  - Produce financial statements in the format used by your industry and type of business.
  - Facilitate the development of a cash budget.
  - Facilitate the task of developing operating and investment budgets.
  - Provide a method for you to define and produce custom reports to meet your management needs.
  - Be able to export financial data in a form that can be used by your accountant and can be imported into tax preparation and spreadsheet programs.
  - Maintain an internal "audit trail" that records all entries and changes to the accounting system in order to facilitate the identification and correction of errors.
  - Have provisions that will either allow the program to grow with your business or to easily export its data into programs that can handle larger businesses.
- Your specific accounting needs are determined by the industry you are in and by the size of your business.
- When a business is large enough to have one or more employees, formal record keeping is a must.
- Essential elements of an accounting system are:
  - *Cash accounting* that is accurate, easy to use, and tracks all checks written and all deposits made.
  - *Accounts payable* records to track what you owe and to make timely payments in order to capture prompt pay discounts and to maintain a good credit rating for your business.
  - *Payroll records* to ensure that payroll and employment taxes are kept current.
  - *Fixed asset* accounting that automatically calculates and accumulates depreciation.

- *Inventory* accounting to facilitate managing inventory.
- *Credit card sales* function to enable reconciling your sales records to those of your credit card provider.
- *Accounts receivable* records if you provide credit to your customers.
- *Insurance register* to ease the problems of keeping necessary insurance coverage current and in force.
- *Investment records* if your business keeps surplus cash invested in securities.
- *Leasehold records* if your business has made improvements to leased property or equipment.

LO 12-3 Explain the content and format of common financial statements.

- The final output of an accounting computer system is a set of six financial statements and reports:
  - Income statement.
  - Statement of comprehensive income.
  - Statement of retained earnings.
  - Statement of owners' equity.
  - Balance sheet.
  - Cash flow statement.
- It is common for these statements to be presented as only three separate documents by combining the statements of retained earnings and owners' equity into the equity section of the balance sheet.
- The income statement is the primary source of information about a business's profitability.
- The primary difficulties in understanding and interpreting the income statement arise from two causes:
  - Disagreements about what should be reported as revenue.
  - Disputes over when to recognize revenues.
- The income statement is used in the following ways:
  - The income statement is used to analyze the effectiveness of business operations.
  - Lenders use operating income as a measure of how much debt a business can support.
  - Equity investors similarly look to operating income as an indication of future sales and thus the value of their investment.
- The balance sheet presents a snapshot of the financial holdings and liabilities at the close of business on a specified date.
- The balance sheet is used in the following ways:
  - The balance sheet is used to determine the liquidity, financial flexibility, and financial strength of the business.
  - These measures are used by owners, lenders, and equity investors in making financial and investment decisions.
- The following are problems in interpreting balance sheet information:
  - All values listed in a balance sheet are *historical* values—the cost of the asset when it was acquired.
  - A balance sheet contains several estimated amounts.
  - Certain assets and liabilities are omitted from the balance sheet.
- The purpose of the cash flow statement is to disclose the sources and uses of cash by the business.
- There are two primary formats of cash flow statement:
  - The direct statement is developed solely from the cash records of the business and does not make any reconciliation to the income statement.
  - The indirect statement of cash flows starts with net income and adjusts the accruals and deferrals to provide cash flow information that can be easily reconciled to the other financial statements.

LO 12-4 Use accounting information as a tool for managing your business effectively.

- Financial accounting is useful for decision making.
- Financial and business managers are familiar with the format, content, and interpretation of financial statements.
- Obtaining loans, answering Internal Revenue Service inquiries, and satisfying the reporting requirements of regulatory agencies are all made easier when an appropriate set of financial statements is provided.
- Financial accounting is used for reporting to outsiders.
- Managerial accounting is used internally for management purposes.
- By mastering managerial accounting techniques, you will become more accurate at forecasting profits, planning operations, and conserving scarce resources.
- Managerial accounting information and reports are used in the conduct of all the managerial functions of planning, organizing, staffing, directing, and controlling.
- The most used managerial accounting technique is cost-volume-profit analysis.
- Accounting data contain the information necessary to create detailed plans of how to achieve a desired level of profit.

- The process of profit planning comprises creating a model of the business that will allow you to test various situations, assumptions, and occurrences, without risking financial loss.
- The most common model used for small businesses planning is the familiar business plan.
- The financial projections in your business plan are a form of a budget that can easily be expanded to be useful for the day-to-day management of your business.

LO 12-5 Create a set of appropriate budgets that support developing pro forma financial statements for your business plan.

- Budgeting is the process through which strategy is mapped into a series of tactical and operational actions.
- Once a budget has been prepared, it becomes a standard against which performance can be measured.
- Business planning is a *simple* process of applying your knowledge of your business to make estimates of future operations and results.
- The most common budget schedules are:
  - The sales budget shows the projected future level of sales in units multiplied by the sales price per unit.
  - The purchases budget shows the number of units expected to be acquired during the budget period.
  - The cost of goods sold budget shows the predicted cost of product actually sold.
  - The labor budget shows both the amount and cost of labor needed to meet required output.
  - The overhead budget details both fixed and variable overhead costs.
  - Selling, general, and administrative expense (SG&A) budget shows both costs that change with production and costs that don't.
- These budget schedules are combined into pro forma financial statements.
- The difference between actual results and budgeted amounts is called a variance.
- Variances occur because either actual prices or volume is different from what was budgeted.
- To understand the effect of price changes, you must answer the following questions:
  - What would I have paid for the amount I actually used, if the price had been what I expected?
  - How much material should I have used to make the number of units that were actually completed?

LO 12-6 Use accounting information to make better business decisions.

- The five primary functions in a business—planning, organizing, staffing, directing, and controlling—are combined as input for decision making.
- To make good decisions we need:
  - Good information.
  - Efficient methods to condense information so it is understandable.
  - Methods to facilitate comparing alternatives.
- Managerial accounting is both a source of information that is used in decision making and a methodology to reduce the complexity of the information used to make a decision.
- Common management decisions that can be aided by the use of accounting information and procedures include investments and outsourcing.
- Managerial accounting uses two primary simplification methods to handle information: differential revenues and expenses and net present value (NPV) analysis.

KEY TERMS

financial accounting, 430

managerial accounting, 430

tax accounting, 430

generally accepted accounting principles (GAAP), 431

income statement, 431

balance sheet, 431

statement of cash flows, 431

standard budgeting, 431

profit planning, 431

pro forma financial statements, 431

business entity concept, 432

going concern concept, 432

accounting equation, 434

asset, 434

DISCUSSION QUESTIONS

1. Which of the three types of accounting is most important to small business? Which is the least? Why do you think so?
2. How does the accounting equation relate to the balance sheet?
3. How are costs and expenses different?
4. Why should you, as a business owner, care about the distinction between costs and expenses?
5. Defend the statement "The function of accounting is to produce information that is useful for decision making."
6. What are the three most important characteristics of a small business computer accounting system? Why do you think these are the most important?
7. What are the three most important functions (think cash, accounts payable, owners' equity, etc.) that a computerized accounting system should have? Why are they the most important?
8. Which financial report is most important for managing a small business? Why?
9. You can sell your product (have revenues) without receiving any money. You can receive money (customer deposits) without having any revenue. Because revenue, expenses, and cash are so different, why should a small business owner care about the income statement?
10. Why would a small business ever need an accounting system more complicated than a simple checkbook register?
11. A budget is a collection of estimates—a big word that means the same thing as "guess." If you are guessing what future results will be, what value can a budget really have?
12. How are budgets related to business plans, as described in Chapter 8?
13. Are there any advantages to making a series of budget schedules, rather than just producing a pro forma income statement and balance sheet? What are the disadvantages, if any?

EXPERIENTIAL EXERCISES

1. Assume that you have decided to purchase a computerized small business accounting system. Visit the website of each of the accounting systems named in this chapter. From the information there determine:
   - **a.** The price of the accounting system.
   - **b.** The minimum computer requirements for the program.
   - **c.** The availability and cost of training to learn to use the program.
   - **d.** The availability of trained accountants and consultants in your geographic area who can be retained to assist you in setting up and using the program.
2. Choose an industry in which you would like to own a small business. Use the Internet, the university library, and the public library to find the names and addresses of industry trade associations. Examine the websites of the trade associations for availability of financial statistics of your industry. Examine governmental agency sites, such as those of the Department of Commerce, Department of the Treasury, Securities and Exchange Commission, and the Small Business Administration, for benchmark statistics.
3. Choose a public business that is in the same industry as the business you would like to own. Go to the company's website and find "investor relations." Download a copy of the business's most recent annual report. Examine the financial statements in the annual report. Make a list of the ways in which their content and format differ from the examples in this text.
4. Either by yourself or in a group of other students, select a business that you could reasonably expect to be able to start and run right now. (This could be as simple as a T-shirt company.) Using the techniques learned in exercises 2 and 3, develop a set of estimates of (a) sales, (b) variable cost of product or service, and (c) the amount of other costs (rent, electricity, transportation, etc.) that you would expect to incur. Using these estimates, create a set of budget schedules through the schedule of cost of goods manufactured and sold.
5. Go to either the QuickBooks or the Sage 50 Accounting website. Download and install a demonstration copy of its accounting program. Using either the budget schedules you developed in exercise 4, or the Red Jett Sweets example from the text, set up the program to do accounting as if this were a real business.
6. Do a Google search for the terms "accounting system" and "small business." Follow the Google returns to the websites of the companies (other than the ones named in the text) that you can find that sell computerized accounting systems. Examine the site to determine if its program would be suitable under the criteria specified in the text.

MINI-CASE

PHIONIA'S FINICKY FELINE GOURMET CAT DINNERS

Phionia Phelps has developed a gourmet cat food. Not only is this food eagerly eaten by the most finicky felines, but it is specially formulated to prevent the many health problems of aging cats. Phionia has been making the food on her kitchen range and selling it at $250 per case only to close acquaintances who are also cat lovers. One of her wealthy acquaintances has now offered to invest in her business if Phionia will begin selling the product through her website. However, the investor wants Phionia to produce a budget for the first six months of operation.

Based on her experience to date, Phionia predicts the following sales in cases:

Nov	Dec	Jan	Feb	Mar	Apr	May	Jun	Jul	Aug
4,300	4,600	5,000	5,500	6,100	6,800	7,000	7,200	7,400	7,500

Each case of Finicky Feline Gourmet Cat Dinner requires 5 pounds of prime lamb meat, 10 pounds of short-grain Chinese rice, 2 pounds of wild caught Alaskan salmon, and 1 pound of secret vitamins and supplements. Phionia plans to maintain end-of-month inventories equal to 10 percent of the next month's projected sales, to meet expected sales growth. All the ingredients inventories are to be maintained at 5 percent of the production needs for the next month, but not to exceed 1,000 pounds of any one ingredient. January will begin with all inventories at the projected levels.

Phionia has the following price quotes good for the following year:

The production process requires direct labor at two skill levels: (1) ingredient preparation, $18 per hour; and (2) cooking and canning, $24 per hour. Two workers are willing to work part time if there is not enough demand for them to work full time. It takes one hour to process one batch. Because of preparation and cleanup time, only six batches can be produced per day. Each batch produces enough food to fill 100 cases. Manufacturing overhead is $6,000 fixed per month plus $15 per case.

Item	$ per pound
Lamb	$15.00
Rice	1.20
Salmon	24.00
Vitamins	45.00

CASE DISCUSSION QUESTIONS

1. Prepare the following budgets for the period January through June:
   - **a.** Sales budget in dollars.
   - **b.** Production budget in units.
   - **c.** Direct materials purchases budget in pounds.
   - **d.** Direct materials purchases budget in dollars.
   - **e.** Direct manufacturing labor budget in dollars.
2. Comment on the viability of this business and the advisability of the investor making a $50,000 investment to get it started.

Your instructor may provide you with a sample solution for this mini-case.

CHAPTER 13

Cash: Lifeblood of the Business

● Thomas Lemery built Creatacor, Inc. from a spin-off of GE's corporate exhibit operations. Between 1987 and 2015, the company grew from 8 employees to more than 50. Jean Hatalsky was one of the most senior of these, having been with the company for 27 years. Who would ever believe that this long-time, loyal employee would steal a half million dollars from its owners?
Creatacor

LEARNING OBJECTIVES

After you complete this chapter, you will be able to:

LO 13-1 Explain the concepts of money, cash, and cash equivalents.

LO 13-2 Explain the importance of managing your business's cash flows.

LO 13-3 Plan for cash needs by developing a cash budget.

LO 13-4 Explain the basics of how cash flows can be kept secured.

LO 13-5 Implement strategies for coping with cash flow problems.

LO 13-6 Appendix A: Reconcile bank and company book balances.

Focus on Small Business: Creatacor, Inc.

Creatacor, Inc. of Clifton Park, New York, designs and builds exhibits for trade shows, sets for live theater, and retail displays. Over the more than 30 years of the company's existence, problems with managing cash flows has caused numerous meetings of managers and several calls for the company to tighten its spending.[1] The problems with cash flows resulted in the company reporting financial irregularities to the police and also hiring Pamela Wickes, a CPA and forensic accountant. By means of an extensive investigation as part of an exhaustive audit of the firm's financial records, Pamela was able to establish that $500,000 had been embezzled across a four-year period.[2]

Soon after the company was started in 1987, Lemery hired a recent high school graduate, 18-year-old Jean Hatalsky, as the receptionist for the new business. During the next 28 years, Jean, a valued and trusted employee, took on more and more responsibility, eventually becoming the firm's office manager.[3] In this position, beginning in 2011, Jean began stealing by using the business credit cards to make personal purchases.[4]

As the office manager, Jean had access to the company's credit cards, and also was responsible for recording the purpose and amount of the transactions. She spent company money on gifts for her family members, a snowmobile, and trips and entertainment for herself and her family. To do this, she had only to falsify the records made for the credit card purchases, incorrectly classifying them as legitimate business expenditures for such items as equipment, inventory, and selling expenses.

Finally, as a result of Pamela's forensic accounting, Jean Hatalsky was confronted with evidence of her fraud and was arrested and arraigned on charges of larceny and falsifying business records. In 2017, she pled guilty to the charges and received a prison sentence of up to six years and a requirement to repay the stolen money.[5]

DISCUSSION QUESTIONS

1. What would you recommend if your business was experiencing continuing cash flow problems?
2. What should a business do to prevent employee theft as was experienced by Creatacor?

LO 13-1 Explain the concepts of money, cash, and cash equivalents.

Money as the Key Idea

Ask someone you know the question, "What is money?"

Most likely the answer you get will tell you about currency—the bills and coins that you use to make purchases. That answer is not completely wrong, but it tells only part of the story because while all currency is money, all money is not currency.

Today we use many electronic forms of money: debit cards, online bill payments, electronic bank drafts, wire transfers, even Bitcoin. These forms of money make an important point—the *essence of money* is that it is a form of *information.*

The U.S. Dallas Federal Reserve Bank provides the following definition:

> Money is a medium of exchange accepted by the community, meaning it's what people buy things with and sell things for. Money provides a standard for measuring value, so that the worth of different goods and services can be compared. And lastly, money is a store of value that can be saved for later purchases.[6]

money
An accepted medium of exchange.

This definition gives us three purposes for **money**:

1. To facilitate exchanges of unlike assets, such as your labor for a grocer's food.
2. To measure the value of things, both tangible, such as jewelry, and intangible, such as pain and suffering.
3. To keep track of wealth.

Most importantly, it defines the essence of money which is contained in the phrase "accepted by the community." Essentially, what makes money "money" is the *belief* users have about the information contained in the money. This belief is the only thing that gives our paper and digital money its value.

Knowing the meaning of money is important so that you can recognize where you have money in your business. For example, are profits money? You might think so at first, but consider: As is discussed in the previous chapter, profit is simply the difference between two accounting items, revenue and expense. Revenue is an accounting entry that is made when you sell your product or service, *whether or not any money changes hands!* Expense is an accounting entry made when you use up some asset for the purpose of producing revenues.

Profits are not money. Profits are information that is useful in predicting when and how much money you may collect. This is shown explicitly later in this chapter when we discuss budgeting for cash flows.

Cash and Cash Equivalents

To this point we've been throwing around the terms *money* and *cash* as if everyone knows just what they are; how they differ. Although we have carefully defined the meaning of money, we have not done so for cash.

cash
Money that is immediately available to be spent.

Cash is money, but it's only one form of money, a subcategory of money that is immediately available to be spent. Not all money is "spendable." For example, think of certificates of deposit. Although you may well have a lot of money in CDs, you may have very little cash because your money is tied up in the CDs and would take time to convert into cash. Cash is composed of the three forms of money that can be immediately used to make payments: currency, demand deposits, and traveler's checks.

cash equivalents
Assets that may be quickly converted to cash.

Businesses, on the other hand, use a concept called **cash equivalents** to measure how much money is available to be spent. Cash equivalents are assets that may be turned into cash in a slightly longer time, from a few hours to a few days, such as marketable securities, commercial paper, and debt investments that mature in less than three months. Businesses use cash equivalents because they provide a better measure of the resources available to pay current bills than is provided by cash alone.

currency
The bills and coins printed by governments to represent money.

Currency is the most familiar form of cash: bills and coins that represent money. On April 2, 2019, the Board of Governors of the Federal Reserve System reported that the supply of currency in circulation was $1.7 trillion as of January 31, 2019,[7] or approximately $5,800 of currency for each individual living in the United States.[8] The Federal Reserve, however, states that more than half of all U.S. currency is being held outside the United States.

Demand deposits make up most of the noncurrency cash. Demand deposits are accounts that let you withdraw (what bankers call demand) any amount of the balance immediately, without any advance notice to the institution: That is, owners may withdraw money on demand by using a check, draft, currency, or electronic transfer. Checking accounts and savings accounts are the two most common forms of demand deposit accounts.

Marketable securities are made up of stocks and bonds for which there is an active auction market, such as the NASDAQ or the New York Stock Exchange. Marketable securities represent either ownership or debt of publicly held firms and government issued debt, in the form of bonds, notes, and bills.

Commercial paper and **short-term debt** are two forms of short-term financing (30 days to 1 year) whereby a company with good credit can issue a note for cash to another company. Commercial paper is issued to be paid to the **bearer** of the note, and thus is fully transferable. Short-term debt is expected to be collected in less than a year, but it can be sold to other investors at any time.

demand deposits
Money held in checking and savings accounts.

marketable securities
Stocks and bonds that are traded on an open market.

commercial paper
Notes issued by creditworthy corporations.

short-term debt
Any debt that must be paid in less than one year from the date of the financial statement on which it is reported.

bearer
Any person or business entity who possesses a security.

The Importance of Cash Management

LO **13-2** Explain the importance of managing your business's cash flows.

There are three very important parts to managing cash in a business. The first part is to collect cash from customers and to have it available when you need it. The second part is to keep the cash safe from misuse and theft. We will discuss both of these issues, especially the issue of securely keeping cash once it has been collected.

Managing the amounts and timing of your business's cash flows is absolutely essential to success. Not doing so may cause you to miss required debt payments and encounter all the problems that missing payments cause. It can cause you to not be able to pay suppliers on time, which can lead to having them refuse to sell essential inventory to your business. It can, in fact, cause your business to fail as happens every year to many small businesses. The problems of not managing cash flows are like avalanches: Once started, they grow and grow until they are overpowering.

Money presents two big problems to owners and managers of small businesses. First is **how much money** the business has, will receive, and must pay to others. Second is **when** the money will be received and **when** the money must be paid. These processes of controlling *how much* and *when* money will come into and go out of the business are referred to as **cash flow management**.

cash flow management
Planning and tracking the amounts and timing of money to be received and paid during the business cycle.

Cash flow management is:	Cash flow management is not:
• having enough cash available to meet business needs	• keeping large sums of cash on hand at all times
• being able to obtain cash quickly from a variety of sources	• obtaining all cash from business operations
• understanding how (and when) cash is used by your business	• assuming that all sales and expenses happen instantly
• closely monitoring accounts receivable for late payments	• trusting customers to pay when the bill comes due
• providing motivation for customers to make prompt payments	• providing lengthy credit terms without charging interest
• taking advantage of prompt payment discount only when it is cheaper than borrowing	• allowing large sums to "sit" in non-interest-paying accounts

The most effective cash flow techniques require budgeting for both the amount and timing of required cash flows in order to know when cash will be available and when it will be needed.

In this chapter we go into detail about how you can know exactly when money is coming in and how much you can expect to receive. Likewise, we explain how you can know when and how much must be paid out for bills. If you are like most people, you will find some surprises. Things that you think you know are going to turn out to be false. Things you might think are trivial will turn out to be of great importance. It is part of what makes cash and money fascinating.

Money In/Money Out—Just How Important Is It?

Approximately 82 percent of small businesses that fail do so because of cash flow problems, not because of lack of profitability.[9] Simply stated, controlling the flows of cash into and out of your business will make the difference between success and failure. The problem reduces to two simple facts: many small businesses have (1) too little money coming into the business and (2) too much money flowing out.

A poll conducted by the National Federation of Independent Business (NFIB) in 2016[10] found that approximately 60 percent of small business owners experienced cash flows to be either a continuing or an occasional problem for their businesses. When asked if cash flow was a greater problem now than in the past, 36 percent reported it to be less of a problem, while 25 percent responded that cash flow was more of a problem than it had been three years earlier. Owners reported that the three primary causes of cash flow problems were (1) difficulty collecting money due from customers, (2) seasonal variation in sales, and (3) requirements to periodically make large capital investments. (See Figure 13.1.)

Cash flow management is a problem for small businesses because of the difficulty of matching the *timing* of the *receipt of cash* to the *timing* of the need to *expend cash.* Figure 13.2 illustrates the flow of money into and out of your business as you buy what you need and sell your product or your service. This repeating flow of money is called the **cash-to-cash cycle** or the **operating cycle** of your business.

cash-to-cash cycle
The time that is required for a business to acquire resources, convert them into product, sell the product, and receive cash from the sale.

operating cycle
See *cash-to-cash cycle.*

FIGURE 13.1

Causes of Cash Shortages

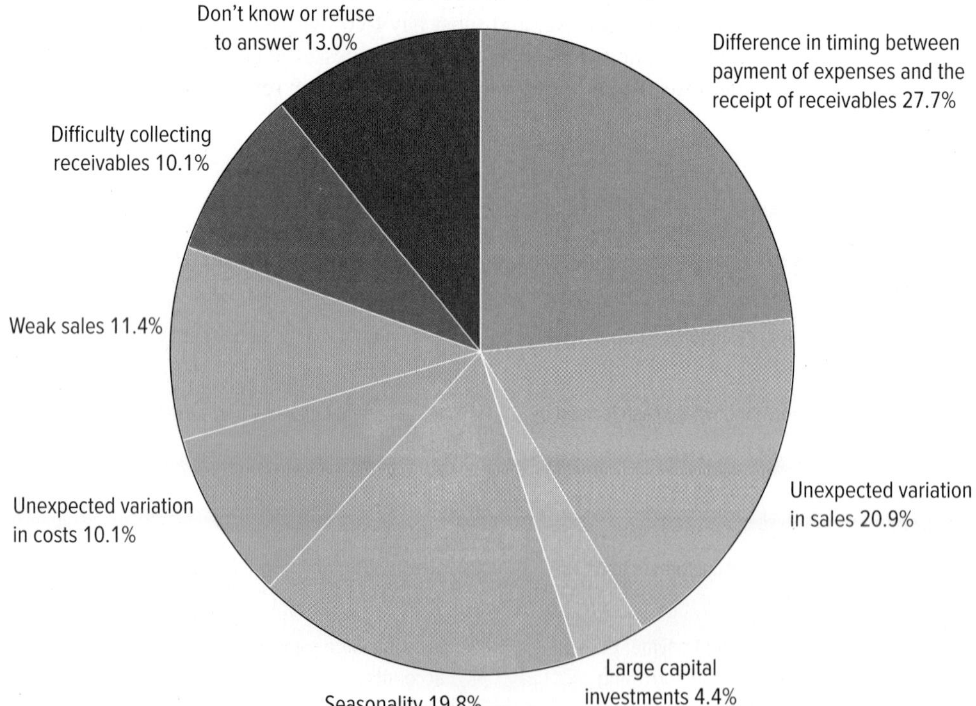

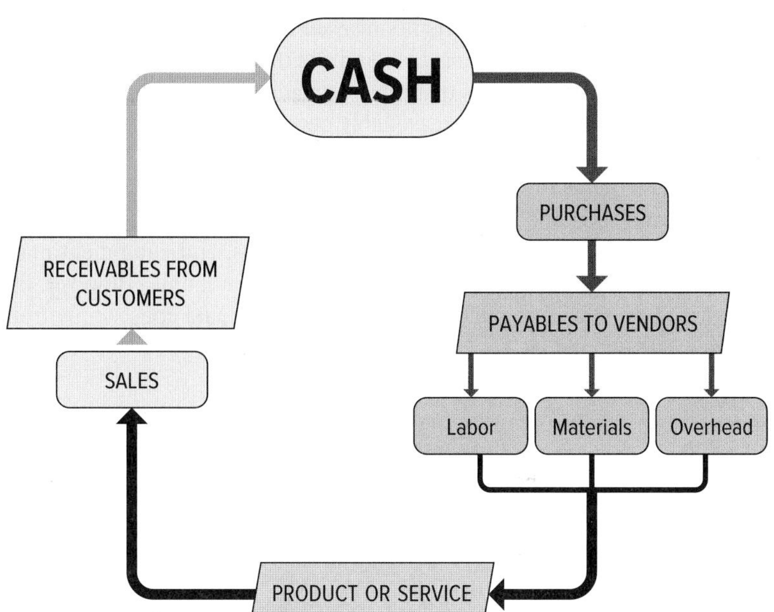

FIGURE 13.2
The Cash-to-Cash Cycle

When you start a new business, you put in some money. You then buy all the things necessary to run the business such as materials, supplies, rent, and labor. Some of these you purchase for cash. Other things you may buy on credit, creating **payables**, which you will have to pay next month. You then use labor to convert materials and supplies into your product or service, which you sell to your customers. Your customers then either pay you immediately, or agree to pay you soon. The promises of your customers to pay are **receivables**, which you will collect in the future. The money you collect will then be used to buy the things necessary to run your business, and thus the cycle repeats.

payables
Amounts owed to vendors for merchandise or services purchased on credit (see also *receivables*).

receivables
Amounts that are owed to a business for merchandise that was sold on credit (see also *payables*).

The time that it takes to complete this cycle can be as short as a few hours or as long as several years, dependent on the type of business you are in. The ubiquitous pushcart vendors of hot dogs in New York City purchase inventory on credit every morning. They sell their product for cash during the day. Each evening they pay for the merchandise sold that day. The cash-to-cash cycle of a pushcart vendor is only a few hours. Construction projects, on the other hand, can easily take years to complete. A contractor will borrow money to begin construction. That money is paid out across the time that it takes to complete the project. The contractor, however, receives from the customer either a single payment upon completion or a few payments as specified completion targets are met.

Pushcart vendors, such as the ones pictured here, enjoy a very short cash-to-cash cycle due to the nature of their business. Each day, their receipt of cash from sales enables them to then expend cash back to their suppliers for exactly what has been sold. Though small in scope, the simplicity of their business setup allows for the immediate assessment of their profitability. Does this kind of setup appeal to you?

Jantira Namwong/Shutterstock

Many small businesses experience difficulty or even failure because of (1) the mismatch in time between receiving cash and spending cash and (2) the mismatch between the size of payments received and the size of payments that must be made. In some businesses, such as restaurants, cash comes into the business in a reasonably dependable pattern that is affected by the state of the economy, the season, the day of the week, and the weather. Expenses, on the other hand, tend to occur less frequently but in larger amounts, as suppliers are paid monthly, employees are paid weekly, and food and beverage wholesalers are paid on delivery. Other businesses, such as construction firms, plumbing contractors, ski resorts, and equipment manufacturers, have cash receipts that tend to occur irregularly but in large amounts. However, the cash payment needs of these businesses are relatively smaller amounts paid consistently from month to month. (See Figures 13.3 and 13.4.)

FIGURE 13.3

Cash-to-Cash Cycle: Many Vendors, Few Customers

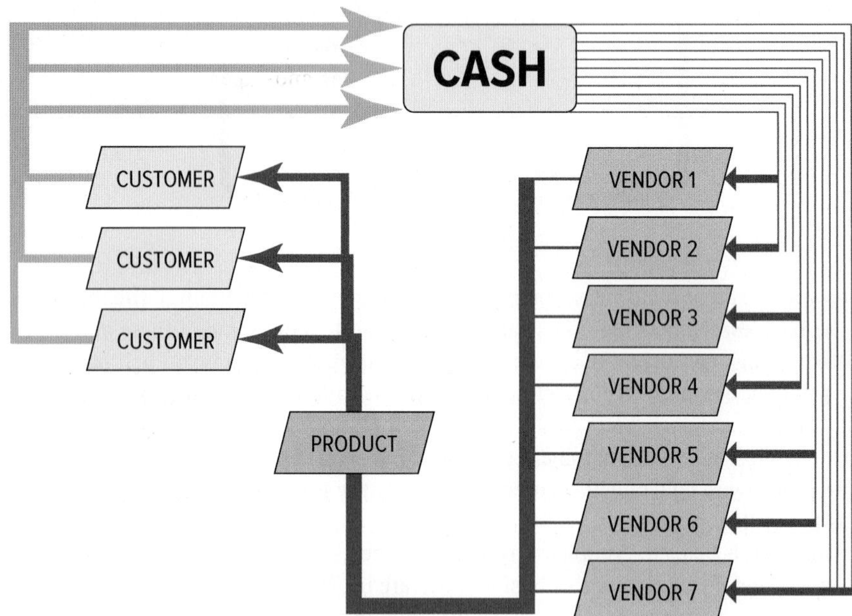

FIGURE 13.4

Cash-to-Cash Cycle: Few Vendors, Many Customers

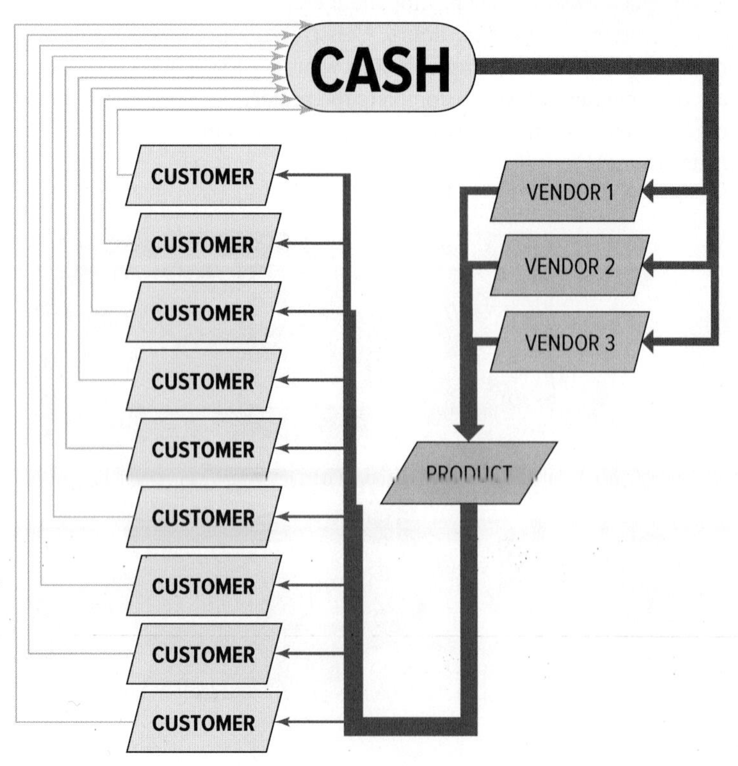

Although maximizing your wealth may not be your highest priority, managing your business's money is critical to succeeding and being able to attain goals that are more important to you.

John Mackey, founder of Whole Foods Market, Inc., said, "Business is the most transformative agency in the world. [Business leaders] can make money and do good. . . . I always wanted to make money. . . . To be sustainable, business has to be profitable."[11]

Planning Cash Needs

LO **13-3** Plan for cash needs by developing a cash budget.

The Sales Budget: Forecasting Sales Receipts

For small businesses, the key to cash planning is the **cash budget**. Simply put, the cash budget identifies when, how, and why cash is expected to come into the business, and when, how, and why it is expected to leave. The quality of those expectations is important. Making more realistic or accurate estimates about expected incomes and expenses means that the budget becomes a more useful tool for understanding and managing your cash flow and financial situation.

cash budget
A cash budget identifies when, how, and why cash is expected to come into the business, and when, how, and why it is expected to leave.

Almost all business budgeting begins with a forecast of sales. As discussed in Chapter 12, several methods are used to make sales forecasts. We will illustrate the process of creating a cash flow budget for the fourth quarter of the year based on the forecast sales for Red Jett Sweets that we used in Chapter 12. This illustrates cash budgeting techniques that will be helpful to you when you write your own business plan. The sales budget developed in Chapter 12 is shown here (with minor modifications) as Table 13.1.

For many small businesses, the sales forecast *is* the cash receipts forecast. Businesses such as barbershops, muffler repair shops, restaurants, and all kinds of retail merchandisers do not provide credit to customers. All sales are made either in cash or by credit card. Despite that, this type of business *can* have cash flow problems created when sales are insufficient to cover required payments. Each type of business has a different pattern of sales and cash receipts. Some businesses, whose customers make heavy use of credit cards, can face serious cash drains as a result (see The Thoughtful Entrepreneur).

TABLE 13.1 Sales Budget

RED JETT Sweets

Sales Budget

	October	November	December	Quarter 4	January
REVENUES					
Unit sales	2,983	2,983	2,712	8,678	3,000
Sales price	$2.75	$2.75	$2.75	$2.75	$2.94
Cash sales	4,389	4,389	4,389	13,167	4,414
Credit card sales	4,389	4,389	4,389	13,167	4,414
Gross Sales	8,778	8,778	8,778	26,334	8,828
Less:					
Credit card fees	88	88	88	263	88
Spoilage & over production	61	61	56	178	62
Sales tax collected	615	615	615	1,845	618
Net sales revenue	8,014	8,014	8,019	24,048	8,060

THE THOUGHTFUL ENTREPRENEUR

THE BUSINESS COSTS OF USING CREDIT CARDS

Credit card use fees quickly add up to material amounts. Consider a successful restaurant that grosses approximately $80,000 per month, with an average per-customer ticket of $20. If 90 percent of customers pay with a credit card, 3,600 credit card charges will be made in a month ($80,000/$20 × 0.9). Assume that the credit card company charges 20 cents per transaction plus 2 percent of the amount charged. The credit card fee for the month will equal $2,160 (3,600 transactions × 0.20) + (80,000 × 0.9 × 0.02). The restaurant will also pay the 2 percent fee on any tips that are added to the bill. If the average tip added is 15 percent, then the added fee on tips charged per month will be another $216. Thus the restaurant will average paying an amount greater than $28,000 in credit card fees per year.

So why, you may ask, do small businesses use credit cards? First, accepting credit cards increases sales. Second, the credit card issuer assumes the cost and risk of determining credit worthiness.

Many businesses have either relatively few large sales events or highly seasonal sales that complicate forecasting cash inflows. Examples include:

- Retailers
- Home builders
- Custom electric sign shops
- Machine shops
- Providers of custom software
- Real estate brokers
- Consultants
- Ski resorts
- Water parks
- All businesses that depend on tourism

The Cash Receipts Budget

As we discussed earlier in this chapter, how much and when money will come into your business is of critical importance. Later, we will discuss specific techniques that you can use to help control both how much and when you will receive money. However, the basis to being able to control your business's money is to understand and be able to predict the patterns of cash flows. Understanding and predicting begin when you prepare a **cash receipts budget**.

cash receipts budget
A schedule of the amounts and timings of the receipt of cash into a business.

If you provide credit to your customers, sales and cash receipts can be very different. If you provide credit, you will always wait some period of time for some of your money—that's what providing credit means, after all. You also, sooner or later, will have some customer who never pays. These two facts about selling on credit create significant differences between the amount of sales and the amount of cash received in any month.

The pattern of collections greatly affects the timing of cash flows. As is customary for food trucks and restaurants, the original Red Jett business plan assumes that all sales are cash or credit card sales. However, this is just not realistic for most businesses. Big-box stores such as Walmart, Safeway, and Home Depot simply do not pay cash for inventory. In fact, the common practice of such retailers is to demand that vendors provide lengthy payment terms for inventory.[12]

So we can demonstrate how to plan for cash receipts from credit sales, we are going to once again depart from the exact Red Jett business plan by assuming that 75 percent of sales will be made directly to consumers and paid for by using credit cards and cash.

The remaining 25 percent of sales will be treated as being sold on credit through big-box outlets, such as Albertsons Grocery or Safeway. The terms provided for payment by the outlets allow a 2 percent discount if the payment is received in 10 days after the sale and all payments are due in 30 days.

In this example we will assume that Red Jett's experience has shown:

- 25 percent of credit customers pay within the discount period.
- 70 percent of credit customers pay on time in 30 days.
- 5 percent of credit customers do not pay until 60 days.

The pattern of cash receipts for the last quarter of 2011 *if 25 percent of sales are made on credit* will look like Table 13.2A. Note that October sales of $8,778 generate three cash inflows: (1) 25 percent of October credit sales, *less the prompt pay discount*, are collected in October; (2) 70 percent of the October credit sales will be collected in November; and (3) the remaining 5 percent of October credit sales will be collected in December.

Once the pattern of cash collections is understood, the numbers may be converted into the cash receipts budget, as shown in Table 13.2B. As you examine this schedule, keep in mind that the numbers do not exactly match the original Red Jett financial projections from the business plan. This is because we have made changes that affect the timing of when cash is received (such as providing direct credit to certain customers). The original business plan tacitly includes the assumption that all cash from sales is received in the month of the sale and all payments are made in the same month as expenses are incurred. In other words, the original Red Jett financial projections are made using cash-based accounting while the examples here and in Chapter 12 are based on accrual-based accounting principles.

TABLE 13.2A Calculate Cash Receipts Schedule

Month of sale	Gross sales	Cash sales (75% of total sales)	Credit sales (25% of total sales)	Prompt pay discount (2% of 25% credit sales collected)	Cash collected on accounts receivable in October	Cash collected on accounts receivable in November	Cash collected on accounts receivable in December	Cash collected on accounts receivable in January 2012	Cash collected on accounts receivable in February 2012
					Oct	Nov	Dec	Jan	
Aug	8,778	6,584	2,195	11	110				
Sep	8,778	6,584	2,195	11	1,536	110			
Oct	8,778	6,584	2,195	11	538	1,536	110		
Nov	8,778	6,584	2,195	11		538	1,536	110	
Dec	8,778	6,584	2,195	11			538	1,536	110
Cash collected form accounts receivab					2,184	2,18	2,184	1,646	
Cash sales during the month					6,584	6,584	6,584		
Total Cash collected from customers					8,768	8,768	8,768		
Balance of account receivable at month end					1,756	1,756	1,756		

5% of customers who purchased in August, pay in October.

70% of customers who purchased in September pay in October.

25% of customers who purchased in October pay in the discount period.

TABLE 13.2B Cash Receipts Budget

RED JETT Sweets

Cash Receipts Budget Fourth Quarter, 2011				
	October	November	December	4th Quarter
Total sales	8,778	8,778	8,778	26,334
Less credit sales (1)	2,195	2,195	2,195	6,585
Cash Sales	6,583	6,583	6,583	19,749
Cash collected on accts receivable (2)	2,184	2,184	2,184	6,552
Total cash receipts	8,767	8,767	8,767	26,301

(1) Credit sales are calculated on the Calculate Cash Receipts Schedule as 25% of gross sales.
(2) Cash collected on receivables include: 25% of the current month's credit sales, less the prompt pay discount, plus the amounts due from the previous two months' credit sales. October amount = (.25 × 2,195 × 0.98) + 1,646.

There is always some uncertainty about exactly when you will collect cash. However, your experience in business, the experience of other businesses in the industry, and careful monitoring of your credit process lets you make very good estimates. For example, while resort owners may on occasion get advance bookings a year or more in advance, on average, deposits are received about one month in advance. Thus a reasonable estimate of their amount and timing can be made.

Forecasting Cash Disbursements

A similar approach is used for the forecasting of cash disbursements. The estimates of expenses that you develop in your budget and your knowledge of your business's payment patterns are combined to predict how much and when cash must be paid out. Table 13.3 illustrates the format of a cash disbursements budget. Note that the payment amounts come from the SG&A (selling, general, and administrative) budget developed in Chapter 12.

The Red Jett business plan specifically reads that inventory will be purchased and consumed each month. We took the liberty of including an ending balance of raw materials to allow us to illustrate the more common budgeting procedure where ending inventory is maintained. However, we did not change the assumption that purchases will be paid in the month that the expense is incurred.

cash disbursements budget
A schedule of the amounts and timings of payments of cash out of a business.

With the cash receipts and **cash disbursements budgets** complete, we need to know only how much money we expect to have on the first day of the accounting period to put together a cash budget for the fourth quarter, as shown in Table 13.4. The amount of cash we will have at the beginning of the quarter is simply the amount of cash we had at the end of the prior quarter. We can get this number from either of two sources: (1) the balance of our cash account after the month-end reconciliation is complete, or (2) the amount of cash shown on our pro forma balance sheet. You will find the beginning cash balance for October 1, 2011, in Appendix B of Chapter 8, Cash Flows–Year 1 in the column for October three lines above the bottom: $3,695.

To illustrate how projected cash shortages may be handled, assume that Red Jett desires to have a minimum ending cash balance of $5,000 each month. If the projected cash balance is less than this, money will be borrowed from a line of credit. If the projected balance exceeds the desired minimum, then the surplus may be used to pay back some or all of the outstanding line of credit. Most business lenders will not make loans for "odd" amounts, so as you complete Skill Module 13.1, assume that any money borrowed will be the amount of the shortage, rounded up to the next higher $1,000, but not less than $3,000.

TABLE 13.3 Illustration of the Format of a Cash Disbursements Budget

Cash Disbursements Budget Fourth Quarter 2011				
	October	November	December	4th Quarter
Cash paid to vendors				
credit card providers	88	88	88	263
sales tax paid to Texas	615	615	615	1,845
raw materials used in production	2,029	2,029	2,029	6,087
Salaries & Wages	4,141	4,141	4,141	12,423
Payroll taxes/benefits	358	358	358	1,074
Rent	1,000	1,000	1,000	3,000
Web site, marketing	100	100	100	300
Telephone	110	110	110	330
Transportation	343	343	343	1,029
Insurance	167	167	167	501
Legal & Accounting	35	35	35	105
Total cash disbursed	8,986	8,986	8,986	26,957

TABLE 13.4 Cash Budget

Cash Budget Fourth Quarter 2011				
	October	November	December	4th Quarter
Beginning cash balance	3,695	6,476	6,257	3,695
Cash receipts	8,767	8,767	8,767	26,301
Total cash available	12,462	15,243	15,024	42,730
Less cash disbursements	(8,986)	(8,986)	(8,986)	(26,957)
Forecast balance	3,476	6,257	6,039	15,772
Desired minimum balance	5,000	5,000	5,000	15,000
Excess (shortage)	(1,524)	1,257	1,039	772
Borrowings (repayments)	3,000	–	–	–
Ending Cash Balance	6,476	6,257	6,039	6,039

It is a fact that no matter how daunting, you will budget, one way or another. The budgeting process presented here is specifically designed to feed directly into your business plan. The final step in this part of business planning is to put everything together to create a complete set of pro forma financial statements that you can use for raising money, for evaluating your operations, and for managing your business. All the budgets from Chapter 12 *and* the cash budget developed here are combined at this point to make the **comprehensive budget**. (Comprehensive budgets are also often referred to as *master budgets*.) The assignment materials included in McGraw-Hill Connect provide you with a chance to practice the techniques explained in Chapter 12 and in this chapter.

comprehensive budget
Comprehensive budgets, also often referred to as *master budgets*, are sets of budgets that detail all projected receipts and spending for the budget period.

The Comprehensive Budget—the Pro Forma Cash Flow Statement

The statement of cash flows, as shown in Table 13.5, is essentially a restatement of the cash budget, but with the cash coming into your business and the cash going out of your business

TABLE 13.5 Statement of Cash Flows

Cash Flows for the Fourth Quarter 2011	
Cash received from customers	26,301
Cash paid to vendors	
credit card providers	263
sales tax paid to Texas	1,845
raw materials used in production	6,087
Salaries & Wages	12,423
Payroll taxes/benefits	1,074
Rent	3,000
Web site, marketing	300
Telephone	330
Transportation	1,029
Insurance	501
Legal & Accounting	105
Net cash flows from operations	(656)
Cash flow from investing activities	
Purchase of Equipment	–
Cash flow from financing activities	
Investment by owners	–
Cash received from borrowing	3,000
Cash paid on loans	
Net cash flow from long-term financing activities	3,000
Beginning cash	3,695
Net cash increase (decrease)	2,344
Ending cash	6,039

A Comprehensive Budget

SKILL MODULE 13.1

Choose a business that you are interested in owning.

1. Prepare a complete list of the costs of operating this business. To determine the costs of your selected business, examine sources such as *Entrepreneur* magazine's start-up manuals (**https://bookstore.entrepreneur.com/product-category/starting-a-business/startup-guides/**) or perform a Google search for the term "business start-up guide" for other books, manuals, and websites. You may also obtain cost information from the Internal Revenue Service, the Small Business Administration, and the audit guides published by the American Institute of Certified Public Accountants (AICPA), franchisers, and industry organizations.
2. Place each cost that you identify into one of the following categories: fixed cost, variable cost, or mixed cost. (Remember: Variable costs are costs that vary with changes in sales or production.)
3. From industry sources, determine what the customary payment terms are from vendors and what terms, if any, your business will be expected to provide to customers.
4. Use this cost information to produce a comprehensive budget, based on the budgeting examples in this chapter.
5. From the cash budget that you have prepared, identify any cash flow shortages. Prepare a plan to deal with the expected shortages.

The solution to this skill module will vary among students.

placed into the categories of cash from operations, cash from investing, and cash from financing. The format illustrated here is the direct method, which is the format now required by GAAP. An example of the indirect method can be found in any of the Intermediate Accounting textbooks, such as McGraw-Hill's *Intermediate Accounting* by David Spiceland et al.

Notice also that although we did the budgeting process to the nearest $1, when pro forma statements are prepared, they are usually stated with an accuracy no greater than $100 dollar amounts. In fact, for businesses that gross in excess of $10 million per year, pro forma amounts are usually rounded to the nearest $1,000. (Showing the numbers to the nearest $1 makes it easier for you to master these techniques.)

This completes the discussion of budgeting for planning and control purposes. The set of budgets created in Chapter 12 and here in Chapter 13 make up the financial projections that outside investors expect from entrepreneurs seeking funding. If you follow the examples given, you will increase the accuracy of your pro forma statements while at the same time making the task of preparing them much easier.

The spreadsheets that were used to prepare the budget examples are available to your instructor to assign for you to use as models to develop other planning spreadsheets appropriate for businesses other than retail. Skill Module 13.1 will let you practice the entire budgeting process, modeling on the example we have provided here.

Managing Cash Flows

LO **13-4** Explain the basics of how cash flows can be kept secured.

Why Worry about Managing Cash Flows?

Once you are the owner of a small business, you will find that suppliers, vendors, employees, and lenders all demand payment in cash. Because of this, a small business must have easy access to cash to be able to remain viable. Cash can come from only three sources: (1) Cash can be obtained by selling the products and services of the business and collecting cash from customers. This is called *cash flow from operations.* (2) Cash can be obtained from investments the business has made such as stocks, bonds, land, buildings, or equipment. This is *cash flow from investing.* (3) Finally, a business may obtain cash through financing. Financing may be in the form of cash donated to the business in return for ownership or in the form of money borrowed from other entities.

To ensure that the cash your business needs is available when the business needs it, you, the owner, must be proactive. If you wait until your business has a cash shortage, you very well may find that it is too late to cope with the shortage. Your business will fail as have innumerable other small businesses that neglected to arrange ready sources of cash before the cash was needed.

Simply put, it is absolutely essential for business success that you stay on top of your cash flows. You really should plan continuously for the cash to be received and the cash to be paid out. A smart owner of a small business will review cash flow requirements once each week at the minimum.

In this section we will look at control methods you should implement to be sure that the cash you collect from customers is properly recorded and is kept safe from theft.

Protecting Cash from Being Stolen

Cash is the most desired asset and easiest asset to steal from your business. While there is some chance that theft will be committed by criminals coming into your business carrying a gun, the vast majority of business theft is committed by employees. This is so for two reasons. First, employees have access to cash in the course of doing their jobs. Second, employees are often in a position to be able to hide the theft.

According to the U.S. Chamber of Commerce,[13] the most common means by which employees steal cash from their employers are through misappropriations of cash accomplished using one of three categories of theft: (1) larceny and embezzlement, which are methods employees use to steal cash after it has been received and recorded in your books; (2) skimming, which is the practice of "pocketing" money from customers and hiding the theft by not recording the sale; and (3) phony disbursements, which are most commonly accomplished by making fake invoices that are subsequently paid by your ordinary cash disbursement procedure. There are many variations on these broad categories, including such practices as creating "phantom employees," whose paychecks go to the accounts of the thieves, tampering with legitimately processed checks, and conducting billing scams.

Of these three broad categories, skimming is the most prevalent. Embezzlement, however, is the means by which the greatest dollar loss occurs. Partly, this is because of the nature of the transactions used in each fraud. Skimming is usually done at the point of sale: a bartender who "forgets" to enter a sale into the register or a salesclerk who scans the code for a $20 jacket while checking out a $500 leather coat for a confederate. Embezzlement, on the other hand, usually happens in your accounting office. Any single skimming incident is limited to the sales amount. A crooked accountant can steal the entire value of your business.

To protect your business from having its cash drained by employees, you need to take specific steps, the first and most important of which is to hire honest and ethical people into your business. Do thorough preemployment background checks including criminal records, previous employer, credit history, official transcripts from colleges, and references. The second and also most important thing is to develop and enforce a system of effective internal control over which employees may handle cash and which employees may account for cash.

When forensic accountants investigate cases of employee embezzlement and theft, they always find that (1) control over cash receipts and disbursements is lax, and (2) a trusted employee is allowed to receive and disburse cash while simultaneously keeping records of the transactions. In almost every case, the loss could have been prevented by having effective separation of duties: making sure that the employee who actually handles the cash is a different employee that the one who has responsibility for recording the cash inflows and outflows.

Other steps you should take are:

- Run credit checks periodically on all employees who have material access to your finances.
- Identify opportunities employees have to steal from you. Examine every aspect of how money flows into and out of your business, and evaluate the inherent risks.
- Investigate budget variances carefully.

- Have a formal audit conducted, including your internal and external control procedures.
- Implement a formal statement of ethics policies.
- Provide coaching, counseling, and training to employees to ensure they understand the ethical standards set for your business.
- Terminate the employment of those who fail to achieve standards within a reasonable time.
- Provide education about the economics of your business to employees. Be sure each understands that the theft of a single dollar means that you will have to increase sales by $10, just to recover the value of the theft.

Preventing Cash Flow Problems

LO 13-5 Implement strategies for coping with cash flow problems.

Benjamin Franklin's adage "An ounce of prevention is worth a pound of cure" truly describes the best way to manage cash flows in a business. It is much easier to prevent such problems than to solve them once they begin.

Several techniques can help prevent getting into a cash flow problem in the first place. The best prevention is attending to and understanding your business's operations–its patterns of generating cash inflows and outflows–which should help you maintain an accurate forecast of cash needs. However, planning alone usually is not sufficient to ensure that cash flow needs are met. The assumptions made may be incorrect. The economy may suffer an unforeseen shock, such as a natural disaster, war, or energy shortages. Fashions and preferences change, often in unexpected and unpredictable ways. As airline pilots often point out, "Careful planning is no substitute for full fuel tanks."

Steps to Take for Effective Cash Flow Management

1. Review your cash needs on a set schedule.

Set aside a specific day and time each week during which you will examine your accounting records and make a list of all cash flows that will occur during the upcoming week. This review is fairly easy to do, if you are using a computerized accounting system. You need only have the system produce an accounts receivable report that lists those accounts that will become due in the next week and those accounts that are currently past their due dates. This report will give you insight into the amounts that should be received. Next, you need to produce an accounts payable report, again listing the amounts that will become due in the next week, and those accounts that are currently due, but not yet paid. The sum of these payables is an important indicator of how much cash will be needed immediately.

The second part of the cash flow report consists of reviewing any recurring payments that you receive such as payments for product you have leased to customers and any principle and interest on product that you have sold to customers on credit. Then you need to include regular payments that you must make such as wages, rent, submissions of taxes collected (employment taxes, sales tax collected, etc.).

2. Arrange a business line of credit or revolving loan before you need it.

It is a rare small business that never experiences cash shortages. So, knowing the likelihood that this will happen, you should act before you have a shortage. If you have an established relationship with a bank, sit down with the business loan officer and explain what you want and why you are seeking it now. It should be no surprise if you discover that the banker is not only sympathetic to your need, but is readily willing to help you make the necessary arrangements.

If for some reason you cannot arrange for a revolving loan or a line of credit at your bank, you should consider setting up an arrangement with a factoring company that will allow you draw funds, with the loan being collateralized with your accounts receivable or your inventory.

3. Obtain a business credit card.

As is shown in Exhibit 13.1, almost two-thirds of small businesses rely on credit cards to cope with cash shortages. Credit cards offer several features that can be very valuable to small business other than just readily available credit. Many business credit cards provide statements that

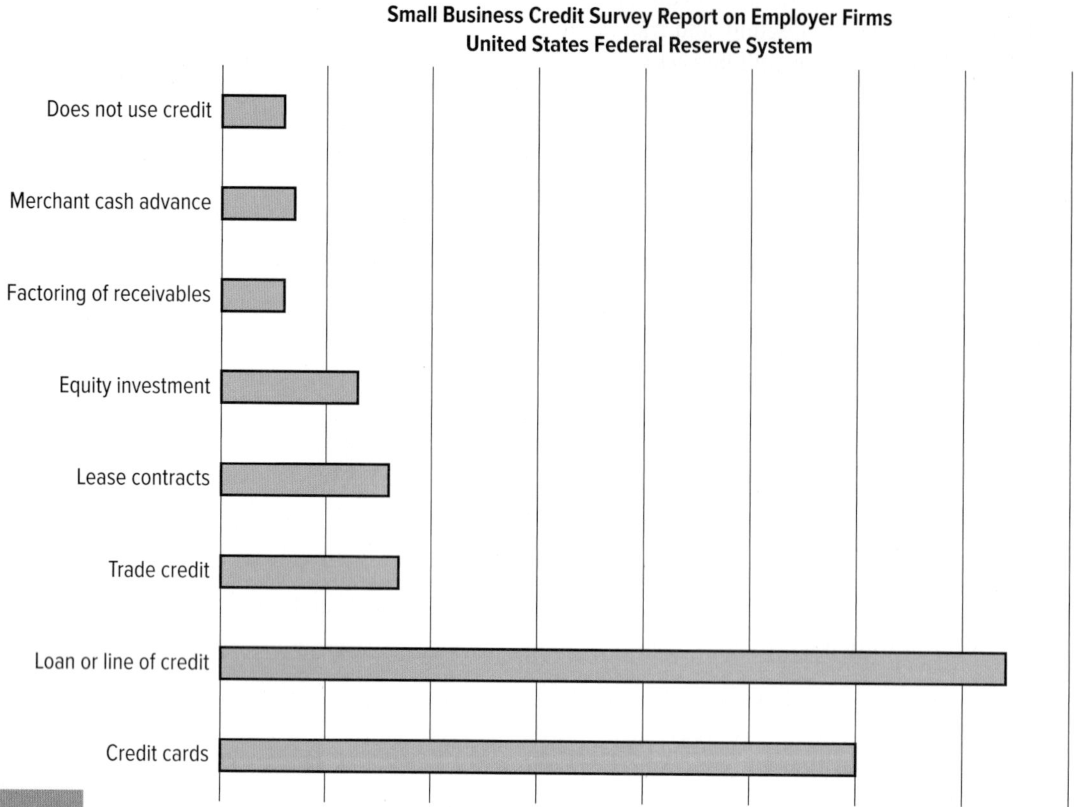

EXHIBIT 13.1

Source: Data from Jessica Battisto, Mels de Zeeuw, Claire Kramer Mills, Scott Lieberman, and Ann Marie Wiersch, *Small Business Credit Survey, Federal Reserve Banks of Atlanta, 2017*, www.fedsmallbusiness.org/medialibrary/FedSmallBusiness/files/2018/SBCS-Employer-Firms-Report.pdf (accessed July 13, 2019).

are highly detailed, showing what was purchased, where it was purchased, and the expense category to which the item belongs. Some even have apps that allow automatic downloading of the statements into small business accounting systems.

4. Collect your receivables–do not become your customers' interest-free bank.

Good sense will tell you that you provide credit only to those customers who will actually pay what they owe. If you allow a customer to take your product for a promise to pay and you do not believe that that customer actually will pay, then you have given a gift, not made a sale! Before you give credit to any customer, establish the credit terms. State exactly when the payment will be due and what late fees or penalties will be assessed if that date is missed. Document each part of the transaction and be sure that you have your customer's signature on all sales agreements, contracts, and delivery receipts.

Offer discounts for early payment. This is a proven incentive for many businesses to pay promptly. Of course, you should do the math and be sure that the discount you offer does not cost you more than the value of getting paid more quickly. (Look to the Learn More Online box for more about this topic.)

Set up and use a billing system. Be sure to send a reminder approximately a week before the bill is due. When a customer misses the due date, send a billing statement. If your customer does not respond to the statement, call the customer and politely ask for payment. Simply asking demonstrates that the payment is important to you and many times the customer will react by paying immediately.

5. Plan and schedule your payments.

This is actually part of the cash budgeting process, which is discussed in this chapter in the section "Planning Cash Needs." Planning to make payments when you know the cash will be available relieves the stress of unexpected cash demands. Also if you have a cash budget and if you regularly compare actual spending to the budgeted spending that will help keep your business from overspending which leads to cash shortfalls.

Unless a vendor offers a significant discount for early payment, examine the credit agreement to determine the last day that payment may be made without incurring a penalty or harming the business relationship with the vendor.

6. Use online collections and payments.

Have your bank make payments for you and receive payments for you through direct bank transfers. These transactions are less expensive than the process of making paper checks. They also offer the advantage of the record keeping and reporting done by the bank. And, finally, they reduce the time between making and receiving payment to very near zero. If your customer pays you with a paper check, you may have to wait up to a full business week before the money is actually available to you. With a direct transfer, once the transaction is recorded, you have full access to the money.

Techniques to Increase Cash Inflows

There are several simple methods that can be used to increase the amount of cash flows while simultaneously reducing the effects of irregular or seasonal patterns of receipts. Five proven techniques are:

- Taking deposits and progress payments.
- Offering discounts for prompt payment.
- Asking for your money.
- Taking on noncore paying projects.
- Factoring receivables.

Deposits and progress payments can greatly smooth the receipt of cash in businesses which otherwise have highly variable levels of cash flows. For example, many businesses that involve summer activities, such as water parks, are open as few as 100 days per year. However, many costs, such as rent, taxes, maintenance, security, and utilities, continue year-round. These types of businesses often choose to obtain cash flow during the closed season by selling season tickets or other forms of advance purchase.[14] Progress payments are payments that are received from your customer as you achieve predetermined goals in a lengthy project. Progress payments are very common in the construction industry where individual projects may take years to complete.

deposits and progress payments
Cash payments received before product is completed or delivered.

Requiring deposits is advisable in many kinds of businesses in which the process to fulfill a contract with a customer requires significant amounts of time or additional capital. Examples of this type of business are building contractors, consultants, and manufacturers of custom machinery.

Discounts for prompt payment will often motivate your customers to make payments in a timely manner. It is common for wholesale suppliers to offer their customers terms of a 2 percent discount for payment within 5 to 10 working days. You must carefully balance the cost of providing the discount with the cost of obtaining needed cash from other sources.[15] The cost of a discount for prompt payment is deceiving. Consider that you are operating a wholesale distributorship of plumbing supplies, with an average margin on sales of 22 percent, and you provide a 2 percent discount for prompt payment. A customer purchases $100 of supplies on account. What is the effect on your profitability? Your profit margin will decline from $22 to $20, a decline in gross margin of 9.1 percent. (See Table 13.6.)

discounts for prompt payment
A reduction in sales price provided to credit customers for paying outstanding amounts in a timely manner.

Asking for your money is at once the most simple and the most effective way to obtain payment from customers.[16] Surprisingly, many owners and managers of small businesses are loath to call customers and request that they pay what they owe. However, you will find that few, if any, businesspeople will be offended by a polite phone call requesting payment. This is especially true of the owners and managers of small businesses who have encountered cash flow difficulties themselves. Very often, a request for prompt payment will be honored, if possible. Of course,

TABLE 13.6 Effect of Prompt Payment Discounts on Gross Margin

Gross sales amount	$100.00
Less cost of goods sold	78.00
Gross margin	22.00
Less prompt pay discount of 2 percent	2.00
Net margin	$ 20.00
Percentage reduction in margin ($2/$22)	9.1%

there is an implied obligation that, if at some time in the future the customers encounter cash flow problems, you will also be understanding and cooperative, helping them through their own rough spot.

noncore projects
Revenue-producing tasks and activities related to, but not part of, the primary strategy of a business.

Taking on **noncore projects** can often provide desperately needed cash during slow business periods. Possibilities are limited only by your imagination. Many sign installers, during slow times in early spring, often will send a crane truck and operator to hoist air-conditioning and other equipment onto the roofs of buildings. Bill Millers's Barbecue of San Antonio, Texas, for a fee, deep-fries whole turkeys for customers during the slow restaurant periods immediately preceding Thanksgiving and Christmas. Rowan Oak House B&B in Salisbury, North Carolina, as do many bed and breakfasts during their slow seasons, sells "murder mystery weekends" that include lodging, breakfast, dinner, and a role-playing mystery game, complete with costumes and props.

Despite the attraction of picking up immediate revenues by taking on a project that is outside the core competencies of your business, the practice is often risky and in extreme cases can result in lessened sales in the core business. The Thoughtful Entrepreneur illustrates this disadvantage.

THE THOUGHTFUL ENTREPRENEUR

DANGERS OF TAKING ON NONCORE BUSINESS PROJECTS

There are several caveats to be considered in taking on noncore projects:

- First, any noncore project should be such that it can be completed in a reasonable time.
- Second, the project should be clearly specified, with clearly defined outcomes or stopping points.
- Third, no noncore project should be taken solely for the purpose of "churning dollars."

Noncore projects can sometimes provide desperately needed cash. However, the time for such projects is taken from time that otherwise would be used for your core business. When the environment for the core business improves, noncore projects can become very costly distractions.

Specifying outcomes and stopping points prevents making noncore projects into permanent business, which then competes for limited resources with the core business.

It is always tempting, when faced with a need for cash, to offer deep discounts to gain cash inflows. This is counterproductive, however, for two reasons: (1) discounting in either your core or in an associated business devalues your product or service, which will limit the price that can be charged when conditions improve; and (2) accepting business that does not provide an adequate margin reduces profitability for the entire year, which can negatively affect your ability to arrange financing and investment when business conditions improve and additional funding is needed for growth.

THE THOUGHTFUL ENTREPRENEUR

EFFECT OF BORROWING AGAINST YOUR RECEIVABLES

It is tempting to use your receivables to obtain immediate cash, but doing so is expensive. Suppose your business has $100,000 in accounts receivable. If you factor these receivables, you will obtain an immediate $75,000. Now suppose a customer who owes $10,000 pays the full amount. The factor will deduct 75 percent in repayment plus 5 percent of the gross payment amount. You will receive the remaining $2,000:

Customer payment	$10,000
Repayment to factor	(7,500)
5% factor fee	(500)
Balance received	2,000

If your factored receivables are all collected within 90 days, you will have paid $5,000 to receive $75,000 immediately plus $20,000 over three months, a total of $95,000. On an annual basis, this is essentially the same as paying 22 percent interest.

factoring receivables Borrowing money secured by a firm's accounts receivable.

Factoring receivables should be considered only if other, less expensive methods to increase cash flows have not been sufficient.[17] Factoring is a method of borrowing against receivables. The factor will usually lend between 75 and 80 percent of the amount of uncollected receivables. As the receivables are collected, the factor deducts a proportional principal amount and remits the remainder, less its fee, typically 5 percent of the gross receivables, to the business.[18]

To factor your receivables, your customers must have good credit ratings. Your credit rating is irrelevant because it is the customers who pay the factor, not you. To provide for losses on uncollectible accounts, some factors either hold back some of the remittances or charge back any uncollected amounts at the end of a specified contract period.

The Thoughtful Entrepreneur illustrates the cost of borrowing against your receivables (factoring).

Techniques to Decrease Cash Outflows

Decreasing cash outflows is as important as increasing cash inflows. Regardless of how much money you're making, conserving cash is essential. All companies have certain costs that cannot be avoided and cannot be financed. Examples of unavoidable cash payments include payroll, rent, utilities, and withholding taxes. If you do not have enough cash to pay your employees, keep the door open, the lights burning, and the tax collector at bay, the business will fail, no matter its potential or paper profits. As with cash inflows there are two factors of cash outflows that must be controlled: (1) the amount of cash being paid out and (2) the timing of cash being paid out.

Controlling the amount of cash being paid out is primarily a function of making good purchasing decisions and avoiding waste. By purchasing in the appropriate quantities with the appropriate quality at the appropriate times, the need to make cash payments can be aligned with the receipt of cash, to the extent that the nature of the business allows.

Every business that maintains inventory has an optimal level that minimizes the total cost of (1) carrying inventory, (2) processing orders, and (3) losing sales due to being out of stock. The optimum level of many other business resources can similarly be determined. Setting reasonable standards and carefully monitoring usage and stocking levels reduce the amount of cash required for these essential business resources while maximizing revenues. The determination of optimum stocking levels is fully discussed in Appendix A of Chapter 15.

Waste also affects cash outflow. Resources that are wasted represent cash that was paid out with no economic benefit. Almost any resource can be wasted. You can waste the time of your employees by requiring procedures such as record keeping and reporting that are not useful for management. You can waste primary materials by inefficient cutting and by allowing materials to spoil, break, or be stolen. You can waste rent by maintaining space that does not produce revenue. The list of potential waste is endless.

Most of us become so accustomed to our ways of doing business that we often do not recognize waste when we see it. For years, restaurants paid people to haul away old cooking oils and grease. If there was no one to haul the oil, it was often dumped onto gravel parking lots or poured into solid waste dumps. The oil was indeed *scrap*–it had no further economic use in the restaurant. The oil was not *waste*, however, until it was poured out. There was an economically valuable use for the oil in making cosmetics, animal feed, paint, and chemicals. Today, the waste oil from restaurants and commercial food manufacturers is so valuable that not only is there an active market for waste oil, but organized bandits often steal the oil at night. Oil that once was considered trash is today a significant source of revenue.

It takes insight into your particular business to determine what constitutes waste.[19] Suppose you have a sizable store of the leftovers from cutting plywood to make your product. It is certain that the plywood pieces are scrap. But are they waste? To determine if these odd pieces of wood are waste, you need to find out (1) if there is a cutting pattern that will reduce the amount of leftover wood; (2) if you cannot reduce the amount of scrap, is there an economically valuable use for it; and (3) what it is costing you to keep the scrap pieces on hand. You may find that the wood is scrap, but the waste is the space that it occupies–space that you could otherwise put to productive use.

In addition to making wise purchasing decisions and avoiding waste of resources, there are several strategies that will provide savings in cash outflows, including:[20]

- Trade discounts.
- Noncash employee incentives.
- Use of temporary agencies.
- Consignment.
- Barter.
- Control of the timing of paying out cash.
- Negotiation of terms with suppliers.
- Timing of purchases.
- Gaming of the payment process.

Some of these should be familiar because they are mentioned in the discussion of bootstrapping in Chapter 6, where bootstrapping is introduced as a way to make possible a part-time business operating on a very limited budget. But the ideas of bootstrapping, as we can see below, also apply to more established kinds of small businesses.

trade discounts
Percentage discounts from gross invoice amounts provided to encourage prompt payment.

Trade discounts are given by suppliers and vendors to encourage customers to make timely payments on account. In effect, you are borrowing from the vendor at the discount rate for the number of days that you may wait to pay after the cutoff date for receiving the discount. The rule of thumb for trade discounts is that you should always capture discounts of 1 percent or greater, if the billing period is less than 30 days.

If the supplier provides payment terms exceeding 30 days, then you must perform a quick analysis to determine whether taking the discount or delaying payment provides the greater value. To decide whether to take the discount, compare the annual effective interest rate of the discount to your cost of borrowing from other sources. Then choose the one with the lower annual effective rate.

The Thoughtful Entrepreneur will guide you through the process of determining the value of accepting or refusing a vendor's offer of a prompt-payment discount.

noncash incentives
Rewards that do not require payment of cash, such as stock options, compensating time off, or added vacation days.

Noncash incentives for employees is the most widely used technique to reduce the amount of cash that must be paid out of the business. The most common such incentive is to grant stock options, which give the employee the right to purchase company stock at a fixed price in the future. The hope of the employee is that the stock will go up significantly in price and, that upon

THE THOUGHTFUL ENTREPRENEUR

SHOULD I TAKE A SUPPLIER'S DISCOUNT FOR PAYMENT?

Assume that Red Jett Sweets can borrow from the bank at 11 percent. The supplier of raw materials for the cupcakes provides credit terms at a 1 percent discount, if paid within 10 days of the receipt of the invoice, and the full amount must be paid in 30 days. To see if the heuristic ("take any discount of 1 percent or greater when the payment period is 30 or fewer days") holds in this case, calculate the annual effective interest rate:

Annual effective rate = Discount/(100% – discount) × 365/(Payment period – Discount period)

AER = 0.01/(1.00 – 0.01) × 365/(30 – 10)

AER = 0.01/0.99 × 365/(20)

AER = 0.01010101 × 18.25

AER = 18.43%

Yes, indeed, the heuristic holds. 18.43 percent is much greater than is 11 percent. Red Jett should pay within 10 days, taking the 1 percent discount on the goods.

Suppose, however, that the vendor's terms were 1 percent discount if paid in 10 days, due in full in 45 days after receipt. If you do the same arithmetic, the result is 10.53 percent. With the more generous terms, it is better for Red Jett to delay payment to the full 45 days.

either selling or exercising the option, the employee will realize large gains. Other noncash incentives include autonomy, a chance to be creative, flexible hours, telecommuting, praise, training, career opportunities, the chance to work with (or learn about) advanced technology, responsibility, benefits packages (health, vacation, retirement, etc.), a supportive or protective culture, and even small prizes and awards.[21]

Use of temporary agencies is another way to reduce the cost of employees. If you do not need a full-time, permanent employee, agencies can provide educated, trained, and skilled workers who will work only as much as you need. It is common today for small businesses to contract with agencies to provide all sorts of temporary employees, from unskilled labor to a chief executive officer.

Consignment is the practice of accepting goods for resale without taking ownership of them and without being responsible to pay prior to their being sold. Consignment sales are the norm in the operation of art galleries. Living artists usually make an exclusive contract with a specific gallery to display their works. When a piece of art is sold, either by the gallery or by the artist, the gallery arranges for receipt of payment, delivery of the art, and guarantee of the provenance of the art, in return for a percentage of the sales price.

consignment The practice of accepting goods for resale, without taking ownership of them and without being responsible to pay prior to their being sold.

Other industries that use consignment sales include the distributors of salty snacks (potato chips, corn chips, peanuts, etc.), specialty food items, used furniture and antiques, sporting goods, and used automobiles. The advantage of receiving goods on consignment is that they remain the property of the consigner and do not have to be paid for until sold, thus matching cash receipts with cash disbursement.

Barter is the practice of trading goods and services without the use of money. For example, an accountant may trade accounting services to a sign company in return for the sign company manufacturing and installing a sign at the accountant's place of business. Barter alleviates the need for cash by trading good for good, service for service, or service for good. Barter is legal in the United States and is widely practiced among small businesses.[22] Although money is not used in the transaction, the legislature, the IRS, and the courts have consistently ruled that barter is a taxable transaction, except in case of trades of "like-kind" goods or services. In other words, you may trade real estate for real estate, or machinery for machinery without creating a taxable transaction. However, if you trade your airplane for real estate or if you use any amount of money in the trade, the transaction is subject to tax.

barter The practice of trading goods and services without the use of money.

Because of the provision for tax-free treatment of like-kind trades, barter transactions are susceptible to misuse to avoid paying taxes. As a result, the rules for reporting barter transactions are restrictive and quite complex. Misuse of barter is usually considered fraud by the IRS and can lead to criminal penalties.

There are numerous services, organizations, and websites that facilitate barter transactions. For example, the Open Directory Project (http://odp.org/Business/International Business and Trade/Barter) lists over 100 online barter clubs, organizations, brokers, exchanges, and for-profit companies that support barter. There are even trade associations for the barter industry such as the International Reciprocal Trade Association (www.irta.com) or the National Association of Trade Exchanges (https://www.natebarter.com/).

Controlling the timing of paying out cash can be accomplished through a number of methods. The strategy is not to unnecessarily delay paying, but to arrange payment schedules in such a way that due dates match the times when cash is available.

Negotiating terms with suppliers is a common, acceptable method for controlling when payment must be made for goods and services. For example, many building contractors who build single-family houses expect to complete and sell a house in a 90-day period. Most builders negotiate with primary suppliers such as lumberyards and plumbing wholesalers to finance the materials needed to build a house. The suppliers are protected by having a lien on the house that must be paid before title of the house can be passed to the buyer.

Similar arrangements are made to finance many types of long-term projects, as well. Often the winning bidder on a large project will make the major suppliers subcontractors who agree to accept payment when the general contractor is paid.

timing purchases
A method of controlling the timing of cash outflows that is invisible to suppliers and vendors.

Timing purchases is a method of controlling the timing of cash outflows that is invisible to suppliers and vendors. Your specific reason for placing any certain order on any certain day is not apparent. However, knowledge of the payment policies of suppliers can provide considerable leeway in when bills must be paid following delivery of goods. For example, it is common for wholesale suppliers to have payment terms that define an on-time payment as being any payment made on or before the tenth day of the month following purchase. Knowing this term, you can gain additional time to pay by delaying purchase until the first day of the month. This provides up to 41 days before payment must be made without being classified as late. Were you to purchase on the last day of the month, you would have only 10 days to make a timely payment.

gaming the payment process
Using methods to appear to be paying bills on time, when in fact payment is being delayed or avoided.

Gaming the payment process is a common, if a bit underhanded, method of controlling cash outflows. Methods range from simply not paying a bill when it is due to sending checks that you've "forgotten" to sign, to sending checks in payment and then stopping payment after the payment has been recorded, but the check has not yet cleared. Very few business owners and managers are proud of taking such measures, but most will, if promised confidentiality, admit to having done one or another in times of cash crises.

Gaming payments can be quite costly, however. You may well get away with any one of these strategies with any single vendor one time. The more often you game payment, the more certain it becomes that your business credit rating and reputation will suffer as a result. Being consistently late in payment, regardless of gaming strategies, will cause a decrease in your business's credit worthiness. It is not uncommon for suppliers and vendors to refuse to do business with customers who regularly attempt to game the process. See the Learn More Online box below for more information on discounts for prompt payment.

LEARN MORE ONLINE

Learn more about the topics above at these sites:

U.S. Small Business Administration (net 30 accounts help conserve cash flow): **www.sba.gov/blog/how-net-30-accounts-help-conserve-*business-cash-flow***

U.S. Department of Treasury (discount formula and calculator): **https://fiscal.treasury.gov/prompt-payment/calculator.html**

U.S. Department of Treasury (prompt payment FAQs): **https://fiscal.treasury.gov/prompt-payment/faqs.html**

Controlling Cash Shortages

No matter how well you plan or how well you manage your business, sooner or later you will experience a significant cash shortage. Causes of cash shortages range from the obvious, a customer fails to make an expected payment or goes out of business without paying at all, to the obscure–an economic shock, such as a plant closing, natural disaster, or political turmoil like an oil embargo or war. During a time of economic shock, you may not attain your sales goals, *and* you may not be able to collect from customers as they suffer from the same bad economy. However, many, if not all, your bills go on, demanding payments that you no longer have the money to make.

Another often overlooked cause of cash shortages is a surplus of good news: Your business has proven to be wildly successful, and sales are growing at an exponential rate. This situation is often referred to as the **growth trap**.[23] Because of increased sales, you need more labor, more materials for your product, more factory space, and more warehouse space to store completed products until they can be shipped to your customers. All this growth requires money, and lots of it. However, as discussed above, sales take time to convert into money. The product must be made and shipped before any customer will pay. If you are offering credit to customers, you will have to wait even longer to receive that payment. You are in a "trap" made by growth: Growing will produce more money, but right now you need money to grow.

growth trap
A financial crisis that is caused by a business growing faster than it can be financed.

There are numerous strategies to handle cash shortfalls, including laying off employees, slowing payments for purchases, stepping up collection efforts, selling investment securities, or using your own money. A survey of small business owners (see Figure 13.5) found that there are at least eight strategies employed by small businesses for handling money shortages. These are, in the order of their frequency of use:

1. Use personal money.
2. Borrow.
3. Adjust scheduled purchases.
4. Adjust scheduled payments.
5. Try to collect money due.
6. Sell investments.
7. Sell receivables.
8. Lay off employees.

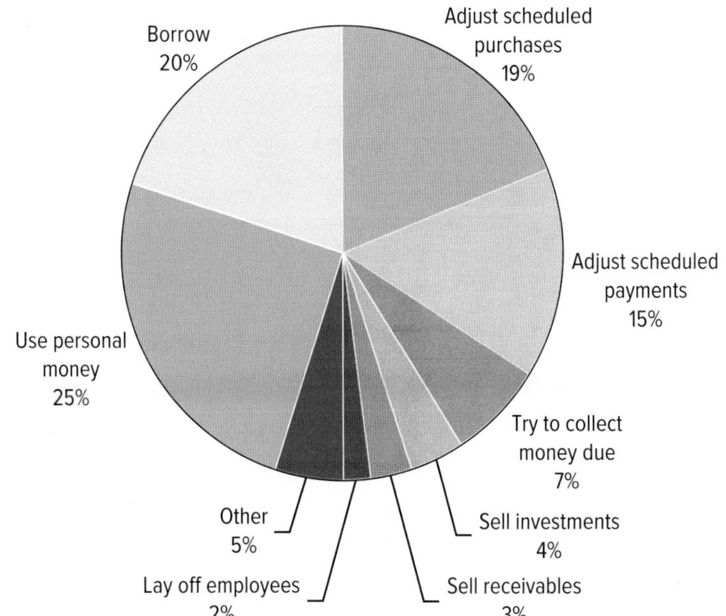

FIGURE 13.5
Eight Top Strategies for Handling Cash Shortages

Of the strategies employed, the three most common, in order of use, are (1) use personal money, (2) borrow, and (3) adjust scheduled purchases. Together, these three strategies were used by over 60 percent of the respondents to the survey.

In Review

Managing cash flows is at the same time the most important and most difficult task faced by owners and managers of small businesses. What makes it so difficult is the constant juggling act between the timing of cash coming into the business and cash going out of the business.

You now have the basics of understanding what constitutes money, cash, revenue, and expense. You know that they are related, but very different concepts. Money and cash are economic realities that are essential for business operation. Revenues and expenses are solely accounting concepts that are used primarily as tools to measure business activities.

Revenues and expenses are used to predict the amounts and timings of cash inflows and outflows primarily through the budgeting process, which starts with forecasting sales and ends in a cash budget.

Since most small businesses depend on their bank checking accounts as a money management tool, the most basic money management skill becomes a bank reconciliation. The best way to go about this is to reconcile the bank balance for items that you know about but are unknown to the bank, and adjust your book balance for those items that are reported by the bank, such as their fees. When done accurately, this type of reconciliation results in the bank and book balances reporting the identical "true" cash position of the firm as of the date of the bank statement.

There are numerous ways that both the amounts and timings of cash flows can be managed, to some extent, by the owner or manager of a small business. Some cash management techniques are very inexpensive and really a matter of common sense, such as not wasting resources and not buying anything that is not absolutely needed for the business. Other techniques incur costs in the form of interest expense and use of management time. All of the techniques discussed in this chapter are used daily by small business managers across the world.

CHAPTER SUMMARY

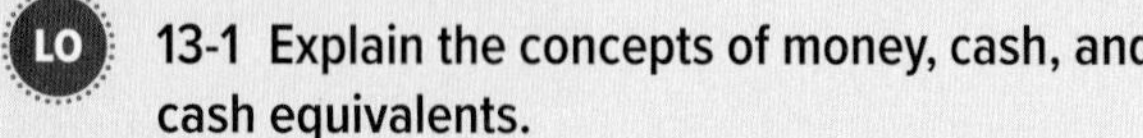

LO 13-1 Explain the concepts of money, cash, and cash equivalents.

- Money is a special type of information with three primary purposes—making exchanges, keeping track of wealth or value, and storing wealth for future use.
  - What makes money "money" is the *belief* users have about the information contained in the money.
  - Profit is not money. Rather, profits are information about money derived from the difference between two accounting items, revenue and expense.
- Cash is composed of the three forms of money that can be immediately used to make payments: currency, demand deposits, and traveler's checks.
- Cash equivalents are assets that may be turned into cash in a few hours to a few days. Cash equivalents include marketable securities, commercial paper, and debt investments that mature in less than three months.
- Currency is the most common form of cash and is composed of bills and coins that represent money.
- Demand deposits, which include checking accounts, savings accounts, and traveler's checks, are the second most common form of cash.
- Marketable securities are made up of stocks and bonds for which there is an active auction market.

LO 13-2 Explain the importance of managing your business's cash flow.

- Almost two-thirds of small businesses experience money problems because of:
  - Difficulty collecting money due from customers.
  - Seasonal variation in sales.
  - Unexpected decreases in sales.

- The cash-to-cash or operating cycle is the time it takes for a business to obtain resources, produce and sell its product, and collect cash from sales.
- Many small businesses experience difficulty or failure, because of:
    - The mismatch in time between receiving cash and spending cash.
    - The mismatch between the size of payments received and the size of payments that must be made.

LO 13-3 Plan for cash needs by developing a cash budget.

- A cash budget identifies when, how, and why cash is expected to come into the business, and when, how, and why it is expected to leave:
    - For businesses that make sales by cash or by credit card, the sales forecast *is* the cash receipts forecast.
    - If you provide credit to your customers, you will always wait some period of time for some of your money. You also, sooner or later, will have some customer who never pays.
- Cash receipts and cash disbursements budgets are used to put together a cash budget.
- All budgets are combined at this point to make the *comprehensive budget.*

LO 13-4 Explain the basics of how cash flows can kept secured.

- You should implement and enforce effective internal controls, especially enforcing separations of duties.
- You must hire ethical employees and monitor their performance.
- You should use a dropbox, or make arrangements with a bank to accept and payments from customers.
- You should review your cash balance at least once weekly.

LO 13-5 Implement strategies for coping with cash flow problems.

- The best way to prevent cash flow problems is to pay attention to and understand your business's operations and patterns of cash flows.
- Five proven techniques to even out cash flows are:
    - Taking deposits and progress payments.
    - Offering discounts for prompt payment.
    - Asking for your money.
    - Taking on noncore paying projects.
    - Factoring receivables.
- Controlling the amount of cash being paid out is primarily a result of making good purchasing decisions and avoiding waste.
- No matter how well you plan or how well you manage your business, sooner or later you will experience a significant cash shortage.
- Causes of cash shortages include a customer failing to pay or going out of business, and economic shocks, such as a natural disaster or war.
- The growth trap causes cash flow problems when the rate of growth is faster than the operating cycle.
- The three most common ways to handle cash shortages are (1) using personal money, (2) borrowing, and (3) adjusting scheduled purchases.

LO Appendix: 13-6 Reconcile bank and company book balances.

- Your business and book balances will often disagree because of differences in the timing and recording of receipts and disbursements.
- Reconciliation gives you a way to estimate the bank's available balance for the purpose of managing your cash flows.
- Regular reconciliation of bank and book balances identifies any mistakes that were made by either the bank or by your own bookkeeper—and those mistakes happen.
- Performing a reconciliation checks the accuracy of both the bank and business records, providing an accurate statement of the value of cash held by the business.
- A reconciliation lets you know about items on the bank statement that would not otherwise be included in the business's accounting records.

KEY TERMS

money, 474
cash, 474
cash equivalents, 474
currency, 474
demand deposits, 475
marketable securities, 475
commercial paper, 475
short-term debt, 475
bearer, 475
cash flow management, 475
cash-to-cash cycle, 476
operating cycle, 476
payables, 477
receivables, 477
cash budget, 479
cash receipts budget, 480
cash disbursements budget, 482
comprehensive budget, 484
deposits and progress payments, 489
discounts for prompt payment, 489
noncore projects, 490
factoring receivables, 491
trade discounts, 492
noncash incentives, 492
consignment, 493
barter, 493
timing purchases, 494
gaming the payment process, 494
growth trap, 495
reconcile, 501
company book balance, 501
bank ledger balance, 501
bank available balance, 501
clearinghouse, 501
overdraft, 502
nonsufficient funds (NSF), 502
charge back, 502

DISCUSSION QUESTIONS

1. Why is it important to plan for the amounts and timing of cash inflows and outflows?
2. What is money, and how does it differ from profits?
3. What are the primary purposes of money?
4. How do the economic and accounting definitions of cash differ?
5. What are the relationships among planning, budgeting, and forecasting?
6. Discuss five methods commonly used to increase cash inflows.
7. Discuss four methods to decrease cash outflows.
8. The text calls the practice of gaming the payment process "underhanded." What is your opinion of this common practice? Does it have any ethical implications?

EXPERIENTIAL EXERCISES

1. Make an appointment with a loan officer at your bank who handles small businesses. Conduct an interview to find out the following:
   a. Will the bank lend to small businesses, using receivables for collateral?
   b. Does the bank ever factor receivables or act as a collection agent for receivables?
2. Form a group from your classmates who completed Exercise 1. Collect your findings into a chart. Compare and contrast bank offerings. Present your findings to your class with a recommendation of which banks in your area offer the best small business support.
3. Do a Google search, using the name of your city and "online banking." Examine the sites returned to determine:
   a. How often is the account balance updated online?
   b. Are monthly account statements available online?
   c. How far back (one month, two months, one year) can you retrieve statements and transactions?

   d. Can you electronically transfer funds among your accounts?
   e. Can you electronically pay bills?
   f. Can you download bank account information into your small business computerized accounting system? If so, which systems are supported?
   g. What is the cost of online banking?

   Make a chart of your findings and report to your class.

4. Do a telephone survey of banks in your area. Ask:
   a. Do they use electronic check clearing?
   b. If they use a clearing bank to manually clear checks, ask what bank they use.
   c. Ask what the average period of float is for the bank.
   d. Ask what the bank's policy is for nonsufficient funds: Does it pay to the limit of ledger balance or to available balance?
   e. What other provisions does the bank make to help small businesses avoid having checks returned NSF?
   f. When does the bank make available funds from deposited checks?

   Write a report of your findings and present it to your class.

5. Form a group from your classmates who completed Exercise 4. Collect your findings into a chart. Compare and contrast bank offerings. Present your findings to your class with a recommendation of which banks in your area offer the best overdraft protection to small businesses.
6. Use the resources of your library and the Internet to identify five credit card processing providers. Contact each and determine the following:
   a. The cost of equipment to be able to accept credit card charges.
   b. The transaction cost, if any.
   c. The amount of discount charged for:
      i. Physically swiped card charges.
      ii. Charges accepted over the telephone.
      iii. Online charges taken on the Internet.
   d. How long does it take between accepting a credit card for payment and receiving the cash in your bank account?

   Report your finding to your class.

7. Assume that you are preparing to open a new business. You need both an on-location sign and professional accounting services. Do a web search and examine your local telephone book to find (a) a sign company and (b) an accountant who is willing to provide its product and services in a barter transaction for the product or service of your business.

MINI-CASE

BULLTUFF STOCK TRAILERS, INC.

Hal Carrier, of Bulltuff Stock Trailers, Inc., has asked you for help. In the last four months, he has had several checks written to suppliers that were refused by his bank because of nonsufficient funds. Now his main supplier, Alcoa Aluminum Supply Co., has cut off credit.

"We're sorry, Hal," Alcoa's credit officer said, "but we simply cannot keep accepting your checks. Every time one bounces, it costs us at least $100 combined in processing fees and the cost of our internal accounting. You simply will have to pay cash or bring a cashier's check for future purchases."

Hal simply cannot understand why his checks keep bouncing. "We've plenty of sales," he said, "and our customers pay pretty much as agreed. Right now, I have only one customer who is as much as 60 days past due. My accountant, Brill Yant, assures me that our cash balance never goes negative. So why are my checks bouncing?"

To try to understand Hal's problem and to advise him how to correct it, you have collected the following information about Hal's business:

1. Cash sales are 10 percent of total sales.
2. Credit card sales are 10 percent of total sales and are collected the week following the sale. The credit card provider deducts 2.5 percent of the gross amount of each credit card sale. (For example, on a $100 sale, $2.50 is deducted.)

3. Sales on account are 80 percent of all sales. All credit sales are to dealers. Terms for dealers are "30-30-30," that is, three equal payments made in each of the three months following the sale. Payments are considered late if they're not received by the tenth of the month in which they are due.
4. Direct materials, primarily aluminum, are 60 percent of the cost of building a trailer. Before credit was cut off, Bulltuff paid 30 percent on delivery and the remainder in 30 days. Now it must pay cash on delivery.
5. Total cost of direct labor is 15 percent of the cost of building a trailer. Workers are paid each Friday for work performed the previous week. Withholding and employment taxes are paid each Friday, also.
6. Variable costs combined (e.g., materials and labor) are 50 percent of gross sales. Fixed costs are *not* allocated to the cost of trailers but are expensed evenly across the year.
7. All other costs combined are treated as fixed costs, and total $1 million per year.
8. Bulltuff leases its building and equipment and has no depreciation.
9. Sales for the year were originally projected to be $2,450,000. However, given the current growth in sales, Hal now estimates that sales will be $5,000,000.
10. Sales for the first four months of the year have been:

January	$208,000
February	261,000
March	293,000
April	328,000

CASE DISCUSSION QUESTIONS

1. What is causing Hal's cash flow problems?
2. Develop a plan to address the problems.

APPENDIX

Reconciling Bank Balances with Company Book Balances

LO 13-6 Reconcile bank and company book balances.

Key to managing your daily cash flow is knowing how much cash is available to you in your bank account at that moment. Some banks report available balances only once a day, so that amount can be misleading. To get a more realistic number, you need to **reconcile** the differences between bank and book balances to know how much cash is currently available and how much will soon be available for your business needs. Most small business managers concentrate their attention on maintaining a positive book balance and assume that this means there will be an adequate available balance. However, when this assumption is not correct, it can lead to a cash flow crisis.

reconcile
An accounting process that identifies the causes of all differences between book and bank balances.

COMPANY AND BANK CASH BALANCES

The balance of the company's cash account and the balance that the bank shows for the company's account are almost always different from each other. Sometimes the difference is significant. This happens because of the difference in timing and amount of entries that are made into the business accounting program, and the actual deposits received and disbursements made by the bank.

The **company book balance** is the name given to the sum of the company's internal accounting record of all transactions that affect cash. This account includes records of all inflows of cash, such as cash from sales, receipts on receivables, and checks received from customers. The cash account also includes records of all outflows of cash, such as checks written to pay for wages, salaries, inventory, services, taxes, and so on. The difference between inflows of cash and outflows of cash is called either *company book balance*, or simply *book balance.*

company book balance
The sum of cash inflows and cash outflows recorded in the firm's accounting records.

Today it is common for many payments to be made directly to your bank from your customers or from your bank to your suppliers. These payments may be set to pay automatically. Thus, you may not know exactly when or how much is transferred by the bank. This is also true when you accept payments by credit card. The company's books will show the payment as of the day the card was swiped. The bank, however, will not receive the payment for up to three working days. Also, the payment that the bank receives will be smaller than what was swiped because of the fees charged by the credit card company.

Now let us consider the bank's side. The **bank ledger balance** is the name given to the bank's accounting system for all recognized transactions that affect the account including deposits, electronic transfers, service fees, and checks presented to the bank for payment. However, just as a company book balance may differ significantly from the actual value of cash of the firm, a bank ledger balance may vary significantly from the actual value of cash that the bank is holding for the depositor because of delays in collecting deposits and delays in making cash transfers.

bank ledger balance
The sum of deposits and withdrawals recorded in a bank's accounting records.

The key measure is called the **bank available balance**, which is the actual cash value of the account and can vary significantly from the ledger balance. The bank available balance is the amount of money that has been received from or on behalf of the customer less all amounts of money that have actually been paid out of the depositor's account by the bank. Bank policies, such as how long checks are held, or when new deposits are added to your account, determine a great deal of the difference between the two balances.

bank available balance
The sum of money that has actually been received and paid out of a depositor's account.

Deposits of cash, electronic transfers, and cash withdrawals result in immediate changes in the available balance because money has been received or disbursed by the bank. Checks, drafts, and automated **clearinghouse** payments result in receipts or disbursements of money only after some delay.

clearinghouse
An entity that processes checks and electronic fund transfers for banks and other financial organizations.

overdraft
A negative balance in a depositor's bank account.

nonsufficient funds (NSF)
A situation that occurs when a check is returned to a depositor because the writer of the check did not have a bank available balance equal to or greater than the amount of the check.

charge back
A reduction in the bank account of a merchant by a credit card company.

Banks differ in how the ledger balance and available balance are used. Some banks will allow established customers to **overdraft** their accounts by paying a check when the available balance is not sufficient to cover the check amount, although the ledger balance is.

The process of reconciling bank balance and book balances is quite simple. There are only two reasons why the balances differ:

1. The bank knows information about your account that you cannot know until the bank tells you.
2. You know information about your account that the bank cannot know, because relevant transactions have not yet reached the bank.

Information that the bank knows about your account that you do not know includes (1) the amount of service charges taken from your account, (2) the amount of any direct payments made to your account by your customers, (3) the amount of any interest received or charged, and (4) the amount of any checks that were returned because of **nonsufficient funds (NSF)**.

Information that you know about your account that the bank does not know includes (1) the number and value of checks that you have written and mailed but that have not been received by the bank, and (2) deposits that you have mailed or made after bank closing.

The process of reconciling the bank and book balances is, therefore, a two-step process:

1. Add (subtract) to the bank balance those things that you know about your account that the bank does not know.
2. Add (subtract) to your book balance those things that the bank knows about your account that you do not know until you receive the bank statement.

When this is done the *corrected* bank balance and the *corrected* book balance will be identical.

Accepting payments by credit card causes significant differences between the bank and book balances for three reasons:

- Your business will record the gross amount of each credit card sale, while the credit card service provider will deposit to your account the sale amount less the credit card service fee.
- Your business will show the amount of the sale deposited on the date of the sale, while the service provider will take up to three working days to actually make the deposit to your account.
- Credit card clearing services also will reduce the amount deposited, or will **charge back** the amount, removing it from the business's account in the event of fraud or customer challenge.

Similar patterns of the timing and the amounts of various deposits, fees, and transfers exist for other electronic transactions. A bank may accept payment, charge a handling fee, and deposit only the net amount, or it may deposit the gross amount and show a separate charge for handling fees. Regardless, the use of electronic payment systems, of all types, creates significant differences between bank and book balances.

Why go to all this trouble? Because reconciling differences in the bank and book balances serves four purposes:

- Reconciliation gives you a way to estimate the bank's available balance for the purpose of managing your cash flows.
- Regular reconciliation of bank and book balances identifies any mistakes that were made by either the bank or by your own bookkeeper–and those mistakes happen.
- Performing a reconciliation checks the accuracy of both the bank and business records, providing an accurate statement of the value of cash held by the business.
- A reconciliation lets you know about items on the bank statement that would not otherwise be included in the business's accounting records.

CHAPTER

14

Small Business Finance: Using Equity, Debt, and Gifts

● While still a college student, Ben Jackson got the idea for a business app that he believed could be developed into a profitable business.

Only problem—he had neither the technical skill necessary to write the app, nor the capital needed to pay for having it developed by others.

Regardless, with a partner (and over his parents' objections) after graduation he worked full time to create a proof of concept of the idea. He also began the task of finding a programmer to develop his app. He soon realized, however, that he was going to need lots of money to make his dream into a reality.

Bungii.com

LEARNING OBJECTIVES

After you complete this chapter, you will be able to:

LO 14-1 Describe the three types of capital financing and their costs and trade-offs.

LO 14-2 Explain the characteristics of a business that determine its ability to raise capital.

LO 14-3 Explain which type of financing is best for your business.

LO 14-4 Describe the differing needs for financial management at each stage of business life.

Focus on Small Business: Bungii—a Pickup Truck on Demand

Quick—where will the next "big thing" tech business be started? What if we had asked you that in 2014? What would your answer have been?

Most likely, you would have answered Silicon Valley or Austin, Texas, or maybe even Cambridge, Massachusetts, or Shanghai, China. You certainly would not have picked a small town in the 35th most populous state in the nation.

Well, you would have been wrong.

Did you even consider that the next-big-thing business got its start in Kansas?

It did; and not in Wichita, home of Learjet; Olathe, home of Garmin GPS systems; or Lawrence, home of Kansas University. Nope, the next big thing got its start in Manhattan, Kansas, at Kansas State University (K-State), home of the Kansas Wildcats Big 12 Conference basketball team.

Still not sold on Manhattan, Kansas, the "Little Apple"? I'll give you a quick rundown.

Manhattan, Kansas, is a city of about 55,000 people (a fifth of which are students at K-State) located in the northeastern corner of the state. The city was founded in 1855 by settlers sponsored by the New England Emigrant Aid Company. Because of its relatively remote location from Missouri (120 miles west of Kansas City, Missouri, and 90 miles south of the Nebraska state line) and its proximity to Fort Riley (only 8 miles away) the town was spared the violence of the Civil War.

Kansas State University was founded there in 1863 as a land-grant college and was the first institution of higher learning in the state. Today K-State is one of the top research universities in the nation.[1]

So maybe it should be no surprise that in 2014, a K-State marketing student had a flash of inspiration that has led to one of the recent entrepreneurial successes. As Ben Jackson told Matt DeCoursey and Matt Watson on their podcast[2] in 2017, the idea came from Ben's experience of being leaned on by friends to help them with moving some bulky furniture.

After spending a full day helping four college friends by donating his black 1999 Ford Ranger pickup truck and his time, Ben found himself lying awake that evening feeling somewhat put upon. "I'd like to consider myself a nice guy," he said, but went on to say that doing these tasks for free left him tired, sore, and feeling put-upon.

The next day as class began he told his story to a casual friend, Harrison Proffitt (his real name; we couldn't make this up). Harrison considered what Ben had told him, and then leaned across the aisle and said, "Let's start a business."[3] When Ben and Harrison walked out of class that day, the idea that would become **Bungii.com** had been conceived.

The idea? As Ben said in the podcast,[4] "We've been compared to popular ride-sharing apps. . . . But instead of moving people, we move stuff."

Now, the main problem was that neither of them had the money nor the technical skills necessary to turn this idea into a real business. So they began to develop a business plan with the idea of raising capital. They entered their business plan in the K-State Launch Competition, where they took first place with an award of $5,000 in the fall of 2015. With this infusion of capital, the partners began trying to develop an app on which the business would run. Their first effort was to try to write an app themselves. Once they realized the scope of knowledge and skills needed for this task, they decided to turn to acquaintances who already had the necessary skills. This, however, also proved to be unworkable, so next they turned to a programming company located in India. After about six months of dealing with the Indian shop, they realized that the business could not be bootstrapped, given their own resources. They would simply have to raise enough capital to pay for the development.

Again, Ben had a serendipitous moment. As he walked from class during his final semester at K-State, he noticed that the entryway of the College of Business building had engraved marble plaques. On these plaques were the names of folks who had donated $250,000 or more to the college. He quickly photographed the names with his smartphone. For the next several days, Ben and Harrison found contact information on the Internet and then asked the donors for appointments, stressing the K-State connection.

They succeeded in raising about $500,000, and Bungii was finally on its way.

In the fall of 2016 the business relocated to Overland Park, Kansas, a suburb of Kansas City, Missouri, and the app was made live. Success was not instantaneous, but succeed they did through a feet-on-the-ground marketing effort made mostly to furniture companies that did not have their own delivery trucks.

Of course, financing for **Bungii.com** does not end here. With success and the desire for growth comes ever more demand for capital. Ben and Harrison received another grant, this time in the amount of $50,000 from the LaunchKC competition of the Economic Development Corp. of Kansas City.[5] But even this was not enough. So in the winter of 2017 they decided on a Series A round of funding to qualified investors. In January 2018 the partners announced that they had not only met their goal of $2 million in equity funding, but that they had surpassed it by more than 50 percent, having closed the funding with more than $3 million.[6]

DISCUSSION QUESTIONS

1. How is funding received from grants different from funding received through equity placements?
2. Why do you suppose that Ben and Harrison decided not to attempt to borrow the capital they needed for start-up?
3. What is your opinion of Ben and Harrison's using the list of donors engraved on the wall of the College of Business to find investors?
4. Why did Ben and Harrison choose to follow a different route to funding than the common reliance on friends, family, and fools?

LO **14-1** Describe the three types of capital financing and their costs and trade-offs.

Sources of Financing for Small Businesses

Getting the money to start or grow a business seems like one of the greatest challenges, but in reality most people who really make the effort, do ultimately find the means to get their business going. There are two reasons for this. First, financing is often easier than people think because

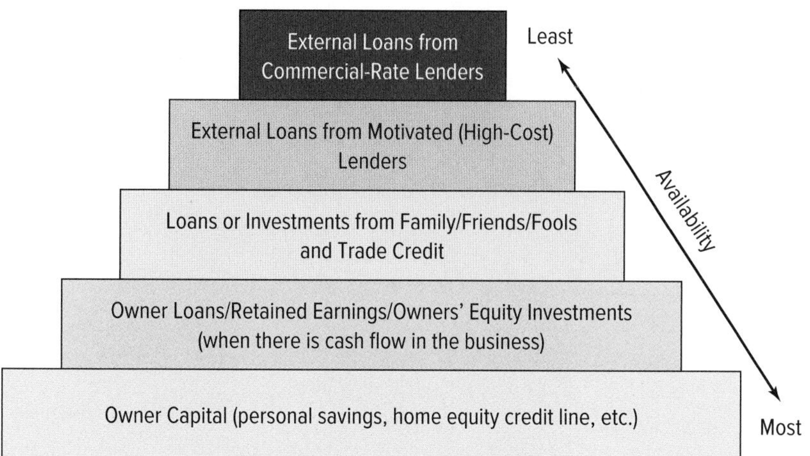

FIGURE 14.1

The Pecking Order of Funding Sources for New Firms

Sources: Adapted from Charles Ou and George W. Haynes, "Uses of Equity Capital by Small Firms—Findings from the Surveys of Small Business Finances (for 1993 & 1998)." Presented at the 14th Annual Conference on Entrepreneurial Finance and Business Ventures at De Paul University, Chicago, IL, April 30–May 2, 2003, www.sba.gov/advo/stats/wkp03co.pdf; and from correspondence with Dr. Ou.

most of us have many assets and financial resources that we take for granted. Second, the range of financing resources available to us is so varied that few people just starting out in business know more than a fraction of the options available to them. The more you learn about your personal finances and your options for financing, the greater your chances of finding the financing you need to start your business.

However, getting money to start is only the tip of the iceberg of finance for small businesses. Once you have started your business, you must continually work to keep up a constant flow of money and capital assets to meet the strategic and operating goals of your business. Constant, careful management of money and other capital resources is essential for success throughout the existence of any business. A business's needs for financial management change as the business develops, as economic conditions vary, and as your needs and goals change. Although the details of financial management are unique to each business, there are patterns that can be seen as a business develops from start-up to exit. We examine these patterns, first getting money for start-up and growth and second using strategic financial management to reach your goals.

Where *does* financing come from for most small businesses? The number one source is from the owners (or potential owners) themselves. (See Figure 14.1.)

The other major sources include family and friends, credit cards, trade credit, banks, and other commercial lenders. There are also a number of other sources that exist but are not commonly used. These include grants from various organizations, angel investors, government programs, community-based financiers, stock sales, and venture capital. As Figure 14.2 shows, start-ups are funded about half from equity and half from debt.

Table 14.1 lists sources of financing as debt, equity, and gifts. **Debt** can take many forms. A business may borrow money directly from banks, development agencies, governments, or individuals. When you sell part of your business, the money you receive is **equity capital**. Any valuable assets or services, including money, that are donated to your business without any obligation to repay or to give any ownership interest is a **gift**. Each of these three types of financing requires a different approach, which we cover next.

debt
A legal obligation to pay money in the future.

equity capital
Money contributed to the businesses in return for part ownership of the business.

gift
Valuable assets or services donated to the business without any obligation to repay or give up any ownership interest.

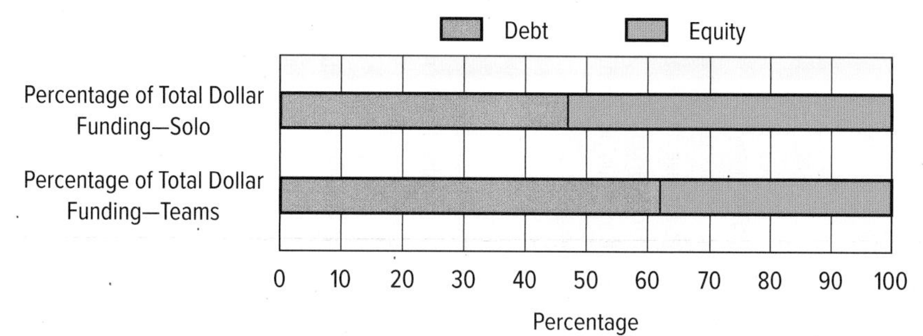

FIGURE 14.2

Use of Debt and Equity in Start-Ups from the PSED

Source: Adapted from Michael Stouder and Bruce Kirchhoff, "Funding the First Year of Business," in William B. Gartner, Kelly G. Shaver, Nancy M. Carter, and Paul D. Reynolds (eds.), *Handbook of Entrepreneurial Dynamics: The Process of Business Creation* (Thousand Oaks, CA: Sage, 2004), p. 368.

TABLE 14.1 Financing for Small Business by Phase, Type, and Source

Phase of Business/ Financial Management Need	Sources of Capital Financing		
	Debt Financing	**Equity Financing**	**Gift Financing**
Financing for start-ups	Consumer banks	Friends, family, and "fools"	Institutional: There are very few grants for start-ups; however, regional economic development agencies occasionally have such funds available
Profits are secondary to cash flow Need cash to pay employees Need cash to pay suppliers Need cash to live on	Commercial banks SBA insured loans Economic development agencies Small business investment companies Incubators Accelerators Leasing companies Personal credit cards	Angels Venture capital Public stock offerings Direct public offerings Crowdfunding (for equity)	Personal: Cash, picking up the tab, accelerated cash-outs, free use, free work/unpaid labor, overpayment, favored status/sweetheart deals, forgiveness, deferral, piggybacking Crowdfunding (nonequity)
Financing for growth Profits consistent with risk levels Funds for investment in equipment Cash for marketing Cash for building inventory levels	Commercial banks Small Business Administration Private placement loans Economic development agencies Small business investment companies Suppliers Leasing companies Personal credit cards	Self-generated funds Venture capital Direct public offerings Mergers Acquisitions	Institutional: SBIR, STTR grants State grants Incubators, accelerators Donated capital Tax abatement Personal: Same as for start-ups
Financing for operations Profits consistent with risk Build owner wealth Cash flow "smoothing" Reinvestment for maintenance	Factor receivables Business credit cards Commercial banks Small Business Administration Private placement loans Suppliers Leasing companies	Self-generated funds Venture capital Direct public offerings	Institutional: Same as for growth Personal: Same as for start-ups
Financing for exit Investing to build equity and firm value Reinvestment to replace worn assets New technology Productivity Quality	Consumer banks Commercial banks Small Business Administration Private placement loans Economic development agencies Small Business investment companies Suppliers Leasing companies Lines of credit	Self-generated funds Venture capital Direct public offerings	Institutional: Same as for growth Personal: Same as for start-ups

Understanding the Three Types of Capital Funding

Before we try to determine which of these types of capital financing is best for your own entrepreneurial venture, we need to discuss the nature and benefits of and the problems caused by each type. We start with a discussion of equity capital because for most businesses the owner's own resources are the first source of funds. Then we consider **debt capital** and conclude with a look at **gift capital**. After that, we look at some of the decisions entrepreneurs make in the financing process.

debt capital
Money borrowed for the purposes of investment in a business.

gift capital
Capital resources that neither provide any ownership nor require any repayment to the giver.

Financing with Equity

Equity can come from the entrepreneur or from others. In general, the entrepreneurs' own pockets are the first source of financing for most businesses. Because of this, understanding your own financial situation and the opportunities available to free up personal capital for use in your business becomes the foundation for any effort to finance using equity.

Personal Equity

The amount that you may contribute to your business from your own resources is very much determined by how much you are worth and how easy it is for you to use what you have. Often people underestimate their personal worth because many parts of their wealth are not cash in a bank account but are made up of things that are rarely seen or thought about, such as retirement funds and the cash value of life insurance policies. Or the value of what they own may seem to be very little because they use it so much that they forget about it having value, like a car, home, or personal collection. Also, not all personal wealth is easily available for use as a source of capital. It can be very difficult and very expensive to draw down retirement funds. You may have a lot of equity in your home, but selling your home to get access to that wealth may be hard to accomplish.

You need to know the amount and type of wealth that you have when you start a business. Your personal wealth is critical not only to your ability to fund yourself but also to show what your net worth consists of if you plan to get equity investments or loans from other people or banks. Your personal financial statements are essential documentation that allows others to understand *your* commitment to the business. Determine your personal financial situation in Skill Module 14.1.

Outside Equity

Outside equity is money from selling part of your business to people who are not and will not be involved in the management of the business. People who buy ownership rights in your business are considered *outside equity investors.*

- *Outside* because they are not part of the management of your business.
- *Equity* because they have legal ownership rights to your business.
- *Investors* because they are letting you use their money now in order to get wealth in the future.

outside equity
Money from selling part of your business to people who are not and will not be involved in the management of the business.

Determining Personal Net Worth

SKILL MODULE 14.1

Use the **Personal Net Worth Calculation Template** from the back of the book. You may either copy the form or your instructor can make a copy available for you.

In the column labeled "Cash Value (A)," enter the amount of money you could get if you were to sell what you own. In the next column, enter any amount that you owe to pay off your debt on the item. Then, in the third column, enter the difference between what you could sell it for and what you owe on it (the difference could be a negative number). After you have listed all that you own and all that you owe, the difference is what you are worth financially.

Lenders and investors usually require that you furnish a personal net worth statement. You can find one common format for the report, published as an Acrobat form, on the website of the Small Business Administration (**www.sba.gov/sites/default/files/forms/SBA_Form_413_7a-504-SBG.pdf**)

Obtaining outside equity financing is done by selling ownership in your business, which you can do only if your business is organized as one of three broad types of legal forms of business: a **partnership**, a **corporation**, or a **limited liability company (LLC)**. A complete discussion of the legal factors you must consider when making a choice of the form of organization that is best for your business is covered in Chapter 17 on small business law.

partnership
Two or more people cooperating to conduct a business enterprise.

corporation
A legal "artificial" entity that is formed by filing specific documents with a state government.

limited liability company (LLC)
A legal form of business organization that is created by filing required documentation with a state government. LLCs have a choice, under federal tax law, of being taxed as either corporations or partnerships.

secured debt
Loans that provide the lender with the legal right to seize specific assets in the event of nonpayment. Most automobile loans are secured debt and if you don't make your payments, your car will be repossessed.

unsecured debt
Loans that do not allow a lender to seize specific assets in the event of nonpayment.

Financing with Debt

Debt is a claim on the value of assets that a business owns. Unlike equity, debts of a business are legally enforceable requirements to pay specific amounts of money at specific times in the future. Debt can be loans from banks, credit unions, economic development agencies, other businesses, or private individuals. Debt can also be the value of inventory or equipment that the business receives right now, but does not have to pay for until some specified time later. **Secured debt** provides a lender with the right to seize specific assets if the loan is not paid back as specified in the loan contract. **Unsecured debt**, on the other hand, does not give a lender the right to seize any specific asset in the event of nonpayment. A lender generally must use court action, a lawsuit, or forced bankruptcy to collect unpaid unsecured debt.

It is usually much easier to obtain capital through borrowing than it is to get it from investors as equity. This is because the repayment of debt can be enforced by repossession of the asset that secures the debt or other action of the courts. Thus a lender has a much lower risk of not getting his or her investment returned than does an owner, who has a right to only whatever money is left over after all lenders and creditors have been paid in full.

Even though debt is easier to obtain than is equity, here are two reasons that cause many owners of small businesses to avoid using debt as a source of capital. First is that debt has repayment obligations that specify exactly how and exactly when the debt must be repaid. Second is the fact that debt gives lenders legal right to enforce payment under the contract terms without any consideration of the business's ability to pay at the time the payment is due. Thus many owners of small businesses prefer equity investment because, unlike debt, equity does not have to be repaid if the business fails or goes through a period of financial difficulty.

The amount of debt financing that your business can raise is limited by the amount of wealth that you have personally, the amount of wealth that your business owns, and your (and your business's) reputation for and history of paying debt when it is due. For a complete discussion of the process of obtaining debt financing, see the section "Financing with Debt: Getting a Loan for Your Business" in this chapter.

Financing with Gifts

Few, if any, small businesses have been able to obtain gift funding for the purpose of start-up. In fact, an extensive search failed to find even one example of a business that has done so. That said, gift capital has been and continues to be a significant source of financing for small businesses.

Gift capital is available (with a few exceptions) only to established businesses that have had several years of successful operations. However, although being established is important to being able to obtain grants, even more important is the fact that a small business will get a grant if, and only if, the business operations are meeting some other desirable societal goal.

Virtually all gift financing available to small business comes either from governments or from private foundations.

Few foundations exist to support small business. However, none exist to specifically provide start-up or working capital funding. The Ewing Marion Kauffman Foundation focuses its efforts on supporting and providing education for entrepreneurs. The National Foundation for Teaching Entrepreneurship provides business education for middle school, high school, and young adult students. SCORE is a nonprofit association that exists to provide advice to entrepreneurs. One of the very few foundations that actually provides cash to entrepreneurs who are trying to start new businesses is Ashoka. However, even Ashoka does not provide funding directly to the business; rather, Ashoka provides fellowships with stipends to cover living expenses for up to three years.

You should also keep in mind that although a capital infusion can be a gift in the sense that there is no requirement to repay the amount or to make any specified return on the investment, gifts come with strings attached. If you win a small business grant, you can bet that there will be, at the minimum, mandatory requirements to make periodic reports that detail how the grant is being used and what impact that use is having on attaining the granting institutions' goals.

The grant process is discussed in depth later in this chapter.

Financing with Equity: Getting Others to Invest in Your Business

LO 14-2 Explain the characteristics of a business that determine its ability to raise capital.

Small businesses get started and stay in business because their owners want to make money. Investors want to make money, too. Lenders expect a return on this money from making loans, by getting back the amount they had plus more money in the form of **interest**. In the same way, people invest in a business to get back the money they invest plus extra money, a **gain on investment**, or a **dividend.** Governments and nongovernmental organizations also expect their tax abatements and gifts of grants to make a return for the people they represent. The only difference is that governments expect to be repaid in the form of the owner creating more jobs and paying more taxes. When a business succeeds and grows, it contributes to the *economic development* of an area.

interest
A charge for the use of money, usually figured as a percentage of the principal.

gain on investment
The percentage amount that the payout of an investment differs from original cost calculated as: (Payout − Investment + Dividends)/Investment.

dividends
Payments of profits to the owners of corporations.

Equity Capital from the Investors' View

Look at it from the investors' point of view. They have money to invest. They may lend it or put it to work by buying a share in someone's business. They do this to make money, so they want to invest in a business that will succeed and thereby provide them with returns. But of course, all businesses are not equal. Every year thousands of people start new restaurants. Every year, thousands shut their doors forever. Of all the businesses that investors could invest in, how do they choose the right one?

One way to decide is by analyzing the business's prospects. Investors want to know just how likely the business is to succeed and produce a gain. In other words, they want to know the business's **risk.** Unfortunately, they can't see risk directly, so they have to look at other things that are associated with risk. Investors know that some of their investments will fail; they just don't know exactly which ones. To protect themselves from losing everything, they **diversify**—invest in several businesses so that the ones that do succeed provide gains that more than offset the losses from those that don't.

risk
The level of probability that an investment will not produce expected gains.

diversify
To invest in multiple investments of differing risk profiles for the purpose of reducing overall investment risk.

To get money from other people, you've got to show them that your business probably can make gains for them. Of course, you're not the only one looking for those investment dollars. You have to convince them that your business is a better place for their dollars than some other business. You do this by promising high enough gains. The minimum potential gain necessary to get people to invest in your business depends mostly on the amount of risk they are taking by purchasing part of your business. Your investors could put their money into a bank savings account earning 1 percent, a CD earning 1.5 percent, or a government bond earning 1 percent. For these vehicles there is no risk at all.[7] Corporate bonds might offer higher rates of return, but they also offer a higher risk of default—think of Payless Shoes, Toys R Us, David's Bridal, or other corporate failures. The riskier the business investment, the higher the return investors expect. Most investors, certainly those who aren't your parents, insist that they take no risk other than the potential loss of their investment. To ensure that nothing other than their investment is at risk, they will invest only if your business is organized to limit the liability of outside owners.

To estimate how much gain they might get from investing in your business, investors consider the growth potential of your business, how long it will take for them to see a return on their investment, and the options they have to receive back the original investment and their gains.

Growth potential is a primary concern for equity investors. Equity investors buy part of a "pie" of a known size. The more slices into which the pie is cut, the smaller each slice is, unless somehow the pie can be made larger. For this reason, it is much easier to get equity financing to develop a new factory to make flexible liquid crystal displays or to produce a treatment for obesity than it is to get someone to invest in a lawn care business in a city of 50,000 people. Lawn care in a small city has a limit to its growth, but there are millions and millions of computer users and people wanting to lose weight. Family and friends may be pleased to get back their investment and a 10 to 50 percent bonus, while business angels and angel groups are looking to receive 5 to 10 times their investment, and preferably even more.

The time required to receive gains can be a deal killer for potential investors. The longer they have to wait, the greater their risk that the business will fail. Also, all other things being equal, an investment that pays sooner is more profitable than one that pays later. Consider two simple situations. You are going to sell 25 percent of your business for $100,000. Your deal with the investor is that you will buy his or her share back at the end of one year for $150,000. In the second situation, you agree to buy back the investor's share for $150,000 in two years. Investors in the first case realize a 50 percent gain on investment, but investors in the second realize only 22 percent.[8] Waiting an extra year reduces the rate of gain by more than half. This is why business angels want to know when you plan to pay the investors their profits (called the **harvest** or exit) before considering investment. Letting family and friends, who may be more financially strapped, know how long it will be until they see a profit is also a nice thing to do, and for everyone, the sooner the better when it comes to getting money back.

harvest
Recover value through a sale of a firm or its assets.

Arrangements for paying gains to owners is an essential, but often ignored, facet of small business finance. Once more than one person owns equity in a small business, it *cannot* be a sole proprietorship. By law, lacking any specific legal business filings, it instantly becomes a general partnership. By making a legal filing, the business entity may become a limited partnership, a corporation, or a limited liability company. Regardless of what business form you choose, the issue of how to pay the owners is suddenly much more complex. Issues arise because of tax considerations, fairness to investors, and compensation for manager-owners. There is certainly no one right way to provide for returning gains to owners. It can take the form of salaries, stipends for serving on the board of directors, dividends, or stock repurchases. In those few cases in which a small business becomes a large business, equity investors often realize their gains by selling stock. Having a plan in place greatly aids in the process of acquiring outside equity capital.

Hybrid Funding—Not Quite Equity, Not Quite a Loan

As discussed in The Thoughtful Entrepreneur, there is a funding method that offers some of the benefits of equity investment but that can be obtained without any of the difficulties of governmental regulation. This hybrid form of investing is called, "Royalty Financing." Although the method is rarely used, it can be a source of funds when more conventional sources cannot be used.

Methods to Obtain Equity Capital

Bootstrapping

The practice of using one's own capital and funds generated by operating the business to finance start-up and growth is generally called **bootstrapping.**[9]

bootstrapping
Using low-cost or free techniques to minimize your cost of doing business.

Bootstrapping is how the great majority of small business start-ups are funded. Various studies completed over the last several years have reported that anywhere from 90 to 95 percent of all start-up businesses are initially funded by the entrepreneur's resources and cash flows from the business.[10]

There are good reasons that bootstrapping is so common among small business start-ups. Consider the following business "facts of life":

- External equity capital is not available for most small business start-ups.
- Banks do not loan to start-up businesses.
- Owners often do not want to share ownership.
- Owners usually want to be their own bosses. They do not want to have to answer to others concerning their businesses.
- Owners typically do not want to be responsible to others for losses of the business.

THE THOUGHTFUL ENTREPRENEUR

ROYALTY FINANCING

There is a method of obtaining financing that is neither equity nor debt, and certainly is not a gift. Rather, it lies somewhere in between these common financing methods. This method is called **royalty financing**. It involves an investor providing funds to a business, but not for ownership or a note requiring a specific rate of interest and repayment terms. Rather, the investor is given a royalty, a contractual percentage of the revenues of the firm for a contractual period.

Because royalty investing is neither the issuance of equity nor the placing of a loan, it is not subject to federal regulation. This means that the deals must be made very carefully because the contract lists all obligations for both parties. The only recourse is a lawsuit.

On the other hand, the owner does not give up any ownership control, and is not committed to any payback, other than the contracted percentage of revenues.

Of course, the owner can expect that this form of financing will be very expensive, should the company's service or product become popular and revenues really take off as a result.

royalty financing
A method of raising capital financing where investors provide money to a business in return for a guaranteed percentage of revenues.

For these reasons, most start-up small businesses get going by some combination of bootstrapping methods. Also, there is a growing body of evidence that highly effective small businesses continue to use bootstrapping for growth throughout operations.[11] Table 14.2 lists the most commonly used bootstrapping techniques.

So, how do you use bootstrapping to get your businesses going and to keep it going?

First, realize that bootstrapping is not simply going without. Rather, as Jeffery Cornwall defines it, bootstrapping is "the process of finding creative ways to exploit opportunities to launch and grow businesses with the limited resources available to most startup ventures."[12] In other words, bootstrapping means getting necessary things done using what you have right now. Here are four areas in which you can profit from bootstrapping.

TABLE 14.2 Percentage of Women Business Owners Who Used Specific Bootstrapping Strategy during 2011

Strategy	Percentage
Delayed purchases	71.3%
Delayed compensation of business owners	64.9
Used credit cards	64.9
Used personal savings	55.3
Delayed hiring employees	54.3
Asked for discounts from vendors	35.1
Used a line of credit	35.1
Used creative compensation (stock, merchandise, etc.)	27.7
Requested vendor or customer financing	22.3
Applied for bank loans	19.2
Received loans from family and friends	17.0
Sold receivables	6.4

Source: *Bootstrapping—Financial Strategies,* Center for Women's Business Research, February 2012.

Minimize Overhead Costs

All the stories that you've heard about businesses being "started in the garage" are examples of entrepreneurs using the bootstrapping method of minimizing overhead. You are already paying for the garage. It costs very little or nothing more to use it for your business. But, there are many, many other ways you might not have thought about, such as the following:

- **Cloud computing** can save your business hundreds, even thousands, of dollars each year. A five-user copy of Microsoft's Office Professional costs at least $1,700. You can use Google Apps for Business (now called, "G Suite") for $6 per employee per month. Or you can use Apache OpenOffice for free on as many computers and with as many users as you want.
- **Virtual storefronts** provide you with a business "location" at a very low cost. Examples for retail are eBay stores and Amazon webstore.
- **Business incubators** often offer office space and services at a very low cost, compared to renting space, obtaining equipment, and hiring workers.
- **Business office co-ops** extend the idea of incubators to established businesses. Businesses rent individual offices, but share common space, business equipment such as high-volume copiers, and sometime clerical help such as phone answering or office assistant services.
- **Co-working spaces** let entrepreneurs rent office space by the day in a setting full of other start-ups.

Maximize Returns from Employee Expense

Maximizing what you get from your employees does not mean that you have to be Dilbert's pointy-haired boss demanding excessive work. Rather, it means that you will match employee costs to getting the optimum levels of services or products.

Here are some examples of maximizing the value of employees:

- **Student interns** often provide high talent and strong motivation at a low cost to you.
- **Overtime** is usually much less expensive than hiring more full-time workers during times of increased business.
- **Contractors** exist to complete tasks that have a clear beginning, middle, and end, such as developing a company website or producing sales reports, brochures, and other advertising materials. When the project is complete, the cost ends.

Minimize Operating Costs

Business space is expensive whether you are getting office, retail, or manufacturing space. Then there are the expenses of licensing, insuring, stocking, and all the other costs of keeping a traditional business operation going. It is easy to set up a business in such manner that it can never generate enough activity to provide you with a profit. You can get a lot of mileage from minimizing these costs, at any level of business. Here are a few tried-and-true ways to do this.

- **Outsource** the production of your service or product. If you outsource, you do not have to maintain inventories of raw materials. You do not have to pay for full-time employees, with all the attendant employee taxes and costs. You do not have to maintain expensive equipment and buildings.
- **Subcontract** parts of your business that are not your core competency. This is a common practice in construction. If you are a carpenter, you most likely will be more efficient if you stick to carpentry and subcontract painting and landscaping.
- **Rent space** that is unused or underutilized by other ongoing businesses. Suppose your business requires freeze-drying product. Rather than spending a half million dollars for your own equipment, you can rent time on the equipment of the biopharma down the street.
- **Rent equipment.** If you have a sign company that rarely makes an outdoor installation, when you do, rent a crane rather than buying one. If you have a catering business and you get a contract for a whole-hog barbeque party, rent a portable cooker/smoker for that one event.

- **Work from home.** This simple bootstrapping method has become widely accepted by Internet and software development businesses. When you allow work from home, you do not have to pay for office space for your employees. You may also be able to negotiate pay for specific output, rather than paying employees by the hour.

Maximize the Results of Marketing

Marketing is a prime area to use bootstrapping techniques. When you are starting and growing your business, it is essential that you make every dollar spent on marketing and advertising count in the form of increased revenue. This pretty much rules out the traditional advertising avenues of radio, television, and print advertising where the typical response rate is only 1 or 2 percent. As noted in Chapter 10, getting free ink or free advertising is the way to get the biggest bang for the buck, so bootstrappers do marketing in tightly focused ways.

- **Word of mouth** is the bootstrapper's best marketing technique. How many times have you purchased something because a friend told you how good it was? When you made that purchase, you were responding to word-of-mouth marketing. The challenge for you is to get your customers to tell other potential customers just how great your service or product actually is. Some ways to encourage your customers to tell others about your business include:
  - **Discounts** for customers who recommend your business to other customers.
  - **Local signage** placed in customer's business locations, such as a web designer placing a notification on a customer's website or a remodeler putting a sign in a customer's yard.
  - **Facebook** "like" links can be done reciprocally–you tell your customer, "I'll 'like' your website, and you 'like' mine."
  - **Cooperative advertising** with your customers and vendors often allows you to reach people likely to become your customers, also.
- **Publicity** can provide a huge boost. "There's no such thing as bad publicity," P. T. Barnum once said. This may not be true in all circumstances, such as the local restaurant that makes the news because of health violations, but regardless, publicity is at the same time cheaper and more effective than advertising. The problem is how to get favorable publicity.
  - **Press releases** often result in media attention. Reporters are always looking both for local news and for good news. A well-designed press kit about your business can provide the 10 o'clock news team with a needed filler item.
  - **Public speaking** will give you an opportunity to stand before an audience and make a pitch for your business. You can present a 10- or 14-minute speech about your business's contribution to the local economy to meetings of the Rotary Club, Kiwanis, chamber of commerce, and the like.
  - **Donate your service or product** to worthy groups and efforts. Is your new restaurant not doing as well as you'd like? Call the local business journal or newspaper and give them a heads up that you will be providing lunches to the Habitat for Humanity workers. Or, for certain exposure, contribute some of your product to your local public television station for inclusion in their annual fund-raising on-air auction.

Crowdfunding for Equity

A new way of getting people to invest in your business is to use the web for crowdfunding. Crowdfunding was created to provide a way for artists to obtain backing for their individual projects.[13] It has, however, emerged as a method for entrepreneurs to obtain public financing.

As is discussed in The Thoughtful Entrepreneur, you can now legally use crowdfunding to raise equity capital. The Jumpstart Our Business Startups (JOBS) Act[14] specifically makes it legal for start-up businesses to use crowdfunding to raise equity capital without having to meet the reporting requirements of the Sarbanes-Oxley Act (SarBox or SOX) or the registration and reporting requirements of the current SEC regulations. In May 2016, the final regulations for Titles II and III of the JOBS Act became effective. This provision of the law allows anyone to invest in a business, but the offering of equity **must** be made by either a licensed broker-dealer or an online funding portal that is registered with the SEC. A complete listing of SEC registered portals can be found on the Financial Industry Regulatory Authority (FINRA) website: www.finra.org/about/funding-portals-we-regulate.

There are still funding opportunities for businesses that are willing to restrict themselves to qualified investors. For example, in the United States you do not have to list your security with the Securities and Exchange Commission (SEC) if you follow certain rules that limit how much money you may raise and that specify the nature of the investors to whom you may sell. Generally, these offerings (described in The Thoughtful Entrepreneur) are limited to accredited investors including members of angel groups and online platforms like AngelList (angel.co), SeedInvest.com, FundersClub.com, and Fundable.com.

THE THOUGHTFUL ENTREPRENEUR

Direct Public Offerings

While initial public offerings (IPOs) are limited to those few start-ups that have billions of dollars in potential sales and a powerful start-up team, other types of public offerings are more accessible to more conventional types of small businesses. They are called direct public offerings (DPOs). These can be used for raising equity by selling stock (for C corporations) or membership units (for LLCs), or for raising debt by selling a note (also known as a bond). There are four forms of DPO: Section 504 or SB-1 offerings (for under $1 million), a 505 offering (for up to $5 million), the more complex 506 or SB-2 offering (for more than $1 million), and the still more complex Small Corporate Offering Registration (SCOR) program for up to $1 million. These are designed for selling securities nationwide and over the Internet. There is also a DPO limited to sales within only one state (i.e., the entrepreneur offering the DPO and the investor both live in the same state) called an Intrastate, or Rule 147, Offering.

On April 5, 2012, the Jumpstart Our Business Startups (JOBS) Act was signed into law. This law specifically provides for raising equity funds by crowdfunding. The final rules for using this new crowdfunding market to raise equity became effective on May 16, 2016. So the provisions are pretty new, and they are very complex.

All offerings, with the exceptions contained in the JOBS regulations, require the creation of a private placement memorandum (a specialized type of business plan discussed in Chapter 8), a subscription agreement, and for a debt offering a promissory note. They also require government filings, sometimes with the federal SEC, often with your own state's security regulations office (a good directory of state offices is given at the North American Securities Administrators Association website (**www.nasaa.org**); search the site for "Directory of Securities Laws." Not many small businesses use this approach because of the extensive regulatory requirements. There is no substitute for engaging a securities lawyer to make sure the filing is done correctly.

The exciting new regulations, Titles II and III of the JOBS Act, provide two major advantages for small businesses. First, small businesses are exempted from the filing requirements if the rules and guidelines of Rule 506 of Regulation D of the Securities Act[15] are followed exactly. Basically, Rule 506 requires that any investor be a **sophisticated investor** or an **accredited investor**. Second, Title III actually allows firms to avoid the restriction that investors must be "sophisticated" or "accredited" by following a different set of rules.

But don't start advertising your offering on the web just yet. The rules you must follow are complex and there is no provision for forgiveness if you err in making your offering. In fact, you may not *just* make an offering, anyway. The offering and all subsequent sales of equity must be conducted through an intermediary that is either a registered broker-dealer, or a new type of entity called a "funding portal." Funding portals are required to register with the SEC, and are bound by the SEC's rulemaking, examination, and enforcement authority.

sophisticated investor
As defined by the SEC, people who "have sufficient knowledge and experience in financial and business matters to make them capable of evaluating the merits and risks of the prospective investment."

accredited investor
As defined by the SEC in Title 17, Chapter II, Part 230, §230.501 of the Code of Federal Regulations (CFR): "Any person who comes within any of the following categories, or who the issuer reasonably believes comes within any of the following categories, at the time of the sale of the securities to that person: banks, business development companies, companies worth more than $5 million, an executive of the firm making the offering, or an individual with a personal net worth of more than $1 million." You may access the regulation at www.ecfr.gov/cgi-bin/retrieveECFR?gp=&SID=8edfd12967d69c024485029d968ee737&r=SECTION&n=17y3.0.1.1.12.0.46.176.

If you think that crowdfunding might work for you, there are some things that every business is going to have to do to succeed in this new market.

- **Document your business.** Your business will have to be either a corporation or an LLC to be able to use JOBS Act equity funding. You should have your articles of incorporation, minutes of the board of directors, and operating rules ready for potential investors to examine.
- **Make a business plan.** You are going to have to show investors how your business will work to make profits and create wealth.
- **Create a compelling story.** You are going to have to convince strangers of the value of your plan and why they should trust you to implement it.
- **Create a professional-looking video.** Crowdfunding has a 15-year history in the arts. One thing that has been shown over and over is that projects that have snappy videos are much more successful raising money than those that don't.
- **Develop a list of potential investors.** Just having a plan, a sales pitch, and an Internet video is not enough to ensure success. You will be competing with thousands of other businesses for funding. You are going to have to work your contacts, and get your contacts to tell others if you are to meet your funding goal.

Angel Investors

For a few very high-quality (or perhaps just very fortunate) business start-ups there is a source of start-up capital beyond the entrepreneur's own resources. A number of high-wealth individuals make a practice of investing in first- and second-stage funding of new businesses. These people are commonly called **angel investors**. Table 14.3 illustrates the characteristics of the three types of angel investors.

angel investor
A wealthy individual who invests in companies in relatively early stages of development.

While it is hard to get angel investment data, there are two major annual efforts, the University of New Hampshire's Center for Venture Research (CVR)[16] and the HALO Report from the Angel Resource Institute at Willamette University.[17] The CVR report is broader in its coverage, so gives us a better idea of what is happening. In 2018, 66,110 companies received angel financing totaling $23.1 billion, or on average $348,000 per firm. It came from 334,565 angels across

TABLE 14.3 Types of Angel Investment

	Individual Angel	Angel Network	Angel Fund
Ease of Finding Angels	Hard to find	Easy to find: formal networks Hard to find: small private networks	Publicly known, so easy to find
Legal Form	Private individual	Formal networks, corporation; informal networks vary	Corporation
Source of Funds	Invests own money	Invests own money	Fund invests on angels' behalf
Typical Size of Investment	$50–100K	$50–$250K	$50–$500K
Geographic Proximity Preferences	Very close proximity preferred	Very close proximity preferred; may invest remotely via syndicate	Very close proximity preferred; may invest remotely via syndicate
Why Invest?	Equity growth and personal interest	Equity growth and personal interest	Equity growth, sometimes regional development
Reporting Requirements	Varies by individual	Varies, set by investing angels	Formal, set by the fund
Involvement Level and Method	Low to extremely high; informal	Low to extremely high; informal	Low to extremely high; more formal
Angels' Exit Expectation	Often unplanned; trade sale	Cash-out when firm bought or VCs invest	Cash-out when firm bought or VCs invest

Source: Parts of this table were adapted from Dirk De Clercq, Vance Fried, Oskari Lehtonen, and Harry J. Sapienza, "An Entrepreneur's Guide to the Venture Capital Galaxy," *Academy of Management Perspectives* 20 (2006), pp. 90–112.

the United States. Recall from Chapter 1 that there are around 400,000 firms with employees started every year, and perhaps as many as 10 to 15 times that many owner-only businesses started. The majority of firms seeking angel investment will be multiperson firms, but angel money goes to all sorts of start-ups and growing firms.

It is not only start-up businesses that seek angel funding. In fact, the CVR study showed that in 2018 about 34 percent of investments went to firms just starting out, with 41 percent going to firms in the next step, called early-stage firms. One of the characteristics of businesses that get funded by angels and angel groups is that the business actually exists: it has a legal form; a product or service; a large market potential; actual customers; a management team; and a plan for growth, success, and ultimate cash-out. About 21 percent of investments were in expanding firms and 4 percent of funding went to later-stage firms. So, a business that successfully gets angel funding may be a start-up or may have been in business for a year, two years, perhaps up to four years.[18]

Although we cannot provide specific numbers, we can confidently say that only a tiny percentage of businesses that seek angel funding actually get it. A typical angel group receives about 30 to 50 business plan submissions each month. Of these unsolicited plans, approximately 5 to 10 will be selected to be presented to the angel group in person. Of the plans that are presented, no more than 1 or 2 will be funded in any quarter. Putting this into percentage terms, we can state that of 600 business plans presented for angel funding, no more than 8 of them will ever get the money.[19] However, this low percentage still amounts to nearly 70,000 angel investments made each year. From these numbers we can infer that some 6 million submissions are made annually, and there must be somewhere around 10,000 individuals and groups making angel investments.

This might lead you to think that an awfully large number of great business ideas and great entrepreneurs are not being funded. That may be so, but consider that of each 100 businesses funded by angel groups, only about half ever repay the original investment. The other 50 percent provide net losses to the angel investor![20] So another way to understand the results of angel investing is to conclude that all worthy business ideas are being funded. In fact, it appears that more than half of the businesses that are funded actually are poor business ideas led by incompetent entrepreneurs.

The truth is most likely somewhere between these two extremes. It's probable that few really good business ideas go undeveloped, and that a large percentage of what seem to be good ideas prove not to be in the long run. It's also likely that some really great ideas fail because of less than stellar entrepreneurs, and that a very few really effective entrepreneurs make a success of a less than wonderful idea.

Equity Capital from the Owner's View

From the point of view of an existing owner, financing with equity is (1) expensive and (2) guaranteed to create problems of control and decision making.

Equity capital is not free, as many entrepreneurs think. Suppose you sell half your business to raise capital. You have just sold half of all your future profits, half of all your future growth, half of all your future wealth. If, on the other hand, you were to borrow the money, your cost will be only the cost of acquiring the loan and making interest payments. In addition, owners of your business (even those who own only a small part) have a legal right to know how you're managing *their* business. As a matter of fact, most equity investors in small businesses insist on having the right to inspect the accounting records *at any time they choose.* Once you accept equity investors, you will find that you'll have to keep careful records of transactions, and you'll have to make regular reports to your investors. If those investors disagree with your running of the business, they can challenge your decisions, even to the point of suing you for supposed damages or replacing you as manager. Many entrepreneurs, including even the late Steve Jobs of Apple Computers, have found themselves forced out of their own businesses by minority equity investors.

Why Use Equity Capital?

There are three primary reasons to use outside equity in your business: (1) you will reduce your own exposure to financial loss, (2) your business will not have increased costs in the form of interest, and (3) bringing outside investors into an existing business can often reenergize it by providing new ideas, procedures, and processes.

Financing with Debt: Getting a Loan for Your Business

The most common source of capital for established ongoing small businesses is borrowed funds. This is the case for several reasons, including all the reasons already discussed, especially the simple fact that small businesses do not have easy access to equity financing. Additionally, national, state, and local governments all encourage small business borrowing. This is done in three ways: (1) direct cash loans, (2) guaranteed loans made by commercial banks, and (3) reduced taxes by allowing interest to be deducted. However, when it comes to borrowing significant amounts of money, all firms are not created equal. Established businesses that have valuable assets that are separable from the owners are able to borrow more easily than are start-up or knowledge businesses.

So, where can a small business actually get loans to start and grow? As you might expect, your best source is the bank where you are currently doing business. After all, it is in the business of making loans. You are a customer. As such, you are a known commodity–you pay your bills, you keep your account balance positive, you don't bounce checks. Start where you're known.

But if your bank turns you down, you are not out of luck. In fact, in the Small Business Administration guaranteed loan programs you *must* be turned down by a bank before you qualify. So maybe your bank did you a favor; having been turned down, you can apply for an SBA-guaranteed loan. Through this avenue you will still borrow from your own bank, but the SBA will guarantee the bank that if your business fails, the SBA will pay off your loan. Other sources for SBA-guaranteed loans include **community development organizations**, and for small loans, **microlenders**, which you can find at www.sba.gov/loans-grants/see-what-sba-offers/sba-loan-programs/microloan-program.

A third source of SBA-guaranteed loans is the **small business investment company (SBIC)**. A directory of SBICs is maintained on the SBA website: www.sba.gov/content/sbic-directory. All SBICs are listed by state. Click on the hot link to open the appropriate list. The directory provides not only a list of active SBICs, but also an outline of the business requirements.

You may also have access to incubators or **accelerators** in your area. These organizations exist solely for the purpose of facilitating the start-up and growth of new businesses. They provide advice for finding loans, and, in some cases, have the ability to make loans to member businesses.

The main things that lenders want to see before they give businesses their money are the Four Cs of Borrowing, listed here and shown in Figure 14.3:

1. Character of the managers of the business.
2. Capacity of the business to repay both principal and interest on time.
3. Conditions of the industry and economy in which the business operates.
4. Collateral that can be used to secure the loan.

No matter how you have organized your business, a lender is going to look at it as an extension of you. The simple fact is that you have the power to make decisions, good or bad, about all facets of operation regardless of its form, whether sole proprietorship, partnership, or corporation. Thus, although technically the loan may be made to the business entity, from the point of view of the lender, a loan is not made to a small business, a loan is made to the *owner* of a small

community development organization
An organization authorized by the SBA to make insured loans to small businesses that are expected to increase economic activity within a specific geographic area.

microlender
SBA-approved partner that offers SBA-guaranteed microloans to eligible small businesses. These loans require much less paperwork than regular SBA or bank loans, and are for amounts under $50,000.

small business investment company (SBIC)
Private business that is authorized to make SBA-insured loans to start-ups and small businesses.

accelerator
An organization that supports start-ups, typically of a particular type (e.g., Internet, biotech, fashion, sports, women-owned firms, etc.) with a financial investment, free or inexpensive office space, mentoring, a variety of free or low-cost support services, and other resources. The goal of an accelerator is to accelerate a start-up from its early stages to being ready to pitch for investment. Most accelerators take an equity stake in the companies they help.

Character of the managers of the business.	**Capacity** of the business to repay both principal and interest on time.
Conditions of the industry and economy in which the business operates.	**Collateral** that can be used to secure the loan.

FIGURE 14.3
The Four Cs of Borrowing

business. The owner's character and business reputation are important considerations for lenders when they decide whether or not to let a business have money.

Owner character is judged largely by the owner's personal credit rating and by that of the business. All lenders want some assurance that a loan will be repaid as agreed. There are several private agencies called consumer **credit reporting agencies (CRAs)** that exist solely to collect, collate, and report the credit histories of individuals and businesses. Lenders pay a fee to join a credit agency, and then pay for each report received. Lenders also promise to provide information about you back to the agency.

credit reporting agency (CRA)
A business that collects, collates, and reports information concerning an entity's use of debt.

There are four primary CRAs: Equifax, Experian, Innovis, and TransUnion. There are also many specialized agencies that provide special services for landlords, medical providers, and resellers of information who create customized reports from data acquired from the four primary CRAs.

The information collected and reported by the CRAs is limited to three areas:

- Identifying information.
- Credit information.
- Public record information.

Race, religious preference, medical history, personal lifestyle choices, political affiliation, criminal record, or anything not related to credit is prohibited from being reported. Of course, for a price all this information can be obtained from sources other than credit reporting agencies.

The **Fair Credit Reporting Act (FCRA)** requires that all information reported by CRAs be accurate. However, the law does not require that CRAs independently confirm any information. It is incumbent upon you, the consumer, to obtain a copy of your credit report and to notify the CRA in writing of any inaccurate information. The CRA has 30 days in which to investigate. The CRA must also forward copies of all relevant information that you provide to the source of the inaccurate information. The source must then make its own investigation and report any inaccuracies to all nationwide CRAs.

Fair Credit Reporting Act (FCRA)
U.S. federal legislation specifying consumers' rights vis-à-vis credit reporting agencies.

Eventually you will get a report of the outcome of the investigation. If the information is still inaccurate, you have to send a notice of dispute to the provider. The provider does not have to change the information, but a copy of your dispute must then be included with any future credit reports. See Skill Module 14.2 for obtaining a credit report.

Commercial credit reporting agencies began in the 1830s when a silk merchant, Lewis Tappan, began to collect extensive records concerning customers of the business. Tappan eventually offered credit reports to other merchants. Through a series of mergers, Tappan's business today is known as Dun & Bradstreet (D&B).

Providers of commercial credit reports are much more entrepreneurial and less rule-bound than are CRAs. For example, Dun & Bradstreet allows businesses to self-report gross sales, profits, numbers and types of customers, numbers of employees, and so on. D&B does, however, make extensive efforts to confirm the accuracy of information and also makes independent investigations of midsize to large businesses, including interviewing management.

SKILL MODULE 14.2 Obtaining Your Credit Report

Under the Fair and Accurate Credit Transactions Act consumers can request one free credit report in every 12-month period from each of the three national credit reporting agencies, Experian, Equifax, and TransUnion. You must use the toll-free telephone number (877-322-8228), the **www.annualcreditreport.com** website, or a special mailing address (Annual Credit Report Request Service, P.O. Box 105281, Atlanta, GA 30348-5281). You will have to supply a Social Security number and date of birth and answer a few personal questions to get instant access online. Credit agencies have up to 15 days to send out reports that are requested by phone or mail.

Use one of the methods listed here to obtain copies of your credit report. Carefully examine each report for accuracy. If you find any incorrect information, contact the CRA and have it corrected.

You can create a credit file for your business with D&B by filling out an online application and paying an initial fee of $500. Once your file is established, D&B maintains it using a sophisticated computer system to confirm accuracy. Visit www.dnbla.com/en/data for an explanation of how D&B collects and verifies its data.

Although D&B is the best-known provider of commercial credit reports, it is by no means the sole provider. Experian provides commercial reports as well as consumer reports. Additionally, there are numerous other commercial credit reporting agencies, including the National Information Bureau, Ltd.; Veritax Business Information, Inc.; and Fair Isaac's Small Business Scoring, to name a few. Finally, there are industry-specific reporting agencies; for example, Seafax provides credit reports for the seafood, poultry, meat, and associated food industries.

The capacity of the business is the most important single factor for being able to borrow significant amounts of money. Your capacity to repay loans is measured primarily by two factors: profitability and cash flows from operations. **Profitability** that has been maintained over time indicates that you are an effective manager who will produce future profits to repay the borrowed money. *Cash flows from operations* that have been constant and reliable indicate that you can reliably convert profits to cash.

profit, profitability
The amount that revenues exceed expenses.

Condition of the industry and economy includes such factors as technology, competition, and economic growth. For example, right now the telecommunications industry is undergoing huge changes. Cable providers are offering telephone service, and telephone companies are offering movies. Satellite operators are adding broadband to their television and radio services. Copper wire connectors are being replaced with fiberoptic cable directly into businesses and homes. Cell phones have rendered pay phones obsolete. Now is not a good time to try to raise money for a telecommunications business.

Collateral value is simply the estimated market value of the assets of your business. Tangible, long-lived assets are the best **collateral**. Auction markets for automobiles, trucks, and commercial machinery provide both a source for estimating value and an immediate market in which they can be sold.

collateral
Something of value given or pledged as security for payment of a loan; collateral may consist of financial instruments, such as stocks, bonds, and negotiable paper, or of physical goods, such as trucks, machinery, land, or buildings.

Intangible assets, other than patents, copyrights, and trademarks, are not good collateral. For example, *goodwill*, the value of a business that exceeds the sum of the value of all individual assets, cannot be sold separately from the business. The same is true of other intangibles, such as experience, education, institutional knowledge, and customer relations. These things can be very valuable, but none can be transferred to a lender to satisfy debt.

Other factors affecting debt worthiness include why you want to borrow the money and just how much money of your own is invested in the business. Lenders eagerly loan money to purchase capital equipment. After all, if you default, they will just repossess your truck and sell it to someone else. If you are willing to pay high enough interest rates, they will even lend you money to finance marketing efforts or business growth. They will not, however, lend you money to make up for financial failure. They will not loan money to finance consumption or extravagance. In fact, it is quite difficult to even borrow working capital to finance ongoing operations of all types. Also, most commercial lenders will not make a loan in an amount greater than that which, when added to existing debt, will bring the debt-to-equity ratio above 50 percent. (See the discussion later in the chapter for an explanation of debt-to-equity.)

Generally, banks don't make loans to start-ups. They will sometimes, however, consider making a personal loan to the entrepreneur creating a start-up, but here again the entrepreneur's ability to pay back the loan from the new business or from your other income will be crucial to the decision to loan you the money. For all loan applicants, the bank will look at what loans you are already committed to paying off, such as student loans, mortgages, car loans, and the balance on your credit cards that remain to be paid. The greater the debt you already have, the harder it is to get loans. You can sometimes arrange to defer or delay paying back student loans, but it takes some preparatory work on your part.[21]

Customer Funding of Your Business

Did you notice in Table 14.2 that one-fifth of women business owners used the specific bootstrapping method of asking vendors and customers for funding?

No? Well, neither do many entrepreneurs. But this technique is a long-established and highly effective method to get operating capital for your business. It is debt because the customer *gives* you the money and you *owe* them the product or service. What it does provide is cash inflows into your business that occur before the necessary outflows must take place. So, customer funding is not per se equity funding, but used properly it can replace some, or all, of your equity funding needs.

Although there is nothing new about using customer funding, it has received little attention from entrepreneurs and from those of us who write about entrepreneurship. This was addressed in 2014 by John W. Mullins, in his book *The Customer-Funded Business.*[22] In this book Mullins identifies five types of funding that get customers to pay first, and get their product or service later:

1. Matchmaker models (like Airbnb)
2. Pay-in-advance models (like Threadless.com)
3. Subscription models (like Netflix)
4. Scarcity-based models (like Groupon or Gilt)
5. Service-to-product models[23] (like BaseCamp or **SaaS** like Office 365)

SaaS

SaaS stands for *Software as a Service* and refers to an Internet-based program that you would use in work or leisure. These are paid for by time frame, project, or some measure of usage.

Each of these models has common examples. Real estate brokers use matchmaker models. A real estate broker does not buy the houses that he or she sells, nor do brokers provide any money to the buyers. Rather, they match willing sellers with willing buyers and receive a percentage fee of the final sales price. Lawyers are experts at pay-in-advance business. Just get yourself embroiled in a lawsuit. When you try to hire an attorney, you will find that you must make a "retainer" in cash, against which the lawyer will charge the costs of representing you. Subscription models are used by many businesses, including magazine publishers, newspapers, amusement parks, and museums to name just a few. For example, Disney sells a variety of annual passes to its theme parks that range from a mere $600 to just under $1,500, depending on the level you buy. You pay up front and may visit the parks as many times as you wish. Scarcity-based models are those where a very limited amount of product is available for a very limited time. For the scarcity model to work, you need to be able to sell the product and collect the cash before you ever have to pay. Finally, the service-to-product model entails developing your product as a service for a single customer who pays the development costs. Later, when the product is proven in the market, it is sold as a product to any buyer who wants it.

The big issue with all these customer-funded models is, Do they work? The answer is a qualified yes!

Matchmaking in the real estate industry has made many people very rich. While it has led to successes like Airbnb and Uber, it has not worked so well in other industries, such as used autos and boats. It seems that the model works only if there is specialized knowledge and skills required to make the match. It also helps if there is a significant barrier to entry such as a licensing requirement.

Pay-in-advance models work when there is an industry standard for prepayment. Thus, this model works well for lawyers, accountants, architects, and engineers, and at the other end of industries, T-shirts and custom clothing. Otherwise it works when the customer sees a financial advantage to paying in advance. Customers of Sam's Club prepay to get lower prices during the year. Michael Dell built his company by getting customers to pay, then making and shipping the computers. A customer who does not see a significant advantage, however, is most unlikely to pay in advance.

Subscription models similarly have a mixed history of success. The model has long driven revenues in the publishing industry, and Netflix and Amazon Prime have made the model work very well. However, many Internet subscription services for things such as precooked meals, house cleaning, and decorating items have failed in the market.

Scarcity-based models have a similar mixed history. A few businesses have experienced spectacular success with the model. For example, when Groupon launched, it became an instant sensation, spawning thousands of imitators, most of whom failed to get the traction of the original because the newcomers offered little advantage. Since scarce items are difficult to come by, many more firms in this industry end up becoming less selective in their offerings, and fail more often than succeed.

There are many example of successful service-to-product models. Microsoft famously developed the original operating system for Intel processors as a contract with IBM. Later, of course,

DOS and Windows were made available to anyone who wanted them. Today Microsoft offers its flagship Office product both as a physical product and an online service called Office 365. Even a superficial search will disclose thousands of products that were originally developed for the U.S. military or space programs that subsequently became common consumer products.

The advantage of these customer-funded approaches is that you don't pay interest on the money advanced to your business, and you have cash flow from the start, which will help with your firm's own cash flow management. These sales are also a validation of your business idea, which helps you prove your idea has market appeal. Just remember, customer funding is a type of debt, and you pay it off by delivering the promised goods or services on time!

Financing with Gifts: Winning Grants for Your Business

Gift financing has a special allure. It seems to many people as if they are getting something for nothing. The impression might be that a government or a foundation hands out money that never has to be repaid, or a family member magnanimously offers a present at just the right time. It is unfortunate that anything that seems too good to be true usually is. Gift capital is anything but free. It costs time and money to obtain; and it requires time and money for accounting and reporting to the granting agency, family members, and government. There are two general sources of gift financing: one is institutional, from government agencies and foundations; the other is personal, from family or occasionally from friends.

Institutional Gifts

The most common form of institutional gift financing is in the form of reduced taxes, either through tax abatement or in the form of a credit against taxes payable. It does seem a misnomer to call reducing the amount taken from a business a gift, but since taxes are a cash cost to businesses, reducing tax burden has the same effect as receiving that same amount of cash. The Thoughtful Entrepreneur provides five examples of the practice.

THE THOUGHTFUL ENTREPRENEUR

WHEN UNCLE SAM IS A SOFT TOUCH

It is hard to even begin to grasp how many government tax abatement programs exist. They are provided to businesses both large and small.

Many small businesses have taken advantage of the U.S. government's program that encourages building low-income housing and rebuilding historic structures through reduced income taxes.

The state of Nevada in 2018 gave Tesla Motors a set of tax abatements that last for 20 years and will provide $1.3 billion in tax savings for the company.

Right now, the state of Wisconsin is promising Foxconn an annual tax break of from $200 to $250 million per year for 15 years, if the company builds a flat-screen factory there.

The city of Flagler, Colorado, and the state of Maine are currently offering commercial land free to businesses that will agree to bring employment to specific areas.

Homestead, Florida, has established an enterprise zone in which there are property tax abatements, a direct refund of sales taxes, direct credits of property tax up to $50,000, as well as tax credits for job creation. Portland, Maine, offers tax increment and tax-exempt bond financing for firms that will relocate to the area.

Waukee, Iowa, and the state of Iowa have promised Apple a tax break of over $207 million across 20 years if the company will build a data center near the town.

Farmers receive gift financing from the U.S. government in the form of direct cash payments and price subsidies for not planting crops, for planting cereal grains, apples (but not peaches), cotton, tobacco, and a plethora of other crops, for raising mohair (angora) goats, and for producing lamb meat and dairy products. Payments for not growing crops are made through a program called "conservation reserve payments," in which farmers contract to not plant specified plots of erosion-prone land for a specific number of years. Direct subsidies and price supports are made through numerous programs, including payments for wetlands protection.

tax abatement
A legal reduction in taxes by a government.

Tax abatements are provided by state and local governments, primarily to encourage specific activities that are expected to improve blighted areas or to provide additional employment. Most governments that impose a tax on real estate have some form of tax reduction to encourage rehabilitating old dwellings, providing housing for low-income citizens, and maintaining buildings that are deemed to be historic. Tax abatements can take many forms, depending on the type of taxes that are imposed.

tax credit
Direct reduction in the amount of taxes that must be paid, dependent on meeting some legal criteria.

Tax credits are provided by the U.S. government and some state governments for the purpose of encouraging investment in specific types of assets, to increase economic activity in specified disadvantaged geographic areas, increase the welfare of specific groups of citizens, or support industries that are held to be of national strategic interest. Credits provided include those for empowerment zone employment, employing American Indians, purchasing electric automobiles, or using ethyl alcohol for fuel. The list of available tax credits and the details of how to claim them is too voluminous to reproduce in this text. Also, the credits change with each Congress, thus any specific information would be sorely out of date by the time this text is published.

grant
Gift of money made to a business for a specific purpose.

Grants of money are available from the U.S. government, most state governments, and semi-private and private economic development agencies. The purpose of the grants varies with the entity that makes the grant. U.S. grant programs for small business are primarily a response to political pressure brought on Congress. The stated purpose of the grant programs is to encourage development of small businesses, thereby increasing the economic activity of the country. Various states also have grant programs. As with the federal program, the rationale for providing grants to small business is to increase economic activity, provide job growth, and provide increases in the overall standard of living of the citizens of the state.

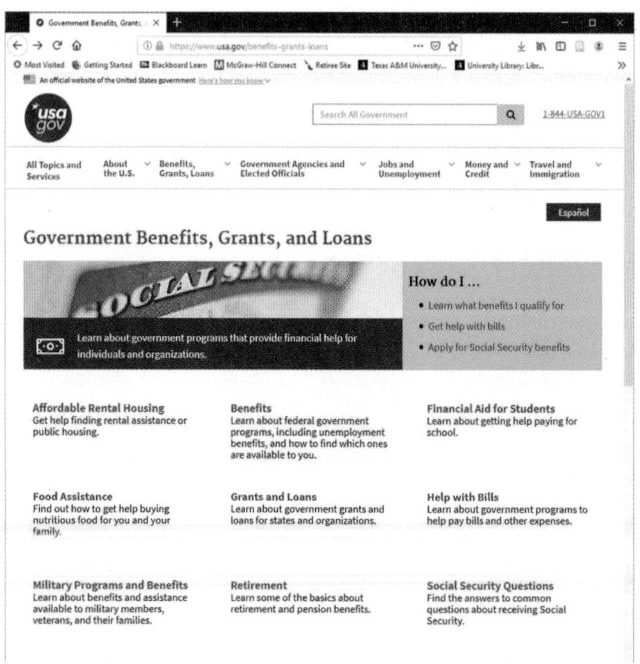

https://www.usa.gov/benefits-grants-loans

To find federal government grants, there are three good sources: (1) The Small Business Administration offers a loan and grant search tool (www.sba.gov/funding-programs/loans) optimized for small businesses. (2) You can go to www.grants.gov and use the basic search. If you type in "small business" you will find hundreds of grants that mention small businesses as potential grantees. (3) Another great resource is www.usa.gov/business. On this site you will find a number of topic hotlinks such as "Start Your Own Business," and "Finance Your Business" that will connect you to federal resources, grants, and support programs. This site also has a tab called "State Business Resources," which will connect you to resources and support organizations in your state.

There is no single website that will direct you to the various state government resources for small business. To find grants in your state, it is best to begin with a Google search, such as "Texas grants for small business."

Grants from governments are highly structured and require very accurate record keeping and reporting. Agencies that issue grants first publish a request for proposal (RFP) that specifies the conditions of the grant. Interested small businesses may then create a proposal, which must be submitted by the specified date and time, in the *exact* format specified. Grant proposals are then judged in a "blind" process. Winning proposals receive notification within about 30 days and funding within six months.

Finding SBIR Grants

SKILL MODULE 14.3

What kind of business are you interested in? Do you have any new ideas or procedures for this business that might lead to better ways of solving problems of health, national security, threats of terrorism, or any other area in which the U.S. government has an interest?

If you do, there is probably an SBIR grant for you.

Assume that you have come up with an idea that might result in stopping would-be terrorists at airports outside the United States. Your idea, if it works, will stop terrorists from getting to the United States in the first place. Do a Google search using the search terms "SBIR grants" and "national security." (Be sure to put in the quotation marks.)

Follow the leads returned by Google (more than 3,000) to identify agencies and programs that will provide funds through SBIR grants for ideas that might help national security.

1. Write a report of your findings to be presented to your class.
2. Use the skill you have now developed to find an SBIR grant that would apply to a business that you are actually interested in starting.

The two largest governmental grant programs that are specifically intended for small business are (1) the Small Business Innovation Research (SBIR) program and the Small Business Technology Transfer (STTR) program. These two programs require that every U.S. agency that makes research grants provide a minimum of 3.2 percent of its grant budget to small businesses, as defined by the SBA. Three percent may not sound like much, but in 2018, the SBIR program resulted in over $3.1 *billion* in grants made to participating small businesses. These programs are each three-phase programs. A winning proposal will initially receive about $200,000 to conduct a feasibility study, as detailed in the grant proposal. Depending on successful completion, additional funds, which can range up into millions of dollars, are provided for stage II and stage III activities. See Skill Module 14.3 for more information on SBIR grants.

Grants from foundations are rarely made to for-profit businesses. **Foundations** exist for the purpose of addressing some identified social need that cannot be adequately met by market forces. The Ewing Marion Kauffman Foundation supports *education* and *research* concerning entrepreneurship and small business. The Ford Foundation supports the arts, including public television programs. The Rotary Foundation supports efforts to eradicate hunger and polio worldwide. All these foundations were founded by successful entrepreneurs and business managers, but they do not specifically support the start-up, expansion, or operation of for-profit enterprises. Rather, their (and those of about 30,000 other private foundations) missions clearly state that grants are made to nonprofit organizations.

foundation
An institution to which private wealth is contributed and from which private wealth is distributed for public purposes.

However, occasionally private foundations will make grants to for-profit businesses *if the purpose of the grant is to address some goal of the foundation*—for example, help for the working poor or youth unemployment. If your business is such that it addresses a pernicious social problem, then you may be able to find private foundation grant funding for specific, limited projects. The Foundation Center offers free access to a directory of large and small foundations at https://fdo.foundationcenter.org/. All of these foundations have to file an annual IRS Form 990, which gives details on the finances of the foundations. These are public records and you can search for them for your locality at http://foundationcenter.org/find-funding/990-finder or at www.guidestar.org/.

Personal Gifts

While the type of gifts governments and foundations offer are relatively consistent, stable, and publicly known, the forms of personal gifts are as varied as human imagination and need can make them. Remember from Chapter 13 that not just money has value; goods and services can provide tremendous value to a start-up business. The most popular forms of gifts are shown in Exhibit 14.1.

EXHIBIT 14.1

Forms of Personal Gifts

Cash—always useful, but also the gift most likely to have tax implications.

Picking up the tab—when someone buys something on behalf of your business and lets you benefit from it.

Accelerated cash-outs—where you might be given the funds for your business from an account your family set up for your future education or first home. Some cash-outs come when family or friends cash out their retirements or home (often via taking out a mortgage).

Free use—your family has an empty storefront, apartment, van, car, or other useful product that they let you use for free, or at a severely reduced price, for your business.

Free work—you get family or friends to help you out in the business for free, or for pizzas and drinks, or for wages significantly below minimum wage. This is sometimes called **unpaid labor**.

Overpayment—where family or friends "hire" you at higher than market rates to help you generate cash for your business. A variant of this is **favored status** or **sweetheart deals** where family or friends give you contracts to help you fund your business, instead of giving their work to the most qualified candidate.

Forgiveness—where family or friends give up on collecting debts you owe them, so you can use the money for the business. A variant of this is **deferral**, where the repayment of debts is delayed until the business is doing well.

Piggybacking—where family or friends let you add (i.e., piggyback) your purchases with theirs in order to get lower prices.

Personal gift financing is tremendously popular. In the Panel Study of Income Dynamics,[24] one-third of the firms reported having unpaid labor contributed by family members. In business plan classes, the same one out of three ratio of personal gifts to start-ups in general is a fairly common occurrence. These gifts range dramatically in size, but the commonality of personal gifts as a major source of funding for start-ups is fairly well known.[25]

Gift giving seems so easy and straightforward that it is hard to imagine how complex it really is—for the giver and the recipient, as well as the business. Consider gifts from the standpoint of the recipient and then the giver.

You are trying to get your business off the ground, and your favorite uncle offers to provide you with start-up capital. Not just any start-up capital, not an investment, not a loan. He is going to *give* you that boost that you need to get into business. It is an entrepreneur's dream—capital without any strings.

Do you take the money? Not so fast. The simple fact is that although Freud may have believed that "sometimes a cigar is just a cigar"[26] you can bet that a gift is *always* much, much more than just a gift. Gifts are loaded with special meanings and hidden purposes. Robert Cialdini wrote that gifts "create and cement alliances, allegiances, and partnerships."[27] Are you ready to enter into an alliance or partnership with your beloved uncle?

Accepting money from family members and friends entails some real risks. That favorite uncle might really mean it when he says that he is *giving* you start-up capital. But gifts like this have a nasty way of morphing into very real expectations that you may quickly come to hate. Meanings, especially in spoken messages, are slippery little devils. Your uncle may well be saying "gift" but thinking "loan," or "investment." If you are successful, you may suddenly find that the "gift" has now transformed (at least in your uncle's mind) into something very different. So here you stand—you *accepted* a gift, but your uncle *gave* you a loan. Lawsuits are made of just such differences of opinion.

Accepting gifts is difficult for many people, especially when the gift is substantial. Before you accept your uncle's offer, you should examine your own feelings. Can you accept a gift? Or do you have some secret plan that you will repay the money when you become successful? If you do not like being beholden to anyone, you probably should think twice about accepting an outright gift. Taking one most likely will lead to guilty feelings and resentment.

No need to immediately refuse your uncle's offer, but you should be absolutely certain that both you and he understand just what is being given and just what is expected in return.

Now turn the example on its head. Assume now that you are the uncle who is going to give a gift of cash to your favorite niece to start her business. Do you just write out a check and forget it? If you wish to keep your niece as a favorite, you probably shouldn't. Giving a gift is risky, just as is receiving one. Any gifts that you make had better be equitable among those who expect to receive from you. It is a simple fact that brothers, sisters, nieces, and nephews all expect to be treated fairly by their parents, grandparents, aunts, and uncles. Overtly favor one heir, and you will trigger resentment in all the others.

Giving a gift also has tax implications. Currently, any gift that exceeds $15,000 may be subject to U.S. gift taxes. Depending on the size of the gift, and your own situation, current gift taxes can be as high as 47 percent of the amount given. So if you are planning to finance your niece's start-up with $500,000, you'll probably need some creative financial planning to avoid the tax implications.

You should carefully consider why you want to make this gift. Perhaps you are one of those very rare people who are true Santa Clauses: You get real satisfaction from giving away your wealth. This is unlikely, however. Komter and Vollebergh showed that gifts given to extended kin are usually made because of feelings of obligation and rarely because of feelings of affection.[28] Probably, you are expecting to receive gratitude. If so, you'll more than likely be disappointed. Or do you think that your niece's business idea is the next Microsoft and that your support will result in untold wealth? In this case, you should not make your support a gift. Structure it as an investment in her business–make it a loan or a purchase of stock.

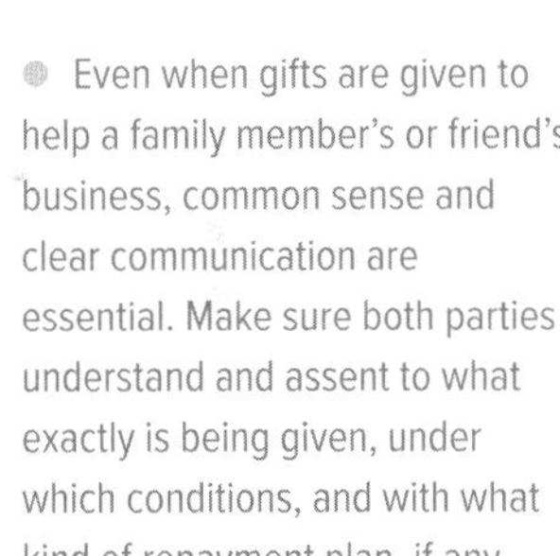

Even when gifts are given to help a family member's or friend's business, common sense and clear communication are essential. Make sure both parties understand and assent to what exactly is being given, under which conditions, and with what kind of repayment plan, if any.

Icatnews/Shutterstock

Given the many problems of gift giving, should you change your mind about supporting your niece's new business?

No, but you should understand exactly what you are giving, and what you expect in return. You should also be sure that your niece also understands.

For both of you to be certain that you agree, you should:

1. **Put your agreement into writing.** As is said in Mexico, "Words walk. Paper talks." This has the same message as the saying "Oral agreements are just as valuable as the paper they're written on!" There simply is no better way to be certain that everyone understands a transaction than to write it out, then have each party read, sign, and date the document. When disagreements arise later, the written agreement provides a permanent, immutable record of your original intentions.
2. **If it is a gift, have the agreement specifically say so.** "This is a gift, freely given between uncle (grantor) and you (recipient). No repayment is expected, and none will be accepted."
3. **If it is a loan, have the agreement specify the exact interest and payment terms.** A good idea from the point of view of the recipient is to make repayment a percentage of positive cash flows. Ideally, payments will be made either (a) until the principal amount plus accrued interest has been paid or (b) until the giver has received a specified return on the original amount. In the real world, loans between family members often go unpaid. Be clear concerning the circumstances under which the loan will be forgiven.
4. **If it is an equity investment, consider nonvoting stock.** One common problem with family and friends as equity investors is that they want to have a say in the management of your business. This may be fine if they have appropriate talents and experience. It can be a kiss of death if they just want to meddle. Nonvoting stock provides the opportunity for capital gains, but pretty much precludes interference in business operations.

Gifts via Crowdfunding

Today you can fund your business online through gifts made to your business. The technique is called crowdfunding, and there are two types: a nonequity model and an equity model. Groups like Kickstarter.com, Indiegogo.com, and GoFundMe.com pioneered the nonequity model. At such sites, you post your business idea, along with descriptions, photos, and if at all possible a video about your business. You set a gift target goal, say $10,000, and a deadline (like 30 days).

For example, the Ramos alarm clock (www.ramosclock.com) is a super-loud alarm clock that can be turned off only by getting out of bed. The inventors posted on Kickstarter seeking $75,000 to develop the product. To get one of the clocks you would have to donate at least $160. Lesser donations received a T-shirt or a listing on the Ramos website. They went out on social media to drum up support and also began to receive some media attention—both of which are best practices you would want to follow. In the end, they had 525 backers from all over the world and had raised $153,585, or more than twice what they sought. This support also helped prove that there was a market for the clock, helping Ramos get the attention of stores and catalogs. Best of all, because the money was received as gifts, the Ramos founders still owned all of their business, plus $153,585 of funding.

LO 14-3 Explain which type of financing is best for your business.

What Type of Financing Is Right for Your Business?

If you were to ask the owner of a small business which kind of financing—equity, debt, or gift—is best you are likely to hear "Gift capital, of course!" This reaction is due to the very meaning of a gift: something given freely with no obligations attached. So, why not? Let me look at that gift: free money just for the taking.

Well, sounds good. In fact, it sounds too good. Even Milton Friedman stated that there's no such thing as a free lunch.[29] And indeed, gift capital can be the least free of all. Even if you choose to raise your free capital on Kickstarter, you are going to be out the time and resources that you will have to use to create and publish a compelling story as to why complete strangers should give their money to you. Which brings us back to the old familiar equity and debt. Suppose you have enough of your own money to start a new business. Because you are such a good risk, you also have the ability to borrow all the money you need to start the business. Which should you do?

To answer this, you must realize that the cost of equity is much greater than the cost of debt. Equity investors routinely expect to earn from 25 to 500 percent on their investment into your business. Debt, on the other hand, is much cheaper. Right now 30-year mortgages are generally less than 4 percent. Car loans are as low as 2 percent through credit unions. And, depending on your credit worthiness, business loans range from the prime rate (currently 5.5 percent) to perhaps as high as 10 percent.

Consider the simplest case in which a small business owner has the alternatives of using personal equity funding or borrowing funds. The business may be 100 percent capitalized by either equity or debt, or any mix of equity and debt. Equity capital costs are estimated to be 20 percent per year—the investors expect $200 in gains or dividends for every $1,000 invested in the business.

Debt capital costs are estimated to be a net of 6 percent after tax, or for every $1,000 borrowed, the entrepreneur owes the bank $60 a year (plus the $1,000 will need to be paid back as agreed).

If the owner chooses to use a capital mix of 70 percent equity and 30 percent debt, the weighted average **cost of capital** is approximately 16 percent. At a 50–50 mix of equity and debt, the **weighted average cost of capital (WAC)** is 13 percent and at 30 percent equity to 70 percent debt, the average cost of capital is approximately 10 percent. The more debt that is included in the capital mix, the lower the weighted average cost will be. The lower your cost of capital, the more profits you can keep for yourself. The more money your business generates for its owners, the more the business is worth. Thus, firm value is inversely related to cost of capital at any level of operations.

cost of capital
The percentage cost of obtaining future funds.

weighted average cost of capital (WAC)
The expected average future cost of funds.

So you probably will do best by using your own equity along with some amount of borrowing. If you invest $100,000 into your business, and make a profit of $25,000, your rate of return (which can be considered to be your cost of equity) is 25 percent. But what if you put up only $50,000 and borrow $50,000 at 5 percent? What is your rate of return now if you have a $25,000 profit? Half of the profit was made using equity, half with debt. You will pay $2,500 in interest on the debt, thus your profit is really only $22,500. But your equity investment is only $50,000. This means that the return on the amount of your own money that you have invested is 45 percent. Compare that to the 25 percent return on a pure equity structure.

As debt increases as a percentage of total investment (called **financial leverage**) returns on equity will also increase at a decreasing rate up to some limit where taking on more debt starts to cause returns to decline. Few, if any, small business owners, however, even attempt to estimate this mix of debt and equity which is called the **optimum capital structure** of their business. Calculating this optimum mix of debt takes too much time for the value it provides.

financial leverage
A measure of the amount of debt relative to total investment.

optimum capital structure
The ratio of debt to equity that provides the maximum level of profits.

What you need to understand is the concept that having some debt in your capital structure works to increase your profits, but having too much debt will decrease profits. So what you want to do is to find that level of debt that works for you.

Owners and managers of small businesses are quite diverse. Entrepreneurs come from all social classes. They have different levels of education ranging from no formal schooling to those with advanced degrees. People of all major religions, of every race, and from every part of the world are represented among small business owners. As you would expect, such a diverse group of people have very diverse attitudes toward work, toward investing, toward management.

Some people gleefully jump out of airplanes; others are determined to "keep one foot on the ground." Business owners similarly differ in their response to financial risk. A few seek risk, thriving on the pressure of attempting to make the big strike. Most prefer to avoid business risk to the extent possible. In academic terms, some business owners are *risk seeking*, although most small business owners are *risk averse*. Because of this, the optimal capital structure for one entrepreneur may well be anathema to another. Each owner of a small business must find the levels of equity, debt, and financial risk with which he or she is comfortable.

Financial risk is the probability of financial loss. Business opportunities, projects, and assets that have a greater chance of producing a loss are considered more risky than those that have a smaller chance. In a very real sense, risk is synonymous with uncertainty. If you purchase a 30-day U.S. Treasury bond, the return is certain. On the thirtieth day the government will issue a check for the amount of the bond plus interest. Because the government has the power to create money, there is no uncertainty and thus no risk of financial loss. If, on the other hand, you use the same amount of money to invest in a business, the return is very uncertain. You might succeed greatly or the business might fail and you lose your entire investment.

financial risk
Uncertainty of returns; the probability of losing money.

Borrowing money increases financial risk. In effect, borrowing money for a business is very much like selling the business to an investor and simultaneously buying back an option to repurchase the business on specific terms of payment. If the terms of payment are not met, the lender has the right to keep the business. The lender may enforce this right through either repossession if business assets were pledged as collateral, or involuntary bankruptcy, mediated by the court system. Payments on debt must be made as agreed without regard to the cash position of the business.

Selling equity in the business provides neither the opportunity to repurchase nor the obligation to make payments to owners. If the business does not provide sufficient profits and cash flows, an equity investor must accept the situation and hope that future operations will be profitable.

FIGURE 14.4

Interaction among Profitability, Control, and Risk

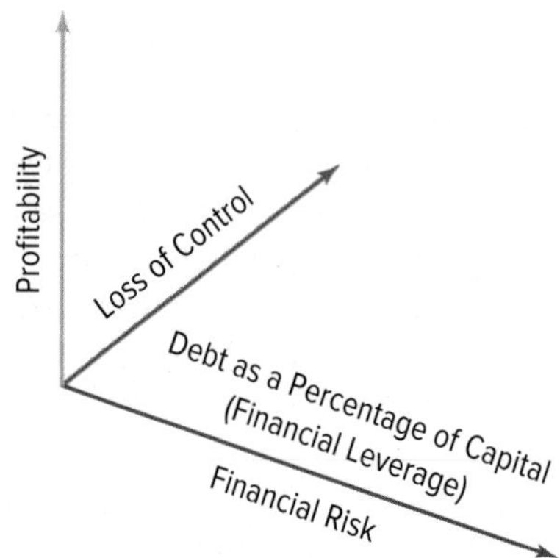

So why should you borrow, if doing so increases the probability of financial loss?

Borrowing money for capital investment provides two benefits: (1) Borrowing enhances the potential for higher rates of return for the owners. (2) Borrowing allows the owners to keep a greater level of control of the business. For these reasons, the majority of small business owners prefer to borrow over accepting outside equity investment.[30] The interaction of the effects of choosing between equity and debt capital results in a small business owner having to compromise among the levels of potential profits, financial risk, and control of the business. This is depicted graphically in Figure 14.4.

Borrowing increases potential profits by (1) lowering the weighted average cost of capital and (2) providing capital funds that allow the business to consider additional opportunities.

However, control issues arise under either alternative of issuing equity to outsiders or borrowing funds. When outside investors acquire equity, they also acquire some level of influence over the operations and strategy of the firm. Should disputes arise among the owners, it is quite possible, depending upon the number of owners and their percentage of ownership, that disgruntled stockholders could form a coalition and take control of the firm from the original founders. Alternatively, disgruntled minority owners may sue majority owners. For these reasons, many owners of small businesses are loath to sell any ownership shares. They prefer to accept the added financial risk of borrowing rather than deal with stockholders.

Borrowing capital, however, is not without its own issues of control. Lenders have to trust your management to operate the business efficiently, generating sufficient cash flow to meet the repayment terms of the loan. It is common, therefore, for lenders to require borrowers to provide regular documentation of the financial condition of the business. Many banks require that a copy of each year's income tax return, income statement, and balance sheet be furnished during the term of the loan. Loan contracts may also impose restrictions on the operation of the business, such as requiring that a specific minimum net worth be maintained, a specific debt-to-equity ratio not be exceeded, no dividends be paid to stockholders, executive salaries not exceed a specified amount, no capital assets be acquired or disposed of without the concurrence of the lender, and so on. These types of restrictions, called *loan covenants*, can seriously limit management's freedom to operate the business and can make taking on shareowners seem like less of a burden. It could also make do-it-yourself funding more attractive.

Financial Management for the Life of Your Business

Tools for Financial Management

Financial management requires that you have some method to measure and compare your financial position and financial results. Your financial position is reflected on your balance sheet, your financial results on your income statement. The problem is how to interpret the information on these two reports.

As with any analysis, you must have something to compare with your position and results. The obvious comparisons are (1) with your planned position and results (your master budget), (2) with prior years' position and results, and (3) with the position and results of other firms. The difficulty is in how to understand the comparison. Suppose last year you had a net business profit of $50,000 and this year your profit was $55,000. Did you do well in the current year? You did make 10 percent more this year than last. But it is often misleading to compare dollars to dollars for a financial result. You did not do well for the year if you invested an additional $100,000 into your business: Your return on your added investment is only 5 percent: Added income/Added investment = $5,000/$100,000 = 0.05.

For these reasons, most financial comparisons are made using ratios. You made $55,000 in profit. You have a competitor who also made a net profit of $55,000. So, were the two of you equally effective business managers? Perhaps so, perhaps not. You made the same profit, but what were your respective inputs to the business? Suppose you had $110,000 invested in your business. Your competitor has $550,000 invested. Your return on investment is $55,000/$110,000, or 50 percent. Your competitor's return is $55,000/$550,000, or 10 percent. It would certainly seem from this analysis that you are the better business manager.

There are four broad categories of financial ratios: (1) activity ratios, (2) profitability ratios, (3) liquidity ratios, and (4) leverage ratios. Activity ratios measure how productive a particular asset is in producing sales activity. Profitability ratios measure management effectiveness in creating wealth from sales and from invested funds. Liquidity ratios measure the business's ability to pay debts and expenses that are due in the current accounting period. Leverage ratios measure the relative risk that a business setback could cause bankruptcy. Commonly used ratios are explained in Table 14.4. The three most commonly used ratios are return on investment (ROI), current ratio, and debt-to-equity ratio. The value of these ratios for management depends to a large extent on the type of business you are conducting and the stage of your business in the business life cycle.

The ratios are the key ways businesses are evaluated. You have seen many of these key ratios in reports from BizStats.com, BizMiner.com, and the Risk Management Association *Annual Statement Studies* mentioned in Chapters 7 and 9. Sources like those can provide important comparisons to help you determine if your key ratios are better or worse than the norms for your industry. While you are in the start-up phase, there can be considerable volatility in your business, and looking over a month or two's results can lead to confusing results using ratios. That is why for start-ups ratios are usually based on annual figures, or at least a six-month period.

In addition, the kinds of ratios that add important information to your business decision making will change as the firm matures. As we have said, initially your concerns are less with profitability and more with having enough cash on hand to meet your immediate needs (what we call the "short term"). That is why initially liquidity ratios are the most important to you. As your firm gets past its initial trial-and-error period and develops its standard operating procedures, activity ratios help tell you if your use of the firm's assets in those standard operating procedures is giving your firm the kind of results it needs to be successful.

As the firm reaches its breakeven point, profits become a reality and profitability ratios become increasingly important to the firm. At this point, leverage ratios also become more important because they look at the longer-term success of the firm, as well as its ability to weather threats leading to bankruptcy. Table 14.4 provides the major financial ratios, and tells you how they are computed and interpreted.

financial management
A set of theories and techniques used to optimize the receipt and use of capital assets.

Financial Management for Start-Up

LO **14-4** Describe the differing needs for financial management at each stage of business life.

During the start-up phase of your business, you will use the **financial management** techniques described in the bootstrapping discussion. The emphasis is on conserving what little cash your new business has.

TABLE 14.4 Common Ratios for Financial Management Using Ratios to Analyze the Income Statement

Ratio Name	Interpretation	Decision Criterion	Formula
Activity ratio	Measures how productive a particular asset was in producing sales activity		
Asset turnover ratio	Measures how efficiently a business uses all its assets to produce sales	Higher ratio is better than a lower ratio	Net sales revenue / Average total assets (Beginning assets + Ending assets) / 2
Accounts receivable turnover ratio	Measures the frequency with which receivables are converted to cash	Higher turnover provides faster access to cash that can be used in the business	Net credit sales / Average net accounts receivable
Inventory turnover ratio	Indicates how quickly inventory is sold and thus the relative efficiency of both the sales and purchasing functions	Higher turnover is preferred	Cost of goods sold / Average merchandise inventory
Average holding period	Indicates the same as inventory turnover, but is easier to understand	Shorter period is preferred	365 days / Inventory turnover ratio
Profitability ratio	Measures management effectiveness in creating wealth from sales and from invested funds		
Gross margin ratio	Measures the percentage of sales revenue available to pay operating costs and to provide profits after paying for inventory	Higher ratio is preferred	Gross margin / Sales revenue
Profit margin ratio, also called return on sales (ROS)	Measures management's effectiveness in managing all costs relative to sales	Higher is preferred	Net income / Sales revenue
Return on equity	Measures management's effectiveness in using investor funds to provide profits	Higher return is preferred	Net income − Preferred stock dividends declared / Average common stockholders' equity
Return on assets	Measures management's effectiveness in using the assets of the business to provide profits	Higher return is preferred	Net income / Average total assets
Return on investment (ROI)	Measures management's effectiveness in using the invested capital of the business to provide profits	Higher return is preferred	Net income / Average investment
Earnings per share	Measures profitability per share investment	Examined over time, a trend of increasing per share earnings is preferred	Net income − preferred stock dividends declared / Weighted average common stock outstanding
Liquidity ratio	Measure the business's ability to pay debts and expenses that are due in the current accounting period		
Current ratio	Measures how much money can be made available to pay obligations within the fiscal year	Higher ratio is preferred	Current assets / Current liabilities

Ratio Name	Interpretation	Decision Criterion	Formula
Acid test or quick ratio	Measures how much money can be made available very quickly to pay obligations within the fiscal year	Higher ratio is preferred	$\frac{\text{Current assets} - (\text{Inventories} + \text{Prepaid assets})}{\text{Current liabilities}}$
Leverage ratio	Measures the relative risk that a business setback could cause bankruptcy		
Debt-to-assets ratio	Measures the extent to which the business can meet its obligations for the long haul	Lower ratio indicates greater solvency; higher ratio indicates increased business risk	$\frac{\text{Total liabilities}}{\text{Total assets}}$
Debt-to-equity ratio	Measures the extent to which the business can meet its obligations for the long haul	Lower ratio indicates greater solvency; higher ratio indicates increased business risk	$\frac{\text{Total liabilities}}{\text{Total owners' equity}}$
Times interest earned	Measures the risk of being forced into bankruptcy for not meeting required interest payments	Higher is preferred	$\frac{\text{Operating income before interest and income tax}}{\text{Interest expense}}$

Financial Management for Growth

Many small businesses successfully start up only to find that the need for financial management is greater than ever as the business enters a phase of rapid growth. This situation is like a lame "bad news-good news" joke. The bad news is that the business has greater capital needs than ever. The good news is that more sources of money are available to meet those needs. The emphasis of financial management during periods of growth is to obtain increasing amounts of cash inflows to pay for added inventory, productive assets, and employees needed to meet growing levels of business operations.

Financial Management for Operations

Most small businesses eventually reach a size that is relatively stable: not too small to generate sufficient profits; not too large for the preferences and abilities of the owners. At this stage of the business, the emphasis of financial management is to build owner wealth, to conserve assets, to match cash inflows to outflows, and to maximize the return on capital assets by making optimal investing decisions.

Financial Management for Business Exit

Eventually, you will face the necessity of leaving the active management of your business. This may be because you want to take advantage of a different opportunity, the business needs professional management, you want to pass ownership to family members, or you want to retire. You might become ill or disabled. Regardless why, successfully leaving your business requires maximizing the value of your business for your successors.

The goals of financial management in preparation for exiting the business depends, in part, on the nature of the exit that is planned. Business exit can entail a transfer to your heirs. Another common exit is to sell the business, either to outside investors or to the employees. Finally, business exit can come from terminating the business through bankruptcy, a "work-out," or simply closing the business and disposing of its assets.

If your plan is to transfer the business to family members, then you will want to ensure that the business is in sound financial condition. You should be working to minimize debt and to increase asset value. It is essential that you establish internal controls over assets by establishing policies and procedures that are clearly stated and understood by everyone involved in management.

If you plan to sell your business, your goals should be to optimize capital structure for profits. Investors usually will not pay to "buy" cash in your business. Therefore, you should be removing all surplus cash and tightening the cash-to-cash cycle to the shortest time possible. The condition and age of assets will greatly affect the final selling price, so now is the time to ensure that all equipment is in good working order, that the facilities are clean and organized, and that accounts receivable and accounts payable are up to date.

Termination of a business is also very common. Many small businesses are extensions of the owner. For example, CPA firms, hair salons, real estate brokerages, indeed any business that provides personal services often depend solely on the reputation and personality of the owner. In reality, there is no business to sell. In cases such as these exit usually involves finishing all outstanding projects, collecting all money due, disposing of all business assets, and finally (if possible) paying off any outstanding debt. Thus, the goals of financial management are to recover all asset value possible, cover any indebtedness, and use the remainder for personal purposes. Refer to Chapter 6 for a more comprehensive discussion of the many issues of business exit.

CHAPTER SUMMARY

LO 14-1 Describe the three types of capital financing and their costs and trade-offs.

- Most people have a number of assets and financial resources that can be used to finance their business.
- Financing can be in the form of equity, debt, or gifts.
- An entrepreneur's own funds are the first source of financing for most small businesses.
- Forms of business organization can be categorized along two dimensions:
    - How the business is taxed.
    - How much responsibility owners have for the liabilities of the business.

LO 14-2 Explain the characteristics of a business that determine its ability to raise capital.

- Investors put money into a business to make money for themselves.
- Lenders expect a return from making loans, by getting back the amount they loan plus more money in the form of interest.
- Equity investors expect to get back the money they invest plus extra money, a gain on investment.
- To get money from other people, owners must show them that their business probably can make gains for them.
- Financing with equity is expensive and creates problems of control and decision making.
- Other than the owner's own funds, the most common source of capital for established ongoing small businesses is borrowed funds.

LO 14-3 Explain which type of financing is best for your business.

- As debt increases as a percentage of total capital, total cost of capital declines.
- Lower cost of capital results in higher firm value, all other things being held equal.
- Borrowing money increases financial risk because payments on debt must be made as agreed without regard to the cash position of the business.

LO 14-4 Describe the differing needs for financial management at each stage of business life.

- You can use financial ratios to evaluate your business.
- There are four broad categories of financial ratios: activity ratios, profitability ratios, liquidity ratios, and leverage ratios.
- During the start-up phase of a small business the primary financial management need is to obtain sufficient funds to pay for equipment, buildings, inventory, and indeed, all the costs of starting and running a business.
- During the growth phase the need for financial management increases to pay for added inventory, productive assets, and employees to meet growing levels of business operations.
- During the mature phase of the business the emphasis of financial management is to build owner wealth, to conserve assets, to match cash inflows to outflows, and to maximize the return on capital assets by making optimal investing decisions.
- Successfully leaving your business requires maximizing its value for your successors by creating effective internal controls and developing business systems to replace your specific skills and knowledge.

KEY TERMS

debt, 507
equity capital, 507
gift, 507
debt capital, 509
gift capital, 509
outside equity, 509
partnership, 510
corporation, 510
limited liability company (LLC), 510
secured debt, 510
unsecured debt, 510
interest, 511
gain on investment, 511
dividends, 511
risk, 511
diversify, 511
harvest, 512
bootstrapping, 512
royalty financing, 513
sophisticated investor, 516
accredited investor, 516
angel investor, 517
community development organization, 519
microlender, 519
small business investment company (SBIC), 519
accelerator, 519
credit reporting agency (CRA), 520
Fair Credit Reporting Act (FCRA), 520
profit, profitability, 521
collateral, 521
SaaS, 522
tax abatement, 524
tax credit, 524
grant, 524
foundation, 525
cost of capital, 529
weighted average cost of capital (WAC), 529
financial leverage, 529
optimum capital structure, 529
financial risk, 529
financial management, 531

DISCUSSION QUESTIONS

1. Why does a business require a constant flow of money and capital assets during its existence?
2. What things do you need to do to convince an investor to make you a loan or purchase equity in your business?
3. In what ways does accepting outside investment change the ways you manage your business?
4. Why do you have to give up more ownership to get outside investment if your business is risky?
5. Explain why investors prefer investments that pay back sooner to those that pay back later.
6. Name four ways that an investor can receive payment from a business. Describe the advantages and disadvantages of each.
7. Many small business owners prefer to borrow money rather than sell equity. Why is this so?
8. In what ways do the Four Cs of Borrowing differ from the requirements for being able to obtain equity capital?
9. Explain why it is easier to borrow money to buy a semitruck than to purchase rights to a business process.
10. Explain how borrowing money (1) increases firm value and (2) makes more money for a business owner.
11. Explain the differing financial management needs of a small business during the start-up, growth, mature, and exit phases.

EXPERIENTIAL EXERCISES

1. Go to the SBA directory of SBICs (**www.sba.gov/content/all-sbic-licensees-state**). Search through the directory, specifically looking for SBICs that will invest in businesses in the industry in which you are interested. Make a chart of the minimum and maximum investments that the SBICs will make, and their requirements to invest. Present your findings to your class.
2. Contact the owner of a business you would like to own. Arrange an interview. Ask how the owner obtained start-up financing. What sources of financing does the owner use today? Report your findings to your class.
3. Find out if your city has an office of economic development. (Almost every city with a population greater than 100,000 does.) Contact the office and inquire about the programs that it supports. Ask specifically how the office would provide support to you for start-up and operations.
4. Find out if your city or county has any tax abatement economic development zones. What must you do to be able to take advantage of the tax abatement?
5. Make an appointment with a commercial bank loan officer who handles business loans. Ask about the bank's documentation requirements. Determine what commitment, if any, the bank has for making loans to local small businesses. Present your findings to your class.
6. Do a search of *Entrepreneur* and *Bloomberg Businessweek Small Business* websites looking for information about businesses that were successful in obtaining financing. Write a report detailing how the businesses arranged financing.

MINI-CASE

EVERLYWELL, INC. IN AUSTIN, TEXAS

Creating a successful startup is always a daunting task. Entrepreneurs risk their savings, their careers, even their reputations when they decide to begin a new business, especially when they use other peoples' money to start. But suppose that in addition to the common challenges of starting a new business, you add being an attractive young woman in a traditionally male industry, and you also add entering a field where there was recently a high-profile failure of just such a female entrepreneur.

That just might make you reconsider the wisdom of your course.

Julia Cheek, however, persisted, and in doing so, has created a startup in the burgeoning field of home-based self-sampling for medical tests. And yes, that is essentially what the recently failed Theranos claimed to be doing. EverlyWell is not another Theranos, however. EverlyWell has not invented a new blood test; it does not manufacture its own testing equipment; it is not located in Silicon Valley, but rather in Austin, Texas; and most importantly, the company does not deal with medical insurance companies. Customers pay directly for any of EverlyWell's diagnostic tests.[31]

So, Julia Cheek is not intimated by the frequent comparisons made of her business, EverlyWell, to the spectacular failure of Theranos. Such comparisons are certainly irritating and as she pointed out in an interview with Jen Wieczner of Fortune magazine, the recent FBI raid on another female-led startup, uBiome, has not helped the situation. She makes a strenuous effort to distinguish EverlyWell as well as herself, and she directs her employees to do the same.[32]

Julia Cheek did not start as an entrepreneur, nor does she have a background in health care. She does have a Harvard MBA however, which she received in 2011. After receiving her degree, she was employed as the Director of Strategy and Operations for the George W. Bush Institute and later as Vice-President of Corporate Strategy and Global Communications for MoneyGram International.[33] Her interest in health care arose because of a perplexing set of symptoms, including fatigue, pain, and a general feeling of lessened cognitive function. Because of these symptoms, she consulted with several physicians, each of whom ordered various medical tests. Despite the time and money that she spent, she remained without a specific diagnosis. Further, she stated that she did not even know what tests had been performed.[34]

Her less-than-wonderful experience as a patient led her to start EverlyWell.

Once she decided to create the business, she followed a familiar path for raising capital. In April 2016, she raised $2.5 million in initial seed funding.[35] Next, in November 2017, Julia Cheek appeared on CBS's program, "Shark Tank," where she won a additional $1 million investment, for which she gave a 5% equity position to the investor. This beginning was followed by other equity investments by venture capitalists, eventually culminating in a $50 million Series B financing award led by Goodwater Capital and Highland Capital Partners.[36]

The company has grown rapidly during its existence. According to the *Wall Street Journal,* EverlyWell has shipped some 275,000 testing kits to date. 2018 revenues are said to be close to $20 million. The company offers 35 different testing kits covering issues ranging across a variety of physical conditions. Kits are sold online and are available at various retailers, including CVS Health Corp. and Target Corp.[37]

CASE DISCUSSION QUESTIONS

1. The case includes a statement that EverlyWell " . . .followed a familiar path for raising capital." How would you describe how Julia Cheek raised development capital for the business?
2. The Shark Tank investor furnished $1 million in seed capital in return for 5% of the ownership of EverlyWell. What total value for the business does this investment imply?
3. The information available about EverlyWell does not mention any borrowed capital. What might be the reasons that EverlyWell has not borrowed any funds for capital?
4. How would you explain the apparent success of Julia Cheek in creating a medical testing business, given her lack of experience in the field of medical care?

CHAPTER

15

Assets: Inventory and Operations Management

● Each month, thousands of businesses experience the theft of inventory. While most inventory theft in retail stores is committed by employees, theft by outside thieves is all too common. The FBI's preliminary report on crime for 2018 states that 441,282 burglaries were committed that year in U.S. cities of 100,000 and greater population.[1] There is no reliable estimate of the value of losses from freight shipments, burglaries, and fraud, but a report by The Hartford insurance company states that such losses hit 20 percent of small businesses and the average loss is approximately $8,000.[2]

Suppose you were to discover a burglary of your business. What would you do?

Robert Kneschke/Shutterstock

LEARNING OBJECTIVES

After you complete this chapter, you will be able to:

LO 15-1 Describe techniques to manage short-term assets.

LO 15-2 Calculate the value of the assets in your business.

LO 15-3 Describe techniques for managing fixed assets.

LO 15-4 Calculate ratios used to analyze capital investment decisions.

LO 15-5 Describe the advantages of renting or leasing capital equipment.

LO 15-6 Describe techniques to manage and improve the operations of your business.

LO 15-7 Be able to discuss the need for and value of documenting your business operations.

Focus on Small Business: Protecting Current Assets—Inventory Theft

Allen and Ginger Record were dismayed when they arrived one Sunday morning in December 2018 at their small business, Fifth Avenue Studio Shop (which sells tattoo supplies). The door had been broken open and the shop had been burglarized overnight.

Once they got over their instant dismay, they began the depressing task of attempting to determine just how much of what had been taken. A quick inspection showed that the criminals had not just randomly taken what was at hand. Rather, they had focused on the expensive tattoo machines and tattoo inks. Twenty thousand dollars' worth of inventory had been stolen.

They also discovered that their security video had captured the entire event. The video clearly showed the door being broken down and the two burglars, wrapped in white coveralls, wearing hoodies, going directly to the most expensive items of inventory.

Then, just to add insult to injury, one of the burglars obtained a copy of the surveillance video and proceeded to post it on social media. This, however, proved to be a less-than-brilliant move. The posting helped point the police to the perpetrators, who later confessed the crime. The machines, however, had been sold and are very unlikely to be recovered.[3]

DISCUSSION QUESTIONS

1. Why do you think burglars would target a small business that sells highly specialized inventory?
2. What could the owners have done to prevent this attack?
3. How do you suppose the cyber criminals obtained the information that allowed them to target only the most valuable inventory?
4. Think of the business that you own or would like to own. How and to what extent would a burglary be a threat to your business?

LO 15-1 Describe techniques to manage short-term assets.

Managing Short-Term Assets

In many ways, you can think of your business as a collection of assets: things you own that will provide value in the future. The things that make up your business include the obvious, such as cash, inventory, tools, machinery, buildings, and land. Less obvious things are also owned, such as legal claims to collect money from customers in the future, patents, copyrights, trademarks, expertise, and your reputation.

Because your business *is* its assets, if you allow them to be damaged, lost, stolen, or destroyed, your wealth diminishes. At some point, if your business loses enough value, it will cease to exist. It will be bankrupt, and you will have lost your investment.

Managing your business assets to obtain their maximum value is critical to ultimate business success. Chapter 13 is dedicated to the issues of managing cash, the most liquid of all business assets. This chapter discusses managing the critical short-term assets of accounts receivable and inventory, and managing the essential long-term assets of property, plant, and equipment.

In the next chapter we will discuss other types of business risk that can often be managed through planning, management, and insurance. These insurable risks include risks to computer assets and critical business data; risks of damage due to events such as storms, floods, and fire; and risks of liability for the well-being of other entities.

In this chapter, we first will look at the issues of maintaining the security of short-term assets (other than cash), and methods for optimizing their value in your business. In the section "Value of Assets in Your Business" we will study the issues involved in determining the value of the short-term assets at any specific point in time. Next, we will look at long-term (capital) assets, briefly discussing their nature and the methods used for planning their acquisition and disposal. Then we will expand on the capital budgeting process and take a more in depth look at the techniques of renting and leasing capital assets. Finally, we will take a very brief look at specific operations management techniques, including the process of documenting business operations.

Accounts Receivable

accounts receivable
Money owed to your business by customers who purchased your product on credit.

Accounts receivable are money that is owed to your business by your customers. As was discussed in Chapter 13, relatively few small businesses today provide credit to customers. Current practice is for small businesses to provide credit only by accepting bank-issued credit cards. However, there are still some small businesses, especially those involved in wholesale distribution, that provide direct credit to customers. For these firms, managing receivables is an essential activity.

The Pros and Cons of Offering Credit to Customers

Have you ever wondered why any business gives credit directly to customers? On the surface the practice of giving credit seems to be a very expensive way to do business.

Think about it: Selling your product and then allowing customers a month or two to pay has three negative effects that are often overlooked when business owners make the decision to extend credit.

- First, providing credit delays the receipt of cash. If your small business is like most, you exist in a state of constant cash shortages. Anything that delays receiving cash makes the problems of meeting payrolls and paying suppliers and vendors even worse.
- Second, you must somehow replace the "missing" cash. Most often this means borrowing. Borrowing, of course, is expensive. You spend time to arrange a loan, and then must make regular payments of interest.
- Third, if you give credit to your customers, sooner or later one of them will not pay. Although you provide credit only to those customers whom you believe will pay, despite careful monitoring and despite strenuous collection efforts, eventually someone won't. The reasons why people don't pay can be almost anything, from inability to pay because they have no money to low ethics to outright fraud. Regardless of the cause, your business loses when customers don't pay.

So, why do it?

Well, there are four big reasons that businesses provide credit to customers:

1. Giving credit increases sales because people who buy on credit tend to buy more.
2. Giving credit increases repeat business.
3. Providing credit reduces the cost of selling because it is much less expensive to obtain repeat business than it is to get new customers.
4. Even though giving credit raises some costs, the increased sales result in increased profit.

So, there are good business reasons to provide credit even though doing so causes many management problems. At least the problems of extending credit are well known in business and there are good methods to maximize the potential benefit while controlling the problems. Some methods to get the best results from offering credit are discussed next.

The ABC's of Extending Credit to Your Customers

The first thing that you should complete before you first extend credit to any customer is a written credit policy. This documented policy replaces having individual contracts between your business and the customers to whom credit is advanced. Because it is a replacement for a unique contract, you want to ensure that each credit customer acknowledges having read the policy statement and agrees to abide by its provisions.

Those provisions, at the absolute minimum, should include:

- Customer permission to complete a credit check and acquire a credit score.
- Payment terms, including the conditions that will make a payment delinquent and any provision for receiving a discount for prompt payment.
- Acceptable forms of payment (cash, checks, credit or debit cards, etc.).
- The specific address to which payments should be remitted.
- Penalties and interest imposed on late payments.
- Collection activities that will be made in the event of late payment.
- Recourse that your business will use in the case of nonpayment, such as the required use of arbitration or selling of the receivable to a third party.

As you can see from this list, creating a credit policy is not anything to be done casually. In fact, you should work with an attorney who is expert in retail and credit operations to assist you in writing an appropriate policy.

As discussed above, extending credit to customers usually will increase sales. The practice does not always increase reliable cash flow, however. To do that, you must be consistent in making collection efforts. One entrepreneur, Dwight Cooper, as described in the nearby Small Business Insight, hit upon a novel method to bring his invoices and statements to the attention of his customers. His technique has worked to speed up the receipt of payments from customers.

If you do choose to provide credit, there are some common sense techniques that will help you make extending credit a value-added activity. These are listed in The Thoughtful Entrepreneur. Also, in Chapter 12, we discussed selecting and installing a computerized accounting system. Many accounting applications for small businesses include applications for managing credit to customers. You should seriously consider using the application if it is included or acquiring a separate credit management application.

Use Your Accounts Receivable as a Source of Financing

You can often get immediate cash from third-party finance companies if you have established and enforced policies to maintain a high quality of receivables. Having high-quality receivables lets you quickly get cash to meet unexpected needs.

You can use your receivables in two ways to quickly lay your hands on cash. First, you can pledge your receivables as collateral for a commercial loan. **Pledging receivables** to a commercial lender is usually less expensive than factoring. When you pledge receivables, your business is liable only for the borrowed amount and accrued interest on the loan, regardless of the amount

pledging receivables
Giving a third party legal rights to debts owed your business in order to provide assurance that borrowed money will be repaid.

SMALL BUSINESS INSIGHT

PUT YOUR BILL ON THE TOP OF THE PILE

Dwight Cooper, CEO of PPR Travel,[4] a nurse-staffing firm in Jacksonville, Florida, was in a quandary. Average time to collect payment on accounts was a crippling 60 days from the time the bill was sent. For two months, Dwight had to cover all the costs of his nurses—wages, benefits, and tax withholdings—as well as his own operating expenses. In effect, Dwight was financing the operations of his customers. On the other hand, if he pressed his clients for payment, he risked creating bad will and perhaps even losing business.

What should I do?, he asked himself.

Owners of small businesses commonly face the same dilemma. A recent study by REL Consultancy Group of Purchase, New York, found that fully one-third of big businesses are habitually late paying vendors' bills.[5] Sooner or later, if you provide credit to customers you too will have difficulties in collecting what is due. Customer accounts will slip ever further into arrears. Past due accounts will accumulate: 90 days, 120 days, even 6 months in arrears. Dwight took a unique approach to his problem: He asked his customers why they paid late and what he could do to help them speed payment.

Dwight Cooper shaved 15 days off his company's average time for collection of bills receivable. Which of his steps could you see yourself imitating in your own business? What ideas might you add in improving your company's collection process?

Courtesy Dwight Cooper

Even more unusually, Dwight *acted* to implement the things that his customers said would help them pay more quickly. First, he established procedures to ensure that every bill was accurate. Second, he issued a single invoice to each hospital for all nurses provided, rather than sending multiple invoices, one for each nurse provided. Third, he started printing his invoices on blue paper, making them immediately recognizable. Fourth, he began sending a reminder when a customer was only one day late. To take the sting from the reminders, each is addressed by hand.

The result of Dwight's efforts is that average collection time has been reduced from 60 days to 45.[6]

that is subsequently collected from your customers. You have the opportunity to collect it all. On the other hand, a commercial lender will loan you only one-half of the amount that can be collected. Depending on the finance company, customer payments on pledged receivables may be collected either by you and forwarded to the lender, or may be directly collected by the lender.

factoring
Selling the rights to collect accounts receivable to an entity outside your business.

Second, you can *sell* your receivables to a finance company in a process called **factoring**. A factoring company will usually pay you about 75 to 80 percent of the total amount that can be collected. The factor then collects the receivables. The difference between the gross amount of the receivables and the amount that is ultimately collected is the factor's profit margin. When you factor receivables, you forever give up all rights to the factor's discount. Of course, for this amount the factoring company assumes your bad debt risk. If a factor does not collect enough to make a profit, it's the factor's problem, not yours.

Skill Module 15.1 gives you a chance to work through the ways a factor might structure a deal for you.

To be able to obtain cash for your accounts receivable, your business must meet the same standards that are needed to be able to borrow money. For example, you must have good credit established, adequate cash flow to meet expected payments, and reliable revenues from sales.

THE THOUGHTFUL ENTREPRENEUR

TECHNIQUES FOR DAY-TO-DAY MANAGEMENT OF ACCOUNTS RECEIVABLE

If you want to collect the money owed you from credit sales, you must be very careful to give credit only to those customers who are likely to pay. To make credit work for your business, you must work consistently to collect what you are owed. The following nine policies are minimum standards for managing customer credit:

1. Make an extensive credit check prior to authorizing credit sales to any individual customer.
2. Promptly bill each customer following each credit purchase.
3. Provide cash discounts for making timely payments.
4. Enforce significant late fees and interest on past due accounts.
5. Maintain constant "aging" of accounts to quickly identify customers who become delinquent.
6. Make consistent, vigorous efforts to collect from customers, including dunning letters and phone calls.
7. Discontinue credit sales to customers who become significantly late in paying.
8. File suits and liens against the assets of customers who default on payment.
9. Use your bank as a **lock box** for the receipt of payments.

lock box
A locked receptacle for money, the keys to which are not available to those who physically handle the receptacle; a common example of a lock box is the coin receptacle for parking meters which cannot be opened by the workers who are responsible for collecting the deposited coins.

Using Receivables to Raise Immediate Cash

SKILL MODULE 15.1

Suppose that you need $50,000 immediately in order to purchase welded steel roof trusses for a building that you have contracted to construct. Normally you would simply purchase the materials on account from an established supplier, but two things prevent this. First, you have reached your credit limit with your supplier, and the supplier refuses to provide more. Second, your regular supplier is operating at maximum possible output and cannot deliver the trusses within the time required by your contract.

You have found a supplier who will manufacture and deliver the trusses when you need them. However, this supplier does not offer credit. Further, the supplier demands an immediate deposit of one-half of the cost of the trusses, $25,000, with the remaining $25,000 paid on delivery. You have approached your bank, but the bank has refused you a loan because (1) you are at your borrowing limit; and (2) the business with which you have contracted is embroiled in a lawsuit with the bank, and the bank therefore will not accept the contract as collateral.

You have current receivables of $67,000. You have contacted a factor in your area that has proposed two financing deals:

1. The factor will purchase your receivables for 75 percent of their collection value. You will receive 95 percent of the cash immediately, and the factor will retain the remaining 5 percent until all the receivables are collected. If the entire $67,000 is collected, then the remaining money will be paid to you. However, the money being held will be reduced by any amount uncollected at the end of 120 days from the date of the factoring contract.
2. The factor will lend you $54,000 discounted at 12 percent interest for 90 days. You must pledge 100 percent of your receivables as collateral for the loan. The factor will collect your receivables, applying 100 percent of the amount collected against the $54,000 until it is completely repaid, dollar for dollar.

What should you do? Show calculations to support your decision.

Your instructor can provide a suggested solution for this skill module.

Additionally, your business' accounts receivable must be well documented with the records up to date. This means that for each business to which you extend credit you will have, at a minimum, the following information:

- The credit check and credit score of each creditor.
- Three to six months' payment history of each creditor.
- The repayment terms that the customer is required to meet.
- The time at which a payment will be deemed to be delinquent.

Managing Inventory

inventory
Products that are held for sale to customers.

Inventory is a constant, everyday problem for most small businesses. It is the largest current asset that most manufacturing, wholesale, and retail firms have. Manufacturing firms, wholesalers, and retailers simply cannot operate effectively without a minimum level of inventory on hand. Even service firms such as restaurants, hair salons, automobile garages, plumbing businesses, electrical contractors, sign companies, and so on also need to have some inventory to function efficiently. It is a rare business indeed that has no inventory at all.

The amount and type of inventory held for resale is important for small businesses because (1) the supply of inventory and demand of customers cannot be precisely matched at all times, and (2) holding inventory requires a nonproductive cash investment. While inventory sits on your shelves, the money required to buy it is tied up and is not making a return for you.

Inventory is also a source of risk for small businesses. As the vignette that opens this chapter relates, inventory is attractive to thieves, including burglars, shop-lifters, hijackers, and even employees. In fact, employees are responsible for the majority of inventory thefts from retail and wholesale outlets.

Specific details of managing the risks to inventory, including the risk of theft, are discussed in the next chapter.

Determining the Appropriate Level of Inventory

The *right* amount of inventory to keep on hand and the *right* amount of inventory to order at one time is determined by (1) the cost of processing an order, (2) the cost of keeping merchandise in inventory, (3) the cost of lost sales if you run out, and (4) the time it takes to receive inventory after it's ordered. These factors vary widely with the location and type of business. Small retailers and service firms that also sell products (such as a hair salon) and are located in urban areas usually have easy access to wholesalers and can make frequent small purchases. If the business is in a small town or if it needs hard-to-get resources, then it may have to keep a lot of merchandise on hand. For example, a manufacturer of fine wooden desks will need hardwood, such as mahogany, teak, or burled maple, which is produced in only a few places and for which there are only a few wholesalers, worldwide. The distribution system for hardwoods is such that, except in very large cities, you have to buy a lot of it at one time and then keep it in stock until it is used.

economic order quantity (EOQ)
A statistical technique that determines the quantity of inventory that a business must hold to minimize total inventory cost.

There is a way to know how much you need to order so that you have an adequate supply of inventory on hand. It is called **economic order quantity (EOQ)**, and it helps you think in terms of ordering costs and carrying costs.

The total cost of keeping inventory is the sum of:

- The cost to buy the inventory.
- The cost to store, protect, and maintain inventory.
- The cost of making an order to purchase inventory.[7]

(See Exhibit 15.1.)

If the cost of carrying inventory were the only factor in making the decision of how much inventory to obtain, it would make the most sense to purchase the smallest number of units possible at any single time. On the other hand, if ordering costs were the only consideration, you would order the largest number that you expect to sell. But if you consider both these *and* purchase price, as we do in Figure 15.1, you get the economic order quantity (EOQ)–the quantity at which the total cost of inventory is minimized.

EXHIBIT 15.1

Inventory Costs

Costs of Carrying Inventory	Costs of Ordering Inventory
1. The opportunity cost of the funds invested in inventory	1. The transaction costs of preparing and transmitting the order
2. The cost of keeping inventory secure and in sellable condition	2. Investigating and selecting an appropriate vendor
3. Cost of warehouse or other storage facilities a. Utilities b. Physically moving inventory into, within, and out of the storage area c. Security guards, fencing, access control, etc.	3. Receiving inventory
4. Insurance and taxes on inventory	4. Time required to travel to suppliers to pick up inventory
5. Inventory shrinkage (i.e., loss from waste, spoilage, and theft)	5. Inspecting shipments
6. The transaction costs for counting and record keeping	6. Record keeping

You do not have to derive the EOQ equation to use it. You can simply substitute your business's projected annual sales demand, cost of placing one order, and cost of holding one unit in inventory to calculate your unique optimum order quantity and the number of orders that you should place each year. If you are interested, Appendix A of this chapter provides a detailed explanation of how the EOC equation can be used.

Scheduling Ordering and Receipt of Inventory

Determining the right quantity to order is only part of the problem of inventory management. You also need to know *when* to place each order. The EOQ tells us only how many units to order and how many orders to make. It does not tell us *when* to place each order. Deciding when to place an order is determined by (1) the rate of sales and (2) the time required to receive new stock.

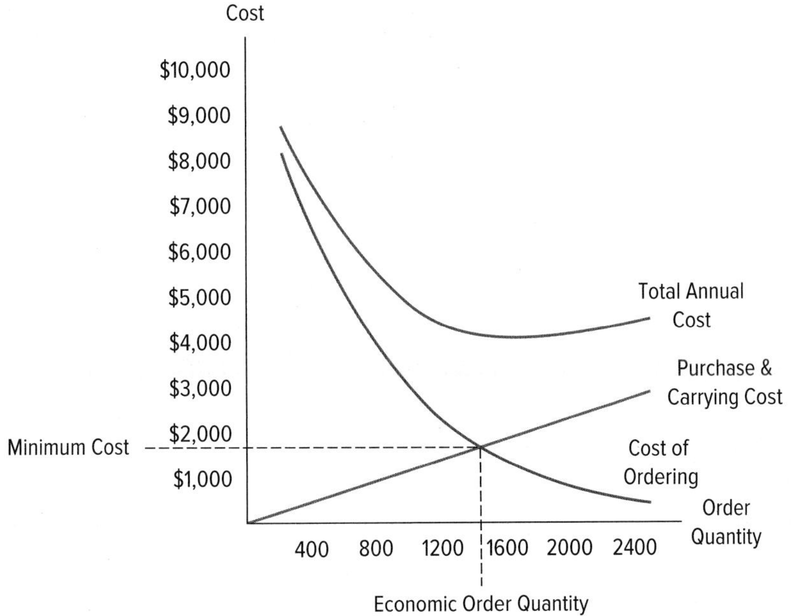

FIGURE 15.1

Economic Order Quantity Graph

Optimum stocking level The amount of inventory that results in the minimum cost, when considering the cost of lost sales resulting from running out of stock, the number of units sold per day, and the number of days required to receive inventory. Also called *reorder point*.

The **optimum stocking level** (also called *reorder point*) is the amount of inventory that results in the minimum cost, considering (1) the cost of lost sales resulting from running out of stock, (2) the number of units sold per day, and (3) the number of days required to receive inventory.

If everything worked perfectly, you would receive new inventory just as you sold the last unit from the prior order. But in business, as in most things in life, things are never perfect. Delivery times vary. Sales volumes are not constant. Sometimes demand exceeds your estimate. Sometimes your estimate exceeds demand.

If you know how demand for a particular product or part changes, you can calculate the probability of being out of stock, given any initial level of inventory and time between receipts of inventory. Computing the reorder point tells you the minimum stock level at which you would place an order. Ordering at that time would ensure that you do not run out of inventory before you run out of customers, and at the same time would minimize your holding unnecessary amounts of stock.

safety stock An amount of inventory carried to ensure that you will not run out of inventory because of fluctuating levels of sales.

pull-through system A term for just-in-time inventory systems in which product is ordered and placed into production only after a sale has been completed.

In practice, managers of small businesses rarely attempt such statistical analyses. Rather, they use a heuristic (rule of thumb) developed from experience. Unless you are selling a product that has very high unit costs, such as automobiles, tractors, or airplanes, the effect of having too little inventory is worse than the effect of having too much. For this reason, most businesses deliberately time the placement of orders to keep some extra amount of inventory on hand as **safety stock** to provide for the possibility that sales might be greater than forecast, or that deliveries might be delayed.

One interesting use of optimum stocking levels comes when an entrepreneur starts to use it as a sales tool directed toward customers. If you compute customers' reorder point, you have an added reason to contact them to find out whether it is time for them to reorder your product.[8]

Just-in-Time Inventory Systems

just-in-time (JIT) inventory The practice of purchasing and accepting delivery of inventory only after it has been sold to the final customer.

The cost of owning and holding inventory is far greater than the cost of ordering inventory. As a result, most businesses try to acquire and keep on hand the minimum amount of inventory possible while still being able to meet customer needs. At the extreme, a few businesses hold no inventory at all. Rather, these businesses order and receive inventory only after a customer purchase has been made.

The practice of acquiring inventory only in response to a completed sale is called a **pull-through system**. Once a customer sale is made, an order is placed to either obtain or produce the product. Each stage of the production process operates in response to this order, ultimately reaching back to the acquisition of the raw materials from which the product is made.

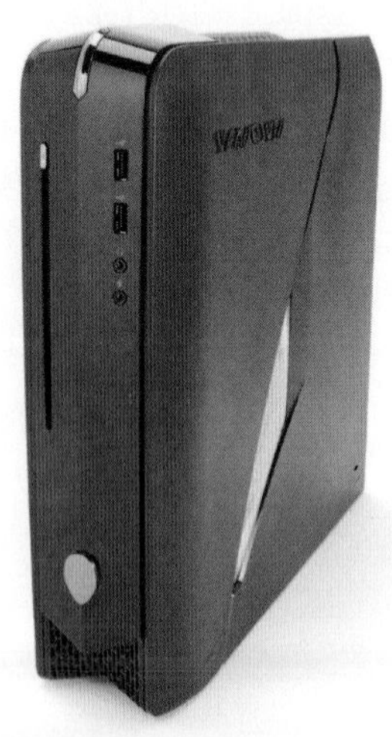

Alienware, a subsidiary of Dell Inc., uses just-in-time inventory management to keep costs of its high-end PCs at a reasonable level.
Official Windows Magazine/Getty Images

The ultimate extension of pull-through processing is **just-in-time (JIT) inventory** management. A just-in-time inventory system attempts to reduce inventory levels to the absolute minimum by (1) accepting inventory only as it is sold, (2) assembling product in the absolute minimum time possible, and (3) shipping product to the customer immediately upon completion. In this way, the three primary inventories of manufacturing, (1) raw materials, (2) work in process, and (3) finished goods, are all kept at the minimum levels possible.

One of the best-known examples of just-in-time manufacturing is Dell Computers.[9] Other small businesses use the approach too. Consider Alienware (now a subsidiary of Dell), a maker of high-end PCs for game enthusiasts. Alienware was started by two lifelong friends, Alex Aguila and Nelson Gonzalez, in Miami, Florida. Their model was simple: "First you pay. Then we build." Having started with only $13,000, they could not afford to spend a lot on inventory. When Alienware received a computer order from its website, a work order was generated that specified each individual component to be assembled. Alienware maintained a just-in-time delivery system for needed parts, and leveraged its relations with suppliers to ensure speedy delivery. With the parts collected, the computer is assembled, tested, and then sent to the packing and shipping department. The use of the JIT approach originally meant that Alienware had no receivables to underwrite, no inventory to depreciate, and no bad debt.[10] Today, Dell, the current owner of Alienware, still gets the same benefits and lowered costs pioneered by Aguila and Gonzalez.

Adoption of JIT inventory management requires an extreme degree of cooperation with your vendors. The location, scheduling, and transportation of inventory must be as carefully choreographed as is a Broadway dance routine. A single misstep in process can result in the shutdown of production and in lost sales. To ensure against this, most businesses that adopt JIT compromise between the theoretical "best way" and the exigencies of real-world business management and maintain some level of safety stock.

The development and growth of the eBay online auction service has provided many small businesses with the ability to practice just-in-time inventory management. Buyers on eBay know that there will be a period of a few days between winning a bid and receiving the product. Numerous eBay sellers use this time to obtain the product. Often, it is shipped directly from the wholesaler to the buyer. This practice is the ultimate just-in-time process: The eBay seller never owns or handles the products being sold. It is called **microinventory** and is a special form of JIT found in Internet-based businesses[11] such as Alienware.

microinventory
The purchase of inventory only after a sale is made; very typical with Internet firms.

Other Approaches to Inventory Control

There are three approaches to maintaining records of inventory that are very common in small businesses: (1) periodic inventory, (2) perpetual inventory, and (3) point-of-sale systems. Any one of these, applied conscientiously, can help control inventory and inventory costs.

Periodic inventory is the process of physically counting business assets on a set schedule. The time between counts is usually one business year, although periodic inventories may be conducted twice per year, quarterly, monthly, or as often as your business needs require. Most small businesses use the periodic inventory method because it is relatively inexpensive and meets the requirements of both local and federal taxing agencies.

periodic inventory
The process of physically counting business assets on a set schedule.

Perpetual inventory is a system of recording the receipt and sale of each item as the receipt and sale occur. A perpetual inventory system maintains a constant record of the amounts and value of inventory that has been sold and the amounts and value of inventory on hand. Perpetual inventory systems provide you with instant access to accurate inventory records, thus greatly easing the problems of managing inventory levels. The main drawback to using perpetual inventory systems is the high cost in time needed for constant record keeping. Keeping perpetual inventory in a manual system usually is accomplished by maintaining a separate record, often called a stock card, for each different type of inventory. Then as inventory is received and sold, the card is updated. (See Figure 15.2.)

perpetual inventory
A system of recording the receipt and sale of each item as it occurs.

Bar coding is one method used to reduce the cost of perpetual inventory systems. Bar codes are computer-readable tags that are unique to each item of inventory. The most common bar codes (those that are used every time your retail purchases are scanned at the register) are called universal product codes (UPCs) in the United States and EANs (European Article Numbers, now called International Article Numbers) elsewhere. The system is administered by a not-for-profit standards organization, GS1, which has a presence in all large countries–for example, GS1 US (www.gs1us.org). Manufacturers pay an annual fee to participate. Each member of the system licenses a "company prefix," a variable-length code unique to that company. To that prefix, the member then adds on a unique code for each product, creating a number that includes all but one digit of the UPC or EAN. A GS1-provided tool creates a final "check digit," which ensures that the number scans correctly. Each UPC or EAN is therefore unique to the product for which it is issued. As a member of GS1, you have access to the database of all codes and the corresponding manufacturer information. The company maintains an extensive website that explains the system, the use of bar codes, and information necessary to join.

bar coding
Obtaining a universal product code number and scan-ready visual tag, and printing it on the product or its packaging. Bar codes can then be scanned and recognized by others.

You may also create private bar codes of any number of digits for your internal use. Because the private codes are for your internal use, they do not have to be registered with GS1 US.

To use bar codes effectively in your business, you need (1) a method to create bar codes, (2) a means to print the codes on the items that you wish to track, (3) a scanner that can read the codes, and (4) a computer software program that can interpret the codes and update a database of information associated with each code. There are hundreds, if not thousands, of businesses that provide all the elements necessary for you to use bar codes internally in your business. A search of the Internet's open directory (DMOZ) for the term "bar codes" returned 229 individual listings for firms that provide bar code software and hardware.

FIGURE 15.2

The Stock Card

Bicycle Buddy Supply, Inc.

STOCK CARD

Supplier Number GM 66062

Supplier Name Garmin, Ltd.

Fiscal Period Fy 2020

Verified By ____________ Date ____________

Item Key	Transaction Date	Inventory Code	Item Name	UPC	Location	Purchase Price	Sales Price	Units Received	Units Sold	Number On Hand	Remarks
20747	12/05/2020	AC10033	GPS Trip Computer	753759142	Bin A3 R5 S3	150.00		100		100	
20748	12/06/2020						300.00		20	80	

Stock Control	
Maximum Qty	
Minimum Qty	
Reorder Level	

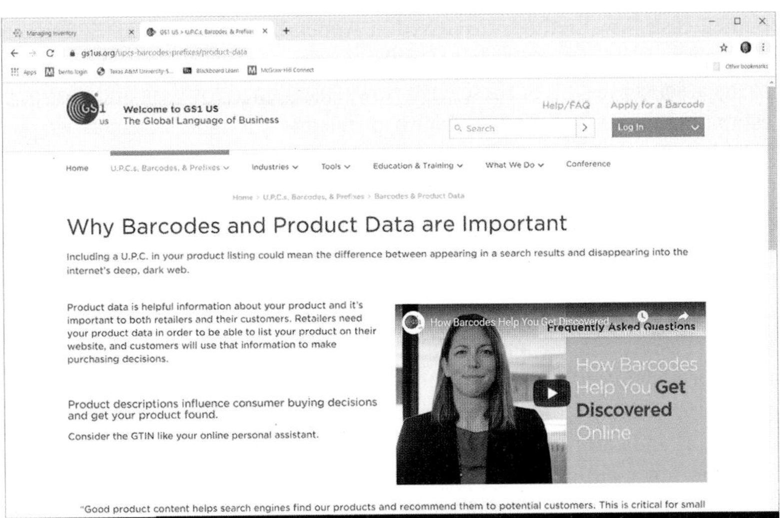

● If it is important to you that your product be recognized universally, be sure to apply with GS1 US to receive your product's UPC.

GS1 US, https://www.gs1us.org/upcs-barcodes-prefixes/product-data

Point-of-sale (POS) systems comprise both hardware and software that integrate inventory management directly into your accounting system. You are very familiar with POS, whether or not you are aware of it. The familiar supermarket scanner and the multibutton registers at fast-food restaurants are examples of POS systems. In these systems, every sale is immediately recorded in the accounting system. Revenue is increased and inventory is decreased simultaneously.

point-of-sale (POS) system Hardware and software combinations that integrate inventory management directly into accounting software.

Point-of-sale systems have recently become inexpensive enough to be used by small businesses. Today, you may acquire complete systems, including a cash drawer, credit card scanner, bar code scanner, computer, monitor, and software for less than $2,000. There are numerous providers of POS systems, including such well-known companies as Intuit, Hewlett-Packard, Sony, and Panasonic.

Value of Assets in Your Business

LO 15-2 Calculate the value of the assets in your business.

There are two fundamental kinds of assets in a business–short-term, which includes inventory and accounts receivable, and operating or **capital assets**. It is necessary for you, as the owner of a small business, to know what the value of these assets is. The value of the business assets your business owns is an important part of the evaluation made by bankers and investors when they are considering making a loan to or investing in your business. The methods for determining the value of each are discussed in the next section.

capital assets Assets that are expected to provide economic benefits for periods of time greater than one year.

Many small businesses need little in the way of capital assets. However, transportation, manufacturing, automobile repair, mining, ranching, and farming businesses all require the use of substantial capital assets in the form of land, buildings, and machinery. The value of such businesses is largely determined by the value of the physical capital assets that they own.

The value to your business of the assets that are used in operations usually far exceeds the value that might be realized if you were to sell them. An example of such an asset is fencing for a ranch or farm. A five-strand barbed-wire fence on steel posts can easily cost $8,000 per mile.[12] However, no rancher can ever realize the value of the fence by selling it. At least half the cost of fencing is in the labor required to install it. Once installed, it would cost a similar amount to uninstall. Used barbed wire and posts will bring only a fraction of their cost new. In fact, farmers and ranchers often cannot even give away old fencing; rather, they incur significant costs to safely dispose of it.

Similar situations exist in other businesses such as manufacturing, in which equipment, especially custom-made machinery, is much more valuable as an operating asset than can ever be realized from disposal. Even restaurant equipment such as deep fryers, cooking grills, and ventilation hoods have a much greater value being used in a restaurant than they do sitting in a restaurant supply store.

Determining the Value of Your Operating Assets

The value of operating assets is a function of their utility. In other words, your assets are worth the sum of the future benefits that the assets will produce. It is this definition that is the source of the discounted cash flow methods discussed in Appendix B of this chapter. Discounted cash flow valuation methods define *utility* as being the net cash inflows that the asset will produce. The value of the asset is the sum of these cash flows discounted for time and cost of capital.

Just as estimating future cash flows is highly problematic for small businesses, predicting future utility of capital assets is so uncertain that it is largely a waste of time. Therefore, most small businesses determine the value of capital assets using some combination of the four common accounting methods of assigning asset value.

The four accounting methods to value capital assets are (1) book value, (2) disposal value, (3) replacement value, and (4) fair market value.

book value
The difference between the original cost of an asset and the total amount of depreciation expense that has been recognized to date.

Book value is an accounting term that describes the difference between the original acquisition cost of capital assets and the amount of depreciation expense that has been recognized for them. Even a superficial consideration of book value discloses that it is simply an accident if book value even approximates the asset's economic value. This is true for two reasons: (1) Purchase price is not an indicator of the current value of any asset, and (2) depreciation is not, nor is it intended to be, any measure of the consumption through use of an asset's value.

Depreciation is an arbitrary, but regular and systematic, method used to take asset value as an expense for the purpose of calculating net income or loss. Depreciation is based on three assumptions: (1) that the asset has a fixed, determinable period of utility (called useful life); (2) that the asset has a fixed, determinable value that will exist when the depreciation process is complete (called *salvage value*); and (3) that the value of the asset will decline in a continuous and predictable manner over the period of utility (e.g., straight line, declining balance, etc.). In fact, none of these assumptions necessarily holds for any capital asset. Thus, depreciation is arbitrary. Book value is generally considered to be not very useful for any purpose other than accounting and income taxes, each of which, through law, regulation, and practice, require its use.

disposal value
The net amount realized after subtracting the costs of getting rid of an asset from its selling price.

arm's-length transaction
A business deal where the parties have a prior relation or affiliation, but where the business is conducted as if they were unrelated. This approach is done to help guard against potential conflicts of interest.

Disposal value is a method of estimating asset value by calculating the net amount that you would realize were you to sell the asset in an **arm's-length transaction.** This is accomplished by subtracting from the estimated sale price the estimated costs of selling, disassembly, shipping, indeed, all costs necessary to dispose of the asset. Disposal value is the residual of many estimates. At best, you must consider the value to be a rough approximation. At worst, the value may hold no relationship to the asset's unknown, "true" economic value.

replacement value
The cost incurred to replace one asset with an identical asset.

Replacement value can be determined with much greater confidence than can be given to either book value or disposal value. In effect, you are estimating the value of a currently owned capital asset by determining the cost that would be incurred to replace it with an identical asset. Unlike disposal value, in which you must estimate an essentially unknowable selling price for a used asset, replacement value is based on determining the price of either a new asset or a used asset for which there is an organized market. For many assets, such as machine tools and vehicles, this is done quite easily by obtaining quotes from dealers. Custom-made assets require a bit more work but still can be accurately priced through an engineering approach.

The primary advantage of replacement value is that you can be quite confident of its accuracy. The disadvantage is that the price of a new asset is often much greater than the price of an essentially identical asset already in your business.

fair market value
The price at which goods and services are bought and sold between willing sellers and buyers in an arm's-length transaction.

Fair market value lies somewhere between disposal value and replacement value. Fair market value is an attempt to determine the price that the asset would bring, in its current location and condition, in an arm's length transaction between a willing buyer and a willing seller. In contrast to disposal value, fair market value is assigned from the point of view of the buyer, and thus includes the selling price and all costs to install, test, and prepare the asset for productive use.

The appropriate valuation method is largely determined by the purpose for which the valuation is being made. As stated, laws, regulations, and GAAP require that book value be used for financial reporting and income tax purposes.

For any other purpose, you may use the valuation method that best meets your needs. If you are offering assets as collateral, lenders are most interested in disposal value, as that best approximates the amount that would be realized if the asset were repossessed. If you are considering an investment opportunity, disposal value provides an estimate of the timing and amounts of cash flows that can be used for net present value and internal rate of return calculations. If you are offering your business for sale, as the seller of a business you would view disposal value as a "lower limit" for the selling price because it approximates the amount that would be realized were the business to be liquidated. On the other hand, potential buyers and investors are most interested in replacement value. Replacement value sets an "upper level" for the value of your business assets as an approximation of the cost that would be incurred to equip a start-up business.

Determining the Value of Inventory

If your business holds inventory for sale, you are faced with the problem of determining its value. The value that you assign to inventory sold and on hand affects (1) the amount of profit that you recognize and (2) the value of your business.

inventory valuation Determination of the amount of assets held by the firm for sale or production.

physical inventory A count of all the inventory being held for sale at a specific point in time.

Inventory valuation begins with knowing *how much* of *what* you are holding. All too often owners of small businesses purchase inventory items which are stored out of sight. These items somehow never get used or sold. Over time such "forgotten" items accumulate, tying up scarce funds. At the minimum, you should conduct a **physical inventory**—a type of periodic inventory—at least once each year identifying and counting all items that your business owns. Items that have not been sold or used for significant periods of time should be disposed of to free up their value for productive use. Slow-moving and dated inventory may be disposed of by discounting or "dumping" it to overstock resellers such as Big Lots, Dollar Stores, or junk dealers.

SMALL BUSINESS INSIGHT

JAMES P. SMITH OF SIGNGRAPHICS, INC.

James P. Smith, owner of Signgraphics, Inc., of Blue Springs, Missouri, had just learned that a contract to produce signs for a chain of convenience stores had been lost to a competitor. As a result, Signgraphics was now stuck with twenty 8 ft. × 12 ft. polycarbonate plastic sign faces. The faces could not be used for any other purpose because they were vacuum molded and internally painted with the logo and name of the store chain. Each sign face, molded and painted, cost over $1,300. That meant Signgraphics had $26,000 of scrap.

Signgraphics, as would most small businesses, would be severely damaged by such a loss. Something had to be done, and done quickly.

Biting the bullet, James called the competitor who had just won the contract. The competitor quickly agreed to purchase the faces for $22,000. Although still a painful loss, $4,000 was not great enough to threaten the survival of the business. In fact, Signgraphics continued to be successful for an additional four years until the business was sold to yet another competitor in the area.

Signgraphics had to make a tough call on selling its extra sign faces inventory to a competitor. Having an inventory handling approach that allows for quick and easy adaptation is key to successfully managing your small business. What are some ways you think owners can build flexibility into their inventory management procedures?

Dennis MacDonald/PhotoEdit

Sooner or later you are likely to be stuck with surplus, slow-moving, or obsolete inventory. If you are like most entrepreneurs, you'll be tempted to keep the inventory "just in case you find a use for it." Over time such surplus inventory can build up to astonishing levels, tying up money that could and should be used in the business.

A better strategy is to constantly monitor the use of inventory and quickly dispose of any "dated" items before they become obsolete or otherwise unsellable. Such inventory items may, as in the case of Signgraphics, find a ready buyer in a competitor. If you are a wholesaler or retailer, you can offer steep discounts to existing customers. You may sell to a company that specializes in buying surplus and distressed items. Finally, as a last resort you may scrap such inventory and take its acquisition cost as a business deduction against profits.

Once you know what inventory you have, you can then assign it a value. One of the unpleasant surprises that many small business owners experience is the discovery that inventory is often worth far less than it cost to acquire. Inventory loses value in many ways. It can lose value because of changes in fashion or changes in technology. Some inventory items, especially food items, spoil with the passage of time. Some things get broken, dented, scratched, dirty, or otherwise shopworn. Determining the value of items being held for sale is essential to efficient inventory management.

acquisition cost
The total cost of acquiring an asset, including such costs as purchase price, transportation, installation, testing, and calibrating in order to ready it for its first productive use.

replacement cost
The total cost of replacing an asset with an essentially identical asset.

property
A general term for real estate, but it can also be applied as a legal term for anything owned or possessed.

As the Small Business Insight above relates, it is rare that inventory has no recoverable value, at all. If you use a bit of ingenuity, you can usually find some way to realize value from even custom-made items, like the sign faces Jim Smith had on hand when he lost his contract with a customer.

The value of inventory items held in stock is highly problematic, especially when prices are rapidly changing. You must answer the questions, "Is inventory worth what I paid for it? Is it worth what I must pay to replace it? Or is it worth only the amount for which I can sell it?" Any of these methods, **acquisition cost**, **replacement cost**, or fair market value, respectively, can reasonably be used to determine the value of your inventory. However, your choice of valuation method affects the profit you recognize and thus the amount of taxes you must pay.

If you assign a high value to inventory, you increase the amount that you deduct for cost of goods sold which results in decreased sales margin and reported profit. Less reported profit means less will be paid in income taxes. However, lowered reported profits makes your business worth less to investors, lenders, and potential buyers. On the other hand, if you assign the lowest acceptable value to inventory, you will make the results of operations of your business look better, but at the price of paying increased income taxes.

LO 15-3 Describe techniques for managing fixed assets.

Property, Plant, and Equipment

plant
A general term for the facilities of a business.

equipment
Machinery, tools, or materials used in the performance of the work of the business.

The importance of the issues of the acquisition and maintenance of real estate, buildings, and machinery varies among businesses. If your business is wholesale or retail merchandising, the issues of **property**, **plant**, and **equipment**, referred to as PPE, are most likely of relatively minor importance to your success. If your business is manufacturing, mining, farming, ranching, or transportation, your greatest investments and your greatest costs are consumed by land, buildings, and machinery. Obtaining, maintaining, and efficiently using these expensive capital assets is critical to your success.

All capital assets cause you to incur four costs over time: (1) the cost of acquiring the asset, (2) the cost of owning the asset, (3) the cost of operating the asset, and (4) the cost of disposing of the asset.

It is common for owners of small businesses to consider only the first of these costs in making an investment decision. This narrow focus on acquiring an asset is unfortunate because although you make such decisions infrequently, the ramifications of the decisions are critical to your success. Making a correct decision will increase the value of your business, and thus your wealth. Making an inappropriate decision will lead to suboptimal returns, even to your business going bankrupt. The probability of making a good capital investment decision is greatly increased when all the costs of the asset, called **whole of life costs**, are included in the decision process. In Skill Module 15.2 you will analyze the whole of life costs for one asset.

whole of life costs
The sum of all costs of capital assets, including acquisition, ownership, operation, and disposal.

Acquisition cost of a capital asset is the sum of *everything* that you spend to acquire and prepare the asset for its first productive use. Thus, the cost of engineering to specify the details of the asset, purchase price, shipping, insurance during shipping, setup, testing, and interest on any borrowed funds are all accumulated to determine the cost of the asset.

cost of owning
Cost incurred in financing, insuring, taxing, or tracking an asset.

cost of operating
The direct cost incurred in using an asset for the purpose for which it was intended.

Costs of owning an asset include interest on funds borrowed and the opportunity costs of funds invested to acquire it. Costs of ownership also include insurance on the asset, property taxes, value of the space that the asset occupies, and the cost of record keeping and security for the asset.

Costs of operating the asset include the energy the asset consumes, maintenance, loss of economic value resulting from wear and obsolescence, and any necessary training of operators.

Understanding Whole of Life Costs for Capital Budgeting

SKILL MODULE 15.2

You are the owner of the Real Wood Furniture Company. Business has grown to the point that a bottleneck has formed where the 4 ft. × 12 ft. lumber-core plywood sheets are cut to finish size. You have identified two automated panel saws that have identical capacity sufficient not only to eliminate the bottleneck, but also to be able to keep up with projected growth for the next 10 years.

Each machine has a useful life of 10 years. However, each will have to be rebuilt at the end of the seventh year to get the final three years of use. At the end of 10 years either machine will be technologically obsolete, thus you will have to dispose of it at that time. Estimated cost data for each saw are shown in the chart.

Real Wood Furniture Co.
Manufacturers of Fine Wood Desks
Data concerning Automatic Panel Saw

	Milwaukee	**Delta**
Purchase price	$110,000	$80,000
Shipping	3,500	1,000
Installation	6,500	4,000
Testing	3,500	4,500
Total acquisition cost	$123,500	$89,500
Maintenance cost per year	$ 12,000	$ 14,900
Energy costs per year	8,500	13,000
Rebuilding in seventh year	25,000	35,000
Disposal cost end of tenth year	4,850	6,000

1. Examine the data in the chart. Without doing any specific mathematical analysis, state which saw you would purchase, and why.
2. Assume that every desk to be produced for the next 10 years will be made from wood that is cut by the saw that is purchased. Sales for the year the saw is purchased are projected at $260,000 and are expected to increase by 15 percent per year for the next 10 years. Use Real Wood Furniture Co.'s cost of capital to perform a discounted cash flow analysis of purchasing each saw. Now which saw would you choose, and why?
3. **Advanced topic:** Assume that Real Wood Furniture Co. is profitable and will pay 30 percent income taxes each year of the life of the saw purchased. Repeat the discounted cash flow analysis, only this time make adjustments for the effect of income taxes. Now which saw would you choose, and why?

Your instructor may provide a suggested solution to this skill module.

Costs of disposition are composed of the value of the activities necessary to get rid of the asset. Such costs include meeting environmental regulations, disassembly, advertising, commissions, shipping, insurance, and fees. The cost of meeting environmental requirements can be huge for some assets. For example, it is nearly impossible to find affordable means to dispose of radioactive tools, anything that contains mercury or lead (e.g., computer monitors), electric motors and transformers that contain polychlorinated biphenyls (PCBs),[13] and personal computers that contain significant quantities of several poisonous heavy metals.[14]

cost of disposition
Cost incurred in the activities necessary to get rid of an asset.

The Capital Budgeting Decision

LO 15-4 Calculate ratios used to analyze capital investment decisions.

Eventually small businesses get to the point where they can begin to make investment choices—do you open a new location or expand the one you have? Do you buy new machinery or invest in real estate? The process of deciding among various investment opportunities to create a specific spending plan is called **capital budgeting**. The goal of capital budgeting is to improve the quality of decisions about how to best use the scarce resources of the business. Capital budgeting works by determining the costs and benefits of each alternative investment, such as machinery or real estate. The question that must be answered to make a decision is, "Which of the available investment alternatives provides the greatest benefit relative to the cost of the investment?"

capital budgeting
The process of deciding among various investment opportunities to create a specific spending plan.

To do this, the alternatives are simultaneously compared by examining various financial ratios or by applying the concepts of the time value of money. The time value of money is the concept that a dollar received today is worth much more than is a dollar to be received at some time in the future.

The two most commonly used financial ratios for comparing investment alternatives are (1) **payback period** and (2) **return on investment (ROI)**. There are also two significantly more complex approaches called *net present value (NPV)* and *internal rate of return (IRR)*, which are discussed in Appendix B at the end of this chapter. Each of these measures has both advantages and disadvantages. Not one of them is appropriate in all circumstances, although each can be useful in the capital budgeting process.

payback period
The amount of time it takes a business to earn back the funds it paid out to obtain a capital asset.

return on investment (ROI)
A capital budgeting equation used to measure the relationship between initial investment and the profits that are expected to be received from making the investment.

To illustrate each of these investment analysis tools, consider the following: The owner of a sign shop has the opportunity to contract with a rapidly growing franchise operator to install signs at all new locations. To be able to complete this contract, she will need to invest in a heavy truck and a truck-mounted crane. She has reduced the decision alternatives to two different truck-crane combinations: a Skyhook 85-foot heavy-duty crane with a service ladder mounted on a Ford diesel truck and a Sponco 87-foot medium-duty crane with a service bucket and remote controls mounted on a GMC diesel truck. The cost of the Ford-Skyhook combination, ready for use, will be $150,000. The cost of the GMC-Sponco combination will be $185,000. Each truck and crane will have a useful life of 10 years.

Each crane has certain advantages and disadvantages. The Skyhook crane can lift 2,000 pounds to its full extension height. However, it does not have remote controls, and thus requires a crew of two people. The Sponco can lift only a 950-pound load, but its service bucket with remote controls allows it to be used by a single operator as a "cherry picker" to lift the operator into position, obviating the need (and dangers) of working from a ladder. Based on these facts, the owner has estimated future cash flows that will be provided by each alternative.

The owner has determined the following criteria to aid in making a decision:

1. The business's weighted average cost of capital is 20 percent.
2. The maximum acceptable payback period is four years.
3. Depreciation is recognized using a **straight line for a useful life of 10 years**.
4. Salvage value of each combination will be $0 (zero).
5. Cash flows and profits will differ by the tax effect of depreciation recognized.[15] Depreciation for the Ford-Skyhook is $15,000 a year, for the GMC-Sponco $18,500 a year.

straight line for a useful life of 10 years
Depreciation is computed using a straight line method over 10 years, so an asset would lose 10 percent of its value each year.

Payback Period

The payback period measure is a statement of how much time must pass before your business receives back the same number of dollars in cash flow as you must pay out to obtain a capital asset. Only cash flows are considered.

Two decision rules are applied in choosing from among alternative investments:

1. Accept only those alternatives for which the time required to recoup the original investment is equal to or less than a maximum allowable time determined by management.
2. Accept the alternative with the shortest payback period among those that meet the first criterion.

Consider the following example: Using the data in Table 15.1, we can calculate that the Ford-Skyhook combination pays back in 2 years and 11 months. In the first year, $35,000 is paid back. Another $60,000 is received in year 2, leaving $55,000 to be recovered. If we assume that the money is received evenly across the year, then it will take 55,000/60,000, or 0.917, of one year to recoup the final $55,000.

Using the same method, we find that the GMC-Sponco combination will require 3 years and 2.7 months to pay back its initial investment.

Following the decision rules, we find that both alternatives meet the minimum hurdle of paying back in four or less years. However, the Ford-Skyhook alternative payback period is 3.7 months shorter, thus we would choose this alternative.

The main advantage to using the payback period analysis is its simplicity. Also, it allows easy comparison of alternatives that are dissimilar in magnitude of cash flows and overall project life.

TABLE 15.1 Data for Capital Budgeting Decisions

Estimated Cash Flows and Accounting Profits of Each Alternative

	Ford–Skyhook		GMC–Sponco	
Years	Cash Flows	Accounting Profits	Cash Flows	Accounting Profits
0	$(150,000)		$(185,000)	
1	35,000	20,000	45,000	26,500
2	60,000	45,000	62,500	44,000
3	60,000	45,000	62,500	44,000
4	65,000	50,000	67,500	49,000
5	70,000	55,000	77,500	59,000
6	75,000	60,000	87,500	69,000
7	75,000	60,000	92,500	74,000
8	80,000	65,000	95,000	76,500
9	80,000	65,000	95,000	76,500
10	80,000	65,000	100,000	81,500

The primary disadvantages of the payback method are that (1) it disregards the time value of money and (2) it disregards all cash flows that occur after the payback period. These disadvantages often result in managers making suboptimal investment decisions.

Rate of Return on Investment

Rate of return on investment (ROI) is a measure of the relationship between the initial investment and the profits that are expected to be received from making the investment. The calculation is straightforward:

$$\text{ROI} = (\text{Average annual profits})/(\text{Average investment})$$

As with the payback method, two decision rules are applied to choose from among alternative investments:

1. Accept only those alternatives for which the return on investment is equal to or greater than the business's weighted average cost of capital, which is the expected average future cost of funds and is discussed in Chapter 14.
2. Accept the alternative with higher ROI among those that meet the first criterion.

We can then calculate the ROI of each alternative:

	Ford–Skyhook	GMC–Sponco
$\frac{\text{(Sum of profits/Length of project)}}{\text{(Initial investment + Salvage value)/2}}$	$\frac{(530{,}000/10)}{(150{,}000 + 0)/2} = 0.707$	$\frac{(600{,}000/10)}{(185{,}000 + 0)/2} = 0.649$

Both alternatives meet the first decision rule as the ROI of each exceeds the business's weighted average cost of capital of 20 percent. We accept the Ford–Skyhook alternative because it has the greater ROI of the two.

Return on investment analysis has two advantages: (1) It is easy to calculate, and (2) it relies on accounting information with which business owners, lenders, and investors are comfortable. ROI's disadvantages are (1) profits are not the same as cash, and (2) the method ignores the time value of money.

Net Present Value

Calculation of net present value (NPV) and its application to this investment decision is explained in Appendix B at the end of this chapter.

LO 15-5 Describe the advantages of renting or leasing capital equipment.

Rent or Buy

It is often not necessary, or even advisable, to purchase capital assets. Many capital assets for which there is an active market, such as real estate, trucks, tractors, and airplanes, can easily be obtained through rental or lease agreements.

renting An agreement between two entities that allows one to use assets of the other in return for a specified payment or series of payments.

leasing A formal agreement, reduced to writing, that specifies the term and conditions that must be met to allow one entity to use a specified asset (or assets) of the other.

Renting and **leasing** are similar, but not identical processes. In each, ownership of the asset remains with the entity from which the asset is rented or leased. The primary difference is that renting is usually a short-term obligation, perhaps as short as one hour, while leasing is usually for a period of a year, or more. Also, unlike a rental agreement, leases may provide for the lessor to take ownership of the asset at the end of the lease term.

Advantages and Drawbacks of Renting

Renting such assets provides several important advantages. First, renting requires little or no cash investment on your part. Purchasing, however, often requires that your business be able to pay cash of 20 percent or more of the purchase price in order to be able to borrow funds to finance your purchase. Second, renting usually does not require an extensive (and expensive) application process as does borrowing money. Third, renting usually protects you from unexpected costs of repairs. If you are renting a truck for your business and it breaks down, you can quickly obtain a replacement vehicle. Fourth, renting capital equipment provides an easy method to avoid ongoing costs if business conditions change. If a sudden loss of business makes the asset uneconomical, you can return it to its owner, thereby avoiding the costs of ownership, operation, and disposal.

Outflow Fund being paid to others by the firm.

Making the decision to rent rather than to buy an asset provides a partial answer to the problem of projecting future cash flows. You may make the same analysis that you would in order to decide to buy. However, in making this analysis, renting provides two advantages over buying: (1) The exact amount and timing of cash **outflows** is specified in the rental contract, and (2) renting provides a fall-back position should your projections prove to be incorrect. If actual cash flows fall short of your projections, you may be able to return the rented property, avoiding future rent payments. If you still wish to pursue the opportunity despite lower cash flows than expected, you can make provisions for a less expensive alternative. Should actual cash flows exceed your projections, you have the options of either purchasing the rented asset or returning the asset and purchasing a higher-capacity replacement.

The disadvantages to rental are, first, you do not have an ownership position. The value of a rented asset does not ever show up on your business's balance sheet. Should you need capital, rented assets cannot be used as collateral to obtain borrowed funds. Second, rental requires that you make regular, timely payments. If you own an asset, you may be able to exercise some control over cash outflows for costs of ownership and operations, such as maintenance and upgrades. These options do not exist for rented assets. Third, the number of dollars paid in rent usually exceeds the number of dollars you would spend to own the asset. The owner of the asset you are renting bears the risk of breakdowns, obsolescence, and disposal costs. Because of these risks, the owner must receive a premium over the costs that you would incur if you were to buy the asset.

Financing with Leases

A lease is simply a rental agreement that specifies a minimum period of time for which you must make rental payments. Lease periods range from as short as a few days to 99 or more years, and leases can include other sorts of provisions or specifications for how the business deal or the leased property is to be handled. Thus, as lessee you may agree to bear the costs of maintenance, insurance, and taxes on leased assets. Alternatively, any of these costs may be born by the lessor. Leases provide a middle ground between renting and owning assets.

There are two basic types of leases, operating leases and capital leases. The two types of leases differ primarily in how the property is disposed of at the end of the lease period.

Operating leases are leases that are similar to renting. In an operating lease, ownership of the asset never passes to you as the lessee. At the end of the lease period, you either return the asset to its owner, or you may purchase the asset at its then current fair market value.

operating lease
A long-term rental in which ownership of the asset never passes to the person paying for the lease.

All other aspects of maintaining and operating the asset can be negotiated between lessor and lessee. Either party may be contractually responsible for maintenance and operating costs.

Capital leases are leases that are essentially the same as buying the asset. At the end of the lease period the asset becomes property of the lessee, either without any additional payment or by the lessee paying a nominal amount. The test to determine if a lease is a capital lease, rather than an operating lease, is the existence of provisions for title of the asset to pass to the lessee at a price less than the asset's fair market value.

capital lease
A lease in which at the end of the lease period the asset becomes the property of the lessee, possibly with an additional payment.

The benefits of leasing are numerous. First, you can usually obtain a very low down payment. Second, the process of negotiating and closing a lease is usually less complicated and expensive than making a purchase and obtaining borrowed funds. A third benefit is that it is usually much easier for you to replace leased assets than it is to replace assets you own.

Because actual ownership of the asset remains with the lessor until the provisions of the lease contract are fulfilled, the owner is not faced with the expensive and time-consuming process of repossession. As owner of the asset, the lessor may simply take it back should you default on the contract. Because of this, a lessor is less concerned with your ability to pay than is a lender and is willing to accept a lower initial investment from you in return for higher periodic lease payments. Similarly, because the lessor is in the business of acquiring and disposing of assets, the lessor assumes the responsibility of disposing of obsolete assets and providing new ones.

The primary disadvantage of leasing is that it usually costs more than would purchasing. A secondary disadvantage is that leased assets are usually subject to numerous restrictions on how they may be used, maintained, and disposed of. Restrictive lease covenants are intended to provide protection to the owner by preventing the lessee from allowing the asset to lose value through misuse, neglect, or abuse. A typical lease restriction is a prohibition on driving or flying leased transportation equipment across an international border. Were you the lessee of a business airplane, such a provision could become a serious inconvenience should you develop business that requires you to regularly travel to Monterrey, Mexico, and no airline offers such service from your home city.

Fractional Ownership and Other Forms of Joint Ventures

A less-used method of reducing the costs and risks of acquiring capital assets is the process of joint venturing. A joint venture is simply a formalized partnership between two or more businesses for some specific purpose. Joint ventures are quite common among medium to large businesses and are growing among small businesses.[16]

Joint venturing makes economic sense when each party to the venture has limited use of an expensive asset or faces major investments that could be sidestepped by partnering with another firm that already has made that investment. One area in which joint ventures are relatively common among small businesses is the ownership of airplanes. Airplanes are quite expensive. Even a 30-year-old Beech King Air turbo prop airplane can easily sell for $1 million. Although old, and by some standards obsolete, a King Air can still produce more than 6 million seat miles per year: the equivalent of 1,600 transcontinental trips. Very few small businesses need even a fraction of the transportation capacity produced by such an airplane. Because of these facts, it is common for airplanes to be owned by partnership arrangements among several businesses that share the costs proportionate to their use of the plane.

Recently, some leasing companies have created an ownership structure similar to joint ventures, called *fractional ownership*. These companies offer buses, airplanes, and yachts under arrangements in which a small business may buy only that share that it can reasonably use during the course of business. In this manner, many small businesses now have access to business jets by having purchased as little as one-sixteenth of the ownership rights.

"Once bought, forgotten" might be the sort of saying that reminds all entrepreneurs about why managing assets is critical to being successful in managing a small business and its finances. Whether inventory or operating assets, most firms have substantial value tied up in the assets of the business. It is possible to make sure that these assets are being managed to be financially useful, and this chapter outlines the techniques–ranging from simple to complex–to do that. The simple techniques of inventory tracking and management can be easily grasped and implemented in a wide variety of settings. The more statistically driven approaches are increasingly workable, because they use functions built into spreadsheets or accounting programs' inventory routines. Like so much in small business, asset management works if you take the time to do it or have it done for you.

Managing Operations

LO **15-6** Describe techniques to manage and improve the operations of your business.

No matter what your business is, the functions of management are always the same: planning, organizing, staffing, directing, and controlling. You and your managers must establish the goals and objectives of your business. Once you have a set of coherent goals, you must make plans on how to attain them. You must organize and direct your business to attain the desired goals. You must also analyze the working of your business to be able to control it and to correct any variations from the planned procedures in order to reach the predetermined goals. These functions interact and it takes skill to coordinate them so you can accomplish your business goals, often through the efforts of others.

Although the preceding paragraph was easy to write, and is easy to read, putting it into practice is far from easy. You must be able to determine which management functions are most important and be able to organize them by priority. Although all five functions are important parts of a manager's job, just how imperative each is varies with changes in the business, such as during the stages of a product life cycle. One simplifying fact for operations management is the fact that operations management is concerned primarily with directing and controlling. Planning, organizing, and staffing are primarily the responsibility of executive management.

Operations management is focused on all of the activities of the business, such as producing product and moving it to customers. Throughout the book you have seen examples of the operations management decisions small business owners must make. These include managing your time in Chapter 5, optimizing your business's value chain in Chapter 7, managing the product and service life cycles in Chapter 9, and optimizing the location and physical layout of your business in Chapter 11. Similarly, much of this chapter deals with optimizing the use of your assets, like inventory and property. Along the way we have mentioned the kinds of strategic operational choices owners have to make about product design, process choice, capacity, quality, productivity, technology, workforce, and job design. The overriding goal of operations management is to be constantly improving the organization, through a more efficient use of resources and through improved or expanded service to customers, where "customer" means the next process as well as the final, external user. Because there is an operations element in every function of your business, people in all jobs should work together to improve their own operation efficiency.

As the Small Business Insight relates, creative thought and a good understanding of your customers' needs is needed in times of business crises.

Inputs into Your Business

inputs
The materials, labor, and energy put into the production of a good or service.

The **inputs** of a business are determined by its objectives. Your business objectives establish which raw materials are needed in what quantities. Your objectives will determine whom and how many people you must hire. For you to keep your business running smoothly, you must have information (feedback) concerning the essential processes that comprise your production system. This is as true for service industries, as it is for retail and manufacturing.

Business Operations Comprise Converting Time and Materials into Services and Products

operations
The process of transforming materials, labor, and energy into goods or services.

Business, to a great degree, comprises **operations**, or taking materials, the time of workers, and the investment of owners and changing these things into a desired product or service.

SMALL BUSINESS INSIGHT

CABOT HOSIERY MILLS: A TURNAROUND STORY

©Darn Tough

Ric Cabot was wrestling with a common business problem: competition from foreign suppliers who had much lower costs than Ric's business, Cabot Hosiery Mills, could ever attain. Long-time customers were choosing other suppliers. Sales and profits were on an unsustainable downward trend.

Ric had few choices. He could close the business. He could contract with sock knitters in China or Thailand. Or he could somehow come up with an idea that would allow him to continue making socks in Northfield, Vermont.

Few hosiery mills remain in the United States, and even fewer of these are in New England. In fact, Cabot Hosiery Mills is the only sock maker left in Vermont. Cabot was primarily a custom manufacturer, producing socks for several apparel firms including Bass Shoes, Eddie Bauer, L.L.Bean, and Orvis. But by the early 2000s most of Cabot's former customers had outsourced their sock knitting to offshore mills, primarily in China and Thailand.[17]

Marketing research conducted for Cabot disclosed that there was a sizable percentage of people engaged in outdoor work and outdoor sports who were less than satisfied with the socks that were then available. To that end, Cabot developed an entirely new line of premium socks made solely from Merino wool, nylon, and Lycra.[18]

"Darn Tough has been a fantastic product for the company all over the United States and Canada. It's our brand and it will propel the company into the fourth generation. It's the most sustainable thing we do. We have wonderful private-brand customers, but the most important thing is to produce our own brand," Ric said.[19]

In fact, the Darn Tough Vermont sock has been way more successful than even the Cabots hoped. In the first quarter of 2012, Cabot Hosiery Mills reported all-time record profits on gross sales that are fully 260 percent higher than in the same quarter of 2010.[20]

Darn Tough continues to succeed today. According to a story posted in VTDigger, a Vermont state-wide news outlet, Darn Tough is currently in expansion mode, and expects to be making a million and a half pair of socks per year by the end of 2020.[21]

Harvey Stabene, R&D director on left, and Ric Cabot, Cabot Hosiery Mills president and CEO on the right, inside Cabot Hosiery Mills in Northfield, Vermont.

©Darn Tough

FIGURE 15.3

The Operations Process

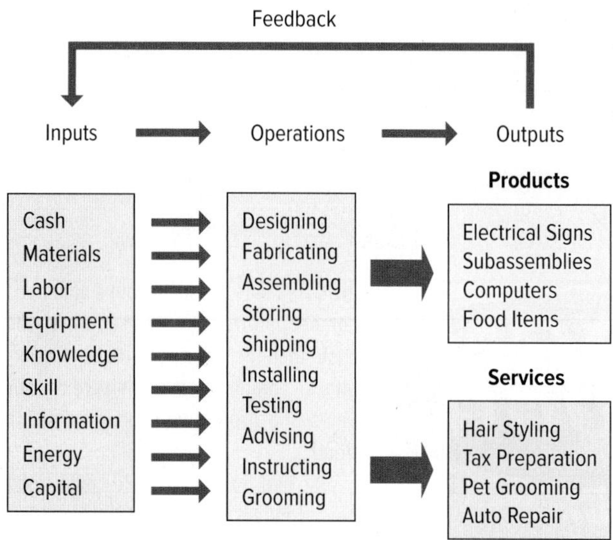

This is illustrated in Figure 15.3. The specifics of your manufacturing, marketing, and distribution must be known in detail. You must also have some understanding of the ways your employees act and react. Some people will be interested in all the fine details. Others will be indifferent to the details as long as the desired result is obtained. For example, a manager may not know or care about the details of how a report is created and circulated. He or she is interested only in the information that the report contains. On the other hand, your accountant will be concerned with the details of each step: gathering data, preparing the report, and communicating it to those who need it.

Business Outputs

outputs
The services or products that are produced for sale.

What constitutes the **outputs** of your business depends on what your business is. The output for a Liberty Tax franchise is completed income tax returns. The output for an automobile garage is properly repaired cars. Generally speaking, output is the quality and quantity of goods and services produced, those things that produce revenue for your business. The entire system of your business should be designed to produce something that is desired in a market. Business customers of all types want goods and services that will make them more efficient, more effective, or more profitable. Individuals as customers will buy those things that provide greater comfort, improved health, enhanced entertainment, and so on.

Feedback

feedback
The process of communicating within or to the organization about how the outputs worked or were received.

Any control system must have **feedback**. All inputs, material, and labor must be compared with a predetermined standard. If there is variation between the output and the standard, management action can be undertaken to correct the situation.

A business that has multiple systems requires complicated feedback. Information must be communicated among all managers and employees who are part of the system. Operations control depends on three types of feedback: (1) informational feedback, (2) corrective feedback, and (3) reinforcing feedback. Informational feedback is just that: information about the processes of your business. Corrective feedback is evaluative and judgmental. It comprises a value judgment about processes and behaviors. Inefficient work processes and undesirable employee behaviors are provided with various correctional actions. The manufacturing line may be redesigned. Misbehaving employees may be given training or punishment. Punishment ranges from a "dressing down" to termination of employment. On the other hand, reinforcing feedback rewards efficient processes and desired employee behaviors and can range from a simple statement, "Good job," to tangibles such as money or paid time off.

Measuring and Improving Productivity

The essence of production management is to ensure that the factors of production—materials, labor, machinery, land, and capital—are used efficiently to produce your business's product or service. Simply put, the major outcome of operations and production management is improved **productivity**. Productivity applies what you have just learned about inputs and outputs because productivity is simply the ratio of outputs to inputs, or:

$$\text{Productivity} = \frac{\text{Outputs}}{\text{Inputs}}$$

productivity
The ratio measure of how well a firm does in using its inputs to create outputs. Literally, productivity is outputs divided by inputs.

If you are creating a product (aka the output of your production process) that you can sell for $10.00 and it costs you $2.50 to make, your productivity ratio is 4:1. If you can cut your production cost to $2.00, you have increased your productivity to 5:1. That increase is hard dollar proof you have improved your productivity. You might have done this by saving money on energy or raw materials or labor. In short, you have increased productivity by improving the **efficiency** of your production process–where efficiency means doing the same with less.

efficiency
The comparison of productivity ratios to see the extent that an organization has generated more outputs with fewer inputs.

There is another way to improve productivity, and that is through improving **quality**. Quality is a product's or service's fitness for use. It is usually measured by characteristics such as durability (how long it lasts), reliability (how consistently does it work), serviceability (how easily can it be repaired), style (how attractive is it), ease of use, and overall dependability (how much you can rely on it). If you can make your product so much better that a customer is now willing to pay $11.00 for the new improved product, your gain is 11:2.50 or 4.4:1. That is a 10 percent gain in productivity due to quality improvements.

quality
A product's or service's fitness for use, measured as durability, reliability, serviceability, style, ease of use, and dependability.

Outsourcing to Improve Productivity

Entrepreneurs have long considered **outsourcing** to be a management method that could be used only by large firms. After all, entrepreneurs reason, where would I get the time, the contacts, the money to be able to oversee foreign contractors?

outsourcing
Contracting with people or companies outside your business to do work for your business.

This reasoning no longer holds for two reasons: First, technology has made outsourcing available, and second, outsourcing does not necessarily require dealing with foreign firms. In fact, your best choice for outsourcing to achieve better productivity for yourself and for your employees just might be in the office next to yours.

To get the greatest benefit from outsourcing, you need to follow four simple rules:

1. **Know yourself.** Nobody is good at everything. This is a truism that is often lost on entrepreneurs who are notorious for believing "if anyone can do it, I can." Misplaced self-confidence has in the past, and will in the future, cause many otherwise excellent ventures to fail. Before you decide what business functions to outsource, you must carefully examine your own weaknesses and strengths.
2. **Keep strategy decisions in-house.** No one is likely to have the knowledge of your business and customers that you do. The success of your business is dependent on strategy. Outsource business functions and businesses activities, but keep strategy at home.
3. **Fully specify tasks that are to be outsourced.** The single greatest cause of failure of outsourcing is lack of clear communications between the entrepreneur and the contractor. You will get the best results when you provide your contractor with exact details of the specifications to be met, methods to be used, outcomes to be delivered.
4. **Know with whom you are contracting.** You will be satisfied with the results of outsourcing if, and only if, you choose competent contractors. Companies and individuals to whom you may outsource have specific competencies, just like you do. Not all CPAs are expert in small business issues. Not all biotech research labs can produce and purify proteins. You must perform careful investigation of the contractors available to choose the best one for your business.

The most commonly outsourced functions of small businesses are legal and accounting. Most entrepreneurs are neither lawyers nor accountants, and many quite frankly will tell you that they have no interest in attempting either area.

There are many functions other than legal and accounting where you could benefit from outsourcing. To identify these functions you need to identify things that you are currently doing in-house that could be done less expensively or more efficiently by expert contractors. In the final analysis all business functions and activities are potential areas for outsourcing.

Finding Outsourcing Contractors

As you would expect, the web provides a multitude of websites to help you find competent companies to which you can outsource services and manufacturing.

The oldest and best-known of these sites for manufacturing is alibaba.com. Alibaba was started in Hangzhou, China, by Jack Ma and a group of 17 other investor-founders. It initially was intended to be a trading platform something like eBay for small Chinese manufacturers to sell their products. Since its founding Alibaba has grown to be the largest business-to-business trading site in the world.

The best-known website for contracting with individuals is Upwork, based in the United States. Upwork claims to have over 10 million registered contractors and to have generated more than $1 billion annually in contracts. The following Learn More Online box lists websites for outsourcing services and manufacturing.

Areas Where Outsourcing May Be Right for Your Business

- Support services
  - Legal
  - Accounting
  - Tax preparation and compliance
  - Website development and maintenance
  - Payroll services
  - Safety and OSHA compliance
  - Human resources/employee benefits
  - Food service
  - Janitorial
- Noncore business functions
  - Marketing and advertising
  - Customer fulfillment/shipping
  - Research and development
  - Customer service
  - Technical support
  - Warranty services
- Repetitive business activities
  - Data entry
  - Day-to-day bookkeeping
  - Accounts payable entry
  - Cold calling for new business leads
- Core business functions
  - Manufacturing
  - Packaging
  - Product design
  - Sales

LEARN MORE ONLINE

Learn more about the topics above at these sites:

Alibaba: www.alibaba.com

Upwork: www.upwork.com

Freelancer: www.freelancer.com

Guru: www.guru.com

Operations Management Challenges for Product-Based Firms

In talking about productivity, the examples were primarily of product-based firms. Product-based firms take some sort of materials–groceries for a restaurant, crude oil for a refinery, or wood and pen parts for a high-end pen manufacturer like Michel Perchin ($1,000 and up) or David Oscarson ($4,000 and up) and add labor and technology to create a product. There are places for efficiencies all along the production process (or as we saw in Chapter 7, along the entire value chain, for that matter).

Consider high-end pens. One way to improve the efficiency of the production process is to use advanced technologies like lasers to help cut and drill quickly and precisely. Or using computerization with the laser to combine several steps into one, making it possible to produce more perfect pens faster. Another approach is to get the latest raw materials first when they are "hot" in the market. If moon rocks became commercially available, imagine what a pen made from moon rock would be worth. As more moon rocks would enter the market, the price would drop, so the best profits would come to the pen maker who gets the moon rock first into production and first into the hands of rich status-conscious buyers.

From this you can see the two major sources of efficiencies for product-based firms. One is to increase the amount, speed, or accuracy of work done for every day of operations. This can be done through scheduling improvements within the firm like those seen in the time management approach described in Chapter 5 or in this chapter's approach to inventory management. Another approach is to improve parts of the **supply chain** outside the firm so that raw materials get into production faster and that finished products get into customers' hands faster too.

suppy chain
A way to think about the line of distribution of a product from its start as materials outside the target firm, to its handling in the target firm, to its handling by sellers, with placement into the hands of customers.

How do you figure out ways to improve operations? There are several sources of expertise you can use. Our reliable friends at the SBA and SCORE can offer help, much of it low-cost or even free. Other major and relatively inexpensive sources are trade and professional associations. They often publicize **best practices** which represent the most productive ways found in your industry.

best practices
Activities identified by authoritative bodies as examples of optimal ways to get things done in a particular industry, profession, or trade.

Often, top-performing firms will share their secrets of success with the rest of the industry to help improve the overall quality. It also does not hurt in advertising to say that "our procedures are now the industry standard, but we know more about them than anyone else!"

Another interesting source of free advice can be your vendors. For example, UPS, DHL, and FedEx will be glad to consult to you (for free) on ways to improve your supply chain. Although many of the answers will end with "we will be glad to do it for you" followed by a price quote, the analyses they can offer, as well as information about how other companies like yours have benefited from supply chain efficiencies, can help open new ideas to you. Similarly, raw material suppliers or equipment vendors will also be glad to consult with you on ways you could improve your productivity in areas where they have expertise–and possibly some equipment or supplies to sell you. The advice is often free and very current. Get it from competing firms to make sure you get the best ideas, and in case you are thinking about buying, also get the best price.

Operations Management Challenges for Service Firms

Service firms face several challenges in obtaining and maintaining efficient processes. Three characteristics of services–intangibility, inseparability, and perishability–impact operations choices and decision making, creating challenges for the managers of service operations. These characteristics confound and limit strategic choices and tactical decisions available to you.

The intangibility of services is a fundamental difference from goods. Services cannot be seen, felt, or tasted in the manner that goods can be. In contrast, tangible goods are produced, shipped, sold, and consumed in separate places. Another characteristic of a service is its inseparability: a service is produced and consumed at the same time. This exposes the entire production process to customer examination. In the manufacturing processes, the customer is rarely present. When producing services, however, the customer is usually present, preventing any clear distinction between the production stage and the consumption stage. Services are also perishable. In services, unused capacity is lost forever. Empty airline seats, vacant motel rooms, and unfilled theater seats not sold cannot be stored and sold later. Because of the characteristic of perishability, providers of services face great difficulty in managing capacity, and scheduling personnel.

However, despite intangibility, inseparability, and perishability, services can be improved. Part of the answer is deciding on a part of the service on which to focus. Services (let's use bowling as an example) tend to have differing degrees of four components. One component is called the explicit service. In bowling, rolling the ball and counting the pins dropped is the explicit service. The bowling takes place in a bowling alley, and that building with its balls and pins and equipment is what is called the supporting facility.

Part of the bowling experience depends on how you are treated–the friendliness of the staff, the process for which you are charged, and the cleanliness of the alley are examples. These aspects of what we usually think of as customer service are called implicit service. The fourth element, called a supporting good, refers to some tangible material outcome (remember that products were called "goods" in Chapter 9) you get from the service. In bowling there are no tangible outcomes, unless you ask for a receipt. Because there is no real supporting goods in bowling, it is an example of a nearly pure service. Recall that in Chapter 9 we talked about pure services, pure goods, and the hybrids that include elements of both.

With these four elements in mind, it can become easier to target a way to improve the service. For a bowling alley, the owner could improve the supporting facility by getting faster pin-setting equipment, or adding more parking. The owner could add lights and sound equipment for "cosmic bowling" to improve (or at least expand) the explicit service. Improving cleanliness of the facility or getting the staff to be friendlier are ways to improve the implicit service, while a supporting good could be offered by giving bowling related tangibles, such as coupons for future games.

Also take a moment to consider innovative ways to improve service. For example, you could use the Internet to expand service delivery. Offering to post bowlers' pictures and high scores online, or sending them an email with their scores, or letting customers network online for scheduling, or offering video analysis of a person's bowling stance are all implicit services that could add value to the customer and improve (as well as expand) the bowling experience.

The techniques for learning more about how to improve services are identical to those discussed for product-based firms. And if you have employees, there is one more great resource for improving productivity–asking them and putting their ideas into action. Employees of your business each have unique skills and knowledge. As your business grows, you most likely will find that certain employees have a greater understanding of certain functions of your business than do you. By including these people in the management process, you (1) ease your own work burden and (2) gain the advantage of expert input into the management process.

The point is that almost every service (and product) can be improved. In the long run, desirable operational improvements make your customers more loyal and your company more able to withstand competitive pressures. Operations management can add to the bottom line through efficiencies, through revenue growth, and when done right, to both at the same time.

LO **15-7** Be able to discuss the need for and value of documenting your business operations.

Documenting the Operations of Your Business

If you are like most owners of small businesses, your most precious resource is your own time. This leads to the common situation where the knowledge of how your business really works is locked up in your own head. This is probably fine if your business is strictly a one-person operation. But it can cause big problems once your business starts to grow and you have to depend on others to make decisions, plan projects, and direct operations.

So, what to do?

First, you are going to have to realize that to effectively use that expensive talent that you are paying your employees for, you are going to have to give up some personal control. This is the requirement that many entrepreneurs find so difficult as to be nearly impossible. But once you are over that hurdle you are more than halfway to getting your business processes documented to the point that the business will continue to run smoothly, even if you are not making every single decision.

process
The business activities necessary to convert inputs into desired outputs.

To put this strategy into effect, you must understand how processes, procedures, and work instructions relate. A **process** is what a business does when it takes some raw material and converts it into a valuable output. This applies evenly to manufacturing and service businesses.

A manufacturer will take materials, use labor to convert it, and make a final output, the product. A service business takes client data, and adds experience and skill to convert the data into the desired output, such as an audit report or an income tax return. Regardless, the process is converting an input to a desired output.

A **procedure** is simply the step-by-step method by which the process is completed. A procedure might entail welding two pieces of steel, grinding the weld, cleaning and etching the part, and applying a corrosion-resistant coating.

procedure
The series of steps and activities required to complete a process.

Work instructions specify how the weld is to be made: by plasma beam, gas envelopment arc welding, gas welding, or brazing. The instructions may specify the shape and thickness of the two edges to be welded, the composition of the flux used, the welding alloy, and so forth. Work instructions can be very large.

work instructions
Specific guidance for completing steps in a process.

Exactly where to start documenting your business processes, and how to proceed with the task, depends on the state of your business. If you are working as a one-person operation, then where you start is right now. As you make the decisions and conduct the transactions that comprise your business operations, just take a few minutes to write down what you just did. A good way to do this is to create a simple document and print out a number of copies. Insert them into a three-ring binder and keep the binder with you all the time. As you solve business problems, write down what you did, how you did it, and what you needed to complete the task. This will take some of your time, and occasionally you will forget to do it. But if you make an effort, it will soon become habit.

Figure 15.4 shows a suggested form for your notebook.

1. What is the task to be done? a. How often is this task done? b. How long does it take? c. When is it done? (order in January, License in April, etc.)	
2. What causes you to do this task?	
3. How is this task completed? a. List the steps. Continue on the back, if needed.	1. 2. 3. 4. 5. 6. 7.
4. What is the result of this task? a. (order is placed, RFP is routed to engineering, etc.)	
5. What documents do you need? a. paper documents? (invoice, bill of lading, etc...) b. database document? (dates, amounts, payment info, etc.)	
6. What documents are created and saved for this task?	

Notes:

FIGURE 15.4

Sample Form for Documenting Business Processes

FIGURE 15.5

Relationship of Process, Procedure, and Work Instructions

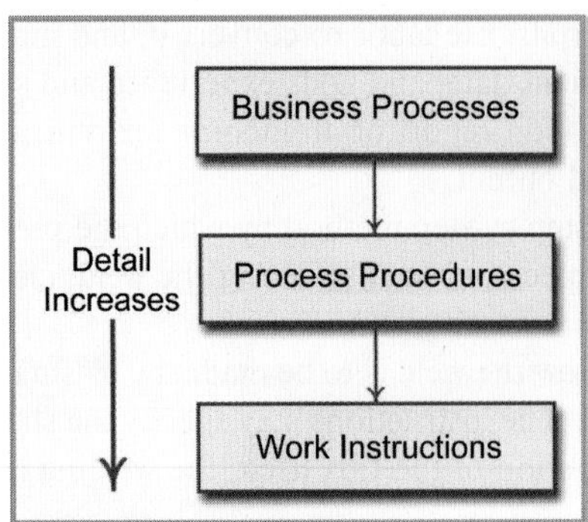

But what if your business has already grown to the size that you have employees and you are outsourcing functions, such as your accounting?

Well, the same process will have to be completed. The big difference is that you will have to enlist the involvement of your employees and consultants. After all, who knows what they are doing better than they do themselves? This is usually accomplished by conducting interviews. (This is a really good task for that intern from your local college.) After the interviews are completed, you can review the sheets and then go back to the involved employee for any additional information that is needed.

For the case of an operating, multipurpose business, there are some techniques of completing the business documentation that are more or less accepted as standard processes. Again, however, the level of detail and the difficulty of completing the task is largely determined by the size and complexity of each individual business.

A typical start to the task of documenting the processes of an operating business is to start from the top down. At the highest level, your business is conducted by conducting specific processes. The processes are completed by conducting necessary procedures, and procedures are done through a set of specific work instructions. Figure 15.5 shows this graphically. The familiar organization chart, shown in Figure 15.6, provides just such an overview.

Finally, it is very important that you realize that every business process does ***not*** have to be extensively documented. Some procedures are so routine that they can easily be programmed into your business computer system for automatic or semiautomatic completion. Some procedures, such as most accounting procedures, are so well documented in statements on best practices, authoritative pronouncements, and regulations that you add no value by rewriting them. This is why most accounting documents produced by CPAs simply state, "This report was compiled using generally accepted accounting principles (GAAP)." GAAP is so well documented that there is no need to specify what it entails.

The procedures that you want to document are those that you must because of governmental regulation and those that are essential to your business. Developing a set of business procedures is time-consuming, and therefore expensive. To have a value greater than their cost they must be carefully reviewed and updated as business processes change. However, if done correctly documenting your business will provide many benefits in the form of fewer employee mistakes and less waste and scrap in your processes.

Oh yes, another point: Having extensive documentation of the essential and unique processes of your business will make selling it much easier when the time comes for you to do so.

FIGURE 15.6

Typical Format for an Organization Chart

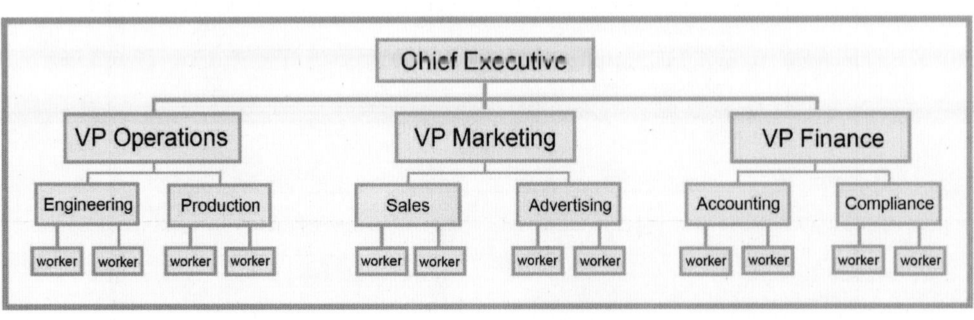

CHAPTER SUMMARY

LO 15-1 Describe techniques to manage short-term assets.

- Two short-term assets other than cash are critical to the success of most small businesses: accounts receivable and inventory.
- Offering credit can benefit a business in many ways, if the credit process is well thought out and carefully managed.
- High-quality receivables provide a means to quickly get cash to meet unexpected opportunities and problems.
- Inventory management is critical because for many small businesses inventory is the single greatest asset.
- Inventory requires significant cash investment that ties up capital that could be used for other business purposes.
- Careful management of inventory involves keeping the right amount of inventory available for sale and ordering the right amount of inventory at the right time to avoid both having too much on hand and running out of inventory, thus losing sales.
- Techniques of inventory management include economic order quantity, just-in-time inventories, optimum stocking level, periodic inventory, perpetual inventory, bar coding, and point-of-sale systems.

LO 15-2 Calculate the value of the assets in your business.

- Assets in use usually have a value greater than can be realized by selling them because of the value present in the assets' future use.
- Because the value of future use is very difficult to determine, accounting methods used to value capital assets are (1) book value, (2) disposal value, (3) replacement value, and (4) fair market value.
- Of these four methods, only book value and replacement value can be accurately determined.
- Each of the four accounting methods is useful in different situations:
  - Book value is used for financial reporting to outsiders.
  - Lenders prefer disposal value for the purpose of accepting collateral for a loan.
  - Disposal value is useful for estimating cash flows for discounted cash flow analysis.
  - Replacement value is useful for estimating sales prices for individual assets and for the business as a whole.

LO 15-3 Describe techniques for managing fixed assets.

- Capital assets create four costs across their useful lives: (1) the cost of acquiring the asset, (2) the cost of owning the asset, (3) the cost of operating the asset, and (4) the cost of disposing of the asset.
- Better decisions result when all the costs previously mentioned, called *whole of life* costs, are considered in the investing analysis.

LO 15-4 Calculate ratios used to analyze capital investment decisions.

- The two most commonly used financial ratios for comparing investment alternatives are (1) payback period and (2) return on investment (ROI).
- There are also two significantly more complex approaches called net present value (NPV) and internal rate of return (IRR).
- Discounted cash flow methods (NPV and IRR) are the most complete because they include the greatest amount of data in the analysis.

LO 15-5 Describe the advantages of renting or leasing capital equipment.

- Renting requires little or no down payment. It therefore preserves cash.
- As a renter, you usually do not bear the costs of maintenance and repair.
- Leasing provides the same advantages as renting, but also provides assurance the asset will remain available for your exclusive use.
- Joint venturing for assets that have limited use allows you to obtain the benefits of the asset, but reduces the cost of ownership by sharing with other businesses.

LO 15-6 Describe techniques to manage and improve the operations of your business.

- Operations management seeks ways to improve productivity.
- Increasing efficiency and increasing quality are the two ways to improve productivity.

- Product-based firms can improve the amount, speed, or accuracy of work, or improve the supply chain.
- Service-based firms can improve their explicit service, implicit service, supporting facility, and supporting good.
- You can get operations management advice from a variety of high-quality free and for-fee sources, as well as your own employees.

15-7 Be able to discuss the need for and value of documenting your business operations.

- Properly documenting the processes of your business will help employees conduct the business without your immediate oversight.
- Documentation may be required by regulation, dependent on the industry in which you operate.
- Documentation provides many benefits, one of which is to aid you in selling your business when the time comes for you to exit.

KEY TERMS

accounts receivable, 540
pledging receivables, 541
factoring, 542
lock box, 543
inventory, 544
economic order quantity (EOQ), 544
optimum stocking level, 546
safety stock, 546
pull-through system, 546
just-in-time (JIT) inventory, 546
microinventory, 547
periodic inventory, 547
perpetual inventory, 547
bar coding, 547
point-of-sale (POS) system, 549
capital assets, 549
book value, 550
disposal value, 550
arm's-length transaction, 550
replacement value, 550
fair market value, 550
inventory valuation, 551
physical inventory, 551
acquisition cost, 552
replacement cost, 552
property, 552
plant, 552
equipment, 552
whole of life costs, 552
cost of owning, 552
cost of operating, 552
cost of disposition, 553
capital budgeting, 553
payback period, 554
return on investment (ROI), 554
straight line for a useful life of 10 years, 554
renting, 556
leasing, 556
outflow, 556
operating lease, 557
capital lease, 557
inputs, 558
operations, 558
outputs, 560
feedback, 560
productivity, 561
efficiency, 561
quality, 561
outsourcing, 561
supply chain, 563
best practices, 563
process, 564
procedure, 565
work instructions, 565

DISCUSSION QUESTIONS

1. Discuss the pros and cons of providing credit to customers. If you do decide to provide credit, what policies should you establish and enforce?
2. Discuss how the use of economic order quantity (EOQ) and reorder calculations can benefit a retail business. What are the drawbacks in using these calculations?
3. Which of the asset valuation methods (book value, disposal value, replacement value, and fair market value) is the best for determining the value of your business's assets? Explain your choice, detailing how your preferred method is better than the other three.
4. How would you estimate the whole of life costs of an expensive capital asset, such as an executive airplane?
5. Discuss the advantages and disadvantages to payback period and to return on investment (ROI) as analysis tools for making capital investment decisions. Which do you prefer and why?
6. Under what circumstances might you be more profitable by outsourcing production?
7. What are the reasons for documenting the processes of your business?
8. Under what circumstances is documentation of processes not necessary?

EXPERIENTIAL EXERCISES

1. Choose a local business in the industry in which you would like to own a firm. Visit the business that you choose, and walk about to observe the amounts and types of inventory on display. Interview the owner or manager. Determine the approximate value of inventory kept on hand. Find out the average time that any single item stays in inventory before it is sold. Also find out the minimum order quantities and delivery times of inventory. Use this information to estimate the amount of working capital necessary to maintain inventory. Make a report to your class.
2. Make a search, using your library, the Internet, and your business contacts, to find factors in your area. Interview the factor and determine the terms offered. Ask what things about the receivables are considered in pricing the factor contract. Contact a commercial banker in your area and find out the bank's policy for lending against receivables. Report your findings to your class.
3. Contact a dealer who sells expensive capital assets, such as earth-moving or transportation equipment. Find out the costs of acquiring, owning, operating, and disposing of the asset. Use a spreadsheet program to estimate the amounts and timing of the whole of life costs of the asset. Estimate the cash inflows that the asset will produce. Use your estimates of costs and cash inflows to calculate the NPV, IRR, ROI, and payback of the asset. Make a presentation to your class, detailing the calculations you have made.
4. Assume that you have a plumbing business that requires the use of a backhoe. Contact equipment rental businesses in your area and find out the rental cost and terms for a suitable machine. Contact leasing companies to find out the cost of leasing a similar backhoe. Assume that, on average, you need the machine for 12 hours weekly. Which is more advantageous, renting or leasing? How would your answer change if you needed the machine an average of 20 hours per week? At what level of usage would renting and leasing not matter?
5. Assume that you own a 2018 Ford F-750 Super Duty truck. The truck has been driven 32,000 miles. What is a reasonable disposal value for this truck? (Be sure to reduce your estimate of sales price by the costs of selling the asset.) What is the replacement value of this truck (in other words, how much would another F-750 with 30,000 miles cost to find, buy, finance, deliver, and license)? Peruse newspaper ads, search the Internet, and talk with truck salespeople to estimate the truck's fair market value. Make a report of your findings to your class.

MINI-CASE

QUALITY SIGN COMPANY

The Quality Sign Co. of Visalia, California, provides credit to customers. The firm is currently averaging receivables of $34,500. The business needs an additional truck-mounted crane to keep up with its rapidly growing business. Quality's owner, George McElroy, has worked up an estimate of the cost of a suitable crane, which is presented in the following chart. Quality's bank is willing to loan 90 percent of the purchase price of the truck, crane, and equipment. All of Quality's currently available cash is needed as working capital and is not available to invest in this project. As a result, Quality must find a way to finance the 10 percent that the bank will not loan, plus the other costs of acquisition.

Quality has contacted a factor who has offered to pay 80 percent for all accounts that are less than 60 days past due. The factor is also willing to act as a collection agency for those accounts that are 60 or more days past due for a fee of 25 percent of the amount collected. Alternatively, Quality's bank has agreed to make a 90-day loan discounted at 12 percent interest in the amount of $32,100, secured by 100 percent of outstanding receivables. The sum of $32,100, which includes accrued interest, is due on the 90th day after the loan is made. During the 90 days, all new receivables will be pledged to the bank as they are incurred. Quality will continue to collect the receivables in the normal course of business. Examine the financial information provided and prepare a recommendation to George McElroy.

Cost of Acquiring Mobile Crane	
Ford F-750 Tandem truck	$ 73,000
120-foot heavy-duty crane	67,000
Hydraulic outriggers	12,500
Hydraulic pump	8,000
30-foot truck bed	5,000
Installation of bed	1,500
Delivery	1,500
Sales tax	12,338
License	1,000
Total acquisition cost	$181,838

Accounts Receivable	
Current	$34,500
>30 days	6,000
>60 days	5,000
>90 days	4,000
Delinquent	4,000
Total receivables	$53,500

APPENDIX A

Economic Order Quantity

To solve for the quantity at which total inventory costs are minimized, consider the following definitions:

EOQ = economic order quantity in units (quantity that minimizes total inventory cost)
Q = quantity in units to be ordered at one time
P = price of one unit of inventory
O = cost of placing one order
C = cost of carrying one unit in inventory for one year
D = number of units to be sold in one year (demand)
D/Q = number of order cycles per year
Q/D = length of one order cycle as a fraction of one year

The total cost of making a single order is calculated as:

$$\text{Total cost of one order} = O + P \times Q$$

The total cost of holding inventory is the cost of holding one unit in inventory times the average number of units held during one order cycle times the number of order cycles in one year. If the number of units at the beginning of an order cycle is Q, and the number at the end of the cycle is 0, and sales are made at a constant rate, then the average number of units held is $(Q + 0)/2$, or simply $Q/2$. The length of one order cycle, as a fraction of one year, lies between 1 and 1 divided by the number of units to be sold in one year.

$$\text{Holding cost per order cycle} = C(Q/2)(Q/D) \text{ which can be simplified to:}$$
$$\text{Holding cost Per cycle} = CQ^2/2D$$

The total cost of ordering and holding inventory for one order cycle is the sum of these two equations. The total cost of inventory for one year is the cost for one cycle times the number of order cycles per year:

$$\text{Total annual cost} = [(O + P \times Q) + (C\,Q^2/2\,D)] \times D/Q = [O(D/Q) + DP + C(Q/2)]$$

The purchase price of inventory (DP) is independent on how many units are ordered at any one time and how many orders are made, and thus may be disregarded. This provides the total cost of ordering and holding inventory:

$$O(D/Q) + C(Q/2)$$

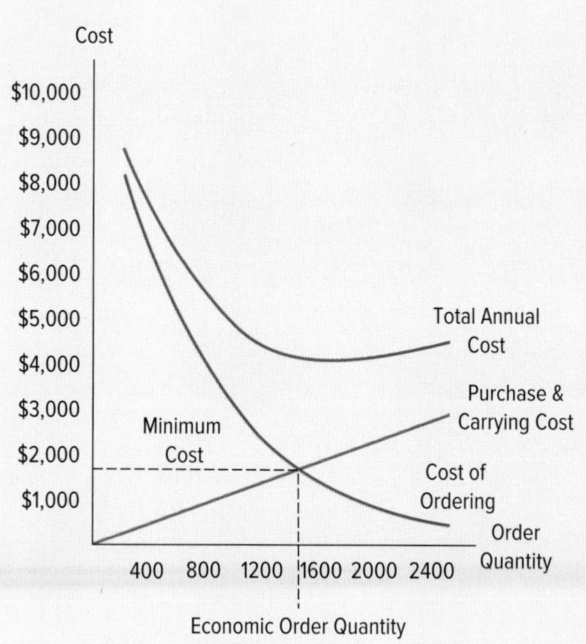

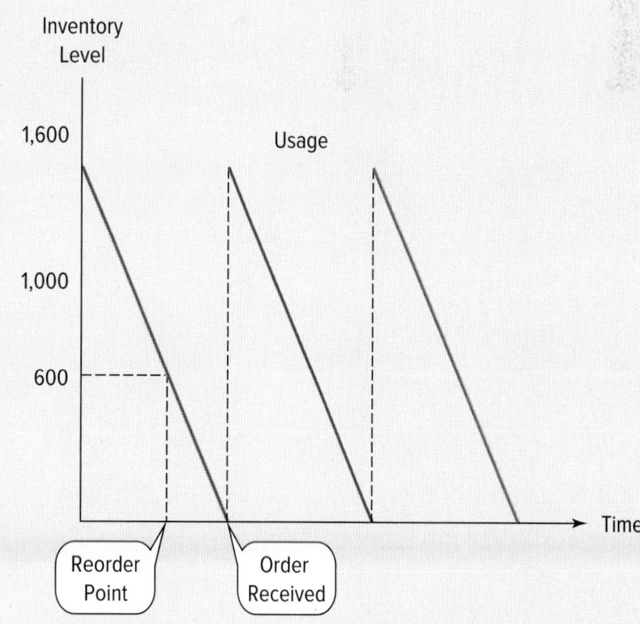

The minimum value of this equation is found by setting the first derivative equal to zero and solving for Q:

$$Q = (20D/C)0.5$$

The EOQ calculation indicates how much to order at one time. It does not tell you when to order, however. To make this decision, you have to know how much time will pass between when the order is placed and when the inventory will be received. Suppose that the lead time is one month and that your business uses 600 units of inventory each month. You therefore must reorder when inventory levels fall to 600 units, leaving you with one month's supply on hand.

But what if your usage fluctuates, say, between 400 and 700 units of product each month? If you wait to reorder until inventory drops to 600 units and you then have a high-sales month, you could run out of inventory long before you run out of month. To protect from this, you can set a policy of maintaining a safety stock of surplus inventory over the minimum. You will reorder when inventory drops to 700 units. This will increase the cost of carrying inventory, but for almost all businesses, the cost of carrying inventory is a fraction of the cost of lost sales. Thus, for you, the cost of holding safety stock is offset by the advantages of not having a stock-out situation.

As you can see from this explanation, deriving the economic order quantity equation requires the use of calculus. Additionally, there are two simplifying assumptions that are unrealistic:

1. Ending inventory quantity is zero for each order cycle.
2. The purchase price of inventory is not affected by the number ordered at one time or by the number of orders placed.

In reality, neither of these assumptions is likely to be true. However, providing for a positive ending inventory and for a price that varies with changes in order quantity and number of orders complicates the solution so much that nobody bothers to do so.

Thus, EOQ determination is another example of an accounting or finance calculation that is approximately true, but precisely wrong. This is why it is necessary to apply common sense to the mathematical solution.

APPENDIX B

Time Value of Money and Discounted Cash Flow Analysis

Which would you prefer: One dollar right now, or one dollar to be received one year from now?

Certainly, you'd prefer to have the dollar today. Anyone would. But consider this: Suppose you were offered the choice between one dollar now or a U.S. savings bond that will pay you $10 one year from now. Which of these would you prefer? Most people immediately see the savings bond as being more valuable.

Now ask yourself, "Why is a dollar right this minute preferable to receiving a dollar in the future, but an iron-clad guarantee of 10 dollars one year from now is preferable to one dollar now?"

Almost everyone, even young children, has an instinctual grasp of the concept that waiting for a benefit somehow lessens the immediate value of that benefit. Given the alternatives of a benefit to be received immediately and a benefit to be received later, the delayed benefit must be of significantly greater value if it is to be chosen. This simple concept is the basis of the concept of the time value of money.

Suppose you knew for a fact that to save your life you would need to have exactly one dollar one year from today. You can make an arrangement with a bank to deposit any amount of money. The bank will pay 10 percent interest. How much must you deposit to have the one dollar when it is needed?

Let x represent the amount that you will deposit. Then $10\%x$ is the amount of interest that the deposit will earn in one year. The sum of the amount you deposit plus the interest earned must equal one dollar:

$$
\begin{aligned}
x + 10\%x &= \$1 \\
1.1x &= \$1 \\
x &= \$1/1.1 \\
x &= \$0.91
\end{aligned}
$$

In finance terms, we would state that the *present value* of one dollar, *discounted at 10 percent for one year*, is $0.91. Alternatively, we could say that the *future value* of 91 cents, *compounded at 10 percent for one year*, is $1.00. The term *present value* simply refers to the amount of money that would have to be deposited now to grow into a specified amount, given an interest rate and period of time. *Future value* is the inverse: the amount that a specific amount of money would grow to be, given a specific interest rate and period of time.

With just a little bit of effort, this concept can easily be expanded to calculate the amount that you must deposit now, at any stated interest rate, to accumulate any amount desired to be received at any time in the future. For example, consider the problem of accumulating for four years:

Value at the End of Year 1	Value at the End of Year 2	Value at the End of Year 3	Value at the End of Year 4
$(1 + r)X$	$(1 + r)(1 + r)X$	$(1 + r)(1 + r)(1 + r)X$	$(1 + r)(1 + r)(1 + r)(1 + r)X$

Where:

X = amount to be deposited
r = interest rate to be earned

The property that in years 2, 3, and 4 interest is being earned on interest from the prior years is called *compounding*.

PRESENT VALUE AND FUTURE VALUE OF 1

Notice that the value at the end of each year is equal to the amount deposited multiplied by 1 plus the interest rate, raised to the power of the number of the period. This allows us to develop an equation that can be easily solved for any amount deposited, any interest rate, and any number of compounding periods:

$$FV_n = PV(1 + r)^n$$

Where:

FV_n = future value of the investment at the end of n years
PV = present value (the amount to be deposited)
r = annual interest rate (also called *compounding rate, or discount rate*)
n = number of periods that the deposit is compounded

By solving the equation for PV, we can develop a general equation that will answer the original question "How much must you deposit now, at a stated interest rate, to accumulate a desired amount at a specified time in the future?"

$$PV = FV_n \times 1/(1 + r)^n$$

Thus, if you need one dollar four years from now, and you can earn 10 percent compounded annually, you must deposit $1/(1.1)^4$ dollars, or 1/1.4641, which equals 68.3 cents.

The calculated value of $(1 + r)^n$ is called the *future value of one*, and can be calculated for any discount rate, r, and any period of time, n. Similarly, the calculated value of $1/(1 + r)^n$ is the *present value of one.* You can easily calculate either the future value or present value of any amount by simply multiplying that amount by the appropriate future value or present value of 1. Thus, if you needed to have available $68,301.50 five years from now and you can earn an interest rate of 8 percent, you would multiply 68,301.50 times the present value of 1 for five years at 8 percent:

$$68{,}301.50 \times 1/(1.08)^5$$
$$68{,}301.50 \times 1/1.4693$$
$$68{,}301.50 \times 0.6806$$

The amount that you would have to deposit today is approximately $46,485.75.

PRESENT VALUE AND FUTURE VALUE OF AN ANNUITY

As the owner of a small business, you will often need to know information about the value of a series of equal payments over time. A series of equal payments made regularly over a set period of time is called an *annuity.*

For example, suppose you know that in three years you will have to replace an essential piece of equipment for your business. Your best estimate is that you can deposit $500 per month for three years at 8 percent interest in order to have sufficient money to make a down payment. How much would you have at the end of three years? The answer to this question can be easily, but tediously, solved by making a series of calculations. First, you must calculate the *monthly* compounding rate by dividing 8 percent by 12 months. Then, you use this monthly rate of 0.00666 to calculate the *future value of each payment*, then simply sum all 36 values:

$$FV = \$500 \times (1 + 0.00667)^{36} + \$500 \times (1 + 0.00667)^{35} + \$500 \times (1 + 0.00667)^{34} + \ldots + \$500 \times (1 + 0.00667)^{1}$$
$$635.119 \quad + \quad 630.912 \quad + \quad 626.734 \quad + \ldots + \quad 503.333$$

There is, however, a much less tedious, although slightly more difficult, means to calculate the future value of an annuity. The above summation equation can be solved algebraically, providing the following:

$$FV = C\left[\frac{(1 + r)^n - 1}{r}\right]$$

Where:

C = cash payment per period
r = number rate
n = number of payments

Substituting values into this equation provides:

$$FV = 500\left[\frac{(1 + 0.00667)^{36} - 1}{0.00667}\right] = \$20{,}403$$

rounded to the nearest whole dollar.

The present value of a series of equal payments may be similarly solved by discounting each payment and summing all the payments. However, this summation equation has also been reduced to a formula:

$$PV = C\left[\frac{(1-(1+r)^{-n}}{r}\right]$$

Thus, by substituting in the appropriate values, you may easily calculate the present value of an installment contract, a lease, indeed, any series of equal payments.

DISCOUNTED CASH FLOW ANALYSIS

These simple concepts and calculations are the basis of all discounted cash flow analyses. Estimated current cash expenditures and net future cash inflows are discounted by some appropriate rate to derive *net present value* and *internal rate of return.*

NET PRESENT VALUE

To perform a net present value analysis, you must:

1. Estimate the *amount* and *timing* of all cash flows of the project.
2. Select an appropriate discount rate.
3. Discount to present value each cash flow using the selected discount rate and timing.
4. Sum the discounted cash flows.

As you can see from the steps above, net present value (NPV) is simply the sum of all cash flows, both negative and positive, discounted by an appropriate discount rate. The difficulty of NPV analysis lies first in accurately estimating future cash flows and second in selecting an appropriate discount rate. Performing the calculations is trivial.

Estimating future cash flows is basically a process of guessing the revenues and expenses that the project will create. Revenues and expenses are then netted for each time period, usually by month, quarter, or year. The estimating process can be as simple or as complex as you believe necessary to produce reliable numbers and dates.

Selecting an appropriate discount rate is absolutely essential to the utility of the analysis. If you select too high a discount rate, desirable projects will be rejected. Select too low a discount rate and money-losing projects will be accepted. Arguments can be made for using any of three very different discount rates: (1) cost of capital of your business, (2) the incremental cost of capital (or marginal cost of capital), and (3) a management-selected minimum acceptable rate of return.

The computation of NPV is accomplished by the following algorithm:

$$NPV = -CF_0 + + + + \ldots + \frac{CF_1}{(1+r)^1} \frac{CF_2}{(1+r)^2} \frac{CF_3}{(1+r)^3} \frac{CF_n}{(1+r)^n}$$

Where:

NPV = net present value of the project
CF_0 = initial investment in the project
CF_n = cash flow at period n
r = discount rate

To illustrate the calculation of *NPV*, consider the following: You are thinking about purchasing for your restaurant a pressurized fryer that will allow you to rapidly prepare spicy deep-fried chicken wings. You believe that the demand for this product will peak within a year, then decrease to zero over three years. The total cost of the fryer, installed and ready for service, is $25,000. The cost of disposing of the fryer at the end of its useful life will be equal to its value at that time.

In order to make an NPV analysis, you have determined that your weighted average cost of capital is 24 percent. You estimate that the fryer will provide the following cash flows to your business:

Cash flows	(\$25,000)	\$20,000	\$8,000	\$4,000	\$2,000
Time period	Right Now (t_0)	One Year from Now (t_1)	Two Years from Now (t_2)	Three Years from Now (t_3)	Four Years from Now (t_4)

Net present value of these cash flows is calculated as follows:

$$\frac{\text{Cash flows}}{\text{Discount factor}} \quad \frac{(\$25{,}000)}{(1+0.24)^0}+\frac{\$20{,}000}{(1+0.24)^1}+\frac{\$8{,}000}{(1+0.24)^2}+\frac{\$4{,}000}{(1+0.24)^3}+\frac{\$2{,}000}{(1+0.24)^4}$$

You may easily calculate the present value of the individual cash flows by using a financial calculator, any calculator that does powers, or a computer spreadsheet such as Lotus 123, Quattro Pro, or Excel.[22] The calculated NPV is (\$724.16). Because the NPV is less than zero (a negative number), you should reject this project because it would not provide a return as great as your business's weighted average cost of capital.

Although the decision rule for NPV indicates that the project should be rejected, remember that all the numbers on which the analysis is made are estimates. No matter how carefully you attempt to estimate future results, you can never do so with certainty. In fact, were you to purchase the fryer, you might find that the product was either much more successful or much less successful than you would ever have expected.

There are several ways to deal with this inevitable uncertainty. You can change your estimates slightly up or down, a process called *sensitivity analysis*, to determine the effects of small changes in your estimates. For example, if you were to increase your estimate of the first year cash flows by just \$898, the decision would change to "accept." If you enjoy doing math, you could adjust each of your estimates for the probability of their being correct, then use the *expected* values in the analysis. You might reconsider using weighted average cost of capital for the discount rate. Perhaps you should consider using the cost at which you can borrow funds. Or you might consider using a discount rate that is the sum of the cost of borrowing and some minimum return that you are willing to accept. In fact, in this example, reducing the discount rate by less than 3/10 of one percent reverses the decision.

INTERNAL RATE OF RETURN

Another way of dealing with the uncertainty of NPV analysis is to ask the question, "If this project does not provide a return equal to the discount rate, then what rate of return does it provide?" Internal rate of return (IRR) provides the answer to this question by disclosing the actual rate of return, based on the amount and timing of the cash flow.

The internal rate of return of a project is that rate at which NPV = zero. In other words, IRR is the discount rate at which the present value of the cash inflows of the project exactly equals the present value of the cash outflows. Thus, in this example, you must solve the following equation for the value of the discount rate (IRR):

$$\frac{(\$25{,}000)}{(1+IRR)^0}+\frac{(\$20{,}000)}{(1+IRR)^1}+\frac{\$8{,}000}{(1+IRR)^2}+\frac{\$4{,}000}{(1+IRR)^3}+\frac{\$2{,}000}{(1+IRR)^4}=\$0$$

It is unfortunate that there is no way to directly solve this equation for IRR. The only way to find the value of IRR is to try different numbers in a reiterative process until you find a number that provides a solution sufficiently close to zero. Financial calculators, such as those provided by Hewlett-Packard and Texas Instruments, all provide an automated means to derive the answer. Computer spreadsheet programs also provide functions to find the IRR of any series of cash flows.

If you do solve the previous equation, you will find that the IRR is approximately 21.59 percent. Compare this number with your estimate of your cost of capital, 24 percent. The question you must answer is, "How confident am I that my cost of capital actually exceeds 21.6 percent?" If you are confident, reject the project. If, on the other hand, you are not so sure, perhaps you should reconsider the assumptions and estimates that you have made.

APPLYING THESE APPROACHES TO THE TRUCK AND CRANE PROBLEM

Earlier in the chapter we discussed the problem of deciding whether to buy a Ford-Skyhook or GMC-Sponco truck and crane combination. We worked through two simple methods for making a capital budgeting decision—the payback period approach and the ROI or rate of return on investment approach. We noted then that NPV and IRR approaches could also be used.

Using either NPV or IRR will avoid the shortcomings of both the payback period and the return on investment methods. Discounted cash flow methods make specific numeric adjustments to approximate the lower value of money to be received as compared to the value of money received now.

Net present value (NPV), like the payback period method, is based upon estimates of the cash flows that an investment will cause and utilizes your business's weighted average cost of capital. It is like ROI in using the weighted cost of capital, but unlike ROI because NPV uses cash flows, not profits. When Warren Buffett is deciding if he will buy a company, he uses this technique. In his case he looks at the cash flow the business generates in a year and then figures how much it would be worth—after being discounted—at some point in the future. For buying businesses, he uses a U.S. Treasury long-term bond rate[23] for the period of time that he decides is appropriate. The final result of NPV calculation is a single dollar value, which can be of any magnitude, even a negative number, although the more positive the number, the better.

For our truck and crane example, the time period is the 10 years the truck and crane would be used. We know from the owner's earlier calculations that her weighted cost of capital is 20 percent, and we saw the cash flows in Table 15.1. The computations are complex, but spreadsheets like Excel can do them quickly and easily.

As with payback period and ROI, two decision rules are applied to decide among alternative investments:

- Accept only those alternatives for which the net present value is equal to or greater than zero.
- Accept the alternative with the greatest value among those that meet the first criterion.

Ford-Skyhook	GMC-Sponco
Net present value = $108,112	Net present value = $107,544

Both alternatives meet the first decision rule. Applying the second, you would accept the Ford-Skyhook alternative because it provides the greater positive net present value.

Internal rate of return (IRR) is a special case of net present value. IRR focuses on the return to the company, but also factors in the cost of the project. What is distinctive about the way IRR does this is that it statistically makes the net present value equal to zero, so the discount rate is thrown out as a consideration.

The decision rules for using IRR are:

1. Accept only those alternatives for which internal rate of return is equal to or greater than the business's weighted cost of capital.
2. Accept the alternative with the greatest IRR among those that meet the first criterion.

Ford-Skyhook	GMC-Sponco
Internal rate of return = 36.520%	Internal rate of return = 33.373%

As with net present value, both alternatives pass the first decision test. Of the two, you would choose the Ford-Skyhook alternative because it has the greater IRR.

It is important to note that NPV and IRR are considered some of the most complex of financial equations. The advantages of discounted cash flow analyses for evaluating investment alternatives are (1) all cash flows of each investment are explicitly included in the analysis, and (2) the time value of money is specifically calculated. Discounted cash flow methods do have serious drawbacks, however. First, a discounted cash flow analysis has the appearance of being extremely accurate. This appearance is highly deceiving, however. Every number in the calculation is, at best, an estimate. The weighted cost of capital, the amounts, and the timings of cash flows cannot ever be known with certainty. Second, the calculation uses a single estimate for each projected cash flow. Although cash flows that will occur soon may be reasonably accurately estimated, the longer the period of time over which projections are made, the greater the uncertainty of each estimate. Third, making good estimates of future cash flows requires considerable expertise and effort. Few owners of small businesses have either the time or the resources to do the necessary projections. All in all, discounted cash flow analyses are theoretically sound but are empirically highly problematic.

CHAPTER

16

Small Business Protection: Risk Management and Insurance

● Each month, thousands of business websites are targeted by cyber criminals. Many small business owners mistakenly believe that they won't be hit because, they reason, "my business is too small for crooks to mess with." The most common types of cyber attacks against businesses are phishing, ransomware, and formjacking. Symantec, a major supplier of anti-malware software, reported that in 2018 an average of 4,800 retail websites were compromised by formjacking code,[1] and there were almost 121,000 ransomware attacks on small and medium-sized businesses.[2]

Suppose you were to find a message similar to the one shown here. What would you do?

A ransomware notification window

Mr.Nngk Phakayaem/iStock/Getty Images

LEARNING OBJECTIVES

After you complete this chapter, you will be able to:

LO 16-1 Explain the meaning and nature of business risk.

LO 16-2 Describe the specific types of risks associated with different aspects of business operations.

LO 16-3 Describe techniques to manage risks to stay within your level of risk tolerance.

LO 16-4 Explain how insurance can be used to manage business risk.

LO 16-5 Describe techniques for sharing risk with other businesses and organizations.

Focus on Small Business: The Threat to Small Business Computer Systems

Cyber crime has become a big business in itself. Cybersecurity Ventures projects that the total cost worldwide will be on the order of $6 trillion (a 6 followed by 12 zeros!) in 2021.[3] The same report states that 58 percent of all victims of cyber crime in 2018 were small businesses. As George Westermann stated in an article for *Forbes* magazine, "Your Business Is Never Too Small for a Cyber Attack."[4] These numbers are alarming, but in fact they probably understate the real problem. Most small business victims of cyber crime do not report the attacks.[5]

So what happens when your business is hit with a ransomware attack?

Although most affected businesses do not discuss their experiences with cyber attacks, a few have. Rick Snow, the owner of one such small business, Maine Indoor Karting, told his business's story in testimony before the U.S. House Small Business Committee.[6]

The hacking of Maine Indoor Karting began with an email alert that appeared to be from the company's bank. The email stated that there had been a suspicious online attempt to access the business account. The email contained instructions to follow an included link. The link opened a site that was identical to the format of the logon page for the bank. Snow clicked on the link and seeing the expected logon page, entered his account data as directed.

Almost immediately, Snow realized that he had been duped. He went to his bank immediately, and with the bank's assistance closed the current account, created a new account, and ordered new checks and debit cards for the business. He stated that it cost about $250 and took three days for the new checks and new business debit cards to be received. It seemed that his prompt action had prevented a business disaster.

Then two weeks later, not long after he distributed the employee paychecks, he discovered that his business checking account balance was zero! Three separate wire transfers had been made from the account. Because the loss was discovered after banking hours, he had to wait a very anxious night before going to the bank to attempt to stop the wire transfers from paying.

Snow was simultaneously unlucky and fabulously fortunate. He was able to prevent the wire transfers from being funded. However, once again he had to close his business account and go through the time-consuming and expensive process to set up a new account.

DISCUSSION QUESTIONS

1. Why do you think that cyber criminals target small and medium-sized businesses more than large businesses?
2. What could Snow have done to prevent this hacking attack?
3. How do you suppose the cyber criminals obtained the information for the new bank account that allowed them to drain it of funds?
4. Think of the business that you own or would like to own. How and to what extent would the theft of money be a threat to your business?

LO **16-1** Explain the meaning and nature of business risk.

Risk in Small Business

We have discussed financial risk that comes from your capital structure and investment risk caused by accepting or providing debt. Within the discussions of the management of cash, accounts receivable, inventory and other business assets we have discussed the issues of employee fraud and theft in its various forms. In this chapter we discuss other kinds of risk that small business owners face.

For business owners, risk can be defined as being the probability that the future will not turn out as planned. Your business may be the target of a lawsuit. Regulatory changes and enforcement may cause you great losses. Floods, fires, earthquakes, tornados, all kind of natural disasters, in fact, can and do happen. While these things are not everyday occurrences, they do occur frequently and your business can suffer as a result.

We all know that people vary widely in their response to risk. Some people will run with the bulls in Pamplona; others will not touch a calf in a petting zoo. As we pointed out in the previous chapter, business owners similarly differ in their response to business risk. Some seek risk, but most prefer to avoid risk to the extent possible. In academic terms, some business owners are *risk seeking*, although most small business owners are *risk-averse.*

To the extent that small business owners are risk-averse, as part of every business decision they consider what they could lose. If they can't reduce the level of risk to where they're comfortable, then they make arrangements to either insure against future losses or to spread the risk among other people or businesses.

Thinking about Risk

We have already defined business risk as the probability that the future state of the business will be less successful than planned, resulting in the loss of value of business assets. No person enters a business for the purpose of losing money, but it can and does happen. The next quarter's business does not meet expectations. Investments go bad. Sales projections are not met. Products do not meet specifications. All of a sudden, investors find themselves the owners of assets that are worth much less than expected. The likelihood of this bleak outcome is the essence of business risk.

Among the most commonly identified sources of risk are:

- Financial risk that is a result of choosing among sources and types of capital investment.[7]
- Theft of business property.
- Nonpayment of debts owed to the business.
- Cyber attacks that disable the firm's computer system or copy sensitive business data.
- Changes in technology that render the business's product or service obsolete.
- Injuries and illnesses suffered by employees as a result of their employment.
- Injuries from accidents incurred by customers, vendors, and others while on business property.

- Loss or harm incurred because of the use of the business's product or service.
- Natural events, such as storms, floods, fire, and earthquakes.
- Violation of any of the multitude of laws and regulations that apply to small business.
- Misbehavior by employees,

In this chapter we will discuss these and other risks, although not in this order. Each discussion will include a description of the risk and a brief discussion of how an owner of a small business may control or lessen the negative effects of each.

Risks Associated with Specific Business Operations

LO **16-2** Describe the specific types of risks associated with different aspects of business operations.

There are three general types of events that cause business risk: (1) events related to the property of the business, (2) events related to personnel, and (3) events related to customers and others.

Risks Related to the Property of the Business

Every business owns things of value such as inventory, production machinery, reputation, skill, and experience. Many businesses own furniture, office equipment, vehicles, buildings, and land. Some businesses own valuable patents, copyrights, trademarks, or trade secrets.

Each type of property involves specific forms of risk. Inventory can be stolen or spoiled or become obsolete. Cyber attacks can destroy critical computer resources. Hacking of databases can cause loss of the trust of customers, vendors, and employees. Production machinery can break down. Institutional skill and experience can be diminished or lost as key employees die, retire, quit, go to work for competitors, or start their own competing businesses. Furniture, office equipment, vehicles, and buildings can be damaged or destroyed by vandalism, accidents, fire, flood, or wind. Land may become contaminated by spills of hazardous materials or rendered unsafe by cave-ins or landslides. Patents may be infringed upon. Trademarks and brand names that are not properly protected may pass into the public domain. A trade secret may be disclosed.

Events Related to Personnel

There are three main types of risk related to events involving personnel: (1) theft, (2) violation of government regulations, and (3) loss of key employees.

Employee Theft

Employee theft is a fact of life for almost all businesses. Theft by personnel may involve direct stealing of money or other assets of the business, or may be the conduct of an illegal act that is intended to provide personal benefit at a cost to the business. The most common form of employee theft is the pilfering of items of small value, such as office supplies and small hand tools, or actions such as making copies for their children to use at school or otherwise using company resources to make personal items. Thought of this way, some experts estimate that 95 percent of small businesses face at least some of this sort of loss annually.[8] Losses of these types are usually insignificant in their effect on the financial results of your business. However, theft losses of cash and inventory can be of such magnitude that your business is significantly damaged or even fails.[9]

employee theft
Misappropriation of business property by employees of that business.

Violation of Government Regulations

Violation of government regulations has become a source of significant business risk over the last 30 years. **Regulation of the workplace** has increased, resulting in employer violations that range from having an employee one time "forget" to use required safety equipment to failing to provide required accommodations for employees with disabilities to discrimination against a protected class (race, religion, color, national origin, age, disability, or gender). The cost of violating any of the many workplace regulations can range from as little as losing a few hours of your time completing paperwork, up to huge dollar fines and judicial awards.

regulation of the workplace
Laws and governmental rules that limit the freedom of business owners to manage their businesses as they please.

Violation of some of the regulations is probably inevitable given the complex, ambiguous, and sometimes contradictory nature of the regulations. The federal rule-making agencies of which employees may run afoul are countless, including the U.S. Food and Drug Administration, the Environmental Protection Agency, the Securities Exchange Commission, the National Transportation Safety Board, the Federal Aviation Agency, the U.S. Coast Guard, and the Department of the Interior, to name only a few. In addition, most states have similar business-regulating agencies that promulgate rules that often conflict with federal standards. The Small Business Administration estimated in 2008 that small businesses that had fewer than 20 employees had to spend roughly $10,585 per employee per year to file and keep up with all the regulatory requirements. This rate was twice what large businesses had to spend.[10]

The study of the costs of regulation on small businesses, cited above, has not been repeated since its release in 2010. However, the National Small Business Association (NSBA) conducted an online survey between November 28, 2016 and January 10, 2017 of 1,000 small business owners. This survey found that the cost of regulation for the average startup was a staggering $83,019.23! The cost of regulation per employee is not reported. On the other hand, the study found that half of all businesses expend approximately $12,000 per year for direct and indirect costs of federal, state, and local regulation, combined.[11]

Equal Employment Opportunity Commission (EEOC)
A commission established to enforce the provisions of the Equal Employment Opportunity Act.

Occupational Safety and Health Administration (OSHA)
A government agency created to enforce safety in the workplace.

protected classes
States of being that are expressly prohibited from suffering discrimination: race, color, religion, sex, national origin, gender, age, or disability.

Age Discrimination in Employment Act (ADEA)
An act of Congress that makes it illegal to discriminate against people who are older than 40 years of age.

Rehabilitation Act of 1973
An act of Congress that provides training for workers who are injured on the job.

Americans with Disabilities Act (ADA) of 1990
An act of Congress that requires that businesses make provisions for access for people with disabilities.

Civil Rights Act of 1991
A series of acts by Congress that prohibit discrimination on the basis of race, color, religion, sex, or national origin.

key employees
Employees whose experience and skills are critical to the success of a business.

Although there are numerous government agencies that issue business regulations, small businesses mostly have trouble with the rules from only three agencies: the Internal Revenue Service, the **Equal Employment Opportunity Commission (EEOC)**, and the **Occupational Safety and Health Administration (OSHA)**. The problems arise because each agency has rules that are so complex that compliance problems are almost a certainty, if enough aspects of the business are reviewed. For example, the Americans with Disabilities Act has rules that govern the furnishings, size, placement, and clear space of public toilets and those run to over four pages and include more than 10 architectural drawings to specify exact maximums and minimums to the inch. Any violation of any of the specific accessibility measurements can result in civil fines or litigation awards. We discuss the IRS and the problems of tax code compliance later in this chapter.

The risk of noncompliance with OSHA and EEOC regulations is further increased by the continual growth in the scope of government regulations. For example, the Equal Employment Opportunity Commission's rule-making authority has grown constantly since the agency's start in 1964. At that time, EEOC established five **protected classes**: race, color, religion, sex, or national origin.[12] Since then the authority of the EEOC has grown through the passage of (1) the **Age Discrimination in Employment Act (ADEA)** of 1967, (2) the **Rehabilitation Act of 1973**, (3) the **Americans with Disabilities Act (ADA) of 1990**, and (4) the **Civil Rights Act of 1991**, all of which grant additional rule-making and enforcement powers. The EEOC has made thousands of rules that are ambiguous and, at times, contradictory.

Loss of Key Employees

Loss of **key employees** is a particularly acute risk for small businesses. Because of the simple fact that there are only a few employees in a small business, invariably one person or a very few people are essential to the successful operation of the business. If such a key employee quits, retires, becomes disabled, or dies, the business faces a crisis. In many cases, the loss of a key employee has led to the bankruptcy and dissolution of the business.

Competition from former employees is also a constant risk. Good employees who understand the business, who successfully sell products and services, and who are skilled at the operations of the business are often tempted to become competitors. This can happen several different ways. A key employee may be "hired away" by an existing competitor who offers a higher salary and greater perks. A key employee may start her or his own business, using the knowledge and skills gained from working in your business. Customers may offer to back a key employee to establish a competing business in order to obtain lower prices and greater negotiating leverage. Vendors may offer a key employee dealerships or exclusive sales territories in a bid to increase sales of their specific products.

This risk is especially acute in knowledge and service businesses, such as accounting practices, medical practices, barber and beauty shops, and restaurants. All of these businesses have relatively low barriers to entry for qualified people. Each type of business depends on personal relationships engendered with customers. When a key employee of a knowledge firm leaves, it is common for several customers to change to the new firm.

Events Related to Customers and Others

Although customers are, by definition, the "reason for being" of any business, they also are the source of considerable business risk. In addition to customers, you are also at risk from vendors and even trespassers on your property. This risk from customers and others primarily arises from (1) injuries suffered while on business property and (2) injury or damage that is caused during the use of the business's products.

Injuries suffered while on business property may or may not be your fault. People at times do stupid things, such as climb on shelves to get items that are "just out of reach." If the shelf collapses and dumps the customer onto the floor, you're going to pay twice: once for the broken shelf and spoiled merchandise, and once for the "pain and suffering" of the customer. A reasonable person might believe that the customer was responsible for his or her own acts and the business should not be liable. It is most unfortunate that juries are composed of "peers" and not of "reasonable persons."

Injuries on business premises may also arise from the actions of trespassers. In many cases, a business has been held responsible for harm experienced by a trespasser, as well as harm inflicted by the trespasser on employees, customers, and vendors. An extreme example of this type of event is robbery and assault that occurs on business property. In many cases, injuries suffered by employees and customers at the hands of the criminals have been held to be the fault of the business. The rationale given has been that the business didn't provide good enough security. Again, the business pays twice: once when the robber steals money and other assets; again when the employees and customers are paid for pain and suffering caused by the robbery.

Payment for injury or damage that occurs during the use of the business's products is referred to as *product liability*. The magnitude of losses resulting from product liability claims has increased greatly in recent years with an increase in class action lawsuits. This is an issue that you must take very seriously if you are a manufacturer. Although individual customers usually get very little money from class action suits, the lawyers who pursue them often receive payments of millions of dollars, as occurred in the case of asbestos producers and tobacco companies. Certainly, the smaller your firm is, the less exposure you have to class action product liability suits. This is true for two reasons: A small business has fewer customers who can claim harm, and a small business does not have the "deep pockets" of cash and other assets that can be raided by rapacious law firms.

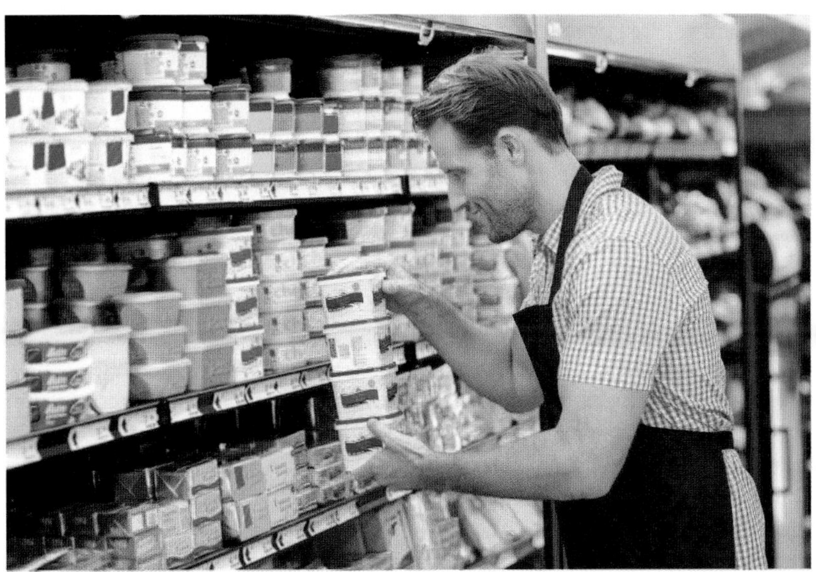

Retailers can be held responsible for damages caused by goods that have been tampered with and placed on the store's shelves. Constant vigilance is required to ensure that inventory is free of any impairment.

Wavebreakmedia/Shutterstock

Individual lawsuits may also be filed when a single user claims to have been harmed by the product. Such lawsuits are actually more common than class action suits. Although the amount paid in settlement is usually a tiny fraction of that of a class action suit, a manufacturer must still take the issue very seriously. In the 1970s a rash of individual lawsuits against manufacturers of small (under 12,000 pounds gross weight) airplanes resulted in the demise of the industry. Many small businesses that either made small airplanes or made parts and subassemblies for airplanes were forced into bankruptcy. The production of small airplanes did not resume in the United States until Congress passed a law that limited the exposure of manufacturers to product liability suits.[13]

LO **16-3** Describe techniques to manage risks to stay within your level of risk tolerance.

Managing Risks

Although none of the risks discussed can be completely avoided, there are strategies you can use to minimize the likelihood and magnitude of losses. The best strategy is to develop a business environment that minimizes (1) the probability of the event occurring and (2) the amount of loss that can be experienced if the event does occur. You do this by (1) making specific plans for and arrangements to deal with foreseeable events, (2) creating and enforcing an appropriate code of conduct for yourself and all employees, (3) ensuring that valuable assets are physically secure, and (4) actively working to get rid of any physical hazards in your workplace.

You should develop disaster plans for events that are unlikely, but that have a finite probability of happening. For example, those businesses that are located in the Missouri and Mississippi River flood plains near St. Louis have a very real probability of significant flooding in any year. Prudent business management for these firms includes creating a plan of action to remove valuable assets to high ground, making plans for temporary business locations, and creating provisions for subcontracting work to minimize the effect of business interruption from the inevitable flood. Disaster planning like this can also work to minimize the effects of fires, storms, and earthquakes on business operations.

A written code of ethics and business conduct (like those discussed in Chapter 3) make explicit what you expect of your employees. By obtaining employee acceptance of the code, you can create an environment in which peer pressure works to discourage inappropriate behavior and works to encourage desired behavior. To be effective it is essential that you abide by the code, leading your employees by your example of integrity and honesty.

Valuable assets of the business must be kept in secure areas. When valuable assets must be used, access to them should be carefully controlled and monitored by management. Only those employees who have a business need should be allowed access to valuable assets at any time.

Working proactively to ensure that your physical place of business is (1) free of potential hazards and (2) secure from intruders to prevent on-premises injuries and violations of EEOC or OSHA rules. It is easier and much less expensive to anticipate and prevent potential lawsuits than it is to defend yourself against them once they have been filed.

Managing Risk to Tangible Property

Protecting Your Business from Theft

Protection from theft of business property also depends on the type of property held. Although land is not subject to being physically stolen, you can lose your property rights through a process called *adverse possession*. Adverse possession occurs when the owner of real property does not enforce property rights and allows a nonowner to use the property as if it were his or her own. Just as land cannot be stolen, buildings and large equipment for which there is no ready market are similarly free from theft because of their physical nature. The property most at risk is cash and small items of high value that can be quickly and easily sold.

separation of duties
A type of internal control that separates the physical control of an asset from the person accounting for that asset.

You need to do two things to protect yourself from theft: (1) physically protect your property, and (2) develop and enforce rules that prevent the employee responsible for the asset from being able to account for the asset. This is called **separation of duties**, and is a core management technique to safeguard money and other valuable assets of a business.[14]

Although separation of duties will keep any single employee from stealing, nothing will keep two or more employees who decide to cooperate from stealing company property. Employee collusion is the source of the largest amount of employee theft.[15] When employees agree to defraud, "one lies, and the other swears to it!" This is the way that common frauds are perpetrated, such as sales of nonexistent advertising, payments to nonexistent vendors, and purchases of inventory and supplies from a vendor who will pay a kickback to the dishonest employees. As Figure 16.1 shows, employees account for the second-largest source of business theft in retail businesses, following shoplifting. The largest source of theft in businesses that do not have retail outlets, such as construction, manufacturing, government, warehousing, is theft by employees.[16]

Managing risk to the tangible properties of your business depends on the nature of the property. Land and buildings aren't subject to theft, but they can be damaged or destroyed by a variety of events. Equipment can be stolen, vandalized, or allowed to fall into disrepair. Small items of high value may be stolen by employees, customers, vendors, or others. The specific measures to control for each type of risk are particular to the specific asset at risk.

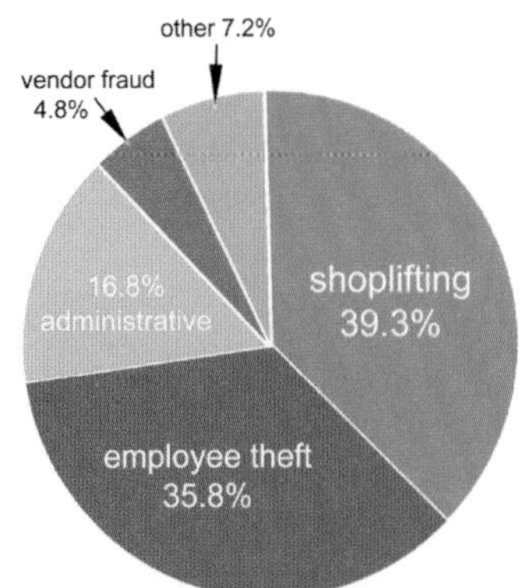

FIGURE 16.1

Source of Theft in Retail Businesses

Source: Richard C. Hollinger and Amanda Adams, *2016 National Retail Security Survey*, University of Florida, 2016, p. 9.

Managing Risk to Inventories

Because inventories are likely to be the most valuable asset of your small business, it's protection and management deserves a close look. Your small business can experience loss of asset value of inventory in several ways;

- As discussed in Chapters 13 and 15, inventory is subject to theft.
- Inventory is often lost—not stolen, not gone, it just can't be found.
- Inventory is frequently damaged during storage or while being moved.
- Inventory can spoil—either physically, as with food products, or technologically, as happened with personal digital assistants.

Theft is the single greatest cause of inventory loss. Inventory is stolen by employees, shoplifters, and burglars. It is extremely difficult to stop any of these three sources of loss. But you can take steps that should greatly reduce the risk.

Reducing theft by employees is accomplished by first educating them in both the cost to the business and the personal cost to the employee of getting caught. Other means of control include being very careful in whom you hire; having a documented policy for dealing with employees who steal; and observing employees especially around the time of closing and inside any break areas.

Reducing shoplifting requires greater efforts than those used to reduce employee theft. Shoplifters usually are relatively experienced thieves. They often "case" a business before performing any theft. They identify surveillance cameras; find weak points in your security; and map out paths in order to be able to escape if detected.

Reasonable approaches to reducing shoplifting include:

- Having security personnel in uniform stationed near exits at peak times and around closing time.
- Carefully monitoring any customers who are wearing bulky clothing such as long raincoats, or who are carrying large handbags or backpacks, and those who are pushing strollers through your business.
- Extensively training checkout clerks to recognize inventory items to allow them to detect label switching.
- Installing and using strategically placed monitoring devices such as video cameras.

Preventing burglary is most difficult of all. The very things that make a retail location desirable, such as glass doors and close parking, also create opportunity for burglars. Determined thieves do not hesitate to break glass doors. And organized thieves will certainly have a getaway vehicle at hand.

The best approach is to ensure that your location has frequent but not regularly spaced drive-bys by police. If your business is large enough, you might consider hiring private security personnel. Entrances, doors, windows, and access hatches to the roof should all be alarmed. The alarm system should automatically call into local police.

Managing Risk to Buildings and Land

Protection from fire for buildings may be obtained through such measures as installing smoke alarms and sprinkler systems and having a fire plug nearby. Other control measures include removing flammable ground cover such as brush, leaves, and fallen branches from proximity to all buildings.

Protection from flood can, first and foremost, be accomplished by not locating on a flood plain. Although this seems like a commonsense directive, unimaginable numbers of businesses are built on flood plains, and new construction continues. In 1993, the entire flood plain of the Missouri and Mississippi Rivers in the St. Louis area, from Kansas City on the west, Hannibal, Missouri, on the north, to the confluence of the Mississippi and Ohio Rivers on the south, was inundated with water up to 50 feet deep. Hundreds of businesses in the areas around St. Louis and St. Charles, Missouri, were destroyed. Despite this experience and despite a second round of severe flooding in 1994, the flood plain of the Missouri River from St. Louis upstream for over 30 miles is the site of extensive building. It is only a matter of time until the river again rises, the levees fail, and hundreds of businesses are flooded with tens of feet of muddy water.

Flooding also occurs for reasons other than streams and rivers overflowing their banks. Floods often occur from breaks in water supply pipes, from accidental activation of fire suppression sprinklers, from blockages in storm and sanitary sewers, and from runoff of water that is sprayed on burning buildings. You may protect yourself from these hazards through performing regular inspection and maintenance of the plumbing and fire suppression systems of your buildings.

Protection from storms can be accomplished by rigorously enforcing building standards concerning attachment of buildings to foundations, types and construction of roofs, and by choice of building materials and construction techniques. The specifics of storm proofing a building depends on the geographic location of the building. Specific storm hazards, wild fire, wind, flood, or snow load are determined primarily by geography. Each geographic area has its own risk. California has frequent floods and mud slides. The mountains of the West are subject to winter snows, spring floods, and summer wild fires. The Gulf and eastern shores south of New York are subject to frequent hurricanes. The Midwest, especially Oklahoma, Kansas, Nebraska, Iowa, Missouri, Illinois, Indiana, and Ohio, experiences thousands of tornadoes every year. On May 22, 2011, a category 5 tornado struck Joplin, Missouri. The storm destroyed homes and businesses in a path nearly 1 mile wide and fully 6 miles long. Total damage has been estimated to be $3 billion. The Small Business Insight relates how one business owner was affected by a force 5 tornado in Joplin, Missouri. The upper Midwest, including northern Ohio, western Pennsylvania, and western New York, is annually buried under tons of snow. Specific building techniques to withstand tornado winds are useless against five feet of snow on the roof, just as structure to withstand snow loading is useless when the entire building slides down the hillside.

Managing Risk to Tools, Equipment, Inventory, and Other Portable Items

Managing risks to tools, equipment, inventory, and other physical assets is largely a function of developing and enforcing appropriate business policies and procedures. Tools and equipment should be maintained on a schedule that prevents serious wear or damage. Frequent inspections should be made to ensure that any problem is detected as soon as possible, allowing repairs to be made in a systematic manner.

Physical assets that can be stolen must be kept in locked storage areas when not in use. Small items of high value should not only be kept locked away, but a procedure should be rigidly enforced that requires employees to sign for removing them from storage. A manager's signature should be required to confirm that the item has been returned to the proper storage when it's no longer needed.

Managing Risk to Computers and Data

One of the riskiest areas of business today involves computers, especially those connected to the Internet. Today hackers use programs that seek out unprotected computers connected to the Internet, and once identified, take them over through spyware programs. Some spyware may use

SMALL BUSINESS INSIGHT

THE MEDICINE SHOPPE IN JOPLIN, MISSOURI

On May 22, 2011, a massive multiple-vortex tornado tore through the midwestern town of Joplin, Missouri. Among the hundreds of business locations destroyed was the Medicine Shoppe, owned by David and Sherree Starrett. All that they could salvage from the wreckage was the safe that held controlled drugs, some computer equipment, and a few filing cabinets. All their pharmacy files were destroyed by being submerged in water.

The Starretts, however, did not give up. Only two days after the storm they managed to lease an undamaged storefront. They moved in the few things salvaged from the storm. With fixtures donated by other Medicine Shoppe owners the Starretts set up for business. The U.S. Drug Enforcement Administration issued a new provider number and the state of Missouri provided a disaster waiver. They received an expedited shipment of drugs and medicines from their supplier. On May 28, six days after the storm, the Starretts reopened for business in their new location.

David and Sherree Starrett recovered from a disaster of a magnititude that few will ever experience. Their resilience, determination, and hard work (along with business insurance and an effective business network) enabled them to literally "rise from the ashes."[17]

Courtesy of David and Sherree Starrett, owners of The Medicine Shoppe of Joplin

your computer to send out advertising spam on behalf of the hacker's clients. Other spyware lets the hacker actually see and even steal data on your PC, including passwords and credit card information. If you have your business data on the computer, your customer lists (including *their* credit card numbers and identifying information) can get hacked.

The best way to think of protecting your PC is a lot like how you think about protecting your car. Locking the door and taking the keys with you prevents the vast majority of car thefts, those done by thieves who find keys in the ignition or open an unlocked door and hot-wire a car. What is the equivalent for a PC?

1. *A firewall:* Firewalls are programs or pieces of equipment called routers that serve as a barrier between your PC and the Internet.
2. *An antivirus program:* Viruses are malicious programs designed to damage PCs. Antivirus software programs prevent, detect, and remove malware from your PC.
3. *Antispyware programs:* Spyware are programs designed to report on your keystrokes or data, or give remote control of your PC to others. Antispyware software programs prevent, detect, and remove spyware programs from your PC.

Windows 10 operating system is delivered with a full set of security features, including a firewall and virus detection and removal. All of the Windows features are configurable. However, configuring the defense apps in Windows can be quite intimidating. You might want to consider hiring a security specialist to set up your business system. Microsoft publishes an extensive set of documentation for the threat protection features of Windows 10.[18]

The simplest answer is to buy an all-in-one collection of security programs like Norton Internet Security or ZoneAlarm Internet Security Suite. You can often find good deals on these packages (usually via rebates) at discounters like Staples or Office Depot. The advantage of these programs is that all their installation and updating is done at the same time, so it is easier to maintain.

The least expensive alternative is to find a free stand-alone program. However, to be ethical in protecting your computer, you need to select programs that are free for use in business (profit-making) situations. Some great programs, like the free version of the ZoneAlarm firewall or AVG's free antivirus, are not free for business use. One company that makes a complete set of programs (firewall, antispyware, and antivirus) is Comodo (www.comodo.com). These programs can be used by businesses for free. The disadvantage of stand-alone programs is that each needs to be installed and updated individually (although many programs can be set to update themselves automatically).

Going back to our car thief analogy, if professional car thieves set out to steal your car, the lock-and-take-keys approach will not deter them. Here you step up to a higher level of deterrence such as the use of an alarm system. The same is true for determined hackers. You may not be able to stop them from getting around a firewall or antispyware program, but you can protect your data by encrypting it. Encryption is the recoding of your data so that only people who know the unlocking code can see the data correctly. Windows comes with a way to encrypt data, but its approach does not let you move or share an encrypted file. A better approach is to use an encryption program like AxCrypt (http://axcrypt.sourceforge.net/) or Inferno (http://inferno.sourceforge.net), both of which are free. One caution, though: If you encrypt a file, make sure you use a password for your encryption that you can easily recall. Once encrypted, if you lose the password you lose the ability to decode the file!

That brings us to the final issue in Internet security–the human element. Many people reading about the problem of password loss probably think, "I'll write down my password." The problem is that most data theft comes from *inside* businesses. Writing down your password and leaving it where others can see it is the equivalent of leaving your keys in the car. Even with all the programs running, a computer can be secure only if the people using it practice safe surfing–using complex passwords, changing them frequently, and keeping passwords to themselves (or written down and hidden away from others); not opening downloads from unknown, unexpected, or untrustworthy sources; and having your PC set to lock itself after a few minutes of inactivity (as when you leave your desk) so others cannot use your computer when you are not there.

Remember the car analogy? If your car is broken it is as useless as when it is stolen. That brings us to one other type of concern you should have about your data–preserving it. We have all heard the line "my computer crashed and took my project." As your contact list in Outlook or your customer database or inventory and accounting records become more important to your business, the cost of a loss of data to *your* business increases. The cost is not just lost revenues–since you cannot charge people if you lost the information on what they owe–it is also lost time. Imagine how long it would take to recreate your complete list of contacts. Now repeat that for all the data files generated by your business. The result is frightening.

Even more threatening is the recent increase in the use of ransomware. This is a computer program that encrypts all the data on your computer with an unknown key. You then receive a ransom demand that you pay an amount to an anonymous account, often through Bitcoin, by a certain time or all your computer contents will be erased.

The solution is having multiple backups. These days it is easier than you might expect. If you have Internet access, you can use Mozy (www.mozy.com), which gives you 2 gigabytes of backup space for free and unlimited space for $50 a year. Its software can be set up for automated backup of key files when you are online. You can find other services by Googling "online

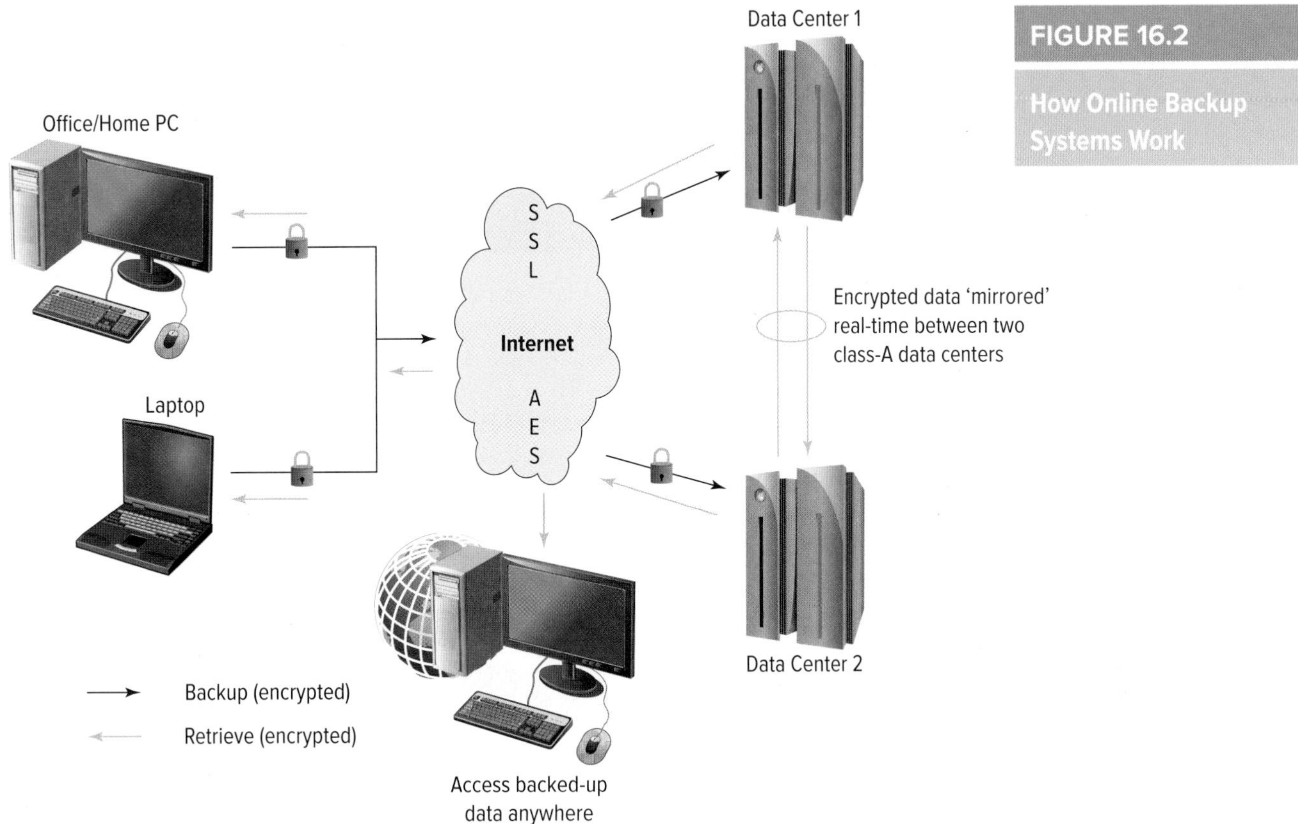

FIGURE 16.2

How Online Backup Systems Work

backup." Many offer a mix of free and for-fee services, including Mozy, Cobian, iDrive, and many others. Each provider offers differing amounts of storage and various levels of security and features. The basic concept of online, cloud-based backup is shown in Figure 16.2, which graphically details this process.

Another alternative is to use an external hard drive that gets its connection and power through a USB cable. Get an external drive that comes with backup software. With these drives, you plug it in once a day to your PC and back up your files. Then disconnect the hard drive. This protects your data from electrical storms or other failures of your PC's power system or motherboard. If the PC does not work, you still have your current (or at worst, day-old) data to work with, and your business can operate almost normally from another computer with the right software.

Today the biggest risk to most businesses comes when using computers, and as more and more of your business's most valuable information is in the files on your computer, the importance of protecting it grows. The basics are relatively simple, but the quality of the protection depends on following through on the basics, and backing them up with behaviors that don't undermine your other efforts to secure your computer and data.

Managing Risk to Intangible Property

Intellectual property rights comprise the legal rights to use unique features of products or services that provide competitive advantage. The rights to use unique features may be legally protected in several ways, including establishing precedence, keeping the process secret, filing for a copyright or trademark, or obtaining a patent. However, if the feature is successful, competitors will eventually find a way to either lessen its competitive advantage or even to render it worthless.

The problem with legal protection methods for intellectual property is that there is no government agency that will assist you, as the owner of a small business, in maintaining your legal rights. Copyrights, trademarks, and patents do not automatically provide any protection. Anyone may copy any of these items at any time. If, and only if, the holder of the intellectual property

SMALL BUSINESS INSIGHT

HARVEY BALL AND THE SMILEY FACE[19]

You see them everywhere—yellow circles with a smiling caricature on them. The amazing thing is that as much of a cultural icon as the smiley face is, its inventor never got any money for it. Harvey Ball was a freelance designer working at State Farm Mutual Insurance in Worcester, Massachusetts, in 1963. He was asked if he could provide a design to boost morale after a merger had left some people upset. He designed the circle and smile, and he added the eyes so disgruntled employees couldn't easily turn the smile into a frown by wearing the button upside down. Harvey was paid $45. He did not trademark it (which, as the designer, he could have done), nor did State Farm. State Farm gave them away—first to the employees, but then to customers who clamored for them. As the buttons spread, the smiley face got copied and copied. Franklin Loufrani of France registered the design in 1971 in over 80 countries and did receive royalties, and eventually Harvey registered a version with his name on it. In the end, Loufrani made the money from the design, while Harvey never got anything else for it, except a lot of satisfaction. As he said, "Never in the history of mankind or art has any single piece of art gotten such widespread favor, pleasure, enjoyment, and nothing has ever been so simply done and so easily understood in art."

How could Harvey Ball have profited from his design? How can a citizen of France register a design created by an American artist?

Paul Connors/AP Images

rights promptly reacts to infringement by making written objections to any and all infractions, can the legal rights be maintained. In other words, holding legal rights to intellectual property provides the owner solely with grounds to pursue lawsuits against infringement. Immediately upon learning of any infringement, a certified letter should be sent to the suspected violator, clearly specifying the nature of the intellectual property rights held and demanding an immediate cease and desist of the infringement. If the infringement continues, a lawsuit is your only recourse. If you do nothing, you get nothing, as was the case for Harvey Ball, the inventor of the smiley face (see the Small Business Insight).

Guarding against obsolescence is best accomplished by maintaining a diligent watch on business intelligence concerning developments within the industry. If you own a small business that depends on valuable intellectual property, you should regularly read the journals and magazines that are unique to your industry. You also should subscribe to clipping services, such as those provided by Westlaw (www.westlaw.com) and Dow Jones (www.dowjones.com).

Additionally, you should carefully listen to customers and vendors for information concerning developments in your industry. Although it sounds paranoid, the truth is that intellectual property is constantly under attack. Very smart people are diligently working to develop better products and processes from which they will gain wealth at your expense if you move too slowly reacting to threats to your business.

Managing Risk Resulting from Events Involving Personnel

Managing risks created by personnel starts with the hiring process, as is discussed in Chapter 18. Efforts must be made to identify people of high moral character and ethical standards. Owners of small businesses are well advised to use employment services to screen potential employees. Employment services can perform background checks, administer drug tests, and conduct psychological tests that are designed to measure an individual's level of integrity.

However, no hiring process is 100 percent foolproof. For that matter, no human being is 100 percent reliable. Ultimately, no one is able to withstand all temptation, regardless of ethical standards. Because all people are fallible, owners of small businesses have an obligation to employees to make theft difficult and honesty easy and rewarding. If you tempt employees with easy access to valuable property and with little likelihood of theft being detected, sooner or later most employees will succumb to temptation in ways great or small.

The Association of Certified Fraud Examiners found in a 2016 study[20] that the most costly employee frauds compared to total business assets occur in businesses with fewer than 100 employees. The median loss to these businesses was a staggering (for the owner of a small business) $180,000. This finding is interesting for two reasons: (1) The vast majority of small businesses have fewer than 100 employees, and (2) it contradicts the belief that people do not steal from people they know.

internal control
A set of rules and procedures that work to limit the opportunity for employee theft or malfeasance.

Internal control is the primary method of ensuring honesty in employees. Internal control is a matter of establishing policies and procedures that work to make dishonesty difficult and honesty easy. The most basic technique of internal control is to separate the duties of maintaining the security of assets from the duties of maintaining records of those assets.

While internal control will reduce the opportunity for employee fraud, it is not sufficient to disclose frauds that are currently taking place. The 2016 Global Fraud Study[21] found that internal controls were responsible for disclosing only a little more than 1 percent of the frauds that were detected during the study period. As Figure 16.3 shows, nearly 40 percent of all frauds that were detected were found because of a tip. About one-sixth of frauds were detected by an internal audit, and one-seventh were found by management review.

Separation of duties is most important for intangible assets—those things of value that have no physical "reality," such as money, accounts receivable, patents, and licensing agreements. Consider the problems of keeping money secure. Money exists primarily as an entry in the accounting records

How Frauds Are Detected

Method of Detection	Percentage
Tip	39.1%
Internal Audit	16.5%
Management Review	13.4%
Accident	5.6%
Account Reconciliation	5.5%
Other	5.5%
Document Examination	3.8%
External Audit	3.8%
Notified by Police	2.4%

FIGURE 16.3

Percentage of Frauds by Method of Detection

Source: Association of Certified Fraud Examiners, *2016 Report to the Nations on Occupational Fraud and Abuse*, 2016.

of your bank. The employee who has authority to write checks and to make deposits has free access to the things related to embezzlement. All that person needs to do is write a check made payable to a fake entity, and then cash the check and pocket the money. If one employee both writes checks and keeps accounts receivable records, theft is even easier to commit and harder to detect.

Such simple frauds can amount to huge amounts of money over time. The *2016 Report to the Nations on Occupational Fraud and Abuse* reports on 2,410 cases of fraud that combined resulted in over $6.3 billion in losses to the defrauded companies. Nearly 93 percent of the frauds detected involved misappropriation of business assets. Fewer than one-fourth of those involved assets other than cash. Fraudulent disbursements of cash comprise 74 percent of all misappropriations with an average loss to a business in the United States of $120,000.[22]

The greatest threat of loss from employee dishonesty occurs when two or more employees *collude:* agree together to defraud your business. Employee collusion is both very common and very difficult to detect. The most common form of employee collusion is the theft of cash and inventory. Cash is most usually stolen by making false disbursements. Inventory is stolen through false employee sales. Many small businesses allow employees to purchase inventory at cost for personal use. When two employees agree to steal, one purchases merchandise from the other. The employee who is "selling" records the sale as being less expensive items than what are actually being bought.

Securing valuable property is a commonsense, but often overlooked, method of keeping honest employees honest. If your business involves small items of high value, such as precision tools, jewelry, laptop computers, data projectors, computer chips, gold, platinum, and so on, those items should be kept locked in secure areas except when being used. Employees who use such items should be required to sign for removing them from storage and obtain a manager's signature when the item is returned to storage. All items of high sensitivity, such as trade secrets, formulas, and employee and customer records, should be protected with locks, access cards, and passwords.

Risk from loss of key personnel and former employees setting up competition against your business can be managed through the contracting process. When a key employee is identified, an employment contract should be negotiated. The contract should include provisions that (1) limit the employee's freedom to go into competition, (2) contain the employee's specific promise not to disclose sensitive or secret information, and (3) offer rewards for providing adequate termination notice and a smooth transition for replacements.

tax codes
Laws and regulations that specify the requirements of taxation.

Additional protection from harm resulting from loss of key employees can be obtained by cross-training among employees. Although any specific employee may not be able to be directly replaced, the needed skills and talents can certainly be found within a group of employees. If employees are cross-trained, the loss of one individual can be alleviated by drawing on the diverse abilities of other employees. Finally, any truly key employee, including yourself as the owner of a small business, should be actively grooming his or her own replacement to be able to step in on an instant's notice.

Managing Risk from Violations of Tax Regulations

It is a rare business that has never run afoul of a taxing agency. Small businesses are subject to taxation from cities, counties, states, and the U.S. government. The **tax codes** of all levels of government have become ever more complex, placing more and more responsibility on businesses for calculating, collecting, and paying various taxes. Taxes imposed on small business include franchise or corporation taxes, income taxes, employee taxes, sales and use taxes, and property taxes. The regulations that relate to all these taxes are so voluminous that it is impossible for any individual to know them all. In fact, the regulations are so complex that even the enforcement personnel of various taxing agencies are often ignorant of the myriad details of the code and regulations. Perhaps then it is not surprising that the government estimates that 15 percent of taxpaying businesses are not complying with the rules.[23]

You won't go to jail for failure to pay your creditors, but you will spend some time behind bars if you do not pay your taxes. Keep your business in financial shape by making timely payment of taxes your first priority.

Danny Johnston/AP Images

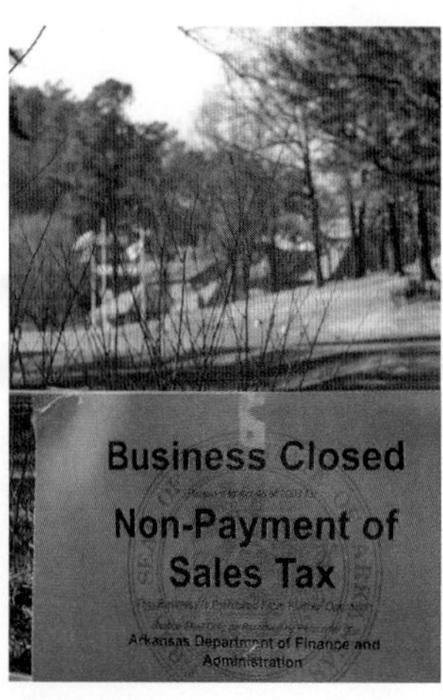

As is related in the Small Business Insight, you can often be fined, even when you have good records and a professional opinion that you are meeting all relevant tax provisions.

Although there is no magic formula that will prevent financial loss that arises from being the subject of a tax audit, there are some fairly simple techniques that will work together to limit your exposure. First, you must keep complete, *accurate* accounting records. If you use a computerized accounting system, be certain that the audit trail function is enabled. Control access to the functions of the accounting system by issuing and regularly changing passwords. File all source documents, such as purchase orders, bills of lading, requisitions, and invoices, in a systematic manner that will provide easy access if you are called on to "prove" any transaction. Carefully document all cash transactions. Ensure that employees properly enter all cash sales into the cash register, and then reconcile the cash register tape to the cash register contents every day. Insist on receiving a *signed* receipt from vendors when you pay in cash.

The simple fact is that many, if not most, owners of small businesses "skim" in ways small and large by taking cash from their businesses before it is recorded as a revenue. Many owners also inappropriately charge personal expenses to the business as a way of extracting money without paying income taxes. Tax agents know these facts very well. As a result, when your business is audited the agent will assume that you have understated your revenues and overstated your deductible expenses. It is your responsibility to prove that you have not.

Second, you should establish a relationship with both an accountant and a lawyer who are expert in tax issues. Although attestation by an accountant or lawyer is not evidence of lack of criminal activity (think Enron), an accountant or lawyer whose practice comprises issues of small business taxation will most likely do a much better job of representing you than you can ever do for yourself.

Third, and most important, make paying your taxes your first financial priority. The temptation to "borrow" from tax money is at times overwhelming, especially when you are being hounded by creditors for payment. Do not give in to this temptation. You can go to prison for not paying employee withholdings, for not paying sales taxes when they are due, for not paying your income taxes. If you do not pay your creditors, your credit rating will suffer. Your business may fail, but you won't go to jail for not paying your bills.

SMALL BUSINESS INSIGHT

WHEN CAREFUL PLANNING AND PREPARATION AREN'T ENOUGH

"Neither Rex nor I expected any problems when we found out that the Texas Sales Tax Commission was going to conduct an audit," said Jay Hall.

Rex said, "When the auditor came, we set up a desk for him. We kept him in coffee and gave him every record he requested. He worked for about three days checking through the last five years of our business."

"We were cool with it. After all, we have always kept our taxes squeaky clean. We knew that we had nothing to worry about."

"Little did we know," said Jay.

Rex Stone and Jay Hall are the owners and managers of Rex Stone Associates. Their business comprises planning, producing, and managing events, primarily in the San Antonio, Texas, area. They have a highly diverse client list, including businesses, unions, academic associations, and church groups. In the last few years they have conducted training sessions, provided trail rides and chuck wagon dinners, conducted motor tours of the Hill Country, and put on numerous balls, dances, and hops for their clients.

"We were stunned when he told us that we owed the state over $125,000 in unpaid taxes, penalties, and accumulated interest. It just couldn't be so!," said Jay.

Rex continued, "When he left, we immediately called our lawyer. The issue boiled down to taxes on the services of bands and combos we had furnished for events. The auditor claimed that we had to collect sales tax on the amount that we charged our client for the music group."

"The problem was," Jay said, "we had already gotten an opinion from the Tax Commission that held that if we did not sell tickets to the event, no sales tax was due. In our business, we never sell tickets. We charge our client a fixed bid price, and only members and guests of the client group attend. Thus, no tax was due, and we had never collected for any music group."

"It took a year and cost us over $24,000 in legal fees, but finally we got a ruling that we had complied with Texas law. We did not owe the tax."

"Of course," Rex said, "we were out the twenty-four thousand. But you know, it could have been a lot worse."

Managing Risk from Employee Violation of Government Regulations

Reducing risk from events involving employees who violate business regulations is best accomplished through a proactive program of training and enforcing appropriate policies and procedures. The courts have consistently ruled that it is the responsibility of the employer to police employee compliance with regulations. Ignorance of either the regulations or of employee violation of regulations is not a defense against administrative action. You are financially responsible for employee violations, intentional or inadvertent. Those few cases where the employer has been held harmless all involve employers who (1) have a written policy provided to each employee, (2) have conducted training of managers and employees concerning those policies, and (3) have immediately and consistently acted on receipt of any complaint.

Risks from violating the requirements of Equal Employment Opportunity Commission are best managed, as with risks from violations of any government regulation, by the owners being proactive:

- Know the EEOC rules that apply to your business.
- Obtain assistance from experts in EEOC regulations to assess the level of your compliance.
- Establish policies and procedures designed to prevent violations.
- Educate and train employees to know the policies and procedures and to understand the importance of following them explicitly.
- Enforce the policies and procedures by immediately dealing in a systematic manner with any employee complaint.

Knowing the EEOC rules is a daunting task for any business owner. As stated earlier, the rules are voluminous, ambiguous, and arcane. There are, however, many sources of information that are written to be easily understood. Most such third-party information is provided by industry associations, and thus is usually specifically written for the problems you are most likely to encounter.

Assistance can be obtained from experts in several different ways. One source that is often overlooked is the employment agency that you use to screen applicants. Employment agencies must be highly knowledgeable of the EEOC rules in order to remain in business. Often such agencies can provide sample policy manuals and advice concerning compliance. Other sources of expert help include SCORE (www.score.org) and the EEOC itself. The EEOC maintains a website that contains myriad resources for small business owners. The commission also publishes numerous books and pamphlets that are available from www.EEOC.gov.

Alleged violations of the Americans with Disabilities Act are best handled through a proactive threefold approach: (1) Determine if you are subject to any of the provisions of the ADA, (2) obtain the services of experts on the ADA to evaluate the level of your compliance, and (3) work diligently to meet the requirements to which you are subject. Although these actions will *not* prevent you from being the target of frivolous lawsuits, you may use records of your actions as evidence of your intent to comply. This is often sufficient to persuade a mediator to pressure the complainant to either reduce the amount demanded or to withdraw the complaint entirely.

The Department of Justice maintains an ADA Technical Assistance Program that provides help directly to interested parties. By using these services, a small business owner can be assured of having current information. The Technical Assistance Program provides specific advice for your business concerning how to comply with the pertinent requirements. This program is specifically aimed at the needs of hotels, motels, restaurants, and other affected small businesses. The program provides an information hotline, printed materials, and a speakers' bureau. It does not provide any inspection or affirmation services. Visit www.usdoj.gov/crt/ada/adahom1.htm for more information.

Managing risk from violations of OSHA standards and regulations is also best accomplished through proactive efforts. As with risks from EEOC and ADA enforcement, you should first ascertain the standards to which your business is subject. The Occupational Safety and Health Act covers all employees except those in mining, transportation, state and local governments, and self-employment. If your business is in any other industry, you are subject to the standards of OSHA for employee health and safety. Also remember that while *you* are self-employed, anyone you hire is not. Thus, while OSHA standards and regulations do not apply to you, they do apply to your employees.

The best way to meet the basic laws of OSHA is to provide a place of employment that is free of recognized hazards and to:

1. Maintain tools and equipment in good condition.
2. Provide appropriate safety equipment and training in its proper use.
3. Provide medical examinations.

OSHA also offers free consultation services to employers who want help in identifying any deficiencies and in developing appropriate solutions. Consultations begin with a conference among the consultants and managers of the business where the scope of the consultation is set, and all parties agree on a set of working rules for the engagement. The conference is followed by an on-site inspection for hazards. The business's health program is also assessed. A final conference is held during which all findings are presented, along with suggested solutions to each identified problem. No report of any deficiency is made to OSHA for enforcement. However, if significant hazards are found, you can count on a follow-up inspection by OSHA after a reasonable time during which you must remedy the problems. A directory of OSHA-funded consultants can be obtained by requesting OSHA Publication No. 3047, *Consultation Services for the Employer.*

You must also keep accurate records of all employee job-related illnesses and injuries. You must report within eight hours any accidents that result in a fatality or in the hospitalization of three or more employees. If your business has fewer than 10 employees or if your business is in one of the OSHA-defined "low-hazard" industries, you are exempt from the record-keeping requirements of the regulations. Low-hazard industries include automobile dealers, apparel and furniture stores, eating and drinking establishments, finance, insurance, real estate, and legal, educational, personal, and business services, as well as cultural and membership organizations.

Using an Internal Audit as a Tool to Manage Risk

A valuable process that can greatly help you with the issues of keeping risks at acceptable levels is completing an internal audit. You probably are somewhat familiar with public business's external audits, which are conducted by CPA firms and which must comply with a set of standards called generally accepted auditing standards (GAAS). An internal audit is similar in conduct; however, because it is strictly a management tool that is not provided to outsiders, it can be structured and conducted in any systematic manner you find acceptable.

It is unlikely that you (or any owner of a small business) have the time, experience, or inclination to attempt to conduct an internal audit on your own. Rather, you should consider outsourcing the conduct of an audit to an expert in the process. Your own accountant may be able to conduct such an audit. But if not, he or she will be able to recommend a reputable and reliable firm that can do so at a reasonable cost.

A properly conducted, independent internal audit will give you:

- An evaluation of your overall level of business risk.
- An objective evaluation of your risk control structure.
- A systematic analysis of your business processes and controls.
- Information on irregularities detected during the audit process.
- A review of your firm's compliance with relevant regulations.
- A review of the existence and value of the assets of your business.
- A review of operational and financial performance.
- Recommendations for more effective and efficient use of resources.
- Assessments of how well your business is accomplishing your goals and objectives.
- Information about your employees' adherence to the organization's values and code of ethics.

As the owner of a small business, you must assume much of the task of conducting oversight of all aspects of your business. Activities that make up oversight include listening, asking questions, assessing and challenging answers. This is exactly what an effective internal audit will do for you. To be sure that the audit effectively meets your goals in having it conducted, you should:

1. Meet (without the presence of other members of your management) with whomever is going to conduct the internal audit.
2. Establish with the auditor that you and your board of directors (if you have a board) have the final authority to review and approve the audit plan.
3. Write an engagement agreement with the auditor that clearly establishes the scope of work to be done.
4. Provide sufficient authority to the auditor to ensure that he or she can accomplish the goals of the audit.

Once the audit is completed, you must make positive steps to address any findings that indicate an unacceptable level of business risk.

LO **16-4** Explain how insurance can be used to manage business risk.

Insuring against Risks

Although it is impossible for the owner of a small business to avoid all business risks, it is possible, through the use of insurance, to minimize the damage that such risks can cause. However, insurance can be expensive. Because of its expense, many small business owners choose too little insurance. When the inevitable occurs, an underinsured business may well face bankruptcy and liquidation.

The key to using insurance is to obtain the "right" amount of insurance at an affordable rate. Having too little insurance leaves the business open to unsupportable losses. Carrying too much insurance wastes money.

Using Insurance to Manage Risks

insurance
A contract between two or more parties in which one party agrees, for a fee, to assume the risk of another.

Insurance is a contract between two businesses in which one, the insurance company, for a fee, agrees to indemnify the other for specific losses that are likely to occur in the future. In other words, the insurance company contracts to pay money to your business if a specific "covered" event occurs that causes your business to suffer financial loss.

Not all risks are insurable. Insurance provides a benefit by requiring a relatively small fee compared to the amount of loss that is possible. The insurance company makes a profit by collecting premiums for coverage from many businesses for the same set of risks. In effect, you and the insurance company are taking opposite gambles. You are betting that your business will be damaged or destroyed. The insurance company is betting that it won't. The insurance company wins by collecting more from all the covered companies combined than it has to pay out to those few businesses that do, indeed, suffer damage. You win (if it can be considered a "win") by having the insurance company pay when your business suffers a covered loss. Thus, the more likely an event is to occur, and the greater the potential amount that the insurance company must pay, the higher the price that you must pay for coverage. For this reason, insurance coverage is either not available or is excessively expensive for common events.

Developing a Comprehensive Insurance Program

Developing an appropriate insurance program for your business requires that you understand the risks to which your business is vulnerable. You must then know the amount of loss that your business could suffer as a result of the adverse events. Finally, you must obtain appropriate rates from reliable insurers, rates that are not too high for your business to pay but that do provide sufficient payouts if the insured event occurs.

Identifying risks is the first task to be completed before a comprehensive insurance program can be developed for your business. Risks, as discussed, vary with the nature of your business. Risks that are common to most small businesses include fire, flood, storm, theft, business interruption, and loss of key personnel. Business-specific risks include product liability claims for manufacturers, malpractice claims for dentists and physicians, and errors and omissions claims for lawyers and accountants.

Determining which risks are to be covered is the next step. Not all identifiable risks can be or should be covered by insurance. The risk of events that are certain to occur cannot be insured at any price. Risks of events that are highly likely to occur but that have indeterminable payouts can be insured, but only at a very high price. Extremely unlikely events (being struck by a meteorite, for example) can be insured, but why would anyone do so? The Thoughtful Entrepreneur Box below discusses this issue in more detail.

Events that should be insured are those that are likely, and the economic cost of which would create a severe burden on the finances of the business. Such events include natural disasters, liability to others, and the death or disability of key employees.

coverages
Contractual provisions of insurance policies that specify what risks the insurance company is assuming.

Coverages required by law exist to provide social protection from harm caused to employees, customers, and uninvolved individuals. The most common mandatory insurance coverages are

THE THOUGHTFUL ENTREPRENEUR

WHAT RISKS CAN BE INSURED?

Not all business risks can be covered by insurance at a reasonable cost. Insurance companies, just like you, are in business to make profits. An insurance company must charge competitive prices to be able to sell policies. At the same time, the insurance company must charge enough to be able to pay legitimate claims of its policyholders. To be able to balance these conflicting needs, an insurance company must be able to accurately predict the amount of payments that will be made to settle claims for insurable events.

The amount that an insurance company must pay out in claims is a function of (1) the frequency with which an event occurs, (2) the amount that must be paid according to the terms of the contract, and (3) the number of policies that have been issued.

- **The risk must be calculable:** An insurance company estimates the amount of potential claims payments by performing statistical analyses of the number and frequency of the occurrence of the event for which the insurance is being provided. For example, the probability of an individual business being flooded can be calculated from information concerning its location relative to sources and frequencies of floods. Although a specific flood may not be predictable, the number of businesses that will encounter floods in any one year can be predicted with reasonable statistical confidence, which allows an insurance company to determine the appropriate price for a flood policy.
- **The value of any loss must be measurable in dollars:** Insurance companies contract to pay only specific amounts of money for specific types and amounts of losses. In order to determine the amount that will be paid, it must be possible for the loss to be stated in a dollar amount. Thus, an insurance company will insure you for physical damage from fire. It will not insure you for the loss of your beautiful view, should the fire burn your neighbor's property across the road.
- **The policyholder must have an insurable financial interest:** Insurance companies will not insure losses for individuals who do not suffer a financial loss from what is being insured. This requirement acts to prevent fraud by persons deliberately "creating" the event in order to profit from it. In the same vein, an insurance company will not pay more than the actual amount of the loss, regardless of the amount of the policy terms.
- **The pool of potential policyholders must be of sufficient size:** Insurance works because the insurance company diversifies its risk by insuring numerous businesses in widely separated locations. This ensures that no single disaster will result in the insurance company having to pay an excessive number of claims at any one time. Of course, this strategy occasionally fails. In August 2005 Hurricane Katrina became the most costly catastrophe on record. The extensive damage to a relatively large area has seriously tested the ability of several insurance companies to pay required claims and to remain in business.

liability for damages caused by vehicle accidents and illness and injury caused by employment. Most businesses are also required to pay for unemployment insurance for employees to help defray the personal cost of having one's employment terminated.

Vehicle liability insurance is mandated by the legislatures of all the states and territories of the United States. Minimum amounts of coverage are specified for property damage caused by the vehicle and for injury suffered by anyone other than the driver of the vehicle.

Workers' compensation insurance is mandatory in some states. In others, it is discretionary. In all states, the workers' compensation laws provide fixed monetary awards to employees who are injured or disabled on the job. Workers' compensation is enforced through administrative procedures which preclude employees suing their employers. Federal statutes are limited to workers who are employed in some interstate commerce.

Unemployment insurance is collected by the IRS and state agencies as a percentage of tax on payroll. The amount collected varies among industries and among businesses within an industry. Industries and businesses that have frequent seasonal layoffs pay higher amounts of unemployment premiums than do those that have stable employment.

Desired coverages beyond mandatory insurance include general liability, product liability, catastrophe, and various types of malpractice coverage. Liability insurance protects your business against claims from harm caused by inadvertent consequences of actions of the business or its employees. The list of potential causes of harm to customers, vendors, or others is nearly endless. Customers fall while on business premises. A careless worker can splatter paint on a stranger's automobile. Sparks from welding can start fires on others' property. A faulty valve can release noxious or even deadly fumes into the atmosphere. Your sewer can plug and cause flooding in your neighbor's place of business. Commercial liability insurance covers losses that are the result of such mishaps and accidents.

Commercial liability insurance can be obtained, at a price for even the businesses with the highest risk of harm to customers. The Thoughtful Entrepreneur Box illustrates the problems of insuring one of the riskiest consumer businesses, that of carnivals.

Product liability insurance covers losses resulting from claims made by persons who use the products of your business. The risk of customers and others being harmed by your product is largely a function of (1) the nature of your product and (2) the intended users. Those products that have historically given rise to the largest claims for injury and illness are (1) transportation equipment, such as automobiles, airplanes, and bicycles; (2) health products, such as pharmaceuticals and body implants; and (3) appliances, such as toasters, vacuum cleaners, and kitchen ranges. However, examples of huge cash settlements for product liability exist for a multitude of products that would seem to be harmless by nature. Examples of such cases include insulating foam that was discovered to emit formaldehyde, asbestos-containing products that are believed to be carcinogenic, and a multitude of toys that are alleged to cause choking and other hazards to children.

Errors and omissions insurance and malpractice insurance are examples of special types of liability insurance that cover losses from harm caused during the performance of your profession. Errors and omissions insurance covers claims made by clients of attorneys, accountants, and other consultants. Malpractice insurance covers claims made by patients of physicians, dentists, nurses, and other medical practitioners. The primary value of this type of insurance is the access to highly competent specialist lawyers that is provided by the insurance company. The insurance companies employ cadres of lawyers to represent professionals who are accused of incompetence or wrongdoing. These lawyers are usually successful in negotiating reasonable settlements with clients who have been harmed. Should a settlement be impossible, the same lawyers will vigorously defend the accused professional in the subsequent court action. Of course, in the event that the professional is held responsible for a client loss, the insurance company will pay the claim, up to the limit of the insurance contract.

You, as an individual owner or manager of a small business, can obtain a general liability insurance, which is often called an *umbrella policy*, or a *success protector policy.* General liability policies exist to pay losses that are not covered by other liability insurance. It is a sad fact of our current legal climate that actual culpability is irrelevant to many damage claims. If you are successful in your business, your success makes you a target for lawsuits because you are considered to be able to pay a judgment, either through your personal wealth or through seizure of your business property. Claims against general liability policies are usually a result of such litigation.

Insuring the Property of the Business

Commercial property insurance covers losses to the business property from causes such as fire, storm, vandalism, and theft. Other property insurance exists to pay losses resulting from floods or earthquakes. The cost of property insurance is determined largely by (1) the property's insurable value, (2) the amount of deductible loss, (3) the amount of co-insurance required, and (4) the loss limits of the policy.

All the value of a property does not have **insurable value**. For example, as a general rule the value of land, excavation, and basement is not insurable. This is because even when a disaster occurs, the land remains. Only a very few types of disasters, such as earthquake or landslide, can change the nature and topography of land.

insurable value
The amount of an asset for which a company will write an insurance policy.

Additionally, some property has value that cannot be stated in dollar amounts. The value of the historical significance of a building often cannot be determined. For example, in Clarksville, Tennessee, the Hachland Hall Bed and Breakfast has a log cabin that was the home of President Andrew Jackson during the time that he was building the famous Hermitage. Were this cabin to burn to the ground, its replacement cost for logs, timber, and finish lumber could be no more than a few tens of thousands of dollars. However, no matter how carefully rebuilt, the replacement would be a replica, not the actual cabin. As such, it might be interesting, but it would not have the special character that now makes it unique. Placing a dollar amount on the historical value of this cabin is highly problematical.

deductible
An amount of loss that will not be paid by an insurance company.

co-insurance
A contract stipulation that requires a policyholder to carry insurance in an amount equal to a stated minimum percentage of the market value of the property insured.

A **deductible** is an amount of loss that is specifically excluded by the insurance contract. It is common for vehicle policies to specify that in the event of loss, the insurance will pay the amount of the loss, less a deductible of $250 to $1,000. Policies on buildings and equipment usually have similar deductibles ranging from $1,000 to $10,000 or more. As a general rule, the higher the deductible, the lower the policy premium payments will be.

Co-insurance is a contract requirement that works to prevent property owners from deliberately under-insuring. Co-insurance requires that the owner carry insurance in an amount equal to a stated minimum percentage of the market value of the property, usually 80 percent. If the owner allows insurance coverage to fall below this amount, then the amount that the insurance company will pay in the event of loss is reduced by an amount proportional to the amount of underinsurance.

The reason for such arcane provisions is to increase the amount of premium that the insurance company collects relative to the risk that the insurance company is taking by insuring the property. The higher the value a property has, the greater the likely payout an insurance company will have to make in the event of loss.

When disasters hit, like this fire, most small businesses depend on insurance to make up for the loss. What factors should you consider when seeking insurance?

rfoxfoto/123RF

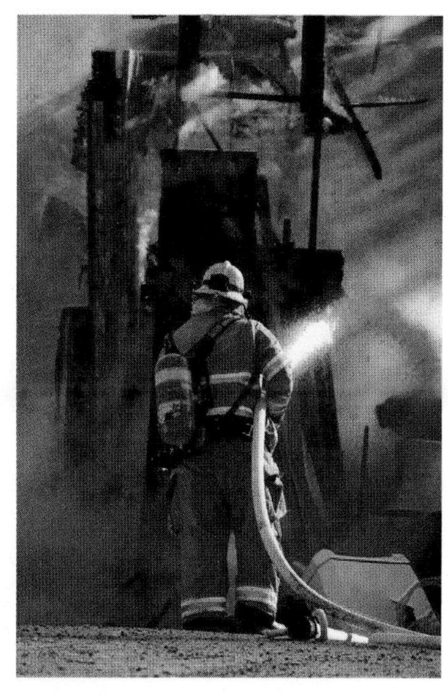

Consider that property losses are highly correlated with the value of the property. At one extreme, the loss can never exceed the market value of the property. At the other extreme, loss cannot be less than zero. In between the two extremes, losses are often a function of the value of the property. For example, suppose two businesses each experienced a fire that destroyed the roof of a warehouse. A 43,000-square-foot warehouse worth $3.5 million has a much more expensive roof than does a 10,000-square-foot warehouse that is worth less than $750,000. Similarly, losing your 1,600-square-foot retail space will be a much greater dollar loss if the store is located on Rodeo Drive in Beverly Hills, California, than if it is located on Main Street in Beckwourth, California.

Business interruption insurance provides funds to pay the ordinary operating expenses of your business should it be forced to close temporarily because of an insured event. Although business interruption insurance can be purchased as a stand-alone policy, it is usually acquired as a provision of commercial property insurance.

Crime insurance offers protection against losses from crimes committed against your business. It is an unfortunate fact that the greatest number of crimes of which you are likely to be victim are committed by trusted employees.

Theft insurance is normally included in insurance on physical assets. However, the greatest threat of loss because of employee dishonesty is the misappropriation of cash, as was discussed earlier. Cash cannot be insured. An approach to obtaining insurance against employee theft of money is to require all employees with access to money or to accounting for money to be *bonded.*

fidelity bonds
Bonds, also called *dishonesty bonds,* that repay employers for losses caused by dishonest or negligent employees.

surety bonds
An agreement with an insurance or bonding company that will pay a specified amount in the event that the entity bonded fails to comply with specified contractual requirements.

Fidelity bonds, also called *dishonesty bonds,* repay employers for losses caused by dishonest or negligent employees. Fidelity bonds cover losses from employee fraud, theft, forgery, and embezzlement. Unlike **surety bonds**, fidelity bonds are purchased only for the employer's benefit.

If you have any employee who handles large amounts of cash or other valuable assets, you should consider bonding that person. Some businesses, including insurance companies, securities brokers, real estate brokers, and businesses that hold escrowed cash, are required by law to carry fidelity bonds. All employees who have direct access to a company's cash, securities, and accounting records, or who handle investment or retirement funds, should be bonded. Bonds are available to cover individual specific key employees, or as blanket bonds that cover all employees.

When obtaining fidelity bonds, you should consider the following:

- The scope of coverage.
- All exclusions.
- Types of employee dishonesty not covered (e.g., salary, benefit, or computer fraud).
- Coverage for employee actions off-premises.

Credit insurance covers abnormal losses from credit customers not paying their bills. Abnormal losses are carefully defined within the insurance contract. Typical covered events include customers who cease business because of bankruptcy or business interruptions caused by fire, storm, wind, floods, and earthquakes. Less common and more expensive coverage exists that will pay for losses that arise from general economic conditions such as recession, war, or trade embargos.

Credit insurance can be obtained that covers all credit accounts or that covers only specific accounts. General credit insurance is expensive, and it is common to choose to cover only very large accounts, the loss of which would threaten survival of the business.

All credit insurance requires the merchant to provide co-insurance in the amount of 10 to 20 percent of the credit loss. The co-insurance provision works to prevent both frivolous claims and to provide a disincentive to companies to issue credit indiscriminately.

Credit insurance companies provide mandatory collection services. The insured business is required to promptly report all past due accounts. When an account is determined to be delinquent, usually after 90 days of no payment, then the account must be assigned to the insurance company which will make vigorous efforts to collect.

Credit insurance is available only for manufacturers and wholesalers. At this time no insurance company will write coverage for retailers who offer credit to customers.

Retailers who provide credit are protected in two ways. First, those few retailers who offer credit directly to customers usually have a large number of relatively small accounts receivable. This provides a greater diversification of the risk of loss than is available to wholesalers who usually have a relatively small number of large value receivables. Second, most retailers today provide credit only through credit cards, including Mastercard, Visa, Discover, and American Express. Credit card companies perform credit checks before issuing cards, and thus limit the risk of nonpayment. Additionally, the credit card companies have developed rules which include checking cards for customer signatures, requiring a government-issued picture ID, and obtaining a transaction authorization prior to providing the credit sale. Retailers who follow the rules are not liable for any future nonpayment by the credit card holder.

Personnel insurance is available to protect both you and your employees from specific risks. Personnel coverages include key person insurance, life, disability, and medical coverage insurance.

Key person insurance protects you in the event that a key employee dies or is disabled and cannot work.

THE THOUGHTFUL ENTREPRENEUR

BRING IN THE CLOWNS

Imagine a fair without a midway. Can a fair even be a fair without a carousel, a roller coaster, or a Ferris wheel? Carnivals are hugely popular entertainments. Over 500 million people attend amusement parks, fairs, and carnivals in the United States each year (which is quite impressive, given that the entire population of the nation is only 300 million).

As you might expect, carnivals experience numerous accidents each year, ranging in severity from bruises and abrasions to permanent maiming and death. According to the U.S. Consumer Product Safety Commission (CPSC),[24] approximately 11,000 people are injured on amusement rides each year. Of these, about 5 die.

There are approximately 500 carnivals that travel the United States each year, ranging in size from 1 to over 100 portable amusement rides. The vast majority of carnivals are small family-owned businesses with second- and third-generation members involved in management and operation.[25]

If your carnival is large enough and you expect to have about 1 million riders in a year, then you should expect to experience approximately 20 to 25 injuries, based on CPSC statistics. If the people injured are representative of the national experience, all of them will be younger than 16. Not one will have an injury severe enough to require more than outpatient treatment. However, there is a small, but measurable risk that you will be among the unfortunate carnival operators who have patrons seriously injured to the point of maiming or death.

As the owner of a carnival, what insurance should you carry to cover the injuries of customers on your rides? Insurance to cover the potential medical expenses for twenty-some minor injuries would be prohibitively expensive. It would, on the other hand, be quite risky for your business to carry no insurance at all. A reasonable strategy is to obtain insurance that will cover only serious injury and death. Your carnival will then absorb the cost of treating minor injuries, the number of which can be reduced by a safety program that prevents customer horseplay, requires operator training, and enforces regular rigid safety inspection of the rides. Taking such measures reduces not only the probability of serious injury but also the cost of accident insurance.

Life insurance is the most common kind of coverage on key persons. Usually key person insurance names you, as the owner, or your business as the beneficiary of the policy. Life insurance also is often provided to employees to provide security for their families. Life insurance provided by you, the employer, is usually term insurance. *Term insurance* is a form of insurance that does not accumulate any value over the contract term. Rather, only specific events, including disability, dismemberment, and death, are insured events. Term insurance is very inexpensive for healthy young people. The premiums increase with age, and with specified risk factors such as obesity, heart problems, and a history of driving while intoxicated.

Disability insurance is usually provided as part of life insurance, although it can be obtained as either a stand-alone policy or as part of medical coverage. You as the owner of a small business should carefully consider obtaining disability coverage not only for key persons but also for yourself. Statistics provided by AARP (formerly the American Association of Retired Persons) show that between the ages of 22 and 65 there is a greater than 25 percent probability that you will be disabled for a period of 12 months or more.[26] Statistics provided by the Social Security Administration indicate that the greatest probability of becoming disabled for this period of time occurs between ages 50 and 65.[27] The probability of shorter periods of disability is, of course, much higher. Given the high probability of temporary disability and the devastating effects it can have upon a small business, it is becoming ever more common for disability coverage to be included in business insurance plans.

Disability insurance can take several forms. The most common disability coverage provides the insured person with funds to replace income lost because of the inability to work. While this coverage is important to the person who becomes disabled, it provides no direct benefit to your business.

Some insurance companies now offer disability coverage that provides direct benefits to small businesses and to owners of small businesses. The most common of such disability coverage is **buyout insurance** which provides funds to purchase the ownership position of an owner who is disabled or deceased. Less common, but of similar value for small business owners, is disability coverage that will pay specific fixed costs of the business, such as rent, salaries, and utilities, in the event that the owner or other named key person becomes disabled. Even less common is disability coverage that will pay specific dollar amounts to the business to replace lost revenue caused by the disability of a key person.

buyout insurance
Insurance that provides funds to purchase the ownership position of an owner who is disabled or deceased.

Medical coverage is the most highly desired form of insurance for most employees. Medical coverage is quite expensive, and the cost has been increasing rapidly in recent years. There are many reasons, however, that you, as the owner of a small business, might wish to provide such coverage for your employees. First, receiving medical coverage is a strong retention incentive for employees. Second, if you provide medical insurance for all employees, you can obtain reduced rates and can include yourself and your family. Third, the least expensive way to obtain key person insurance is as a part of a comprehensive medical insurance plan that covers all employees.

Of more immediate concern, however, are the provisions of the Patient Protection and Affordable Care Act (PPACA), and the Health Care and Education Reconciliation Act, which together are often called, "Obamacare." The provisions of these acts require that businesses with 50 or more full-time equivalent employees pay a substantial part of the cost of medical insurance. For businesses with 25 or fewer full-time equivalent employees, there are tax credits to help offset the cost of providing health insurance.

Today, more than 10 years after its passage, the entire PPACA remains highly controversial. Numerous unsuccessful attempts have been made to repeal the law, while at the same time, many politicians have campaigned to extend its scope. What the ultimate costs and benefits will be are yet to be determined. Regardless, the act and subsequent regulations are highly complex and generally not well understood. Owners of small businesses are well advised to seek expert assistance in this area.

LO **16-5** Describe techniques for sharing risk with other businesses and organizations.

Sharing Risk

One very effective method to reduce and to control business risk is to share that risk with other entities. As discussed previously, one way to share risk is through insurance programs that, in effect, diversify risk across industries, businesses, and geographic areas. Additionally, risk can be directly shared without the intermediary of an insurance company, by forming joint ventures, by joining industry groups, and by obtaining government grants and guarantees.

Joint Ventures

joint venture
An agreement between two or more entities to pool resources in order to complete a project.

Joint ventures are partnerships through which two or more businesses combine to undertake a specific economic activity. Each business involved in a joint venture keeps its own identity and conducts its own business separately from that of the other partners. The businesses are partners only for the activities specified in the joint venture contract.

Joint ventures are most usually formed and taxed as partnerships. This allows for disproportionate allocation of revenues and expenses among the partner businesses. The ability to assign tax items to the partner for which they are most advantageous eases the problems of dissimilar businesses forming a partnership. A relatively large, profitable partner can be assigned the deductible costs of the joint venture, while revenues are simultaneously assigned to the smaller, less profitable (or even unprofitable) partner who will pay taxes at a lower rate.

Another advantage of joint ventures is that each partner can lose no more than its investment in the venture. The joint venture is a separate entity from any of the partners that own it. Thus, if the joint venture fails, only the resources of the joint venture are lost. The partner companies can continue in their individual businesses.

Industry Groups for Insurance Coverage

One of the primary reasons that there is at least one organized group for every conceivable industry is that joining in groups provides benefits of scale to members. The most common benefit is low-cost group insurance. The cost of insurance, as discussed, is partly a function of the risk that the insurance provider assumes. Insurance companies diversify risk by insuring large numbers of similar businesses. It is obvious that the International Sign Association can provide a much larger pool of people to be insured than can any single sign shop member. Because of the larger pool of potential insured people and because of its greater bargaining power, the ISA can obtain much lower insurance rates for its members than the members can obtain individually.

Government Funding of Risky Ventures

The final source for sharing risk is governments. Townships up to the federal government have programs to encourage economic activity. Governments do not have the profit-making requirements of businesses, but they do have the power to extract money from citizens. As a result, risk for a government is very different from risk for private business. Governments often subsidize very risky ventures that private companies would otherwise never attempt.

One example of government subsidizing risky ventures can be seen in the building of sports arenas, convention centers, and convention hotels. Cities across the nation have imposed taxes on citizens and tourists to subsidize the building of such facilities. St. Louis has three such publicly funded arenas: one for the Cardinals baseball team, one previously for the Rams football team, and a half-million-square-foot convention center. Houston recently demolished an old facility and built a new one for the Houston Oilers football team. The city of San Antonio, Texas, and Bexar County recently enacted one of the nation's highest taxes on hotel rooms and rental cars to finance a new arena for the Spurs basketball team, despite having the largely unused Alamodome.

Small businesses can also obtain their share of government subsidies through direct contracting and grants. Opportunities exist for small businesses to obtain government funding for recycling of waste materials, for research and development of products for health, security, and defense, and for providing services directly to government entities.

In Conclusion

Although business risk cannot be eliminated, it can be controlled. Management techniques including security devices and internal controls can reduce the risk of misappropriation of business assets. Those risks that cannot be controlled can be insured. Insurance works to reduce the amount of loss that any individual business experiences because of natural events, dishonesty, or negligence. Because the environment in which business operates is constantly changing, you, as the owner and manager of a small business, must constantly reassess your risk controls, your exposure to disaster, and your insurance coverage.

Ben Franklin said long ago, "A penny saved is a penny earned," and that adage is truly important for small businesses. Money saved means more flexibility and more profit. The point of spending time on risk and insurance and protecting yourself and your business is to help you identify the ways to minimize your losses. Often, thinking about the potential sources of risk and loss ahead of time makes it possible for you to take action to minimize the risk or handle the loss should it come. The whole concept of insuring against risk works best when you can think objectively about the potential risk, loss, and cost to your firm. Only then can you be sure that you are spending your insurance dollars wisely. Despite all the talk about financial loss, it is important to note the human and emotional cost of loss. Whether through injury or criminal action, loss focuses our attention and can make us sad, angry, guilty, or a combination of the three. When it causes harm to employees or customers, it can derail a business and its owner. For all these reasons, taking the time to protect your business, its assets, and people always makes sense.

CHAPTER SUMMARY

LO 16-1 Explain the meaning and nature of business risk.

- Business risk comes from many sources, including financial risk from capital structure, economic risks from business decisions, and the environment.
- Business risk is the probability that the future economic state of the business will be worse than is projected.

LO 16-2 Describe the specific types of risks associated with different aspects of business operations.

- Economic risks arise from events related to the property of the business, to the personnel of the business, and to the customers, vendors, and visitors to the business.
- Violation of government regulations has become a significant business risk due to the many laws, rules, and regulations of the ADA, OSHA, the EEOC, and various tax agencies.
- Businesses are usually held liable for injuries suffered on business property, regardless of the cause.

LO 16-3 Describe techniques to manage risks to stay within your level of risk tolerance.

- The loss from various events can be reduced by making specific plans and arrangements to deal with them, should they occur.
- Disaster plans can reduce losses by reducing the time that business operations are interrupted when the event occurs.
- Following building codes, locating away from flood plains, and keeping property clear of flammables can reduce loss from natural events.
- Risk to computers and data can be controlled by protection software, backups, and password use.
- The best control for risks from personnel is to hire qualified people of high integrity.
- Conducting an internal audit can provide an independent analysis of the levels and types of business risk.

LO 16-4 Explain how insurance can be used to manage business risk.

- Keeping the right types and levels of insurance can minimize a business's loss from adverse events.
- You should not try to insure against all risks, rather only those that have economic consequences great enough to threaten the survival of your business.
- Some insurance coverages are required by law.

LO 16-5 Describe techniques for sharing risk with other businesses and organizations.

- Risk may be reduced and insurance made affordable by joining with other similar businesses.
- The risky activity can be separated from the main part of your business through joint ventures and placing the risky activity into a separate legal entity.
- Industry groups can obtain lower insurance rates than can a single business.
- Government agencies can provide protection from risk by limiting the potential loss and by subsidizing risky ventures.

KEY TERMS

employee theft, 581

regulation of the workplace, 581

Equal Employment Opportunity Commission (EEOC), 582

Occupational Safety and Health Administration (OSHA), 582

protected classes, 582

Age Discrimination in Employment Act (ADEA), 582

Rehabilitation Act of 1973, 582

Americans with Disabilities Act (ADA) of 1990, 582

Civil Rights Act of 1991, 582

key employees, 582

separation of duties, 584

internal control, 591

tax codes, 592

insurance, 596
coverages, 597
insurable value, 599
deductible, 599
co-insurance, 599
fidelity bonds, 600
surety bonds, 600
buyout insurance, 602
joint venture, 602

DISCUSSION QUESTIONS

1. Discuss the types of risk encountered by small businesses. Are these risks different in any way from risks facing big business?
2. What are the risks to small businesses caused by personnel issues?
3. How are the risks from personnel affected by government business regulations?
4. How does disaster planning help a small business cope with risk?
5. The text discusses methods to protect against weather. What might a business do to protect itself against an earthquake?
6. Which is easier to steal, money from an employer's bank account or secret business processes? Why?
7. What types of insurance should a small business have? Give your reasons for maintaining each type of coverage.
8. Suppose you are in the business of making ladders. A customer places a board plank between two of your ladders as a scaffold. One of the ladders fails, causing your customer to fall and break a leg. Are you responsible for your customer's losses? How can you protect yourself from lawsuits in such cases?
9. You are considering offering credit to good customers to increase sales. What things should you consider to limit your risks if you do?
10. One of your partners has special skills that would be very difficult to replace. His great joy in life is single-track bicycle racing. How can you protect yourself from the probability that he will be injured and unable to work?

EXPERIENTIAL EXERCISES

1. Identify a business you would like to own. Make a list of the risks that are specific to that business. Contact an insurance broker to find out what coverages are available and what they would cost. Make a report to your class of your findings.
2. Identify a business you would like to own. Go to the OSHA website and find out what rules and regulations apply to this business. Create a chart of hazards of this business and the applicable OSHA rules. Make a report to your class of your findings.
3. Suppose you are going to open a consulting business. You are going to finish half of your garage to use as an office. Go to the ADA site and determine what accessibility requirements you must meet. Make a report to your class of your findings.
4. Identify a specific location (street address) where you would like to operate a business. Visit your city's planning and zoning office (or its website, if it has one) and determine if this site is in a flood plain. Make a copy of the city's map of flood plains. Then make a report to your class of your findings.
5. Identify a business you want to own. Use the resources of your library and the Internet to identify what insurance you are legally required to carry. Contact an insurance broker to determine how and for how much you can obtain the required coverage. Make a report to your class of your findings.

MINI-CASE

RISKY BUSINESS

Vicky Volare fell in love with motor scooters on her vacation trip to Aruba. "They're a blast!," Vicky said. "They are convenient, safe, inexpensive, and fun to ride." Now she is planning to buy 30 Vespa Scooters to provide scooter rental in Vail, Colorado. Vicky will need four employees, in addition to her own services. She has completed a business plan, except for determining what types and amounts of insurance coverage she should have. As soon as she completes the insurance planning, she can complete the financial section of her business plan. Vicky will invest $50,000 of her own funds and is borrowing $230,000. $180,000 of the loan will be secured with the 30 scooters. The other $50,000 is a personal note to her from her bank. She hopes to start her business within 90 days, to catch the beginning of the summer.

CASE DISCUSSION QUESTIONS

1. What financial risks is Vicky assuming?
2. What are the risks specific to renting motor scooters?
3. What are the risks specific to motor scooters as physical assets?
4. What risks will Vicky face because she is hiring four people?
5. What regulatory risks will Vicky face in operating a vehicle rental service in the state of Colorado?
6. What insurance coverage will Colorado require Vicky to have?
7. What insurance must Vicky have for her employees?
8. How should Vicky structure her business to minimize the potential loss she can suffer if a customer or bystander is injured or killed by one of her scooters?

5

PART FIVE

Management and Organization in the Small Business

CHAPTER

17

Legal Issues: Recognizing Your Small Business Needs

● A top-notch turntable scratcher, like B-Money Hughes, could make a good royalty income from getting one of his tracks included on a commercial CD. But in order to get that royalty, you need a good lawyer negotiating on your behalf. How could you tell if a lawyer is right for the negotiation you face?
Chuck Savage/Corbis/Getty Images

LEARNING OBJECTIVES

After you complete this chapter you will be able to:

LO 17-1 Know when you need legal information and how to get it.

LO 17-2 Understand legal structures in setting up a new business.

LO 17-3 Learn how to master the process of negotiating.

LO 17-4 Recognize potential legal liabilities for your business.

LO 17-5 Know contract terms and when a contract is needed.

LO 17-6 Understand the basics of intellectual property.

Focus on Small Business: Brian "B-Money" Hughes[1]

Brian "B-Money" Hughes has a tip for budding hip-hop producers: "The best advice I can give to anyone that's coming up: Make sure you get yourself a good lawyer." He knows of what he speaks.

B-Money was a turntable scratcher good enough to get credits on Jennifer Lopez and Murphy Lee CDs. He scored big in street cred when he produced 50 Cent's "Hustler's Ambition," the lead track to the soundtrack of *Get Rich or Die Trying*. This did not translate into much money, though. Two weeks before the film's release, 50 Cent's team offered a small flat fee rather than a larger royalty. B-Money was told to take it or leave it, but do it now. An experienced lawyer would have realized that the cost to 50 Cent to redo the film's soundtrack without B-Money's contribution would have been a lot more than what was offered. But as B-Money put it, "I had way more leverage, but my lawyer wasn't poised and let it slide."

B-Money took the flat fee offered, but he replaced that lawyer with an industry veteran. So later, when Jay-Z's producer asked for a B-Money-produced track called "The Prelude," this time the artist and lawyer were ready to negotiate. The track was the lead for Jay-Z's *Kingdom Come* CD. The new lawyer delivered, and B-Money finally came into some of the money he deserved for his work.

DISCUSSION QUESTIONS

1. Given B-Money's experience, if you were interviewing a potential lawyer, what sort of questions would you want to ask?
2. Can you think of anything you could have said to your lawyer to get a better outcome during the negotiation with 50 Cent?
3. Did B-Money have any recourse when it turned out his first lawyer was just not very good at the music business?

LO **17-1** Know when you need legal information and how to get it.

You and the Law

Business and law are inseparable. For B-Money, the two predictably merged when he was negotiating a deal for his tracks. At other times, the merger is unpredictable, like when your business faces an unexpected auto accident, product recall, or government regulation change. In either type of situation, when business owners know the law, they can better protect themselves and sometimes even avoid the problems completely. This chapter will help you spot important legal issues for small businesses and provide guidance for dealing effectively with those issues.

The United States is one of the most *litigious* (from the word *litigate*, meaning "to sue") societies in the world, along with countries such as Germany, Sweden, Israel, and Austria. On the other hand, a 2005 SBA study suggested that just 30,000 small businesses (out of a population of 27 million small firms) had been sued that year.[2] No matter what the perception, the law affects everything about business. Despite all the negative comments about attorneys, attorney jokes, and general resentment of the legal profession, the fact remains that if you are going to start a small business, you are going to be stuck with the legal system—virtues and faults both.

Because of that, it is important for you as a prospective small business owner to understand our legal system. Understanding the legal system will help you be less intimidated by attorneys and the law. And that knowledge can help move you from being a passive victim of the legal system, merely reacting to legal threats, to an empowered owner able to use the law to your advantage in a proactive way. Starting a business is risky enough. With the right knowledge about the law and the use of legal counsel, many of those risks can be significantly reduced or eliminated altogether.

It is easy to underestimate the number of laws that apply to a new small business because it is hard to believe how many laws apply—federal laws, state laws, even county and city laws. Let us take a moment and get an overview of the laws most likely to apply.

Table 17.1 provides an overview of some major federal laws in the areas of taxation and environmental health and safety. Intellectual property laws are considered later in this chapter, and labor and employment laws will be considered in Chapter 18. Even so, what Table 17.1 does not consider are state laws. There are some areas that only states legislate, for example, workers' compensation and employment security, which we will cover in Chapter 18. There can also be areas where there are overlapping state and federal laws, most typically in civil rights, and in such cases, the more demanding law is the one you should obey.

While the scope can be overwhelming, the good news is that not all laws apply to your business on the day you open. Many laws start to apply only as you reach certain thresholds. For example, tax laws tend to focus on financial thresholds, while environmental laws look at how much waste you produce.

Meanwhile, the state laws applicable to a small business are extraordinarily varied. It is truly a case where one size does not fit all. In Chapter 18 you will see the additional state laws that apply to labor and employment. For any category of laws, it is important to check what is applicable in your state. State laws can vary dramatically, so one state's laws are unlikely to be of much use anywhere else.

There are commercial and government sources of information for finding the relevant state laws. The major commercial source is the legal website Nolo (www.nolo.com/legal-encyclopedia/business-permits). The major government source is the SBA, which has its link to federal and state legal requirements at www.sba.gov/starting-business/business-licenses-permits. If you want a more personal consultation on local laws, one of the best ways to get a complete rundown of the relevant laws is to contact your closest state Small Business Development Center (to find it, click "Local Assistance" at the SBA website, www.sba.gov). Also, your local SCORE chapter (www.score.org) should be able to help, or at least point you to the right resources. Obviously, you can also work with an attorney to get expert help personalized for your business.

In the next portion of this chapter we start with your key legal expert—your attorney. We talk about how to select and work with an attorney. We also cover how to make some key legal decisions that come up in business, such as choosing a legal form for your business, how to negotiate, liability issues, and contracts (in person and online). We conclude the chapter with a discussion of the latest hot topic in law—intellectual property.

TABLE 17.1 Selected Laws Applicable to Growing Businesses

Benchmark	Law/Regulation	Ramification
	Business and Taxation	
In general, you must deposit federal income tax withheld and both the employer and employee Social Security and Medicare taxes; the timing of the deposit depends on the amount of the total tax liability (TTL): • If TTL is less than $2,500 during a quarter. • Under $50,000 during the four quarters in the "lookback period" applicable to the calendar year of withholding. • More than $50,000 during the "lookback period." • $100,000 or more during a monthly or semiweekly period.	Circular E-Employer's Tax Guide	Employer must deposit withheld taxes: • Quarterly (if paying with Form 941) • Monthly • Semiweekly • Next banking day after $100,000 threshold is reached
Gross receipts up to $5,000,000.	Section 448 of Internal Revenue Code	The business may qualify for an exception that allows it to compute taxable income using the cash method of accounting rather than the accrual method.
More than 100 shareholders of a corporation, more than one class of stock, certain prohibited shareholders.	Section 1361 of Internal Revenue Code	Corporation could lose or be ineligible to elect "Subchapter S" status.
Filing requirements for an employee benefit plan with: • One participant (if the total of the plan's assets and assets of all other one-participant plans maintained by the employer exceed $250,000 at the end of the year). • 2–99 participants. • 100 or more participants. • Reporting to participants: Summary Annual Report.	Internal Revenue Service/ Department of Labor Reg. §2520.104(b)-10	• Generally must file form 5500EZ annually with IRS. • Form 5500 or Form 5500-SF must be filed annually with IRS, with some exceptions if the plan is unfunded or insured. • Form 5500, with some exceptions, must be filed annually including a report by an independent qualified accountant. • Annually provide to participants within 9 months after the end of plan year.
Qualifying depreciable tangible personal property (and certain computer software) purchased for use in the active conduct of a trade or business.	Section 179 of the Internal Revenue Code	The total amount you can elect to deduct for most property placed in service in tax years beginning in 2015 generally cannot be more than $500,000.
	Environmental/Health and Safety	
Conditionally Exempt Small Quantity Generators of Hazardous Waste: • Generators of less than 1 kilogram/month of acute hazardous waste, or less than 100 kilograms/month of hazardous waste may accumulate up to 1 kilogram of acute hazardous waste or 1,000 kilograms of hazardous waste on-site.	EPA Hazardous Waste Regulations under RCRA (40 CFR Section 261 et seq.) and Missouri Hazardous Waste Law, Chapter 260 et seq. RSMo and 10 CSR 25-1.010 et seq.	• Do not require an EPA Hazardous Waste ID number • Manifests, reporting, personnel training, contingency planning, emergency procedures are not required. • DOT transport labeling, however, is generally required.

(Continued)

TABLE 17.1 (Continued)

Benchmark	Law/Regulation	Ramification
	Environmental/Health and Safety	
Process involves 1 of over 130 listed chemicals in an amount exceeding a listed threshold level or involves any flammable gas or liquid in a quantity of 10,000 pounds or more.	Process Safety Management Rule under the OSH Act 29 CFR 1910.119	Requires owners to perform a process hazard analysis and develop written operating procedures, employee training, emergency action plans, evaluation of mechanical integrity of critical equipment and written procedures for managing changes in process or procedures.
Employs 100 or fewer individuals on a companywide basis.	EPA's Interim Policy on Compliance Incentives for Small Businesses	EPA will eliminate or mitigate its settlement penalty demands against small businesses based on: • Good faith effort to comply with applicable environmental requirements. • This is the business's first violation of this requirement (no previous enforcement of that requirement within last 3 years). • The violation has not caused or does not pose a serious harm or threat to health or the environment. • The violation does not involve criminal conduct. • The violation is corrected within a specified period.
An employer with more than 10 employees on a companywide basis (except those in Standard Industrial Classification codes 52–89).	OSHA's Recording and Reporting of Occupational Injuries and Illnesses	Employer is required to record occupational injuries and illness on a log with a separate supporting record for each injury or illness and post in the workplace the log for the previous calendar year during the following month of February.

Note: The chart is not, nor is it intended to be, a comprehensive summary of the threshold levels at which the statutes and regulations cited therein take effect, and it is qualified in its entirety by reference to the appropriate statute and regulations.

Source: Chart compiled in August 2016 by Armstrong Teasdale attorneys: Michael B. Kass, Julie O'Keefe, Robert B. Reeser III, and Robert J. Browning.

You Need a Good Attorney

Setting up a business requires some familiarity with several areas of law—forms of organization, contracts, and licensing, for example. Usually with legal issues, as with health issues, it is best to confront potential problems before they have a chance to get serious. Timely decisions and action may avoid a problem altogether or may make solving the problem much easier and cheaper. Think of legal knowledge as a form of insurance. The key is finding the right lawyer.

First, look for an attorney who is experienced in forming new business entities and handling the needs of small businesses.[3] Where can you find such a person? If you do not have someone in mind, get suggestions from small business owners you know and respect. Bankers involved in commercial financing on a regular basis often know which attorneys handle small businesses well. In addition, a trade association for your industry may have suggestions. A less certain way to find a *good* lawyer is to look online searching with the term "start-up attorney [your town]" or "small business attorney [your town]." You can search lawyer directories like Martindale-Hubbell (www.martindale.com) or the American Bar Association'(www.americanbar.org/groups/legal_services/flh-home/) because the lawyers themselves control those listings.

You can use these sites to learn more about the attorneys (like degrees or specialty areas), but to find out the negative reports, like disbarment or ethics violations, you need to check with the state bar association where the lawyer is based. Look at the ABA's "Resources for the Public" page at www.americanbar.org/groups/professional_responsibility/services/databank/ for a Directory of State Disciplinary Agencies, and a link to the ABA's National Lawyer Regulatory Databank (to whom you need to send a written request for information).

These days, it is typical to be involved with more than one attorney. As with doctors, where you might work with one generalist and several specialists, today most businesses need to depend on one general-purpose lawyer and several specialists. The law is so complex that no one can be an expert in all areas. Beware of the attorney who tells you he or she can handle all your legal needs. However, if the attorney is in a group practice, there may well be others in the firm who specialize in the other areas where you need specialized help. Ask about the legal specialties covered within the firm when you call to make an appointment. You may make several calls and visits. If one attorney does not meet your needs in terms of qualifications, work ethic, or pricing, there are many others who would like to have your business.

Again, like with physicians, once you have chosen an attorney, having an ongoing relationship helps him or her to know you and your situation when something comes up and you need legal advice on short notice.

Clients and attorneys start with a natural conflict of interest. The attorney wants to make money for the services, and you would like the services for as little cost as possible. In reality, all entrepreneurs know they will have to pay, so the key issues are how and how much you will be charged for legal services.

Typically you and the attorney will discuss and decide on the type and rate of charges up front, before you engage his or her professional services. The attorney–client agreement should definitely be in writing and signed by both parties.[4] Take the time to read the agreement before signing. Ask for it to be sent to you to review. If the agreement is hard to understand, think about what other work from the attorney will look like, and consider whether that attorney is right for you. There are four ways attorneys typically charge:

1. **Hourly fees:** **Hourly fees** can vary greatly from one part of the country to another, as well as from firm to firm and even within a firm. Attorneys with more experience often charge more than new law school graduates. Prestigious law firms often charge more than smaller, less recognized firms.
2. **Flat fees:** **Flat fees** are a fixed amount paid for a certain task. For example, an attorney may have a flat fee for handling all the paperwork to establish a corporation.
3. **Retainers:** When using a **retainer**, the attorney will be paid a specified amount every month regardless of the workload for that month. Usually there is a retainer agreement that specifies what types of work the monthly fee covers and when and how much additional fees are when circumstances change.
4. **Contingency fees:** You have seen the attorney ads on television announcing, "I don't get paid unless you get paid." That ad is describing a contingency fee. **Contingency fees** are typical in accident (especially personal injury) situations, but are not usually used in everyday contract and business-related matters. With a contingency fee, the attorney will take a percentage of your recovery (if your side wins) as his or her fee.

hourly fees
A basis for legal charges in which the rate is based on a price per hour. Often lawyers will charge for fractions of an hour.

flat fees
A method of billing for lawyers in which a fixed amount is paid for a certain task.

retainer
A fee paid by a client to an attorney to engage the attorney's services.

contingency fee
Fee paid by a client to an attorney for legal services that is dependent on the outcome of a case.

Just like anything else, pricing of legal services is based on supply and demand, especially your negotiating demands. Do not be intimidated by having to negotiate price with an attorney. Regardless of what the attorney says, the attorney's fee schedule in all four types of pricing of services may be negotiable, particularly if the attorney is a more senior member of the firm with the authority to negotiate. Diplomacy is recommended in these negotiations because once the original issue of pricing is resolved, it is in your best interest for you and your attorney to have a positive working relationship.

Can I Do This for Free?

There are three elements to most aspects of business law—finding the right information, negotiating the specific outcome you want, and then taking care of the paperwork associated with it. The three elements are what you pay your lawyer to do, but when you look at paying lawyer's fees, you probably want to know if there are things you can do yourself. The good news is that you can.

These days there are many sources of reliable legal information on the Internet for small business owners who want to do the legal work themselves. Also be aware that your local library and bookstores are brimming with titles on business law and how to start your own business.

There are two basic categories of information available to small business owners: free and paid. If you are paying a nonattorney for legal services, such as using an Internet company to set up your business as a corporation, you may not be saving that much money over what an attorney would charge. Consider whether you would be better served in seeking out an attorney and getting individual, custom-tailored advice. Falling between free and paid are the do-it-yourself products. Nolo (www.nolo.com) and LegalZoom (www.legalzoom.com) are well-known companies that have been established for some time and offer do-it-yourself products.

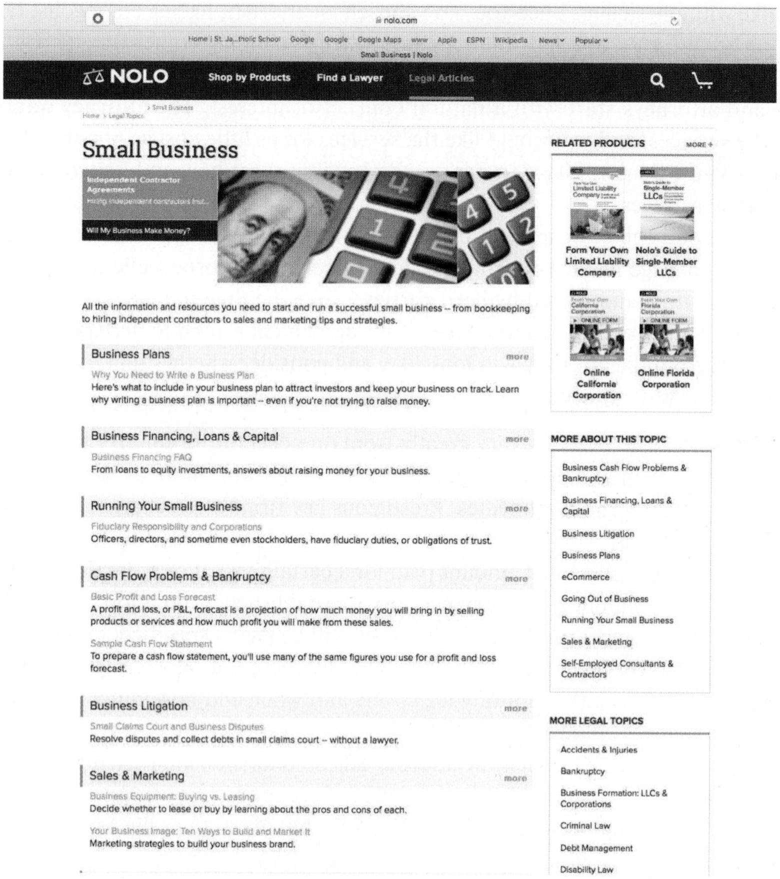

● Visit **www.nolo.com/legal-encyclopedia/small-business** to take advantage of Nolo's compilation of the government's free legal resources. Looking at this and related websites can help you determine which legal aspects you can manage on your own and which require a paid attorney's involvement.

Source: Nolo

NOLO Shop by Products Find a Lawyer Legal Articles

Small Business

Independent Contractor Agreements

Will My Business Make Money?

All the information and resources you need to start and run a successful small business – from bookkeeping to hiring independent contractors to sales and marketing tips and strategies.

Business Plans

Here's what to include in your business plan to attract investors and keep your business on track. Learn why writing a business plan is important – even if you're not trying to raise money.

Business Financing, Loans & Capital

From loans to equity investments, answers about raising money for your business.

Running Your Small Business

Officers, directors, and sometime even stockholders, have fiduciary duties, or obligations of trust.

Cash Flow Problems & Bankruptcy

A profit and loss, or P&L, forecast is a projection of how much money you will bring in by selling products or services and how much profit you will make from these sales.

To prepare a cash flow statement, you'll use many of the same figures you use for a profit and loss forecast.

Business Litigation

Resolve disputes and collect debts in small claims court – without a lawyer.

Sales & Marketing

Decide whether to lease or buy by learning about the pros and cons of each.

Marketing strategies to build your business brand.

RELATED PRODUCTS

Form Your Own Limited Liability Company

Nolo's Guide to Single-Member LLCs

Online California Corporation

Online Florida Corporation

MORE ABOUT THIS TOPIC

Business Cash Flow Problems & Bankruptcy

Business Financing, Loans & Capital

Business Litigation

Business Plans

eCommerce

Going Out of Business

Running Your Small Business

Sales & Marketing

Self-Employed Consultants & Contractors

MORE LEGAL TOPICS

Accidents & Injuries

Bankruptcy

Business Formation: LLCs & Corporations

Criminal Law

Debt Management

Disability Law

Of the free information sources available, some are more reliable than others. Government websites are at the top of the list for reliability because the government does not have the conflict of interest of wishing to make money from the business owner. And what the government says usually has the force of law behind it. Major examples include:

- www.dol.gov (for labor laws)
- www.irs.gov/businesses/small-businesses-self-employed (for small business-related help)
- www.sba.gov (the Small Business Administration site)
- www.uspto.gov (for patent and copyright help)

Remember the SBA and Nolo links given previously for state-level licensing and assistance websites. In addition you can go to www.usa.gov/business?source=busa to find resources near you, or the commercial site Coordinated Legal Tech's listing at www.coordinatedlegal.com/SecretaryOfState.html. Skill Module 17.1 offers help on finding legal information.

Getting Started on Legal Issues Online

SKILL MODULE 17.1

The Internet can be a great source of information in helping you determine which various governmental requirements apply to a business. On the state level you can go to the website for the state and obtain all sorts of information on starting a business in that state, required licenses, and the like.

Usually starting with government information sources makes sense since they are the source for all things legal, and you can be sure they are not being paid by one side or the other. In this case, start at **www.usa.gov/business**, the government's key small business page. Click on "State Business Resources."

Pretend that you wish to start a business in Lexington, Kentucky. So select "Kentucky" from the drop-down box. On the resulting page, you can download a "Small Business Resource Guide for Kentucky" or you can look at Kentucky's One Stop Business Portal which would walk you through the actual steps to start you business with the state, and connect you to city level resources.

Note that while the USA.gov site lists all states, each state's own website is different. So if you try this with a different state, what it might offer or what information is asked of you will probably differ.

Trade associations are another source of information for business start-ups. Many trade associations compile legal information for their members, including laws particularly applicable to certain types of businesses in various jurisdictions and proposals for changing the laws that affect your industry. As you may be aware, these organizations also hire lobbyists to push the agenda of an industry or trade group within the various branches of government, both federal and state. Because of the limited resources of small businesses, membership in one of these organizations can be particularly valuable in informing the business owners and giving them more power as a group to influence legislation that affects them. In addition, through these trade associations it is possible to meet others in your industry and make noncompetitive connections that help you network and keep up with industry trends. Remember that you learned how to find your relevant trade, industry, or professional association in Skill Module 3.1.

Be wary of legal information on matters such as statutes or agency regulations offered by individuals who seek to profit from doing business with you. For instance, if you are looking for space to locate your business, be wary of what real estate agents tell you regarding the law. Never forget, these folks make their money when you buy something or if they arrange some lease agreement for you. It may not be in your best interest to buy property, but real estate agents are not likely to tell you that because they will make money by getting a percentage when you buy.

For example, in the issue of zoning, go to your local governmental unit and check on the zoning of the property before you seriously consider it.[5] Do not take the real estate agent's word on the zoning. Be sure that the business you plan may be legally operated in that location. If the building will need any remodeling to suit your purposes, be sure to contact the local government regarding safety standards, exits, entrances, etc., so that the property will pass inspection once the remodeling is done. In the contract with your remodeler, it is best to insert a provision that the remodeling has to be done according to applicable building codes before the contractor is fully paid.

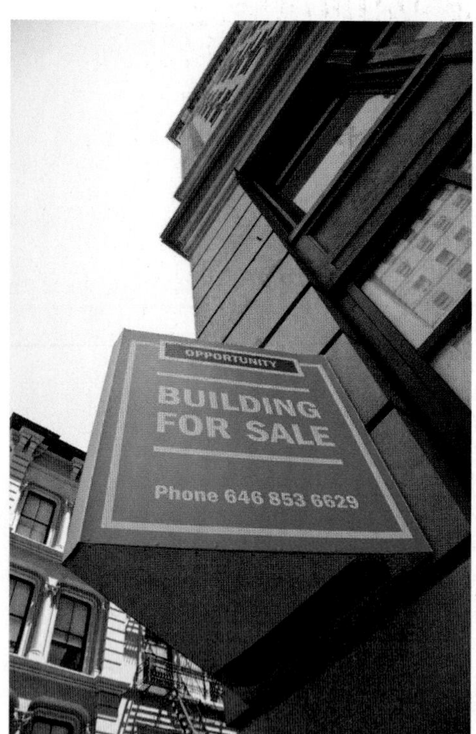

● One key legal issue for small business owners is the matter of real estate. Before you purchase a space for any of your business's activities, make sure the site is zoned appropriately and that you can legally undertake any planned remodeling, expansion, or rezoning of the area.

James Leynse/Corbis/Getty Images

In the contract to purchase or lease the property, insert a provision that the property has to be zoned such that your business can be legally operated in that location. By contacting the local government, you should be able to get guidelines on zoning, placement, and size of signage, parking, property tax, and other matters related to the location.[6] Also, be sure to inquire about future plans regarding street repairs, expansions, and closures in the area that could affect your ability to do business. Do not rely on the real estate agent for any of this information.

As noted at the start of this section, there are three elements to the law—finding the right information, negotiating the specific outcome you want, and then taking care of the paperwork associated with it. Often, as businesspeople become familiar with the legal specifics of their business, they take on more of the responsibilities. Most often they do the negotiating themselves (you will see how later in this chapter), and where the paperwork is standardized (as we see when we discuss standard contracts), even handle aspects of the paperwork themselves. Some legal research can be done, especially when the business owner is made aware of new legal concerns by the trade or professional association. But for all of these things you can eventually do for yourself, when learning the business or when facing a new or unusual situation, it makes sense to go with the pro. When in doubt, call your lawyer.

Small-Claims Court

There is also a legal option available to entrepreneurs that does not involve an attorney. It is typically called small-claims court. Despite the name, many of these courts will accept cases where the stakes are as large as $10,000. Most are designed so that ordinary citizens can bring in their cases. Yes, this is the sort of court you see on afternoon television—*Judge Judy, The People's Court, Judge Mathis*, and the like.

Believe it or not, you can learn something about preparing yourself for small-claims court by watching the television shows: (1) evidence helps, (2) have everything ready and with you when you go to court, (3) practice your explanation, (4) be on time, (5) stay calm, and (6) above all, stay respectful to the judge and court.

Small-claims courts work only when you are owed money, can prove it (proof you did the work, and that your customer did not pay—think of purchase orders, contracts, invoices, past-due letters, etc.), and have exhausted other procedures like calls and letters to the customer. If there is a reason the other party did not pay—for example, he or she said your work was late, shoddy, or not as promised—you need to prove you are in the right; otherwise you will have a tough day in court.

The typical next step starts with finding the right court—either where your business is located or where the person (or business) you want to sue lives or works. Realize this means small-claims court is not useful for problems in other states, unless it is a short drive for you. To find the right court for your state, look at www.nolo.com/legal-encyclopedia/lawsuits-court. Most state bar associations also have pamphlets on small-claims courts.

Contact the court to find out the specifics and costs of filing. These fees are typically less than $50, and are something you can charge the customer for if you win. You will probably have to fill out a form and give a written explanation of the problem. Make copies of your evidence to include in the packet. If you have potential witnesses, list them and get their testimony written down. Take the packet and the originals of your evidence to court to file the complaint with the clerk.

When you get to court, the TV lessons apply. Look the judge in the eye as you talk. Speak up and sound confident. Stick to what you wrote. Answer questions directly, briefly, and politely. Don't get angry at the other party, especially if they get angry or they insult you or the court. If you have a court date, be there no matter what. In case of emergency, it might be possible to get one postponement (called a continuance)—if the other party agrees. Otherwise, the case will be thrown out and you cannot refile it.

If you win, the court will give you official support to get your money; however, it remains mostly up to you to collect payment. The customer will have a fixed amount of time to pay up. If he or she doesn't, you can get the clerk to serve the losing party with a certified letter reminding the customer of the court order. A personal delivery can often be arranged for an additional fee. If that doesn't get the job done, the court can help garnish the loser's income or attach assets of the losing party, making them yours until you get the payment the court ordered. But realize that a defendant with little income and few assets will be difficult to collect from, regardless of the decision, so it only makes sense to go to small-claims court if you think you will be able to collect, should you win.

Choosing a Business Name

As we saw in Chapter 10 your business name is one of the key owned media elements for any business. In addition, the name is tied closely to your business's brand and identity. For businesses, names are vitally important. But in addition to the features that make up a name that is distinctive, memorable, and descriptive, for everything to work, that name needs to be legal and protected. That is the focus of this section.

The legal issue for your business is protecting the business's name or idea from copycats. This is an issue of intellectual property. At this point, we will consider the ways you can protect the identity of your business, while later in the chapter we will consider the other forms of intellectual property that can protect your idea.

The name of your business is called its **trade name**. It can also be called an **assumed name** or a **doing business as (dba) name**. If you use something other than your own name (e.g., The Jerome Katz Company), then the trade name must be registered in the states in which your firm does business. The filing is typically called an **assumed name filing** or a **fictitious name filing**. In most states, this filing is made with the secretary of state's office. You can find this information at the SBA website (www.sba.gov/starting-business/choose-register-your-business/register-your-business-name). The same office usually offers a public database to see the names of the people behind other businesses using trade names.

trade name or assumed name or doing business as (dba) name
The name under which a business is operated.

assumed name filing or fictitious name filing
Filing made with a state(s) in which the business operates disclosing the trade name or assumed name of the business along with the owners of the business.

There may be more than one business using the same name within a state. Most states allow several firms to use the same trade name, as long as the firms are in different parts of the state, or are in different lines of business (e.g., Courtesy Cleaners, Courtesy Pharmacy, etc.) in the same town, and as long as none of the firms have received a trademark or service mark in that name. You can check this using the secretary of state database just mentioned, as well as the trademark search at the U.S. Patent Office (www.uspto.gov).

When selecting a trade name, you want to find one that is memorable and descriptive. "Social Networking Experts, LLC" tells customers who you are, better than "Darlene Jones, LLC" does. If you have plans to grow, factor that in too. Since St. Louis is known for baseball and beer, but not bread, the founders of the Saint Louis Bread Company had to create a new name when it left its home market. Now the country knows the company as Panera Bread. Given how Panera's menu has grown, it is possible that "Bread" may someday get dropped from the title, too.

Saint Louis Bread Company® really did start out in St. Louis, but when it wanted to expand outside the region, it felt it needed a name that was place-neutral. It came up with Panera Bread, which is what the company is known as everywhere except in St. Louis, Missouri, where the original name is still used.

Panera, LLC.

In the end, the other key element in picking a trade name is your own goals. It can be very satisfying to have your name on a successful business–think of Donald Trump! But also realize that it can make it hard to sell the business. Imagine the Trump Companies without Trump. On the other hand, for a family-owned business, having the family name visible can be a benefit. Part of what makes Ford a bit more personal brand compared to General Motors is that there are members of the Ford family who own stock, sit on the board, and occasionally even run the place. The Ford family stands behind the Ford line, even today.

LO **17-2** Understand legal structures in setting up a new business.

legal entity
A being, human or nonhuman, such as a corporation, that is recognized as having rights and duties, such as the right to own property.

plaintiff
Person or other entity filing a lawsuit.

defendant
Person or other entity being sued.

Choosing a Business Form

Most often choosing the *form* of your business is the next legal decision you need to make. Except for sole proprietorships, business forms are types of separate, legal entities. A **legal entity** is a unit recognized as having rights and duties apart from the owners of the company. Legal entities can own property, sue, and be sued.

The original type of legal entity recognized in England, the source of U.S. law, was the individual. An individual may hold property ownership and be a **plaintiff** (the party who files a lawsuit) or a **defendant** (the party who is sued) in a lawsuit. As time passed, the law recognized other legal entities that were not human beings. For example, in about 1600 the corporation was recognized as a separate entity in England. In other words, a corporation itself, without its shareholders (or owners), could hold title to property and could sue or be sued in its own name, without its owners being sued.

Today there are seven general types of business form for for-profit organizations–sole proprietorships, general partnerships, limited partnerships, C corporations (commonly known as just "corporations"), S corporations (also known as Subchapter S corporations), professional corporations (which the IRS calls Personal Service Corporations), and limited liability companies (commonly known as LLCs). Each general form has advantages and disadvantages, which are outlined in Tables 17.2, 17.3, 17.4, and 17.5. For start-ups, the most popular form is the sole proprietorship, although the approach is not always optimal for a small start-up, as we see in the tables. General partnerships are the second most popular, and C corporations are third. These results are shown in Figure 17.1.

TABLE 17.2 Advantages and Disadvantages of Corporations

Advantages	Disadvantages
Can have representative management	Impersonal
Ease of raising large amounts of capital	Owners have limited interest in firm's activities—except profits
Legal entity separate and distinct from its owners as individuals	High incorporation fees and high taxes, especially double income taxation
Relatively permanent, since life of firm not affected by loss of any shareholder	Burdensome procedures, reports, and statements required by governments
Owners' liability for the firm's debt limited to their investment in it	Powers limited to those stated in charters—may be difficult to do business in another state

Source: Adapted from Mary Jane Byrd and Leon C. Megginson, *Small Business Management: An Entrepreneur's Guidebook* (New York: McGraw-Hill Education, 2017).

TABLE 17.3 Advantages and Disadvantages of Sole Proprietorships

Advantages	Disadvantages
Secrecy	Limited capital
Unique tax advantages	Difficulty in obtaining credit
Owner doesn't have to share profits	Inadequate management and employee skills
Relative freedom of action and control	Unlimited liability for the firm's debts
Easiest and simplest form to organize, operate, and dissolve	Limited life because business and owner are legally the same

Source: Adapted from Mary Jane Byrd and Leon C. Megginson, *Small Business Management: An Entrepreneur's Guidebook* (New York: McGraw-Hill Education, 2017).

TABLE 17.4 **Advantages and Disadvantages of Partnerships**

Advantages	Disadvantages
Easy to form	Limited life
Division of labor and management responsibility	Unlimited liability for debts of the firm
Can use ideas and plans of more than one person	Each partner is responsible for the acts of every other partner
Specialized skills available from individual partners	An impasse may develop if the partners become incompatible
Can raise more capital since good credit may be available	Death of any one of the partners terminates the partnership
Obtains financial resources from more than one person	A partner cannot obtain bonding protection against the acts of the other partner(s)

Source: Adapted from Mary Jane Byrd and Leon C. Megginson, *Small Business Management: An Entrepreneur's Guidebook* (New York: McGraw-Hill Education, 2017).

TABLE 17.5 **Advantages and Disadvantages of Limited Liability Companies (LLCs)**

Advantages	Disadvantages
More flexible paperwork and reporting requirements than C corporations	More paperwork and fees than sole proprietorships and partnerships
Corporate protection—legal entity separate and distinct from its owners as individuals	LLC (in some states) can cease if a LLC member departs
LLC a pass-through entity, so no double taxation	Personal tax rates may be higher than corporate tax rates
Limited liability—owners' liability for the firm's debt limited to their investment in it	Adding or reducing members requires all members' consent

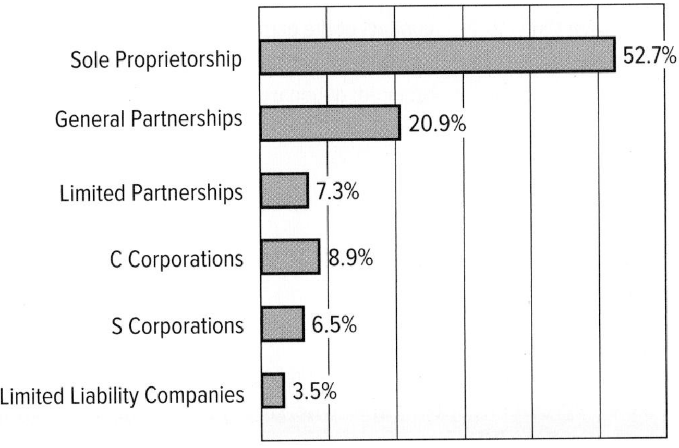

FIGURE 17.1

Legal Forms of Start-Ups from the PSED

Source: Based on an original computation done by Paul D. Reynolds for *Entrepreneurial Small Business* using the PSED dataset (weighted sample data), March 8, 2016.

Unless you are going to see a lawyer for advice on what legal form of business makes sense in your situation, or you are using an interactive guide (like the "Incorporation Wizard" at https://www.bizfilings.com/toolkit/tools/incorporation-wizard) to get a general idea about the best type of business form to use, the best choice for a new small business is a limited liability company (LLC). This is because, as noted above, LLCs are simple to set up and relatively easy to maintain

TABLE 17.6 Forms of Legal Organization

Factors	Sole Proprietorship	General Partnership	Limited Partnership
Personal liability of owners	Unlimited personal liability.	Unlimited personal liability of partners if partnership has insufficient assets to cover partnership liabilities.	A limited partnership has to have at least one general partner and one limited partner. The general partner has unlimited personal liability. The limited partner can lose "only" his or her investment in the business.
Taxation	**Single taxation** of income to sole proprietor.	Single taxation of income to individual partners.	Single taxation of income to individual partners.
Control or management of business	Complete control by sole proprietor.	Authority shared equally between partners unless otherwise stated in articles of partnership.	Written articles of partnership generally are required for limited partnerships. Authority of various partners is set forth in the articles.
Continuity of business	Ends at death of sole proprietor.	Whenever mix of partners is changed, that partnership is dissolved.	Whenever mix of partners is changed, that partnership is dissolved.
Raising capital	Dependent on assets and credit of sole proprietor.	Dependent on capital contributions of the partners, credit of the partnership, and credit of the individual partners.	Dependent on capital contributions of the partners, credit of the partnership, and credit of individual partners.
Complexity of setup and maintenance of business form	No government permission required; few (if any) legal costs.	May be formed by conduct of the parties; no government permission required; optional cost of articles of partnership.	Limited partnerships have to meet state statutory requirements which may vary from state to state. Filings with the state are generally required. In addition, states usually require that the business always identify itself to the public as a limited partnership.

single taxation
Earnings of the business are taxed once with the owners paying the taxes.

double taxation
Earnings of the business are taxed twice with the business as well as its owners being subject to tax.

pass through (taxation)
Earnings of the business are distributed to the business owners and those owners (rather than the business) pay individual tax on the earnings.

check the box taxation
A choice LLCs can make on their tax returns to be taxed as a corporation or a partnership.

operating agreement
A contract among LLC members outlining how the LLC will conduct itself.

once started. They can be used for an individual or a group of partners. If you have partners, it makes sense to create an agreement specifying ownership, profit splitting, buyouts, and the like called **articles of organization**. When properly structured, an LLC offers legal protection to owners for assets they personally hold outside the LLC. It also gives the owners the benefits of single taxation, if they choose to go that route. (See Table 17.6.)

articles of organization
Document setting forth information about a limited liability company that is filed with the state to establish an LLC.

The major advantage of the sole proprietorship is that it is extremely easy to set up. There are no forms to file; you just start doing business. The problem is one mentioned in Chapter 16 when discussing risk. In a sole proprietorship, the owner and the firm are one and the same. If an employee has an accident while at work, the business is liable for the damages–*and the owner*

Corporation	S Corporation	Professional Corporation	Limited Liability Company
Shareholders are not responsible for debts of the corporation. If the corporation fails, the shareholders can lose, at most, the value of their investment in the corporation.	Shareholders are not responsible for debts of the corporation. If the corporation fails, the shareholders can lose, at most, the value of their investment in the corporation.	Shareholders are not responsible for debts of the corporation. If the corporation fails, shareholders can lose, at most, the value of their investment in the corporation.	Members (owners) are not responsible for debts of the LLC. If the LLC fails, the members can lose, at most, the value of their investment in the LLC.
Double taxation of earnings generated by the corporation. Corporation is taxed on its income at the corporate rate, and shareholders are taxed on dividends at their individual rate.	There is no taxation of the S corporation, itself. The earnings are **passed through** to the shareholders who are taxed at their individual rate on their individual tax returns.	There is no taxation of the professional corporation (PC) itself. The earnings are passed through to the shareholders who are taxed at their individual rate on their individual tax returns.	**Check the box taxation** means an LLC can choose whether to be taxed as a corporation or as a partnership (pass through taxation).
Shareholders elect directors who set broad corporate policy. Directors appoint officers to carry out that policy, aided by employees.	Shareholders elect directors who set broad corporate policy. Directors appoint officers to carry out that policy, aided by employees.	Shareholders elect directors who set broad corporate policy. Directors appoint officers to carry out that policy, aided by employees.	Members enter into an **operating agreement** under which the division of management rights (e.g., committees, voting) is established.
The corporate entity can continue indefinitely if the corporation is properly formed, regardless of changes in ownership of shares.	S corporations may continue as long as the business qualifies under the federal tax code and the rules and regulations of the Internal Revenue Service.	PC can continue as long as the business qualifies under state law.	Depends on state statute creating LLCs. Some states allow perpetual existence.
Corporations may issue securities such as stocks and bonds, and/or borrow money based on the corporation's credit.	S corporations may issue securities such as stocks and bonds, and/or borrow money based on the corporation's credit.	PC may issue stock, although ownership may be limited by state law.	In addition to the capital contributions paid in by members, the LLC can borrow money as a separate entity.
Corporations are created by the state. Incorporators must submit articles of incorporation and pay appropriate fees to the state.	S corporations are created by the state. Incorporators must submit articles of incorporation and pay appropriate fees to the state. In addition, the S corporation must elect this tax status with the Internal Revenue Service.	Professional corporations are created by the state. The incorporators must qualify under state law. An application and fees are submitted to the state.	In some states a single individual may form an LLC. In other states two or more members are required. To form the LLC, articles of organization must be filed with the state. The members also need an operating agreement. There will be minimal state filing fees.

is personally responsible too. This means the sole proprietor's home, stocks, savings, and even personal property could be taken to pay damages. (See Table 17.3.)[7]

Partnerships can vary dramatically. They can be set up quickly with nothing more than a handshake or with a formal legal agreement called **articles of partnership** (the latter is **highly recommended**). They can be set up so all partners are equally and fully responsible for the business's obligations (called a *general partnership*) or where most partners are liable only for the amount they invested in the partnership (called a *limited partnership*—but every limited partnership has at least one general partner). The total liability issue in general partnerships is like that of sole proprietorships, so although easy to start, partnerships are something to avoid. (See Table 17.4.)

articles of partnership
Agreement between the partners of a firm on matters pertaining to the formation and operation of the partnership.

Maybe you are not sure that an LLC is right for your situation, or your lawyer has suggested another form. How do you go about thinking through the issues? There are six major factors at play in the decision on the form of a business organization to set up:

1. Personal liability of the business owner–how much the owner can lose if there are problems arising from the business.
2. Taxation of both the entity and its owners–do owners get taxed as well as the business?
3. Complexity and organizational costs in setting up the business and maintaining that entity–how difficult and costly is it for the owner to maintain the legal form of the business?
4. Control of the business–who runs the business and how is decision making split among various people?
5. Continuity of the business–how long that particular form of business can continue and under what conditions the business could end.
6. Ability of the business to raise capital–can the business borrow money, issue stock, or issue bonds?

Table 17.6 provides a simple summary of how the forms of legal organization differ on the six issues. After going through the characteristics of these various entities, you can easily see how some of the newer and nontraditional business forms, such as S corporations and LLCs, can offer the best of both worlds–that is, limited liability of owners as well as single taxation. Of these newer forms, the easiest to form and the most user-friendly is the LLC, or limited liability company. As a result, LLCs should be viewed as a default of sorts, so select an LLC unless there is a compelling reason to choose another form.

If you choose any of the forms other than the sole proprietorship, please be careful to treat your legal form of business as if it were a being separate from the owner or owners. When you keep the business separate from you personally, that business entity can have liability apart from its owners. If you fail to keep them separate, such as using personal funds for business purposes or using the business's car or equipment for personal purposes, there is a chance that a court may hold that there is no distinction between the entity and its owners in practice. If this happens, called **piercing the veil**, the court may hold that the owners have some personal liability for debts of that business entity. A good place to start in this area is to keep the finances of the business entity and those of its owners entirely separate. Company bills should never be paid from the owners' personal accounts using an owner's personal check. An asset of the business, such as a car, should not be used for personal use without accounting for that nonbusiness use.

piercing the veil
The dissolution of a corporate form, making it back into a sole proprietorship or general partnership, if the court finds that the owner carelessly mixed up personal and business assets or finances.

Another essential caution comes from recognizing that *no* form of LLC or corporation will make the owner(s) bulletproof. No matter what form of business a person owns, if he or she causes a traffic accident or accidentally hurts another person in some way (causes a tort), that person may be found "personally liable" in a lawsuit. That person may have to sell his or her car, home, or other assets (including the business) to pay the judgment. On the other hand, if the owner's employee causes the loss, as mentioned before, the business may be held liable. This is when it makes a huge difference what the structure of the business is in terms of what the owner can lose. If the business is a sole proprietorship or a partnership, the owner may lose personal assets as well as business interests. If the business is a corporation or an LLC, the owner can lose "only" what he or she has in that business.

Similarly, for a newly created LLC or C corporation going to the bank for a loan, it is unlikely that the new corporation will have the collateral base, asset base, or cash flow to convince a banker to issue a loan to the corporation. Regardless of your efforts to shield yourself from liability, the likelihood is that a bank giving a loan to your new corporation will require that you *personally* sign for the loan, in addition to the corporation's signing for it. From a banker's view, a corporation is only as strong as its balance sheet.

Taxation Issues

As you can see in Table 17.6, the legal form of organization you choose can have an impact on the taxes you pay. For every type of legal form except the C corporation and limited liability company, the taxes are paid by the owner on the basis of the income received from the business. This income can consist of a salary you pay yourself and any profits made by the firm. In these cases, you are being taxed at the applicable personal rate, shown in Table 17.7.

TABLE 17.7 2019 Tax Rates

Sole Proprietors, General Partnerships, Limited Partnerships, S Corporations, and LLCs Not Filing Form 8832	C Corporations, Professional Corporations, and LLCs Filing Form 8832
10% on amount up to $9,700	21% on all income
12% on amount between $9,701 and $39,475	
22% on amount between $39,476 and $84,200	
24% on amount between $84,201 and $160,725	
32% on amount between $160,726 and $204,100	
35% on amount between $204,101 and $510,300	
37% on amount above $510,300	

Note: The tax rates on the left-hand side are given for unmarried individuals. Rates differ for married filers. The tax rates above are for regular income, such as salaries, wages, and commissions. Dividends paid from your company's stock are taxed differently (Google "corporate dividend rate" for specifics). Also note that pass-through entities (like S corporations and possibly LLCs) may also be able to apply a *qualified business income* deduction if the individual taxpayer qualifies.

Sources: IRS, "IRS Provides Tax inflation Adjustments for Tax Year 2019," November 15, 2018, www.irs.gov/newsroom/irs-provides-tax-inflation-adjustments-for-tax-year-2019; IRS, "2018 Instructions for Form 1120," January 16, 2019, www.irs.gov/pub/irs-pdf/i1120.pdf.

For C corporations and professional corporations, as a shareholder, you get taxed on the income you receive from the firm. This income can be in the form of dividends and profits. The good news is that tax rates for these are lower than for individuals. The bad news is that those profits face double taxation. C corporations and professional corporations file taxes as entities, and pay taxes on their profits and dividends. When the remaining posttax profits are paid to you as the owner or shareholder, you personally pay taxes again on the income at your individual rate. In 2018, dividends had a rate fixed at zero for the people making $38,600 or less, 15 percent for people making between $38,601 to $425,801, and 20 percent for those earning beyond $425,801. But for dividends or profits you are looking at the double taxation mentioned in Table 17.6.

For the other forms of organization (except the LLC), the money you take out of the business is taxed at your individual rate. The firm itself does not pay taxes. This is the idea of single taxation. The good news here is when your business is unprofitable, these losses can also be applied to your personal taxes. So if you are employed somewhere else full time, and run your own business part time, the loss you have from your small business can be used to reduce your overall taxable income for the year.

One thing to watch for is the issue of paying yourself a salary. In a C corporation and S corporation, the IRS expects you to pay yourself a salary that is roughly at market rates. Why would you pay yourself less in salary? Because salary has the added costs of Social Security and Medicare taxes. But paying no salary is one of the red flags that draws IRS auditor attention.

The LLC has been curiously absent in this discussion, but it can operate using either of the approaches described here. To use the C corporation taxation approach, you need to file a Form 8832 with the IRS. Otherwise, a one-person LLC is taxed as a sole proprietorship and a multi-person LLC like a general partnership. Once a Form 8832 is filed, you can't change it for 60 months, unless the business changes ownership and the IRS agrees.

Note that in addition to the income tax or its corporate equivalent, entrepreneurs can also be liable for self-employment tax, estimated tax, Social Security tax, Medicare tax, and even federal unemployment tax. The IRS provides a basic guide based on the legal form of organization you have, at www.irs.gov/businesses/small-businesses-self-employed/business-structures. The IRS even provides an online tax calendar with reminders to help you keep track of your federal tax filings at www.irs.gov/businesses/small-businesses-self-employed/irs-tax-calendar-for-businesses-and-self-employed.

Because the legal form of organization can make a difference in the taxes you (and the firm) pay, it makes sense to think about which legal form can make the most difference in your annual income. For many small businesses in their first years, losses are typical and profits are not, so it helps to have a form that provides for single taxation. As the firm becomes profitable, the advantages of the C corporation or LLC organized with Form 8832 as a check the box corporation can make a lot of sense.

Nonprofits and Social Benefit Organizations

For social entrepreneurs, or for-profit entrepreneurs who want to pursue a mix of for-profit and social outcomes, there are special forms of organization available. For nonprofits that see themselves as charities that will raise money and secure grants in order to fund themselves, states offer a **nonprofit corporation** legal form of organization. In most states this is a legal form by itself, although some states have started permitting nonprofit LLCs.

nonprofit corporation
A business form specific to charitable organizations (i.e., organizations that do not make a profit for their owners). Nonprofit business charters differ in the kinds of responsibilities the nonprofit has, compared to the other forms of for-profit business forms. Nonprofits are the only form of business that can seek 501(c)(3) status from the IRS, which permits donations to the nonprofit to be considered tax-deductible to the donor.

501(c)(3)
501(c)(3) refers to a section of the U.S. Tax Code that specifies the conditions for a nonprofit organization to be certified tax-exempt, meaning it does not pay any federal income taxes. In addition to saving taxes, 501(c)(3) status gives the recipient organization the ability to legally tell donors that their donations are also tax-exempt, which makes such donations a way to decrease the amount on which taxpayers would have to pay income taxes. This is one of the big incentives to nonprofits to increase the attractiveness of getting donations.

Whichever legal form you choose, you file the forms and your articles of incorporation in your base state of operations, and then need to typically file with the federal IRS for what is called a **501(c)(3)** tax exemption (or for very small nonprofits a Form 1023-EZ). States also have tax exemptions for nonprofits, and you'll have to fill out those forms too. Nolo has a list of state government websites for nonprofit filings at www.nolo.com/legal-encyclopedia/form-nonprofit-501c3-corporation-30228.html. In addition to these filings, you'll create bylaws and get necessary licenses and permits, similarly to the way for-profit firms do.

For social ventures, where the firm is a for-profit but uses some or all of its profits to fund or underwrite social benefits, the standard legal forms of organization pose a problem. They assume the role of the firm is to make profits and distribute them to their owners or shareholders. In such a case, diverting profits to do some social good could be seen as contrary to the firm's obligation to owners, and the regular for-profit corporate forms of organization back these up legally.

So to make it possible for firms to be for-profit and pro-social-benefit, some new legal forms of organization have emerged including low-profit limited liability companies (L3Cs) and benefit corporations. Ten states have L3Cs and 35 have benefit corporations as legal forms you can use.[8] Using either of these approaches, you can use profits for social benefits, and investors will be able to see this up front because of the legal form of organization you have pursued.

But it is also possible to telegraph this sort of intent through a certification process available nationwide, called a certified B corp. This is available even in states lacking L3C or benefit corporation laws. The certification involves the issuing authority, B Lab (www.bcorporation.net), reviewing the firm every two years to make sure the firm's directors consider impact on all stakeholders (which include the environment, customers, suppliers, workers, and communities); that the firm's actions and performance are public and based on third-party standards; and that the firm achieves a passing score on B Lab's "B Impact Assessment." The assessment measures the impact of a business on all of its stakeholders (as mentioned); the firm's best practices regarding mission, measurement, and governance; and the firm's impact business model, which shows how the firm's social benefit role seeks to benefit a particular stakeholder through products and services or internal practices.

The B corp certification is a way to publicly inform potential investors that a for-profit firm is pursuing a social benefit role. While this doesn't negate the legal responsibility for making and distributing a profit, it does provide a way to publicly strike a different balance between profit and benefit in a way that is transparent enough that investors could not complain to the state about having their profits diverted to a social benefit.

LO **17-3** Learn how to master the process of negotiating.

Everything Is Negotiable, and Negotiation Is Everything

Some people argue that business is all about negotiation. While customers go into stores, find price tags, and pay the amount all the time, deals between businesses and even deals between businesses and consumers are often handled through a negotiation. Negotiations are discussions aimed at coming to an agreement about a particular outcome.

The ideal goal in a business negotiation is for each side to feel it got what it wanted. Leaving one side feeling a loss, particularly if someone thinks he or she lost and the other side won, only paves the way for future bad feelings, bad reputations, and bad negotiations. Often small businesses entering into negotiations worry that their youth, lack of experience, lack of track record, or lack of resources mean that there is no way they can win. Experience has shown that small businesses, even *new* small businesses, can do well in negotiations.

Use these four steps to structure a negotiation to achieve a winning solution for you and the other party: prepare, position, propose, and pounce.[9]

- **Prepare** what you need to achieve, what you are ready to give up, and what it takes to close rapidly once agreement is reached. Learn as much as you can about the other side, its track record, current situation, and possible needs.
- **Position** by putting your best foot forward, show confidence in yourself, your firm, and your prospects. Don't lie or mislead, but do not apologize. All businesses started small. With the right deals some small businesses grow large and bring their trading partners along with them. Talk about where you see your business in a couple of months or years. Position your firm as a good partner with which the other firm can ally.
- **Propose** solutions that provide value and balance for both you and the other party. This is often the hardest part of the negotiating process, but it is also the aspect that has received the most attention. Consider using these techniques for finding mutually winning propositions:
  - **Seek to create value:** Listen to what *drives* the other side's needs and seek alternative ways to solve the problem. For example, it says it needs money, but it may be able to work with more time, more flexibility, or a preferred treatment later. Adding new acceptable factors enlarges the negotiated pie.
  - **Seek long-term solutions:** Today you are small, but tomorrow you may be bigger, so think longer term.
  - **Seek balance:** Ideally, each side's contributions should closely balance. Where close balance is not easily achieved initially, structure contingent contracts to ensure balance later. For example, pay a small amount now to get started, but agree to pay a larger amount (e.g., a balloon payment) or a percentage of sales when sales reach a higher level.
  - **Seek mutual safety:** Where risk is faced, consider sharing risks and rewards so each party is providing some of the safety net for the other, and each shows commitment to the deal working out.
  - **Seek outcomes commensurate with investment:** Scale returns or considerations according to the size of the contribution of the party to your success. Aim to satisfy people or organizations that are major factors in your business, and realize you cannot accommodate every small contributors' every need.
- **Pounce** when agreement on any part of the negotiation appears at hand; move to close the deal on that issue. When you have an agreement, even on small issues, pounce on it as a positive outcome, an indicator of future deals to be made. Then get the deal down in writing. When stalled, ask the other party how to move forward.

One fear some people have is being dealt a dirty trick by the other side. Preparation and a long-term view help here. A dirty trick works only when the other party can be confident you will not be able to retaliate or tell others about the dirty trick, since publicizing it will ruin negotiations with others. One-time deals are more prone to dirty tricks; long-term arrangements make them harder to sustain. Also, knowing if the other party has done dirty tricks in the past can help you prepare for them. Being well networked (and letting the other party know you are) can also help since if you are tricked, you can let others know, minimizing the chance of the other party playing dirty tricks on others.

What makes all negotiations work is honesty. No one expects you to give up your secrets, but to build trust, you need to offer some information that helps the other side determine where to start negotiating. The optimal strategy is called *tit-tit-tat.*[10] Give up one piece of information on what you need or are willing to offer. Wait for an equal response. If you get one, your negotiation is off to a good start. If you do not get a response, offer one more piece of information. Wait for a response. If you do not get one, bring up the point that so far in the negotiation you have made all the overtures. If the other side is serious about coming to a fair deal, it needs to step up to the table and start talking seriously. If not, then it is clear it is not interested in striking a fair deal, and the negotiation must obviously be over.[11]

Along these lines, another negotiating tactic that lets you be open about your goals without giving away your secrets involves prioritizing your goals. Let us say you know three key goals you hope to achieve. Go into the negotiations asking for 5 or even 10 goals. In the bargaining process, you can "give up" some of your demands to show the other side you are willing to compromise. As long as you gain some or all of the three key goals you wanted, you are ahead of the game by negotiating.[12]

Always keep issues of legality in the back of your mind when negotiating without a lawyer present. Let's say you negotiate a trade of services with another business–you print its ad brochure, it waterproofs your parking lot. Legal? Yes, *but* in barter arrangements, you are trading something of value. That means you need to count it when tax time rolls around. If you fail to account for it, you *have* done something illegal. Twists like that are a good reason to get lawyerly advice until you know enough to go solo.

LO **17-4** Recognize potential legal liabilities for your business.

Legal Liabilities

A huge concern for business owners is liability arising from the business. The simplest form of liability is direct liability. Simply put this means the business entity is responsible for something the entity has done. For example, when a customer goes into a fast-food restaurant and places an order, the restaurant employee is there representing the restaurant. The contract formed is between the customer and the restaurant, not between the customer and the employee. The employee is an agent of the entity, in this case the restaurant. The employee represents the entity. Through that employee's actions, the restaurant is now bound in contract to provide certain food at a certain price. Failure of the restaurant to honor its contractual obligations will bring direct liability on the restaurant. The liability could apply through contract or tort law, each of which is described next.

Torts: Responsibility for Your Actions and the Actions of Employees

Torts here are not fancy French desserts, but are civil (not criminal) wrongs. Torts can arise when a person's legal rights are violated in ways other than from a breach of contract. For example, where a person is hurt in a car accident caused by your driver, the tort issue is that the victim's right to travel down the road was impaired by the wrongful actions of your driver. Often when this happens the driver faces direct liability for causing the accident, but the employer can also be sued by the injured party for what is called **vicarious (indirect) liability**. Vicarious liability against a business is possible if the employee involved was an agent of the business and at the time of the accident doing work for the employer.

vicarious (indirect) liability Indirect liability or responsibility for the actions of another.

If your business is facing vicarious liability, there are two typical arguments you can try to deflect the liability: (1) the actor is not an employee, but an independent contractor; and (2) the actions were outside the scope of agency/employment. If you can prove that either one applies, your firm is not likely to be held for vicarious liability. The employee as an individual would face the liability alone.

The Independent Contractor Argument

Sidestepping the problem of agency is one of the reasons businesses often use **independent contractors**. If your firm publishes a cookbook series, and you sell it door-to-door through independent contractors, and one of those contractors accidentally damages a person's home while doing the sales pitch, your publishing company is not responsible for the damages–the independent contractor is.

independent contractors Persons working to achieve a certain goal without being subjected to substantial controls by another.

That kind of distancing makes independent contracting attractive to small businesses. The fact that the entrepreneur doesn't pay benefits for an independent contractor makes it even more attractive. It is so attractive that the IRS takes claims of independent contractor arrangements very seriously. According to the IRS, to be an independent contractor the person has to display three characteristics:[13]

1. **Behavioral:** The contractor solely decides how the work is to be done.
2. **Financial:** The contractor pays his or her own expenses (e.g., benefits, tools, purchases) directly rather than having the employer pay them.
3. **Relational:** The independent contractor is employed for a project or a distinct term and the service the contractor provides is not central to the operation of the business.

There are many ways to show these three characteristics, and the IRS can look beyond the three. For example, if the entrepreneur is not paying the contractor benefits, but also pays no or almost no benefits to employees, the contractor could look to the IRS like another employee. If the IRS classifies the independent contractor as an employee, the firm becomes responsible for damages, but also for benefits not paid, and for the taxes and workers' compensation sidestepped–the latter two with penalties possibly added. Check with a lawyer ahead of time to make sure you are using independent contractors correctly.

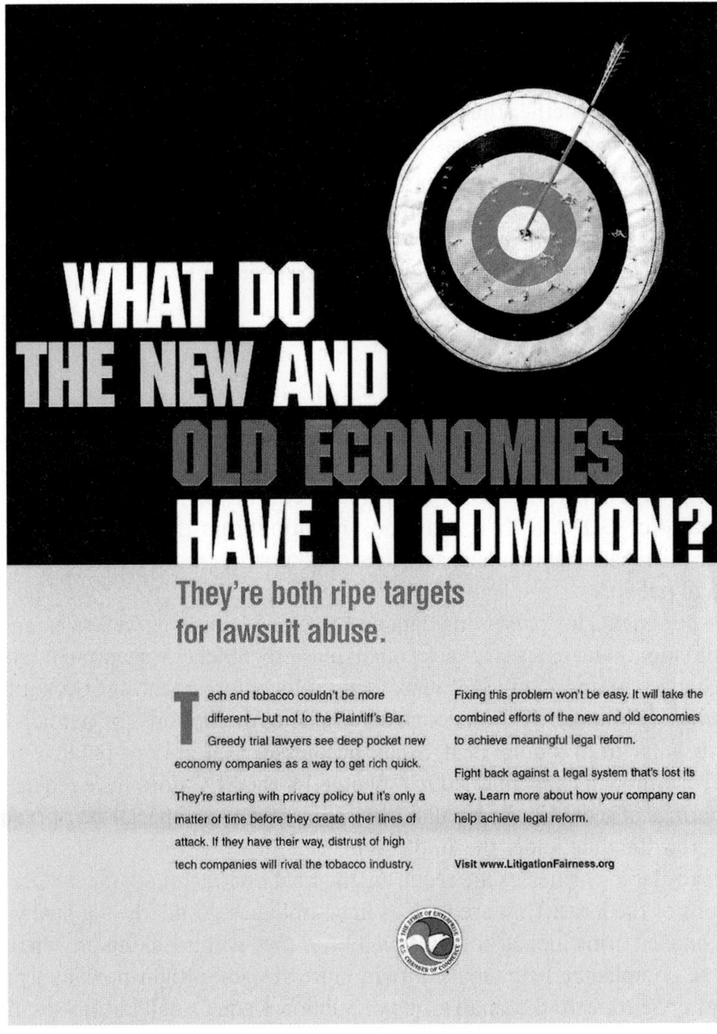

Protect yourself and your business from unnecessary lawsuits, which can quickly cripple your best-laid plans. The very first step in doing so is to develop clear guidelines for your employees to follow in regulating their conduct on the job and give them complete training programs on how to apply the guidelines.

Litigation Fairness

Another approach to protection against liability is to train employees to avoid problems. Training employees on diverse issues such as safety measures, including spotting hazards at the business and how to treat customers, can drastically lower the exposure to liability for a business.

The Scope of Authority Argument

Another important part of agency law involves the amount of authority given to each agent. Employees differ in their job descriptions and responsibilities, so it is common for them to also differ in the amount of authority they have to handle their jobs. In practice this relates to the activities an employee can do and make decisions about without checking with their boss for approval. If employees make a decision requiring more authority than they really possess, the business can argue it was not liable for the problem.

For this argument to work, the firm needs to show that it fully trains or informs the employees of the exact authority they possess–when they can decide for themselves, and when they need approval from higher-ups. It also helps to include informing employees that they may face personal liability for problems that arise from their exceeding their authority. The business also ought to take steps to convey to its customers what the authority level of an employee is. For example, calling a salesclerk a "retail manager" would give the wrong impression of how much authority the clerk possesses.

Similarly it is important that management take appropriate steps to listen to employees. This is because one of the rules of agency law is that notice to an agent can serve as notice to the business itself. For example, if a customer comes into a retail store and announces to the employees that sleet has started falling on the steps outside, the business itself is now on notice that there is a hazard. If someone subsequently falls on that slick, frozen surface, the question may arise as to whether the business was negligent in clearing the icy area. The business will be unable to argue that it was unaware of the hazard. The court will be looking at what would be reasonable to expect of the business in terms of how quickly the area was cleaned up after any member of the business had notice of this problem. It is important to note that these issues work only where the concerns revolve around civil law. If it is a case of criminal law (see the following Thoughtful Entrepreneur), another, tougher standard applies.

SOX and Dealing with Big Businesses

Sarbanes-Oxley Act (SOX) A federal law describing the steps publicly traded businesses must take to protect and provide their key financial information.

If you have involved business dealings with a publicly traded company, or are subcontracting with one, partnering with one, or being bought by one, or if you have plans to become a publicly traded company, or even if you have government contracts, you need to be aware of the **Sarbanes-Oxley Act (SOX)**. SOX is legislation resulting from the Enron and other scandals, and its purpose is to make the financial activities of companies more visible to the shareholders, government, and public.

SOX has requirements for preserving data and tracking its use, as well as extensive financial reporting requirements and external checks on all of these. Since its inception in 2002, the Securities and Exchange Commission (SEC) has focused its enforcement of SOX on large publicly traded businesses. While the SEC has considered giving exemptions for publicly traded small businesses, this is far from a done deal. Small businesses that are not publicly traded are not covered by SOX, although as mentioned in Chapter 14, the SEC does have requirements for direct public offerings of securities by small businesses, as well as a special set of requirements for firms seeking crowdfunding under the JOBS Act.

However, many large businesses are requiring their subcontractors to meet SOX standards, so all of the actions of the larger firm are seen as in compliance. Similarly, big businesses thinking about buying smaller firms look at the SOX liabilities they will be taking on when they buy the smaller firm, so compliance helps make a firm more saleable. Right now, at a practical level, SOX officially applies only to the small group of publicly traded small businesses, but if you find you are being asked by big corporate partners or investors to start operating under SOX rules,

THE THOUGHTFUL ENTREPRENEUR

Dealing with Criminal Companies

Here's an example to think about. Suppose a business markets some sort of medical device used to close wounds. Assuming this device is widely sold and used, many thousands of patients may come in contact with the device. If the device is poorly designed or manufactured, one can imagine situations in which infections could result from the use of this product. Assume further that employees of the business know of the problem and do nothing to improve the product or to warn the users of this product. Perhaps the company has even been issued a warning of some sort from a governmental agency on this matter.

Even though the business entity itself cannot form criminal intent like a human being, if that entity produces or sells a product that is widely used, the potential to harm a great number of people is certainly present. The prevailing thought is that such businesses are subject to criminal prosecution in order to protect the public from harm and secondarily as a warning to others who might contemplate similar actions.

In other words, nowadays, there are cases in which the business itself (e.g., the corporation, partnership, or LLC) or management can be held *criminally* liable for damages caused by the actions of its employees. If management directs, encourages, knows of, or in some cases should have known of criminal behavior of others in the organization, the company and management may be held criminally liable. Of course, a nonhuman business form cannot be put in jail, but in such cases the business can be, and often is, fined a substantial amount of money as punishment.

There are also specific statutes that provide criminal penalties against businesses (as well as managers and, under certain circumstances, owners) if those statutes are violated. Examples of these statutes are laws that protect the public health and environment, certain tax laws, and certain employment laws protecting employees from sexual discrimination and harassment.

the only way to handle it is to get legal and accounting advice on how to do it correctly. It is not something that works as a do-it-yourself project.

What Is the Right Level of Paranoia?

Considering all the ways a firm can face legal threats can bring any entrepreneur to a point of paranoia. Is there any way to avoid being sued or taken to court? In reality the longer you are in business, the greater the likelihood that something will happen. But there are ways to think about your business and risks to help you manage and deal with any propensities you have for paranoia. The keys are:

1. **Plan to do good:** Planning to be honest and open from the start means you have less to hide, and probably will automatically take steps to do things the right way from the start.
2. **Check with a lawyer early on:** Talking to a lawyer early in the start-up process can help you learn what issues you need to deal with, and when you need to deal with them.
3. **Recognize the predictable surprises of business and life:** In life, you or an employee will get sick or injured or need to take time off for some reason; you will face an angry customer or get a threatening letter from a customer or his or her lawyer; you will fire some employee; or you will have someone renege on you. Thinking about these predictable surprises ahead of time gives you a chance to figure out what you will need to do and what preparatory steps to take so the surprise isn't so surprising–doing preparatory work, changing the way you do something, insuring your firm, or taking some other approach..

The point is that as the entrepreneur you need to think about liability, but your goal should be to think about it ahead of time, take steps to manage or prepare for it, and then stop worrying because you've done what you needed to.

Litigation versus Arbitration versus Mediation

litigation
A formal dispute resolution method that operates using the court system, typically with a lawyer representing each party.

Problems of contract or tort law can be handled either through litigation, through arbitration, or through mediation. **Litigation** uses the court system to settle differences. Whether you go to a small-claims court or go through a lawyer and the regular courts, the litigation approach is draining, both financially and emotionally, on both sides in a lawsuit. So before pursuing the litigation route, think through these issues to decide if litigation is right for you.

Either form of litigation means that prior efforts—letters, calls, or even visits—have failed. That will increase the emotional stakes for the entrepreneur and the defendant. While small-claims court is lawyer-free, it is not stress-free. It is a rare entrepreneur who really wants to play attorney when his or her own money and reputation is on the line. It is true that litigating going the lawyer route in the regular courts will cost money, time, and aggravation. It can cost to have the attorney handle correspondence and recovery efforts. If these don't solve the problem, you will pay additional fees for your attorney to take the case to court. And if you lose in regular court, you can be responsible for both sides' attorney's fees.

Our approach here is to recommend using an attorney from the start when creating contracts and setting up major deals or deals new to you and your firm. Why? There are four good reasons. First, in litigation, the only guaranteed winners are the attorneys. That is how they make their living, and particularly in business litigation, the case is not emotionally draining for them. Second, remember that good attorneys keep their clients *out* of court by writing better contracts and negotiating on behalf of their clients. If you are going to court, it means you have failed to win at the bargaining table. Third, remember that since litigation is so expensive, large, well-funded companies have a definite advantage over small businesses. And finally, beware of any attorney who guarantees a certain outcome in a case, particularly a jury trial. Human beings are not always predictable, and it is not all that unusual for a case to be decided in an unforeseen way. Of course, litigation can have wonderful outcomes for participants, but the point is that litigation can be risky, it often is expensive, and it always is emotionally demanding for the small business owner.

arbitration
A dispute resolution process held instead of court cases in which both sides present their case to a legal professional.

Given these cautions, if litigation does not make sense, a growing alternative is called *arbitration*. **Arbitration** is a way of settling disputes in place of going to court. Often it involves the two sides of a case presenting their perspective, facts, and materials to a private judge. If you agree to submit your dispute to arbitration, you are giving up a legal right to sue if you do not like the result. For that reason, an agreement to arbitrate should be in writing and should be given in exchange for something (a contract) if it is to be enforceable. Many of us unwittingly sign such agreements all the time. In a standard contract, such as an agreement with a brokerage firm to open an account, a contract for wireless service, and even in employment agreements, a closer look at the written contract terms may show that the parties have agreed, as part of the contract, to settle their disputes by the use of an arbitrator rather than by litigation.

mediation
A dispute resolution process held instead of court cases in which both sides present their case to a neutral third party who is not a judge. Unlike arbitration and court decisions, mediation decisions are not binding on the two parties.

A third choice is **mediation,** in which the dispute is put to a neutral third party who is not a judge. While arbitration and court cases have decisions that are binding, mediation works only if the two sides agree to the decision and settlement. If mediation fails, arbitration and litigation are still possible. Mediations are generally much faster to complete than either arbitration or litigation, and it is the least expensive of the three approaches. Mediation can even be used with the government, based on the rules set out in the Administrative Dispute Resolution Act, which is handled by the Federal Mediation and Conciliation Service (www.fmcs.gov). Outside of government, mediators and arbitrators generally come from the same sources, such as the American Arbitration Association (www.adr.org). A comparison of the three approaches is given in Table 17.8.

Generally, the optimal situation is to include a clause in your contracts requiring binding arbitration. If an issue arises, you can see if you can handle it yourself. If you cannot get satisfaction, think about asking for mediation, since it is the fastest and cheapest of the

TABLE 17.8 Litigation versus Arbitration versus Mediation

Litigation		Arbitration	Mediation
Regular Courts	**Small-Claims Court**		
Uses court system	Uses court system	Works outside the court system	Works outside the court system
Both parties represented by attorneys	Both sides represent themselves	Both sides represent themselves	Both sides represent themselves
Formal	Informal	Informal	Informal
Public judges	Public judges	Private judges	Attorneys or mediation specialists
Multiple levels of postdecision appeal	Appeal to regular court possible (varies by state)	Limited appeal possibilities	Full range of appeals
Can force the other party into court	Can force the other party into court	Occurs by agreement or accepting clause to arbitrate	Occurs only by mutual agreement
Binding decisions	Binding decision	Binding decision if agreed to beforehand	Nonbinding decision
Public	Public	Confidential	Confidential
Most costly	Least costly	Costly	Less costly
Slowest	Moderately fast	Moderately fast	Fastest
Favors those with more money for legal help	Friendly format for small businesses	More balanced than courts	Friendly format for small businesses

Sources: Adapted from John R. McGinley Jr., "Arbitration or Litigation? Having Trouble Choosing between the Two? Here Are Some Factors to Consider When Making Your Decision," *Entrepreneur*, April 1, 2002, www.entrepreneur.com/article/50350; A. Murad, "Mediation, Arbitration or Trial? Information to Make Your Decision With," *Entrepreneur*, February 19, 2016, www.entrepreneur.com/article/270724.

procedures. If mediation does not work, exercise the binding arbitration clause. If there was no clause, the best route is to negotiate on your own, mediate if possible, and then go to litigation.

Commonsense Ways to Avoid Torts

In addition to the obvious ways of avoiding being sued, such as making sure there are no hazards on your property, not infringing upon another's trademark, and impressing upon your employees the importance of safe driving, there is another method to avoid a lawsuit that is rarely mentioned. When it comes down to it, transactions between businesses and customers are an interchange of communications between people.

You know from personal experience that there are various ways of dealing with conflicts besides suing, the most obvious being communication and negotiation. You might think that lawsuits come as the result of a careful decision-making process, since they are so costly and time-consuming, but in reality lawsuits are often filed out of frustration or anger. It sounds simplistic, but people are less likely to sue someone they like or someone they perceive to be willing to work out the problem with them.

Take a moment to think about the actor Tom Hanks and former *American Idol* judge Simon Cowell. Both are wealthy. Imagine each caused a car wreck. Which one do you think is more likely to be sued? If Hanks and Cowell are at all like their screen personalities, Hanks is much less likely to be sued. Being perceived as a likable and genuinely concerned person can sometimes save you from an angry reaction. How do you achieve this? Try to develop client loyalty and give personal service. Listen to your customers. Besides helping the bottom line of your business, developing such relationships can keep you out of court.

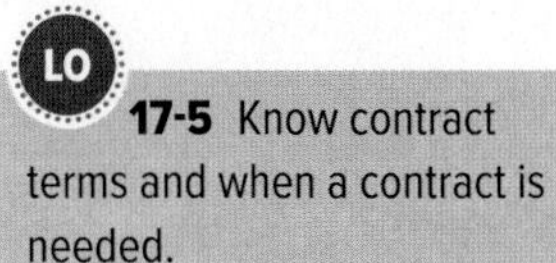

LO
17-5 Know contract terms and when a contract is needed.

Contracting

The vast majority of business law in the everyday operations of a business is contract law. Contracts are essentially agreements in which the parties exchange promises. Not all contracts have to be in writing to be enforceable. For example, one neighbor wishes to buy a snowblower from the other neighbor who is relocating to Hawaii. The two discuss the purchase agreement and decide on a price of $800. Nothing is put in writing. It is a spoken promise to pay $800 in exchange for a spoken promise to give possession and title to the snowblower. If it works out as described, fine. But if there is a problem, how can it be resolved? There is likely to be a difference of opinion on what was intended. Without a written contract, there is no way to be sure what should have happened.

Oral agreements are as legally binding as written ones, but when the two sides disagree, how can a court decide which of the two versions to believe? In reality, it is very difficult to enforce oral agreements (also called handshake agreements). Sometimes oral agreements are unavoidable, but even in those cases, you can make the oral agreement written.

It works best if you specify you will write up the agreement and send it to the other person as you are shaking hands on the deal, but even if you did not mention it, write up what you thought the two of you agreed to and mail (use certified mail if possible), fax, or email it to the other person. Mention in a note or letter accompanying the written form of the agreement that if the other person's recollection of the agreement is different, you would like to clarify what he or she thought was agreed to before either of you go further on the business deal–putting a deadline on the response can help move the work along. Follow up with the other person (preferably by certified mail or email so there is a record of your sending it) if you don't hear back by the deadline. Should you continue the business if the other person does not respond? That is up to you, but at least you know that the situation is risky, and you have also taken the initiative to clarify what the responsibilities are for you and the other person.

In business, there are several kinds of situations in which you want a lawyer to take charge in making things work; for example:

- **Standard contracts:** If you are going to use one type of contract over and over, such as a purchase order, have your attorney draft that contract so that agents of the company can just fill in the blanks as needed.
- **Specialty contracts:** Unique contract terms and/or large dollar amounts at stake usually require careful drafting and legal counsel.
- **Interstate contracts:** When doing business outside your home state, it makes sense to have your lawyer draw up the contract because state laws vary. Charging 20 percent interest on financed purchases may be all right in your state, but this rate may be illegally high in another.
- **Noncompete clauses:** In a **noncompete clause** someone promises not to open a competing business or to go to work for a competitor.[14] Such clauses are tricky because they need to be part of another agreement and cannot stand alone. They also have to be reasonable. You cannot keep people out of their line of business forever, nor can you force them to leave town to practice their business. A lawyer can tell you what is reasonable for the kind of situation you face.
- **Exculpatory clauses:** **Exculpatory clauses** say that a party to the contract will not be responsible for certain things. An example of an exculpatory agreement is the statement on the claim check for dry cleaning that says the dry cleaner will not be responsible for any damages to clothing. This may not be true, but such statements are "cheap" to make, just the cost of the ink and paper. The only chance for having one that works is to have a lawyer draft it.
- **Hold harmless agreements:** By agreeing to a **hold harmless** clause in a contract (also called a **waiver**), one party is agreeing not to hold the other responsible for his or her actions. In other words, one party is giving up legal rights to sue or otherwise enforce his or her rights. Courts tend not to like such agreements, so again the best chance to have an agreement that holds up in court is to have a lawyer draft it. If you see such a clause in a contract, let *your* lawyer advise you what to do. A workable clause makes it possible for Ann Williams to run a children's gym (see the following Small Business Insight).

noncompete clause
Part of a contract in which a person agrees not to open a certain type business or seek employment doing certain things in a particular area for a period of time.

exculpatory clause
Part of a contract in which a party to the contract states that he or she will not be responsible for certain actions.

hold harmless
A type of waiver in which a party agrees not to hold another party responsible for certain events.

waiver
Part of a contract in which a party intentionally gives up legal rights or claims.

Contracting often seems intimidating, with all the small print and often official-sounding language. But the point in contracting is to make sure *your* needs and goals are covered. Three

SMALL BUSINESS INSIGHT

ANN WILLIAMS AND HEAD OVER HEELS[15]

Ann Williams and her husband Craig bought Head Over Heels, a children's gym in Birmingham, Alabama, in 2000. Ann had been a gymnast at Auburn University and had worked for another gym in town gaining experience. A key problem facing any gym—but especially one that focuses on children—is liability. Young bones and muscles are easily hurt, and while children are resilient, parents often are not.

The Williamses have liability insurance, but to keep it reasonably priced and to provide assurance to the parents (which is far more important in the long run), Ann makes sure parents know that every instructor is trained on safety issues and puts the safety of the children first. Additionally the gym has only the finest equipment. With all these in place, it is easier for Ann to get parents to sign a lawyer-drafted agreement, in which parents recognize the possibility of injury to their child and hold the business harmless for injuries.

ways to help take some of the fear out of contracting include:[16]

- Put in a binding arbitration clause to minimize the possibility of court expenses (and because small businesses often do better before arbitrators than judges).
- When sued, call your insurance agent first. Your business liability insurance may cover not only the settlement costs, but often even your legal fees.
- Consider getting extra liability insurance if you fear you will be facing added business risks. For example, if you expand your business into a wealthy neighborhood, you might want to have an extra $1 million in insurance coverage.

Subcontracting

As the term indicates, a **subcontract** may be necessary to fulfill the promises of a "larger" contract. Particularly in small businesses, many support types of tasks such as human resources and marketing are often subcontracted, thereby allowing for fewer employees and thus lower salary and benefit costs to the business. Generally speaking, the same contract principles apply to both regular and subcontracts.

subcontract
A contract by which a new party agrees to perform a duty that one of the original parties to a contract was already legally obligated to perform.

Subcontracting has one unique aspect: Saying that the subcontractor did not perform does not get you off the hook. Imagine you get a contract from Ford to make rearview mirrors. You subcontract out making the glass, while you concentrate on the housing. Your subcontractor does not deliver. Who gets sued? It is you. Your firm signed the Ford contract, so you are responsible. You can sue the subcontractor, but you still have obligations to Ford, and can be sued by Ford.

Internet Issues in Contracting

Small businesses have blossomed through the Internet. They have taken their place in commerce alongside brick-and-mortar establishments. Contract law that has existed for hundreds of years is now being applied to Internet transactions. Courts are being asked to apply this old, standard contract law to new situations arising in e-commerce as legislatures try to enact new statutes specifically addressing contract law as applied to e-commerce. In the meantime, certain problems can be anticipated.

In **business-to-business (B2B)** transactions, contracts often involve electronic data interchange (EDI). These systems link suppliers of raw materials and components with wholesalers and retailers, usually using the Internet but occasionally using dedicated lines or satellites. In this way, for example, an order for new inventory may be submitted electronically. B2B systems are generally used in situations in which repeat transactions are entered into and there is generally a master contract or umbrella contract that states the terms of the transactions covered, leaving, for example, quantity and prices to be determined in each transaction. These master agreements between the parties are known as *trading partner agreements.* You need to have your lawyer review these before you enter into any major EDI effort.

business-to-business (B2B)
Business-to-business transactions using e-commerce.

business-to-consumer (B2C)
Business-to-consumer transactions using e-commerce.

Another type of Internet contract is the **business-to-consumer (B2C)** contract. This is commonly used by small businesses to sell over the Internet. Here are a couple of pointers for setting up the websites. First, if you want to ensure control over the selling process, make it very clear on the website that the representations of merchandise or services are not actual offers to the buyer. Direct wording to that effect is common on many websites. The reason for this is so that the seller is not tied into a certain price and that the buyer cannot create the contract simply by accepting in the form of placing an order. In setting up a website, in addition to stating that information on the site is merely informational and not an offer, the site might also contain a statement to the effect that the seller reserves the right not to sell to everyone and that the website seller need not accept the buyer's offer. This gives the seller some control over pricing and also, in this new world of terrorism, allows the seller to not sell certain merchandise if he or she considers it a risk.

Another issue with online contracting is how to handle contracts that are required to be in writing to be enforceable. Historically contracts needed a "wet signature" of the party to be held responsible. That has extended to legally permit e-signature technologies. Permissible techniques include click-through agreements or signature pads or electronic signatures. You can get an e-signature from many vendors (search online for "e-signature") like DocuSign.com. You can even search for "free e-signature," which will turn up https://esignatures.com/ offering two free per month, www.digisigner.com offering three free per month, and Hellosign.com also giving you three free per month.

Although not an issue in business contracting, there is one other Internet-related issue with legal overtones–how a business handles email. As business email becomes more important, more problems have arisen with employee misuse of these tools. For that reason, it is very important that businesses, big and small, establish policies for employees on usage of the Internet and email.

If your employees have access to the Internet at work, make it very clear how that access can be used both in terms of amount of time spent and sites visited. Employees should be informed (ideally through a written communication such as an employee handbook or written notice) about the company's policy regarding usage of the Internet for personal business. For example, are employees allowed to access Internet sites for sports scores, sexually explicit materials, stock quotes, and online shopping while "on the clock"? If not, you need to specify this.

For email, the essential message that must be conveyed (again, ideally through a written communication such as an employee handbook or written notice) to employees is that the business owns the email system and has full rights to monitor that system. This even includes email in outside Internet service providers (ISPs) (like a personal email account) that is accessed from work. In fact, over 50 percent of U.S. companies monitor employee email, and 22 percent of companies have terminated an employee for misuse.[17]

Employees should be informed of policy regarding personal use of the email system at work. For example, are employees allowed to send emails at work informing co-workers that their children are selling cookies for scouts or candy bars for the baseball team? In addition, employees should be told explicitly what is considered inappropriate content of emails. Clearly, unauthorized transfer of trade secrets is a huge concern of business owners and should be prohibited as well as email that contains offensive sexual, ethnic, or racial messages. Besides monitoring email for misuse by employees, it can be very beneficial for a company to monitor its system as a way to ensure proper customer service. A good rule of thumb is that nothing should be sent by email that you wouldn't be embarrassed to read on the front page of the newspaper. Once that send button is clicked, it may be impossible to limit access to that message.

intangible property
Property that has no value of its own but that represents value, such as a stock certificate.

patent
A grant by the U.S. government to an inventor for an idea that is new, useful, and nonobvious, giving the inventor the exclusive right to make, use, or sell his or her idea.

trade secret
Confidential information within a company that gives that company a competitive advantage.

copyright
Exclusive right given to the creator of a literary or artistic work to make use of that work.

trademark
Distinctive word, slogan, or image that identifies a product and its origin.

Intellectual Property

LO **17-6** Understand the basics of intellectual property.

When you worry about making copies of books or songs, you are dealing with issues of intellectual property (IP). Intellectual property is a type of **intangible property** in which what is being protected is an idea or a form of expression. This includes the law of **patents**, **trade secrets**, **copyrights**, and **trademarks**. It also touches on the creation of a trade name for a business. In reality, a start-up will create a large number of properties that could be protected. Table 17.9 provides a checklist of many of the most common sorts of intellectual properties a start-up might create and

TABLE 17.9 IP Checklist: Finding and Protecting IP in Your Business

Aspect of Your Business	Form of IP Protection
Business Identity	
Business name, logos, and hashtags	Trademark/service mark
	Fictitious name registration, incorporation (C corp, LLC, etc.—consider in your home state versus an "away" state)
	URL in multiple domains (.com, .net, .org, .biz, .us, etc.), digital watermarking for logos, TM/SM, register hashtags at **twubs.com**
Business Materials	
Brochures, sales materials, publicly visible pages on your website	Copyright (or Creative Commons), digital watermarking for your photos, logos, audio, and video
Documents, forms, and spreadsheets used internally by your firm to make decisions or perform evaluations	Trade secret
Your customer list or database	Trade secret
Your catalog	Copyright (or Creative Commons) (design may be covered by trade dress), digital watermarking for the electronic copy
Your price list	Trade secret
Your investors or funding sources	Trade secret (except where disclosure is required by law)
Interactive web elements like tweets, postings, blogs, videos, podcasts, etc.	Copyright (or Creative Commons) (design elements may be protected by trade dress or design patents or both), digital watermarking for your photos, logos, audio, and video
Uniforms or decor specialized for your business	Trade dress
Specialized designs used elsewhere in your business (e.g., magazine covers, custom packaging)	Trade dress
Product/Service and Its Design	
Name of your product or service	Trademark/service mark, URL in multiple domains (e.g., **dietcoke.com**, .net, etc.)
Distinctive product design (e.g., a Coke bottle)	Design patent
Your product (if it does something new or in a new way)	Patent
Your type of business service if it is new or different (e.g., Amazon's one-click ordering)	Business method patent
The process underlying your service (if it is new or does things in a new way)	Business method patent
Internal code of your website, especially code that "does the work" of the website	Trade secret (also use techniques like server-side scripting so the user cannot see the code that contains your "secret sauce") Patent (where possible)
Web mash-ups, widgets, gadgets (if it does something new or different)	Business method patent, permission from data sources

(Continued)

TABLE 17.9 (Continued)

Your method for legally decreasing or deferring taxes	Tax patent
A new chemical process or product	Chemical patent
A new circuit or computer chip	Electrical patent
A biological organism or a new gene sequence	Biological/gene patent
Business Partnering	
Use of brand names (and/or logos) of components or services used by your firm	Permission of the vendor
Use of brand names (and/or logos) of customers of your firm	Permission of the customer

Note: Consider getting common misspellings of your business name to protect it, along with [business name]online, my[business name], or [business name]isgreat.

design patent
A 14-year patent for a new, original, and ornamental design for an article of manufacture.

utility patent
A 20-year patent covering a process, machine, article of manufacture, composition of matter, or any new or useful improvement of an existing one.

plant patent
A 20-year patent that covers new strains of living plant organisms, algae, or macro fungi.

opinion of patentability
A report (typically written as a letter) from a patent attorney or patent agent that is his or her professional opinion of the possibility of obtaining a patent for an idea that you have explained. The opinion is based on the attorney's or agent's research of patents for similar or related ideas. Typically the first official step in the patenting process.

provisional patent
A preliminary description of your idea submitted to the U.S. Patent Office according to its specifications. It is intended to serve as a sort of placeholder for a full (or regular) patent, which needs to be filed within one year of the filing of the provisional patent.

infringer
Someone who uses intellectual property without the permission of the owner.

offers some of the ways these typically get protected. Intellectual property laws are most active at the federal level, although trademarks and service marks can be registered with any state also. Remember, state level laws vary dramatically, so check what laws apply (and how) in your state.

Patents and Trade Secrets

To protect new ideas from being used by others, the owner can obtain a patent issued by the U.S. Patent Office (www.uspto.gov) or keep the information as a trade secret. A **design patent** (which lasts 14 years) covers the look of a product and those parts that are essential or part of the design. **Utility patents** cover processes and functions and last 20 years. There are even **plant patents** for newly created strains of living matter, which last 20 years from when the patent application is filed. A great first stop at the Patent Office website (www.uspto.gov) is the "Inventor and Entrepreneur Resources" page at www.uspto.gov/learning-and-resources/inventors-entrepreneurs-resources. It can tell you most of what you will want to know.

The patent process generally starts with a patent search to see if others have invented what you propose. You can try this yourself at www.uspto.gov or commercial sites like SumoBrain.com, but in reality the only way to be sure is to have a patent attorney or registered patent agent do the search. He or she should give you an **opinion of patentability**, which is an analysis of the potential for your idea being patentable. If you get a favorable opinion, the next step is usually to file a **provisional patent** as soon as possible. This is a placeholder for the idea that gives you one year to file the regular patent, like those types described previously. Again, this is something you can try yourself, but is much more likely to work better if you have a patent attorney do it. The final stage is to file that full patent application within the year while the provisional is in force.

Because of the complexity in this area of the law (starting with the question of whether an idea *is* patentable), it is highly unlikely that an inventor could obtain a patent without the services of a patent attorney. To get an idea of how complex patent applications are, look at the patent application in Figure 17.2 for the patent granted to Joe Fischer, whose story started Chapter 7. This patent application is for the basic design of a Greetabl gift box. It is important to remember that patents don't require the item to be high tech, just a new way of doing something useful.

Patents are essentially monopolies granted to inventors by the U.S. government giving patent owners the exclusive rights to make, use, or sell that invention for a certain period of time. Once the patent is issued, anyone can have access to the information covered by the patent, but people cannot make use of that information without the consent of the patent holder. Persons doing so are known as **infringers** and are subject to being sued by the patent holder.

Whether an idea is patentable and whether it should be patented or whether an idea can or should be protected as a trade secret are questions for a patent attorney. There are certain ideas that can be patented and also would be suitable for protection as a trade secret.[18] The kinds of issues the lawyer considers include whether the idea might be useful past the 20-year expiration of a patent, the ease of reverse engineering the process or product, if the idea under consideration is

FIGURE 17.2

Section of a Patent Application

Source: Joseph M. Fischer

US00D727144S

(12) **United States Design Patent**
Fischer

(10) **Patent No.:** **US D727,144 S**
(45) **Date of Patent:** ** **Apr. 21, 2015**

(54) **CUBE-SHAPED BOX AND BLANK**

(71) Applicant: **GreetingQUBE, LLC**, Washington, MO (US)

(72) Inventor: **Joseph M. Fischer**, Washington, MO (US)

(73) Assignee: **GreetingQUBE, LLC**, Washington, MO (US)

(**) Term: **14 Years**

(21) Appl. No.: **29/446,948**

(22) Filed: **Feb. 28, 2013**

(51) **LOC (10) Cl.** **09-03**

(52) **U.S. Cl.**
USPC **D9/433**

(58) **Field of Classification Search**
CPC B65D 5/00; B65D 5/0015; B65D 5/0045; B65D 5/18; B65D 5/40; B65D 5/2033; B65D 1/22; B65D 1/225; B65D 1/24; B65D 1/34; B65D 1/38
USPC D9/414–433, 444–445, 456, 711, 715, D9/718, 748; D7/601, 602, 538, 540, D7/550.1; D3/203.5, 202, 207, 210
See application file for complete search history.

(56) **References Cited**

U.S. PATENT DOCUMENTS

1,847,598 A * 3/1932 Cornell 229/120

(Continued)

Primary Examiner — Susan Bennett Hattan
Assistant Examiner — Vy Koenig
(74) *Attorney, Agent, or Firm* — Thompson Coburn LLP

(57) **CLAIM**

The ornamental design for a cube-shaped box and blank, as shown and described.

DESCRIPTION

FIG. **1** is a top plan view of a first configuration of a cube-shaped box and blank showing my new design;
FIG. **2** is a bottom view of the cube-shaped box and blank of FIG. **1**;
FIG. **3** is a left side view of the cube-shaped box and blank of FIG. **1**;
FIG. **4** is a right side view of the cube-shaped box and blank of FIG. **1**;
FIG. **5** is a front view of the cube-shaped box and blank of FIG. **1**;
FIG. **6** is a rear view of the cube-shaped box and blank of FIG. **1**;
FIG. **7** is a perspective view of an alternate configuration of the cube-shaped box and blank of FIG. **1** folded along fold lines to form a cube-shaped box;
FIG. **8** is a top plan view of a first configuration of an alternate embodiment of a cube-shaped box and blank showing my new design;
FIG. **9** is a bottom view of the cube-shaped box and blank of FIG. **8**;
FIG. **10** is a left side view of the cube-shaped box and blank of FIG. **8**;
FIG. **11** is a right side view of the cube-shaped box and blank of FIG. **8**;
FIG. **12** is a front view of the cube-shaped box and blank of FIG. **8**;
FIG. **13** is a rear view of the cube-shaped box and blank of FIG. **8**; and
FIG. **14** is a perspective view of an alternate configuration of the cube-shaped box and blank of FIG. **8** folded along fold lines to form a cube-shaped box;
FIG. **15** is a top plan view of a first configuration of an alternate embodiment of a cube-shaped box and blank showing my new design;
FIG. **16** is a bottom view of the cube-shaped box and blank of FIG. **15**;
FIG. **17** is a left side view of the cube-shaped box and blank of FIG. **15**;
FIG. **18** is a right side view of the cube-shaped box and blank of FIG. **15**;
FIG. **19** is a front view of the cube-shaped box and blank of FIG. **15**;
FIG. **20** is a rear view of the cube-shaped box and blank of FIG. **15**; and,
FIG. **21** is a perspective view of an alternate configuration of the cube-shaped box and blank of FIG. **15** folded along fold lines to form a cube-shaped box.
In the drawings, the light weight lines identify creases or fold lines of the cube-shaped box and blank. The heavy weight lines define the outer periphery of the cube-shaped box and blank. The dashed lines define areas which form no part of the claimed design and identify area(s) where a greeting or other indicia may be displayed.

1 Claim, 12 Drawing Sheets

easily visible to competitors (or buried in other aspects of the process or product), or if it is likely someone will invent it independently. Obviously, if an invention would not be eligible for a patent, its only protection might be as a trade secret. Once again, a patent attorney is the appropriate source to help the business owner make that determination.

Here is an important word of warning: Be extremely wary of companies stating that they will assist you in finding financial backers to develop your new idea or that they will assist you in patenting your new idea. Do not deal with these companies. They are often out to steal unprotected, new ideas from inventors. Before sharing information on a new idea to obtain financing or marketing assistance, that idea must first be protected as a trade secret or by a patent.

grace period
An idea in patent law that says disclosing the idea starts a one-year clock for filing a provisional or regular patent, where the disclosure would not count as "prior art" and disqualify the idea from being patented (since as "prior art" it was already publicly known). These grace period disclosures are strongest if they are limited to specific people (versus publicizing an idea on the Internet or in mass media).

Also be aware that the United States and the rest of the world run with different laws regarding patents. One of the key differences between the two approaches is when you need to file your patent applications in order to qualify for patent protection if and when a patent is granted. In the United States you have what is called a **grace period**, one year from the first time you disclose your idea outside your firm or to the public (via the web, printing, or a public presentation). In the rest of the world, you need to file your patent application *before* you disclose it publicly. So if you plan to file patents in Europe, Asia, Africa, or South America, start your patent filings before you disclose to the public. Also check the World Intellectual Property Organization's database at www.wipo.int/reference/en/ to see if your idea has popped up elsewhere. Outside the United States, patent applications are publicly available while in the United States, only granted patents can be searched.

In general, it makes a lot of sense to file before you talk about your idea to anyone, other than a patent attorney. Anyone to whom you disclose an idea could beat you to a filing, and then you could well be out of luck because since the 2013 America Invents Act, America has switched to a first-to-file approach. So filing a provisional patent application electronically with the U.S. Patent Office is a good way to start–*after* you talk to a patent attorney (the U.S. Patent Office lists them). Do not worry, talking to your attorney does not count as a public disclosure. While there are books showing patent filing as a do-it-yourself project, in reality the vast majority of patents granted to individuals are those filed by professional patent attorneys and patent agents. To give your patent the best chance of surviving, this is a case where you want to go with the pros.

A *trade secret* is not created by the government but is information known to certain people in the company that makes that company more competitive. Trade secrets include more than patents. A trade secret can be a formula (e.g., the formula for the KFC "11 herbs and spices" chicken coating), the name of the company's top salesperson, or details of (or even acknowledgment of) the upcoming ad campaign. One rule of thumb when considering whether certain information is a trade secret is to ask whether a competitor would be willing to pay for that information. If the answer is yes, then you may have an idea that is protectable as a trade secret.

To protect a trade secret, the secret literally must be kept a secret from all except those who need to know to operate the business. The most famous example of a trade secret is the formula for Coca-Cola Classic. Had that recipe been patented back in the late 1800s, the company would have had exclusive rights to it for 17 years under the patent laws in effect at that time (today it would have had the rights for 20 years). Then, after 17 years, anyone could follow the recipe and make the beverage known to us as Coca-Cola. However, by treating the formula as a trade secret and successfully keeping the formula a secret from outsiders for all these many years, Coca-Cola still has exclusive rights to its use. There is no expiration date for trade secrets. There are five steps to protecting trade secrets:[19]

1. **Ensure that the trade secrets are really secrets:** They cannot be shared with others or be likely to be known by others.
2. **Use warning labels:** Put "confidential" on *every* page that contains trade secrets. The full legal version can go on the front page of the document, and it looks like this:
   This item/document/material contains CONFIDENTIAL TRADE SECRET INFORMATION owned by [THE LEGAL NAME OF YOUR COMPANY] and/or its affiliated companies. This information is protected by applicable state law and may be protected by the federal Economic Espionage Act of 1996 (18 U.S.C. Sec. 1831), which provides for criminal penalties of up to 15 years in prison and/or a $5 million fine for stealing, receiving, possessing and/or duplicating any information contained herein.
3. **Restrict physical access:** Coca-Cola has a big vault. You can get by with a locked cabinet or a password protected file, but if you have a secret, it should be locked up when not in use.
4. **Get signed confidentiality agreements:** Only people who sign one of these (have your lawyer draft it) get to handle, see, or hear the trade secret material.
5. **Keep doing steps 1 through 4:** A trade secret is enforceable only as long as you take positive steps to protect it. If you get lazy, the secret may get out and you have no protection.

Wrongful acquisition of a trade secret is a tort and if certain behavior, such as trespassing or bribery, is involved in getting the information, criminal violations may also have taken place. Concern over protection of trade secrets can justify use of a noncompete agreement to help protect against former employees taking that information to new employers.

Copyright

Copyright involves the expression of ideas, not (as with patents and trade secrets) the ideas themselves. For example, if a greeting card company creates a picture of a single sunflower for use on a greeting card, what can be copyrighted is that particular rendition of a single sunflower. Copyright does not mean that no one else can create a card with a single sunflower (which would use that idea). That *particular* image of a sunflower is protected, so another person or company cannot use that same image without permission. Copyrights for new works last for the creator's life plus 70 years. If it is a "work for hire" bought from the creator, the copyright lasts for 120 years after creation or 95 years after its first publication, whichever is less.

Writers, artists, and others who create unique expressions of ideas automatically copyright those expressions by creating their work. Even though it is not now required, it is a very good idea to place a notice on your original creation such as a book, painting, sculpture, computer program, or musical score that the work is copyrighted. Placing a notice on the work is done by using the word *copyright*, *copr.*, or ©, the creator's name, and the year of creation. Because original works are automatically copyrighted, this notice does not create the copyright, but it puts others on notice that the materials cannot be copied without permission of the copyright holder and will prevent any infringer from successfully arguing that he or she didn't know the materials were copyrighted.

The government does not create copyrights. However, copyrights on works can be registered with the federal government (www.copyright.gov) for more complete protection of the work(s). Registration with the government of copyrighted materials will establish a presumption as to ownership of the work. However, registration is not generally done unless wide distribution of those materials is planned.

One of the recurring issues for self-employed professionals, web designers, and artists is who owns the work they do for others. Unless there is a contract giving the hiring individual rights to the material (making the project into a "work for hire" in copyright law), the creator owns the material. Often freelancers have developed a set of materials, templates, or designs that they adapt for a variety of clients. If that is your plan, you need to make sure you retain the intellectual property rights to the materials you develop. You can grant the client rights to the specific products from your project, while retaining the rights to the underlying intellectual property for use in other projects. In these work-for-hire contracts, the typical approach is to license to the hiring party the particular creative materials produced. The license can be limited by duration (it is yours for a year), territory (you can use it in your city), media (you can use it only on the web), or exclusivity (others may not have a logo similar to the one made for you). There are work-for-hire templates available, and it is a good idea to get with a lawyer early in your business to sort out how to create a standard contract to protect your ideas and your business.

Trademarks

One last area of intellectual property, *trademark*, can be of particular significance to small business owners. Trademarks identify certain goods. A trademark will indicate the source of particular goods, for example, a Mini Cooper automobile, and not just any automobile. A related concept using the same law is a service mark. Service marks identify services. Some words or groups of words such as WW® can be both trademarks (applicable to foods sold under this name) and service marks (identifying services such as programs of instruction on dietary management).

Once a mark is established as identifying certain goods or services, the owner of the mark can keep others from using a similar or identical mark to identify similar or identical goods. As with other intellectual property, anyone using the mark without permission is an infringer and is subject to legal action, such as Ty, Inc. learned in 2004 when it was sued by a small business (see the following Small Business Insight). A trademark once granted lasts for 10 years and can continue to be renewed for another 10 years at a time.

Trademark issues can come up at the very beginning when a name is being chosen for a new business. It is important to check to see what marks are already being used to identify goods and

SMALL BUSINESS INSIGHT

PEACEABLE PLANET AND "NILES"[20]

Peaceable Planet is a very small toy maker from Savannah, Georgia, that makes a line of plush toy dolls. In 1999 it created a camel it called "Niles," named for the Egyptian river. Niles had a name card with information on it about Egypt. Peaceable Planet trademarked the name, and it sold a few thousand in the first year. The next year, Ty, Inc., the maker of Beanie Babies bean bag dolls, introduced its camel, who also happened to be named Niles, and sold more than 1 million of them in the first year.

Peaceable Planet sued for trademark infringement, and lost in the U.S. district court. Peaceable Planet appealed and won. In the complex world of intellectual property protection, what this meant was that Peaceable Planet got another chance to prove in district court that Ty took advantage of the Niles name. Peaceable Planet faced another round in court, with the attendant legal fees and time spent on depositions and briefings. However, in pursuing the case to the appeals court and getting a favorable ruling, the chance of getting an out-of-court settlement increases. In reality, sometimes that is what a "win" in intellectual property lawsuits looks like. In the case of Peaceable Planet, it did win on the rehearing of the case.

services similar or identical to yours *before* a mark is selected. Skill Module 17.2 can help you get a start on this.

Entrepreneurs often don't realize the power of a trademark. Let's say you have a process for filling basketballs with nitrogen instead of regular air. It is too obvious to be patented (there is already nitrogen inflation for auto tires), but a lot of teams and players think the balls bounce more consistently. So you call it *NitroBounce* and get trademark protection for it. If anyone comes up with the same process and calls it NitrogenBounce, you could sue the newcomer for infringing on your trademark and causing confusion in the eyes of customers. Where a patent or trade secret might not be able to work, a trademark could give you protection–if you know to get it.

On the other hand, all too often with small businesses a name is chosen and used and the business incurs all sorts of expenses in terms of labels, signs, and even advertising without considering trademark issues. Before selecting a business name, an Internet address, or the mark for products or services, an attorney should be consulted. An attorney can do a trademark search to determine what use is being made of the words or groups of words a business may want to use. Researching the desired name(s) ahead of time can avoid liability for infringement in which

SKILL MODULE 17.2

Checking Out Trademarks Online

Before you settle on a name for your business or product, it is very important to determine how that word or group of words is already being used in the United States to avoid trademark infringement challenges. Assume you are starting a business doing detailing work on vehicles. You are considering the name "Clean as a Whistle." In checkinq the name, one source of information is the U.S. Patent and Trademark Office listing of federally registered trademarks. While that list shows only federally registered marks and there may be an identical or similar name used that is not registered, this listing is a start. Go to the U.S. Patent and Trademark website, **www.uspto.gov**, click on "Trademarks" in the top navigation bar, select "Search trademarks," and then click on the "Search our trademark database (TESS)" button. Select "Basic Word Mark Search (New User)" and search for "Clean as a Whistle." Trademarks listed as "DEAD" could be claimed anew. Your focus should be on trademarks listed as "LIVE." According to the information in this site, is this name currently being used for a car detailing business?

someone already using or having rights to that name sues the business, as well as financial costs (including loss of goodwill) in changing names. Once an attorney has established that it is unlikely that your choice of name is infringing on another's, consideration can be given to obtaining state or federal trademark registration to get additional rights for your mark.

Any size business may own valuable intellectual property such as patents, trade secrets, copyrights, and trademarks. Understanding and protecting these assets by seeking qualified, professional counsel cannot be overemphasized.

This brings up something you should be thinking about right now. Colleges vary in their intellectual property ownership rules. In many colleges, students own the ideas they create in classes (and outside), but in many other colleges, the college owns the student's idea. And even in colleges where the student owns the idea, if the college thinks it put in significant additional resources over the usual, it may claim part or even all of the ownership. For nearly all schools, a student can apply to obtain ownership of his or her idea, but the rules for this differ. So if clearly owning your idea is important, check with the college's lawyer (often called the *general counsel*) and see what the policy is and how to get done what you want.

Whether you think we have too many laws or not enough, the stability and success of the United States' business community is based, in large part, on our legal system. Laws guarantee rights to individuals and companies. Those rights are upheld every day in courtrooms across America. Caveat emptor (let the buyer beware) is *not* the motto in twenty-first-century America. Knowing the law or even knowing when to ask for advice concerning the law gives business owners more power in pursuing their dreams. Knowledge is power. After reading this chapter, you should have a greater understanding of our legal system and particular areas of interest for business owners. This should give you more confidence in pursuing those dreams.

CHAPTER SUMMARY

LO 17-1 Know when you need legal information and how to get it.

- There are many federal, state, and local laws applicable to any small business.
- Get a good attorney with experience in your areas of concern. You may need more than one attorney for various issues that arise over time.
- You can use online sources from the government or trade associations for certain legal information.

LO 17-2 Understand legal structures in setting up a new business.

- Trade names exist when a firm uses something other than the owner's name as the name of the business.
- The most common business forms are sole proprietorships, general partnerships, limited partnerships, C corporations, S corporations, professional corporations, and limited liability companies.
- Each of various types of business entities has pros and cons in terms of personal liability of the owners, creation and maintenance of the organization, management of the organization, continuity of the organization, the raising of capital, and taxation.
- Unless there is a compelling reason to do otherwise, an LLC is probably the best choice of business entity because of its ease of formation, limited liability of owners, and flexibility in taxation.

LO 17-3 Learn how to master the process of negotiating.

- Nearly everything in business is negotiable.
- Negotiating successfully depends on mastering four steps: prepare, position, propose, and pounce.
- The goal is to create outcomes where you and the other party win.
- Be honest in your presentation and balanced in your approach.

LO 17-4 Recognize potential legal liabilities for your business.

- You and your business may be held responsible for the actions of agents, including employees.
- Avoid lawsuits by properly training employees, using independent contractors, or submitting disputes to arbitration.

LO 17-5 Know contract terms and when a contract is needed.

- You are free to contract for anything that is not illegal or unethical.
- Put agreements in writing and have them reviewed by legal counsel.
- Make use of special contract terms such as noncompete clauses, exculpatory clauses, and hold harmless agreements to avoid litigation.
- The primary contractor is responsible for a subcontractor's failure.
- On the Internet make sure to specify that your site is informational and arrange for secure alternatives to "wet signatures."
- Design and implement a company email policy.

LO 17-6 Understand the basics of intellectual property.

- Intellectual property is composed of patents, trade secrets, copyrights, trademarks, and trade names.
- Ideas can be protected as patents or trade secrets.
- Expression of ideas can be protected as copyrights.
- Trademarks uniquely identify products and their origin.
- Intellectual property is a business asset and can be extremely valuable. For that reason protection of intellectual property should be taken seriously.

KEY TERMS

hourly fees, 613
flat fees, 613
retainer, 613
contingency fee, 613
trade name or assumed name or doing business as (dba) name, 617
assumed name filing or fictitious name filing, 617
legal entity, 618
plaintiff, 618
defendant, 618
articles of organization, 620
single taxation, 620
double taxation, 620
pass through (taxation), 620
check the box taxation, 620
operating agreement, 620
articles of partnership, 621
piercing the veil, 622
nonprofit corporation, 624
501(c)(3), 624
vicarious (indirect) liability, 626
independent contractors, 626
Sarbanes-Oxley Act (SOX), 628
litigation, 630
arbitration, 630
mediation, 630
noncompete clause, 632
exculpatory clause, 632
hold harmless, 632
waiver, 632
subcontract, 633
business-to-business (B2B), 633
business-to-consumer (B2C), 634
intangible property, 634
patent, 634
trade secret, 634
copyright, 634
trademark, 634
design patent, 636
utility patent, 636
plant patent, 636
opinion of patentability, 636
provisional patent, 636
infringer, 636
grace period, 638

DISCUSSION QUESTIONS

1. How would you go about finding a lawyer for your business?
2. Which form of business structure would be best for your new business, and why?
3. In what ways could the owner of a parking lot limit his or her potential liability?
4. How could you keep your employees from going to your competitors after you have trained them?
5. How can you protect your company's trade secrets?
6. What issues should be addressed in a company policy on email?

EXPERIENTIAL EXERCISES

1. Find your state's secretary of state home page on the Internet. Find information on forming LLCs. Can the form(s) be submitted online? If not, can the form(s) be downloaded or filled in using the computer?
2. In most states you can contact the state bar, the state supreme court, or a state commission to check on whether a particular attorney has been disciplined for professional conduct violations. To find out whom to contact in your state, go to the American Bar Association listing at **www.americanbar.org/groups/professional_responsibility/services/databank/**, find the link to *Directory of State Disciplinary Agencies,* and locate the group for your state. Almost all states have a website. Check your state's site to learn how you would find a local lawyer.
3. You may be able to represent yourself on small matters by going to small-claims court. These courts of limited jurisdiction have different names in different states. Go to **www.nolo.com/legal-encyclopedia/lawsuits-court**. Scroll down and look for 50-State Chart of Small Claims Court Dollar Limits and select the state of Indiana as an example. There you will find information on small-claims courts in Indiana.
4. Would you like more information on LLCs? Go to **www.nolo.com/**, scroll down toward the bottom of the page and, under "Popular Categories," click on "LLCs & Corporations" to learn more.

MINI-CASE

VIVID SKY AND MAJOR LEAGUE TROUBLE

Entrepreneur Tim Hayden, CEO of Vivid Sky, had created a service called SkyBOX that could stream videos and statistics to sports fans over their 3G cell phones (like the iPhone). It had taken four years to launch the service, which originally was going to require military-grade hardened wireless PDAs and wiring stadiums for Wi-Fi, but had been reconfigured to run on Internet-ready cell phones.

Professional teams in baseball, football, basketball, and hockey had seen SkyBOX and were enthusiastic about its deployment. However, there were competitors to the SkyBOX. One of the largest was Major League Baseball, which was developing its own iPhone application to tie fans into MLB video feeds and statistics.

Executives at Apple liked the SkyBOX so much they made it their Feature Product on the iTunes home page.

It wasn't clear if MLB's team saw this or not, but it was at that moment that it served Vivid Sky with a cease-and-desist claiming that the SkyBOX used content that was copyrighted. In addition, MLB contacted Apple and demanded that the SkyBOX application be pulled from the iTunes Store. Executives from Apple refused to pull the SkyBOX application. However, they wanted Vivid Sky to work out a solution with MLB.

While Tim knew that Vivid Sky conformed to all copyright issues and was legally within its rights, he suspected that MLB might be going this route to disrupt Vivid Sky and the sale of its applications in the iTunes Store. He could make a stand and hire lawyers, which would cost a small business like his lots of money. Or he could look for a mutually agreeable solution.

Tim thought, What is an entrepreneurial way to handle this?

CASE DISCUSSION QUESTIONS

1. What are Tim's choices at this point?
2. What do you think Tim means when he asks if there is an "entrepreneurial way to handle this"?
3. If there is no infringement, but the injunction was brought to slow down a fast-moving new competitor, would it make any difference in the strategy Tim should employ?

CHAPTER

18 Human Resource Management: Small Business Considerations

● Jesse Mecham started as a solo entrepreneur, but hired his first employee as a virtual employee when the programmer with useful ideas lived 1,350 miles away. How do you think that went?

Piotr Swat/Shutterstock

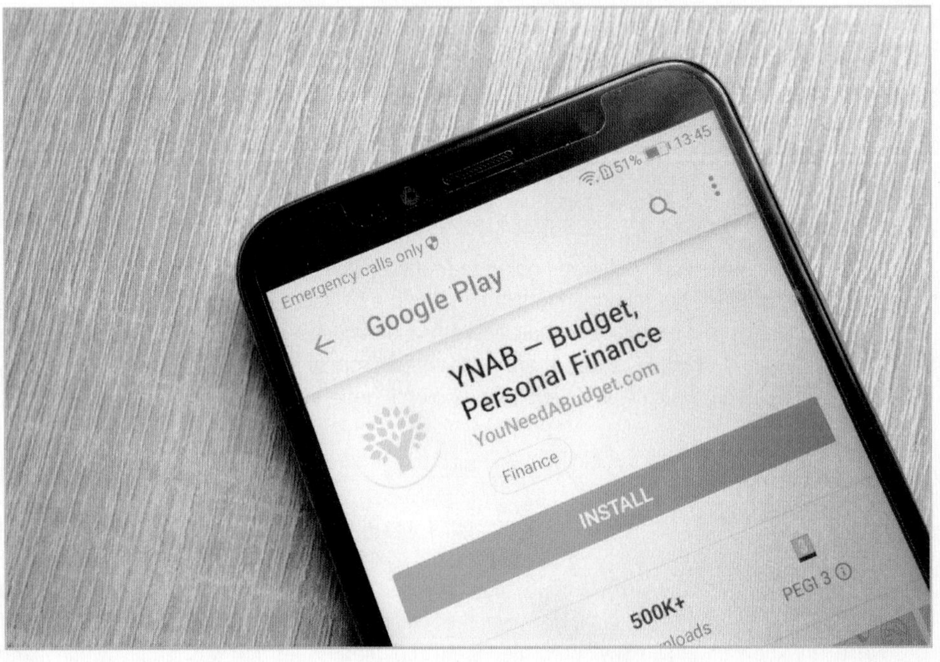

LEARNING OBJECTIVES

After you complete this chapter, you will be able to:

LO 18-1 Evaluate the decision to hire full-time or part-time help.

LO 18-2 Understand how to recruit good employees on your budget.

LO 18-3 Know how to match the right person to the job.

LO 18-4 Describe employee training methods and resources.

LO 18-5 Recognize how to meet employees' needs and expectations.

LO 18-6 Develop a fair compensation and benefit plan.

LO 18-7 Explain the complexities of managing family within your business.

Focus on Small Business: Jesse Mecham and You Need A Budget.[1]

Jesse and Julie Mecham were undergrads and newly married, living paycheck to paycheck in Provo, Utah. Well, maybe not quite living; more like scraping by, sometimes making it, sometimes missing it. The newlyweds knew they needed to do something, so they came up with a decision to budget—seriously budget. They followed four principles:

1. We decided what we wanted our money to do before we spent it.
2. We broke up larger, less-frequent expenses into manageable "monthly bills."
3. We changed our budget as needed.
4. We only spent money that was at least thirty days "old."

This worked so well for them that Jesse created an online service called You Need A Budget (YNAB for short) applying the principles. A CPA by training, he inadvertently got into hiring virtual (remote) employees when a programmer from Austin wrote him and offered to improve YNAB's software. Using phone and email, the two worked together for more than a year. With such a positive initial experience, when Jesse searched for YNAB's third employee, he searched widely and hired someone based in Australia.

By 2019, YNAB had 84 employees, scattered "from Boston to Brazil and Portland to Pakistan and everything in between." Jesse expected people to move around and work on their own schedule, but he also learned a few things along the way.

One thing was to hire people who are able to work remotely. An early hire had always worked in offices and knew she benefited from the energy of working around others. Now when Jesse interviews potential employees, he makes sure the interviewees have strategies for getting that infusion of energy from being around others (e.g., working from a Starbucks or a co-working space). YNAB also no longer uses email, preferring video chats in order to get things done in the moment. Jesse also learned that some in-person contact is important, so YNAB's executive team meets quarterly and the whole company shares an annual retreat to maintain their team spirit.

All of this has paid off for the company. YNAB is one of the top-rated personal finance apps, and the book *You Need A Budget* was a *Wall Street Journal* bestseller and the number six book in budgeting on Amazon. In 2015, YNAB was ranked 2,538th on the *Inc. 5000* list of fastest-growing small businesses.

DISCUSSION QUESTIONS

1. What are some potential advantages as well as drawbacks of having virtual employees like You Need A Budget?
2. Do you agree with the company dropping email in favor of real-time video chats? Why or why not?
3. Are you the sort of person who works most productively around others? If you had to work as a virtual employee, doing occasional video chats, where could you go to do your work and get your daily dose of people power?
4. Are there concerns you would have about being a virtual employee?

LO **18-1** Evaluate the decision to hire full-time or part-time help.

The Bigger Small Business: Hiring Employees

Of all the decisions that differentiate the types of small businesses, no decision is as important or complex as the decision to hire an employee. Many small businesses never do. Of the more than 30.2 million businesses in the United States in 2015, over 24.3 million had no employees at all–only the owner. Another 5.9 million firms had one or more employees.[2] For the economy, those firms that hire employees are an important source of job generation.[3]

For the owner, adding employees is important for several reasons. Adding employees increases the amount of work that can be done–serving more customers, producing more, or staying open longer. It also increases the demands on the owner. Now sales need to be made to cover the employees' wages or salary, and, when adding employees, the owner and business become responsible for the safety and well-being of the employees, as well as face legal requirements as an employer. Some owners look at the pluses and minuses and decide to stay a solo operation for as long as possible, like Jesse Mecham in the early stages of his business. Others take on the opportunity and responsibility from the start. For those entrepreneurs, the next key decision is what work should be done, who the best people are to do that work, and how the firm should take care of them. This is where the field of human resource management comes into small business. In this chapter we look at those three areas.

Let's start with the decision of what kind of work needs to be done. Generally we start by thinking about how much work we want to cover. As a small business owner, you can hire either part-time or full-time employees. Which will be best for you? You need to consider the pros and cons and expand with care. Full-time employees make it possible for you to take significant time away from the business. They get to understand the business sooner, and often are willing to take on more responsibility. They provide the ability to dramatically increase your hours open, material produced, or sales. But there are many additional expenses to having full-time employees on staff as opposed to part-time employees. The costs of adding employees include compensation, training time, and employee tax and accounting costs. Presumably such costs are outweighed by greater productivity, but you need to carefully balance the ledger. "Probably the biggest mistake I made in my early hires was hiring too early," says Louis Gudema, former president of Magic Hour Communications, a marketing agency in Watertown, Massachusetts, that was acquired in 2017 by Finalsite (www.finalsite.com/magic-hour). "As a result, we were not as profitable as we might have been if I had been slower to hire."[4]

"While every business has its own rhythm, it's usually wise to go through the first year without hiring. Get a feel for the sales cycle and the downturns. Measure the 'just right' temperature of income and outgo. Experts suggest squirreling away at least a year's worth of expenses and overhead before hiring in order to see you through any rough patches," says Joanna Krotz, co-author of the *Microsoft Small Business Kit*.[5]

employee fit
The match between the needs, expectations, and culture of the small business with the expectations and the skills of the individual employee.

Not only are there additional expenses to consider, but also **employee fit**.[6] You can ease into an eventual full-time employee by first hiring part-time help and if he or she works well and the demand for additional help is present, you can ease into a full-time position weighing the additional expense. Before making a full-time offer, let the applicant work part time for a while so you can see how she or he fits. Likely as not, this will be learning period for you, too. You can ease someone into the business as a part-time worker. Or, if you go ahead and hire a full-time applicant, set up a **probationary period**, or set up the job as an internship or a temporary one.[7] Usually, state law dictates how long such trials may last, so check with your state employment office. Typically, a probationary period lasts 30–180 days. A trial period can be important, and if your first choice turns memorable in all the wrong ways, chalk it up to experience and keep recruiting.[8]

probationary period Trial period in which an employee has temporary status before a formal offer to work full time is presented.

Whether you hire a part-time or full-time employee, it is important that each type of employee values your company's mission. Don Dymer, a former Scotland Yard police inspector, started his preemployment screening business in Jacksonville Beach, Florida, in 1995. He emphasizes the need for "employees to take on the mission and values that you want the business to take on." You do that by setting an example and making sure to define those values for every new hire.[9]

Recall in Chapter 9 we talked about "the perfect customer"; that discussion also included what would make the perfect employee, namely the kind who gives outstanding customer service. Your being able to articulate what your firm's values are, in a way that can inspire a potential employee, is crucial to making a value-driven selection work. An employee who can't get excited about your values when hungry for a job is certainly not likely to "grow into" being passionate about your business.

One of the challenges facing entrepreneurs who want to grow is understanding the many laws that apply to small businesses as their number of employees grows. We talked about this a bit in Chapter 17, but Figure 18.1 provides a simple graphic to see which employment laws begin to apply at what size of firm, while Table 18.1 gives a quick rundown of the major federal laws.

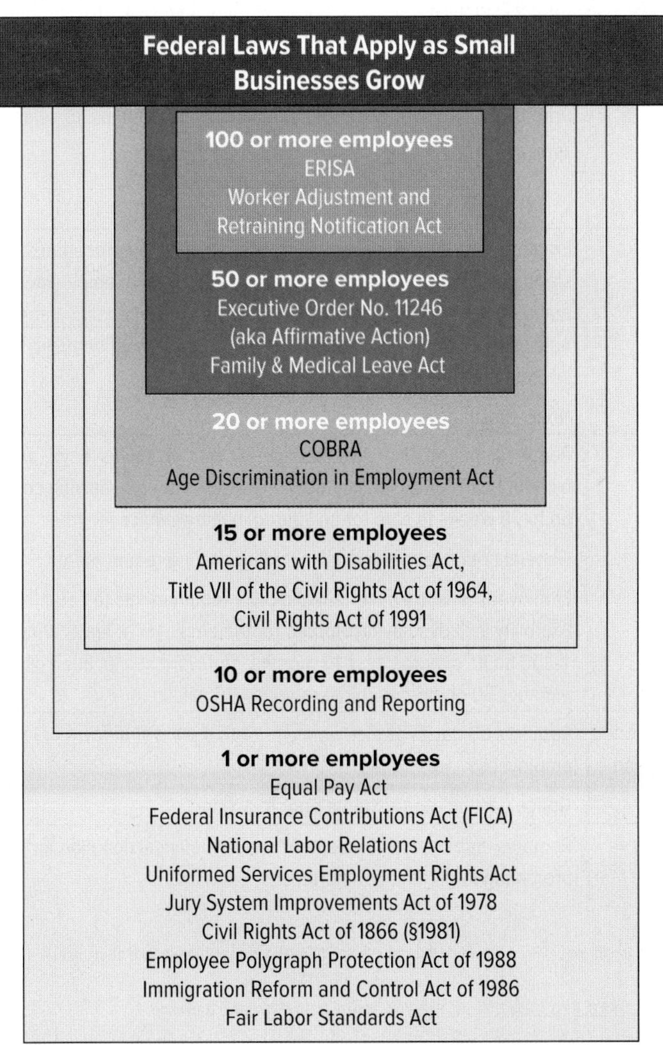

Federal Laws That Apply as Small Businesses Grow
100 or more employees
ERISA
Worker Adjustment and Retraining Notification Act
50 or more employees
Executive Order No. 11246
(aka Affirmative Action)
Family & Medical Leave Act
20 or more employees
COBRA
Age Discrimination in Employment Act
15 or more employees
Americans with Disabilities Act,
Title VII of the Civil Rights Act of 1964,
Civil Rights Act of 1991
10 or more employees
OSHA Recording and Reporting
1 or more employees
Equal Pay Act
Federal Insurance Contributions Act (FICA)
National Labor Relations Act
Uniformed Services Employment Rights Act
Jury System Improvements Act of 1978
Civil Rights Act of 1866 (§1981)
Employee Polygraph Protection Act of 1988
Immigration Reform and Control Act of 1986
Fair Labor Standards Act

FIGURE 18.1

Federal Laws That Apply as Small Businesses Grow

TABLE 18.1 Federal Employment and Labor Laws Applicable to Growing Businesses

Labor and Employment		
Employers engaged in interstate commerce or engaged in the production of goods for interstate commerce (almost all employers).	Fair Labor Standards Act	Requires payment to most hourly employees of minimum wage and time and a half for overtime hours. Requires payment of same wage to males and females for work requiring equal skill, effort, and responsibility in similar working conditions. Notice posting requirements.
Employers who have 15 or more employees for each workday in each of at least 20 calendar weeks in the current or preceding calendar year (federal).	Title VII of the Civil Rights Act of 1964	Prohibits discrimination with respect to any condition of employment based on race, color, sex, religion, or national origin, except where religion, sex, or national origin is a bona fide occupational qualification that is reasonably necessary to the conduct of a particular business. Includes a prohibition on harassment, including sexual harassment. Notice posting requirements. The Equal Employment Opportunity Commission has taken the position that gender identity and sexual orientation are covered under the protected category of "sex," but federal courts have not agreed with that interpretation.
All employers.	Immigration Reform and Control Act of 1986	Prohibits hiring of unauthorized aliens. Prohibits employment discrimination based on national origin or citizenship status. Requires employers to complete I-9 forms for each employee. Notice posting requirements.
All employers.	Employee Polygraph Protection Act of 1988	Prohibits employers from using polygraph results as basis for employment action with limited exceptions. Notice posting requirements.
Employers with 20 or more employees for each working day in each of 20 or more calendar weeks (federal).	Age Discrimination in Employment Act	Prohibits employment discrimination against individuals 40 years old and older. Notice posting requirements.
Employers with 15 or more employees (federal).	Americans with Disabilities Act	Employers must have nondiscriminatory application procedures, qualification standards, selection criteria, terms and conditions of employment. Employers must make reasonable accommodation for limitations of qualified applicant or employee unless to do so creates undue hardship. Governs confidentiality of medical information. Notice posting requirements.
Employers with 50 or more employees each working day for 20 weeks in the current or preceding calendar year.	Family and Medical Leave Act	Requires employers to give employees up to 12 weeks leave, paid or unpaid, without loss of position, seniority, or benefits, for a qualifying condition or event, or up to 26 weeks to care for an injured military service member. General notice requirements, including posting requirements. Employees must meet certain eligibility requirements to be entitled to leave. Eligibility includes having worked for the employer at least 12 months, at least 1,250 hours over the past 12 months, and work at a location where the company employs 50 or more employees within 75 miles.
Employers with 100 or more employees.	Worker Adjustment and Retraining Notification Act	Requires 60 days advance notice prior to a plant shutdown or layoff of 50 or more employees. Notice posting requirements prior to action.
50 or more employees and contracts or subcontracts of $50,000 plus.	Executive Order No. 11246	Requires employers to implement an affirmative action plan for hiring and promoting females and minorities.

Note: The chart is not, nor is it intended to be, a comprehensive summary of the threshold levels at which the statutes and regulations cited therein take effect, and it is qualified in its entirety by reference to the appropriate statute and regulations.

Source: Chart compiled in August 2016 by Armstrong Teasdale attorneys: Michael B. Kass, Julie O'Keefe, Robert B. Reeser III, and Robert J. Browning.

There is some help for determining if the federal employment laws will or do apply to your business. The U.S. Department of Labor has created a set of interactive online exercises to help you determine which laws apply in your situation at webapps.dol.gov/elaws/. In particular, use the "*FirstStep* Employment Law Advisor" (https://webapps.dol.gov/elaws/FirstStep/) to get an overview of which laws apply. The website elaws also provides a host of other interactive advisers to help you determine eligibility for more than two dozen laws and programs.

To be fair, there are always more laws that apply. In addition to those detailed in Table 18.1, there are related laws that apply to small businesses. For example, the Civil Rights Act of 1991 kicks in at 15 employees. Some of the other laws applicable as soon as you hire one employee include at least two big issues–the Federal Insurance Contributions Act (FICA) which is the Social Security and Medicare withholding law, and the Uniformed Services Employment and Reemployment Rights Act (USERRA) of 1994, which gives veterans the right to the jobs they left behind when called up for service.

Meanwhile, the state laws applicable to a small business are extraordinarily varied. For example, in Missouri there are laws such as the Missouri Genetic Testing Law, jury-release laws, a Voting Leave Act, the Political Activities of Employees Act, the Final Wage Payment Statute, Missouri's own Equal Pay Act, an Indoor Clean Air Act, and at the other extreme a Smokers and Alcohol Users Rights Law. This is by no means a comprehensive list, but it gives you an idea of the range of laws that apply to businesses.

When it comes to state law, it is truly a case where one size does not fit all. Even when two states use similar names for laws, the specifics of the law in each state are likely to differ. Being in the same region doesn't mean two nearby states will be similar. To give you an idea of the laws you might have to deal with, take the example of two adjoining states, Missouri and Illinois. There are a lot of firms in either state that might consider expanding into the adjoining state, but the laws to run firms in the two states differ. Table 18.2 shows laws from the two states for three types of human resource practices a small business typically would need to consider.

Remember, most states have laws protecting citizens in the same general ways. But the names of these laws can differ and–more to the point–have slightly different minimum employee headcounts, requirements, processes, and penalties. You want to be sure to determine the laws that apply to you as you start hiring.

To find this out, as noted in Chapter 17, you can get help from your local Small Business Development Center or SCORE chapter (both searchable at www.sba.gov/local-assistance/find/), the local chamber of commerce, or the local branch of the trade or professional association for your line of business (see Skill Module 3.1). Probably the best source for employment law questions is the state employment security office for your area. The federal government provides a comprehensive national online listing of state department of employment sites at www.careeronestop.org/LocalHelp/local-help.aspx.

TABLE 18.2 Differences in State Laws: The Case of Two Adjoining States

	Illinois	Missouri
Legal holidays	Traditional holidays	Traditional holidays plus Truman Day
Minimum wage	$8.25	$7.65
Wages must be paid	Monthly (for executive, administrative, and professional personnel) or biweekly (for everyone else)	Biweekly

Sources: "Minimum Wage Laws in the States," U.S. Department of Labor, 2019., www.dol.gov/whd/minwage/america.htm; "Public holidays in the United States," Wikimedia Foundation, Inc, https://en.wikipedia.org/wiki/Public_holidays_in_the_United_States.

The point is that hiring more employees makes your organization a more professional one, and with that professionalism comes a need to deal with more laws and regulations. While the best way is to work with a lawyer to make sure all issues are covered, these days you can get much of the work done at little or no cost by yourself, using the resources and free advice available to you. For example, RocketLawyer.com offers a free basic employee handbook you can develop online (www.rocketlawyer.com/document/employee-manual.rl#/), as well as dozens of other letters and forms for your business. Whereas it is not a replacement for having lawyer's advice specific to your company, the free handbook can be useful as a way to start thinking about the issues you will need to deal with when you start hiring. With the legal side under control, you are ready to go out and find those employees who will help your business grow.

LO 18-2 Understand how to recruit good employees on your budget.

Attracting Employees

A lot of the time a smaller firm can actually outperform large businesses in attracting high-quality employees.[10] To attract and hire new talent into a medium to large growing organization, help wanted ads in regional newspapers or the use of an employment service have been traditional methods. For small business owners, these methods tend to be expensive and have a long turnaround time. Today there are less expensive alternatives to consider.

Networking is a relatively low-cost, although time-intensive, method of recruiting. There are many benefits such as receiving a credible critique of a potential candidate's work experience and personal character. People to network with include colleagues, business professionals (your attorney or accountant), friends, vendors you have strong relationships with, alumni, and advisory board members. You can also use online social networking sites like LinkedIn (introduced in Chapter 3) to recruit, either by directly posting for a job or asking if people on LinkedIn know someone who might want the job you are offering.

Internet recruiting
Method of recruiting that allows you to search a résumé database or post a job description to the web; a small business owner who knows exactly what he or she wants can use filters to search vast numbers of résumés with pinpoint accuracy.

employee referral
An underused, low-cost method for finding workers that rewards your employees for recommending potential candidates who would be a great employee fit.

Internet recruiting allows you to search a résumé database or post a job description to the web. The main contribution of recruiting websites, such as Monster.com, Indeed.com, CareerBuilder.com, and Glassdoor.com, has been to speed up hiring and vastly increase the accuracy of the job-search process. You can post a job at 2 P.M. and get your first response a minute later. An employer who knows exactly what he or she wants can use filters to search vast numbers of résumés with pinpoint accuracy.[11]

Employee referral is an underused, low-cost method that rewards your employees for recommending potential candidates who would be a great fit. Even for small businesses, to work successfully, referrals should be handled formally, with guidelines such as following up on all leads within 24 hours.[12]

Company websites can be used to post job openings. This method would be effective if your site receives a fair amount of traffic, and it would incur only a small incremental cost to your website budget.[13] If your business does not have a company website, the investment of website development and maintenance may be a limiting factor, but when a website can cost $50 a year, it is a worthwhile investment. Search Google for "cheap web hosting" and you will find plenty of services offering template-based design and hosting services.

Many universities have *career service offices* that encourage companies to post openings to their job bank to recruit at both the undergraduate and the graduate levels. This service is commonly offered at no cost to companies and allows businesses to set up an account to manage résumé selection. Universities can often help you evaluate if it makes sense to offer an internship to their students. Internships are jobs in businesses like yours, arranged through the university. Some internships are done as a for-credit class; some are not. Some internships are paid by the employer; some are not. Interns usually work for only one semester, and the best internships involve a mix of simple and challenging work as well as time to talk with you, the entrepreneur, about what they are learning and what is the best way to do things. If you feel like teaching a little and working a little, an internship could work for you.

Professional groups can be a resource for recruiting new talent. Many associations publish newsletters or post openings online or at their meeting locations. Try sending a one-page job description to associations to which you belong.[14] Along these lines, professional networking

Attracting the best talent to your company can be encouraged by the strategic use of networking. Spend time in conversation with colleagues in the field, friends, vendors, and others to learn of possible employee leads.

Rawpixel.com/Shutterstock

websites like LinkedIn.com can also be a way to publicize jobs. LinkedIn has groups organized around professions, which can make it easier to figure out where to post.

Outsourcing may be the answer if your small business is not ready to hire employees, but you have a growing need to meet workload demand. Consider, as an example, outsourcing to an assistant who is an independent entrepreneur and provides administration, creative, or technical support. The assistant, often called a **virtual employee**, works on a contractual basis online and handles such functions as keeping your schedule, customer intelligence, or database up to speed.[15] Rather than having to provide additional office space and be responsible for the development and supervision of an employee, you can enjoy the support and assistance of a professional without the headaches of hiring and managing employees.[16] Assistants can be people from your neighborhood or city, or virtual assistants working over the Internet. The nonprofit International Virtual Assistants Association can be found at www.ivaa.org, and the major websites for outsourcing are Upwork (www.upwork.com) and Fiverr.com.

virtual employee
An independent contractor who provides specialized business services or support from a distance, through the Internet, telephone, fax, or another method of communication.

Here are some guidelines and methods for managing and fostering productivity among virtual employees:[17]

- Hire virtual employees who have experience with being self-motivated and disciplined, including former consultants, freelancers, and salespeople who are accustomed to dealing with deadlines and working independently. As a small business owner, this is critical, given that you already have multiple deadlines and responsibilities.
- As you manage your virtual employees, make sure to spend time developing a system of task lists, schedules, and goals with varying time frames and clear deadlines. Invest in spreadsheets and project scheduling software that will help your virtual employees organize tasks. Be sure to consistently review status reports with virtual employees to ensure that tasks are completed on time and on budget.
- Maintain communication with virtual workers via voice, fax, and other electronic methods. Don't become reliant on email since it is too easy to misinterpret or misunderstand the written word. Speak on the phone and schedule face-to-face meetings occasionally.
- Micromanagement is nearly impossible with a remote staff, and it will unnerve anyone who attempts it. Trust that your employees are doing the right thing until evidence proves otherwise. If you are paranoid about slacking, hire salaried, rather than hourly, workers or pay per project.

You can see how this approach plays out in the following Small Business Insight.

Employee leasing is a hybrid between outsourcing and having a paid staff. In employee leasing, your "employees" actually work for the leasing company, which handles recruiting, training, compensation, and government filings. You lease employees from the leasing company, paying a

SMALL BUSINESS INSIGHT

Mavens & Moguls, a Marketing Strategy Consulting Firm[18]

I feel like my role is to connect the dots. . . . I'm a conductor of a world class orchestra.

—Paige Arnof-Fenn

Paige Arnof-Fenn, founder and CEO of Mavens & Moguls, launched her company in 2001. Paige had worked with companies at all stages that needed expert marketing advice, including projects for start-ups, authors, professional service firms, the Sundance Film Festival, Merrill Lynch, Sprint, and Delta Air Lines. With Mavens & Moguls she has assembled a team of marketing all-stars, the best people whom she has encountered in her career across all marketing disciplines. They are spread across the United States and as far away as Bangkok.

As the sole business owner of Mavens & Moguls, Paige relies on her virtual employees to knit together the network of experienced professionals who have actually "done it" for the top companies across a variety of industries. Working from their own offices, homes, or other private work spaces, they provide marketing strategy, planning, and execution. The real mavens and moguls specialize in promotion, PR, direct marketing, media, pricing strategy, positioning, customer acquisition, and new product launches. In many ways, all the areas of the marketing mix are covered that can be used to build a brand and grow a client's business.

fixed amount for the employee as well as an annual fee, usually 2 to 7 percent of the dollar value of your annual payroll. Leases can be set for periods of a few weeks to a year or more. For employing the same people part time but repeatedly over a long period of time, or keeping the total number of full-time employees low, this can be a good way to handle the complexities of employment. Other ways to have employees without spending a lot are described in The Thoughtful Entrepreneur box that follows.

Other traditional and nontraditional hiring sources to consider include:

- Contact *local churches* and the pastors to see if they have parishioners who are looking for a new job.
- Check with local *senior centers* to see if there are residents who might like to work.
- Visit local *high schools* for entry-level jobs, and local *community colleges* for those interested in management or a technical career.
- Finally, *state unemployment offices* are a great resource, with no cost to the employer.

LO **18-3** Know how to match the right person to the job.

Matching the Worker to the Work

Even before your first hire, you will need to know what your basic needs are and what roles this new employee will fit into. Ultimately, you would like to "match" the job with the ideal individual who can fulfill the responsibilities of the job and grow with the business. Your first step is to define and describe all the work that will be part of the new job. Then you'll need to know how to evaluate the potential employees to see how well they match your ideal set of requirements.

job description
Defines and discusses all the essential knowledge, skills, and abilities that are needed to fill a position.

Writing a Job Description

Your **job description** needs to define and discuss all the essential knowledge, skills, and abilities that are needed to fill the position. In addition, you will need to describe what kind of

THE THOUGHTFUL ENTREPRENEUR

LOW-COST AND NO-COST EMPLOYEES

If your budget does not allow for a paid employee, consider three alternative methods to hire an employee at no cost.[19]

1. **Barter:** Trade your products or services for those of another business; for example, a maid service trading its house-cleaning services to a designer in return for a new logo. For this method of recruiting, you must be flexible in services rendered and received. Bartered services may add great value to a particular function of your small business and can be particularly useful when money is in short supply.
2. **Internships:** Hiring students to work at little or even no cost in exchange for work experience may be a great way to get the assistance you need. Generally, students who intern are looking to use specific skill sets or be exposed to a particular functional area of a business. If you can provide valuable work experience, offering internships may be an appealing way to attract temporary help.
3. **Volunteers:** Volunteers are a wonderful resource if your business is strapped for cash, although the search process may be time-consuming. Who will work for free? Family members are always the first source, with friends a close second, although people who need relevant work experience might give a few hours to have an entry on their job applications, such as stay-at-home spouses who are looking for work experience while children are at school. Also, individuals committed to your company's mission are possible candidates. If your firm is doing a promotion for a charitable organization (like operating a stand at a fair), you may be able to get customers or members of the charity to contribute their help.

personality, experience, and education you believe a person who performs the job should have. To determine some of these attributes, sit down and do a job analysis covering the following areas:[20]

- The job itself: the work being done, job goals, and how these relate to other positions in the company.
- The tasks of the job: the components that make up the work.
- The critical tasks: what are the most important elements.
- The critical competencies: what the person absolutely has to be able to do to get the job done.

If you have difficulty defining and describing your hiring needs, consider talking to other small business owners in your area. You may also discuss these issues with employees and supervisors at other noncompeting small businesses that offer similar positions.

To get started, write down the job title and whom that person will report to (define how the job relates to you or other positions in the small business). Next, develop a job statement or summary describing the position's major and minor duties. List any educational requirements, desired experience, and specialized skills or knowledge required. Include salary range and benefits (see the section on compensation later in this chapter). Finish by listing any physical or other special requirements associated with the job.

Figure 18.2 gives you an example of a job description for an internship in a growing small business. For a one-person business hiring its first employee, these guidelines may seem unnecessary. But remember, you are laying the foundation for your personnel policy, which will be essential as your small business grows. Keeping detailed records from the time you hire your first employee will make things a lot easier when you hire your tenth, twentieth, and so on.

JOIN THE REVOLUTION: BUSINESS/ENTREPRENEURSHIP/MANAGEMENT INTERNSHIP

Company or Recruiter	Better Weekdays	**Position Level**	Entry Level
Industry	Internet	**Position Type**	School Year Internship
Function	Community Engager Intern	**Intern Paid**	Yes
Location	St. Louis, MO	**Intern Type**	Undergraduate

COMMUNITY ENGAGER INTERN

Please email your résumé and cover letter to: joinus@betterweekdays.com

Better Weekdays is a job-matching platform that helps universities measure and improve their graduates' job outcomes. The software enables businesses to effectively target their employer brands and jobs to candidates most compatible in professional experience and corporate culture.

Job Description

- As a Community Engager, you will effectively have as much responsibility as a full-time member of the team. There will be defined goals that you will pursue. At the end of the internship you will be able to look back and codify your impact in the organization to any prospective employer.
- Management will spend one-on-one time with you. We will get you up to speed by teaching you key concepts about our business, and explain how things work across our business model. Basically, we'll make sure you connect the dots in what it takes to be an entrepreneur and run a company.
- We have a "team mentality." There is camaraderie and you can expect to feel an "us against the world" attitude. You will be part of a group of people who are trying hard to live up to their potential to accomplish something very important for colleges and universities.
- The product we are building reduces friction out of the internship/job search and recruiting process. You will help shape product direction based on user feedback.

Desired Qualifications

- Support planning and organization for industry conferences in the summer.
- Support our university customer on-boarding process.
- Propose and execute new customer success activities to engage students using the job matching application.
- Help manage social media channels with content for students and career services professionals.
- Create content for our blog for employers and career services.
- Track overall engagement and generate qualitative insights from users on our platform.

FIGURE 18.2

Sample Job Description

Source: Chris Motley, CEO, BetterWeekdays.com. Ad was posted at www.stltechjobs.org/jobs/community-engager-intern/.

Also, writing the job description will help you determine whether you need a part time or full time employee, whether the person should be permanent or temporary, and whether you could use an independent contractor to fill the position. The specifics for crafting a job description are given in Skill Module 18.1.

One thing that might help is to look for examples of job descriptions to get an idea what is involved. It turns out there are a lot of published job descriptions of all sorts across the Internet. A great listing is maintained by HR-Guide at https://hr-guide.com/Documents/Job_Descriptions.htm. See the websites in the Learn More Online box for some of the best job descriptions.

Crafting a Job Description

SKILL MODULE 18.1

In this skill module, you have the opportunity to write job descriptions for a student worker and for an instructor on your campus. Write a job description for the role of student worker, and ask one of your instructors about his or her job and write a description. In your instructor interview or when thinking about the student job, cover many of the areas and questions discussed to get a full view and perspective of the positions. Write a half-page job description using the following how-to steps:[21]

1. **Start with a Title:** Provide a job title for the position (two or three words). Beneath the title you want to include important information related to the job such as the status (**exempt** versus **nonexempt**) and to whom the employee reports. For example:

   Intern: A nonexempt summer position reporting to the CEO.
2. **Give a Job Overview (or Summary of the Job):** Be sure that this section is not more than three to four sentences long and that it explains the level and basic nature of this job position. You will be outlining details of the job in the following sections. For example:

   An entry-level job position providing administrative support to a technology business with three employees.
3. **Define the Duties and Responsibilities:** Write down all the tasks that the employee will be doing in this position. Be flexible in writing the duties and responsibilities to accommodate growth of the position. Be clear, concise, and complete. For example:

   Main duties include: scheduling appointments, giving information to callers, and generally relieving staff of clerical work and minor administrative and business detail.
4. **State the Knowledge, Skills, and Abilities Desired:** These are basic qualities that the employee should possess. They could include:

   Knowledge of computer software, including PowerPoint, Excel.
   Skilled at performing multiple tasks simultaneously.
   Ability to relate to people and make them feel comfortable.
5. **List the Credentials and Experience Desired:** List the level of educational and professional experience the person should have (possibly allow for additional experience to make up for the lack of an educational degree). For example:

   Minimum two years of college with coursework in business or related fields. Prior business experience desirable.
6. **State Special Requirements:** Anything that may not have been covered up until this point should go here. For example:

   Frequent travel required to other universities and conferences.
   Job includes some evening and weekend hours.
   Ability to lift 15 pounds or more.

exempt
A federal government descriptor of employees who are exempt from the Fair Labor Standards Act and are generally paid salaries.

nonexempt
A federal government descriptor of employees under the Fair Labor Standards Act who get an hourly wage and time-and-a-half for overtime.

Then compare the descriptions with those of other students. You might also try to find the official job description for an instructor from your school. When comparing your description with the other ones, consider the following:

1. How difficult was it to define and narrow the many responsibilities of the position?
2. Were there differences between your description and the actual description?
3. How many similarities were there between your description and the actual description?
4. If there were discrepancies, where were the "gaps" between the two?
5. As a small business owner, what can you do to ensure there is a mutual understanding between you and the employee in describing the job/position as your business grows?
6. How can you get both formal and informal feedback from employees regarding the job on a continual basis?

LEARN MORE ONLINE

Learn more about the topics above at these sites:

Proven.com blog: **blog.proven.com/job-descriptions**

Best Job Descriptions: **www.bestjobdescriptions.com**

Department of Labor's *Occupational Outlook Handbook* (gives detailed job activities for thousands of jobs): **www.bls.gov/ooh/**

Evaluating Job Prospects

Once you have a job description, you can use it to help you evaluate whether an individual would be the right match for the position and your small business. So what can you do to make sure you hire the right person for the job? This is probably one of the most difficult decisions you may be faced with making, especially since we are all not trained in the art and science of hiring employees. In making successful hiring decisions, rely on the information developed in your job description to identify the most important knowledge areas, skills, and abilities the ideal candidate should possess.

One of the realities of the job market these days is that it is possible you post a job locally or online and find yourself flooded with applications. What you need to do is think about how to screen the applicants. Look at your job description and think about what one to three aspects are most important, and use those to screen the applicants to narrow down the number you will look at in greater depth. If you still have too many applicants in the pool, add additional factors from the job description. If there are still too many, you may need to consider creating more job elements to help you narrow down your candidates.

Once you have a pool of screened applicants, go back to the job description and create a set of specific questions that you will ask of all candidates. Pick questions that will clearly and behaviorally demonstrate to you that the applicants have these critical factors. Do not simply accept the candidate's word that he or she possesses a certain skill or knowledge base. Ask that person to demonstrate the skill, solve a problem, or write or create something that clearly and concretely provides you with the proof you need to make an informed decision.

We recommend the behavioral-interviewing approach because it is one that entrepreneurs can do a good job on by themselves, and because the kinds of information it generates is something an entrepreneur can directly understand and relate to the applicant and the job in question.

You have heard of selection tests for jobs, and there are a variety of tests and simulations that can be used. Originally, these techniques required major up-front costs for training, validation, and the materials themselves. Work simulations hold many of the same issues, but are even more complex and costly. Either approach usually accounts for no more than 50 percent of the variation in performance among multiple candidates, and in real-world situations, often can account for only 10 percent of performance.[22] That said, there are a lot of online services offering skill-based and job-based pre-employment tests online. Examples are given in the Learn More Online box below.

LEARN MORE ONLINE

Learn more about the topics above at these sites:

Capterra preemployment testing software: **www.capterra.com/pre-employment-testing-software/**

eSkill: **www.eskill.com**

TalentLMS: **www.talentlms.com**

Success Performance Solutions: **www.successperformancesolutions.com**

ClassMarker: **www.classmarker.com/online-testing/pre-employment-tests/** (to make and administer your own tests online)

TABLE 18.3 Typical Types of Behaviorally Based Interview Questions[23]

1. *Tell me about a time when:*
   You worked effectively under pressure.
   You were creative in solving a problem.
   You had to deal with an irate customer.
   You were unable to complete a project on time.
2. *Describe:*
   One of your strengths and one of your weaknesses.
   Your three most important work-related values (and an example of where you demonstrated each value at work).
   A decision you made that was unpopular and how you implemented it.
   A time when you were tolerant of an opinion that was different than your own.
3. *Give an example of:*
   A goal you reached and tell me how you achieved it.
   An occasion when you used logic to solve a problem.
   A time when you anticipated potential problems and developed preventive measures.
   A time when you had to make an important decision with limited facts.
4. *The last time it happened, how did you:*
   Adapt to a difficult situation?
   Persuade team members to do things your way?
   Overcome a major obstacle at work?
   Preserve your integrity when it was put to the test at work?

Remember: (1) You can replace "work" with "school," "church," "club," or "dorm" depending on the experience you think the interviewee is likely to have. (2) Questions that ask what they have done give a better indication than questions asking what they would do.

Note: These help match the right person to the job based on questions tied to the demonstrated knowledge, skills, abilities, and experiences of the applicant.`

For most small businesses, the owner will probably do more of a do-it-yourself approach, and the best way to organize this is to focus on using a behaviorally based interview (along with application forms and references) as the centerpiece of the selection process.

Develop questions structured like those shown in Table 18.3. These use slightly different techniques to obtain descriptions of situations the interviewee had encountered before. You will notice that the questions are designed so a "yes" or "no" answer is not applicable, and that most questions lend themselves to follow-up questions from you about the specifics of the experience. In the process, you are observing how the candidate analyzes situations, how rationally or logically the situation is presented, and whether or not, to the best of your judgment, the person is being truthful. Also notice what kinds of questions are not being asked—those about a person's race, religion, age, citizenship, marital status, disabilities, or arrest record—because such questions are illegal.

If at all possible, consider involving one or two other interviewers (if possible from within your small business, if not, ask people whose judgment you trust) to look at a candidate who seems promising. This helps you be sure that you understand the individual as well as possible. In that way, you can all share your insights and impressions of the candidate. Furthermore, one interviewer can add an aspect to a question that another one (or even you as the owner) may have overlooked.

One of the temptations these days is to look up an applicant's profile on Facebook or LinkedIn. If you do this, keep a few key points in mind. First, if you do it for one person, you need to do it for everyone. Second, LinkedIn is generally a more relevant source than Facebook since people post their professional profiles on LinkedIn, while Facebook can be very personally focused and not necessarily job relevant. If you see a Facebook photo of a person with a cup of some drink, what do you actually *know* about the applicant? What was he or she drinking? Was the applicant drunk? Even if the person was, can you prove it would make him or her a bad employee? You can see the legal problems that diving into social media to supplement your decision making could create. So if you use it, be careful and consistent. Checking on this—and how best to do background checks—with your lawyer is a good idea.

Interviewing can be a nervewracking experience for both interviewer and candidate. As an interviewer, be prepared as fully as possible, with specific questions to ask and a clear communication of job details. See Table 18.3 to glean sample interview questions and start you thinking of additional questions you might want to ask in your own company setting.

fizkes/Shutterstock

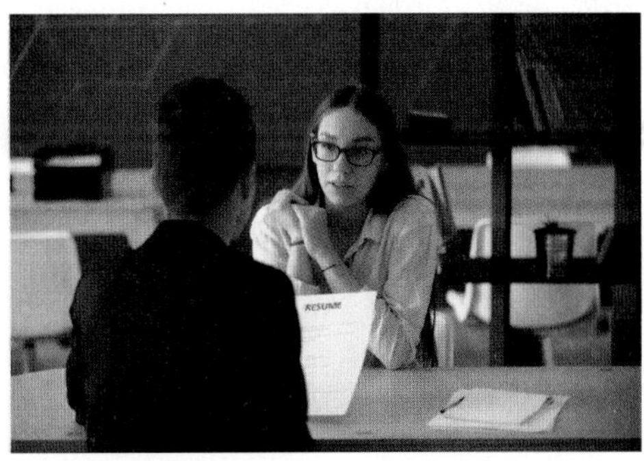

Finally, make sure you know enough about a candidate before you hire that person, and never, ever hire even a moderately qualified person just because you need someone now. You want to be sure you haven't hired a problem. It can be long and painful to terminate someone and advertise, screen, interview, and hire another person. Take your time to make sure you have the best person that best matches the position for your small business.

Selecting the Right Person

Imagine you have crafted the job description, sought candidates from several sources, and interviewed the candidates using the same set of basic questions. If you are hiring your first employee, you probably learned a bit about yourself, your business, and your employee needs as you went through this process. You run a consulting business that helps local companies identify promising markets overseas. You split your time between your clients' offices, learning about their businesses, and your own office, where you work up prospects using the Internet and phone.

You started looking for someone to handle the office phone and email when you were out, and to prepare reports for clients and sales catalogs for overseas customers from the templates you've developed. As you started talking to prospective employees, you realized that you could go any one of several ways: (1) Since you have an orderly process, you could hire someone relatively inexperienced (and inexpensive) and quickly get him or her up to speed doing the above tasks; or (2) you could hire someone with more experience in international sales (and would need higher pay) who could actually handle finding overseas customers and negotiate pieces of deals while you are soliciting more business. You have a top candidate for either approach. How do you decide?

Recall the idea of fit introduced earlier. As the owner, you decide how the firm should be run and what will be important. Both people seem nice enough and you think you could get along well with either one. So look at something different. Do you like your current pace of business? If yes, the inexperienced person should help take off some of the stress you're facing now, and will cost you less in wages, so is less of a burden. You should be able to grow your business at your own rate, but you will also be responsible for training and checking up on this person until she or he gets experienced in the job and your approach to it.

If you want to grow the business more quickly, the experienced person can be of more help. The experienced person should be able to do more things upon starting and learn new ways more quickly because he or she understands the underlying ideas of your industry, but that person will require more money from you and may have ideas about the best way to do something that do not match your preferred way.

Notice that a lot of the decisions about hiring really involve the entrepreneurs' realization of what they want to see happen in the business. Sometimes this becomes apparent only by going through the hiring process. In fact, for first-time hiring situations, it can be a good thing to try someone in the job part time in order to have a chance to refine what you want to see in the job description and in the business. In other situations, making use of the probationary period mentioned earlier can help define the job's potential end point, leaving you a graceful way out of having the wrong person in the job, or the wrong job described.

Training Your Employees

LO **18-4** Describe employee training methods and resources.

Of course, it would be great if employees came to work fully prepared to meet your business needs. However, most employees (even the most ideal new hires) need training. The time and money you spend teaching employees how to do their jobs could turn out to be your small company's wisest investment.

To begin, you should first assess your small firm's training needs from the perspective of the business, the job itself (job description), and the needs of the employees. This assessment will provide answers to the following questions:

- *Where* is training needed? What key areas need the most attention?
- *What* specifically must an employee learn in order to be more productive?
- *Who* needs to be trained?

Once you have answered these questions, you can then design your training program. There are two different types of training: initial training and ongoing training. When employees first join your small business or start a new role, offering them the training they need to handle the position makes them feel valued, challenged, and rewarded.

Initial and Ongoing Training Methods

There are two broad types of training available to small businesses: on-the-job and off-the-job techniques. Individual circumstances and the where, what, and who of your training program determine which method to use.

On-the-job training is delivered to employees while they perform their regular jobs. In this way, they do not lose time while they are learning. After a plan is developed for what should be taught, employees should be informed of the details. On-the-job techniques include orientations, job instruction training, apprenticeships, internships and assistantships, job rotation, and coaching.[24]

on-the-job training Delivered to employees while they perform their regular jobs; techniques include orientations, job instruction training, apprenticeships, internships and assistantships, job rotation, and coaching.

For on-the-job training in a small business, you need to stay abreast of all the jobs that need doing and define them so others can be trained in doing parts of the job. It is critical to design a job to make sure that nothing important is missed. To give you an idea on how to design on-the-job instruction that gives an employee a method to complete a certain task in a job, consider Skill Module 18.2,

Along with on-the-job training techniques, off-the-job methods such as lectures, special study, videos, television conferences or discussions, case studies, role-playing, simulation, programmed instruction, and laboratory training are all possible. Most of these techniques can be used by small businesses, although some may be too costly.[25] Other affordable and ongoing training methods can be less formal. In fact, training can be as simple as encouraging employees to meet regularly to discuss issues and share new ideas and perspectives. If your firm is large enough, you can also assign mentors to junior employees. Mentors give less experienced employees the opportunity to learn from seasoned veterans. Employees will be more comfortable in the face of new challenges if they know where to go for help. Mentors can inspire employees to strive for greater levels of success, help them channel their ambitions, and teach them new ways of handling ongoing problems more effectively.

Three Guidelines for Training[26]

1. **Give your employees opportunities to use their new skills:** Many small business owners complain that it is sometimes useless to train employees. Owners may argue that employees will take the knowledge and leave for a higher-paying job at another firm. While this may happen, small business owners can help prevent it. Once your employees are trained, give them opportunities to use their new skills.

Writing Instructions and Procedures[27]

SKILL MODULE 18.2

- Give the instruction/procedure a clear heading that summarizes the task.
- Show clearly who does what.
- Start each step or instruction with a verb that tells the reader to do something: "Open the valve. . . ." "Press the emergency button. . . ." "Tell your supervisor. . . ."
- Use a numbered list when the order in which tasks are to be performed is important. Use a bulleted list (like this one) when the order is not important.
- Put notes, warnings, and prerequisite conditions at the start, or *before* the list item to which they refer.
- Don't mix instructions with conceptual information. Present any necessary background information before the instructions.
- Use a level of detail that is appropriate to your employees' skill level and will ensure they will be able to know how to complete the job task.

2. **Make training an ongoing process:** Good employees want to learn, and you should provide them with opportunities to do so. Give employees encouragement to talk to you when their learning curve goes flat and then find ways to provide them with challenges and the knowledge to meet them successfully.
3. **Think of training as an investment (as opposed to an expense):** Many small business owners hesitate to invest too much energy, time, or money in training employees. Feeling that the expense does not justify the end results, they choose instead to give new hires a crash course and then put them right to work. Results of that sink-or-swim approach include costly mistakes, unhappy workers, and low productivity.

LO **18-5** Recognize how to meet employees' needs and expectations.

Rewarding Employees

Congratulations! Your business is growing and you have hired your first employee(s), either full time, part time, or on a virtual basis. Most likely the hiring process was time-consuming to ensure a perfect fit between your new employee and your company. So how are you going to retain your first employee and ensure you are meeting his or her needs? To retain productive employees and increase their job satisfaction, the simplest answer is to ask them what their needs are. Next, create an environment that appeals to them.

But when you do not have employees to ask, where do you start? In thinking about how to reward employees, know that for most employees surveyed, salary rewards, bonuses, and perks were not as important as autonomy and personal growth. For many, job security and responsibility can be as important as benefits. A lot of research[28] and practice[29] has been devoted to this, and six recurring factors that seem to be among the most valuable to employees are:

1. **Teamwork:** Fostering a sense of teamwork allows people to interact with one another on a professional level. Sharing ideas, working toward a common goal, analyzing one another's work, and communicating cross functionally help build stronger professional bonds that increase a sense of belonging and company fit.
2. **Recognition:** Showing appreciation for a job well done or giving credit to an employee who introduced a great idea can go a long way in making your employee feel valued. Recognition can be given in person, by voice mail, through email, or written in a memo or letter. You can also incorporate a reward system. Do you have star performers? Increase their motivation by recognizing their accomplishment with a certificate, plaque, or personal bonus such as a dinner or movie gift certificate. This will help them feel valued for their hard work and dedication and encourage them to continue this behavior.[30]
3. **Training:** A common reason people leave a company is that they feel they are not developing professionally. Providing learning opportunities at every level of the organization through on-the-job training or professional training will increase your employees' capabilities, allow them to expand their job responsibility, and help increase job satisfaction. Commitment to employees' development and growth is one way to ensure an employee is growing and will stay longer.[31]
4. **Empowerment:** This means letting employees make on-the-spot decisions for the companies' best interest. Making empowerment work requires giving employees permission to act, the knowledge to act, and the skill to act.[32] When empowerment works, it increases employees' personal feelings of responsibility and increases their commitment to the company.
5. **Contribution:** Providing meaningful work for employees gives them the feeling or belief that the day's work was a valuable contribution to the company and that they made a difference.[33] Employees have to believe that the decisions they make and the work they perform have a direct impact on the product or service you provide.[34]
6. **Communication:** Employees want to know what the company is trying to do, where it is going, and what it stands for.[35] Share your vision and the mission of the business. To be sure your employees feel valued, it is important to make time to talk about the direction of the company. Make sure *you* understand how they see what you have said and what they think you have promised.[36]

Supporting these rewards, entrepreneurs need to make job offers and manage based on an **open-book policy**. If you work this way and your company hits a downturn and promises cannot be met, employees are less likely to react badly since they have a better understanding of the firm's situation. It is also important to be aware that small business owners often implicitly or explicitly communicate conflicting terms when making **psychological contracts** with employees. To avoid this, denote strict limits on what you promise employees and how and when those promises will be delivered. Put what you agree to in writing to prevent problems when it comes time to evaluate whether you've delivered on the contract.

open-book policy
Concept that key employees should be able to see and understand a firm's financials, that they should have a part in moving the numbers in the right direction, and that they should have a direct stake in the strategy and success of the firm.

psychological contract
Refers to employees' beliefs about the promises between the employee and the firm. These beliefs are based on the perception that promises have been made (e.g., competitive wages, promotional opportunities, job training) in exchange for certain employee obligations such as giving of their energy, time, and technical skills.

Increasingly, small entrepreneurial companies are implementing formal performance appraisals. Reviewing employees' performance is an ongoing process. Owners and managers need to communicate with employees and give year-round feedback to employees on the job regarding performance and company goals. Before conducting a formal review, it is important to understand that there are two parts to a review: (1) the performance review and (2) the pay review. These reviews should be held at different times of the year.

The performance review typically occurs once a year to monitor your employees' job satisfaction, overall performance, and set career objectives. The goal of the performance review is to identify employee strengths, formally recognize performance, set goals to utilize the skills identified as strengths, and set direction for the upcoming year. It is also a time to identify areas of development and communicate with employees concerning how you will support them and the necessary steps they need to take to develop identified areas. It is a time to plan and set goals for the year ahead and to review work from the year past. The goal of the pay review is to reward your employees if they have performed all duties and met general requirements as discussed in initial job description conversations.

Small business owners with fewer than five employees may find formal performance reviews unnecessary or impersonal—taking away the strength of a small firm. But it is a good idea to conduct written reviews to track employee performance. This gives you an out if their performance becomes unsatisfactory after coaching or retraining. To successfully conduct an employee review, you should have a clear understanding of the position.[37] Next you should create a list of questions and issues that will be discussed in preparation for creating an evaluation sheet.[38] This list can include what the current responsibilities are, how well they are performing in the identified responsibilities, what needs to be improved or learned to be successful in position, and where employees are headed in their career. The evaluation sheet should include open-ended questions for the employees to fill out regarding job performance, strengths, areas of development, and what gets in the way of accomplishing the job.[39] For a sample appraisal and type of questions you may want to begin with, go to https://uptickapp.com/blog/free-performance-review-templates or https://www.sampleforms.com/sample-performance-appraisal-forms.html.

An appraisal form should be filled out and returned to you before the scheduled performance review so that you can learn the employees' goals, interests, and self-evaluation when you are crafting your comments.[40] Your comments during the review should address how the employee can grow, improve, and build on his or her current set of successes to contribute to the company, what you can do as a leader to provide resources, guidance, and opportunities, and what the individual needs to do on his or her own to continue to grow and succeed.[41]

Fair Labor Standards Act (FLSA)
A federal law which establishes minimum wage, overtime pay eligibility, recordkeeping, and child labor standards affecting full-time and part-time workers in the private sector (including small businesses) and in federal, state, and local governments.

Compensation, Benefits, and Perks

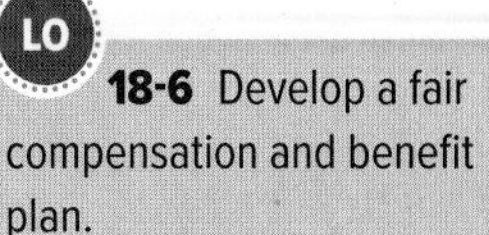
LO 18-6 Develop a fair compensation and benefit plan.

One of the first steps in developing a compensation plan is to determine whether you are hiring someone for an hourly or salaried position. The federal government defined nonexempt and exempt employees in the **Fair Labor Standards Act (FLSA)** (www.dol.gov/agencies/whd/compliance-assistance/handy-reference-guide-flsa). Nonexempt (from FLSA) employees get an hourly wage and time-and-a-half for overtime. Employees exempt from FLSA are generally paid salaries (there are exceptions). Look how these positions are paid in other businesses like yours, and strongly consider making this one of the questions you ask your lawyer. Misclassifying a worker can lead to legal problems with the state and even the federal government.[42]

The next step in figuring compensation is determining your organization's compensation philosophy. Do you believe in raising the level of base salaries in your organization or do you appreciate the flexibility of variable pay? A small business, with variable sales and income, may be better off controlling the levels of base salaries. When times are good, the business can tie bonus dollars to goals achieved.

The next step is to find comparison factors for salary. Research the salary range for similar positions and job descriptions. Determine whether you are competitive with organizations of similar size, sales, and markets. If you can find companies in the same industry, especially in your area or region, that is another good comparison source. You can check salary surveys and want ads, and scout out competitors to see if they are underpaying or overpaying their employees. You can get a start by searching Google for "salary comparison." Probably the best-known site for comparison information is Salary.com shown in Skill Module 18.3. Paying too much is an unnecessary drain on your resources, but paying too little will make it difficult for you to find and keep the best people.

SKILL MODULE 18.3

Finding Local Salaries and Benefits Information Online

There are two possible sources of online information on salaries and benefits specific to your locality. One is governments. To find the state employment security office for your area, check the locator at **www.careeronestop.org/LocalHelp/local-help.aspx**. The federal Department of Labor has a salary and skill finder at **www.careeronestop.org/businesscenter/SkillsGapFinder/SkillsGapFinder.aspx**. The FLSA Guide is at **www.dol.gov/whd/regs/compliance/hrg.htm**.

Salary.com offers a wealth of information on salary and benefits, organized by type of job and locality. Over the years, more and more of its information has become available only for a fee, but basic information remains free and useful. Go to **www.salary.com** to get started. Let's pick Provo, Utah, as our location and "retail cashier" as our position of interest. Then click the Get my salary estimate button.

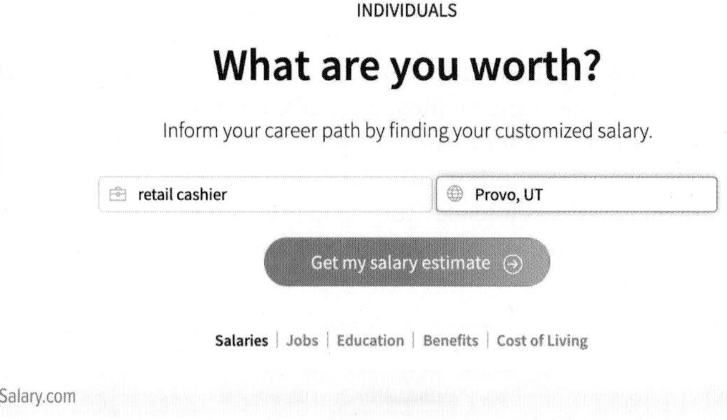

Salary.com

The resulting page gives you several job positions. Choose the one that says "Retail Cashier—Full-Time". The resulting report shows the median (50 percent of people above, 50 percent of people below this level) salary for the position, for example, $21,520. The graphic also gives you the range of the salary by percentile (a 75th percentile means 75 percent of people have lower numbers, and 25 percent have higher).

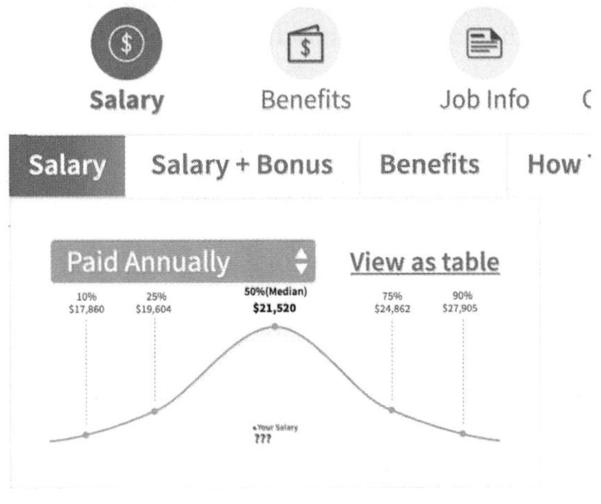

Salary.com

Next, click on "Benefits" to the right of "Salary". Here you will find the median salary as well as the median additional amount of money spent by the employer to provide the benefits typical in that zip code. See an example below.

Core Compensation	Median	% of Total
Base Salary	$ 21,520	62.1%
Bonus	$ 60	0.2%
Value of Benefits		
Social Security	$ 1,651	4.8%
401K/403B	$ 1,057	3.1%
Disability	$ 345	1.0%
Healthcare	$ 6,371	18.4%
Pension	$ 906	2.6%
Time Off	$ 2,739	7.9%
Total Compensation	**$34,650**	**100%**

Salary.com

As a potential employer, you need to keep both the base salary and the total salary in mind. Often potential employees screen jobs based on the base salary, so it is important to offer a competitive wage. But as an employer, that position can cost you as much as the total wage, which can be from 25 to even 50 percent higher than the base wage. For the job above the total is 62 percent above the base wage.

The last place to check online is the Living Wage Calculator at MIT (**http://livingwage.mit.edu/**). A **living wage** is the amount needed for a person (or family of a particular size) to meet the basic necessities of life from a single job. In Provo, Utah, the 2020 living wage for one person was $24,336, so the median salary for a cashier given above puts the person about $54 a week below the living wage level. Even for a person with no family responsibilities, the median cashier job's pay may be too low.

living wage
The amount needed for a person (or family of a particular size) to meet the basic necessities of life from a single job.

When deciding on a wage, it is important to remember that some benefits are required, like Social Security and Disability, while others may be up to the entrepreneur's choice, like health care or retirement plans. If the job is covered by a contract with a labor union (see The Thoughtful Entrepreneur), there are likely to be additional requirements around pay, benefits, and working conditions. If you expect the job you offer to be the employee's full-time job, it is important, and when you think about it, only fair, to make sure you cover his or her basic needs.

Moreover, salary should be tied to a person's skills and experience. Subsequent increases need to be based on an employee's performance, value, and contribution to the small business. Use the information from the employee's performance appraisal form to help you determine the appropriate increase. You will also want to consider percentages of increase in salary in similar jobs in your local area.[43]

Bonuses and Long-Term Incentives[44]

Employee bonuses, usually paid in a single lump at the end of the year, are one way of providing performance incentives. Profit-sharing plans, stock options, or stock grants not only provide long-term incentives to employees, but they can also help retain valuable team members through your small business start-up phase. However, you also may want to consider these options once you are beyond the start-up phase and have stability in your business earnings overall.

Health Insurance[45]

Employer-sponsored health insurance is fairly standard among medium-sized companies, but not among small businesses. While an employer-sponsored plan saves employees money and gives them peace of mind in knowing that they won't be denied coverage, it is not always affordable to the small business owner. However, providing insurance to your employees sends the message that you care about their health and the health of their families. The Patient Protection and Affordable Care Act (popularly called Obamacare) does not require health insurance for small businesses with fewer than 50 employees. But to encourage health care coverage for as many as possible, it offers tax credits for firms with fewer than 25 employees. This is called the Small Business Health Options Program (SHOP) with details at www.healthcare.gov/small-businesses/. In addition, the health care exchanges (also called marketplaces) provide new options for lower-cost coverage for all small businesses. To minimize costs, consider having employees pick up part of the tab. Employees who have coverage through a spouse may want to opt out of a plan, particularly if there's a cost associated with it. The Affordable Care Act has been the focus of political debate at the federal level, so be sure to check out the latest details when you are looking for health care options for your small business.

Retirement Plans[46]

401(k) plans have become popular because they are relatively easy to administer and are less expensive than traditional pension plans. Many employees like these plans because they maintain some control over the amount of their contribution and how the money is invested. Most small companies try to put some kind of savings or 401(k) plan in place, even if they don't contribute money to them. Other incentives that you may want to consider include time off and flexible schedules such as holidays, vacations, sick days, and personal days. An employer unable to offer competitive salaries may close part of the gap by offering more time off or flexible work hours. Some employers make no distinction between sick, vacation, and personal days and allow employees a set number of days off each year to be used at their discretion. This prevents employees from abusing sick days and keeps employees from feeling that they need to lie when a child is ill or a personal emergency arises.

Perks

Perk is short for *perquisite* and refers to the privileges, services, or even tangible items given to employees as part of the overall compensation and benefits package. Perks are a great way to provide short-term boosts in motivation—in effect a psychological pick-me-up. Good perks do not have to cost a lot; in fact, some perks can be powerful, even if free. Consider the list of perk ideas given in Table 18.4.

The rule of thumb is that perks like these should take no more than 3 percent of the annual personnel budget. That said, a bagel and coffee breakfast for your staff may be a very inexpensive way to say you care about them, as well as being a great way to position them for a more productive day. In the long term, that is what compensation and benefits are supposed to achieve.

THE THOUGHTFUL ENTREPRENEUR

LABOR UNIONS

Today a tiny percentage of small business employees are members of labor unions. A labor union is an organization of employees that usually work for the same employer at the same workplace. Labor unions try to get a "collective" contract for their members. The labor laws governing unions can be very complicated. If you are faced with a union organizing drive, you should contact a labor lawyer immediately to make sure that your response to the organizing drive is legal.

If your employees belong to a labor union they probably already made a "union contract," which is also called a "collective bargaining agreement," with you. This agreement and contract covers wages, working conditions, and procedures for complaining about problems on the job.

Union contracts usually provide that employees cannot be fired, suspended, or disciplined without "good cause." This rule is usually found in a section of the contract titled "Grievance Procedure" or "Discipline." If an employee thinks you didn't have "good cause" to fire or discipline, he or she generally contacts the union. The union may decide to file a grievance for the worker against you. If the union files a grievance against you, you should see an attorney who specializes in labor law, who should help you decide how to defend against the grievance. If you have questions about labor unions, contact a business lawyer near you, or you can start some of the research yourself by contacting the U.S. Department of Labor's Office of Labor-Management Standards, **www.dol.gov/olms**. Its main goal is to help employers and employees comply with Department of Labor laws and regulations as well as to give you additional information related to your state's laws and compliance issues specific to managing and operating your small business.

TABLE 18.4 Innovative Low-Cost and Free Perks for Your Employees[47]

- Give time off and provide flexible scheduling (especially for families with children and older adults at home). Consider reinstating "recess."
- Arrange discounts with local and online merchants for your employees.
- Offer free seminars onsite or online (your insurers, banks, and HMOs will often do this for free onsite and might have videos to share).
- Arrange pickups and deliveries at your location for your employees (like dry cleaning, car washing, etc.).
- Offer supplemental services administered through payroll—but paid for by the employee (e.g., supplemental health insurance or retirement programs, prepaid legal services, etc.).
- Offer credit union memberships.
- Let employees buy excess inventory at a big discount.
- Feature special days (work-from-home days, family days, community service days, bring-your-dog-to-work days, pizza lunch days, etc.).
- Offer a group perk like two tickets to a movie that weekend.
- Offer free car washes in the lot (detailers will charge around $5 per car for external washes bought in bulk).
- Let employees expense work clothing bought for sales efforts.
- Hold an after-work party.
- Bring a continental breakfast for all.
- Set up a nap room, or a video and board game meeting space.
- Offer massages (Silicon Valley start-ups do)
- Offer a volunteer day off or a service day for the firm.

HRM at the Founder's Level

Founding entrepreneurs face some internal human resource management issues as they think about and create their firm, and connect with the first people who will be central to the firm. There are three issues to think about: the leadership you provide, the advisers you secure, and the partners you select.

The Leadership You Provide

In most general management and business classes, when we talk about "leadership," what we really mean is administration. In fact, the two key factors in traditional leadership theories are task and person. If you are getting the job done, and you are keeping your people happy with each other and the firm, then you have achieved the primary goals of "leadership." Neither one of these key factors does much to explain what we commonly think of when we talk about leaders like Washington or Jobs or Musk. The disconnect is exactly the difference between everyday administration of your team and project, and that beyond the regular increment of energy that we imagine around people with entrepreneurial leadership.

Leadership is essential to the growth of any small business. If you intend to have employees, you need to be able to provide the skills of the entrepreneurial leader. In any year, about 79 percent of the businesses in the United States consist of only their owner. There are no employees. This remains true for most one-person businesses, and when larger small businesses are studied, we often find that businesses freeze their employee growth at particular levels. Some of this can be explained by a desire to avoid ever-increasing levels of federal and state laws, with their complexities and costs, but an even more powerful reason is that many entrepreneurs realize that there is an optimal size of firm for them to manage. It is central to your evaluating your potential for entrepreneurial leadership.

Entrepreneurial leadership looks at how you operate as the chief executive of your business. It has three key components over and above task and person—innovation, operation, and inspiration. Innovation is the idea that we look to the leader of a small business as its key visionary. The owner should be the person thinking about the future of the business, how to compete better, how to grow, what next new thing should be tried. Employees can contribute ideas, but in the end, the boss is the key to innovation. If you spend all your time worrying about today and spend no time thinking about tomorrow, eventually your business will lose.

Operation is often the scariest of the three components—although it is the one most closely related to the task and person elements of administrative leadership. Operation refers to the ability to manage the business as it grows. Some people have trouble delegating. Those people often feel out of control when they start to employ others, and the business suffers as a result. They may not know how to delegate, or even if they do, they want to rush in and take over when things "go bad" (i.e., "It was not done the way *I* would have done it.") and thus undermine the employees. Some bosses are just so personally disorganized that it can be difficult to explain or find or share with others the key information of the business, and so the business is locked inside their heads or on their piled-high desktop. If you have employees and they are unhappy, the most likely problem is one of operation.

Inspiration is the third component, and stems from the very reasonable expectation among employees and customers that the entrepreneur should be the business's biggest booster and champion. If you do not have 100 percent iron-clad belief in your business, its product and services, its people, and your ability to make it all work, how can anyone else? While the ability to deliver a stirring speech is an admirable inspirational skill, it is not necessary. Speaking quietly from the heart can work just as well, as long as it is apparent that it *is* from the heart, and it is backed by your own passion. Think of retired basketball coaches Phil Jackson and Bobby Knight. Both inspire, but one is quietly intense, and one is loudly bombastic.

How do you know if you have what it takes in terms of entrepreneurial leadership? Your past experience is the best indicator. If you have been a leader of teams, study groups, shifts at work, or church projects, and people seemed to get the job done and liked each other and you—you probably have what it takes to cover the operation. If you could keep them working when problems arose or times were tough, then you probably have what it takes in terms of inspiration.

If you have not had these sorts of opportunities, college is a great place to get them–in classes, in student organizations, and at work. If you have had these opportunities and they have not been positive, then you want to enroll in workshops and classes on leadership and supervision, and develop the behaviors you need to be successful. You can test out how well you are learning by volunteering to lead on and off campus. Innovation is often easy for entrepreneurs because the process of creating and growing a business is a natural application of the innovative component of leadership.

The Advisers You Secure

One special area of hiring concerns your advisers. Small businesses organized as corporations will have share owners who belong to a board of directors, and who are ultimately responsible for the business. You pick those directors by taking their investment in your business.

But there is another type of board many founders create regardless of the ownership structure of the business. This is called your **advisory board**. This is a group of people you assemble because you trust their judgment and goodwill toward you and your firm.[48] These may be current or retired entrepreneurs, managers, or professionals. They may meet with you as a group, or individually, and meetings may be scheduled or impromptu.

advisory board
A group of formal or informal people offering advice and a sounding board to the owner or manager of a business. Unlike boards of directors, advisory boards (or single advisors) do not have legal or fiduciary responsibilities for the business.

There is an old saying "It's lonely at the top," and the owner often can't discuss problems or prospects in the business with employees. Having advisers to talk with gives the entrepreneur a chance to articulate his or her thoughts, try them out on others, and get feedback and possible suggestions on how to handle events. Generally professionals supporting your business, your attorney and accountant, are automatically advisers, albeit paid ones. Most successful entrepreneurs supplement these professionals with advisers who don't have a formal relationship with and responsibility to the firm.

Advisers may be recruited from people you know from business, school, church, civic organizations, anywhere. What is important is whether you think they have knowledge or connections that can help you do your business better, and if you trust them enough and feel comfortable enough around them to tell them your troubles. Many advising relationships are unpaid. Some advisers are paid a stipend of a couple of hundred dollars a year (or every quarter if your business is doing well).

Advisers serve at your pleasure. You can set a time limit, which you can extend, or keep in place to remind yourself to get some fresh perspectives.

The Partners You Select

Selecting partners is probably the greatest challenge an entrepreneur faces. We talked about entrepreneurial teams in Chapter 2, but left the discussion of partner selection for here. Partnership is very much like marriage. In fact, the partnership legal form of organizing is just like a marriage in the joint ownership and responsibility of the partners! But even for partnerships organized with different legal forms, the issues of mutual responsibility and support remain very much intact.

Research[49] has shown that there is a simple model for success in partnerships in business and life–*shared core values and complementary skills*. In fact, here is one of the best-known definitions of a team: "A team is a small number of people with complementary skills who are committed to a common purpose, performance goals, and approach for which they hold themselves mutually accountable."[50] The core values of business build from that definition and relate to:

1. **Mission:** Why are you in business? For financial reasons? To bring a product or service to life? Because you need to keep busy? Because you have a burning passion? Partners driven by different reasons for being in the business will rarely be pulling hard in the same direction, so the business will always seem a bit unfocused or diffuse. Partners who agree on the "why" of the business are more likely to share and generate passion in the firm and agree on more, more often.
2. **Money:** How much is enough? If one person is happy making $50,000 a year and another wants to become a millionaire ASAP, you can see where trouble will come up. Will you go after every dime? Do you want to pitch a business for high-rollers or everyday people? When

times are bad, how do you react–tighten your belt and wait it out, or get out and sell more or take a bigger risk in hopes of a win? Disagreements over money are the number one reason for divorces, and its close to the same in business.

3. **Method:** Money and mission represent the "ends" of your business–method represents the "means." How will you treat your customers, your employees, your suppliers, your competitors, your community, your environment, and each other? How focused are you on what's happening today and how much do you think about and plan for the future? How professionalized (from Chapter 1) do you want to get? Method is the most involved of the three core values, and it can better handle differences among partners than mission and money, but partners with very different thoughts about method will face more tough times in their business.

Complementary skills relate to what you are good at, and what you partner brings to the relationship. Your firm is stronger the more skills, forms of expertise, resources, and connections its principals have. If you are a classic inventor–thoughtful, thorough, methodical–your firm might benefit from having a classic sales type–intuitive, spontaneous, adaptive–on the team. If the partners have differing (i.e., complementary) skills but share their core values, they will be able to handle more kinds of situations, and benefit from the differing expertise each partner brings to the business.

Note that *partners* can be more than a legal term. You can apply the same thinking to employees, looking for employees whose skills add to the capabilities of the firm, and who share your core values. They may not share ownership of the firm, but using this approach, you may hire employees who psychologically are partners in the firm and its success–literally, passionate members of your company team. To the extent that your employees share in the core values and share their skills, your passion for your firm becomes something shared by everyone in the firm.

LO **18-7** Explain the complexities of managing family within your business.

Human Resource Issues in the Family Business

Family business is a catchall term covering tens of millions of firms. In fact, some researchers estimate that 95 percent of all businesses are indeed family businesses.[51] From a one-person business with occasional infusions of free help from family members to larger family firms employing multiple generations of family members along with nonfamily employees, there are two key human resource management issues that continually surface in family businesses: striking a balance between nepotism and meritocracy as well as managing privilege. There are basic human resource management "best practices" that help whether the business is a family firm or a business with no family ties that get covered next, with a moment spent revisiting the issues of managing compensation and benefits within the family business and the family.

Nepotism, Meritocracy, and the Family Business

nepotism
A management philosophy of selecting and promoting people based on family ties.

meritocracy
A management philosophy of selecting and promoting people based solely on their being the most capable person for the job.

As a family business owner, you need to make a decision about how you feel about two ideas that at first do not fit easily together–nepotism and meritocracy. **Nepotism** is the management philosophy of selecting and promoting people based on family ties. Nepotism's advantages are involving people you know and hopefully trust in your business, being able to involve the person more completely (in terms of work time and family time) in the business, and having loyalty and support from your worker and their family in return. **Meritocracy**, on the other hand, is the management philosophy of selecting and promoting people based solely on their being the most capable person for the job.

When the family member is also the most capable person for the job, the two philosophies live in harmony. But what if you want to hire your son as manager and hopeful heir to the business, but there is a more capable person available to you? If you can afford to employ and use both, you may be able to eventually create a strong top management team using both people. If you can afford to hire only one person, this is when you have to make a hard decision as to which philosophy wins out.[52]

If you are extremely lucky, your family member might make life easy by saying that you hired the best person and that is the best for all in the long run. But it is just as likely that hiring meritocratically is seen as showing no loyalty to kin, and results in estranged relationships in the family. In a family business, if the family is stressed out, it almost always spills over into the business in negative and sometimes disastrous ways.

Sometimes it is important to recognize that "good enough" may well be just that. If the family member is good enough to do the job well (but perhaps not *as well* as the nonfamily candidate), hiring from the family may well make the most sense in the long run, to build the family and the family business. It is one situation where it might make sense to favor a slightly nepotistic philosophy over a strictly meritocratic one.

If you make that nepotistic decision, what you as the decision maker must do is avoid comparisons of the family member you hired to the "one that got away." It is your job to make every employee, including family members you hire, best able to contribute to the business. Part of being the boss is taking responsibility for your decisions, especially when that is difficult.[53]

The nepotism versus meritocracy issues also comes up when the child of a family business owner considers coming into the family business. If this happens right after graduating, the nagging question for the owner, the potential heir, and the employees is whether the young person gets ahead because of his or her skill or family tie. The answer to this is simple and often highly beneficial to everyone–work somewhere else first.[54]

In particular, seek a job in a related industry, or with a customer, or even with a competitor with whom your family's business is friendly (e.g., a similar company operating in a different market). A job in one of these areas will give you insight into groups important to your business. It can expand your contacts in key areas like new customers or suppliers, and it can help you learn new ways of getting things done to bring back to the family business.

If you take a job elsewhere, and do a good job there, you return to the family business a proven winner in a more objective situation. You know you have done well, your new fellow employees know it, and your boss knows it. It helps by giving you a stronger basis for what you say, and what you say you are worth.

Managing Privilege

Nepotism has the potential to play a role in the everyday operations of your business and its human resource activities. In fact, many entrepreneurs purposely create a family business in order to give their family members jobs, a sense of purpose, incomes for now with the possibility of future ownership, *and* the privileges of flexibility. Part of the advantage they imagine for a family business is that it can accommodate family needs better than an impersonal, nonfamily business. So the boss's son, who works in the family business, needs time off to coach the grandson's hockey team. In a family business, a doting grandparent can give the time off. You can see how this could be great for the family, but come across as unfair to nonfamily employees.[55]

There is a way to handle this that is easy to say and hard to do–separate family and business. In those everyday occurrences at work, family members should be treated just like anyone else, with no special status or privileges. Making decisions based on what is best for the firm (a meritocratic philosophy) and what is fair to other employees (the basic idea of equality) is a great way to operate if you can do so without totally alienating your family.

Giving all employees similar privileges, or denying favorable treatment to your family are the options most likely to work overall. When looking at "similar privileges," realize that they do not have to be identical. Letting family and nonfamily members pick and choose from a set of privileges or benefits helps create a situation where people in the firm can opt for working (or not working) in a way that best fits with their needs.

Sometimes, the opposite can happen. Some owners hold expectations that their family should work longer and harder than anyone else, because, after all, it is the family's business.[56] If the family members are working harder without the promise of eventual ownership, they are unlikely to upset nonfamily members. If those family members are believed to be making a down payment of sweat equity for future ownership of the firm, there is a greater possibility of negative employee reaction, since the family members' harder work looks like it could have a large payout in the future. Realize that such situations reflect the creation of a type of career

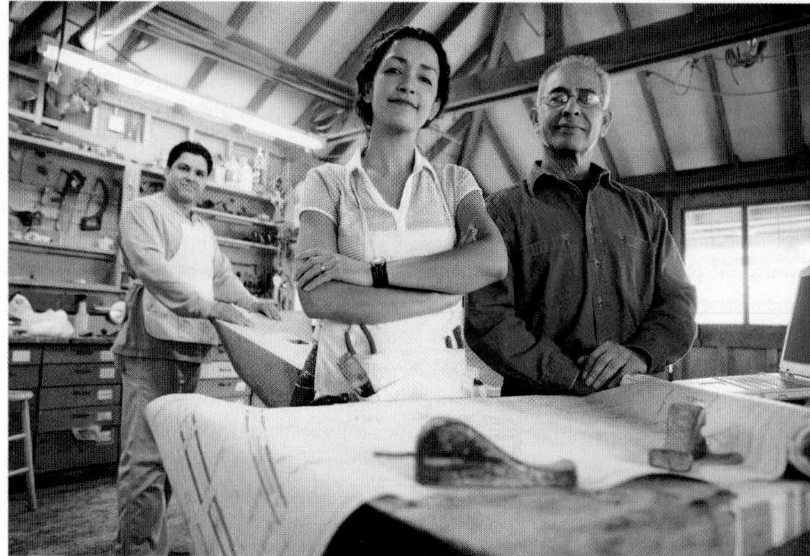

When it is working well, having multiple generations together in a family business is a great experience. What sort of HR actions are most likely to minimize problems in a family business?

ColorBlind Images/Blend Images LLC

ladder—a sequence of increasingly responsible positions—for family members, with ownership at the top.

In the end, while sales to employees or to an outsider are possibilities, they are relatively rare events. Family firms most often stay in the family. But to treat family and nonfamily as similarly as possible, it becomes especially important to create career ladders for nonfamily members. These may not lead to ownership, but can lead to increased skills, responsibilities, and income. Having career ladders for all employees is a way to help minimize the differences and show how important every employee's contribution is seen to be.

While talking about handling employees, let us jump from the best to the worst. Have you heard the phrase "With privilege comes responsibility"? Where that applies in a family business is when other family members want to saddle your firm with family members who are not a good fit to your business.[57]

If you can find a place where their skills would be a good fit, then you may be able to sidestep a problem. There is another old saying that "For every pot, there is a lid," and that may be the best solution. If you end up saddled with this person, consider putting him or her to work where the individual can do the least harm to the business and to your employees. Also, since the family may have guilted you into hiring the person, don't be shy about reversing the process to guilt those same people into helping you make the new family employee toe the line. Obviously, if mentoring, coaching, or training can work to help the person do well, those are great ways to resolve a tricky problem.

In the end, disciplining and even firing the relative may be necessary. "Sometimes people think just because they're family, they can take advantage of the rules," says Leon Eastmond, president of A. L. Eastmond & Sons Inc., a second-generation, family-run boiler/tank manufacturing and repair company in New York City. "But I won't tolerate such foolishness. Business is business, and I tell them that I don't dictate the terms of their behavior; the business does. If they don't act properly on the job, they'll be on a slippery banana with this company—even if they're members of the family."[58]

Good Human Resource Practices for All Businesses

As you have seen, there are times when a family business may need to reflect a bit of nepotism but that we recommend a general philosophy of meritocracy in handling employees, both family and nonfamily. This is true for most of the key elements of a good human resource (HR) approach. The professional way to craft a consistent HR process depends on a set of key elements:[59]

- *Transparent procedures with consistent application:* There should be procedures in place to handle the major human resource activities of a firm. They should be publicly known and they should be consistently and fairly applied.

- *Job basics:* The basics for every job should consist of the job description, which we talked about earlier in the chapter. The version of that job description used after the hire should also explain how this position relates to other jobs, so all people in the firm can be sure what is (and is not) the individual's responsibility.
- *Job metrics:* It should be possible to objectively evaluate how well someone is doing his or her job. It is ideal if the metric is clear enough for the employee to be certain that he or she did the job well or poorly. Note that metrics are not just for after the job. Knowing the metrics to be applied help employees know what is expected on the job.
- *Task repair:* People will make mistakes. That is true of everyone in business. When that happens, are there processes in place to help the mistake-maker learn what went wrong, and how to do a better job the next time? Knowing that learning (even trial-and-error learning) is a part of the job helps the mistake-maker feel less threatened and helps employees take the initiative when needed.
- *Lines of communication:* Even good employees can have a valid complaint about something in the firm and need an outlet to express their views. This can be as simple as a suggestion box (wooden or electronic), an open-door policy to hear complaints and suggestions, a special time set aside with your people to talk about their ideas and issues, or an ombudsperson or go-between who confidentially receives the complaints and suggestions and forwards them to the owner.
- *Clear termination rules:* Mistakes can happen, and will. Some will repeat, and if they do, it may be necessary to fire someone. Other mistakes will be so enormous that firing the person responsible may be the only way to save the firm. When firing is necessary, are the reasons for it clear to all? Are the rules and procedures used known to all, and applied the same way to all people, family and nonfamily alike? Firing is emotionally difficult for everyone, but having procedures that are known, known to be fair, and followed consistently help the process go more smoothly.
- *Lines of appeal:* Lines of appeal means having a way for the person who has failed to meet a metric, or made a mistake, or is facing firing to have their side of the story heard. In small businesses this can be tough since the owner might be the disciplinarian. In such cases, having a trusted employee (or even an entrepreneur outside the business who knows the business and people and is trusted by the owner) serve as the go-between can help.

Dividing Up Ownership and Dividends

Family businesses can also add complexity to compensation and benefit packages. This typically occurs when family members working in the business receive a compensation or benefits package that looks like it was modeled after the owners' packages instead of the other employees' packages. For example, owners of corporations often receive the base of their compensation as a salary as the CEO of the corporation. In addition, they receive a dividend from the corporation based on company profits and amount of stock owned.

Family members working in the business may also receive a similar package, which raises their annual salary above nonfamily employees in similar positions. The best ways to handle this are to create profit-sharing plans or a bonus system for nonfamily employees based on performance.[60] These approaches help give everyone in the firm a stake in the outcome and a tangible benefit for good performance. There is often a temptation to declare salaries and dividends secret and assume you are done with the problem, but in reality few pay plans are secret, and HR-related secrets in most businesses are usually counterproductive.

The benefits problem is tougher to solve. Today, with health benefits so costly and so important to people, family businesses can end up with different levels of health care benefits for owners and employees. That type of difference is a bit easier to take than differences between family and nonfamily employees, since the health of the business directly depends on the health of the owner, not necessarily the other family members.

Obviously the best solution is treating family and nonfamily members the same. There are several possible ways to do this. Offering the higher level of benefits to all employees at a subsidized rate may make it easier for family members to get a superior benefits package without discriminating against other employees. Along these lines, the cost of these higher level of benefits can be paid for employees who are family members using money from the owner's or family's stock dividends.

Dividing Ownership in Nonfamily Start-Ups

While considering the particular complexities of equity splits in the family business, realize that even when it is not family involved in a start-up, there can be major questions about who gets how much equity and for what contribution. There are many ways to think about it, but one that has received wide attention and positive reviews builds on the idea of "Slicing Pie" by Mike Moyer at slicingpie.com. In his model employees' share of the rewards should equal their share of their at-risk contributions. His model counts not only money invested but time, equipment and supplies, facilities, intellectual property, and relationships (which are ties to sales and commissions). Everything is converted to its cash equivalent at fair market value, and each person's share divided by the total of all shares, determines the employee's share of ownership, called his or her slice.

Models like this clarify the value of what each person brings to the business, and provides a relatively transparent way to build out the equity shares. While no model is always going to be perfect,[61] the Slicing Pie model helps account for most of the situations of businesses built from the ground up without outside money. And if the participants decide to include other factors, they can. You will find there are several variants of this approach, and it will be worth your time to look at them to find the model that best fits what you and your start-up team members think is fairest.[62]

You may notice that a recurring theme in this section is to treat people as close to the same as possible, and to be transparent and open in policies and communications in general.[63] That open, transparent, equal, and communicative approach is essential to a successful HR policy in the small business or family business. The natural human resource and competitive advantage of a small or family business is realized when the firm treats all of its people "like family." That usually reflects a personal touch, a focus on personal needs, and the flexibility to treat people equally well, even if that does not mean treating each person identically (which is how big businesses end up applying the idea of "equal treatment"). Small businesses and family businesses, especially in their early years, may not be able to afford the compensation and benefit packages of larger businesses, but they often have exceptionally loyal and hardworking employees. Why? Because that "like family" atmosphere in the small or family business makes a tremendous difference for good in a lot of employees. That atmosphere is driven more by open communication and personal concern than through other policies or payouts. That is why the key to successful human resource management in *every* type of small or family business rests with open communication.

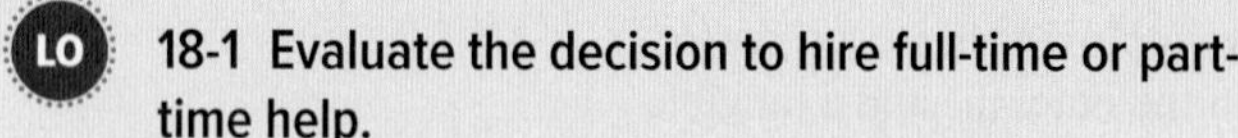

CHAPTER SUMMARY

LO 18-1 Evaluate the decision to hire full-time or part-time help.

- There are many additional expenses to having a full-time employee as opposed to a part-time employee. You need to consider the pros and cons and expand cautiously.
- The cost of adding an employee includes compensation, training time, employee taxes, and accounting costs.
- Whether you hire a part-time or full-time employee, it is important that the employee values your company's mission.

LO 18-2 Understand how to recruit good employees on your budget.

- For the small business owner, there are inexpensive, alternative methods to consider in attracting and recruiting key employees.
- Networking, Internet recruiting, employee referrals, and company websites are several ways to look for talent for your small business. Also consider bartering and internships for part-time employees.
- Hire virtual employees who have experience with being self-motivated and disciplined, including former consultants and freelancers who are accustomed to dealing with deadlines and working independently.

- As you manage your virtual employees, make sure to spend time developing a system of task lists, schedules, and goals with varying time frames and clear deadlines.

LO 18-3 Know how to match the right person to the job.

- The first step in hiring is writing a job description that discusses and reveals all the essential knowledge, skills, and abilities that are needed to fill the position.
- Use the job description to help you evaluate whether an individual would be the right match for the position and your small business.
- Use the information developed in the job description to identify the most important knowledge areas, skills, and abilities the ideal candidate should possess. Next, create specific questions that you will ask of all candidates that will clearly and behaviorally demonstrate to you that they have these critical factors.

LO 18-4 Describe employee training methods and resources.

- To begin, you should first assess your small firm's training needs from the perspective of the business, the job itself (job description), and the needs of the employees.
- There are two different types of training: initial training and ongoing training.
- There are two broad types of training available to small businesses: on-the-job and off-the-job techniques. Individual circumstances and the where, what, and who of your training program determine which method to use.

LO 18-5 Recognize how to meet employees' needs and expectations.

- Factors conducive to a positive and rewarding work environment include communication, teamwork, recognition, training, empowerment, and contribution.
- Increasingly, small entrepreneurial companies are implementing formal performance appraisals. Reviewing employees' performance is an ongoing process.
- The performance appraisal sheet should include open-ended questions for the employee to fill out regarding job performance, strengths, areas of development, and what gets in the way of accomplishing the job.

LO 18-6 Develop a fair compensation and benefit plan.

- One of the first steps in developing a compensation plan is to determine your organization's salary philosophy. The next step is to find comparison factors for salary. Subsequent increases need to be based on employee performance, value, and contribution to the small business.
- Employee bonuses, usually paid in a single lump at the end of the year, are one way of providing performance incentives (consider also profit-sharing plans, stock options, or stock grants early or later on).
- While an employer-sponsored medical insurance plan saves employees money and gives them peace of mind in knowing that they won't be denied coverage, it may not always be affordable to the small business owner.

LO 18-7 Explain the complexities of managing family within your business.

- Family business owners need to strike a balance between nepotism and meritocracy that they can live with.
- Treating everyone in the business the same is the best approach for minimizing the problems arising from favoring family members.
- Having open and transparent human resource policies and practices can help family and nonfamily businesses run more effectively.
- In all businesses, open communication is the key to effective human resource management.

KEY TERMS

employee fit, 646
probationary period, 647
Internet recruiting, 650
employee referral, 650
virtual employee, 651
job description, 652
exempt, 655
nonexempt, 655
on-the-job training, 659
open-book policy, 661
psychological contract, 661
Fair Labor Standards Act (FLSA), 661
living wage, 663
advisory board, 667
nepotism, 668
meritocracy, 668

DISCUSSION QUESTIONS

1. As a small business owner, you will most likely have the opportunity to hire either part-time or full-time employees. What do you need to consider in determining which one will be best for you and when to hire the first or another employee for your business?
2. Whether you hire a part-time or full-time employee, in what ways can you ensure that each type of employee knows and values your company's mission?
3. While a smaller firm can actually outperform large businesses in attracting high-quality employees, how can you communicate to the job market the multiple benefits of working within your firm? How can you get the word out about these advantages in a cost-effective manner?
4. What are the multiple benefits of hiring virtual employees for your small business? What are some of the ways to manage and foster productivity among your virtual employees? Are there any drawbacks to these methods?
5. What recommendations or suggestions would you give Paige Arnof-Fenn, founder and CEO of Mavens & Moguls, on how to manage and "orchestrate" her multiple virtual employees?
6. What are some of the different ways small business owners can write a job description for the first time? How can they ensure that they cover all the essential knowledge, skills, and abilities that are needed for the position? Why is this important?
7. As a new small business owner, what can you do to make sure you hire the right person for the job? This is probably one of the most difficult decisions you may be faced with making, especially since we all are not trained in the art and science of hiring employees.
8. What specific training guidelines would you incorporate into your business? What inexpensive techniques (on-the-job training) can you use after you make the first hire? Did the owner of the business where you are employed use any of these techniques with you? If so, how beneficial were they to your own development and learning?
9. What are creative ways that you can retain your first employee and ensure you are meeting his or her needs? Consider how you can meet or exceed the employee's "psychological contract."
10. Consider your previous employment position; did the firm have an open-book philosophy? How much information was shared regarding the strategy and financials of the business? What are the advantages and disadvantages of sharing too much or too little information with employees, particularly from a small business owner perspective?
11. Managing health care costs is one of the biggest concerns for small business owners; what are some creative ways that they can minimize some of these costs? In your own community, how have owners confronted these concerns and costs? Be specific with types and the size of the small firms you believe are being innovative in how they manage health care costs.
12. Dr. David Gage, a clinical psychologist, has argued that "Families don't need written guidelines to operate, but family businesses do."[64] What are some initial guidelines that should be defined in the family business?
13. As mentioned, one of the most common problems in a family business is the hiring of relatives who do not have talent to fulfill the necessary job responsibilities. What can you do if you are "stuck" with an unproductive family member to ensure that he or she does not disturb the work and interfere with the operations of the business?

EXPERIENTIAL EXERCISES

1. At ReCellular, Inc., a cellular phone remanufacturing company in Ann Arbor, Michigan, the small business owner put together a list of interview questions that immediately improved the hiring process. The owner first defined the qualities, characteristics, and basic aptitude he wanted to find in a potential remanufacturing employee. The owner wanted to find people who shared these characteristics:
   - Excellent attendance and dependability
   - Flexibility
   - Integrity and honesty
   - Motivated and dedicated
   - Detail-oriented
   - Team-oriented
   - Strong work ethic
   - Positive, polite, and approachable
   - Continuous improvement–oriented

- Good communication skills
- Actual hands-on demonstration of capability to sort phones and identify cosmetic problems with phones

The owner then worked with several online resources to structure questions that would indicate whether candidates had these characteristics. No list of questions is totally comprehensive; however, these questions are helping the interviewers find better candidates:

- What made you decide to apply at ReCellular?
- Tell me about yourself and your last/current job/class.
- When we call your previous employer for references, what is he or she likely to tell us in regard to your dependability/attendance?
- Tell me about a time when you demonstrated your trustworthiness or integrity in school or at work.

This is, of course, a start—your job is to think of other questions that the small business owner may want to ask a potential employee (either for a full-time, part-time, or virtual assistant position).

2. Let's say the federal minimum wage in your state is $7.25 an hour, or $ 14,500 a year (although there are places where it is higher (see **www.minimum-wage.org/wage-by-state**). As an entrepreneur, it can look attractive to pay the minimum wage because it gives your firm more financial cushion. But what does paying the minimum wage do for any cushion of the employee? The *New York Times* has an online interactive budgeting tool to let you see how well you could live on the federal minimum wage at **www.nytimes.com/interactive/2014/02/09/opinion/minimum-wage.html**. Try it out and report on your results.

3. Small business owner Jeff Birdsell opened Shauncey's Gourmet Ice Cream, Inc. in Battlefield Shopping Center in Springfield, Missouri. Like any small business owner, Jeff realized that starting this venture would entail a tremendous commitment of time and energy. He had expected to work 60–80 hours a week indefinitely, and finds he works at least that. He estimates that he and his parents frequently tally up to 250 hours per week in the organization. Employee turnover at Shauncey's runs at 100 percent per year. What creative and innovative hiring and retention recommendations would you give Jeff as he manages both his family and part-time workers (especially with 100 percent employee turnover)?

4. Go to **Salary.com** and look for a position in *retail sales* in *Lincoln, NE*. Look for a listing for "Retail Sales Staff—Full Time" and check out the job description as well as the salary and benefits. What is the most typical educational level of people with this job? Including salary and benefits, what will you need to spend on this position per year, if you were aiming to pay the median wage?

MINI-CASE

VIVID SKY EMPLOYEE WAVE 3

It was 2006 and Vivid Sky's sole product, SkyBOX, had survived its pilot test. Designed as an in-stadium information service for fans, SkyBOX offered video feeds, statistics, infographics (like graphics of the last 10 pitches, last 10 hits, etc.), maps, live chats and voting, and in-seat ordering. All of this was delivered by wireless PDAs (personal digital assistant; think of a PalmPilot) "hardened" to withstand dropping and spilled liquids.

SkyBOX got to this stage because of three different waves of employees. Founder Tim Hayden was tech-savvy, but lacked the skills to write the code that would meld all of these different streams of data into one application. The first wave of programmers worked with Tim at his full-time employer. They shared Tim's love of sports and passion for using technology to revitalize the stadium experience. Together they created the overall design of the program and an interactive demo to show potential investors. These employees worked nights and weekends with no expectations. Since they couldn't put more time (and money) into the project, they decided to move on to other projects once Tim had a working model.

Tim used the local network he built as SkyBOX developed to recruit the next group of programmers. This group was even more skilled, and they were able to dedicate the time to build a "basic" application. For this, Tim was able to pay them a small amount as he continued to bootstrap the company. Unfortunately, they found that they lacked the time to take SkyBOX to the level of refinement customers and investors were asking for. Lacking equity in the business, they left on their own when Tim asked them to.

The third wave of programmers had more time and wanted to take the "basic" SkyBOX to the next level. This group, recruited from across the country based on Tim's SkyBOX promotional trips, created a highly interactive application that was used for Vivid Sky's first stadium deployment. Because of their dedication, Tim decided to give the developers a bonus in the form of equity.

But the third wave of programmers faced two major challenges. Vivid Sky was receiving requests from numerous sports properties for national and international events, and the current development team couldn't keep up with the new opportunities. Also, the current programmers were untested developers for the iPhone and iPod touch platform, which was the future of the company.

Tim faced the prospect of asking the third wave of programmers to leave Vivid Sky and give up their salaries and equity. He wasn't sure all of them would do this voluntarily, and he wasn't sure he could afford to share more of his own equity with a fourth wave of programmers. On the other hand, he knew his current programmers couldn't handle the conversion to the new platform. If he fires the programmers who don't go voluntarily, will it hamper efforts to recruit the fourth wave of programmers?

CASE DISCUSSION QUESTIONS

1. What were the differences in the sources of employees for Vivid Sky as it developed?
2. What are the benefits and problems of using equity to compensate employees? What about using pay?
3. How could Tim have managed the third wave of employees if he had hired them right off the bat?
4. Should Tim replace the third wave of programmers? If yes, how do you recommend he go about this doing this? Can you find a way for him to protect his share of the equity he has in the business?

PERSONAL NET WORTH CALCULATION TEMPLATE

	Cash Value (A)	Amount Owed to Others (B)	Net Value (A – B)
Cash			
Your personal checking account		0	
Your spouse's checking account		0	
Other checking accounts you own		0	
Money in all savings accounts		0	
Cash value of money market account		0	
Total money in other accounts		0	
TOTAL CASH			
Cash Equivalents			
Cash value of stocks owned (net of selling commissions)			
Cash value of bonds owned			
Cash value of annuity			
Cash value of IRAs			
Cash value of other retirement funds			
Cash value of life insurance			
TOTAL CASH EQUIVALENTS			
Personal Property			
Automobile 1			
Automobile 2			
Motorcycle			
Bicycles			
Personal watercraft			
Boat and motor			
Airplane			
Guns and rifles			
Cameras			
Sports equipment (binoculars, skis, parachutes, etc.)			
Art and collectibles			
Antiques			
Jewelry			
Shop tools			
Furniture			
TOTAL PERSONAL PROPERTY			

(Continued)

	Cash Value (A)	Amount Owed to Others (B)	Net Value (A – B)
Real Estate			
Primary dwelling			
Second or vacation home			
Lot at the lake			
Farms, ranches, development property			
Houses, duplexes, apartment buildings that you rent to others			
Business lots and commercial buildings			
TOTAL REAL ESTATE			
Intangible Assets			
Copyrights on books, songs, videos, movies, etc. that you own			
Patents you own			
Trademarks			
URLs			
TOTAL INTANGIBLE ASSETS			
Unsecured Debt			
American Express credit card			
Mastercard 1			
Mastercard 2			
Visa card 1			
Visa card 2			
Discover card			
Unsecured loan from credit union			
Unsecured loan from bank			
Loan from your brother-in-law			
TOTALS			

GLOSSARY

4 Ps of marketing The four major components of a marketing effort—product, price, promotion, and placement. Sometimes called the marketing mix.

501(c)(3) 501(c)(3) refers to a section of the U.S. Tax Code that specifies the conditions for a nonprofit organization to be certified tax-exempt, meaning it does not pay any federal income taxes. In addition to saving taxes, 501(c)(3) status gives the recipient organization the ability to legally tell donors that their donations are also tax-exempt, which makes such donations a way to decrease the amount on which taxpayers would have to pay income taxes. This is one of the big incentives to nonprofits to increase the attractiveness of getting donations.

A/B testing A way to check customer reaction to websites describing your product or service. Two versions (version "A" and version "B") of the site are posted and are served up randomly to prospective customers. The version of the website that gets the most commitments from customers is the one kept and the less attractive site is revised and the two versions tested until one revision gets consistently superior customer reactions.

accelerator An organization that supports start-ups, typically of a particular type (e.g., Internet, biotech, fashion, sports, women-owned firms, etc.) with a financial investment, free or inexpensive office space, mentoring, a variety of free or low-cost support services, and other resources. The goal of an accelerator is to accelerate a start-up from its early stages to being ready to pitch for investment. Most accelerators take an equity stake in the companies they help.

account In terms of accounting practice, an account is a chronological list of all additions to and subtractions from a single type of asset (e.g., cash, receivables, loans outstanding).

accounting equation The statement that assets equal liabilities plus owners' equity (Assets = Liabilities + Owners' Equity).

accounts receivable Money owed to your business by customers who purchased your product on credit.

accredited investor As defined by the SEC in Title 17, Chapter II, Part 230, §230.501 of the Code of Federal Regulations (CFR): "Any person who comes within any of the following categories, or who the issuer reasonably believes comes within any of the following categories, at the time of the sale of the securities to that person: banks, business development companies, companies worth more than $5 million, an executive of the firm making the offering, or an individual with a personal net worth of more than $1 million." You may access the regulation at https://www.ecfr.gov/cgi-bin/text-idx?SID=e00bd1562536c556bceb30e9c098f2bd&mc=true&node=se17.3.230_1501&rgn=div8.

acquisition cost The total cost of acquiring an asset, including such costs as purchase price, transportation, installation, testing, and calibrating in order to ready it for its first productive use.

action The visible behavior a person takes.

advertising Often used to support the corporate identity and value propositions that are established through public relations efforts. Part of conveying your message to your customers, advertising outlets include newspapers, magazines, billboards, television, and Internet banner ads, to name a few.

advertorial Typically a paid advertisement from a company written in the form of an editorial, making the company's point about an issue, and published in the mass media.

advisory board A group of formal or informal people offering advice and a sounding board to the owner or manager of a business. Unlike boards of directors, advisory boards (or single advisors) do not have legal or fiduciary responsibilities for the business.

affiliate marketing Partnerships between firms where a firm (often a content creator) mentions the product or service of another firm. That mention includes a link to purchase the product or service, and each time the link is clicked and produces the agreed-upon outcome (seeing the website, having a cookie placed, leaving their email, requesting information, buying the product) the content creator gets paid by the other firm.

affordable loss The minimum possible expenditure of capital and other resources in order to bring an entrepreneurial idea to market.

Age Discrimination in Employment Act (ADEA) An act of Congress that makes it illegal to discriminate against people who are older than 40 years of age.

agent An intermediary business that represents a manufacturer's product or service to other business-to-business intermediary firms.

aggrandizing Attempting to make your business or yourself seem more accomplished or grander than reality.

Americans with Disabilities Act (ADA) of 1990 An act of Congress that requires that businesses make provisions for access for people with disabilities.

angel investor A wealthy individual who invests in companies in relatively early stages of development.

arbitration A dispute resolution process held instead of court cases in which both sides present their case to a legal professional.

arm's-length transaction A business deal where the parties have a prior relation or affiliation, but where the business is conducted as if they were unrelated. This approach is done to help guard against potential conflicts of interest.

articles of organization Document setting forth information about a limited liability company that is filed with the state to establish an LLC.

articles of partnership Agreement between the partners of a firm on matters pertaining to the formation and operation of the partnership.

articulate The concept that information flows from the income statement through the statements of retained earnings and owners' equity to the balance sheet.

asset Something the business owns that is expected to have economic value in the future.

assumed name filing or fictitious name filing Filing made with a state(s) in which the business operates disclosing the trade name or assumed name of the business along with the owners of the business.

augmented product Core product plus features that tend to differentiate it from the competition.

balance sheet A statement of what a business owns (assets), what it owes to others (liabilities), and how much value the owners have invested in it (equity).

Baldrige Award The Malcolm Baldrige National Quality Award is given by the U.S. government to businesses and nonprofit organizations that have been judged outstanding in seven measures of quality leadership; strategic planning; customer and market focus; measurement, analysis, and knowledge management; human resource focus; process management; and results (see www.quality.nist.gov).

bank available balance The sum of money that has actually been received and paid out of a depositor's account.

bank ledger balance The sum of deposits and withdrawals recorded in a bank's accounting records.

bankruptcy An extreme form of business termination that uses a legal method for closing a business and paying off creditors when debts are substantially greater than assets.

bar coding Obtaining a universal product code number and scan-ready visual tag, and printing it on the product or its packaging. Bar codes can then be scanned and recognized by others.

barter The practice of trading goods and services without the use of money.

BASIC An acronym for Beginner's All-purpose Symbolic Instruction Code, a computer programming language.

BATNA An acronym for Best Alternative to a Negotiated Agreement in which the second-best outcome is identified by the parties in a negotiation to help clarify the value of achieving a successful negotiation.

bearer Any person or business entity who possesses a security.

best practices Activities identified by authoritative bodies as examples of optimal ways to get things done in a particular industry, profession, or trade.

billboard principle An ethical model that asks whether someone would be comfortable having his or her decision and name advertised on a billboard for the public to see.

blog A web page in which entries are posted in reverse chronological order (i.e., the most recent at the top of the page).

blue ocean strategy A strategy based on creating a new product or service that has no competitors.

board of directors A formal group within a company that is legally responsible for the decisions and actions of the company. The directors sit above the president or chief executive officer of the company.

book value The difference between the original acquisition cost and the amount of accumulated depreciation.

book value The difference between the original cost of an asset and the total amount of depreciation expense that has been recognized to date.

boom A type of life cycle growth stage marked by a very rapid increase in sales in a relatively short time.

bootstrapping Using low-cost or free techniques to minimize your cost of doing business.

born international A new firm that opens a website immediately, thus being exposed to customers from around the world.

bot A web-based program that uses artificial intelligence techniques to automate tasks such as searches.

Brainstorming A group thinking technique where you ask participants about a situation or a product or service. You ask them to tell you all the things that come to mind when they think of that situation, product, or service. You can ask for specifics, like ways to make something better, or ways to create new versions, or ways to imagine how it would be used at other times or in other situations. In this group discussion, criticism is suspended in order to generate the maximum number of ideas.

brand The name a firm puts on itself and its products to differentiate them from competitors' offerings.

brand ambassador A person who represents your brand, company, product, or service to others to increase brand awareness, sales, and positive attitudes among the public. They can be paid or volunteer. They often receive your products and services to use and show off to the public. Also called a spokesperson.

brand promise The gains provided (i.e., the benefits) or the help given (i.e., the pains removed) by the product or service your firm offers.

bricolage A word derived from the French verb *bricoler* ("to tinker"). In entrepreneurial usage bricolage refers to the process of analyzing the resources available and creating a product or service from them.

budget A financial plan for the future based on a single level of operations; a quantitative expression of the use of resources necessary to achieve a business's strategic goals.

budget cycle A term applied to the schedule and the process for setting the schedule for making purchases by an individual or an organization.

bundling Combining two or more products in one unit and pricing it less than if the units were sold separately.

business directory sites Online services that provide the equivalent of the old telephone directory, listing businesses, their websites, phone numbers, and other information for prospective customers.

business entity concept The concept that a business has an existence separate from that of its owners.

business format franchising An agreement that provides a complete business format, including trade name, operational procedures, marketing, and products or services to sell.

business life cycle The sequence or pattern of developmental stages any business goes through during its life span.

business model A way to identify and organize key information on a business and how it achieves its goals. Business models can be analytic tools (like a business model canvas) or a way to do business (like the "razor and blade" business model).

business plan A document designed to detail the *major* characteristics of a firm—its product or service, its industry, its market, its manner of operating (production, marketing, management), and its financial outcomes on the firm's *present* and *future*.

business profile kit The name for the media kit you create for your own business (to distinguish it in your mind from the media kits of other organizations).

business-to-business (B2B) Business-to-business transactions using e-commerce.

business-to-consumer (B2C) Business-to-consumer transactions using e-commerce.

buy-in The purchase of substantially less than 100 percent of a business.

buyers People who purchase an existing business.

buyout The purchase of substantially all of an existing business.

buyout insurance Insurance that provides funds to purchase the ownership position of an owner who is disabled or deceased.

C

cannibalizing Taking business away from your employer.

capital assets Assets that are expected to provide economic benefits for periods of time greater than one year.

capital budgeting The process of deciding among various investment opportunities to create a specific spending plan.

capital lease A lease in which at the end of the lease period the asset becomes the property of the lessee, possibly with an additional payment.

captive pricing Setting the price for an item relatively low and then charging much higher prices for the expendables it uses.

cash Money that is immediately available to be spent.

cash budget A cash budget identifies when, how, and why cash is expected to come into the business, and when, how, and why it is expected to leave.

cash disbursements budget A schedule of the amounts and timings of payments of cash out of a business.

cash equivalents Assets that may be quickly converted to cash.

cash flow management Planning and tracking the amounts and timing of money to be received and paid during the business cycle.

cash receipts budget A schedule of the amounts and timings of the receipt of cash into a business.

cash-to-cash cycle The time that is required for a business to acquire resources, convert them into product, sell the product, and receive cash from the sale.

categorical question Question that is answered by selecting the proper category; for example, "What is your ethnicity? White, African American, Hispanic, Asian, American Indian, Other."

causal (predictive) reasoning The process of setting a goal and then determining the strategy and resources required to attain the goal.

causal model of entrepreneurship One of two approaches to thinking about entrepreneurship (the other is effectuation). The causal approach is one in which you want to create a particular product or service that does not yet exist, and to achieve that end, you have to cause the product or service to exist. This can mean you will have to learn new skills, or find others to help you achieve your end.

caveat emptor A Latin expression that means "let the buyer beware," which has been made into a philosophy sometimes used by businesses to put the burden for consumer protection onto the customer.

certification An examination-based acknowledgment that the firm is owned and operated as specified.

channels People and firms who connect producers of goods and services with customers.

charge back A reduction in the bank account of a merchant by a credit card company.

check the box taxation A choice LLCs can make on their tax returns to be taxed as a corporation or a partnership.

churn The turnover rate for your customers—the percentage of customers you typically lose after their first purchase from you.

Civil Rights Act of 1991 A series of acts by Congress that prohibit discrimination on the basis of race, color, religion, sex, or national origin.

clearinghouse An entity that processes checks and electronic fund transfers for banks and other financial organizations.

co-branding When two companies or brands combine to create a new product or service that combines both brands, such as Nike's LeBron sneakers.

co-insurance A contract stipulation that requires a policyholder to carry insurance in an amount equal to a stated minimum percentage of the market value of the property insured.

co-marketing A type of media partnership where two products jointly pay to advertise together. Usually this is when customers use the two products together, like chips and salsa.

co-working space A type of "incubator lite" offering low-cost shared space and basic business services (Wi-Fi, desks, coffee, conference room, copier, etc.) for a daily, weekly, or monthly rental fee. Unlike incubators, co-working spaces rarely get any equity in the businesses using the space.

cognition A person's way of perceiving and thinking about his or her experience.

cognitive dissonance Doubt that occurs after a purchase has been made. An inconsistency between experience and belief.

collateral Something of value given or pledged as security for payment of a loan; collateral may consist of financial instruments, such as stocks, bonds, and negotiable paper, or of physical goods, such as trucks, machinery, land, or buildings.

commercial paper Notes issued by credit-worthy corporations.

commercialization The process of making the new products ready for use by consumers by achieving standards of durability and performance suitable for the market and comparable to (if not better than) the competition.

community development organization An organization authorized by the SBA to make insured loans to small businesses that are expected to increase economic activity within a specific geographic area.

community service Activities undertaken to help support, repair or improve the community, its institutions, infrastructures, or people. Examples include clean-up days, disaster relief, or helping-your-neighbor efforts, among others.

company book balance The sum of cash inflows and cash outflows recorded in the firm's accounting records.

competencies Forms of business-related expertise.

competitive advantage The particular way a firm implements customer benefits that keeps the firm ahead of other firms in the industry.

competitor Any other business in the same industry as yours.

comprehensive budget Comprehensive budgets, also often referred to as *master budgets,* are sets of budgets that detail all projected receipts and spending for the budget period.

comprehensive planners Entrepreneurs who develop long-range plans for all aspects of the business.

conflict of interest A situation in which a person faces two or more competing standards or goals.

consignment The practice of accepting goods for resale, without taking ownership of them and without being responsible to pay prior to their being sold.

consumer A private individual or household that is the end user of (the entity that "consumes") a product or service.

contingency fee Fee paid by a client to an attorney for legal services that is dependent on the outcome of a case.

contract manufacturing An existing firm with the correct manufacturing capabilities makes your product for you.

conversion franchising An agreement that provides an organization through which independent businesses may combine recourses.

conversion rate The measure of how many visitors to your website (or people who click on your online advertisement) are actually willing to make a commitment to the product or service promoted on the site.

copyright Exclusive right given to the creator of a literary or artistic work to make use of that work.

core competency The main work of a firm in a particular line of business.

core product The basic description of what a product is—a bar of soap, a housecleaning service, and so on.

corporate entrepreneurship The form of entrepreneurship that takes place in existing businesses around new products, services, or markets.

corporation A legal "artificial" entity that is formed by filing specific documents with a state government.

corridor principle A theory in entrepreneurship and occupational theory that says that as you start pursuing one line of work or opportunity (which is like going down a corridor) you will encounter other opportunities.

cost of capital The percentage cost of obtaining future funds.

cost of disposition Cost incurred in the activities necessary to get rid of an asset.

cost of goods sold An expense recognized at the time of a sale of merchandise in the amount of the cost of the merchandise to the seller.

cost of operating The direct cost incurred in using an asset for the purpose for which it was intended.

cost of owning Cost incurred in financing, insuring, taxing, or tracking an asset.

cost strategy A generic strategy aimed at mass markets in which a firm offers a combination of cost benefits that appeals to the customer.

cost to start up The amount of money it takes to start a new business.

cost-volume-profit analysis A method for planning operations necessary to attain a specific profit goal. Break-even analysis is a specific application of cost-profit-volume analysis.

covenant The limitations imposed on an individual's property by the neighborhood group.

cover letter A one-page document on business stationery (also called *letterhead*) that introduces the business plan and the business owner to the recipient and indicates why the recipient is being asked to read the plan.

coverages Contractual provisions of insurance policies that specify what risks the insurance company is assuming.

creative destruction The way that newly created goods, services, or firms can hurt existing goods, services, or firms.

creativity A process producing an idea or opportunity that is novel and useful, frequently derived from making connections among distinct ideas or opportunities.

credit reporting agency (CRA) A business that collects, collates, and reports information concerning an entity's use of debt.

critical point planners Entrepreneurs who develop plans focused on the most important aspect of the business first.

cross-selling To sell related products.

crowdfunding Funding a business online through the collective involvement of others who provide donations, loans, or investments.

crowdsourcing Techniques often based on Internet services to get opinions or ideas through the collective involvement of others.

CSI entrepreneurship The identification of three settings in which entrepreneurship can be pursued, corporate settings, social (charitable) settings, and independent settings.

currency (1) A concept in public importance that alludes to the degree to which the issue is immediate to its impact (2) The bills and coins printed by governments to represent money.

current ratio The value of current assets divided by current liabilities.

customer development process The procedure to organize and pursue the finding, obtaining, and keeping of new customers.

customer job The term given to what a potential customer is trying to do—perform or complete some sort of task, solve some problem, or try to achieve some outcome. The target of the job is often the key to what a proposed product or service is intended to help.

customer lifetime value A marketing concept that refers to the revenue (or profit) generated by one customer over his or her lifetime dealing with one firm. Higher long-term value is usually preferred. CLV is also known as long-term value or LTV.

customer profile A detailed description of an archetypical or hypothetical potential customer for a product or service, also called a customer persona.

customer relationship management (CRM) The process of tracking the customer's different contacts with the firm, and using these data to help improve sales as well as the customer's experience.

customer retention (CR) Techniques that focus on efforts to promote satisfaction with and interest in the firm.

customer segment A group or subgroup of potential purchasers that can be approached in a coherent manner.

customer vector report A type of CRM report that segments by customer (or customer group) on purchases or dates of purchase.

D

data room An online repository (e.g., Dropbox, Box, ShareVault) for the documentation that backs up and details the specifics of your business and business plan. The contents of the data room are very similar to those of the three-ring-binder personal edition of the plan held and used by the founder.

debt A legal obligation to pay money in the future.

debt capital Money borrowed for the purposes of investment in a business.

decision maker A customer role that describes a person in an organization who is responsible for choosing which product or service will be obtained.

decline stage A life cycle stage in which sales and profits of the firm begin a falling trend.

deductible An amount of loss that will not be paid by an insurance company.

defendant Person or other entity being sued.

degree of similarity The extent to which a product or service is like another.

delegation The assignment of work to others over whom you have power.

demand deposits Money held in checking and savings accounts.

deposits and progress payments Cash payments received before product is completed or delivered.

depreciation Regular and systematic reduction in income that transfers asset value to expense over time.

design patent A 14-year patent for a new, original, and ornamental design for an article of manufacture.

design thinking A customer-focused approach using interviews, observation, and exercises to create products and services that provide demonstrated evidence of solving customers' problems.

determination competencies Skills identified with the energy and focus needed to bring a business into existence.

dichotomous question Question that has only two possible choices; for example, "Have you shopped here before?"

differentiation strategy A type of generic strategy aimed at clarifying how one product is unlike another in a mass market.

direct exporting Exporting using no intermediaries.

direct mail A method of selling in which catalogs, brochures, letters, videos, and other pieces of marketing materials are mailed directly to customers from which they can mail in, call in, or email an order. Direct faxing and direct emailing are more modern forms of direct mail.

direct marketing Selling your goods or services to consumers without intermediaries, typically to select customer groups and typically with tracking of the results.

direct response advertising Placing an advertisement in a magazine or newspaper, on television or radio, or in any other media. The ad contains an order blank with a phone number and email or regular mail address with the intent of having the customer place an immediate order.

direct sales Methods of going directly to your customer in order to sell your product. Vending machines, door-to-door salespeople, leasing space at a craft fair, farmer's markets, party sales, and most industrial sales are methods of direct selling.

discounted cash flows Cash flows that have been reduced in value because they are to be received in the future.

discounts for prompt payment A reduction in sales price provided to credit customers for paying outstanding amounts in a timely manner.

disposal value The net amount realized after subtracting the costs of getting rid of an asset from its selling price.

distinctive competence Those features, benefits, or aspect of your business that are unique to your firm, or more strongly identified with your firm than with your competitors. This is the specialty for which your firm is best known.

distinctive competence map A graphic display that compares your company's product or service to that of your competitors, in order to identify your core (shared) competencies and those unique to you and to your competitor.

diversification A strategy whose goal is growth based on adding new products or services to the firm's existing collection of offerings.

diversify To invest in multiple investments of differing risk profiles for the purpose of reducing overall investment risk.

dividends Payments of profits to the owners of corporations.

documentary draft A draft that can be exercised only when presented with specified shipping documents.

Domain name The specific name of an Internet site, consisting of a name followed by *.com*, *.net*, or a similar code.

donations Monetary or other gifts to organizations or people who are in need.

door-to-door selling The practice of taking products directly to the homes or places of business of potential customers and attempting to sell the products immediately.

double taxation Earnings of the business are taxed twice with the business as well as its owners being subject to tax.

drop-shipping A business in which you sell items in person or online, but you hold no inventory. You refer sales to a third party who handles the shipping, and very often the financial transaction, in your name.

due diligence The process of investigating a business to determine its value and potential for investment.

E

e-commerce The general term for conducting business on the Internet.

e-tailer An electronic retailer; a store that exists only on the Internet.

earned media Generally what has been called publicity or press or public relations, these refer to do-it-yourself and paid efforts to get the message of your brand, business, product, or service out to the general public or the mass media (TV, radio, print) in hopes it gets repeated by them.

earnings multiple The ratio of the value of a firm to its annual earnings.

economic order quantity (EOQ) A statistical technique that determines the quantity of inventory that a business must hold to minimize total inventory cost.

effectual reasoning A logical process in which one analyzes the resources available and restraints on the use of resources to create an attainable goal.

effectuation An approach used to create alternatives in uncertain environments.

efficiency (1) The entrepreneurial focus that refers to doing the most work with the fewest resources (2) The comparison of productivity ratios to see the extent that an organization has generated more outputs with fewer inputs.

efficiency-driven economy A nation where industrialization is becoming the major force providing jobs, revenues, and taxes, and where minimizing costs while maximizing productivity (i.e., efficiency) is a major goal.

elastic product Product for which there are any number of substitutes and for which a change in price makes a difference in quantity purchased.

elasticity From economics, the idea that the market's demand for a product or service is sensitive to changes in its price.

elevator pitch A 30-second (100 words or less) action-oriented description of a business designed to sell the idea of the business to another.

emergence stage The first stage of the small business life cycle, where the entrepreneur moves from thinking about starting the business to actually starting the business.

employee fit The match between the needs, expectations, and culture of the small business with the expectations and the skills of the individual employee.

employee referral An underused, low-cost method for finding workers that rewards your employees for recommending potential candidates who would be a great employee fit.

employee stock ownership plan (ESOP) A formalized legal method to transfer some or all of the ownership of a business to its employees.

employee theft Misappropriation of business property by employees of that business.

end user A customer role that describes the person who eventually makes actual use of a product or service in his or her personal or work life.

entrepreneur A person who owns or starts an organization, such as a business.

entrepreneurial alertness A special set of observational and thinking skills that help entrepreneurs identify good opportunities; the ability to notice things that have been overlooked, without actually launching a formal search for opportunities, and the motivation to look for opportunities.

entrepreneurial ecosystem A specific configuration of the environment that reflects the components that are most central to developing a strong and active community of start-up businesses. The components are entrepreneurs, government, universities, investors, service people, mentors, and large organizations.

entrepreneurial mindset The motivations, cognitions, attitudes, aptitudes, and behaviors that lead to a propensity to create solutions to problems or seek opportunities to do something new or better.

entry wedge An opportunity that makes it possible for a new business to gain a foothold in a market.

environment The sum of all the forces outside the firm or entrepreneur.

episodic business A temporary, project-based, or sporadically operating business.

Equal Employment Opportunity Commission (EEOC) A commission established to enforce the provisions of the Equal Employment Opportunity Act.

equipment Machinery, tools, or materials used in the performance of the work of the business.

equity capital Money contributed to the businesses in return for part ownership of the business.

ethical dilemma A situation that occurs when a person's values are in conflict, making it unclear whether a particular decision is the right thing to do.

ethics A system of values that people consider in determining whether actions are right or wrong.

ethnographic research Data gathered by simple observation—seeing what consumers do, rather than asking them.

exculpatory clause Part of a contract in which a party to the contract states that he or she will not be responsible for certain actions.

executive summary A one- to two-page (250–500 words) overview of the business, its business model, market, expectations, and immediate goals. It is typically put at the start of a business plan and is the most popular summary form for a business plan.

exempt A federal government descriptor of employees who are exempt from the Fair Labor Standards Act and are generally paid salaries.

existence stage The second stage of the business life cycle marked by the business being in operation but not yet stable in terms of markets, operations, or finances.

expense A decrease in owners' equity caused by consuming your product or service.

expert business professionalization A situation that occurs when all the major functions of a firm are conducted according to the standard business practices of its industry.

exporting Taking products or services made in your home country and selling them in other countries.

external (cost) factors Aspects of the world outside the business that could cause the business's costs to change.

external environment The forces, institutions, and people (i.e., the rest of the world) outside the boundary of the firm.

external legitimacy The extent to which a small business is taken for granted, accepted, or treated as viable by organizations or people outside the small business or the owner's family.

external reference price An estimation of what a price should be based on information external to a consumer, such as advice, advertisements, or comparison shopping.

external relations The general description for the processes and skills used in the management of a firm's interactions with people, organizations, and institutions outside of its boundary.

F

factor-driven economy A nation where the major forces for jobs, revenues, and taxes come from farming or extractive industries like forestry, mining, or oil production.

factoring Selling the rights to collect accounts receivable to an entity outside your business.

factoring receivables Borrowing money secured by a firm's accounts receivable.

Fair Credit Reporting Act (FCRA) U.S. federal legislation specifying consumers' rights vis-à-vis credit reporting agencies.

Fair Labor Standards Act (FLSA) A federal law which establishes minimum wage, overtime pay eligibility, recordkeeping, and child labor standards affecting full-time and part-time workers in the private sector (including small businesses) and in federal, state, and local governments.

fair market value The price at which goods and services are bought and sold between willing sellers and buyers in an arm's-length transaction.

family business A firm in which one family owns a majority stake and is involved in the daily management of the business.

feasibility The extent to which an idea is viable and realistic and the extent to which you are aware of internal (to your business) and external (industry, market, and regulatory environment) forces that could affect your business.

feasibility study Evaluates the potential of a business opportunity by studying five primary areas in depth: the overall business idea, the product/service, the industry and market, financial projections (profitability), and the plan for future action.

feedback The process of communicating within or to the organization about how the outputs worked or were received.

fidelity bonds Bonds, also called *dishonesty bonds,* that repay employers for losses caused by dishonest or negligent employees.

financial accounting A formal, rule-based set of accounting principles and procedures intended for use by outside owners, investors, banks, and regulators.

financial flexibility A business's ability to manage cash flows in such a manner that the company can respond appropriately to unexpected opportunities and needs.

financial leverage A measure of the amount of debt relative to total investment.

financial management A set of theories and techniques used to optimize the receipt and use of capital assets.

financial risk Uncertainty of returns; the probability of losing money.

financial statements Formal summaries of the content of an accounting system's records of transactions.

financial strength The ability of a business to survive adverse financial events.

financing activities Activities through which cash is obtained from and paid to lenders, owners, and investors.

firm An organization that sells to or trades with others.

fixed costs Those costs that remain constant regardless of quantity of output, for example, rent.

flat fees A method of billing for lawyers in which a fixed amount is paid for a certain task.

flexibility rewards The ability of business owners to structure life in the way that suits their needs best.

focus group A form of data gathering from a small group led by a moderator.

focus strategy A generic strategy that targets a portion of the market, called a *segment* or *niche*.

forms of entrepreneurship The settings in which the entrepreneurial effort takes place.

foundation An institution to which private wealth is contributed and from which private wealth is distributed for public purposes.

founders People who create or start new businesses.

franchise A prepackaged business bought, rented, or leased from a company called a *franchisor*.

free ink Mentions of your company or products in the media for which your firm did not pay.

freemium An approach to pricing, and a business model, that connects free and premium products or services. Typically a free version is offered and users have the option to pay to move up to premium features. Popular examples include Dropbox (5 GB of space for free, with more space or services at a price) and Angry Birds (free ad-supported version; paid version removes ads).

freight forwarders Firms specializing in arranging international shipments—packaging, transportation, and paperwork.

full-time employment Working more than 35 hours a week.

G

gain Any sort of outcome (a product, service, outcome, or situation) customers or potential customers would like to encounter or be able to depend on. It is one of two driving forces of creating new products or services, with the other driving force being pain.

gain on investment The percentage amount that the payout of an investment differs from original cost calculated as: (Payout − Investment + Dividends)/Investment.

gaming the payment process Using methods to appear to be paying bills on time, when in fact payment is being delayed or avoided.

general environment A part of the external environment made up of sectors of major forces that shape the people and institutions of the task and internal environments, such as the economic sector or the demographic sector.

generally accepted accounting principles (GAAP) The standardized rules for accounting procedures set out by the Financial Accounting Standards Board and used in all audits and submissions of accounting reports to the government.

generic strategies Three widely applicable classic strategies for businesses of all types—differentiation, cost, and focus.

gift Valuable assets or services donated to the business without any obligation to repay or give up any ownership interest.

gift capital Capital resources that neither provide any ownership nor require any repayment to the giver.

goal An intended outcome for your business.

going concern concept The accounting concept that a business is expected to continue in existence for the foreseeable future.

Golden Rule An ethical model that suggests you treat others in the manner you wish to be treated.

goods Physical products.

goods or services The tangible things (goods) or intangible commodities (services) created for sale.

grace period An idea in patent law that says disclosing the idea starts a one-year clock for filing a provisional or regular patent, where the disclosure would not count as "prior art" and disqualify the idea from being patented (since as "prior art" it was already publicly known). These grace period disclosures are strongest if they are limited to specific people (versus publicizing an idea on the Internet or in mass media).

grant Gift of money made to a business for a specific purpose.

green entrepreneurship Another term for sustainable entrepreneurship taken from the popular belief that green is the color of a healthy environment, as in forests or fields.

gross profit Funds left over after deducting the cost of goods sold.

growth rewards What people get from facing and beating challenges.

growth stage An industry life cycle stage in which customer purchases increase at a dramatic rate.

growth trap A financial crisis that is caused by a business growing faster than it can be financed.

guerrilla marketing The use of creative and relatively inexpensive ways to reach your customer. Examples include doorknob hangers, flyers under windshield wipers, T-shirts, balloons, and messages written on sidewalks.

H

habit-based planners Entrepreneurs who do not plan, preferring to let all actions be dictated by their routines.

harvest Recover value through a sale of a firm or its assets.

hashtag A term developed to be easily searched on the Internet. Hashtags are words or multiword phrases (without spaces) preceded by a "#" sign (called a *hash*) that is associated with an idea, person, product, service, brand, firm, event, or the like.

heir A person who becomes an owner through inheriting or being given a stake in a family business.

heterogeneity A quality of a service in which each time it is provided it will be slightly different from the previous time.

heuristic A commonsense rule; a rule of thumb.

high-growth venture A firm started with the intent of eventually going public, following the pattern of growth and operations of a big business.

high-performing small business A firm intended to provide the owner with a high income through sales or profits superior to those of the traditional small business.

hit rate How many prospects or leads you need to approach in order to make one sale. Also called the *conversion rate*.

hold harmless A type of waiver in which a party agrees not to hold another party responsible for certain events.

home party A business model in which the entrepreneur arranges a customer to host a party, inviting friends, family, and neighbors. During the party, the entrepreneur demonstrates products and accepts orders for future delivery.

hourly fees A basis for legal charges in which the rate is based on a price per hour. Often lawyers will charge for fractions of an hour.

hybrid entrepreneurship The process of initiating a business while simultaneously remaining employed for wages or salary.

I

IDEO screen A technique for conducting a fast initial analysis of ideas for their potential. An IDEO screen looks at three elements—market desirability, technical feasibility, and organizational viability.

imitative Characterized by being like or copying something that already exists.

imitative strategy An overall strategic approach in which the entrepreneur does more or less what others are already doing.

importing Buying products or services from a place not your home country, and selling them in your home country.

impression What it is called when someone notices a promotional effort.

incentive media The overlap of paid and owned media reflects the partnerships where you are paying for connections useful to your business. This includes affiliate marketing, brand ambassadors, native advertising, and sponsored content.

income rewards The money made by owning one's own business.

income statement A statement that lists revenues and expenses and shows the amount of profit a business makes for a specified period of time.

incremental innovation An overall strategic approach in which a firm patterns itself on other firms, with the exception of one or two key areas.

incremental strategy Taking an idea and offering a way to do something slightly better than it is done presently.

incubator A facility that offers subsidized space and business advice to companies in their earliest stages of operation.

independent contractors Persons working to achieve a certain goal without being subjected to substantial controls by another.

independent entrepreneurship The form of entrepreneurship in which a person or group owns a for-profit business.

independent small business A business owned by an individual or small group.

indirect exporting Exporting using intermediaries such as agents, export management companies, or export trading companies.

industry The general name for the line of product or service being sold, or the firms in that line of business.

industry analysis (IA) A research process that provides the entrepreneur with key information about the industry, such as its current situation and trends.

industry dynamics Changes in competitors, sales, and profits in an industry over time.

Industry-specific knowledge Activities, knowledge, and skills specific to businesses in a particular industry.

inelastic product Product for which there are few substitutes and for which a change in price makes very little difference in quantity purchased.

influencer A customer role describing a person or group who can make credible or recognized suggestions or recommendations to others regarding purchase choices.

informational plan A business plan that gives potential customers or suppliers information about the company and its product or service.

informational website An Internet site designed to introduce and explain a business to others.

infringer Someone who uses intellectual property without the permission of the owner.

innovation-driven economy A nation where the major forces for jobs, revenues, and taxes come from high-value-added production based on new ideas and technologies and from professional services based on higher education.

innovative strategy An overall strategic approach in which a firm seeks to do something that is very different from what others in the industry are doing.

innovativeness Refers to how important a role new ideas, products, services, processes, or markets play in an organization.

inputs The materials, labor, and energy put into the production of a good or service.

inseparability A quality of a service in which the service being done cannot be disconnected from the provider of the service.

insurable value The amount of an asset for which a company will write an insurance policy.

insurance A contract between two or more parties in which one party agrees, for a fee, to assume the risk of another.

intangible property Property that has no value of its own but that represents value, such as a stock certificate.

intangibles Assets, such as patents or trademarks, and liabilities, such as accounts payable, that have no physical existence.

intellectual property (IP) Property coming from some sort of original thought; for example, patents, trade secrets, trademarks, and copyrights.

interest A charge for the use of money, usually figured as a percentage of the principal.

internal (cost) factors Aspects of or choices within the business that could cause the business's costs to change.

internal control A set of rules and procedures that work to limit the opportunity for employee theft or malfeasance.

internal environment The people and groups within the boundary of a firm, including the owners, managers, employees, and board members of the firm.

internal reference price A consumer's mental image of what a product's price should be based on experience and the consumer's estimate of what the comparative value might be.

internal understanding The extent to which employees, investors, and family members involved in the business know the business's purposes and operations.

Internet recruiting Method of recruiting that allows you to search a résumé database or post a job description to the web; a small business owner who knows exactly what he or she wants can use filters to search vast numbers of résumés with pinpoint accuracy.

introduction stage The life cycle stage in which the product or service is being invented and initially developed.

invention plan A business plan that provides information to potential licensees. Invention plans focus on the details of an invention, including intellectual property rights.

inventory Products that are held for sale to customers.

inventory valuation Determination of the amount of assets held by the firm for sale or production.

investing activities The purchase and sale of land, buildings, equipment, and securities.

investment An asset that is acquired for the purpose of either generating future incomes and cash flows or appreciating in value to provide an increase in future wealth.

ISO Stands for the International Organization for Standardization, and refers to certification for having met a standard of quality that is consistently evaluated around the world (see www.iso.org).

ISO 14001 certification A certification awarded to organizations for creating and implementing an environmental management system that meets the requirement of the International Organization for Standardization.

J

job description Defines and discusses all the essential knowledge, skills, and abilities that are needed to fill a position.

joint venture An agreement between two or more entities to pool resources in order to complete a project.

just-in-time (JIT) inventory The practice of purchasing and accepting delivery of inventory only after it has been sold to the final customer.

K

key business functions Activities common to all businesses such as sales, operations (also called *production*), accounting, finance, and human resources.

key employee/partner plan A business plan that provides information on the company, product/service, market, and critical risks to prospective business or marketing partners or to prospective key employees.

key employees Employees whose experience and skills are critical to the success of a business.

key performance indicators (KPIs) Measures or metrics that identify the outcomes that are most important to the success of a business. While outcomes like sales or products produced are KPIs, events leading up to these are also usually considered key, like customers coming to your store or website for sales, or number of products started.

keywords and description tags Terms included in the hidden portion of a web page (called the *document head*) that are used by search engines such as Yahoo! and Google to describe your website and evaluate its focus and category placement.

L

law of supply and demand The economic theory that describes how the demand for products (or services) and the supply of them affect each other.

lead generation The promotional technique of obtaining prospective customers through paid and unpaid efforts to obtain contact information from people with the plan to send these prospects advertisements or other messages in hopes of getting them to become customers.

lean business practices An application created by Eric Ries that addresses the specifics of new business creation, particularly Internet-based businesses, where rapid experimentation and constant monitoring of viewers' choices are possible.

leasing A formal agreement, reduced to writing, that specifies the term and conditions that must be met to allow one entity to use a specified asset (or assets) of the other.

legal entity A being, human or nonhuman, such as a corporation, that is recognized as having rights and duties, such as the right to own property.

legitimacy The belief that a firm is worthy of consideration or doing business with because of the impressions or opinions of customers, suppliers, investors, or competitors.

letter of credit A document issued by a bank that guarantees a buyer's payment for a specified period of time upon compliance with specified terms.

leveraging contingencies The practice of and ability to seize upon novel opportunities that become apparent during the conduct of business.

liabilities Legal obligations to give up things of value in the future.

liability of newness The set of risks faced by firms early in their life cycles that comes from a lack of knowledge by the owners about the business they are in and by customers about the new business.

license A legal agreement granting you rights to use a particular piece of intellectual property.

licensee The person or firm that is obtaining the rights to use a particular piece of intellectual property.

licensing Documented permission from the government to run your business.

licensor The person or organization that is offering the rights to use a particular piece of intellectual property.

lifestyle or part-time firm A small business primarily intended to provide partial or subsistence financial support for the existing lifestyle of the owner, most often through operations that fit the owner's schedule and way of working.

limited liability company (LLC) A legal form of business organization that is created by filing required documentation with a state government. LLCs have a choice, under federal tax law, of being taxed as either corporations or partnerships.

liquidity A measure of how quickly a company can raise money through internal sources by converting assets to cash.

litigation A formal dispute resolution method that operates using the court system, typically with a lawyer representing each party.

living wage The amount needed for a person (or family of a particular size) to meet the basic necessities of life from a single job.

lock box A locked receptacle for money, the keys to which are not available to those who physically handle the receptacle; a common example of a lock box is the coin receptacle for parking meters which cannot be opened by the workers who are responsible for collecting the deposited coins.

long-term value (LTV) A marketing concept that refers to the revenue (or profit) generated by one customer over his or her lifetime dealing with one firm. Higher long-term value is usually preferred. LTV is also known as customer lifetime value or CLV.

M

MACRS rate An Internal Revenue Service acronym for the Modified Accelerated Cost Recovery System. The MACRS approach lets taxpayers depreciate more of the cost earlier in the life of a capital expense.

magic number The posttax income the entrepreneur personally seeks from the business.

mail order Sales made from ads in newspapers or magazines, with purchases taken online or by phone as well as by mail.

main street businesses A popular term for small businesses reflecting the idea that these are the kinds of firms you would expect to find on the main street of a typical American city, and are the opposite of big business or "Wall Street" businesses.

maker A modern term for an inventor, in particular, an inventor who uses modern techniques like 3-D software and 3-D printers or do-it-yourself electronics to create new items.

managerial accounting Accounting methods that are specifically intended to be used by managers for planning, directing, and controlling a business.

manufacturer The entity that produces a product or service to be sold.

manufacturer's suggested retail price A target price set by a manufacturer for a product or service intended to provide profit for each intermediary in the distribution channel.

margin The amount of profit, usually stated as a percentage of the total price.

market The business term for the population of customers for your product or service.

market expansion A strategy whose goal is growth, based on selling in areas or to groups previously not served by the business.

market penetration A strategy whose goal is growth, based on selling more of the firm's product or service to the existing customer base.

market segmentation The process of dividing the market into groups that have somewhat homogeneous needs for a product or service.

marketable securities Stocks and bonds that are traded on an open market.

marketing The actions of a business related to promoting and selling products or services.

marketing funnel The rule of thumb in marketing that it takes a large number of people to be made aware of your product in order to find a purchaser.

marketing research Systematic collection and interpretation of data to support future marketing decisions.

markup The amount an entrepreneur adds to costs to provide a profit.

markup pricing A price-setting method where an amount is added to the cost of a product to set the retail price and provide a profit.

mass market A customer group that involves large portions of the population.

mat release A news release that is typeset and thus may be photographically reproduced for inclusion in a newspaper.

maturity stage The third life cycle stage, marked by a stabilization of demand, with firms in the industry moving to stabilize or improve profits through cost strategies.

me-too products Products essentially similar to something already on the market.

media content strategy plan A document, for the managers and employees of the firm to see, that details the specifics of the firm's marketing efforts including the goals, target audiences, distribution channels, keywords, content types, calendar, publishing procedures, action items, KPIs, and analytics across all the different types of marketing efforts the firm will attempt.

media integration The overlap of paid and earned media is based on generating leads through three paid types of efforts: advertorials (editorials written by a company as a type of ad), lead generation purchases (e.g., mailing or subscriber lists or contests), and contests or sweepstakes.

media kit A type of specialized web page or sales-material-based package (hard copy or PDF) sent to media outlets that is focused on telling them about your company and its story. These are often built around a press release for something of potential current interest to the media outlet. Also called a *press kit*.

media partnerships These occur at the overlap of shared and earned media and represent the paid and unpaid arrangements made by your brand, company, product, or service with outside individuals or organizations to promote your brand to the public or their own social media or public bases. These partnerships include influencer marketing (also called brand ambassadors), trade and professional organizational memberships, local organization memberships, sponsorships, co-branding, co-advertising, donations, and community service.

mediation A dispute resolution process held instead of court cases in which both sides present their case to a neutral third party who is not a judge. Unlike arbitration and court decisions, mediation decisions are not binding on the two parties.

meritocracy A management philosophy of selecting and promoting people based solely on their being the most capable person for the job.

micro-commitment An online action that is quick and easy to make and connects you to the message, but does not require a substantial personal or financial commitment, such a liking or favoriting a post or reposting it to your own social media account.

microinventory The purchase of inventory only after a sale is made; very typical with Internet firms.

microlender SBA-approved partner that offers SBA-guaranteed microloans to eligible small businesses. These loans require much less paperwork than regular SBA or bank loans, and are for amounts under $50,000.

minimalized business professionalization A situation that occurs when the entrepreneur does nearly everything in the simplest way possible, rather than in a professional way.

minimum viable product A concept central to lean business practices where you make a minimum product, but one that can be sold. By selling to customers and collecting feedback, an entrepreneur can develop a product at minimum cost.

mission statement A paragraph that describes the firm's goals and competitive advantages.

money An accepted medium of exchange.

moonlighting Working on your own part time after your regular job.

multichannel marketing The use of several different channels to reach your customers; for example, a website, direct mail, and traditional retailing.

multiple or bonus pack Combining more than one unit of the same product and pricing it lower than if each unit were sold separately.

mutuality The action of each person helping another.

N

native advertising Native advertising are forms of ads inserted into the regular flow of noncommercial web pages so that it appears to be "native" to the page. The FTC regulates that native advertising carry an identifier (such as "Sponsored" in front of the item) to show it is an ad and not a statement by the page's content creator.

necessity-driven entrepreneurship Creating a firm as an alternative to unemployment.

nepotism A management philosophy of selecting and promoting people based on family ties.

net present value (NPV) The difference between the present value of cash inflows and the present value of cash outflows over a specified period of time.

net profit The amount of money left after operating expenses are deducted from the business.

net realizable value The amount for which an asset will sell, less the costs of selling.

network marketing An approach to selling in which the salesperson recruits customers to become distributors of the product or service to others.

networking Interacting with others in order to build relationships useful to a business.

new entrant business A firm whose product or service is established elsewhere, but is new to this market.

newsworthy events To garner serious attention from the media and the public, a news story needs to deliver certain essentials that will hold their attention and keep your news in their thoughts. It should have public recognition, importance, and interest.

niche market A narrowly defined segment of the population that is likely to share interests or concerns.

noncash incentives Rewards that do not require payment of cash, such as stock options, compensating time off, or added vacation days.

noncompete clause Part of a contract in which a person agrees not to open a certain type business or seek employment doing certain things in a particular area for a period of time.

noncore projects Revenue-producing tasks and activities related to, but not part of, the primary strategy of a business.

nonexempt A federal government descriptor of employees under the Fair Labor Standards Act who get an hourly wage and time-and-a-half for overtime.

nonprofit corporation A business form specific to charitable organizations (i.e., organizations that do not make a profit for their owners). Nonprofit business charters differ in the kinds of responsibilities the nonprofit has, compared to the other forms of for-profit business forms. Nonprofits are the only form of business that can seek 501(c)(3) status from the IRS, which permits donations to the nonprofit to be considered tax-deductible to the donor.

nonsufficient funds (NSF) A situation that occurs when a check is returned to a depositor because the writer of the check did not have a bank available balance equal to or greater than the amount of the check.

novelty Characterized by being different or new.

O

occupation The type of activity a person does regularly for pay.

Occupational Safety and Health Administration (OSHA) A government agency created to enforce safety in the workplace.

odd-even pricing Setting a price that ends in the number 5, 7, or 9.

off-peak pricing Charging lower prices at certain times to encourage customers to come during slack periods.

offering circular (OC) A legal document required by firms seeking funding through equity crowdfunding platforms created under the JOBS Act. An OC contains SEC required forms, an offering memorandum (which is almost identical to a PPM), and the financial statements of the firm.

on account Merchandise purchased or sold with payment due in the future, usually within one month.

on-the-job training Delivered to employees while they perform their regular jobs; techniques include orientations, job instruction training, apprenticeships, internships and assistantships, job rotation, and coaching.

OOH Stands for "out of home" and refers to advertising people will encounter when away from home. This includes posters, digital and print ads in transit shelters, at airports and venues with major foot traffic, and digital and conventional billboards and signage.

open-book policy Concept that key employees should be able to see and understand a firm's financials, that they should have a part in moving the numbers in the right direction, and that they should have a direct stake in the strategy and success of the firm.

open-ended question Question that allows respondents to express themselves as they choose; for example, "What do you like about this book?"

operating activities Activities involved in producing and selling goods and services.

operating agreement A contract among LLC members outlining how the LLC will conduct itself.

operating cycle See *cash-to-cash cycle*.

operating income The amount of income earned by the regular operations of the business.

operating lease A long-term rental in which ownership of the asset never passes to the person paying for the lease.

operational plan A business plan designed to be used internally for management purposes.

operations The process of transforming materials, labor, and energy into goods or services.

opinion of patentability A report (typically written as a letter) from a patent attorney or patent agent that is his or her professional opinion of the possibility of obtaining a patent for an idea that you have explained. The opinion is based on the attorney's or agent's research of patents for similar or related ideas. Typically the first official step in the patenting process.

opportunistic planners Entrepreneurs who start with a goal instead of a plan and look for opportunities to achieve it.

opportunity competencies Skills necessary to identify and exploit elements of the business environment that can lead to a profitable and sustainable business.

opportunity recognition Searching and capturing new ideas that lead to business opportunities. This process often involves creative thinking that leads to discovery of new and useful ideas.

opportunity-driven entrepreneurship Creating a firm to improve one's income or a product or service.

optimum capital structure The ratio of debt to equity that provides the maximum level of profits.

optimum price The highest price that will produce your desired level of sales in your intended market.

optimum stocking level The amount of inventory that results in the minimum cost, when considering the cost of lost sales resulting from running out of stock, the number of units sold per day, and the number of days required to receive inventory. Also called *reorder point*.

organic traffic People who come to your website based on their own actions (e.g., typing in your URL, clicking on a link mentioning your site on a web page, or clicking on a search engine finding based on where your site naturally—or "organically"—appears in the search results) where you have not paid for the link. It is also called *unpaid search*.

organizational culture A set of shared beliefs, basic assumptions, or common, accepted ways of dealing with problems and challenges within a company that demonstrate how things get done.

organizational identity Part of the BRIE model; composed of the name, description, and distinctive elements of a firm, such as trademarks, uniforms, logos, characters, and stories.

outflow Fund being paid to others by the firm.

outputs The services or products that are produced for sale.

outside equity Money from selling part of your business to people who are not and will not be involved in the management of the business.

outsourcing Contracting with people or companies outside your business to do work for your business.

outstanding customer service The idea of "going all out" for the customer or providing over-the-top service, not just the basic help, professionalism, and friendliness we all expect in any business transaction; an employee or manager who is trying to make sure the customer walks away with an exceptional experience.

overall growth strategy One of four general ways to position a business based on the rate and level of growth entrepreneurs anticipate for their firm.

overdraft A negative balance in a depositor's bank account.

owned media These are promotional materials directly and wholly owned by your company, like your name, your websites, your signage, and the like.

owner-managed firm A business run by the individual who owns it.

owners' equity The difference between assets and liabilities of a business.

P

P2P lending Loans made from one or more individuals to the entrepreneur, rather than through a conventional bank. This can be as simple as a loan to a friend, or formally handled through a dedicated P2P website.

paid media Generally referred to as bought or paid advertising, paid media are promotions where your firm pays another for the placement and distribution of the material.

pain Any sort of problem, annoyance, source of aggravation, shortcoming, or suboptimal situation customers or potential customers face. It is one of two driving forces of creating new products or services, with the other driving force being gain.

painstorming A group thinking technique where you ask participants about a situation, product, or service they experienced. You ask them to tell you all the things about that experience that were suboptimal—what was wrong, what didn't work well, what caused pain or discomfort, what could have been better. Their results can help describe how to improve the product, service, or situation, or possibly even provide alternatives to the original.

parallel competition An imitative business that competes locally with others in the same industry.

part-time business A business in which the owner either participates fewer than 35 hours per week or operates on a temporary or seasonal basis while maintaining employment elsewhere for wages or salary.

part-time employment Working for 35 or fewer hours a week.

partitioned pricing Setting the price for a base item and then charging extra for each additional component.

partnership Two or more people cooperating to conduct a business enterprise.

pass off A type of business transfer where the owner gives the business to someone else without a payment. This is most often done to maintain employment for the staff and service for the customers, but the business is not profitable enough to give the original owner any revenue.

pass through (taxation) Earnings of the business are distributed to the business owners and those owners (rather than the business) pay individual tax on the earnings.

passion An intense positive feeling an entrepreneur has toward the business or the idea behind the business.

patent A grant by the U.S. government to an inventor for an idea that is new, useful, and nonobvious, giving the inventor the exclusive right to make, use, or sell his or her idea.

payables Amounts owed to vendors for merchandise or services purchased on credit (see also *receivables*).

payback period The amount of time it takes a business to earn back the funds it paid out to obtain a capital asset.

penetrated market (PM) A marketing term that describes the actual number of customers of an operating firm, divided by the size of the target market, which gives a percentage of the market the firm (or product/service) has attained so far.

periodic discounting Sales conducted at predictable intervals, such as before major holidays.

periodic inventory The process of physically counting business assets on a set schedule.

perishability A service exhibits perishability in that if it is not used when offered, it cannot be saved for later use.

permanance The impression of long-term continuity a business gives others.

permanent accounts The accounts of assets, liabilities, and owners' equity, excluding accounts for revenues and expenses.

perpetual inventory A system of recording the receipt and sale of each item as it occurs.

perseverance The behavior of continued effort to achieve a goal.

personal selling The process of selling your products and services; includes prospect and evaluate, prepare, present, close, and follow up.

physical inventory A count of all the inventory being held for sale at a specific point in time.

piercing the veil The dissolution of a corporate form, making it back into a sole proprietorship or general partnership, if the court finds that the owner carelessly mixed up personal and business assets or finances.

pilot test A preliminary run of a business, sales effort, program, or website with the goal of assessing how well the overall approach works and what problems it might have.

pioneering business A firm whose product or service is new to the industry or is itself creating a new industry.

pitch The name given to the formal presentation of a slideshow summarizing your business plan given before judges or potential investors or partners.

pitch deck The name of a slideshow presentation that summarizes a business or more often a business plan.

pivot Typically, a term describing a change of direction in the thinking of an entrepreneur or a firm, often based on new data or other findings.

plaintiff Person or other entity filing a lawsuit.

plant A general term for the facilities of a business.

plant patent A 20-year patent that covers new strains of living plant organisms, algae, or macro fungi.

pledging receivables Giving a third party legal rights to debts owed your business in order to provide assurance that borrowed money will be repaid.

point of indifference The price at which a buyer is indifferent about buying or not buying the business.

point-of-sale (POS) system Hardware and software combinations that integrate inventory management directly into accounting software.

poisoning the well Creating a negative impression among your employers' customers.

pop-up business A temporary business that offers services or products in a variety of locations for a brief period at a time. What characterizes a pop-up business from any other is its *temporary* nature.

predetermined market segments Professionally compiled target audiences based on shared demographic, financial, shopping, and psychographic characteristics.

premium pricing Setting a price above that of the competition to indicate a higher quality.

preselling Involves introducing your future product to potential customers and taking orders for later delivery.

press relations Activities used to establish and promote a favorable opinion by the media.

press release A written announcement intended to draw news media attention to a specific event.

prestige pricing Setting a price above that of the competition to indicate your product is a status symbol.

prevention focus An entrepreneur's attention to minimizing losses, with a bias toward inaction or protective action to prevent loss.

price gouging Charging an outrageously high price for something.

price lining The practice of setting (usually) three price points: good quality, better quality, best quality.

primary research An approach to researching based on the gathering of new information, using techniques such as interviewing, surveying, and observation.

private placement memorandum (PPM) A specialized legal form of business plan crafted by lawyers for the purpose of soliciting formal investments.

pro forma financial statements Planning documents for future business activities that are formatted to look like the common financial statements of the income statement, balance sheet, and statement of cash flows.

probationary period Trial period in which an employee has temporary status before a formal offer to work full time is presented.

procedure The series of steps and activities required to complete a process.

process The business activities necessary to convert inputs into desired outputs.

product development process The procedure to organize and pursue the creation of new goods or services.

product distribution franchising An agreement that provides specific brand-name products that are resold by the franchisee in a specified territory.

product expansion A strategy whose goal is growth, based on selling existing customers a product or service they have never bought before.

productivity The ratio measure of how well a firm does in using its inputs to create outputs. Literally, productivity is outputs divided by inputs.

professionalization The extent to which a firm meets or exceeds the standard business practices for its industry.

profit before taxes The amount of profit earned by a business before calculating the amount of income tax owed.

profit planning The process of creating a set of interconnected budgets that combine into a master budget that can be used for assessing and controlling the business processes.

profit, profitability The amount that revenues exceed expenses.

promotion focus An entrepreneur's attention to maximizing gains and pursuing opportunities likely to lead to gains.

promotional mix How much of each message conveyance you will use to sell your product as well as your objective in using each one.

proof-of-concept website An Internet-based type of business plan providing information or demonstration of a product or service designed to solicit information on customer interest.

property A general term for real estate, but it can also be applied as a legal term for anything owned or possessed.

proprietary technology A product or service or an aspect of one that is kept as a trade secret or is protected legally using patent, copyright, trademark, or service mark.

prospects Sales leads who actually make some sort of effort to learn more about the product, service, or business in anticipation of a possible purchase.

protected classes States of being that are expressly prohibited from suffering discrimination: race, color, religion, sex, national origin, gender, age, or disability.

prototype The name given to the first model of a product or service. Some prototypes may be functioning, but built in a way that no consumer would buy it (e.g., with exposed wires and sharp edges) but shows the product can do what is promised. Some prototypes look like the final product, but might not be functional. Prototypes are made to prove aspects of the idea and are seen as the first stop along the path of product/service creation.

provisional patent A preliminary description of your idea submitted to the U.S. Patent Office according to its specifications. It is intended to serve as a sort of placeholder for a full (or regular) patent, which needs to be filed within one year of the filing of the provisional patent.

psychological contract Refers to employees' beliefs about the promises between the employee and the firm. These beliefs are based on the perception that promises have been made (e.g., competitive wages, promotional opportunities, job training) in exchange for certain employee obligations such as giving of their energy, time, and technical skills.

public relations Activities used to establish and promote a favorable opinion by the public.

publicity Information about your company and its activities that is disseminated to the public in order to gain their good opinion.

pull-through system A term for just-in-time inventory systems in which product is ordered and placed into production only after a sale has been completed.

purchaser A customer role that describes an individual or institution that pays for or obtains a product or service.

purchasing process The sequence of steps an individual or organization goes through in making a decision to buy a product or service.

pure innovation The process of creating new products or services, which results in a previously unseen product or service.

Q

quality A product's or service's fitness for use, measured as durability, reliability, serviceability, style, ease of use, and dependability.

R

"real options" approach An idea in entrepreneurship popularized by Rita Gunther McGrath and Ian Macmillan that suggests thinking of entrepreneurial opportunities (like start-ups) in terms similar to buying a stock option, putting a small amount of money down now to let you invest more at favorable rates later. This approach minimizes the amount you can lose and gives you a chance to make a decision later, based on the start-up's track record and prospects.

radical innovation strategy Rejecting existing ideas, and presenting a way to do things differently.

random discounting A sale run on a schedule that is unpredictable to the customer.

reactive planners Entrepreneurs with a passive approach, who wait for cues from the environment to determine what actions to take.

receivables Amounts that are owed to a business for merchandise that was sold on credit (see also *payables*).

reciprocal link A listed, live connection to a different website, which in turn displays a similar link to the first website.

reconcile An accounting process that identifies the causes of all differences between book and bank balances.

referral discount A discount given to a customer who refers a friend to the business.

referrals Getting customers to refer their friends to you.

registration Information provided to the government concerning the existence of, name of, nature of, and contact information for your business.

regulation of the workplace Laws and governmental rules that limit the freedom of business owners to manage their businesses as they please.

Rehabilitation Act of 1973 An act of Congress that provides training for workers who are injured on the job.

renting An agreement between two entities that allows one to use assets of the other in return for a specified payment or series of payments.

replacement cost The total cost of replacing an asset with an essentially identical asset.

replacement value The cost to acquire an essentially identical asset.

replacement value The cost incurred to replace one asset with an identical asset.

research and development (R&D) The part of a business (and a business plan) that is focused on creating new products or services and preparing new technologies, ideas, products, or services for the firm's market.

reserve price A minimum acceptable selling price in an auction. If the bidding does not exceed the price, the sale will not go through.

resource competencies The ability or skill of the entrepreneur at finding expendable components necessary to the operation of the business such as time, information, location, financing, raw materials, and expertise.

resource maturity The resource maturity stage is the most typical fourth stage of the small business. It is characterized by relatively stable or slowly rising sales and profits over several years. In a firm that has a takeoff stage following the success stage, the resource maturity stage occurs after takeoff.

retail arbitrage An approach to business where the entrepreneur buys something at a severely reduced retail price (like clearance or closeout merchandise from a retailer) and then resells it (most typically online) at a price closer to the typical retail price.

retailer An intermediary business that sells to consumers or end users of a product (typically in single or small quantities).

retained earnings (1) The sum of all the profits and losses that the business experiences from formation (2) A balance sheet item in owners' equity that reflects the wealth created by the business from its formation.

retainer A fee paid by a client to an attorney to engage the attorney's services.

retrenchment An organizational life cycle stage in which established firms must find new approaches to improve the business and its chances for survival.

return on investment (ROI) A capital budgeting equation used to measure the relationship between initial investment and the profits that are expected to be received from making the investment.

revenue An increase in owners' equity caused by selling your product or service.

reverse auction An auction in which the low bid gets the business or wins.

revolving credit A credit agreement that allows the borrower to pay all or part of the balance at any time; as the loan balance is paid off, it becomes available to be borrowed again.

risk The level of probability that an investment will not produce expected gains.

risks The parts of a business or business plan that expose the firm to any kind of loss—profits, sales, reputation, assets, customers, and so on.

role conflict The kind of problem that arises when people have multiple responsibilities, such as parent and boss, and the different responsibilities make different demands on them.

royalty A payment to a licensor based on the number or value of licensed items sold.

royalty financing A method of raising capital financing where investors provide money to a business in return for a guaranteed percentage of revenues.

RSS feed An Internet messaging service that pushes (sends) whatever web material you specify to subscribers to that feed.

S

SaaS SaaS stands for *Software as a Service* and refers to an Internet-based program that you would use in work or leisure. These are paid for by time frame, project, or some measure of usage.

safety stock An amount of inventory carried to ensure that you will not run out of inventory because of fluctuating levels of sales.

sales leads People who receive a promotional impression and who give some thought to buying the product.

sales promotion A form of communication that encourages the customer to act immediately, such as coupons, sales, or contests.

Sarbanes-Oxley Act (SOX) A federal law describing the steps publicly traded businesses must take to protect and provide their key financial information.

scalar question Question that is answered by some sort of scale; for example, "On a scale of 1 to 5, how do you like this book?"

scale A characteristic of a market that describes the size of the market—a mass market or a niche market.

scope A characteristic of a market that defines the geographic range covered by the market—from local to global.

screening plan Also called a *mini-plan,* gives the basic overview of the firm and a detailed look at the financials.

search engine optimization (SEO) A general approach to website design intended to result in the site being displayed toward the beginning of a search engine's (e.g., Google, Yahoo!, etc.) listing for that term.

second career entrepreneur Person who begins a business after having left, retired, or resigned from work. Can include veterans of the armed forces and civilians from a broad range of industries.

secondary research An approach to researching based on the use of existing information, often from government, commercial, or academic databases and research efforts.

secured debt Loans that provide the lender with the legal right to seize specific assets in the event of nonpayment. Most automobile loans are secured debt and if you don't make your payments, your car will be repossessed.

segmentation The process of dividing the market into smaller portions of people who have common characteristics.

self-efficacy A person's belief in his or her ability to achieve a goal.

self-employed Working for yourself.

sell off A type of business transfer where the seller gets only a fraction of the value of the business. This is most often done to maintain employment for the staff and service for the customers, but the business can generate only a small amount of profit with which the original owner can be paid, or the new owner does not have much money to buy the business.

separation of duties A type of internal control that separates the physical control of an asset from the person accounting for that asset.

serial entrepreneur A person who opens multiple businesses throughout his or her career.

serviceable available market (SAM) A marketing term that refers to the customers within the geographic reach of a firm.

serviceable obtainable market (SOM) A marketing term (also called the target market) that represents the customers that a firm expects to be interested in its particular product or service, and able to be serviced by the firm.

services Nonphysical products.

set-asides Government contracting funds that are earmarked for particular kinds of firms, such as small businesses, minority-owned firms, women-owned firms, and the like.

shake-out A type of life cycle stage following a boom in which there is a rapid decrease in the number of firms in an industry.

shared media Generally called word-of-mouth or referral advertising, these are promotional mentions of your brand, firm, product, services, or user experiences with them made by customers and others and posted or shared through their social media sites.

sheltered workshop A nonprofit organization or institution that provides business services by using workers who have disabilities or who are rehabilitated.

short-term debt Any debt that must be paid in less than one year from the date of the financial statement on which it is reported.

signature block A snippet of text (or text and images), typically inserted at the bottom of an email, that contains contact information for the sender of the email.

single taxation Earnings of the business are taxed once with the owners paying the taxes.

skimming Setting a price at the highest level the market will bear, usually because there is no competition at the time.

slack resources Profits that are available to be used to satisfy the preferences of the owner in how the business is run.

small and medium enterprise (SME) The international term for a small business.

small business Involves 1–50 people and has its owner managing the business on a day-to-day basis.

Small Business Administration (SBA) A part of the U.S. government that provides support and advocacy for small businesses.

small business investment company (SBIC) Private business that is authorized to make SBA-insured loans to start-ups and small businesses.

social capital Characteristics of a business, such as trust, consistency, and networks, that represent potential social obligations that are assets of the firm or entrepreneur.

social entrepreneurship The form of entrepreneurship involving the creation of self-sustaining charitable and civic organizations, for-profit organizations that invest significant profits in charitable activities, or the creators of nonprofit charitable or service organizations.

social media embassies These combine elements of owned and shared media and represent the social media platforms on which your brand, business, products, or services have a formal presence (like a company page). The page belongs to you, but it exists on a media platform that you don't own or control.

social media management platform An online service that captures and displays the feeds from your social media platforms and makes it easy to post across multiple platforms, schedule posts on different platforms, and help you see social media statistics. Free and freemium examples include Hootsuite, Buffer, Tweetdeck, SocialOomph, and Followerwonk.

social ventures Businesses that are organized as for-profit entities but are also solving or supporting solutions to social problems.

sophisticated investor As defined by the SEC, people who "have sufficient knowledge and experience in financial and business matters to make them capable of evaluating the merits and risks of the prospective investment."

specialized business professionalization A situation that occurs when businesses have founders or owners who are passionate about one or two of the key business functions, such as sales, operations, accounting, finance, or human resources, and pursues those functions in a professional manner.

spin-off A business that is created by separating part of an operating business into a separate entity.

sponsored content Sponsored content is material you develop or have developed to present to customers information about your company, brand, products, or services. Links to this material are placed on other people or brand websites or social media feeds, in hopes potential customers will click on the links and learn more about your offering.

sponsored link A form of paid advertising that gets your company's website at the top of a search list.

sponsorships Paying for a local organization's needs in exchange for recognition.

stakeholder A person, organization, or entity that has an interest or concern in a particular business or decision.

standard budgeting A method for business forecasting and control in which specific expected volumes and prices per unit are used.

standard business practice A business action that has been widely adopted within an industry or occupation.

start-up A new business that is started from scratch.

statement of cash flows A statement of the sources and uses of cash in a business for a specific period of time. Also called a cash flow statement.

storytelling arcs There are several classic structures to stories, such as beginning, middle, and end, or a multiple-step journey, or a situation-complication-resolution.

straight line for a useful life of 10 years Depreciation is computed using a straight line method over 10 years, so an asset would lose 10 percent of its value each year.

strategic actions Competitive responses requiring a major commitment of resources.

strategic partnerships Formal or informal relationships with customers, vendors, or mentors to ensure the success of an entrepreneurial venture.

subcontract A contract by which a new party agrees to perform a duty that one of the original parties to a contract was already legally obligated to perform.

success stage The third stage of the business life cycle marked by the firm being established in its market, operation, and finances.

succession The process of intergenerational transfer of a business.

succinct message The key point in as few and as memorable words as possible.

suppy chain A way to think about the line of distribution of a product from its start as materials outside the target firm, to its handling in the target firm, to its handling by sellers, with placement into the hands of customers.

surety bonds An agreement with an insurance or bonding company that will pay a specified amount in the event that the entity bonded fails to comply with specified contractual requirements.

survey A data-collection method using a questionnaire—in person, on the phone, on paper, or on the Internet.

sustainable entrepreneurship An approach to operating a firm or a line of business that identifies, creates, and exploits opportunities to make a profit in a way that can minimize the depletion of natural resources, maximize the use of a recycled material, or improve the environment.

synergy A combination in which the whole is greater than the sum of its component parts.

T

tactical actions Competitive responses with low resource requirements.

tagline Memorable catchphrase that captures the key idea of a business, its service, product, or customer (also known as a slogan).

takeoff This stage occurs after the success stage for a small percentage of businesses. It is characterized by rapid growth (5–10 percent a month or more). When this growth levels off, the firm enters the resource maturity stage.

takeover The seizing of control of a business by purchasing its stock to be able to select the board of directors.

tangibility An item's capability of being touched, seen, tasted, or felt.

target market A marketing term (also called serviceable obtainable market, or SOM) that refers to the group of customers in the area you plan to serve who would be likely to be interested in your product, or those of competitors. Target markets can refer to individuals or market groups called segments.

task environment A part of the external environment made up of those components that the firm deals with directly such as customers, suppliers, consultants, media, interest groups, and the like.

tax abatement A legal reduction in taxes by a government.

tax accounting An accounting approach based on specific accounting requirements set by governmental taxing agencies.

tax codes Laws and regulations that specify the requirements of taxation.

tax credit Direct reduction in the amount of taxes that must be paid, dependent on meeting some legal criteria.

telemarketing Contact via telephone for the express purpose of selling a product or service. Telemarketing can either be inbound (customer calls company) or outbound (company calls customer).

termination An endgame strategy in which the owner closes down a business.

test marketing Selling your product or service in a limited area, for a limited time.

testimonial Statement made that is allowed to be publicly repeated and attributed to the person that made it.

time management The organizing process to help make the most efficient use of the day.

time to start up How long it takes to start a new business.

timing purchases A method of controlling the timing of cash outflows that is invisible to suppliers and vendors.

total available market (TAM) A marketing term that refers to all of the people or organizations (in one nation, region, or the world) who might consider a product or service being offered.

total cost Total costs are simply the sum of all costs that are incurred within an accounting period. For the purposes of cost-volume-profit analysis, total costs are set equal to the sum of fixed costs and variable costs.

total product The entire bundle of products, services, and meanings of your offering; includes extras like service, warranty, or delivery, as well as what the product means to the customer.

traction Those characteristics of your business that show it is making progress, such as making sales, recruiting customers, being sold in more locations, or achieving milestones that reflect a firm's growth or development.

trade association (also known as *professional association*). A group of people in the same industry who band together to gather and share information and present and represent the industry to the public and government.

trade discounts Percentage discounts from gross invoice amounts provided to encourage prompt payment.

trade magazines The magazines that target specific industries and professions.

trade name franchising An agreement that provides to the franchisee only the rights to use the franchisor's trade name and/or trademarks.

trade name or assumed name or doing business as (dba) name The name under which a business is operated.

trade secret Confidential information within a company that gives that company a competitive advantage.

trademark Distinctive word, slogan, or image that identifies a product and its origin.

traditional small business A firm intended to provide a living income to the owner, and operating in a manner and on a schedule consistent with other firms in the industry and market.

traffic generators Other businesses that bring customers (generate traffic) to the area.

transfer *An endgame strategy in which* ownership is moved from one person or group to another.

tweet A 140-character-or-less message sent using the Twitter web service.

U

unbundle To break apart a product or service into components.

unicorns The most successful high-growth ventures, those with a valuation of $1 billion or more.

universalism An ethical model that suggests that there is a code of right and wrong that everyone can see and follow.

unsecured debt Loans that do not allow a lender to seize specific assets in the event of nonpayment.

up-selling Selling additional accessories or higher-quality versions of the product at a higher cost.

user review sites Online sites where customers and users of products and services can post their opinions, rating, and experiences for others to see. Smart companies track these sites and respond to customers' reviews on these sites.

utilitarianism An ethical model that supports seeking the greatest good for the greatest number of people.

utility patent A 20-year patent covering a process, machine, article of manufacture, composition of matter, or any new or useful improvement of an existing one.

V

value proposition Small business owners' unique selling points (also known as benefits) that customers can expect from your goods or services, including benefits that differentiate your offering from those of the competition.

variable costs Those costs that change with each unit produced, for example, raw materials.

variance (1) The difference between an actual and budgeted revenue or cost (2) Permission from a government organization to act differently than the laws state.

variance analysis The process of determining the effect of price and quantity changes on revenues and expenses.

venue A place where something takes place. For example, a theater is the venue for a play; a stadium is the venue for a football game.

veteran entrepreneur Individual who was formerly in military service who decides to become self-employed as a subsequent career. (Not to be confused with serial entrepreneur.)

vicarious (indirect) liability Indirect liability or responsibility for the actions of another.

viral marketing Any electronic equivalent of word-of-mouth advertising, in which the advertiser's message spreads quickly and widely via email, website, blogs, and other online tools.

virtual employee An independent contractor who provides specialized business services or support from a distance, through the Internet, telephone, fax, or another method of communication.

virtual instant global entrepreneurship (VIGE) A process that uses the Internet to quickly create businesses with a worldwide reach.

virtuous cycle Situations where one good turn invites a another one from someone else are called virtuous cycles.

vision statement A very simple 5- to 10-word sentence or tagline that expresses the fundamental idea or goal of the firm.

volatility The frequency of business starts and stops.

waiver Part of a contract in which a party intentionally gives up legal rights or claims.

walkaway Business termination in which the entrepreneur ends the business with its obligations met.

weighted average cost of capital (WAC) The expected average future cost of funds.

whole of life costs The sum of all costs of capital assets, including acquisition, ownership, operation, and disposal.

wholesaler An intermediary business that buys (typically in large quantities) and sells (typically in smaller quantities) to businesses rather than consumers.

word of mouth A means of spreading information about your business through the comments friends and customers make to other potential customers.

work instructions Specific guidance for completing steps in a process.

working capital The cash immediately available to the firm for the day-to-day expenses and operations of the firm.

workout A form of business termination in which the firm's legal or financial obligations are not fully met at closing.

Z

zoning laws Government specifications for acceptable use of land and buildings in particular areas.

ENDNOTES

Chapter 1

1. This is based on interviews with Robin Rath as well as the Pixelpress.com website and its YouTube channel (www.youtube.com/channel/UC0a1xM2o6KcbcpE-C00kaYg), and articles on Rath and Pixel Press such as the following; E. Morrissey, "What You Can Learn from the Successful Pixel Press Kickstarter," *Integrity*, May 19, 2015, https://integritystl.com/pixel-press-kickstarter/; D. Nicklaus, "Mattel Deal Is Breakthrough for St. Louis Startup Pixel Press," *Stltoday.com*, December 30, 2016, www.stltoday.com/business/columns/david-nicklaus/mattel-deal-is-breakthrough-for-st-louis-startup-pixel-press/article_edecea96-0b63-5aea-adfc-32fd48747eb7.html; M. Halstead, "Murphysboro Men Develop Video Game Creation Technology," *The Southern*, December 23, 2014, https://thesouthern.com/news/local/murphysboro-men-develop-video-game-creation-technology/article_b78a790a-6d8b-594c-80fa-33a1c9405ed4.html.
2. Self-efficacy has a long history in predicting entrepreneurial intention and action. The key work for many is N. Krueger and P. R. Dickson, "How Believing in Ourselves Increases Risk Taking: Perceived Self-Efficacy and Opportunity Recognition," *Decision Sciences* 25, no. 3 (May 1, 1994), pp. 385–400. Other relevant works include C. C. Chen, P. G. Greene, and A. Crick, "Does Entrepreneurial Self-Efficacy Distinguish Entrepreneurs from Managers?," *Journal of Business Venturing* 13, no. 4 (July 1998), pp. 295–316; C. P. Neck et al., "'I Think I Can; I Think I Can': A Self-Leadership Perspective toward Enhancing Entrepreneur Thought Patterns, Self-Efficacy, and Performance," *Journal of Managerial Psychology* 14, no. 6 (January 11, 1999), pp. 477–501; F. Wilson, J. Kickul, and D. Marlino, "Gender, Entrepreneurial Self-Efficacy, and Entrepreneurial Career Intentions: Implications for Entrepreneurship Education," *Entrepreneurship Theory and Practice* 31, no. 3 (2007), pp. 387–406.
3. This link between planning and success has been shown worldwide in the works of Michael Frese and his colleagues in their studies of "action strategies." Their work shows that the intensity of the planning you do can make a difference between success and failure. M. Frese, M. van Gelderen, and M. Ombach, "How to Plan as a Small Scale Business Owner: Psychological Process Characteristics of Action Strategies and Success," *Journal of Small Business Management* 38, no. 2 (April 2000), pp. 1–18; J.-L. Van Gelder et al., "Differences in Psychological Strategies of Failed and Operational Business Owners in the Fiji Islands," *Journal of Small Business Management* 45, no. 3 (May 26, 2007), pp. 388–400.
4. For help from experts, the key findings have come from James Chrisman and colleagues. In their latest study they reported that expert counseling improved performance whereas entrepreneurship classes increased the likelihood of venture creation. J. J. Chrisman et al., "Counseling Assistance, Entrepreneurship Education, and New Venture Performance," *Journal of Entrepreneurship and Public Policy* 1, no. 1 (April 20, 2012), pp. 63–83. The key study for education effects remains A. Charney and G. Libecap, *Impact of Entrepreneurship Education* (Kansas City, MO: Kauffman Center for Entrepreneurial Leadership, 2000), although there are now dozens of studies of individual programs.
5. B. Bucar, M. Glas, and R. D. Hisrich, "Ethics and Entrepreneurs: An International Comparative Study," *Journal of Business Venturing* 18, no. 2 (March 2003), pp. 261–281.
6. The Kauffman Index provides an annual estimate of new firms each year. For 2016, it reported that 0.31 percent of the over-20-year-old population Americans started new businesses each month. With 186 million people, that reflects the creation of 6,919,200 businesses in 2016. In email discussions with Index researchers Robert Fairlie, Arnobio Morelix, and E. J. Reedy, it was pointed out that this number is probably an overestimate because of individuals who are contractors and go in and out of business several times a year as contracts end and new ones start. The 6 million figure represents an estimate that attempts to account for this, and is a relatively good fit to the rates for several recent years. See www.kauffman.org/kauffman-index/profile?loc=US&name=united-states&breakdowns=growth|overall,startup-activity|overall,main-street|overall#indicator-panel-se-index.
7. The 15.5 million estimate comes from the U.S. Census Bureau's Current Population Survey (www.census.gov/programs-surveys/cps.html), which does a detailed analysis of occupations and jobs every March. These data are from the March 2015 CPS, and were originally analyzed using DataFerrett (http://dataferrett.census.gov/). Note this is also the dataset used by the Kauffman Index of Entrepreneurship (www.kauffman.org/microsites/kauffman-index) to report on entrepreneurship rates across the United States.
8. Upwork, "Freelancing in America: 2018 Survey—Upwork," 2019, www.upwork.com/i/freelancing-in-america/2018/.
9. These computations were based on the March 2015 Current Population Survey. The variables were analyzed using DataFerrett. "Owner-managers" is a combination of the CPS occupations of "Managers, All Other" and "Chief Executives"; Construction combines "Construction Managers," "Construction Laborers," and "Carpenters." All analyses were done by Jerome Katz.
10. Even among small business owners, calling someone an entrepreneur can be problematic. About one owner in eight was offended by the term in a 2001 poll, although "small business owner" was almost universally accepted. *NFIB—National Small Business Poll—Success, Satisfaction and Growth* (Washington, DC: NFIB Research Foundation, 2001).
11. This fight among professors seems to have settled down to three competing camps—wealth creation, opportunity recognition, and firm creation. Wealth creation proponents usually define *entrepreneurship* as efforts to create wealth, especially through high-growth new ventures. Major centers for this approach are Harvard University and Babson College. The opportunity recognition approach is centered at the University of Chicago and University of Virginia. This approach sees entrepreneurship occurring when an individual finds and exploits some technological, economic, or market mismatch. The firm creation approach says that starting a business is where entrepreneurship occurs, and it is the favored model at Clemson University and Saint Louis University.
12. The ideas for independent businesses come from Jerome A. Katz and William B. Gartner, "Properties of Emerging Organizations," *Academy of Management Review* 13, no. 3 (July 1988), pp. 429–441; William B. Gartner, "A Conceptual Framework for Describing the Phenomenon of New Venture Creation," *Academy of Management Review* 10, no. 4 (October 1985), pp. 696–706. The social entrepreneurship ideas are built from a number of sources including L. Gregory Dees and Beth Battle Anderson, "For-Profit Social Ventures," *International Journal of Entrepreneurship Education* 2, no. 1 (2002), www.senatehall.com/journals.php?journal=1; Douglas Henton, John Melville, and Kimberly Walesh, "The Age of the Civic Entrepreneur: Restoring Civil Society and Building Economic Community," *National Civic Review* 6, no. 2 (1997), pp. 149–156; Janna Mair and Ignasti Marti, "Social Entrepreneurship Research: A Source of Explanation, Prediction, and Delight," *Journal of World Business* 41 (2006), pp. 36–44; Julia Sass Rubin and Gregory M. Stankiewicz, "The Los Angeles Community Development Bank: The Possible Pitfalls of Public-Private Partnerships," *Journal of Urban Affaris* 23, no. 2 (2001), pp. 133–153; Sandra A. Waddock and James E. Post, "Social Entrepreneurs and Catalytic Change," *Public Administration Review* 51 (1991), pp. 393–401. The material on corporate entrepreneurs comes from Peter Drucker, "What Business Can Learn from Nonprofits," *Harvard Business Review* 67, no. 4 (1989), pp. 88–93; Steven Klepper, "Employee Start-ups in High-Tech Industries,"

Industrial and Corporate Change 10 (2001), pp. 639–674; Donald F. Kuratko, R. Duane Ireland, Jeffrey G. Covin, and Jeffrey S. Hornsby, "A Model of Middle-Level Managers' Entrepreneurial Behavior," *Entrepreneurship Theory and Practice* 29, no. 6 (2005), pp. 699–716.

13. This is based on interviews with Jim McKelvey and additional sources such as J. McKelvey, "Blog," *Jim McKelvey*, March 14, 2013, www.fullscreendirect.com/JimMcKelvey/blog/technology/337197/why-square-s-jim-mckelvey-is-crazy-about-st-louis; https://third-degreeglassfactory.com/connect/about/; L. Calhoun, "Why Square Co-Founder Jim McKelvey Says Be Wary of Advice from Successful People," *Inc.*, June 8, 2016, www.inc.com/lisa-calhoun/why-squares-founder-jim-mckelvey-says-be-wary-of-advice-from-successful-people.html.
14. D. J. Kelly, S. Singer, and M. Herrington, *Global Entrepreneurship Monitor: 2011 Global Report* (Babson Park, USA/Santiago, Chile/Kuala Lampur, Malaysia: Babson College/Universidad del Desarrollo/Universiti Tun Abdul Razak, 2012), www.gemconsortium.org/docs/2201/gem-2011-global-report.
15. This number comes from estimates for 2015 included in the Small Business Administration Office of Advocacy, "Frequently Asked Questions about Small Business," www.sba.gov/sites/default/files/advocacy/Frequently-Asked-Questions-Small-Business-2018.pdf.
16. Also called "habitual entrepreneurs"; see D. Ucbasaran, M. Wright, P. Westhead, and L. W. Busenitz, "The Impact of Entrepreneurial Experience on Opportunity Identification and Exploitation: Habitual and Novice Entrepreneurs," *Advances in Entrepreneurship, Firm Emergence and Growth,* no. 6 (December 9, 2003), pp. 231–263; A. Amaral, R. Baptista, and F. Lima, "Serial Entrepreneurship: Impact of Human Capital on Time to Re-entry," *Small Business Economics* 37, no. 1 (2011), pp. 1–21.
17. M. Dell and C. Freedman, *Direct from Dell: Strategies That Revolutionized an Industry* (New York: Harper Business, 2000), www.amazon.com/exec/obidos/tg/detail//0756718775/102-2417352-1853726?v=qlance&vi=excerpt.
18. Robert X. Cringley, *Accidental Empires: How the Boys of Silicon Valley Make Their Millions, Battle Foreign Competition, and Still Can't Get a Date* (New York: HarperInformation, 2000).
19. The count comes from *Fortune* magazine's online "The Unicorn List," checked January 22, 2016, and filtering for U.S.-only firms.
20. The 56 percent number comes from U.S. respondents aged 15–25 from InSites global survey, J. Van den Bergh, "Generation Y around the World: Global Youth Research by InSites," *Business & Management,* February 15, 2012, www.slideshare.net/joerivandenbergh/generation-y-around-the-world-by-insites-consulting. The 14.7 percent number reflects youth 18–24 and comes from N. Bosma and D. Kelley, *GEM 2018/2019 Global Report* (Babson Park, MA: Babson College, 2019), www.gemconsortium.org/report/50213, Appendix Table 4.
21. U.S. Small Business Administration, Office of Advocacy, "Frequently Asked Questions about Small Business Finance, 2018," September 2018, www.sba.gov/sites/default/files/Finance-FAQ-2016_WEB.pdf.
22. U.S. Small Business Administration, Office of Advocacy, "Frequently Asked Questions about Small Business Finance, 2018," September 2018, www.sba.gov/sites/default/files/Finance-FAQ-2016_WEB.pdf.
23. M. Segal, *Peer-to-Peer Lending: A Financing Alternative for Small Businesses*. Issue Brief. Washington, DC: US SBA Office of Advocacy, September 9, 2015, www.sba.gov/sites/default/files/advocacy/Issue-Brief-10-P2P-Lending_0.pdf.
24. Benjamins, S. "The Top 10 Free Website Builders | Reviews & Comparison (2019)," January 1, 2019. https://www.sitebuilderreport.com/free-website-builders.
25. J. Cornwall, *Bootstrapping* (Upper Saddle River, NJ: Prentice Hall, 2010); Center for Women's Business Research, *Bootstrapping—Financial Strategies* (McLean, VA: Center for Women's Business Research, February 2012), www.womensbusinessresearchcenter.org/Data/research/february2012survey/february_2012_short_survey.pdf.
26. M. E. Biery, "The 20 Most-Profitable Industries," October 28, 2011, www3.cfo.com/article/2011/10/growth-strategies_most-profitable-ndustries-sageworks-private-companies; Sageworks, "The 20 Most Profitable Industries," Sageworks, Inc., October 28, 2011, www.sageworksinc.com/pressroom.aspx?article=627&title=The-20-Most-Profitable-Industries&date=October-28-2011. For 2015, Sageworks, "The Most Profitable Industries in the U.S.," August 28, 2015, www.sageworks.com/datareleases.aspx?article=329&title=The-Most-Profitable-Industries-in-the-U.S.&date=August-28-2015-.
27. David Rottenberg and Jeffrey Shuman, "Loser Chic," Entrepreneur.com, February 1999, www.entrepreneur.com/article/17228.
28. Mindy Carson, "Famous Mompreneurs and How They Made Their Fortunes," *Associated Content—Business & Finance,* April 21, 2009, www.associatedcontent.com/article/1662719/famous_mompreneurs_and_how_they_made.html; E. C. Hoffman III, "10 Famous Career Switchers," Businessweek.com, June 28, 2007, http://images.businessweek.com/ss/07/06/0628_second_careers/index_01.htm.
29. The closure rates come from the Office of Advocacy, U.S. Small Business Administration, "SBA Frequently Asked Questions" (U.S. Small Business Administration, January 2011), www.sba.gov/sites/default/files/sbfaq.pdf. The analysis of closings come from B. Headd, "Redefining Business Success: Distinguishing between Closure and Failure," *Small Business Economics* 21, no. 1 (2003), pp. 51–61.
30. Jerome Katz and William B. Gartner, "Properties of Emerging Organizations," *Academy of Management Review* 13, no. 3 (July 1988), pp. 429–441; Jerome A. Katz and Scott Safranski, "Standardization in the Midst of Innovation: Structural Implications of the Internet for SMEs," *Futures: The Journal of Policy, Planning and Future Studies* 35, no. 4 (May 2003), pp. 323–340; Sumit K. Kundu and Jerome A. Katz, "Born-International SMEs: Bi-Level Impacts of Resources and Intentions," *Small Business Economics* 20, no. 1 (February 2003), pp. 25–47; Jerome A. Katz and Susan Peters, "Understanding the Entrepreneur in the Growth Process of SMEs," *The International Journal of Entrepreneurship and Innovation Management* 1, nos. 3–4 (2001), pp. 366–380; Nancy M. Carter, William B. Gartner, and Paul D. Reynolds, "Exploring Start-Up Sequences," *Journal of Business Venturing* 11, no. 3 (May 1996), pp. 151–166.
31. Jeffrey Pfeffer and Robert I. Sutton, *The Knowing-Doing Gap: How Smart Companies Turn Knowledge into Action* (Cambridge, MA: Harvard Business School Press, 1999); or see Alan M. Webber, "Why Can't We Get Anything Done?," *Fast Company,* June 2000, www.fastcompany.com/magazine/35/pfeffer.html.
32. The theory was developed in the article: Jerome Katz and William B. Gartner, "Properties of Emerging Organizations," *Academy of Management Review* 13, no. 3 (July 1988), pp. 429–441; and extended in J. A. Katz and S. Peters, "Understanding the Entrepreneur in the Growth Process of SMEs," *The International Journal of Entrepreneurship and Innovation Management* 1, nos. 3–4 (2001), pp. 366–380. Empirical work in the PSED study was reported in Nancy M. Carter, William B. Gartner, and Paul D. Reynolds, "Exploring Start-Up Sequences," *Journal of Business Venturing* 11, no. 3 (May 1996), pp. 151–166. An independent confirmation was reported in Sumit K. Kundu and Jerome A. Katz, "Born-International SMEs: Bi-Level Impacts of Resources and Intentions," *Small Business Economics* 20, no. 1 (February 2003), pp. 25–47; and C. G. Brush, T. S. Manolova, and L. F. Edelman, "Properties of Emerging Organizations: An Empirical Test," *Journal of Business Venturing* 23, no. 5 (September 2008), pp. 547–566. A shortened form of the scale they developed for the PSED remains in use in the Global Entrepreneurship Monitor.
33. Nancy M. Carter, William B. Gartner, and Paul D. Reynolds, "Exploring Start-Up Sequences," *Journal of Business Venturing* 11, no. 3 (May 1996), pp. 151–166.

34. Nancy M. Carter, William B. Gartner, and Paul D. Reynolds, "Exploring Start-Up Sequences," *Journal of Business Venturing* 11, no. 3 (May 1996), pp. 151–166; Monica Diochon, Yvon Gasse, Teresa Menzies, and Denis Garand, "From Conception to Inception: Initial Findings from the Canadian Study on Entrepreneurial Emergence," ASAC 2001 Annual Meeting, www.sauder.ubc.ca/research/research_centres/era/arena5/papers/ASAC2001Revised%20Submission.pdf.
35. U.S. Small Business Administration, Office of Advocacy, "SBA Frequently Asked Questions," August 2018, www.sba.gov/category/advocacy-navigation-structure/faqs.
36. SBA Office of Advocacy, *Small Business by the Numbers,* www.sba.gov/advo/stats/sbfaq.pdf; Z. J. Acs and C. Armington, "Endogenous Growth and Entrepreneurial Activity in Cities," Center for Economic Studies, U.S. Bureau of the Census, Working Paper #CES-WP-03-2, January 2003.
37. Jeffrey Pfeffer and Robert I. Sutton, *The Knowing-Doing Gap: How Smart Companies Turn Knowledge into Action* (Cambridge, MA: Harvard Business School Press, 1999); or see Alan M. Webber, "Why Can't We Get Anything Done?," *Fast Company,* June 2000, www.fastcompany.com/magazine/35/pfeffer.html.
38. Joseph A. Schumpeter, *The Theory of Economic Development* (New York: Oxford, 1961) (originally published 1934).
39. Scott A. Shane, "Is the Independent Entrepreneur a Valuable Organizational Form?," *RISEbusiness*, www.riseb.org/shane.html.
40. Jeffrey Pfeffer and Robert I. Sutton, *The Knowing-Doing Gap: How Smart Companies Turn Knowledge into Action* (Cambridge, MA: Harvard Business School Press, 1999); or see Alan M. Webber, "Why Can't We Get Anything Done?," *Fast Company,* June 2000, www.fastcompany.com/magazine/35/pfeffer.html.
41. History of Snowboarding website, www.sbhistorv.de/.
42. "Behind the Earmuff," *Kids World,* www.kidzworld.com/site/p880.htm; Mary Bellis, "Chester Greenwood, Earmuffs," *Inventors,* About.com, http://inventors.about.com/library/inventors/blgreenwood.htm; "Fascinating Facts about the Invention of Earmuffs by Chester Greenwood in 1873," *The Great Idea Finder,* www.ideafinder.com/history/inventions/story091.htm.
43. Krisztina Holly, "Visual Voice (TM) Telephony Software," *Thinkquest,* http://library.thinkquest.org/26451/contents/inventors/krisztinaholly.htm?tqskip1=1; Mary Bellis, About.com, Inventors "Krisztina Holly," http://inventors.about.com/library/inventors/blholly.htm.
44. Don Debelak, "A Novel Dilemma: To Reach Potential Customers with an Avant-Garde Product, You'll Need to Have a Few Tricks Up Your Sleeve," *Entrepreneur,* June 2003, www.entrepreneur.com/article/61972; Drinksafe Technologies website, www.drinksafetech.com.
45. "Our Founders: Ed Lowe and Darlene Lowe," http://edwardlowe.org/index.peer?paqe=FDNfounders, July 9, 2005; Jenny Kee, "Author Mark Baven on Being Extreme: Do You Have What It Takes to Be an Extreme Entrepreneur? Let Mark Baven Show You the Ropes of Rule-Breaking, Risk-Taking Entrepreneurship," *Entrepreneur,* June 18, 2001, www.entrepreneur.com/article/41484.
46. This table was inspired by a table on small business innovation in *The State of Small Business: A Report of the President, 1994* (Washington, DC: U.S. Government Printing Office, 1995), p. 114. We tracked down the inventors of several of the small business innovations listed in the report and added several new ones, as well as all the student-started innovations. We found the video laryngoscope in Melnie Reid, "How a Shop Assistant Saw the Light and Saved Lives," *The Times,* July 17, 2008, www.timesonline.co.uk/tol/news/uk/scotland/article4354048-ece.
47. Small Business Administration, *The New American Revolution: The Role and Impact of Small Firms* (Washington, DC: U.S. Small Business Administration, Office of Economic Research, 1998).
48. Small Business Administration, *Rural and Urban Areas by Firm Size, 1990–1995* (Washington, DC: Office of Advocacy, 1999), www.sbaonline.sba.gov/advo/stats/urb_rur.pdf.
49. Economic development experts call these *central place theorems,* with the efforts to figure out how many stores a population can support called *demand-threshold studies*. Examples tend to be fairly localized and include Thomas R. Harris and J. Scott Shonkwiler, "Interdependence of Retail Businesses," *Growth and Change* 28, no. 4 (Fall 1997), pp. 520–533; J. Scott Shonkwiler and Thomas R. Harris, "Rural Retail Thresholds and Interdependencies," *Journal of Regional Studies* 36 (1996), pp. 617–630; H. Gale Jr., "Retail Sales Pull Factors in U.S. Counties," *The Review of Regional Studies* 26 (1996), pp. 177–196; David Darling and Stephen Tubene, "Determining the Population Thresholds of Minor Trade Centers: A Benchmark Study of Non-Metropolitan Cities in Kansas," *Review of Agricultural Economics* 18, no. 1 (January 1996), pp. 95–102; G. Ebai and T. Harris, "Factors Influencing Trade Area Activity in the Great Basin Area," *The Review of Regional Studies* 27 (1997), pp. 251–276.
50. The idea that living spaces are important to creativity (such as the kind we find in entrepreneurial and high-growth ventures) comes from Richard Florida, *The Rise of the Creative Class: And How It's Transforming Work, Leisure, Community and Everyday Life* (New York: Basic Books, 2004).
51. Robert Berner, "P&G: New and Improved: How A.G. Lafley Is Revolutionizing a Bastion of Corporate Conservatism," *BusinessWeek,* July 7, 2003, www.businessweek.com/magazine/content/03_27/b3840001_mz001.htm. You can find information about Trillium Health Care Products at www.brockville.com/newsdetails.cfm?IDIn=172_01.htm or at its corporate website, www.trilliumhealth_care.com.
52. U.S. Census Bureau, *A Profile of U.S. Importing and Exporting Companies, 2015–2016* (Washington, DC: Author, April 5, 2018), www.census.gov/foreign-trade/Press-Release/edb/2016/text.pdf.
53. GT's Living Foods, "Our Story—Founder GT Dave," n.d., retrieved January 15, 2019, from https://gtslivingfoods.com/our-story/; T. Foster, "Meet GT Dave, the King of Kombucha," February 18, 2015, retrieved January 15, 2019, www.inc.com/magazine/201503/tom-foster/the-king-of-kombucha.html; S. J. Bronner, "The Creator of the Kombucha Category Says the Term 'Serial Entrepreneur' Makes Him Sick to His Stomach," January 14, 2019, retrieved January 15, 2019, from www.entrepreneur.com/article/326155.
54. Sumit K. Kundu and Jerome A. Katz, "Born-International SMEs: Bi-Level Impacts of Resources and Intentions," *Small Business Economics* 20, no. 1 (2003), p. 25.
55. Jerome A. Katz, Scott R. Safranski, and Omar Khan, "Virtual Instant Global Entrepreneurship," *Journal of International Entrepreneurship* 1, no. 1 (2003), p. 43.
56. Stuart Read, Saras Sarasvathy, Nick Dew, Robert Wiltbank, and Anne-Valérie Ohlsson, *Effectual Entrepreneurship* (London: Routledge, 2010).
57. Wrigley Company, "Juicy Fruit," *Wrigley: A Subsidiary of Mars, Incorporated,* n.d., www.wrigley.com/global/brands/juicy-fruit.aspx; Wrigley Company. "Heritage Timeline," *Wrigley: A Subsidiary of Mars, Incorporated,* n.d., www.wrigley.com/global/about-us/heritage-timeline.aspx.
58. The corridor principle comes from R. Ronstadt, "The Corridor Principle," *Journal of Business Venturing* 3, no. 1 (1989), pp. 31–40. The same idea was called the "open systems" model of occupational choice by S. H. Osipow and L. F. Fitzgerald, *Theories of Career Development* (Englewood Cliffs, NJ: Prentice Hall, 1973).
59. This is a composite based on several students' efforts to fight food insecurity in St. Louis. The source for the 25 percent insecurity rate was https://map.feedingamerica.org/county/2016/overall/missouri/county/st-louis-city.

Chapter 2

1. This profile is based on interviews with Khalia (whom Jerome works with at Saint Louis University) and several articles about her and her team such as the following: P. Brown, "Persons of Interest: Khalia Collier," *Ladue News*, September 17, 2015, www.laduenews.com/business/columns/persons-of-interest-khalia-collier/article_07f97cce-828c-5d59-88b7-598d8ea36181.html; E. Austin, "At Age 23, Khalia Collier Owns Her Own Basketball Franchise," *St. Louis American*, n.d., www.stlamerican.com/sports/local_sports/at-age-khalia-collier-owns-her-own-basketball-franchise/article_525342b0-ad91-11e0-8723-001cc4c03286.html; "Khalia Collier Archives," *The Vital Voice*, n.d. http://thevitalvoice.com/tag/khalia-collier/.
2. The description here looks at behavior in the founder (vs. inventor or developer) role and comes from Melissa Cardon, Joakim Wincent, Jagdip Singh, and Mateja Drnovsek, "The Nature and Experience of Entrepreneurial Passion," *Academy of Management Review ARCHIVE* 34, no. 3 (July 1, 2009), pp. 511–532. The impact of passion on employees comes from Melissa S. Cardon, "Is Passion Contagious? The Transference of Entrepreneurial Passion to Employees," *Human Resource Management Review* 18, no. 2 (June 2008), pp. 77–86; Nicola Breugst, Anne Domurath, Holger Patzelt, and Anja Klaukien, "Perceptions of Entrepreneurial Passion and Employees' Commitment to Entrepreneurial Ventures," *Entrepreneurship: Theory and Practice* 36, no. 1 (January 2012), pp. 171–192. The impact on investors comes from Xiao-Ping Chen, Xin Yao, and Suresh Kotha, "Entrepreneur Passion and Preparedness in Business Plan Presentations: A Persuasion Analysis of Venture Capitalists' Funding Decisions," *Academy of Management Journal ARCHIVE* 52, no. 1 (February 1, 2009), pp. 199–214. However, while Chen et al. suggest that passion is important, planning can trump it.
3. This approach to perseverance as learned optimism (also known as resilience) comes from Daniel Seligman's thinking, specifically as applied by Norris F. Krueger Jr., "Entrepreneurial Resilience: Real and Perceived Barriers to Implementing Entrepreneurial Intentions," *SSRN eLibrary* (July 3, 2008), http://papers.ssrn.com/sol3/papers.cfm?abstract_id=1155269.
4. For example, in one group of entrepreneurs, the higher the perseverance scores, the higher their annual earnings. See Gideon D. Markman, Robert A. Baron, and David B. Balkin, "Are Perseverance and Self-Efficacy Costless? Assessing Entrepreneurs' Regretful Thinking," *Journal of Organizational Behavior* 26, no. 1 (2005), pp. 1–19.
5. In addition to Krueger's work, an effectuation-grounded approach can be seen in Mathew L. A. Hayward, William R. Forster, Saras D. Sarasvathy, and Barbara L. Fredrickson, "Beyond Hubris: How Highly Confident Entrepreneurs Rebound to Venture Again," *Journal of Business Venturing* 25, no. 6 (November 2010), pp. 569–578.
6. Joel Brockner, E. Tory Higgins, and Murray B. Low, "Regulatory Focus Theory and the Entrepreneurial Process," *Journal of Business Venturing* 19, no. 2 (March 2004), pp. 203–220.
7. Keith M. Hmieleski and Robert A. Baron, "Regulatory Focus and New Venture Performance: A Study of Entrepreneurial Opportunity Exploitation under Conditions of Risk Versus Uncertainty," *Strategic Entrepreneurship Journal* 2, no. 4 (March 23, 2009), pp. 285–299; Jintong Tang, "Exploring the Constitution of Entrepreneurial Alertness: The Regulatory Focus View," *Journal of Small Business and Entrepreneurship* 22, no. 3 (2009), pp. 221–238.
8. Gideon D. Markman, Robert A. Baron, and David B. Balkin, "The Role of Regretful Thinking, Perseverance, and Self-Efficacy in Venture Formation," *Advances in Entrepreneurship, Firm Emergence and Growth*, no. 6 (December 9, 2003), pp. 73–104; Gideon D. Markman, Robert A. Baron, and David B. Balkin, "Are Perseverance and Self-Efficacy Costless? Assessing Entrepreneurs' Regretful Thinking," *Journal of Organizational Behavior* 26, no. 1 (2005), pp. 1–19.
9. These are inspired by the concept of action strategies from M. Frese, M. van Gelderen, and M. Ombach, "How to Plan as a Small Scale Business Owner: Psychological Process Characteristics of Action Strategies and Success," *Journal of Small Business Management* 38, no. 2 (April 2000), pp. 1–18. Frese and his colleagues do not have a survey to assess action strategies, so the concepts and the questions offered in Skill Module 2.1 reflect an application of their idea. A related idea is the proactive personality: T. S. Bateman and J. M. Crant, "The Proactive Component of Organizational Behavior: A Measure and Correlates," *Journal of Organizational Behavior* 14, no. 2 (March 1, 1993), pp. 103–118.
10. S. Escher et al., "The Moderator Effect of Cognitive Ability on the Relationship between Planning Strategies and Business Success of Small Scale Business Owners in South Africa: A Longitudinal Study,"*Journal of Developmental Entrepreneurship* 7, no. 3 (October 2002), pp. 305–318; A. M. F. Hiemstra, K. G. Van Der Kooy, and M. Frese, "Entrepreneurship in the Street Food Sector of Vietnam—Assessment of Psychological Success and Failure Factors,"*Journal of Small Business Management* 44, no. 3 (June 15, 2006), pp. 474–481; J. Van Gelder et al., "Differences in Psychological Strategies of Failed and Operational Business Owners in the Fiji Islands,"*Journal of Small Business Management* 45, no. 3 (May 26, 2007), pp. 388–400; M. von Gelderen, M. Frese, and R. Thurik, "Strategies, Uncertainty and Performance of Small Business Startups,"*Small Business Economics* 15, no. 3 (2000), pp. 165–181.
11. H. Chang, "Atiba Is the Success of a Self-Taught Man,"*The Tennessean,* September 10, 2003; "Enterprise Executive Profile: J. J. Rosen, Chief Executive Officer," *Nashville Business Journal,* March 2, 2001, http://nashville.bizjournals.com/nashville/stories/2001/03/05/smallb1.html; M. Capps, "Bootstrapping Atiba Software Adds C-Level Exec," *Venture Nashville,* February 13, 2009, www.venturenashville.com/news.php?viewstory=238.
12. J. Plazonja and A. Zildjian, "Avedis Zildjian: The Father of Cymbals," 2003, www.zildjian.com/adaa/adaa_2003_legacy_6.asp; "Historical Timeline," July 10, 2005, Zildjian Company website, www.zildjian.com/EN-US/about/timeline.ad2.
13. The self-efficacy questions are adapted from F. Wilson, J. Kickul, and D. Marlino, "Gender, Entrepreneurial Self-Efficacy, and Entrepreneurial Career Intentions: Implications for Entrepreneurship Education," *Entrepreneurship Theory and Practice* 31, no. 3 (2007), pp. 387–406. The passion questions are from N. Breugst, A. Domurath, H. Patzelt, and A. Klaukien, "Perceptions of Entrepreneurial Passion and Employees' Commitment to Entrepreneurial Ventures," *Entrepreneurship: Theory and Practice* 36, no. 1 (January 2012), pp. 171–192. The perseverance questions were called "Entrepreneurial Intensity" in the Panel Study of Entrepreneurial Dynamics, from W. B. Gartner et al. (eds.), *Handbook of Entrepreneurial Dynamics: The Process of Business Creation* (Thousand Oaks, CA: Sage, 2004), pp. 186–195. The promotion–prevention focus comes from P. Lockwood, C. H. Jordan, and Z. Kunda, "Motivation by Positive or Negative Role Models: Regulatory Focus Determines Who Will Best Inspire Us," *Journal of Personality and Social Psychology* 83, no. 4 (October 2002), pp. 854–864, based on the suggestions of Keith Hmieleski and Robert Baron. The questions for planning style are inspired by the work on action styles by Michael Frese, while the questions on professionalization were inspired by the work on professionalization by Edgar Schein.
14. Scoring the Entrepreneurial Personality Overview is done is sections. Questions 1 through 4 measure self-efficacy from Chapter 1. Add up your score on these four items. The higher the score, the stronger your self-efficacy. Successful entrepreneurs tend to have above-average levels of self-efficacy. Questions 5 through 9 measure your level of passion as a founder. Add up your score on these five items. The higher your score, the stronger your level of passion. Successful

entrepreneurs demonstrate high levels of passion for their business. Note that there are two other roles entrepreneurs find themselves in—as inventors and as business developers in established firms. There are different scales for measuring passion in those roles. Questions 10 through 13 measure your perseverance. Add up your score on these four items. The higher the score, the stronger your perseverance, and successful entrepreneurs have above-average perseverance levels. Questions 14 and 15 measure your promotion focus. Add up your score on these two items. The higher the score, the stronger your promotion focus. Questions 16 and 17 measure your prevention focus. Add up your score on these two items. The higher the score, the stronger your prevention focus. The best entrepreneurs show both promotion and prevention orientations. The ABCDE ranking shows your planning style: "A" is a comprehensive planning style, "B" is a critical-point planning style, "C" is an opportunistic planning style, "D" is a reactive planning style, and "E" is a habitual planning style. Entrepreneurial success is greatest for comprehensive planners and decreases for each successive style. The FGH ranking shows your level of professionalization: "F" is the expert professionalization, "G" is specialized, and "H" is minimalized professionalization.

15. For a detailed review of the underlying theories and research see Allan Gray Orbis Foundation. "A Study of Entrepreneurial Mindset: Its Origins and How Best to Measure It." *Allan Gray Orbis Foundation*, September 19, 2017. https://www.allangrayorbis.org/entrepreneurship-blog/anatomy/study-entrepreneurial-mindset-origins-best-measure/. This paper is tied to the questionaire offered in the USA by Mindcette.com, and developed by Kelly Shaver of the College of Charleston. One of the most accessible books about the mindset was one of the first: McGrath, R. G. and I. C. MacMillan. *The Entrepreneurial Mindset: Strategies for Continuously Creating Opportunity in an Age of Uncertainty*. Harvard Business Press, 2000.
16. Looking at Google Trends for the two terms, "entrepreneurial mindset" has been searched more often than "entrepreneurial personality" for most of the period since 2014. Check for yourself at https://trends.google.com/trends/explore?date=all&geo=US&q=entrepreneurial%20mindset,entrepreneurial%20personality.
17. The link is https://www.bdc.ca/en/articles-tools/entrepreneur-toolkit/business-assessments/pages/self-assessment-test-your-entrepreneurial-potential.aspx.
18. There are two major models of entrepreneurial competency—Mitchell et al. and Chandler/Hanks models. The Mitchell et al. model has been validated cross-culturally, with very strong results, while the Chandler/Hanks model has seen wider use in U.S. studies. Although each model labels the competencies differently, the content of the competencies is very similar. The model presented here builds from the Mitchell et al. and Chandler/Hanks models, mapping their specific competencies to the BRIE model of Katz and Gartner introduced in Chapter 1. The key article on competencies is Ronald K. Mitchell, J. Brock Smith, Eric A. Morse, Kristie W.Seawright, Ana Maria Peredo, and Brian McKenzie, "Are Entrepreneurial Cognitions Universal? Assessing Entrepreneurial Cognitions across Cultures," *Entrepreneurship: Theory & Practice* 26, no. 4 (Summer 2002), pp. 9–32. Note that what are called *competencies* in this text are called *scripts* in the Mitchell works. The scripts are observed through their related cognitions: Gaylen N. Chandler and Steven H. Hanks, "Founder Competence, the Environment, and Venture Performance," *Entrepreneurship: Theory & Practice* 18, no. 3 (Spring 1994), pp. 77–89.
19. This skill is called *business ability competency* by Mitchell et al. and *managerial competency* by Chandler and Hanks.
20. This is called *organizational resources and capabilities* by Chandler and Hanks, while in the Mitchell et al. model resources are part of arrangement competencies. The social competencies that make these easier or harder for the entrepreneur come from R. A. Baron and G. D. Markman, "Beyond Social Capital: The Role of Entrepreneurs' Social Competence in Their Financial Success," *Journal of Business Venturing* 18, no. 1 (January 2003), pp. 41–60.
21. In the Mitchell et al. model these are called *willingness competencies*, while in the Chandler/Hanks approach they make up a part of the entrepreneurial competence factor.
22. In the Chandler/Hanks model, this is called the *quality of the opportunity*, while opportunity factors make up much of the arrangements competency cluster.
23. See R. Mitchell and S. Chesteen, "Enhancing Entrepreneurial Expertise: Experiential Pedagogy and the Entrepreneurial Expert Script," *Simulation & Gaming* 26, no. 3 (September 1995), pp. 288–306.
24. William Gartner (W. B. Gartner, "A Conceptual Framework for Describing the Phenomenon of New Venture Creation," *Academy of Management Review* 10, no. 4 [October 1985], pp. 696–706) defined the entrepreneurial event as the interaction of the entrepreneur, the business itself, the process by which it is started, and the context or environment in which all this happens. Other works that have built on the Gartner idea include L. Herron and H. J. Sapienza, "The Entrepreneur and the Initiation of New Venture Launch Activities," *Entrepreneurship: Theory & Practice* 17, no. 1 (Fall 1992), pp. 49–55; Douglas W. Naffziger, Jeffrey S. Hornsby, and Donald F. Kuratko, "A Proposed Research Model of Entrepreneurial Motivation," *Entrepreneurship: Theory & Practice* 18, no. 3 (Spring 1994), pp. 29–42; Carolyn Y. Woo, U. Daellenbach, and C. Nicholls-Nixon, "Theory Building in the Presence of 'Randomness': The Case of Venture Creation and Performance," *Journal of Management Studies* 31, no. 4 (July 1994), pp. 507–524; Richard C. Becherer and John G. Maurer, "The Proactive Personality Disposition and Entrepreneurial Behavior among Small Company Presidents," *Journal of Small Business Management* 37, no. 1 (January 1999), pp. 28–36. The term *entrepreneurial settings* follows the idea of environment in these studies. However, neither Gartner nor the subsequent researchers specified the exact nature of different types of settings. The settings described here are chosen because of their frequency.
25. American Express OPEN, Ventureneer, and Corewoman, *The 2018 State of Women-Owned Businesses Report,* 2018, https://about.americanexpress.com/files/doc_library/file/2018-state-of-women-owned-businesses-report.pdf.
26. American Express OPEN, *The 2015 State of Women-Owned Businesses Report,* May 2015, www.womenable.com/content/userfiles/Amex_OPEN_State_of_WOBs_2015_Executive_Report_finalsm.pdf.
27. American Express OPEN, Ventureneer, and Corewoman, *The 2018 State of Women-Owned Businesses Report, 2018*, https://about.americanexpress.com/files/doc_library/file/2018-state-of-women-owned-businesses-report.pdf.
28. American Express OPEN, Ventureneer, and Corewoman, *The 2018 State of Women-Owned Businesses Report, 2018*, https://about.americanexpress.com/files/doc_library/file/2018-state-of-women-owned-businesses-report.pdf.
29. All of these results about gender-driven entrepreneur differences are taken from E. Kepler and S. Shane, "Are Male and Female Entrepreneurs Really That Different?," Office of Advocacy Working Paper (Shaker Heights, OH: U.S. SBA Office of Advocacy, September 2007), http://archive.sba.gov/advo/research/rs309tot.pdf.
30. D. J. Kelly, C. G. Brush, P. C. Greene, and Y. Litvosky, *Global Entrepreneurship Monitor 2010 Women's Report,* Global Entrepreneurship Monitor (Babson Park, MA: Babson College, 2011), www.babson.edu/Academics/centers/blank-center/global-research/gem/Documents/GEM%202010%20 Womens%20Report%20V2.pdf.
31. These results were from the Kepler and Shane study, updated using the industries from the American Express OPEN 2012 report: E. Kepler and S. Shane, "Are Male and Female Entrepreneurs Really That

Different?," Office of Advocacy Working Paper (Shaker Heights, OH: U.S. SBA Office of Advocacy, September 2007), http://archive.sba.gov/advo/research/rs309tot.pdf; American Express OPEN, *The American Express OPEN State of End Notes E-7 Women-Owned Businesses Report—A Summary of Important Trends, 1997–2012* (New York: American Express OPEN, March 2012), http://media.nucleus.naprojects.com/pdf/State_of_Women-Owned_Businesses-Report_FINAL.pdf.

32. American Express OPEN, *The American Express OPEN State of Women-Owned Businesses Report—A Summary of Important Trends, 1997–2012* (New York: American Express OPEN, March 2012), http://media.nucleus.naprojects.com/pdf/State_of_Women-Owned_Businesses-Report_FINAL.pdf.
33. U.S. Small Business Administration, Office of Advocacy, "Frequently Asked Questions about Small Business Finance, 2018," August 2018, www.sba.gov/sites/default/files/advocacy/Frequently-Asked-Questions-Small-Business-2018.pdf.
34. American Express OPEN, *The 2015 State of Women-Owned Businesses Report,* May 2015, www.womenable.com/content/userfiles/Amex_OPEN_State_of_WOBs_2015_Executive_Report_finalsm.pdf.
35. U.S. Small Business Administration, Office of Advocacy, "Frequently Asked Questions about Small Business, 2018," 2018, www.sba.gov/sites/default/files/advocacy/Frequently-Asked-Questions-Small-Business-2018.pdf.
36. Alicia M. Robb, "Entrepreneurial Performance by Women and Minorities: The Case of New Firms," *Journal of Developmental Entrepreneurship* 7, no. 4 (December 2002), pp. 383–397.
37. Karen E. Klein, "Women, the Loan Strangers," *BusinessWeek*, May 28, 2004, www.businessweek.com/smallbiz/content/may2004/sb20040528_5382_sb010.htm; A. M. Robb, "Entrepreneurial Performance by Women and Minorities: The Case of New Firms," *Journal of Developmental Entrepreneurship* 7, no. 4 (December 2002), pp. 383–397.
38. Center for Women's Business Research, *Access to Markets: Perspectives from Large Corporations and Women's Business Enterprises* (Washington, DC: Author, 2003), www.womens businessresearch.org/pressreleases/2-4-2003/2-4-2003.htm.
39. K. S. Cavalluzzo and L. C. Cavalluzzo, "Market Structure and Discrimination: The Case of Small Business," *Journal of Money, Credit and Banking* 30, no. 4 (November 1998), pp. 771–792.
40. National Contract Management Association, *Annual Review of Government Contracting 2016* (Washington, DC: Author, 2017), www.ncmahq.org/docs/default-source/default-document-library/pdfs/exec16—book—annual-review-of-government-contracting_lowres.
41. National Minority Supply and Diversity Council, MBE—Certification NMSDC website, 2005, www.nmsdc.org/MBEs/tool_kit_certification.html.
42. National Minority Supply and Diversity Council, MBE—Certification NMSDC website, 2005, www.nmsdc.org/MBEs/tool_kit_certification.html.
43. Stephen Roper, "Entrepreneurial Characteristics, Strategic Choice and Small Business Performance," *Small Business Economics* 11, no. 1 (1998), pp. 11–24; Gangaram Singh and Alex DeNoble, "Early Retirees as the Next Generation of Entrepreneurs," *Entrepreneurship: Theory and Practice* 27, no. 3 (Spring 2003), pp. 207–226.
44. Joshua Kurlantzick, "About Face: The Face of Entrepreneurship Has Evolved over the Years, and Today, It's Dramatically Different. But What Will the Entrepreneur of the Future Look Like?," *Entrepreneur*, January 2004, www.Entrepreneur.eom/article/0,4621,312260,00.html; David A. Baucus and Sherrie E. Human, "Second Career Entrepreneurs: A Multiple Case Study Analysis of Entrepreneurial Processes and Antecendent Variables," *Entrepreneurship: Theory and Practice* 18, no. 2 (Winter 1994), pp. 41–71; Wallace N. Davidson, Dan L. Worrell, and J. Fox, B. Jercary, "Early Retirement Programs and Firm Performance," *Academy of Management Journal* 39, no. 4 (August 1996), pp. 970–984.
45. Gangaram Singh and Anil Verma, "Is There Life after Career Employment? Labour Market Experience of Early Retires," in Victor W. Marshall, Walter R. Heinz, Helga Krueger, and Anil Verma (eds.), *Restructuring Work and the Life Course* (Toronto: University of Toronto Press, 2001).
46. The change was from 4.2 percent in 1988 to 5.4 percent in 2015 among people aged 62 and older. D. Wilmoth, *The Ascent of the Senior Entrepreneur* (Washington, DC: SBA Office of Advocacy, August 18, 2016), www.sba.gov/sites/default/files/advocacy/Ascent-Senior-Entrepreneur.pdf.
47. Gangaram Singh and Alex DeNoble, "Early Retirees as the Next Generation of Entrepreneurs," *Entrepreneurship: Theory and Practice* 27, no. 3 (Spring 2003), pp. 207–226.
48. Andrea C. Poe, "Start a Business . . . Even after 50: Neither Shy nor Retiring, People over 50 Are Proving There's Life—and Profits—after Retirement as They Launch Second Careers as Entrepreneurs," *Entrepreneur*, August 19, 2003, www.Entrepreneur.com/article/0,4621,310607,00.html.
49. Andrea C. Poe, "Start a Business . . . Even after 50: Neither Shy nor Retiring, People over 50 Are Proving There's Life—and Profits—after Retirement as They Launch Second Careers as Entrepreneurs," *Entrepreneur*, August 19, 2003, www.Entrepreneur.com/article/0,4621,310607,00.html.
50. Andrea C. Poe, "Start a Business . . . Even after 50: Neither Shy nor Retiring, People over 50 Are Proving There's Life—and Profits—after Retirement as They Launch Second Careers as Entrepreneurs," *Entrepreneur*, August 19, 2003, www.Entrepreneur.com/article/0,4621,310607,00.html; L. Strang. "Downsized Designer Shuns Corporate Life–and Finds Success," *Late Blooming Entrepreneurs*, November 3, 2011, https://latebloomingentrepreneurs.wordpress.com/2011/11/03/downsized-designer-shuns-corporate-life-%e2%80%93-and-finds-success/; K. Sauers, "A Single Mom Takes the Jump to Being Own Boss, Finds Success," August 30, 2011, *North Hills, PA Patch,* http://patch.com/pennsylvania/northhills/a-single-mom-takes-the-jump-to-being-own-boss-finds-success.
51. Howard E. Aldrich, Nancy M. Carter, and Martin Ruef, "Teams," in William B. Gartner, Kelly G. Shaver, Nancy M. Carter, and Paul D. Reynolds (eds.), *Handbook of Entrepreneurial Dynamics: The Process of Business Creation* (Thousand Oaks, CA: Sage, 2004), Table 27.1, p. 307.
52. In Chapter 1, endnote 6, we explored the number of new firms annually. Applying the PSED findings from endnote 32, we have about 400,000 new firms started by firms with more than one person involved.
53. The term *equity* comes from the J. Stacy Adams motivational model called equity theory, which is often discussed in Introduction to Psychology courses. Two examples of applying it in partner situations include Brian Tracy, "Is a Business Partnership Right for You?," *Entrepreneur*, February 21, 2005, www.entrepreneur.com/article/76362; John A. Gromala and David F. Gage, "Mediating Personality Differences behind Internal Business Disputes," *The CPA Journal* 72, no. 3 (March 2002), pp. 68–69.
54. Paige Arnof-Fenn, "The Partner Track: How to Decide If You Should Fly Solo or Not: The Second in a Two-Part Series on Business Partnerships," *Entrepreneur*, July 14, 2005, www.entrepreneur.com/author/978-2.
55. Robert D. Hisrich, *Small Business Solutions: How to Fix & Prevent the 13 Biggest Problems That Derail Business* (New York: McGraw-Hill, 2004), pp. 70–71; Joe A. Cox, Kris K. Moore, and Philip M. Van Auken, "Working Couples in Small Business," *Journal of Small Business Management* 22, no. 4 (October 1984), pp. 24–30.

56. S. L. Wright and J. A. Katz, "Protecting Student Intellectual Property in the Entrepreneurial Classroom,"*Journal of Management Education* 40, no. 2 (April 1, 2016), pp. 152–169.
57. J. N. Baron and M. T. Hannan. "Organizational Blueprints for Success in High-Tech Start-Ups: Lessons from the Stanford Project on Emerging Companies," *California Management Review* 44, no. 3 (April 1, 2002), pp. 8–36; T. Blumentritt, J. Kickul, and L. K. Gundry, "Building an Inclusive Entrepreneurial Culture: Effects of Employee Involvement on Venture Performance and Innovation," *The International Journal of Entrepreneurship and Innovation* 6, no. 2 (May 1, 2005), pp. 77–84; A. Leung, J. Zhang, P. K. Wong, and M. D. Foo, "The Use of Networks in Human Resource Acquisition for Entrepreneurial Firms: Multiple 'Fit' Considerations," *Journal of Business Venturing* 21, no. 5 (September 2006), pp. 664–686.
58. This builds on the concepts of firm-level entrepreneurial orientation (G. T. Lumpkin and G. G. Dess, "Clarifying the Entrepreneurial Orientation Construct and Linking It to Performance," *Academy of Management Review* 21, no. 1 (January 1, 1996), pp. 135–172) and a strong analysis of entrepreneurial culture (D. Kariv, *Entrepreneurship: An International Introduction* (London: Taylor & Francis, 2011), as well as entrepreneurs' own ideas on the topic like J. Lawton, "Creating an Entrepreneurial Culture," Entrepreneurship.org, n.d., www.entrepreneurship.org/resource-center/creating-an-entrepreneurial-culture.aspx.
59. There has been a great deal of literature about this over the years. My favorites include R. M. Bramson, *Coping with Difficult People* (New York: Random House, 2012); R. I. Sutton, "Why I Wrote the No Asshole Rule," *Harvard Business Review*, March 17, 2007, https://hbr.org/2007/03/why-i-wrote-the-no-asshole-rule; M. Housman and D. Minor, "Toxic Workers," Harvard Business School, November 2015, www.hbs.edu/faculty/Publication%20Files/16-057_d45c0b4f-fa19-49de-8f1b-4b12fe054fea.pdf. The popular version of the toxic worker working paper can be found at N. Torres, "It's Better to Avoid a Toxic Employee Than Hire a Superstar," *Harvard Business Review*, December 9, 2015, https://hbr.org/2015/12/its-better-to-avoid-a-toxic-employee-than-hire-a-superstar.
60. Joseph Weber and Louis Lavelle, "Family, Inc.," *BusinessWeek*, November 10, 2003, www.businessweek.com:/print/magazine/content/03_45/b3857002.htm?mz.
61. R. Kurtz, "When Business Is in the Blood," *BusinessWeek*, January 25, 2005, http://yahoo.businessweek.com/smallbiz/content/jan2005/sb20050125_3409.htm; D. Miller and I. Le Breton-Miller, *Managing for the Long Run: Lessons in Competitive Advantage from Great Family Businesses* (Boston: Harvard Business School Press, 2005).
62. Joseph Astrachan and Melissa C. Shanker, "Family Businesses' Contribution to the U.S. Economy: A Closer Look," *Family Business Review* 16, no. 3 (September 2003), pp. 211–219.
63. Joseph Weber and Louis Lavelle, "Family, Inc.," *BusinessWeek*, November 10, 2003, www.businessweek.com:/print/magazine/content/03_45/b3857002.htm?mz.
64. W. Gibb Dyer and Wendy Handler, "Entrepreneurship and Family Business: Exploring the Connections," *Entrepreneurship: Theory & Practice* 18, no. 1 (Fall 1994), pp. 71–83.
65. W. Gibb Dyer and Wendy Handler, "Entrepreneurship and Family Business: Exploring the Connections," *Entrepreneurship: Theory & Practice*18, no. 1 (Fall 1994), pp. 71–83; Frank Hoy and Trudy Verser, "Emerging Business, Emerging Field: Entrepreneurship and the Family Firm," *Entrepreneurship: Theory & Practice* 18, no. 1 (Fall 1994), pp. 9–23.
66. David N. Laband and Bernard F. Lentz, "Like Father Like Son: Towards an Economic Theory of Occupational Following," *Southern Economic Journal* 50, no. 2 (October 1983), pp. 474–493; Bernard F. Lentz and David N. Laband, "Entrepreneurial Success and Occupational Inheritance among Proprietors," *Canadian Journal of Economics* 23, no. 3 (August 1990), pp. 563–579; Robert F. Scherer, James D. Bordzinski, and Frank A. Weibe, "Assessing Perception of Career Role-Model Performance: The Self-Employed Parent," *Perceptual and Motor Skills* 72, no. 2 (1991), pp. 555–560; Robert F. Scherer, James D. Brodzinski, and Frank A. Wiebe, "Entrepreneurship Career Selection and Gender: A Socialization Approach," *Journal of Small Business Management* 28, no. 2 (April 1990), pp. 37–44.
67. A. P. Sherman, "Connect the Daughters: Sons Aren't the Only Off-Spring Taking Over Family Businesses," *Entrepreneur* 30, no. 2 (December 2002), p. 36. Enstrom sales come from www.manta.com/c/mmc7wrw/enstrom-candies-inc.
68. John L. Ward, *Perpetuating the Family Business: 50 Lessons Learned from Long Lasting, Successful Families in Business* (New York: Palgrave Macmillan, 2004).
69. Charles R. Stoner, Richard I. Hartman, and Raj Arora, "Work-Home Role Conflict in Female Owners of Small Business: An Exploration Study," *Journal of Small Business Management* 28, no. 1 (January 1990), pp. 30–38.
70. E. H. Updike, "How to Avoid a Dysfunctional Family Business," *BusinessWeek*, March 2, 1998, p. 3; K. E. Gersick, J. A. Davis, M. McCollom Hampton, and I. Lansberg, *Generation to Generation: Life Cycles of the Family Business* (Boston: Harvard Business School Press, 1997).
71. Nancy J. Miller, Mary Winter, Margaret A. Fitzgerald, and Jennifer Paul, "Family Microenterprises: Strategies for Coping with Overlapping Family and Business Demands," *Journal of Developmental Entrepreneurship* 5, no. 2 (August 2000), pp. 87–114; Frank Hoy and Trody Verser, "Emerging Business, Emerging Field: Entrepreneurship and the Family Firm," *Entrepreneurship: Theory & Practice* 18, no. 1 (Fall 1994), pp. 9–23; Eric G. Flamholtz, *How to Make the Transition from an Entrepreneurship to a Professionally Managed Firm* (San Francisco: Jossey-Bass, 1986).
72. W. Gibb Dyer Jr., *The Entrepreneurial Experience: Confronting Career Dilemmas of the Start-Up Executive* (San Francisco: Jossey-Bass, 1992), p. 184.
73. Paul Edwards and Sarah Edwards, "How to Manage Your Home-based Time," Entrepreneur.com, May 13, 2003, www.entrepreneur.com/homebasedbiz/worklifebalance/advicefrompaulandsarahedwards/article61974.html; Lisa Kanarek, "Keeping Time," Home-OfficeMag.com, January 2001, www.entrepreneur.com/worklife/worklifebalanceadvice/timemanagementandorganization/article35806.html; Rosalind Resnick, "Secrets to Staying Focused in Your Home Office," Entrepreneur.com, May 17, 2004, www.entrepreneur.com/homebasedbiz/worklifebalance/timemanaqement/article70836.html; Sonja Treven and Vojko Potocan, "Training Programmes for Stress Management in Small Businesses," *Education + Training* 47, nos. 8–9 (2005), pp. 640–652; Howard Van Auken and James Werbel, "Family Dynamic and Family Business Financial Performance: Spousal Commitment," *Family Business Review* 19, no. 1 (2006), pp. 49–63.
74. Joseph Astrachan and Melissa C. Shanker, "Family Businesses' Contribution to the U.S. Economy: A Closer Look," *Family Business Review* 16, no. 3 (September 2003), pp. 211–219; Arthur Andersen Center for Family Business, *American Family Business Survey* (St. Charles, IL: Arthur Andersen Center for Family Business 1995); John Ward, *Keeping the Family Business Healthy: How to Plan for Continuing Growth, Profitability and Family Leadership* (San Francisco: Jossey-Bass, 1987). Ward suggested that around 88 percent of family firms fail by the third generation, with family infighting, rather than a lack of succession planning, taking a toll in later generations. Ward's sample was relatively small. A very large, multigenerational study of family firms in France suggested a much higher survival rate (see Dean Savage, *Founders, Heirs and Managers: French Industrial Leadership in Transition* [Beverly Hills: Sage, 1979]).

75. W. Gibb Dyer Jr., *The Entrepreneurial Experience: Confronting Career Dilemmas of the Start-Up Executive* (San Francisco: Jossey-Bass, 1992), p. 184.
76. Ernesto J. Poza, *Family Business* (Mason, OH: South-Western, 2004), pp. 28–29, 33.
77. Ernesto J. Poza, *Family Business* (Mason, OH: South-Western, 2004), p. 33.
78. John Ward, *Keeping the Family Business Healthy: How to Plan for Continuing Growth, Profitability and Family Leadership* (San Francisco: Jossey-Bass, 1987). Ward suggested that around 88 percent of family firms fail by the third generation, with family infighting, rather than a lack of succession planning, taking a toll in later generations. Ward's sample was relatively small. A very large, multigenerational study of family firms in France suggested a much higher survival rate (see Dean Savage, *Founders, Heirs and Managers: French Industrial Leadership in Transition* [Beverly Hills: Sage, 1979]).
79. William G. Shuster, "Family Business in Crisis: Letting Go," *Jewelers Circular Keystone,* March 2003, p. 84.
80. David Whitford, "Century-Old Companies Built to Last," *Fortune Small Business* 12, no. 5 (2002), pp. 28–34.
81. Eric G. Flamholtz and Yvonne Randle, *Growing Pains: Transitioning from an Entrepreneurship to a Professionally Managed Firm* (San Francisco: Jossey-Bass, 2000), pp. 64–65.
82. Joseph Weber and Louis Lavelle, "Family, Inc." *BusinessWeek*, November 10, 2003, www.businessweek.com:/print/magazine/content/03_45/b3857002.html?mz.
83. W. Gibb Dyer Jr., *The Entrepreneurial Experience: Confronting Career Dilemmas of the Start-Up Executive* (San Francisco: Jossey-Bass, 1992), p. 184.
84. Barnett Helzberg Jr., "Sage Counsel for All Seasons," *BusinessWeek*, August 13, 2003, www.businessweek.com:/print/smallbiz/content/aug2003/sb20030813_2077 htm?sb.
85. Ernesto J. Poza, *Family Business* (Mason, OH: South-Western, 2004), pp. 28–29, 33.
86. Ibid.
87. D. Bork, D. T. Jaffee, S. H. Lane, L. Dashew, and Q. G. Heisler, *Working with Family Businesses: A Guide for Professionals* (San Francisco: Jossey-Bass, 1996); N. C. Churchill and K. J. Hatten, "Non-Market Based Transfers of Wealth and Power: A Research Framework for Family Businesses," *American Journal of Small Business* 11, no. 3 (Spring 1987), p. 51; E. G. Flamholtz, *How to Make the Transition from an Entrepreneurship to a Professionally Managed Firm* (San Francisco: Jossey-Bass, 1986); R. Beckhard and W. G. Dyer, "Managing Continuity in the Family-Owned Business," *Organizational Dynamics* 12, no. 1 (Summer 1983), pp. 5–12.
88. S. Foley and G. N. Powell, "Reconceptualizing Work--Family Conflict for Business/Marriage Partners: A Theoretical Model," *Journal of Small Business Management* 35, no. 4 (October 1997), pp. 36–47.
89. Linda Moraski, "When a Partnership Turns Toxic," *BusinessWeek*, December 17, 2003, www.businessweek.com:/print/smallbiz/content/dec2003/sb20031217_7845.htm?sb.
90. Robert D. Hisrich, *Small Business Solutions: How to Fix & Prevent the 13 Biggest Problems That Derail Business* (New York: McGraw-Hill, 2004), pp. 70–71; J. A. Cox, K. K. Moore, and P. M. Van Auken, "Working Couples in Small Business," *Journal of Small Business Management* 22, no. 4 (October 1984), pp. 24–30.
91. Look at Mark Hendricks, "Stage Right: Make Smarter Management Decisions by Knowing What Stage Your Company's In," *Entrepreneur*, April 1997, www.entrepreneur.com/article/14090. The most famous model comes from Larry Greiner, "Evolution and Revolution as Organizations Grow," *Harvard Business Review* 76, no. 3 (May 1998), pp. 55–68, a revisiting of Greiner's 1972 *HBR* article of the same name. Neil C. Churchill and Virginia L. Lewis adapted Greiner's model in "The Five Stages of Small Business Growth," *Harvard Business Review*, May–June 1983. A three-stage simplification follows the ideas expressed by Kelin E. Gersick, Ivan Lansberg, Michele Desjardins, and Barbara Dunn, "Stages and Transitions: Managing Change in the Family Business," *Family Business Review* 12, no. 4 (1999), pp. 287–297, www.lgassoc.com/library/articles/112-Stages&Transitions.pdf; and in their book, Kelin Gersick, John Davis, Marion McCollum Hampton, and Ivan Lansberg, *Generation to Generation: Life Cycles of the Family Business* (Cambridge, MA: Harvard University Press, 1997).
92. The model is derived from four major works on small business life stages: William J. Baumol, "Entrepreneurship in Economic Theory," *American Economic Review* 58, no. 2 (May 1968), pp. 64–71; Gaylen Chandler and Steven H. Hanks, "Market Attractiveness, Resource-Based Capabilities; Venture Strategies and Venture Performance," *Journal of Business Venturing* 9, no. 4 (1994), pp. 331–349; Neil C. Churchill and Virginia L. Lewis, "The Five Stages of Small Business Growth," *Harvard Business Review* 61 (June 1983), pp. 30–40; Jerome Katz and William B. Gartner "Properties of Emerging Organizations," *Academy of Management Review* 13, no. 3 (July 1988), pp. 429–441.
93. As noted in Chapter 1, the 56 percent rate among 15- to 25-year-olds comes from Joeri Van den Bergh, "Generation Y around the World: Global Youth Research by InSites Consulting," February 15, 2012, www.slideshare.net/joerivandenbergh/generation-y-around-the-worldby-insites-consulting. The 13.6 percent number comes from N. Bosma and D. J. Kelley,"GEM 2018/2019 Global Report," Global Entrepreneurship Monitor, January 21, 2019, www.gemconsortium.org/report/50213, Table 3's TEA number for the USA.
94. Rieva Lesonsky, "It's Never Too Late," *Entrepreneur*, November 2003, www.entrepreneur.com/article/65024; Jacquelyn Lynn, "Don't Be Afraid: Are You a Big Scaredy-Cat? Here's How to Turn Terror into Super-Confidence," *Entrepreneur*, June 2000, www.entrepreneur.com/article/28316; Rieva Lesonsky, "What's the Big Idea? Start-Up Ideas Are All Around . . . Once You Know Where to Look," *Business Start-Ups*, November 1998, www.entrepreneur.com/author/311-3; J. Katz, "Longitudinal Analysis of Entrepreneurial Follow-Through," *Journal of Entrepreneurship and Regional Development* 2, no. 1 (1990), pp. 15–25.
95. D. A. Shepherd and M. Shanley, *New Venture Strategy* (Newbury Park, CA: Sage, 1998); D. A. Shepherd, E. J. Douglas, and M. Shanley, "New Venture Survival: Ignorance, External Shocks, and Risk Reduction Strategies," *Journal of Business Venturing* 15 (2000), pp. 393–410; H. Robert Dodge, Sam Fullerton, and John E. Robbins, "Stage of the Organizational Life Cycle and Competition as Mediators of Problem Perception for Small Businesses," *Strategic Management Journal* 15, no. 2 (February 1994), pp. 121–135.
96. Mark Henricks, "Staying Power: Zero Defections Strategy Keeps Customers Coming Back," *Entrepreneur*, July 1997, www.entrepreneur.com/article/15786; Frederick F. Reichheld, *The Loyalty Effect, The Hidden Force behind Growth, Profits, and Lasting Value* (Cambridge, MA: Harvard Business School Press, 1996); Robert C. Blattberg, Gary Getz, and Jacquelyn S. Thomas, *Customer Equity: Building and Managing Relationships as Valuable Assets* (Boston: Harvard Business School Press, 2001); Roland T. Rust and R. L. Oliver, "Should We Delight the Customer?," *Journal of the Academy of Marketing Sciences* 28, no. 1 (2000), pp. 86–94; Sandy D. Jap, "Control Mechanisms and the Relationship Life Cycle: Implications for Safeguarding Specific Investments and Developing Commitment," *Journal of Marketing Research* 37, no. 2 (May 2000), p. 227; F. F. Reichheld and W. E. Sasser, "Zero Defections: Quality Comes to Services," *Harvard Business Review,* 1990, pp. 105–111; R. T. Rust, A. J. Zahorik, and T. L. Keiningham, "Return on Quality (ROQ): Making Service Quality Financially Accountable," *Journal of Marketing* 59 (1995), pp. 58–70; Valarie A. Zeithaml, "Service Quality, Profitability, and the Economic Worth of Customers: What We

Know and What We Need to Learn," *Academy of Marketing Science Journal* 28, no. 1 (2000), p. 67.

97. Zig Ziglar, *Zig Ziglar's Secrets of Closing the Sale* (New York: Berkeley Publishing Group, 1985). The ideas came from the long-out-of-print Australian series, "10 Sales Cassettes by Dr. Joseph Braysich." Other good sources for this approach include Kim T. Gordon, "Building Customer Relationships: Increase Your Sales through Better Relationships with Your Existing Customers," *Entrepreneur*, January 1, 2001, www.entrepreneur.com/article/35876; Nichole L. Torres, "Marketing Buzz 09/02: Sell Better by Understanding the Six Different Customer Types; How to Respond to Bad Press," *Entrepreneur*, September 2002, www.entrepreneur.com/article/54530.
98. M. Stefanik, "The Power of Micro Commitments," *The Lifestyle Architect*, June 7, 2016, https://thelifestylearchitect.com/power-micro-commitments/; R. Levesque, "Kaizen in Action: 8 Types of Micro-Commitments and How You Can Use Them in Your Sales Process to Increase Conversions," *American Writers & Artists Inc.*, July 8, 2018, www.awai.com/2018/07/8-micro-commitments-to-use-in-your-sales-process/; P. Williams, "Five Examples of Profitable Marketing with Micro-Commitments [Conversions]," *Preneur Marketing Blog*, July 14, 2014, http://preneurmarketing.com/essays/micro-commitments/.
99. D. Guithues-Amrhein and J. A. Katz, "Assessing the Mortality Risk of a Business," *Journal of Enterprising Culture* 7, no. 3 (1999) or www.sbaer.uca.edu/Research/1998/ICSB/n004.htm; Joan Stableford, "Business Notes: It's Here: The Great Pumpkin," *Time* 136, no. 21 (November 12, 1990), p. 64; Joan Stableford, "For Sun-Hill Industries, Success Last Year Was in the Bag," *Fairfield County Business Journal* 22, no 19 (May 27, 1991), p. 10. The pirate pursuit resulted in a legal battle, which was decided in Zinbarg's favor in 1999; see United States Court of Appeals for the Federal Circuit, 98-1498 (Serial No. 08/427,732), *in Re Anita Dembiczak and Benson Zinbarg*, www.law.emory.edu/fedcircuit/apr99/98-1498.wp.html.
100. mereChina, "Fun Chinese Lessons—9: Danger and Opportunity: The Chinese Expression for Crisis," www.merechina.com/language/chineselesson9.shtml.
101. Marc Fleury, "Doing It Wrong, Getting It Right," Entrepreneur's Byline, *BusinessWeek*, September 3, 2003, www.businessweek.com/smallbiz/content/sep2003/sb2003093_8638.htm.
102. Thomas J. Stanley, *The Millionaire Mind* (Kansas City, MO: Andrews McNeel, 2001); Thomas J. Stanley and William D. Danko, *The Millionaire Next Door* (New York: Pocket Books, 1996).
103. Devlin Smith, "Women of Substance—Experience: A Secret to Success," *Entrepreneur,* November 2003, www.entrepreneur.com/article/65012.
104. The "universally mentioned" rewards were those mentioned by 75 percent or more of potential or new small business owners—a much higher rate than working people in general mention. The "occasionally mentioned" rewards were those mentioned by less than 50 percent of potential or new small business owners, but were still mentioned more often than by working people. The "rarely mentioned" rewards were those in which entrepreneurs mention a reward significantly less often than working people do in general. The sample was 871 potential and new entrepreneurs, compared to a control group of 431 individuals. For details on the measures see Nancy M. Carter, William B. Gartner, and Kelly G. Shaver, "Career Reasons," in William B. Gartner, Kelly G. Shaver, Nancy M. Carter, and Paul D. Reynolds (eds.), *Handbook of Entrepreneurial Dynamics: The Process of Business Creation* (Thousand Oaks, CA: Sage, 2004), pp. 142–152. The PSED analyses reported here were custom analyses performed by Dr. Jennifer Shaver.
105. "America's First Businessman: George Washington's Business Acumen," The Businessweek Video Library, http://feedroom.businessweek.com/; Associated Press, "A Taste of George Washington's Whiskey," msnbc.com, April 9, 2007, www.msnbc.msn.com/id/18025413/; Lisa Brown, "Washington's Whiskey Hits the Barrel after 200 Year Hiatus," *USA Today*, April 15, 2009, www.usatodav.com/travel/destinations/2009-04-15-mount-vernon-whiskey_N.htm; John Fund, "Moonshine Patriot: George Washington, Whiskey Entrepreneur," *The Wall Street Journal*, February 21, 2007, www.opinionjournal.com/la/?id=110009692; George Washington's Distillers, "Making George Washington's Whiskey," n.d., http://makinggeorgewashingtonswhiskey.blogspot.com/; Thane Peterson, "Washington Sipped Here," *BusinessWeek*, June 17, 2003, www.businessweek.com/bwdaily/dnflash/un2003/nf20030617_2197_db028.htm; Marta Roberts, "George Washington Slept It Off Here," *BusinessWeek*, May 21, 2001, www.businessweek.com/bwdaily/dnflash/may2001/nf20010522_060.htm.

Chapter 3

1. Summer was an undergraduate student at Saint Louis University's Chaifetz School of Business. She started blogging in 2012. The story told here about the collaboration with Mimu Maxi and the aftermath comes from interviews with Summer and from the media posts about it, including Lumsden, L. "A Jewish Fashion Line Was Attacked for Their Photo of a Muslim." Mail Online, July 18, 2014. https://www.dailymail.co.uk/femail/article-2697479/Orthodox-Jewish-design-duo-branded-appalling-shameful-posting-photo-Muslim-fashion-blogger-wearing-modest-chic-designs.html and Basu, T. "How the Internet Made Modest Fashion Cool." The Atlantic, February 27, 2015. https://www.theatlantic.com/entertainment/archive/2015/02/making-modest-fashion-cool/385789/, and Ghert-Z, R. "A Muslim Models a Jewish Brand." The Times of Israel, July 14, 2014. http://www.timesofisrael.com/no-skirting-the-issue/. Summer continues to get press such as: Sarkar, M. "It's Time We Stop Ignoring Modest Fashion Influencers." Forbes, n.d. https://www.forbes.com/sites/meghnasarkar/2019/04/04/its-time-we-stop-ignoring-modest-fashion-influencers/ and Laneri, R. "Conservative Women Pushing Back on Skimpy Bikini Culture." New York Post, June 5, 2019. https://nypost.com/2019/06/05/conservative-women-pushing-back-on-skimpy-bikini-culture/.
2. Anna Merlan, "An Orthodox Brooklyn Clothing Line Shared a Photo of a Woman in a Hijab, and Their Customers Flipped Out," *The Village Voice,* July 15, 2014, www.villagevoice.com/2014/07/15/an-orthodox-brooklyn-clothing-line-shared-a-photo-of-a-woman-in-a-hijab-and-their-customers-flipped-out/.
3. The formal name for this overlap of entrepreneur and firm is called partial inclusion and was original to Daniel Katz and Robert L. Kahn, *The Social Psychology of Organizations,* 2nd ed. (New York: Wiley, 1978). A better-known approach for many comes from Karl E. Weick, *The Social Psychology of Organizing,* 2nd ed. (Reading, MA: Addison-Wesley, 1979).
4. Definition is a paraphrase from Steve Robbins, *Essentials of Organizational Behavior,* 7th ed. (Upper Saddle River, NJ: Prentice-Hall, 2003), p. 231; Edgar Schein, "The Role of the Founder in Creating Organizational Culture," *Organizational Dynamics,* Summer 1983, p. 14.
5. "Horizon-Chamber Collaboration Brings Wellness to Workplace," *The Business Monthly,* December 2007, http://209.116.252.254/12_2007/9.shtm; "Workplace Wellness Award," *The Horizon Foundation 2007,* www.thehorizonfoundation.org/ht/d/sp/i/1152/pid/1152; "Jolles Insurance," www.jollesinsurance.com/index.php; www.wepromotehealth.com/.
6. These ideas come from B. Feld and D. Kaplan, *Startup Communities: Building an Entrepreneurial Ecosystem in Your City,* Unabridged edition (Brilliance Audio, 2013); J. Bell-Masterson and D. Stangler, *Measuring an Entrepreneurial Ecosystem,* SSRN Scholarly Paper (Rochester, NY: Social Science Research Network, March 1, 2015), http://papers.ssrn.com/abstract=2580336.

7. The profile is created from a series of interviews by *ESB* co-author Jerome Katz with Jim Allsup. The final version was approved by Allsup on May 30, 2009. It was updated with the number of people helped in February 2019 using material from www.truehelp.com/our-story/.
8. Kendra S. Albright, "Environmental Scanning: Radar for Success," Entrepreneur.com, July 5, 2004, https://www.researchgate.net/publication/239970846_Environmental_Scanning_Radar_for_Success; Donald L. Lester and John A. Parnell, "Firm Size and Environmental Scanning Pursuits across Organizational Life Cycle Stages," *Journal of Small Business and Enterprise Development* 15, no. 3 (2008), pp. 540–554.
9. R. G. McGrath, "Falling Forward: Real Options Reasoning and Entrepreneurial Failure," *Academy of Management Review* 24, no. 1 (January 1, 1999), pp. 13–30; R. G. McGrath, "Options and the Enterprise: Toward a Strategic Theory of Entrepreneurial Wealth Creation," *Academy of Management Proceedings* 1996, no. 1 (August 1, 1996), pp. 101–105; A. M. Pettigrew, H. Thomas, and R. Whittington, *Handbook of Strategy and Management* (Thousand Oaks, CA: Sage, 2002).
10. M. H. Morris, D. F. Kuratko, and M. Schindehutte, "Towards Integration: Understanding Entrepreneurship through Frameworks," *The International Journal of Entrepreneurship and Innovation* 2, no. 1 (February 1, 2001), pp. 35–49.
11. Patricia Carr, "Revisiting the Protestant Ethic and the Spirit of Capitalism: Understanding the Relationship between Ethics and Enterprise," *Journal of Business Ethics* 47, no. 1 (September 2003), pp. 7–16; Jeffrey R. Cornwall and Michael J. Naughton, "Who Is the Good Entrepreneur? An Exploration within the Catholic Social Tradition," *Journal of Business Ethics* 44, no. 1 (April 2003), pp. 61–75.
12. This is the concept of cognitive legitimacy as discussed in John Freeman, Glenn R. Carroll, and Michael T. Hannan, "The Liability of Newness: Age Dependence in Organizational Death Rates," *American Sociological Review* 48, no. 5 (October 1983), pp. 692–710; Michael T. Hannan and John Freeman, "Structural Inertia and Organizational Change," *American Sociological Review* 49, no. 2 (April 1984), pp. 149–164: Howard E. Aldrich and C. Marlene Fiol, "Fools Rush In? The Institutional Context of Industry Creation," *Academy of Management Review* 19, no. 4 (October 1994), pp. 645–670.
13. Dean Shepherd and Andrew Zacharakis, "A New-Venture's Cognitive Legitimacy: An Assessment by Customers," *Journal of Small Business Management* 41, no. 2 (April 2003), pp. 148–167.
14. By the way, the fact that outsiders see entrepreneurs as a key source of legitimacy, while the entrepreneurs look outside themselves to their product as the legitimacy source, is a wonderful example of the classic psychological idea of causal attribution. People tend to see causes as being outside themselves, while outsiders are more likely to attribute cause to a person. For more on this in general, see Richard Nisbet and Lee Ross, *Human Inference: Strategies and Shortcomings of Social Judgement* (Englewood Cliffs, NJ: Prentice Hall, 1980). For an example in entrepreneurship, see Kelly G. Shaver, William B. Gartner, Elizabeth Crosby, Karolina Bakalarova, and Elizabeth J. Gatewood, "Attributions about Entrepreneurship: A Framework and Process for Analyzing Reasons for Starting a Business," *Entrepreneurship: Theory and Practice* 26, no. 2 (Winter 2001), pp. 5–32.
15. F. R. David, "An Empirical Study of Codes of Business Ethics: A Strategic Perspective," paper presented at the 48th Annual Academy of Management Conference, Anaheim, California, August 1988.
16. Kim T. Gordon, "Cross-Training: Join the Multichannel Marketing Revolution, and Get Ready to Pump Up Your Sales," *Entrepreneur,* July 2003, www.entrepreneur.com/article/62766.
17. Anat BarNir and Ken A. Smith, "Interfirm Alliances in the Small Business: The Role of Social Networks," *Journal of Small Business Management* 40, no. 3 (July 2002), pp. 219–232; T. A. Ostgaard and S. Birley, "Personal Networks and Firm Competitive Strategy—A Strategic or Coincidental Match?," *Journal of Business Venturing* 9, no. 4 (July 1994), pp. 281–305; Herminia Ibarra, "Personal Networks of Women and Minorities in Management: A Conceptual Framework," *Academy of Management Review* 18, no. 1 (January 1993), pp. 56–87; Sue Birley, "The Role of Networks in the Entrepreneurial Process," *Journal of Business Venturing* 1, no. 1 (Winter 1985), pp. 107–117.
18. Heidi M. Neck, G. Dale Meyer, Boyd Cohen, and Andrew C. Corbett, "An Entrepreneurial System View of New Venture Creation," *Journal of Small Business Management* 42, no. 2 (April 2004), pp. 190–209; Danny Mackinnon, Keith Chapman, and Andrew Cumbers, "Networking, Trust and Embeddedness amongst SMEs in the Aberdeen Oil Complex," *Entrepreneurship and Regional Development* 16, no. 2 (March 2004), pp. 87–106; Robert A. Baron and Gideon D. Markman, "Beyond Social Capital: The Role of Entrepreneurs' Social Competence in Their Financial Success," *Journal of Business Venturing* 18, no. 1 (January 2003), pp. 41–60; Sarah D. Dodd, "Social Network Membership and Activity Rates: Some Comparative Data," *International Small Business Journal* 15, no. 4 (July–September 1997), pp. 80–87; Eric L. Hansen, "Entrepreneurial Networks and New Organization Growth," *Entrepreneurship Theory and Practice* 19, no. 4 (Summer 1995), pp. 7–20; Tone A. Ostgaard and Sue Birley, "Personal Networks and Firm Competitive Strategy—A Strategic or Coincidental Match?," *Journal of Business Venturing* 9, no. 4 (July 1994), pp. 281–306; Howard E. Aldrich and Carlos Zimmer, "Entrepreneurship through Social Networks," in Donald L. Sexton and Ray W. Smilor (eds.), *The Art and Science of Entrepreneurship* (Cambridge, MA: Ballinger, 1986), pp. 3–24; Sue Birley, "The Role of Networks in the Entrepreneurial Process," *Journal of Business Venturing* 1, no. 1 (Winter 1985), pp. 107–117.
19. David A. Whetten and Alison Mackey, "A Social Actor Conception of Organizational Identity and Its Implications for the Study of Organizational Reputation," *Business & Society* 41, no. 4 (December 2002), pp. 393–414. Concept taken from p. 394.
20. L. Denworth, "How Do You Make or Maintain Friends? Put in the Time," *Psychology Today*, March 30, 2018, www.psychologytoday.com/blog/brain-waves/201803/how-do-you-make-or-maintain-friends-put-in-the-time; J. A. Hall, "How Many Hours Does It Take to Make a Friend?," *Journal of Social and Personal Relationships* 26 (March 15, 2018), pp. 347-369.
21. Howard E. Aldrich and Nancy M. Carter, "Social Networks," in William B. Gartner, Kelly G. Shaver, Nancy M. Carter, and Paul D. Reynolds (eds.), *Handbook of Entrepreneurial Dynamics: The Process of Business Creation* (Thousand Oaks, CA: Sage, 2004).
22. V. K. Bohns, "A Face-to-Face Request Is 34 Times More Successful Than an Email," *Harvard Business Review*, April 11, 2017, https://hbr.org/2017/04/a-face-to-face-request-is-34-times-more-successful-than-an-email; J. Rampton, "Email Is Great but Face-to-Face Meetings Are 34 Times More Successful," *Entrepreneur*, July 14, 2017, www.entrepreneur.com/article/296590.
23. S. Rainer, "How Best to Communicate: Phone Call, Email, Text, Social Media," *Sam Rainer*, February 29, 2016, https://samrainer.com/2016/02/how-best-to-communicate-phone-call-email-text-social-media/; J. DeMers, "Communication in 2015: Text, Voice, Video or In-Person?," *Inc.*, January 29, 2015, www.inc.com/jayson-demers/communication-in-2015-text-voice-video-or-in-person.html.
24. Paula Caproni, *The Practical Coach: Management Skills for Everyday Life* (Upper Saddle River, NJ: Prentice Hall, 2000). Other articles that use similar approaches and show positive effects include Jeff Gold, Dave Devins, and Alistair Johnson, "What Is the Value of Mentoring in a Small Business? Using Narrative Evaluation to Find Out," *British Journal of Guidance & Counselling* 31, no. 1 (February 2003), pp. 51–62; Tony Kent, Charles Dennis, and Sue Tanton, "An Evaluation of Mentoring for SME Retailers," *International Journal of Retail & Distribution Management* 31, nos. 8–9 (2003), pp. 440–465;

R. Sullivan, "Entrepreneurial Learning and Mentoring," *International Journal of Entrepreneurial Behaviour & Research* 6, no. 3 (2000), pp. 160–175.

25. Ivan Misner, "Start by Learning How to Tailor Your Networking Approach for Different Occasions," *Entrepreneur–Sales & Marketing*, March 22, 2004, www.entrepreneur.com/article/0,4621,314878,00.html; Kim T. Gordon, "Attracting Customers: Use Your Business's Assets to Bring in More Clients, *Entrepreneur*, August 7, 2000, www.entrepreneur.com/article/31152; Dorothy P. Moore, *Careerpreneurs–Lessons from Leading Women Entrepreneurs on Building a Career without Boundaries* (Palo Alto, CA: Davies-Black, 2001); Cynthia E. Griffin, "Gender Blender: Boys Don't Have Cooties, So Don't Be Afraid to Mingle at Mixed-Gender Functions," *Entrepreneur*, October 2001, www.entrepreneur.com/article/44294; Erin Chambers, "A Warm Reception for Female Execs," *BusinessWeek* online, December 9, 2004, www.businessweek.com/smallbiz/content/dec2004/sb2004129-3272-sb013.htm; Sherry Alpert, "Making a Network Connection," *BusinessWeek* online, September 18, 2003, www.businessweek.com/smallbiz/content/sep2003/sb20030918_4557.htm.
26. C. Reisenwitz, "The 8 Best Free and Open Source CRM Software Solutions," *Capterra Blog*, May 9, 2018, https://blog.capterra.com/free-and-open-source-crm/. Or, Google "free crm" to find the latest reviews.
27. *BusinessWeek*, "A Guide to Social Networking: Tip Sheet (CEO Guide to Technology: Tip Sheet)," n.d., www.businessweek.com/technology/ceo_tipsheet/2006_5.htm; Pat Thomas and Susan Moisey, "Women Entrepreneurs: Informal Learning and the Internet," *Journal of Small Business & Entrepreneurship* 19, no. 2 (2006) pp. 183–201; Lena L. West, "Becoming More Social," Entrepreneur.com, April 9, 2007, www.entrepreneur.com/article/176798.
28. Ian I. Mitroff and Murat C. Alpaslan, "Preparing for Evil," *Harvard Business Review* 81, no. 4 (April 2003), p. 109; Ian I. Mitroff, *Crisis Leadership: Preparing for the Unthinkable* (New York: Wiley, 2003); D. Creelman, "Interview: Ian Mitroff on Crisis Leadership," 2004, HR.com, http://hradmin1.hr.com/HRcom/index.cfm/WeeklyMag/9A954EE7-B500-4AC4-A13DF077B83214E2?ost=wmFeature.
29. Norman R. Augustine, "Managing the Crisis You Tried to Prevent," *Harvard Business Review* 73, no. 6 (November–December 1995), pp. 147–158.
30. Dan Millar, "ICM Crisis Report: News Coverage of Business Crises during 2002," May 2003, the Institute for Crisis Management, www.crisisexperts.com/02creport.htm; Theresa Forsman, "Contemplating the Unthinkable: An Entrepreneur Who Lacks a Plan for Coping with Catastrophe Is a Victim in the Making, Says Crisis-Management Expert Debra Traverso," *BusinessWeek*, October 2, 2001, www.businessweek.com/smallbiz/content/oct2001/sb20011003_514.htm;Michael Seid and Kay Marie Ainsley, "Managing Your Reputation: Follow These Tips to Save Your Brand during a Crisis," *Entrepreneur*, October 22, 2001, www.entrepreneur.com/article/45572; Christopher D. Lancette, "Critical Thinking: A Crisis Has Hit. Now What?," *Entrepreneur*, June 1999, www.entrepreneur.com/article/17788.
31. Daniel Tynan, "In Case of Emergency: A Smoke Alarm or a Life Preserver May Save Your Life, but They Won't Save Your Business. You Need a Real Disaster Plan Now. Your Business's Survival Depends on It," *Entrepreneur*, April 2003, www.Entrepreneur.com/article/0,4621,307161,00.html; Institute for Crisis Management, "Crisis Management and Crisis Communications" (Louisville, KY: The Institute for Crisis Management, 2000), www.crisisexperts.com/management.htm; Michael Seid and Kay Marie Ainsley, "Managing Your Reputation: Follow These Tips to Save Your Brand during a Crisis," *Entrepreneur*, October 22, 2001, www.entrepreneur.com/article/4557; Christopher D. Lancette, "Critical Thinking: A Crisis Has Hit. Now What?," *Entrepreneur* June 1999, www.entrepreneur.com/article/17788.
32. M. Lynch, "Preparing a Dark Website for Crisis Management | LinkedIn," *LinkedIn*, November 25, 2015, www.linkedin.com/pulse/preparing-dark-website-crisis-management-matt-lynch/; T. Lloyd, "Dark Sites in Crisis Communication: Six Reasons to Consider," *Social Simulator*, March 9, 2015, https://socialsimulator.com/dark-sites-fad-fundamental/.
33. Scott J. Vitell, Erin B. Dickerson, and Troy A. Festervand, "Ethical Problems, Conflicts and Beliefs of Small Business Professionals," *Journal of Business Ethics* 28, no. 1 (November 2000), pp. 15–24; Ruth Clark and John Aram, "Universal Values, Behavioral Ethics and Entrepreneurship," *Journal of Business Ethics* 16, no. 5 (April 1997), pp. 561–572.
34. LaRue T. Hosmer, *The Ethics of Management*, 6th ed. (Boston: McGraw-Hill/Irwin, 2008).
35. Nichole L. Torres, "Ethically Speaking," *Entrepreneur*, December 2005, www.entrepreneur.com/magazine/entrepreneur/2005/december/81076.html.
36. Lawrence M. Salinger and Gilbert Geis, "Caveat Emptor," *Encyclopedia of White-Collar & Corporate Crime* (Thousand Oaks, CA: Sage, 2004), pp. 145–146, http://books.google.com/books?id=0f7yTNb_V3QC&pg=PA146&lpg=PA146&dq=%22caveat+emptor%22,+corporate&source=bl&ots=OeLuQT8JSV&sig=a6Wp4JC30KZrd77RDJQHdnopL6o&hl=en&ei=7JlcSqDHDoryMr_NsZIP&sa=X&oi=book_result&ct=result&resnum=6#PPA146,M1.
37. The negotiation approaches used here are adapted from Roger Fisher, William Ury, and Bruce Patton, *Getting to Yes: Negotiating Agreement without Giving In*, 2nd ed. (New York: Houghton Mifflin Harcourt, 1991).
38. Dave's story comes from B. Snyder, "United Feels the Pain When Complaints Go Viral," *CBS News*, July 8, 2009, www.cbsnews.com/news/united-feels-the-pain-when-complaints-go-viral/; R. Wilson, "A Public Relations Disaster—How Saving $1,200 Cost United Airlines 10,772,839 Negative Views on YouTube," *Marketing Rocket Fuel*, 2011, http://sentium.com/a-public-relations-disaster-how-saving-1200-cost-united-airlines-10772839-negative-views-on-youtube/; Wikipedia, "Sons of Maxwell," July 2, 2018, https://en.wikipedia.org/w/index.php?title=Sons_of_Maxwell&oldid=848594594; Wikipedia. "United Breaks Guitars," July 24, 2019, https://en.wikipedia.org/w/index.php?title=United_Breaks_Guitars&oldid=907633658. The American Express information comes from American Express, "#WellActually, Americans Say Customer Service Is Better Than Ever," December 15, 2017, https://about.americanexpress.com/press-release/wellactually-americans-say-customer-service-better-ever. And a great list of consumer complaint sites can be found at Alex's (No Last Name), "Best Complaint Websites 2018," *Medium*, March 8, 2018.
39. M. H. Morris, M. Schindehutte, J. Walton, and J. Allen, "The Ethical Context of Entrepreneurship: Proposing and Testing a Developmental Framework," *Journal of Business Ethics* 40, no. 4 (November 2002), pp. 331–361; Hai Y. Teoh and Siang L. Foo, "Moderating Effects of Tolerance of Ambiguity and Risk Taking Propensity on the Role Conflict-Perceived Performance Relationship: Evidence from Singaporean Entrepreneurs," *Journal of Business Venturing* 12, no. 1 (January 1997), pp. 67–81.
40. C. Lagorio-Chafkin, "Resistance Is Futile: Uber Loves a Good Fight," *Inc.*, July 1, 2013, www.inc.com/magazine/201307/christine-lagorio/uber-the-car-service-explosive-growth.html; J. D. Sapienza, "Uber under Siege: These Cities Are Its Biggest Enemies," *The Cheat Sheet*, March 29, 2018, www.cheatsheet.com/money-career/uber-under-siege-cities-biggest-enemies.html/; O. Solon, "How Uber Conquers a City in Seven Steps," *The Guardian*, April 12, 2017, www.theguardian.com/technology/2017/apr/12/why-everyone-hates-uber-seven-step-playbook; "How Uber Enters New Markets," *61-Bit*, November 28, 2017, www.61-bit.com/how-uber-enters-new-markets/; "The Aggressive Processes Uber Uses for Global Expansion," *Process Street*, April 21, 2017, www.process.st/global-expansion/.

41. Melissa S. Baucus and Caryn L. Beck-Dudley. "Designing Ethical Organizations: Avoiding the Long-Term Negative Effects of Rewards and Punishments." *Journal of Business Ethics* 56 (2005), pp. 355–370; Small Biz—Features, Online Extra: "How to Play with the Big Guys," BusinessWeek.com, September 10, 2001, www.businessweek.com/magazine/content/01_37/b3748628.htm; Brenda Joyner, E. Dinah Payne, and Cecily A. Raiborn, "Building Values, Business Ethics and Corporate Social Responsibility into the Developing Organization," *Journal of Developmental Enterpreneurship* 7, no. 1 (April 2002), pp. 113–131; Robert J. McGarvey, "Lords of Discipline: 'Gimme 10!' Is Not the Way to Change Your Employees' Behavior," *Entrepreneur,* January 2000, www.entrepreneur.com/magazine/entrepreneur/2000/January/18856.html.
42. This case is built from several newspaper and magazine accounts about the introduction of P2P services into localities, especially when these services are initially illegal. See O. Solon, "How Uber Conquers a City in Seven Steps." *The Guardian*, April 12, 2017, www.theguardian.com/technology/2017/apr/12/why-everyone-hates-uber-seven-step-playbook; "How Uber Enters New Markets," *61-Bit*, November 28, 2017, www.61-bit.com/how-uber-enters-new-markets/; P. D. Guttentag, "What Airbnb Really Does to a Neighbourhood," August 30, 2018, www.bbc.com/news/business-45083954.

Chapter 4

1. This case is based on interviews with Mary Elizabeth Coleman by Jerome Katz, as well as her websites, https://house.mo.gov/MemberDetails.aspx?year=2019&code=R&district=097 and www.maryelizabethcoleman.com/.
2. Mary Elizabeth was a student of Jerome Katz (the lead author of this textbook) at Saint Louis University (SLU). She stayed in contact and helped over the years in SLU's angel network as well as lecturing on the law to entrepreneurship classes at SLU.
3. D. J. Hansen, R. Shrader, and J. Monllor, "Defragmenting Definitions of Entrepreneurial Opportunity," *Journal of Small Business Management* 49, no. 2 (April 1, 2011), pp. 283–304.
4. C. M. Gaglio, "Opportunity Identification: Review, Critique and Suggested Research Directions," in J. A. Katz (ed.), *Advances in Entrepreneurship, Firm Emergence and Growth*, vol. 3 (Greenwich, CT: JAI Press, 1997), pp. 139–202; S. Venkataraman, "The Distinctive Domain of Entrepreneurship Research," in J. A. Katz (ed.), *Advances in Entrepreneurship, Firm Emergence and Growth*, vol. 3 (Greenwich, CT: JAI Press, 1997), pp. 119–138; I. Kirzner, *Perception, Opportunity, and Profit* (Chicago: University of Chicago Press, 1979); H. H. Stevenson and J. C. Jarillo, "A Paradigm of Entrepreneurship: Entrepreneurial Management," *Strategic Management Journal* 11 (Summer 1990), pp. 17–27.
5. I. Kirzner, *Competition and Entrepreneurship* (Chicago: University of Chicago Press, 1973); I. Kirzner, *Perception, Opportunity, and Profit* (Chicago: University of Chicago Press, 1979); I. Kirzner, *Discovery and the Capitalist Process* (Chicago: University of Chicago Press, 1985).
6. C. M. Gaglio and J. A. Katz, "The Psychological Basis of Opportunity Identification: Entrepreneurial Alertness," *Small Business Economics* 16, no. 2, 2001, pp. 95–111.
7. Connie M. Gaglio and Jerome A. Katz, "The Psychological Basis of Opportunity Identification: Entrepreneurial Alertness," *Small Business Economics* 16 no. 2 (2001), pp. 95–111.
8. G. A. Stevens and J. Burley, "3,000 Raw Ideas Equals 1 Commercial Success!," *Research Technology Management* 40, no. 3 (June 1997), pp. 16–27.
9. S. D. Sarasvathy, "Effectual Reasoning in Entrepreneurial Decision Making: Existence and Bounds," *Academy of Management Proceedings* 2001, no. 1 (August 1, 2001), pp. D1–D6; S. D. Sarasvathy, "Causation and Effectuation: Toward a Theoretical Shift from Economic Inevitability to Entrepreneurial Contingency," *Academy of Management Review* 26, no. 2 (April 1, 2001), pp. 243–263.
10. G. E. Hills and R. P. Singh, "Opportunity Recognition," in W. B. Gartner, K. G. Shaver, N. M. Carter, and P. D. Reynolds (eds.), *Handbook of Entrepreneurial Dynamics: The Process of Business Creation* (Thousand Oaks, CA: Sage, 2004), Table 24.1, p. 266.
11. R. Siegel, R. "'Flesh and Blood Robots for Amazon': They Raid Clearance Aisles and Resell It All Online for a Profit," *The Washington Post,* February 8, 2019, www.washingtonpost.com/business/economy/flesh-and-blood-robots-for-amazon-they-raid-clearance-aisles-and-resell-it-all-online-for-a-profit/2019/02/08/f71bff72-2a60-11e9-984d-9b8fba003e81_story.html?wpisrc=nl_most&wpmm=1; "Retail Arbitrage 101—The Ultimate Guide for Buying Retail and Reselling on Amazon," *The Selling Family*, July 19, 2018. https://thesellingfamily.com/retail-arbitrage-101-the-ultimate-guide-for-buying-retail-and-reselling-on-amazon/.
12. "Ideation 4: Brainstorming Solutions," *Technovation*, n.d., https://technovationchallenge.org/curriculum/ideation-4/.
13. M. Michalko, *Thinkertoys: A Handbook of Business Creativity* (Berkeley, CA: Ten Speed Press, 1991).
14. G. Wallas, *The Art of Thought* (New York: Franklin Watts, 1926).
15. S. G. Isaksen, K. B. Dorval, and D. J. Treffinger, *Creative Approaches to Problem Solving* (New York: Kendall-Hunt, 2000).
16. C. W. Prather and L. K. Gundry, *Blueprints for Innovation* (New York: American Management Association, 1995).
17. IDEO, ed. *The Field Guide to Human-Centered Design: Design Kit* (San Francisco: IDEO, 2015); K. Guppta, "A Quick Guide to Asking Good Customer Questions," *Strategyzer*, November 30, 2015, https://blog.strategyzer.com/posts/2015/11/26/a-quick-guide-for-asking-good-customer-questions; I. Jeffries, "BMC Part One: How to Use the Business Model Canvas," *Isaac Jeffries*, n.d., https://isaacjeffries.com/blog/2017/3/3/bmc-part-one-how-to-use-the-business-model-canvas; C. Constable, *Talking to Humans (*New York: NYU Entrepreneurial Institute, 2014), www.talkingtohumans.com/; J. Wilcox, "How to Do Customer Interviews," *Customer Development Labs*, November 5, 2013, https://customerdevlabs.com/2013/11/05/how-i-interview-customers/.
18. This idea comes from the impact graph developed by Alex Bruton as part of his "Idea Model" screening process: A. Bruton, "The Idea Model," The Straight Up Business Institute, n.d., www.straightupbusiness.institute/tools/idea-model/.
19. The original business model canvas came from A. Osterwalder and Y. Pigneur, *Business Model Generation: A Handbook for Visionaries, Game Changers, and Challengers* (Hoboken, NJ: Wiley, 2010). The variant displayed here adds the solution and problem at the top of the canvas. We do this so it is clear to students what problem they are solving and how they are solving it (both may change as they fine-tune their research). This approach reflects the wisdom of Ash Muraya's lean canvas: A. Muraya, *Running Lean: Iterate from Plan A to a Plan That Works,* 2nd ed. (Sebastopol, CA: O'Reilly Media, 2012). The mapping of the IDEO model to the canvas comes from Isaac Jeffries: I. Jeffries, "BMC Part One: How to Use the Business Model Canvas," n.d., https://isaacjeffries.com/blog/2017/3/3/bmc-part-one-how-to-use-the-business-model-canvas.
20. While this ordering is a typical or likely one, it isn't cast in stone. You might start out in any of the boxes. The person who discovered the *source Perrier* probably started with the key resource and then built out the other elements.
21. The elements before the Solution/Problem row come from A. Osterwalder and Y. Pigneur, *Business Model Generation: A Handbook for Visionaries, Game Changers, and Challengers* (Hoboken NJ: Wiley, 2010). The addition of the problem and solution are similar to elements from A. Maurya, *Running Lean: Iterate from Plan A to a Plan That Works* (Sebastopol, CA: O'Reilly, 2012). The blue boxes come

from I. Jeffries, "BMC Part One: How to Use the Business Model Canvas," n.d., https://isaacjeffries.com/blog/2017/3/3/bmc-part-one-how-to-use-the-business-model-canvas.

22. The SBA's website in 2018 started showing a "Lean Startup Format" business plan as an option. Their choice of a name is confusing, because there is a Lean Canvas created by Ash Muraya, but it has different boxes than the SBA canvas. The SBA canvas is the same as the Osterwalder and Pigneur canvas shown above. But while they offer a template for the traditional business plan like the one we cover in Chapter 8, they don't offer the same for the canvas. We list several sources for online canvases and templates in the associated Learn More Online box.
23. A detailed source for the steps in doing this online test (including names of website providers, templates for websites, and great advice and step-by-step procedures) is Professor Craig Armstrong's "10 (Or So) Steps from New Venture Opportunity to Crowdfunding Campaign," available at docs.google.com/document/d/1RdIs9ZRR20o05-GkXJfj4_zRmFV67iE7QIdw8WBLVpg/edit#heading=h.ef6u3w47928g or by searching the Internet with the note's title.
24. This outline is adapted from Ewing Marion Kauffman Foundation, *The Business Mentor CD-ROM* (Kansas City, MO: Ewing Marion Kauffman Foundation, 2001) and its predecessors, R. H. Buskirk, C. H. Price, and R. M. Davis, "Entrepreneurial Education Foundation, and Premier Fast-Trac," *The Entrepreneur's Planning Handbook* (Denver, CO: Entrepreneurial Education Foundation, 1997); Entrepreneurial Education Foundation, ed. *The Entrepreneur's FastTrac I Handbook,* Rev. ed. (Denver, CO: Entrepreneurial Education Foundation, 1998). It also builds on related materials from Missouri Small Business & Technology Development Centers, "Evaluating Your Business Idea," Curators of the University of Missouri and the Missouri Small Business & Technology Development Centers, March 19, 2016, http://missouribusiness.net/wp-content/uploads/evaluating-business.pdf; D. Kehrer, "A 6-Step Checklist for New Business Ideas: SCORE," SCORE, December 8, 2015, www.score.org/resources/6-step-checklist-new-business-ideas.
25. A. Daniels, "Generating Great Ideas from Employees," *Entrepreneur,* September 18, 2000.
26. L. K. Gundry and M. LaMantia, *Breakthrough Teams for Breakneck Times: Unlocking the Genius of Creative Collaboration* (New York: Dearborn Books, 2001).
27. Ibid.
28. Tim Hayden's story came from a 2003 classroom presentation in an Advanced Business Planning class Tim took with ESB co-author Jerome Katz at Saint Louis University.
29. American Pet Products Association, "Pet Industry Market Size & Ownership Statistics," https://www.americanpetproducts.org/press_industrytrends.asp
30. Joseph Tarnowski, "Pet Project: Giant Eagle Mixes Creative Merchandising, Special Events, and Just Plain Love to Create a Pet Program that Caters to Owners as Much as Animals," *Progressive Grocer* 83, no. 13 (September 15, 2004), p. 68.
31. U.S. Census Bureau, American Fact Finder for Zip Code 60657, Profile of General Demographic Characteristics: 2000, Census 2000 Summary File 1 (SF 1) 100-Percent Data, https://factfinder.census.gov/bkmk/table/1.0/en/DEC/00_SF1/DP1/8600000US60657.
32. egov.cityofchicago.org/webportal/COCWebPortal/COC_EDITORIAL/RetailChicago_2004_North_2.pdf.
33. American Pet Products Association, "Fact Sheet: Industry Statistics & Trends," site05.fuzweb2.fuzint.com/press_industrytrends.asp.
34. April Y. Pennington, "Hot Stuff: Want to Know What's Hot for 2004? We've Got the Businesses, Markets and Trends You Shouldn't Miss Out On," *Entrepreneur,* December 2003, www.entrepreneur.com/article/0,4621,311833,00.html; Steve Cooper, "Fever Pitch," *Entrepreneur,* December 2004, www.entrepreneur.com/article/0,4621,318038,00.html.
35. Alicia Suman, "Pet Owners," *Target Marketing* 26, no. 8 (August 2003), pp. 61–62.
36. "Americans Are Spending More on Pets Than Ever Before: $72 Billion," *Cision PR Newswire,* 5/21/2019, https://www.prnewswire.com/news-releases/americans-are-spending-more-on-pets-than-ever-before-72-billion-300816835.html.
37. "Organic Pet Food Gets Paws Up: Niche Grows Fast, Despite High Prices," *USA Today,* July 14, 2004, www.usatoday.com/money/industries/food/2004-07-13-organicx.htm.
38. R. Gardyn, "Animal Magnetism," *Ad Age,* May 1, 2002, https://adage.com/article/american-demographics/animal-magnetism/43901.
39. www.newmansownorganics.com/pet/home/index.php.
40. www.naturapet.com.
41. www.castorpolluxpet.com.
42. www.omhpet.com.
43. www.threedog.com.
44. www.flintriver.com.
45. www.howlinghound.com.
46. www.happydogtoys.com.
47. www.kongcompany.com.
48. www.fatcats.com.
49. www.woofonline.com. The company has gone out of business since the feasibility study was written.
50. www.dogztogz.com.
51. www.ruffruffandmeow.com.
52. American Pet Products Association, "Pet Industry Market Size & Ownership Statistics," https://www.americanpetproducts.org/press_industrytrends.asp
53. www.petco.com.
54. www.petsmart.com.
55. www.samandwillys.com.
56. www.sba.gov/starting/regulations.html.
57. www.illinoisbiz.biz/bus/step_by_step.html.

Chapter 5

1. T. B. Folta, F. Delmar, and K. Wennberg, "Hybrid Entrepreneurship," *Management Science* 56 (2010), pp. 253–269.
2. PSED, question 331a asks people starting a business if they work for someone else more or less than 35 hours a week; 74.4 percent reported working for others full time (more than 35 hours a week).
3. Joseph J. Fucini and Suzy Fucini, *Entrepreneurs: The Men and Women behind Famous Brand Names and How They Made It* (Boston: G. K. Hall, 1985); Brendan Howard, "Making Time: Not Ready for the Burden of a Full-Time Business? How Do Your Evenings and Weekends Look?," *Entrepreneur,* June 2000, www.entrepreneur.com/article/28442; Adam Cohen, *The Perfect Store: Inside eBay* (Boston: Back Bay Books, 2003), www.businessknowhow.com/manage/perfectstore2.htm.
4. U.S. Census Bureau, 2012 Survey of Business Owners.
5. U.S. Census Bureau, *Business Formation Statistics (BFS)*, www.census.gov/programs-surveys/bfs/technical-documentation/methodology.html#par_textimage_1 (accessed February 15, 2019).
6. David Gumpert (in *Burn Your Business Plan* [Needham, MA: Lauson Publishing, 2002]) suggests 100 hours, but the range is given as rules of thumb in government (http://bellzinc.sympatico.ca/en/content/503613?skin=sli) and commercial (e.g., www.capital-connection.com/bpconsulting.html).
7. Computed from numbers provided in U.S. Census American Fact Finder, 2012 data, http://factfinder.census.gov/faces/tableservices/jsf/pages/productview.xhtml?pid=SBO_2012_00CSCB19&prodType=table.
8. The material in this section is based on the following articles: Broderick Perkins, "Create the Ideal Space for Business at Home," 2001, www.startupjournal.com/howto/workhome/20011012-perkins.html;

Meredith Gould, "Space Quest," *Entrepreneur,* 2000, www.Entrepreneur.com/article/0,4621,280012,00.html; Broderick Perkins, "Realize the Dream of a Home-Based Business," 2001, www.startupjournal.com/howto/workhome/20011026-perkins.html; Cliff Ennico, "The Reality of Working from Home," *Entrepreneur,* 2002, www.entrepreneur.com/article/53186; Paul Edwards and Sarah Edwards, "Handling Houseguests in Your Home Office," *Entrepreneur,* August 2003, www.entrepreneur.com/article/63922; Owen Thomas, "You, Incorporated," *Business 2.0,* December 2002–January 2003.

9. An old listing can be found at www.cyburbia.org/directory/index.php?t=sub_pages&cat=217, but it is no longer being updated. A good listing of practical zoning help can be found at the Realtors' site at www.realtor.org/library/library/fg803.
10. Cliff Ennico, "Avoiding the Zoning Trap," Entrepreneur.com, August 15, 2005, www.entrepreneur.com/article/79464.
11. Paul and Sarah Edwards, "Dealing with Zoning Restrictions," HomeOfficeMag.com, December 2001, www.entrepreneur.com/article/46816; Paul and Sarah Edwards, "Bad Zoning Laws? Get 'Em Changed!," HomeOfficeMag.com, June 1, 2003, www.entrepreneur.com/article/62418; Entrepreneur.com, 2007, "Zoning: Home Is Where the Business Is, and It's also Where a Lot of Regulations Are," Entrepreneur.com, www.entrepreneur.com/article/38884; Karen E. Spaeder, "Is Your Home Zoned for Business?," Entrepreneur.com, January 26, 2004, www.entrepreneur.com/article/68844.
12. Paul and Sarah Edwards, "Bad Zoning Laws? Get 'Em Changed!," HomeOfficeMag.com, June 1, 2003, www.entrepreneur.com/article/62418; Karen E. Spaeder, "Is Your Home Zoned for Business?," Entrepreneur.com, January 26, 2004, www.entrepreneur.com/article/38884.
13. Azreila Jaffe, "When Is It Time to Move the Office out of the Home?," www.jbsa.com/content/suites/hb_teleworking/time_to_move.shtml.
14. For more information regarding the impact of the Internet on small and medium businesses see Hee Dae Kim, In Lee, and Choong Kwon Lee, "Building Web 2.0 Enterprises: A Study of Small and Medium Enterprises in the United States," *International Small Business Journal* 29, no. 4 (August 2011), http://isb.sagepub.com/content/early/2011/08/12/0266242611409785.abst);act (accessed June 5, 2012); Judith Jeffcote, Caroline Chappel, and Sylvia Feindt, "Best Practice in SME Adoption of E-Commerce," *Benchmarking* 9, no. 2 (2002), pp. 122–132; S. McCue, "Small Firms and the Internet: Force or Farce?," *International Business Trade Forum,* 1999; B. Kleindl, "Competitive Dynamics and New Business Models for SMEs in the Virtual Marketplace," *Journal of Developmental Entrepreneurship* 5, no. 1 (2000), pp. 73–85; C. Chappel and S. Feindt, "Analysis of E-Commerce Practice in SMEs," 1999, http://kite/tsa/de; P. Haynes, R. Becherer, and M. L. Helms, "Small and Mid-Sized Businesses and Internet Use: Unrealized Potential?," *Internet Research: Electronic Networking Applications and Policy* 8, no. 3 (1990); Dick Anderson, "Marketplace: Creating and Nurturing a Premier E-Business," *Journal of Interactive Marketing* 14, no. 3 (2000), pp. 67–78.
15. Google website, n.d., www.internetlivestats.com/google-search-statistics/ (accessed February 24, 2019).
16. U.S. Census Bureau, Annual Retail Trade Survey—2018, n.d., www.census.gov/retail/index.html (accessed February 24, 2019).
17. David S. Evans, Scott Murray, and Richard Schmalensee, "Why Online Retail Sales Are Much Larger Than U.S. Census Data Report," February 7, 2016, https://ssrn.com/abstract=2716266 or http://dx.doi.org/10.2139/ssrn.2716266 (accessed February 21, 2019).
18. U.S. Census Bureau, Annual Wholesale Trade Report—2014, n.d., www.census.gov/wholesale/index.html.
19. Conversation with David W. Peters, vice president of Letrah, used with permission, June 20, 2005.
20. Don Debelak, "Working the Web," *Entrepreneur,* 1998, www.entrepreneur.com/article/16130.
21. Gerry Grant, "Search Optimization Campaigns Build Brand," *Marketing News,* September 29, 2003; Yong Seck Sohn, Hangun Houn, and Dae Ryon Chang, "A Model of Consumer Information Search and Online Network Externality," *Journal of Interactive Marketing* 16, no. 4 (2002), pp. 2–14.
22. Nancy Einhart, "How to Get Them Buzzing to Your Site," *Business 2.0,* October 2003.
23. Philippa Gamse, "Are Search Engines Worth It Any More?," 2003, www.jbsba.com/cgi-bin/articlesbybtsub.cgi?art=441.
24. U.S. Census Bureau, "E-Stats 2013: Measuring the Electronic Economy," May 28, 2015, www.census.gov/econ/estats/e13-estats.pdf.
25. Savanna Dance, Archive Selling, "How Many Sellers on eBay?," eBay community member since June 30, 2014, posted April 4, 29, 2015, https://community.ebay.com/t5/Archive-Selling/How-Many-Sellers-on-eBay/td-p/23914701 (accessed March 22, 2016).
26. The listing fees on eBay came from a search of eBay on June 7, 2009.
27. Miniwatts Marketing Group, "World Internet Usage and Population Statistics," *Internet World Stats: Usage and Population Statistics,* n.d., www.internetworldstats.com/stats.htm.
28. Melissa Campanelli, "Anti-Fraud Measures for Your Site," *Entrepreneur,* September 2006, www.entrepreneur.com/ebusiness/operations/article166010.html; Amanda C. Kooser, "Card Tricks," *Entrepreneur,* February 2002, www.entrepreneur.com/magazine/entrepreneur/2002/february/48322.html; Tim Miller, "Chargebacks: A Huge Price to Pay," *Entrepreneur,* June 25, 2001, www.entrepreneur.com/money/paymentsandcollections/acceptingpayments/article41670.html.
29. Sandy D. Jap, "An Exploratory Study of the Introduction of Online Reverse Auctions," *Journal of Marketing* 67 (July 2003) pp. 96–107.
30. Melissa Campanelli, "Help Wanted," *Entrepreneur,* 2003, www.entrepreneur.com/article/63816.
31. Cliff Ennico, "Selling Your Specialty Merchandise Online," *Entrepreneur,* 2003.
32. Jacquelyn Lynn, "Let the Bidding Begin," *Entrepreneur,* 2003, www.entrepreneur.com/article/0,4621,310583,00.html.
33. Tim W. Knox, "The Secret to eBay Success," *Entrepreneur,* 2003, www.entrepreneur.com/article/71112.
34. Compiled from information from Tim W. Knox, "The Secret to eBay Success," *Entrepreneur,* 2003, www.entrepreneur.com/article/71112; Marsha Collier, *eBay for Dummies,* 7th ed. (New York: Wiley, 2011).
35. Jacquelyn Lynn, "Let the Bidding Begin," *Entrepreneur*, 2003, www.entrepreneur.com/article/0,4621,310583,00.html.
36. Michael Krauss, "EBay 'Bids' on Small-Biz Firms to Sustain Growth," *Marketing News,* December 8, 2003.
37. www.marketwired.com/press-release/stanley-home-products-75-years-of-excellence-and-a-place-in-direct-selling-history-nasdaq-cpak-687872.htm (accessed February 24, 2019).
38. Michael L. Sheffield, "Closing the Sale as a Network Marketer: How to Get a Commitment Out of Prospective Customers," *Entrepreneur*, April 21, 2003, www.entrepreneur.com/article/61244.
39. Multilevel marketing resources are also available at *Entrepreneur,* www.entrepreneur.com/businessopportunities/networkmarketing/archive114792.html.
40. Chris Penttila, "Retaliatory Strike: Don't Let the Big Boxes Win without a Fight. There's Plenty of Room for Start-Ups to Make Their Mark in Retail," *Entrepreneur,* December 2002, www.Entrepreneur.com/article/0,4621,304515,00.html.
41. Jan Kingaard, "How to Select a Shopping Center Location: Your Plan for Retail Success Requires a Shopping Center or Mall Location," *Entrepreneur,* February 10, 2005, www.entrepreneur.com/article/0,4621,319969,00.html.
42. Ibid.

43. Paul Edwards and Sarah Edwards, "Treasure Hunt: Hit the Mark When You're Hunting for Products to Sell," *Entrepreneur,* December 2003, www.entrepreneur.com/article/65678.
44. en.wikipedia.org/wiki/Pop-up_retail (accessed March 18, 2016).
45. lelandchamber.com/page/Frogfest (accessed January 12, 2016).
46. www.opensanantonio.com/ (accessed March 22, 2016).
47. www.ciarestaurantgroup.com/ (accessed March 22, 2016).
48. Eileen Cunniffe, "Art Center Offers 'Pop Up' Conceptual Art Experiences," *Non Profit Quarterly*, June 1, 2015, nonprofitquarterly.org/2015/06/01/art-center-offers-pop-up-conceptual-art-experiences/ (accessed March 22, 2016).
49. Nichole L. Torres, "Juggling Multiple Tasks: How to Find the Time to Do All You Need to Do—and Then Some," *Entrepreneur,* July 6, 2004, www.entrepreneur.com/article/71688.
50. Lisa Druxman, "Mama Needs to Get out of the Home Office," *Entrepreneur*, August 21, 2008, www.entrepreneur.com/startingabusiness/mompreneur/mompreneurcolumnistlisadruxman/article196600.html.
51. J. A. Katz and W. B. Gartner, "Properties of Emerging Organizations," *Academy of Management Review* 13, no. 3 (July 1988), pp. 429–441.
52. PSED, question 331a asks people starting a business if they work for someone else more or less than 35 hours a week; 74.4 percent reported working for others full time (more than 35 hours a week).
53. Mark Henricks, "Just To-Do It: Having Trouble Getting Organized?," *Entrepreneur,* August 2004, www.entrepreneur.com/article/71810.
54. Margaret Jackson, "30 Under 30: Courtney Hopson, Codi Jewelry," www.bizjournals.com/stlouis/stories/2004/07/19/focus18.html, July 18, 2004; Danielle Montgomery, "In Store-Bead By Bead," *St. Louis Magazine,* www.stlmag.com/In-Store-Bead-By-Bead/, April 17, 2007; www.facebook.com/courtney.hopson.14, (accessed February 24, 2020).
55. Nichole L. Torres, "Juggling Multiple Tasks: How to Find the Time to Do All You Need to Do—and Then Some," *Entrepreneur,* July 6, 2004, www.entrepreneur.com/article/71688.
56. Another useful site is maintained by the U.S. Small Business Administration at www.sba.gov/hotlist/license.html.
57. American Express—The Open Network, "Learning to Delegate," *Entrepreneur,* December 9, 2002, www.entrepreneur.com/article/0.4621.305082.00.html; M. A. Johnston, "Delegation and Organizational Structure in Small Businesses: Influence of Managers Attachment Patterns," *Group & Organization Management* 25, no. 1 (March 1, 2000), pp. 4–22; Robert McGarvey, "To the Rescue: Always Stepping in to Save the Day?," *Entrepreneur,* March 2000, www.entrepreneur.com/article/17326; Alexander Ardichvili, Brian Harmon, Richard N. Cardozo, Paul D. Reynolds, and Mary L. Williams, "The New Venture Growth: Functional Differentiation and the Need for Human Resource Development Interventions," *Human Resource Development Quarterly* 9, no. 1 (Spring 1998), pp. 55–70; Robert McGarvey, "Ready, Set, Delegate! Handing Out Tasks Is the Key to Growing Your Business," *Entrepreneur,* July 1998, www.entrepreneur.com/article/16046; Glenn H. Matthews, "Run Your Business or Build an Organization?," *Harvard Business Review* 62, no. 2 (March–April 1984), pp. 34–39.
58. Chris Penttila, "Close the Loop: If You're Outsourcing Projects Right and Left, Make Sure the Information You Need Is Rolling Back to You," *Entrepreneur,* October 2003, www.entrepreneur.com/article/64532; P. Jacobs, "So You Want to Be a Mountain Climber—Changing Careers One New Experience at a Time," *Global Career Coaching* (corporate website), www.gccoach.com/documents/SoYouWanttoBeAMountainClimberOct03_000.pdf. Additional information was also obtained from the Gourmet Gatherings corporate website, www.gourmetgatherings.com.
59. J. Finegan, "Bootstrapping: Great Companies Started with Less Than a Thousand Dollars: CEOs from 11 Different Companies Share Tips and Suggestions on How to Fund a Start-Up with under $1,000," *Inc.*, August 1995, www.inc.com/magazine/19950801/2363.html; Jerry Useem, "Should You Lie? Permissible or Not, Lying Has a Hallowed Place in the World of Business," *Fortune Small Business,* October 14, 1999, www.fortune.com/fortune/smallbusiness/managing/articles/0,15114,360720,00.html; MSGI Security Solutions Inc., "Board of Directors," MSGI Security Solutions, Inc. (corporate website), www.media-services.com/about/board.cfm.
60. Carla Goodman, "The Big Time: You've Tested the Part-Time Waters; Now Take the Full-Time Plunge," *Business Start-Ups,* August 1998, www.entrepreneur.com/article/16124.
61. K. Petrova, "Part-Time Entrepreneurship and Wealth Effects: New Evidence from the Panel Study of Entrepreneurial Dynamics," Working Paper, Boston College Department of Economics, September 2004, www..bc.edu/~petrovak/html/research/jmp.pdf.

Chapter 6

1. Saras D. Sarasvathy, "What Makes Entrepreneurs Entrepreneurial?," 2008, ssrn.com/abstract=909038.
2. https://blog.skratchlabs.com/blog/sports-hydration-as-simple-as-it-gets; https://cyclingtips.com/2017/01/origins-how-a-tainted-yellow-jersey-and-bird-poop-led-skratch-labs-to-a-new-mindset-in-exercise-nutrition/; https://www.skratchlabs.com/pages/about-us.
3. Dave Munday, "Charleston Student's Business Plan for Makeup Remover Wins National Prize," *The Post and Courier,* October 13, 2017, https://www.postandcourier.com/business/charleston-student-s-business-plan-for-makeup-remover-wins-national/article_23c5989e-b01e-11e7-982a-5b068ac66967.html; http://smudgiesllc.com/about.html. Michael Chidbachian, "Happy Accident: How A Makeup Disaster Launched One Teen's Business Career," https://yr.media/news/happy-accident-how-a-makeup-disaster-launched-one-teens-business-career/
4. Alan et al., *The Future of the Automobile: The Report of MIT's International Automobile Program* (Cambridge, MA: MIT Press, 1984).
5. R. N. Lussier, "A Nonfinancial Business Success versus Failure Prediction Model for Young Firms," *Journal of Small Business Management* 33, no. 1 (January 1995), pp. 8–20; R. N. Lussier, and S. Pfeifer. "A Crossnational Prediction Model for Business Success," *Journal of Small Business Management* 39, no. 3 (July 2001), pp. 228–239.
6. This saying has deep roots. The oldest known version dates to perhaps 700 BCE during the reign of Hezekiah. It was written in Hebrew in the book of Proverbs, chapter 19, verse 2. The current rhyming statement in English, "haste maketh waste," was printed in 1546 in *The Workes of John Heiwood. Namelie a Dialogue, wherein are Pleasantle Contrived the Number of all the Effectuall Proverbs in our English Tongue: Compact in a Matter Concerning two Maner of Mariages* [original spelling]. This English language book was reprinted many times over the next 50 years. A modern version edited by Julian Sharman can be found on Google Books: *"The proverbs of John Heywood. Being the "Proverbes" of that Author printed 1546. Edited, with Notes and Introduction.* (1874).
7. Lynn Neeley, "Bootstrap Finance," Coleman Foundation White Paper, 2002, www.colemanchairs.org/files/documents/4/Neeley.pdf; Verne Harnish, "Finding Money You Didn't Know You Had," *Fortune Small Business* 12, no. 5 (June 2002), pp. 67–68; Mary Kay Sullivan, "Small Business Familiarity with Sources of Financing: Impact of Location and Size," U.S. Association for Small Business and Entrepreneurship, annual meeting, 2000, www.usasbe.org/knowledge/proceedings/2000/sullivan.pdf; Bob Weinstein, "Walk This Way: Lessons in the Fine Art of Bootstrapping," *Entrepreneur*, October 1998, www.entrepreneur.com/article/0,4621,229429,00.html; Howard E. Van Auken and Lynn Neeley, "Evidence of Bootstrap Financing among Small Start-Up Firms," *Journal of Entrepreneurial and Small Business Finance* 5, no. 3 (1996), pp. 235–249.

8. basecamp.com/about (accessed March 26, 2016).
9. Stephanie Clifford, "How to Start a Business for (Almost) Nothing," *Inc.*, July 2006, www.inc.com/magazine/20060701/bootstrapping-intro.html (accessed April 29, 2007); Michael Fitzgerald, "CRM Made Simple," *Inc.*, January 2007, www.inc.com/magazine/20070101/technology-tools.html (accessed April 29, 2007); Mike Fitzgerald, "Something for Nothing," *Inc.*, November 2006, www.inc.com/magazine/20061101/handsontechnology.html (accessed April 29, 2007); Derek Gehl, "12 Free Tools for Online Businesses," *Entrepreneur*, June 27, 2005, www.entrepreneur.com/ebusiness/ebusinesscolumnist/article78504.html (accessed April 29, 2007); *Inc.* staff, "The Open-Source Advantage," *Inc.*, January 2007, www.inc.com/magazine /20070101/technology-software-adv.html (accessed April 29, 2007); Gwen Moran, "If You Build It," *Entrepreneur*, April 1, 2007, www.entrepreneur.com/ebusiness/ebaycenter/boostingyoursales/article176310.html (accessed April 29, 2007).
10. Eric Ries, *The Lean Startup: How Today's Entrepreneurs Use Continuous Innovation to Create Radically Successful Businesses* (New York: Crown, 2011), p. 103.
11. D. A. Veasley, "Incubators Build Economies, Benefit communities," *Birmingham Business Journal*, August 15, 2003, birmingham.bizjournals.com/birmingham/stories/2003/08/11/focus6.html.
12. For example, see Oregon SBDC Network, *ASBDC Accreditation Self-Study* (Eugene, OR: SBDC Network, November 2002); *Journal of Small Business Management* 37, no. 4 (1999), pp. 42–58; J. J. Chrisman and W. E. McMullan, "A Preliminary Assessment of Outsider Assistance as a Knowledge Resource: The Longer-Term Impact of New Venture Counseling," *Entrepreneurship Theory and Practice* 24, no. 3 (2000), pp. 37–53; James J. Chrisman and W. Ed McMullan, "Outsider Assistance as a Knowledge Resource for New Venture Survival," *Journal of Small Business Management* 42, no. 3 (2004), pp. 229–244; A. Charney and G. Libecap, *Impact of Entrepreneurship Education* (Kansas City, MO: Kauffman Center for Entrepreneurial Leadership, 2000); L. Kolvereid and O. Moen, "Entrepreneurship among Business Graduates: Does a Major in Entrepreneurship Make a Difference?," *Journal of European Industrial Training* 21, no. 4 (1997), pp. 154–160; W. E. McMullan and L. M. Gillin, "Entrepreneurship Education: Developing Technological Start-Up Entrepreneurs: A Case Study of a Graduate Entrepreneurship Programme at Swinburne University," *Technovation* 18, no. 4 (1998), pp. 275–286; T. V. Menzies and J. C. Paradi, "Encouraging Technology-Based Ventures: Entrepreneurship Education and Engineering Graduates," *New England Journal of Entrepreneurship* 5, no. 2 (2002), pp. 57–64; T. V. Menzies and J. C. Paradi, "Entrepreneurship Education and Engineering Students: Career Path and Business Performance," *International Journal of Entrepreneurship and Innovation* 6, no. 2 (2003), pp. 85–96; N. B. Upton, D. L. Sexton, and C. Moore, "Have We Made a Difference? An Examination of Career Activity of Entrepreneurship Majors since 1981" (abstract), *Frontiers of Entrepreneurship Research,* 1995 edition, pp. 727–728.
13. Brian Headd, "Redefining Business Success: Distinguishing between Closure and Failure," *Small Business Economics* 21, no. 1 (2003) pp. 51–61.
14. Recorded interview with Josh Fraser, February 13, 2010, www.onlineaspect.com/2010/02/15/mixergy-interview/.
15. "Failed Startups: The Other Side to Entrepreneurship," EventVue, failedstartups.wordpress.com/page/2/.
16. Blog written by Rob Johnson, Friday, February 5, 2010, blog.eventvue.com/post/372936164/post-mortem.
17. Ibid.
18. These statistics come from the Panel Study of Entrepreneurial Dynamics, William B. Gartner, Kelly G. Shaver, Nancy M. Carter, and Paul D. Reynolds (eds.), *Handbook of Entrepreneurial Dynamics: The Process of Business Creation* (Thousand Oaks, CA: Sage, 2004).
19. McDonald's Corporation, *Annual Report*, 2002, p. 10.
20. Jimmy John's website, "About Us," n.d., www.jimmyjohns.com/about-us/our-owner-founder/; *Entrepreneur*, "Our 40th Annual 2019 Franchise 500 Ranking," n.d., www.entrepreneur.com/franchise500; Jimmy John's Gourmet Sandwiches website, n.d., www.google.com/?gws_rd=ssl#q=jimmy+john%27s (all accessed March 1, 2019).
21. *Entrepreneur*, "Our 40th Annual 2019 Franchise 500 Ranking," n.d., www.entrepreneur.com/franchise500 (accessed July 8, 2019).
22. www.google.com (accessed July 8, 2019).
23. Sarah E. Lockyer, "One Year Later: Ground Round Sizzles under Franchisee Co-op," *Nation's Restaurant News,* February 28, 2005; Carlye Adler, "The Ground Round Rebound: Stunned by a Sudden Bankruptcy, Stubborn Franchisees Step in to Buy Their Parent Company," *Fortune Small Business Magazine,* February 2005; Michael Peña, "Richmond's Job Center Gets Downsized," *East Bay Business Times,* April 2004.
24. R. Green and J. J. Carroll, *Investigating Entrepreneurial Opportunities* (Thousand Oaks, CA: Sage 2000).
25. Professional Association of Innkeepers International (PAII), *Eighth Biennial Industry Study of Bed-and-Breakfast & Country Inns* (Santa Barbara, CA, 2003).
26. Bizstats.com gets its heuristics from T. West, *2016 Business Reference Guide,* 26th ed. (Worcester, MA: Business Brokerage Press, 2016).
27. L. Marx and G. Shaler, "Bargaining Power in Sequential Contracting," Duke/UNC Micro-Theory Working Paper 3, 2002.
28. Financial Accounting Standards Board, "Statement of Financial Accounting Standards No. 142," *Goodwill and Other Intangible Assets* (2001).
29. Sandra King, "Organizational Performance and Conceptual Capability: The Relationship between Organizational Performance and Successors' Capability in a Family-Owned Firm," *Family Business Review* 16, no. 3 (September 2003), pp. 173–182; Patricia Schiff Estess, "Class Acts: Family Business Forums Are a One-Stop Education Resource," *Entrepreneur,* December 1996, www.entrepreneur.com/article/13568; A. Ibrahim and W. Ellis, *Family Business Management: Concepts and Practices* (Dubuque, IA: Kendall/Hunt, 1994).
30. Rod P. Burkert, "A Good Deal Depends on Preparation," *Journal of Accountancy* 196, no. 5 (November 2003), pp. 47–52.
31. Stephen Weinstein, "Add a New Owner to Your Firm," *Journal of Accountancy* 196, no. 2 (August 2003), pp. 43–48.
32. The ideas here are derived from Chris Kelleher, "Preventing Feuds in the Family Business: Handling Delicate Topics—Like Succession Planning— with Care Is Key to Keeping the Peace in Any Family Business," *Entrepreneur*, June 14, 2004, www.entrepreneur.com/article/71132; Nichole L. Torres, "Family Affair When Business and Family Mix, the Key to Success is Communication," *Entrepreneur*, September 2004, www.entrepreneur.com/article/72314; Patricia Schiff Estess, "Class Acts: Family Business Forums Are a One-Stop Education Resource," *Entrepreneur*, December 1996, www.entrepreneur.com/article/13568.
33. Dominique Besson and Slimane Haddadj, "Dysfunctions in Owner-Manager Succession Process in Family Firms and How a SEAM Intervener-Researcher Can Address Them," *Journal of Organizational Change Management* 16, no. 1 (2003), pp. 83–89.
34. Isabelle Le Breton-Miller, Danny Miller, and Lloyd P. Steier, "Toward an Integrative Model of Effective FOB Succession," *Entrepreneurship: Theory & Practice* 28, no. 4 (Summer 2004), pp. 305–328; William S. White, Timothy D. Krinke, and David L. Geller, "Family Business Succession Planning: Devising an Overall Strategy," *Journal of Financial Service Professionals* 58, no. 3 (May 2004), pp. 67–86.
35. Scott Bernard Nelson, "Leave It to Them: Make Sure Your Family Gets What It Needs by Including a Disclaimer Provision in Your Estate Plan," *Entrepreneur,* August 2004, www.entrepreneur.com/article/71782; Paul DeCeglie, "State of the Estate: What Is Estate Planning and Why

Should You Be Doing It Now?," *Entrepreneur's Start-Ups,* January 2001, www.entrepreneur.com/article/77778.

36. N. Upton and B. Petty, "Funding Options for Transferring the Family-Held Firm: A Comparative Analysis," presented at the 18th annual meeting of the Babson Research Conference, Ghent, Belgium, April 1998; N. Upton and B. Petty, "Venture Capital Funding of Family Business Transition: An Exploratory Analysis," *Proceedings of the United States Association of Small Business and Entrepreneurship*, 1998, pp. 94–101; Neil C. Churchill and Kenneth J. Hatten, "Non-Market-Based Transfers of Wealth and Power: A Research Framework for Family Businesses," *American Journal of Small Business* 12, no. 2 (Fall 1987), pp. 53–66.
37. Rod P. Burkert, "A Good Deal Depends on Preparation," *Journal of Accountancy* 196, no. 5 (November 2003), pp. 47–52.
38. Dominique Besson and Slimane Haddadj, "Dysfunctions in Owner-Manager Succession Process in Family Firms and How a SEAM Intervener-Researcher Can Address Them," *Journal of Organizational Change Management* 16, no. 1 (2003), pp. 83–89.
39. Scott Bernard Nelson, "Leave It to Them: Make Sure Your Family Gets What It Needs by Including a Disclaimer Provision in Your Estate Plan," *Entrepreneur*, August 2004, www.Entrepreneur.com/article/0,4621,316380,00.html. Paul DeCeglie, "State of the Estate: What Is Estate Planning and Why Should You Be Doing It Now?" *Entrepreneur's Start-Ups*, January 2001, www.entrepreneur.com/article/0,4621,284549,00.html; Dominique Besson and Slimane Haddadj, "Dysfunctions in Owner-Manager Succession Process in Family Firms and How a SEAM Intervener-Researcher Can Address Them," *Journal of Organizational Change Management* 16, no. 1 (2003), pp. 83–89.
40. United States Courts website, "June 2018 Bankruptcy Filings Fall 2.6 Percent," July 24, 2018, www.uscourts.gov/news/2018/07/24/june-2018-bankruptcy-filings-fall-26-percent (accessed March 1, 2019).
41. J. Warrillow, *Built to Sell: Creating a Business That Can Thrive without You* (New York: Portfolio Hardcover, 2011).

Chapter 7

1. This was built from interviews with Joe Fischer, the video "Startup Snapshot #1: Greetabl" (www.youtube.com/watch?v=u2xvN4op4YA) as well as articles such as: D. Nicklaus, "E-commerce Startup Greetabl Aims to Simplify Gift-Giving," *Stltoday.Com*, October 20, 2015, www.stltoday.com/business/columns/david-nicklaus/e-commerce-startup-greetabl-aims-to-simplify-gift-giving/article_4ae432be-030b-510a-92a2-8e70e43d6152.html; *Entrepreneur Quarterly* staff, "Greetabl Raises $1.5M Funding Round to Expand Platform and Break into New Markets," *Entrepreneur Quarterly*, June 5, 2017, https://eqstl.com/greetabl-raises-1-5m-funding-round-expand-platform-break-new-markets/; D. Velázquez, "Cards That Transform into Gifts Are an Antidote to the Facebook Age," *Fast Company*, December 16, 2014, www.fastcompany.com/3039218/engineering-a-better-christmas-card.
2. A. Kaczanowska, "IBISworld Industry Report 51119—Greeting Cards & Other Publishing in the US," July 2012 (accessed March 18, 2019).
3. G. E. Hills and R. P. Singh, "Opportunity Recognition," in *Handbook of Entrepreneurial Dynamics: The Process of Business Creation,* ed. W. B. Gartner, K. G. Shaver, N. M. Carter, and P. D. Reynolds (Thousands Oaks, CA: Sage, 2004), Table 24.1, p. 266.
4. The North American Industry Classification System (NAICS) uses a six-digit code and offers original categories reflecting newer industries, such as those related to the Internet. For NAICS information, check out the NAICS page at the Census Bureau, www.census.gov/econ/isp/. The NAICS replaced the Standard Industrial Classification (SIC) codes but you'll sometimes see SIC codes (which go up to 4 digits) being used.
5. Thomas J. Stanley and William D. Danko, *The Millionaire Next Door* (New York: Pocket Books, 1996).
6. Anita Campbell, "Top 30 Most Profitable Small Businesses during 2008," *Small Business Trends,* February 2009, small biztrends.com/2009/02/top-30-most-profitable-small-businesses-2008.html; Anita Campbell, "What Are the Most profitable Small Businesses in a Recession?," *Small Business Trends,* January 27, 2009, smallbiztrends.com/2009/01/profitable-small-businesses-recession.html; Maureen Farrell, "The Most and Least Profitable Businesses to Start," *Forbes,* January 18, 2008, www.forbes.com/2008/01/18/citigroup-sageworks-nyu-ent-fin=cx_mf_0118mostprofitable.html; Scott Shane, "Are There Recession-Proof Industries for Small Businesses?," *Small Business Trends,* December 1, 2008, smallbiztrends.com/2008/12/recession-proofsmall-businesses.html; Mindy Woolen, "Industry Trends: Most Profitable Industries of 2008," January 28, 2009, www.sageworksinc.com/industrytrends/index.php/mostprofitable industries-of-2008/.
7. Sarah Caron, "14 Big Businesses That Started in a Recession," insidecrm.com, May 24, 2009, www.insidecrm.com/features/businessesstarted-slump-111108/; Michael Mandel, "Starting Successful New Companies in Recessions," *BusinessWeek*, May 3, 2009, www.businessweek.com/the_thread/economicsunbound/archives/2009/05/starting_succes.html. This list of airlines was based on Michael Masouras, "Companies Founded after 2000," *Freebase*, May 24, 2009, www.freebase.com/view/user/masouras/default_domain/views/companies_founded_after_2000, compared to operating airlines shown in "List of Airlines—Planes," *Plane Spotting World,* May 24, 2009,plane.spottingworld.com/List_of_airlines.
8. Thomas J. Stanley and William D. Danko, *The Millionaire Next Door* (New York: Pocket Books, 1996).
9. PSED Q327, "If someone asked you which kind of person you are, would you say that you preferred doing things better or doing things differently?" Of respondents, 63.3 percent said doing things better, while 32.4 percent said doing things differently.
10. The ideas in this section build on three works. Michael Porter talked about the topic in general in his 1980 masterpiece *Competitive Strategy* (Free Press). Karl Vesper really gave the first detailed workup of imitation-innovation strategies in his 1990 book *New Venture Strategy* (Prentice Hall). The most advanced thinking on the topic can be found in Dean Shepherd and Mark Shanley's 1998 book *New Venture Strategy* (Sage).
11. Blue ocean strategy was originated by W. Chan Kim and Renée Mauborgne, *Blue Ocean Strategy: How to Create Uncontested Market Space and Make Competition Irrelevant* (Brighton, MA: Harvard Business Review Press, 2005). The firm's website gives the Cirque du Soleil example: Blue Ocean Strategy website, "Cirque du Soleil," n.d., www.blueoceanstrategy.com/bos-moves/cirque-du-soleil/. Additional material came from B. Halligan, "Blue Ocean Strategy: A Small Business Case Study," n.d., https://blog.hubspot.com/blog/tabid/6307/bid/54/blue-ocean-strategy-a-small-business-case-study.aspx; "Ringling Bros. and Barnum & Bailey Circus," Wikipedia, February 2, 2019, https://en.wikipedia.org/w/index.php?title=Ringling_Bros._and_Barnum_%26_Bailey_Circus&oldid=881357919; "Circus," Wikipedia, April 26, 2019, https://en.wikipedia.org/w/index.php?title=Circus&oldid=894291439.
12. "Consumer Web Services DVD Movie Rental Plot Pits Tiny Netflix vs. Blockbuster," *Investor's Business Daily*, March 21, 2001, p. A08; "DVD Renter Netflix Crafts New Plot Line, Molding Itself after HBO: The Distribution Company Foresees Its Subscribers Getting a Host of Content," *Investor's Business Daily,* November 26, 2003, p. A04; "Blockbuster Battles Netflix," *Variety* 395, no. 13 (August 16, 2004), p. 2; Tara Lemmey, "Push the Positive for Customers: Any Revenue Model That Takes Advantage of Human Frailty Is Vulnerable. Case in Point: Blockbuster. Opportunist: Netflix," *BusinessWeek*, September 13, 2005.

13. Michael V. Copeland, "Start Last, Finish First," *Business 2.0*, February 2, 2006, money.cnn.com/magazines/business2/business2_archive/2006/01/01/8368119/index.htm; Mauro F. Guillén, "Structural Inertia, Imitation, and Foreign Expansion: South Korean Firms and Business Groups in China, 1987–95," *Academy of Management Journal* 45 (2002), pp. 509–525; Henrik Barth, "Fit among Competitive Strategy, Administrative Mechanisms, and Performance: A Comparative Study of Small Firms in Mature and New Industries," *Journal of Small Business Management* 41, no. 2 (April 2003), pp. 133–147; David Newton, "To Spark Business Growth, Follow the Leader in Your Industry," *Entrepreneur*, October 2003, www.entrepreneur.com/magazine/entrepreneur/2003/october/64478.html.
14. Nichole L. Torres, "Designing Women—A 'by Women, for Women, about Women' Attitude Is Making This Greeting Card Company a Success," *Entrepreneur,* July 2001, www.entrepreneur.com/article/41436.
15. This is question Q291 in the PSED, "Within the first three to four years, what percentage of your customers do you expect to be ... located within x miles?" Because the numbers are averages of percentages reported, they don't necessarily add up to 100 percent. Some firms aimed for more than one market.
16. Pot, J. "How to Spot Fake Reviews on Amazon, Yelp, and Other Sites." *How-To Geek*, December 6, 2016. https://www.howtogeek.com/282802/how-to-spot-fake-reviews-on-amazon-yelp-and-other-sites/. Liu, B. "Opinion Spam Detection: Detect Fake Reviews and Reviewers." *Fake Reviews*, 2017 2008. https://www.cs.uic.edu/~liub/FBS/fake-reviews.html.
17. Adapted from discussion of the drivers of value and costs in Gordon Walker, *Modern Competitive Strategy* (Boston: McGraw-Hill, 2004) and in Michael Porter, *Competitive Strategy: Techniques for Analyzing Industries and Competitors* (New York: Free Press, 1980).
18. The model for life cycle comes from strategy texts like Gordon Walker, *Modern Competitive Strategy* (Boston: McGraw-Hill, 2004); and Gregory G. Dess and G. T. Lumpkin, *Strategic Management: Creating Competitive Advantage* (Boston: McGraw-Hill/Irwin, 2003). The discussion of the auto industry's growth comes from Renato Bertodo, "The Strategic Alliance: Automotive Paradigm of the 1990s," *International Journal of Technology Management* 5, no. 4 (1990), pp. 375–388; Edward K. Miller, *Century on Wheels: The Story of the American Automotive Industry* (Houston, TX: Pioneer Publications, 1987); H. Eugene Weiss, *Chrysler, Ford, Durant, and Sloan: Founding Giants of the American Automotive Industry* (Jefferson, NC: McFarland, 2003).
19. These generic strategies for business come from Michael E. Porter, *Competitive Strategy: Techniques for Analyzing Industries and Competitors* (New York: Free Press, 1980).
20. This list adapts and labels Shepherd and Shanley (Dean A. Shepherd and Mark Shanley, *New Venture Strategy* [Thousand Oaks, CA: Sage, 1998], p. 59) with two exceptions. One of their categories, "Products with special features appealing to specific niches," is treated here as a variant of customization. Second, the comprehensiveness suprastrategy (p. 61) is provided; Michael Porter, *Competitive Strategy: Techniques for Analyzing Industries and Competitors* (New York: Free Press, 1980).
21. Gary Nabham, "Food for Thought: Eating In—the Benefits of Locally Grown Food," *Sierra*, November–December 2002, www.sierraclub.org/sierra/200211/food.asp.
22. James Carpenter, "Little Guy Is No. 1 Volume Car Dealer," *The Salt Lake Tribune and Deseret Morning News*, www.utahbusinessandindustry.com/2003article/menlove2.asp. The sale was noted in T. Busselberg, "The Davis Clipper–Menlove Family Still Tied to Area Despite Dealership Sale," February 11, 2011, davisclipper.com/bookmark/11329976-Menlove-family-still-tied-to-area-despite-dealership-sale (accessed April 9, 2016).
23. Karl Vesper, *New Venture Strategy* (Prentice Hall, 1990).
24. Tax Resources, Inc., www.taxaudit.com.
25. Initiative for a Competitive Inner City, Inner City 100 Winners 2003 SLR Contracting, www.icic.org/vsh/oin/smRenderfs.php?phpsessid=b5238b 7a7e0007c805caf97833ab6fda&cerror; Fred O. Williams, "Inner-City Success Story," *Buffalo News*, April 26, 2003, www.buffaloniagara.org/news.asp?ID=25&ARCHIVED=1.
26. Vazquez Commercial Construction website, "About Vazquez Commercial Contracting," n.d., www.vazquezcc.com/about/; *Fortune* magazine and Initiative for a Competitive Inner City, "100 Fastest-Growing Inner City Companies," *Fortune*, October 3, 2018, http://fortune.com/inner-city-100/; Missouri Business Development Program website, "Vazquez Commercial Contracting, LLC–Kansas City," January 2013, https://missouribusiness.net/2013/01/vazquez-commercial-contracting-kansas-city/; Missouri Business Development Program website, "Vazquez Commercial Contracting, LLC–Kansas City (Where Are They Now?)," July 17, 2017, https://missouribusiness.net/2015/05/vazquez-commercial-contracting-kc-2015/.
27. Michael Porter, *Competitive Strategy: Techniques for Analyzing Industries and Competitors* (New York: Free Press, 1980).

Chapter 8

1. Krista was a MBA student at Saint Louis University's Chaifetz School of Business. This case comes from her telling her story in classes and club meetings, as well as from the press (https://news.google.com/search?q=%22helper+helper%22) and online materials included below. You can see Helper Helper's videos at https://vimeo.com/helper-helper, and read more about its NCAA Service Challenge results at Helper Helper NCAA Service Challenge Results: https://static.helper-helper.com/files/ncaa/2018-2019-NCAA-HelperHelper-Report.pdf. A great article about her and Helper Helper is at https://mgoblue.com/news/2017/7/21/womens-basketball-alumna-clement-bridging-communities-one-helper-at-a-time.aspx.
2. Lisa K. Gundry and Aaron A. Buchko, *Field Casework: Methods for Consulting to Small and Startup Businesses* (Thousand Oaks, CA: Sage, 1996); B. Honig, "Who Gets the Goodies? An Examination of Microenterprise Credit in Jamaica," *Entrepreneurship and Regional Development* 10 (1998), pp. 313–334.
3. The ideas in this table come from David Gumpert, *How to Really Create a Successful Business Plan: Step-by-Step Guide,* 4th ed. (Needham, MA: Lauson Publishing, 2003), chap. 10; D. A. Shepherd and A. L. Zacharakis, "A New Venture's Cognitive Legitimacy: An Assessment by Customers," *Journal of Small Business Management* 41, no. 2 (April 2003), pp. 148–167; D. A. Shepherd and A. L. Zacharakis, "Venture Capitalists' Expertise: A Call for Research into Decision Aids and Cognitive Feedback," *Journal of Business Venturing* 17, no. 1 (January 2002), pp. 1–20; Dean Shepherd and Evan Douglas, *Attracting Equity Investors* (Thousand Oaks, CA: Sage, 1999); J. Hall and C. W. Hofer, "Venture Capitalists' Decision Criteria in New Venture Evaluation," *Journal of Business Venturing* 8, no. 1 (January 1993), pp. 25–42; Robert Ronstadt, *Entrepreneurial Finance* (Gilmanton, NH: Lord Publishing, 1988), chap. 10.
4. Examples of this focus on the start-up team and venture management come from G. H. Smart, "Management Assessment Methods in Venture Capital: An Empirical Analysis of Human Capital Valuation," *Venture Capital* 1, no. 1 (January 1, 1999), pp. 59–82; D. A. Shepherd, "Venture Capitalists' Assessment of New Venture Survival," *Management Science* 45, no. 5 (May 1, 1999), pp. 621–632.
5. The venture capital numbers come from PWC Moneytree, "Current Quarter Data by State," *PWC Moneytree Report*, 2015, www.pwcmoneytree.com/CurrentQuarter/ByState. The angel results come from "Released Halo Reports—Angel Resource Institute—2015 Annual HALO Report," Angel Resource Institute at Willamette University website, n.d., www.angelresourceinstitute.org/research/halo-report/halo-report.aspx.

6. DocSend, "What We Learned from 200 Startups Who Raised $360M," *DocSend*, June 2015, https://docsend.com/. The insights about the details of the study and the comparison of Silicon Valley to Boston came from an email discussion with study author and Harvard Business School professor Tom Eisenmann by ESB co-author Jerome Katz in June 2015.
7. John L. Nesheim, *High Tech Start-Up* (revised and updated ed.) (New York: Free Press, 2000).
8. Twenty-eight percent of owners wrote a formal plan while 26 percent had an informal or partial plan. Sarah Bartlett, "Seat of the Pants," *Inc.*, October 2002, www.inc.com/magazine/20021015/24772.html.
9. F. Delmar and S. Shane, "Does Business Planning Facilitate the Development of New Ventures?," *Strategic Management Journal* 24, no. 12 (December 2003), p. 1165; Nancy Upton, Elisabeth J. Teal, and Joe T. Felan, "Strategic and Business Planning Practices of Fast Growth Family Firms," *Journal of Small Business Management* 39, no. 1 (January 2001), pp. 60–72; Brian Gibson and Gavin Cassar, "Planning Behavior Variables in Small Firms," *Journal of Small Business Management* 40, no. 3 (July 2002), pp. 171–187.
10. F. Delmar and S. Shane, "Does Business Planning Facilitate the Development of New Ventures?," *Strategic Management Journal* 24, no. 12 (December 2003), p. 1165; B. Honig and T. Karlsson, "Institutional Forces and the Written Business Plan," *Journal of Management* 30, no. 1 (2004), pp. 29–48; B. J. Orser, S. Hogarth-Scott, and A. L. Riding, "Performance, Firm Size, and Management Problem Solving," *Journal of Small Business Management* 38, no. 4 (October 2000), pp. 42–58; Stephen C. Perry, "The Relationship between Written Business Plans and the Failure of Small Businesses in the U.S.," *Journal of Small Business Management* 39, no. 3 (July 2001), pp. 201–209.
11. B. Honig and T. Karlsson, "Institutional Forces and the Written Business Plan," *Journal of Management* 30, no. 1 (2004), pp. 29–48.
12. John L. Nesheim, *High Tech Start-Up* (rev. and updated ed.) (New York: Free Press, 2000).
13. Question 114 in the PSED: What is the current form of your business plan: unwritten or in your head, informally written, formally prepared, or something else?
14. Sources for this section: Cliff Ennico, "The 30-Second Business Plan: Want to Impress a Potential Investor Quickly? Here's Exactly What to Say," *Entrepreneur*, January 20, 2003, www.entrepreneur.com/article/58946; Ben Casnocha, "Perfecting the Elevator Pitch: Learn to Rattle Off a Spiel Quickly about Your Company, and Soon You'll Have More Contacts Than You'll Know What to Do With," TeenStartUps.com, February 2003, www.entrepreneur.com/article/59274; Stan Mandel, "The Elevator Pitch: Engage People, Move to Action ... in 2 Minutes," Wake Forest University, 2003.
15. A. L. Zacharakis, "Writing a Business Plan," in W. Bygrave and A. Zacharakis (eds.), *The Portable MBA in Entrepreneurship*, 3rd ed. (New York: Wiley, 2003).
16. Gregory G. Dess and G. T. Lumpkin, *Strategic Management: Creating Competitive Advantage* (Boston: McGraw-Hill/Irwin, 2003), pp. 27–29; Gordon Walker, *Modern Competitive Strategy* (Burr Ridge, IL: McGraw-Hill/Irwin, 2003), pp. 263–264; Guy Kawasaki, *The Art of the Start* (New York: Penguin Group, 2004).
17. Gregory G. Dess and G. T. Lumpkin, *Strategic Management: Creating Competitive Advantage* (Boston: McGraw-Hill/Irwin, 2003), p. 27.
18. Robert X. Cringley, *Accidental Empires* (New York: HarperBusiness, 1996).
19. Mark Henricks, "Words to Live By," *Entrepreneur*, September 1998, www.entrepreneur.com/article/16392.
20. There is no standard time for elevator pitches. For example, the Wake Forest Elevator Pitch Competition allows two minutes for the pitch, but that is one of the longest times. For the MIT Enterprise Forums, the pitch is limited to one minute. Outside of these formal settings, communications experts tell us that listeners lose interest after 30 seconds. That in large part explains why 30 seconds is the length of the typical television commercial.
21. These come from the advertising slogan database at http://www.textart.ru/database/slogan/list-advertising-slogans.html. Another source for slogans is Slogan's Hub at https://sloganshub.org/. If you'd like to try making your own slogan, you can use online slogan generators. There is a review of these at https://www.oberlo.com/blog/slogan-generator.
22. Real examples of such businesses described this way include www.outdooraccess.com, www.hipcamp.com/, https://privateacre.com/, and www.tentrr.com/. You can search using the phrase "airbnb for the outdoors."
23. The traditional 25 pages (double-spaced) of text in a business plan would contain around 6,250 words. The University of Texas competition model of 15 pages (double-spaced) of text would come to 3,750 words. The Georgia Bowl competition model of 10 pages of text (1.5-line spacing) would come in at around 3,300 words. The model used in *Entrepreneurial Small Business* comes in as 10 pages (single-spaced) of text with around 4,000 words maximum. The point is, in a world with more business plans than ever before, there is greater need for plans to be shorter, faster, and easier to deal with.
24. This outline for the full business plan was developed specifically for small businesses, but its roots are in a number of works on business planning. These include Jeffry Timmons and Stephen Spinelli, *New Venture Creation: Entrepreneurship for the 21st Century* (Boston: McGraw-Hill/Irwin, 2003); David Gumpert, *How to Really Create a Successful Business Plan: Step-By-Step Guide,* 4th ed. (Needham, MA: Lauson Publishing, 2003); Edward G. Rogoff, *Bankable Business Plans* (Mason, OH: Thompson/Texere, 2004); Kauffman Foundation, *New Business Mentor* (Kansas City, MO: Kauffman Foundation, 2002); J. D. Ryan and Gail Hyduke, *Small Business: An Entrepreneur's Plan* (Cincinnati, OH: South-Western, 2003); C. W. Hofer, "The Evolution of Business Plans in International Business Plan Competitions," in J. A. Katz and A. Corbett (eds.), *Advances in Entrepreneurship, Firm Emergence and Growth,* vol. 18 (Bingley, UK: Emerald, 2016). Hofer discusses how the length of business plans has shortened to the current cover + 10 + 7 page range, which is close to what most competitions and the SBA online business plan maker typically produce.
25. These numbers are fairly standard in many settings. For example, Linda Pinson and Jerry Jinnett gave these numbers in their SBA how-to guide "How to Write a Business Plan" (Managing and Planning Series, MP-32, 1993), www.sba.gov/library/pubs/mp-32.txt or www.sba.gov/library/pubs/mp-32.pdf. The same numbers are consistently used in the major business plan competitions.
26. Edward G. Rogoff, *Bankable Business Plans* (Mason, OH: Thompson/Texere, 2004); David Gumpert, *How to Really Create a Successful Business Plan: Step-By-Step Guide*, 4th ed. (Needham, MA: Lauson Publishing, 2003); David Gumpert, *Burn Your Business Plan* (Needham, MA: Lauson Publishing, 2002).
27. Dean Shepherd and Mark Shanley, *New Venture Strategy* (Thousand Oaks, CA: Sage, 1998).
28. These days you can cut and paste or add files with Excel spreadsheets to Word documents and position everything for readability to get started. Once the plan looks right, you can either go File > Save As and select PDF from the drop-down box showing file formats, or do File > Print and select PDF on the Print Dialog box. If your word processing software doesn't do this, you can use an online converter. To find one, Google "convert to pdf."
29. You can find ratings of data room services at sites such as https://datarooms.org/, https://dataroom-review.com/, or www.capterra.com/virtual-data-room-software/.
30. There is a tremendous range of models for different types of plans. Examples include Edward G. Rogoff, *Bankable Business Plans* (Mason,

OH: Thompson/Texere, 2004); A. L. Zacharakis, "Writing a Business Plan," in W. Bygrave and A. Zacharakis (eds.), *The Portable MBA in Entrepreneurship*, 3rd ed. (New York: Wiley, 2003); David Gumpert, *How to Really Create a Successful Business Plan: Step-by-Step Guide,* 4th ed. (Needham, MA: Lauson Publishing, 2003); Jill E. Kapron, *Biz-Plan Builder* (Mountain View, CA: JIAN/South-Western, 1999); the ICVE model developed through R. K. Mitchell, J. B. Smith, K. W. Seawright, and E. A. Morse, "Cross-Cultural Cognitions and the Venture Creation Decision," *Academy of Management Journal,* 43 no. 5 (October 2000) pp. 974–993; Dean Shepherd and Evan Douglas, *Attracting Equity Investors* (Thousand Oaks, CA: Sage, 1999).

31. Michael McMyne and Nicole Amare, *Student Entrepreneurs: 14 Undergraduate All Stars Tell Their Stories* (St. Louis: Saint Louis University/Premium Press, 2003).
32. The approach here is inspired by three sources on the critical analysis of business plans: Robert C. Ronstadt, *Entrepreneurial Finance: Taking Control of Your Financial Decision Making* (Gilmanton NH: Lord Publishing, 1988); David Gumpert, *Burn Your Business Plan* (Needham, MA: Lauson Publishing, 2002); and most of all Dean Shepherd and Evan Douglas, *Attracting Equity Investors* (Thousand Oaks, CA: Sage, 1999).
33. R. K. Mitchell, J. B. Smith, K. W. Seawright, and E. A. Morse, "Cross-Cultural Cognitions and the Venture Creation Decision," *Academy of Management Journal* 43, no. 5 (October 2000), pp. 974–993; G. N. Chandler and S. H. Hanks, "Founder Competence, the Environment, and Venture Performance," *Entrepreneurship Theory and Practice* 19 (1999), pp. 77–89; G. N. Chandler, and E. Jansen, "The Founder's Self-Assessed Competence and Venture Performance," *Journal of Business Venturing* 7 (1992), pp. 223–236.
34. DocSend commissioned a study looking at the data it had on 200 companies that raised funds through the site, which presents pitch decks and tracks viewers' habits. You can find the study at https://docsend.com/view/p8jxsqr, or find a story about the study at http://techcrunch.com/2015/06/08/lessons-from-a-study-of-perfect-pitch-decks-vcs-spend-an-average-of-3-minutes-44-seconds-on-them/. While the DocSend study looks at businesses trying to raise around $1 million each, the wisdom seems to work well for start-up businesses of all sizes.
35. I came to Aristotle's model through a circuitous route. Bill Gartner of Babson and Steven Harowitz of Campfire (http://cmpfr.com/) both talked to me about storytelling. The first time I saw storytelling models was in Visme's *A Non-Designer's Guide to Creating Visually Captivating Presentations* (https://visme.co/blog/presentation-design/). From this free e-book I went to fassforward.com's blog about storytelling models (www.fassforward.com/blog/use-these-story-structures-to-make-messages-people-talk-about), where I learned about other model collections like those of Christopher Booker, Kurt Vonnegut, and Dan Roam, as well as the classic models of Aristotle, Joseph Campbell, and Nancy Duarte. Their approach to Aristotle resonated with the approach I've been teaching, and it became the basis for this section.
36. Margaret Fletcher and Simon Harris, "Seven Aspects of Strategy Formation," *International Small Business Journal* 20, no. 3 (August 2002), p. 297–313.
37. C. L. Nicholls-Nixon, A. C. Cooper, and C. Y. Woo, "Strategic Experimentation: Understanding Change and Performance in New Ventures," *Journal of Business Venturing* 15, no. 5–6 (September–November 2000), pp. 493–521.
38. Adapted from "Michael Cain," in Michael McMyne and Nicole Amare, *Student Entrepreneurs: 14 Undergraduate All Stars Tell Their Stories* (St. Louis: Saint Louis University/Premium Press, 2003), pp. 59–67.
39. www.slu.edu/services/cc/jobsearch/chronologicalresume.pdf. Used with permission.
40. U.S. Census, (2008), 2007 Economic Census of the United States - Accommodation and Food Services: Geographic Area Series: Summary Statistics for the United States, States, Metro Areas, Counties, and Places: 2007 (for Texas). URL: https://factfinder.census.gov/faces/tableservices/jsf/pages/productview.xhtml?src=bkmk.

Chapter 9

1. Like the opening vignette in Chapter 7 "Joe Fischer, Zoë Scharf, and the Strategy behind Greetabl," this vignette was built from interviews with Joe Fischer, the video "Startup Snapshot #1: Greetabl (www.youtube.com/watch?v=u2xvN4op4YA), as well as articles such as: D. Nicklaus, "E-Commerce Startup Greetabl Aims to Simplify Gift-Giving," *Stltoday.Com*, October 20, 2015, www.stltoday.com/business/columns/david-nicklaus/e-commerce-startup-greetabl-aims-to-simplify-gift-giving/article_4ae432be-030b-510a-92a2-8e70e43d6152.html; EQ staff, "Greetabl Raises $1.5M Funding Round to Expand Platform and Break into New Markets," *Entrepreneur Quarterly,* June 5, 2017, https://eqstl.com/greetabl-raises-1-5m-funding-round-expand-platform-break-new-markets/; D. Velázquez, "Cards That Transform into Gifts Are an Antidote to the Facebook Age," *Fast Company*, December 16, 2014, www.fastcompany.com/3039218/engineering-a-better-christmas-card.
2. Tomima Edmark, "On Your Mark ...," *Entrepreneur*, April 1999, www.entrepreneur.com/article/0,4621,230153,00.html.
3. Robert G. Cooper and Elko J. Kleinschmidt, "Benchmarking the Firm's Critical Success Factors in New Business Development," *The Journal of Product Innovation Management* 12 (1995), pp. 374–391.
4. R. Nelson, "94% of U.S. App Store Revenue Comes from the Top 1% of Monetizing Publishers—Sensor Tower App Marketing Blog," May 10, 2016, Sensortower.com, https://sensortower.com/blog/app-store-one-percent.
5. This typical conversion rate comes from B. Brandall, "Freemium Conversion Rate: Why Spotify Destroys Dropbox by 667%," *Process Street*, March 29, 2016, www.process.st/freemium-conversion-rate/.
6. This idea originally comes from the concept of customer jobs to be done (JTBDs) from Harvard professor Clayton Christensen (C. M. Christensen and M. E. Raynor, *The Innovator's Solution: Creating and Sustaining Successful Growth* [Boston, MA: Harvard Business School Press, 2003]) and was summarized most usefully in D. Silverstein, P. Samuel, and N. DeCarlo. "Technique 1—Jobs to Be Done: The Innovator's Toolkit," *The Innovator's Toolkit*, n.d., http://innovatorstoolkit.com/content/technique-1-jobs-be-done. It was recently made popular again in the Osterwalder *et al.* book on value propositions: A. Osterwalder, Y. Pigneur, G. Bernarda, A. Smith, and T. Papadakos, *Value Proposition Design: How to Create Products and Services Customers Want* (Hoboken, NJ: Wiley, 2014).
7. The figures come from N. Patel, "How to Calculate Lifetime Value—The Infographic," *Neil Patel*, August 18, 2011, https://neilpatel.com/blog/how-to-calculate-lifetime-value/, although the computation was unique to this example. Other useful places to learn about LTV/CLV are B. Sugars, "How to Calculate the Lifetime Value of a Customer," *Entrepreneur*, August 8, 2012, www.entrepreneur.com/article/224153; A. Kucheriavy, "How to Calculate Customer Lifetime Value (CLV) to Market to High Value Customers," *Intechnic*, 2017, www.intechnic.com/blog/how-to-calculate-customer-lifetime-value-clv-to-market-to-high-value-customers/, which also offers a free Excel template to compute CLV/LTV for B2B and B2C businesses; and T. Walker, "How to Calculate & Increase Customer Lifetime Value," *CXL*, March 5, 2014, http://conversionxl.com/blog/customer-lifetime-value/.
8. This list is hardly comprehensive or exhaustive, but it reflects the convergence of several great thinkers about customer service in small business including, K. Blanchard, S. Bowles, and H. Mackay. *Raving*

Fans: A Revolutionary Approach to Customer Service (New York: William Morrow, 1993); S. Godin, *Permission Marketing: Turning Strangers into Friends and Friends into Customers* (New York: Simon & Schuster, 1999); A. Weinzweig, *Zingerman's Guide to Giving Great Service* (New York: Hyperion, 2004); B. Burlingham, *Small Giants: Companies That Choose to Be Great Instead of Big*, updated ed. (New York: Portfolio, 2007); T. Hsieh, *Delivering Happiness: A Path to Profits, Passion, and Purpose* (New York: Grand Central Publishing, 2010).

9. See, for example, William O. Bearden, Thomas N. Ingram, and Raymond W. LaForge, *Marketing: Principles & Perspectives,* 4th ed. (Boston: McGraw-Hill, 2004), pp. 147–176.
10. Sumit K. Kundu and Jerome A. Katz, "Born-International SMEs: Bi-level Impacts of Resources and Intentions," *Small Business Economics* 20, no. 1 (2003), pp. 25–47.
11. Karen E. Spaeder, "Who Is Your Market—and What Do They Want?," *Entrepreneur*, March 18, 2002, www.entrepreneur.com/article/50024.
12. Cliff Ennico, "Expanding Your Target Market," *Entrepreneur*, October 28, 2002, www.entrepreneur.com/article/56528.
13. Laura Clampitt Douglas, "Landing Customers," *Entrepreneur,* March 2, 2002, www.entrepreneur.com/article/49568.
14. Laura Tiffany, "Researching Your Market," *Entrepreneur*, August 7, 2001, www.entrepreneur.com/article/43024.
15. S. Hogarth-Scott, K. Watson, and N. Wilson, "Do Small Businesses Have to Practice Marketing to Survive and Grow?," *Marketing Intelligence and Planning* 14, no. 1 (1996).
16. Data for this table were extracted from www.websurveyor.com in 2012. The site has since gone out of business, but the costs remain approximately right.
17. See Gerald Zaltman, "Rethinking Market Research: Putting People Back In," *Journal of Marketing Research*, November 1997, pp. 424–437; Stephen Groves and Raymond P. Fisk, "Observational Data Collection Methods for Services Marketing: An Overview," *Journal of the Academy of Marketing Science*, Summer 1992, pp. 216–224; Rebecca Piirto, "Socks, Ties, Videotapes," *American Demographics,* September 1991.
18. Stever Robbins, "Down and Dirty Market Research," *Entrepreneur,* August 12, 2002, www.entrepreneur.com/article/54550.
19. Judith Langer, "15 Myths of Qualitative Research: It's Conventional, but Is It Wisdom?," *Marketing News*, March 1, 1999, pp. 13–14.
20. See Janet Ilieva, Steve Baron, and Nigel M. Healey, "Online Surveys in Marketing Research: Pros and Cons," *International Journal of Marketing Research* 44, no. 3 (2002), pp. 361–376; Michael P. Cronin, "On-the-Cheap Market Research," *Inc.,* June 1992, p. 108; Robert Hayes, "Internet-Based Surveys Provide Fast Results," *Marketing News*, April 13, 1998, p. 13; Phil Levine, Bill Ahlauser, Dale Kulp, and Rick Hunter, "Internet Interviewing," *Marketing Research*, Summer 1999, pp. 33–36.
21. Paul E. Green, Yoram Wind, Abba M. Krieger, and Paul Saatsoglou, "Applying Qualitative Data," *Marketing Research*, Spring 2000, pp. 17–25.
22. Don Debelek, "Want Some of This?," *Entrepreneur*, June 2002, www.entrepreneur.com/article/51926.
23. Phaedra Hise, "Grandma Got Run Over by Bad Research," *Inc.*, January 1998, www.inc.com/magazine/19980101/851.html.
24. Prior to 2019, County Business Patterns included information on annual sales (called "receipts") for businesses by NAICS number. That seems to have stopped, but you can find the successor datasets and tables at www.census.gov/topics/business-economy/production.html.
25. Sherri Dorfman, "Value Proposition," *Marketing News,* March 2, 2006, 54; John Williams, "Building a Money-Making Brand," February 6, 2006, www.entrepreneur.com/marketing/branding/imageandbrandingcolumnistjohnwilliams/article83258.html; Dodo Zu Knyphausen-Aufsess, "Corporate Venture Capital: Who Adds Value?," *Venture Capital: An International Journal of Entrepreneurial Finance* 7, no. 1 (January–March 2005), pp. 23–49.
26. The details of the canvas can be found in A. Osterwalder, Y. Pigneur, G. Bernarda, A. Smith, and T. Papadakos, *Value Proposition Design: How to Create Products and Services Customers Want* (Hoboken, NJ: Wiley, 2014). It can also be found online at http://businessmodelgeneration.com/canvas/vpc. The graphic displayed in the skill module is downloaded from that URL.
27. This is the customer "job to be done" approach developed by the Strategyn Group (T. Ulwick, "Strategyn," Strategyn, n.d., https://strategyn.com/jobs-to-be-done/) and popularized by Clayton Christensen and Michael Raynor in C. M. Christensen, and M. E. Raynor, *The Innovator's Solution: Creating and Sustaining Successful Growth* (Boston, MA: Harvard Business School Press, 2003). I first learned about the practical approach to this from D. Silverstein, P. Samuel, and N. DeCarlo, "Technique 1—Jobs to Be Done: The Innovator's Toolkit," The Innovator's Toolkit, n.d. http://innovatorstoolkit.com/content/technique-1-jobs-be-done.
28. I found these suggestions and several others in a wonderful blog post, T. Grønsund, "7 Proven Templates for Writing Value Propositions That Work," *Tor on Tech*, November 29, 2011, http://torgronsund.com/2011/11/29/7-proven-templates-for-creating-value-propositions-that-work/. Tor, in turn, pulled ideas from E. Sink, "Marketing Is Not a Post-Processing Step," June 6, 2003, http://ericsink.com/Positioning.html; S. Blank, "How To Build a Web Startup—Lean LaunchPad Edition," *Steve Blank*, September 22, 2011, https://steveblank.com/2011/09/22/how-to-build-a-web-startup-lean-launchpad-edition/; "Pitching Hacks Preview," www.slideshare.net/venturehacks/pitching-hacks-preview.
29. The ESB version model has been developed from several sources. The oldest work I've seen for this model was J. E. Urbany and J. H. Davis, "Strategic Insight in Three Circles," *Harvard Business Review*, November 1, 2007, https://hbr.org/2007/11/strategic-insight-in-three-circles. Another version of this work was Joel E. Urbany and James H. Davis, *Growth and Competitive Strategy in 3 Circles 1.0: Flat World Education*, 2011, Figure 5.3, http://catalog.flatworldknowledge.com/bookhub/reader/5581. A slightly different version can be found in D. Grewal and M. Levy, *M: Marketing,* 5th ed. (Burr Ridge, IL: McGraw-Hill, 2016), Exhibit 9.8, p. 186; Grewal and Levy cite that they built on the work of John Bers of Vanderbilt and Ronald Goodstein of Georgetown.
30. Laura Tiffany, "How to Create a Marketing Plan," *Entrepreneur*, August 7, 2001, www.entrepreneur.com/article/0,4621,291706,00.html.
31. Larry Chiagouris and Brant Wansley "Start-Up Marketing," *Marketing Management* 12, no. 5 (September–October 2003), p. 39.
32. Donald Lehmann and Russell Winer, *Analysis for Market Planning*, 6th ed. (Burr Ridge, IL: McGraw-Hill, 2005).
33. Gwen Moran, "23 Hours to a Great Marketing Plan," *Entrepreneur*, June 1, 2006, www.entrepreneur.com/article/159816.
34. C. Ratcliff, "Telling Stories: Five Successful Marketing Examples," Econsultancy, n.d., http://econsultancy.com/blog/63710-telling-stories-five-successful-marketing-examples/?utm_campaign=bloglikes&utm_medium=socialnetwork&utm_source=facebook; N. Bahadur, "How Dove Tried to Change the Conversation about Female Beauty," *The Huffington Post*, February 6, 2014, www.huffingtonpost.com/2014/01/21/dove-real-beauty-campaign-turns-10_n_4575940.html; Dove, "The Dove Campaign for Real Beauty," n.d., www.dove.us/Social-Mission/campaign-for-real-beauty.aspx.
35. You can learn about working with colleges on small business research in Gundry, L. K. and A. A. Buchko. *Field Casework: Methods for Consulting to Small and Startup Businesses* (Thousand Oaks: SAGE Publications, Inc, 1996). For the general process, look at Research, I. R. N. and G. Giddings. "How to Commission a Market Research Study | IRN Research," n.d. http://www.irn-research.com/howtoguides/howtocommission/.

36. Robert G. Cooper and Elko J. Kleinschmidt, "Benchmarking the Firm's Critical Success Factors in New Business Development," *The Journal of Product Innovation Management* 12 (1995), pp. 374–391.
37. Laura Tiffany, "Got a Lemon?," *Entrepreneur*, May 1999, www.entrepreneur.com/article/17646; Tim W. Know, "Evaluating Your e-Business Idea," *Entrepreneur,* May 26, 2003, www.entrepreneur.com/article/184990.
38. Albert H. Rubenstein, "At the Front End of the R&D/Innovation Process: Idea Development and Entrepreneurship," *International Journal of Technology* 9, nos. 5, 6, 7 (1994), pp. 652–678.
39. Don Debelak, "Inspired Minds Want to Know," *Entrepreneur*, January 1999, www.entrepreneur.com/article/17050.
40. Don Debelak, "Testing the Waters," *Entrepreneur*, February 1998, www.entrepreneur.com/article/0,4621,228009,00.html.
41. D. Taylor, "How Do I Create a Private, Closed Facebook Group?," AskDaveTaylor.com, January 2010, www.askdavetaylor.com/how_to_create_private_closed_facebook_group.html.
42. Greg A. Stevens and James Burley, "Piloting the Rocket of Radical Innovation," *Research Technology Management* 46, no. 2 (March–April 2003), pp. 16–26. See also Greg A. Stevens and James Burley, "3000 Raw Ideas, 1 Commercial Success!," *Research Technology Management* 40, no. 3 (May–June 1997), pp. 16–27.
43. Phillip Kotler and Gary Armstrong, *Principles of Marketing*, 9th ed. (New York: Prentice Hall, 2000).
44. Don Debelak, "I Needed That," *Entrepreneur*, May 2002, www.entrepreneur.com/article/51140.
45. Robert McMath and Thom Forbes, "Look Before You Leap," *Entrepreneur*, April 1998, www.entrepreneur.com/article/15414.
46. Teresa McUsic, "Differentiate Those Differences to Stay Competitive," *St. Louis Post Dispatch*, April 17, 2000, p. BP17.
47. Kim T. Gordon, "Pros and Cons of Expanding Your Product Line," *Entrepreneur*, June 7, 2004, www.entrepreneur.com/article/71094.
48. Rosabeth Moss Kantor, "The 15-Minute Competitive Advantage," *Business 2.0*, February 2002, p. 87.
49. R. McMath, "Inventions, Profitability—Look Before You Leap," *Entrepreneur*, April 1, 1998, www.entrepreneur.com/article/15414.
50. Arundhati Parmar, "Where Are They Now?," *Marketing News*, April 14, 2003, pp. 1, 13, 14.
51. Statista reported 1 million units sold in 2007 and 16.8 million sold in 2018: Medium, "LP/Vinyl Album Sales in the United States from 1993 to 2018 (in million units)," www-statista-com.ezp.slu.edu/statistics/188822/lp-album-sales-in-the-united-states-since-2009/ (accessed May 16, 2019). Also see: Wikipedia, "Phonograph Record," n.d., https://en.wikipedia.org/w/index.php?title=Phonograph_record&oldid=895694602 (accessed May 16, 2019).
52. Adam Barak and Geoffrey Wilson, "Pricing Policies to Handle Patent Loss or Expiry," *International Journal of Medical Marketing* 3, no. 3, June 2003, p. 245.
53. Adam Barak and Geoffrey Wilson, "Pricing Policies to Handle Patent Loss or Expiry," *International Journal of Medical Marketing* 3, no. 3, June 2003, p. 245.
54. Personal interviews with Dongzhou Gongbu and from a business plan for the Aba Sichuan Dairy Company written by Dr. Susan D. Peters, July 2002.

Chapter 10

1. This vignette was developed using material taken from an interview with Addie Swartz, conducted by Jill Kickul in April 2004, as well as excerpted from the Beacon Street Girls press release, "Introducing The Beacon Street Girls, Entrepreneur/Mother of Two Creates Fun, Values-oriented Books and Accessories for Girls Who Are, Between Toys and Boys'," written by Ellen Miller and Alan Ryan.
2. For this we use a CTR (click-through rate) of 3.17 percent and a CVR (conversion rate) of 3.75 percent, so the number would be 1000 × 0.0317 × 0.0375, or 1.18 purchases per 1,000 impressions. These numbers are 2018 averages across industries. Source: M. Irvine, "Google Ads Benchmarks for YOUR Industry [Updated!]," WordStream, April 10, 2019, www.wordstream.com/blog/ws/2016/02/29/google-adwords-industry-benchmarks.
3. William O. Bearden, Thomas N. Ingram, and Raymond W. LaForge, *Marketing,* 4th ed. (Boston, MA: McGraw-Hill, 2004); Robert L. Desatnick, *Managing to Keep the Customer: How to Achieve and Maintain Superior Customer Service throughout the Organization* (San Francisco, CA: Jossey-Bass,1988); Rafi A. Mohammed, Robert J. Fisher, Bernard J. Jaworski, and Gordon J. Paddison, *Internet Marketing: Building Advantage in a Networked Economy,* 2nd ed. (Boston: McGraw-Hill/Irwin-MarketSpaceU, 2004).
4. Story, L. "Anywhere the Eye Can See, It's Likely to See an Ad." *The New York Times*, January 15, 2007, sec. Media. https://www.nytimes.com/2007/01/15/business/media/15everywhere.html. Bloor, R. "The Crazed Battle For Your Attention." *Medium*, October 18, 2019. https://medium.com/permissionio/the-crazed-battle-for-your-attention-7d207f31d688.
5. Lance E. Brouthers and George Nakos, "The Role of Systematic International Market Selection on Small Firms Export Performance," *Journal of Small Business Management* 43, no. 4 (2005), pp. 363–381; Roy Williams, "Target Your Market with Appropriate Ad Copy," *Entrepreneur*, April 11, 2005, www.entrepreneur.com/advertising/adcolumnistroyhwilliams/article76978.html.
6. The sources for these numbers are: (number of websites) Internet Live Stats, "Total Number of Websites—Internet Live Stats," May 24, 2019, www.internetlivestats.com/total-number-of-websites/; (social media users) Statista, "Topic: Social Media Statistics," n.d., www.statista.com/topics/1164/social-networks/=; (bloggers) Statista, "U.S. Number of Bloggers 2020," n.d., www.statista.com/statistics/187267/number-of-bloggers-in-usa/: (newspapers) Statista, "Number of Daily Newspapers in the U.S. 2016," n.d., www.statista.com/statistics/183408/number-of-us-daily-newspapers-since-1975/; (magazines) Statista, "Number of Magazines in the United States 2002–2017," n.d., www.statista.com/statistics/238589/number-of-magazines-in-the-united-states/; (television channels) Wikipedia, "List of United States Pay Television Channels," May 18, 2019, https://en.wikipedia.org/w/index.php?title=List_of_United_States_pay_television_channels&oldid=897687678.
7. This idea was initially presented in G. Dietrich, "The Differences between Paid, Earned, Owned, and Shared Media," AllBusiness.Com, June 7, 2013, www.allbusiness.com/the-differences-between-paid-earned-owned-and-shared-media-4246-1.html; G. Dietrich, "The Four Different Types of Media," *Spin Sucks*, June 24, 2013, https://spinsucks.com/communication/the-four-different-types-of-media/. Dietrich expanded the idea in her book G. Dietrich, *Spin Sucks: Communication and Reputation Management in the Digital Age* (Indianapolis, IN: Que Publishing, 2014). A blogging website called https://spinsucks.com was built from her book.
8. In addition to Dietrich's original versions noted in the immediate prior footnote, we also were informed by other marketing experts' takes on the PESO Model including L. Goldsberry, "How the PESO Model May Change the Way You Think about PR," n.d. www.axiapr.com/blog/how-the-peso-model-may-change-the-way-you-think-about-pr; N. Ochieng, "What the PESO Model Got Wrong," March 20, 2018, www.axiapr.com/blog/what-the-peso-model-got-wrong (which both have a much more involved earned media section given Axia's expertise in PR); S. Robinson, "What Is the PESO Model for Marketing?," *Iterative Marketing*, November 2, 2016, https://iterativemarketing.net/peso-model-marketing/, who builds from Dietrich's model but offers some analytic

differences, especially his "Pros and Cons" list; J. Macnamara, M. Lwin, A. Adi, and A. Zerfass, "'PESO' Media Strategy Shifts to 'SOEP': Opportunities and Ethical Dilemmas," *Public Relations Review* 42, no. 3 (September 1, 2016), pp. 377–385, which gives a marketing professor's take on the fine points of the model.

9. Roy E. Disney, "Shareholders Meeting Remarks," in a report of the U.S. Securities and Exchange Commission, March 3, 2004, www.sec.gov/Archives/edgar/data/1001039/000089534504000132/drpx14a6g-disney_disney.txt.
10. This approach builds from a convergence of academic and practitioner sources including K. Punjaisri and A. Wilson, "The Role of Internal Branding in the Delivery of Employee Brand Promise," *The Journal of Brand Management* 15, no. 1 (September 1, 2007), pp. 57–70; A. Rao, "Value Promise versus Value Delivery," *Journal of Creating Value* 1, no. 1 (May 1, 2015), pp. 91–100; S. Kirchner, "How to Write a Killer Brand Promise That Helps You Stand Out from the Crowd," *The Work at Home Woman*, March 10, 2011, www.theworkathomewoman.com/how-to-write-a-killer-brand-promise-that-helps-you-stand-out-from-the-crowd/; K. Leifer, "The Best Brand Promise Examples We've Seen," *LinkedIn Pulse*, April 27, 2015, www.linkedin.com/pulse/best-brand-promise-examples-weve-seen-kevin-leifer; T. Tyrell-Smith, "What's Your Brand Promise? Fix, Build And Drive™," June 9, 2011, http://fixbuildanddrive.com/whats-your-brand-promise/.
11. S. Kirchner, "How to Write a Killer Brand Promise That Helps You Stand Out from the Crowd," *The Work at Home Woman*, March 10, 2011, www.theworkathomewoman.com/how-to-write-a-killer-brand-promise-that-helps-you-stand-out-from-the-crowd/.
12. Rule number 8 of "Norman Ray Lambert's 13 Golden Rules," www.throwedrolls.com/shopcontent.asp?type=13Rules.
13. This follows a quote attributed to Richard Branson of Virgin Companies, "Brands always mean something. If you don't define what the brand means, your competitors will," www.azquotes.com/quote/875385.
14. Susan Fournier, "Consumers and Their Brands: Developing Relationship Theory in Consumer Research," *Journal of Consumer Research*, March 1998, pp. 343–373.
15. Chiranjeev Kohli and Douglas W. LaBahn, "Creating Effective Brand Names: A Study of the Naming Process," *Journal of Advertising Research*, January–February 1997, pp. 67–75. See also Leonard L. Berry, Edwin F. Lefkowith, and Terry Clark, "In Services, What's in a Name?," *Harvard Business Review*, September–October 1998, pp. 28–30.
16. One caveat when you check on a name: Whois.net and most of the other places you can check for domain name availability sell their daily searches to hundreds of individuals and companies. Those buyers look at the names and decide which domain names to buy up before the searcher buys the name they searched for. So when you search, search from a site where you can buy domain names inexpensively ($8/year is a good price on average), and if you see a name you like, don't wait! Buy it today. It could be on sale for $200 tomorrow.
17. Anonymous, "SCORE's Top Marketing and Public Relations Tips," *Entrepreneur,* December 6, 2006, www.entrepreneur.com/grow/score/index.html#market.
18. Michael Myser, "Marketing Made Easy," *Business 2.0,* June 2006, pp. 43–45.
19. The range of social media sites you could be on is truly staggering. The Conversation Prism 5.0 shows 28 different categories of social media platforms with a couple of hundred entries total. See this at https://conversationprism.com/. Your goal should be to have a presence where enough of your target customers are to make a difference in sales.
20. Terri Lammers Prior (ed.), *301 Great Ideas for Selling Smarter* (Boston, MA: Inc. Publishing, 1998).
21. Geyser, W. "8 Influencer Marketing Platforms to Amplify Your Campaigns." *Influencer Marketing Hub*, January 18, 2017. https://influencermarketinghub.com/8-top-influencer-marketing-platforms/. Bannister, K. "Influencer Marketing Tools for Finding Influencers." *Brandwatch*, January 23, 2019. https://www.brandwatch.com/blog/find-influencers-marketing-tools/.
22. C. Ziles, "How to Negotiate Macro and Micro Influencer Deals," *Social Media HQ*, February 4, 2019, https://socialmediahq.com/how-to-negotiate-macro-and-micro-influencer-deals/; J. Chen, "An Expert's Guide to Influencer Marketing," *Sprout Social*, May 5, 2019, https://sproutsocial.com/insights/influencer-marketing/.
23. K. Bodnar, "10 Simple Strategies for Business Blog Content," *HubSpot Blog*, June 1, 2010, http://blog.hubspot.com/blog/tabid/6307/bid/6023/10-Simple-Strategies-for-Business-Blog-Content.aspx?utm_source=feedburner.
24. Michael V. Copeland and Andrew Tilin, "The New Instant Companies," *Business 2.0*, June 2005, pp. 82–94.
25. Today there is a lot of discussion online about "paid blogger reviews" (search for the term), and some of the best includes: H. Agrawal, "How Much You Should Charge for Paid Reviews?," *ShoutMeLoud*, February 19, 2010, www.shoutmeloud.com/how-much-you-should-charge-for-paid-reviews.html; S. A. Dunleview, "Are You Being Conned? Fair Sponsored Blog Post Rates and Best Practice Guidelines," *Successful Blogging*, July 20, 2012, www.successfulblogging.com/sponsored-blog-post-rates/; J. A. Miller, "The Ethical Freelancer: Charging Fees for a Product Review?," June 3, 2014, http://jenamiller.com/notes-from-a-hired-pen/the-ethical-freelancer-two-big-no-nos/; K. McKibbin, "Reader Q & A: How Much Should I Charge for a Blog Post or Sponsored Post?: Make Money Blogging," *Secret Bloggers' Business: Make Money Blogging*, June 18, 2014, www.secretbloggers-business.com/how-much-should-i-charge-for-a-blog-post/.
26. Anonymous, "SCORE's Top Marketing and Public Relations Tips," *Entrepreneur,* December 6, 2006, www.entrepreneur.com/article/0,4621,324728,00.html.
27. Nichole L. Torres, "Almost Famous," *Entrepreneur*, June 2003, www.entrepreneur.com/magazine/entreperneursstartupsmagazine/2003/june/62194.html; Anonymous, "60-Second Guide to Generating Publicity for Your Business," *Entrepreneur,* 2007, www.entrepreneur.com/growyourbusiness/scoreresources/60secondguides/article81348.html.
28. Al Lautenslager, "The Ingredients of a Press Kit," *Entrepreneur*, 2007, www.entrepreneur.com/marketing/publicrelations/prbasics/article57260.html; J. Callahn, "Press Pages and Media Kits: Include These 7 Items to Please Reporters," *Zapier*, March 26, 2015, https://zapier.com/blog/best-press-kit/.
29. Based on information from the following: Al Lautenslager, "A Press Release Primer," *Entrepreneur*, 2007, www.entrepreneur.com/marketing/publicrelations/gettingpress/article62050.html; Randall Hansen, *A Barebones Guide to Writing Successful Press Releases* (Deland, FL: Stetson Marketing Department, 2005), www.stetson.edu/~rhansen/prhowto.html.
30. This is an actual title of a case study by Richard P. Green II and Susan D. Peters.
31. Catherine Seda, "Make a Great First Impression," *Entrepreneur*, October 2006, www.entrepreneur.com/ebusiness/gettingtraffic/article167634.html.
32. S. Gunelius, "Find Blogs You Want to Read," *Lifewire*, December 15, 2018, www.lifewire.com/how-to-find-blogs-3476351.
33. J. Wilcox, "MTurk + Google News API = Press," *Customer Development Labs*, September 24, 2013, http://customerdevlabs.com/2013/09/24/google-news-api-mturk-press/.
34. Deborah L. Vence, "Cookie Dough," *Marketing News,* October 27, 2003, p. 10.

35. For all her tips and more details, see Margie Fisher, "10 Creative Ways to Get PR," *Entrepreneur,* February 6, 2006, www.entrepreneur.com/marketing/publicrelations/article83268.html.
36. G. Kimbrell, "7 Ways to Build Rock-Solid Relationships with Your Investors," *Entrepreneur*, March 12, 2015, www.entrepreneur.com/article/243456; E. Cachette, "5 Steps to Good Investor Relations," *Inc.*, November 12, 2013, www.inc.com/ellie-cachette/springboard-five-steps-to-good-investor-relations.html.
37. The ideas here come from several sources: T. Giannattasio, "Need to Get People Paying Attention to Your Brand? Hold a Contest," *Entrepreneur*, July 10, 2018, www.entrepreneur.com/article/315042; W. Keller, "How a Contest or Giveaway Can Attract Business Prospects," *Entrepreneur*, December 20, 2016, www.entrepreneur.com/article/284851; M. Konigsmark, "You Win When Using Giveaways to Grow Your Social Audience," *Entrepreneur*, June 6, 2014, www.entrepreneur.com/article/234558.
38. T. Giannattasio, "Need to Get People Paying Attention to Your Brand? Hold a Contest," *Entrepreneur*, July 10, 2018, www.entrepreneur.com/article/315042.
39. "How to Create a Simple Small Business Lead Generation Process," *Insider Group Member: Making Money Online Blog*, March 4, 2019, www.insidergroupmember.com/2019/03/04/how-to-create-a-simple-small-business-lead-generation-process/; R. Myers, "How to Create a Simple Small Business Lead Generation Process," *Bplans Blog*, March 4, 2019, https://articles.bplans.com/how-to-create-a-simple-small-business-lead-generation-process/.
40. G. Burrus, "Advertorial? Can It Help Your Small Business as a Solo Entrepreneur?," *EzineArticles*, September 23, 2008, https://ezinearticles.com/?Advertorial?-Can-it-Help-Your-Small-Business-As-a-Solo-Entrepreneur?&id=1522663; "10 Pointers for Crafting an Effective Advertorial," *Entrepreneur*, January 9, 2007, www.entrepreneur.com/article/172780; Y. Grauer, "4 Steps to Creating Advantageous Advertorials," *VerticalResponse Blog*, August 11, 2014, www.verticalresponse.com/blog/4-steps-to-creating-advantageous-advertorials/; V. Michener, "Sample Advertorials to Spark Your Marketing," *MyFavoriteMarketer*, October 15, 2012, https://myfavoritemarketer.com/sample-advertorials/.
41. You can get additional details on doing this in the lean start-up way at B. Dorf and S. Blank, "Startup Owner's Manual: How to 'Get' Customers," *Entrepreneur*, June 13, 2012, www.entrepreneur.com/article/223770; S. G. Blank and B. Dorf, *The Startup Owner's Manual: The Step-by-Step Guide for Building a Great Company,* vol. 1 (Pescadero, California: K & S Ranch, Inc, 2012).
42. Michael Warshaw," A Web Strategy Runs through It," *Inc.*, November 1, 2001, www.inc.com/magazine/20011101/23622.html.
43. The video is at www.youtube.com/watch?v=9D_UXPPYTql. The story came from J. Niesen, "St. Louis-Style Pizza Deserves More Respect," SI.Com, November 29, 2017, www.si.com/eats/2017/11/29/jayson-tatum-st-louis-style-pizza-imos; Staff writer, "Imo's Adds Jayson Tatum as Spokesman," *St. Louis Business Journal*, August 22, 2017, www.bizjournals.com/stlouis/news/2017/08/22/imos-adds-jayson-tatum-as-spokesman.html; Staff writer, "Jayson Tatum Joins Imo's Pizza as New Spokesperson," *St. Louis American*, August 22, 2017, www.stlamerican.com/sports/local_sports/jayson-tatum-joins-imo-s-pizza-as-new-spokesperson/article_d48880f6-8774-11e7-abe8-0328600e4287.html.
44. Two great resources for understanding content marketing and its issues are J. Sonderman and M. Tran, "The Rise of Sponsored Content and Native Advertising in News," *American Press Institute*, November 14, 2013, www.americanpressinstitute.org/publications/reports/white-papers/understanding-rise-sponsored-content/; C. Pollitt, "Everything You Need to Know about Sponsored Content," *Moz*, January 20, 2015, https://moz.com/blog/everything-you-need-to-know-about-sponsored-content. A good source for practical applications is Mediakix Team, "What Is Sponsored Content? Definition, Application, & Examples," Mediakix, September 28, 2015, http://mediakix.com/2015/09/what-is-sponsored-content/.
45. Based on the following: Jack Ferrari, "Selling 101," *Entrepreneur*, November 1, 2005; *Principles of Advertising & IMC,* 2nd ed. (Boston, MA: McGraw-Hill, 2005), pp. 523–527; Barry Farber, "On the Horizon" *Entrepreneur,* January 2001, p. 119; Brian Caulfield, "How to Land the Deal," *Business 2.0,* April 2004, p. 85.
46. Alan J. Zell "Business Etiquette—The Rule for Business Survival," http://sellingselling.com/articles/bizetq.html.
47. Cord Cooper, "The Art of Closing a Deal," *Investor's Business Daily*, March 2, 2003; Cord Cooper, "Deal with People Effectively—Stressing Value over Cost," *Investor's Business Daily*, January 27, 2005, p. A3; Cord Cooper, "Deal with People Effectively—Sidestep Sales Slip-Ups," *Investor's Business Daily*, February 24, 2005, p. A3; Cord Cooper, "Deal and Communicate Effectively—Hit Your Mark Each Time," *Investor's Business Daily*, July 14, 2005, p. A4; Cord Cooper, "Take Action—Art of a Successful Deal," *Investor's Business Daily*, November 23, 2005, p. A4; Cord Cooper, "Deal with People Effectively—How to Clinch the Deal," *Investors Business Daily,* September 7, 2006, p. A3; Cord Cooper, "Cut New Deals, and Win," *Investor's Business Daily*, March 27, 2007, p. A3.
48. For more information on the steps of personal selling, visit www.udel.edu/alex/chapt20.html and Sales & Marketing Top Secrets at www.entrepreneur.com.
49. William O. Bearden, Thomas N. Ingram, and Raymond W. LaForge, *Marketing,* 4th ed. (Boston, MA: McGraw-Hill, 2004); Frederick F. Reichheld and W. Earl Sasser Jr., "Zero Defections: Quality Comes to Services," *Harvard Business Review* 5 (1990), pp. 105–111; Rafi A. Mohammed, Robert J. Fisher, Bernard J. Jaworski, and Gordon J. Paddison, *Internet Marketing: Building Advantage in a Networked Economy,* 2nd ed. (Boston, MA: McGraw-Hill/Irwin-MarketSpaceU, 2004).
50. LoyaltyOne Consulting, Verde Group, and D. Small, "2015 Customer Experience Risk Study—Executive Summary," 2015, www.verdegroup.com/whitepapers/2015-Customer-Experience-Risk-Study-Verde-Group.pdf.
51. Ibid.
52. Charles M. Futrell, *Fundamentals of Selling: Customers for Life through Service* (Boston, MA: McGraw-Hill/Irwin, 2006).
53. This process was built by the authors from several sources: C. Futrell, *Fundamentals of Selling: Customers for Life through Service,* 13th ed. (New York: McGraw-Hill/Irwin, 2013); D. Grewal and M. Levy, *M: Marketing,* 5th ed. (Burr Ridge, IL: McGraw-Hill/Irwin, 2016); W. Bearden, T. Ingram, and R. LaForge, *Marketing: Principles and Perspectives,* 4th ed. (New York: McGraw-Hill/Irwin, 2003); Newtek—The Small Business Authority, "7 Steps for Dealing with Angry Customers," *Forbes*, August 2, 2013, www.forbes.com/sites/thesba/2013/08/02/7-steps-for-dealing-with-angry-customers/; Young Entrepreneur Council, "17 Ways to Deal with Unhappy Customers," Inc.com, September 30, 2013, www.inc.com/young-entrepreneur-council/17-ways-to-deal-with-unhappy-customers.html; T. Hopkins, "How to Handle an Angry Client," *Entrepreneur*, May 2, 2005, www.entrepreneur.com/article/77404; C. Tice, "Seven Ways to Keep Angry Customers (Like Me) Happy," *Entrepreneur*, February 22, 2012, www.entrepreneur.com/article/222860.
54. William O. Bearden, Thomas N. Ingram, and Raymond W. LaForge, *Marketing*, 4th ed. (Boston, MA: McGraw-Hill, 2004); Charles M. Futrell, *Fundamentals of Selling: Customers for Life through Service* (Boston, MA: McGraw-Hill/Irwin, 2006); Vince Pesce, *A Complete Manual of Professional Selling* (New York: Prentice Hall, 1989).
55. D. Mikkelson, "Nordstrom Tire Return," Snopes, n.d., www.snopes.com/business/consumer/nordstrom.asp; H. Khan, "How Nordstrom Made Its Brand Synonymous with Customer Service (and How You

Can Too)—Shopify," *Retail Marketing Blog—Retail News, Trends, Store Tips, and More by Shopify*, May 2, 2016, www.shopify.com/retail/119531651-how-nordstrom-made-its-brand-synonymous-with-customer-service-and-how-you-can-too; K. Grind, "REI, Nordstrom and the Perils of No-Questions-Asked Returns," *The Wall Street Journal*, September 18, 2013, http://blogs.wsj.com/moneybeat/2013/09/18/rei-nordstrom-and-the-perils-of-no-questions-asked-returns/.

56. The findings have been fairly consistent for several years, see LoyaltyOne Consulting, Verde Group, and D. Small, "2015 Customer Experience Risk Study—Executive Summary," 2015, www.verdegroup.com/whitepapers/2015-Customer-Experience-Risk-Study-Verde-Group.pdf, vs. RightNow Technologies. "RightNow's Annual Research Shows 86 Percent of U.S. Adults Will Pay More For A Better Customer Experience | Business Wire," January 11, 2012, which was summarized at http://www.businesswire.com/news/home/20120111005284/en/RightNow%E2%80%99s-Annual-Research-Shows-86-Percent-U.S.
57. Adapted from Rafi A. Mohammed, Robert J. Fisher, Bernard J. Jaworski, and Gordon J. Paddison, *Internet Marketing: Building Advantage in a Networked Economy*, 2nd ed. (Boston, MA: McGraw-Hill/Irwin-MarketSpaceU, 2004), p. 664.
58. You can get additional ideas on how to keep customers from B. Dorf and S. Blank, "How a Lean Startup Can Keep Customers," *Entrepreneur*, June 19, 2012, www.entrepreneur.com/article/223826; S. G. Blank and B. Dorf, *The Startup Owner's Manual: The Step-by-Step Guide for Building a Great Company*, vol. 1 (Pescadero, California: K & S Ranch, Inc., 2012).
59. You can also find some additional ideas on growing customers at B. Dorf and S. Blank, "Simple Sales Tips for Growing Your Customer Base," *Entrepreneur*, June 27, 2012, www.entrepreneur.com/article/223884; S. G. Blank and B. Dorf, *The Startup Owner's Manual: The Step-by-Step Guide for Building a Great Company*, vol. 1 (Pescadero, California: K & S Ranch, Inc., 2012).
60. See, for example, David M. Georgoff and Robert G. Murdock, "Manager's Guide to Forecasting," *Harvard Business Review*, January–February 1986, pp. 110–120; Angelo Guadagno, "Mastering the 'Magic' of Sales Forecasting," *American Salesman*, November 1, 1995; Carlo D. Smith, "An Integrated Model of Factors Affecting Sales Forecasting Management," *Academy of Marketing Science* 90, 1999; Donald McBane, "Benchmarking Sales Forecasting Performance Measures," *Journal of Personal Selling and Sales Management*, 2001.
61. Stever Robbins, "Down and Dirty Market Research," *Entrepreneur*, August 12, 2002, www.entrepreneur.com/article/0,4621,302407,00.html.
62. You can learn about shopping using bots and getting around them from I. S. Mangla, "3 Tricks to Help You Snag the Best Deals Online," *Time*, September 8, 2014, http://time.com/money/3136612/dynamic-pricing-amazon-best-buy-walmart/; Chandra Steele, "The 11 Best Shopping Apps to Compare Prices," *PCMAG*, July 10, 2019, www.pcmag.com/slideshow/story/290959/the-11-best-shopping-apps-to-compare-prices.
63. Steven K. Baker, "Forecasting Your Sales Revenue," *Entrepreneur*, May 7, 2001, www.entrepreneur.com/article/0,4621,389242,00.html.
64. A lot of the wisdom underlying this approach to sales forecasting and connecting it to the key financial drivers of the business comes from D. Rao, *Avoid VC Intelligently* (Minneapolis, MN: InterFinance Corporation, 2015); as well as Dileep's presentations at the Experiential Classroom.
65. Orabrush, "Story of Orabrush," Orabrush.com, www.orabrush.com/story; T. Wasserman, "Orabrush Parlays YouTube Success into Walmart Deal," Mashable, September 20, 2011, mashable.com/2011/09/20/orabrush-walmar/; L. Shackleton, "The Orabrush Story: How a Utah Man Used YouTube to Build a Multi-Million Dollar Business," *Google: Official Blog*, November 15, 2011, http://googleblog.blogspot.com/2011/11/orabrush-story-how-utah-man-used.html; J. Neff, "How Orabrush Got National Walmart Deal with YouTube Videos: News—Advertising Age," *Advertising Age*, September 20, 2011, http://adage.com/article/news/orabrush-national-walmart-deal-youtube-videos/229914/.

Chapter 11

1. Don Debelak, "Rookie Rules,"*Entrepreneur*, September 1999, www.entrepreneur.com/article/18240.
2. www.kyptonitelock.com; www.kryptonitelock.com/inetisscripts/abtinetis.exe/templateform@psublic?tn=aboout_media.
3. *Wine Cellar Insider*, "Screaming Eagle Napa California Cabernet Sauvignon Sauvignon Blanc," n.d., www.thewinecellarinsider.com/california-wine/screaming-eagle-california-wine-cabernet-sauvignon/.
4. S. N. Lewis, "The Chateau Mouton Lockdown," *The Wall Street Journal Weekend Journal* (2007), pp. W1 and W8.
5. O. C. Ferrell and M. D. Hartline, *Marketing Strategy* (Mason, OH: Thomson/South-Western, 2005), p. 193.
6. Robert McGarvey and Babs S. Harrison, "Name Your Price," *Entrepreneur*, July 2000, www.entrepreneur.com/article/29222; Beverly Williams, "The Price Is Right," *Entrepreneur*, October 3, 2000, www.entrepreneur.com/article/0,4621,280990,00.html; Ian Benoliel, "Pricing Your Product," *Entrepreneur*, July 22, 2002, www.entrepreneur.com/article/0,4621,301698,00.html; Rosalind Resnick, "Setting the Right Price," *Entrepreneur*, November 10, 2003, www.entrepreneur.com/ article/65484; Tim W. Knox, "Secrets to Setting Your Price," *Entrepreneur*, April 2, 2004, www.entrepreneur.com/article/70174; C. Beesley, "How to Price Your Small Business' Products and Services," U.S. Small Business Administration, September 19, 2012, www.sba.gov/blogs/how-price-your-small-business-products-and-services; B. W. Pollack, "What to Consider Before You Price Your Products," U.S. Small Business Administration, January 7, 2016, www.sba.gov/blogs/what-consider-you-price-your-products; telephone communication with Screaming Eagle Winery staff, June 22, 2012.
7. S. Seget, *Pharmaceutical Pricing Strategies* (London: Reuters Business Insight Healthcare, 2005).
8. W. W. Haynes, *Pricing Decisions in Small Business* (Lexington: University Press of Kentucky, 2015); George J. Avlonitis and Kostis A. Indounas. "Pricing Objectives and Pricing Methods in the Services Sector," *Journal of Services Marketing* 19, no. 1 (January 1, 2005), pp. 47–57; Charles R. Duke, "Matching Appropriate Pricing Strategy with Markets and Objectives," *Journal of Product & Brand Management* 3, no. 2 (June 1, 1994), pp. 15–27.
9. Darrell Zahorsky, "Super Charge Your Business with Profit Pricing Strategies," 2004, http://sbinformation.about.com/cs/marketresearch/a/pricing_p.htm.
10. "Inventing Success," *Business 2.0*, April 2003, p. 105.
11. Marty Nemko, "Perfecting Your Pricing Strategies," *Entrepreneur*, March 2000, *The Review of Financial Studies* 14, no. 2 (Summer 2001), pp. 433–458; Michel A. Habib and Alexander P. Ljungqvist, "Underpricing and Entrepreneurial Wealth Losses in IPOs: Theory and Evidence," *The Review of Financial Studies* 14, no. 2 (Summer 2001), pp. 433–458.
12. Cliff Ennico, "Set the Right Price for Your Product or Service," *Entrepreneur*, June 1, 2003, www.entrepreneur.com/article/62382.
13. J. R. Baum, E. A. Locke, and K. G. Smith, "A Multidimensional Model of Venture Growth," *Academy of Management Journal* 44, no. 2 (2001), pp. 292–303; Elisabeth J. Teal, Nancy Upton, and Samuel L. Seaman, "A Comparative Analysis of Strategic Marketing Practices of High-Growth U.S. Family and Nonfamily Firms," *Journal of Developmental Entrepreneurship* 8, no. 2 (August 2003), p. 177.

14. Timothy Matanovich, Gary L. Lillien, and Arvind Rangaswamy, "Engineering the Price-Value Relationship," *Marketing Management*, Spring 1999, pp. 48–53.
15. Julie Monahan, "Name Your Price," *Entrepreneur*, December 1999, www.entrepreneur.com/article/0,4621,231863,00.htm.
16. Cliff Ennico, "Set the Right Price for Your Product or Service," *Entrepreneur*, June 1, 2003, www.entrepreneur.com/article/62382; Tim W. Knox, "Secrets to Setting Your Price," *Entrepreneur,* April 2, 2004, www.entrepreneur.com/article/70174.
17. Bob Weinstein, "What Price Success," *Entrepreneur*, March 1999, www.entrepreneur.com/article/17366; Kim T. Gordon, "How to Price Your Product," *Entrepreneur*, March 5, 2001, www.entrepreneur.com/article/0,4621,287402,00.html; Julie Monahan, "Name Your Price," *Entrepreneur*, December 1999, www.entrepreneur.com/article/0,4621,231863,00.htm.
18. Don Debelak, "Look What I Found!," *Entrepreneur*, July 2002, www.entrepreneur.com/article/0,4621,300831,00.html.
19. K. Carroll and D. Coates, "Teaching Price Discrimination: Some Clarifications," *Southern Economic Journal* 66 (1999), pp. 466–480.
20. Mark Hendricks, "The Art of (Price) War," *Entrepreneur*, April 2002, www.entrepreneur.com/article/0,4621,297992,00.html.
21. Kim T. Gordon, "How to Price Your Product," *Entrepreneur*, March 5, 2001, www.entrepreneur.com/article/0,4621,287402,00.html.
22. Roberta Maynard, "Take the Guesswork Out of Pricing," *Nation's Business*, December 1997, pp. 27–30.
23. Bob Weinstein, "What Price Success," *Entrepreneur*, March 1999, www.entrepreneur.com/article/17366.
24. Jacquelyn Lynn, "The Middle of the Road," *Business Start-Ups*, December 1996, p. 33.
25. Julie Monahan, "Name Your Price," *Entrepreneur*, December 1999, www.entrepreneur.com/article/0,4621,231863,00.htm.
26. C. Beesley, "How to Price Your Small Business' Products and Services," U.S. Small Business Administration, September 19, 2012, www.sba.gov/blogs/how-price-your-small-business-products-and-services; B. W. Pollack, "What to Consider Before You Price Your Products," U.S. Small Business Administration, January 7, 2016, www.sba.gov/blogs/what-consider-you-price-your-products.
27. Eric Anderson and Duncan Simester, "Mind Your Pricing Cues," *Harvard Business Review* 81, no. 9 (September 2003), p. 96.
28. Joel Dean, "Pricing Policies for New Products," *Harvard Business Review* (November–December 1976), p. 141–153.
29. Jean-Noel Kapferer, "Managing Luxury Brands," *Journal of Brand Management*, July 1999, pp. 251–260.
30. Bob Weinstein, "What Price Success," *Entrepreneur*, March 1999, www.entrepreneur.com/article/17366.
31. Robert M. Schindler and Thomas Kilbarian, "Increased Consumer Sales Response through Use of 99-Ending Prices," *Journal of Retailing*, Summer 1996, pp. 187–199. See also Robert M. Schindler, "Patterns of Rightmost Digits Used in Advertising Prices: Implications for Nine-Ending Effects," *Journal of Consumer Research*, September 1997, pp. 192–201.
32. "When the Price Is Right," *Entrepreneur*, www.entrepreneur.com/article/54994.
33. Barbara Kiviat, "Sneaky Pricing," *Time*, September 19, 2003.
34. www.makersmarkcollector.com/home.shtml.
35. Priya Raghubir and Kim Corfman, "When Do Price Promotions Affect Pretrial Brand Evaluations?," *Journal of Marketing Research* 36 (1999), pp. 211–222.
36. Barbara Kiviat, "Sneaky Pricing," *Time*, September 19, 2003.
37. Thea Singer, "Upstarts: Children's Hair Salons," *Inc.*, July 2001, http://pf.inc.com/magazine/20010701/22874.html.
38. Antonio used one from Freelanceswitch, but that site merged with another firm's. However, there are several online website design price calculators. One of the best is DesignQuote's (www.designquote.net/html/dq_estimate_wizard.cfm), with Mazuzu's (https://mazuzu.com/pricing.html#pages=0&layouts=0&complexity=0&emails=0&options) a close second. Note there are also calculators designed to help you arrive at an hourly rate as a freelancer, which is another way to approach your pricing efforts. Good examples of this type of calculator include BeeWits (https://hourlyrate.beewits.com/) and Motiv (https://motivapp.com/freelance-hourly-rate-calculator).
39. HOW Staff, "Designers' Hourly Rates: Are You Charging Enough?," February 12, 2008, www.howdesign.com/design-business/pricing/hourly-rates/. The 2014 version staff (HOW, "Designers' Hourly Rates: Pricing Design Work," *HOW Design*, February 12, 2014, www.howdesign.com/design-business/pricing/hourly-rates/) worked with pretty much the same average figures.
40. Good examples include http://platowebdesign.com/web-design-pricing-calculator.php; www.designquote.net/; and www.buyerzone.com/internet/web-site-design. You can get some general guidelines for high-end efforts from R. Parr, "How Much Does a Website Cost in 2016?," *Executionists: Web Design, Development and Marketing Agency*, December 14, 2015, http://executionists.com/much-website-cost-2016/.
41. Ellen Rohr, "Keep Your Business from Closing," *Entrepreneur*, July 3, 2000, www.entrepreneur.com/article/29980.
42. Gwen Moran, "Flash!," *Entrepreneur*, June 2000, www.entrepreneur.com/article/29646.
43. Cliff Ennico, "Set the Right Price for Your Product or Service," *Entrepreneur,* June 1, 2003, www.entrepreneur.com/article/62382; Tony Parinello, "Should You Offer Extra Services or Lower Prices?," *Entrepreneur*, July 1, 2002, www.entrepreneur.com/article/53310.
44. See G. Bruce Friesen, "Dynamic Pricing: Teaching Your Clients to Dance," *Consulting to Management* 14, no. 1 (March 2003), pp. 33–38; Ellen Garbarino and Olivia F. Lee, "Dynamic Pricing in Internet Retail: Effects on Consumer Trust," *Psychology & Marketing* 20, no. 6 (June 2003), pp. 495–513.
45. "Sweepstakes, Contests, and Giveaway Laws," *Sara Hawkins*, May 10, 2011, http://sarafhawkins.com/blog-law-is-your-giveaway-legal/.
46. Corliss L. Green, "Media Exposure's Impact on Perceived Availability and Redemption of Coupons by Ethnic Customers," *Journal of Advertising Research* 25, no. 2 (March–April 1995), pp. 55–64.
47. Kapil Bawa and Srini S. Srinivasan, "Coupon Attractiveness and Coupon Proneness: A Framework for Modeling Coupon Redemption," *Journal of Marketing Research* 14, no. 4 (November 1997), pp. 517–525.
48. Peter Tat, William A. Cunningham III, and Emin Babakus, "Consumer Perceptions of Rebates," *Journal of Advertising Research* 28, no. 40 (August–September 1994), pp. 45–50.
49. John Burtzloff, "Keep Customers Coming Back for More," *Entrepreneur*, June 10, 2002, www.entrepreneur.com/article/52780.
50. Advice for these efforts is built on the suggestions of C. Zorzini, "Tips for Hosting Successful Giveaways & Competitions," Ecommerce Platforms, January 7, 2016, http://ecommerce-platforms.com/ecommerce-selling-advice/tips-hosting-successful-giveaways-competitions; C. Harrington, "How to Host a Successful, Stress-Free Blog Giveaway: 7 Things to Remember," *Independent Fashion Blogger*, May 23, 2013, http://heartifb.com/2013/05/23/how-to-host-a-successful-stress-free-blog-giveaway-7-things-to-remember/; "Sweepstakes, Contests, and Giveaway Laws," Sara Hawkins website, May 10, 2011, http://sarafhawkins.com/blog-law-is-your-giveaway-legal/.
51. If you're thinking about putting a contest together, check out these resources: Y. Grauer, "12 Tips to Running a Winning Social Media Contest," *Vertical Response Blog*, June 16, 2014, www.verticalresponse.com/blog/12-tips-to-running-a-winning-social-media-contest/; B. Matthew, "The Ultimate Guide to Running Online Competitions,"

Matthew Barby, September 19, 2013, www.matthewbarby.com/running-online-competitions/; J. Ledgard, "Step-by-Step Guide on How to Run Successful Contests," KickoffLabs, June 16, 2014, https://kickofflabs.com/blog/step-by-step-guide-on-running-successful-contests/; "Sweepstakes, Contests, and Giveaway Laws," Sara Hawkins website, May 10, 2011, http://sarafhawkins.com/blog-law-is-your-giveaway-legal/.

52. This advice is built from several sources: "Loyalty Marketing Best Practices," CRMtrends, n.d., www.crmtrends.com/loyalty.html; M.-C. Nideau and M. Singer, "The Secret to Creating Loyalty Programs That Actually Work," *Business Insider*, March 21, 2014, www.businessinsider.com/effective-loyalty-programs-2014-3; T. Caporaso, "3 Crucial Steps to Developing an Effective Loyalty Program," *Momentology*, April 16, 2015, www.momentology.com/6081-developing-effective-loyalty-program/; L. Kolowich, "7 Customer Loyalty Programs That Actually Add Value," n.d., http://blog.hubspot.com/blog/tabid/6307/bid/31990/7-Customer-Loyalty-Programs-That-Actually-Add-Value.aspx; R. L. Brooks, "Four Steps to Launching a Loyalty Program," *Entrepreneur*, December 10, 2010, www.entrepreneur.com/article/217741.

53. In addition to many of the sources for loyalty programs, there are some good sources dedicated to referral programs. These include E. Siemasko, "Referral Programs 101: Everything Needed to Build a Program," ReferralRock.com, n.d., https://referralrock.com/blog/referral-programs-101-everything-you-need-to-build-a-referral-marketing-program/; V. Veerasamy, "Referral Program Examples—an Epic List of 47 Referral Programs," *Word-of-Mouth and Referral Marketing Blog*, August 9, 2015, www.referralcandy.com/blog/47-referral-programs/; J. Jantsch, "How to Boost Your Customer Referrals in 7 Simple Steps," *Duct Tape Marketing*, March 12, 2010, www.ducttapemarketing.com/blog/how-to-boost-your-customer-referrals-in-7-simple-steps/; Masjedi, "5 Tips for a Successful Customer Referral Program," *Salesforce Blog*, August 29, 2013, www.salesforce.com/blog/2013/08/customer-referral-program.html; B. Gains, "6 Ways You Can Create a Referral Program That Works," *Referral SaaSquatch*, October 8, 2014, www.referralsaasquatch.com/6-ways-create-referral-program-that-works/.

54. Gary L. Frazier, "Organizing and Managing Channels of Distribution," *Journal of the Academy of Marketing Science* 27, no. 2 (1999), pp. 226–240.

55. E. Rosen, *The Anatomy of Buzz: How to Create Word of Mouth Marketing* (New York: Doubleday, 2000).

56. David Stokes, "Entrepreneurial Marketing: A Conceptualisation from Qualitative Research," *Qualitative Market Research* 3, no. 1 (2000), pp. 47–54.

57. You can find door-to-door and party-sale-based companies at the following sites: "Home Party Company and Direct Sales Company Rankings," Homepartyrankings.com, n.d., http://homepartyrankings.com/; Biz Ops, "160+ Party Plan Businesses," Business Opportunities, April 13, 2009, www.business-opportunities.biz/2009/04/13/160-party-plan-businesses/.

58. You can learn more about the at-home party business at K. E. Spaeder, "It's Your Party," *Entrepreneur*, May 1, 2007, www.entrepreneur.com/article/177884; R. Nichols, "Marketing through Home Parties," *Entrepreneur*, March 30, 2007, www.entrepreneur.com/article/176460; K. E. Spaeder, "Start a Home Party Business," *Entrepreneur*, November 17, 2006, www.entrepreneur.com/article/170740.

59. Lissan Levin and Jacob Zhavi, "The Economics of Selection of Mail Orders," *Journal of Interactive Marketing* 15, no. 3 (2001), pp. 53–71; F. Gonul Fusan and Byung-Do Kim, "Mailing Smarter to Catalog Customers," *Journal of Interactive Marketing* 14, no. 2 (2000), pp. 2–16.

60. Sean M. Lyden, "Make Newspaper Ads Work for You," *Entrepreneur*, May 27, 2002, www.entrepreneur.com/article/52098. Reprinted with permission of Entrepreneur.com.

61. The original source is US-FTC, "CAN-SPAM Act: A Compliance Guide for Business," Federal Trade Commission website, September 2009, www.ftc.gov/tips-advice/business-center/guidance/can-spam-act-compliance-guide-business. Useful sites expanding on and applying the CAN-SPAM Act include C. Wainwright, "What Is CAN-SPAM? [FAQs]," n.d., http://blog.hubspot.com/marketing/what-is-can-spam-ht; B. Barron, "10 Email Marketing Spam Laws You Need to Know About," *Elegant Themes*, April 15, 2015, www.elegantthemes.com/blog/resources/10-email-marketing-spam-laws-you-need-to-know-about; L-Soft, "Opt-In Laws in North America and Europe," L-Soft, n.d., www.lsoft.com/resources/optinlaws.asp; MailChimp, "Terms of Use and Anti-Spam Requirements," MailChimp.com, June 14, 2016, http://127.0.0.1/site/accounts/compliance-tips/terms-of-use-and-anti-spam-requirements.

62. State of California Department of Justice and Office of the Attorney General, "SPAM," Office of the Attorney General, n.d., https://oag.ca.gov/consumers/general/spam10.

63. Kristin Zhivago, "You and CAN-SPAM," January 23, 2004, www.marketing-technology.com/MT/canspam.cfm.

64. Don Debelak, "Lights, Camera, Action," *Entrepreneur*, April 2003, www.entrepreneur.com/article/72148.

65. M. Trusov, R. E. Bucklin, and K. Pauwels, "Effects of Word-of-Mouth versus Traditional Marketing: Findings from an Internet Social Networking Site," *Journal of Marketing* 73, no. 5 (September 2009), pp. 90–102.

66. Michael H. Morris, Minet Schindehutte, and Raymond W. LaForge, "Entrepreneurial Marketing: A Construct for Integrating Emerging Entrepreneurship and Marketing Perspectives," *Journal of Marketing Theory and Practice* 10, no. 4 (2002), pp. 1–19; K. J. Clancy and P. C. Krieg, *Counterintuitive Marketing: Achieve Great Results Using Uncommon Sense* (New York: Free Press, 2000).

67. Michael McMyne, *Student Entrepreneurs* (St. Louis: Premium Press America, 2003).

68. Personal story, used with permission.

69. Kim T. Gordon, "Cross-Training," *Entrepreneur*, July 2003, www.entrepreneur.com/article/62766.

70. C. Bosdal, "Pros and Cons of UPS SurePost, FedEx SmartPost," *Practical Ecommerce*, May 20, 2014, www.practicalecommerce.com/Pros-and-Cons-of-UPS-SurePost-FedEx-SmartPost.

71. G. Marion, "Are You Optimizing Costs and Customer Delivery with a Supply Chain?," *The Balance Small Business*, n.d., www.thebalancesmb.com/is-supply-chain-your-competitive-advantage-2221295; A. Roggio, "Ship-from-Store Fulfillment a Must for Brick-and-Click Retailers," *Practical Ecommerce*, June 5, 2017, www.practicalecommerce.com/ship-from-store-fulfillment-a-must-for-brick-and-click-retailers.

72. Melissa Campanelli, "Fulfilling Orders," *Entrepreneur*, 2000, www.entrepreneur.com/article/27696.

73. Art Avery, "Order Fulfillment for Your Small E-business: Should You Beg, Borrow or Buy?," 2000, www.etailersdigest.com/resources/Specials/BegBorrow.htm.

74. George Matyjewicz, 'Doc' Don Avery, Kris Campbell, and Dave Campbell, "Online Logistics and Order Fulfillment Solutions for E-Tailers," 1999, www.etailersdigest.com/resources/Specials/Logistics.htm.

75. Andy Gibbs, "How to Sell Your Product," IPFrontline.com, November 17, 2000, www.ipfrontline.com/depts/article.aspx?id=256&deptid=2.

76. Paul Edwards and Sarah Edwards, "It's in the Mail," *Entrepreneur*, 2003, www.entrepreneur.com/article/60430. If you want to hear the story from the Orabrush people themselves, look at this YouTube video: www.youtube.com/watch?v=4oKYeWf3dPA&index=20&list=PLB73276F91DD26C78.

77. "MBA Case Study: How Orabrush Got into Walmart," 2011, www.youtube.com/watch?v=4oKYeWf3dPA&feature=youtube gdata player; J. Neff, "How Orabrush Got National Walmart Deal with YouTube

Videos," *Advertising Age,* September 20, 2011, http://adage.com/article/news/orabrush-national-walmart-deal-youtube-videos/229914/; T. Wasserman, "Orabrush Parlays YouTube Success into Walmart Deal," *Mashable,* September 20, 2011, http://mashable.com/2011/09/20/orabrush-walmar/. You can also see a video from Orabrush about this episode at www.youtube.com/watch?v=4oKYeWf3dPA&feature=player_embedded.

78. For academic studies on e-tailers, see Heiko de B. Wijnolds and Michael W. Little, "Regulatory Issues for Global E-Tailers: Marketing Implications," *Academy of Marketing Science Review*, 2001, pp. 1–17; Gary J. Stockport, George Kunnarth, and Rashida Sedik, "Boo.com, the Path to Failure," *Journal of Interactive Marketing* 15, no. 4 (2001), pp. 56–70.
79. Don Debelak, "Who Needs 'Em?," *Entrepreneur*, 2000, www.entrepreneur.com/article/29558.
80. P. Delehanty, "Small Businesses Key Players in International Trade," *SBA Office of Advocacy Issue Brief*, no. 11 (2015), p. 4; U.S. Department of Commerce, International Trade Administration, "Exporting Is Good for Your Bottom Line," n.d., www.trade.gov/cs/factsheet.asp.
81. Oystein Moen, "The Relationship between Firm Size, Competitive Advantages, and Export Performance Revisited," *International Small Business Journal* 18, no. 1 (1999), pp. 53–72.
82. Ibid.
83. Benjamin M. Oviatt and Patricia Phillips McDougall, "Towards a Theory of International New Ventures," *Journal of International Business Studies* 25, no.1 (1994), pp. 45–65. S. K. Kundu and J. A. Katz, "Born-International SMEs: Bi-level Impacts of Resources and Intentions," *Small Business Economics* 20, no. 1 (2003), pp. 25–47.
84. For more about SMEs and exporting, see Pierre-Andre Julien and Charles Ramagalahy, "Competitive Strategy and Performance of Exporting SMEs: An Empirical Investigation of the Impact of Their Export Information Search and Competency," *Entrepreneurship Theory and Practice* 27, no. 3 (2003), pp. 227–246; Neil A. Morgan, Anna Kaleka, and Constantine S. Katsikeas, "Antecedents of Export Venture Performance: A Theoretical Model and Empirical Assessment," *Journal of Marketing* 68 (January 2004), pp. 90–108.
85. Carla Goodman, "Going Global," *Entrepreneur*, 1996, www.entrepreneur.com/article/13480.
86. C. Smith, "85 Amazing EBay Stats and Facts (2019)," *DMR*, January 7, 2015, https://expandedramblings.com/index.php/ebay-stats/. Originally we reported one-fifth based on Jerome A. Katz, Scott R. Safranski, and Omar Khan, "Virtual Instant Global Entrepreneurship: Cybermediation for Born International Service Firms," *Journal of International Entrepreneurship* 1 (2003), pp. 43–57.
87. S. K. Kundu and J. A. Katz, "Born-International SMEs: Bi-level Impacts of Resources and Intentions," *Small Business Economics* 20, no. 1 (2003), pp. 25–47.
88. "How to Take Your Country Global," *Entrepreneur*, 2003, www.entrepreneur.com/article/0,4621,312297,00.html.
89. Laura Tiffany, "Researching Your Market," *Entrepreneur,* August 7, 2001, www.entrepreneur.com/article/43024.
90. Carla Goodman, "Going Global," *Entrepreneur,* 1996, www.entrepreneur.com/article/13480.
91. Beverley Williams, "Zoning Information and Resources," www.jbsja.com/content/suites/hb_teleworking/zoning.shtml.
92. Virginia Baldwin Gilbert, "Start-Ups Are Poised to Fly Away from Incubator Nest," *St. Louis Post-Dispatch*, February 2, 2002, www.niduscenter.com/m arts_html/post 02-25-02a.html.
93. Michael H. Seid and Kay Marie Ainsley, "What Makes a Location Great?," *Entrepreneur*, March 2001, www.entrepreneur.com/article/0,4621,287982,00.html.
94. Julie Bennett, "Location Is Everything to Franchise Hopefuls," http://startupjournal.com/columnist/franchiseinsight/20020814-bennett.html.
95. Michael H. Seid and Kay Marie Ainsley, "Finding a Great Location," *Entrepreneur*, April 2001, www.entrepreneur.com/article/0,4621,288851,00.html.
96. Rieva Lesonsky, "Cart Blanche," *Entrepreneur*, 2003, www.entrepreneur.com/article/63244.
97. Michael H. Seid and Kay Marie Ainsley, "Finding a Great Location," *Entrepreneur*, April 2001, www.entrepreneur.com/article/39848.
98. Julie Bennett, "Location Is Everything to Franchise Hopefuls," http://startupjournal.com/columnist/franchiseinsight/20020814-bennett.html.
99. Peter Carbonara and Maggie Overfelt, "The Dot-Com Factories," *Fortune,* 2000, www.fortune.com/fortune/print/0,15935,360353,00.html.
100. Michael H. Seid and Kay Marie Ainsley, "Finding a Great Location," *Entrepreneur*, April 2001, www.entrepreneur.com/article/39848.
101. Michael H. Seid and Kay Marie Ainsley, "What Makes a Location Great?," *Entrepreneur*, March 2001, www.entrepreneur.com/article/0,4621,287982,00.html.
102. Cliff Ennico, "Franchise Business—Finding Space for Your Franchised Business," *Entrepreneur*, April 26, 2004, June 26, 2009, www.entrepreneur.com/management/operations/location/article70514.html.
103. The advice in the bullet points in this section come from Cliff Ennico, "Franchise Business—Finding Space for Your Franchised Business," *Entrepreneur,* April 26, 2004, www.entrepereneur.com/management/operations/location/article70514.html; Cliff Ennico, "Retail Business—Negotiating Your Shopping Center Lease," *Entrepreneur*, October 17, 2005, www.entrepreneur.com/management/operations/location/article80604.html; Rieva Lesonsky, "Commercial Leases," *Entrepreneur*, 1998, June 26, 2009, www.entrepreneur.com/management/operations/location/article21886.html; Jeffrey Steinberger, "How to Get out of a Commercial Lease," *Entrepreneur*, January 24, 2007, June 26, 2009, www.entrepreneur.com/management/legalcenter/legalissuescolumnistjeffreysteinberger/article173568.html; Nichole L. Torres, "Small Business—Lease Lessons," *Entrepreneur,* December 2004, www.entrepreneur.com/startingabusiness/startupbasics/location//article73744.html.
104. Rieva Lesonsky, "Commercial Leases," *Entrepreneur*, 1998, www.entrepreneur.com/management/operations/location/article21886.html.
105. "Release Me?," *Entrepreneur*, 1998, www.entrepreneur.com/article/22564.
106. Julie Baker, A. Parasuraman, Dhruv Grewal, and Glenn B. Voss, "The influence of Multiple Store Environment Cues of Perceived Merchandise Value and Patronage Intentions," *Journal of Marketing* 66 (April 2002), pp. 120–140.
107. This comes from a write-up of the history of Flipoutz by cofounder Lachlan Johnson, done in May 2016.

Chapter 12

1. https://yec.co/members/profile/Justin-Beegel-Founder-President-Infographic-World-Inc/18414f4d-df0e-4ae4-bc7b-2a2fab621c3b (accessed April 16, 2019).
2. Ibid.
3. www.entrepreneur.com/slideshow/237370#14 (accessed April 16, 2019).
4. https://yfsmagazine.com/2012/05/10/cash-and-burn-how-i-saved-my-business-from-financial-failure/ (accessed April 16, 2019).
5. Ibid.
6. www.businessbewareshow.com/2012/05/03/humble-modest-entrepreneur-interview-justin-beegal-infographic-world/ last (accessed April 16, 2019).
7. www.linkedin.com/in/justinbeegel/ (accessed April 16, 2019).
8. P. Danner, "'Bad Accounting' or Illegal?," *San Antonio Express-News*," n.d., www.mysanantonio.com/business/article/Bad-accounting-or-illegal-1334193.php.

9. Ibid.
10. J. Davenport, "12-Year Sentence for Developer," *San Antonio Express-News*, n.d., www.mysanantonio.com/default/article/12-year-sentence-for-developer-1337478.php.
11. *Statement of Financial Accounting Concepts No. 8* as amended (August 2018), Chapter 3, p. 16.
12. A complete description of the quality of financial accounting information is presented in Concepts Statement No. 6, "Elements of Financial Statements," available in PDF format at www.fasb.org/jsp/FASB/Page/SectionPage&cid=1176156317989.
13. The Microsoft Accounting Express programs were discontinued in 2009, although users received support through 2019. Microsoft has replaced the program with Microsoft Dynamics GP which can be a stand-alone installation, a cloud-based installation, or some hybrid of the two. Available at www.microsoft.com/en-us/dynamics/erp-gp-overview.aspx (accessed April 16, 2016).
14. Vindu Goel, "Intuit Sheds Its PC Roots and Reinvents Itself as a Cloud-Based Service," *The New York Times*, April 11, 2016.
15. Gene Marks, "Will the Cloud Kill Intuit?," *Fox News*, November 18, 2015, www.foxbusiness.com/features/2015/11/18/will-cloud-kill-intuit.html.
16. The website accountingweb.com claims 88 different programs exist, but when duplicate entries were removed, only 75 remained. Available at www.accountingweb.com/technology/accounting-software/small-business-accounting-software-market-expanding (accessed April 15, 2016).
17. It is common for these statements to be presented as only three separate documents by combining the statements of retained earnings and owners' equity into the equity section of the balance sheet. Regardless of whether they are combined or presented as separate statements, they contain the same information and follow the same general format.
18. An economist defines *income* as a change in wealth. This implies, for example, that if a business purchased a plot of land some time ago for $100,000, and today, because of the development of adjacent property, several potential buyers each offered to pay $200,000 to purchase the land, then the business has income equal to the $100,000 increase in the value of the real estate. Accounting does not, however, recognize as income the increase in wealth caused by the increase in value of the land. If, and only if, the land is sold to an outside party will the increase in value be recognized as income in the accounting statements. For accounting purposes, income, gains, expenses, and losses are recognized only when a transaction takes place between nonrelated entities.
19. An economist would say that it is converted without facing any discount from the true economic value of the asset.
20. C. Koornhof, "Accounting Information on Flexibility," Dissertation, University of Pretoria, 1997.
21. Rebecca Cooper, "Marketing from the Inside Out: A Coach's Perspective," *Entrepreneur*, May 20, 2002, www.entrepreneur.com/article/52006.
22. M. J. Peel and J. Bridge, "Planning Business Objectives and Capital Budgeting in Japanese, German and Domestic SMEs: Some Evidence from the UK Manufacturing Sector," *Journal of Small Business and Enterprise Development* 6, no. 4 (2000), pp. 350–365.
23. Dorothy A. Davis, "Internal Controls for the Small Owner-Operated Business," Small Business Institute Directors Association National Meeting, www.Sbaer.Uca.Edu/Research/Sbida/1991/Pdf/03.Pdf.
24. R. N. Lussier and S. Pfeifer, "A Cross-National Prediction Model for Business Success," *Journal of Small Business Management* 39, no. 3 (2001), pp. 228–239.
25. M. J. Peel, "Timeliness of Private Company Accounts and Predicting Corporate Failure," *The Investment Analyst: The Journal of the Society of Investment Analysts*, no. 83, pp. 23–27.
26. This definition is deliberately simple. The analysis as presented overstates both the price variance and the efficiency variance by ignoring the common variance. In practice this analysis is sufficient for all but the most sophisticated cost analysis systems.
27. H. A. Simon, "Rational Decision Making in Business Organizations," in L. Green and J. H. Kagel (eds.), *Advances in Behavioral Economics*, vol. 1 (Norwood, NJ: Ablex, 1987), pp. 18–47.
28. In practice, an outsourcing decision should not be made based solely on a financial analysis. Multiple factors, especially the effect on the strategy of the business, should be considered. See J. Bowles, "Outsourcing for Competitive Advantage," *Forbes*, June 7, 2004, p. 101.

Chapter 13

1. www.timesunion.com/local/article/She-embezzled-500K-Now-she-faces-prison-12255234.php#photo-14292693 (accessed May 20, 2019).
2. Robert Gavin, "Mechanicville woman 'ashamed' over $500,000 theft," Timesunion, October 5, 2017, (https://www.timesunion.com/local/article/She-embezzled-500K-Now-she-faces-prison-12255234.php, last accessed May 20, 2018).
3. Chelsea Diana, "Is your 'trusted employee' stealing from you?," Albany Business Review, March 1, 2018 (accessed May 20, 2018).
4. Ibid.
5. Kassie Parisi, "Mechanicville woman gets 6 years for stealing $500,000 from employer," *The Daily Gazette,* October 5, 2017. (https://dailygazette.com/article/2017/10/05/mechanicville-woman-gets-6-years-for-stealing-500-000-from-employer, last accessed May 20, 2018).
6. Federal Reserve Bank of Dallas, *Money, Banking and Monetary Policy*, 1995, p. 1.
7. www.federalreserve.gov/faqs/currency_12773.htm (accessed April 24, 2019).
8. $1.7 trillion divided by 328.8 million = $5,170
9. Widely quoted figure attributed to U.S. Bank. See www.nfib.com/content/resources/start-a-business/why-do-small-businesses-fail/ (accessed April 24, 2019).
10. Holly S. Wade, *NFIB National Small Business Poll: Cash Flow,* Vol 13, Issue 2, 2016, www.nfib.com/content/resources/money/the-state-of-cash-flow/ (accessed April 28, 2019).
11. Evan Smith, "John Mackey," *Texas Monthly* 33, no. 3 (2005), pp. 122–132.
12. "Big Box Retailers Squeeze Smaller Suppliers by Borrowing from Them," *Yale Insights*, November 26, 2014, http://insights.som.yale.edu/insights/big-box-retailers-squeeze-smaller-suppliers-borrowing-them (accessed June 6, 2016); "Wal-Mart Puts the Squeeze on Suppliers to Share Its Pain as Earnings Sag," Reuters, October 19, 2015, www.reuters.com/article/us-wal-mart-suppliers-insight-idUSKCN0S-D0CZ20151019 (accessed June 6, 2016).
13. http://business.uschamber.com/P14/P14_1105.asp.
14. Paul Deceglie, "Fun with Funding: If You Left Your Creativity Somewhere with Your Coloring Books, You're Not Ready to Find Financing in the Post-Dot-com Era," *Entrepreneur*, BizOpp Zone, September 14, 2001, www.entrepreneur.com/article/44428; John F. Dalrymple, *International Business Profile Benchmarking for the SME Sector—Does It Work?* (RMIT University, Centre for Quality Management Research, 2001), www.cmqr.rmit.edu.au/publications/jdimprov.pdf; S. Mian and C. Smith, "Accounts Receivable Management Policy: Theory and Evidence," *Journal of Finance* 47 (1992), pp. 169–200.
15. Jonathan A. Scott and Morris G. Danielson, "Bank Loan Availability and Trade Credit Demand," *The Financial Review* 39 (2004), pp. 579–600, www.blackwell-synergy.com/links/doi/10.1111/j.07328516.2004.00089.x/pdf; A. N. Berger and G. F. Udell, "Small Business Credit Availability and

Relationship Lending: The Importance of Bank Organizational Structure," *Economic Journal* 112 (2002), pp. 32–53.

16. Judy Gedge, "Does Your Collections System Need a Checkup?," *Entrepreneur*, March 29, 2004, www.entrepreneur.com/article/70086; Paul DeCeglie, "Gimme My Money: Steps You Can Take to Collect on Past Due Accounts Receivable," *Business Start-Ups*, August 2000, www.entrepreneur.com/article/30200; W. Lim and M. Rashid, "An Operational Theory Integrating Cash Discount and Product Pricing Policies," *Journal of American Academy of Business* 2 (2002), pp. 282–288; W. Beranek, "Behavioral Relations, Operating Factors and the Optimal Cash Discount," the 7th International Symposium on Cash, Treasury and Working Capital Management, Chicago, Illinois, October 1991.
17. See G. Udell, *Asset-Based Finance* (New York: The Commercial Finance Association, 2004); A. N. Berger and G. F. Udell, "Small Business and Debt Finance," in Zoltan J. Acs and David B. Audretsch (eds.), *Handbook of Entrepreneurship* (Norwell, MA: Kluwer Academic Publishing, 2003); M. R. Bakker, L. Klapper, and G. F. Udell, "The Role of Factoring in Commercial Finance: The Case of Eastern Europe," Working Paper, 2004.
18. See Mie-Yun Lee, "Factor Your Receivables for More Cash: Need a Quick Cash Infusion? A Factoring Service Can Help You Out," *Entrepreneur*, June 03, 2002, www.entrepreneur.com/article/52344; Jan Norman, "How to Factor: Get Money to Grow!," *Business Start-Ups*, November 1998, www.entrepreneur.com/article/16636.
19. One other approach is called *activity-based costing* (or ABC), which looks at which services, products, or internal operations add to your profits or add to your costs. It is used most often for companies with several different types of products, services, or markets and can help you pare down to those things that can truly make a positive difference in your bottom line. For an introduction, see Mark Henricks, "Beneath the Surface: Suspicious Not All Areas of Your Company Are Bringing in a Profit? Break It Down with Activity-Based Costing," *Entrepreneur*, October 1999, www.entrepreneur.com/article/18388.
20. For some other ideas, look at Jan Norman, "How to Manage Your Cash Flow: You're Making Sales, But Are You Making Money?," *Business Start-Ups*, June 1998, www.entrepreneur.com/article/15728.
21. Nancy R. Lockwood, "Work-Life Balance: Challenges and Solutions," Society for Human Resource Management, *2003 SHRM Research Quarterly*, 2003, www.ispi.org/pdf/suggestedReading/11_Lockwood_WorkLife Balance.pdf; Aubrey C. Daniels, "Choosing an Employee Incentive Program: With So Many Choices Out There, How Do You Pick the Best One for Your Business?," *Entrepreneur*, September 2, 2002, www.entrepreneur.com/article/54952; G. A. Marken, "Ten Low-Cost Steps to Keep Employees from Job Hunting," *Water Quality Products* 7, no. 4 (April 2002), www.wwdmag.com/wwd/index.cfm/powergrid/rfah=%7Ccfap=/CFID/2522697/CFTKEN/34858572/fuseaction/showArticle/articleID/3032; Marvin Collins, *The Human Use of Human Resources* (New York: McGraw-Hill, 1981).
22. Mark Henricks, "Trading Up: No Cash? No Problem," *Entrepreneur's Be Your Own Boss*, February 2005, www.entrepreneur.com/article/76128; Kirk Whisler and Nichole Torres, "Barter to the Cause: Does Cutting Costs Sound Like a Good Start-Up Idea?," *Entrepreneur*, October 2002, www.entrepreneur.com/article/55484; Kurt J. Samson, "Better Business? Think Barter Business Why Trading for Products and Services Makes Great Financial Sense," *Home Office*, August 1999, www.entrepreneur.com/article/25704.
23. See C. O'Gorman, "The Sustainability of Growth in Small- and Medium-Sized Enterprises," *International Journal of Entrepreneurial Behaviour and Research* 7, no. 2 (February 2001), pp. 60–75; Kevin Mole, "Business Advice to Fast Growth Small Firms" (Telford: University of Wolverhampton, 1999), http://mubs.mdx.ac.uk/research/Discussion_Papers/Business_and_Management/dpapmsno_4.pdf.

Chapter 14

1. V. Lombardi, C. Abbey, and D. Craig, *The Top American Research Universities, 2017 Annual Report*, The Center for Measuring University Performance, 2017.
2. Matt DeCoursey and Matt Watson, *Startup Hustle.XYZ* [Audio podcast], Ben Jackson, Bungii, December 27, 2017, www.startuphustle.xyz/episode-10-ben-jackson-bungii/ (accessed June 12, 2019).
3. Ibid.
4. Ibid.
5. L. Collins, "LaunchKC's 2018 Winners Include Five Local Startups," *Kansas City Business Journal*, October 12, 2018 www-bizjournals-com.tamusa.idm.oclc.org/kansascity/news/2018/10/12/launchkcs-2018-winners-include-five-local-startups.html (accessed June 12, 2019).
6. Bobby Burch, "Truck Hailing Tech Firm Bungii Straps Down $3M in Oversubscribed Round," *Startland News*, January 18, 2018, www.startlandnews.com/2018/01/truck-hailing-tech-firm-bungii-straps-3m-oversubscribed-round/ (accessed June 12, 2019).
7. Certainly, these investment vehicles are not truly risk-free. At the minimum, they have term risk. A full discussion of the elements of investment is far beyond the scope of this text.
8. The actual annual effective interest rate is 22.47 percent: $r = [fv/c]^{1/n} - 1$ $r = (150{,}000/100{,}000)^{1/2} - 1$ $r = 0.224745$
9. Bootstrapping comes from an old saying that a person started poor and became successful through diligence and hard work had "pulled himself up by his bootstraps."
10. P. D. Reynolds, "Informal and Early Formal Financial Support in the Business Creation Process: Exploration with PSED II Data Set," n.d., http://web.ebscohost.com.tamusa.idm.oclc.org/ehost/pdfviewer/pdfviewer?sid=be77b594-7bc9-4230-bdea-9617eb8c482b%40sessionmgr11&vid=1&hid=10.
11. J. Cornwall, *Bootstrapping* (Upper Saddle River, NJ: Prentice Hall, 2010).
12. Ibid, p. 2.
13. Othmar Lehner, "A Literature Review and Research Agenda for Crowdfunding of Social Ventures," SSRN website, July 6, 2012, http://papers.ssrn.com/sol3/papers.cfm?abstract_id=2102525.
14. H. R. Huhman, "JOBS Act to Jumpstart the Job Market," *Forbes*, n.d., www.forbes.com/sites/work-inprogress/2012/04/05/jobsact-to-jumpstart-the-job-market/.
15. The following link will take you directly to the Securities and Exchange Commission website discussion of the use of Rule 506 "safe harbor" provisions: www.sec.gov/answers/rule506.htm.
16. https://paulcollege.unh.edu/resources/all?combine&resource_type=All&field_resource_category_tid=107&field_resource_topic_tid=105 (accessed June 12, 2019).
17. www.angelresourceinstitute.org/research/halo-report/halo-report.aspx (accessed July 25, 2016).
18. Jeffrey Sohl, "The Angel Market in 2018: More Angels Investing in More Deals at Lower Valuations," Center for Venture Research, May 9, 2019.
19. M. Hudson, "Important Things for Entrepreneurs to Know about Angel Investors," n.d., www.angelresourceinstitute.org/data/Documents/Resources/AngelCapitalEducation/What_Ents_Should_Know_About_Angels.pdf.
20. R. Wiltbank and W. Boeker, *Returns to Angel Investors in Groups*, Angel Capital Education Foundation (Kansas City, MO: Kauffman Foundation of Entrepreneurship, November 2007), www.angelresourceinstitute.org/data/Documents/Resources/AngelCapitalEducation/RSCH_-_ACEF_-_Returns_to_Angel_Investor_in_Groups.pdf.
21. https://studentaid.ed.gov/sa/repay-loans/deferment-forbearance (accessed July 25, 2016).
22. J. Mullins, *The Customer-Funded Business: Start, Finance, or Grow Your Company with Your Customers' Cash* (New York: Wiley, 2014).

23. Ibid, p. 11.
24. J. A. Katz, "Modelling Entrepreneurial Career Progressions: Concepts and Considerations," *Entrepreneurship: Theory and Practice* 19, no. 2 (Winter 1994), pp. 23–40; J. A. Katz, "A Psychosocial Cognitive Model of Employment Status Choice," *Entrepreneurship: Theory and Practice* 17, no. 1 (1992), pp. 29–37; J. A. Katz, "Secondary Analysis in Entrepreneurship: An Introduction to Data Bases and Data Management," *Journal of Small Business Management* 30, no. 20 (1992), pp. 74–86.
25. Crystal Detamore-Rodman, "The Search Is On: Entrepreneurs and Experts All Agree: If You're Willing to Hunt Around, You Can Score Financing to Get Your Home-Based Business Off the Ground," *Entrepreneur's Be Your Own Boss*, June 2003, www.entrepreneur.com/article/62238; Cliff Ennico, "Accepting Money from Friends & Family: 4 Ways to Get Your Cash without Wreaking Havoc on Your Personal Relationships," *Entrepreneur*, Money & Finance, May 6, 2002, www.entrepreneur.com/article/51542; Stever Robbins, "Asking Friends and Family for Financing: Heed Our Warnings Before You Play This Dangerous Game," *Entrepreneur*, October 1, 2001, www.entrepreneur.com/article/44612.
26. Actually, Freud most likely never made this statement; however, it has entered popular folklore and is usually attributed to him.
27. R. Cialdini, *Influence: The Psychology of Persuasion* (New York: William Morrow and Company, 1993).
28. A. Komter and W. Vollebergh, "Gift-Giving and the Emotional Significance of Family and Friends," *Journal of Marriage and the Family* 59, no. 3 (August 1997), pp. 747–757.
29. Milton Friedman, *There's No Such Thing as a Free Lunch* (LaSalle, IL: Open Court Publishing, 1975).
30. R. Pettit and R. Singer, "Small Business Finance: A Research Agenda," *Financial Management*, Autumn 1985, pp. 47–60.
31. Wieczner, Jen, "WeWork, Theranos Scandals Haunt Female Startup CEOs," Fortune,com /2019/10/22/wework-theranos-female-startup-ceo/, October 22, 2019. Last accessed Dec. 9, 2019.
32. Ibid.
33. Lundin, Katie, "13 Women Entrepreneurs Who Are Changing the World," https://www.crowdspring.com/blog/13-women-entrepreneurs-who-are-changing-the-world/. Last accessed Dec. 9, 2019.
34. Lagorio-Chafkin, Christine, " This Entrepreneur Wants to Change How You Get Blood Tests (and Make You Forget About Theranos)," https://www.inc.com/christine-lagorio-chafkin/everlywell-democratizing-health-information.html. Last accessed Dec. 9, 2019.
35. Calnan, Christopher, " Health care tech startup raises big chunk of seed funding," *Austin Business Journal*, https://www-bizjournals-com.tamusa.idm.oclc.org/austin/blog/techflash/2016/04/health-care-tech-startup-raises-big-seed-funding.html, April 19, 2015. Last accessed Dec. 9, 2019.
36. Mack, Heather, "Venture Investors Bet $50 Million on Test-Kit Startup EverlyWell." *The Wall Street Journal*, April 16, 2019, https://www.wsj.com/articles/venture-investors-bet-50-million-on-test-kit-startup-everlywell-11555414200. Last accessed Dec. 9, 2019.
37. Ibid.

Chapter 15

1. FBI, *Preliminary Semiannual Uniform Crime Report*, February 25, 2019, www.fbi.gov/news/stories/2018-preliminary-semiannual-uniform-crime-report-released-022519.
2. M. Bonner, "10 Most Common Types of Business Insurance Claims and the Most Costly," *The Balance Small Business*, n.d., www.thebalancesmb.com/common-insurance-claims-462673 (accessed June 15, 2019).
3. https://fox13now.com/2018/12/09/utah-couple-out-20000-dollars-after-tattoo-supply-shop-burglary/ (accessed June 15, 2019); https://newsblaze.com/usnews/crime/utah-burglars-steal-20000-from-tattoo-supply-shop-get-caught_148948/ (accessed June 15, 2019); www.abc4.com/news/local-news/alleged-burglar-shares-surveillance-video-of-crime-on-social-media-then-turns-himself-in/ (accessed June 15, 2019).
4. www.pprhealthcare.com/index.shtml.
5. REL's Annual Working Capital surveys, 2004, www.relconsult.com/website/website.nsf/Articles/.
6. Ellyn Spragins, "Get Paid First!," *Fortune Small Business* 15, no. 1 (February 2005), p. 85.
7. Rieva Lesonsky, "Inventory Control: When It Comes to Inventory, the Key Is Striking a Balance between Too Little and Too Much," *Entrepreneur*, 2006. www.entrepreneur.com/article/21842.
8. Gwen Moran, "Cover Your Bases: If You Thought Database Marketing Was Just Wasting Your Time with Fliers and Mailing Lists, Take Another Look—at the Net," *Entrepreneur*, February 2000, www.entrepreneur.com/article/18988.
9. "Dell Does What Others Have Given Up," *Forbes World Media Digest*, 2005, www.forbes.com/technology.
10. Mike Hogan, "The Outer Limits: With Larger PC-Makers Struggling, Why Is Alienware Doing So Well?," *Entrepreneur*, March 2005, www.entrepreneur.com/article/76244; "Cutting the Edge Hardware," interview with Alex Aguila, www.ownt.com/hardware/interviews/2003/alienware/alienware.shtm; Ed Duggan, "Alienware, a Miami Computer Maker, Could Top Sales of $50 million," *South Florida Business Journal*, August 16, 2002, www.bizjournals.com/southflorida/stories/2002/08/19/smallb1.html?t5printable.
11. Jerome A. Katz, Scott R. Safranski, and Omar Khan, "Virtual Instant Global Entrepreneurship: Cybermediation for Born International Service Firms," *Journal of International Entrepreneurship* 1, no. 1 (March 2003), pp. 43–57.
12. "What Will a New Fence Cost This Year?," n.d., www.agriculture.com/news/livestock/what-will-a-new-fence-cost-this-year_3-ar22518 (accessed June 6, 2016).
13. Stephen Barlas, "Industrial Cleanser: The EPA Is Targeting Small Business for Pollution Cleanup," *Entrepreneur*, January 2000, www.Entrepreneur.com/article/0,4621,232505,00.html.
14. Amanda C. Kooser, "Who's Paying for Computer Recycling: The Newest Standard for Modems," *Entrepreneur*, August 2, 2002, www.entrepreneur.com/article/53730.
15. Because depreciation is a noncash expense, it causes net operating profit to be an amount less than net cash inflows, all other things being equal. (Refer to Chapter 12 for a more complete discussion of depreciation.)
16. David A. Kirby and Stefan Kaiser, "Joint Ventures as an Internationalisation Strategy for SMEs," *Small Business Economics* 21, no. 3 (Spring 2003), pp. 229–242; Marc J. Dollinger, Peggy A. Golden, and Todd Saxton, "The Effect of Reputation on the Decision to Joint Venture," *Strategic Management Journal* 18, no. 2 (1997), pp. 127–140.
17. I. Groves, "Vermont Sock Maker Looking for Experienced Workers Cabot, Company, Socks, Top News," *Burlington Times News*, n.d., www.thetimesnews.com/news/cabot-10499-company-socks.html.
18. Ibid.
19. R. Graham, "Business People—Vermont: Cabot Hosiery Mills," Mill Publishing, Inc., 2019, www.vermontguides.com/2006/11-nov/cobot_mills.html.
20. "Making it in Vermont: Darn Tough doubles down on Northfield facilities," *VTDigger*.org, https://vtdigger.org/2019/03/31/making-vermont-darn-tough-doubles-northfield-facilities/. Last accessed 12/9/2019.
21. Ibid.

22. There is a caveat if you use Excel, however. The built-in net present value function of Excel does not provide for time period 0. Therefore, you must calculate the present value of the cash flows of periods 1, 2, 3 *n* and then add the initial negative investment cash flow to the number provided by the Excel function.
23. Stever Robbins, "How Much Is This Business Worth? If You're Interested in Purchasing an Existing Business, Here Are a Few Ways to Gauge Its Value," *Entrepreneur*, January 12, 2004, www.entrepreneur.com/article/66442.

Chapter 16

1. https://interactive.symantec.com/istr24-web (accessed June 15, 2019).
2. Malwarebytes Labs, *Cybercrime Tactics and Techniques Q1 2019*, n.d., https://resources.malwarebytes.com/resource/cybercrime-tactics-techniques-2019-q1-report/ (accessed June 15, 2019).
3. Verizon, *2019 Data Breach Investigations Report*, n.d., https://enterprise.verizon.com/resources/reports/dbir/ (accessed June 15, 2019).
4. G. Westermann, "Your Business Is Never Too Small for a Cyber Attack: Here's How to Protect Yourself," *Forbes*, May 13, 2013, www.forbes.com/sites/forbesleadershipforum/2013/05/13/your-business-is-never-too-small-for-a-cyber-attack-heres-how-to-protect-yourself/#2a49f58e54f6 (accessed June 14, 2019).
5. K. Bernhard, "Ransomware Attacks on Businesses Happen Frequently but Often Go Unreported," *Philadelphia Business Journal*, August 3, 2018, www-bizjournals-com.tamusa.idm.oclc.org/philadelphia/news/2018/10/03/ransomware-attacks-on-businesses-happen-frequently.html (accessed June 14, 2019).
6. R. Snow, *Testimony before the House Small Business Committee*, National Small Business Association, April 20, 2016, www.nsba.biz/wp.../Rick-Snow-HSBC-Testimony-Cybersecurity-4.20.16.pdf (accessed June 15, 2019).
7. Financial risk is discussed in detail in Chapter 14.
8. Doris A. Christopher, "Small Business Pilfering: The "Trusted" Employee(s)," *Business Ethics: A European Review* 12, no. 3 (2003), pp. 284–297. Note that there is a lot of disagreement on how much theft there is. In an SBA-sponsored survey, only 2 percent of small businesses reported employee theft in the prior year, but it is better to be safe than sorry. The SBA study was Bonnie Fisher, *Small Businesses, Big Burdens: The Nature and Incidence of Crime within and against Small Business and Its Customers and Employees, Their Causes, Their Effects, and Their Prevention*, U.S. Small Business Administration, Office of Advocacy Research Report no. 176, March 1997, www.sba.gov/advo/research/rs176.pdf.
9. Anita Dennis, "The Downside of Good Times," *Journal of Accountancy* 190, no. 5 (2002), pp. 53–55; Neil H. Snyder, O. Whitfield Broome, and Karen Zimmerman, "Using Internal Controls to Reduce Employee Theft in Small Businesses," *Journal of Small Business Management* 27, no. 3 (July 1989), pp. 48–55.
10. Nicole V. Crain and W. Mark Crain, "The Impact of Regulatory Costs on Small Firms," Small Business Administration, Office of Advocacy, 2010, www.sba.gov/sites/default/files/advocacy/The%20Impact%20of%20Regulatory%20Costs%20on%20Small%20Firms%20(Full)_0.pdf (accessed November 21, 2016).
11. "2017 NSBA Small Business Regulations Survey, "National Small Business Association, https://www.nsba.biz/wp-content/uploads/2017/01/Regulatory-Survey-2017.pdf (accessed November 11, 2019).
12. 42 USC Pub. L. 88-352, Title VII, Sec. 701(b).
13. General Aviation Revitalization Act (GARA), 1994.
14. Separation of duties is discussed more fully in Chapter 15.
15. R. Hollinger, "National Retail Security Survey Final Report," University of Florida, 2001.
16. Association of Certified Fraud Examiners, Inc., *2016 ACFE Report to the Nations on Occupational Fraud and Abuse*, www.acfe.com/rttn2016.aspx (accessed August 15, 2016).
17. M. Shelton, "Businesses in Joplin, MO, Find Economic Opportunity," n.d., www.wbez.org/story/2011-09-13/businesses-joplin-mo-find-economic-opportunity-91935; "Joplin Open Business: Relocated Businesses," n.d., http://joplintornado.info/joplin_open_for_business/joplin_open_for_business.htm.
18. https://docs.microsoft.com/en-us/windows/security/threat-protection/overview-of-threat-mitigations-in-windows-10.
19. Gene Gable (ed.), "Heavy Metal Madness: Put on a Happy Face!," Creativepro.com, April 22, 2004, www.creativepro.com/story/feature/21223.html. See also Yahoo!'s answer at http://ask.yahoo.com/ask/20011213.html, and the international angle on the "smiley face" story at www.goodbyemag.com/apr01/ball.html.
20. Association of Certified Fraud Examiners, Inc., *2016 ACFE Report to the Nations on Occupational Fraud and Abuse*, www.acfe.com/rttn2016.aspx (accessed August 15, 2016).
21. Ibid.
22. Association of Certified Fraud Examiners, *2016 Report to the Nations on Occupational Fraud and Abuse*, 2016, www.acfe.com/rttn2016.aspx.
23. Thomas M. Sullivan, "Closing the Tax Gap and the Impact on Small Business," Testimony of the Chief Counsel for Advocacy to the U.S. House of Representatives, Committee on Small Business, April 27, 2005, www.sba.gov/advo/laws/test05_0427.html.
24. U.S. Consumer Product Safety Commission, "Amusement Ride-Related Injuries and Deaths in the United States: 1987–2000," Bethesda, MD, 2001.
25. The Outdoor Amusement Association website, November 27, 2004, www.oaba.org/facts2.htm/.
26. M. Holmer, "The Value of Social Security Disability Insurance," Public Policy Institute of AARP, Washington, DC, 2001.
27. T. Zayatz, "Social Security Disability Insurance Program Worker Experience: Actuarial Study No. 114," Social Security Administration, Washington, DC, 1999.

Chapter 17

1. This article is based on Randall Roberts, "B-Money in the Bank: St. Louis Native B-Money Is Hanging with Rap's Heavy Hitters," *Riverfront Times* (St. Louis, MO), December 6, 2006, www.riverfronttimes.com/2006-12-06/music/b-money-in-the-bank/ (all quotes come from this article and are used with permission); Kevin C. Johnson, "St. Louisan Wins Grammy for Work with Beyonce," *St. Louis Post-Dispatch*, February 22, 2007, www.stltoday.com/stltoday/entertainment/columnists.nsf/kevinjohnson/story/6E9B89B710A94682862572880082B63D?OpenDocument; Randall Roberts, "STLOG: B-Money's Beat Kicks Off the New Jay-Z," November 21, 2006, http://blogs.riverfronttimes.com/stlog/2006/11/bmoneys_beat_kicks_off_the_new.php.
2. For cross-national litigation rates see Robert A. Kagan, "On Surveying the Whole Legal Forest," *Law and Social Inquiry* 28 (2003), pp. 833–872, www.journals.uchicago.edu/cgi-bin/resolve?id=doi:10.1086/380082&erFrom=445040558813465220Guest; Christian Wollschlager, "Exploring the Global Landscapes of Litigation Rates," in Jurgen Brand and Dieter Stempel (eds.), Soziologie des Rechts: Fetschrift fur Erhard Blankenburg zum 60, Geburtstag (Baden-Baden, Germany: Nomos Berlagsgesellschaft, 1998), pp. 587–588. For the 2005 SBA study see SBA Office of Advocacy and Klemm Analysis Group. "Impact of Litigation on Small Business," October 2005. https://www.sba.gov/sites/default/files/files/rs265tot.pdf.

3. Pamela Rohland, "Follow Suit: What to Do When You Get Sued," *Entrepreneur-Business Start-Ups*, April 2000, www.entrepreneur.com/article/25032.
4. Cliff Ennico, "How to Hire an Attorney: Hiring a Good Lawyer Is Crucial to Any Successful Business," *Entrepreneur*, January 20, 2003, www.entrepreneur.com/article/58326.
5. Karen E. Spaeder, "Is Your Home Zoned for Business? How to Research, Comply with and Change Local Zoning Laws in Your Home-Based Business's Favor," *Entrepreneur—Home Office*, January 26, 2004, www.entrepreneur.com/article/0,4621,313950,00.html.
6. Christopher L. Hansen, "Special Report: Home-Based Zoning: What Issues Are at Stake for Homebased Businesses Fighting Zoning Ordinances?," *Entrepreneur—Home Office*, January 1, 2001; Laura Tiffany, "Zoning: Home Is Where the Business Is, and It's Also Where a Lot of Regulations Are," *Entrepreneur—Home Office*, March 21, 2001.
7. "The Basics of Sole Proprietorships: Chances Are, You're Already Running a Sole Proprietorship," *Entrepreneur*, May 12, 2005, www.entrepreneur.com/article/77798.
8. Benefit Corporation. "State by State Status of Legislation | Benefit Corporation." *Benefit Corporation*, 2016. http://benefitcorp.net/policymakers/state-by-state-status. InterSector Partners. "Latest L3C Tally | interSector Partners, L3C." *InterSector Partners, L3C*, June 14, 2016. http://www.intersectorl3c.com/l3c_tally.html. Cooney, K., J. Koushyar, M. Lee, and J. H. Murray. "Benefit Corporation and L3C Adoption: A Survey (SSIR)." *Stanford Social Innovation Review*, December 4, 2014. http://ssir.org/articles/entry/benefit_corporation_and_l3c_adoption_a_survey.
9. These tips are adapted from Asheesh Advani, "Negotiation Tips for Start-Ups: Follow These Suggestions for Negotiating with Employees, Investors and Suppliers When Your Business Has No Revenue," *Entrepreneur*, April 4, 2005, www.entrepreneur.com/article/76894; Max H. Bazerman, "Creating Value, Weighing Values," *Negotiation*, April 2005, pp. 3–5; Tony Parinello, "Dealmaking Basics: Tips for Negotiating Your Way to a Smooth Sale," *Entrepreneur*, May 12, 2003, www.entrepreneur.com/node/sales/212-17; Sean Silverthorne, "Five Questions for Max Bazerman," *HBS Working Knowledge*, September 4, 2001, http://hbswk.hbs.edu/item.jhtml?id=247 2&t=negotiation&noseek=one; Max H. Bazerman and James J. Gillespie, "Betting on the Future: The Virtues of Contingent Contracts," *Harvard Business Review* 77, no. 5 (September–October 1999), pp. 155–160.
10. This is a variation of the idea of "tit for tat," where two parties immediately achieve balance.
11. Robert Axelrod, *The Evolution of Cooperation* (New York: Basic Books, 1984). See also the Evolution of Cooperation website at http://pscs.physics.lsa.umich.edu/Software/CC/ECHome.html. For a business-oriented approach, consider looking at John Stewart, *Evolution's Arrow: The Direction of Evolution and the Future of Humanity* (Steamboat Springs, CO: Chapman Press, 2000). The entire text is available for a free download at http://users.tpg.com.au/users/jes999/index.htm.
12. The key books on negotiating come from the Program on Negotiating at Harvard Law School (www.pon.harvard.edu/main/home/index.php3). They are R. Fisher, W. Ury, and B. Patton, *Getting to Yes: Negotiating without Giving In* (New York: Penguin Books, 1991); W. Ury, *Getting Past No: Negotiating Your Way from Confrontation to Cooperation* (New York: Bantam Books, 1993). Another book you might find useful for working with very problematic types is R. M. Bramson, *Coping with Difficult People* (New York: Dell, 1981).
13. Internal Revenue Service, "Independent Contractor (Self-Employed) or Employee?," Internal Revenue Service, June 15, 2009, and July 17, 2009, www.irs.gov/businesses/small/article/0,,id=99921,00.html.
14. Steven C. Bahls and Jane Easter Bahls, "RA-A-A-ID! Creepy Competitors Raiding Your Work Force? The Law Can Be the Perfect Bug Spray," *Entrepreneur*, September 2000, www.entrepreneur.com/article/31548.
15. David Rountree, "Head Over Heels: Former Auburn Gymnast and Husband Turn Her Talent into Success," *Birmingham Business Journal*, June 6, 2005, http://birmingham.bizjournals.com/birmingham/stories/2005/06/06/smallb1.html.
16. Chris Kelleher, "5 Litigation Secrets: These Tips May Keep Your Business Out of Court—or Possibly Help You Win If You Get There," *Entrepreneur,* July 12, 2004, www.entrepreneur.com/article/71770.
17. W. Michael Hoffman, Laura P. Hartman, and Mark Rowe, "You've Got Mail . . . and the Boss Knows: A Survey by the Center for Business Ethics of Companies' Email and Internet Monitoring," *Business and Society Review* 108, no. 3 (2003), pp. 285–307; American Marketing Association with the ePolicy Institute and Clearswift, *2003 E-Mail Rules, Policies and Practices Survey* (New York: American Marketing Association, 2003), www.amanet.org/research/pdfs/Email_Policies_Practices.pdf; Robert McGarvey, "Watch and Learn . . . or Watch and Feel Like a Slimy Interloper," *Entrepreneur*, December 2000, www.entrepreneur.com/article/45374.
18. For a discussion of these (which are complex enough that having a patent attorney or patent agent talk with you about strategy is the best approach) look at D. W. Russell, J. F. Bogan, and K. M. Crall. "Choosing between Trade Secret and Patent Protection: Intellectual Property Desk Reference," Kilpatrick, Townsend & Stockton website, May 1, 2015, www.kilpatricktownsend.com/en/Knowledge_Center/Publications/Books/2015/05/~/media/IP%20Desk%20Reference%202015/Choosing%20Between%20Trade%20Secret%20and%20Patent%20Protection.ashx; R. M. or Halligan, "Trade Secrets v. Patents: The New Calculus," August 2010, American Bar Association website, www.americanbar.org/content/dam/aba/migrated/intelprop/magazine/LandslideJuly2010_halligan.authcheckdam.pdf.
19. Chris Kelleher, "How to Protect Your Business's Trade Secrets: These Five Rules Will Help Safeguard Some of Your Company's Most Important Assets," *Entrepreneur*, May 1, 2005, www.entrepreneur.com/article/77680.
20. Jane Easter Bahls, "The Name Game: You Can Shield Your Trade Name from Being Ripped Off by a Larger Company—If It's Distinctive Enough," *Entrepreneur*, January 2005, www.entrepreneur.com/article/77322; "The Source of the Nile(s): Trademark Law's Personal Name Rule Shows Flexibility," *Ideas on Intellectual Property Law* (Manchester, NH: McLane Intellectual Property Practice Group, October–November 2004), pp. 2–3; Eugene R. Quinn Jr., *Beanie Babies Trademark Infringement?* (Albany, NY: Hiscock & Barclay, LLP, 2004), www.hiscockbarclay.com/pdf/IPnewsletter_hb_0504.pdf.

Chapter 18

1. This starts with the YNAB website, www.youneedabudget.com/, but also includes coverage of YNAB in places like: K. Rockwood, "Can't Find Great Talent in Your Backyard? How Great Bosses Hire from Any ZIP Code or Country," *Inc.*, May 30, 2018, www.inc.com/magazine/201806/kate-rockwood/remote-employees-telecommuting-long-distance.html; M. L. Turner, "Remote Control: The Tools and Tactics You Need to Manage a Far-Flung Workforce," *Entrepreneur*, January 13, 2016, www.entrepreneur.com/article/253731; K. Luckett, "Don't Let Student Debt Hogtie Your Business," *Entrepreneur*, March 18, 2015, www.entrepreneur.com/article/243567; *Inc.*,"INC 5000," 2015, www.inc.com/profile/interactive-education-concepts; B. W. Reynolds, "26 Virtual Companies That Thrive on Remote Work," *FlexJobs Job Search Tips and Blog*, March 14, 2014, www.flexjobs.com/blog/post/25-virtual-companies-that-thrive-on-remote-work/ and Flexjobs.com Staff; "You Need A Budget—YNAB Jobs with Remote, Part-Time or

Freelance Options," n.d., www.flexjobs.com/jobs/telecommuting-jobs-at-you_need_a_budget_-_ynab.

2. These numbers come from estimates for 2015 in the SBA's "Frequently Asked Questions," U.S. Small Business Administration, Office of Advocacy; U.S. Small Business Administration, Office of Advocacy, "Frequently Asked Questions about Small Business, 2018," August 2018, www.sba.gov/sites/default/files/advocacy/Frequently-Asked-Questions-Small-Business-2018.pdf.
3. B. A. Kirchhoff, *Entrepreneurship and Dynamic Captalism* (Westport, CT: Quorum Books, 1994); B. Phillips and B. A. Kirchhoff, "Formation, Growth and Survival Small Firm Dynamics in the U.S. Economy," *Small Business Economics* 1 (1989), pp. 65–74; D. Birch, *Job Creation in America* (New York: Free Press, 1987).
4. Joanna L. Krotz, "5 Tips for Hiring Your First Employee," Microsoft Small Business Center (2005), www.microsoft.com/smallbusiness/issues/management/recruiting_Staffing/5_tips_for_hiring_your_first_employee.mspx.
5. Ibid.
6. Gideon D. Markman and Robert A. Baron, "Individual Differences and the Pursuit of New Ventures: A Model of Person-Entrepreneurship Fit," in Jerome A. Katz and Theresa M. Welbourne (eds.), *Advances in Entrepreneurship, Firm Emergence and Growth*, vol. 5 (Oxford: JAI/Elsevier, 2002), pp. 23–54.
7. Allbusiness.com, "Is Employee Probation a Good Idea?," 2005, www.allbusiness.com/articles/EmploymentHR/749-33-1817.html; Wayne F. Cascio and Herman Aguinis, "Chapter 3: Staffing Twenty-First-Century Organizations," *Academy of Management Annals* 2, no. 1 (2008), pp. 133–165.
8. Joanna L. Krotz, "5 Tips for Hiring Your First Employee," Microsoft Small Business Center (2005), www.microsoft.com/smallbusiness/issues/management/recruiting_Staffing/5_tips_for_hiring_your_first_employee.mspx.
9. Joanna L. Krotz, "Are You a Control Freak? 5 Ways to Stop," Microsoft Small Business Center, 2005, www.microsoft.com/smallbusiness/issues/management/leadership_training/are_you_a_control_freak_5_ways_to_stop.mspx.
10. Ian O. Williamson, Daniel M. Cable, and Howard E. Aldrich, "Smaller but Not Necessarily Weaker: How Small Businesses Can Overcome Barriers to Recruitment. Managing People in Entrepreneurial Organizations," in *Advances in the Study of Entrepreneurship Firm Emergence and Growth,* vol. 5 (Greenwich, CT: JAI Press, 2002), pp. 83–106.
11. Jeff Taylor, "A Monster Success," *The Economist* 307, no. 8368 (March 27, 2004), p. 66.
12. Chris Penttila, "How Embarrassing! Highly Publicized Dry Spells Are Poor Recruiting Tools," *Entrepreneur*, August 2002, p. 66.
13. Dale Duncan and Peter Hausdorf, "Firm Size and Internet Recruiting in Canada," *Journal of Small Business Management* 42, no. 3 (July 2004), p. 325.
14. Businesstown.com, "Hiring Top Performers," n.d., www.businesstown.com/hiring/hiring-top.asp, adapted from Bob Adams and Peter Veruki, *Adams Streetwise Hiring Top Performers: 600 Ready-to-Ask Interview Questions and Everything Else You Need to Hire Right* (Cincinnati: Adams Media Corporation, 1997).
15. Joanna L. Krotz, "Tips for Outsourcing Your Small-Business Needs," Microsoft Small Business Center, 2005, www.microsoft.com/smallbusiness/resources/management/recruiting_staffing/tips_for_outsourcing_your_small_business_needs.mspx.
16. Jerome A. Katz, Scott R. Safranski, and Omar Khan, "Virtual Instant Global Entrepreneurship: Cybermediation for Born International Service Firms," *Journal of International Entrepreneurship* 1 (2003), pp. 43–57; Robyn Greenspan, "Managing Virtual Employees," February 28, 2002, e-commerceguide.com/news/news/article.php/983281.
17. Gisela M. Pedroza, "Hiring Telecommuters, Before You Set Up Employees in Their Own Home Offices, Make Sure You Can Handle the Costs," *Entrepreneur*, January 2002, www.entrepreneur.com/article/47760.
18. Adapted from the Mavens & Mogul website, www.mavensandmoguls.com/, and from *Inc.* magazine, "Entrepreneur of the Year: The Accidental Entrepreneur—Paige Arnof-Fenn," www.inc.com/entrepreneur/profile/index.php? arnof-fenn52.
19. Katz et al., "Virtual Instant Global Entrepreneurship"; I. O. Williamson, D. M. Cable, and H. E. Aldrich. "Smaller but Not Necessarily Weaker: How Small Businesses Can Overcome Barriers to Recruitment," in *Advances in Entrepreneurship, Firm Emergence and Growth*, vol. 5 (Bingley, UK: Emerald/ MCB University Press, 2002), pp. 83–106, www.emeraldinsight.com.ezp.slu.edu/books.htm?issn=1074-7540&volume=5&chapterid=1781504&show=abstract; P. Silver, "How to Get Free Employees for Your Business." *Entrepreneur*, November 15, 2004, www.entrepreneur.com/article/73776.
20. U.S. Office of Personnel Management, "Six Steps to Conducting a Job Analysis," www.opm.gov/policy-data-oversight/assessment-and-selection/job-analysis/job_analysis_checklist.pdf.
21. Chris Kelleher, "Writing Great Job Descriptions," *Entrepreneur*, May 10, 2004, www.entrepreneur.com/article/0,4621, 315429,00.html.
22. Wayne F. Cascio and Herman Aguinis, "Chapter 3: Staffing Twenty-First-Century Organizations," *Academy of Management Annals* 2, no. 1 (2008), pp. 133–165. Cascio and Aguinis argue that most studies of selection device effectiveness using actual (versus adjusted) statistics show results indicating a statistically significant but very small (low-power) improvement in predictive power. Meanwhile, using adjusted results has not been shown to work in real-world selection situations. They contend using *in situ* approaches such as internships and contingent work is the best way to sample. Cascio in earlier works (as well as Schmitt) have pointed out that behavioral interviewing is the next best approach.
23. Alison Doyle, "Behavioral Interview—Behavioral-Based Interviewing," About.com, July 20, 2009, http://jobsearch.about.com/cs/interviews/a/behavioral.htm. Susan M. Heathfield, "Behavioral Interviews: Use Behavioral Interviewing to Select the Best," About.com, July 20, 2009, http://humanresources.about.com/od/interviewing/a/behavior_interv_2.htm; Elaine D. Pulakos and Neal Schmitt, "Experience-Based and Situational Interview Questions: Studies of Validity," *Personnel Psychology* 48, no. 2 (1995), pp. 289–308; U.K. Work Ministry, "Work Ministry—The Interview," *Work Ministry,* 2004, July 20, 2009, www.workministry.com/resources/Interview3.shtml.
24. The ideas here are excerpted and adapted from Gary Roberts, Gary Seldon, and Carlotta Roberts, "Human Resources Management," Emerging Business Series, Monograph EB-4 (Washington, DC: U.S. Small Business Administration), www.sba.gov/library/pubs/eb-4.txt.
25. Excerpted from Roberts et al., "Human Resources Management."
26. Allbusiness.com, "Secrets of Effective Employee Training," 2005, www.allbusiness.com/articles/EmploymentHR/1465-33-1817.html.
27. Adapted from "TechScribe Writing," in *How to Write Instructions* (Sheffield, South Yorkshire, UK, 2004), www.techscribe.co.uk/ta/how_to_write_instructions.htm.
28. F. Herzberg, *The Motivation to Work* (New York: Wiley, 1959); A. E. Burke, F. R. FitzRoy, and M. A. Nolan, "Self-Employment Wealth and Job Creation: The Roles of Gender, Non-Pecuniary Motivation and Entrepreneurial Ability," *Small Business Economics* 19, no. 3 (November 2002), pp. 255–270; J. Worth, "Should You Pay Employees an Hourly Wage or a Salary?," *Entrepreneur*, July 9, 2014, www.entrepreneur.com/article/234949.
29. M. Michalowicz, "51 Ways to Reward Employees without Money,"*Open Forum*, March 22, 2011, www.openforum.com/articles/51-ways-to-reward-employees-without-money-1/; Insperity Staff,

"52 Epic Ways to Reward Your Employees,"*Insperity*, October 13, 2015, www.insperity.com/blog/52-epic-ways-to-reward-your-employees/; K. Kruse, "25 Low-Cost Ways to Reward Employees,"*Forbes*, March 1, 2013, www.forbes.com/sites/kevinkruse/2013/03/01/25-low-cost-ways-to-reward-employees/; M. Michalowicz, "101 Ways to Reward Employees (without Giving Them Cash): American Express Canada," n.d., https://smallbusiness.americanexpress.com/ca/en/big-ideas-for-small-business/employee-retention-and-engagement/101-ways-to-reward-employees-without-giving-them-cash; A. Bell, "33 Amazing Employee Recognition Ideas You Need to Be Using." *SnackNation*, August 21, 2015, www.snacknation.com/blog/employee-recognition-ideas/.

30. Adapted from Commerce Clearing House, "Building Employee Involvement," *Business Owners Toolkit* (Riverwoods, IL: Commerce Clearing House, 2005), www.toolkit.cch.com/text/P05_7200.asp.
31. Elcha Shain Buckman, "Motivating and Retaining Non-Family Employees in a Family-Owned Business," *The UMASS Family Business Center Online Newsletter* (Hadley, MA: The UMASS Family Business Center, 1998), www.umass.edu/fambiz/motivate_key_employees.htm.
32. This well-put concept was contributed by an anonymous user and reviewer of *Entrepreneurial Small Business.*
33. Elcha Shain Buckman, "Motivating and Retaining Non-Family Employees in a Family-Owned Business," The UMASS Family Business Center Online Newsletter (Hadley, MA: The UMASS Family Business Center, 1998), www.umass.edu/fambiz/motivate_key_employees.htm.
34. Building Employees' Involvement, www.toolkit.cch.com.
35. Alison Stein Wellner, "What Makes Employees Want to Stick Around?," *BusinessWeek*, March 2000, www.businessweek.com/smallbiz/content/mar2000/sb000320a.htm.
36. David Newton, "Of One Mind: Keep Employees by Getting on the Same Page from the Get-Go," *Entrepreneur*, August 2003, p. 23, www.entrepreneur.com/article/63276.
37. Peter L. Allen, "Performance Appraisal Question and Answer Book," *Harvard Management Communication Letter* 6, no. 3 (March 2003), p. 3.
38. BizHelp23.com, "Employee Appraisal," 2005, www.bizhelp24.com/personaldevelopment/employee_appraisal.shtml.
39. Gina Imperato, "How to Give Good Feedback," *Fast Company*, September 17, 1998, p. 144.
40. Allbusiness.com, "Making Performance Appraisals Work," 2005, www.allbusiness.com/articles/content/1383-33-1817.html.
41. David G. Javitch, "Establishing an Employee Review System," Entrepreneur.com, April 5, 2004, www.entrepreneur.com/article/70172.
42. J. Worth, "Should You Pay Employees an Hourly Wage or a Salary?," *Entrepreneur*, July 9, 2014, www.entrepreneur.com/article/234949; FindLaw, "Exempt Employees vs. Nonexempt Employees," n.d., http://employment.findlaw.com/wages-and-benefits/exempt-employees-vs-nonexempt-employees.html.
43. Staff of *Family Business*, "The Power of Base Pay," *Inc.*, October 1999, www.inc.com/articles/1999/10/19037.html.
44. Allbusiness.com, "Key Compensation Components,"n.d., www.allbusiness.com/articles/EmploymentHR/794-33-1773.html.
45. Allbusiness.com, "Key Compensation Components," n.d., www.allbusiness.com/articles/EmploymentHR/794-33-1773.html; The Henry J. Kaiser Family Foundation, "Implementation Timeline," Health Reform Source, 2013, http://healthreform.kff.org/timeline.aspx.
46. Ibid.
47. S. Lucas, "10 Perks Your Company Can Afford," *Inc.*, March 25, 2013, www.inc.com/suzanne-lucas/10-perks-your-small-business-can-afford.html; Rich Mintzer, "20 Low-Cost Employee Perks," December 8, 2006, www.entrepreneur.com/humanresources/compensationand-benefits/article171630.html; *Entrepreneur*, "Low-Cost Benefits That'll Make Your Employees Happy," October 23, 2002, www.entrepreneur.com/humanresources/compensationandbenefits/article 56492.html; Aliza Pilar Sherman, "How Women Business Owners Reward Their Staff," *Entrepreneur*, September 2005, www.entrepreneur.com/humanresources/managingemployees/motivationandretention/article79320.html.
48. C. E. Aronoff and J. L. Ward. *How to Choose & Use Advisors: Getting the Best Professional Family Business Advice* (Marietta, GA: Family Enterprise Publisher, 1994); T. Lahti, "The Value-Added Contribution of Advisors in the Process of Acquiring Venture Capital," *International Small Business Journal,* October 29, 2012; D. R. Soriano and G. J. Castrogiovanni, "The Impact of Education, Experience and Inner Circle Advisors on SME Performance: Insights from a Study of Public Development Centers," *Small Business Economics* 38, no. 3 (March 17, 2010), pp. 333–349; T. Kautonen, R. Zolin, A. Kuckertz, and A. Viljamaa. "Ties That Blind? How Strong Ties Affect Small Business Owner-Managers' Perceived Trustworthiness of Their Advisors," *Entrepreneurship & Regional Development* 22, no. 2 (March 1, 2010), pp. 189–209.
49. This model was espoused in classes by Edgar Schein of MIT and Harry Levinson of Harvard in the 1970s and 1980s. In working with clinical psychologists, this model is common to help couples understand what is necessary to make marriages work. And there continue to be studies and reports coming to the same conclusion in a variety of business situations: R. Erwee, *Business Networks: Spanning Boundaries and Incorporating Teams* (Toowoomba, Australia: University of Southern Queensland, 2001), https://eprints.usq.edu.au/2851/; D. Devigne and S. Manigart, "Investment Strategies of Cross-Border Venture Capital Investors," *Frontiers of Entrepreneurship Research* 33, no. 2 (June 8, 2013), http://digitalknowledge.babson.edu/fer/vol33/iss2/1.
50. Jon R. Katzenbach and Douglas K. Smith, *The Wisdom of Teams: Creating the High-Performance Organization* (Boston: Harvard Business School Press, 1993), p. 45.
51. Catherine M. Daily and Marc J. Dollinger, *Alternative Methodologies for Identifying Family—versus Nonfamily-Managed Businesses* (Columbus, Ohio: Max M. Fisher College of Business, Ohio State University, 1994); John Ward and Christina Dolan, "Defining and Describing Family Business Ownership Configurations," *Family Business Review* 11 (1998), pp. 305–310.
52. Eric Flamholtz and Yvonne Randle, *Growing Pains: How to Make the Transition from an Entrepreneurship to a Professionally Managed Firm* (San Francisco: Jossey-Bass, 2007).
53. Barbara Blouin, Katherine Gibson, and Margaret Kiersted, *The Legacy of Inherited Wealth: Interviews with Heirs* (Halifax, Nova Scotia: Trio Press, 1995); Paul C. Rosenblatt, Leni de Mik, Roxanne Marie Anderson, and Patricia A. Johnson, *The Family in Business* (San Francisco: Jossey-Bass Publishers, 1985).
54. Dennis T. Jaffe, *Working with the Ones You Love: Conflict Resolution & Problem Solving Strategies for a Successful Family Business* (Berkeley, CA: Conari Press, 1990); David Javitch, "David Javitch: Employee Management—How to Earn Employees' Respect," June 2, 2003, www.entrepreneur.com/humanresources/employeemanagementcolumnistdavidjavitch/article62284.html.
55. Eric Flamholtz and Yvonne Randle, *Growing Pains: How to Make the Transition from an Entrepreneurship to a Professionally Managed Firm* (San Francisco: Jossey-Bass, 2007).
56. Paul C. Rosenblatt, Leni de Mik, Roxanne Marie Anderson, and Patricia A. Johnson, *The Family in Business* (San Francisco: Jossey-Bass, 1985).
57. David Bork, *Family Business, Risky Business: How to Make It Work* (New York: AMACOM, American Management Association, 1986); Gideon Maas and Andre Diederichs, *Manage Family in Your Family Business* (Northcliff, South Africa: Frontrunner, 2007); U.S. Small

Business Administration, *Challenges in Managing a Family Business*, Management and Planning Series, Monograph MP-3 (Washington, DC: U.S. Small Business Administration), www.sba.gov/library/pubs/mp-3.txt; Jeff Wuorio, "How to Fire a Family Member," Microsoft Small Business Center, 2005, www.microsoft.com/smallbusiness/issues/management/employee_relations/how_to_fire_a_family_member.mspx.

58. Patricia Schiff Estess, "Don't Get Personal: Taking the Personal out of Personnel Isn't Easy When You're Talking about Family," *Entrepreneur*, January 2000, www.entrepreneur.com/article/18852.

59. Craig E. Aronoff and John L. Ward, *From Siblings to Cousins: Prospering in the Third Generation and Beyond*, Family Business Leadership Series, no. 22 (Marietta, GA: Family Enterprise Publishers, 2007); David Bork, *Family Business, Risky Business: How to Make It Work* (New York: AMACOM, American Management Association, 1986); Flamholtz and Randle, *Growing Pains;* David G. Javitch, "By Setting Clear Standards and Involving Employees in the Review Process, Your Entire Company Can Benefit from Formal Appraisals," April 5, 2004, www.entrepreneur.com/article/0,4621,314968,00.html; Sandra W. King, George T. Solomon, and Lloyd W. Fernald Jr., "Issues in Growing a Family Business: A Strategic Human Resource Model," *Journal of Small Business Management* 39, no. 1 (January 2001), pp. 3–13; Paul C. Rosenblatt, Leni de Mik, Roxanne Marie Anderson, and Patricia A. Johnson, *The Family in Business* (San Francisco: Jossey-Bass, 1985).

60. Patricia Schiff Estess, "Theory of Un-Relativity: How to Keep Nonfamily Managers Happy in Order to Grow Your Business," *Entrepreneur*, March 1999, www.entrepreneur.com/magazine/entrepreneur/1999/march/17328.html; Patricia Schiff Estess, "Attracting Non-Family Employees: As Appealing as the Cozy Atmosphere of a Family Business May Be, You Can't Beat Incentives for Hooking Good Managers," *Entrepreneur*, December 1999, www.entrepreneur.com/magazine/entrepreneur/1999/december/18656.html; Paul C. Rosenblatt, Leni de Mik, Roxanne Marie Anderson, and Patricia A. Johnson, *The Family in Business* (San Francisco: Jossey-Bass, 1985).

61. Various authors. "What Are the Pros and Cons of the 'Slicing Pie' Method of Dynamic Startup Equity Distribution?," Quora, n.d., www.quora.com/What-are-the-pros-and-cons-of-the-slicing-pie-method-of-dynamic-startup-equity-distribution; J. Carter, "Dividing the Equity Pie | Points and Figures," *Points and Figures*, October 23, 2017, http://pointsandfigures.com/2017/10/23/dividing-the-equity-pie/; C. Gatewood, "Startup Equity--Dividing the Pie," Threshold Counsel, PC, December 7, 2015, http://threshold.cc/startup-equity-dividing-the-pie/; L. Hower, "How to Divide Founder Equity: 4 Criteria to Discuss," *NextView Ventures*, December 4, 2014, https://nextviewventures.com/blog/how-to-divide-founder-equity/.

62. M. Volker, "Business Basics—Equity: Dividing the Pie," *Business Basics for Engineers*, October 15, 1997, www.sfu.ca/~mvolker/biz/equity.htm F. Demmler, "Cutting Up the Founders' Pie," 2009, www.cmu.edu/swartz-center-for-entrepreneurship/assets/Connect%20Spring%202017/Frank%20Demmler%20-%20Equity%20Pie/Founders_Pie_Final.pdf. Also look at the online calculator at http://foundrs.com/.

63. Aronoff and Ward, *From Siblings to Cousins;* Dennis T. Jaffe, *Working with the Ones You Love: Conflict Resolution & Problem Solving Strategies for a Successful Family Business* (Berkeley, CA: Conari Press, 1990); Nichole L. Torres, "Family Affair: When Business and Family Mix, the Key to Success Is Communication," *Entrepreneur's Start-Ups*, September 2004, www.entrepreneur.com/magazine/entrepreneursstartupsmagazine/2004/september/72314.html; Paul C. Rosenblatt, Leni de Mik, Roxanne Marie Anderson, and Patricia A. Johnson, *The Family in Business* (San Francisco: Jossey-Bass, 1985).

64. Estess, P. S. "Don't Get Personal." *Entrepreneur,* January 1, 2000. https://www.entrepreneur.com/article/18852.

NAME INDEX

O

P

R

S

T

V

W

Y

Z

COMPANY INDEX

M

N

O

P

Q

R

S

T

U

V

W

X

Y

Z

SUBJECT INDEX

C

D

E

G

H

I

J

K